ARBA Guide
to Biographical Resources
1986–1997

ARBA Guide
to Biographical Resources 1986–1997

ROBERT L. WICK
and
TERRY ANN MOOD
Editors

LIBRARIES UNLIMITED, INC.
Englewood, Colorado
1998

Libraries Unlimited, Inc.
P.O. Box 6633
Englewood, CO 80155-6633
1-800-237-6124
www.lu.com

Production Editor: Judy Gay Matthews
Proofreader: Jason Cook
Typesetter: Michael Florman

Library of Congress Cataloging-in-Publication Data

ARBA guide to biographical resources 1986-1997 / Robert L. Wick and
  Terry Ann Mood, editors.
    xxxiv, 604 p. 17x25 cm.
    Includes indexes.
    ISBN 1-56308-453-8 (hc.)
    1. Biography--Dictionaries--Bibliography. I. Wick, Robert L.,
  1938- . II. Mood, Terry Ann, 1945- . III. American reference
books annual.
Z5301.A82 1998
[CT103]
016.92--dc21   98-39503
                                                         CIP

Contents

Journals Cited

The following is a list of journals cited at the end of the reviews. They are abbreviated following the letter "R"; for example: [R: Choice, 15 Oct 91, p. 237; WLB, Oct 94, p. 74].

Form of Citation	Journal Title
BL	Booklist
BR	Book Report
Choice	Choice
C&RL	College & Research Libraries
CLJ	Canadian Library Journal
EL	Emergency Librarian
JAL	Journal of Academic Librarianship
JOYS	Journal of Youth Services in Libraries
LAR	Library Association Record
LJ	Library Journal
RBB	Reference Books Bulletin
RQ	RQ
SBF	Science Books & Films
SLJ	School Library Journal
SLMQ	School Library Media Quarterly
TN	Top of the News
VOYA	Voice of Youth Advocates
WLB	Wilson Library Bulletin

Preface

The *ARBA Guide to Biographical Resources* is intended to provide a representative selection of biographical dictionaries and related works that will be useful to the reference and information process in libraries of all types. It is also expected that the work will be of assistance to the selection and collection development processes. More than 1,100 sources have been included. Three basic inclusion criteria were used in selection: 1) each item included was published within the past 12 years, 2) each item has either been published in *American Reference Books Annual* (*ARBA*) or has been selected due to the importance of the work, and 3) each item contains substantial biographical information. Some of the books included were not in print at the time of publication, but in these cases the editors felt that they were either unique in the type of biographical information contained, or that the works are considered "standard" in the field even though they are temporarily listed out of stock by the publisher. If newer editions of annual publications were not substantially changed in format or inclusion criteria from an earlier edition that appeared in *ARBA,* they have been left unchanged. The original additional review information included in the original *ARBA* reviews has been included at the end of the reviews of the *ARBA Guide to Biographical Resources* (see p. xiii for list and key to abbreviations). In many cases the arrangement of the subjects and the headings within subject areas have been changed from the original *ARBA* publication. This has been done to bring together biographical sources covering the same groups, professions, or historical periods.

When a critical review was updated or changed in any way from that of the original, an editor's name has been included at the bottom along with the original reviewer. Each entry provides complete bibliographic information (i.e., author or editor, title, publisher, date of publication, price, ISSN/ISBN and LC numbers if available, and a complete critical evaluation of the work). Most of the entries have been selected from the past 12 years of *ARBA*. In many cases the original reviews have been rewritten to reflect the most recent edition, or they have been changed to open entries to reflect the serial nature of the publications. More than 20,000 books were reviewed in order to find all that contain significant biographical information.

The *ARBA Guide to Biographical Resources* is divided into two major parts: Part I, **International and National Biographies**, and Part II, **Biographies in Professional Fields**. International and national biographies are divided generally by works that include all geographical areas both current and retrospective and works that are restricted to a single country, group of countries, or area. In many cases these divisions are somewhat arbitrary in that some books include both international and national biographies. In these cases the works may be found in National and Regional Sources. In Part II, **Biographies in Professional Fields**, there are 22 subcategories by professional fields, including **History; Geography; Political Science; Military Science; Pyschology, Sociology and Social Work; Law; Business and Economics; Women's Studies; Ethnic Studies; Education; Literature; Applied Arts; Fine Arts; Music; Communications and Mass Media; Performing Arts; Folklore and Mythology; Philosophy and Religion; Library and Information Science; Science and Technology; Health Sciences;** and **Sports and Recreation**. For the most part books listed in these subcategories are obvious, but in a few cases particular works have biographical sources that cross designated subject areas. In these cases, it was determined what the subject of the "majority" of the biographical sources in the work are, and the book has been placed in that subject category. There is a brief introduction at the beginning of Part II. Introductions provide organizational notes and list specific sources of interest in some sections, including recent works that are unique in their inclusion. The number of sources in the various subject divisions range from more than 285 books in the chapter **Literature** to fewer than 10 books in **Applied Arts**.

The editors have attempted to include all books included in past *ARBA*s that contain substantial biographical information. Individual biographies have not been included, although some selections may contain biographies of only a few individuals. In some cases, biographical sources have been included that have received less than positive reviews because they contain information on individuals not generally covered in other works. Books that have been reviewed as completely unacceptable from the standpoint of accuracy have not been included.

The editors would like to thank all of the *ARBA* reviewers who have contributed to this volume; without their work, this book could not have been completed. A list of reviewers has been included following this preface. Also, thanks should go to the staff of Libraries Unlimited, who have not only written a number of reviews themselves, which, as is the tradition with the original *ARBA*s, are included here, but also for their careful editing and attractive design of the book. Special thanks go to Ed Volz, Ron Maas, and *ARBA* editor Bohdan S. Wynar, Libraries Unlimited, who provided advice and support for the project. Finally, the editors would like to thank the Auraria Library, University of Colorado at Denver, for both financial support of the project and release time for editing of the manuscript. Without the University of Colorado's support for scholarly activities, it would not have been possible to complete this work.

Robert L. Wick
Terry Ann Mood
Denver, Colorado

List of Contributors

The affiliation shown by the contributor's name was in effect
at the time of the book review, if known.

Diana Accurso, Bibliographic Instruction Coordinator/Reference Librarian, Denison
  University Libraries, Granville, OH
Robert D. Adamshick, Librarian, U.S. Army Corps of Engineers, Chicago, IL
Sandra Adell, Asst. Professor, Dept. of Afro-American Studies, University of
  Wisconsin, Madison, WI
Robert Aken, (formerly) Head of Reference, Margaret I. King Library, University of
  Kentucky, Lexington, KY
Walter C. Allen, Assoc. Professor Emeritus, Graduate School of Library and
  Information Science, University of Illinois, Urbana, IL
Mohammed M. Aman, Education Librarian, Gola Meir Library, Univ. of Wisconsin,
  Milwaukee, WI
Elizabeth L. Anderson, Part-time Instructor, Lansing Community College, MI
Frank J. Anderson, Librarian Emeritus, Sandor Teszler Library, Wofford College,
  Spartanburg. SC
James D. Anderson, Assoc. Dean and Professor, School of Communication,
  Information, and Library Studies, Rutgers Univ. New Brunswick, NJ
Margaret Anderson, Assoc. Professor, Faculty of Library and Information Science,
  University of Toronto, Toronto, Canada
Charles R. Andrews, Dean of Library Services, Hofstra University, Hempstead, NY
Theodora Andrews, Professor of Library Science and Special Bibliographer,
  Pharmacy, Nursing and Health Science Librarian, Purdue University, West
  Lafayette, IN
Susan B. Ardis, Head, McKinney Engineering Library, University of Texas, Austin,
  TX
Bill Bailey, Head of Reference, Newton Gresham Library, Sam Houston State Univ.,
  Huntsville, TX
Jack Bales, Reference Librarian, Mary Washington College Library, Fredericksburg,
  VA
JoAnn Balingit, Library Media Specialist, Avon Grove High School, West Grove, PA
Robert M. Ballard, Professor, School of Library and Information Science, North
  Carolina Central University, Durham, NC
Betty Bankhead, Library Media Coordinator, Cherry Creek High School Library,
  Englewood, CO
Gary D. Barber, Head of Reference, Daniel A. Reed Library, State Univ. of New
  York, Fredonia, NY
Helen M. Barber, Reference Librarian, New Mexico State Univ., Las Cruces, Denver,
  CO
Suzanne I. Barchers, Author/Consultant, Denver, CO
Ruth E. Bauner.
Craig W. Beard, Reference Librarian, Mervyn H. Steme Library, Univ. of Alabama,
  Birmingham, AL
Sandra E. Belanger, Reference Librarian, San Jose State University Library, San Jose,
  CA
Carol Willsey Bell, Head, Local History and Genealogy Dept., Warren-Trumbull
  County Public Library, Warren, OH

Helen Carol Bennett.
Bernice Bergup, Humanities Reference Librarian, Davis Library, University of North Carolina, Chapel Hill, NC
John B. Beston, Professor of English, Nazareth College of Rochester, NY
Barbara M. Bibel, Reference Librarian, Science/Business/Sociology Dept., Main Library, Oakland Public Library, CA
Kerranne G. Riley, Reference Librarian, Auraria Library, University of Colorado at Denver, Denver, CO
Terry D. Bilhartz, Assoc. Professor of History, Sam Houston State Univ., Huntsville, TX
John D. Blackwell, Coordinator of Information Services, Arthur A. Wishart Library, Algoma University College, Sault Ste. Marie, Ontario, Canada
Daniel K. Blewett, Reference Librarian, Cudahy Library, Loyola Univ., Chicago, IL
Marjorie E. Bloss, Director, Technical Services Division, Center for Research Libraries, Chicago, IL
Edna M. Boardman, Library Media Specialist, Minot High School, Magic City Campus, Minot, ND
George S. Bobinski, Dean and Professor, School of Information and Library Studies, State Univ. of New York, Buffalo, NY
Melvin M. Bowie, Assoc. Professor, Dept. of Instructional Technology, Univ. of Georgia, Athens, GA
Mary L. Bowman, Reference Librarian, Noel Memorial Library, Louisiana State Univ., Shreveport, LA
James K. Bracken, Head, Second Floor Main Library Information Services, Ohio State University, Columbus, OH
William Bright, Research Associate in Linguistics, Univ. of Colorado, Boulder, CO
Robert N. Broadus, Professor, School of Library Science, University of North Carolina, Chapel Hill, NC
William S. Brockman, English Librarian, University of Illinois, Urbana, IL
Ellen Broidy, Publications Coordinator, Library, University of California, Irvine, CA
Simon J. Bronner, Distinguished Professor of Folklore and American Studies, Capitol College, Pennsylvania State University, Middletown, PA
Barbara E. Brown, Former Head, General Cataloging Section, Library of Parliament, Ottawa, Ontario, Canada
Judith M. Brugger, Books/Journals Team, Library, Los Alamos National Laboratory, NM
Richard M. Buck.
John R. Burch, Jr. Technical Services Librarian, Hagan Memorial Library, Cumberland College, Williamsburg, KY
Robert H. Burger, Head, Slavic and East European Library, University of Illinois, Urbana-Champaign, IL
Ingrid Schierling Burnett Reference Librarian, University of Southern Colorado Library, Pueblo, CO
Debbie Burnham-Kidwell.
G. Joan Burns, Principal Art Librarian, Art and Music Department, Newark Public Library, Newark, NJ
Lois J. Buttlar, Assoc. Professor, School of Library and Information Science, Kent State University, OH
Hans E. Bynagle, Library Director and Professor of Philosophy, Whitworth College, Spokane, WA
Diane M. Calabrese, Research Assoc. for Planning and Eisenhower Grant Programs, Coordinating Board for Higher Education, Jefferson City, MO
John Lewis Campbell, Asst. Head of Reference Department, University of Georgia Libraries, Athens, GA

Joseph L. Carlson, Library Director, Vandenberg Air Force Base, CA

Kathleen W. Carver.

James A. Casada, Professor of History, Winthrop College, Rock Hill, SC

Jefferson D. Caskey, Professor of Library Science and Instructional Media, Western Kentucky University, Bowling Green, KY

G. A. Cevasco, Assoc. Professor of English, St. John's University, West Lafayette, IN

Bert Chapman, Government Publications Coordinator, Purdue University, West Lafayette, IN

John Y. Cheung, Assoc. Professor, University of Oklahoma, Norman, OK

Boyd Childress, Reference Librarian, Ralph B. Draughon Library, Auburn University, AL

Eric H. Christianson, Assoc. Professor of History, University of Kentucky, Lexington, KY

Diane J. Cimbala.

Dene L. Clark, Reference Librarian, Auraria Library, University of Colorado at Denver, Denver, CO

Stella T. Clark, Professor, Foreign Languages, California State University, San Marcos, CA

Beth Clewis, Collection Specialist, Prince William Public Library, VI

Harriette M. Cluxton, Former Director of Medical Library Services, Illinois Masonic Medical Center, Chicago, IL

Donald E. Collins, Assoc. Professor, History Department, East Carolina University, Greenville, NC

Kay O. Cornelius, (formerly) Teacher and Magnet School Lead Teacher, Huntsville City Schools, Huntsville, AL

Paul B. Cors, Catalog Librarian, University of Wyoming, Laramie, WY

Angelo Costanzo, Professor of English, Shippensburgh University, PA

Nancy Courtney.

Brian E. Coutts, Head, Dept. of Library Public Services, Helm-Cravens Library, Western Kentucky University, Bowling Green, KY

Kathleen W. Craver, Head Librarian, National Cathedral School, Washington, D.C.

Milton H. Crouch, Asst. Director for Reader Services, Bailey/Howe Library, University of Vermont, Burlington, VT

John Cudd.

Gregory Curtis, Director, Northern Maine Technical College, Presque Isle, ME

Mark Cyzyk, Reference Librarian, Albert S. Cook Library, Towson State University, MI

William J. Dane, Supervising Librarian, Special Libraries, Newark Public Library, Newark, NJ

Joseph W. Dauben, Professor of History, and History of Science, City University of New York, New York, NY

Estelle A. Davis, Reference Librarian and Asst. Professor, Science/Engineering Library , City College of the City University of New York, New York, NY

Geraldo U. de Sousa.

Anna L. DeMiller, Social Sciences/Humanities Librarian, Morgan Library, Colorado State University, Ft. Collins, CO

Barbara Van Deventer.

Donald C. Dickinson, Professor Emeritus, Graduate Library School, University of Arizona, Tucson, AZ

Dennis Dillon, Asst. for Reference Services Operations, General Libraries, University of Texas, Austin, TX

Carol A. Doll, Asst. Professor, Graduate School of Library and Information Science, University of Washington, Seattle, WA

David A. Doman, PA Instruction Specialist, Pikes Peak Library District, Colorado Springs, CO

Dominique-René de Lerma, Professor, Conservatory of Music, Lawrence University, Appleton, WI

Margaret F. Dominy, Head, Mathematics-Physics-Astronomy Library, University of Pennsylvania, Philadelphia, PA

G. Kim Dority, Assoc. Director/Project Manager, The Library, National Cable Television Center and Museum, Denver, CO

Kristin Doty, Freelance librarian

John A. Drobnicki, Librarian, Queens Library, Jamaica, NY

John E. Druesedow, Jr., Director of the Music Library/Adjunct Asst. Professor of Music, Duke University, Durham NC

Joe P. Dunn, Charles A. Dana Professor of History and Politics, Converse College, Spartanburg, SC

Susan Ebershoff-Coles, Supervisor, Technical Services, Indianapolis-Marion Country Public Library, IN

David Eggenberger, Freelance Writer and Editor, Vienna, VA

Garabed Eknoyan, Professor of Medicine, Baylor College of Medicine, Houston, TX

Jennifer Comi Ellard, Young Adult Librarian, San Antonio Public Library, San Antonio, TX

Marie Ellis, English and American Literature Bibliographer, University of Georgia Libraries, Athens, GA

Ray English, Director of Libraries, Oberlin College, Oberlin, OH

Edward Erazo, Reference/Outreach Librarian, New Mexico State University, Las Cruces, NM

Jonathon Erlen, Curator, History of Medicine, University of Pittsburgh, Pittsburgh, PA

Judith A. Erlen, Curator, History of Medicine, University of Pittsburgh, Pittsburgh, PA

G. Edward Evans, University Librarian, Charles Von der Ahe Library, Loyola Marymount University, Los Angeles, CA

Andrew Ezergailis, Professor of History, Ithaca College, Ithaca, NY

Ian Fairclough, Serials Cataloger, Coe Library, Lararnie, WY

Joyce Duncan Falk, Independent Scholar, Santa Barbara, CA

Kathleen Farago, Reference Librarian, Lakewood Public Library, Lakewood, OH

Megan S. Farrell, Collection Development Librarian and Asst. Professor, Dupre Library, University of Southwestern Louisiana, Lafayette, LA

Adele M. Fasick, Dean and Professor, School of Library and Information Science, University of Toronto, Toronto, Canada

Robin Riley Fast, Assoc. Professor, Division of Writing, Literature, and Publishing, Emerson College, Boston, MA

Joan B. Fiscella, Bibliographer for Professional Studies, Library, University of Illinois, Chicago, IL

Virginia S. Fischer, Reference/Documents Librarian, University of Maine, Prewque Isle, ME

Jerry D. Flack, Assoc. Professor of Education, University of Colorado, Colorado Springs, CO

Patricia Fleming, Professor, Faculty of Library and Information Science, University of Toronto, Toronto, Canada

Michael A. Foley, Honors Director, Marywood College, Scranton, PA

Harold O. Forshey, Assoc. Dean, Miami University, Oxford, OH

A. David Franklin, Professor of Music, Winthrop University, Rock Hill, SC

David K. Frasier, Asst. Librarian, Reference Department, Indiana University, Bloomington, IN

Suzanne G. Frayser, Social Science Research Consultant and Faculty, University College, University of Denver, Denver, CO

Susan J. Freiband, Assoc. Professor, Graduate School of Librarianship, University of Puerto Rico, San Juan, Puerto Rico

Lewis Fried.

Ronald H. Fritze, Assoc. Professor, Dept. of History, Lamar University, Beaumont, TX

Paula Frosch, Assoc. Museum Librarian, Thomas J. Watson Library, Metropolitan Museum of Art, New York City, NY

Sherrilynne Fuller, Director, Health Sciences Library, University of Washington, Seattle, WA

Monica Fusich, Reference and Instruction Librarian, Henry Madden Library, Fresno, CA

Elizabeth Futas, Professor/Director, Graduate School of Library and Information Studies, University of Rhode Island, Kingston, RI

Ahmad Gamaluddin, Professor, School of Library Science, Clarion State College, PA

Vera Gao, Catalog Librarian, Auraria Library, University of Colorado at Denver, Denver, CO

Jack I. Gardner, Administrator, Central Library, Las Vegas, NV

Gregg S. Geary, Music Librarian, Sinclair Library, University of Hawaii, Honolulu, HI

Tom Gilson, Head, Reference Services, Robert Scott Small Library, College of Charleston, Charleston, SC

Elizabeth A. Ginno, Coordinator of Library Computer Information Resources, Univ. Library, California State University Hayward, CA

Edwin S. Gleaves, State Librarian and Archivist, Tennessee State Library and Archives, Nashville, TN

Lisha E. Goldberg, Technical Writer, Safety Insurance Co., Boston, MA

Barbara B. Goldstein, Media Specialist, Magothy River Middle School, Arnold, MD

Joanne M. Goode, Head, Lexmark Technical Library, IPD Technical Library, University of Kentucky, Lexington, KY

Helen M. Gothberg, Assoc. Professor, Graduate Library School, University of Arizona, Tucson, AZ

Allie Wise Goudy, Professor, Western Illinois University, Macomb, IL

Frank Wm. Goudy, Professor, Western Illinois University, Macomb, IL

M. Patrick Graham, Director, Pitts Theology Library, Emory University, Atlanta, GA

Bonnie Gratch.

Richard A. Gray.

Marilynn Green, Librarian, NASA Johnson Space Center, Scientific and Technical Information Center, Houston, TX

Richard W. Grefrath, Reference Librarian, University of Nevada, Reno, NV

Arthur Gribben, Professor, Union Institute, Los Angeles, CA

Margaret A. Grift, Public Service Librarian, Redeemer College, Ancaster, Ontario, Canada

Leonard Grundt, Professor, A. Holly Patterson Library, Nassau Community College, Garden City, NY

M. David Guttman.

L. Hallewell, Visiting Professor, UNESP, Marilia, Brazil

Deborah Hammer, Head, History, Travel and Biography Div., Queens Borough Public Library, Jamaica, NY

Joseph Hannibal, Curator of Invertebrate Paleontology, Cleveland Museum of Natural History, Cleveland, OH

Roland C. Hansen, Readers' Services Librarian, The School of the Art Institute of Chicago, Chicago, IL

Beverley Hanson, Office Manager, Midwest Ultrasound, Cincinnati, OH

Constance Hardesty, Twenty-first Century Communications, Denver, CO

Thomas S. Harding.

Roberto P. Haro, Director and Professor, San Francisco State University, San Francisco, CA

Chauncy D. Harris, Samuel N. Harper Distinguished Service Professor Emeritus of Geography, University of Chicago, Chicago, IL

Linda Suttle Harris, Business Librarian, University of Alabama, Birmingham, AL

Thomas L. Hart, Professor, School of Library and Information Studies, Florida State University, Tallahassee, FL

Ann L. Hartman.

Ann Hartness, Asst. Head Librarian, Benson Latin American Collection, University of Texas, Austin, TX

Ralph Hartsock, Senior Music Catalog Librarian, University of North Texas, Denton, TX

Karen D. Harvey, Assoc. Dean for Academic Affairs, Univ. College, University of Denver, Denver, CO

Robert J. Havlik, Librarian Emeritus and Exhibit Coordinator, University of Notre Dame, IN

Fred J. Hay, Librarian of the W. L. Eury Appalachian Collection and Assoc. Professor, Center for Appalachian Studies, Appalachian State University, Boone, NC

Mary Hemmings, Technical Services Librarian, Law Library, University of Calgary, Canada

David Henige, African Studies Bibliographer, Memorial Library, University of Wisconsin, Madison, WI

Carol D. Henry, Librarian, Lyons Township High School, LaGrange, IL

Mark Y. Herring, Dean of Libraries, Oklahoma Baptist University, Shawnee, OK

Susan Davis Herring, Reference Librarian, University of Alabama Library, Huntsville, AL

Nancy L. Herron, Head Librarian, J. Clarence Kelly Library, Pennsylvania State University, McKeesport, PA

George R. Hill.

Marquita Hill, Cooperating Professor of Chemical Engineering, University of Maine, Orono, ME

V. W. Hill, Social Sciences Bibliographer, Memorial Library, University of Wisconsin, Madison, WI

Robert Clyde Hodges, (formerly) Instructor University of Kentucky, Lexington, KY

Paul E. Hoffman, Assoc. Professor of History, Louisiana State University, Baton Rouge, LA

Richard E. Holl, Asst. Professor, History Dept., Lees College, Jackson, KY

Susan Tower Hollis, Assoc. Dean and Center Director, Central New York Center of the State University of New York, NY

Curtis D. Holmes, Instructor, Aurora Hinkley High School, Aurora, CO

Shirley L. Hopkinson, Professor, Div. of Library and Information Science, San Jose State University, San Jose, CA

Renee B. Horowitz, Professor, Dept. of Technology, College of Engineering, Arizona State University, San Jose, CA

Valerie R. Hotchkiss, Director, Bridwell Library, Perkins School of Theology, Southern Methodist University, Dallas, TX

John H. Hunter, Reference/Collection Development Librarian, Fondren Library, Rice University, Houston, TX

Jonathan F. Husband, Program Chair of the Library/Reader Services Librarian, Fondren Library, Rice University, Houston, TX

Hwa-Wei Lee, Dean of Libraries, Ohio University, Athens, OH

David Isaacson, Asst. Head of Reference and Humanities Librarian, Waldo Library, Western Michigan University, Kalamazoo, MI

Barbara Ittner, Staff, Libraries Unlimited, Inc., Englewood, CO

Janet R. Ivey, (deceased) Automation Services Librarian, Boynton Beach City Library, FL

Eugene B. Jackson, Professor Emeritus, Graduate School of Library and Information Sciences, University of Texas, Austin, TX

Janet M. Jaguszewski, Mathematics Librarian, University of Minnesota, Minneapolis, MN

D. Barton Johnson, Professor Emeritus of Russian, University of California, Santa Barbara, CA

Jennie S. Johnson, Reference Librarian, University of Toledo, OH

Marie F. Jones, Reference and Bibliographic Instruction Librarian, Muskingum College, New Concord, OH

Raymond E. Jones, Assoc. Professor of English, University of Alberta, Edmonton, Canada

Rebecca Jordan, Director of Composition, Division of English, Emporia State University, KS

Jane Jurgens, Reference Librarian, St. Cloud State University, St. Cloud, MN

Elia Kacapyr, Asst. Professor Economics, Ithaca College, Ithaca, NY

Thomas A. Karel, Assoc. Director for Public Services, Shadek-Fackenthal Library, Franklin and Marshall College, Lancaster, PA

Sydney Starr Keaveney.

John Laurence Kelland, Reference Bibliographer for Life Sciences, University of Rhode Island Library, Kingston, RI

Joanne Kelly, Champaign, IL

Barbara E. Kemp, Asst. Director, Dewey Graduate Library, State University of New York, Albany, NY

Kathleen Kenny, Science Librarian, Auraria Library, University of Colorado at Denver, Denver, CO

Caroline M. Kent, Head of Research Services, Widener Library, Harvard University, Cambridge, MA

Michael Keresztesi, Professor Emeritus, Wayne State University, Detroit, MI

Cheryl Kern-Simirenko, Asst. University Librarian for Collection Development and Resource Services, University of Oregon Library, University of Oregon, Eugene, OR

Jackson Kesler, Professor of Theatre and Dance, Western Kentucky University, Bowling Green, KY

Vicki J. Killion, Asst. Professor of Library Science and Pharmacy, Nursing and Health Sciences Librarian, Purdue University, West Lafayette, IN

Sun Ok Kim, Senior Asst. Librarian/Social Sciences Cataloging Librarian, Cornell University, Ithaca, NY

Sharon Kincaide, Production Supervisor/Supplement Editor, Wiley Law Publications, Colorado Springs, CO

Christine E. King, Reference Music Library, State University of New York, Stony Brook, NY

Jeffrey C. Kinkley, Professor of History, St. John's University, New York, NY

Zsuzsa Koltay, Mann Library, Cornell University, Ithaca, NY

Johan Koren, Lecturer, Library Science Program, Wayne State University, Detroit, MI

Lori D. Kranz, Freelance Editor; Assoc. Editor, *The Bloomsbury Review,* Denver, CO

Kerry L. Kresse, Head, Physics Library, University of Wisconsin, Madison, WI

Linda A. Krikos, Head, Women's Studies Library, Ohio State University, Columbus, OH

Ramsdell Kristin.

Colby H. Kullman, Assoc. Professor and Editor, Studies in American Drama, University of Mississippi, MS

Natalie Kupferbert, Health Sciences Library Coordinator, Ferris State University, Big Rapids, MI

Robert V. Labaree, Reference/Public Services Librarian, Von KleinSmid Library, University of Southern California, Los Angeles, CA

Linda L. Lam-Easton, Assoc. Professor, Dept. of Religious Studies, California State University, North Ridge, CA

Shirley Lambert, Staff, Libraries Unlimited, Englewood, CO

Sharon Langworthy, Production Supervisor/Supplement Editor, Wiley Law Publications, Colorado Springs, CO

Binh P. Le, Reference Librarian, Abington College, Pennsylvania State University, University Park, PA

Brad R. Leach, Records Manager, Northern Colorado Water Conservancy District, Loveland, CO

Patricia M. Leach, Editorial Technician Training Leader, Group Publishing, Loveland, CO

Mary Lou LeCompte, Asst. Professor, Kinesiology and Health Education, University of Texas, Austin, TX

R. S. Lehmann, Rocky Mountain BankCard System, Colorado National Bank, Denver, CO

John A. Lent, Drexel Hill, PA

Charlotte Lindgren, Professor Emerita of English, Emerson College, Boston, MA

Dorothy E. Litt.

Janet H. Littlefield.

Koraljka Lockhart, Publications Editor, San Francisco Opera, San Francisco, CA

Catherine R. Loeb.

David V. Loertscher, (formerly) Staff, Libraries Unlimited, Inc., Englewood, CO

David Lonergan.

Jeffrey E. Long, Interlibrary Loan/Photocopy Services Library Assistant, Lamar Soutter Library/University of Massachusetts Medical Center, Worcester, MA

Koert C. Loomis, Jr..

Jeffrey R. Luttrell, Leader, Humanities Cataloging Team, Princeton University, Library, NJ

Sara R. Mack, Professor Emerita, Dept. of Library Science, Kutztown University, PA

Linda Main, Assoc. Professor, San Jose State University, San Jose, CA

Donald J. Marion, Reference/Bibliographer, Science and Technology Library, University of Minnesota, Minneapolis, MN

S. D. Markman, Professor Emeritus, Art Department, Duke University, Durham, NC

Lorraine Mathies.

Judy Gay Matthews, Staff, Libraries Unlimited, Inc., Englewood, CO

George Louis Mayer, (formerly) Senior Principal Librarian New York Public Library and Part-Time Librarian, Adelphi, Manhattan Center and Brooklyn College, NY

James P. McCabe, Univ. Librarian, Fordham University, Brooklyn, NY

James R. McDonald, Professor of Geography, Eastern Michigan University, Ypsilanti, MI

Dana McDougald, Lead Media Specialist, Learning Resources Center, Cedar Shoals High School, Athens, GA

T. McKimmie, Reference Librarian, New Mexico State University, Las Cruces, NM

Margaret McKinley, Head, Serials Dept., University Library, University of California, Los Angeles, CA

Maria O'Neil McMahon, (deceased) Professor, School of Social Work, East Carolina University, Greenville, NC

Jean C. McManus, Asst. Reference Librarian, Tisch Library, Tufts University, Medford, MA

Lillian R. Mesner, Technical Services Librarian, Agricultural Library, University of Kentucky, Lexington, KY

Philip A. Metzger, Curator of Special Collections and Director, Lehigh University Press, Lehigh University, Bethlehem, PA

G. Douglas Meyers, Chair, Dept. of English, University of Texas, El Paso, TX

Jeffrey Meyers, Self-Employed Professional Worker, Kensington, CA

Bogdan Mieezkowski, Professor of Economics, Ithaca College, Ithaca, NY

Zbigniew Mieezkowski, (deceased) Assoc. Professor Dept. of Geography, University of Manitoba, Winnipeg, Canada

Bogdan Mieezkowaski, Professor of Economics, Ithaca College, Ithaca, NY

Jerome K. Miller, (deceased) President, Copyright Information Services, Friday Harbor, WA

Richard A. Miller, Director of Libraries, Florida Atlantic University, Boca Raton, FL

Shirley Miller.

Paul A. Mogren, Head of Reference, Marriott Library, University of Utah, Salt Lake City, UT

Terry Ann Mood, Assoc. Professor & Humanities Bibliographer, Auraria Library, University of Colorado at Denver, Denver, CO

Gerald D. Moran, Director, McCartney Library, Geneva College, Beaver Falls, PA

Michael Ann Moskowitz, Library Director, Emerson College, Boston, MA

K. Mulliner, Asst. to the Director of Libraries, Ohio University Library, Athens, OH

Craig A. Munsart, Teacher, Jefferson County Public Schools, Golden, CO

James M. Murray, Director, East Bonner Country Library, Sandpoint, ID

Necia A. Musser, Head, Acquisitions and Collection Development, Western Michigan University, Kalamazoo, MI

Linda A. Naru, Planning and Development Officer, Center for Research Libraries, Chicago, IL

Charles Neuringer, Professor of Psychology and Theatre and Film, University of Kansas, Lawrence, KS

Robert Neville, Asst. Director for Technical Services, College of Charleston Library, Charleston, SC

Danuta A. Nitecki, Assoc. University Librarian, Yale University, New Haven, CT

Eric R. Nitschke, Reference Librarian, Robert W. Woodruff Library, Emory University, Atlanta, GA

Christopher W. Nolan, Head, Reference Services, Maddux Library, Trinity University San Antonio, TX

Carol L. Noll, Plano, TX

Marilyn Strong Noronha, Reference Librarian, Harleigh B. Tracker Library, University of Connecticut, West Hartford, CT

Marshall E. Nunn, Professor, Dept. of History, Glendale Community College, Glendale, CA

Barbara J. O'Hara, Adult Services Librarian, Free Library of Philadelphia, Philadelphia, PA

Lawrence Olszewski, Manager, OCLC Information Center, Dublin, OH

John Howard Oxley, Halifax, Nova Scotia, Canada

Mark Padnos, Humanities Reference Librarian, Mina Rees Library, Graduate School and University Center, City University of New York, New York, NY

Roberta R. Palen.

Robert Palmieri, Professor Emeritus, School of Music, Kent State University, OH

Penny Papangelis, Health Sciences Librarian, Western Kentucky University, Bowling Green, KY

Jean M. Parker, Asst. Director, Rolvaag Memorial Library, St. Olaf College, Northfield, MN

Maureen Pastine, University Librarian, Paley Library, Temple University, Philadelphia, PA

Anna Grace Patterson, Staff, Libraries Unlimited, Inc., Englewood, CO

Elizabeth Patterson, Head, Reference and Computer Reference Services, Robert W. Woodruff Library, Emory University, Atlanta, GA

Thomas H. Patterson.

Gari-Anne Patzwald, Freelance Editor and Indexer, Lexington, KY

Harry E. Pence, Professor of Chemistry, State University of New York, Oneonta, N

Karin Pendle, Professor of Musicology, University of Cincinnati, Cincinnati, OH

Susan R. Penney, (formerly) Staff, Libraries Unlimited, Englewood, CO

Dennis J. Phillips, Head Librarian, Library Learning Resource Center, Pennsylvania State University, Fogelsville, PA

Edwin D. Posey, Engineering Librarian, Purdue University Libraries, West Lafayette, IN

Phillip P. Powell, Asst. Reference Librarian, Robert Scott Small Library, College of Charleston, Charleston, SC

Carl Pracht, Reference Librarian, Southeast Missouri State University, Cape Girardeau, MI

William S. Proudfoot, Asst. Librarian, Science Library, University of California, Santa Cruz, CA

Richard H. Quay, Social Science Librarian, Miami University Libraries, Oxford, OH

Randall Rafferty, Reference Librarian, Mississippi State University, MS

Varadaraja V. Raman, Professor of Physics and Humanities, Rochester Institute of Technology, Rochester, NY

Kristin Ramsdell, Assoc. Librarian, California State University, Hayward, CA

Octavia Porter Randolph, Architectural Scribe, Nahant, MA

Lisé Rasmussen, Reference Librarian, Dowling College, Oakdale, NY

Jack Ray, Asst. Director, Loyola/Notre Dame Library, Baltimore, MD

Ronald Rayman.

Nancy P. Reed, Media Specialist, St. Mary Middle/High School, Paducah, KY

Lorna K. Rees-Potter, Asst. Professor, Graduate School of Library and Information Studies, McGill University, Montreal, Canada

Shulamit Reinharz, Assoc. Professor, Dept. of Sociology and Director, Women's Studies, Brandeis University, Waltham, MA

James Rettig, Asst. Univ. Librarian for Reference and Information Services, Swern Library, College of William and Mary, Williamsburg, VA

Sara J. Richardson.

Philip R. Rider, Instructor of English, Northern Illinois University, De Kalb, IL

Anne F. Roberts, Adjunct Prof., School of Education, State University of New York, Albany, NY

Ilene F. Rockman, Assoc. Dean of Library Services, California Polytechnic State University, San Luis Obispo, CA

Antonio Rodriguez-Buckingham.

Anne C. Roess, Librarian, Peoples Gas, Light & Coke Co., Chicago, IL

Deborah V. Rollins, Reference Librarian, University of Maine, Orono, ME

Melissa Rae Root, Staff, Libraries Unlimited, Inc., Englewood, CO

David Rosenbaum, Reference Librarian, Education Library, Wayne State University Libraries, Detroit, MI

D. Aviva Rothschild, Independent Scholar, Freelance Editor, and Author, Aurora, CO

Louis R. Ruybal, Project Editor, ABC-Clio, Denver, CO

Laurie Saboll, Reference Librarian, Jerome Library, Bowling Green State University, Bowling Green, OH

Edmund F. SantaVicca, Librarian, Information Commons, Estrella Mountain Community College Center, Litchfield Park, AZ

Jay Schafer, Coordinator for Bibliographic Services, Auraria Library, University of Colorado at Denver, Denver, CO

Willa Schmidt, Reference Librarian, University of Wisconsin, Madison, WI

John P. Schmitt, Librarian, Regis University Library, Denver, CO

Isabel Schon, Director, Center for the Study of Books in Spanish, California State University, San Marcos, CA

L. L. Schroyer, Professor, University Libraries, Northern Illinois University, De Kalb, IL

Eleanor Elving Schwartz.

LeRoy C. Schwarzkopf, (formerly) Government Documents Librarian, University of Maryland, College Park, MD

Ralph Lee Scott, Assoc. Professor, East Carolina University Library, Greenville, NC

Robert A. Seal, University Librarian, Texas Christian University Library, Fort Worth, TX

Cathy Seitz.

Ravindra Nath Sharma, Library Director, West Virginia State College, Institute, WV

Bruce A. Shuman, Adjunct Professor, University of South Florida, Tampa, FL

Kari Sidles.

Stephanie C. Sigala, Head Librarian, Richardson Memorial Library, St. Louis Art Museum, St. Louis, MO

Linda Keir Simons, Head of Client Services, University of Dayton Library, Dayton, OH

Esther R. Sinofsky, Library Media Teacher, Alexander Hamilton High School, Los Angeles, CA

Robert Skinner, Technology Development Librarian, Central University Libraries, Southern Methodist University, Dallas, TX

Jeanette C. Smith, Head, Government Documents, New Mexico State University Library, Las Cruces, NM

John David Smith, Alumni Distinguished Professor of History, North Carolina State University, Raleigh, NC

Mary Ellen Snodgrass, Freelance Writer, Charlotte, NC

Miluse A. Soudek.

Lawrence E. Spellman.

Paul H. Spence.

Howard Spring, Asst. Professor, University of Guelph, Ontario, Canada

Steven J. Squires, Bibliographic Access Librarian, Health Sciences Library, University of North Carolina, Chapel Hill, NC

Karen Y. Stabler, Head of Information Services, New Mexico State University Library, Las Cruces, NM

Kay M. Stebbins, Coordinator Librarian, Louisiana State University, Baton Rouge, LA
James Edgar Stephenson, Cataloger, Society of the Cincinnati Library, Washington, DC
Norman D. Stevens, Director Emeritus, University of Connecticut Libraries, Storrs, CT
John P. Stierman, Reference Librarian, Western Illinois University, Macomb, IL
John W. Storey, Professor of History, Lamar University, Beaumont, TX
Bruce Stuart, Professor and Parke-Davis Chair, University of Maryland at Baltimore, Baltimore, MD
Mila C. Su, Senior Assistant Librarian, Pennsylvania State University, Altoona, PA
Timothy E. Sullivan, Asst. Professor of Economics, Towson State University, MD
Richard H. Swain, Reference Librarian, West Chester University, West Chester, PA
James H. Sweetland, Assoc. Professor, School of Library and Information Science, University of Wisconsin, Milwaukee, WI
Nigel Tappin, (formerly) General Librarian North York Public Library, Ontario, Canada
Deborah A. Taylor, Staff, Libraries Unlimited, Englewood, CO
Warren G. Taylor, Manager, Office of Facilities Use, Auraria Higher Education Center, Denver, CO
Glynys R. Thomas, Sawyer Library, Suffolk University, Boston, MA
Paul H. Thomas, Head, Catalog Dept., Hoover Institution Library, Stanford University, CA
Christine E. Thompson, Head, Catalog Dept. and Assoc. Professor, University of Alabama Libraries, Tuscaloosa, AL
Angela Marie Thor, Librarian, Simmons Institute of Funeral Service, Syracuse, NY
Peter Thorpe, Professor Emeritus, University of Colorado at Denver, Denver, CO
Bruce H. Tiffney, Assoc. Professor of Geology and Biological Sciences, University of California, Santa Barbara, CA
Cheryl Todd-Simirenko.
Andrew G. Torok, Assoc. Professor, Northern Illinois University, De Kalb, IL
John U. Trefny, Head and Professor, Dept. of Physics, Colorado School of Mines, Golden, CO
Carol Truett, Assoc. Professor, Appalachian State University, Boone, NC
John Mark Tucker, Senior Reference Librarian, Humanities, Social Science and Education Library, Purdue University, West Lafayette, IN
Dean Tudor, Professor, School of Journalism, Ryerson Polytechnical Institute, Toronto, Canada
Elias H. Tuma, Professor of Economics, University of California, Davis, CA
Robert L. Turner, Jr., Librarian and Asst. Professor, Radford University, Radford, VA
Michele Tyrrell, Media Specialist, Arundel Senior High School, Gambrills, MD
Daniel Uchitelle, Manager, Online and Special Services, Modern Language Association, New York, NY
Felix Emer Unaeze, Head, Reference and Instructional Services, Timme Library, Ferris State University, Big Rapids, MI
Arthur R. Upgren, Professor of Astronomy and Director, Van Vleck Observatory, Wesleyan University, Middletown, CT
Judith A. Valdez, Reference Librarian, Auraria Library, University of Colorado at Denver, Denver, CO
Robert F. Van Benthuysen, Library Director, Monmouth College, West Long Branch, NJ
Vandelia L. VanMeter, Assoc. Professor and Library Director, Spalding University, Louisville, KY

Carole Franklin Vidali, Adjunct Asst. Professor, Dept. of Fine Arts, Syracuse University, NY

Dario J. Villa, Reference Librarian/Bibliographer, Ronald Williams Library, Northeastern Illinois University, Chicago, IL

Kathleen J. Voigt, Head, Reference Dept., Carlson Library, University of Toledo, Toledo, OH

Bridget Volz, Freelance Librarian and Weaver, Denver, CO

Ed Volz, Staff, Libraries Unlimited, Inc., Englewood, CO

Louis Vyhnanek, Reference Librarian, Holland Library, Washington State University, Pullman, WA

David V. Waller, Asst. Professor of Sociology, Dept. of Sociology and Anthropology, University of Texas, Arlington, TX

Jeff Wanser, Coordinator, Reference and Government Documents, Hiram College Library, Hiram College, OH

Lydia W. Wasylenko, Assoc. Librarian, Syracuse University Library, Syracuse University, Syracuse, NY

J. E. Weaver, Dept. of Economics, Drake University, Des Moines, IA

Bruce H. Webb, Librarian/Asst. Professor, Rena M. Carlson Library, Clarion University of Pennsylvania, PA

Michael Weinberg, Reference Librarian, Ronald Williams Library, Northeastern Illinois Library, Chicago, IL

Lynda Welborn, Director of Libraries, Colorado Academy, Denver, CO

Erwin K. Welsch.

Emily L. Werrell, Reference/Instructional Services Librarian, Northern Kentucky University, Highland Heights, KY

Lucille Whalen, Dean of Graduate Programs, Immaculate Heart College Center, Los Angeles, CA

Carol Wheeler, Government Documents Reference Librarian, University of Georgia Libraries, Athens, GA

Cathy Seitz Whitaker, (formerly) Social Work Librarian Hillman Library, University of Pittsburgh, Pittsburgh, PA

Marilyn Domas White, Assoc. Professor, College of Library and Information Services, University of Maryland, College Park, MD

Robert L. Wick, Asst. Professor & Fine Arts Bibliographer, Auraria Library, University of Colorado at Denver, Denver, CO

Wayne A. Wiegand, Professor, History Dept., Appalachian State University, Boone, NC

Albert Wilhelm, Professor of English, Tennessee Technological University, Cookeville, TN

Lynn F. Williams, Professor, Div. of Writing, Literature, and Publishing, Emerson College, Boston, MA

Wiley J. Williams, Professor Emeritus, School of Library Science, Kent State University, OH

Frank L. Wilson, Professor and Head, Dept. of Political Science, Purdue University, West Lafayette, IN

Wayne Wilson, Director, Research and Library Services, Amateur Athlete Foundation, Los Angeles, CA

Patty Wood.

Raymund F. Wood, Editor, *The Westerners,* Encino, CA

Ross Wood, Music Librarian, Wellesley College, MA

Hensley C. Woodbridge, Professor of Spanish, Dept. of Foreign Languages, Southern Illinois University, Carbondale, IL

Anna T. Wynar, Certified Rehabilitation Counselor, Ravenna, OH

Bohdan S. Wynar, Staff, Libraries Unlimited, Inc., Englewood, CO

Christine L. Wynar.

Lubomyr R. Wynar, Professor, School of Library Science and Director, Center for Ethnic Studies, Kent State University, OH

Virginia E. Yagello, Head, Chemistry, Perkins Observatory and Physics Libraries, Ohio State University, Columbus, OH

Eveline L. Yang, Interlibrary-Loan Librarian, Auraria Library, University of Colorado at Denver, Denver, CO

Hope Yelich, Reference Librarian, Earl Gregg Swem Library, College of William and Mary, Williamsburg, VA

Mark R. Yerburgh, Library Director, Trinity College, Burlington, VT

Henry E. York, Head, Collection Management, Cleveland State University, Cleveland, OH

Arthur P. Young, Director, Northern Illinois Libraries, Northern Illinois University, De Kalb, IL

Ahmet Yücel, Manager of Operations, OEA, Inc., Denver, CO

Louis G. Zelenka, Public Services Librarian, Southwest Georgia Regional Library, Bainbridge, GA

Magda Zelinska-Feri, Professor/Faculty Advisor, Union Institute, Los Angeles, CA

Susan Zernial, Staff, Libraries Unlimited, Englewood, CO

Oleg Zinam, (deceased) Professor of Economics, University of Cincinnati, OH

Anita Zutis, Adjunct Librarian, Queensborough Community Collete, Bayside, NY

Introduction

Part I, **International and National Biographies**, is the smaller of the two parts of this book. The chapter on international sources is divided into "current" and "retrospective" biographies, but this designation is somewhat arbitrary. A number of the works included contain both current and retrospective biographies, making it difficult to place them in current or retrospective sections; in these cases, it has been determined which category dominates the work, and it was placed in that section. The chapter **National and Regional Sources** is divided by geographical area, and more than 20 countries or geographical areas are included. In cases where a country has many biographical dictionaries written on its people, further subdivisions have been used, such as Great Britain and the Commonwealth, with subdivisions of General Works, Current Biographies, Retrospective Biographies, Ireland, and Northern Ireland.

Because indexes to biographical sources are not included, it is important to point out some significant sources for locating biographical materials in general. Of course, two major sources are *Books in Print* and OCLC's *FirstSearch* (online), which both provide in-depth listings of biographical sources. Also, *American Reference Books Annual (ARBA)* (Libraries Unlimited, 1970-), the basic source for this volume, provides one of the most in-depth listings of biographical sources available. In addition, a number of other sources for biographies that will be of use include *Index to Who's Who Books* (Marquis Who's Who/Reed Publishing, 1992. 476p. $79.50. ISBN 0-8379-1429-9), which contains more than 379,000 entries for biographical sketches published in various Marquis Who's Who publications; *Biography: An Annotated Bibliography* by Carl Rollyson (Salem Press, 1992. 215p. $40.00. ISBN 0-89356-678-0), which surveys and annotates the literature of biography in English; and the *Biography Index: A Cumulative Index to Biographical Material in Books and Magazines* (H. W. Wilson 1946-), which provides a yearly update of biographical information found in more than 2,500 periodicals indexed by H. W. Wilson and of current books, including juvenile. Also, the *Biography Index* is now available on CD-ROM (H. W. Wilson, 1991- . Requirements: IBM or compatible, ISO 9660 compatible CD-ROM drive with interface cards, MS-DOS CD-ROM extensions 2.0 or later, 640K RAM and 1.2MB hard disk space. $1,260.00 for 1995 edition), which contains the same basic information as the paper edition but allows for advanced searching techniques including personal name, subject, and browse by an unlimited number of search terms. Finally, the *World Biographical Index, Internationaler Biographischer Index*, 2d ed. CD-ROM (K. G. Saur/Reed Reference Electronic Publishing, 1995 Requirements: IBM or compatible, ISO 9660 compatible CD-ROM drive with interface cards, Windows 3.1. 4 MB RAM, 5MB hard disk space. $1,235.00), provides biographical information on more than 1,700 reference works from the late sixteenth to the early twentieth centuries in English, Spanish, French, Italian, and German. Two additional biographical sources, now somewhat older but still of significance, include the *Current Biography Cumulated Index 1940–1990* (see entry 5 for review of *Current Biography*), which provides indexing to more than 15,000 biographies included in *Current Biography* during the 46 years from its founding to publication in 1985, and the *International Bibliography of Biography 1970 to 1987* (K. G. Saur, 1988. 4pts. $2500.00/set. ISBN 0-86291-750-6), which offers a subject, author, and title approach to over 100,000 monographic biographies and autobiographies.

There are also some important indexes that provide access to more retrospective biographies, including *Biography and Genealogy Master Index 1986: A Consolidated Index to More Than 255,000 Biographical Sketches in over 35 Current and Retrospective Biographical Dictionaries*, CD-ROM (Gale, 1993. Requirements: IBM PC or compatible, MS-DOS or PC-DOS 3.1 or higher, MS-DOS CD-ROM, 640K RAM, hard disk with 1MB free. $1,2500.00 [1st year]; $350.00/yr. ISBN 0-8103-4965-5), which allows for advanced searching by name and other additional entry points, and *Biographical Dictionaries and Related Works: An International Bibliography of More Than 16,000*

Collective Biographies, Biobibliographies, Collections of Epitaphs ... (Gale, 1986, 2 vols. $140.00/set. ISBN 0-8103-0234-8), which is the first full revision of the work first published in 1967 and updated with two supplements in 1972 and 1978, which provides access to biographical information in more than 12,094 titles, and includes 16,000 sources. Finally, an additional source of note is the *Index to Biographies for Young Readers* (R. R. Bowker, 1988, 494p. $34.95, ISBN 0-8352-2348-5), which is a valuable source for biographical materials written for children that includes listings of more than 9,000 individuals.

Indexes to biographies on a national and regional level are less prominent but a number of important works stand out, including, of course, the *British Biographical Index* (K. G. Saur, 1990. 4v. $995.00/set. ISBN 0-86291-390-X),which provides more than 170,000 biographies on personalities who lived in Britain between 1601 and 1926. Also, there are indexes covering Canadians and Chinese, represented by the *Dictionary of Canadian Biography: Index: Volumes I to XII, 1000 to 1900* (University of Toronto Press, 1991. 557p. $85.00. ISBN 0-8020-3464-0), which indexes the 12 volumes of the *Dictionary of Canadian Biography* and covers biographies of more than 6,000 Canadians, and the *Biographical Dictionary of Republican China* (vols. 1-5) (Columbia University Press, 1979. $50.00. ISBN 0-231-08958-9), which concentrates on the period 1911 through 1949 and includes 600 biographies. A number of biographical indexes cover Americans. Several important publications indexing biographical dictionaries contained later in this book include the *Dictionary of American Biography: Comprehensive Index: Complete Through Supplement Eight* (Scribner's, 1990, 1001p. $85.00, ISBN 0-684-19114-8), which is the index to the *Dictionary of American Biography* (*DAB*) and provides indexing for all 18,110 biographical entries. *Who's Who in America Indexes* (covering 1898 on), provides access to these annual volumes that are among the most important biographical sources for Americans. Also, *Who Was Who in America with World Notables: Index, 1607-1985, Volumes I-VIII and Historical Volume* (Marquis Who's Who, 1985. 260p. $34.00. ISBN 0-8379-0215-0) provides an index to this work and provides 112,000 biographical sketches. The *St. James Guide to Biography* (St. James Press, 1991, 870p. $125.00, ISBN 1-55862-146-6) indexes the *St. James Guide to Biography* and provides access to just over 700 signed reviews included there. Finally, the *Index to Who's Who Books* (Marquis Who's Who Series) provides access to several of the Marquis titles, including *Who's Who in the World*; *American Law*; *Entertainment*; *Finance and Industry*; *Who's Who of Emerging Leaders in America*; *American Women*; *Who Was Who in America*, and others. This work is published yearly, and the latest compilation covering 1986-1990 indexes nearly 2 million entries in 250 biographical sources.

Though general encyclopedias are not included in the *ARBA Guide to Biographical Resources*, there are several of these works that provide important biographical information. *The Encyclopedia Americana* (Grolier, 1989. 30v. $1,200.00/set. ISBN 0-7172-0120-1) contains more than 1,130 biographical entries. Both *Academic American Encyclopedia* and *Concise Columbia Encyclopedia* are excellent sources for biographies, and of course, *Encyclopaedia Britannica* can be an important source for biographical information worldwide.

There are a total of 121 sources in Part I, **International and National Biographies**, with the chapter **International Sources** containing 52 (15 current and 38 retrospective), and the chapter **National and Regional Sources** containing 68, divided into various countries and regions. Current international biographical sources include a number of important sources, such as *Who's Who: An Annual Biographical Dictionary* (St. Martin's Press, 1949-), which provides more than 29,000 separate biographical entries of persons in all walks of life worldwide; *Current Biography Yearbook* (H. W. Wilson, 1940-) (see entry 5), which provides a yearly list of biographies of artists, politicians, business people, journalists, actors, authors, scientists, and other people who have made the headlines; and *Encyclopedia of World Biography* (Jack Heraty & Associates, 1987-88) (see entry 7), which was first published in 1973 and is now updated with more than 900 entries of some 950 subjects. Some additional sources of particular interest include *Earl Blackwell's Celebrity Register 1990* (Detroit, Gale, 1990) (see entry 6), which is a register of brief essays on well-known personalities; the *People in the News* series (Macmillan, 1994) (see entry 4), for which each volume profiles approximately 700 people worldwide whose accomplishments have made the mainstream news. Also, *Current World Leaders Almanac* (Academy at Santa Barbara, 1957-) (see entry 5a), which has been published since 1957, provides biographies of important world leaders.

There are also a number of important sources in the retrospective sections, including *The Cambridge Biographical Dictionary* (Cambridge University Press, 1996) (see entry 18), which includes more than 15,000 brief biographies of important figures in all walks of life worldwide; *A Dictionary of Twentieth Century World Biography* (Oxford University Press, 1992) (see entry 23), which includes an astonishing 1,750 people who have gained prominence in the twentieth century; *The HarperCollins Dictionary of Biography* (HarperCollins, 1994) (see entry 28), which contains more than 8,000 biographical entries; and the *Merriam-Webster's Biographical Dictionary* (Merriam-Webster, 1995) (see entry 32), which provides an inexpensive, single-volume biographical dictionary of notable figures worldwide. There are several additional sources of particular interest in the section on retrospective international biographies, including *Nobel Prize Winners* (H. W. Wilson, 1997) (see entry 35), which provides the names of all Nobel Prize winners from the beginning of the award to the present; *Born This Day: A Daily Celebration of Famous Beginnings* (Citadel Press/Carol Publishing Group, 1995) (see entry 34), which lists famous and not-so-famous individuals who were born on each calendar day, along with brief biographies; and *Icons: An A-Z Guide to the People Who Shaped Our Time* (Collier Books/Macmillan, 1991) (see entry 37), which provides an offbeat and unusual list of biographies of individuals who influenced the twentieth century.

In addition, the chapter **National and Regional Sources** contains biographical dictionaries including individuals of various countries and regions around the world. The countries covered include Africa (with 7 sources), Asia and the Pacific Rim (with 1 source), Australia and New Zealand (with 3 sources), Canada (with 4 sources), Europe (with 2 sources), France (with 1 source), Great Britain and the Commonwealth (with 12 sources), India (with 2 sources), Iran (with 1 source), Italy (with 1 source), Japan (with 1 source), Latin America (with 1 source), Lebanon (with 1 source), Mexico (with 1 source), the Middle East (with 2 sources), Newfoundland and Labrador (with 1 source), People's Republic of China (with 2 sources), Romania (with 1 source), Russia and CIS Republic (with 6 sources), Spain (with 1 source), and the United States (with 21 sources). Several works merit special mention, including the recently published *An African Biographical Dictionary* (ABC-CLIO, 1994) (see entry 53), which provides biographical sketches for nearly 500 people who are prominent in sub-Saharan Africa; *Australian Dictionary of Biography* (International Scholarly Book Services, 1966-) (see entry 61), which is still in progress and is projected to be a 12-volume compilation of biographical sketches that will cover thousands of Australians; the monumental *Dictionary of Canadian Biography* (University of Toronto Press, 1994) (see entry 65), which was begun in 1966 and covers from the sixteenth century to the present; the 148-year-old *Who's Who: An Annual Biographical Dictionary* [Great Britain and the Commonwealth] (St. Martin's Press, 1849-) (see entry 73), which continues to be a major source for British biographical information; the multivolumed *Dictionary of National Biography* [Great Britain] (Oxford University Press), which is probably the most impressive biographical series ever published, *Who's Who in Japan* (CRC Press, 1984/85-) (see entry 85), which provides brief biographical information on more than 27,000 Japanese in all walks of life, *Who's Who in Mexico Today* (Westview Press, 1993) (see entry 88), which provides an impressive number of biographies of Mexican citizens in English; and *Who's Who in the Arab World* (Publitec Publications/Gale, 1966-) (see entry 90), which includes profiles of individuals in several Arab countries.

The coverage of the United States is represented by a number of well-known and important biographical sources of living persons, including several Marquis publications: *Who's Who in America*, *Who's Who in the East*, *Who's Who in the Midwest*, *Who's Who in the West*, and *Who's Who of Emerging Leaders in America*. The Marquis publications began more than 20 years ago, follow similar formats, and remain among the most important biographical sources on Americans. For retrospective biographies, an important source remains the *Dictionary of American Biography* (Scribner's) series (see entry115), which is an indispensable biographical tool and provides more than 20,000 biographical sketches.

Finally, more unusual biographical sources may be found in the **National and Regional Sources**. Books covering individuals the compilers consider "great" or "outstanding" abound, including *100 Great Africans* (Scarecrow, 1994) (see entry 57), which contains chapters titled "Saints and Sinners," "The Golden Kings," and "Hannibal and Rome," among others; *Great Britons: Twentieth-Century Lives* (Oxford University Press, 1985) (see entry 71), which provides short biographies of individuals by occupation and interests; and *Longman Biographical Directory of Decision-Makers in Russia and the Successor States* (Detroit, Gale, 1993) (see entry 95), which provides brief biographical sketches on decision makers in Russia and the successor states, listing some 600-700 individuals. Also, obituaries are found in *The Canadian Obituary Record: A Biographical Dictionary of Canadians Who Died in 1992* (Dundurn Press, 1993) (see entry 66), which is published annually and provides approximately 500 obituaries.

PART I
International and National Biographies

1 International Sources

CURRENT BIOGRAPHIES

1. Andersen, Christopher P. **The New Book of People: Photographs, Capsule Biographies and Vital Statistics of over 500 Celebrities**. New York, Perigee Books/Putnam, 1986. 463p. illus. index. $13.95pa. LC 85-25862. ISBN 0-399-51223-3.

The foreword to *The New Book of People* (the first *BoP* was published in 1981) states that its purpose is to answer "compelling" questions such as: "How much do they make? What do they spend it on? Whom do they sleep with? How do they live?" Compiled from an edition of *People* magazine, *The New Book of People* is a checkout-line version of a current biographical dictionary. Those included call to mind Cleveland Amory's introduction to the *Celebrity Register*, a similarly gossipy work, in which he defines a celebrity as "a name which, once made by news, now makes news by itself." Media personalities and film and rock stars dominate the 500-plus entries. Each alphabetical entry includes a paragraph describing the highs and lows of the individual's career and personal life, followed by a list of "factual" data ranging from birth date, height, weight, and hair and eye color to habits (a category including information on food, beverage and drug preferences, number of facelifts, etc.), marriages, religion, and income. Most include a photograph, and all include one (usually outrageous) quotation by the subject.

Marquis's *Who's Who, Current Biography,* and *Biography Index* collectively provide access to a more dependable compilation of biographical information on the currently famous; however, for the avid reader of *People, US,* and other periodicals of that ilk, *The New Book of People* may indeed be preferable. As it is relatively inexpensive as biographical reference works go, it is recommended, with reservations, for public library collections. [R: RBB, 15 Nov 86, p. 495]—**Diane J. Cimbala**

2. **Biography Today: Profiles of People of Interest to Young Readers**. Volume 1, Issue 1- . Laurie Lanzen Harris, ed. Detroit, Omnigraphics, 1992- . illus. index. $10.00pa. (4 issues/yr.); $39.50 (cumulative). ISSN 1058-2347.

This quarterly provides short, interestingly written biographies of celebrities, primarily for the use of school children. It has a mixture of individuals of lasting importance and others who are currently enjoying what Andy Warhol termed their "15 minutes" of fame. This 1st issue contains 29 profiles and a list of future subjects. The great majority are actors, athletes, authors, and musicians. Each profile, a few of which are autobiographical, is accompanied by a photograph and an address where the celebrity can be contacted. The magazine-format reference book provides basic information and the subjects' own views on their lives, without avoiding controversy. The editor does not take sides; for example, the account of Clarence Thomas's confirmation hearings in the Senate mentions Anita Hill's allegations of sexual harassment, but it does not attempt to defend or attack either side's stand. Many of the biographees can be found in other sources, but the choice of celebrities profiled and the tone taken in the essays make *Biography Today* particularly appropriate for young readers. [R: RBB, 15 June 92, p. 1880]—**David Lonergan and Robert L. Wick**

3. Browne, Ray B., with Glenn J. Browne et al. **Contemporary Heroes and Heroines**. Detroit, Gale, 1990. 451p. illus. index. $49.95. ISBN 0-8103-4860-8.

This book reminds us that the world abounds with great people doing wonderful things to improve society. In concise, well-written biographical sketches, Browne presents almost 100 people, principally from the twentieth century. Individuals such as Billy Graham, Jackie Joyner-Kersee, Helen Keller, Anne Frank, and Desmond Tutu are included. Each sketch begins with an excellent photograph followed by several pages of biographical information that gives an analysis of the person's contribution to society. Accomplishments are not blown out of proportion or described didactically. Several books and periodical sources for further information are included at the end of each sketch.

Written in a clear style with easy-to-read type, *Heroes* will appeal to junior and senior high school students and adults who want to spend a pleasurable hour associating with great contemporaries. For libraries not subscribing to *Current Biography,* this volume might come in handy although its price is high. Perhaps it will be best used by reluctant or below-average readers who need quick, uncomplicated information on modern heroes. [R: RBB, 1 May 90, p. 1732; RQ, Fall 90, pp. 110-12; WLB, May 90, p. 124]—**David V. Loertscher**

4. Brownstone, David, and Irene Franck. **People in the News 1994**. New York, Macmillan, 1994. 442p. illus. index. $75.00. CT120.B76. 920. LC 91-14962. ISBN 0-02-897057-8. ISSN 1062-2713.

This volume profiles some 700 persons worldwide whose 1993 accomplishments, notoriety, or death attracted coverage by America's mainstream news media. Notables include such disparate figures as Paula Abdul, Stephen Hawking, and John Gotti. About one-third of the articles include a photograph of the subject. Entries conclude with a list of supplemental readings, mainly drawn from recent issues of popular magazines. Two cumulative indexes—by surname and occupation—complete the work. Because of the greater number of newly compiled and updated sketches in an annual volume modest in heft and cost, *People in the News* (*PIN*) does not provide as thorough biographical treatment as *Newsmakers, Current Biography,* and the infrequently published *Earl Blackwell's Celebrity Register.* Articles have balance, and no factual errors are apparent.

Celebrity achieved through victimization usually excludes candidates from consideration (e.g., the Bobbitts, Gennifer Flowers, female Citadel enrollee Shanon Faulkner). *PIN* intentionally shuns those icons, superstars, and glitterati who have slipped from regular public view (e.g., Bob Hope, George Wallace, Saul Bellow, Mark Harmon, Jimmy Stewart). However, a number of headliners from sports are unaccountably absent, such as Paul Molitor, Andres Galarraga, Chris Webber, Julie Krone, Oksana Baiul, and Jerry Jones. Also omitted are obituaries of racers Davey Allison and Alan Kulwicki.

The exclusion of celebrities' addresses is a definite minus; also, it would be helpful if obituary entries were separately indexed. This book is a marginal purchase, useful only for libraries lacking two or more of the rival publications cited above. [R: BR, Jan/Feb 95, p. 59]—**Jeffrey E. Long**

5. **Current Biography Yearbook**. Bronx, N.Y., H. W. Wilson, 1940- . illus. index. $72.00 for recent edition. LC 40-25432. ISSN 0084-9499.

Current Biography has been published as a monthly journal each year since 1940. In recent issues it provides biographies on artists, politicians, business people, journalists, actors, authors, sports figures, scientists, and other people who have made headlines, or who have been prominent in their field of endeavor during the past year. It is published every month except December. The *Current Biography Yearbook* is published yearly and based on the monthly issues of *Current Biography.*

Each entry includes date of birth, an address for contacting the individual (usually the publisher or publicist), the profession or occupation, a biographical sketch, and a picture of the subject. The biographical articles tend to be about three pages long and are generally well written. There are references at the end indicating where the information was obtained, e.g., printed sources, personal interview, etc. Since the 1990 edition there has been an alphabetical list of the individuals included in the front making it easier to locate biographies. Each volume includes a list of obituaries for individuals included in previous volumes, and an index. There is also a pronunciation key and a key to abbreviations. A separate publication: *Current Biography Cumulated Index 1940-1990* (Jill Kadetsky, ed. Bronx, N. Y., H. W. Wilson, 1991. 133p. $25.00. LC 40-27432. ISBN 0-8242-0722-X) (see ARBA 92, entry 58) provides an index from the beginning of the series.—**Robert L. Wick**

5a. **Current World Leaders Almanac**. Santa Barbara, Calif., International Academy at Santa Barbara, 1957- . $245.00pa./yr. for recent edition. (4-year colleges/universities, corporate libraries); $190.00pa./yr. (2-year colleges, public libraries, high schools, individuals). ISSN 0192-6802.

Current World Leaders has been published since 1957, and since 1981 has consisted of two parts, each alternately issued three times a year. There is the *Almanac* (issued in February, June, and

October), *International Issues* (issued in April, August, and December, and formerly entitled *Biography & News/Speeches & Reports*), which contains original articles on a broad topic, along with a cumulative index. The major portion of the almanac, "National Governments" (191 of them), gives the name of the state/government, the ministers, and other important officials, with addresses and telephone numbers of the country's top leaders and the embassy in Washington, D.C. Also included are selected vital statistics regarding the economy, demographics, religion, and so on, and membership in international organizations. The "area" line compares the country to some portion of the United States.

In addition, there are directory sections for 35 major international organizations and "Colonies and Dependent Territories" (numbering 29), plus a list of acronyms and abbreviations. Information is mostly obtained from official sources; those items culled from the international news media are indicated with asterisks. The International Academy at Santa Barbara (est. 1960; e-mail: iasb@igc.org; http://www.isab.org/intacad/) promotes interdisciplinary research in the social sciences and international relations and has recently been involved in environmental research.

The price for this work is steep, but one is paying for an updating service to keep the information current. Many libraries probably already own other standard annual sources, such as the (more expensive) *Europa World Year Book* (see ARBA 94, entry 82), *The CIA World Factbook* (see ARBA 95, entry 8), and *The World Almanac* (see ARBA 95, entry 6). This work is suitable for those libraries not owning or not able to afford the more expensive sources.—**Daniel K. Blewett and Robert L. Wick**

6. **Earl Blackwell's Celebrity Register 1990**. Compiled by Celebrity Services International, Inc. Detroit, Gale, 1990. 484p. illus. index. $80.00. LC 85-51472. ISBN 0-8103-6875-7.

Previously published in 1959, 1963, 1973, and 1986, this register is a simple alphabetical list of brief essays on well-known personalities. Although "celebrity" is not defined, entries are predominantly American (with some European) entertainers and sports figures, although some politicians, businessmen, literary figures, and similar individuals are included. Some omissions, however, are curious. George Bush, the Reagans, and Richard Nixon are listed, yet Margaret Thatcher and Mikhael Gorbachev are not to be found. The entries are not uniform in style and tend to be chatty, often with quotations from the celebrity. Each entry is accompanied by a photograph, but no address is given. The index is cumulative for all the previous volumes.

The entries often seem more appropriate to a fan magazine, and the lack of addresses is a drawback. However, the register does provide information about some personalities who are often ignored by standard biographical directories or are too new to be included elsewhere. Therefore, the book would be helpful in a collection serving those interested in entertainment, sports, and popular culture. [R: LJ, 1 Oct 90, p. 123; RBB, 15 Oct 90, p. 468]—**Barbara E. Kemp**

7. **Encyclopedia of World Biography. 20th Century Supplement. Volume 13: A-F**. David Eggenberger, ed.-in-chief. Palatine, Ill., Jack Heraty & Associates, 1987. 518p. illus. $85.00. LC 86-63173. ISBN 0-910081-02-6.

> **Encyclopedia of World Biography. 20th Century Supplement. Volume 14: G-M**. David Eggenberger, ed.-in-chief. Palatine, Ill., Jack Heraty, 1987. 544p. illus. maps. $249.50/set (3 vols.). LC 86-63173. ISBN 0-910081-02-6.

> **Encyclopedia of World Biography. 20th Century Supplement. Volume 15: N-Z**. David Eggenberger, ed.-in-chief. Palatine, Ill., Jack Heraty, 1988. 598p. illus. maps. $249.50/set (3 vols.). LC 86-63173. ISBN 0-910081-02-6.

When first published in 1973, the original twelve-volume edition of the *Encyclopedia of World Biography* was rather well received. Popular demand for additional articles on contemporary world figures, the publishers of *EWB* maintain, has been responsible for a four-volume supplement featuring individuals of the present century—three volumes of text divided alphabetically (A through F, G through M, N through Z), and a fourth volume consisting of study guides and an index. Subjects were judiciously selected because of the impact they have had thus far in this century and the influence they will continue to exert well into the next century.

The supplement is meant to serve both as a self-contained reference tool and to enhance the overall usefulness of the *EWB* itself. Its format, style, and design accord with the appearance of the basic encyclopedia, and like all *EWB* entries, each biography was newly planned, written by one of 400 academic experts or other specialists, and illustrated with a photograph or drawing of the subject. Biographies of painters, sculptors, architects, and photographers contain an illustration of the artist's work. Accompanying the entries of individuals from the Third World are helpful locator maps to show the approximate position and relative size of the subject's country.

This first supplemental volume, A through F, contains some 300 of the total 950 subjects making up the complete supplement. Each entry is about 1,000 words in length and is enhanced by a final "Further Reading" paragraph keyed to one or more of the study guides and to related biographies within the supplement. Following each entry is a bibliographic essay of some 200 words for the reader intent upon pursuing the subject further. Of special interest is the large number of women included from the arts, the sciences, and other areas of human endeavor who have often been seriously neglected or insufficiently recognized.

While hardly essential to large university collections, where much of this biographical material is readily available in other standard reference works, this supplement can be warmly recommended to secondary schools and public libraries, for it is certain to be put to frequent use.—**G. A. Cevasco and Robert L. Wick**

8.   **The International Who's Who**. London, Europa; distr., Detroit, Gale, 1935- . $275.00 for recent edition. LC 35-10257. ISSN 0074-9613.

Considered a reliable reference source throughout the world, *The International Who's Who 1994-95* has once again brought together many gifted contemporaries. The work is now in its 58th edition and is often the only source for individuals in some countries. There are more than 20,000 entries in this edition, including 700 new entries for famous people from practically every country of the world. The list includes distinguished personalities in every field, including heads of state; religious leaders; diplomats; politicians; ambassadors; business officials; doctors; lawyers; and leading personalities of film, music, sports, fashion, media, literature, and the performing arts.

The book is arranged in alphabetical order. Each entry includes name, date of birth, nationality, career details, honors received by the person, current address, telephone number, place of birth, parentage, marital status, children, and leisure interests. Royal families are listed in a separate section. The book includes a list of people whose names appeared in the last edition of the book, but who have since died. A majority of the countries of the world have been represented.

This excellent book is perhaps the best single source for obtaining brief information about the famous and influential humans of the world. Highly recommended for all types of libraries. —**Ravindra Nath Sharma and Robert L. Wick**

9.   **Newsmakers 1994: The People Behind Today's Headlines**. Louise Mooney Collins, ed. Detroit, Gale, 1994. 4v. (subscription includes 3 quarterly paperback issues and 1 cumulative hardback). illus. index. $95.00/yr. ISBN 0-8103-8560-0.

Newsmakers, which was renamed from *Contemporary Newsmakers* with the 1988 edition, uses a format resembling that of *Current Biography*. The quarterly frequency of this title enhances its value by providing relatively current information regarding names and personalities in a variety of venues: business, education, technology, law, politics, religion, entertainment, labor, sports, medicine, and other fields. Entries are arranged alphabetically, with an average of 30 new biographees included in each quarterly issue. In addition, obituaries appear in a separate section, detailing the achievements of those noteworthy individuals who are recently deceased.

Information presented for biographees includes vital personal statistics, accompanied by address; a description of career and sidelights; a list of honors and awards; a list of works by and about the individual; and sources for further information. A photograph of the individual (or group) is also included. Essays are quite readable and informative, presenting the basic information one might expect in a brief profile (1,500-3,000 words).

Most school, public, and academic libraries should seriously consider this serial as an addition to the ready-reference collection. Students, instructors, and the general public will find value in the information presented. As necessary, information can be supplemented through electronic sources.—**Edmund F. Santa Vicca and Robert L. Wick**

10. **Notable Hispanic American Women**. Diane Telgren and Jim Kamp, eds. Detroit, Gale, 1993. 448p. illus. index. $59.95. E184.S75N68. 920.72'089'68073. LC 92-42483. ISBN 0-8103-7578-8.

As part of a new series of books from Gale, which includes *Who's Who Among Hispanic Americans* (see ARBA 92, entry 357), *Hispanic Americans Information Directors* (see ARBA 93, entry 428), and *The Hispanic-American Almanac* (1993), this attractively designed work contains 300 biographical sketches of prominent women. Represented are women of Mexican, Puerto Rican, Cuban, Spanish, Central American, and South American heritage; they were selected by an eight-person advisory board.

The work begins with an alphabetical list of entrants, followed by an occupation index and an ethnicity index. Biographical sketches range from 500 to 2,500 words, often accompanied by photographs. The sketches, written and signed by contributing authors, drew their data from telephone interviews or previously published information. They focus on personal, career, and family influences that have contributed to the success of these women. From politician Polly Baca to entertainer Raquel Welch, the work includes women from all walks of life who have not abandoned their Hispanic roots. Personal information is not glossed over, and biographees are often candid in the obstacles that they had to overcome to achieve their goals. A 19-page subject index concludes the book.

The work is easy to use and well conceived, and it will inspire young women to achieve excellence in their chosen professions. It deserves a place on the shelves of all libraries. [R: Choice, July/Aug 93, p. 1753; LJ, Aug 93, p. 96; RBB, 15 Oct 93, p. 474; RQ, Fall 93, pp. 132-33; WLB, June 93, pp. 126-29]—**Ilene F. Rockman**

11. **People to Know**. Chicago, World Book, 1989. 256p. illus. index. $15.95. LC 65-25105. ISBN 0-7166-0689-5.

Each year World Book issues a volume to complement Childcraft's basic set on topics of interest to young children. The current volume is a collection of biographical stories about prominent people, both living and deceased, who have made a contribution to American life. The 30 stories consist of a picture and short biographical information, followed by a narrative of an incident from the person's life. The reader learns of the difficulty Stephen Hawking, the physicist, had writing a book when impaired by ALS (Amyotrophic Lateral Sclerosis), Sally Ride's first journey into space, and Rosa Parks's famous day on a city bus. Some of the other persons featured include Beverly Cleary, Mother Teresa, Martin Luther King, Jr., Jim Thorpe, Clara Barton, and Sequoyah. Interesting sketches are written at a second-grade reading level. The volume is an excellent introduction to biography for the first few grades of school. Recommended for home, school, and public libraries. [R: RBB, 15 Feb 90, p. 1188]—**David V. Loertscher**

12. Straub, Deborah Gillan. **Contemporary Heroes and Heroines**. Detroit, Gale, 1992. 559p. illus. index. $49.95. CT120.C662. 920'.009'04. LC 90-132617. ISBN 0-8103-8336-5.

First published in 1990, *Contemporary Heroes and Heroines* (see entry 3) was revised and enlarged in the 1992 edition. Pop-culture authority Ray B. Browne introduces this collection of biographical sketches. He points out that knowledge of heroism provides models of behavior, defines our world, bolsters democracy, nourishes our ideal selves, makes the world one, and inspires us with faith while strengthening our resolve. Straub's sketches demonstrate how these attributes of heroism infuse a life and, in doing so, touch all hearts. The sketches are each approximately five pages in length, with sources listed. A half-page photographic portrait and a compelling quotation preface each entry. The variety of people covered makes for an eclectic but balanced gathering. Grandma Moses, Jim Henson, the Dalai Lama, Vaclav Havel, Simon Wiesenthal, and Stevie Wonder differ dramatically from one another, but all have the common link of heroism. Most of the names will be familiar, although some might not be, such as Corrie ten Boom (she sheltered Jews from the Nazis), Chico Mendes (he fought against the destruction of the Amazon rain forest), and Ben Carson (the black neurosurgeon). The subjects are as contemporary as Elizabeth Glaser, the AIDS activist, and as renowned as Clarence Darrow. School and public libraries will want to own this book and the previous volume for general reading and classroom assignments.—**Bill Bailey and Robert L. Wick**

13.   **Who's Who in the World**. New Providence, N.J., Marquis Who's Who/Reed Reference Publishing, 1971- . $339.95 for recent edition. ISSN 0083-9825.

The 13th edition of *Who's Who in the World* (1995) provides a choice of "38,000 globally noteworthy persons" is a daunting and necessarily subjective task. Nearly every country is represented, although there are 143 Smiths, against a mere 43 Kims (only 32 from Korea), 31 Garcias (7 from the United States), 16 Singhs (4 from the United States), and 14 Zhangs (only from China). Entries for librarians are overwhelmingly American. There is excellent international coverage of public officials—down to the attorney general of Western Samoa—but only of those currently in office. Immediate past presidents of Brazil, Colombia, Peru, and Venezuela, and all recent ex-prime ministers of Japan, are lacking, as are monarchical pretenders. Among business people, neither Great Britain's Richard Branson nor Brazil's Jose Mindlin is mentioned. Brazilian literature is represented by Jorge Amado and Nelida Pinon, but not by world best-seller Paulo Cole. Louis Farrakhan, Vuk Stefanovic' Karadzi, Oliver North, Pol Pot, Raul Salinas, O. J. Simpson, Donald Trump, and Kurt Waldheim are other notable omissions.

The solidly factual nature of the entries determines their length. Barbara Cartland's multitudinous publications give her an entire column; President Carlos Saul Menem gets just eight lines. Reliance on questionnaires allows such idiosyncrasies as V. S. Naipaul's entry omitting his knighthood. Most leave their religious affiliation blank. An asterisked entry shows when the Marquis Who's Who staff had to compile the entry. Cross-references are few. This reviewer nearly overlooked Gerry Adams (under "Adams, Gerard"); Sarah Ferguson (under "York"); and Afghan president Gulbuddin Hekmalyar (under his first name), while the all-through alphabetization almost lost King Juan Carlos I (following "Juana"). Nevertheless, its convenient access to basic data on so many of the world's currently prominent citizens makes this biennial standby an essential reference library purchase.
—**L. Hallewell and Robert L. Wick**

14.   **Who's Who: An Annual Biographical Dictionary**. New York, St. Martin's Press, 1849- . $195.00. ISSN 0083-937X.

The 1995 edition contains more than 29,000 separate biographical entries, arranged in alphabetic order according to last name. Each entry includes the person's current position, date of birth, family members, educational background, clubs, recreational activities, and an address. These individuals come from all disciplines (e.g., the arts, athletics, business, entertainment, politics, science) and from every continent. *Who's Who* also provides an obituary of entrants who died from September to September each year, and a complete roster of the British royal family.

An anonymous editorial board chooses the individuals appearing in *Who's Who*, seeking to recognize men and women of achievement and influence. Many selections are outstanding, others only adequate. Unfortunately, traditional biases remain. The entrants hail disproportionately from Great Britain, and the vast majority are males. To cite one example, British singer Elton John is listed, while United States pop star Whitney Houston is not. Other omissions are even more glaring: Newt Gingrich, the U.S. Speaker of the House of Representatives, is nowhere to be found, nor is Vladimir Volfovich Zhirinovsky, the Russian ultranationalist. *Who's Who* is a valuable work, rich in detail, but other biographical sources should be consulted in order to fill in gaps. This volume is recommended for college, university, and public libraries.—**Richard E. Holl and Robert L. Wick**

15.   Ziegler, Ronald. **Celebrity Sources: Guide to Biographical Information about Famous People in Show Business and Sports Today**. New York, Garland, 1990. 578p. index. (Garland Reference Library of the Humanities, v.1176). $57.00. Z5304.C44Z53. 016.9202. LC 89-11762. ISBN 0-8240-5946-8.

This guide covers a wide range of sources, some specific to a particular celebrity, others general sources of information to current personalities. People covered are those listed in the *Celebrity Register* (4th ed., 1986, and selectively from the 3d ed., 1973), so a few of those whose stars have recently risen are included.

Most of the celebrities come from the motion picture, television, music, and sports fields (excluding television journalists). An introductory section covers general sources in the following formats: reference books, collective biographies, periodicals, computerized databases, organizations (e.g., libraries, museums, halls of fame), commercial sources and services (e.g., those who purchase and/or sell biography books, artifacts, memorabilia), fan clubs, individual biographies, and general books about celebrity and fame. Separate sections on film and television, music, and sports cover the same formats. The weakest sections by far are those on periodicals, primarily because individual references to articles on the celebrities are not included. The listings of magazine titles are supplemented by brief descriptions and indexing sources. More useful are the fan club, organizational, and commercial sources of information. Name, title, and subject indexes complete the work, and the name index includes listings from the annotations as well as the general entries to the 900 celebrities covered. Although not containing nearly the number of references as *Biography Index* (see ARBA 88, entry 75) or *Biography and Genealogy Master Index* (see ARBA 87, entry 420), *Celebrity Sources* suggests a wide range of sources useful to those seeking biographical information on the most well-known figures in the present entertainment fields. [R: Choice, June 90, p. 1665; LJ, 15 Feb 90, p. 182; RBB, 15 May 90, p. 1838; WLB, Apr 90, p. 118]—**Robert Aken**

RETROSPECTIVE BIOGRAPHIES

16.   **Almanac of Famous People: A Comprehensive Reference Guide to More Than 27,000 Famous and Infamous Newsmakers from Biblical Times to the Present**. 5th ed. Detroit, Gale, 1994. 2v. index. ISBN 0-8103-698-5.

The previous edition was the *Almanac of Famous People: A Comprehensive Reference Guide to More Than 25,000 Famous and Infamous Newsmakers from Biblical Times to the Present* (4th ed. Susan L. Stetler, ed. Detroit, Gale, 1989. 3v. index. $90.00/set. ISBN 0-8103-278-8. ISSN 1040-127X). The general content of this almanac has changed little over previous editions. Formerly *Biography Almanac*, this 1994 edition is published in two volumes and covers a wide range of persons who have achieved fame in a variety of areas, from television to science. Many additional names that have become well known since the publication of the last edition have been added, and most entries have been updated in some fashion, though in some cases the update is merely a new one-line descriptor.

Each of the entries provides the name of the individual; pseudonym, real name, or nickname; one-line descriptor; occupation; birth and death dates and places; and abbreviated citations to biographical dictionaries containing entries on that individual. New entries include Steffi Graf (winner of Wimbledon in 1988); Dick Rutan and Jeanna Yeager (first to fly around the world without refueling); and Fawn Hall (participant in the Iran-Contra controversy).

As a biographical dictionary, *Almanac of Famous People* is not meant to be a substitute for Gale's *Biography and Genealogy Master Index,* though it may serve as an easier means of locating sources of biographical information. In addition, it serves as an excellent source for easily locating a minimum of information on a vast array of individuals, from the biblical character Deborah to restaurateur Lorerizo Delmonico. The index volume assists the reader in locating each individual occupationally, chronologically, and geographically.—**Susan R. Penney and Robert L. Wick**

17.   **The Annual Obituary**. Louise Mooney Collins and Lorna Mpho Mabunda, eds. Detroit, St. James Press, 1980- . index. $95.00 for recent edition.

This series, begun in 1980, provides biographical information on notable persons who died during the year. The first volume contained 450 entries, of which many included pictures, while the latest volume has 340 entries and no pictures. Although international in scope, the 1993 volume contains over 60 percent U.S. entrants, about 10 percent from the British Isles, and the rest from various parts of the world. Criteria for inclusion are not provided. The entries vary in length from just over one page to seven pages. Examples of short biographies are those for Davis Roberts, Leo Manso, and Anwar Al-Khatib. There are longer biographies of six to seven pages on such persons as Cyril Cusack and Norman Vincent Peal. Others, such as those for Thurgood Marshall, Myrna Loy, and David Koresh, are from three to four pages long, which is the normal length. Contributors are identified only by name.

Although this biographical information can be found in other standard reference sources, this series is convenient to use, and entries are generally well written. Particularly helpful are the two cumulative indexes providing the year (volume) where various entries are found. Recommended for academic and public libraries.—**Karen Y. Stabler and Robert L. Wick**

18.   **The Cambridge Biographical Dictionary**. David Crystal, ed. New York, Cambridge University Press, 1996. 495p. $16.95pa. ISBN 0-521-56780-7.

The 15,000 entries in this paperback biographical dictionary are largely derived from the previously published *Cambridge Biographical Encyclopedia* (see ARBA 95, entry 25); both titles share the same editor. Surprisingly, *The Cambridge Biographical Dictionary*, first published in 1996, is more selective than the previous book with the same title published in 1990 (see ARBA 92, entry 25) (also published as Chambers' *Biographical Dictionary*), which contains 19,000 entries. After reviewing the different titles, Chambers versus Cambridge, and dictionary versus encyclopedia, this reviewer became confused and questioned the reasoning behind the choice of titles.

Each entry, usually of no more than 50 words, includes the person's full name in bold typeface; year of birth (and death if relevant); place of birth; nationality; occupation; chief achievement; pronunciation (for difficult names); and, at times, cross-references to other personalities found in the book. No illustrations are provided. The scope is international, largely twentieth century, and an additional effort has been made to include often overlooked groups, such as women and African Americans. Libraries already owning any of the above titles do not need to purchase this book unless they want a more up-to-date source; otherwise, libraries wanting an easy-to-use, inexpensive, general biographical dictionary providing only brief information on a modest number of individuals would find this title useful. [R: Choice, Dec 96, p. 587]—**Carl Pracht**

19.   **The Cambridge Biographical Encyclopedia**. By David Crystal. New York, Cambridge University Press, 1994. 1304p. illus. maps. $49.95. CT103.C26.920'.003. LC 94-6218. ISBN 0-521-43421-1.

Those responsible for developing a reference collection must decide what information a new title will add to that provided by titles already in stock. In considering *The Cambridge Biographical Encyclopedia* (*CBE*), the selector will find some unique features but much that is simply taken word for word from *The Cambridge Biographical Dictionary* (*CBD*) (published as *Chambers Biographical Dictionary* in the United Kingdom). Of the first 10 entries of the *CBE*, 8 are duplicated from and often amplified by entries in the *CBD*. In the *CBE*, for example, we learn that Alvar Aalto, the Finnish architect, designed "numerous public and industrial buildings including the Finlandia concert hall." In the *CBD*, we are told he also designed the library at Viipuri and the Sunila mill and, in the United States, he built the Baker House residence at MIT. In order to augment the straight alphabetical approach traditionally found in biographical dictionaries, the *CBE* editors have included three special sections: 145 pages of tables listing kings, popes, athletic notables, and the like; 110 pages of "Connections" (a series of brief essays on topics such as science, the arts, and exploration); and 16 pages of contemporary events, with mention of the people who were involved in those events. The information in these supplements increases the usefulness of the volume, but the facts could easily be found in most general encyclopedias.

The *CBE* provides pronunciation for difficult names and a scattering of 250 illustrations—both features lacking in the *CBD*. As to the number of names included, the *CBE* has 15,000, the *CBD* 19,000, and *Webster's New Biographical Dictionary* 30,000. In some cases, the *CBE* supplies current information, so that L. I. Abalkin is identified as a "Russian" economist instead of his designation in *CBD* as a "Soviet" economist. The *CBE* does include a small number of names not given in the *CBD*, but the reverse is also true.

Selectors in libraries that already own the *CBD* will need to think carefully before they invest in *CBE*. It is disappointing that the editors of the *CBE* felt no obligation to make a statement of acknowledgment as to the extremely close textual connection between this volume and the previous work. That kind of statement would have helped selectors judge the current volume on a more accurate basis. [R: WLB, Oct 94, p. 78]—**Donald C. Dickinson**

20.   **The Cambridge Encyclopedia**. 2d ed. David Crystal, ed. New York, Cambridge University Press, 1994. 1347p. illus. maps. $49.95. ISBN 0-521-44429-2.

Compared to its softcover offspring (see ARBA 95, entry 45), this one-volume reference is more comprehensive—if a bit more dated—in its subject coverage. It boasts nearly 8,000 additional entries: Its alphabetical listing accounts for more than 5,000 of these, with the other additions appearing in the 126-page ready-reference section. The editor states in his preface that this work contains approximately 1,500 more entries than its predecessor, and that about 30 percent of the entries carried forward into this edition have undergone revision. Crystal pledges subject currency through 1993 for all entries. An attractive 24-page, full-color world atlas follows the preface.

In this edition more space has been awarded to entries pertaining to popular culture, philosophy, mathematics, religion, and computer science, among other disciplines. The natural sciences remain well represented, with abundant entries on plant and animal species of the world. Impressive as well is the treatment given the performing arts, architecture, and music. Although entries average 125 words apiece, longer articles appear for countries, wars, major historical leaders, and broad subjects such as "Renaissance" and "ship."

With 6,000 biographical entries, *The Cambridge Encyclopedia* assembles persons from diverse backgrounds; for example, Raquel Welch, Simone Weil, John Coltrane, and Winnie Mandela. Some unfortunate absences include James Earl Jones, Cab Calloway, Nelson Rockefeller, and Donald Trump. Particularly troubling, however, is the absence of entries for notables who passed away before the book went to press; also, while death dates are provided for such personalities as Jacqueline Kennedy Onassis and Erich Honecker, none are given for such predeceased individuals as Helen Hayes, Peter Quennell, and Marian Anderson.

Although all of this edition's entries were examined for British bias by a specialist, a number of problems persist. Under such bicultural head words as *sheriff* and *cabinet*, extended British definitions routinely tamp down American meanings into the lower third of the entry. Furthermore, *turnpike* is defined as "a gate across a road," and *salsa* is said only to be "a type of popular music of Cuban origin." Errors seem to be rare in this edition, although there are exceptions. Under *Denver,* the Forney Transportation Museum is misspelled as "Fornery Transport Museum." Also, embedded in the article on the Three Stooges is "(b. 1909)," after the name Joe de Rita; it is only after readers look at the end of the entry that they learn de Rita is actually deceased. Cross-references are profuse; there is no cross-reference, however, from "mythology" to a chart of "The 12 Major Gods of Olympus," nearly 200 pages removed.

Despite their drabness, *The Cambridge Encyclopedia*'s illustrations, charts, panels, and maps (now totaling 1,000) are clean, uncluttered, and usually informative. Regrettably, the compass rose seems to have become an endangered cartographic element, as it is absent from maps throughout this work. Overall, however, this is a remarkably accomplished piece of scholarship by diverse hands. For its asking price, no library should forgo its purchase.—**Jeffrey E. Long**

21. **The Complete Marquis Who's Who on CD-ROM**. [CD-ROM] (2 discs). New Providence, N.J., Marquis Who's Who/Reed Reference Publishing, 1996. Minimum system requirements (Windows version): IBM or compatible 386. CD-ROM drive. Windows 3.1. 4MB RAM. Hard disk. Minimum system requirements (Macintosh version): 68020 processor. CD-ROM drive. 6MB RAM. Hard disk. $995.00.

Marquis Who's Who biographical works are essential for academic libraries and businesses for which data on people are important. Therefore, when this reference standard appears in a new form (i.e., on CD-ROM) for the first time, it is an occasion to be noticed. Unfortunately, this premier edition does not live up to the print volumes' distinguished history.

The Complete Marquis Who's Who on CD-ROM consists of two discs, one for current volumes and a second for previous entries, each of which must be searched separately. In many ways, this electronic version is a tremendous improvement over the book-bound data in print format. Simple name and address searching is easier than ever before, although the latter occasionally suffers from an inconsistency in the use of abbreviations. Approximately 750,000 biographical sketches published during the past 10 years in the 18 regional and specialized titles issued by Marquis Who's Who are now searchable via only 2 CD-ROMs. Entries are updated every six months with the inclusion of new biographees as well as selected updates of previous entries. The CD-ROMs include every entry from *Who's Who in America* and *Who Was Who in America*, as well as volumes covering the East, West, Midwest, South and Southwest, the world, education, U.S. nursing, entertainment, finance and industry, religion, advertising, U.S. law, women, human services professionals, science and engineering, and emerging leaders in the United States. The price of the electronic version was recently cut in half, thereby reducing it to within the budgets of many libraries that may not have been able to purchase it otherwise.

Marquis Who's Who has obviously put much work, thought, and effort into producing this electronic version. Searchers may retrieve the desired biographies by using any number of search methods: keyword(s), Boolean, wild card, and field searching, among others. The basic search is simple. Through the use of a series of fill-in-the-blank templates, data may be retrieved according to a biographee's name, birthplace, birth year, death date, address, zip code, educational background, place of employment, professional and other organizations, occupation, family name of wife, and so on. Searchers may highlight records, add notes to individual entries, and compile edited versions of specific records via shadow files. Installation is easy, but access to records suffers severe limitations.

Several significant additional problems were found in using this work. Many of the problems are a result of the way in which records were compiled. Rather than going for uniformity, Marquis used two types of biographical record formats: 90 percent are in category form, and 10 percent are in sketch format. With some exceptions, each of these categories must be searched separately in order to ensure that a biographee is, or is not, included. In most instances, searches do not permit the inclusion of both city and state. Because of this, users attempting to find persons born in Miami, Oklahoma, are subjected to a long list of hits that includes every individual born in Miami, Florida, and Miami, Ohio. Inconsistency in the use of abbreviations is fairly widespread.

In addition to difficulties in retrieval because of lack of consistency, this tool is disappointing for other reasons. The expertise necessary to effectively search the database necessitates the thorough study of the 112-page printed guide that accompanies the two discs; unfortunately, this guide has no index. The brief lifespan of this CD-ROM, which is timed to cease functioning after 248 days, requires the lease of expensive updates every 8 months. The necessity to continually lease updates, combined with the fact that the discs are limited to a 10-year time span, almost requires that university libraries must also purchase the hardcover print volumes. The cumulative effect of these problems is that, despite the inclusion of so much data, much will be missed through searches that have too many unnecessary impediments to them.

Despite its faults, libraries for which biographical searches form a major part of their reference services should consider inclusion of this work. Marquis Who's Who states that changes are planned that will alleviate some of the above problems, and other modifications are being discussed.—**Donald E. Collins**

22.   Cowan, Thomas. **Gay Men and Women Who Enriched the World**. New Canaan, Conn., William Mulvey; distr., Chicago, Independent Publishers Group, 1988. 257p. $17.95. HQ75.2.C69. 306. 7'66'0922. LC 88-43401. ISBN 0-934791-16-3.

Cowan, a professional writer with a doctorate in history and literature from St. Louis University, has chosen 9 lesbians and 31 gay men as subjects of brief biographical essays. Spanning more than 2,000 years from Alexander the Great, Plato, and Sappho to Michael Bennett, creator of the Broadway hit *A Chorus Line,* all are western European or North American except for Peter Ilyich Tchaikovsky of Russia and Yukio Mishima of Japan. All are Caucasian except Mishima, Bessie Smith, and James Baldwin. The essays, arranged for the most part in chronological order, are each approximately six pages in length. They read well, emphasizing the artistic, musical, literary, military, and intellectual contributions of their subjects, with minimal information on their sexual lives.

As a reference work, this volume has a serious defect in its complete absence of references to sources. Not only does this absence weaken the authority of the essays, but readers are also deprived of leads for further reading if their interest is piqued by the essays. Also missing is a subject index, making it impractical, if not impossible, to find themes that cut across the lives of these persons.

In a lead essay on "purpose and meaning in the gay experience," the author claims, again without reference to sources, that the sexuality of each of the subjects has been "established by solid historical and biographical evidence." Nevertheless, the only common thread among all subjects is that they are known, or are believed, to have had intimate sexual or affectionate relations with persons of their own gender. Beyond that, no evidence is offered that they shared any common conception of what it meant to be gay. What they do have in common, especially those from the Renaissance to the present, is the will to be different from the stereotypes of their cultures. The essays suggest that this may be a possible cause for extraordinary contributions to society. For this reason, they are valuable examples for lesbian and gay people of today. All general libraries serving lesbian and gay people should add this book to their collections. [R: BL, 1 Mar 89, p. 1073]—**James D. Anderson**

23.   **A Dictionary of Twentieth Century World Biography**. Asa Briggs, ed. New York, Oxford University Press, 1992. 615p. $30.00. ISBN 0-19-211679-7.

Biographical dictionaries rise or fall on the basis of the clarity and logic of their selection criteria. In the preface, the editor states that the object of this work is to include those who have had an impact, either directly or indirectly, on the rest of us. This vague announcement is not strengthened by a statement in the foreword that people "about whom it is useful to be able to have easily accessible information" are included.

The editor has listed 1,750 people from all walks of life who have gained prominence in the twentieth century. While the sketches are well written and seem accurate, there are too few of them, particularly when considered against the 5,650 notables in a comparable work, *The International Dictionary of 20th Century Biography* (see ARBA 88, entry 35). For example, the work under review fails to include James Weldon Johnson, W. E. B. DuBois, Langston Hughes, or Richard Wright. All are included in the older volume. Finally, the book lacks indexing of any kind—a serious flaw. *A Dictionary of Twentieth Century World Biography* cannot be recommended. [R: Choice, Dec 92, p. 600; LAR, Oct 92, p. 672; RBB, 1 Nov 92, p. 545]—**Donald C. Dickinson**

24.   Fradin, Dennis Brindell. **Remarkable Children: Twenty Who Made History**. Boston, Little, Brown, 1987. 207p. $14.95. LC 87-3820. ISBN 0-316-29126-9.

Twenty child achievers, each of whom made a rare accomplishment or discovery at a young age and left their mark on history, are featured here. The author has an impressive personal look into the remarkable lives of these children, some of whom are very well known and some of whom are relatively obscure. Among the famous included are Mozart, Picasso, Helen Keller, Louis Braille, and Anne Frank. The relatively unknown include Hilda Conkling, a young poetess; Maria de Sautuola, who discovered rare cave paintings in northern Spain; and Zerah Colburn, son of a Vermont farmer, who was not quite six when he first showed an ability to do complex mathematical equations in his head.

The author was able to talk to several of the persons featured and to individuals who knew them, including Shirley Temple, Pelé, Bobby Fischer, Nadia Comaneci, and Tracy Austin.

Public and school libraries will want this as a biographical and inspirational reference.
—**Beverley Hanson**

25.   Gay, Kathlyn, and Martin K. Gay. **Heroes of Conscience: A Biographical Dictionary**. Santa Barbara, Calif., ABC-CLIO, 1996. 482p. illus. index. $65.00. ISBN 0-87436-874-X.

The authors have established a definitive biographical dictionary of individuals through the late 1800s to the present day. Listed alphabetically, each entry contains a vivid description of the person's achievements through life and how they have benefited the world. A few—Clara Barton, Jimmy Carter, Albert Einstein, Jane Fonda, Mohandas Gandhi, and Edward R. Murrow—depict the variety of the individuals included.

The dictionary is international in scope, with no preference as to the geographic location or classification of their endeavor, whether it is animal rights, artistic or athletic achievements, entertainment, musicians, or politicians. Each entry is complete with references, and some also have a photograph of the individual. The work is well documented with a bibliography and a thorough index.

This dictionary contains ample information that should be expanded. It is highly recommended for academic (arts, history, public affairs, or sociology), public, and special libraries.
—**Lisé Rasmussen**

26.   **The Grolier Library of International Biographies**. Danbury, Conn., Grolier, 1996. 10v. illus. index. $319.00/set. ISBN 0-7172-7527-2.

This 10-volume set of biographies covers activists; athletes; entrepreneurs, inventors, and discoverers; explorers; performing artists; political and military leaders; scholars and educators; scientists; visual artists; and writers. It is a beautifully organized and well-written set for children and young adults; adults may find it useful as well. The inclusiveness of its contents speaks well for the research efforts of the editors; as they state in the introduction, the set is a "mosaic that spans time and geography while overcoming boundaries of gender, race, and class."

Entries are arranged alphabetically in each volume, sometimes including a photograph of or a quotation from the subject. The life achievements of each are placed in a historical context, and the necessary facts are summarized in a concise fashion. One of the attractive features of this set is the brevity and clarity of the writing, along with the ease of use. Appendixes include a glossary that refers to the words in bold typeface in each entry (for performers, for instance, there is a definition of *glitter rock* and *diva*; for explorers, there is *avalanche* and *malaria*). Another appendix provides a "Sources and Further Reading" list for each person profiled, and a general index includes locations, types of occupations, and people.

Whether the set is describing Italian mountaineers or Mongolian cosmonauts, French actors or African musicians, the editors succeed in supplying a well-rounded and readable addition to any library. It is highly recommended. [R: BR, Sept/Oct 96, p. 57; RBB, 1 Apr 96, p. 1388; SLJ, May 96, p. 145]—**Barbara J. O'Hara**

27.   **The Grolier Library of North American Biographies**. Danbury, Conn., Grolier, 1994. 10v. illus. index. $299.00/set. ISBN 0-7172-7246-X.

This 10-volume set provides basic information about approximately 2,000 famous North Americans, with emphasis on nineteenth- and twentieth-century figures. Each volume focuses on a theme: activists, athletes, entrepreneurs and inventors, explorers, performance artists, political and military leaders, scholars and educators, scientists, visual artists, and writers. The biographies, arranged alphabetically within each volume, range from one to four pages per entry. They include the person's birth and death date(s) if applicable, pertinent family background, and why the person is of historical significance. Some entries contain a small black-and-white photograph or illustration. Each volume has a glossary of appropriate words, sources, and further reading arranged by entry, and a volume-only index. The master index is in volume 10.

While females and minorities are well represented, North America translates into the United States with a Canadian flavoring. Is not Mexico still part of North America? Of course, this type of work is great for playing the "why" game. Why is Johnny Cash not listed in the performance artists volume alongside Willie Nelson? What about Charlton Heston? Also, a typographical error appeared in the John Brown entry: 1932 was printed instead of 1832. People famous in more than one category (e.g., Benjamin Franklin) must be tracked down via the master index or by checking several tables of contents—a minor inconvenience.

The page layout, typeface size, and prose style will make this work popular with students in grades 5-10, and those in English as a Second Language classes. It should be purchased by libraries that never have enough biographical information to go around.—**Esther R. Sinofsky**

28.   **The HarperCollins Dictionary of Biography**. New York, HarperCollins, 1994. illus. index. $45.00. ISBN 0-06-270098-7.

This work of over 8,000 cross-referenced entries covers historical personages and newsworthy contemporaries—not only national and religious leaders, writers, artists, composers, scientists, inventors, and explorers but also architects, directors, photographers, conductors, dancers, singers (rock and rap more than country or Broadway), designers, gardeners, actors (in media up to but not including television), and sports figures. Originally compiled for a British audience by Hutchinson, this dictionary shines when it comes to the Commonwealth and Europe as far east as Finland. U.S. presidents, Hollywood and Wild West figures, and pop culture heroes and villains also get generous coverage (there are three paragraphs on Oliver North), next only to royalty, British mystery writers, and Booker Prize nominees. This is the place to find St. Columbia and St. Columban, Myra Hess (but not Isaac Stern), world authors writing in English (but not Amy Tan or Sue Grafton), and soccer stars (but not Chinese painters; Asian and Third World authors such as Kobo Abe, Lao She, and Isabel Allende). Abolhassan Bani-Sadr, Mohammed Mahathir, Jerry Rawlings, and noted Vietnamese and Filipinos are absent. So are our recent culture critics. William F. Buckley is in, but not George Will or Garry Wills, Cornel West, Helen Vendler, William Bennett, Frederic Jameson, or Jacques Derrida.

Entries, typically two lines to two paragraphs, are briefer and often drier than those in big encyclopedias. The Columbus entry ends with rediscovery of the *Santa Maria* in 1968, not recent flak over his post-colonial symbolism. However, this work, also strong on medieval and nineteenth-century figures, is more topical than *The Cambridge Biographical Dictionary* (see entry 18). Here Benazir Bhutto rates more space than her father Zulfikar, and Rajiv Gandhi as much as Indira or Mohandas K. Nearly every page has a famous person's portrait or memorable quotation. All this, and the name indexes by field and accomplishment, make this work a home reference that can be browsed consecutively or topically for "cultural literacy," a work with more popular appeal—if less enduring reference value—than the solid *Cambridge*, which has more than twice as many entries. Pronunciations of difficult names are helpful, but U.S. readers need a gloss of the international phonetic symbols used. [R: WLB, June 94, pp. 98-99]—**Jeffrey C. Kinkley**

29. Hyamson, Albert M. **Dictionary of Universal Biography of All Ages and of All Peoples**. 2nd ed. New York, E. P. Dutton, 1951; repr., Detroit, Omnigraphics, 1994. 679p. $65.00. CT103.H9. 920.02. LC 93-27120. ISBN 0-7808-0010-9.

This is at least the fourth reprint of this edition of Hyamson's work. The original appeared in 1951, published by Dutton in the United States and by Routledge and Kegan Paul in the United Kingdom. The latter reprinted it in 1962 and 1966, and Gale reprinted it in 1981. Although "biographical dictionary" is implied by the title, this source contains only minimal biographical information. It is really a compact master index to biographical information contained in 23 reference works published prior to 1950. There are 110,000 alphabetized entries for persons "of eminence" from the United States, the United Kingdom, Europe, and Africa who died prior to 1950. A typical entry includes the person's name and country, why the person was famous, birth and death dates, and alphabetical codes indicating in which of 23 titles a biographical sketch of the figure is included.

This was doubtless a useful source when it appeared in 1951, but it is not very useful anymore. First, the publisher claims that the 23 reference titles are "standard reference titles," but 44 years later, most are standard in only the largest research collections. (This reviewer's library has only 8 of the 23 sources, and most of these are later editions.) Second, a lot of libraries already own either the 1951 edition or a reprint. Third, since 1951, Gale's much more comprehensive *Biography and Genealogy Master Index* has become available in print and on CD-ROM and online. These three factors raise the question as to why this title was reprinted. Recommended only for large research collections that missed acquiring it in any of its previous incarnations.—**Diana Accurso**

30. Marzollo, Jean. **My First Book of Biographies: Great Men and Women Every Child Should Know**. New York, Scholastic, 1994. 78p. illus. $14.95. ISBN 0-590-45014-X.

My First Book of Biographies is a unique, international biographical book for girls and boys aged 6-10. Marzollo lists biographies of people from various fields of endeavor in one volume, along with vivid and entertaining illustrations in color. It should be included in all children's libraries.

Marzollo chose 45 people who can be role models for children who aspire to greatness of their own. These men and women are both historical and contemporary people, including political leaders, scientists, artists, and athletes (e.g., George Washington, Marie Curie, Leonardo da Vinci, and Jesse Owens). Simple language to describe each person and full-page illustrations by Irene Trivas are good features for younger children. Yet, unlike *Twenty Names* series (Marshall Cavendish, 1988), this book lacks a glossary and a bibliography for further reading for older children aged 9-10. Older children may need independent reading and a more detailed biographical book after they read these introductory stories. Trivas's pictures would also be more effective if accompanied by explanatory captions similar to those provided in the *Twenty Names* series. However. Marzollo's book is eye-catching and truly valuable for every child.—**Sung Ok Kim**

31. **The McGraw-Hill Encyclopedia of World Biography**. David I. Eggenberger, ed.-in-chief. New York, McGraw-Hill, 1973. 12v. illus. (part col.). index. $550.00. 342. LC 70-37402. ISBN 0-07-079633-5.

Though now somewhat older, this monumental work is still a valuable source. It is kept up-to-date through the use of annual supplements. According to the introduction, this encyclopedia "has been designed to meet a growing need in school and college libraries as well as in public libraries. Written entirely by academic authorities and other specialists, and enriched with illustrations, bibliographies, Study Guides, and Index, this work, we believe, combines more useful features for the student than any other multivolume biographical encyclopedia" (Vol. 1, p.v). In other words, *EWB* was conceived primarily for the use of students. The editors have provided 5,000 biographies, averaging about 800 words in length, with a curriculum orientation. Each article concludes with a "further reading" section, consisting of references to Study Guides in Volume 12 and to related articles in other volumes. An annotated bibliography of English-language books is appended to each article. Access to the material is enhanced by the 100,000-entry index located in the last volume; the last volume also contains a list of contributors, showing their institutional affiliation.

It is almost impossible to provide a formula for selection of 5,000 biographees who might be "universally appealing" to students. Inclusions (or exclusions) can be debated. With respect to politicians, Beria, head of the Soviet secret police until his execution, is included (although with an inadequate bibliography), as is Trotsky (who is provided much better coverage). Benesh, however, the president of Czechoslovakia from 1935 to 1938 and 1940 to 1948, is treated in less detail. A comparison of the *EWB* with *Dictionary of Scientific Biography* shows that the coverage of famous scientists who have a popular appeal is quite adequate.

This set will be very useful in public schools; college students, however, will often need more detailed information and will have to rely on more specialized biographical directories, such as *Dictionary of Scientific Biography*.—**Bohdan S. Wynar and Robert L. Wick**

32.   **Merriam-Webster's Biographical Dictionary**. Springfield, Mass., Merriam-Webster, 1995. 1170p. $27.95. ISBN 0-87779-743-9.

This is a revised edition of *Webster's New Biographical Dictionary* published in 1988 (see ARBA 90, entry 34). Almost 40 pages have been added to the new edition. Important characteristics have been maintained from the earlier edition. These are no restrictions concerning the time, place, or country of origin of individuals selected for inclusion; clearly stated explanatory and pronunciation guides provide easy understanding of the book's contents; entries remain succinct and informative. The original preface is included in the new edition, so it remains unclear precisely what has been added or otherwise enhanced. Direct consultation with the publisher indicates that 287 new entries of deceased individuals have been added, all previous entries have been reviewed by the editorial staff, the size has been recomposed to make the volume easier to handle, and the book has been assigned a new copyright date. Given the low price, the comprehensive inclusion criteria, and the quality of presentation, this work remains a core research tool that must be considered an essential part of every library collection.—**Robert V. Labaree**

33.   **Merriam-Webster's Pocket Biographical Dictionary**. Springfield, Mass., Merriam-Webster, 1996. 372p. $3.95pa. ISBN 0-87779-507-X.

Moses's brother Aaron is the first entry; the sixteenth-century Swiss Reformation leader Huldrych Zwingli is the last. Nearly 7,000 notable people, living and dead, fit in between. There are authors and athletes, composers and heads of state. Missing is a clarification about how compilers decided who got mention and who did not. The delineator used for contemporary authors is particularly murky. Jorge Luis Borges and Gabriel Garefa Marquez are in; A. S. Byatt, Seamus Heaney, and Vikram Seth are out. Given that Byatt, Heaney, and Seth reached their pinnacles in the last decade, the explanation might be "newness"—but then how did sports figures Wayne Gretzky and Michael Jordan merit spaces?

Inevitably, telegraphic synopses sometimes (and inadvertently) mislead. For example, "psychological insight" is too modern a label to hang on Jane Austen's prose. Also, the shorthand "genes sometimes behave unexpectedly inside cells" is not so much an untrue characterization of Barbara McClintoek's transposing ("jumping genes") work as an uninformative one. On the whole, however, this small book is sheer fun. Those who like to test their knowledge with dense and inexpensive compendiums ought to snatch up the pocket-size volume—and keep it at arm's reach to quickly break a crossword impasse or get fast help recalling the real name of Stendhal (Marie-Henri Beyle).—**Diane M. Calabrese**

34.   Morrow, Ed. **Born This Day: A Daily Celebration of Famous Beginnings**. New York, Citadel Press/Carol Publishing Group, 1995. 407p. index. $12.95pa. ISBN 0-8065-1648-8.

Books of days are fun for students, teachers, media specialists, and lay readers to turn to for finding out the famous as well as the infamous persons with whom their birthdays are shared. People born on April 6, for example, may be fascinated to learn that they celebrate their birthday with Merle Haggard, Billy Dee Williams, and Michelle Phillips. The majority of *Born This Day* is devoted to short vignettes about one famous person born on each of the 366 respective days of the calendar year (February 29 is included). All other prominent persons are listed only by name and the year of their birth. For example, January 1 features a short profile of Paul Revere and then lists the birth years of eight others, including Betsy Ross, J. Edgar Hoover, and Barry Goldwater.

School personnel need to be circumspect in their use of this resource. The author appears often to favor titillation more than good taste. How else to explain an account of John Barrymore's drunkenness and laziness as the profile of choice for February 14 birthdays while simply noting that Susan B. Anthony was born on the same day in 1820? The same question arises for the June 8 entries. Is Joan Rivers a more significant figure for young people to know than Frank Lloyd Wright or Barbara Bush? Of course, all such decisions are subjective. Nevertheless, the author seems to elect sensationalism over substance.

Even when the subject of the daily profile is justifiably famed, Morrow's source of information may be more appropriately geared to college youth than elementary or secondary school students. It may be interesting for some people to learn that pop singer Madonna scraped by early in her career by posing nude for artists at $7 per hour, but that is hardly the information teachers and parents have in mind when they send youth to the library. Although the book contains an index, only those persons fully profiled are listed. The reader will find Rivers in the index, but not Bush or Wright.

This limitation further weakens the value of the book as a reference tool. Morrow credits many sources he used, but he must have missed some vital ones. April 6 birthday celebrators will need to look elsewhere to learn that French revolutionary Maximilien de Robespierre and magician Harry Houdini celebrated their birthdays that day, as does Nobel Prize-winning geneticist James Watson, who constructed the first model of DNA.—**Jerry D. Flack**

35.   **Nobel Prize Winners: An H. W. Wilson Biographical Dictionary**. Tyler Wasson, ed. Bronx, N.Y., H. W. Wilson, 1987. 1165p. illus. $90.00. LC 87-16468. ISBN 0-8242-0756-4.

Nobel Prize Winners: Supplement 1987-1991. Paula McGuire, ed. Bronx, N.Y., H. W. Wilson, 1992. 143p. illus. $35.00. AS911.N9N59. 001.4'4'0922. LC 92-12197. ISBN 0-8242-0834-X.

Nobel Prize Winners: Supplement 1992-1996. Clifford Thompson, Edward Moran, and Selma Yampolsky, eds. An H. W. Wilson Biographical Dictionary. Bronx, N.Y., H. W. Wilson, 1997. 165p. illus. $35.00. ISBN 0-8242-0906-0.

This is a comprehensive work which addresses the research needs of a large audience, including students, teachers, and general readers. Nobel Prize recipients from 1901 to 1996 (in the supplements) in every category are included.

The general format of the book is similar to Wilson's *World Authors* and *Current Biography* (1940-). Entries are arranged alphabetically by last name and include not only the standard biographical information such as birth, family history, education, and the work for which the Nobel Prize was awarded, but also an assessment of the work's impact and significance, such as the launching of a new era of medicine from Gerhard Domagk's discovery of the antibacterial agent Prontosil. Though the essays are somewhat brief, limited to 1,200 to 1,500 words, they focus on the height of the laureate's career and provide cross-references to other Nobel Prize recipients playing a part in the individual's life or in the overall development of the field or specialty. For instance, in the entry for Hans A. Bethe, winner of the Nobel Prize for physics in 1967, there is reference to Werner Heisenberg (physics, 1932), Erwin Schrodinger (physics, 1933), P. A. M. Dirac (physics, 1933), Max Planck (physics, 1918), Albert Einstein (physics, 1921), Niels Bohr (physics, 1922), and Clinton J. Davisson (physics, 1937), whose works illustrate the development of the quantum theory.

Access to information is made simple by the arrangement and cross-referencing, and the bibliographies which follow each entry lead the researcher to major works by and about the subject. Works about the subject are selective and include both older and more recent works. A list provided in the front of the book directs the reader to laureates by year and category.

As a whole, the comprehensive coverage and timelessness of this reference work make it a useful tool for public and school libraries.—**Susan R. Penney and Robert L. Wick**

36. **Obituaries from *The Times* 1951-1960;** including an index to all obituaries and tributes appearing in *The Times* during the years 1951-1960. Reading, England, Newspaper Archive Developments Ltd.; Westport, Conn., Meckler Books, 1979. 896p. index. $85.00.

> **Obituaries from *The Times* 1961-1970;** including an index to all obituaries and tributes appearing in *The Times* during the years 1961-1970. Reading, England, Newspaper Archive Developments Ltd., 1975. 952p. index. $60.00.

> **Obituaries from *The Times* 1971-1975;** including an index to all obituaries and tributes appearing in *The Times* during the years 1971-1975. Reading, England, Newspaper Archive Developments Ltd.; Westport, Conn., Meckler Books, 1978. 647p. index. $60.00.

The first volume provides a full text of selected obituaries from *The Times* of London plus an index to all obituaries covered during 1951-1960. According to the preface, "In this volume, there are 1,450 entries. There is of course some overlap with the relevant volume of the *Dictionary of National Biography*, but 28 percent of the notices refer to British subjects who do not appear in the *Dictionary of National Biography* and 29 percent are foreign subjects."

The 2nd volume (1961-1970) reprints a selection of 1,500 obituaries. And the third, according to the preface, contains an index of all entries appearing in the obituary columns of *The Times* from 1971-1975. The first part of this volume reprints in full an alphabetically arranged selection of about 1,000 obituary notices of the period.

The selection for these volumes has been made with regard to the public importance of the subject of the obituary, the intrinsic interest of what was written about him/her, and the need to reflect the wide range of nationalities and walks of life that *The Times* obituary columns encompass. After 1978, this series ceased publication.—**Bohdan S. Wynar**

37. Park, James. **Icons: An A-Z Guide to the People Who Shaped Our Time**. New York, Collier Books/Macmillan, 1991. 469p. index. $12.00pa. CT103.P157. 920'.009'04. LC 91-36769. ISBN 0-02-047100-9.

Not a typical reference book, with its offbeat tone and unusual contributors, this new biographical dictionary includes a decidedly different array of information about a wide range of political, social, and cultural figures. Symbols scattered throughout indicate such characteristics as "necromantic love-icon" and "almost ended up behind bars." Entries focus on the meaning of an individual's work or the influence someone had on society and history rather than on straight, dry biographical facts.

Intended to serve as a "route map through this postwar world" and to "encapsulate the essence of what 1000 or so" people did to be considered famous, the book's bias is left of center. Also, the varied mix of subjects contains many people who might not be considered quite as famous by the U.S. reader as by the creators of this book (e.g., playwright Dario Fo). But the inclusion of these not-so-obviously influential types is the strong point of this source; information about many of them may not be easy to locate elsewhere. This work will be of interest to those college and university libraries that serve strong programs in twentieth-century history and popular culture. [R: LJ, 1 Sept 92, p. 168; RBB, 15 Nov 92, pp. 626-27]—**Sharon Langworthy**

38. **The Pocket Factfile of 20th Century People**. St. Catharines, Ont., Vanwell Publishing, 1996. 208p. illus. (The Pocket Factfile Series). $10.95pa. ISBN 1-55068-083-8.

The editors state that when selecting the 500 key figures of the twentieth century to be included in this small volume, they tried to present a rounded picture of the times. Politicians form the largest group represented, followed by entertainers, business and industrial tycoons, writers, artists and musicians, and sports figures. This alphabetic arrangement of brief biographies includes photographs (some in color). The pocket size (4 by 6 inches) of this work severely limits coverage, but this type of book has appeal to individuals interested in trivia. Libraries would do better to select more traditional biographical reference tools.—**Vandelia L. VanMeter**

39.   **Prominent Women of the 20th Century**. Peggy Saari, ed. Detroit, U*X*L/Gale, 1996. 4v. illus. index. $115.00/set. ISBN 0-7876-0646-4.

Until recently, history books have focused almost exclusively on the achievements of men. Although recent publications have made an effort to include women and minorities, it is still sometimes difficult to find information about female heroes. This new reference work remedies that to a great extent. Aimed at students in grades 5-12, it gives young readers a glimpse at the many facets of greatness achieved by women around the world in the past century.

The 200 alphabetically arranged biographical sketches tell the stories of such great women as Aung San Suu Kyi, the political activist and human-rights advocate from Myanmar (formerly Burma); African American poet Maya Angelou; and Ida Tarbell, the American writer who exposed corrupt practices in the oil industry in the early 1900s. Many of the names are familiar—Marie Curie, Anne Frank, Madonna, Gloria Steinem, Mother Teresa, Margaret Thatcher—but others are relatively unknown. For example, the book tells the story of Annie Dodge Wauneka, the tribal leader who eradicated tuberculosis among the Navajo, and Rosalind Franklin, who co-discovered the structure of DNA.

Emphasis is on U.S. women (encompassing African American, Asian American, Hispanic American, and Native American), but the work also covers women from other countries—China, France, Germany, Japan, India, Palestine, Poland, Russia, the former Yugoslavia, and so on. There are representatives from a variety of fields, such as sports, politics, social issues, the arts, and science. A nationality/ethnicity index and an index to fields of endeavor enable readers to access specific information. The profiles (approximately 5-8 pages in length) are written in journalistic style, and what they lack in finesse is made up for with factual information. Boldfaced headlines and handsome black-and-white photographs will spark the interest of casual browsers, and lists of resources will lead them to further study.

It seems inevitable in such a work as this one that there are some obvious names missing—Angela Davis, Judy Chicago, Billie Jean King—and one might wish for less of a U.S. bias or for a more thorough index. However, this ambitious endeavor is one that should be applauded. The stories will be sources of information and inspiration to students, and the work will supplement the information offered in history textbooks and other resources. While not affordable to all school and public libraries, the price is reasonable. Those seeking a less expensive alternative that covers U.S. women throughout history may consider *Amazing American Women* (Libraries Unlimited, 1995). [R: BR, Sept/Oct 96, p. 50; RBB, 1 May 96, pp. 1534-38; SLJ, May 96, p. 146]—**Barbara Ittner**

40.   Russell, Paul. **The Gay 100: A Ranking of the Most Influential Gay Men and Lesbians, Past and Present**. New York, Carol Publishing Group, 1995. 386p. illus. index. $24.95. ISBN 0-8065-1591-0.

Those in search of a definitive "who's who" of gay men and lesbians will find this book vexing in its subjectivity, but taken as one man's idiosyncratic collection of 100 gay men and lesbians who have made the most influential contributions to American/European gay/lesbian identity, it provides a good deal of interesting information. It begins with an introduction outlining the project and touching on key questions about the meaning of such terms as *influential, gay, lesbian*, and *gay/lesbian identity*. It ends with a selected bibliography of 57 sources and an index.

Most of the book consists of the author's essays about his subjects. These are arranged by ranking, starting with #1 in importance (Socrates) to #100 (Michelangelo Signorile). Activists, artists, authors, military leaders, politicians, and thinkers spanning 2,400 years are discussed for their important contributions to history in general, and to gay/lesbian identity in particular. Of the 100 entries, 60 are about men, sketching such figures as Magnus Hirschfeld (#4), Alexander the Great (#14), Jean Genet (#45), Francis Bacon (#81), and Ian McKellen (#97). Thirty-eight entries are about women, from Sappho (#2) to Susan B. Anthony (#12), Adrienne Rich (#47), Mary Renault (#80), and Ethel

Smyth (#94). Two entries are shared by men and women—the Patrons of the Stonewall Inn (#5) and Harold Nicolson/Vita Sackville West (#64). This is a well-researched and highly readable book; while not a rigorous scholarly work, *The Gay 100* deserves a place in any library that takes seriously the ideal of diversity.—**G. Douglas Meyers**

41.   Snodgrass, Mary Ellen. **Crossing Barriers: People Who Overcame**. Englewood, Colo., Libraries Unlimited, 1993. 248p. index. $32.50. CT120.S588. 920'.009'04. LC 92-39789. ISBN 0-87287-992-5.

This eclectic mix of 38 biographical sketches will appeal to secondary school students for its "examples of admirable courage and determination" in many different people. Individuals span several centuries and reflect a multitude of occupations and ethnicities. Some surprises pop up, such as the inclusion of Nelson Rockefeller (for having dyslexia), the late actor Herve Villechaize (for overcoming height discrimination), and author Gary Paulsen (for battling poverty, alcoholism, and low self-esteem).

All entrants were selected by the author, but each seems to reflect the fact that no obstacle can prevent success. Yet, the title would not lead one to expect biographical sketches of the likes of Marian Anderson, Corazon Aquino, Joan Baez, Johnny Cash, Jack London, Claude Pepper, Renee Richards, Gloria Steinem, and Elie Wesley in the same source. Each descriptive, in-depth sketch is approximately six to seven pages in length, and an appended bibliography lists sources for further information. No photographs are included. The price of this source, coupled with its unusual mix of popular and lesser-known individuals, will cause librarians to carefully consider its purchase. [R: RBB, 1 Nov 93, p. 561; VOYA, Dec 93, p. 326]—**Ilene F. Rockman**

42.   Snodgrass, Mary Ellen. **Late Achievers: Famous People Who Succeeded Late in Life**. Englewood, Colo., Libraries Unlimited, 1992. 286p. $26.00. CT 120.S59. 920.02. LC 91-32136. ISBN 0-87287-937-2.

Many books have been written about people who have achieved success, but this book concentrates on those who "took on new challenges in their thirties, their forties, even their sixties and seventies" (p.ix). Some changed careers to become successful, while others started careers or new ventures later in life. This book contains 40 alphabetically arranged biographies of people, both living and deceased, from the eighteenth through the twentieth centuries in Europe and the United States. In many cases, readers will be familiar with the subject's achievement (e.g., dumpsters, McDonald's, Outward Bound), but they may not know the name behind the achievement (e.g., George Dempster, Ray Kroc, Kurt Hahn). Others in the volume represent equally diverse fields, such as Peter Mark Roget (thesaurus), Wally Amos (cookies), Vaclav Havel (president), Ethel Waters (actress), and William Griffin Wilson (Alcoholics Anonymous founder).

Six-part narratives about the biographees describe their lives and include important dates. These are followed by footnotes and sources consulted. For recent biographees the sources are mainly magazine and newspaper articles, while for the others the sources are books.

There are some flaws in the work. The date of death for some deceased biographees are omitted; there are several typographical errors; and at times the narrative jumps back and forth in the person's life, making the sequence of events hard to follow. But on the whole, this is a well done, easy to read, and often (with the exception of G. Gordon Liddy) inspiring work. It can be useful as a reference source because information on many of the living biographees is hard to locate elsewhere.—**Kathleen Farago**

43.   **The Oxford Children's Book of Famous People**. New York, Oxford University Press, 1994. 384p. illus. maps. $35.00. ISBN 0-19-910171-X.

Arranged alphabetically, this lavishly illustrated biographical dictionary contains sketches of 1,000 historical (e.g., Charlemagne) and popular (e.g., Madonna) individuals chosen by a team of consultants and authors. With an emphasis on politicians, writers, scientists, and actors, the result is a more representative selection of internationally known figures (e.g., Gabriel Garcia Marquez, Imran Khan). Women represent approximately 20 percent of newer personalities, but significantly less from earlier eras.

Entries of varying lengths identify the role and achievements or failures for which the person is known, with appropriate *see also* references. Entries for well-known partnerships (e.g., [Meriwether] Lewis and [William] Clark) appear in a combined entry, a technique that fails when the appellation (e.g., [John] Lennon and [Paul] McCartney) is confusing and the expected cross-reference (Beatles) is missing. The thematic and chronological directories, with individuals listed by achievement and date of birth, are useful features but contain some errors.

Intended as an inspiring collection for family reference or browsing, this work is disappointing. The use of "children" in the title is misleading as the vocabulary employed is clearly beyond the scope of most elementary students, while middle school students require a level of detail or additional references that are absent here.—**Sandra E. Belanger**

44. **Thinkers of the Twentieth Century**. Roland Turner, ed. 2d ed. Chicago, St. James Press, 1987. 977p. index. $75.00. ISBN 0-912289-83-X.

This 2nd edition includes all entries from the 1st edition (see ARBA 85, entry 1276) plus some fifty new additions. Each entry consists of a brief biographical sketch, bibliography, listing of critical studies, and critical essay on each of those individuals selected as prominent "thinkers" in the fields of science, mathematics, literature, philosophy, art, history, law, sociology, theology, economics, psychology, architecture, politics, and others.

Criteria for inclusion are not outlined in the volume, and selection appears to be almost random at times. For instance, information is provided for French artist Wassily Kandinsky, yet Pablo Picasso has been omitted from the volume; George Bernard Shaw is included, yet Nobel Prize winner Eugene O'Neill is not to be found; entries are provided for Karl Kautsky, Leon Trotsky, and V. I. Lenin, yet Joseph Stalin has been excluded.

The biographical sketches are brief, and include only the standard information on birth date, education, and professional positions. The signed critical essays provide more in-depth coverage of the individual's work and, for the most part, prove to be well written and researched.

The list of publications by each entrant is extensive, but the inclusion of several selected articles in addition to the books would have created a more well-rounded bibliography. As was the case with the 1st edition, the lack of a subject index poses a problem and makes access extremely difficult. In addition, potential users will not find this collection through subject-area listings or encyclopedias.

Though the information and bibliography provided for each entrant may be of use to the searcher, the volume's lack of selection criteria, subject index, and scope detract from its usefulness as a library reference source.—**Susan R. Penney**

45. **U*X*L Biographies: Biographies and Portraits of 1,500 High-Interest People**. [CD-ROM]. Detroit, U*X*L/Gale, 1996. Minimum system requirements: IBM or compatible 286 (486SX or faster recommended). ISO 9660-compatible CD-ROM drive with cables, interface card, and MS-DOS CD-ROM. Extensions 2.1 (double-speed drive or faster recommended). MS-DOS or PC-DOS 3.3. 640K RAM. 3MB hard disk space. VGA monitor and graphics card. Mouse (optional). Printer (optional). $325.00/stand-alone version; $450.00/2-8 users. ISBN 0-7876-0538-7. [Also available in Macintosh version.]

Designed for students in upper-elementary through middle school, *U*X*L Biographies* profiles 1,500 current and historical figures who represent an extremely broad range of endeavor. Although, as one would expect, there is strong representation of celebrities (especially athletes and entertainers), there are also entries for Black Elk, St. Francis of Assisi, Amelia Earhart, Vincent van Gogh, Vaclav Havel, Dean Koontz, Colin Powell, and Faye Wattleton. The entries range in length from 1,000 to 3,000 words and describe the individual's early years, key experiences, and adult careers. Sidebars highlight important events and provide factual summaries of each individual's career. Portraits are included with each entry, and many entries include not only other illustrations but also "fact boxes" that feature additional interesting information about the individual. Happily, the entries reflect the solid, consistent writing style found throughout the U*X*L series, and clearly are designed to engage the reader's interest. Each profile concludes with a list of sources to check for further information.

The software and search engine are simple to use and provide many options for "getting at" the kind of information students would be likely to look up. The main menu offers four search options: by name, by subject term, by personal data, and by custom search. Personal data include birth and death information; gender; nationality; ethnic group (African American, Arabic, Asian American, Hispanic American, and Native American); and occupation. Subject terms are derived from the subject term assigned to each individual based on his or her field(s) of endeavor. *Biographies* supports use of Boolean operators and truncation, as well as offering full-text search options, printing and downloading (especially useful with the photographs and other illustrations), on-screen tutorials, and context-sensitive help buttons.

This is a well-executed, high-quality resource that belongs in every school and public library. Although an expensive purchase, it provides exceptionally strong value for its cost. It should prove to be a popular research tool for its target audience. [R: RBB, 1 Feb 96, p. 948; SLJ, Aug 96, p. 60]—**G. Kim Dority**

46.   Vernoff, Edward, and Rima Shore. **The International Dictionary of 20th Century Biography**. New York, New American Library, 1987. 819p. index. $24.50. LC 86-21885. ISBN 0-453-00529-2.

The editors of this dictionary, Vernoff, a history teacher, and Shore, a Russian-language teacher, have taken on a considerable task—to provide sketches of notable men and women, living and dead, who have "made significant contributions during the century" (Introduction). The 5,650 notables have been drawn from all areas of endeavor with particular emphasis on politics and literature. Personalities from these fields represent half of the total. Although the sketches are brief they tell more than the typical who's who entry and give a sense of the person's contributions. Ray Kroc, founder of the McDonald's hamburger chain, is included (100 words), as are Rod Laver, Australian tennis star (115 words), and Ernesto Maserati, Italian car designer (50 words). The emphasis seems to be on the more popular figures as indicated by the inclusion of forty-two cartoonists and only nineteen political scientists.

In the case of writers, chief works are noted along with, frequently, one or two critical studies. An index by professional area helps to organize the names, but the lack of running heads on the page tops makes the index less useful. The binding, unfortunately, does not look as if it will withstand extended active reference use. This dictionary will serve as a supplement, for quick identification, to fuller sources, such as *Current Biography* and *Contemporary Newsmakers*. Certainly, few librarians will find fault with the price.—**Donald C. Dickinson**

47.   **Webster's Biographical Dictionary**. Springfield, Mass., G. & C. Merriam, 1980. 1697p. (A Merriam-Webster Co.). $15.00. LC 79-23607. ISBN 0-87779-443-X.

The aim of *Webster's Biographical Dictionary* "is to provide in a single handy volume a work of biographical reference not restricted in its selection of names by considerations of historical period, nationality, race, religion, or occupation." In this effort, the work is successful, and it has become a standard on the ready-reference shelf. Some 40,000 names have been amassed in the volume, approximately the same number as in the original 1943 edition. It is interesting that this volume carries a 1980 copyright, but it is not a numbered edition, nor are previous copyright years listed. In fact, remarkably little is revealed about the selection processes used to update the volume. "Only in certain classes of contemporaries may some consultants feel an inadequacy. The names of persons prominent (sometimes only briefly) in sports, in motion pictures, in the contemporary theater, and in radio are so numerous that the editors were compelled, however reluctantly, to curtail their representation to the minimum" (preface). In reality, the omissions are a little more widespread than in the areas stated. Jimmy Carter and Walter Mondale are included; Ronald Reagan and George Bush are not. Also missing are Golda Meir, Ian Smith, and Suharto.

Because the process of updating is not explained, and the editors do not claim comprehensive coverage of current notables, a library might carefully consider ordering each new edition. Nonetheless, *Webster's Biographical Dictionary* is an excellent single-source reference, and every library should own a recent edition.

An abridged version advertised as *Webster's New Biographical Dictionary*, covering 30,000 biographies (1148p.), sells for $18.95. [R: BL, 15 July 70, p. 1353; RQ, Summer 73, p. 411; WLB, Jan 70, p. 563]—**Janet H. Littlefield**

48.   **Who Was Who Volume IX: Who Was Who 1991-1995**. New York, St. Martin's Press, 1996. 619p. $99.95. ISBN 0-312-16246-4.

With the publication of this edition, St. Martin's Press has stepped up this necrology's publication rate, from a decennial to a quinquennial basis. As in earlier volumes, alphabetically arranged profiles largely consist of a death-date tagline appended to the subject's most recent appearance in the relevant sister publication of *Who's Who*. Cross-references remain plentiful and helpful, although some heraldic nomenclature will be an impediment for many (information on British government leader Harold Wilson is buried under the entry "Wilson of Rievaulx," for example).

Librarians on this side of the Atlantic will be pleased to find entries for Helen Hayes, Kay Boyle, Frank Capra, John Connolly, and Jonas Salk, but will be disappointed with the omission of such figures as Colleen Dewhurst, Wallace Stegner, George Abbott (New York City mayor), Robert Wagner, and Jean Mayer. The demise of such international figures as Northrop Frye and Natalia Ginzburg also is unrecorded, as is the passing of noted women Jacqueline Kennedy Onassis, Sylvia Porter, and Ginger Rogers. U.S. athletes missing from this edition's pages include Mickey Mantle, Leo Durocher, and Arthur Ashe. Given its content and price, this reference tool is optional for all but the most comprehensive of U.S. and Canadian biographical collections.—**Jeffrey E. Long**

49.   **The Who's Who of Nobel Prize Winners 1901-1995**. 3d ed. Bernard S. Schlessinger and June H. Schlessinger, eds. Phoenix, Ariz., Oryx Press, 1996. 251p. index. $49.95. ISBN 0-89774-899-9.

When Alfred Nobel invented dynamite, little did he know that his ticket to fortune would be the least explosive of his inventions. The Nobel Prizes, especially in literature, have proven time and again not only to be volcanic, but also highly controversial. This new edition of those famous winners is now the most up-to-date source (barring those online) on all Nobel winners from chemistry and economics to literature, medicine, peace, and physics. Within each subject area, winners are listed chronologically. A brief vita follows, with a selected bibliography and a comment from the award itself. Name, education, citizenship, and religion indexes follow. As sources go, this is about as pedestrian as it gets. Yet such a source, when needed, is the only thing that will suffice. Trying to locate this much information in other sources is easy; trying to find that information in the space of a few hours is humanly impossible. [R: Choice, Dec 96, p. 596]—**Mark Y. Herring**

50.   Wigoder, Geoffrey. **They Made History: A Biographical Dictionary**. New York, Simon & Schuster Academic Reference Division, 1993. 711p. illus. $55.00. CT103.W54. 920.02. LC 93-25031. ISBN 0-13-915257-1.

Including such luminaries as Franklin D. Roosevelt, Alexander the Great, Homer, Sigmund Freud, George Gershwin, and Oliver Cromwell, Wigoder has compiled a who's who of some 750 deceased figures who have contributed, either positively or negatively, to the making of history. Freely admitting that any selections in such a work must be subjective, he has defined history as the broad spectrum of human endeavor that has "advanced the march of civilization and broadened the human experience." Entries vary as to the significance of the individual, but most are roughly 750 words long. Interestingly enough, Adolf Hitler receives almost 1,775 words, while Jesus Christ merits only about 900. Numerous essays feature boxed inserts that provide either anecdotes about or quotations by the highlighted person, and all individuals warrant a bibliography for additional research. Many of the biographies are illustrated with portraits or black-and-white photographs.

None of the entries are signed, although the book includes a list of contributors. Although the lack of a broad occupation index that would provide some frame of reference for users is excusable, the omission of an alphabetical name index is not. Small libraries may find the volume handy, but most libraries will be better served by any number of other biographical reference works, such as *The McGraw-Hill Encyclopedia of World Biography* (see entry 31).—**Jack Bales**

51.   **World Leaders: People Who Shaped the World**. Rob Nagel and Anne Commire, eds. Detroit, U*X*L/Gale, 1994. 3v. illus. maps. index. $57.00/set. D107.W65.920.02. LC 94-20544. ISBN 0-8103-9768-4.

This collection of 120 leaders is a useful reference tool for young people in the middle and early secondary grades. The individual entries, typically spanning three to four pages, do not have exceptional depth, but they do introduce young people to a broad range of historical figures who have shaped the last 4,000 years of recorded history. Chiefly, political and military leaders are profiled, although there are social and religious figures such as Jesus of Nazareth, Siddhartha, Lao-tzu, Francis of Assisi, Mother Ann Lee (founder of the Shakers), Jane Addams, Eleanor Roosevelt, and Booker T. Washington. The attention paid to leaders from Asia and Africa is an especially positive feature of this collection at a time when schools are paying greater attention to multicultural education. This is not to say, however, that this reference work is free of bias. The United States is represented by 30 lives, one-fourth of the total number of lives present to represent the great leaders of all recorded history. While it is a positive feature that this list of 30 notable Americans includes seven women, seven African Americans, and four Native Americans, it is also surprising that Greece, generally considered to be the cradle of Western civilization, is not represented by a single historical figure.

The work consists of three volumes, each presenting forty profiles. Volume 1 presents leaders from Asia and Africa; volume 2 covers Europe; and volume 3 presents North and South American leaders. Several standard features are repeated in each of the three volumes. Biographical listings are located in the opening pages of each volume. So too is an alphabetized country-by-country list of the 120 featured leaders. A 14-page timeline ranging from 3000 B.C. and projected to A.D. 2000 is provided. All 120 subjects are placed on the timeline. The earliest person profiled is the Egyptian woman ruler Hatshepsut, and the most recent is Mikhail Gorbachev. The master index is repeated in all three volumes and includes bold typeface entries noting the leaders profiled.

Individual entries of most leaders are illustrated with portraits or photographs. Each entry starts with the name and dates and places of birth and death for the subject, plus a brief overview stating his or her significance to history. The remainder of each entry provides a chronological overview of the subject's life. Maps are featured in profiles of leaders such as Genghis Khan, who conquered vast territories. Sidebars often provide extensions of learning. For example, a sidebar briefly outlines the philosophy of Taoism in the profile of the Chinese philosopher Lao-tzu. *World Leaders* is a fine and useful resource that should help both teachers and library media specialists connect today's youth with the vital leaders who have influenced and shaped the world they will inherit. [R: RBB, 1 Oct 94, p. 364]—**Jerry D. Flack**

52.   Yenne, Bill. **100 Men Who Shaped World History**. San Francisco, Calif., Bluewood, 1994. 112p. illus. maps. index. $7.95pa. ISBN 0-912517-05-0.

This work also has a companion volume entitled *100 Women Who Shaped World History* by Bill Yenne (San Francisco, Calif., Bluewood 1994. 112p. illus. maps. index. $7.95pa. ISBN 0-912517-06-9). These two slim companion volumes provide capsule views of 100 men and 100 women who made their mark in history. Each volume includes a table of contents with a timeline along the bottom showing the entry's place in history, an introduction, the individual entries arranged in chronological order, a trivia quiz based upon the entries, and an index. The one-page entries include at least one illustration (usually of the individual under discussion); a small map indicating the person's country; and a brief overview of the person's life, with an emphasis on his or her contribution. The men's volume basically covers individuals who are readily found in general reference sources (e.g., Homer, William Shakespeare, Simon Bolivar, Thomas Edison, and Stephen Hawking). Similarly, the women's volume covers many predictable names (e.g., Harriet Beecher Stowe, Helen Keller, Golda Meir), but also highlights less well-known influences such as Marquise du Chatelet, Madame Lavoisier, and Mary Wortley Montagu. No bibliography or further reading list is furnished. These paperbacks would work best as circulating copies in the children's young adult section, or as supplemental texts in history or English as a Second Language classes.—**Esther R. Sinofsky and Robert L. Wick**

2 National and Regional Sources

AFRICA

53. Brockman, Norbert C. **An African Biographical Dictionary**. Santa Barbara, Calif., ABC-CLIO, 1994. 440p. illus. maps. index. $54.00. ISBN 0-87436-748-4.

This book provides biographical sketches of nearly 500 people who figure prominently in the history of sub-Saharan Africa. It includes non-Africans as well as Africans. The emphasis is on post-colonial contemporary history. North African states of the Mediterranean basin are not included; the island nations of the Indian Ocean are.

A listing of the entries under the following categories is given: politics, culture, economics, science and technology, religion, and geography and history. For example, under politics, there are traditional rulers, imperialists, anti-colonial resistance leaders, post-independence heads of state or government, civil servants, political figures, and guerrilla leaders. Under culture, entries include sculptors and painters, novelists and writers, musicians, sports figures, and feminist activists and thinkers. Within economics, some subcategories are business people and entrepreneurs, traders, and labor leaders. Science and technology is broken down into such subdivisions as physicists and mathematicians, wildlife and environmental advocates, engineers, medical and health care specialists, and paleontologists and archaeologists. The area of religion includes traditional religious leaders, Islamic leaders, African Christian leaders, Christian missionaries, and prophets and leaders of new religious movements. Finally, under geography and history, there are chroniclers and historians, and geographers and explorers.

An individual is sometimes listed under more than one heading. The headings indicate the spheres of activity of those included in this dictionary. Each entry starts with a short statement of the person's significance, followed by a chronological biographical sketch. Brief evaluations of their work are given for the cultural figures. Many of the entries refer the reader to one or more of 34 works listed in the book. Some entries list an autobiography and principal biographies, where relevant. Several appendixes are given to aid the reader, and there is also an index.—**J. E. Weaver**

54. **Dictionary of African Historical Biography**. 2nd ed. Mark R. Lipschutz and R. Kent Rasmussen, eds. Berkeley, Calif., University of California Press, 1986. 328p. bibliog. index. $40.00. LC 86-19157. ISBN 0-520-05179-3.

The authors of this book call it a handbook of the general literature, saying that "our primary criterion for choosing each name is its prominence in that literature." The 850 primarily biographical entries consequently focus on precolonial political leaders from much-studied regions of sub-Saharan Africa and on nineteenth-century events. The entries are arranged alphabetically, with additional access provided by an index of subjects and an index of names, variant names, and variant spellings. Each entry cites at least one work listed in the extensive bibliography. The 2nd edition is almost identical to the 1st (see ARBA 80, entry 292), but while the earlier edition only covered events through 1960, the later one contains a supplement of entries making the work current through 1980.

Biographical sketches of those people who have been significant since 1960 have been updated from the 1st edition. Yet oddly enough, other presumably less important entries have been shortened so that the revised section of the 2nd edition is the same length as its counterpart in the original work. Nevertheless, the concise yet detailed biographies, large bold headings for each entry, inclusion of maps, and the two indexes make this a well-rounded reference book. The lack of other convenient sources of biographical information about African personalities further increases its usefulness.—**Cathy Seitz**

55. **The Encyclopaedia Africana Dictionary of African Biography (in 20 Volumes).** New York, Reference Publications, 1977- . In progress. illus. maps. index. $59.95/vol. LC 76-17954. ISSN 0013-712X.

The appearance in 1977 of the first volume (*Ethiopa-Ghana*) under the aegis of the *Encyclopaedia Africana* is a major publishing event. It is the first tangible outcome of W. E. B. DuBois's dream (conceived in 1909) of a monumental synoptic work devoted to the contributions of Africa and Africans to civilization. The idea has been kept alive for more than half a century, but not until 1961 was it possible to translate it into a concrete plan. That year, DuBois moved to Ghana to organize and direct the project with Nkrumah's financial and moral support. Following DuBois's death in 1963, the editorial board of the *Encyclopaedia* decided to implement the plan by initially publishing volumes of biographical articles on a country-by-country basis covering the entire sweep of African history. Subsequent financial support came from some African governments and from American and West German foundations.

The first volume brings together 146 Ethiopian and 138 Ghanian biographies spanning many centuries. They include rulers, statesmen, politicians, religious leaders, intellectuals, and people from all walks of life who have influenced the course of events in these countries in one way or another. Many of the people highlighted had been previously overlooked by Western literature. All biographies are treated in a broad historical framework in the context of events contemporary with the biographee. Consequently, the whole historical epoch comes alive through the vivid individual portraiture.

The articles resulted from meticulous research carried out by leading Africanists in the world, half of whom are African nationals associated with leading universities on the continent. Uniformly, the tone of discourse is elevated. Attempts to assess objectively a person's significance and efforts to present historical events in a balanced manner are in evidence throughout the whole work. The articles dealing with Grazianiin Ethiopia and Padmore in Ghana could be cited as examples. Collectively, these biographies accomplish the project's objective, which Kenneth Kaunda, president of the Republic of Zambia, defined in the *Dictionary*'s prefatory note: "to reveal the genius of her [Africa's] people, their history, culture and institutions, their achievements as well as their shortcomings."

The articles are cross-referenced and followed by substantial bibliographies both of materials in various Western languages and of citations to local source materials when available. A detailed index at the end of the volume provides excellent topical penetration into the contents of the articles, making the *Dictionary* a superb tool for researching many aspects of Ethiopia and Ghana. A large number of the biographies are accompanied by portraits and illustrations. Each section of the work is preceded by a twenty-page overview of the history of these two countries. Other features include a glossary of unfamiliar terms and maps of provinces, principal rivers, towns, and ethnic distribution of the population.

In 1979, the second volume was published (*Sierra Leone-Zaire*), and again the articles were based on materials ranging from archival resources to standard treatises listed in the source bibliographies that follow each biography. The third volume (*South Africa, Botswana-Lesotho Swaziland*) was published in 1985.

The *Dictionary of African Biography* should be hailed as a landmark achievement in every respect. When completed, it will close a vast gap in our knowledge. In restoring the dignity of Africa's contribution to the civilization of mankind, it will become an effective instrument for the promotion of cultural understanding between Africa and the West. [R: BL, 1 Mar 78, p. 1127; Choice, Dec 78, p. 1346]—**Michael Keresztesi**

56. Naylor, Phillip Chiviges, and Alf Andrew Heggoy. **Historical Dictionary of Algeria.** 2d ed. Metuchen, N.J., Scarecrow, 1994. 443p. maps. (African Historical Dictionaries, no. 66). $55.00. ISBN 0-8108-2748-4.

This is another volume in the second round of historical dictionaries relating to Africa. As with other 2d editions in the series, it is superior to its predecessor, being in fact a combination of new and old. (See ARBA 82, entry 326, for a review of the previous edition.)

By the standards of the series, this is a large volume, and it possesses the usual accouterments: a list of acronyms, a glossary, and tables of colonial and independence governments. There is also a

50-page bibliography that contains an appropriately large list of French-language materials, as well as a 40-page introduction providing some background. There is more on the precolonial period than in most of the African Historical Dictionaries, but this volume still remains largely biographical and contemporary in its focus. Chronologically, coverage extends back to pre-Roman times; geographically, there is relatively little on interior Algeria.

The entries seem accurate and internally well balanced, and it is a pity that the lack of an index—common to all volumes in this series—precludes convenient access to the materials in them. Although there is a good degree of cross-referencing (the entry for *Vandals* serves as an example), it remains that only luck or unnecessary persistence will bring users to much of the information in the work, and opportunities to discern patterns and commonalities are all but lost. Smaller print throughout would have permitted an index to be accommodated without additional pages.—**David Henige**

57. Rake, Alan. **100 Great Africans**. Metuchen, N.J., Scarecrow, 1994. 431p. maps. index. $59.50. ISBN 0-8108-2929-0.

The subjects in this book are arranged into 11 topical chapters, with titles such as "Saints and Sinners," "Struggle Against Colonialism," and "Modern Rulers." There are nine maps for topics such as "Egypt and Kush," "The Golden Kings," and "Hannibal and Rome." The entries, averaging four pages each, are longer than those found in the older *Dictionary of Africa Historical Biography* (see ARBA 87, entry 96). The text in Rake's book flows a little better as well, but there are no source notes or bibliographies, a serious omission. Illustrations of these people would also have been nice, although that would have raised the book's price. Rake selected people whose significance was in Africa, regardless of their color or place of birth. He leaves out those whom he considered "essentially visitors doing a job on behalf of themselves or external powers" (p.viii), such as Henry Stanley and David Livingstone, General Charles Gordon, and Albert Schweitzer. The author is the managing editor of *New African* magazine, and also wrote *Who's Who in Africa: Leaders for the 1990s* (see ARBA 93, entry 760), which complements his newer title. Rake writes in the preface that "this book is essentially journalistic, not based on profound academic research." This biographical dictionary is suitable for the reference collections of all academic, high school, and public libraries. [R: WLB, Feb 95, p. 70]—**Daniel K. Blewett**

58. **Who's Who of Southern Africa: An Illustrated Biographical Record**. S. V. Hayes and W. A. C. van Niekerk, eds. Johannesburg, South Africa, Who's Who of Southern Africa; distr., Bristol, Pa., Taylor & Francis, 1907- . illus. $130.00. for recent edition.

The present 1993 edition of this annual, first published since 1907, contains some 3,500 to 4,500 biographical entries ranging in length from 100 to 300 words, most being shorter rather than longer. All the countries of southern Africa are covered, as well as Mauritius, but South Africa captures the lion's share of attention.

The work is as much a paean to South African entrepreneurial enterprise as it is a reference work. In the preface, for instance, the publisher foresees that "the struggle in South Africa will be to eliminate government from the daily business of the people," and adds that "prosperity follows economic freedom," so that "South Africa will flourish as government is unbundled." The brief introduction to Namibia is written by the managing director of Standard Bank Namibia; color advertisement festoon the landscape; and the biographees are overwhelmingly white, overwhelmingly male, and overwhelmingly in business.

The work is not without value, however. There are useful government, diplomatic, and educational directories, and addresses are provided for all entrants. And there are innumerable gems for the finding, such as that Canaan Banana, the former president of Zimbabwe, is by avocation a soccer referee! Even so, *Who's Who of Southern Africa* belies its expansive name, is largely unconcerned with today's interests in and about South Africa, and will be more at home in a business than in a general reference collection.—**David Henige**

59. **Who's Who of Southern Africa**. S. V. Hayes, ed. Bristol, Pa., Taylor & Francis, 1989. 674p. illus. maps. index. $130.00. ISSN 0083-9876.

This is a crucial reference for anyone interested in southern Africa. Coverage is not limited just to the Republic of South Africa; Botswana, Mauritius, Namibia, Swaziland, and Zimbabwe are also covered. The heart of the work consists of biographical sketches of notable men and women in the areas of geographical coverage. In virtually all instances there is a photograph of the biographee.

Unfortunately, there is no indication of how those listed are chosen, although inclusion is by invitation only. There are some obvious omissions, but that is inevitable in a work of this scope. Still, the coverage is impressive, and the utility of the work goes well beyond provision of basic biographical data. Its first 108 pages are devoted to useful information on the administrators and faculties of universities, representatives of foreign governments in South Africa, political office holders and those in key government posts, and more. In this sense the book is also an official guide to the Republic of South Africa. This is a work of vital importance for any academic library supporting study or research in African studies.—**James A. Casada**

ASIA AND THE PACIFIC RIM

60. **Who's Who of the Asian Pacific Rim**. 1992 ed. Laguna Beach, Calif., Barons Who's Who, 1991. 705p. index. $175.00. LC 91-061765. ISBN 0-9620943-5-8. ISSN 1059-5392.

More than a who's who, this volume is an up-to-date source of information on business and government leaders; principal Asian Rim corporations; government agencies; and religious organizations in China, Hong Kong, Indonesia, Japan, Malaysia, the Philippines, Singapore, South Korea, Taiwan, and Thailand. The 6,145 biographies of leaders are alphabetized by surname in the first and largest section. They include business addresses, telephone and fax numbers, current job title, and function. Many also give personal and professional data, and a few are accompanied by a photograph of the biographee. The corporation directory lists 4,262 corporations grouped by country. Each entry gives address, telephone and fax numbers, and names and titles of the chief executives. Government agencies are provided in a third section by country and include ministries, consulates, embassies, officials, and courts. Major religious organizations and churches of each country appear in a separate section. An index to the directory sections is organized under 68 professional or subject categories, then by country, and finally by corporate name. No page references are given; the user must look under the appropriate section and under each country. Because the directories are basically alphabetical in arrangement, this should cause no major difficulty.

This compilation will be extremely useful for persons in business and commerce who need to make contact with or learn about key individuals and corporations in the Asian Rim countries. It will be an essential part of any business collection and also of use in general reference or Asian studies collections.—**Shirley L. Hopkinson**

AUSTRALIA AND NEW ZEALAND

61. **Australian Dictionary of Biography**. Carlton, Victoria, Melbourne University Press; distr., Portland, Oreg., International Scholarly Book Services, 1966- . In progress. (To be published in 12v.) $41.00/vol.

The *Australian Dictionary of Biography* is a projected twelve-volume compilation of biographical sketches, of which nine volumes have already been published. The first two volumes cover 1788-1850; volumes 3, 4, 5, and 6, 1851-1890; volumes 5 and 6, 1851-1890; volumes 7, 8, and 9, 1891-1939. The volume which covers 1940-1980 was completed and published in 1993. At this time, there is no indication when this work will be completed. Sketches range in length from under a page to seven pages, and when completed, the project will include some 7,000 biographies. All articles are signed and include a short list of reference sources, personal data, and information on careers and other contributions. According to the preface, this scholarly work is based on consultation and cooperation, and the "burden of writing has been shared by university historians and by members of historical and genealogical societies and other specialists." Some 2,000 contributors are involved in this project, and "the placing of each individual's name in the appropriate section has been generally determined by when he did his most important work. For articles that overlap the chronological division, preference has usually been given to the earlier period, although all the important Federationists will appear in the third section, 1891-1939." A complete index of names will be published in the last volume.

A related title is *Who's Who in Australia* (23rd ed. Philadelphia, International Publications Service, 1980. 925p. $67.50. ISBN 0-8002-2541-4), that started in 1922 and was published by Herald and Weekly Times in Melbourne. The title and frequency of this current biography vary. The twentieth edition incorporated John's *Notable Australians,* first published in 1906. Occasionally, this work carries an *Australian Biographical Dictionary and Register of Titled Persons.*

Most larger libraries may also have *Debrett's Handbook of Australia and New Zealand* (2nd ed. distr., Chicago, Marquis Who's Who, 1984. $85.00. ISBN 0-949-137-006), that contains 800 brief biographies of prominent people in Australia and New Zealand. In addition to biographical sketches, this handbook provides gazetteer-type information on both countries.—**Bohdan S. Wynar and Robert L. Wick**

62. **Bateman New Zealand Encyclopedia**. 2d ed. Gordon McLauchlan, ed. Auckland, New Zealand, David Bateman; distr., Boston, G. K. Hall, 1987. 640p. illus. (part col.). maps. index. $49.00. ISBN 0-908610-21-1.

As a reference volume, this encyclopedia is intended for a wide range of readers in age and background. The topics range across a standard array; geography, explorers, arts (writers, musicians, artists), agriculture, sports, and natural history, with particular strength in individuals (of all sorts—explorers; artists; politicians; sports figures, particularly in rugby; religious leaders), Maori culture (individuals, names, places, history), flora, fauna, and whaling, but with less extensive coverage of business and commerce, history (as connected with Europe), demographics, and politics. General or popular knowledge for an interested general reader, from fifth grade up, is stressed, so this encyclopedia, while accurate and authoritative, does not provide the detail or world coverage one expects in *Encyclopaedia Britannica* or *The Encyclopedia Americana.*

The coverage in this 2nd edition goes through mid-1987, including Prime Minister Lange's reelection, which is mentioned in the eighteen-page historical chronology (from A.D. 925) but not in his personal entry. A subject index (twelve pages) covers only the headings of the approximately 1,900 entries but not topics or people who merit mention but no individual entry. Colored maps cover climate, vegetation, forest, minerals, land use, soils, and New Zealand's Antarctic claim. A foldout map shows topography, cities, and major roads. Forty-eight pages of colored plates depict stamps; flags; coats of arms; war ribbons; Maori artifacts; geothermal, geologic, glacial, and river features; sheep; industries; art; insects, birds, flowers, fruits, and butterflies.

This volume is a delight to browse. The text is extremely readable, a popular as distinguished from a technical approach to New Zealand. With a wealth of information, this extremely useful single-volume work for libraries and individuals serves as a quick reference on New Zealand. [R: RBB, 1 Dec 88, pp. 628, 630]—**Richard A. Miller**

63. **Monash Biographical Dictionary of 20th Century Australia**. John Arnold and Deirdre Morris, eds. New Providence, N.J., Reed Reference Publishing, 1994. 568p. $50.00. ISBN 1-875589-19-8.

Compiled under the direction of the Australian Research Council and Monash University, this work provides brief biographies on more than "2200 Australians who have achieved prominence and/or made a contribution to their country this century" (foreword). It is another imprint in an unofficial series from Monash University, which has already produced *Who's Who of Australian Writers* (1991) and other reference works. Previous biographical works on Australians have included John Henniker Heaton's *Australian Dictionary of Dates and Men of the Time* (1879), Fred Johns's who's who series beginning with *Who's Who in Australia* (1906), and *Australian Dictionary of Biography* (1906-). While the *Australian Dictionary of Biography* has been updated through the years, this new twentieth-century dictionary is a welcome addition to the biographical information on Australians.

The criteria for inclusion in the *Monash Biographical Dictionary* do not require that each individual be of Australian birth or an Australian citizen, but that each has made a significant contribution to Australian society. In this respect, Australians who have simply gained a certain amount of fame for one reason or another are not necessarily included. Standard bibliographical form has been followed for each entry, which includes full name (including any nicknames or aliases), dates of birth and death, an indication of the occupation of the individual, and a brief biographical sketch. At the end of each entry, there is a reference code that corresponds to a chart of acronyms and abbreviations in the front of the volume referring to various organizations, associations, or honors common for Australians. In addition, there is a bibliography of works (67 items) used in the compilation of the volume. No other appendixes are provided.

This book will be an invaluable reference for biographical information on twentieth-century Australians, and it will act as a complement to the older Australian biographical dictionaries. It should be considered for personal collections and for all larger public and academic libraries worldwide.—**Robert L. Wick**

CANADA

64. **Canadian Who's Who**. Elizabeth Lumley, ed. Toronto and Buffalo, N.Y., University of Toronto Press, 1910, 1936, 1978- . [1996 edition: 1338p. $165.00 (U.S.).] ISSN 0068-9963.

The 1st edition of *Canadian Who's Who* was published in 1910 by the Times Publishing Company (London), with the 2nd edition appearing in 1936. It has been published every third year since. In 1978, Tunnell sold it to the University of Toronto Press, which has continued the publishing schedule. The University of Toronto Press has been known for its reference list in Canadiana.

Canadian Who's Who is the standard source for current biography. This edition includes entries for more than 15,000 Canadians. Each year, those already listed are twice invited to update their biographies, and questionnaires are mailed to new candidates for inclusion. More than 5,000 individuals were invited to submit new listings for the 1996 edition. Each biography follows a standard format of occupation, personal data, education, career, with current position usefully picked out in capitals, publications, honors, awards, religion, recreations, clubs, and addresses. Entries vary in length from four lines to half of a three-column page.

Sample checking of musicians, writers, aboriginal and labor leaders, and even expatriates such as Peter Jennings and John Kenneth Galbraith indicates coverage that is both comprehensive and current. To measure occupational and gender inclusion, the first 50 names starting with C were examined. Of these, 11 are women, 20 work in business and finance, 10 are academics, 5 are in law, and another 5 are writers. The remaining 10 include a family-planning advocate, a retired aboriginal leader, a singer, an artist, an actress, a museum curator, and a politician. Thirty-nine of the listings include a home address. Design and production are appropriate for this essential annual reference source.—**Patricia Fleming and Robert L. Wick**

65. **Dictionary of Canadian Biography**. Frances G. Halpenny, ed. Toronto and Buffalo, N.Y., University of Toronto Press, 1966- . In progress. $60.00 for recent volumes. ISSN 0070-4717.

Also published in French under the title *Dictionnaire biographique du Canada*, by Les Presses de l'Université Laval, Quebec. This is the most important Canadian retrospective biography patterned after *DNB* and *DAB*. It should be noted that the *Dictionary of Canadian Biography* is not published in sequence. Volume 1, covering subjects who died before 1701, was published in 1966; volume 2, for the period 1701-1740, appeared in 1969; volume 5, 1801-1820, was published in 1983; volume 8, 1851-1860, was published in 1985; volume 10, for the decade 1871-1880, was published in 1972. The other volumes published at this writing are: volume 3, 1741-1770, in 1974; volume 4, 1771-1800, in 1979; volume 9, 1861-1870, in 1976; volume 11, 1881-1890, in 1982. A limited deluxe edition, Laurentian Edition, is also available at $100/volume, bound in morocco and buckram.

There is a major difference between *DCB* and the *DNB* and *DAB*. The Canadian work is being produced on the premise that coverage of a segment of time creates the most coherent frame for the consideration of a nation's major figures. In contrast, *DNB* and *DAB* were, in their main volumes, issued in straight alphabetical order. Their supplementary volumes, however, are appearing on a time-segment basis.

Editorial policy as stated in the preface includes the "Directives" supplied to contributors: "Each biography should be an informative and stimulating treatment of its subject, presented in readable form. All factual information should be precise and accurate, and be based upon reliable (preferably primary) sources. Biographies should not, however, be mere catalogues of dates and events, or compilations of previous studies of the same subject. The biographer should try to give the reader an orderly account of the personality and achievements of the subject against the background of the period in which the person lived and the events in which he or she participated."

Thus, for example, to reinforce the background of 1741-1770, the editor has included two clearly written historical review essays on the French forces and the British forces in the Seven Years War, written by W. J. Eccles and C. P. Stacey, respectively. These essays are particularly apposite because most of the 550 figures who died between 1741 and 1770 and are therefore treated in this volume were in one way or another involved in that eighteenth-century struggle between Britain and France for commercial dominance of North America. Persons qualified for inclusion are those who took an active part or exerted major influences in that part of North America which later became Canada. Thus, we find many prominent French officers (e.g., the Marquis de Montcalm), British officers (e.g., General James Wolfe), and Indian chiefs (e.g., Pontiac).

An examination of sample biographies shows that the editors have accomplished their main goal: The sketches do indeed "give the reader an orderly account of the personality and achievements of the subject against the background of the period."

On the average, each volume contains some 500 biographies ranging from 400 to 1,200 words in length. There are copious bibliographies, a full-name index, and cross-references to other people and other volumes. A new feature in the eleventh volume is a regional index, subdivided by primary area of occupation. In short, *DCB* is an irreplaceable source of documentation on Canada and should find its place in any respectable library.—**Bohdan S. Wynar and Robert L. Wick**

66.   Stamp, Robert M. **The Canadian Obituary Record: A Biographical Dictionary of Canadians Who Died in 1992**. Toronto, Dundurn Press, 1993. 288p. index. $39.99. ISBN 1-55002-193-1.

Begun in 1988, *The Canadian Obituary Record* is published annually to "provide brief, interpretive biographies of over 500 Canadians who died in the previous twelve months—persons prominent in all fields of endeavor and all parts of the country" (introduction to the 1988 edition). The selection of individuals provides a wide representation of Canadian society in all walks of life.

Canada lacks an encyclopedia yearbook, and obituaries are not included in that country's almanacs and current biographical sources. Now in its sixth year, *The Canadian Obituary Record* (*COR*) offers interpretive biographies, ranging in length from 100 to 800 words, of 500 Canadians "prominent in all fields of endeavor and all parts of the country" who died in 1992. In this volume, the short subjects include local politicians and community volunteers. The style is crisp and uncompromising, providing such details as the discovery of marijuana in a politician's suitcase during a royal visit. Each biography concludes with citations to one or more of 70 sources, mostly newspapers or reference books.

The geographical index, arranged by province and then city (with a second section for other countries), includes places of birth, death, and major work activity. The identification index uses 19 categories, many subdivided (e.g., "Academia" is broken into 26 disciplines). A cumulative nominal index for 1988-1991 concludes the volume. Printed in two-column format with pleasant type and a clearly lettered binding, *The Canadian Obituary Record* fills a need admirably.—**Patricia Fleming and Robert L. Wick**

67.   **Who's Who in Canada: An Illustrated Biographical Record**. Catherine Brown and Kimberley Lund, eds. Agincourt, Ont., Global Press; distr., Bristol, Pa., Taylor & Francis, 1911- . illus. Annual. $125.00 for recent volumes.

The initial edition of this reference tool was published in 1911 and concentrated on prominent people from Western Canada. While the early editions of the work included mostly Canadians from business, the professions, government, and academia, and represented mostly men, more recent editions have attempted a more balanced representation of both men and women. Each entry contains the standard features for such a dictionary: brief information on education, career history, memberships, honors, publications, and residence. Photographs accompany most entries. The dictionary is organized in alphabetical order, and it also contains an index of entries, a list of abbreviations, and a cross-reference listing by corporation or professional body.

There is some inconsistency in the language of presentation. Some entries are in one language (English of French); some are in both. The language used does not appear to depend on the linguistic background of the individual. This publication is not the best biographical dictionary of Canadians available, but it is useful for the information it provides on the business community.—**Lorna K. Rees-Potter and Robert L. Wick**

EUROPE

68.   **International Biographical Dictionary of Central European Emigrés 1933-1945**. Herbert A. Strauss and Werner Röder, eds. Munich, New York, K. G. Saur, 1980-1983. 3v. $375.00. ISBN 3-598-10089-2.

Publication of these three volumes completes an important project concerning the emigrés that fled Nazi Germany between the years 1933 and 1945. It is a representative sampling of 8,700 individuals who achieved prominence in the arts, science, and literature among the more than 500,000 who fled. Each entry provides a brief paragraph of vital statistics (including religion, emigration information, and destination), a more descriptive paragraph describing activities, and a bibliography. Volume 3 is a complete index to volumes 1 and 2.

As far as could be determined, the information is accurate and complete and is marred only by occasional typographical errors that closer proofreading might have found but that do not interfere with the works' usefulness. Since a number of the individuals are listed in other sources, this may not be an essential source for all libraries. But for those interested in the period, in Central European history, or in American intellectual history, this is a vital publication. [R: Choice, Sept 84, p. 64]—**Erwin K. Welsch**

69.   **Who's Who in European Institutions and Enterprises: A Biographical Directory**. John C. Dove, ed. Zurich, Switzerland, Verlag AG; distr., Hauppauge, N.Y., Ballen Booksellers International, 1992. 2298p. illus. maps. index. (Sutter's International Red Series). $230.00. ISBN 88-85246-18-4.

Although this volume is titled *Who's Who*, it also includes considerable information of the sort found in *Statesman's Year-Book* (see ARBA 92, entry 77). One-half of the book consists of biographical entries on European politicians and government officials, while the other half is descriptive and statistical information about the European Community and the various nations of the Council of Europe. More than 4,000 people connected with the European Community, the governments of the nations of the Council of Europe, and industry and commerce form the biographical entries. They range from well-known figures, such as Lech Walsea and John Major, to obscure banking executives and members of national Olympic committees. An anonymous committee of experts has picked the biographees, who must be living to be included. The biographical information supplies the normal vital and family information as well as education, career, publications, awards, memberships, and recreational activities.

The second part of the volume begins with a section describing the various components of the government of the European Community and the Council of Europe and listing the names of the various officials. This information is followed by a country-by-country survey of the 27 nations of the Council of Europe, which includes a map, a brief history, a description of politics and government, and an economic overview. A third section provides an industry-by-industry survey of the European economy, while the fourth and fifth sections deal with cultural and social matters. A brief index allows individual companies or government agencies to be located. As a current source of European information, this title is quite useful and has been considerably expanded beyond earlier editions. [R: Choice, Oct 93, p. 274; LJ, 15 Sept 93, p. 70]—**Ronald H. Fritze**

FRANCE

70.   **Who's Who in France. Qui est qui en France: Dictionnaire biographique**. Paris, Editions Jacclues Lafitte; distr., Detroit, Gale, 1953- . $190.00 for recent edition. ISSN 0083-9531.

The 1st edition was published in 1953, covering 1953-1954 and providing some 5,000 biographical sketches of Who's Who type. Subsequently, it became a biennial, and the present edition contains some 20,000 biographies covering a wide range of prominent personalities in France, including not just those in the metropolitan area of Paris as it did in the 1950s. Recent editions of this well-known work have many new entries and now contain more than 20,000 total biographies. It remains the standard source for biographical information about notable French nationals living in France, its overseas territories, or abroad, and foreigners living in France. Particular attention has been paid to the scientific, industrial, and regional political sectors, as well as to women. Typical entries provide full name, title if applicable, occupation, date and place of birth, family data, education, career, major works, honors and awards, hobbies, and home and/or office addresses. Although the bulk of the work is devoted to this purpose, there are several special sections, of varying worth, such as lists of sovereigns and chiefs of state since A.D. 751, current members of the National Assembly and Senate, and the diplomatic corps. Additional sections cover business, investments, professional societies and associations, media, arts and leisure, tourism, forms of address, and even how to serve wine. As a comprehensive source, this title remains indispensable to anyone needing biographical information on contemporary French personages.—**Barbara E. Kemp and Robert L. Wick**

GREAT BRITAIN AND THE COMMONWEALTH

General Works

71.   Oxbury, Harold. **Great Britons: Twentieth-Century Lives**. New York, Oxford University Press, 1985. 370p. illus. index. $29.95. LC 84-27214. ISBN 0-19-211599-5.

Great Britons states that its purpose is to "portray the history and character of modern Britain" by means of short biographies of well-known individuals. The volume contains 645 entries. All of the people selected died between 1915 and 1980. As a result, there is also a large amount of material on late-nineteenth-century Britain. The people chosen for inclusion come from all fields and include native-born and naturalized British subjects. Decisions regarding an individual's inclusion or exclusion are based on the informed personal judgment of Harold Oxbury, the author. However, as principal editor of the *Concise Dictionary of National Biography, 1901-1970* (Oxford University Press, 1982), he possesses an excellent background for such a difficult and sensitive task. Over 200 well-chosen photos and illustrations accompany the entries. The tone of the entries is dispassionate, and gossipy details are avoided or passed over quickly. Information is primarily based on the *Dictionary of National Biography*, with some updating and new research. There is an index of biographies by occupation and interests.

Readers of *Great Britons* will find it a fascinating and attractively produced collection of information on the famous personalities of modern Britain. Subjects range from the Beatle John Lennon and the comedian George Formby to the classicist A. E. Houseman and the politician Keir Hardie. Most important, the modest price makes this excellent volume a readily affordable reference book for small libraries and individuals. [R: Choice, Mar 86, p. 1042; LJ, 15 Feb 86, p. 174; RBB, 1 May 86, p. 1295]—**Ronald H. Fritze**

72.   Sakol, Jeannie, and Caroline Latham. **The Royals**. New York, Congdon & Weed; distr., Chicago, Contemporary Books, 1987. 377p. illus. bibliog. $19.95. ISBN 0-86553-194-3.

Less a serious reference work than a hodgepodge of trivia about the British royal family, this book seems to contain as much gossip as documented fact. Among the brief biographies and tidbits about royal affairs and family ghosts can be found such information as the names of Queen Elizabeth's Corgis, the shoe size Princess Margaret wears, and the Queen Mother's favorite drink.

The arrangement is alphabetical, but not particularly useful. For example, Prince Philip is entered under "His Royal Highness the Prince Philip, Duke of Edinburgh" and filed in the "P" section under "Prince." Most people probably remember Princess Margaret's former husband as Lord Snowdon, but there is no entry under his title. They would have to look under "Her Royal Highness Princess Margaret" in the "P" section, then see Antony Armstrong-Jones in the "A" section to find biographical information about him. There are no cross-references in the book. Many of the entries have intriguing but not very enlightening headings such as "Omen of the Orchid," "One Hip Chick," and "Over the Moon." There is a bibliography of books and magazines, including special and commemorative issues, at the end. Throughout the book are attractive black-and-white photographs. Sprinkled throughout the text are the British addresses of suppliers of clothing and other items to the royal family, and also sources for souvenirs such as postcards and books in both the United States and the United Kingdom.

Probably more appropriate for the coffee table than the reference collection, this work might nevertheless prove useful in public libraries. There seems to be an insatiable interest in the royal family, and this book would answer many possible questions about the British monarchy. [R: RBB, 15 Nov 88, p. 556]—**Christine E. King**

Current Biographies

73. **Who's Who: An Annual Biographical Dictionary**. New York, St. Martin's Press, 1849- . $225.00 for 1998 edition. LC 4-16933. ISSN 0083-937X.

The 148th edition (1996) of the original British *Who's Who* series continues to be a major source for British biographical information. The work contains biographies of British nobility and prominent people in British society. Entries include address, education, positions held, date of birth, spouse's and children's names, hobbies, and a list of works if the person is an author. Recent editions of the work have seen changes in the print size and format of the book. The publishers have used larger print, which makes it easier to read. The work continues to be easy to use and remains an important source for British biography. The 1996 volume contains more than 2,000 pages in the larger format which is considerably more than the 2,537 pages of the 1984 smaller-format edition, or the 1986 format, which is the same as 1996 with its 1,939 pages.—**Robert L. Wick**

Ireland

74. Boylan, Henry. **A Dictionary of Irish Biography**. 2d ed. New York, St. Martin's Press, 1988. 420p. $35.00. LC 88-25142. ISBN 0-312-02497-5.

This revised edition of Boylan's 1978 work (see ARBA 80, entry 110) is a welcome update indeed. Following the same format as the 1st edition, this new volume adds 200 more names, bringing the total to 1,300. Among the new entries are names which were omitted from the earlier volume due to lack of space. Some entries have been expanded or corrected, based on recently released research data. In a few selected entries, Boylan also has added a new feature—a quotation that gives a flavor of the person's style or philosophy. A select bibliography of resources used in compiling this new edition also is provided.

As with the 1st edition, this labor of love will prove a valuable addition to the literature. Criteria for inclusion are well laid out, the research is thorough, and only space limitations hinder what could develop into a comprehensive, basic biographical tool. [R: LJ, 15 Mar 89, p. 66; RBB, 1 June 89, p. 1703]—**Elizabeth Patterson**

Northern Ireland

75. Byrne, Art, and Sean McMahon. **Great Northerners**. Swords, Ireland, Poolbeg Press; distr., Chester Springs, Pa., Dufour, 1991. 226p. $13.95pa. ISBN 1-85371-106-3.

This book contains brief biographies of 100 notable men and women from Ulster. These persons range from St. Colum Cille, who led a mission to Christianize Scotland in the seventh century, to contemporary political and literary figures, such as Brian Faulkner and C. S. Lewis. The authors contend that the tensions that have divided Ulster for 300 years have produced vitality, inventiveness, and energy in its people. There are biographies on figures from both sides of the bitter dispute, with the major focus on individuals from the nineteenth and twentieth centuries.

The selection of people included in this book is admittedly idiosyncratic. In the absence of a more comprehensive dictionary of Ulster biography, *Great Northerners* offers the people of Northern Ireland short descriptions of some of their illustrious compatriots.—**Frank L. Wilson**

Retrospective Biographies

76.   The Concise Dictionary of National Biography: From Earliest Times to 1985. New York, Oxford University Press, 1992. 3v. $195.00/set. ISBN 0-19-865305-0.

The Dictionary of National Biography (*DNB*) is a major set of volumes containing biographical sketches of notable persons from Great Britain and the Commonwealth from the beginning of time until 1985. The main set consists of a basic group of volumes first published in 1908 and supplemented at 10-year (now 5-year) intervals, the latest supplement being issued in 1990 (see ARBA 91, entry 13). From the entire main set, including the supplements, the concise *DNB* has been created. Twice before, concise versions have appeared, so this current work might be thought of as a 3rd edition of the *Concise*, although it is not labeled as such.

The work contains every name listed in the entire set, but biographical material has been condensed anywhere from a few lines to a few column inches. The *Concise* is uneven in its treatment of individuals. The longest sketches are for those people who appeared in the *DNB* supplements, and brief sketches are used for persons in the main volumes. Very important people, such as kings and William Shakespeare, are treated extensively no matter when they appeared in the original volumes. One can understand the differences in editorial practice over the decades, but the result is inconsistency.

The advantage to a smaller library of the *Concise* is the extensive coverage for a reasonable cost. If a person is found in the *Concise,* the user knows that the main volumes can be consulted at another library with the major set for more complete information. No cross-references to the main set are provided, however, so one is uncertain whether to begin looking in the main volumes or one of the supplements.

The *Concise* is a first source to consult if the person sought is British and died before 1985. Because the *DNB* is biased toward men in politics and the humanities, other sources will be needed to help with women and people in the sciences if a first search is unsuccessful. If an individual is located, users can be certain that they have the most authoritative information.

Recommended for libraries needing British biographical information that cannot afford the main volumes, or branch libraries that want some coverage but have access to the whole set at a central location. It is also great for telephone reference centers. [R: Choice, May 93, p. 1436; RBB, 1 Mar 93, p. 1251; WLB, May 93, p. 114]—**David V. Loertscher**

77.   Dictionary of Labour Biography. Bellamy, Joyce M., and John Saville, eds. Fairfield, N.J., Augustus M. Kelley, 1972- . Vol. 1- . In progress. $37.50/vol. LC 78-185417.

The dictionary continues as a multivolume project, each volume of which will be a self-contained unit with a comprehensive subject index and a cumulative index of entries. The most recent volume published is volume 9 (London, Macmillan) in 1993. The time span of the dictionary covers the period of modern industrialism—from the last decades of the eighteenth century to the present. Living persons are excluded. Its aim is to include anyone who was active, at any level, in the organizations and institutions of the British labour movement, as well as those who influenced the development of radical and socialist ideas.

So far, nine volumes have been published. Each volume contains between 70 and 100 entries, from 600 to 8,000 words each, with 2,500 to 3,000 being a typical length. Entries are based on primary sources, with heavy drafts, where possible, on personal information from colleagues, friends, and relatives (among whom the authors of the sketches, when not subject specialists, are frequently found). The unique opportunity presented here to give full treatment to hitherto neglected or local figures is not lost. Also admirable are the bibliographies, a treasure trove of manuscript and archival sources, newspaper references, pamphlets, documents, and lists of personal informants. The biographee's own writings are listed in full, and secondary sources are also well represented.

The editors foresee no end to this project either by number of volumes or by closing date. The project will continue until all potential biographees have been written up. The volumes follow no alphabetic or chronologic sequence, the entries in each volume clustering loosely around a variety of movements or periods. The present volume, for instance, contains (to quote the dust jacket) "entries concerned with the Chartist, Secularist, and Clarion movements, with New Unionism, and with a cross-section of MPs, trade unionists and others active in the labour movement in the late nineteenth and twentieth centuries."—**David Rosenbaum and Robert L. Wick**

78.   **The Dictionary of National Biography: Missing Persons.** C. S. Nicholls, ed. New York, Oxford University Press, 1993. 768p. index. $115.00. DA28.D5254. 920.041. LC 92-9744. ISBN 0-19-865211-9.

For biographical sources of persons of the British Isles (and some Commonwealth individuals) from the beginning of time until 1985, no source has equaled the *Dictionary of National Biography* (*DNB*) (see ARBA 91, entry 13). The main set of 63 volumes covered 29,120 persons, and supplements (first 10-year, now 5-year) keep the set up-to-date. Now, because of changing times and differing societal values on what constitutes importance, the publishers of *DNB* have added 1,086 biographical sketches of people who, for one reason or another, did not get into the original set. These missing persons span the entire time period form the beginning of recorded history to 1985 and include many women, business persons, and engineers and scientists. As in the other volumes, each biographical sketch is carefully researched and approximately half a page in length (unless the person is of particular importance). A must purchase for libraries owning the set. [R: Choice, Oct 93, p. 265; RBB, 1 Sept 93, p. 82; WLB, Sept 93, p. 116]—**David V. Loertscher**

78a.   **Dictionary of National Biography, From the Earliest Times to 1900.** Edited by Sir Leslie Stephen and Sir Sidney Lee. London, Smith, Elder; repr., New York, Oxford University Press, 1938- . 22v. $998.00. ISBN 0-19-865101-5.

> **Dictionary of National Biography. Supplements (The Twentieth Century D.N.B.): The D.N.B. 1901-1911.** Edited by Sir Sidney Lee. 1912. 2084p. $89.00. ISBN 0-19-865201-1; The D.N.B. 1912-1921. Edited by W. H. C. Davis and J. R. Weaver. With a cumulative index covering 1901-1921. 1927. 650p. $89.00. ISBN 0-19-865202-X; The D.N.B. 1922-1930. Edited by J. R. Weaver. With a cumulative index covering 1901-1930. 1937. 976p. $65.00. ISBN 0-19-856203-8; The D.N.B. 1931-1940. Edited by L. O. Wickham Legg. With a cumulative index covering 1901-1940. 1949. 984p. $89.00. ISBN 0-19-865204-6; The D.N.B. 1941-1950. Edited by L. O. Wickham Legg and E. T. Williams. With a cumulative index covering 1901-1950. 1959. 1054p. $89.00. ISBN 0-19-865205-4; The D.N.B. 1951-1960. Edited by E. T. Williams and Helen M. Palmer. With a cumulative index covering 1901-1960. 1971. 1171p. $89.00. ISBN 0-19-865206-2; The D.N.B. 1961-1970. Edited by E. T. Williams and C. S. Nichols. 1981. 1178p. $74.00. ISBN 0-19-865207-0; The D.N.B. 1981-1985. 518p. Edited by Robert Blake and C. S. Nichols. ISBN 0-19-865210-0; The D.N.B. 1986-1990. 607p. Edited by C. S. Nichols. ISBN 0-19-865212-7.

Founded in 1882 by George Smith, the *Dictionary of National Biography (DNB)* is the first major biographical tool of the English-speaking world. There were other British biographies, but none whose scope or completeness could match the *DNB*. At first, the plan was to make a universal biography, but it was decided that such an undertaking would be too impractical. The project was begun by George Smith, the publisher who took on the financial responsibility, and Sir Leslie Stephen, the editor. In 1889, Stephen resigned because of poor health and was succeeded by Sir Sidney Lee. After his retirement Stephen continued to be a major contributor; in all, he wrote 820 biographies consisting of over 1,370 pages.

The editors intended to include all noteworthy inhabitants of Great Britain, Ireland, and the Colonies, exclusive of living persons, from the earliest historical period to the time of publication. Included are Britons who lived abroad and foreigners who became British subjects during their lifetime. Names of important legendary figures, such as Robin Hood, are also listed. Among the names included are the very famous, the famous, and the infamous.

The *DNB* staff gathered names from a wide range of sources in historical and scientific literature and from an endless amount of miscellaneous records and reports. A preliminary list was compiled and sent to specialists of literary experience competent to write articles for the proposed dictionary. Subsequent lists were published in the Athenaeum, and readers' comments were invited.

Included in the basic set are 29,120 articles. The contributors were urged to get their information from original sources whenever possible, especially from unpublished papers. The articles had to be accompanied by bibliographies. The average length of a biography is a little less than one page, although some run much longer (Shakespeare, forty-nine pages) and others are less than one column. The articles are signed with the initials of the contributor, and a key to their names is included in every volume.

The original work was completed in 1900, and decennial supplements have covered the lives of those who died during the decade, making it possible to have the lives written by persons many of whom knew their subjects intimately. So, for example, in the most recent supplement covering 1961-1970, we find records of lives of 745 British men and women who died between 1961 and 1970. Like the previous supplements and the _DNB_ itself, this volume is an outstanding model for all biographical dictionaries. It shows careful scholarship, providing lengthy, well-researched biographies of prominent individuals from the vast field of human endeavor. Bibliographical notes listing important secondary and primary sources follow each signed biography. The biographies have been written by people, often as eminent as their subjects, who knew their subjects personally and who could often add private knowledge to the biographical facts. Thus, the sketches of Winston Churchill, T. S. Eliot, Vivian Leigh, Bernard Russell, Dame Edith Sitwell, Charles Onions, Mervyn Peake, Clement Attlee, Nancy Astor, and the others come alive, making this a reference work of great interest to the general reader as well as the historian.—**Bohdan S. Wynar and Robert L. Wick**

79. Jones, Barry, and M. V. Dixon. **The St. Martin's Press Dictionary of Biography**. New York, St. Martin's Press, 1986. 917p. $35.00. LC 85-30393. ISBN 0-312-69733-3.

This large volume is made up of 6,500 to 7,000 biographical sketches of persons in science, the arts, literature, politics, religion, sports, and many other fields, including murder. Most of the entries are short (less than 200 words); hence, only essential information is given. For about half the articles, there is a bibliographical note, typically consisting of one book, but now and then two or three. A number of the articles include cross-references to associated persons.

The overwhelming majority of the names are represented in widely held reference works such as _Encyclopaedia Britannica_ or _Encyclopedia Americana_. Only the very smallest libraries will find that this work adds enough in formation to justify its purchase. It is a more useful item for home or office. [R: RBB, 15 Mar 87, pp. 1104, 1106]—**Robert N. Broadus**

80. **Who Was Who**. London, Block; New York, St. Martin's Press, 1897- . Vol. I. 1897-1915. $69.50. ISBN 0-312-87570-3. Vol. II. 1916-1928. $69.50. ISBN 1-312-87605-X. Vol. III. 1929-1940. $69.50. ISBN 0-312-87640-8. Vol. IV. 1941-1950. $69.50. ISBN 0-312-87675-0. Vol. V. 1951-1960. $69.50. ISBN 0-312-87710-2. Vol. VI. 1961-1970. $69.50. ISBN 0-312-87745-5. Vol. VII. 1971-1980. $74.50. ISBN 0-312-87746-3. Vol. VIII. 1981-1992. ISBN 0-312-06818-2.

Who Was Who consists mainly of original sketches as they appeared in _Who's Who_. They have been reprinted with the date of death added. In some instances additional information is added.

Who Was Who was first published in 1920 and covered the period from 1897 through 1915. A new edition was published in 1929. Volumes II-VIII cover the years 1916-1928, 1929-1940, 1941-1950, 1951-1960, 1961-1970, 1971-1980, and 1981-1992, respectively. The editors indicate that they plan to publish a new volume at the close of each decade. According to this plan the next volume should cover 1993-2004.—**Bohdan S. Wynar and Robert L. Wick**

INDIA

81. Buckland, C. E. **Dictionary of Indian Biography**. London, Sonnenschein, 1906; repr., New York, Greenwood Press, 1969. 494p. bibliog. $21.00. LC 69-13848. ISBN 8371-0331-2.

Contains 2,600 biographical sketches of Who's Who type for Indian, English, and foreign persons "who have been conspicuous in the history of India, or distinguished in the administration of the country," covering the period 1750-1905. In addition to biographical listings, this volume includes a brief bibliography of reference works consulted and a bibliography of biographical works on some prominent personalities arranged under the name of the biographee or subject. This biographical dictionary is a valuable reference work for historical research; it is supplemented by other biographical dictionaries, such as *Who's Who in India* (Lucknow, Newul Kishore Press, 1911-1914) and *The Times of India Directory and Year Book* (Bombay, The Times of India, 1915- . Annual). [R: RQ, Summer 69, p. 288; WLB, June 69, p. 1019]—**Bohdan S. Wynar**

82. **Dictionary of National Biography [India]**. Edited by Siba Pada Sen. Calcutta, Institute of Historical Studies; distr., Columbia, Mo., South Asia Books, 1974. 4v. $90.00. **1947-1972 Supplement**. Edited by Siba Pada Sen and Nisith Ranjan Ray. Calcutta, Institute of Historical Studies, 1986.

According to the preface, this four-volume dictionary is "the first attempt of its kind in India, on the lines of similar works in other countries." Its purpose is to cover "people from all walks of life—politics, religious and social reform, education, journalism, literature, science, law, business and industry, etc.—who made some tangible contribution to national life from the beginning of the nineteenth century to the achievement of independence" (1800-1947). In fact, this dictionary includes among its 1,400 entries quite a few personalities of only regional importance, omitting, however, many artists and sports figures who achieved national importance. Promised supplementary volumes that may rectify some of these omissions have not yet been published. The supplement to the *Dictionary of National Biography* covers the years 1947 through 1972. The editorial policy of the original volume is continued in that it covers people from all walks of life. Many additional entries bring the original volume up-to-date. [R: Choice, June 73, p. 596]—**Bohdan S. Wynar and Robert L. Wick**

IRAN

83. **Encyclopedia Iranica**. Ehsan Yarshater, ed. Costa Mesa, Calif., Mazda, 1990. 1v. (various paging). illus. maps. $28.00pa. ISBN 0-939214-69-5.

The first fascicle of this authoritative, comprehensive reference work appeared in 1982. Eight years later, with the publication of the fascicles reviewed here, the alphabetical entries have progressed only partially through the letter "C." A reader waiting for the entry on Zoroaster will need to be patient. Yarshater, affiliated with the Center for Iranian Studies at Columbia University, is assisted by an array of expert advisors, editors, and consultants from all over the world. The list of contributors, composed of some 300 recognized scholars, reads like a virtual "who's who" of Iranianists.

The signed entries are extensively documented, with primary sources cited in the text and additional references listed at the end. Charts, pictures, drawings, maps, and tables can be found throughout. Editorial policy for Islamic proper names is to list under shohra and *nesba* rather than the given name or *konya*. Exceptions exist, but cross-references are liberally inserted to assist the user. The transliteration system requires careful attention, particularly where there is an alphabetical sequence, as the editors have revised the system most often used by English speakers of Arabic in an effort to more accurately render Persian words.

This work's scope is truly encyclopedic, encompassing not only Iran but also the surrounding areas and their cultural relations with Iran. It extends from prehistory to the present with articles on topics of archaeological, geographic, ethnographic, historical, artistic, literary, religious, linguistic, philosophical, scientific, and folkloric interest. It is particularly rich in biographical material, although biographies of living persons are specifically excluded. There is a certain amount of duplication with the well-established *Encyclopaedia of Islam* (E. J. Brill, 1991), but not as much as might be expected given the parallels in general organization and overlap of geographic and subject coverage.

For scholars and specialists in Iranian studies and related fields, this publication fills a gap by providing information on neglected subjects. It should also prove of use to students who need a comprehensive work or survey of major aspects of Iranian culture and civilization.—**Anna L. DeMiller**

ITALY

84. **Who's Who in Italy: A Biographical Encyclopaedia**. 1957/58- . John C. Dove, ed. Bresso/Milano, Italy, Who's Who in Italy; distr., Hauppauge, N.Y., Ballen Booksellers International. 2 vols. (Sutter's International Red Series). $260.00/set for recent edition.

"Biographical encyclopaedia" describes this set fairly well. In the 1992 edition there are 11,000 biographical sketches of all manner of prominent living Italians, with all entries attractively laid out and written in a little more lively fashion than one generally encounters in similar volumes. Where the sketches stop, midway through volume 2, a fascinating section begins: Italy-related information that starts with a historical survey (from prehistory to today) and a breakdown of the government structure with the names of all currently relevant politicians and addresses for their offices. The economic section is broken down into several parts, ranging from the aerospace industry to transportation. Cultural life covers institutions of learning, miscellaneous awards, broadcasting, publishing, and more. Social life includes information on associations and trade unions, social security, and sports organizations. The section on religious life provides an overview of the Vatican state and other Italian religious organizations. The entire nonbiographical section is generously interlaced with advertisements, most of them from industrial establishments. The set is handsomely printed and bound in red cloth with gold lettering. Any business organization that frequently deals with Italian clients or organizations will find this work an indispensable aid in day-to-day dealings with their transatlantic counterparts.—**Koraljka Lockhart and Robert L. Wick**

JAPAN

85.   **Who's Who in Japan**. Tokyo, Asia Press; distr., Boca Raton, Fla., CRC Press, 1984/85- . index. $250.00 for the 1991/92 edition.

Who's Who in Japan contains more than 27,000 entries, mostly from business, academia, politics, and administration. Information on the order of entries and on abbreviations used precedes the main part. The 12 possible items of information in the entries are rarely complete, but current position, education, and address are emphasized. An index to the volume is arranged by categories, such as diet members, government, bureaucrat/legal, registered or nonregistered company, communications, culture, natural science, literature, art, music/dance, sports, and fashion/beauty/cooking/hobbies. Under the legal category, the Chief Justice of the Japanese Supreme Court is included, but a check for several other justices revealed a lack of coverage. A directory of public and private institutions completes the volume. The usefulness of this reference source is enhanced by the increasingly close relations between Japan and the rest of the world. It can be recommended to journalists, academicians, business and government executives, and researchers.—**Bogdan Mieczkowski and Robert L. Wick**

LATIN AMERICA

86.   **National Directory of Latin Americanists: Biographies of 4,915 Specialists**. 3d ed. Inge Maria Harman, ed. Washington, D.C., Library of Congress; distr., Washington, D.C., GPO, 1985. 1011p. index. $34.00. LC 84-600356. ISBN 0-8444-0491-8.

This is the first revision of the *National Directory of Latin Americanists* since 1971, and its coverage has been expanded accordingly. The 1st edition (1966) included bio-bibliographical information on 1,884 specialists on Latin America in the humanities and social sciences; the 2nd edition encompassed 2,695 persons; and the present edition covers no fewer than 4,915 authorities in many fields. In fact, one of the strengths of this biographical dictionary is that it cuts across many disciplinary lines: agriculture, anthropology, archaeology, architecture, art, bibliography, biological sciences, business, communication, computer science, demography, economics, education, folklore, geography, history, journalism, language, Latin American studies, law, library science and archives, linguistics, literature, musicology, natural resources, nutrition, philosophy, physical sciences, political science, psychology, public administration, public health, religion and theology, sociology, urban and regional planning, urban studies, and women's studies. One index lists scholars by these fields and their subfields (over 100 appear under "Library Science and Archives"), the other by country or region. The main entries appear alphabetically by last name, and each entry provides the following information: name, birthplace, date; major discipline; degrees, including honorary ones; professional career; fellowships, honors, consultantships, officerships, editorships; membership in professional and honorary organizations; research specialties (limited to three); publications (limited to three); language knowledge; and home and/or office address.

Inclusion in this directory is not automatic; 976 of the respondents were excluded because they did not meet the criteria set by the editorial board. According to the introduction, "Eligibility was limited to Latin Americanists of professional status, generally those individuals who hold the highest degrees in their disciplines. Final determination of eligibility was made by a panel composed of the editor and senior Hispanic Division staff."

An important tool for Latin American reference collections in research libraries, the 1,000-page *National Directory of Latin Americanists* is a bargain at $34.00 and should be affordable to many liberal arts college libraries and medium-sized public libraries.—**Edwin S. Gleaves**

LEBANON

87. **Who's Who in Lebanon**. Gabriel M. Bustros, ed. Beirut, Lebanon, Publitec Publications; distr., Detroit, Gale, 1981- . $155.00 for recent edition. ISSN 0083-9612.

First published in 1981, recent editions (1995-96) include more than 250 pages of detailed biographical entries and about an equal number of broad survey pages covering history, geography, government, economy, education, international organizations, and cultural agencies. Individuals profiled appear to have widely varied professional backgrounds ranging from surgeons to former diplomats. Entries describe personal and professional background data, including a current address and telephone number. The survey section is well organized and provides extensive background information on Lebanon, as well as useful directory listings for consulates, companies, libraries, museums, and the media. This book will be helpful to individuals with a need for a concise overview of Lebanon, or a need to make contact with agencies or well-known leaders in Lebanon.—**Ahmad Gamaluddin and Robert L. Wick**

MEXICO

88. Camp, Roderic Ai. **Who's Who in Mexico Today**. 2d ed. Boulder, Colo., Westview Press, 1993. 197p. $65.00. CT552.C36.920.072. LC 92-35773. ISBN 0-8133-8452-4.

The 1st edition of this work, published in 1988, contained 391 entries. This new edition is only 12 pages longer. The biographies are usefully arranged in 12 categories: date of birth, birthplace, education, elected office, political party offices, governmental appointments, leadership in national organizations, private-sector position, family information, military activities, national awards, and sources of information. The word *letter* at the end of an entry indicates that Camp either interviewed the biographee or received information in writing. Although Camp does not explain why a few entries from the 1st edition are omitted, it is assumed that these persons are no longer living. It is stated that more that half of the entries have been updated, but most appear to be the same, with additional information for occurrences after 1988. Thirteen additional sources for background information were used in this 2d edition. Camp notes that the book is not comprehensive because viable information is not always available. All sectors of society, especially decision makers, are included, as well as people usually omitted from this type of work, such as clergy and women (whom the author categorized as pioneers).

This volume fills a gap with current Mexican biographies in English. It is essential for those libraries with emphasis on Latin American studies. Recommended for public and academic libraries.—**Karen Y. Stabler**

MIDDLE EAST

89. **The Encyclopaedia of Islam. Encyclopedie de L'Islam**. New ed. H. Pearson and I. D. Pearson, comps., and E. van Donzel, ed. Leiden, Netherlands, E. J. Brill; distr., New York, Macmillan, 1954- . $871.00/set.

Begun in 1954, the new edition of *The Encyclopaedia of Islam* brings together scholarly information about the Islamic world covering every aspect of its religious, cultural, and legal traditions. Volumes 1 and 2, first published in 1965 (with subsequent reprintings in 1970 and 1983), include articles originally appearing in fascicles, dating from 1954. Volume 5, the latest addition to the projected ten-volume set, contains materials from fascicles 79-98, spanning 1979-1985. In 1979 the editors compiled a subject index to volumes 1, 2, and 3. An additional subject index is expected shortly.

The Encyclopaedia of Islam (new edition) is a massive undertaking. The articles are written by world-renowned scholars, both in the Middle East and in Europe and the United States. Each article is signed, and to aid the serious scholar even further, each volume includes a list of authors with the page numbers of his or her signed article(s). Names in brackets indicate those authors whose articles have been reprinted or revised from the earlier *Encyclopaedia of Islam* or the one-volume *Shorter Encyclopaedia of Islam*. Bibliographies of major sources follow each article, and the encyclopedia makes liberal use of cross-references. Articles dealing with art and architecture are illustrated, often with photographs, and excellent maps accompany discussions of major geographic areas.

Although clearly designed for a scholarly audience, particularly for scholars with excellent reading knowledge of Arabic, Persian, or Turkish, the articles are accessible to the nonspecialist willing to take the time to read carefully and analytically. Although articles on more secular subjects (politicians, geographical locations, etc.) tend to include references to works in English, French, or German, the majority of the bibliographies cite scholarly treatises in Middle Eastern languages. Whereas this encyclopedia is an excellent beginning point for the lay reader (often the only place where information may be located in a concise and readable fashion), it is less useful as a guide to finding additional sources of information on the topic.

One major difficulty for the Western reader is actually locating the articles within the five volumes. The index to volumes 1-3 and the projected new index help enormously, but the problems that the Arabic alphabet and language, even when transliterated, present for the uninitiated reader cannot be ignored. Even with the aid of the index, few undergraduates would know that *DIMASHK* was the entry for information on the Syrian city of Damascus, or that Cairo was listed under "K," as *al-KAHIRA*. The difficulty is not limited to place-names. The excellent discussion on newspapers in the Muslim world appears under the Arabic term *DJARIDA*. Since the N volume hasn't been issued yet, the user must refer to the index, but the index only covers articles in the first three volumes. This is one encyclopedia that demands careful examination, and some explanation, prior to sending a student off to use it.

In spite of these difficulties, *The Encyclopaedia of Islam* is an invaluable resource, well worth the time and effort required to master whatever linguistic difficulties it might present. The articles, even those simply providing brief dictionary-like definitions, are works of scholarship (and are signed). In terms of bibliographic control, the lengthy time span between the appearance of the volumes has resulted in the publication of, to date, three supplements dealing with material in volumes 1 and 2. It is important that research libraries be aware of the publication sequence of *The Encyclopaedia of Islam,* particularly the fact that, along with the bound volumes, fascicles, supplements, and indexes (all in paper) are crucial components of the set. These difficulties notwithstanding, the *Encyclopaedia of Islam* (new edition) is a landmark publication, a most worthy successor to the earlier *Encyclopaedia of Islam.*—**Ellen Broidy**

90. **Who's Who in the Arab World**. Gabriel M. Bustros, ed. Beirut, Lebanon, Publitec Publications; distr., Detroit, Gale, 1966- . index. $310.00 for recent edition. ISSN 0083-9752.

The most recent volume of *Who's Who in the Arab World* is the 1995-96 edition. The hefty volume deserves a more descriptive title, such as "Who's Who and What's What in the Arab World." In its three parts it covers biographies, profiles of countries, a brief historical survey, and essays and documents relating to specific topics, such as the Suez Canal, the Gulf Cooperation Council, and the Palestinian issue. There is a detailed index and a selected bibliography. The book is printed on good paper and looks elegant enough to (almost) justify its relatively high price. Having been reprinted each year since 1966, it no doubt serves a useful function. The work would, however, be much more useful as a "dictionary" of the Arab world if edited more carefully. Three kinds of problems should and can be removed: inadequate updating, imbalance in selection, and uncontrolled space and content of biographies. This reviewer's position and address are 12 years out-of-date. The profiles of Algeria, Iraq, and Palestine are other examples. The imbalance of coverage is shown by the 10-page index of individual biographies of Saudi Arabians, compared with less than 7 pages for Egyptians and 22 pages for Syrians. Prominent people such as Galal Amin, Heba Handoussa, Haseeb Sabbagh, and Antoine Zahian are missing. The third problem relates to space and content of biographies. One biography fills four-and-a-half pages, most of which is useless detail. To admit that no editing or control of space for biographies was exercised is not an adequate explanation. More careful editing would minimize these defects, enhance the volume, and make it more useful.—**Elias H**. **Tuma and Robert L**. **Wick**

NEWFOUNDLAND AND LABRADOR

91.   Cuff, Robert H., Melvin Baker, and Robert D. W. Pitt, eds. **Dictionary of Newfoundland and Labrador Biography**. St. John's, Nfld., Harry Cuff, 1990. 408p. index. $49.95. 920.0718. ISBN 0-921191-51-0.

Envisioned as an initial attempt to provide a regional bibliographic reference source, this volume is an outgrowth of the upcoming *Encyclopedia of Newfoundland and Labrador.* The editors were, in fact, involved in the research for that project and have drawn upon it as a source.

The book includes around 1,500 individual biographies. Criteria for inclusion were established by defining occupational categories with a wide variety of objective and some rather subjective guidelines. House of Assembly members must have served for a 10-year period to be included, while a journalist or artist may have been included on the basis of significant contributions. Inclusion was not limited to well-known individuals. Community histories and newspapers yielded information about a number of people, often from rural areas, who had not been treated before. Excluded are native-born Newfoundlanders whose primary influence was outside the Province. While the resulting outcome is somewhat uneven, and there are gaps in the coverage of women and minorities, the editors hope that further research will be encouraged.

The compact style of the dictionary limits the length of articles, but each entry includes full name, birth/death dates, birthplace, and a list of accomplishments. A paragraph or two explains the individual's participation in the development of Newfoundland and Labrador. Contributors are noted. A summary list of sources consulted is included as a "bibliographic note." There are geographic and identification indexes. While this volume has some significant omissions and weaknesses and may be of limited interest outside the province, it is a laudable contribution to the historical and cultural information about Newfoundland and Labrador.—**Virginia S**. **Fischer**

PEOPLE'S REPUBLIC OF CHINA

92.   Bartke, Wolfgang. **Who's Who in the People's Republic of China**. 3d ed. Munich, New Providence, N.J., K. G. Saur, 1991. 2v. illus. $250.00/set. ISBN 3-598-10771-4.

This comprehensive biographical dictionary of China follows the high standards of previous editions (see ARBA 88, entry 41, and ARBA 82, entry 335). It has been extensively revised and expanded to include the biographies of 4,100 current Chinese political and cultural leaders, more than half of whom are new additions. About 2,400 of the biographies are accompanied by photographs. Compared with *Who's Who in China: Current Leaders* (China Books, 1989) by the Chinese government, this work has twice as many entries and much broader coverage, including leaders in fields outside the government. Despite its high price, it continues to be an essential reference work to key leaders in China and is recommended for all major reference collections.—**Hwa-Wei Lee**

93.   **Who's Who in China 1918-1950**. Hong Kong, Chinese Materials Center; distr., San Francisco, Calif., Chinese Materials Center, 1982. 3v. illus. index. $130.00/set. ISBN 0-89644-626-3.

Probably the first modern English-language publication of the Who's Who genre for China, this work was originally published in nine volumes (consisting of six editions and three supplements) issued between 1919 and 1950. It was begun by *Millard's Review of the Far East,* better known by its later name, the *China Weekly Review*, a leading English-language newspaper published in China from June 1907 until it went out of existence in July 1953. This current work, published in 1982 by the Chinese Materials Center in Hong Kong, is a reprint in three volumes of the entire original with a cumulative index prepared by Jerome Cavanaugh. This index contains 2,908 names of some of the best-known personalities in China. For many, biographical sketches were updated in subsequent editions. The cumulative index also incorporates the names, in alphabetical order, of about 580 alumni of Tsing-Hua College who studied in the United States on funds from the American remission of the

Boxer Indemnity. These names were included in "Directory of American Returned Scholars," which was appended to the 3rd edition published in 1925.

When begun, *Who's Who in China* was intended to be an annual, but successive wars and chaotic conditions within China frequently delayed publishing schedules, resulting in the nine volumes over a thirty-one-year span. In the early editions, the biographies were taken from a regular column in the weekly newspapers and were published in the order in which they appeared. With the 3rd edition, all entries were arranged in alphabetical order by surname and the scope of the coverage was greatly expanded. For example, the 1st edition included only fifty-nine biographies while the third contained over 100,000 and the fifth over 1,500. To permit this expanded scope, biographies were sought from sources such as newspaper stories, official records, and individually submitted autobiographies.

Although other biographical works have appeared in recent years, such as Howard L. Boorman's *Biographical Dictionary of Republican China* in four volumes, for which a separate index was published, and the two-volume *Biographic Dictionary of Chinese Communism, 1921-1965,* this *Who's Who in China 1918-1950* remains the original and contemporary biographical publication on leading Chinese personalities in the first half of the twentieth century. The cumulative index greatly enhances the utility of this reprint.—**Hwa-Wei Lee**

ROMANIA

94.   Ionescu, Şerban N. **Who Was Who in Twentieth Century Romania**. Boulder, Colo., East European Monographs; distr., New York, Columbia University Press, 1994. 318p. (East European Monographs, no. 395). $59.00. LC 94-71278. ISBN 0-88033-292-1.

This volume provides information about Romanian personalities who have had an impact, either positive or negative, during the twentieth century. Two works that are precursors of Ionescu's work are *Enciclopedia Cugetareau* (The Encyclopedia of Thought) (1940) and *Mica Enciclopedie Româna* (Little Romanian Encyclopedia) (1972). There are approximately 3,000 entries, plus a list of presidents of the Romanian Academy and prime ministers. Also included are the names of principal Romanian political parties, a Romanian chronology, and important twentieth-century dates. Finally, there are a pronunciation key and bibliography.

The minimum entry requirement is name and nickname, dates and places of birth and death, education and titles, important works and achievements, and political affiliation if relevant. However, many entries in the present volume lack this information. (Ionescu appeals for data to update his work.) Such omissions leave a question regarding inclusion, since there is only a vague reference to standards and criteria. Also, there is no governing order for entries that would create a uniform data key. Additionally, it would be helpful if there were a geographic and occupational index for cross-reference, which would make the volume a more accessible source of life and career data on noteworthy individuals. Since there are very few English sources regarding Romanian personages, this compendium will serve well the varied needs of libraries, schools, universities, media and research organizations, and individual researchers.—**Magda Zelinska-Feri**

RUSSIA AND CIS REPUBLIC

95.   **Longman Biographical Directory of Decision-Makers in Russia and the Successor States**. Martin McCauley, ed. Harlow, England, Longman; distr., Detroit, Gale, 1993. 726p. maps. index. $152.00. ISBN 0-582-20999-4.

Published in Great Britain and distributed by Gale, this biographical directory provides brief biographical sketches on decision-makers in Russia and the successor states, listing some 600-700 individuals. The information is recent as of 1992 (in some cases, as of the first half of 1993), with an emphasis on Russia and, to some extent, Ukraine. Contrary to the statement in the preface, Belarus is not well worked (25 listings), and neither are some other countries: Armenia (2 listings), Estonia (3 listings), Lithuania (3 listings), and Kyrgyztan (6 listings). The introduction is dated July 1993, and 50 percent of the material is now somewhat obsolete. For example, there are only two entries for Chechnya (Husayn Akhmadov and Dzhokhar Dudaev) without any comment about Dudaev's role in the conflict with Russia (before the current war with Russia, Chechnya proclaimed its independence in 1991), and information on Ukraine's political leaders is also in many cases obsolete (Boris Morozov, Vasyl Durdynets, and many others).

Nevertheless, the historical information provided for many individuals is interesting, describing important steps in their careers, political affiliations, imprisonment history (for former dissidents), educational background, and so on. This is an adequate dictionary and hopefully subsequent editions or supplements can be published in electronic form.—**Bohdan S. Wynar**

96.   Morozov, Vladimir. **Who's Who in Russia and the CIS Republics**. New York, Henry Holt, 1995. 328p. index. $60.00. ISBN 0-8050-2691-6.

With the breakup of the Soviet Union and the ensuing establishment of the independent republics, many biographical sources are being published. Morozov's *Who's Who in Russia and the CIS Republics* is one example of such a compilation, but the reader will find a more comprehensive treatment of this topic in *Who's Who in Russia and the New States* (see ARBA 94, entry 136). The present volume provides brief biographical sketches of some 1,000 individuals, including political leaders, military commanders, scholars, artists, educators, sports stars, and prominent religious leaders. Morozov is a journalist and editor of *V.I.P. Magazine* who specializes in Russian foreign affairs. The treatment is sketchy, covering more than 25 academicians, 6 actors, 4 correspondents, 1 economist, and so forth. This work needs to be used with caution.—**Bohdan S. Wynar**

97.   **The Soviet Union: A Biographical Dictionary**. Archie Brown, ed. New York, Macmillan, 1991. 489p. $60.00. CT1213.S65. 920.047. LC 91-10812. ISBN 0-02-897071-3.

This selective biographical dictionary, edited by a well-known British scholar, covers some 1,400 prominent personalities from 1917 to the present. All entries are arranged alphabetically and provide essential information (e.g., dates of birth and death, brief family history, education, major contributions, accomplishments). The emphasis is on the most recent period, with only selective coverage of important post-revolutionary personalities (e.g., members of the Politburo or Secretariat of the Communist Party, very important artists or writers). Since 1989, major new political institutions have emerged, and for this period the coverage of leading personalities of perestroika and glasnost is quite adequate. The volume concludes with five appendixes—a list of entries by subject and profession, a key to acronyms and abbreviations, a guide to the changing Soviet institutional structure, suggested further reading (mostly British books), and new Politburo members. As often happens with such "timely" works, this volume is already out-of-date; with the abolishment of the Communist Party, a new biographical volume might be in order. Nevertheless, this book will be of substantial assistance to all students of Soviet affairs. [R: LJ, Aug 91, pp. 90-92]—**Bohdan S. Wynar**

98.   Vronskaya, Jeanne, with Vladimir Chuguev. **A Biographical Dictionary of the Soviet Union 1917-1988**. Munich, New York, K. G. Saur, 1989. 525p. index. $240.00. CT1213.V76. 920'.047. LC 88-39417. ISBN 0-86291-470-1.

This companion volume to *Who's Who in the Socialist Countries in Europe*, also published by K. C. Saur, contains some 5,000 biographical sketches of significant individuals in the Soviet Union. According to the author's note, a number of sources were consulted for this compilation, primarily Russian, including some emigre sources (e.g., *Novoe Russkoe Slovo* [New Russian World], *Novyi Zhurnal* [New Magazine]) and the Soviet press. No mention is made of several other biographical sources published in previous years by a number of publishers in the West. The author apparently relied on her previous specialization in Russian films (filmmakers are well represented) as well as her firsthand knowledge of Soviet sources.

As a result, we have a rather uneven treatment of Soviet personalities, with an emphasis on fine arts and performing arts and the inclusion of only a few politicians and literary figures. Thus, for example, there are long articles on such figures as Lenin, Stalin, and even Gorbachev, but nothing on the former first secretary of the Communist Party of Ukraine, P. Shelest, or such well-known figures as Skrypnyk. There is a lot of information on Bohdan Stashinsky, the SMERSH agent who killed Rebetand Bandera, but nothing on such very prominent Ukrainian writers as Rylsky or Stel'mach. Scholars, including academicians, are poorly represented, often with misleading information. For example, Boris Grekov, one of the leading Russian medievalists, is given only 12 lines, but nothing is given to Rybakov, an equally important Russian scholar in medieval studies. Academician Kryms'kyi (not Krimskii) is included, but the author provides misleading information on Hrushevs'kyi (again, not Hrushevskii), the most important Ukrainian historian. Information on Hrushevs'kyi was simply taken from Soviet sources published during the Stalin or Brezhnev periods. Such examples are numerous; this potentially useful biographical dictionary has to be used with caution. [R: Choice, Dec 89, pp. 617-18; LJ, Aug 89, pp. 126-28; RBB, 15 Dec 89, pp. 852-54; RQ, Winter 89, pp. 283-84]—**Bohdan S. Wynar**

99.   **Who's Who in Russia and the New States**. Leonard Geron and Alex Pravda, eds. London, I. B. Tauris; distr., New York, St. Martin's Press, 1993. 1v. (unpaged). $185.00. ISBN 1-85043-487-5.

A revised, expanded edition of a 1989 publication, this directory is billed as "the most comprehensive and up-to-date guide to organizations and individuals in the political, economic, social and military life of the independent states that previously made up the Soviet Union" (dust jacket). The independent states include Armenia, Azerbaijan, Belarus, Estonia, Georgia Kazakhstan, Kyrgyzstan, Latvia, Lithuania, Moldova, the Russian Federation, Tajikistan, Turkmenistan, Ukraine, and Uzbekistan.

The book is divided into two main parts, the first of which is relatively brief. Fifteen country entries list heads of state and key government officials, along with ministries, state committees, and other national bodies. Part 2 lists almost 7,000 significant public figures. While individuals from Russia predominate, the other states are certainly covered. As might be expected, entries for politicians, government officials, diplomats, and military officers abound, but virtually every field is represented. Among those featured are managers, historians, clergy, cosmonauts, engineers, physicists, physicians, ballet dancers, composers, writers, and at least one "worker." The fullness of biographical entries varies, depending on the prominence of and data available on individuals. Examples range from 3 lines for Arif Gadzhiev, an Azerbaijani politician, to 44 lines for Yevgeny Aleksandrovich Yevtushenko, the Russian poet, actor, and filmmaker. A typical entry may include full name and occupation; family information; education and career history; lists of publications, affiliations, and honors; address; and telephone, telex, and fax numbers.

Who's Who in Russia and the New States, a high-quality publication compiled with care, is a source of much information not yet available elsewhere. Some of the details cited may quickly become out-of-date, especially give Eastern Europe's current state of upheaval. But this fascinating work is potentially invaluable to anyone with a serious interest in contemporary Russia or the new states. [R: Choice, Nov 93, p. 440; WLB, Dec 93, p. 123]—**Lydia W. Wasylenko**

100.   **Who's Who in the Socialist Countries of Europe: A Biographical Encyclopedia of More Than 12,600 Leading Personalities**. Juliusz Stroynowski, ed. New York, K. G. Saur, 1989. 3v. $350.00/set. ISBN 3-598-10636-X.

This work is a dinosaur of publishing in 1990. There was no way that Stroynowski and K. G. Saur could have anticipated the sudden collapse of Communist-dominated Eastern Europe and the descent of most of the dignitaries selected for biographical sketches into insignificance. The covers of the volumes are graced by six formerly dominant Eastern European statesmen; all but one, Lech Valesa, are now in disgrace, and Ceaucescu was executed.

The work covers over 13,000 dignitaries from Albania, Bulgaria, Czechoslovakia, the German Democratic Republic, Hungary, Poland, Romania, and Yugoslavia. The entries contain the individual's full name, nationality, profession, place and date of birth, family background, brief biographical data, publications, honors, decorations, and prizes. The misfortune of the editor was that his subjects were largely members of the establishment, and the people from the power structure were the first to be swept out by the revolution. Figures from the arts and letters are perhaps the least scathed by the revolution, but they were few to begin with. The volume also contains 350 names of dissidents. One use researchers may have for this set, other than for antiquarian purposes, is to look up Communists who managed to survive the democratic revolution. [R: C&RL, Mar 90, pp. 130-31]—**Andrew Ezergailis**

SPAIN

101. **Who's Who in Spain: A Biographical Encyclopedia of Sutter's International Red Series. . . .** 1992 ed. John C. Dove, ed. Barcelona, Who's Who in Spain; distr., Hauppauge, N.Y., Ballen Booksellers International, 1992. 1927p. Index. (Who's Who the International Red Series). $230.00. ISBN 88-85246-14-1.

This welcome contribution provides key biographical facts for 7,500 prominent personalities currently residing in Spain and also includes selected foreign nationals who are actively contributing to Spanish life. Alphabetically arranged by last name, the clear and easy-to-read entries generally include title, field, pseudonym (if any), place and date of birth, family details, home and business address, education and career, publications and awards, professional memberships, and recreation. Some entries refer the user to the excellent survey section, which provides background information, including some statistical data, on the economic, cultural, social, and political aspects of Spain. This section, divided into four chapters, includes a sketchy but useful index and provides directory information on major companies by type, museums, libraries, universities, all levels of government, diplomatic representation, chambers of commerce, and much more. The few advertisements found in this latter section are somewhat distracting but do not take away from the outstanding value of this reference work. As Spain continues to enjoy international prominence, purchase of this work is a must for any large public and academic library.—**Isabel Schon**

UNITED STATES

Current Biographies

102. Holloway, Charles M. **Profiles in Achievement**. New York, College Board, 1987. 173p. illus. index. $9.95pa. LC 87-072157. ISBN 0-87447-285-7.

Many contemporary books have signaled a decline in educational standards in America. Authors have written warningly that contemporary youth lack writing, math, and science skills and demonstrate appalling gaps in their knowledge of geography, history, and the humanities. All of these books speak to adults. Finally, there is a book which is written for and speaks to youth. Moreover, it is not a tirade of words bemoaning all that is wrong, but rather a celebration of education and the opportunities it continues to provide youth who are willing to work hard and learn. *Profiles in Achievement* should be *required* reading for every high school freshman in the land.

The eight profiles found in Holloway's immensely readable book are truly inspiring. Yes, there are two famous figures, Arthur Ashe and San Antonio Mayor Henry Cisneros, but perhaps more important, there are six other success stories here about people who are not famous and whose stories are probably more inspiring and relevant to the vast majority of young readers because they are lives cut from the fabric of the possible. Most young people do not aspire to great fame and fortune, which are so often based upon chance factors, but do want to lead good, productive lives, and Holloway's insightful profiles of television writer Karen Hall, Navajo engineer Anthony Kahn, refugee honor graduate Winston Hong Lieu, attorney Suzanne Saunders, Oklahoma Representative Carolyn Thompson, and corporate executive Sybil Jordan Stevenson suggest patterns young people can follow to fashion such lives.

It is not surprising that Holloway was drawn to subjects who have made their mark on life through hard work. His own work is evidence of the same work ethic he obviously admires in others. Here is no collection of profiles written by someone sitting in a library gleaning facts from *Current Biography* and recent news files. Holloway traveled 30,000 miles to talk to not only the subjects but their parents, siblings, teachers, bosses, colleagues, and friends. Each profile is a celebration of the tenacity, determination, and personal courage of its subject, and collectively the profiles celebrate the joy of being human, offering proof positive of the accomplishment of which human beings are capable when their will is to succeed. *Profiles in Achievement* is both fascinating and inspirational reading.—**Jerry D. Flack**

103.   Ward, Geoffrey C. **American Originals: The Private Worlds of Some Singular Men and Women**. New York, HarperCollins, 1991. 277p. index. $23.00. CT215.W37. 920.073. LC 90-56401. ISBN 0-06-016694-0.

This collection of well-written short biographical works will interest even readers who usually avoid biography. Most of the pieces were originally written for publication in the monthly *American Heritage*. In the preface, Ward identifies and, in some cases, critically discusses the published biographies that helped him in his research. He does not attempt to dryly chronicle entire lives in the 4- to 14-page articles but instead focuses on the private (and not always flattering) side of more than 40 famous Americans. For example, the piece on photographer Margaret Bourke-White illuminates her single-minded dedication to her work, even when "seduction seemed part of the job description." The article on Mark Twain centers on the happy and productive years (1874-1891) Twain spent in the "big curious house" he built for himself and his family in Hartford, Connecticut, before financial woes forced him to move. Ward organizes his subjects mainly by profession: politics, entertainment, writing and art, and the military. There are also sections on "bad men and liars" and the "Delanos and Roosevelts." (Three articles discuss different aspects of Franklin D. Roosevelt, about whom Ward has written two books.) The work is well indexed.

The writing in *American Originals* is fluid and energetic, with warmth and respect for the subjects as human beings. It deserves a place in both public and academic libraries.—**Kerranne G. Biley**

104.   **Who's Who in America**. New Providence, N.J., Marquis Who's Who/Reed Reference Publishing, 1900- . (Biennial). 3v. index. $459.95/set for recent edition. ISSN 0083-9396.

Who's Who in America is a classic reference to current, prominent individuals. The 50th edition (1996) is reviewed here. Typical information consists of the person's name, occupation, place and date of birth, parents, spouse and children, education, accomplishments, memberships, and address (usually office). This standard biographical reference source was reviewed in ARBA on many occasions. It was last reviewed in ARBA 94. The 49th edition contained more than 80,000 biographies, using identical criteria as compared to previous volumes. The present edition substantially increases coverage, and now one discovers 92,000 entries, including prominent scholars, educators, industrialists, government officials, artists, and so forth.

All entries are updated every year, and deceased individuals are removed to the companion volume, *Who Was Who in America with World Notables* (see ARBA 94, entry 23). This source should be found in all major libraries.—**Bohdan S. Wynar and Robert L. Wick**

105.   **Who's Who in America: Junior & Senior High School Version**. Wilmette, Ill., Marquis Who's Who, 1991. 4v. index. $87.00pa./set. LC 04-16934. ISBN 0-8379-1251-2.

These four books are a continuation of the title introduced in 1989 (see ARBA 91, entry 21). The new volumes have the same virtues as the old. In addition, the type size has been more than doubled, and abbreviations have been held to a minimum, making them easier for students to access and to read. The first four volumes provide nearly 6,000 entries about subjects from the fields of science and technology, politics and government, sports, and entertainment. The new volumes have 5,000 more entries on business and industry, literary and visual arts, and world leaders. The final volume also contains a complete index to the subjects of all eight volumes.

Each volume contains a 20-point key to information found in each entry, a table of abbreviations, and an explanation of the alphabetizing practices used. Each entry contains subject's name; vital statistics; occupation; parents; marital status and children; education; professional certification; career patterns and achievements; writings and creative works; civic and political activities; military record; awards and fellowships; political, religious, social, and club affiliations; avocations; and home and office addresses. The business and industry volume profiles such notables as designer Ralph Lauren and Disney head Michael Eisner. In the literary arts volume, students will learn about Madeleine L'Engle, Lloyd Alexander, Alice Walker, and Chaim Potok. Andrew and Jamie Wyeth, Peter Max, Yves Saint-Laurent, and Christo are among the subjects in the visual arts volume. World leaders include Boris Yeltsin, Elie Wiesel, Lech Walesa, and Desmond Tutu. The complete set is an excellent resource work. [R: RBB, 15 Mar 92, p. 1400]—**Jerry D. Flack**

106. **Who's Who in the East**. 24th ed. New Providence, N.J., Marquis Who's Who/Reed Reference Publishing, 1943- . $259.00 for recent edition. LC 43-18522. ISSN 0083-9760.

This directory offers biographical sketches of distinguished people whose influence is concentrated in the eastern United States (Maine to Washington, D.C.) and eastern Canada. The 1993/94 edition contains approximately 26,750 names of persons in a wide range of fields. Admission to the volume is based on the extent of the person's reference interest, judged on either the position of responsibility held or the level of achievement attained by the individual. For most sketches, information is provided by the biographees; for some, the publisher's staff compiled the data. Entries are short but highlight 19 data points, including information on personal, education, and professional factors. A random check of a few persons fitting the admission criteria confirmed the work's broad coverage of positions, except for the omission of the president of the flagship public university in one of the states covered.

Each edition of this regional directory expands the coverage of the previous year; this edition contains 1,250 more names than its immediate predecessor. The entry format and the alphabetical arrangement have remained constant since the 1st edition; the present layout has been retained since the early 1970s. There is some overlap between this volume and *Who's Who in America* (Reed Reference Publishing, 1993).

The key advantage of using this directory is the convenience of a single-volume list of notable people in one geographical region across disciplines. Other sources offer access to persons from a geographical region by special index listings, but no other print directory makes geographical orientation integral to the volume and has coverage across disciplines. Access to this biographical data can also be achieved through searching the Dialog file of *Who's Who in America*; the electronic alternative may be of greater value than the print to libraries where there is infrequent need for this data. However, in most eastern larger academic and public libraries, the print format could be used more often.—**Danuta A. Nitecki and Robert L. Wick**

107. **Who's Who in the Midwest**. New Providence, N.J., Marquis Who's Who/Reed Reference Publishing, 1970- . index. $249.95 for recent edition. ISSN 0083-9787.

The 1995 edition of *Who's Who in the Midwest* is similar to previous editions. The Midwest is defined as Illinois, Indiana, Iowa, Kansas, Michigan, Minnesota, Missouri, Nebraska, North Dakota, Ohio, South Dakota, Wisconsin, and Manitoba and western Ontario in Canada. There are approximately 23,100 entries in this volume, compared to 21,700 in the 23d edition. There is some overlap with the 23d edition, but a spot check shows that as many as 70 percent of the entries on some pages are new. Also new in this edition is a professional index arranged alphabetically by categories from agriculture to social science. The entries under each category are alphabetical by states, then alphabetical by cities, and under these alphabetical by names of individuals. This is a helpful feature for identifying professionals in one's own locality.

As with other Marquis publications, most of the information in this volume is provided by the biographees, so it is as accurate as they choose to be. Although criteria are supplied for the inclusion of the biographees, it is still hard to figure out why some people are included and others with similar qualifications are not.—**Kathleen Farago and Robert L. Wick**

108. **Who Was Who in America with World Notables**. **Volume X: 1989-1993**. New Providence, N.J., Marquis Who's Who/Reed Reference Publishing, 1993. 402p. $75.00. LC 93-3788. ISBN 0-8379-0220-7.

It has been 50 years since *Who Was Who* was first published. The tradition continues with the publication of this volume. As always, it serves as a complement to *Who's Who in America,* providing much personal and professional information (which is often unique) in the succinct format for which Marquis Who's Who publications are noted. For those users who are not familiar with the format and the many abbreviations used, there are a key to information and a table of abbreviations.

This has been a standard work for many years and should continue to be a part of almost any reference collection. However, it has some quirks that could occasionally make usage inconvenient, such as the inclusion of people found in *Who's Who* who are more than 93 years old at the time of publication, whether they are dead or not. Also, the compilers, although generally adhering to the established 1989-1993 limit for a person's death, occasionally include individuals whose deaths occurred long before 1988. There is no indication of such a policy in the preface.—**Phillip P. Powell**

109. **Who's Who in the West**. 24th ed. New Providence, N.J., Marquis Who's Who/Reed Reference Publishing, 1971- . $249.95 for recent edition. ISSN 0083-9817.

Following the typical pattern of other volumes in this series, *Who's Who in the West* (1995) (24th edition) provides brief biographical annotations on some 23,500 people in the western United States, and the Canadian provinces of Alberta, British Columbia, and Saskatchewan. While most individuals listed have achieved fame or prominence, it is questionable if all have attained the "conspicuous achievement" the editors set as a criterion for inclusion, and many who have seem to be missing. Bill McCartney, football coach at the University of Colorado in Boulder for 13 years and one of the founders of the national organization Promise Keepers, is just one of several who come to mind. The accuracy of the information provided generally rests with the biographee who submitted it; information on nonrespondents has been gleaned from public sources. Therefore, data vary greatly in amount, content, and importance. Long a standard shelf item in libraries, this series of books is well used by patrons and would be missed if omitted from the collection.—**Jo Anne H. Ricca**

110. **Who's Who in the South and Southwest**. New Providence, N.J., Marquis Who's Who/Reed Reference Publishing, 1971- . index. $229.95 for recent edition. ISSN 0083-9809.

As with the previous editions, the 24th edition (1995) of this regional *Who's Who* contains entries of individuals whose occupational stature or achievement are regionally noteworthy by the standards set by the editorial staff. Although the number of entries remains basically the same as the previous editions (see ARBA 94, entry 26), the present work is 80 pages longer than the 1994 edition and displays a typeface that is noticeably finer. The South and Southwest are defined as those states from Virginia to Florida on the Atlantic Coast, running westward through Texas, and taking in a couple of the border states—Kentucky and West Virginia. On an extremely selective level, representatives from Puerto Rico, the United States Virgin Islands, and Mexico are included. Marquis Who's Who continues its policy of soliciting biographical information directly from qualified individuals. The amount of information to be included is at the biographee's discretion, and that variation is easily discernible and sometimes irritating.

A useful addition to this edition is the professional-area index, which provides a level of access to the work not previously available. A list of professions has been established, and biographees are listed under the one that most closely applies to them. Additional detail is given by the further listing of them by state and city under the professional heading. This may be a double-edged sword for the editors regarding their inclusion policies. Such facile access allowed these reviewers to locate familiar names, and to ask themselves "Why" occasionally when encountering and reading about certain names.

For a reference collection in either a southern or southwestern library, the inclusion of this work is important. The hefty price of a single volume, however, may cause libraries with tight budgets to weigh the work's merits before purchasing it.—**Phillip P. Powell and Robert L. Wick**

111. **Who's Who of Emerging Leaders in America**. 4th ed. New Providence, N.J., Marquis Who's Who/Reed Reference Publishing, 1987- . $229.00. LC 86-63225.

Originally published in 1987, this Marquis Who's Who is another excellent reference volume worthy of shelf space in both municipal and research libraries. Unfortunately, this work is not among those volumes. This 4th (1993) edition of *Who's Who of Emerging Leaders in America* provides up to 19 pieces of information on approximately 20,500 individuals who, according to the editors, "warrant entry into this valuable reference source" (p.vi). The biographical data provided on each listee is similar to the information supplied in other Marquis Who's Who directories. Each entry, for instance, includes vital statistics, education, career history, awards and publications, and address. The information was obtained from the biographees.

The limitation of this particular volume is in the selections of the listees. Although the editors insist individuals "became eligible for listing because their positions and/or noteworthy accomplishments proved to be of significant value to society, and, thus, rendered them reference-worthy" (p.vi), an inspection of the selectees arouses suspicion. Nearly 90 percent of those included have surnames beginning with the first 13 letters of the alphabet, while the N-Z listees warranted only about 10 percent of the space in the volume. No explanation is given for this apparent discrepancy in coverage.

Unless a library wishes to specialize in reference materials that cover only the first half of the alphabet, it would be prudent to save the cost of this volume and wait for the next edition, which one hopes will be more complete in its coverage.—**Terry D. Bilhartz and Robert L. Wick**

Retrospective Biographies

112. **The Cambridge Dictionary of American Biography**. John S. Bowman, ed. New York, Cambridge University Press, 1995. 903p. index. $44.95. ISBN 0-521-40258-1.

Librarians have long lamented that biographical dictionaries are often lacking. For instance, necrologies such as *Merriam-Webster's Biographical Dictionary* bar the living, celebrity registers eschew the noncharismatic, and few works sufficiently accommodate the lives of important women and minorities.

Now joining the fray are editor Bowman and 94 subject consultants, who in an affordable volume have profiled 9,000 notable U.S. residents, past and present, many of whom are women or members of various ethnic groups. Of the total number of biographees, more than 200 were born before 1800, and more than 2,200 were alive at the time of publication. Unfortunately, despite the book's title, Canadians and Latin Americans are poorly represented. However, many of the covered subjects (e.g., Marlene Dietrich, Captain Kidd, and Sonja Henie) are not U.S. natives, but are people who have impacted U.S. culture. The breadth of this work is further widened by its 40-page names index, in which the main entries include individuals receiving mention within articles, as well as those accorded their own entries in the text.

Entries, which are unsigned, fall largely into the 75- to 250-word range, with articles on such figures as Jesse Jackson, Thomas Jefferson, and Elvis Presley, each exceeding 400 words. Besides year of birth and (when deceased) death, the entries scrupulously provide birthplace information, even giving birthplace name changes. Birth names, pen names, and nicknames are supplied, followed by highlights of the subject's life, including educational attainments, awards, publications, and his or her overall influence on the United States.

The publisher and editor deserve commendation for offering such a wide cross-section of occupation holders. Here are criminals, judges and legal scholars, financiers, musicians, social activists, manufacturers and inventors, athletes and coaches, writers, and soldiers. Among the more obscure vocations covered are hat manufacturer, cartoon animator, army scout, and horse trainer. An occupational index affords access to the work's entries through more than 60 broad categories (e.g., theater, psychiatry, and journalism).

Significant omissions are few for a reference work of such ambitious compass. However, unaccountable absences include Jerry Brown, George Burns, John Dean III, Eliot Ness, John Wesley Hardin, Clarence Brigham, and Harry Combs. Also, it is noted that the entry for Robert Dworkin misspells "Worcester" as "Wooster." Despite such imperfections, this is the best one-volume biographical dictionary on the market today, and is strongly recommended for all libraries.—**Jeffrey E. Long**

113. **Concise Dictionary of American Biography**. 4th ed. New York, Scribner's, 1990. 1536p. index. $150.00. E176.D564. 920.073. LC 90-8951. ISBN 0-684-19188-1.

Containing abridged entries on all 18,110 individuals who appeared in the basic set of the *Dictionary of American Biography* (*DAB*) and its 8 supplements, this concise edition of the *DAB* provides coverage of prominent Americans who died prior to 1971. By including two additional supplements, it extends coverage a decade beyond that of the 3d edition (see ARBA 81, entry 112). Unlike its predecessor, which had two separate sections of entries, this edition incorporates all entries into a single alphabetical sequence. As with previous editions, the ratio of reduction for articles is generally 14 to 1. The length of the condensed entries varies from a few lines to several pages for notable figures such as major U.S. presidents.

A welcome feature—new to this edition—is an index to occupations. Offering a fascinating perspective into the lives of individuals whose achievements merited their inclusion in the DAB, this index lists such interesting pursuits as "balloonist," "desperado," and "restaurant critic" along with more traditional professions. While this type of access is available through the *Dictionary of*

American Biography. Comprehensive Index: Complete Through Supplement Eight (see ARBA 91, entry 51), it enhances the condensed volume's usefulness as well. Based on a work of outstanding authority, this latest edition of the *Concise DAB* is a valuable biographical resource, particularly for small libraries that do not have the complete *DAB* and its supplements. [R: LJ, 15 Mar 91, pp. 83-84; RBB, 15 Mar 91, pp. 1520-22; RQ, Spring 91, p. 15]—**Marie Ellis**

114.   Culbertson, Judi, and Tom Randall. **Permanent New Yorkers: A Biographical Guide to the Cemeteries of New York**. Chelsea, Vt., Chelsea Green, 1987. 405p. illus. maps. bibliog. index. $16.95pa. LC 8-17663. ISBN 0-930031-11-3.

This is an intriguing guide to a selective number of cemeteries located in four of New York City's boroughs (Staten Island is not included), on Long Island, and in Westchester and Rockland counties. Some may consider visiting burial grounds a morbid pastime; after reading this volume, the visitor will have a greater appreciation of the history, art, architecture, and cultural features such places contain.

Emphasis is on the burial places of the rich and famous, with 350 featured in brief biographies. The biographical sketches, running two to three pages, have a whimsical, witty tone. Each section of the work is introduced by directions on how to reach the particular cemetery, followed by instructions for walking tours; twelve maps, 112 photographs, a bibliography, and an index supplement the text. The biographical subjects range from the seventeenth century to modern times, with many twentieth-century figures featured.

This work is the second in a series of guides to "the most interesting cemeteries of the world's great cities." The first, *Permanent Parisians,* appeared in 1986. Both are of interest to armchair as well as actual visitors.—**Robert Van Benthuysen**

115.   **Dictionary of American Biography**. John A. Garraty and Mark C. Carnes, eds. New York, Scribner's, 1928- . index. $80.00 for recent edition.

This is a standard, indispensable reference tool. Its purpose, as stated in the first volume (published in December 1928), is to provide scholarly biographical essays on persons "who have made some significant contribution to American life in its manifold aspects." Supplement 7 was reviewed in ARBA 82 (see entry 126); the review of supplement 6 appeared in ARBA 81 (see entry 113); and supplement 5 was reviewed in ARBA 78 (see entry 115). Supplement 8 contains biographies of 454 persons and extends the period of coverage through 1970, raising the total number of biographical sketches to 18,110. Supplement 9 (1994) contains biographies of 544 individuals bringing the grand total to 18,645 sketches in both the primary volumes and the supplements. The most recent supplement is Supplement 10 (1995), which covers 1976-1980 and includes 519 individuals. With a nod to our tabloid society, the editors have allotted space for personalities such as Bob Crane and Freddie Prinze. Users primarily familiar with the pre-supplement *Dictionary of American Biography* (*DAB*) may also be surprised to encounter sketches of Carlo Gambino, Sally Rand, and Jim Jones. A check against concurrent editions of *Current Biography* revealed some omissions (e.g., George R. Stewart, Mary Jo Shelly, Arnold Gingrich, and Ted Mack). It should be noted that the percentage of women in this book is three times that of the *DAB* 20 years ago.

Only about 15 percent of those profiled in supplement 10 are women, and this scholarly neglect of women's history in the *DAB* brought about the publication of *Notable American Women, 1607-1950* (see ARBA 72, entry 221). Women covered in supplement 8 include Alice B. Toklas, Sonja Henie, Dorothy Gish, Judy Garland, Janis Joplin, and Hedda Hopper. Men profiled include Jack Kerouac, Dwight D. Eisenhower, Herbert Hoover, Basil Rathbone, Martin Luther King, Jr., Joseph P. Kennedy, Robert F. Kennedy, Jack L. Ruby, and Woody Guthrie.

Readers expecting persons' "significant contributions to American life" to be positive ones may be surprised to read the biographical sketch of "reputed Cosa Nostra boss" Vito Genovese. Also a bit surprising is the inclusion of "wealthy eccentric and playboy" Thomas Franklyn Manville, Jr., whose numerous marriages and divorces were "his only claim to public attention."

The book concludes with an index guide to the supplements that covers all ten volumes.—**Jack Bales and Robert L. Wick**

116.   **Dictionary of North Carolina Biography**. Volume 1: A-D; Volume 2: E-G. Chapel Hill, University of North Carolina Press, 1979. ISBN 0-8078-1329-X (vol. 1); ISBN 0-8078-1656-6 (vol. 2). Volume 3: H-K. William S. Powell, ed. Chapel Hill, University of North Carolina Press, 1988. 384p. ISBN 0-8078-1806-2. Volume 4: L-O. William S. Powell, ed. Chapel Hill, N.C., University of North Carolina Press, 1991. 415p. $49.95. CT252.D5. 920'.0756. LC 79-10106. ISBN 0-8078-1918-2. Volume 5: P-S. William S. Powell, ed. Chapel Hill, University of North Carolina Press, 1994. 494p. $49.95. CT252.D5. 920'.0756. LC 79-10106. ISBN 0-8078-2100-4.

With the fifth volume, the *Dictionary of North Carolina Biography* is nearing completion; six volumes are now projected. As in the initial volume (see ARBA 81, entry 380) and those already published, this one continues the same high standards of scholarly research initially outlined for the project by Powell and carried out under his capable editorship. This volume contains almost 700 biographies of people who were born or who lived in North Carolina, or who otherwise contributed in some significant way to the Tar Heel state, from colonial times to the twentieth century. In keeping with its scope, no person living at the time of publication is included.

This unique project is a collaborative effort, both in the selection of the biographees and in the research and writing of the actual biographies—all the work of volunteers recruited for this enterprise. Similar to the subjects about whom they write, they come from varied backgrounds. Some are well known scholars in their respective fields; others are students and nonprofessionals. All are united by their interest in the makers of North Carolina's history: politicians, physicians, artists, educators, lawyers, journalists, crafts people, authors, and ministers. Where possible, these volunteer biographers have consulted both primary and secondary sources, which are identified at the conclusion of each signed article. Powell has written a number of articles, but his major contribution is the careful direction and consistent editing that make this a landmark biographical work.—**Bernice Bergup and Robert L. Wick**

116a.   **Encyclopedia of American Biography**. 2d ed. John A. Garraty and Jerome L. Sternstein, eds. New York, Harper Reference/Harper Collins, 1996. 1263p. $50.00. ISBN 0-06-270017-0.

First published in 1974 (see ARBA 75, entry 124), this 2d edition provides information on more than 1,000 significant and famous Americans. Each entry consists of two parts. The first section is factual, chronological information (two or three paragraphs) compiled by Columbia University graduate students. The second, much longer part, written by an expert on that person, is subjective, evaluating and interpreting the biographee's accomplishments. Although each article is signed, there is no list of contributors or indication as to the individual authors' qualifications, which may confuse general readers.

Selection criteria are questionable; for example, Ida Tarbell is included, but not Upton Sinclair. While strong on politicians, the reference is weak on entertainers—the Marx Brothers are in, but not Lucille Ball, Jack Benny, or Milton Berle. Each entry lists one or two standard biographies for further reading, but there is no index. *The Cambridge Dictionary of American Biography* (see ARBA 96, entry 35) provides less information on many more (9,000) people, and also has the benefit of name and occupational indexes. Nevertheless, this is a convenient source for both factual and critical material, although limited in scope.—**John A. Drobnicki**

117.   **The Faces of America**. Carter Smith, ed. New York, Facts on File, 1988. 1v. (various paging). illus. index. (American Historical Images on File). $125.00 looseleaf with binder. LC 87-6707. ISBN 0-8160-1608-9.

This is the third in the Facts on File American Historical Images on File series, a looseleaf service containing a wide range of pictorial Americana, and *The Faces of America* seems the best suited to the format. The volume has 300 portraits, including paintings, sculpture, and photographs of a diverse group of Americans from earliest times to the present. Among those included are presidents (Washington, Kennedy, Reagan), artists (Longfellow, Cassett, O'Keefe), and reformers (Debs, DuBois, Dix). The large portraits (6 by 8 inches) are on heavy paper, copyright-free, and easy to reproduce. At the bottom of each is an annotation that places the person in historical perspective. Each portrait is identified with artist, medium, date, and source.

The format should come in handy for reference librarians and students in academic, school, and public libraries. The price may preclude smaller libraries from purchase, but the volume will be valuable for those who can afford it. The problem will be retaining the contents, which, because of the binding, may be filched most easily. Many volumes contain portraits or photographs of famous people, but they do not have as large or as easily copyable a selection as this one. *The Dictionary of American Portraits* (Dover, 1967) contains 4,045 pictures of important Americans, but all are small (2 by 3 inches). The *Catalogue of American Portraits* (see ARBA 76, entry 918) contains many paintings (oil, watercolor, etc.), but is also small and not for copying purposes. This is a very useful volume, with an index by artist and subject, including events as subjects, but it would benefit from an occupations index. [R: BR, Sept/Oct 88, p. 52; RBB, 1 Oct 88, p. 238; WLB, June 88, p. 137]—**Elizabeth Futas**

118.   Filler, Louis. **Distinguished Shades: Americans Whose Lives Live On**. Ovid, Mich., Belfry, 1992. 278p. illus. index. $24.95; $12.95pa. LC 91-077228. ISBN 0-961527-1-8.

"Distinguished Shades" are Americans who made a difference in history but who were often misunderstood and, in some cases, forgotten. The book consists of 56 biographies of men and women of various races who were born between 1745 and 1903. They were progressives, liberals, politicians, and feminists who were active in civil rights, woman suffrage, and social reform movements. Filler has chosen them because they represent aspects of today's national life and dilemmas. He asserts that we should not forget our "shades," for they offer insights to humanity, even today.

The biographies are concise and readable, generally three to five pages long, and include bibliographic notes. Each begins with a statement that covers the impact on society that the person made and continues with a synopsis of the individual's life story. Filler's account goes beyond a factual listing of events; he reiterates the opinions and misconceptions of society at the time and provides the reader with a thought-provoking biography. A comprehensive bibliography would be helpful for those interested in further research, but this makes a good beginning guide.—**Deborah A. Taylor**

119.   Koykka, Arthur S. **Project Remember: A National Index of Gravesites of Notable Americans**. Algonac, Mich., Reference Publications, 1986. 597p. maps. bibliog. index. $59.95. LC 83-42530. ISBN 0-917256-22-0.

Following in the same genre as another publication by Reference Publications, *Final Placement* (1982) by Robert Dickerson, Jr., this index provides a fascinating, if a bit morbid, guide to the final resting places of a number of famous and not-so-famous Americans. Comprehensive in its coverage, the work contains information on over 5,300 persons and is based on extensive research into state, local, private-association, and historical-society collections, as well as an examination of cemetery files and vital records.

Each entry contains the person's name, birth and death dates, a brief statement of the person's significance, and the name of the cemetery or other burial place. Following the main categories are special sections on mass and animal burials and maps showing locations of cemeteries in New York and Los Angeles. Entries are indexed by name and listed by state and cemetery.

Project Remember can be compared to another recent work, Jean Arbeiter and Linda G. Cirino's *Permanent Addresses* (M. Evans, 1983). Koykka's work is much more comprehensive and better researched. However, the earlier work is written in a more anecdotal style and does contain exact addresses, hours, and sections of the cemetery where individuals are buried, which *Project Remember* does not.

While sometimes quite subjective in its criteria for inclusion, this index is certainly the most complete study on the final resting places of individual Americans yet available. The information, while interesting, is mainly useful to genealogists and trivia buffs. The work makes fascinating reading, but many librarians will have to consider whether, given its cost, *Project Remember* is really an essential addition to their reference collections. [R: Choice, Oct 86, p. 282; LJ, Aug 86, p. 136; RBB, 1 Nov 86, p. 399; WLB, Sept 86, p. 81]—**Louis Vyhnanek**

120.   Roberts, Gary Boyd. **The Royal Descents of 500 Immigrants to the American Colonies or the United States Who Were Themselves Notable or Left Descendants Notable in American History**. Baltimore, Md., Genealogical Publishing, 1993. 622p. index. $45.00. LC 93-79085. ISBN 0-8063-1395-1.

The author explains in his lengthy introduction that the notables treated in his work include merchants, lords mayor, clergy, bishops, lawyers, Puritan leaders, and professional soldiers who became the New England Yankees, Pennsylvania Quakers, and Tidewater planters who settled early in U.S. history. These settlers, to be included, must have been descended from royalty, and they must have left notable descendants. One standard for notability is inclusion in the *Dictionary of American Biography* (see ARBA 89, entry 25), *Who's Who in America* (Marquis Who's Who, annual), or the *National Encyclopedia of American Biography*. Included among the present-day notables are George Herbert Walker Busch, whose ancestor was Robert II, king of Scotland; actor Peter Lawford, long-distant relative of Edward III, king of England; and Franklin Delanor Roosevelt, traced to Louis IV, king of France. Roberts takes obvious pleasure in connecting more than one notable descendant to the same ancestor. Sources are cited for each chapter and are explained in the list of abbreviated sources.

Thoroughly indexed, the book is a joy to use. Recommended for libraries with serious genealogical collections.—**Carol Willsey Bell**

121.   **Who Was Who in America with World Notables**. Chicago, Marquis Who's Who, 1942- . $67.50 for recent edition. LC 43-3789. ISSN 0146-8081.

This title, a companion volume to the publisher's *Who's Who in America*, certainly requires no introduction and will be considered an essential purchase for most general reference collections. It is made up of brief biographical sketches of deceased entrants from *Who's Who in America*. The preface stresses the autobiographical nature of much of the data provided and the personality of *Who's Who* is clearly reflected in the *Was* volume. The typical Marquis entries conclude with date of death and place of interment. Entries are arranged in alphabetical order by the decedent's last name. There are no indexes.

Included are not only prominent Americans, but world figures such as Pierre Mendes France, Glenn Gould, Indira Gandhi, and Sir Michael Redgrave. Although it covers thousands of personalities, *Who Was Who* is not exhaustive, even for notable Americans. Helen Clay Frick, Ruth Carter Stapleton, Thelonious Monk, Sally Stanford, Stringfellow Barr, and others cannot be found here and must be pursued elsewhere. *Who Was Who* is not perfect, but it remains a primary reference source. Recommended.—**Thomas H. Patterson and Robert L. Wick**

PART II
Biographies in Professional Fields

3 History

INTRODUCTION

History is a difficult area to define. In a sense, all written accounts of the world can be considered history. That difficulty has been felt in compiling this chapter. Here are books on various historical world leaders, books on the classical world, books on ancient times in other countries and in the United States, and books that simply profile historical figures. However, many books that might be categorized as historical sources will not be found here, but in other chapters. Look in the chapter **International Sources** for many biographical sources of world leaders and for such classic sources as *Dictionary of National Biography* and *Encyclopedia of World Biography*. Look in the **Political Science** chapter for many sources listing and profiling political leaders. The chapter **Women's Studies** has information on prominent women—although some sources will also be found here—while the chapter **Ethnic Studies** does the same for African-Americans, Hispanics, Asian-Americans, and other groups. In the end, many decisions on where to place certain titles were difficult and could have been answered in more than one way.

What is included in this chapter is subdivided into the following categories: General Works, Canada, China, Classical World, Europe, Germany, Great Britain, Historians, Japan, Jewish History, Russia, United States, and Vietnam. The United States category is subdivided into General Works, Civil War and Reconstruction, Historians, Revolutionary War, South, and West.

A Magill series, from the publisher of the *Masterplots* volumes, details *Great Lives from History*. International titles in the series are *Great Lives from History: Ancient and Medieval Series* (Salem Press, 1988) (see entry 126)*; Great Lives from History: Renaissance to 1900 Series* (Salem Press, 1989) (see entry 127); and *Great Lives from History: Twentieth Century Series* (Salem Press, 1990) (see entry 128). There is also a United States title in the series: *Great Lives from History: American Series* (Salem Press, 1987) (see entry 161). Other general sources concentrate on world rulers, some more notorious than famous. *Dictators and Tyrants: Absolute Rulers and Would-Be Rulers in World History* (Facts on File, 1995) (see entry 122) is one such title. Women rulers are also covered, in *Women Who Ruled* by Guida M. Jackson (ABC-Clio, 1990) (see entry 130).

The pre-modern world, from classical times up through the Renaissance, is covered in a variety of sources. *Contemporaries of Erasmus*, from the University of Toronto Press (1985-1987) (see entry 125), was conceived as a companion volume to the collected works of Erasmus, an attempt to avoid explaining the many people who appear in those works. *The Roman Emperors: A Biographical Guide to the Rulers of Imperial Rome, 31 BC-AD 476* by Michael Grant (Scribner's, 1985) (see entry 136); and *Who Was Who in the Greek World: 776 BC-30 BC* edited by Diana Bowder (Phaidon Book/Cornell University Press, 1982) (see entry 137), chronicle the Greek and Roman worlds. Facts on File offers the *Encyclopedia of the Renaissance* (1987) (see entry 138) for a look at that world.

British history is particularly well documented. The series *Who's Who in British History*, from St. James Press, offers a number of volumes: *Who's Who in Roman Britain and Anglo-Saxon England* (St. James Press, c.1989) (see entry 143); *Who's Who in Tudor England* (St. James Press, 1990) (see entry 143); *Who's Who in Stuart Britain* (St. James Press, c.1988) (see entry 143); *Who's Who in Late Medieval England (1272-1485)* (St. James Press, 1991) (see entry 144); *Who's Who in Shakespeare's England* (St. Martin's Press, 1981) (see entry 149); and *Who's Who in Early Hanoverian Britain* (St. James Press, 1992) (see entry 150). All these offer maps, portraits, and genealogical tables as well as biographical sketches, for a wide look at the times. Most people are familiar with *Debrett's Peerage*; here we find *Debrett's Kings and Queens of Britain* (Salem House/Merrimack Publishers' Circle, 1986) (see entry 151), which gives short, readable biographies of rulers of Britain back to Anglo-Saxon times. An unusual but nonetheless fascinating work is *A Biographical Register of the University of Oxford A.D. 1501 to 1540* (Oxford University Press, 1974) (see entry 142). This 742-page volume is a supplement to a previous three volume set and contains 15,000 entries of Oxonians.

By far the greatest number of sources fall under the United States category. Aside from the *Great Lives from History: American Series*, mentioned previously, other general works include Gale's *Profiles in American History: Significant Events and the People Who Shaped Them* (U*X*L/Gale, 1994) (see entry 164); and—also from Gale—*Notable Americans: What They Did, from 1620 to the Present: Chronological and Organizational Listings of Leaders . . .* (Gale, 1988) (see entry 165). While many sources emphasize political leaders, one source takes an unusual approach, listing cultural leaders: Justin Harmon's *American Cultural Leaders from Colonial Times to the Present* (ABC-Clio, 1993) (see entry 163).

Students of military history, whether specializing in the Revolutionary War or the Civil War, can find ample material here; look in the appropriate category for specific titles. Books in this chapter look at these wars in a broad context, with information on politicians, journalists, and historians of the particular period as well as on military leaders. Look in the chapter **Military Science** for material geared only to military personnel.

GENERAL WORKS

122. Axelrod, Alan, and Charles Phillips. **Dictators and Tyrants: Absolute Rulers and Would-Be Rulers in World History**. New York, Facts on File, 1995. 340p. illus. index. $45.00. ISBN 0-8160-2866-4.

For those who have ever drawn a blank on where to begin researching a Hapsburg prince or a Middle Eastern tyrant, this unique single-volume reference book would be a good place to start. The comprehensive text profiles nearly 600 tyrants and would-be tyrants from world history. People chosen for inclusion by the editors are those who ruled unlawfully according to the standards of the society in which they originally came to power. Beginning as far back as King David of Israel and Genghis Khan, the coverage extends to the modern day with dictators such as Adolf Hitler, Muammar Muhammad al-Qadhafi, and Manuel Antonio Noriega.

Arranged alphabetically by name, each entry is 3 to 15 paragraphs long and begins with an explanation of how the rulers overstepped their power, a description of their rise to power, and their final demise. The writing is easy to read, particularly for the junior high and high school student. Most entries end with suggestions for further reading and many have black-and-white photographs, often of sculptures or paintings. The book concludes with a useful index that not only lists the biographical entries, but also includes subjects such as biblical figures, English monarchs, massacres, political purges, and poison. This is a well-made reference book with an unorthodox slant on world history.—**Carol D. Henry**

123. Boatner, Mark M. III. **Biographical Dictionary of World War II**. Novato, Calif., Presidio Press, 1996. 733p. $50.00. ISBN 0-89141-548-3.

Boatner, the author of several historical reference works, worked for many years on this biographical dictionary of the Second World War. Using an objective counting method, he selected 1,000 key people to be included. The entries vary in length depending on the importance of the person, and the writing is colorful and entertaining. A glossary of places, events, documents, and other relevant information allows the user to read a biographical entry and refer to the glossary, effectively avoiding repetitive descriptions within each entry.

While considerably greater in scope than earlier biographical dictionaries of World War II, such as those edited by David Mason (Routledge, 1978) and Christopher Tunney (see ARBA 74, entry 303), Boatner's dictionary contains no illustrations. The entries conclude with bibliographic references for further reading. An annotated bibliography of sources and authorities consulted is given at the end of the work. Coverage includes people from all parts of the globe related to World War II, from entertainers to military and political figures. Selected from existing printed reference works as well as firsthand eyewitness accounts, this reference work is particularly useful for the entries on

Russian officials and officers. Boatner, a colonel in the U.S. Army (Ret.), served in Europe during World War II and taught military history at West Point from 1959 to 1963.

This otherwise outstanding work is slightly flawed by typographic errors (e.g., "Pasadina," "Reichssicherheitshauptnamt," "Sach[s]enhausen," "subver[si]ve"). Sloppy errors in editing, as in the entry for Joseph Goebbels that refers to him alternately as [Hermann] Göring, are also unfortunate. In addition, some readers may be offended by such language as "the little cripple" and "the strident dwarf" (p. 187).

Aficionados of the history of World War II will find this dictionary to be an indispensable browsing tool. Most libraries will want to add it to their reference collections; smaller libraries that already have one of the earlier biographical dictionaries may choose not to add this, as price may be a factor.—**Ingrid Schierling Burnett**

124.   Chambers, Steven D. **Political Leaders and Military Figures of the Second World War: A Bibliography**. Brookfield, Vt., Dartmouth Publishing/Ashgate Publishing, 1996. 440p. index. $84.95. ISBN 1-85521-646-9.

Chambers has provided an interesting bibliography of important names in the political and military era of World War II. This work is a classed bibliography with five main classes: Allied political leaders, Axis political leaders, Allied military leaders, Axis military leaders, and other notable figures and miscellaneous entries. The military leaders are further divided by country, and political leaders are listed by name and appear to cover only the major players: Winston Churchill, Joseph Stalin, Franklin Roosevelt, Adolf Hitler, and others.

Each leader is covered by a brief one- or two-page biographical introduction and bibliography. The bibliographies are preceded by a paragraph of annotations of suggested readings, with the annotations referring only to the more well-known biographies. It is a puzzle to the reader what criteria were used for selection. Only books are cited, leaving readers to locate the many periodical articles on their own. In general, the volume seems to have been compiled by searching several large computer library catalogs. This results in a bibliography that is neither complete nor annotated. In addition, choices of titles are sometimes odd; for example, detailed Ph.D. dissertations on the speech patterns of World War II political leaders and a correspondence collection between FDR and Pope Pius XII.

The biographical sketches, although balanced, are rather simplistic. For example, the Roosevelt entry reads, "during his terms as president, Roosevelt had his admirers and his detractors." Hitler is similarly described as "the catalyst for change in Europe in the 1930s." Charles de Gaulle's entry covers a scant two paragraphs and lacks the concise phrasing accorded the other leaders as cited above. There are numerous minor inaccuracies in the Stalin thumbnail sketch. Military leaders are arranged alphabetically within the country of their command. Maurice-Gustave Gamelin is given a mere five sentences. There is a miscellaneous grouping at the end that lists collected biographies by class. An author index is provided for each cited biography. There is no general index other than the table of contents. For example, when looking for Klaus Barbie, one can only search through the book. Only when the subject of the biography is a cited author will the person be found in the index, for example Churchill, Dwight Eisenhower, and so on.

Although this is an interesting point of view on World War II, it is better covered by other bibliographers, which the author cites. Most of the information can also be obtained by searching a major library catalog or encyclopedia. In addition, the price seems rather steep for the value.—**Ralph Lee Scott**

125.   **Contemporaries of Erasmus: A Biographical Register of the Renaissance and Reformation**. 3 vols. Peter G. Bietenholz and Thomas B. Deutscher, eds. Buffalo, N.Y., University of Toronto Press, 1985-1987. illus. Vol. 1, $72.50. Vol. 2, $95.00. Vol. 3, $100.00. ISBN 0-8020-2507-2; 0-8020-2571-4; 0-8020-2575-7.

These handsome volumes are offshoots of the project to publish the collected works of Erasmus. To avoid the necessity of the editors having to fully and repetitiously identify the many persons who appear in the works and the correspondence, the decision was made to publish a separate biographical register.

As with the collected works themselves, this is a joint project. Scholars from many nations contributed biographies of persons great and small. The size of each biography is generally proportional to the person's importance and the availability of information. Thus, figures such as Pope Adrian VI, Martin Bucer, and John Colet have entries of approximately three double-column pages each, while others have only a line or two to indicate that they are mentioned by Erasmus but cannot be otherwise identified. For each entry, there is reference to where the person is named by Erasmus, and wherever possible, there is a bibliography directing the reader to further information.

This is very much a work for specialists. Its narrow scope and high price will keep it out of most undergraduate and public libraries. Specialists in the Reformation and early Renaissance will find it helpful, and for Erasmus scholars it will be indispensable.—**Philip R. Rider and Terry Ann Mood**

126.   **Great Lives from History: Ancient and Medieval Series**. Frank N. Magill, ed. Englewood Cliffs, N.J., Salem Press, 1988. 5v. index. $325.00/set. LC 88-18514. ISBN 0-89356-545-8.

The latest addition to the Magill stable of summaries, this is the third of a projected five-set series. Sets already published are the *American Series* (see ARBA 88, entry 513) and the *British and Commonwealth Series*. This *Ancient and Medieval Series* covers non-British persons from antiquity through the Middle Ages (mid fifteenth century). There are 455 articles of 2,000 to 3,000 words in length, in the characteristic Magill format. A brief factual summary is at the beginning, including dates of birth and death, the subject's areas of achievement, and major contributions to history. The main portion of each entry is divided into three parts: early life, life's work, and a summary, which is "an overview of the individual's place in history" (p.v). Finally, an annotated list of references for further study is included. Each entry is signed and written "by an academician who specializes in the area of discussion" (p.v). The biographies are clear and readable, suitable for undergraduates or general readers.—**Nancy Courtney**

127.   **Great Lives from History: Renaissance to 1900 Series**. Frank N. Magill, ed. Englewood Cliffs, N.J., Salem Press, 1989. 5v. index. $325.00/set. CT104.G68. 920'.009'03. LC 89-24039. ISBN 0-89356-551-2.

This is the fourth in a series of five sets that, when completed, will cover the lives of significant individuals throughout the world from ancient times through the twentieth century. The *American Series* (see ARBA 88, entry 513), the *British and Commonwealth Series* (see ARBA 89, entry 463), and the *Ancient and Medieval Series* (see entry 126) have already been published, and the *Twentieth Century Series* (see entry 128) was scheduled for publication in 1990.

The current set contains 481 articles on 495 individuals. The signed articles, written by experts from academic institutions, are arranged alphabetically and cover prominent people in fields such as science, politics, the arts, architecture, and religion. Each article (about 1,500 to 2,000 words in length) is arranged in a set format—birth and death dates, area of achievement, short statement on the individual's contribution to society, brief information on early life, major events and accomplishments, and evaluation of the individual's contributions. Because the articles emphasize positive achievements, however, negative aspects are glossed over. A brief, critical annotated bibliography accompanies each article. Volume 5 contains an alphabetical biographical index, an index by areas of achievement, and a geographical index.

The well-written articles provide concise information on the accomplishments of each individual. While shorter biographies are available in *The McGraw-Hill Encyclopedia of World Biography* (see ARBA 74, entry 106) and in general encyclopedias, *Great Lives'* clear format, readable writing, and suggestions for further reading make it useful and desirable for high school students and the general reader. [R: Choice, Apr 90, p. 1298; WLB, Mar 90, p. 128]—**Kathleen Farago**

128.   **Great Lives from History: Twentieth Century Series**. Frank N. Magill, ed. Pasadena, Calif., Salem Press, 1990. 5v. index. $325.00/set. CT120.G69. 920'.009'04. LC 90-8613. ISBN 0-89356-565-2.

This is the fifth set of biographical reference works to be published by Salem Press. Previous sets have dealt with the United States, Great Britain and the Commonwealth, and the rest of the world to 1900. As a result, there are no British and American figures among the 475 biographees in this set, and it is confined to people whose careers predominantly took place since 1900.

The selection is quite cosmopolitan and includes statesmen, artists, scientists, philosophers, religious leaders and thinkers, filmmakers, and musicians. Biographees may still be alive. Each entry is presented in the standard format developed by Salem Press: a brief head note with vital information and a brief description of the individual, early life, life's work, summary, and a selected bibliography of six to eight items in English.

Unlike the previous volumes, this set has some competition worth mentioning: *Twentieth Century Culture: A Biographical Companion*, edited by Alan Bullock and R. B. Wooding (Harper & Row, 1983), with about 2,000 entries; and *The International Dictionary of 20th Century Biography* by Edward Vernoff and Rima Shore (see ARBA 88, entry 35), with over 5,600 entries. Both of these titles are single volumes that are more suited for ready-reference, but they generally lack bibliographies. The Salem Press set complements those works by providing detail while remaining reasonably concise. Furthermore, the Salem Press entries are well written and researched.

Everyone will note some favorite individuals that have been left out of this set (e.g., Lucien Febvre, Marc Bloch), but that situation could be remedied by publishing a second series of *Great Lives from History.*—**Ronald H. Fritze**

129.   Hamilton, Neil A. **Founders of Modern Nations: A Biographical Dictionary**. Santa Barbara, Calif., ABC-CLIO, 1995. 505p. illus. maps. index. $60.00. ISBN 0-87436-750-6.

This is an intriguing title. According to the preface, *Founders of Modern Nations* is divided into two parts: biographical entries and national entries. There is an explanation of criteria that, unfortunately, can only add to the confusion. Who is a "modern" founder in Russia? According to the entry locator, there are the following political figures: Catherine II (the Great), Mikhail Gorbachev, Ivan III (the Great), Peter (the Great), and Boris Yeltsin. For the United States, John Adams, Samuel Adams, Benjamin Franklin, Alexander Hamilton, Thomas Jefferson, James Madison, Thomas Paine, and George Washington are listed. Indeed, as the preface indicates, "exhaustive coverage of the United States would, in itself, require a dictionary of formidable size." Yes, there are several scholarly dictionaries for the United States, but why include Gorbachev and Yeltsin and omit Franklin Roosevelt? The second part, "Country Profiles," is simply not sufficient for any user, including the elementary school student. Hamilton is an associate professor of history at Spring Hill College in Mobile, Alabama. It is difficult to recommend this book to even the uninitiated.—**Bohdan S. Wynar**

130.   Jackson, Guida M. **Women Who Ruled**. Santa Barbara, Calif., ABC-Clio, 1990. 190p. illus. $35.00. D107.J33. 920.72. LC 89-28282. ISBN 0-87436-560-0.

This biographical dictionary lists more than 360 women sovereigns, including selected legendary rulers. The scope is comprehensive with respect to both time and place. The introduction surveys major world regions and the historical conditions in which women ruled. A century-by-century chronology provides a useful overview.

Entries are arranged alphabetically, with each letter treated as a chapter. Source materials are not listed in the individual entries; instead, notes are numbered consecutively within chapters and appear at the end of the volume. Entries added just prior to publication are without notes, and sources are listed in the preface. The rules followed in alphabetizing and in standardizing spellings are neither stated nor obvious. Variant names/titles are included in the entries, but cross-references are not consistently provided. A bibliography of cited sources completes the volume.

Despite these obstacles to easy use, this compendium is valuable as a single source of information not readily available elsewhere. As such, it is a welcome addition to the range of biographical sources on women. [R: LJ, Dec 90, p. 118; WLB, Dec 90, p. 158]—**Cheryl Kern-Simirenko**

131.   Matthews, Rupert. **Power Brokers: Kingmakers & Usurpers Throughout History**. New York, Facts on File, 1989. 326p. illus. index. $24.95. CT9970.M38. 920.02. ISBN 0-8160-21562.

The subject of this mediocre work is people who became rulers by means other than the normal process (usually by violence) or aided others to positions of rule. About 300 men and women from Sneferu (c.2900 B.C.) to Idi Amin are profiled in essays of around 350 words each. No references to sources accompany the articles, but there are a bibliography of general works and an index at the end.

The book jacket suggests that this work is for the reader "from young student to historian," but it is clearly not written for adults, and such writing is not acceptable for young people. In many articles it is difficult to make sense out of the information given. Just as it is hard to know for what audience this book was written, so it is impossible to imagine what library would want to purchase it. Since 89 percent of the entry subjects can be found as full articles in either *Encyclopedia Americana* or *Encyclopaedia Britannica* (and more appear as parts of other subject articles), libraries already have the information at hand and can ignore this title.—**Eric R. Nitschke**

132.   **Scholastic Encyclopedia of Women in the United States**. By Sheila Keenan. New York, Scholastic, 1996. 206p. illus. index. $17.95. ISBN 0-590-22792-0.

Scholastic Encyclopedia of Women in the United States is a valuable illustrated profile of women who have made a difference in U.S. history, from Pocahontas to Hillary Rodham Clinton. The biographies are brief and represent a broad range of women's lives. Women treated are from every walk of life and from every ethnic group. A significant number are included because they filled nontraditional roles.

Entries are divided into six broad categories covering a period from the 1500s through the 1990s. Most entries are biographical, but a significant number of cameos are included that highlight women whose broader lives are not detailed. A section called "Women's Words" presents quotations by and about women. A section entitled "Women's Sphere" is a sidebar that provides information on what women's lives were really like during a certain period.

This source contains both a topical and an alphabetic index. It is recommended for both public and school libraries.—**Mary L. Bowman**

CANADA

133.   Bercuson, David J., and J. L. Granatstein. **The Collins Dictionary of Canadian History: 1867 to the Present**. Don Mills, Ont., Collins, 1988. 270p. illus. maps. $24.95. ISBN 0-00-217758-7.

This new reference work on Canadian history since Confederation is an important addition to recent reference works on Canada, including the *Canadian Encyclopedia*, 2d ed., and the *Historical Atlas of Canada* (see ARBA 88, entry 529). It represents the combined talents of two of Canada's most prominent historians, David Bercuson, of the University of Calgary, and J. L. Granatstein, of York University. Bercuson has written extensively on labor history, while Granatstein has published on topics ranging from conscription to foreign policy. The present volume includes some 1,600 alphabetized entries on topics ranging from politics to agriculture. There are numerous cross-references, some black-and-white illustrations, a helpful timeline, and numerous appendices listing governors general, prime ministers, provincial premiers, election results, immigration statistics, etc. The entries are short and in some cases critical. Pierre Trudeau warrants one and one-fourth pages and no picture, while René Lévesque gets one-half page and likewise no picture. There are entries for such widely diverse topics as the Group of Seven (artists), *Saturday Night* (literary magazine), and the Munsinger Affair (political scandal). Politics and labor are extensively covered, but coverage of the arts and sports is a bit eclectic. For example, there is an entry for Jean Beliveau, former Montreal Canadien, but none for Wayne Gretzky. Singers Paul Anka, Neil Young, and Anne Murray are included, but Gordon Lightfoot and Joni Mitchell are not. Despite these shortcomings, this new volume should prove helpful for students of Canadian history and culture.—**Brian E. Coutts**

134.   **People in History: An Index to U.S. and Canadian Biographies in History Journals and Dissertations**. Susan K. Kinnell, ed. Santa Barbara, Calif., ABC-Clio, 1988. 2v. $125.00/set. ISBN 0-87436-493-0. ISSN 0894-0916.

When an organization labors as diligently as ABC-Clio does to produce its widely used and respected bibliographic volumes, *America: History and Life,* its editors are perpetually faced with the temptation to skim off a small portion of the database, repackage it, and market it as a brand-new, "how-did-you-get-along-without-it" product. ABC-Clio has succumbed to this temptation with the publication of its latest reference work, *People in History.*

This work is being marketed as a "unique new reference tool . . . a landmark two-volume publication . . . a rich, new vein of exploration for historians, genealogists, and scholars concerned with the history of specific ethnic or religious groups, schools of thought, or occupations in the United States and Canada." In fact, *People in History* is simply a selection of citations and abstracts for biographical materials, journal articles, and dissertations culled from the *America: History and Life* database. The biographee's name is the main entry, and each article is assigned one or more subject terms, which then appear in the index at the end of the second volume. This will all be quite familiar to users of the print version of *America: History and Life,* as it employs the same indexing system.

Since *America: History and Life* is available online through DIALOG, it would be difficult to justify the purchase of this work in a library that provided adept database searching for its patrons; it would be still harder to justify if the library already possessed the print version of *America: History and Life.* [R: Choice, Oct 88, pp. 294-95; LJ, Aug 88, p. 151; WLB, June 88, p. 143]—**Daniel Uchitelle**

CHINA

135. Association for Asian Studies. Ming Biographical History Project Committee. **Dictionary of Ming Biography, 1368-1644**. L. Carrington Goodrich, ed. New York, Columbia University Press, 1976. 2v. illus. index. $140.00/set. LC 75-26938. ISBN 0-231-03801-1(v.1); 0-231-03833-X(v.2).

This excellent, scholarly biographical dictionary complements two other compilations, *Eminent Chinese of the Ch'ing Period (1644-1912)*, edited by Arthur W. Hummel, and *Biographical Dictionary of Republican China*, edited by Howard L. Boorman and Richard C. Howard, and extends their coverage back to the fourteenth century. Together they constitute the most authoritative source for Chinese biographical information in the English language, and perhaps in any language. The *Dictionary of Ming Biography* includes some 650 biographies ranging from one page to thirteen pages in length. Although rulers and officials predominate, persons of many other occupations are included—especially artists, writers, and scholars. Most of the subjects are of Chinese nationality, but Europeans, as well as persons of other East Asian nationalities who were important in Chinese history, are included. Very few women are included, probably because historical records for women, other than those related to rulers, are very rare for this period. The biographies are written in a clear, unpretentious style. The important aspects of each subject's life are described, and an effort is made to evaluate the contribution to Chinese society. The biographies are signed by their authors, all eminently suited for this task, and conclude with extensive but highly abbreviated bibliographies of basic sources, most of which are in East Asian languages.

Among the most valuable contributions of this work are its extensive indexes. An index of names includes not only the names of the biographees, but some 6,000 other persons described in the biographies. The value of this work for bibliographical research is greatly enhanced by a title index to some 3,500 books mentioned in the biographical articles. The subject index locates discussions of some 2,500 specific events and topics.

This fundamental tool is an indispensable addition to any library that has an interest in China and its history. [R: BL, 1 Nov 76, p. 424; Choice, Sept 76, p. 794; LJ, 1 June 76, p. 1275]—**James D. Anderson**

CLASSICAL WORLD

136. Grant, Michael. **The Roman Emperors: A Biographical Guide to the Rulers of Imperial Rome, 31 BC-AD 476**. New York, Scribner's, 1985. 367p. illus. maps. index. $25.00. LC 85-8391. ISBN 0-684-18388-9.

All of the knowledge and expertise accumulated by Michael Grant has gone into this work. Grant has provided us with short biographies of 92 Roman emperors from Augustus, the first of the imperial rulers, to Romulus, Emperor of the West, who abdicated in 476. During this period, Rome ruled a vast empire ranging from Britain to the Sahara, and from the Atlantic to the Euphrates.

The men portrayed here are those who had ultimate authority over that empire and whose decisions shaped the destiny of that empire and in many ways shaped our own time. These men were a diverse and colorful group with many levels of ability. None of them were dull. Grant has used ancient manuscripts, coins, medallions, inscriptions, and archaeology to re-create a time almost 2,000 years removed from our own. Most of the sketches are two to three pages long but provide a considerable amount of information. We learn how each man came to the purple, something about his early life and family, and his contributions—or lack thereof—to the growth and stability of the Roman Empire. Each ruling family is given a genealogical table and each sketch is headed by a photo of a coin or medallion dating from that individual's reign.

A number of maps and plans are included. The maps show the territories ruled by Rome at various times. A key to Latin terms, an index of Greek and Latin authors, and a detailed index to the maps and place names are also provided. The key to Latin terms gives brief explanations of terms used in the book as well as some other common expressions. It is cross-referenced to assist the reader. An example is "Chief Priest. *See* Pontifex Maximus." The index to authors is also cross-referenced. In the index to the maps, the modern equivalents of ancient place names mentioned in the text are included. This is a good basic source for the study of Imperial Rome. [R: Choice, Jan 86, pp. 725-26]—**Susan Ebershoff-Coles**

137.   **Who Was Who in the Greek World: 776 BC-30 BC**. Diana Bowder, ed. Ithaca, N.Y., Phaidon Book/Cornell University Press, 1982. 227p. illus. maps. bibliog. index. $29.95; $8.50pa. LC 82-71594. ISBN 0-8014-1538-1; 0-671-50159-3pa.

This title is the companion volume to *Who Was Who in the Roman World, 753 B.C.-A.D. 476.* Alphabetically arranged, the entries contain biographical information about important Greeks and non-Greeks who were important in Greek history. With each biographical sketch, the length of which varies from very brief to extensive, there is at least one bibliographic citation. Well illustrated with pertinent maps, the book also contains a helpful glossary and bibliography. [R: BL, 1 Feb 83, p. 712; Choice, Apr 83, p. 1116; LJ, Jan 83, p. 122]—**Bohdan S. Wynar**

EUROPE

138.   **Encyclopedia of the Renaissance**. Thomas G. Bergin and Jennifer Speake, eds. New York, Facts on File, 1987. 454p. illus. (part col.). bibliog. $40.00. LC 87-13433. ISBN 0-8160-1315-2.

For the person interested in a preliminary view of the Renaissance, this encyclopedia suits the purpose. Continental in scope, over 2,500 entries cover several disciplines: literature, philosophy, religion, art, science, and music, as well as architecture and exploration. Full-color and black-and-white illustrations reveal the artistic glory of the age, and the work is wrapped up with a selective bibliography and brief chronology.

It is the opinion of this reviewer, however, that the editors of this encyclopedia, by choosing to cover only the fourteenth through sixteenth centuries, have cheated the reader. Much of the late English Renaissance, particularly literature, is ignored. For example, while the editors include Ben Jonson, they fail to note two of his famous contemporaries, John Donne and George Herbert, both metaphysical poets. As a matter of fact, metaphysical poetry doesn't even earn an entry. Yet a more disappointing omission is John Milton, whom *The Norton Anthology of English Literature* (W. W. Norton, 1975) places in the late Renaissance, and whose style it deems characteristic of the period.

Another disappointment lies in the fact that few portraits, a mere handful, accompany the biographical entries. For an artist as famous and favored as Michelangelo, just one colored plate of an obscure section of the Sistine Chapel is illustrated.

With the caveat that this encyclopedia suffices only as a starting point for research or as a quick reference, it may be useful.—**Patricia M. Leach**

139. Opfell, Olga S. **Queens, Empresses, Grand Duchesses and Regents: Women Rulers of Europe, A.D. 1328-1989**. Jefferson, N.C., McFarland, 1989. 282p. illus. index. $25.95. D107.064. 920.72'094. LC 88-43484. ISBN 0-89950-385-3.

Nearly 40 royal women are featured in this collection. Included are European women who reigned not merely as consorts but either as sitting monarchs or as regents with actual power, from the fourteenth century through the present. Arranged chronologically, each biographical sketch is four to eight pages long and includes a picture of the subject. A selected bibliography listing two to thirteen titles about each woman and an index, primarily of names, complete the volume.

These lively sketches provide more information than encyclopedia entries and highlight those women who actually exercised royal power. This collective biography seems useful for school, public, and college libraries. [R: BR, Nov/Dec 89, p. 50; RBB, 1 Oct 89, pp. 395-96]—**Cheryl Kern-Simirenk**

140. **Women in Western European History, First Supplement: A Select Chronological, Geographical, and Topical Bibliography**. Linda Frey, Marsha Frey, and Joanne Schneider, comps. and eds. Westport, Conn., Greenwood Press, 1986. 699p. index. $65.00. LC 86-22777. ISBN 0-313-25109-6.

This hefty *First Supplement* continues the excellent work Frey, et al. began in 1982 with *Women in Western European History* (see ARBA 83, entry 396) and its 1984 companion volume covering the nineteenth and twentieth centuries. Following the same format as those earlier volumes, this bibliography supplements and updates the earlier compilations, providing record of recent or newly discovered research as well as later editions or translations of some 100 earlier entries. Like its predecessors, this work uses a detailed historical outline and topical guide as its main access point for over 6,500 listings. A subject, name, and author index are included, as well as a brief guide to the quotations which preface most sections.

As in the earlier volumes, this bibliography includes listings of published materials focusing on the historical condition of women in Western Europe from antiquity to the present. Primary source materials such as manuscripts and letters are not included. Wherever possible, English-language works or English translations are used, and only titles available in the United States are included.

Perhaps the only shortcoming of the earlier volumes was the brevity of their subject indexes. This new volume is made considerably easier to use by its greatly expanded subject index, now including geographical subdivisions. However, much more work needs to be put into this section to make it a truly helpful tool. The uneven use of cross-references continues to be confusing. Why, when the compilers use the subdivision "Literature" throughout their historical outline section, do they omit the term from their subject index? Readers looking for entries under this topic will find no cross-references to the only listing that is used—"Novelists—women." Despite these problems this supplementary volume should prove a great asset to researchers in the field of women's history, and it is a welcome addition to the literature. [R: Choice, May 87, p. 1378; WLB, Mar 87, p. 68]—**Elizabeth Patterson**

GERMANY

141. Wistrich, Robert. **Who's Who in Nazi Germany**. New York, Macmillan, 1982. 359p. bibliog. $17.75. LC 82-4704. ISBN 0-02-630600-X.

Essentially a biographical dictionary of almost 350 figures who exerted significant influence during the rise, zenith, and demise of Nazi power in Germany, this work should be titled *Who Was Who*. Narrative-style entries average 300 words, and the treatment in each is chronological. Personalities include both friends and foes of Nazism. Many represent the military, but more than a few were notable in contemporary art, science, academia, industry, and entertainment. Career highlights are delineated succinctly, footnotes are eschewed, and q.v. cross-referencing is frequent. The author attempts, with mixed success, to link each biographee to the Third Reich and the enormously intricate machine that was Hitlerian Germany. His admittedly subjective opinion of de-Nazification court actions is not complimentary. In all other aspects, however, his approach is relatively unbiased. Much background data has been drawn from German publications, which form the bulk of an appended bibliography. In addition, there are a glossary of terms plus a comparative list of ranks vis-a-vis U.S. and British counterparts.

Targeted for the lay reader or tyro researcher, this work is both readable and informative. It constitutes a valuable basic insight into the Nazi phenomenon. [R: BL, 1 Oct 82, p. 187; LJ, 15 Sept 82, p. 1745; WLB, Dec 82, p. 352]—**Lawrence E. Spellman**

GREAT BRITAIN

142.   Emden, A. B. **A Biographical Register of the University of Oxford A.D. 1501 to 1540**. New York, Oxford University Press, 1974. 742p. o.p. ISBN 0-19-951008-3.

This is a supplementary volume to the author's three-volume set, *A Biographical Register of the University of Oxford to A.D. 1500*. Published by Oxford University Press from 1957 to 1959, this work contains some 15,000 biographical entries. The present volume uses an identical structure for the biographical entries, and also provides a brief historical introduction for the period covered. There are two older compilations on the same subject, by Joseph Foster: *Alumni Oxonienses: The Members of the University of Oxford, 1500-1714* (4v. Oxford, Parker, 1891-1892); and its continuation, *Alumni Oxonienses, 1715-1886* (4v. 1888). Mr. Emden is also the author of *A Biographical Register of the University of Cambridge to 1500* (Cambridge University Press, 1963).

The present register is an essential biographical history for the period; it will be indispensable to all scholars interested in the history of this great university and the political influence of its alumni.—**Bohdan S. Wynar**

143.   Fletcher, Richard. **Who's Who in Roman Britain and Anglo-Saxon England**. Chicago, St. James Press, c.1989, 1990. 245p. illus. index. (Who's Who in British History, v.1). $45.00. LC 90-63659. ISBN 1-55862-131-8.

> Routh, C. R. N. **Who's Who in Tudor England**. Chicago, St. James Press, 1990. 476p. illus. index. (Who's Who in British History, v.4). $45.00. LC 90-63661. ISBN 1-55862-133-4.

> Hill, C. P. **Who's Who in Stuart Britain**. Chicago, St. James Press, c.1988, 1990. 466p. illus. index. (Who's Who in British History, v.5). $45.00. LC 90-63660. ISBN 1-55862-132-6.

These three works are the first volumes published in the revised Who's Who in British History series. The original five volumes, published in the 1960s, covered British history from 55 B.C. to A.D. 1837. All will be revised to reflect more recent scholarship and research. The new series has more detailed and broader coverage as well. For example, the original series had only one volume covering 55 B.C. to A.D. 1485; in the new series, three volumes will cover the same period. More prominence will also be given to Scottish, Irish, and Welsh individuals than in the earlier works.

This series has an unusual arrangement for a biographical source; the entries are not arranged in alphabetical order but chronologically by the dates of the persons discussed. Also, similar classes of people (e.g., clergy, explorers, scholars) are grouped together. An index at the end of each volume provides alphabetical access. Each book contains a short glossary of historical terminology for the lay reader and illustrations such as maps, genealogies, and portraits.

The entries vary in length according to the authors' evaluation of the importance of each individual in British history. For example, in *Who's Who in Roman Britain and Anglo-Saxon England*, Julius Caesar only receives two pages. (He only visited England briefly on two occasions.) However, St. Bede and King Alfred both have 11 pages devoted to them. The entries try to give a sense of the character of the individuals as well as an account of their historical importance. Many include interesting anecdotal material and titles of books for further reading. This series would be a useful addition to large reference collections, and it would also be of interest to browsers wishing to get a feel for British history. [R: Choice, June 91, pp. 1616, 1623; Choice, July/Aug 91, p. 1758; RBB, Aug 91, p. 2176]—**Christine E. King**

144.   Hicks, Michael A. **Who's Who in Late Medieval England (1272-1485)**. Chicago, St. James Press, 1991. 382p. illus. index. (Who's Who in British History, v.3). $45.00. LC 90-64267. ISBN 1-55862-135-0.

This work provides biographical sketches of prominent figures in English history, from Henry III's death in 1272 to the 1485 death of Richard III and the subsequent accession of the Tudors. After introductory statements, Hicks provides a list of illustrations, a chronological guide to prominent events during this period, genealogical tables of monarchical families, biographical entries, a selective bibliography, and a useful glossary of pertinent terminology. Individual portraits cover a broad societal swath. Monarchs such as Edward III, authors Geoffrey Chaucer and Thomas Malory, publisher William Caxton, historical chronicler Jean Froissart, the 1381 Peasant Revolt leader Wat Tyler, religious figures John Wyclif and Archbishop of Canterbury John Stratford, philosopher William Ockham, and prominent women such as Joan of Kent and Margery Kempe are all included. These portraits, incisive and judicious, strive to use scholarship of optimal currency.

Unfortunately, the book is weakened by its awkward organization. The biographical portraits appear to be arranged in loose chronological order instead of more logically by subject, alphabet, or tightly focused historical period. This, coupled with the absence of a biographical table of contents, requires readers to spend excessive time jumping to and from the index in order to find the location of individual biographical materials.

This work remains of sufficient utility for undergraduates. It would be enhanced with a more structured biographical arrangement and a substantive, concise, contextual historical analysis of the late Medieval epoch. [R: Choice, Dec 91, p. 574]—**Bert Chapman**

145.   Kanner, Barbara. **Women in English Social History 1800-1914: A Guide to Research**. Volume I. New York, Garland, 1990. 871p. index. (Garland Reference Library of Social Science). $100.00. Z7964.G7K36. 016. 3054'0942. LC 82-49189. ISBN 0-8240-9201-5.

This bibliography is part of a three-volume set, of which *Volume III: Autobiographical Writings* appeared in 1987. Although lacking a formal scope note, the preface suggests an effort to be comprehensive—but not definitive—for published primary and secondary materials, including contemporary dissertations. Random scanning of entries indicates that U.K. and U.S. publications are covered. Kanner defines her approach as "bibliomethodology" rather than "traditional bibliography," stressing the analytical and contextual style of presentation. The volume is thus an extended, and unwieldy, bibliographic essay.

An essay on feminist scholarship appears as the introduction, supported by a bibliography of some 300 entries. The contents of volume I are organized into 6 chapters covering opinion on "woman," marriage and family, sickness and health care, law, religion, and education. Entries are numbered consecutively within chapters, and about one-half are annotated, often with quotations. Monograph citations include author, title, date, and sometimes place of publication, but not publisher.

The 6,100 entries are in chronological order within chapters, but many entries include multiple citations. Entries may include several publications by the same author as well as relevant reviews and articles about the works and biographies. Articles appearing in a particular journal over several decades are included in a single block entry under the journal title and placed by the first date. Punctuation in these block entries is confusing. An article title is separated by a period from its annotation, while this annotation is separated by a semicolon from the next article title.

The index includes authors, subjects (both names and topics), and journal (but not book) titles. While its organization makes this volume difficult to use, it is nonetheless an impressive compilation of sources for women's history.—**Cheryl Kern-Simirenko**

146.   Kanner, Barbara. **Women in English Social History 1800-1914: A Guide to Research**. Volume III: Autobiographical Writings. New York, Garland, 1987. 215p. index. (Autobiographical Writings, Vol. 3; Garland Reference Library of Social Science, vol. 155). $30.00. LC 82-49189. ISBN 0-8240-9168-X.

This bibliography is the third volume of a *Women in English Social History* set. Volume III is reviewed here as an independent work. For a review of volume I, see entry 145.

The volume is divided into two chapters. The first 104 citations appear in chapter 1, with an introductory essay that discusses the general theory and methodology of using autobiographies, diaries, memoirs, and letters as sources for social history and women's studies. Included are works discussing working-class authors, personal diaries, and the application of social science methods to their analysis; the changing nature of autobiographical writings over time and culture; the differences between women's and men's autobiography; the absence of attention to women's autobiography; and the unique contributions of women's writings to the genre.

The second chapter cites approximately 670 autobiographical works written by English women during the nineteenth and early twentieth centuries. Entries are arranged alphabetically by author. Full citations are provided and, in most cases, a brief annotation tells something about the woman, often through quotes taken from the work itself. Dates of birth and death are provided to the extent known.

Some of the writers are famous; some are not. Common to all the women is the resistance they express to the social prescriptions of the time that dictated that women remain passive, innocent, weak, and dependent. [R: Choice, Nov 87, p. 456]—**Debbie Burnham-Kidwell**

147. **The Makers of English History**. Norman Stone, ed. New York, Macmillan, 1987. 288p. illus. (part col.). bibliog. index. $40.00. LC 86-12821. ISBN 0-02-931650-2.

This collection of 45 essays covers the lives and accomplishments of a wide variety of British historical figures from the seventh century A.D. to the present. The editor, Norman Stone, Professor of Modern History and a Fellow of Worcester College, Oxford, asked in the introduction what had made England great and who were the major individuals responsible for this greatness. The essays written by nine British historians offer one answer in terms of biography. Together these profiles attempt to present a composite portrait of the English.

The subjects cover many fields, though politics, the monarchy, and the military are very heavily represented. There are two painters, one musician, and only five women. Pondering those included (James I and Tennyson) and those excluded (Charles I and Wordsworth) is an inevitable part of examining this book. Each essay covers four to five pages, with the main events and circumstances of the subjects' lives reviewed in chronological fashion. There is also always a statement offering a comprehensive view of the importance of each individual. For example, Bede "invented the concept of English history" (p.11) and Turner was "Britain's greatest artist" (p.183). While some may wish to dissent from these judgments, these capsule evaluations can be useful in reference work when facts alone are not sufficient to readily place a person in historical context.

In addition to the 45 portraits, there are a guide to further reading for each subject, a brief chronology of British history, and an index. The book is written in an engaging style, with 25 full-color and 125 black-and-white illustrations.—**Henry E. York**

148. **Outlines of English History: Dates, Facts, Events, People**. rev. ed. George Carter, comp. London, Ward Lock; distr., North Pomfret, Vt., David & Charles, 1987. $9.95pa. ISBN 0-7063-6582-8pa.

This convenient handbook covers, in chronological order, key events in English history from the Roman invasion in 55 B.C. through 1986. A brief description of each event is included. The work also features genealogical tables for all of England's ruling dynasties, and some fifty pages of short biographical sketches. This is a revised, updated, and expanded version of a work which has been around since 1962, and the fact that it has gone through several previous revisions is suggestive in regard to its value. Students of English history, those who want a convenient, inexpensive reference work covering a broad range of events, and certainly public and academic libraries will find this book quite useful.—**James A. Casada**

149.   Palmer, Alan, and Veronica Palmer. **Who's Who in Shakespeare's England**. New York, St. Martin's Press, 1981. 280p. illus. $32.50. ISBN 0-312-87096-5.

This is a guide to some 700 persons who were important in England or to Shakespeare during the years 1590 to 1623. Entries are brief, with, in some cases, one to three bibliographical citations or a portrait of the subject. Women are given generous inclusion as subjects. There are maps of London and Stratford-on-Avon; an index of names by occupation and relation to Shakespeare: for family, legends, London and Stratford connections; and a brief glossary of terms.

The book reveals good planning for usefulness and ease in locating information. A sample check of biographies found them to be accurate, albeit somewhat telescoped, as is, of course, to be expected in this type of guide. *Who's Who in Shakespeare's England* should make an excellent introductory work of reference. [R: BL, 1 Sept 82, p. 69; Choice, Feb 82, p. 746]—**Dorothy E. Litt**

150. Treasure, Geoffrey. **Who's Who In Early Hanoverian Britain (1714-1789)**. Detroit, St. James Press, 1992. 450p. illus. index. (Who's Who in British History, v.6). $45.00. LC 90-64266. ISBN 1-55862-136-9.

Nearly 200 men and women who achieved leadership across a wide spectrum of society are covered in this biographical dictionary. The Early Hanoverian period for this volume begins with the accession of King George I and ends with the French Revolution. No claim is made for comprehensiveness. Some individuals were included because they were interesting and contributed to providing a "portrait of the age"—one of the goals of this series. In the same vein, the biographical essays are not in alphabetical order but arranged in a loose chronological fashion, with groups composed of subjects in similar fields. There is no guide to this arrangement. The index provides direct access for readers who prefer to locate a specific subject rather than read through the volume.

The biographical sketches vary in length from one paragraph to eight pages. In addition to kings, politicians, soldiers, and clergy, there are also authors, artists, musicians, scientists, and merchants. These are rounded off with such eminent Hanoverians as Lancelot Brown, Josiah Wedgewood, Edmund Burke, and several prominent criminals. This series attempts to put each life examined into perspective rather than merely reciting basic biographical facts.

This makes the biographies interesting to read, with their emphasis on character and the place of the subjects in the age. Judgments tend to be carefully balanced: Treasure provides positive elements for the three early Hanoverian kings as well as the negative elements commonly found in contemporary public opinion and history books. Another goal of this series, to provide the "latest findings of scholarship," is more difficult to judge, as the bibliographies appended to the end of the essays are limited to several standard works, very few with recent publication dates.—**Henry E. York**

151. Williamson, David. **Debrett's Kings and Queens of Britain**. Topsfield, Mass., Salem House/Merrimack Publishers' Circle, 1986. 240p. illus. (part col.). bibliog. index. $27.50. LC 86-60918. ISBN 0-88162-213-3.

This book contains three sections: introductory essays on kingship in ancient Britain, biographical sketches on each sovereign and consort from Egbert in the ninth century to the present queen, and an appendix with genealogical tables. The biographies vary in length from a paragraph to several pages. They are preceded by a table giving the dates and places of birth, accession, marriage, death and burial, plus a list of children. The genealogies, which trace all lines related to the present royal family, are especially useful for the tables delineating the rulers of the early Anglo-Saxon kingdoms, the heptarchy, and those showing the descent of the royal family from the ancient Irish, Scottish, and Welsh rulers.

The author states in the introduction that this book is not a biographical dictionary or a history. The aim was to illustrate the character of the royal individuals with anecdotes and personal details to reveal them "as ordinary human beings with the same feelings, passions, and failings as any other man or woman" (p.7). It is this emphasis on personality and personal events, rather than historical facts or political analysis, that distinguishes these short biographies from others readily available in such sources as the *Encyclopaedia Britannica* or the *Dictionary of National Biography*. For an exhaustive account of the British royal lineage, listing all kings and known descendants since Cerdic of Wessex of the sixth century, *Burke's Guide to the Royal Family* is the most complete source.

Anglophiles, especially those interested in the royal family, will find this new survey of the monarchs of England fascinating. It is lavishly illustrated and written in popular style. The tables listing the "vital statistics" may be the most valuable aspect of this book for reference use as they conveniently assemble much biographical data which might otherwise be illusive, especially in regard to early or minor royal figures.—**Henry E. York**

HISTORIANS

152.   **The Blackwell Dictionary of Historians**. John Cannon and others, eds. New York, Basil Blackwell; distr., New York, Harper & Row, 1988. 480p. index. $75.00. Dl4.B58. 907'.202'2. LC 88-19361. ISBN 0-631-14708-X.

This is a British publication presenting an unabashedly English point of view of those who have written about the human experience. One would expect a smattering of non-English contributors among its 200-plus authors, yet they are virtually absent, as are female contributors. The 450 historians considered are presented alphabetically and are joined by essays on 25 nations and 40 historiographical subjects. As a group, the entries are written in remarkably stuffy prose.

While this volume may be lauded for its attempt at comprehensiveness, the convenience that it might afford is more than offset by the turgid presentations and national singularity of authorship. The major value of this dictionary may be that it represents current yet incomplete English views of how non-English historians have plied their craft. At its price, it should do more than that. Most general and academic libraries contain journals with historiographical essays markedly superior to this collection. Likewise, various national encyclopedias contain better entries. The general library patron will derive much more benefit from these workhorses: E. H. Carr, *What Is History* (Random House, 1967) and Robert Shafer, A *Guide to Historical Method* (Dorsey, 1980).—**Eric H. Christianson**

153.   **Great Historians from Antiquity to 1800: An International Dictionary**. Lucian Boia, and others, eds. Westport, Conn., Greenwood Press, 1989. 417p. index. $65.00. D14.G74. 907'.2022. LC 88-25089. ISBN 0-313-24517-7.

Historians and students of history have a strong curiosity about the people who wrote classic works of history. This is an admirable attitude, since a history book can often be fully understood only when something is known about the beliefs and prejudices of the author. Boia, a Romanian scholar, edited this new biographical dictionary of historians that helps to satisfy this curiosity. It provides brief descriptive and analytical essays of 500 to 2,000 words for some 600 historians worldwide who wrote before 1800.

Each essay includes a brief bibliography for further reading and was written and signed by an expert on the subject. The essays are organized into 37 geographical categories, some of which contain large numbers of historians: Byzantium (18), China (20), England (23), France (22), and Arabia and Persia (24). Others, such as Austria, Bulgaria, Iceland, and Serbia, only list one or two. There are separate indexes for historians and subjects. A second volume will be published for historians of the nineteenth and twentieth centuries.

This volume is an excellent reference for well-known historians, such as Thucydides and Edward Gibbon, and historians who are relatively unfamiliar in the English-speaking world. The criteria for selecting the historians was their "absolute" contribution to general historical writing and their place in the historiography of their own culture. Many readers will discover that some favorite historian was left out, but the work still remains highly useful and comprehensive. Particularly impressive is the coverage of Eastern European, Islamic, and East Asian historians. Unfortunately, India and North America were completely neglected. Early American historians William Bradford and Cotton Mather, and medieval and early modern Indian historians Kalhana and Ziauddin Barani, deserve inclusion.

Compared with *The Blackwell Dictionary of Historians* (see ARBA 90, entry 530), there is some overlap, but Boia's volume contains far more unique entries. It is well worth adding to the collection of any library where history is studied. [R: WLB, May 90, p. 128]—**Ronald H. Fritze**

154.   **Great Historians of the Modern Age: An International Dictionary**. Lucian Boia and others, eds. Westport, Conn., Greenwood Press, 1991. 841p. index. $95.00. D14.G75. 907'.2022. LC 89-26009. ISBN 0-313-27328-6.

A multinational cast of over 200 scholars has contributed to this dictionary edited by Boia, a lecturer at the University of Bucharest in Romania. Sponsored by the International Committee on the Historical Sciences, it is the second volume in a two-volume series on historians from antiquity to the present. It includes an introductory essay on historiography in the modern period and about 700 entries (400 to 600 words each) on the careers and major works of notable nineteenth- and twentieth-century historians. The entries are organized in 38 geographical or national areas and then alphabetized by name within each regional section. This arrangement enables the reader to use the volume as a reference for comparative national historiography as well as a handy guide on prominent modern historians.

Although the "great historians" included in the project have been selected by a team of regional consultants, the volume has definite European and male biases. Roughly 63 percent of the work covers historians from Europe or Russia, 13 percent from Asia, 10 percent from North America, 8 percent from South America, 3 percent from Africa, and 2 percent from Australia and New Zealand. Also, some readers will question the national balance of the volume. Why, for instance, do Italian historians receive 66 pages (about the same weight given to United States historians) while English historians receive only 31 pages? Boia's policy of excluding living historians and those who have died since 1987 also mars this book's usefulness as a comprehensive reference tool of modern historians. In fact, only 3 percent of those listed were born in this century. A dictionary designed to cover historians of the modern age, but lacking entries for such persons as Barbara Tuchman, C. V. Wedgewood, G. R. Elton, and Manning Clark, is obsolete even before it is published.

Despite these criticisms, the volume contains much fascinating and hard-to-find information about an international sample of distinguished historians. Recommended for college and university libraries. [R: Choice, Nov 91, p. 416; WLB, Dec 91, p. 123]—**Terry D. Bilhartz**

JAPAN

155.   Hata, Ikuhiko, and Yasuho Izawa. **Japanese Naval Aces and Fighter Units in World War II**. Annapolis, Md., Naval Institute Press, 1989. 442p. illus. index. $46.95. D767.23.H36413. 940.54'1352. LC 89-33201. ISBN 0-87021-315-6.

Co-authored by a well-known Japanese military historian and a researcher, this definitive work on Japan's naval fighter pilots, units, aircraft, and battles in World War II is a translation of the revised and enlarged 1975 edition in Japanese. Divided into three parts, the book opens with rare photographs and brief descriptions of the principal Japanese naval aircraft. This part is followed by concise histories of the air units in the Imperial Navy and important battles from the early 1930s to 1945. The third part captures Japan's leading naval aces (defined as any pilot destroying 11 or more aircraft) in photographs and individual biographical sketches. Besides name and unit indexes, the book includes a section on Japanese naval terminology and abbreviations. There are several appendixes containing tables of names and records of the aces, dates of those killed in action, graduating classes of naval fighter pilots, and dates of major air battles.

This incomparable collection of information on the naval portion of the air war over China and the Pacific is based on Japanese official reports and private interviews and documents. In presenting the Japanese view, this data is an essential counterpoint to the more accessible Allied data and interpretations previously available.—**Hwa-Wei Lee**

JEWISH HISTORY

156.   Comay, Joan. **Who's Who in Jewish History after the Period of the Old Testament**. New York, McKay, 1974. 448p. illus. (part col.). index. o.p. LC 73-93915. ISBN 0-679-50455-9.

Karpman's *Who's Who in World Jewry: A Biographical Dictionary of Outstanding Jews* (Pitman, 1972. 999p.) includes some 10,000 biographies written in a standard Who's Who format. The present work, actually a sequel to Comay's *Who's Who in the Old Testament,* is quite different in format as well as in execution. As a general rule, persons alive at the time of writing have been omitted, except for some Israeli leaders and persons who have gained international reputations in scholarship, the arts, or politics. Entries vary in length from fifty words to more than a page, depending on the relative importance of the subject. One of the longest entries is for Dr. Theodor Herzl, founder of the modern Zionist movement.

A questionable editorial policy is the inclusion of non-Jewish leaders—Hitler is listed, as is Winston Churchill, who "early in his political career . . . took a sympathetic interest in Jewish matters" (p.114). One finds here also entries for King Hussein, Boris Pasternak (whose mother, Rosa Kaufmann, was of Jewish origin), and Joseph Pulitzer, whose father was a Jew. Marcel Proust, a Catholic, was "clearly influenced by his half-Jewish background" (p.326). Instead of concentrating on such entries, this dictionary might better serve its purpose by including entries for such persons as Kantor, founder of the first Hebrew daily newspaper, and Kaplansky, the Zionist labor leader, to suggest only two examples.

The reviewer thinks that this dictionary is trying to do too much. Most scholars will prefer to consult the biographical material in the prestigious *Encyclopaedia Judaica*; nevertheless, this compilation can be a handy, ready-reference tool for smaller institutions, if it is used with caution.—**Bohdan S. Wynar**

RUSSIA

157.   **The Blackwell Encyclopedia of the Russian Revolution**. Harold Shukman, ed. New York, Basil Blackwell, 1988. 418p. illus. index. $65.00. LC 88-10360. ISBN 0-631-15238-5.

The purpose of this encyclopedic work is to describe and analyze the revolutionary events in the Russian empire in order to show how they affected the political, social, economic, and ethnic history of the old empire. Over fifty contributors, primarily from England, contributed a variety of unsigned articles. Most longer articles, such as "The Ukrainian Revolution and the Civil War," contain brief bibliographies, but unfortunately the authors are occasionally unfamiliar with a specific language (see nine citations under "Further Reading," p. 225; one in Ukrainian, with a number of errors). Beginning on page 297, brief biographies of prominent personalities are provided, including one paragraph on Petliura, a prominent Ukrainian leader, and two pages on Plekhanov, a well-known leader of Russian communism.

The reviewer is not familiar with Harold Shukman, the editor of this volume, and a brief introduction written by him unfortunately tells us very little about the scope of this work, the authority, or the sources used. For example, there are many encyclopedic works covering the Civil War and the October Revolution written in several languages in the Soviet Union, plus encyclopedias and dictionaries published in other Eastern European countries, such as Poland and Czechoslovakia. None of these works is mentioned here, nor is there any mention of the rather impressive American output on all aspects of the Civil War and the Revolution.

All in all, this is a handy volume for the uninitiated, but will be of marginal assistance to scholars and advanced students of Soviet affairs. [R: RBB, 1 Nov 88, p. 460]—**Bohdan S. Wynar**

UNITED STATES

General Works

158.   **The Abridged Compendium of American Genealogy: First Families of America. A Genealogical Encyclopedia of the United States**. Frederick A. Virkus, ed. Baltimore, Md., Genealogical Publishing, c.1970, 1987. 7v. index. $325.00/set. LC 68-27449. ISBN 0-8063-1171-1.

This monumental work began in 1916, to provide background information to "assist persons in their quest for war-related employment." Material was submitted by individuals, and volume 1 contained 5,000 records and 10,000 lineages. The first volume did not appear until 1925, with the second volume published in 1926. Volume 7 appeared in 1942, and the editor once more mentioned the need for evidence for national service. While this series may be classed in the "mug book" category, it is fair to mention that the material submitted was carefully edited, verification was attempted, and much material was discarded. Most of the subjects were born in the latter half of the nineteenth century, and could be expected to have firsthand knowledge at least of their grandparents.

Entries appear in paragraph style, with numerals indicating the degree of descent from a particular ancestor. Biographies contain thumbnail sketches of the submitters, as well as varying data on both maternal and paternal ancestors. Of necessity, the entries are heavily abbreviated, and an extensive list of abbreviations appears in each volume. An every-name index provides easy access to all information.

While this series boasts a subtitle of "First Families of America," it should be pointed out that Virkus explained that "first" meant "earliest." Consequently, many lineages appear for common folks, as well as for the more prominent. The entries are very valuable as clues to pursue for further verification. The work is recommended as an important addition to any genealogical collection.—**Carol Willsey Bell**

159.   Benson, Michael. **Who's Who in the JFK Assassination: An A-to-Z Encyclopedia**. New York, Citadel Press/Carol Publishing Group, 1993. 511p. $18.95pa. E842.9.B46. 364.1'524'0973. LC 93-27949. ISBN 0-8065-1444-2.

This is basically a handbook for John F. Kennedy assassination conspiracy buffs, but its coverage is so broad, and the biographies so detailed in regard to the topic, that anyone with an interest in Kennedy will find it to be a valuable resource. Benson provides an impressive collection of data, conspiracy theories, and biographical information relating to the assassination and to more than 1,400 suspects, victims, witnesses, law enforcement officials, investigators, and others who were involved in any way. For example, entries are included for such persons as CBS newsman Dan Rather, presidential aide H. R. Haldeman, Cuban dictator Fidel Castro, and columnist Dorothy Kilgallen. Entries range from a sentence to 20 pages, depending on the significance of the individual to the event.

There is no index. However, the arrangement lends itself to easy use. An introduction explains how to use the book and includes a five-page essay that details the events surrounding the assassination and discusses some of the conspiracy theories that developed from it. The biographies are alphabetically arranged. Each provides quick identification of the individual (e.g., Ruby witness, suspicious death), how that person ties into the assassination, *see also* references leading to related people, and a list of sources.

The price is very reasonable, and the book is highly recommended for all libraries and individuals with an interest in the subject. The paper cover will have to be reinforced to withstand the heavy use the book will receive.—**Donald E. Collins**

160.   Downs, Robert B., John T. Flanagan, and Harold W. Scott. **Memorable Americans 1750-1950**. Littleton, Colo., Libraries Unlimited, 1983. index. $23.50. LC 82-22871. ISBN 0-87287-360-9.

This book focuses on 150 men and women whose achievements and actions made a permanent impression on the nation's culture and history. Literature, science, and invention, business and industry, social reform, the arts, and politics are but a few of the fields represented by the biographees in this work, who include Ernest Hemingway, Cyrus McCormick, Margaret Sanger, Frederic Remington, and Horace Greeley. Names nominated for inclusion by specialists in various fields were carefully screened by the authors to determine those persons whose impact was permanent and whose contributions indicated something of the richness and variety of U.S. history and culture. The authors have excluded individuals who died after 1950, whose great work was accomplished prior to coming to the United States, or whose work had little impact on their successors. The sketches are arranged alphabetically and include basic dates related to the person, the individual's major writings, and selected references. Lists of the individuals, arranged both by birth date and field of endeavor, are offered in the appendix. This one-volume source of biographical information on selected notable Americans can be used for ready reference and by U.S. history teachers to supplement the curriculum. It can also be enjoyed by anyone interested in obtaining an overview of U.S. history through the accomplishments of some of the nation's most prominent personalities. [R: WLB, June 83, p. 883]—**Ann Hartman**

161.   **Great Lives from History: American Series**. Frank N. Magill, ed. Englewood Cliffs, N.J., Salem Press, 1987. 5v. index. $325.00/set. LC 86-31561. ISBN 0-89356-529-6.

This is the first set of a series which will soon extend to British history, and ultimately the history of the rest of the world. The *American Series* covers 456 individuals (living and dead) who have influenced American society and culture from the discovery of the New World to the present day. Coverage is spread over five volumes, extending to 2,500 pages. Sketches range from 2,000 to 3,000 words in length, and follow a standard outline: (1) birth and death dates and locations, followed by one to seven words targeting area(s) of achievement, then one or two sentences summarizing the subjects' contributions; (2) the text of the sketch, which is further subdivided into two sections—"Early Life" (generally covering parents and grandparents, formal education and relevant early work experiences) and "Life's Work"; (3) a two- to three-paragraph summary analysis relating subjects' contributions to a broader cultural context; and (4) an annotated six- to eight-item bibliography of major works on the subject.

Two indexes conclude the fifth volume—a biographical index, which alphabetically lists the subjects covered, and an "areas of achievement" index, which mimes a subject index but is constrained by the controlled vocabulary editors apply to the first section of each entry. All index entries refer users back to volume and page numbers. Lack of a general index is disappointing and will limit usefulness of the work.

To the conventional criteria for inclusion in any biographical reference work as selective as this must be, the editors have added what they consider one criterion for inclusion which distinguishes *Great Lives* from others: "Will this individual be judged historically to have gone beyond his or her own immediate field of endeavor to affect the everyday lives of most, if not all, Americans?" (p.vi). By specifically addressing this question, the editors feel justified to include more athletes and artists, entertainers and scientists, explorers and astronauts, conservationists and inventors, than their competitors. But questions remain. Why Billy Sunday, but not Billy Graham or Oral Roberts? Earl Warren but not Warren Burger? Vernon L. Parrington but not Richard Hofstadter? Sandra Day O'Connor but not Betty Friedan? Elvis Presley but not Frank Sinatra? All the presidents are here, but among the missing notables are Lee Harvey Oswald, Bob Woodward, and Carl Bernstein, each of whom helped force tremendous change on American society in a unique way.

The army of contributors is impressive if not distinguished, and represents a generous sampling of scholars from colleges and universities across the country. Many are listed as "independent scholars." Format is adequate, margins slightly crowded, paper a bit underweight. Unfortunately, the series includes no photographs or portraits, certainly a surprise given the price of the set. Generally, *Great Lives* is written for the layperson, and its easy organization should make it a handy reference work, if librarians determine it fits a gap between more scholarly standard works such as *Dictionary of American Biography* (*DAB*) and the more entertaining standard series such as *Current Biography* (*CB*). Obviously, bibliographies in *Great Lives* are more up-to-date than the *DAB,* more scholarly than *CB*; naturally, its entries are less substantive than *DAB,* but more reliable than *CB.* As always for librarians, it comes down to spending limited resources prudently: Can they afford $325.00 for five volumes on 456 individuals undoubtedly covered variously elsewhere in their collections? [R: LJ, 1 June 87, p. 103; RBB, 15 Oct 87, p. 378; WLB, Sept 87, pp. 92-93]—**Wayne A. Wiegand**

162. **Great Lives from History: American Women Series**. Frank N. Magill, ed. Pasadena, Calif., Salem Press, 1995. 5v. index. $365.00/set. ISBN 0-89356-892-9.

One of the myriad Magill compendiums, this set profiles 409 women who had a major impact on North American society and culture. White Anglo-Saxon women from the United States overwhelmingly predominate, but readers will also find entries for 45 African Americans, 11 Asian Americans, 8 Hispanic Americans, 8 Native Americans, and 7 Canadians. As would be expected in a Magill series, the women draw from diverse walks of life, including education; business; government, diplomacy, and politics; arts, architecture, literature, music, theater, and entertainment; medicine; religion; and social reform. Coverage is both interesting and eclectic; although one never knows whether a particular woman being sought after is likely to appear within this set's pages, the exploration is always enlightening. For example, those who have always wondered just how much Ariel contributed to the Durants' *The Story of Civilization*—and at what cost to her own professional goals—will find just this information sensitively presented in volume 2.

A typical 2,000-word entry begins with birth and death dates, areas of achievement, and a short statement on the individual's primary contribution. Three narrative overviews follow: "early life" (two to three paragraphs), "life's work" (about two pages), and "summary" (two to three paragraphs). A bibliography of 5 to 10 works concludes each profile. Concluding materials include a biographical index, an index by areas of achievement, and a timeline (starting with Anne Hutchins on, b. 1591, and ending with Kristi Yamaguchi, b. 1971). Although serious researchers will need to look elsewhere for scholarly materials, this Magill series provides solid, basic information that will meet the needs of most school and public libraries.—**G. Kim Dority**

163. Harmon, Justin, and others. **American Cultural Leaders from Colonial Times to the Present**. Santa Barbara, Calif., ABC-Clio, 1993. 550p. index. (Biographies of American Leaders). $65.00. NX503.A49. 700' .92'273. LC 93-36284. ISBN 0-87436-673-9.

This third volume in a series that presents brief biographical information about leaders of the United States includes 360 individuals—men and women, living and dead, foreign and native-born—who have made significant contributions to American culture. Specific fields encompassed are art, dance, film, literature, music, and theater. Omitted are television, radio, other forms of entertainment, journalism, and criticism.

Arranged in alphabetical order, the entries contain a brief identification of the individual and the area of significant achievement or contribution. This is followed by short biographical profiles (750-1,500 words) that highlight specific achievements. Cross-references are given as appropriate. Concluding each entry is a one- to four-item bibliography for further reading. A list of entries, a preface, and a user guide to entry format prove useful not only to clarify the nature of the information supplied but also to elucidate why certain key contributors to American culture have been omitted from the work.

Given the brevity of information, this volume likely will prove most useful to secondary school students and college freshmen and sophomores. Public libraries with limited budgets might also avail themselves of it, especially for those whose collections are weak in biography. The work will function well in the general reference setting, complemented as necessary by more advanced and specialized biographical tools.—**Edmund F. SantaVicca**

164. Moss, Joyce, and George Wilson. **Profiles in American History: Significant Events and the People Who Shaped Them**. Detroit, U*X*L/Gale, 1994. 8v. $225.00/set. ISBN 0-8103-9207-0.

Profiles in American History is a set of literary short biographies arranged chronologically in eight volumes. Individual volumes cover colonization, the Constitutional period, Indian displacement, westward expansion, Reconstruction, the early twentieth century, the Great Depression to the New Deal, and the late twentieth century. The set presents history from the point of view that people make a difference and determine what happens when crises catapult them into the public eye. Each chapter is the biography of an important person and a significant event that changed the course of history. For example, in volume 7, we learn of Franklin Delano Roosevelt, John Steinbeck, Dorothea Lang, Minoru Yasui, J. Robert Oppenheimer, Douglas MacArthur, Joseph McCarthy, Julius and Ethel Rosenberg, Rosa Parks, Thurgood Marshall, and others. An attempt has been made to include a few multicultural notables, but for the most part the traditional historical point of view is taken.

The essays, written with upper elementary/junior high school readers in mind, are presented in a story-like literary form, giving life to the characters, times, and events. Each sketch is complemented with photographs, drawings, and interesting sidebars. Individual essays cover several points of view. For example, the issue of the Spaniards versus the native peoples is covered from each culture's point of view, with a major discussion of Antonio de Montesinos and Las Casas's attempts to right wrongs against the Indians. It is clear that the Spanish felt they were contributing to the civilization of indigenous peoples, but the tragic result is clearly represented.

The set meets the needs and desires of students: short sketches, interesting writing, factual information with a late-twentieth-century touch of political correctness, and sources for further information. However, the set's format poses problems. Having numerous people in a single volume limits its usefulness because teachers cover a specific period in their units, and many students will need access to the same volume at the same time. If the set were on CD-ROM or in pamphlet form, its use would be increased. As it is, this source may be a shelf-sitter unless librarians duplicate volumes. It is hoped that the treasures here, for which the authors should be congratulated, will be discovered in libraries and classrooms, including the home classroom. [R: BR, Nov/Dec 94, p. 55; RBB, 1 Apr 94, p. 1477; VOYA, Oct 94, p. 245]—**David V. Loertscher**

165.   **Notable Americans: What They Did, from 1620 to the Present: Chronological and Organizational Listings of Leaders**. . . . 4th ed. Linda S. Hubbard, ed. Detroit, Gale, 1988. 733p. index. $150.00. LC 87-32671. ISBN 0-8103-2534-9.

The *Conspectus of American Biography,* first issued in 1906, has undergone numerous revisions and title changes over the years. This new 4th edition bears both a new name and a new look, updating the 1973 edition, *Notable Names in American History.* Coverage now extends from 1620 through 1986. As with previous editions, this register is divided into nineteen broad subject sections providing chronological listings of over 42,000 notable persons and organizations in such areas as government, education, religion, business, and labor. A personal-name index is provided for easy access. New with this edition is an organizational index allowing for access to personal names by institutional or other type of affiliation.

Some sections simply have been updated, while others, such as the "Corporate Executive's Action," have undergone substantial redesign in criteria for inclusion and scope of coverage. So many name changes have occurred in the organization listings that notes indicating previous institution/group names often are included.

As with previous editions, this register is best used in conjunction with biographical directories such as the *National Cyclopaedia of American Biography* (White, 1892-) and comparable historical biographical listings. Topical access continues to be the greatest value of this research tool, but without access to the detailed biographical information available in the *Cyclopaedia* and related works, this register on its own can provide only brief data on Americans of note. [R: BR, May/June 88, pp. 47-48; RBB, 15 May 88, pp.1585-86]—**Elizabeth Patterson**

166.   **Research Guide to American Historical Biography**. Robert Muccigrosso, ed. Washington, D.C., Beacham Publishing, 1988. 3v. illus. index. $189.00/set. CT214.R47. 920'.073. LC 88-19316. ISBN 0-933833-09-1.

This work provides a bio-bibliographic guide to the lives of 278 prominent Americans. The emphasis is on men and women "most often studied in the areas of politics and statecraft, business and labor, education, journalism, religion and the military." In general, literary figures have been omitted. (Beacham Publishing's earlier *Research Guide to Biography and Criticism* [see ARBA 87, entry 1067] covers literary figures.)

Geared to undergraduates and advanced high school students, the *Research Guide* breaks down each entry into several sections. A chronology lists the major events of the subject's life and is followed by activities of historical significance that attempt to place the person's accomplishments in context. The next section is an overview of biographical sources that notes the development of and the changes in the biographical treatment of the subject over the years. It is followed by an evaluation of principal biographical sources that lists and evaluates the major secondary sources covering the subject and then rates each source for its appropriate audience. This same treatment is afforded primary sources in the next section. Other sections include fiction and adaptations; museums, historical landmarks, and societies; and other sources.

While it is not an in-depth scholarly treatment, the *Research Guide* is a fine starting point. It gives solid factual information about each subject and useful evaluations of basic biographical sources. In addition, the section on fiction and adaptations, which describes "novels, films, plays and other creative interpretations," provides lists of nontypical sources that show how the subject has been popularly portrayed. The writing is usually clear and precise, and the text is organized logically and well presented. One concern, however, is the quality of the binding. The review copy of volume 3 was already beginning to separate from its covers. [R: Choice, June 89, p. 1666; LJ, 15 Mar 89, p. 68; WLB, Apr 89, p. 127]—**Tom Gilson**

167.   **Roots of the Republic**. Danbury, Conn., Grolier, 1996. 6v. illus. maps. index. $159.00/set. ISBN 0-7172-7608-2.

This set pulls together, in an attractive, hardbound format, basic information about the founding of and the "movers and shakers" in the U.S. government. The major portion of the material consists of biographical sketches 1.5 to 3 pages in length, with black-and-white photographs or pen-and-ink drawings of most persons profiled. This information is usually available only in scattered sources.

Unfortunately, the set lacks a clear sense of audience. The first two volumes especially need to be read with a book on U.S. history at hand. Plenty of adjectives describe the biographees, but there is often a paucity of hard information. Too many references will be puzzling to young readers. Few are likely to know the meaning of "born to the purple" or "straight-laced" in a day when class and behavior are defined so differently from what they were 200 years ago. Occasionally, someone is described in terms of political outlook without defining phrases; for example, ". . . it was equally difficult to decide whether he was a Federalist or a Democrat." The remainder of the set is stronger, with personalities and achievements of the chief justices of the United States more clearly defined. The sketch of Bill Clinton sounds partisan. All books have useful essays, such as "The Accomplishments of the First Congress" and "The Power of Judicial Review." The set needs a firmer editorial hand.

These volumes could serve as supplementary material for U.S. history classes. The set possesses thorough indexes and scholarly bibliographies. [R: BL, 15 Oct 96, p. 452]—**Edna M. Boardman**

Civil War and Reconstruction

168. **Biographical Dictionary of the Union: Northern Leaders of the Civil War.** John T. Hubbell and James W. Geary, eds. Westport, Conn., Greenwood Press, 1995. 683p. index. $99.50. ISBN 0-313-20920-0.

Researching individual leaders of the U.S. Civil War has never been easy due to the large variety of possible sources. This biographical dictionary goes a long way toward solving this problem. *Biographical Dictionary of the Union* provides information on more than 800 individuals who are considered leaders in the Union army, as well as civilians. The editors point out, "The main criterion used in determining the final choice of biographical entries centered on those men and women who influenced the course of public policy, opinion, and events. The list is comprehensive for political leaders (presidents, congressmen, senators, governors, cabinet officers, Supreme Court justices) and selective for others (e.g., foreign service officials, editors, photographers, abolitionists)" (introduction).

Military leaders were selected based on their contribution to the Union cause and, for the most part, include division commanders and other officers who became prominent. The entries have been written by numerous Civil War historians, scholars, and enthusiasts. Each entry contains the individual's name, employment (e.g., officer, senator, congressman), birth and death dates, education, positions held, and a brief biography based on the person's activities during and after the Civil War. In most cases, the source of the information is also included. Most references are to standard works such as the *Dictionary of American Biography* or *Generals in Blue* by Ezra Warner. In a few instances, the references are to primary sources that may be out-of-print. There are entries to some individuals "whose obscurity is breathtaking" (introduction), but the documentation available is always provided.

Even though it is a reference work, this book is a delight to peruse. The entries are uneven and vary in their approach due to the use of dozens of authors, but this adds to the work's charm. The entries are loaded with fascinating information and serve to point out how the nation was consumed by the war. Appendixes furnish an extensive bibliography, an index, and a list of contributors. This book is especially recommended for all larger academic and public libraries with special Civil War collections. It will also be a valuable resource for historians and Civil War enthusiasts.—**Robert L. Wick**

169. Foner, Eric. **Freedom's Lawmakers: A Directory of Black Office Holders during Reconstruction.** New York, published in cooperation with the Schomburg Center for Research in Black Culture by Oxford University Press, 1993. 290p. illus. $75.00. E185.96.F64. 920'009296073. LC 92-31777. ISBN 0-19-507406-8.

Foner, a leading historian, has done much to revive the historical memory of the tribulations and positive accomplishments of black Americans during Reconstruction. With *Freedom's Lawmakers*, he has supplied a biographical dictionary of 1,465 black officials from the Reconstruction era of 1863-1877. In it he has included all individuals who served as major state officials, delegates to constitutional conventions, and legislators, even if only a name and the fact that they held such an office is known. For local officials, Foner lists only those that have some additional biographical information, a decision that eliminated several hundred people for whom only their name and the fact that they held an office has survived.

Individual entries are arranged alphabetically by surname. Each begins with a head note that supplies, when known, the state where the person held office; the person's occupation; and whether the person was born in freedom or slavery, was pp. or mulatto, or was literate. A biographical sketch then follows, and it concludes with a list of sources used in compiling the entry. Foner begins the directory with a detailed introduction that summarizes the collective conclusions that can be drawn about these officeholders. For example, 933 of them were literate while only 195 were known to be illiterate. This information dispels the prevalent historical myth that black officials during Reconstruction were largely ignorant or illiterate. Several separate indexes for states, occupations, offices, birth status, and topics conclude the work.

There is some minor and necessary overlap with the coverage of existing reference works, particularly the *Dictionary of American Negro Biography* (see ARBA 84, entry 381). Still, Foner has produced a unique and scholarly work that belongs in any library interested in the Civil War and Reconstruction or African American history. [R: Choice, Sept 93, pp. 80-82]—**Ronald H. Fritze**

170.   Sifakis, Stewart. **Who Was Who in the Civil War**. New York, Facts on File, 1988. 766p. illus. bibliog. index. $45.00. LC 84-1596. ISBN 0-8160-1055-2.

This comprehensive, illustrated biographical dictionary contains nearly 2,500 entries of principal Union and Confederate military participants in the Civil War. All officers—583 Union and 425 Confederate—of the rank of general are included, plus lower rank officers who led forces larger than a regiment for a lengthy period in a major action or in distinguished service. Also treated are federal and state officials, congressional members, political activists, journalists, artists-correspondents, medical personnel, diplomats, religious commissioners, relevant foreign leaders and observers, and engineers. The data in each entry concentrate on the respective subject's actions during the period of the war and generally omit pre- and postwar activities unless pertinent to the conflict. The entries are concise, supplying such information as birth/death dates, ranks and positions, major contributions, and historical perspective. One valuable feature is the inclusion for each entry of further sources of information when available. Approximately 250 primary source illustrations and photographs are furnished. There are two appendices: a monthly chronology of the major events of the war and a listing of officers who received the thanks of the U.S. Congress. A selected bibliography includes annotations of valuable books and periodicals. There is an index of people and places as well as headings of interest relative to the war for the respective entries (e.g., abolitionists and artillerists). This is an interesting source containing much accessible, comprehensive data. It provides adequate, condensed information with suggestions for more in-depth research if desired. [R: LJ, July 88, pp. 72-73; RBB, 1 Oct 88, p. 245; WLB, Dec 88, pp. 115-16]—**Jackson Kesler**

Historians

171.   **American Historians, 1607-1865**. Wilson, Clyde N., ed. Detroit, Gale, 1984. 382p. illus. index. (Dictionary of Literary Biography, Vol. 30). $82.00. LC 84-10262. ISBN 0-8103-1708-7.

A handsome addition to the Dictionary of Literary Biography, volume 30 contains biographical and critical essays on forty-six early American historians. The signed articles differ somewhat in format, but all give basic biographical information, criticism, and/or commentary on the writer's works, a selected bibliography of the above, and a list of references for further research. The writing style is sometimes heavy, but easily accessible to the student for whom the book is intended; illustrations are appropriate and attractive. Volume 30 complements previous ones in the series focusing on colonial and early American and antebellum literature. Several people included here are also mentioned in those previous volumes, but the current articles are fresh and the concentration is on their historical writings rather than the popular or other work they may have done. This is an excellent reference book, valuable to all early-American history and literature collections.—**Deborah Hammer**

172.   **American Historians, 1866-1912**. Clyde N. Wilson, ed. Detroit, Gale, 1986. 427p. illus. bibliog. index. (Dictionary of Literary Biography, vol. 47). $88.00. LC 85-29245. ISBN 0-8103-1725-7.

American Historians, 1866-1912 completes the Dictionary of Literary Biography's (DLB) coverage of American historians by presenting full-length critical essays on forty-eight important

American writers of history whose first works were published between the end of the Civil War and 1912. Previous DLB volumes which treat American historians are *Twentieth-Century American Historians* (Gale, 1983) and *American Historians, 1607-1865* (Gale, 1984).

The forty-eight critical essays by forty contributors encompass historians of U.S. history and other twentieth-century historians who specialized in fields outside of U.S. history. Five master essays delineate the careers and contributions of James Henry Breasted, Charles Homer Haskins, James Harvey Robinson, Henry Adams, and John Bach McMaster. Among the other historians selected for inclusion are W. E. B. DuBois, John Fiske, Gustavus Myers, Theodore Roosevelt, Reuben Gold Thwaites, Andrew Dickson White, and Woodrow Wilson. Additional essays in the appendix examine the significant Civil War publications *The Official Records of the Rebellion* and *Battles and Leaders of the Civil War*. Individual essays combine biography and critical scholarship to discuss each subject's life and work within a chronological framework. Accompanying the essays are extensive bibliographies, illustrations, and documentary reproductions. The quality of writing and interpretive orientation are uniformly high.

The late nineteenth century was a dynamic period of professionalization for the historian in America. A new caste of professional scholars emerged dedicated to research methods, objective history, and exhaustive use of primary sources. This transitional epoch is well served by the editor and contributors. Recommended for the specialist and the amateur alike.—**Arthur P. Young**

173. **Historians of the American Frontier: A Bio-Bibliographical Sourcebook**. John Wunder, ed. Westport, Conn., Greenwood Press, 1988. 814p. index. $75.00. LC 88-5637. ISBN 0-313-24899-0.

The word *sourcebook* in the subtitle of this work is well deserved. Presented here are 57 famous and not-quite-so-famous historians of the West (though only five of them are women), and both the biographical sketches and the bibliographical listings are excellent. Arrangement is alphabetical by name, and the time span is from the 1850s (with Bancroft's Pacific Handbook of 1859 as a very early contribution) to the present; several historians listed are still living or, as is the case of Ray Billington, only recently deceased. Frederick Jackson Turner and Frederic Logan Paxson are included, but Francis Parkman and Reuben Gold Thwaites are not, because, so the editor tells us, the writers assigned to these two were unable to complete their work in time.

Each essay is by a different contributor, but each includes a biography of one or two pages in length; a discussion of themes in the historian's writings; a longer discussion of his importance in the field of history; a bibliography consisting of books, articles, or in some cases only selected articles and reviews by the historian; and finally, in some cases, studies of the historian. These listings, except when noted as "selected," appear to be reasonably complete and are therefore valuable bibliographies.

Because each essay is by a different author, there is considerable variation in style. Tighter editorial control might have eliminated a few lapses in syntax, especially noticeable in the essay on Bernard Augustine DeVoto, where the reader finds *lay* for *lie*, *who* for *whom*, and an omitted comma, which makes the sentence hard to understand at first reading. Also, birth and death dates might have been added since many of the historians are not exactly household names, even among scholars. [R: Choice, May 89, p. 1493]—**Raymund F. Wood**

174. Scanlon, Jennifer, and Shaaron Cosner. **American Women Historians, 1700s-1990s: A Biographical Dictionary**. Westport, Conn., Greenwood Press, 1996. 269p. illus. index. $75.00. ISBN 0-313-29664-2.

Scanlon and Cosner, both educators, have compiled the first biographical dictionary of U.S. women historians. Two hundred women of diverse backgrounds were selected for inclusion based on their publications and their participation in defining a certain field of study. Hence, the specific historical fields covered range from architectural history, religious history, and the history of sexuality to world history and local history of various regions and states. Each historian is given a one- to two-page biography with emphasis on her educational background and career, especially her publications; personal information is minimal. Each entry includes a bibliography of the historian's publications as well as a list of when further information about her can be located. There is a general bibliography for the entire volume and an index by name and historical-subject specialty.

While many of the names, such as Ariel Durant, Alice Morse Earle, and Barbara Tuchman, are familiar to many, other women are listed here for the first time, such as Sarah Elbert, a cultural historian of the nineteenth-century United States, and Bettye M. Collier-Thomas, who studied African American social history. A collection of photographs adds to the work. This is a unique, valuable reference source that should be available in college, university, and public library reference centers.—**Deborah Hammer**

175.   **Twentieth-Century American Historians**. Clyde N. Wilson, ed. Detroit, Gale, 1983. 519p. illus. bibliog. index. (Dictionary of Literary Biography, vol. 17). $80.00. LC 82-24210. ISBN 0-8103-1144-5.

Twentieth-Century American Historians (volume 17 of Gale's Dictionary of Literary Biography) contains biographical and critical essays on 59 historical writers. Most of these authors are academic and professional historians. Twenty are still living. To be eligible for inclusion, writers had to be American; their historical writings had to be concentrated chiefly upon the United States; and their most important work had to fall within the twentieth century. Fourteen major writers have been selected for extended treatment, including Charles A. Beard, Daniel J. Boorstin, Richard Hofstadter, Allan Nevins, and Frederick Jackson Turner. A photograph of each historian is given, as well as a bibliography of the historian's books and a bibliography of secondary sources. The volume includes a supplementary reading list and a cumulative index to the Dictionary of Literary Biography.

The criteria for inclusion rule out historians like Captain Alfred Thayer Mahan, whose history of sea power was largely concentrated on Europe, and J. Fred Rippy, whose writings were mainly on U.S. foreign policy in relation to Hispanic America. On the other hand, there are some rather surprising omissions among U.S. historians: Eugene C. Barker, Dexter Perkins, and Julius W. Pratt, to name a few. However, the editor had to draw a line somewhere, and these omissions do not in any way downgrade the historical writers who were not selected.

A total of 54 contributors wrote the essays (three contributors wrote two biographies each). Of these, 36 (or two-thirds) are from Southern states. While this does not reflect on the competence of the contributors, it shows a rather surprising disproportion. The essays themselves are of high quality and follow the dictum of Allan Nevins that historical writing should be readable as well as factually accurate. [R: Choice, Dec 83, p. 559; WLB, Sept 83, p. 68]—**Thomas S. Harding**

Revolutionary War

176.   Barthelmas, Della Gray. **The Signers of the Declaration of Independence: A Biographical and Genealogical Reference**. Jefferson, N.C., McFarland, 1997. 334p. illus. index. $55.00. ISBN 0-7864-0318-7.

The premise of this book is simple: to provide concise biographical and genealogical information on the lives of the signers of the Declaration of Independence. Each of the 56 signers, plus Charles Thomson, the Secretary of the Continental Congress, receives several pages. Well-known signers, such as Thomas Jefferson and Benjamin Franklin, receive the most coverage. For each signer, information is divided into three parts. The first section is a brief look at his life, with particular emphasis on his participation in events of the Revolution; the second gives supplementary information, such as physical appearance, anecdotes, and present-day markers or memorials that commemorate his life; and the third section traces the signer's lineage back several generations. Genealogical information concerns the paternal line of the signer. Each biography is preceded by a portrait.

Although the collection of information about these individuals, who are bound together in history by their participation in a momentous happening, is attractive, informative, and well written, it is difficult to know where this book would fit in library collection policies. The genealogical information is rather difficult reading, as such information always is for those not practiced in following the tangled paths of family descent. Most of the biographical information is available in standard sources, such as the stalwart *Dictionary of American Biography* (see ARBA 96, entry 36), although of course not so conveniently packaged. Libraries with a specialized interest in either American history or in genealogy will be interested in its purchase.—**Terry Ann Mood**

177.   Claghorn, Charles E. **Women Patriots of the American Revolution: A Biographical Dictionary**. Metuchen, N.J., Scarecrow, 1991. 499p. $52.50. E276.CS. 973.3'15042. LC 91-15495. ISBN 0-8108-2421-3.

This dictionary, divided into two alphabetical parts, includes women who "performed patriotic acts or services" during the Revolutionary War. The first section contains brief biographies of 600 women. The second section lists more than 5,000 women, including those who appear in the first section, and describes them in 10 to 50 words. Both sections include the state and usually the town or county where the individual lived, as well as where the information was found. Together with newspapers of the period and personal communications, 61 books have been used as sources. However, not every source in which a name appears is listed under each entry.

While it is handy to have one source that contains so many names, it is a drawback, especially in the first section, that the information found under each entry varies so greatly. In some entries, complete dates are given for the woman and her husband and children, together with other relevant information. In others, only one line mentions the woman; the rest of the data is about the fighting in the area or about some famous male relative or the fact that George Washington stayed at her house. This may be a useful book for genealogists trying to trace people to a certain locality, but it is much less useful for school reports or for answering general reference questions.—**Kathleen Farago**

178.   Purcell, L. Edward. **Who Was Who in the American Revolution**. New York, Facts on File, 1993. 548p. illus. index. $60.00. E206.P87. 973.3'092'2. LC 92-19831. ISBN 0-8160-2107-4.

Several Reference books on the American Revolution have been published in recent years, including *The Blackwell Encyclopedia of the American Revolution* (see ARBA 92, entry 470), *The Encyclopedia of Colonial and Revolutionary America* (see ARBA 91, entry 504), Purcell's own *The World Almanac of the American Revolution* (St. Martin's Press, 1992), and *Women Patriots of the American Revolution* (see ARBA 92, entry 461). This new book fills a void in Revolutionary scholarship by supplying biographical information on more than 1,500 men and women who played major and supporting roles during these turbulent years. Purcell profiles American patriots, Loyalists, French allies, and British foes, and highlights military commanders, foot soldiers, diplomats, politicians, and government officeholders.

The alphabetically arranged entries each include birth and death dates and a brief descriptor. The biographies range in length from a brief paragraph of about 60 or 70 words, such as the one for soldier, jurist, and teacher Nathaniel Chipman, to some 1,500 words, such as the lengthy profile of Benedict Arnold. Cross-references are included where appropriate.

Many entries include a brief bibliography for further reading, and Purcell's meticulously detailed guide to biographical sources will aid serious researchers as well as high school or college students. Regrettably, however, the bibliographies are uneven in quality. For example, renowned frontiersman and general George Rogers Clark has been the subject of several scholarly and well-received biographies, yet Percell mentions only a brief volume that focuses on one aspect of Clark's career. [R: Choice, Dec 93, p. 589; JAL, Sept 93, p. 275; RBB, 15 Oct 93, p. 465; RQ, Winter 93, pp. 297-98; WLB, Oct 93, p. 134]—**Jack Bales**

South

179.   **Biographical Cyclopedia of the Commonwealth of Kentucky: Embracing Biographies of Many of the Prominent Men and Families of the State**. Chicago, John M. Gresham, 1896; repr., Easley, S.C., Southern Historical Press, 1980. 631p. illus. index. $40.00. ISBN 0-89308-193-0.

Most any biographical dictionary can be useful if the reader knows the limitations and caveats in its use. Many of the southern and Midwestern works of the last century are execrable as reference works, but they often contain information not readily available elsewhere. They were frequently based on interviews with a publisher's representative, who collected a fee for inclusion.

The special value of this reprint is not only the fact that it lists 1,104 biographical sketches, but also that it includes an index of names, both of biographees and others. The text of the original edition is in miscellaneous alphabetical order, indexed by biographee only. The present reprint provides an index of other names, prepared by Eileene Sandlin, of 35 unnumbered pages at the end. The information is generally, but not invariably, accurate, and, by the standards of inclusion, the work could be expanded several times. It would be a genuine service to historians and genealogists if dozens of other similar works could have a new index similar to Sandlin's.—**Lawrence S. Thompson**

180.   **Encyclopedia of Southern Culture**. Charles Reagan Wilson and William Ferris, eds. Chapel Hill, University of North Carolina Press, 1989. 1634p. illus. maps. index. $59.95. F209.E53. 975'.003'21. LC 88-17084. ISBN 08078-1823-2.

Both figuratively and literally, this is a monumental work. This hefty compendium, weighing eight pounds, was conceived and developed at the University of Mississippi's Center for the Study of Southern Culture and took a decade to complete. Coordinated by historian Wilson and anthropologist Ferris, both faculty members at the University of Mississippi, this ambitious project drew on the knowledge and expertise of more than 800 scholars and other professionals, including lawyers, journalists, and architects. Subscribing to the broad definition of culture espoused by T. S. Eliot, the editors have attempted not only to identify the interests, activities, and cultural traits that reflect the South's regional distinctiveness but also to represent a way of life that is uniquely Southern. While focusing primarily on the geographical area that encompasses the 11 states that were members of the Confederacy, the editors define "the South" as "wherever southern culture is found" (p. xv) and extend their coverage accordingly.

The volume is organized into 24 alphabetically arranged sections according to academic fields or cultural themes (e.g., agriculture, pp. life, language, history and manners, violence). Each section consists of three parts: an interpretive essay contributed by the consultant for that section; thematic articles, arranged alphabetically; and briefer biographical and topical entries, also alphabetically arranged. For example, following the eight-page introductory essay in the music section are 23 thematic articles treating types of music and musical activities (e.g., bluegrass, jazz, spirituals, square dancing, clogging). An additional 80 entries focus on individuals, musical instruments, and other topics pertinent to the music industry (e.g., banjo, Stephen Foster, Grand Ole Opry, Leontyne Price, Sun Records). All entries are signed and are followed by bibliographical references to sources of further information. Citations to journal articles are notably skimpy, providing only author, journal title, and date of issue. Many articles provide cross-references to related entries in other sections of the encyclopedia. Complementing the text throughout the work are numerous black-and-white photographs and other illustrations, such as maps and drawings. Much of the illustrative material depicts the South prior to 1950. Concluding the volume are both a general index and an index to contributors.

One of the encyclopedia's most impressive features is its breadth of coverage. The approximately 1,300 articles touch on all aspects of Southern life, such as historical events, educational institutions, societies, social concerns, customs, industries, and the arts. Entries span the spectrum from serious topics, such as illiteracy, the Great Depression, and race relations, to lighter subjects, such as fried chicken, Goo Clusters, and pickup trucks. Approximately 350 (not 250 as noted in the introduction) biographical articles cover both living and deceased individuals. The editors indicate that their goal was not to include every prominent Southerner but to choose representative individuals who made contributions to the region or who exemplify characteristic aspects of Southern culture. Thus, being born or having lived in the South is not the principal criterion, as is evidenced by articles on such non-Southerners as British actress Vivien Leigh, noted for her portrayal of Southern women in *Gone with the Wind* and A *Streetcar Named Desire*, and the New England artist Winslow Homer, whose work sometimes incorporated Southern themes. This representative approach leads to choices for inclusion that are debatable in light of individuals omitted. For example, why Herschel Walker but not Fran Tarkenton, Martha Mitchell but not Oveta Culp Hobby, Harry Crews but not Elizabeth Spencer? Possibly because the volume has been so long in the making, the coverage of individuals or groups who have come to prominence in the last 10 years is particularly sparse. Thus, there are no entries for Beth Henley, Charlayne Hunter-Gault, Anne Tyler, or the rock group REM.

While the sectional arrangement has the advantage of bringing related articles together, it also creates inconsistencies in coverage and results in rather arbitrary decisions regarding the placement of articles in appropriate categories. For example, actress Tallulah Bankhead is covered under "Women's Life" rather than "Media," "Motherhood" is treated under "Mythic South" instead of "Women's Life," and "House Types" is under "Folklife," not "Art and Architecture." In addition, the arrangement seems to have led to some anomalies regarding not only subjects covered but also the extent of treatment. While there is no entry for either Harper Lee or her Pulitzer Prize-winning novel *To Kill a Mockingbird*, Lee's fictional lawyer, Atticus Finch, is accorded an article in the law section. In contrast, *Uncle Tom's Cabin* has entries under "Media" and "Mythic South," one dealing with film versions, the other with the novel; Kyle Onstott's sensationalized *Mandingo* not only is treated in an article in the media category but also has five additional references in the index.

Although this work contains a wealth of information about the South and its culture, access to that information is not without flaws. Only the 24 broad subject categories appear in the table of contents at the front of the volume; to identify the articles within each section the user must consult the separate contents pages that precede each category. The lack of an overall table of contents hinders efforts to obtain an accurate overview of the volume's scope and arrangement and forces the user to rely heavily on the general index. Fortunately, the index is extensive and quite detailed; however, it has its limitations and faults. First, the subentries under primary headings in the index are arranged numerically according to page reference rather than alphabetically. Thus, the subcategories under Virginia begin with "Religion" and end with "Family Dynasties." In addition, some articles are not indexed under the terms that would appear to be most appropriate for locating them. For instance, the entry on "Speech Black" is not indexed under either "Black English" or "Blacks," but under the more general headings "Language" and "Speech." Also, although there is an index entry for "Oil," it does not include a reference to the article "Oil Industry," which instead appears under the index heading "Industry, Oil." The article on the railroad industry is, however, indexed under "Railroads."

As a scholarly endeavor that provides an authoritative synthesis of knowledge about the South, its history, its culture, and its institutions, the *Encyclopedia of Southern Culture* is a remarkable achievement. Unfortunately, its value as a reference work is diminished by its somewhat cumbersome arrangement and the sometimes imperfect access offered by the index. However, in these days of exorbitantly priced reference books, it is a bargain. This significant work belongs in most public and academic libraries. In addition, it would be useful in many high school libraries, particularly those in Southern states. [R: BR, Nov/Dec 89, p. 58; Choice, Nov 89, p. 458; LJ, July 89, p. 72; RBB, 1 Sept 89, pp. 97-98; WLB, Oct 89, pp. 133-35]—**Marie Ellis**

West

181.   Cusic, Don. **Cowboys and the Wild West: An A-Z Guide from the Chisholm Trail to the Silver Screen**. New York, Facts on File, 1994. 356p. illus. index. $40.00. F596.C957. 987' .003. LC 93-45584. ISBN 0-8160-2783-8.

This work is a good mix of three major interests: the meaning (and sometimes the origin) of items of cowboy lingo; biographies of hundreds of famous cowboys and other Westerners, such as Jesse James; and information about cowboy (or just plain Western) movies, television shows, songs, and related topics. In between are informative articles on Indian tribes, the Pony Express, the Mormons, Jedediah Smith and William Sublette, the Chisholm Trail, and similar items of interest to aficionados of the Old West.

Since there exist several other dictionaries of Western words, as well as directories of outlaws, gunfighters, and so on, the major contribution of the work under review is its emphasis on western films. On the other hand, it is not a complete list of the hundreds of B-movies (mostly westerns) that have been made during the past half-century. It is selective, but the selection is good, whether it be for movies, songs, or television shows. For example, 16 lines are devoted to the song "Cool Water," reputed to be "the best-known western song of all time." The text states that it was originally written as a poem by its author, Bob Nolan, while he was a student at Tucson High School. There are more than 100 black-and-white illustrations, some full-page, and many of them stills from movies. There are a 12-page, double-columned bibliography, and an excellent index of names and topics. A surprising omission is any mention of the Gene Autry Western Heritage Museum in Los Angeles, especially in view of its excellent and permanent exhibit of the history of the cowboy in the movies. While not an exhaustive reference source for any of the three major topics that it covers, the work is recommended for any library with Western interests. [R: RBB, 1 Jan 95, p. 840]—**Raymund F. Wood**

182.   **Encyclopedia of Frontier Biography on CD-ROM**. [CD-ROM]. Lincoln, University of Nebraska Press, 1995. Minimum system requirements: IBM or compatible. Double-speed CD-ROM drive (recommended). VGA monitor (color recommended). $150.00.

A catalog of significant persons and personalities of the U.S. West, this menu-driven CD-ROM contains some 5,700 biographical entries that can be accessed by both alphabetical and chronological listings. Clearly, the principal advantage of creating a CD-ROM from what was initially published as a three-volume set of books (by Dan L. Thrapp [1991-1994]) is that its digital format encourages searches of any and all of these entries for similar themes, words, or phrases, or to cross-reference persons and events.

The individuals included in this reference work were chosen for the significance of their actions and lives on the U.S. frontier. The people selected include a wide variety of men, women, and Native Americans who were settlers, explorers, outlaws and desperadoes, writers, scientists, and military figures. Entries are linked together and identified by name (and aliases if any), fields of significance, dates of birth and death (if known), summaries of their careers, and various facts and places of interest. Entries also typically provide useful biographical notes to guide further research.

The entries in this encyclopedia are concise and informative and reflect Thrapp's background not only as a historian but also as a journalist. He has achieved his objective of creating a permanent record of a fascinating era of U.S. history and legend. The lives and times of the famous and the infamous, the recognizable and the obscure, reveal much about who people are and how they became what they are. Students and researchers alike will benefit from either casually browsing or thoroughly studying this practical reference work.—**Timothy E. Sullivan**

183.   **Encyclopedia of Frontier Biography**. Dan L. Thrapp. Glendale, Calif., Arthur H. Clark, 1988. 3v. index. $175.00/set. LC 88-71686. ISBN 0-87062-191-2.

Encyclopedia of Frontier Biography. **Volume 4: Supplemental Volume**. Dan. L. Thrapp. Spokane, Wash., Arthur H. Clark, 1994. 610p. index. $65.00. LC 92-75560. ISBN 0-87062-222-6.

This three-volume set and supplemental volume contain approximately 5,500 names of Western pioneers—4,500 in the original set, another 1,000 in the supplement. For the basic set, though it does include seventeenth- and eighteenth-century frontier settlers in both New France and New England as well as the trans-Appalachia country, the vast majority of entries are for nineteenth-century men and women who discovered, settled, fought for, governed, or merely lived in the unsettled lands west of the Mississippi River. This lack has been corrected by the supplement.

Each alphabetical entry begins with a one-word descriptor—frontiersman, desperado, Indian chief, cowboy, or sometimes just "character." The average length of each biography is about one-half of a double-columned page, shorter or longer for Westerners such as Custer or Kearny. It offers no illustrations or pronunciations, but accents are sometimes given. A bibliography follows each entry. For famous persons, "literature abundant" appears in place of bibliography.

Coverage for the plains and mountain states is very good: Cochise, Sacajawea, Escalante, Kino, Laframboise, Jedediah Smith, Carrie Nation, "Calamity Jane," and so forth, are discussed. Coverage of California is less complete, omitting many Hispanic names. Most of the Franciscan missionaries, as well as Consul Thomas O. Larkin, pioneer enthusiast John Marsh, and alcalde Edwin Bryant, are left out. Also omitted is the name of New Mexico's Archbishop Lamy. Coverage of Alaska is even less complete—Baranoff, Bering, Rezanov, and Wrangel do not appear, though Baranoff is referred to in passing as "a Russian official."

The supplement expands coverage both in geographical space and in time. The Russians of Alaska are plentiful, notably in the K section—Kalinin, Kashevarov, Kotzbue, and so on. For California and nearby areas, there are many new Hispanic names; in Thrapp's own words, "there (now) appear virtually all those who explored for Spain, Mexico, or Russia. . . ." There is also more detailed coverage of the old Northwest, as well as of Kentucky, Tennessee, and Texas. As for time, this has been brought forward to the 1990s and expanded to include more names of writers about the frontier, both fiction and nonfiction. We now find Horace Albright, John Kemble, Louis L'Amour, and Oscar Lewis. One final addition: The supplement frequently uses *see entry* whenever, in a person's biography, another name is mentioned that might add more knowledge about the biographee. This feature is not found in the basic three-volume set.

The index to the basic set, over 70 double-columned pages, is valuable. It covers many topics—gunmen, Mormons, vigilantes, Indian tribes, many names, including those listed and others having any relationship to persons appearing in the book. Thus, "Wild Bill" Hickok has 27 citations to other persons; Custer and Geronimo each have about 100 citations. This feature adds to the reference value of the book.

Both the basic set and the index are highly recommended and will be invaluable to all Western-history buffs as well as to reference librarians with a similar clientele. The supplement, bound to match the basic set, is a must buy for all who have the earlier work. It rounds the set out, fills in the gaps, brings it up-to-date, and is in itself fascinating reading.

The *Encyclopedia of Frontier Biography* is also available as a CD-ROM product.—**Raymund F. Wood and Terry Ann Mood**

184. **Encyclopedia of the American West**. Charles Phillips and Alan Axelrod, eds. New York, Macmillan Library Reference/Simon & Schuster Macmillan, 1996. 4v. illus. maps. index. $375.00/set. ISBN 0-02-897495-6.

This four-volume work is truly encyclopedic in its coverage of the West's history during the eighteenth and nineteenth centuries. The preface states that all the 23 states west of the Missouri River are covered in the more than 1,700 entries, written by approximately 400 authors. However, it should be noted that of these 1,700 entries, about 290 were written by the editors, and 145 by a single, other person. The time limits of the set are given as from c.1803 (the Louisiana Purchase, Daniel Boone, the American Fur Company, and so forth) to the end of the nineteenth century, with occasional spill over into the twentieth century (cowboys, Roy Rogers and Dale Evans, Theodore Roosevelt). Following the preface is a list of all contributors and their affiliations.

The text is a judicious mix of subject and biographical articles, about equal in number, although the former are generally longer. Typical biographies run from about three-quarters of a page (e.g., Calamity Jane, Chief Joseph, Peter Ogden), while a few run to a full page or more (e.g., George Armstrong Custer, John C. Frémont, John Muir). More than 1,000 black-and-white photographs and maps illustrate the articles. Topical articles are interestingly written, on such subjects as disease, divorce, the fur trade, intermarriage, and the noble savage theory (although this article makes no mention of either Jean-Jacques Rousseau or Francois-Auguste-René de Chateaubriand). Also, articles on specific subjects (e.g., Ghost Dance, Penitentes, Virginia City) are done well. Instead of brief articles on the separate Indian tribes or peoples, all are included in a rather top-heavy omnibus article, "Native American Peoples," with nine subdivisions—not quite so useful.

The usage of maps is peculiar and somewhat unsatisfactory. With rare exceptions, there is but one map used throughout. This is a reduction of the map of the United States as a whole, which forms the endpapers. It is a natural-features-only map. For each western state, this map is reused, with the outline of the pertinent state drawn upon it. The only city named on each map is the state capital. Thus, the map of Nevada locates neither Reno nor Las Vegas.

Each article is signed, and most have a bibliography attached. There are *see also* references, and cross-references within the text are printed in "capitol" (sic) letters. In a work of this magnitude, some inconsistency is bound to occur. One article claims that Zane Grey "invented the popular western novel." Elsewhere, the same author says that Grey "established and refined the genre that Owen Wister had created." Biographical articles repeat information normally found for prominent people in standard encyclopedias, but errors may occur for lesser-known names. The entry for Jedediah Smith contains three of them: the words "Because of [problems with Mexicans]" should read "Despite [the problems] he was able to rejoin his men." The year 1839 is a misprint for 1830 (Smith died in 1831). Finally, the words "the California" in the bibliography should read "the Californians."

This encyclopedic work, with its excellent index and with a listing of all biographees arranged by occupation or profession, brings together a tremendous amount of condensed information—names, dates, trends, conflicts, heroes and villains: all the wide variety of Western lifestyles—and presents it all to the public in alphabetic order. Easy to use, well illustrated, and well written, the set is recommended for any academic or public library in the United States. [R: LJ, 1 Nov 96, p. 58; RBB, 1 Dec 96, p. 680]—**Raymund F. Wood**

185. O'Neal, Bill. **Encyclopedia of Western Gunfighters**. 1st ed. Norman, University of Oklahoma Press, 1979. 386p. illus. bibliog. index. $29.95. LC 78-21380. ISBN 0-8061-1508-4.

This encyclopedia contains a wealth of information, listing a total of 255 Western gunfighters and 587 gunfights under an alphabetical arrangement by name of gunfighter. Each entry provides the gunfighter's name, any known aliases and/or nicknames, a short biographical sketch with birth and death dates if known, and descriptions of all verified gunfights, including the date and location of each if known. An abbreviated list of sources used to write and verify each entry follows, referring the reader to a bibliography at the end of the book. Introductory material is brief but useful, and very interesting. O'Neal provides a definition of *gunfighter* as a yardstick to determine whether an individual is truly a gunfighter and merits inclusion in the book. Also provided is comprehensive information on the listed gunfighters' vital statistics, causes of death, occupations pursued, number of gunfights, and so on.

O'Neal's writing style is interesting, smooth, and well suited to his subject matter. Well-placed photographs (some of which are extraordinary and unforgettable) help to relieve the repetitive format of the entries, although extended reading of this encyclopedia is not difficult. This is a first-rate effort and fascinating reading. [R: BL, 1 June 80; p. 1437; WLB, Jan 80, p. 332]—**Ronald Rayman**

186. O'Neal, Bill. **Fighting Men of the Indian Wars: A Biographical Encyclopedia of the Mountain Men, Soldiers, Cowboys, and Pioneers**. . . . Stillwater, Okla., Barbed Wire Press, 1991. 255p. illus. index. $26.95. E81.053. 978'.00992. LC 91-36114. ISBN 0-935269-07-X.

Although this work is billed as an encyclopedia, O'Neal admits that it is an arbitrary selection of more than 100 men who fought Native Americans during the nineteenth century. Even so, it is a valuable collection of biographies, made even more interesting by the frequent inclusion of graphic details of the fighting and occasionally of actual conversations, as recorded in Army field notes or diaries.

Preceding the biographical sketches are some interesting preliminaries: an introduction; an essay on "What the Indians Called Them"; chronological statistics from 1810 to 1898; "Extraordinary Exploits of Warriors, and of Indians"; combat techniques; and "The Medal of Honor," with tables of recipients by year. After all this (and yet another short introduction), the biographies begin, running from one double-columned page to three or four pages in length, although George Custer is assigned nearly eight pages.

Each entry starts with biographical information, followed by detailed combat data. Each combat has a separate entry; some have three or four paragraphs. At the end of each biographee's entry is a brief list of sources; there is also a full-length bibliography at the end of the book. In addition, a good index lists not only the biographees but also cross-references to other persons. For example, William T. Sherman does not have an entry, but there are 10 cross-references from his name in the index. A few other omissions were noted. Marcus Reno does not have an entry, although he has eight cross references in the index; the cases are similar for Edward Canby (perhaps because he was pursuing peace when he was killed in the Modoc War) and John Chivington (perhaps because his men slaughtered defenseless women and children at Sand Creek). Some 35 black-and-white illustrations, mostly of individual fighters but occasionally of groups, add to the value of the book. [R: RBB, July 92, pp. 1958-60]—**Raymund F. Wood**

VIETNAM

187. Duiker, William J. **Historical Dictionary of Vietnam**. Metuchen, N.J., Scarecrow, 1989. 269p. maps. (Asian Historical Dictionaries, no. 1). $32.50. DS556.25.D85. 959.7'003'21. LC 88-29721. ISBN 0-8108-2164-8.

Duiker, professor of East Asian history at Pennsylvania State University and an authority in modern Vietnamese history, is the author of this first volume of the Asian Historical Dictionaries series. The format is similar to the titles in the African Historical Dictionaries series.

The heart of the work consists of an excellent introduction to the history of Vietnam; over 400 alphabetically arranged entries comprised mainly of major historical figures, events, movements, organizations, literary figures and works, and other important events relating to Vietnamese history; and a well-organized, selective, and lengthy (43 pages) bibliography. Each entry averages about a half-page in length; in particular, major historical figures such as kings are extensively covered. Accompanying the main entries where appropriate, cross-references are provided and prove to be extremely useful. The dictionary entries seem appropriately chosen and the information presented is accurate and balanced. Also included in the text are a brief chronology of events in Vietnamese history starting from the Paleolithic Era (10,000 B.C.) to the resignation of Pham Van Dong (prime minister) in 1988; tables providing statistical data of population, industry, agriculture, and foreign trade; and four maps.

An index of names, titles, and subjects would be helpful. On the whole, this work is a solid one, and despite its limited coverage, this volume compares favorably with the work of Danny J. Whitfield entitled *Historical and Cultural Dictionary of Vietnam* (see ARBA 77, entry 332). The price is reasonable for an important work such as this. It is a worthy addition for every reference collection, especially where the history of the Vietnam War is being taught. [R: Choice, Oct 89, p. 284]—**Binh P. Le**

4   Geography

INTRODUCTION

This chapter contains biographical sources in the areas of Geographers, Demographers, and Explorers. Additional biographical dictionaries which contain biographies on geographers can be found in other chapters including **Business and Economics**, **Ethnic Studies**, **History**, and of course, **International Sources** and **National and Regional Sources**. General encyclopedias also contain biographical information on geographers. The Geographers section contains the important biographical sources, *Biographical Dictionary of Geography* (Greenwood Press, 1993) (see entry 189), which contains biographies on more than 75 geographers worldwide, and *Geographers: Biobibliographical Studies* (H. W. Wilson, 1977-) (see entry 188), which is a series of works that provide biographies on geographers in various countries.

The section Demographers contains only one entry: *Dictionary of Demography: Biographies* (Greenwood Press, 1985) (see entry 190), which provides biographical information including name, dates, nationality, career positions, main publications on population, and one or more references to sources of additional biographical information.

The final section, Explorers, contains the majority of the sources. *World Explorers and Discoverers* (Macmillan, 1992) (see entry 193) includes significant explorers from all times and places, such as the Arab Ibn Battuta (1304-1368/9), the Chinese Zhang Qian (d. 107 B.C.), the English Mary Henrietta Kingsley (1862-1900), and the Norwegian Thor Heyerdahl (1914-present). History seems to be the story of change and discovery, and two volumes in this chapter speak to this specifically: Milton Lomask's *Great Lives: Exploration* (Scribners, 1988) (see entry 192), and *Explorers & Discoverers: From Alexander the Great to Sally Ride* (U*X*L/Gale, 1995) (see entry 194). Although these two specifically deal with the theme of exploration, in one sense all the books in this chapter can be said to do so.

GEOGRAPHERS

188. **Geographers: Biobibliographical Studies**. T. W. Freeman, ed. London, Mansell; distr., New York, H. W. Wilson, 1977- . Price varies. ISSN 0308-6992.

As part of a wider program of studying the history of geography, the Commission on the History of Geographical Thought of the International Geographical Union sponsored the writing of a series of biographical sketches of geographers who have played seminal roles in the development of this field. Each biobibliography includes a brief summary of the subject's education, life, and work; scientific ideas and geographical thought; influence and spread of the person's ideas; sources and bibliography; and a chronological table of the life, career, activities, field work, and publications of the individual, as well as contemporary events. In an average of 6 pages, the life, contributions, and influence of each person are succinctly summarized.

Volume 1 (published in 1977) contains eighteen biographies. In this initial volume, geographers of the United States (4), United Kingdom (5), and France (4) are well represented, and individuals from Poland, Rumania, the Soviet Union, Japan, and Malaya are also included. The authors of the sketches typically come from the same countries as the biographees and are intimately acquainted with their contributions and impact. The biobibliographies are convenient and authoritative summaries in accessible form, more objective and evaluative than some memorials written immediately after the death of an eminent figure and more concise than the full biographies that appear in book form.

Volume 13 (1991) continues the high quality and international coverage of earlier volumes. Volume 13 contains 18 short essays that discuss the lives, intellectual contributions, and influence of persons who contributed significantly to the field of geography, even though several were not geographers per se. The authors of the essays have apparently submitted manuscripts based on their interests in the subject rather than having been assigned articles. As a result, they often show intimate knowledge of the individuals and display access to special and archival materials. Volume 14, published in 1992, updates the set again with a number of new biographical essays.—**Chauncy D. Harris and Robert L. Wick**

189. Larkin, Robert P., and Gary L. Peters. **Biographical Dictionary of Geography**. Westport, Conn., Greenwood Press, 1993. 361p. index. $69.50. G67.L37. 910.922. LC 92-18364. ISBN 0-313-27622-6.

Apart from a generalized appreciation that their subject involves the consideration of space and place, and an acceptance of a few basic technologies such as cartography, remote sensing, and information systems, modern geographers are an increasingly diverse group with little common ground. Given the increasing need to specialize, geography continues to witness a sort of "big bang," as individuals move steadily away from an always-minimal core of agreed knowledge to the cutting edges of various physical, cultural, and economic specialties. As a result, efforts to identify historically important contributors to the science are increasingly fraught with difficulty.

The present work, for example, offers basic biographical information on 77 geographers. Arranged in alphabetical order, the entries range chronologically from Thales of Miletus (6th century B.C.) to a dozen still-living professionals. Each entry—they range from two to seven pages—consists of a biographical sketch, a select bibliography, a personal chronology, and a few references to more detailed works. The biographies are unadorned and make little effort to place the subjects in the larger context of their times.

This book will be of interest to students of the history of geographic ideas, but it will also, based on the necessarily limited number of inclusions, be controversial in the profession despite the authors' statement that their purpose is to include representatives from as many subfields as possible. Several famous names more commonly associated with other disciplines (e.g., Charles Darwin, John Muir) seem questionable, but it is undoubtedly the composition of the still-living group that will raise the most eyebrows. [R: Choice, June 93, p. 1606; RBB, 15 Apr 93, p. 1532]—**James R. McDonald**

DEMOGRAPHERS

190. Petersen, William, and Renee Petersen, with an international panel of demographers. **Dictionary of Demography: Biographies**. Westport, Conn., Greenwood Press, 1985. 2v. bibliog. index. $125.00/set. LC 83-12567. ISBN 0-313-21419-0.

Companion volumes to this set are *Dictionary of Demography: Terms, Concepts, and Institutions* (Greenwood Press, 1986) and *Dictionary of Demography: Multilingual Glossary*. The *Biographies* set has been compiled with the help of fifty-seven collaborators throughout the world. The joint author, William Petersen, is professor emeritus of demography at Ohio State University. "Demography" is interpreted here to include population analysis as well as formal demography, the presentation of population data. Consequently, many of the subjects of the biographies are from other disciplines, such as biology, sociology, economics, public health, etc. Since demography is a recent science, the emphasis is on contemporary persons.

The information given for each person includes name, dates, nationality, career positions, main publications on population, and one or more references to sources of additional biographical information. The scope of the work is truly worldwide. Biographies of 3,363 nationals from ninety-nine countries ranging from Afghanistan to Zimbabwe are presented. The United States leads with 823 entries; the United Kingdom has 291; France, 260; and Russia, 148. The arrangement is alphabetical by name, with an appendix classifying the entries by country. There is a ten-page list of references, and a very full sixty-five-page index. This comprehensive set is a valuable reference source for a relatively new discipline. It is a mine of information on persons and publications in population analysis. The extensive index provides a good subject approach to the material.—**Necia A. Musser**

EXPLORERS

191. Dunmore, John. **Who's Who in Pacific Navigation**. Honolulu, University of Hawaii Press, 1991. 312p. index. $34.00. DU19.D78. 910'.91823. LC 91-19280. ISBN 0-8248-1350-2.

The term *navigation* as used as a criterion for inclusion in this biographical dictionary is restricted to those who led or played a major role in voyages of exploration and research in the Pacific Ocean. Some secondary figures whose names occur in accounts of voyages, their origin or aftermath, are also included. Well-known names, such as Bligh, Bougainville, Cook, Drake, and La Perouse, will be found as well as those of lesser-known explorers. American, British, Dutch, French, Spanish, and other nationalities are represented. Sketches are mostly short, the longest being about two pages in length; they are not complete biographies. When available, information on date and place of birth, parentage, education, and notable accomplishments is given, but the entries are mainly devoted to the person's Pacific explorations and discoveries. A selected bibliography lists general works and reference sources as well as specific titles that are alphabetically arranged under the country with which the voyage is associated. A name index provides reference access not only to the main entries but also to places within the sketches where the explorer is mentioned. There are also indexes to the names of ships and to broad subjects. This thoroughly researched and well-prepared work will be an excellent source of information for historians, subject specialists, and others who are interested in the Pacific area. [R: Choice, July/Aug 92, p. 1653]—**Shirley L. Hopkinson**

192. Lomask, Milton. **Great Lives: Exploration**. New York, Scribners, 1988. 258p. illus. maps. index. $22.95. G200.L66. 910'.922. LC 88-15744. ISBN 0-684-18511-3.

Biography is happily enjoying a renaissance in the world of children's book publishing. *Great Lives: Exploration* is one of many new biographical collections available to youth in the middle school years. The lives of 15 explorers are described in this third volume of a series that also includes volumes of biographical essays about famous men and women in government and sports. Author Lomask colorfully describes the lives and explorations of such famed explorers as Marco Polo, Christopher Columbus, Roald Amundsen, David Livingstone, Richard Byrd, and Robert Peary. Readers also learn about lesser-known, but highly significant explorers such as Hoei-shin, a Chinese Buddhist monk who is believed to have explored North America in the fifth century, and Mary Kingsley, a Victorian Englishwoman who explored Africa.

While Lomask's profiles make fascinating reading, they should be read critically. In the profile of Hoei-shin, for example, he refers to two books written in 1875 and 1885 as being from the "late eighteenth century." At times he uses florid prose to describe the emotional states of the subjects without marshaling the facts to substantiate his claims. He describes Mary Kingsley thus: "She laughed at herself, not at others. It was her way of sparing others sadness, the sense of being a loner and a misfit, that lay at the core of her being" (p.132).

Lomask does provide a detailed and useful chronology of significant dates in the exploration of the world, and his profiles make fine reading for young people. The essays are brief, but will probably serve to whet the appetites of young readers, who will be inspired to look for further readings about these unique people. [R: BR, May/June 89, p. 56]—**Jerry D. Flack**

193. **World Explorers and Discoverers**. Richard E. Bohlander, ed. New York, Macmillan, 1992. 331p. illus. maps. index. $83.00. G200.W67. 910'.922. LC 91-23136. ISBN 0-02-897443-X.

Exploration and *discovery* are words that conjure up images of adventure. It is therefore not surprising that many readers seek biographical information about explorers. Fortunately, *World Explorers and Discovers,* with its 313 entries, will help fulfill that demand. Significant explorers from all times and places have been included, such as the Chinese Zhang Qian (d. 107 B.C.), the Arab Ibn Battuta (1304-1368/9), the English Mary Henrietta Kingsley (1862-1900), and the Norwegian Thor Heyerdahl (1914-present). People involved in space exploration, aviation, and mountaineering are excluded (except for Sir Edmund Hillary), while people whose work as geographers, inventors, and historians has helped advance exploration are included (e.g., the historian Herodotus).

Individual entries are listed alphabetically and vary in length from about 400 to 4,000 words. All entries have a head note that supplies the person's nationality, vital dates, and major accomplishments. Longer entries include a bibliography. Also supplied are a glossary of terms, a list of explorers by nationality, a list of explorers by area of exploration, and a bibliography that is further subdivided by the names of some explorers. In this regard, it would have been better if each entry included at least one item of bibliography. (This reviewer has no idea where to find more information on the fascinating Johan Schiltberger [1380-1440?], and the main bibliography is not much help.) Finally, an index of personal names, places, and subjects concludes the volume.

On the surface, *World Explorers and Discovers* appears to be quite similar to *The Discoverers* (see ARBA 81, entry 3), which contains about 200 mostly biographical entries (although many are topical). In fact, the two books should be seen as complements rather than as rivals. For example, *The Discoverers* lists 13 entries in the letter D and *World Explorers* contains 17, but only 8 entries are common to both volumes. The amount of unique material in *World Explorers* makes it worth purchasing even if a library already owns *The Discoverers*. [R: BR, Sept/Oct 92, p. 68; RBB, 1 June 92, p. 1780; WLB, June 92, p. 158]—**Ronald H. Fritze**

194.   Saari, Peggy, and Daniel B. Baker. **Explorers & Discoverers: From Alexander the Great to Sally Ride**. Detroit, U*X*L/Gale, 1995. 4v. illus. maps. index. $76.00/set. ISBN 0-8103-9787-8.

This series breaks former molds of the stodgy reference book by offering young researchers a cornucopia of information in an attractive, vigorous worldview of exploration and discovers. A simple but exacting preface explains the authors' working method—study of lives and times, including women and non-European adventurers whom former histories have passed over. A single sentence expresses to the user a researcher's most valuable tool—an inquiring attitude toward who, when, and how alongside why and what consequences resulted. Following the introduction and picture credits are rather spare maps devoid of the minutiae that often mar or obscure cartography in adult reference works.

Similar in style and scope to U*X*L's *Performing Artists* series, this attractive work summarizes lives and expeditions along with black-and-white photographs, line drawings, portraits, and sidebars. For example, the entry on Abu Abdallah Ibn Battutah cites a significant issue of the Middle Ages—the influence of bubonic plague on travelers, city officials, and whole nations devastated by the disease. Each volume concludes with a timeline by global regions, explorers by country of origin, and an index of minor and major figures, with the most important appearing in boldface. Along with the *de rigueur* Marco Polo, Jacques Cousteau, and Captain Cook, U*X*L juxtaposes the flight of Beryl Markham, Will Steger's study of the North Pole, and Herodotus, who become a father of history. For no obvious reason, certain prominent travelers receive no mention, notably Margaret Mead, Heinrich Schliemann, and Louis S. B. and Mary Leakey. Detailed views of Christopher Columbus's landfalls in the Caribbean and the shape and record of *Sputnik I* fill in many gaps for a generation still learning that exploration has always been a global project.—**Mary Ellen Snodgrass**

195.   Waldman, Carl, and Alan Wexler. **Who Was Who in World Exploration**. New York, Facts on File, 1992. 712p. illus. maps. $65.00. G200.W24. 910'.922. LC 91-21277. ISBN 0-8160-2172-4.

More than 800 entries and 120 illustrations make up this timely and easy-to-read biographical dictionary. Its scope extends from ancient to modern times, but most of the entries deal with those persons from the so-called "Age of Exploration" (the fifteenth to the nineteenth centuries). Fortunately, the authors consider cartographers important to the history of discovery and have included them in this volume. With each person's name are given the years of birth and death, a sentence or two that describes the person's place of origin and importance, and a brief chronological list of the highlights of the individual's contributions to world exploration. The real meat of the book lies in several paragraphs of historical narrative about the person. Cross-references to other entries in the book are in heavier type. However, the entries lack suggested readings. Appendix 1 lists the explorers by region of exploration, while Appendix 2 is composed of 15 maps of the world that show countries and important locations in the history of exploration. Additionally, black-and-white prints of old maps are scattered throughout the volume. A 14-page bibliography arranged by geographic region rounds out the book, but there is no index.

Reference librarians will want to compare the coverage of the item under review with that of two other new publications: *World Explorers and Discoverers*, edited by Richard E. Bohlander (Macmillan, 1992), and *Old Worlds to New: Age of Exploration and Discovery*, edited by Steven Anzovin and Janet Podell (H. W. Wilson, 1992). Recommended for the reference collection of all libraries. [R: RBB, 15 Oct 92, p. 460; SLJ, Nov 92, p. 146; WLB, Oct 92, p. 115]—**Daniel K. Blewett**

5 Political Science

INTRODUCTION

The subcategories in the **Political Science** chapter include both geographical and topical subdivisions. Geographical subdivisions are self explanatory—categories such as Africa, Asia, and Europe—and include information on leaders and politics of these countries or regions. One special note is that there is a category both for the old Soviet Union and the new Russia. In the category Soviet Union, there are such sources as *A Biographical Directory of 100 Leading Soviet Officials*, compiled by Alexander Rahr (Westview Press, 1990) (see entry 248) and *The Soviet Nomenklatura: A Comprehensive Roster of Soviet Civilian and Military Officials*, 3d ed. compiled by Albert L. Weeks (Washington Institute Press, 1991) (see entry 249). Under Russia are listed, among other sources, *Who Is Who in the Russian Government*, compiled by Pavel Gazukin and edited by Andrei Vasilevsky (Panorama of Russia; distr., Somerville, Mass., Panorama of Russia, 1992) (see entry 246), and its supplement, *Who Is Who in the Russian Government. Supplement I* (Panorama of Russia; distr., Somerville, Mass., Panorama of Russia, 1993) (see entry 246).

Some of the items in the various geographical subdivisions are listings of contemporary leaders, such as Alan Rake's *Who's Who in Africa: Leaders for the 1990s* (Scarecrow, 1992) (see entry 209), or *Political Leaders of Contemporary Western Europe: A Biographical Dictionary*, edited by David Wilsford (Greenwood Press, 1995) (see entry 222). Others are important for their historical perspective, such as A. H. M. Kirk-Greene's *A Biographical Dictionary of the British Colonial Service, 1939-1966* (Hans Zell/K. G. Saur, 1991) (see entry 227), or Peter D. Stachura's *Political Leaders in Weimar Germany: A Biographical Study* (Simon & Schuster Academic Reference Division, 1993) (see entry 225).

Some unusual categories are among the topical subdivisions. Espionage is one of these. Here one finds Richard Deacon's *Spyclopedia: The Complete Handbook of Espionage* (Silver Arrow Books/William Morrow, 1988) (see entry 217). Listings are both for spies and for such topics as "certain espionage 'operations,' codes and ciphers, fake defectors, lie detectors, and nuclear spies. . . ." Lest one suspect that this section is sexist and concentrates only on the male of the species, there is M. H. Mahoney's *Women in Espionage: A Biographical Dictionary* (ABC-CLIO, 1993) (see entry 218). This work "contains short biographies of 150 female spies that cover all time periods and many nationalities." Most of this book's entries, however, are for twentieth-century European and American women.

A category on a somewhat loftier plane than espionage and spying is International Organizations. Here are listed books on personnel in organizations such as the United Nations: *Who's Who in the United Nations and Related Agencies*, 2d ed. (Omnigraphics, 1992) (see entry 235); and the Peace Corps: *Who's Who in the Peace Corps*, 1993 ed. (Reference Press International, 1993) (see entry 234). Also listed are more general directories of people involved in various world organizations: *Who's Who in International Organizations: A Biographical Encyclopedia of More Than 12,000 Leading Personalities*, edited by Jon C. Jenkins, with Cecile Vanden Bloock (K. G. Saur, 1992) (see entry 233).

Another interesting category is Peace Movement. While so much of history and political science involves the study of war, here are books that celebrate people involved in the peace movement. The 1960s are documented in *Leaders from the 1960s: A Biographical Sourcebook of American Activism*, edited by David DeLeon (Greenwood Press, 1994) (see entry 242). The long history of the Nobel Peace Prize is commemorated in Irwin Abrams's *The Nobel Peace Prize and the Laureates: An Illustrated Biographical History, 1901-1987* (G. K. Hall, 1988) (see entry 241); while a more general work, the four-volume *World Encyclopedia of Peace*, edited by Ervin Laszlo and Jong Youl Yoo (Pergamon Press, 1986) (see entry 244), covers both people and peace-related topics.

Of all the geographical subdivisions, the United States, perhaps not surprisingly, has the most entries. Personnel in all three branches of the federal government are documented, although for personnel in the judicial branch, one should consult the chapter **Law**. Both Executive and Legislative branch material is located in this chapter, and both elected and staff personnel are represented. Such standards as *Federal Staff Directory* (CQ Directories, 1982-) (see entry 261) and *Who's Who in the Federal Executive Branch* (Congressional Quarterly, 1993-) (see entry 262) appear under the subdivision United States Politics and Government—Executive Branch, as do more specific and topical titles such as *The Clinton 500: The New Team Running America 1994*, edited by Jeffrey B. Trammell and Gary P. Osifchin (Almanac Publishing, 1994) (see entry 260) and *Notable U.S. Ambassadors Since 1775* (Greenwood Press, 1997) (see entry 254). Under United States Politics and Government—Legislative Branch, there appear other standards: *The Almanac of the Unelected: Staff of the U.S. Congress*, edited by Jeffrey B. Trammell and Steve Piacente (Almanac Publishing, 1988-) (see entry 277) *Congressional Yellow Book: Who's Who in Congress, Including Committees and Key Staff* (Monitor Leadership Directories, 1976-) (see entry 284); and *Who's Who in Congress* (Congressional Quarterly, 1992-) (see entry 287).

Both presidents and first ladies have their own categories, although in the case of Presidents the category is shared with their seconds in command: United States Politics and Government—Presidents and Vice-Presidents and United States Politics and Government—First Ladies are both subdivisions in this chapter. Under the Presidents and Vice-Presidents subdivision are frequently updated titles such as William A. DeGregorio's *The Complete Book of U.S. Presidents* (Dembner Book/Barricade Books, 1991) (see entry 292), described by its reviewer as "a trivia buff's delight and a treasure for reference librarians in search of otherwise difficult-to-find information on U.S. presidents." *The Presidents*, edited by Fred L. Israel (Grolier, 1997) (see entry 301), contains information on the daily life of the presidents and their first ladies. One book speaks specifically to presidential families rather than to the presidents themselves: *America's Royalty: All the Presidents' Children* (Greenwood Press, 1995) (see entry 303). One book of Vice-Presidents also includes their wives: Leslie W. Dunlap's *Our Vice-Presidents and Second Ladies* (Scarecrow, 1988) (see entry 294).

While it may not be surprising that U.S. presidents have so many books written about them, perhaps it is a bit surprising to see the number of titles in the First Ladies category: a total of five. Some have a personal slant, such as Margaret Brown Klapthor's *The First Ladies*, 6th ed. (White House Historical Association; distr., Sewall, 1989) (see entry 265), which includes both a portrait of each first lady and "a warm, personal account of each woman's private and political life." One is more scholarly: *American First Ladies: Their Lives and Their Legacy*, edited by Lewis L. Gould, (Garland, 1996) (see entry 263), uses the first lady's own writings as well as articles and scholarly writings about her to give "a well-rounded account that presents the problems, controversies, and perceptions by her peers that each first lady faced." This book also contains information on where the first lady's personal papers and other manuscript sources can be found.

Clearly, political science is an interdisciplinary study. Other items of interest to collection builders in this area can be found in the chapters **History**, **Law**, and **Business and Economics**.

GENERAL WORKS

196. **Chambers Dictionary of Political Biography**. John Ransley, ed. New York, Chambers Kingfisher Graham, 1991. 436p. $30.00. ISBN 0-550-17251-3.

In one concise volume, the editor has brought together short biographies of 1,150 prominent political leaders who have had or are having lasting effects on world politics, from Alexander the Great to John Smith. The biographies are very short but nonetheless useful in identifying key figures and their relationships with other political leaders. There is also a separate collection of quotations from some of the leaders in the biographical dictionary. Finally, Ransley provides a glossary of terms and foreign phrases often used in political discourse.

In a book as small as this with as large a scope, there is often concern about the selection criteria and comprehensiveness. This is not a problem with the current volume. There is a slight bias toward contemporary political figures and Anglo-American leaders, but there is still very good coverage of politicians from other parts of the world, including a respectable number of important leaders in Asia and Africa. The quotations are highly selective but useful. The glossary is even more discriminating and most useful in understanding foreign phrases that are not usually included in other political dictionaries. This volume is recommended for all libraries and the personal collections of historians, political scientists, and others interested in political history.—**Frank L. Wilson**

197. **The Columbia Dictionary of Political Biography**. New York, Columbia University Press, 1991. 335p. index. $40.00. D108.C65. 920.02. LC 90-24439. ISBN 0-231-07586-3.

This reference offers brief biographical sketches of over 2,000 current world political leaders who represent more than 165 countries. Heads of state, top ministers, party leaders, influential legislators, state and local officials, union leaders, prominent dissidents, and other important figures are listed. Each sketch is basic and concise and includes the individual's country of origin, birthplace and date, and career profile. However, the entries are somewhat uneven. Educational backgrounds are given for some individuals but not for others, and little or no family information is given in any of the entries.

The emphasis is on the prominence and influence individuals have had in their nation's political life. In many cases an attempt is made to hint at future prospects. For example, Senator Albert Gore is "well positioned for another White House bid in the 1990's"; Nelson Mandela has held up to "his punishing schedule . . . and his status remains undiminished"; and Yasser Arafat has been done "great damage" by the PLO's refusal to condemn the invasion of Kuwait. This volume also contains a brief glossary, a list that defines the abbreviations used, and an index of individuals by country.

Overall, this reference is more popular than scholarly. The writing style is typical of news magazines: precise, easily understood, and opinionated. However, the book provides quick access to basic information about political figures not readily available in other sources and as such is a worthwhile purchase for both public and undergraduate libraries. [R: Choice, Nov 91, p. 412; RBB, 15 Sept 91, p. 192; WLB, Dec 91, pp. 117-18]—**Tom Gilson**

198. Foner, Eric. **Freedom's Lawmakers: A Directory of Black Officeholders during Reconstruction**. rev. ed. Baton Rouge, Louisiana State University Press, 1996. 298p. illus. index. $19.95pa. ISBN 0-8071-2082-0.

Before the American Civil War, the Supreme Court decreed that no black person could be a citizen of the United States. In 1860, only five Northern states allowed blacks to vote on an equal basis with whites. Virtually unheard of was blacks holding office. However, after the war, large numbers of black Americans were elected to office only a few years after the destruction of slavery. *Freedom's Lawmakers*, a product of painstaking research, is a monument to the formerly forgotten black officials of the Reconstruction period and to their struggle for equality before the law of all citizens of the United States.

The introduction to this biographical directory provides an interesting and meaningful historical perspective and includes several tables noting the public offices held by blacks after Reconstruction, occupations, literacy status, and many other details. A list of general sources is followed by a section of several group portraits. The directory consists of 1,510 short biographical entries in alphabetic order, many accompanied by portraits. Complete entries (many entries are incomplete because of lack of documented information) contain dates of birth and death, state, free or slave status at birth, black or mulatto status, literacy status, occupation(s), a biographical sketch, service as an elected official, and a list of sources. Several new entries were added to this revised edition. The book concludes with several indexes: by state; by occupation; by office; by birth status (free or slave); and by topic, such as "Abolitionist Movement" or "Freedman's Savings Bank."

Freedom's Lawmakers is a substantial contribution to Reconstruction history. Its compilation of facts is useful in dispelling stereotypes critical of the qualifications of black officeholders, such as illiteracy (in fact, 83 percent were able to read and write). In addition, the volume brings to life the memory of many black officials whose lives were formerly shrouded in obscurity. The reference is recommended for historical research in public and university libraries. [The original edition of this book is reviewed in entry 169.] [R: RBB, 15 Feb 97, p. 1041]—**Penny Papangelis**

199.   **Great Leaders, Great Tyrants? Contemporary Views of World Leaders Who Made History**. Arnold Blumberg, ed. Westport, Conn., Greenwood Press, 1995. 354p. index. $49.95. ISBN 0-313-28751-1.

The distinction between leadership and tyranny has produced debates among historians and political scientists concerning numerous contemporary and historical figures. This compilation, edited by Towson State University history professor Arnold Blumberg, is an attempt to synthesize such debate over the political assets and tyrannical liabilities personified by numerous historical leaders.

Blumberg presents succinct portraits of 52 historical rulers. Personalities examined include Fidel Castro, King Charles I of England, Mikhail Gorbachev, Ho Chi Minh, Mao Tse-tung, Maximillien, Robespierre, and the Roman emperor Vespasian. Entries begin with contextual introductions and proceed with concise biographical portraits. The principal features of each entry include assessments of why the individual should be regarded as a great leader or great tyrant. Portraits conclude with a bibliography of selected readings.

This work can serve as a useful introduction to the lives and policies of numerous historically prominent rulers. Some will object to the exclusion of figures such as Kim Il Sung and Ayatollah Ruhollah Khomeini, as well as other historically significant leaders. Nevertheless, *Great Leaders, Great Tyrants?* should initiate study and analysis, and lead to consultation of more substantive works describing and analyzing the lives and policies of these individuals.—**Bert Chapman**

200.   Lentz, Harris M. III. **Heads of States and Governments: A Worldwide Encyclopedia of Over 2,300 Leaders, 1945 Through 1992**. Jefferson, N.C., McFarland, 1994. 912p. index. $95.00. D412.L46.920.02. LC 94-13310. ISBN 0-89950-926-6.

This important reference tool provides biographical information on 2,300 leaders of 174 countries between the end of World War II and the end of 1992. Included are minor states (e.g., Andorra), the former South African homelands, nations that ceased to exist (e.g., East Germany), and those that emerged (e.g., component parts of the Soviet Union). States formed after 1992 are outside the book's scope. Officeholders in power in 1992 but who have since left are not indicted.

Entries are arranged by country and then into sections for heads of state and of government. In a few cases where important leaders did not fill one of these roles (e.g., Manuel Noriega in Panama), there is a section for other leaders. Information given includes birth and death dates where ascertainable, full names, and a public career summary. Entries are relatively long. For well-known figures one may cover a double-columned page or more, and reasonably prominent people typically get more than a column. Only little-known figures have short paragraphs. People are listed in chronological order of office holding, with references to previous entries for people who held one or both offices and who are covered more than once. Two sentences at the start of each country section indicate the geographical location and time of the country's creation, where applicable. A table of contents lists the countries, and an extensive index provides further access by name, place, and subject.

This is a valuable political, historical, and biographical tool for the postwar period. Large- and medium-sized libraries should purchase it if budget limitations permit. Smaller institutions and specialized collections should also consider it if appropriate.—**Nigel Tappin**

201.   Morin, Isobel V. **Women Who Reformed Politics**. Minneapolis, Minn., Oliver Press, 1994. 160p. illus. index. $14.95. ISBN 1-881508-16-1.

Women Who Reformed Politics is a concise and affordable guide to the political lives of eight noteworthy, although not necessarily well-known, U.S. women. Profiled women are those who overcame various forms of discrimination, and whose efforts clearly demonstrate that despite some very real prohibitions, women have long been politically active in the United States. Despite the fact that women do not now nor have they historically spoken with a solitary voice, women as a group and individually have often been on the forefront of social reforms. The women outlined in this guide are women who, though themselves not public officeholders, did nevertheless champion efforts to end mob violence, abolish slavery, curb alcohol consumption, regulate and improve working conditions, and provide women with increased access to education and political rights. The women profiled in this compact and accessible guide are: Abby Kelley Foster, Frances Willard, Ida Wells-Barnett, Carrie Chapman Catt, Molly Dewson, Pauli Murray, Fannie Lou Hamer, and Gloria Steinem.

The issues and policies that these women advocated were and remain ones that affect the economic and social lives of all U.S. citizens. However, because not all citizens share equally in political and economic power, those who fight for reform invariably encounter harsh opposition and criticism. In the face of such opposition, reforms often require years of struggle along with the voices and efforts of many people. This insightful and useful guide places these interesting and courageous reformers within the context of U.S. history and the evolution of U.S. society.—**Timothy E. Sullivan**

202.   Opfell, Olga S. **Women Prime Ministers and Presidents**. Jefferson, N.C., McFarland, 1993. 237p. illus. index. $29.95. LC 92-56675. ISBN 0-89950-790-5.

This unusual volume includes articles on each of 21 women who have been prime ministers or presidents of their countries. It is not "a book of profiles," as stated on page ix, but rather a book of essays detailing both the subjects and the politics of their times. The Golda Meir and Margaret Thatcher essays are excellent. Photographs of the women and an index are included. The selected bibliography includes works on only 11 of the 21; there are no relevant books on the other 10. Some of the subjects held only the title and not the power; Domitien in the Central African Republic and Pintasilgo of Portugal held office for only six months. Eight were still in office at the time of publication (four of those only since 1990). Badly needed are maps identifying problem areas in each country and separate listings of the other main governmental and political officials and parties, especially for the longer articles. This volume will be especially useful for women's studies programs. [R: BR, Nov/Dec 93, p. 36; VOYA, Dec 93, p. 333]—**Karen Y. Stabler**

203.   **The Routledge Dictionary of Twentieth-Century Political Thinkers**. Robert Benewick and Philip Green, eds. New York, Routledge, Chapman & Hall, 1992. 244p. $59.95. ISBN 0-415-04371-9.

This volume examines political thought during the twentieth century through a biographical approach. Altogether, 159 short biographies appear, written by more than 85 contributors. Arranged in alphabetical order, the entries run from Max Adler, W. E. B. DuBois, and Josef Stalin through Clara Zetkin. The individuals selected fall into three overlapping groups: politicians with ideas of their own, persons who have influenced political movements, and political theorists. The editors made a special effort to include individuals whose contributions have related ethnicity, gender, or the environment to political action. Each biography comes with a sketch of the person, an analysis of the person's ideas, and a brief list of references. Among other things, readers learn that Milovan Djilas "epitomizes the rise and fall of Soviet/East European communism" and that Susan Griffin's work tries "to show how scientific paradigms that assume the need to conquer nature coincide . . . with patriarchal customs that depend on the oppression of women."

The biographical essays are generally well written, concise, and sophisticated, and the minibibliographies are helpful. The intelligent layperson will want to read this book, and even the expert will find valuable information here. Of course, some important political thinkers have been omitted. What about the ideas and actions of Mikhail Gorbachev or Lech Walesa? Why include Adolf A. Berle but not fellow New Dealer Rex Tugwell? Why Michael Harrington but not Rachel Carson, especially if the environment is a prime concern? Perhaps this extremely useful dictionary should have been longer. Recommended strongly for university, college, and public libraries. [R: Choice, Sept 93, p. 88; LAR, May 93, p. 294; RBB, 1 Nov 93, p. 569-70]—**Richard E. Holl**

204.   **Statesmen Who Changed the World: A Bio-Bibliographical Dictionary of Diplomacy**. Frank W. Thackeray and John E. Findling, eds. Westport, Conn., Greenwood Press, 1993. 669p. index. $85.00. D108.S73. 909.08'0922. LC 92-14616. ISBN 0-313-27380-4.

This volume contains 62 essays on Western statesmen, arranged in alphabetical order. The individuals selected include Dean Acheson, Konrad Adenauer, Adolf Hitler, Carlos R Tobar, Chales-Maurice de Talleyrand, and Woodrow Wilson. Each entry comes with a brief biographical sketch and an annotated bibliography. Five useful appendixes follow. An index and a list of contributors complete the work.

The biographies are concise, balanced, and generally well written. Contributors devoted more than the usual effort to summing up their subject's significance in a final paragraph. William Earl

Weeks, for example, tells us that, in many ways, John Quincy Adams's career paralleled the history of the American republic: "A life that had begun at the birth of independence had ended in the shadow of civil war." Prospective researchers will also find the annotated bibliographies extremely helpful, because they document both original and secondary sources and are fairly comprehensive. As is normal in a reference book of this type, selection is critically important. Editors Thackeray and Findling are to be congratulated for their choices, but reasonable users can disagree over particulars, as the editors note when they observe that other scholars might "arrive at a somewhat different lineup. . . ." That being the case, why James G. Blaine but not John Hay? Why Mikhail Gorbachev but not Ronald Reagan? And most startling, where is Venezuelan general and statesman Simon Bolivar? Surely he and a few more Latin Americans deserve inclusion. Nevertheless, the vast majority of editorial selections are sound, making *Statesmen Who Changed the World* a valuable acquisition. Highly recommended for high school, college, university, and public libraries. [R: Choice, Oct 93, p. 273; RBB, July 93, p. 2005]—**Richard E. Holl**

205.   **Who's Who in Democracy**. Seymour Martin Lipset, ed. Washington, D.C., Congressional Quarterly, 1997. 247p. illus. index. $85.00. ISBN 1-56802-121-6.

This slim volume contains a preface, an introduction, 156 short biographical sketches, and an index. Men and women from all over the globe appear in alphabetical order, from John Adams, John Locke, and Nelson Mandela through Roh Tae Woo, Elizabeth Cady Stanton, and Boris Yeltsin. Some of these people were (or are) political leaders, others revolutionaries, academics, or reformers. Each contributed in a meaningful way to the spread of democracy or to the common understanding of it. Mandela, to cite just one example, fought for decades against apartheid in South Africa and ultimately became the first president of that country to be elected by a vote of blacks and whites alike. The various composite portraits, taken together, illustrate the richness and complexity of democratic theory and reality.

Who's Who in Democracy succeeds at the most fundamental level. The reader comes away with a better grasp of democracy in all its varieties. The focus on the part that the individual has played in the democratic past is particularly helpful, counteracting the recent preoccupation with structural factors. Lipset shows knowledge that a true understanding of democracy must take into account not only broad, underlying forces such as economics and culture but also the decisions of outstanding leaders. Yet if this conceptual approach is sound, then why is the book not more comprehensive? For example, why include Frederick Douglass but not Harriet Tubman or William Lloyd Garrison? One may properly question the short length of such an important project as well as the selection of certain individuals over others. Still, the virtues of *Who's Who in Democracy* outweigh the faults. The reference is recommended for high school, college, university, and all public libraries.—**Richard E. Holl**

206.   **Who's Who in International Affairs**. London, Europa; distr., Detroit, Gale, 1990. 590p. index. $295.00. ISBN 0-946653-63-1. ISSN 0956-7984.

The dust jacket of this new biographical directory gives more information about the volume's coverage than does the very brief foreword. Approximately 7,000 leading personalities in both large and small international organizations are included, as are diplomats, politicians, and government officials who regularly participate in intergovernmental meetings. In addition, academics and writers who are influential in the field of international affairs are listed.

The entries vary greatly in length. Some include only name, position held, and address. Entries for more significant figures include information such as academic degrees and honors, career history, titles of major publications, and family. Useful indexes by organization and nationality close the volume. The user should be forewarned that organizations are listed in the index under the acronym (if well known) or under the full form of the name, but not under both (e.g., EFTA, not European Free Trade Association). The typeface is large enough that entries can be easily read, sometimes a problem with directories of this kind. The information was gathered through questionnaires; one is not told how entries were compiled if the questionnaires were not returned. No details on the process of selecting the names are given. (Involvement in international affairs on an unofficial basis must not meet the requirements, since Jesse Jackson is not included.)

A random check of some less well-known names shows that they are listed here and not in other biographical directories. However, information on major figures seems to be slightly more complete in *Europa's International Who's Who* (54th ed., 1990); the fact that both Willi Brandt and Lech Walesa received the Nobel Peace Prize is noted in *Who's Who* but not in *International Affairs*. There is overlap with other specialized directories, including individual country directories and subject-specific directories such as *Who's Who in European Politics* (K. G. Saur, 1990) and the *International Year Book and Statesmen's Who's Who* (Reed Information Services, 1990). More general directories, such as *Who's Who in the World* (10th ed., Marquis Who's Who, 1990), also compete for shelf space. Libraries must decide how much specialization their budgets can support. [R: Choice, June 91, p. 1627; RBB, 15 May 91, p. 1836]—**V. W. Hill**

207. **Who's Who of Women in World Politics**. Munich, New Providence, N.J., Bowker-Saur, 1991. 311p. index. $95.00. 323.34. ISBN 0-86291-627-5.

This reference work contains more than 1,500 alphabetized, single-paragraph biographies of women in positions of political influence in 115 countries. Biographees are heads of state, members of governments or national legislatures, leaders of parties or trade union federations, and regional leaders. The volume includes a map, a preface by U.S. political scientist Ruth Mandel, a five-language key to the biographies, a list of abbreviations, and a very useful set of statistical appendixes based on a compilation of data from the biographies. The volume concludes with an index of names by country.

There are many uses for this fascinating compendium of information about women's occupancy of political leadership roles. There are some spelling errors in the book, however. Shulamit Aloni, for example, is listed as Shumalit both in her biographical entry and in the index. Although problems such as this are likely when reference works are based on many languages, users must be sure, nevertheless, to double-check the information in this volume before considering it definitive. [R: Choice, June 92, pp. 1530-31; RBB, 1 May 92, p. 1637; RQ, Fall, pp. 123-25; WLB, Mar 92, pp. 122-23]—**Shulamit Reinharz**

AFRICA

208. Gastrow, Shelagh. **Who's Who in South African Politics, Number 5**. Johannesburg, South Africa, Ravan Press; distr., Athens, Ohio University Press, 1995. 319p. illus. $24.95pa. ISBN 0-86975-458-0.

The differences between this title and the 4th edition of *Who's Who in South African Politics* (Johannesburg, South Africa, Ravan Press; distr., New York, Harper & Row, 1985) (see ARBA 94, entry 762) reflect the political changes in South Africa under majority government. Many of the leaders listed in the previous edition who had been active in "civil" institutions, such as the anti-apartheid movement, voter education, or women's organizations, have now become active in party politics or have moved into the state bureaucracy. The result is that this edition focuses, as one would expect in a political who's who, almost exclusively (with the exception of about 5-10 entries) on those in positions of power in political parties or the government (e.g., ministers, members of parliament). There is also a slight increase in women represented in this edition (from 6 to 12).

Of the 103 people listed, 46 appeared in the previous edition (69 who were in the last edition were deleted) and 57 names are new. Each entry includes a portrait, the person's current title, a biographical sketch, and the sources used to compile the information. There is also a listing (current as of June 1995) of major national- and regional-level government officials and political party officials.

This is a useful, inexpensive reference source for any library that collects material on the current political situation in South Africa. Although many of the persons listed here (21 out of a sample of 30) are also found in *Who's Who of Southern Africa*, 1995/1996 ed. (Johannesburg, Jonathan Ball, 1996), the listings are more detailed in the work under review, making it a valuable complement to the larger, more general work or simply useful by itself. [R: RBB, 15 Apr 96, p. 1460]—**Paul H. Thomas and Terry Ann Mood**

209. Rake, Alan. **Who's Who in Africa: Leaders for the 1990s**. Metuchen, N.J., Scarecrow, 1992. 448p. index. $59.50. DT18.R35. 920.067. LC 92-8166. ISBN 0-8108-2557-0.

Biographical sketches of political and military leaders from 47 African nations and principalities are presented in this handbook-size volume. Sketches range in length from several paragraphs to fewer than 200 words. It is stated that the book treats the most important and the most populated countries in greater depth than it does smaller and island nations. No sketch, however, is longer than two-and-a-half pages, even those of Nelson Mandela and Desmond Tutu. In most instances the biographies resemble news reports from the Associated Press or other news agency. Rake is the managing editor of New African (based in London), so the journalistic flavor is understandable.

This edition is the first such work from Rake since 1973, when many African countries had just won independence from European colonial powers. Since that earlier volume, many new leaders have been swept in and out of power. The biographees represent countries and political principalities south of the Sahara Desert. Many of these countries are prominent in today's international headlines; thus, informed citizens need to become better acquainted with the personalities shaping events in those countries. This volume covers those who currently hold political leadership roles, those who were leaders in the recent past, and those who stand on the immediate horizon. Rake takes particular pride in having been able to build profiles of figures from some Marxist countries (e.g., Angola, Mozambique, Ethiopia, Somalia) where published information about such personalities is practically nonexistent. Cultural, artistic, religious, and business leaders are not included unless they are visibly concerned with politics. Apparently no women met either of these criteria as none are included in the book.

Who's Who in Africa is arranged alphabetically by country and then alphabetically by last names of persons within the country. Each country receives a brief profile with essential facts about population and type of government. Biographies are chronological in nature, highlighting the subject's major accomplishments so the reader can quickly scan the discussions. An italicized paragraph at the beginning of each biography summarizes the political or military activities that established the person as a central figure in his country. As a serious spectator of African affairs, Rake has interspersed editorial comments throughout the biographical data.

One of the real values of this volume is that when taken collectively, the biographies provide a sweeping view of the turmoil and political intrigue that have engulfed this part of the world over the last 35 to 40 years. At the same time, many of the personalities have contributed much to the social and economic progress of their countries. This is particularly true of people such as Kwesi Botchwey of Ghana, who is credited with turning the collapsing Ghanian economy around and who has seemingly helped to create a stable society in spite of many adverse conditions. Serious students of world history should gain valuable insight and knowledge about not only the political history of this part of Africa but also about the men and the circumstances that are directly and indirectly contributing to these conditions.

There is no map of Africa in this work, so the reader must turn to an up-to-date atlas to locate countries. Nor are there photographs of the personalities discussed. Otherwise, this is a well-done book. It should be a welcome addition to most reference collections in secondary school, college, university, and public libraries. [R: Choice, Oct 92, p. 280; LJ, 1 June 92, p. 116; RBB, 1 Sept 92, p. 92; WLB, Sept 92, p. 122]—**Melvin M. Bowie**

210. Wiseman, John A. **Political Leaders in Black Africa: A Biographical Dictionary of the Major Politicians since Independence**. Brookfield, Vt., Edward Elgar/Gower Publishing, 1991. 248p. index. $74.95. DT352.8.W57. 967.03'2'0922. LC 91-3753. ISBN 1-85278-047-9.

Prosopographical studies of current political leaders run the risk of becoming rapidly obsolete. The present work diminishes that risk by incorporating individuals from the 1950s to the present, thereby retaining a historical dimension. Every African country is represented in the 485 brief biographies, 3 of them (Cape Verde, Djibouti, and Sao Tome and Principe) only once and 2 of them (South Africa and Nigeria) a total of 105 times. This apparently disproportionate coverage simply reflects the relative population, importance, and intrinsic interest of the respective countries. Although the selection of entries is not likely to satisfy every potential user, this reviewer was able to find an entry for every political figure sought. However, information is not as current as it might be and seems to end about two years before the date of imprint.

In addition to the biographies, *Political Leaders in Black Africa* includes an alphabetical list of entries, which merely wastes eight pages by duplicating the listings of the biographies themselves; a much more useful list of some 225 acronyms; and an even more useful index of leaders arranged by country. A country-by-country political chronology, too sketchy to be helpful, completes the work. Unfortunately, all accents are missing from French names, and there is no bibliography, nor cross-references. As it is, libraries will need to decide whether the volume is worth the price, even though there is no comparable source for quick information on such a large array of post-independence political figures in Africa. [R: Choice, May 92, p. 1378]—**David Henige**

ASIA

211. **Who's Who in Asian and Australasian Politics**. Munich, New Providence, N.J., Bowker-Saur, 1991. 475p. $175.00. D535.2.W48. 920.05. LC 91-15868. ISBN 0-86291-593-7.

This fine tool combines a political who's who and a government directory for Asia, Australasia, and Oceania, excluding the Middle East and the former Soviet Union. The main body of the work is divided into two parts. The first is an alphabetical biography section with over 3,000 entries. Entry criteria limit subjects to current heads of state, members of governments or national legislatures, leaders of parties or trade-union federations, regional leaders, and a few other prominent figures. Information on each entrant is arranged under 24 categories and includes birth date; education; family; career; offices and honors; recreations; address; and telephone, telex, and fax numbers when possible. The cutoff for updates was late March 1991.

The second part is organized by country name. Under each state there is a governmental list with addresses of major ministries and then a list of the legislature, the main parties, and union federations, again with directory data. There is an index to the country's entries in the biography section. The directory part seems to contain fewer fax and telephone numbers than such sources as the *International Directory of Government* (see ARBA 91, entry 719) or the *Europa World Yearbook* (see ARBA 90, entry 91), but it is still a very useful feature in a basically biographical tool.

The prefatory material is well done and the physical production is good with high-contrast printing, although the print is a little small. This work is an important, well-executed source and deserves serious consideration as an acquisition where budgets allow. [R: Choice, Apr 92, p. 1214; LJ, 1 Feb 92, p. 82]—**Nigel Tappin**

CANADA

212. **Canadian Parliamentary Guide. Guide Parlementaire Canadien**. Toronto, Info Globe, 1909- . index. $59.95. ISSN 0315-6168.

Under its new publisher, the *Canadian Parliamentary Guide* retains its status as an essential resource for information about Canadian federal, provincial, and territorial legislators. The guide is fully bilingual and features comprehensive biographical information about the royal family; the Governor General; members of the Privy Council, Senate, House of Commons, and provincial and territorial legislatures; and the Supreme, Federal, and Tax Courts. Facts provided are dates of birth and marriage, education, highlights of public and private careers, religion, party affiliation, and address. The 1990 guide also includes federal election results from 1867 through 1988, a list of members of the parliamentary press gallery, and a name index.

The larger page format of this latest guide makes it slimmer and easier to handle and shelve. A new typeface and effective use of boldface type make it easier to scan entries for specific types of information. This work is a necessary purchase where there is interest in Canadian government or politics.—**Gari-Anne Patzwald**

213. **Canadian Parliamentary Handbook. Repertoire Parlementaire Canadien**. 1988 ed. John Bejermi, comp. Ottawa, Borealis Press, 1988. 512p. illus. index. $43.95. ISBN 0-88887-902-4. ISSN 0714-8143.

Revised in February 1988 and issued late the same year, this handbook is a victim of the November 1988 Canadian election. Its largest single component is composed of biographies of members of the House of Commons, but the election resulted in the addition of 13 new seats to the House and the redistribution of existing seats among the three major political parties (e.g., the Progressive Conservative party held 211 seats before the election and 169 after; some of these seats were newly obtained). Consequently, the handbook's value as a current reference work is severely limited. However, it is still useful for its biographies of Senate members (who are appointed and serve until age 75) and for its general information about Canadian government. The biographies vary but generally include party affiliation, date and place of birth, location and composition of constituency, home and office addresses, profession, interests, and a photograph. The general information includes a discussion of the role of the Governor General, a history and description of the Senate, a history of the House and descriptions of its components (e.g., appointed staff, committees), and a discussion of the electoral process. The text is bilingual.

This handbook is an excellent source of concise information about the Canadian government, particularly about members of Parliament and other government officials. One hopes a revision is forthcoming that will bring it up-to-date and make it the essential resource it could be.—**Gari-Anne Patzwald**

CHINA

214.   Bartke, Wolfgang. **Biographical Dictionary and Analysis of China's Party Leadership 1922-1988**. Munich and New Providence, N.J., K. G. Saur, 1990. 482p. illus. $200.00. ISBN 3-598-10876-1.

More than 10 years of painstaking research is clearly evident in this massive compilation, which is actually two reference works in one. The first two-thirds of the volume is a biographical directory that outlines the lives and careers of 1,094 Community Party cadres who held positions in the Second through the Thirteenth Central Committees. Each sketch contains the birth date (if known) or estimated birth date, place of birth, father's social status, party service, government posts held, offices in mass organizations, minority status (if applicable), education, and visits abroad. The amount of information varies. Some entries contain short textual statements that give further information. There are passport-sized, black-and-white photographs for 539 of the subjects; over 300 cadres have multiple photographs that show them at various ages. Most of the photographs are clear or at least of a quality adequate for identification.

The final third of the work consists of detailed historical and social analyses of the membership of the Politburo and the Central Committees in text and tabular form. Age, sex, education at home and abroad, military background, minority status, participation in the Long March, father's social status, and years of service are all included. One section discusses nepotism among the cadres. This unique compendium of information, most of which is not readily obtainable elsewhere in English, will be an essential acquisition for subject collections. [R: Choice, Oct 91, p. 253]
—**Shirley L. Hopkinson**

215.   **Biographical Dictionary of Chinese Communism, 1921-1965**. Donald W. Klein and Anne B. Clark, eds. Cambridge, Mass., Harvard University Press, 1971. 2v. $65.00. LC 69-12725. ISBN 0-674-07410-6.

Taking into consideration the political realities of these times, this biographical directory with a selected listing of 433 biographical sketches of prominent leaders of the People's Republic of China will probably be one of the most popular reference books. Biographical sketches vary in length, depending on the relative importance of a given individual and, as one can expect, the availability of information. Appended to the biographical sketches is a list of sources used, occasionally even interviews, but primarily secondary sources—books and articles in many languages including Russian. There is also a selected bibliography and a glossary-name index, which lists 1,750 persons found in the text. The many appendixes show that all information gathered in this work is current to 1965. Thus, the events of the Cultural Revolution are not included. Perhaps there will be a supplement to update some of the information.

This is truly a work of significant proportion—the first such undertaking in the West. In comparison to the monumental *Biographical Dictionary of Republican China*, this work is obviously not as detailed, and its biographical sketches often lack the wealth of documentation provided by its counterpart on Republican China. But again, at this point in our study of Chinese Communism, it might be impossible to prepare such a work, with so much information simply not available. In the meantime this is by far the best biographical source on this important subject.

Not as elaborate, Robert Elegant's *China's Red Masters: Political Biographies of the Chinese Communist Leaders* (New York, Twayne, 1951; repr., Westport, Conn., Greenwood Press, 1971) contains informal biographical information on twelve Chinese Communist leaders and includes a four-page bibliography. [R: Choice, Nov 71, p. 1162; LJ, 15 June 71, p. 2071]—**Bohdan S. Wynar**

216. **Who's Who in China: Current Leaders**. Compiled by the editorial board of Who's Who in China. Beijing, China, Foreign Languages Press; distr., San Francisco, Calif., China Books and Periodicals, 1989. 1126p. illus. index. $90.00. ISBN 0-8351-2352-9.

This full-length biographical dictionary of current political leaders and government officials in China is the first such authoritative publication from that country written in both Chinese and English. It is an important biographical tool for hard-to-find references in central and local governments, political parties, and the armed forces. Each entry contains detailed information on the political figure and has a personal photograph. For the Chinese text, traditional Chinese characters are used instead of the simplified characters. Useful features include lists of abbreviations and categories of individuals, a table of major organizations and their leading officials, and a Chinese name index. This initial edition is one of three principal biographical works published in China under government auspices. The other two covered prominent individuals in China before and after 1949. Together, they include over 30,000 biographies. Recommended for all major reference collections.—**Hwa-Wei Lee**

ESPIONAGE

217. Deacon, Richard. **Spyclopedia: The Complete Handbook of Espionage**. New York, Silver Arrow Books/William Morrow, 1988. 416p. illus. $20.95. UB250.D43. 327.1'2'0321. LC 88-31266. ISBN 0-688-08631-4.

This is a readable book on a highly interesting subject. However, the subtitle is an exaggerated claim. The two most absorbing parts are the short essays on the world's secret services and the glossary of what the author terms "spy jargon." The main sections of the book give short biographical sketches of spies divided chronologically from 510 B.C. to A.D. 1918, 1919 to 1945, and 1946 to 1987. The spies are arranged alphabetically within these three main sections. However, important subjects such as certain espionage "operations," codes and ciphers, fake defectors, lie detectors, and nuclear spies are interlaced within these sections. Inclusions possibly surprising to nonspecialists are Baden-Powell of the Boy Scouts, Daniel Defoe, W. Somerset Maugham, and the "Jesuit Connection" (which claims that at least 25 Jesuit priests are active KGB agents today).

Probably the prime shortcomings of this work are the limited citations for further reading at the end of the biographical sketches. For example, R. Harris Smith's *OSS* (University of California Press, 1972) is not cited for further reading in the summary of U.S. espionage; nor is Bob Woodward's *Veil* (Simon & Schuster, 1987). Further reading for J. Edgar Hoover cites only his book *Masters of Deceit* (Holt, Rinehart and Winston, 1951), ignoring Ovid Demaris's *The Director* (Harper's Magazine Press, 1975). There is no index and the table of contents is brief. More useful reference books on espionage would include *Spy/Counter Spy* (see ARBA 83, entry 496) and *The Encyclopedia of American Intelligence and Espionage* (see ARBA 89, entry 639). [R: BL, 1 Mar 89, p. 1074; LJ, 1 Mar 89, p. 66]—**Karen Y. Stabler**

218. Mahoney, M. H. **Women in Espionage: A Biographical Dictionary**. Santa Barbara, Calif., ABC-CLIO, 1993. 253p. illus. $65.00. JF1525.I6M25. 327.1'2'082. LC 93-36559. ISBN 0-87436-743-3.

This book makes fascinating reading. It contains short biographies of 150 female spies that cover all time periods and many nationalities. There is, however, an emphasis on twentieth-century European and American women. The subject index includes not just names but also topics. Mahoney, a former CIA agent, could be clearer about his sources and credentials. He writes that he "consulted experts" when selecting women to profile but made the final selections himself. He does not state his sources of information, although each entry has at least one reference. If these references are his sole source of data, it means that many of the profiles are based upon a single work.

This is a welcome addition to the literature on espionage, most of which focuses on men. *Who's Who in Espionage* (see ARBA 1986, entry 660) contains fewer than 20 women. While narrow in scope, this could be a handy book in any collection supporting research on famous women. [R: Choice, June 94, p. 1558; SLJ, May 94, p.140; WLB, Apr 94, p. 92]—**Cathy Seitz Whitaker**

219.   Minnick, Wendell L. **Spies and Provocateurs: A Worldwide Encyclopedia of Persons Conducting Espionage and Covert Action, 1946-1991**. Jefferson, N.C., McFarland, 1992. 310p. index. $45.00. JF1525.I6M56. 321.1 '2'0922. LC 92-50312. ISBN 0-89950-746-8.

This work contains biographical sketches of individuals who have engaged in or have influenced intelligence operations in the four-and-a-half decades since World War II. Entries are arranged alphabetically and provide succinct portraits of the key activities of these individuals of various nationalities. Figures listed include Rudolph Abel, Peter Deriabin, Klaus Fuchs, Oleg Gordievsky, William King Harvey, Vladimir Petrov, Edwin Wilson, and Greville Wynne. The book concludes with a selective glossary of intelligence terminology, an annual summary of selected intelligence developments from 1946 to 1991, and a bibliography of pertinent works.

Minnick has produced a fairly straightforward and relatively unpolemical work on the complexities and ambiguities that affect participants in this profession. Weaknesses include the uncritical acceptance of Alger Hiss's innocence and the description of James Angleton's concern over possible Soviet penetration of the CIA as "hysterical." The bibliographic use of undocumented or conspiratorial fantasies, such as Leslie Cockburn's *Out of Control* (Atlantic Monthly, 1987) and Bob Woodward's *Veil: The Secret Wars of the CIA* (Pocket Books, 1988), diminishes the generally substantive and authoritative approach of this work. Despite these flaws, *Spies and Provocateurs* is an adequate introduction to some of the prominent personalities involved in recent historical intelligence operations. [R: Choice, May 93, p. 1445; LJ, Jan 93, p. 102; RBB, 15 Feb 93, pp.1084-85]—**Bert Chapman**

EUROPE

220.   **Biographical Dictionary of Modern European Radicals and Socialists. Volume 1: 1780-1815**. David Nicholls and Peter Marsh, eds. New York, St. Martin's Press, 1988. 291p. index. $49.95. LC 87-36961. ISBN 0-312-01968-8.

Because Britons are included in a companion set, *Biographical Dictionary of Modern British Radicals* (see ARBA 80, entry 396), they are excluded from this volume, the first of seven projected volumes on European radicals and socialists active between 1780 and 1980. While volume 1 covers 1780 to 1815, subsequent volumes will treat the following periods: 1816-1848,1849-1870, 1871-1890, 1891-1914, 1915-1939, and 1940-1980. A supplementary volume will contain entries for those originally omitted.

Edited by two historians at Manchester Polytechnic, volume 1 includes signed articles on 187 men and women, 86 of them French, 43 German, 14 Italian, 8 Austrian, 7 Dutch, 6 Polish, 6 Swiss, 5 Hungarian, 5 Russian, 3 Belgian, and 1 each Czech, Greek, Norwegian, and Spanish. Written by 48 scholars worldwide, the biographies are arranged alphabetically from Abbamonti to Zschokke, and vary in length from less than one page to more than five pages.

Each article describes the radical's life, highlights major contributions, and concludes with a bibliography in narrative form. Although the entries are in English, most of the bibliographic works cited are in other languages. To assist the reader, cross-references are supplied in the articles. The index, unfortunately, is limited to names of biographees. Nevertheless, this useful, well-produced publication belongs in all research libraries serving students of European history and politics. [R: Choice, Nov 88, p. 455; WLB, Oct 88, p. 106]—**Leonard Grundt**

221.   Cook, Chris, and Geoff Pugh. **Sources in European Political History**. **Volumes 1-3**. New York, Facts on File, 1987-1991. 237p. bibliog. (Sources in European Political History). LC 82-7365. ISBN 0-8160-1016-1 (vol. 1); 0-3332-7775-9 (vol. 2); 0-3334-2369-0 (vol. 3).

Volume 1 of this series is titled *The European Left*; Volume 2, *Diplomacy and International Affairs;* Volume 3, *War and Resistance*. The series is similar in intent (and format) to Cook's *Sources in British Political History 1900-1951* (see ARBA 78, entry 477, and ARBA 80, entry 397). The entire series is a rich resource for anyone researching topics in European history. For example, volume 1 provides an "outline guide to the surviving personal papers of over 1000 individuals active in the socialist, labor, radical and revolutionary movements in Europe," focusing on the years between 1848 and 1945.

Cook notes several important limitations in this compilation. Personal papers of the British and Irish Left are excluded (these have already been documented in the series mentioned above), as have most collections found in Eastern Europe (which are not easily accessible to scholars). Yet, important archival collections have migrated to unexpected places (such as the Hoover Institution in California), and Cook identifies these locations.

The arrangement is a simple alphabetical listing of personal names. There are a brief identification of the individual and a location (with brief description) of the papers. Some individuals (Rosa Luxemburg, Leon Trotsky, Peter Kropotkin, Ernst Reuter, Georgii Plekhanov) receive at least half a page of text; most entries, however, are quite brief. A typical page in this compilation will include information on five or six people. Major figures (Marx, Engels) are treated very briefly, since ample biographical material is available elsewhere. Lenin is not even listed, probably because Cook identifies Trotsky as "the only prominent Bolshevik to have left extensive and uncensored private papers."

This resource will be a valuable addition to reference collections in major research libraries, though it is also recommended (and affordable) for smaller academic collections.—**Thomas A. Karel and Terry Ann Mood**

222.   **Political Leaders of Contemporary Western Europe: A Biographical Dictionary**. David Wilsford, ed. Westport, Conn., Greenwood Press, 1995. 514p. index. $115.00. ISBN 0-313-28623-X.

This volume contains 71 biographical essays on politicians in postwar Europe. Subjects come from 14 of the 15 European Union countries and Norway. Contributors are academics with affiliations in the United States and Europe. The articles are arranged alphabetically from Konrad Adenauer through Harold Wilson, with the leaders also listed by country. Darkly influential figures, such as Jean-Marie Le Pen, are included. Papers average just under seven pages. One anomaly is the short (three-page) entry for the colorful Bavarian Franz-Josef Strauss. Brief bibliographies are appended. Many entries sampled seem detailed and make fascinating reading. Francois Mitterrand's biography, for example, accurately matches this reviewer's memories of his career as reflected in the "Le Monde" section of the Manchester *Guardian Weekly* from 1977 to the present. There is also an introductory essay on influential theories of leadership by the editor. The leaders are also listed by country.

The selection of subjects is a difficult and thankless task. Thus, Winston Churchill was excluded as a politician whose main impact was prior to 1945, while Neil Kinnock was included among the few British politicians, presumably because he started the reform of the Labour Party in order to restore it as a credible party of government. Why was John XXIII discussed, but not John Paul II? On the whole, however, the selection is good.

There is an index, but it does not seem to be complete—odd in this age of computer-assisted indexing. For example, the entry for Helmut Kohl lists his profile, with references to those on Hans-Dietrich Genscher, Ruud Lubbers, and Helmut Schmidt, but not those on Mitterand or Strauss. This work should be purchased by research libraries with the relevant client interests and other large libraries if budgets permit.—**Nigel Tappin**

223.   **Who's Who in European Politics**. 2d ed. New Providence, N.J., K. G. Saur/Reed Reference Publishing, 1993. 1016p. index. $265.00. ISBN 1-8573-9021-0.

Three years after the 1st edition was published (see ARBA 92, entry 719), a substantially revised and expanded edition of this work has appeared. This edition provides short biographical sketches on more than 8,000 politicians and "political personalities" in the European nations, approximately 2,000 more entries than were contained in the 1st edition. The entries follow a typical who's-who format, and some, for major political figures such as Boris Yeltsin, are surprisingly brief. The coverage is impressive, however. In addition to heads of state and leaders of political parties, other entries are for members of parliaments or legislative bodies, bureaucratic departments, and other political organizations. Most former heads of state, such as Margaret Thatcher or Vaclav Havel, are no longer included in the directory unless they currently hold another political position.

The second, and shorter, part of this volume is a political directory, arranged by country. This section now includes a separate listing for all of the former Soviet republics, as well as the Czech Republic, the Slovak Republic, and the various portions of Yugoslavia. A listing for the European Community is also found here. The directory lists the head of state, the governmental departments, the legislature, main political parties, trade unions, and the central bank. A biographical index lists the names of individuals who are associated with that country, the person's position, and a page number. Additional features of the volume include a glossary of terms and institutions, a detailed key to the biographical entry, and a list of abbreviations. This resource is highly recommended for most academic libraries and is an excellent companion to such standard political sources as the *Europa World Year Book* (Gale, 1992).—**Thomas A. Karel**

FRANCE

224.   **Biographical Dictionary of French Political Leaders since 1870**. David S. Bell, Douglas Johnson, and Peter Morris, eds. New York, Simon & Schuster, 1990. 463p. index. $85.00. DC342.B56. 944.08'092'2. LC 90-9662. ISBN 0-13-084690-2.

This biographical dictionary is intended to provide concise information on French political leaders, from 1870 to the present, for researchers and general readers who do not read French. Over 400 individuals are covered in signed articles ranging from 1 to 12 columns of text. The contributors are primarily British scholars. As well as government and party officials, leaders of social movements and trade unions are included, as are political thinkers (e.g., Jean-Paul Sartre) and writers who were heavily involved in politics (e.g., Emile Zola). The length of an article reflects the importance of the figure being discussed. Each is followed by a brief but useful bibliography of books by and about the subject, with an indication of why the works cited are valuable. The articles are well written and interesting. Four appendixes list the presidents and prime ministers for the time period covered, as well as post-World War II union leaders and the leaders of political parties during the Fifth Republic. A name and subject index closes the volume.

The Historical Dictionary of the Third French Republic, 1870-1940, edited by Patrick H. Hutton (see ARBA 87, entry 513), also covers this earlier period well, but the entries are less comprehensive. There is no comparable work on the Fifth Republic—entries include, for example, Daniel Cohn-Bendit, Jack Lang, Alain Krivine, Jean-Marie LePen, and many others. The introduction is too brief; there is no elaboration of the criteria for inclusion, which would have been helpful in explaining why some political thinkers were included and others were omitted. In addition, a promised glossary of terms does not appear. Nevertheless, there is nothing quite like this work, which will be essential for libraries with an interest in contemporary French history. [R: LJ, Aug 90, p. 100; RBB, 15 Sept 90, p. 188]—**V. W. Hill**

GERMANY

225.   Stachura, Peter D. **Political Leaders in Weimar Germany: A Biographical Study**. New York, Simon & Schuster Academic Reference Division, 1993. 230p. index. $45.00. DD244.S64. 920.043. LC 92-30716. ISBN 0-13-020330-0.

Weimar Germany represents the transitional era in German history between the fall of the Wilhelmine monarchy and the rise of the Third Reich. A complicated period in German historical development, this era produced many figures who assumed or would eventually obtain prominence in Germany's modern political development. Many of these figures are profiled in *Political Leaders in Weimar Germany*.

The volume opens with an alphabetical list of individuals profiled and an introductory explanation. The principal portion of this volume consists of biographical portraits of politically prominent figures of the Weimar era and those whose rise began during this period. Individuals profiled here include personalities as diverse as Konrad Adenauer, Walther Ulbricht, Walter Rathenau, Rosa Luxemburg, Gustav Stresemann, Ernst Roehm, and others who represent the diverse ideological perspectives characteristic of the Weimarian polity. Biographical entries include sources for more substantive portrayals of these individuals and their careers. Subsequent sections include a chronology of key events in Weimar Germany, abbreviations, a glossary of important organizations and concepts, and a selective bibliography of works on Weimar Germany.

Stachura has produced a concise and substantive work that should help stimulate study on the personalities and events of this crucial period in twentieth-century German and world history. Especially recommended for academic libraries. [R: Choice, May 93, p. 1450; RBB, 1 May 93, pp. 1630-32; WLB, Apr 93, pp. 122-24]—**Bert Chapman**

GREAT BRITAIN AND THE COMMONWEALTH

226.   Englefield, Dermot, Janet Seaton, and Isobel White. **Facts about the British Prime Ministers: A Compilation of Biographical and Historical Information**. New York, H. W. Wilson, 1995. 439p. illus. index. $55.00. ISBN 0-8242-0863-3.

This is a new addition to H. W. Wilson's Facts About . . . series, and it closely resembles *Facts about the Presidents* (6th ed.; see ARBA 94, entry 499) in format and scope. However, while there are numerous reference books on U.S. presidents, there are few on British prime ministers, making this an important new work. All 50 prime ministers, from Sir Robert Walpole in 1721 to the present John Major, are profiled. The first and main section of the book consists of chronological entries, each about seven pages in small typeface. Following a brief overview of the individual's career is a section on family members, Parliamentary elections and experience, governments formed, and a list of important dates in the person's life. The sketches end with background information on the PMs, including appearance; education; hobbies; memorable quotes; locations of portraits, statues, and personal papers; and a short bibliography.

In the second part of the book, information on the prime ministers is rearranged into 80 tables that compare personal and professional characteristics. Here is a playground for trivia fans. Where else can one find out easily that "since 1730, a Prime Minister has been born on average every 5 years and 69 days" (p. 371)? Other features of the book are an introduction to the role of the prime minister in the twentieth century, a discussion of the official residences, a glossary, and a subject index.

The authors are all affiliated with the Library of the House of Commons, and they share a librarian's love of detail. They have done an excellent job presenting their facts in an attractive, logically organized format, but with enough anecdotes to make the work entertaining. *Facts about the British Prime Ministers* is recommended for high school, public, and academic libraries that field questions on recent British history.—**Hope Yelich**

227.   Kirk-Greene, A. H. M. **A Biographical Dictionary of the British Colonial Service 1939-1966**. Munich, New Providence, N.J., Hans Zell/K. G. Saur, 1991. 403p. $165.00. DA16.8. K57. 325'. 341'0922. LC 90-26027. ISBN 0-905450-96-5.

This specialized work covers the gradual decline of the British Colonial Service up to its official closing in 1966. Nearly 15,000 individuals are included from the more than 40 colonial territories that had been under British rule (mostly in Africa, Southeast Asia, the Pacific, and the Caribbean). The various Professional Services and Administrative Services personnel are listed, as well as senior Colonial Office officials.

The biographical information in this volume is taken directly from the official Colonial Office Lists, which were compiled annually. Hence, this dictionary "represents a cumulative and composite reproduction" of the biographical entries from 1939 through 1966. Each entry contains the following information: birth date (but not date of death), decorations or professional qualifications, education, dates of military service, date of first colonial service post, subsequent transfers and promotions, a brief reference to any important special work, and major publications. This data has not been updated in any way, so that later accomplishments by these officials are not noted in this volume.

Kirk-Greene's lengthy introduction gives useful background on the Colonial Service and its recruitment practices, a discussion of the Colonial Office Lists, and a detailed explanation of the biographical entry information. Truly a one-of-a-kind resource, this work will be an important acquisition for libraries with strong British and African history collections. [R: Choice, Dec 91, p. 575]—**Thomas A. Karel**

228.   Powell, John. **Art, Truth, and High Politics: A Bibliographic Study of the Official Lives of Queen Victoria's Ministers in Cabinet, 1843-1969**. Pasadena, Calif., Salem Press and Lanham, Md., Scarecrow, 1996. 221p. index. (Magill Bibliographies). $36.00. ISBN 0-8108-3139-2.

The *Official Lives* of British Cabinet members during the reign of Queen Victoria were a series of 70 biographies written over a period of more than 120 years by many different authors. Although much maligned for their dry style and lack of critical objectivity, they are nevertheless an essential source of information on nineteenth-century politics. They contain documents, illustrations, family pedigrees, and background details, all vital to gaining an understanding of each cabinet minister. Many of the diaries and letters consulted in compiling them are no longer extant.

A long introductory essay critically examines the scholarly value of the *Official Lives*. The majority of this work is a series of studies on the biography of each cabinet member, arranged alphabetically by the name of the biographee. They include bibliographic data and a biographical sketch of the author. All editions and the principal primary materials incorporated into each work are listed. To aid in judging the reliability of each biography, archival sources and selected published works on both the biographee and the biographer (if available) are also given. Illustrations, political cartoons, and any other materials, such as maps or lists, included in the biography are listed. Various appendixes with statistics about the publication of the *Official Lives* and a subject index complete the bibliography.

Powell's work is an impressive accomplishment. With great thoroughness, he demystifies the role of the *Official Lives* as a significant source of information about Victorian polities and society. This resource belongs in all graduate-level collections on British history.—**Christine E. King**

IDEOLOGIES

229.   **Biographical Dictionary of Marxism**. Robert A. Gorman, ed. Westport, Conn., Greenwood Press, 1986. 388p. index. $55.00. LC 84-29016. ISBN 0-313-24851-6.

Virtually identical in format to its companion volume, *Biographical Dictionary of Neo-Marxism* (see entry 230), this title highlights the lives and ideas of mainstream Marxist thinkers and activists (i.e., those who adhere[d] to the principles of historical materialism).

As Marxists represent a more plentiful species than the Neo-Marxist variant, selection of the more than 200 individuals represented in this work has been more problematic. Those included do seem appropriate, however, and range from Lenin, Castro, Tito, and Maoto to a wide cross-section of important, lesser-known luminaries (past and present) from both industrialized and developing nations. Many of the contributors to this volume provided essays for the companion volume, too. Length of entry frequently does not correspond to importance of subject—Rudolf Hilferding, for example, receives greater coverage than Joseph Stalin.

The biographical entries are alphabetically arranged and supported by a comprehensive index and a listing of entrants by nationality. Brief bibliographic statements are appended to each entry.

This work will probably appeal to a wider audience than the *Biographical Dictionary of Neo-Marxism*, though it could be argued that information on the traditional Marxists is generally easier to obtain. Regardless, both volumes represent useful, well-conceived reference sources. [R: Choice, July/Aug 86, p. 1651; LJ, 1 Feb 86, p. 73; RBB, 1 June 86, p. 1444]—**Mark R. Yerburgh**

230.   **Biographical Dictionary of Neo-Marxism**. Robert A. Gorman, ed. Westport, Conn., Greenwood Press, 1985. 463p. index. $55.00. LC 84-27968. ISBN 0-313-23513-9.

With its companion volume, *Biographical Dictionary of Marxism* (see entry 229), this well-produced though somewhat specialized reference source offers brief overviews of the lives and ideas of those past and present who have become the leading intellectual heirs of Karl Marx.

Neo-Marxists are not easy to categorize. Generally, they are revisionists who have rejected historical materialism but who still adhere to the Marxist philosophical tradition. In a lengthy introductory essay, the editor presents the major schools of Neo-Marxist thought. It is very difficult reading.

The biographical entries number over 200 and average about 2 pages each. Some of the more familiar subjects include Adorno, Bernstein, Fanon, Medvedev, Djilas, Lukacs, DuBois, Debs, and Foucault. Coverage is global and knows no chronological constraints. The seventy-one contributors have adhered to high editorial standards; the essays are well written and informative. Several topical entries—considered vital for an understanding of the evolution of Neo-Marxism—have been included as well: for example, the "Prague Spring," "Praxis," "Liberation Theology," and "Structural Marxism."

Appended to each entry is a list of writing by and about these 200 odd (and some of them are rather odd) individuals. The entries are arranged alphabetically. There are also a very comprehensive index and a listing of entrants by nationality.

Within its rather narrow field of vision, the *Biographical Dictionary of Neo-Marxism* does what it sets out to do and does so in a competent, professional manner. [R: Choice, May 86, p. 1368; RBB, 1 June 86, p. 1444]—**Mark R. Yerburgh**

231.   Lazitch, Branko, with Milorad M. Drachkovitch. **Biographical Dictionary of the Comintern**. new, rev. ed. Stanford, Calif., Hoover Institution Press, 1986. 532p. $44.95. LC 86-7466. ISBN 0-8179-8401-1.

Better known as the Comintern, the Communist International served as a vehicle to promote international solidarity and worldwide revolution during the period 1919 to 1943. It was founded on militant Bolshevik principles and, though frequently choreographed by Moscow, coordinated communist activities regardless of geographical setting. *Biographical Dictionary of the Comintern* will be a useful reference work for scholars wishing to penetrate its shadowy, turbulent milieu.

Though many libraries may not feel compelled to purchase this volume if they already possess its somewhat less comprehensive 1973 predecessor, those with specialized needs undoubtedly will. It includes 753 biographies. Arranged alphabetically, they average two-thirds of a page in length. Useful auxiliary features include an introduction, a list of pseudonyms, and a guide to abbreviations (for which communists seem to have a special predilection).

The biographical entries, though professional and informative, are exceedingly colorless and unremittingly non-evaluative. The utilization of other contributors might have helped in this regard. Biographical source listings at the end of each entry would have been useful, too. Many potential users might also have profited from a brief essay on the history of the Comintern or, at the very least, a clear statement of the organization's scope and principles.

Despite these limitations, *Biographical Dictionary of the Comintern* is a useful, scholarly work. While its appeal is narrow, those it serves will be well served. It is a unique reference title—the product of years of painstaking research. [R: Choice, June 87, pp. 1534-35]—**Mark R. Yerburgh**

INTERNATIONAL ORGANIZATIONS

232.   **Biographical Dictionary of Internationalists**. Warren F. Kuehl, ed. Westport, Conn., Greenwood Press, 1983. 934p. index. $75.00. LC 82-15416. ISBN 0-313-22129-4.

This is a valuable new addition to the shelf of biographical reference works. Its 680 sketches deal with the men and women who have stood out in history as advocates of world organization. The selections range from internationally famous activists to little-known visionaries.

The first subjects to be treated are individuals who were alive after 1800. For the first century or so, the predominance of entries from the United States and Great Britain reflects the flourishing of internationalist thought in democracies. After 1914, continental Europe, Asia, and Latin America produced an increased number of such leaders. Unfortunately many persons active since 1945 have been omitted by the decision to include only the deceased. The postwar period, however, does provide an imposing list: for example, Ralph Bunche, Jean Monnett, Hans Morgenthau, Paul Henri Spaak, U Thant, and Arnold Toynbee.

Each entry opens with basic information on birth, death, education, and career. Many traditional details are omitted in favor of concentration on the subject's work, ideas, or activity as an internationalist. The bibliography also emphasizes this career bent.

The back matter is rich in reference material. A chronology traces trends and developments from the 1815 Congress of Vienna to the 1979 first general elections to the European Parliament. Appendixes provide the nation of birth for each subject, the primary career of each, and the type of approach (for example, African unity, health, food, interdependence). There is a good index and a helpful identification of contributors, most of whom are academics, including editor Warren Kuehl. The more than 250 authors include such figures as Fred Israel, Richard Leopold, Forrest Pogue, and David Trask. The one blemish on the volume is the lack of illustrations. [R: Choice, May 84, p. 1271]—**David Eggenberger**

233. **Who's Who in International Organizations: A Biographical Encyclopedia of More Than 12,000 Leading Personalities**. Jon C. Jenkins, with Cecile Vanden Bloock, eds. Munich and New Providence, N.J., K. G. Saur, 1992. 3v. index. $400.00/set. ISBN 3-598-10908-3.

More than 12,000 entries for eminent individuals appear in this set prepared by the Union of International Associations. These people are many of the principals involved in the management and operation of the institutions and networks listed in the association's *Yearbook of International Organizations* (K. G. Saur, 1991). Many of them are not well known enough to appear in most of the standard international biographical reference works.

To develop this publication, questionnaires were sent to 10,000 major international organizations. The editors had difficulties with incomplete and illegible returns, and in some cases did not receive any. This 1st edition, therefore, does not claim to be complete or representative of all important organizations that could have been included. Complete entries for individuals consist of full name and title, nationality, date and place of birth, spouse's name, number of children, religion, languages spoken, education, current positions in international organizations, main field of work, career, publications, memberships, honors, and residential and mailing addresses. The minimum acceptable entry provides name, organization, position, and address.

The first two volumes contain the alphabetical entries for the individuals. Volume 3 indexes their names by country, profession, and organization. Given the price of this set, it would seem to be most appropriate in collections with a particular focus on international organizations for which the standard international biographical sources are not sufficient.—**Henry E. York**

234. **Who's Who in the Peace Corps**. 1993 ed. Cheryl Klein Lacoff, ed. Greenwich, Conn., Reference Press International, 1993. 724p. index. $95.00; $75.00pa. ISBN 1-879583-03-8; 1-879583-02-Xpa. ISSN 1065-8459.

This directory provides information on about 50,000 of the 120,000 people who have served in the Peace Corps since its establishment in 1961. It is divided into six sections. The first is an alphabetical list of current and returned Peace Corps volunteers (RPCVs) with biographical data. The most complete entries list such data as country of service, birth and marriage dates, names of spouse and children, education, memberships, and business and residence addresses. However, most entries contain only a few pieces of information, usually country of service and current address. Other sections list deceased volunteers and Peace Corps staff; organizations serving RPCVs; RPCVs by state, city, or country of residence; and RPCVs by country of service.

The stated purposes of the directory are to help RPCVs locate each other and to familiarize them with organizations that serve RPCVs. The book might also be useful to educators, journalists, and social service workers seeking people with knowledge of Third World countries and their cultures and languages. Some larger libraries and businesses or agencies involved in the Third World may want to acquire it. [R: Choice, July/Aug 93, p. 1756; RBB, June 93, p. 1906; WLB, May 93, p. 122]—**Gari-Anne Patzwald**

235. **Who's Who in the United Nations and Related Agencies**. 2d ed. Stanley R. Greenfield, ed. Detroit, Omnigraphics, 1992. 850p. index. $185.00. JX1977.W467. 341.23'092'2. LC 92-28304. ISBN 1-55888-762-8.

This directory provides brief biographical information, most of which cannot be found in other sources. The criteria for inclusion have changed slightly since the 1975 edition (see ARBA 76, entry 471). Retired officials now seem to be excluded. Individuals who served the United Nations (UN) in 1991 are covered, including high-level officials of the Secretariat, agencies, and UN missions of specific countries, as well as a few leaders of related organizations. Also included are the book's editor and most of the members of its advisory panel, some of whom do not meet other criteria for inclusion. Two appendixes describe the 1992 reorganization of the UN Secretariat and list new senior officials.

In addition to biographical entries, this work provides a number of listings (e.g., presidents of the General Assembly; secretaries-general of the UN; permanent missions to the UN in New York, Geneva, and Vienna; UN depository libraries). The most extensive and useful listings are those for the UN system of organizations and specialized agencies and related organizations, which provide directory type information and list individuals in specific positions. The 1st edition had a list of UN offices by country all over the world, including liaisons of specialized agencies at UN headquarters in New York and in other countries. It is unfortunate that this hard-to-find information has been omitted from the new edition.

Additional access to the alphabetically arranged biographical entries is provided through indexes by organization (new to this edition) and by nationality. It would be helpful if the indexes indicated an individual's specific position, because the names in the index by organization do not necessarily match the names in the lists of organizations and specialized agencies, and also because the index by nationality includes at least one nationality with more than 300 names.—**Carol Wheeler**

LATIN AMERICA

236. Adams, Jerome R. **Liberators and Patriots of Latin America: Biographies of 23 Leaders**. . . . Jefferson, N.C., McFarland, 1991. 289p. illus. index. $25.95. F1407.A33. 980'.00992. LC 91-52511. ISBN 0-89950-602-X.

"There is an embarrassing difference," says Adams, "between how much Latin Americans know about the United States and how little curiosity flows in the other direction." These biographical essays help to lift the curtain of ignorance that has long rendered Latin American leaders as little more than silhouettes and caricatures. Few North Americans possess more than mere surface knowledge of such individuals as Simon Bolivar, the "Liberator of the North"; Benito Juarez, Mexico's "Builder of Democracy"; or Pancho Villa, who followed as Mexico's "Political Warrior." Three key figures in the development of modern Central America—Augusto Sandino of Nicaragua (the inspiration behind the Sandinistas), Jose (Pepe) Figueres of Costa Rica, and Bishop Romero of El Salvador (assassinated in his own church in 1980)—are mere shadows to many North American observers.

Other "liberators and patriots" profiled in this book include Pierre Francois Dominique L'Ouverture of Haiti; Manuela Saenz of Ecuador; Bernardo O'Higgins of Chile; and Dolores Jimenez y Muro, Juana Belen Gutierrez de Mendoza, and Hermila Galindo de Topete, three women of the Mexican revolution. The fact that Adams has chosen to include a number of women is evidence of the balance that he tries (with success) to achieve.

The essays are devoid both of partisan political rhetoric and scholastic pedantry; they should make compelling reading for high school and college students, as well as the general public. The entries on Figueres and Fidel Castro disappoint in that they do not cover recent events—in Castro's case, little after the Revolution of 1959 is provided. In any case, this book, long overdue and reasonably priced, deserves a place in all libraries that intend to give Latin America its due on their shelves. [R: LJ, 15 Sept 91, p. 68]—**Edwin S. Gleaves**

237.　Alexander, Robert J. **Biographical Dictionary of Latin American and Caribbean Political Leaders**. Westport, Conn., Greenwood Press, 1988. 509p. index. $75.00. LC 87-17803. ISBN 0-313-24353-0.

These 460 biographical sketches by 15 contributors were intended to provide basic data on the family backgrounds, education, and especially the political significance of persons selected as the "most important political figures" in the nineteenth and twentieth centuries in Latin America and the Caribbean (p. ix). Living and dead persons are profiled. Entries are of variable length; most are less than a page but a few exceed two pages. All entries include as many as five bibliographic items for those wanting further information. A chronology of significant political events 1804-1985, a list of biographees by country, an analytical index, and short biographies of the contributors complete the presentation. Most of the contributors are political scientists.

Criteria for selection of biographees are not stated except to say that twentieth-century figures were favored. Review of the country list confirms this bias and shows that at least two biographees were selected for each nation-state or territory. Country coverage does not have any apparent correlation to size or traditional notions of historical importance. Thus, Chile has thirty-eight entries; Barbados has nine, and Brazil, Costa Rica, Cuba, and Mexico have twenty-three each. Presidents and leaders of twentieth-century leftist parties and unions dominate the lists.

This work will be of value in any library whose patrons have an interest in Latin America and the Caribbean, especially in recent decades. [R: Choice, Dec 88, p. 622; RBB, 1 Nov 88, p. 460]—**Paul E. Hoffman**

238.　Camp, Roderic Ai. **Mexican Political Biographies, 1935-1993**. 3d ed. Austin, University of Texas Press, 1995. 985p. $75.00; $24.95pa. ISBN 0-292-71174-3; 0-292-71181-6pa.

This 3d edition provides nearly 2,000 brief biographical sketches of Mexican political figures prominent since 1935. The 1st edition, printed in 1976, contained approximately 900 entries, and the 2d edition (1982) provided 1,350 entries. Significant updates have been made to many of the original entries. The author used more than 200 sources to identify and update this information. The criteria for inclusion combined using Frank Brandenberg's top six levels of political prestige outlined in *Making of Modern Mexico* (1964) and cross-referencing of data from at least two sources.

This book is a continuation of the author's 1991 book entitled *Mexican Political Biographies 1884-1934*. Both books, organized in the same manner, contain such information as birth date; birthplace; education; elective and party positions; appointive governmental and private positions; interest group activities; parents, spouses, and friends; military experience; and additional sources of information. Ten helpful appendixes provide a chronological list of Supreme Court justices; senators; federal deputies; directors of federal departments, agencies, and banks; major ambassadorial posts; governors; rectors of the national universities; national executive committees of the Partido Nacional Revolucionario (PNR), the Partido de la Revolucion Mexicana (PRM), and the Partido Revolucionario Institucional (PRI); presidents of major parties; and secretaries-general of large labor organizations. This excellent, up-to-date, ready-reference book includes reliable biographical information that is extremely difficult to locate, and is highly recommended for large public and academic libraries.—**Karen Y. Stabler**

239.　**Who Is Who [in] Government, Politics, Banking and Industry: In Latin America**. 4th ed. Bettina Corke, ed. New York, Norman Ross Publishing, 1997. 2v. index. $149.00. ISBN 0-88354-225-0.

This biographical dictionary gives information in English about more than 2,400 contemporary leaders, from South America (vol. 1), Central America, and the Caribbean (vol. 2), including birth date, present and past positions, education, publications, and address and telephone number when available. Bankers, business leaders, economists, government officials, and journalists are included. Data are arranged alphabetically by country and then by last name. A general index provides an alphabetical listing of all biographees in one list. Each volume may be purchased separately.—**Ann Hartness and Terry Ann Mood**

MIDDLE EAST AND NORTH AFRICA

240. **Political Leaders of the Contemporary Middle East and North Africa: A Biographical Dictionary**. Bernard Reich, ed. Westport, Conn., Greenwood Press, 1990. 557p. index. $79.95. DS61.5.P65. 920'.056. LC 89-7498. ISBN 0-313-26213-6.

Included here are biographical profiles of 70 political leaders "who have been instrumental in the evolution of political life in their own states or other political systems in the Middle East, North Africa and beyond" (preface). All were actively involved in political affairs in their part of the world after World War II, and many still retain power. The 69 men and 1 woman (Golda Meir) were variously rulers, politicians, or organizers of resistance or liberation movements, and there is at least one person representing each country. Basic "who's who" information is provided for each person, but the essays also provide a serious, probing, detailed analysis of the contributions and achievements of each. A short bibliography is appended to each entry and provides both additional references and a list of works by the profiled individual.

A chronology of events is given, stretching from 1869 when Imam Yahya of Yemen was born, through 1989 and the death of the Ayatollah Khomeini. Greater coverage is accorded to the years from 1945, beginning with the formation of the Arab League. A general bibliography of materials focusing more broadly on the political elite of the Middle East and North Africa is supplied for the edification of the general reader.

Each essay is written by an acknowledged specialist in the history of the country or movement whose leader is profiled. All are well researched and well written, making the entire work a pleasure to read. [R: Choice, July/Aug 90, p. 1810; LJ, 15 Feb 90, p. 180; RBB, 15 May 90, p. 1843]—**Margaret Anderson**

PEACE MOVEMENT

241. Abrams, Irwin. **The Nobel Peace Prize and the Laureates: An Illustrated Biographical History, 1901-1987**. Boston, G. K. Hall, 1988. 269p. illus. index. $39.95. LC 88-16313. ISBN 0-8161-8609-X.

One cannot help wondering if this book, focusing on peace as it does, is not yet one more sign of the times. Whatever the motivation, Irwin Abrams has provided readers with a good beginning for exploring the peace prize awardees.

Perhaps more important than the actual entries are the first three chapters. Here Abrams discusses Alfred Nobel, the Norwegian Nobel Committee, and the transformation of the prize over the years from a strict interpretation of Nobel's wishes, to a more liberal interpretation. Written in a lively style, the reader is taken behind the scenes as a witness to the establishment of the prize, what is done with the money, how it has helped establish the peace movement, and more.

The individual biographies of awardees are less satisfying to this reviewer. For example, the entry for the 1973 prize jointly awarded to Henry Kissinger and Le Duc Tho is written with gloves on. The award was considered controversial not only in the United States, but also in Norway. The prize winner for 1987, Oscar Arias Sanchez, might not be considered a peace giant. And the Arias plan was criticized at the time, and has subsequently been shown to be a failure. Some discussion of the merits of the plan, both pro and con, would have been more helpful.

Despite the occasional hagiographical tone of the entries, however, the volume should find its way into libraries of every description. While such information is likely to be there already, no one source will be able to offer more.—**Mark Y. Herring**

242. **Leaders from the 1960s: A Biographical Sourcebook of American Activism**. David De-Leon, ed. Westport, Conn., Greenwood Press, 1994. 601p. illus. index. $75.00. Z7164.S66L43. 016.30348'4'09730922. LC 93-31603. ISBN 0-313-27414-2.

This volume provides short biographical entries on the leading figures of the dissident movements of the 1960s. The figures are organized by type of movement: racial democracy, peace and freedom, radical culture, and the like. Each section is introduced by a brief essay on the movement and a lengthy bibliography. This is followed by short (4- to 10-page) biographies of the leaders from that movement organized in alphabetical order. The range of personalities included is impressive: from Dr. Spock to Drs. Masters and Johnson, Joan Baez to Angela Davis, and Gore Vidal to I. F. Stone. Each biography is centered on the individual's ideas and contributions to the movements of the 1960s, but there is also an update on what the person is doing now. The biographical entries end with a short bibliography for further information on the individual.

There are some curious omissions; for example, there is no entry on Abbie Hoffman. Biographies are often hard to find since many personalities might fit into several of the categories. But this is a useful addition for public libraries and essential for college and university libraries. [R: BR, Jan/Feb 95, p. 52; Choice, Dec 94, pp. 576-77; LJ, Oct 94, p. 52; RBB, 1 June 94, p. 1878; SLMQ, Fall 94, p. 67; WLB, Nov 94, pp. 94-97]—**Frank L. Wilson**

243.   Roberts, Nancy L. **American Peace Writers, Editors, and Periodicals: A Dictionary**. Westport, Conn., Greenwood Press, 1991. 362p. index. $65.00. JX1962.A2R63. 327.1'72'092273. LC 90-23169. ISBN 0-313-26842-8.

Roberts provides a valuable biographical collection of over 400 peace activists and writers from the colonial period to the present. Additionally, she has included an extensive annotated bibliography of peace publications, a chronology of U.S. peace movements, and an extensive bibliography of scholarly peace-related studies. The biographical sketches of peace writers and the bibliography of peace publications are the most useful components of the book.

The biographies are remarkably informative. They include extensive personal information, peace activities and publications, and scholarly works about the individuals. When possible, the subjects were consulted for information, and some sketches, such as those on Daniel Berrigan and Philip Berrigan, are quite impressive. Yet the choice of whom to include as peace writers is often perplexing. Roberts includes a sketch on one of America's foremost militarists, Alfred T. Mahan, whose most influential work, *The Influence of Sea Power upon History* (1894, reissued under various titles) provided justification for the Spanish American War and American imperialism. Anti-imperialist E. L. Godkin, on the other hand, is omitted. The bibliography of peace publications is useful but fails to include the information researchers value most: libraries that have copies of these often hard-to-find publications.

Despite these limitations, this book remains an impressive reference tool. It is recommended for graduate and theological libraries and, considering the continuing interest in peace topics, for undergraduate institutions as well. [R: Choice, Oct 91, pp. 264-65]—**Robert Clyde Hodges**

244.   **World Encyclopedia of Peace**. Ervin Laszlo and Jong Youl Yoo, eds. Elmsford, N.Y., Pergamon Press, 1986. 4v. bibliog. index. $375.00/set. LC 86-25520. ISBN 0-08-032685-4.

With the distinguished scientist and peace advocate Linus Pauling as honorary editor-in-chief, and with the dedication by the Secretary General of the United Nations, this is a prestigious set, very handsomely produced, on peace research and peace activism. The editors view it as not merely another reference work but as "tangible testimony to the rise of the human spirit to the challenge of life and well-being in the nuclear age" (preface). This set is considered the first comprehensive encyclopedia to present an integrated overview of peace in all its aspects.

To achieve the goal of contributing to peace through this publication, the editors have assembled a wide variety of information in four volumes. The core of the work is in the first two volumes, which contain some 500 signed articles written by more than 300 scholars. These cover topics such as aggression, Buddhism, conscientious objection, East-West conflict, limited war, and peace museums. There are also biographical articles on such disparate persons as Che Guevara and St. Francis of Assisi, Albert Einstein, and Albert Camus. Each article very definitely approaches the subject from the general perspective of peace, though each also carries, to varying degrees, the attitudes of the authors. There are short bibliographies of major sources, averaging several pages in length, appended to these articles.

Volume 3 contains the text of thirty-nine major international treaties. There are also a chronology of the peace movement (reprinted as acknowledged from the *Biographical Dictionary of Modern Peace Leaders* by Harold Josephson) and biographical sketches of Nobel Peace Prize winners through 1985. The fourth volume contains an international directory of peace research institutes, a sixty-page unannotated bibliography of the literature of peace studies, and a list of peace-related journals. There are name and subject indexes which cover all the sections of the encyclopedia.

These sections in the last two volumes provide much information, such as the bibliography, the chronology, and the list of peace institutes, which is readily available elsewhere. Explanatory articles rather than the full text might have been a better choice for the treaty section, where the Treaty of Versailles is followed by the treaty on the Archipelago of Spitsbergen. The worth of this set rests principally with the first two volumes of encyclopedic articles. These provide a valuable overview and analysis of the persons, events, and philosophies involved in the search for peace. [R: C&RL, July 87, pp. 358-59; Choice, Oct 87, p. 292; RBB, 15 Sept 87, p.128]—**Henry E. York**

RUSSIA

245. **Directory of Russian MPs: People's Deputies of the Supreme Soviet of Russia-Russian Federation**. Martin McCauley, ed. Harlow, England, Longman; distr., Detroit, Gale, 1992. 326p. $260.00. ISBN 0-582-09647-2.

For students of and writers covering the present political scene in Russia, this reference work is invaluable. It consists of 252 short biographies, including the voting records, of all deputies of the Russian Supreme Soviet, otherwise known as a parliament. The persons described in the directory are the movers and shakers of present-day Russia. McCauley has written an informative introduction, explaining the genesis and procedures of the Supreme Soviet. The major parties, factions, tendencies, and measures passed are also noted.

For those who wish well to democratic Russia, this volume makes for sad reading, because most of the deputies listed are individuals with roots in the old order. Although the Supreme Soviet was elected by majority vote, the pasts and the voting records of the members do not, on the whole, convey the sense that they are democrats. There is no substitute for this work in English, and it is recommended for all reference desks with one caveat: Should the Supreme Soviet, for whatever reason, be dissolved, the volume will instantly become one of antiquarian interest. [R: Choice, June 93, p. 1600; RBB, Aug 93, p. 2088]—**Andrew Ezergailis**

246. **Who Is Who in the Russian Government**. Pavel Gazukin, comp., and Andrei Vasilevsky, ed. Moscow, Panorama of Russia; distr., Somerville, Mass., Panorama of Russia, 1992. 96p. illus. $25.00pa. ISBN 5-85895-001-9.

Who Is Who in the Russian Government. **Supplement I**. Moscow, Panorama of Russia; distr., Somerville, Mass., Panorama of Russia, 1993. 23p. $10.00pa.

Panorama calls itself an "information-expert group" and during 1992-1993 published a number of reference sources dealing with several aspects of life in the former Soviet Union. *Who Is Who in the Russian Government* offers some 30 biographical sketches in the main volume, plus 11 in the supplement. In most cases the biographical narrative is accompanied by a picture, and besides the usual personal information it includes a brief description of education and career and a list of most important positions held. All in all, it provides basic facts for the uninitiated. It must be used with caution because, in view of rapid changes in Russia, career information becomes dated quickly.—**Bohdan S. Wynar**

SOVIET UNION

247. **Biographical Dictionary of Dissidents in the Soviet Union, 1956-1975**. S. P. de Boer, E. J. Driessen, and H. L. Verhaar, comps and eds. Boston, Martinus Nijhoff, 1982. 679p. bibliog. $165.00. LC 81-22433. ISBN 90-247-2538-0.

Unlike other biographical dictionaries, this unique biographical source includes biographies only of unofficial, oppositionist Soviet citizens of various social backgrounds and nationalities. The dictionary is the result of a project started in 1975 at the Institute of Eastern European Studies of the University of Amsterdam, and it is dedicated to Sergei Dedjulin, Leningrad biographer of the dissident movement in the Soviet Union, whose files were confiscated by the KGB in 1979. Many sources were used in this compilation, including such well-known documents as the thirty-volume *Sobranie dokumentov samizdata*, published in Munich by Radio Liberty, and thirty-eight issues of *Khronika tekus Ycvikh sobytij.* This well-edited work will complement such standard sources as *Who's Who in the Socialist Countries: A Biographical Encyclopedia of 10,000 Leading Personalities in 16 Communist Countries* (Verlag Dokumentation, 1978) and should be recommended as a priority purchase to all larger libraries.—**Bohdan S. Wynar**

248.   **A Biographical Directory of 100 Leading Soviet Officials**. Alexander Rahr, comp. Boulder, Colo., Westview Press, 1990. 210p. illus. index. $42.85. JN6521.R34. 354.47002. LC 90-32130. ISBN 0-8133-8015-4.

Accessible biographical information on leading Soviet policy makers is to be found in this directory. Rahr's compendium is current as of summer 1990, and most of the individuals were contacted directly in order to verify the accuracy of their biographical portraits. Entries list current position, birth dates, nationality, education, career, political life, speeches and publications, foreign travel, and awards and honors received. Of the 100 policy makers, 74 are Russians; their positions range from figures of national influence and international recognition to provincial party bosses. Photographs are provided of 56 officials, 19 of whom verified their biographies.

Individual officials include Abel Aganbegyan, Georgi Arbatov, Alexander Bessmertnykh, Boris Yeltsin, Mikhail Gorbachev, Vladimir Kryuchkov, Vladlen Mikhailovich, Eduard Shevardnadze, Yevgeny Velikov, and Yevgeny Primakov (whom Americans will recall from his efforts to limit the scope of Saddam Hussein's defeat during the Gulf War). Shortcomings include the vague standards given for including speeches and publications; the questionable reliability of officially verified sketches, particularly those of intelligence officers; and the omission of Anatoly Dobrynin. However, the more numerous strengths of Rahr's compilation include its scope of coverage, as it lists prominent non-Russian officials; the efforts to verify the information; and the concluding official affiliations index. One hopes that this work will be continually updated to reflect the systemic fluidity of domestic Soviet politics. [R: Choice, Sept 91, p. 68; LJ, 1 Sept 91, p. 182; RBB, 1 June 91, pp. 1894-96]—**Bert Chapman**

249.   **The Soviet Nomenklatura: A Comprehensive Roster of Soviet Civilian and Military Officials.** 3d ed. Albert L. Weeks, comp. Washington, D.C., Slevin & Associates for Washington Institute Press, 1991. 133p. index. $84.50 spiralbound. JN6521.W43. 354.47002. LC 87-18954. ISBN 0-88702-030-5.

This reference book on the Soviet Nomenklatura (top party bureaucracy) has been compiled by painstaking examination of Soviet official publications, as was the earlier, 1987 edition (Washington Institute Press, 1987). It opens with an introductory essay that explains the history, nature, and presumed future of the top tier of Soviet Nomenklatura. The main body of the directory consists of five chapters that list the apparatchiks of the Communist Party of the Soviet Union; the Communist Party of the Republics, Krais, and Oblasts; the Government of the Soviet Union; the Ministry of Foreign Affairs; and the Ministry of Defense. The total list of nomenklaturists contains 1,427 names. Important entries include year of birth, former position, current position, and date of appointment or election. Auxiliary materials of the directory consist of a list of abbreviations, two maps (political and military districts), and an index. Very interesting are four charts that illustrate the interlocking nature of the party, government, and military systems.

The market for this directory is relatively limited, mainly Sovietologists, scientists, and businesspeople dealing commercially with the Soviet Union. At first glance, the material presented seems obsolete, especially after the abortive military coup of August 19, 1991. However, it is the opinion of these reviewers that, despite the defeat of the party and some considerable political attrition and reshuffling among the Nomenklatura, many of these people, after leaving the party, will be able to retain positions of influence because of their administrative experience, connections, and instincts for self preservation.—**Zbigniew Mieczkowski and Terry Ann Mood**

TERRORISM

250.   Rosie, George. **The Directory of International Terrorism**. New York, Paragon House, 1987. 310p. bibliog. $18.95. LC 86-25211. ISBN 0-913729-29-9.

Many useful reference books have been published lately on the subject of terrorism. Most of these have been bibliographies; see the review of Suzanne Ontiveros's *Global Terrorism: A Historical*

Bibliography (ARBA 87, entry 685) for an overview of these titles. Now there is a good mini-encyclopedia of terrorism available, Rosie's *Directory of International Terrorism*. The major portion of this book consists of an alphabetical listing of personal names, places, organizations, and terrorist incidents. Most of the entries are one or two paragraphs in length and contain cross-references to other entries in the book.

A notorious event, such as the Achille Lauro hijacking (October 1985), receives two pages of text, with separate entries for Leon Klinghoffer, the Delta Force Group, the four Palestinian hijackers, and the Palestine Liberation Front. The emphasis of this volume is on recent, post-World War II terrorist activities (Rosie's compilation ends in July 1986). However, some early-twentieth-century names and incidents are included. There is, for example, nearly a full page on the Okhrana, the secret police of Tsarist Russia, and a brief entry for Engelbert Dollfuss, the chancellor of Austria who was assassinated by the Nazis in 1934.

Among the names that appear in the directory are some American political assassins, or would-be assassins: Lee Harvey Oswald, Sirhan Sirhan, James Earl Ray, Sarah Jane Moore, Lynette Fromme—but not, for some reason, John Hinckley, Jr. or Arthur Bremer. Prominent victims of terrorist acts are also listed: Aldo Moro, Anwar Sadat, Indira Gandhi, Benigno Aquino, Patricia Hearst, General James Dozier, and even Mahatma Gandhi. Yet the real value of this book is in the quick access it provides to background information on the known terrorist groups. Some of these entries are listed under the original language (e.g., "Red Brigades" is found under "Brigate Rosse").

Rosie's introduction takes the form of a good scholarly essay, in which various aspects of terrorism are examined: definitions and categories, a short history of modern terrorism, the media and terrorism, weapons technology, the rule of law and the terrorist states, and hijacking. This kind of overview adds to the overall value of the directory. This book is highly recommended for all public and academic library reference collections. [R: Choice, Apr 87, p. 1203]—**Thomas A. Karel**

U.S. POLITICS AND GOVERNMENT

General Works

251. American Leaders 1789-1994: A Biographical Summary. updated ed. Colleen McGuiness, ed. Washington, D.C., Congressional Quarterly, 1994. 546p. $39.95. E176.A59. 920.073. LC 94-27169. ISBN 0-87187-841-0.

An update of *American Leaders 1789-1987: A Biographical Summary*, and *American Leaders 1789-1991: A Biographical Summary*, this title brings Congressional Quarterly's list of U.S. presidents, vice presidents, cabinet members, Supreme Court justices, members of Congress, and state governors up to the Clinton administration. With the exception of the state governors list, the six lists are arranged alphabetically by name. (The governors list is arranged by state name.) The biographical information contains only these items: name; relationship to other persons in the lists; political party; state elected from; and dates of birth, death, and service. Since there is no other information given in the biographical summaries, this title is not very useful as a biographical source.

Also included are numerous short essays, sidebars, charts, and lists that cover such topics as the presidential line of succession, minority members of Congress, first ladies throughout history, and congressional members who have been elected president or vice president since 1789. This information is placed at the beginning of the most logical section or in the appendix, making it relatively easy to find.

The information in this volume and its predecessors is readily available and more in-depth in other sources, making this volume useful only for quick identification. There is no index for any of the lists except the list of governors. The lack of an overall index to all names makes the information difficult to find.—**Christine E. Thompson and Terry Ann Mood**

252.   **Federal Yellow Book: Who's Who in Federal Departments and Agencies**. New York, Monitor Leadership Directories, 1976- . 1v. (various paging). illus. index. $225.00pa./yr. (4 issues; 1994). JK6.F45. ISSN 0145-6202.

Federal Yellow Book provides a directory of personnel and addresses for senior officials in the federal civil service. There are very brief descriptions of the cabinet secretaries and department or agency directors: birth date, date service began, education, and career highlights. The directory's central purpose, though, is to provide names, addresses, and telephone numbers of key federal officials. Presidential appointees that require Senate confirmation are marked, as are other presidential appointments.

Each department and agency is introduced by a table of contents that helps users quickly identify key offices and divisions. The directory lists general telephone numbers for each department and agency and provides a list of addresses in the Washington, D.C., area. Indexes at the end of the directory provide quick reference for specific offices and agencies and for individuals by name. The directory focuses on Washington-area offices.

This is a very useful directory for businesses, lobbyists, and others who make regular contacts with the federal government. It is also available on CD-ROM.—**Frank L. Wilson**

253.   **Government Affairs Yellow Book: Who's Who in Government Affairs**. Winter 1995: Vol. 1, No. 1. New York, Leadership Directories, 1995. 1024p. index. $180.00pa. ISSN 1078-9812.

The 11th title to be added to the Leadership Directory series, this book is a semiannual directory of government affairs experts who are employed by the leading business, government, and professional organizations to represent them before federal, state, and local governments. The directory covers 18,000 experts and gives their names, addresses, e-mail addresses, telephone and fax numbers, backgrounds, and the legislative issues in which they specialize. Corporations, financial institutions, trade associations, as well as subsidiaries, divisions, and joint ventures that run their own government affairs operations are profiled.

A large part of the directory includes listings of the executive office of the federal government, as well as key departments and agencies in the states and U.S. territories, major cities and counties, and authorities. The lobbying firms given in the other sections of the volume are also profiled separately. Excellent indexes conclude the directory; they are broken down by legislative issues, industries, government subject areas, geography, personnel, and a master index. A user's guide is helpful for the first-time user of the directory. The work is a needed title in every reference collection of public and academic libraries.—**Kathleen J. Voigt**

254.   **Notable U.S. Ambassadors Since 1775: A Biographical Dictionary**. Cathal J. Nolan, ed. Westport, Conn., Greenwood Press, 1997. 430p. index. $95.00. ISBN 0-313-29195-0.

Implementation of U.S. foreign policy depends on many factors, including the personalities of its executors. U.S. ambassadors to countries around the world have often proven to be crucial architects of U.S. foreign policy interests in these countries. *Notable U.S. Ambassadors since 1775* provides biographical portraits of a select, but diverse, group of individuals who, in the editor's viewpoint, have represented U.S. diplomatic interests with noteworthiness.

Following an introduction, this work presents six- to eight-page biographical vignettes of diplomatic personnel that the editor sees as being significant in the transaction of U.S. foreign policy. Individuals covered include current U.S. Secretary of State, Madeleine Albright; nineteenth-century historian, George Bancroft; twentieth-century economist, John Kenneth Galbraith, a U.S. Ambassador to India; Thomas Jefferson; George Kennan; former U.S. Ambassador to the United Nations, Jeane Kirkpatrick; Reagan Administration Assistant Secretary of State for Near Eastern and African Affairs, Richard Murphy; and Soviet Union specialist, Llewellyn Thompson Jr. Biographical entries also feature listings of works by and about these ambassadors. A select bibliography of primary and secondary sources concludes this volume.

This is a valuable introduction to some of the individuals influencing U.S. diplomatic history. Scholars in this field may quibble about the inclusion or omission of individuals they consider important. Nevertheless, *Notable U.S. Ambassadors since 1775* will prove useful to students and scholars desiring to learn more about some of the personalities who have shaped U.S. foreign policy.—**Bert Chapman**

255.   O'Brien, Steven G. **American Political Leaders from Colonial Times to the Present**. Santa Barbara, Calif., ABC-Clio, 1991. 473p. illus. (Biographies of American Leaders). $65.00. E176.027. 973'.0992. LC 91-30755. ISBN 0-87436-570-8.

A masterpiece in almost every regard, *American Political Leaders* is an excellent source of biographical information on over 400 key American political figures. The sketches range from a few hundred to well over 1,000 words, depending on the importance of the individual discussed. Portraits are included in a good number of the entries, as are short bibliographies of important works about each individual.

Factually accurate, attractively printed, and written with a lucid verve usually absent from such books, this work is sure to capture the imagination of almost every precollege student and interest the general public library reader. Beyond this, the biographies are historically interpretative. They provide the reader with more than a bland collection of facts and dates; they give meaning and significance to the life of each individual. The author also deserves praise for the judicious choice of subjects covered. Ranging from the well known, such as Franklin Roosevelt, to the obscure (yet important), such as George Mason, the work includes most significant American political figures, not just those who held high office. It does not include intellectual, scientific, cultural, or social reform movement leaders, but such was not its goal. A must buy for all high school and public libraries, this work is highly recommended for high school history and American government teachers. [R: LJ, 1 Oct 91, p. 90; RBB, 15 Nov 91, p. 639]—**Robert Clyde Hodges**

256.   Utter, Glenn H., and Charles Lockhart. **American Political Scientists: A Dictionary**. Westport, Conn., Greenwood Press, 1993. 374p. index. $85.00. JA61.A525. 320'.092'273. LC 92-35938. ISBN 0-313-27849-0.

This dictionary presents a collection of short bio-bibliographical sketches of 171 scholars in all subdisciplines of political science. Each of the signed articles includes a summary of the most significant intellectual contributions of the subject as well as an enumeration of institutional affiliations and academic honors; there is little or no information about the personal lives of the subjects. A bibliography of selected works and, where appropriate, "Works About" close each article. The articles are uniformly well written and to the point. A brief bibliography at the end of the volume primarily includes works on the history of the discipline.

The authors outline the methods (reputational studies, directories, and expert advice) and criteria (e.g., an active professional life in the United States, identification with political science rather than another social science discipline) used in selecting the men and women included. This reviewer was surprised at the exclusion of Michael Harrington, who was a professor of political science as well as a political theorist, but this may simply illustrate the volume's emphasis on mainline academic, institutional political science. Of the 171 scholars included, an interesting list by degree-granting institutions at the end of the volume shows that 62 percent received their doctorates from Columbia, Harvard, Yale, or the University of Chicago. A list of political scientists by subfield and an index complete the volume.

There is no other biographical dictionary exactly like this one. It will be a useful addition to any library with an interest in the history of academic political science. [R: Choice, Nov 94, p. 421]—**V. W. Hill**

257.   **Who's Who in American Politics**. New Providence, N.J., R. R. Bowker/Reed Reference Publishing, 1967-68- . 2v. index. $225.00/set. ISSN 0000-0205.

The 16th edition of this biographical directory (1997-98), provides in two volumes more than 27,000 entries for individuals active in U.S. politics. Included are the president; vice-president; cabinet members; key presidential appointees; members of Congress and their administrative assistants; key members of the judiciary at the federal and state levels; ambassadors; top-level elected state officials; members of state legislatures; key people in political parties at the national, state, and country levels; mayors of cities with populations over 50,000; and others. The data elements of entries have not changed from previous editions, and include party affiliation; birth date and place; names of parents, spouse, and children; education; current and past political, government, and business positions; military service; honors and awards; publications; memberships; religion; legal residence; and current mailing address. Entries vary from two lines to more than thirty, depending on information provided by biographees or other available data. Some entries have not been updated to reflect any current political involvement or current positions that fit the criteria for inclusion.

The most significant problem with this work is the arrangement of entries by state. Many biographees apparently failed to indicate their legal states of residence and are listed under the states of their mailing addresses. Hillary Rodham Clinton appears under "District of Columbia," while Bill Clinton appears under "Arkansas." Even more serious is the appearance of many current members of Congress under "District of Columbia," instead of under the states they represent. If entries were in one alphabetical sequence, instead of by state, the index of names that covers more than 100 pages at the end of this work would be unnecessary. The brief information provided at the beginning of each state would not be greatly missed either. In spite of the problems noted, this reference work is a valuable source of brief information about individuals involved in U.S. politics at many different levels. [R: RBB, 1 Feb 94, p. 1029]—**Carol Wheeler and Terry Ann Mood**

Executive Branch

258. **Biographical Dictionary of the United States Secretaries of the Treasury, 1789-1995**. Bernard S. Katz and C. Daniel Vencill, eds. Westport, Conn., Greenwood Press, 1996. 403p. index. $115.00. ISBN 0-313-28012-6.

This biographical dictionary is a highly readable collection of 67 biographies covering the Secretaries of the Treasury, from Alexander Hamilton in 1789 to Robert E. Rubin in 1995. Written and signed primarily by academic economists, whose credentials are listed in an appendix, each biography covers not only the particulars of the individual's life (e.g., education, family and professional background, personality) but also the problems he faced during his term, and assesses his contributions during his tenure. The biographies vary in length, usually according to the importance of the individual. Albert Gallatin's entry, for example, is 12 pages long. Each entry is documented by a list of about 5 to 15 articles and books, usually secondary sources. The book would be even more valuable if, as in *Notable American Women* (see ARBA 72, entry 221), the authors had identified the major manuscript collections for each individual.

The book begins with a list, by presidential administration, of the names and tenures of the various secretaries; then the individual biographies are arranged alphabetically. This arrangement is supplemented by an extensive subject index. The editors have published a similar publication, *Biographical Dictionary of the Board of Governors of the Federal Reserve* (see ARBA 93, entry 240), with many of the same authors. Katz is professor emeritus of economics at Lafayette College and now a lecturer at San Francisco State University, where Vencill is a professor of economics.

Although the subjects were prominent in their day, not all are covered well in modern reference sources. The authors have done a good job of presenting current thinking on the secretaries' lives and tenure as Secretary of the Treasury in short essays that are intelligible, even to those with limited economics backgrounds—**Marilyn Domas White**

259. **Biographical Directory of the United States Executive Branch, 1774-1989**. Robert Sobel, ed. Westport, Conn., Greenwood Press, 1990. 567p. $75.00. E176.B578. 353.04'092'2. LC 89-25779. ISBN 0-313-26593-3.

Sobel compiled this collection to provide quick access to biographical information about all cabinet officials, especially the more obscure officials for whom access cannot be easily obtained from other sources. It contains brief biographies (200-1,000 words) of the U.S. presidents, vice-presidents, and cabinet officers—over 650 in all. Most can be found in the *Dictionary of American Biography*.

While a biographical guide to obscure executive branch officials is potentially useful to specialists, Sobel's directory omits undersecretaries, deputy and assistant secretaries, and secretaries of the individual services after they were brought under the Defense Department. Neither does the work provide biographies of critical appointments that were not cabinet-level. As National Security Advisor, Henry Kissinger would not have been included, yet, in this reviewer's opinion, his contribution in that role was greater than his contribution as Secretary of State. By leaving such individuals out,

Sobel's work fails to recognize the political realities of the modern executive branch. The research quality is also questionable. The sketch on Cordell Hull states that he lived to 1955, but "was published posthumously in 1948" (p. 188). It is difficult to recommend a work that is flawed in both design and execution. [R: RBB, 1 Dec 90, p. 774; WLB, Nov 90, p. 147]—**Robert C. Hodges**

260. **The Clinton 500: The New Team Running America 1994**. Jeffrey B. Trammell and Gary P. Osifchin, eds. Washington, D.C., Almanac Publishing, 1994. illus. index. $125.00. ISBN 0-9626134-8-7.

This new biographical directory includes Clinton appointees in charge of 29 areas within the Executive Office of the President, 14 governmental departments (Agriculture to Veterans Affairs), and 37 independent agencies, such as the Civil Rights Commission, Federal Reserve Board, and the General Services Administration. Approximately one page is devoted to each person, with a photograph (if available), information on education and work experience, and a brief outline of the person's role within the current administration. Separate name and subject indexes are provided.

Some of the information is tentative or already out-of-date. For example, Warren Zimmerman, director of Bureau of Refugee Programs, announced his retirement as of January 6, 1994; Thomas F. "Mack" McClarty, Chief of Staff, was replaced in June 1994; and Ricki R. Tigert, Chairman-Designate of the Federal Deposit Insurance Corporation, was yet to be confirmed by Congress six months after being nominated. While the editors are planning to publish updated editions every January, a quarterly updating service would be even more useful to reference librarians and general users.

This unique source fills an important gap by providing biographical information on individuals often difficult to trace. The book's excellent binding and typography will further justify its expense for most libraries. [R: Choice, July/Aug 94, p. 1699]—**Gary D. Barber**

261. **Federal Staff Directory**. P. Wayne Walker, ed. Alexandria, Va., CQ Directories, 1982- . 670p. index. $79.00. LC 59-13987. ISSN 0735-3324.

Now published twice a year in January and August, this useful directory provides timely and accurate access to 40,000 key executives in the Executive Branch. It is similar to the *Congressional Staff Directory* (Congressional Staff Directory, Ltd.), but with an emphasis on the Executive branch. Independent agencies such as the Federal Trade Commission and presidential advisory organizations are also listed, while a separate section covers quasi-official, international, and nongovernmental organizations (e.g., the International Monetary Fund). Most of the book is arranged by agency and identifies important officials, titles, mailing and office addresses, and direct-dial telephone numbers. Additional access is provided by an excellent keyword subject index and a separate individual index. Pages are color coded for ease in distinguishing sections.

A separate section provides brief biographical information for key federal executives selected on the basis of interest to readers. Biographical information, usually submitted by the entrants themselves, includes present position, birth, marriage, children, career, organization memberships (including church affiliation), and interests. Not all information is available for each person. An individual with a biography is indicated by a star next to his name in the agency listing.

While sources such as the *Washington Information Directory* (see ARBA 90, entry 702), *U.S. Government Manual* (see ARBA 84, entry 456), and the *Federal Regulatory Directory* (see ARBA 87, entry 704) provide similar information, they concentrate more on information on agencies and offices, and give somewhat limited biographical information. By contrast, *Federal Staff Directory* offers more comprehensive biographical coverage of individuals.—**Marilyn Domas White and Terry Ann Mood**

262. **Who's Who in the Federal Executive Branch**. Washington, D.C., Congressional Quarterly, 1993- . ISSN 1069-6946.

This sourcebook contains the names, titles, and telephone numbers of important executive branch officials. Bill Clinton is named first, and thousands of others follow. Part 1 includes information on the executive office of the president, beginning with a diagram showing office assignments in the west wing of the White House. Part 2 covers the 14 cabinet departments; part 3, a host of federal agencies, boards, bureaus, commissions, and corporations. Accompanying each cabinet department and the other organizations is a headquarters address and a telephone number for information. An appendix of regional federal information sources completes this guide. Within the various parts and the appendix, material is arranged alphabetically.

Who's Who in the Federal Executive Branch (1993) provides easy access to high-ranking individuals within the executive branch and their assistants. Information on almost any subject can be gathered in a relatively efficient manner by dialing a few telephone numbers. Unfortunately, the compilers did not distinguish between civil service employees and Clinton political appointees. An asterisk used to denote the latter would have been quite helpful. Regardless, all citizens of the United States who have questions for their government, including researchers, can make valuable use of this little book; it remains a handy reference. Recommended for college, university, and public libraries.—**Richard E. Holl**

First Ladies

263.   **American First Ladies: Their Lives and Their Legacy**. Lewis L. Gould, ed. New York, Garland, 1996. 686p. illus. index. $95.00. ISBN 0-8153-1479-5.

This is a fascinating account of the first ladies of the United States, from Martha Washington to Hillary Rodham Clinton. A separate chapter is devoted to each first lady, and each is written by a different scholar. For all first ladies there are a portrait, a chronological account of her life, an evaluation of her place in developing the role of first lady, selections from her own writings, recollections of family and friends, important newspaper articles and scholarly writings, and the location of her personal papers and other manuscript sources.

The book successfully gives a sense of the personality and appeal of each first lady and discusses and precedents she set while occupying the White House. This is a well-rounded account that presents the problems, controversies, and perceptions by her peers that each first lady faced. One can also get a picture of how the role of first lady has changed from the beginning of the country to the present and how it reflects the period in which she lived. A lengthy subject index at the back of the volume, which includes topics such as assassinations, artists who performed at the White House, health of first ladies, and so forth, enables the reader to find specific information quickly. This book will be of value both to the casual reader who simply wishes to read interesting accounts of first ladies and to the scholar who is doing serious research. It belongs on the shelves of all libraries. [R: Choice, Oct 96, p. 247; RBB, Aug 96, p. 1920; SLJ, Aug 96, p. 186; VOYA, Dec 96, p. 297]—**Marilyn Strong Noronha**

264.   Healy, Diana Dixon. **America's First Ladies: Private Lives of the Presidential Wives**. New York, Atheneum, 1988. 254p. illus. $18.95. LC 88-3365. ISBN 0-689-11873-2.

This book, by the author of *America's Vice-Presidents: Our First Forty-three Vice Presidents and How They Got to Be Number Two* (see ARBA 85, entry 648), contains brief (three to nine pages) biographies of the forty-one "First Ladies," mostly wives of the presidents, but in some cases other women who served as official hostesses. Arranged chronologically by administrations, the biographies give brief background information (date and place of birth, early life, etc.), but concentrate on each woman's role, attitude, and behavior during the presidency. A black-and-white picture of almost all of the first ladies is included. The biographies are well written, witty, interesting, and compassionate. They capture each personality and the social atmosphere during each administration. There are many tidbits of information in this work which would be useful in answering trivia questions, but due to the lack of an index they are not readily accessible. Although it cannot be recommended as a reference work, it can serve as a lively addition to general collections. Paul F. Boller, Jr.'s *Presidential Wives* (Oxford University Press, 1988) covers much of the same material in more detail, but only deals with wives; and while it does contain a name index, its use is also limited by the lack of a subject index.—**Kathleen Farago**

265. Klapthor, Margaret Brown. **The First Ladies**. 6th ed. Washington, D.C., White House Historical Association; distr., Lincoln, Mass., Sewall, 1989. 90p. illus. $9.95pa. LC 89-050706. ISBN 0-912308-39-7.

A joint venture of the White House Historical Association and the National Geographic Society, this book maintains the quality that readers expect from these institutions. A double-page spread on each of the first ladies includes a full-page portrait and a page of text. The majority of the attractive reproductions are in color; the succinct text provides a warm, personal account of each woman's private and political life. In those instances where circumstances caused a woman other than a president's wife to serve as his official hostess, that woman's portrait is inset, and brief information is provided about her.

The First Ladies is suitable for junior high students as well as adults. More extensive coverage of the first ladies, suitable for the same audience, is provided by the thematically arranged brief biographies in Diana D. Healy's *America's First Ladies* (see ARBA 89, entry 443); longer sketches of the biographees' personal lives, each approximately eight pages in length, can be found in Carole Waldrup's *Presidents' Wives* (see ARBA 90, entry 485). Paul F. Boller's *Presidential Wives* (Oxford University Press, 1988) provides anecdotal essays, while Peter Hay's *All the Presidents' Ladies* (Viking, 1988) supplies humor, lively gossip, and intriguing detail.—**Vandelia L. VanMeter**

266. **Modern First Ladies: Their Documentary Legacy**. Nancy Kegan Smith and Mary C. Ryan, comps and eds. Washington, D.C., National Archives and Records Administration, 1989. 184p. illus. index. $12.00. CD3029.82M63. 973.9'092'2. LC 88-15263. ISBN 0-911333-73-8.

Profiled in this collection of essays are 14 first ladies. The essays are intended to explore the historical significance of individual presidential wives as well as the changing role of the first lady. They provide an overview of each first lady's activities and highlight the range of primary source material available.

Edith Roosevelt, Helen Taft, Ellen Wilson, and Edith Wilson, whose papers are housed in the Manuscript Division of the Library of Congress, are treated briefly in a collective essay. Individual essays are devoted to the remaining first ladies, from Lou Henry Hoover to Nancy Reagan. The information available varies from essay to essay, depending on whether or not records are processed and open for research. The essay on Nancy Reagan was prepared while her husband was still in office, and so is largely speculative on the nature of the documentary record to be preserved. Suggestions for further reading and an index complete the volume.

A popular book rather than a reference work, it is likely to be of more interest to the general reader than to those engaged in historical research. Scholars will no doubt find the *National Inventory of Documentary Sources. Federal Records* (Chadwyck-Healey, 1984-), which includes materials in seven presidential libraries, a more detailed source of information on the first ladies' papers.—**Cheryl Todd-Simirenko**

267. Waldrup, Carole Chandler. **Presidents' Wives: The Lives of 44 American Women of Strength**. Jefferson, N.C., McFarland, 1989. 381p. illus. index. $24.95. E176.2.W35. 973'.09'92. LC 89-42572. ISBN 0-89950-393-4.

Most people know comparatively little about the personal lives of the wives of U.S. presidents. If the First Lady happens to be particularly active, such as Eleanor Roosevelt or Nancy Reagan were, her public image is projected but her personal story is largely ignored. *Presidents' Wives* is an effort to get behind the headlines and present these women as persons in their own right, but Waldrup does not wholly succeed in this endeavor.

The individual biographies read as if they were written for a popular magazine's column on fascinating people. Composed of extremely brief factual paragraphs and presented in staccato style, the biographies lack depth. Although the subtitle calls them "women of strength," nothing in these capsule accounts provides any real indication of why and how these women were strong. Most of them gained prominence through an accident of marriage. Some did more than others, due in large measure to circumstances not of their making. As biography, even encyclopedia-style biography, the work is disappointing. As history, there are some serious shortcomings.

The most interesting piece of historical interpretation (or misinterpretation) appears in the chapter on Pat Nixon (Thelma Catherine [Patricia] Ryan Nixon). Waldrup describes the 1950 California senatorial race by ascribing the "ruthless, smear-tactic type of campaign" to Nixon's opponent, Helen Gahagan Douglas. Given that Nixon defeated Douglas handily, Waldrup's interpretation of events seems rather biased, if not inaccurate.

On a more favorable note, the author is to be congratulated for not shying away from some of the more difficult facts about America's first ladies. She records problem marriages, alcoholism, and drug dependency, dealing sympathetically with these tough issues. Unfortunately, given the general lack of substance in the biographies, these problem areas stand out in sharp contrast to the rest of the narrative. [R: RBB, 1 Nov 89, p. 611]—**Ellen Broidy**

Governors

268.   Cook, James F. **The Governors of Georgia, 1754-1995**. rev. ed. Macon, Ga., Mercer University Press, 1995. 341p. illus. index. $25.00. ISBN 0-86554-480-8.

Cook, professor of history at Floyd College in Rome, Georgia, offers an interesting and useful resource in this revised and expanded edition of a work originally published in 1979. He provides in-depth sketches on each of the 76 men who have served as the chief executive of the state, from the first Royal Governor John Reynolds in 1754 to the incumbent Zell Miller. The individuals are an eclectic lot, from obscure figures to national leaders, including a president of the United States. Sixteen governors also served as U.S. senators, seventeen served in the U.S. House of Representatives, several held cabinet positions, and Alexander Stephens was vice president of the Confederacy. The composite biographies provide a history of a state that was founded as a haven for the destitute and remained abjectly poor throughout much of its history until its emergence in the last two or three decades as the center and capital of the upscale Sunbelt South.

The chronologically arranged sketches focus on the major achievements of each governor's administration, but also include references to the individual's family, background, personal traits, and subsequent political or professional career. All the entries are well researched, judicious, and compactly written. Most of the entries supply a picture of the governor. The selected bibliography is outstanding, as it lists all the significant books, dissertations and theses, and articles on the governors and other major works on Georgia history. It would be wonderful if a book such as this existed on every state. In the meantime, this valuable volume should be in all libraries with significant collections on Southern history; in every academic, school, and public library in Georgia; and in larger collections in surrounding states.

Similar volumes have been produced for other states. The following list provides some examples.

Governors of Alabama. John C. Stewart. 1975. 232p. $13.95. LC 75-8763. ISBN 0-88289-067-0.

Governors of Arkansas: Essays in Political Biography. 2d ed. Edited by Timothy P. Donovan. 1995. 376p. $36.00. LC 81-50374. ISBN 1-557283-31-1.

Governors of Georgia. James F. Cook. 1979. 320p. $12.95. LC 77-71397. ISBN 0-686-83449-6.

Governors of Louisiana. 3rd ed. Miriam G. Reeves. Edited by James Calhoun. 1980. 128p. $13.95. LC 72-89969. ISBN 0-911116-71-0.

Governors of Maryland, 1777-1970. Frank F. White, Jr. 1970. $12.00. ISBN 0-942370-01-5.

Governors of Minnesota: 1849-1971. Committee for the Inauguration of Wendell R. Anderson. 1971. 22p. $2.00pa. ISBN 0-685-47097-0.

Governors of Mississippi. Cecil L. Sumners. 1980. 164p. $13.95. ISBN 0-88289-237-1.

Governors of Texas. Ross Phares. 1976. 184p. $13.95. LC 76-7013. ISBN 0-88289-078-6.

Governors of Virginia. 1860-1978. Edited by Edward Younger and James T. Moore. 1982. 428p. $17.95. LC 81-16359. ISBN 0-8139-0920-1.

—**Joe P. Dunn and Terry Ann Mood**

269. Hendrickson, Kenneth E. Jr. **The Chief Executives of Texas: From Stephen F. Austin to John B. Connally Jr**. College Station, Texas A&M University Press, 1995. 246p. illus. index. (Centennial Series of the Association of Former Students, Texas A&M University, no. 55). $29.00. ISBN 0-89096-641-9.

Outside the Lone Star State, this reference tool will be of only marginal value. Inside the "whole other country" of Texas, this tome will be viewed with skepticism, dismay, and outright regret. No little part of the skepticism exhibited by Texans will reside in the one small but significant fact that the author was educated at none other than the University of Oklahoma, longtime longhorn rival, and therefore the bane of all "true" Texans.

Hendrickson has attempted to combine scholarship with diatribe and has come up with this volume. Trying to avoid commonplace hagiography in the treatment of former governors of Texas, the author careens to the other side of the road, smashing spades into spades, and wrecking jackanapes into jackanapes. The sore contention of this volume is that Texas has not been blessed with good leadership; on the contrary, it has been cursed with knaves and only by the grace of God has not fallen into mediocrity, although its leadership has weltered in it.

Forty-four heads of state appear in this volume posthumously. Of the six living governors, only the scantiest mention is made of five. The text reads hotter than a Texas pepper in the Rio Grande. For example, of the sainted Coke Stevenson, Hendrickson writes, "Throughout his political career, Stevenson . . . exhibited no liberal tendencies . . . and few that could be even described as constructive. [H]e was reactionary, penurious, and in some cases downright cruel." Ouch! Do not look for this to get the Texas Popular Book of the Year award.—**Mark Y. Herring**

270. **The Louisiana Governors: From Iberville to Edwards**. Joseph G. Dawson, III, ed. Baton Rouge, Louisiana State University Press, 1990. 297p. illus. index. $29.95. F368.L68. 976.3'0092'2. LC 89-27333. ISBN 0-8071-1527-4.

This political and biographical history of Louisiana's governors is better than a novel. It features intrigue, bargaining and political maneuvering, graft, and corruption, as well as the governors' good qualities. An unofficial policy of breaking and ignoring laws by the governors of Louisiana was started by the first colonial governor, Pierre Lemoyne, Sieur d'Iberville. Iberville realized that if the new French colony was to survive economically, it would be wise for him to look the other way and allow the smuggling of needed supplies. Such executive leniency is thoroughly chronicled in this text, as is the tradition of a strong and influential executive. Political adroitness, often accompanied by great administrative abilities and leadership qualities, was necessary for one to successfully govern this state.

Over 30 contributors, each of whom is established in historical and related fields, have combined forces to cover nearly 300 years of Louisiana political history. They chronicle each governor and provide a brief insight into his politics and economic policies. Arranged chronologically, entries give a brief biographical sketch of each governor. An evaluation of his administration is worked into the sketch, and most have an accompanying portrait. A bibliography follows each biography.

The biographer of Governor David Treen (1980-1984) points out that "Louisianians like their politicians like their food: hot and spicy" (p. 279). In addition to being a serious reference, this work offers some hot and spicy politics in a historical framework. It is highly readable and strongly recommended for public, high school, and college libraries, as well as for personal collections. [R: LJ, 1 June 90, p. 118]—**Louis G. Zelenka**

271. Mullaney, Marie Marmo. **Biographical Directory of the Governors of the United States 1988-1994**. Westport, Conn., Greenwood Press, 1994. 425p. illus. index. $75.00. JK2447.M86. 353.9'1313'0922. LC 93-37875. ISBN 0-313-28312-5.

This is the latest in a series of biographical directories of U.S. governors that stretches back to 1607. Arranged alphabetically by state, it lists the recent governors by state, including both the incumbents and those who served earlier in the period 1988-1994. Arrangement within the state is chronological. Each governor has a short biography covering such information as birth date and place, prior career, residences, education, family, and political activities. Special attention is paid to the governor's election campaign, with vote totals for both primary and general elections. Major programs and initiatives pursued by the governors are also briefly listed. The entries show an awareness of the political setting and subtleties that are often missing in official biographies. Each entry is accompanied by a photograph of the governor. In addition, there is a brief bibliography to assist those wanting additional information, including not only formal biographies but biographical articles from the *New York Times* and other newspapers and periodicals. This is a valuable resource for journalists and those interested in state politics. [R: Choice, Oct 94, p. 263]—**Frank L. Wilson and Terry Ann Mood**

272.   Raimo, John W. **Biographical Directory of American Colonial and Revolutionary Governors, 1607-1789**. Westport, Conn., Meckler Books/Microform Review, 1980. 521p. maps. index. $75.00. LC 80-13279. ISBN 0-930466-07-1.

The format of *Biographical Directory of American Colonial and Revolutionary Governors, 1607-1789* makes the volume accessible to both students and the lay reader. The colonies are presented in alphabetical order, while the biographies within a colony appear chronologically. A chronological listing of each colony's governors is given, but page numbers are not included. The index, therefore, is the only key to the location of the material. A general bibliography of pertinent works appears at the beginning of each colony, while a concise bibliography follows each entry. The entries provide dates of birth and death, place of birth, names of parents, family, religion, political and private careers, and some accomplishments in office. However, if a governor served in more than one colony (e.g., Sir Edmund Andros—nine colonies), the identical information is published for each colony. It would have been more beneficial to the user if pertinent achievements in each colony had been given rather than redundant material.

The term *governor* is interpreted to include "anyone who held effective executive power in those British colonies which in 1776 became the first thirteen states." Thus, the volume contains the lives and careers of approximately 400 individuals who met this criterion. Of these men, roughly 50 percent are not represented in either the *Dictionary of American Biography* (*DAB*) or the *Dictionary of National Biography* (*DNB*). For those who are listed in the *DAB* and *DNB*, considerable new information has been added by the discovery of additional genealogical and historical data. This could account for the differences in length of the biographies; some contain more information than others. Nevertheless, any college or university library whose faculty or students do research in American history should obtain this volume. In addition, large public libraries would do well to add this to their collections of reference works. [R: BL, 15 Apr 81, p. 1168; Choice, Dec 80, p. 510; LJ, 15 Sept 80, p. 1849]—**Irene Wood Bell**

273.   Socolofsky, Homer E. **Kansas Governors**. Lawrence, University Press of Kansas, 1990. 255p. illus. index. $22.50. F680.S63. 978.1'00992. LC 89-29123. ISBN 0-7006-0421-9.

Drawing on a wide variety of primary and secondary resources, the author presents a set of biographical sketches of governors of the territory (1854 to 1861) and state of Kansas. Each sketch contains genealogical and voting data as well as an account of the events occurring during the incumbent's term of office. The biographical sketches are preceded by an excellent essay on the territorial governor selection process (territorial governors were selected by the president) and voting patterns for governors when Kansas became a state. The volume is profusely illustrated and a bibliography and index are supplied. This reference work is a critical tool for those interested in the history of Kansas.—**Charles Neuringer**

Ideologies

274.   **Biographical Dictionary of the American Left**. Bernard K. Johnpoll and Harvey Klehr, eds. Westport, Conn., Greenwood Press, 1986. 493p. index. $65.00. LC 85-27252. ISBN 0-313-24200-3.

The history of American radicalism is one of chronic failure and abandoned dreams. Yet it is not without interest or importance; from 1820 on, an incredible array of parties, movements, and factions has offered noncompetitive alternatives to the inequalities forged by laissez-faire capitalism. This useful work contains biographical entries for over 250 leaders of the American Left.

Though data for most of these individuals can be gleaned from a variety of available sources, this volume conveniently brings them together for the first time. Forty-eight contributors have helped the editors prepare these biographical entries, which range in length from less than one page to more than seven. Though not every subject is a household name, each played a significant role in creating and maintaining anti-establishment alternatives. Taken collectively, they represent every hue of the American Left over time—utopian communitarians, socialists, communists, anarchists, etc. They range from Robert Owen to David Dellinger, from Victoria Woodhull to Abbie Hoffman. Twenty-six of them are women.

The biographical entries are arranged alphabetically and provide sources for further study. The appendixes offer a number of useful breakdowns (e.g., by party affiliation, place of birth, birth/death date). These features are followed by a serviceable index.

Biographical Dictionary of the American Left is an informative, well-executed reference tool. It serves a wide range of interests and levels of interest. The visionaries, ideologues, and activists presented in its pages represent important and frequently fascinating tributaries of the American mainstream.—**Mark R. Yerburgh**

275. Filler, Louis. **Dictionary of American Conservatism**. New York, Philosophical Library, 1987. 380p. $29.95. LC 86-22665. ISBN 0-8022-2506-3.

This is a lively, and somewhat controversial, compilation that serves as a companion volume to the author's *A Dictionary of American Social Change* (see ARBA 84, entry 285). Broad subjects, specific issues, slogans, prominent individuals (both political and cultural), and titles of books are included in this dictionary. Filler's intent is not to attempt a comprehensive encyclopedia or biographical register of conservatism. Rather, he casts his net to include "representative figures, visible personalities, and symbolic slogans and ideas" (p. 11). Filler also highlights what he calls "transitional figures," individuals whose careers involved major political and philosophical changes (e.g., John Dos Passos, James Burnham, Garry Wills). Most entries consist of one substantial paragraph, though some fill two columns of text. Many of the entries contain one or more bibliographical references, which lead the user to a mixture of scholarly and popular works on the subject.

While the entries are useful in providing quick background information on a subject, or an individual, a distinct ideological bias permeates the writing in this book. For example, "Gun Control" is defined as "a cause generally identified with liberals" (p. 143). Yet the author makes no claim of objectivity and his opinions contribute greatly to the readability of the dictionary. Also, one finds many off-beat and unexpected headings here. There is a listing for the Amway Corporation (nearly a column in length, half of which consists of an explanation of its legal problems with the Canadian government); an entry for "Labor Faker," which refers to Samuel Gompers (this is the kind of cross-reference you won't find in most reference sources!); and an entry for the phrase "There you go again," which Ronald Reagan used so effectively in his 1980 debate with Jimmy Carter. Longer entries are provided for such diversely influential people as Herbert Hoover, Ronald Reagan, T. S. Eliot, H. L. Mencken, and Benjamin Disraeli; and for broad areas like conservatism, liberalism, education, and minorities. The lengthy entry on *The National Review* contains a capsule history of that journal.

Influential and controversial books (not all written by conservatives) receive separate entries; in most cases there is also an entry for the author. Predictable books are included, such as Barry Goldwater's *The Conscience of a Conservative* (1960) and George Gilder's *Wealth and Poverty* (1981), as well as some classic works of political fiction like George Orwell's *1984* (1949). There is even an entry for Mario Puzo's novel *The Godfather*!

A good indication of the lasting value of this work is that Peter Viereck (the poet, scholar, and conservative theorist) receives more than twice as much space as Richard Viguerie (the well-known fundraiser and writer). Also, among influential journalists, Garry Wills receives more space than George Will. In spite of the ideological bias noted above, and some minor inaccuracies (e.g., Orwell's *Homage to Catalonia* is cited as *Homage to Barcelona* in the entry on Lionel Trilling), this is a well-written and well-intentioned dictionary. It belongs in most academic libraries—right next to a work in a similar vein, Safire's *Political Dictionary* (see ARBA 80, entry 468). [R: BL, Aug 87, p. 1726; Choice, July/Aug 87, p. 1676]—**Thomas A. Karel**

276. Rees, Philip. **Biographical Dictionary of the Extreme Right since 1890**. New York, Simon & Schuster, 1990. 418p. $60.00. D412.6.R39. 920'.009'04. LC 90-47107. ISBN 0-13-089301-3.

Rees, acquisition librarian at J. B. Morrel Library, University of York, and author of two previous reference books on fascism, has prepared a biographical dictionary of approximately 500 people, from 1890 to the present, associated with the extreme Right. Rees's definition of extreme Right includes three distinct strains of conservatism: fascism, the radical Right, and the conservative authoritarian Right. Also, the candidate for inclusion must fit into the Left/Right dichotomy used to classify ideologists. This excludes many theocrats in the Middle East and civic or military dictators in Africa, Asia, and Latin America (e.g., Pinochet, Stroessner). About one-tenth of the biographees are still living.

Of the 500 A-Z biographical entries, approximately 50 do not cover individuals from the European continent. This is not surprising since fascism and National Socialism, two exemplars of the extreme Right, originated and were most active in Europe. Other continents and countries represented are the Americas, Ireland, Great Britain, Japan, South Africa, and Israel. Because so many countries are included, the author might have provided a country index, which would have made it easier, for example, to find the handful of people from the United States.

The average entry is between 500 and 1,000 words long. Each begins with a one-line biographical summary. The main body of the entry contains factual information, including significant achievements, associations, and failures. A detailed discussion of the biographee's political ideas is beyond the scope of this work. Following the entry is a short bibliography, often with no references to sources in English. In some cases this work provides what is probably the biographee's first treatment in English, making it invaluable to researchers needing to know about obscure members of the extreme Right. However, a standard reference collection should suffice for the well-known far Rightists. [R: Choice, May 91, p. 1466; RBB, 1 Mar 91, p. l420]—**John P. Stierman**

Legislative Branch

277. **The Almanac of the Unelected: Staff of the U.S. Congress**. Jeffrey B. Trammell and Steve Piacente, eds. Washington, D.C., Almanac Publishing, 1988- . illus. index. $250.00. ISSN 1047-0999.

This biographical sourcebook is a welcome volume that profiles staffers working with congressional members and committees. Staff people in Congress play very important roles in the U. S. governmental process. Usually they are the first contacts a person or group has with a representative or senator on a topic of mutual interest. Their assistance and expertise can expedite access to information on key issues and legislation.

More than 700 key members of the congressional staff are profiled, with information on their professional background, areas of expertise, specific legislative contributions, ideological or political orientations, and opinions of colleagues and observers. A photograph is provided for most of the staffers.

One drawback to this type of biographical reference book is that congressional staff change often. To address this concern, the publishers plan to update this work annually. Also, the book could be improved by adding a subject index that lists key personnel dealing with such broad issues as education and the environment. Currently its organization compels the user to search through each committee that may seem appropriate in the separate listings for the House of Representatives and the Senate.

Still, it is strongly recommended for large public libraries, colleges and universities, and specialized collections focusing on congressional activities and legislation.—**Roberto P. Haro**

278. **Beacham's Guide to Key Lobbyists: An Analysis of Their Issues and Impact**. Walton Beacham, Margaret Roberts, and C. Peter Kesler, eds. Washington, D.C., Beacham Publishing, 1989. 632p. illus. index. $195.00; $95.00 (school, public, and academic libraries). JK1118.B3924. 328.73'078'0202. LC 89-380. ISBN 0-933833-13-X.

Although expensive, this new reference book provides important information on people who significantly influence the legislative and policy development agenda for our nation. This new compilation of key lobbyists in Washington will be a welcome addition to library users who are interested in government, public policy, the legislative policy, and the activities of major national organizations concerned with the behavior of the federal government.

Profiled in this three-part book are 125 lobbyists. The first part includes narrative material on lobbyists that stresses roles they play and their long-term influence. The second part provides biographical information about the lobbyists, including the name of the firm or group, title of the lobbyist, telephone and fax numbers, issues, clients, party affiliation, a narrative statement on lobbying activities, background, firm profile (if appropriate), donations, and personal data. Each entry includes a picture and a subject heading. The final section includes appendixes for selected contributions during 1987-1988, 1987 honoraria paid to members of congress, lobbyists grouped by issue areas, and an index.

Overall this work is a welcome addition to the materials dealing with government, legislation, and the policy process. There are a few weaknesses in this compilation: a limited index, the omission of key terms to identify major efforts such as Mothers Against Drunk Driving and the Sierra Club, and the exclusion of connections with foreign groups. Recommended for large academic libraries, major public libraries, and research collections with a focus on government and the legislative process at the national level. [R: Choice, Nov 89, p. 455; RBB, 1 Oct 89, pp. 387-88; WLB, Sept 89, pp. 131-32]—**Roberto P. Haro**

279.   Biographical Directory of the American Congress, 1774-1996. Alexandria, Va., CQ Staff Directories, 1997. 2108p. illus. $295.00. ISBN 0-87289-124-0. ISSN 1091-0859.

The 16th edition of the *Biographical Directory of the American Congress*, like its predecessors, will continue to be an indispensable reference tool for students and scholars of U.S. history and politics. It is the most comprehensive biographical source on congressional members. The directory provides brief biographical and career information on the 11,400 men and women who served in the U.S. and Continental Congresses between 1774 and 1996.

The directory is divided into sections. The first section, under separate headings, contains the executive officers, which include vice presidents and cabinet members of each administration from 1789 to 1996; the delegates to the Continental Congress; and the members of each Congress, which include congressional leaders and officers from the 1st to the 104th Congress. Neither biographical information nor party affiliation on these individuals is provided. Also included in this section is the "Representatives Under Each Apportionment" table showing the number of congressional seats allotted to each state of the past 21 censuses. The second section, the main text, contains biographical information on members of Congress. Each entry contains date and place of birth, education, employment (prior to and after governmental service), record of governmental service, party affiliation, and date and place of death; entries for living members contain present occupation and place of residency. The information provided for each entry is rather brief; however, it is accurate. At the end of many entries, biographical references are provided for notable congressional figures. Additional biographical references should have been included for certain entries, however. For example, no biographical references are provided for such major figures as Richard Gephardt, Newt Gingrich, and Albert Gore.

The printing, binding, cover, and organization are excellent. Overall, this is an outstanding reference tool. College, public, and school libraries should acquire this work.—**Binh P. Le**

280.   Congressional Quarterly's Green Guide. 100th Congress pocket ed. Washington, D.C., Congressional Quarterly, 1987. 292p. illus. maps. $11.95pa. LC 87-5321. ISBN 0-87187-435-0.

This handbook provides uniform, brief information (including a photograph) on each member of the 100th Congress (6 January 1987-). It is designed to help to "identify members of Congress in committee, in official or informal meetings, and while watching C-SPAN." Entries for senators appear alphabetically before those of representatives. For each member the order of information is as follows: name, party affiliation/state, city of residence, year elected to the house of current membership (e.g., Brock Adams [D-Wash.] of Seattle—elected 1986); birth date and place; college education; military career; occupation; family (marital status, spouse's name, number of children); religion; political career prior to present position; U.S. Capitol office and telephone number; and statewide vote percentages for Ronald Reagan in 1984 and 1980 (with senatorial entries). Then follow committee (but not subcommittee) assignments; general and primary election percentages for the member's last two elections (if applicable); three voting studies in percentages for 1985 and 1986 (presidential support score, party unity score, voting participation) prepared by Congressional Quarterly; and 1985 and 1986 ratings of the member by four interest groups representing liberal, conservative, labor, and business viewpoints (Americans for Democratic Action, American Conservative Union, AFL-CIO, and the Chamber of Commerce of the United States).

These profiles are followed by a roster of members of Congress by state, including the name of each member's chief aide. The work concludes with sections on how to watch the Senate and House on C-SPAN, a brief glossary of congressional terms, and a map of Capitol Hill. A pronunciation guide to members' names often mispronounced precedes the Senate profiles. An envelope in the review copy includes cards providing certain changes in House and Senate membership and committee assignments, key official Washington and Congressional Quarterly telephone numbers.

Finally, it is clear that the *Green Guide* draws heavily on information published later in 1987 in Congressional Quarterly's comprehensive *Politics in America* (see ARBA 86, entry 694) and other CQ services. There is, of course, no mention of National Journal's compendium, *The Almanac of American Politics* (see review of 1986 edition in ARBA 86, entry 695).—**Wiley J. Williams**

281.   Kaptur, Marcy. **Women of Congress: A Twentieth-Century Odyssey**. Washington, D.C., Congressional Quarterly, 1996. 256p. illus. index. $23.95. ISBN 0-87187-989-1.

Since the founding of the United States, fewer than 200 members of Congress have been women. Of these, only 42 served longer than a decade. Presently only 11 percent of the members of Congress are women. It is interesting to note that twice as many of these women have been Democrats as Republicans. This book was written to pay homage to these women and their perseverance over adversity in politics. They are trailblazers and pioneers in U.S. politics. The author, a congresswoman herself, includes the profiles of 15 tenured congresswomen and overviews of other women lawmakers during 3 periods of the twentieth century. The first period, covering 1917 to World War II, includes such pioneers as Jeannette Rankin and Mary Teresa Norton. The second period, called "The Greening Years," covers World War II through the 1960s and features long-serving Frances Payne Bolton and Margaret Chase Smith. The third period, "The Modern Era," profiles some contemporary leaders, such as Shirley Chisholm, Pat Schroeder, and Nancy Kassebaum. These congresswomen's legislative records are sufficiently rich and significantly influential in U.S. society. The overviews in each section are particularly informative because they summarize and assess the triumph and struggle of women politicians in that era. The articles provide biographical information, data on the political career, and some of the notable issues and viewpoints of these congresswomen. The entries end with a brief evaluation of their contributions to Congress and society.

As one can expect, the roles that women have been able to play in Congress have varied widely and have assumed greater significance over time. Only a few women rose to positions of seniority and chaired important committees—Julia Butler Hansen and Barbara Vucanovich are still the only women to have chaired House Appropriations subcommittees. Barbara Mikulski of Maryland is the only woman to have chaired a Senate Appropriations subcommittee. The pattern of few women in leadership positions in Congress is slowly changing. The influence of women in Congress has been mostly in the traditionally feminine areas of interest, such as family, children, health, and literacy. Overall, these women are often less concerned with the attainment of a position and more concerned with the well-being of the nation than are their male counterparts. The author predicts that in the twenty-first century, more U.S. women will be unleashed from the previous conventions and commit their potentials and energy to ensure the survival and advancement of the United States.

The reference materials section presents charts and tables that list the women in Congress by their names, dates and length of service, a brief profile, professional background, key committees they served on, and political interests. This is not only an informative resource book about congresswomen in the United States but is also remarkably entertaining reading for those who are interested in the personal biographies of these remarkable women. The volume is highly recommended for libraries supporting women's studies and political science programs. [R: RBB, 15 Feb 97, p. 1043]—**Eveline L. Yang**

282.   **Politics in America**. Washington, D.C., Congressional Quarterly, 1965- . illus. index. $79.95. JK1010.P64. 328.73'073'025. LC 89-7405. ISSN 1064-6809.

Politics in America provides students and other researchers with valuable background on members of Congress. Arranged alphabetically by state, each section presents a table of statistics for the state, brief information on the governor, a map of the state's congressional districts, and extensive information on its senators and representatives. The information on each member of Congress includes an analytical essay, listings of committee assignments, election results, campaign financing, key votes, voting studies, and interest group ratings. House members for each state appear in order by the number of the district they represent; background information on the district is also provided.

Additional features of the work include a detailed table of contents, an informative introduction covering the leadership and concerns of the current Congress, membership listings of Congressional committees, and an index of personal names and states. New sections added in the 1990 edition are a table of seniority by party, a listing of close House races in the last election, and a helpful guide to pronunciation of members' names. The 1990 edition is presented in a larger size, making the text and Congressional district maps easier to read.

A comparison with the 1988 *Almanac of American Politics* (see ARBA 86, entry 695 for a review of the 1986 edition) reveals that the almanac covers more territory. It provides a broader survey of the nation, regions, presidency, House, Senate, governors, demographics, and campaign finance, as well as providing useful metropolitan area district maps for selected areas and ratings of more interest groups. Nevertheless, *Politics in America* does an excellent job covering its more limited territory. Its well-researched and highly readable assessments of individual members of Congress make this an important reference work.—**Carol Wheeler and Terry Ann Mood**

283.   **Congressional Staff Directory, Summer: Containing, in a convenient arrangement, useful information concerning the Congress, with emphasis on the staffs of the Members and of the committees and subcommittees, together with staff biographies**. Joel D. Treese, ed. Alexandria, Va., CQ Staff Directories, 1959- . index. $89.00. LC 59-13987. ISSN 0069-8938.

For more than thirty-five years, the *Congressional Staff Directory* has provided biographical and locational information on the staffs of the members of Congress. The *Directory* is now published three times each year, spring, summer, and fall, and is available as a subscription as well as individually. Each directory is particularly useful for its listing of names, room locations, phone numbers, and positions of all (not just selected!) staff members. In addition, names, positions, and phone numbers of key personnel of executive departments and independent agencies are listed.

Biographical information on key congressional staff experts is provided by the staff members themselves. Not all staff are included in this section and there are no stated criteria concerning the selection of "key experts."

The directory contains a wealth of other information, much of which is found in other sources. There is merit, however, in having all of this information in one volume.

Biographical information about state delegations in Congress includes names of cities within each district and addresses and telephone numbers of district offices. One section lists all cities with more than 1,500 population and their congressional district number and name of representative. Another section lists governors and their office addresses and phone numbers.

In addition to the expected index of names, there is a keyword subject index which, for example, leads the user to any executive agency or committee concerned with nuclear energy. Each section of the *Directory* is printed on a different color paper, providing easier access to information. The directory can be useful in any library.—**Roberta R. Palen and Terry Ann Mood**

284.   **Congressional Yellow Book: Who's Who in Congress, Including Committees and Key Staff**. New York, Monitor Leadership Directories, 1976- . 1v. (various paging). illus. maps. index. $265.00pa./yr. (4 issues). JK1010.C68. ISSN 0191-1422.

Formerly subtitled *A Directory of Members of Congress, Including Their Committees and Key Staff Aides*, the *Congressional Yellow Book* provides basic information on members of the Senate and House of Representatives: birth date, home city, education, and religion. Political information is also provided: year first elected to Congress, committee assignments, and other legislative and party responsibilities. It also lists key staff aides and their areas of legislative responsibility, although it gives no biographical information on staff. The directory also gives office addresses in Washington and in the home district and (where available) fax numbers and E-mail addresses. Quarterly updates keep the directory accurate.

The directory includes maps of each congressional district and zip codes by district. A complete listing of congressional committees and subcommittees provides their membership, staff, addresses, and a brief description of their jurisdiction. Congressional caucuses, party groups, and leadership offices are also listed with their members and addresses.

This is a very useful resource on Congress. While the biographical material is limited, the directory is comprehensive. The book is also available on CD-ROM.—**Frank L. Wilson and Terry Ann Mood**

285.   Morin, Isobel V. **Women of the U.S. Congress**. Minneapolis, Minn., Oliver Press, 1994. 160p. illus. index. $14.95. E840.6.M66. 328.73'0082. LC 93-26068. ISBN 1-881508-12-9.

This slim volume selects seven of the most important congresswomen and gives them just over 10 pages apiece. This group of biographies is sandwiched in between introductory and concluding chapters on American politics, women's places therein, and 1992 (the Year of the Woman). One of the excellent facets of this book is the numerous full-page black-and-white photographs. Not just head shots, these portraits capture the spirits of the women and the times. There are also a serviceable index, a bibliography, and a chronological list of all 159 women who have served in the U.S. Congress. The typeface is large and the prose simple, so that one has the impression the text is intended for schoolchildren or early undergraduates. For example, in the entry on Barbara Jordan, who served on the Judiciary Committee during Watergate, one reads: "Representative Jordan was convinced that impeachment was necessary. Her speech began with a resounding affirmation of her faith in the Constitution. . . . The 'gentlelady from Texas' became an instant celebrity. *Newsweek* magazine reported that her speech was the most memorable indictment of the president to come out of the impeachment hearings" (pp. 93-94). There is no citation to *Newsweek*, and no mention of *Newsweek* appears in the bibliography.

The only book with which this title competes, *Women in Congress*, was put out by the House of Representatives in 1989. This book is not cited in the bibliography either. There are some similarities of format between the two texts: Both feature large photographs, and both use a large font. However, the biographies in *Women in Congress*, although there is one for every woman who served in Congress, are much briefer. They are also equally unsophisticated.

Readers would be well served by having a one-volume collection of biographies of all the women in Congress that were of the caliber of those in the *Dictionary of American Biography*, with a complete scholarly apparatus and a deeper level of analysis. This being said, it must also be said that *Women of the U. S. Congress* is a delightful and well-written narrative. [R: BL, July 94, pp. 1934-35; SLJ, May 94, p. 125]—**Judith M. Brugger**

286.   **Congressional Directory**. Washington, D.C., GPO, 1809- . index. $23.95pa. ISSN 0160-9890.

Published since 1809, the *Official Congressional Directory* is one of the two indispensable directory reference sources for the U.S. government (the other is the *United States Government [Organization] Manual*). Although there is substantial overlapping between the two works, a point that cost-conscious government officials might well investigate further, each is essential for the unique elements it contains. Although both works have listings of executive agencies, the *Congressional Directory*, as would be expected, has much fuller coverage of matters pertaining to the Congress: personnel of Congressional committee staffs, maps of Congressional districts, representatives of the press and other media officially accredited to the Congress, zip codes for Congressional offices and committees, etc. It also includes brief biographies of members of Congress, arranged by state. Some non-Congressional information is also included: information about the Federal Judiciary, for example, and consular offices here in the United States. Despite the steadily escalating costs of the biennial volumes, this work is still a bargain.—**Richard A. Gray and Terry Ann Mood**

287. **Who's Who in Congress**. Washington, D.C., Congressional Quarterly, 1992- . illus. $7.95pa. ISSN 1054-9234.

This is the perfect directory to Congress for virtually all except the largest public libraries. The Congressional Quarterly (CQ) staff have provided a comprehensive, usable, and reasonably priced guide to Congress. For each member of Congress, it contains birth date, educational background, occupation, political background, office address, telephone number, key staff positions, committee assignments, CQ voting analysis, key interest group ratings (Americans for Democratic Action, American Conservative Union, AFL-CIO, and Chamber of Commerce of the United States), and basic election statistics. It also contains lists of all congressional committees and their members, a list of the leadership of both houses, and a breakdown of how each member voted on key issues.

For all of this, the work does have limitations, mainly the result of the small format. A number of interest group ratings are omitted, and not even the majority and minority committee staff directors are listed. The book lacks the comprehensiveness of more extensive guides, such as the *Congressional Staff Directory* (see ARBA 91, entry 735). Nevertheless, this is a well-done and useful reference book. While it might not meet all the needs of college and university libraries, for those libraries without a larger guide to Congress, this is an affordable "must buy."—**Robert Clyde Hodges and Terry Ann Mood**

Presidents and Vice Presidents

288. **The American Presidents: The Office and the Men**. Frank N. Magill, ed. Englewood Cliffs, N.J., Salem Press, 1986. 3v. illus. maps. index. $119.00/set. LC 85-30338. ISBN 0-89356-525-3.

The American Presidents is a collection of biographical essays and commentaries on all U.S. presidents and their administrations from Washington to Reagan. As Frank Magill says in his introduction, "the objective has been to interpret the impact of the man on the office, to stress his contributions to . . . the nation and to show whether the tenor of the office was changed by his administration." The essays were produced by professors from academic institutions throughout the country and vary considerably in length. The essay on Chester A. Arthur rates six pages of text while Franklin D. Roosevelt merits forty-seven. Each essay concludes with a brief annotated bibliography. An index to the entire work is at the end of the third volume.

American Presidents cannot be used as a quick reference guide. William DeGregorio's *The Complete Book of U.S. Presidents* (see entry 292) and Joseph Kane's *Facts about the Presidents* (see entry 297) are far better ready-reference tools. *American Presidents* is quite similar to Henry F. Graff's *The Presidents: A Reference History* (see ARBA 85, entry 448). Both provide rather detailed introductory reviews of U.S. presidential administrations together with recommended sources for additional information. The single-volume Graff work has larger print and is more convenient to use, and its bibliographies tend to be more detailed. Unlike Graff's, the Magill work is well illustrated. *The Presidents* stops with the Carter years, while *The American Presidents* continues up to the beginning of Reagan's second term, although the ultimate value of this final chapter might be questioned pending the completion of the Reagan presidency.

The American Presidents is certainly a useful work. However, it is not a new idea, and at $119.00 it is considerably more expensive than the $65.00 Graff volume. Recommended for larger collections and for consideration by those not already owning *The Presidents*. [R: RQ, Fall 86, pp. 106-7]—**Thomas H. Patterson**

289. Beard, Charles A., with William Beard and Detlev Vagts. **Charles A. Beard's The Presidents in American History: George Washington to George Bush**. rev. ed. Englewood Cliffs, N.J., Julian Messner/Silver Burdett Press, 1989. 227p. illus. $12.98; $5.95pa. E176.8.B43. 973'.09'92. LC 89-3241. ISBN 0-671-68574-0; 0-671-68575-9pa.

The initial edition of this book appeared in 1935 and was revised several times by Beard before his death in 1948. Since that time, two children and a grandson (Vagts) have made updates and minor corrections.

Each presidential sketch consists of a picture of the president and a brief biographical essay. The essay is a political portrait with a recognizable Beardian slant for those familiar with his many historical works. At the end of the book, a biographical digest section lists each president and includes data on birth, death, marriages, public career, and terms of office. This data is followed by a list of cabinet members who served that president and information on popular and electoral votes for those who ran for the presidency.

While there are many other works about the presidents that contain more factual information, the unique style and flavor of Beard's work demand a presence on library shelves. Librarians should add this volume if they have not purchased an edition recently.—**David V. Loertscher**

290.   **The Complete History of Our Presidents**. Vero Beach, Fla., Rourke Enterprises, 1997. 13v. illus. maps. index. $239.95/set. ISBN 0-86593-405-3.

The Complete History of Our Presidents is an excellent encyclopedic history of the U.S. presidency for juveniles. Numerous illustrations, maps, and photographs highlight the easy-to-read text. Each volume contains a glossary with clear, simple explanations of pertinent terms used in the text. In addition, each book has its own index and bibliography, a general chronology and timeline, and a list of all the presidents.

Each volume covers the terms of several chief executives, and students will readily see the larger historical picture. In addition to the general historical information about the presidents, a brief article appears about each first lady and vice president, accompanied by illustrations or photographs. Throughout the series there are selected topics that are covered in one or two pages; for example: "Immigration in the 1850s" (v. 4, p. 29); "African Americans After Reconstruction" (v. 6, p. 47); and "The Space Race" (v. 10, pp. 52-53).

The final volume consists of a 64-page alphabetic index of the entire set. Again, large typeface and generous illustrations make it easy to read. The series is highly recommended for collections that provide service for students in middle school through junior high and the lower high school grades.—**Bruce H. Webb**

291.   Cunningham, Homer F. **The Presidents' Last Years: George Washington to Lyndon B. Johnson**. Jefferson, N.C., McFarland, 1989. 335p. index. $25.95. E176.l.C95. 973'.09'92. LC 88-35089. ISBN 0-89950-408-6.

As former president John Adams breathed his last, he muttered, "Thomas Jefferson survives," although Jefferson had passed away earlier that same day—July 4, 1826, exactly 50 years after the nation's independence day. This represents one of the stories in Cunningham's collection of essays on the deaths of 36 presidents. Averaging about 10 pages for each, the rather uneven text relates the post-presidential period of each and their deaths. Ulysses S. Grant, for example, suffered terribly and depended on morphine and cocaine to relieve his pain. James Monroe died in poverty, having often used his own funds to travel between diplomatic posts. The attractiveness of the book is that the stories of the chief executives are collected in one volume. [R: BR, Nov/Dec 89, p. 54]—**Boyd Childress**

292.   DeGregorio, William A. **The Complete Book of U.S. Presidents**. 3d ed. New York, Dembner Book/Barricade Books, 1991. 740p. illus. index. $30.00; $19.95pa. E176.1.D43. 973'.0992. LC 91-19325. ISBN 0-942637-37-2; 0-942637-38-0pa.

This book is a trivia buff's delight and a treasure for reference librarians in search of otherwise difficult-to-find information on U.S. presidents. In a well-organized, easy-to-use format, historian DeGregorio presents major and minor facts about the presidents, from Washington through the first 27 months of the Bush administration. Subcategories for each president provide answers to questions about name, physical description, personality, family, ancestry, relatives, childhood, education, religion, recreation, romances (including extramarital), marriage, and career prior to the presidency. History students will be pleased with the detail provided on presidential administrations, including campaigns, campaign issues, political opponents, cabinet members, Supreme Court appointments, and other historically pertinent information (both favorable and unfavorable). Articles are footnoted and identify books for further reading. Three appendixes give data on the political composition of Congresses from 1789 to the present, presidential curiosities, and historians' rankings of the presidents. Access is excellent through the logical arrangement of chapters and a good subject index.

Historians and individuals may disagree with some of the author's interpretations of history. Lincoln himself would disagree that slavery was the main cause of the Civil War (p. 238). Also, considering the importance of secession to his administration, Lincoln's little-known 1848 argument in favor of the right of revolution in general, and the right of Texas to separate from Mexico in particular, perhaps should be included. Nevertheless, the book is quite good, and historians do not always present varying viewpoints. As valuable as is *Facts About the Presidents* (see entry 297), *The Complete Book of U.S. Presidents* is highly recommended for anyone with an interest in American history and for school, public, college, and university libraries.—**Donald E. Collins and Terry Ann Mood**

293. Diller, Daniel C., and Stephen L. Robertson. **The Presidents, First Ladies, and Vice Presidents: White House Biographies, 1789-1997**. Washington, D.C., Congressional Quarterly, 1997. 180p. illus. index. $24.95pa. ISBN 1-56802-311-1.

At first glance, Congressional Quarterly's new volume of presidential biographies seems just another one of the large group of reference books that present presidential information in readily accessible form. Yet closer examination shows that this highly respected publisher of governmental information has again gathered into one handy reference book information that is available elsewhere only in scattered locations. The first chapter makes fascinating reading. "The Daily Life of the President" covers briefly the work habits of the various presidents, the changing roles of the first ladies, and the role of the Secret Service in protecting the first family. This chapter contains two gems of information: a copy of President Clinton's typical daily work schedule and a one-column explanation of the role of the Chief Usher of the White House, taken from J. B. West's book *Upstairs at the White House*.

The White House biographies start with illustrated biographies of every president, running approximately two pages in length. Under the picture of each man is a facsimile of his signature, which is an interesting touch. The wives of the presidents receive one-page coverage with a picture. An interesting insertion in this section is a two-page spread covering "White House Hostesses: Surrogate First Ladies" (pp.118-19). Biographies, even brief ones, of the 11 women covered here—sisters, daughters, and nieces of the chief executives—are difficult to find. The last group of biographies covers all the vice presidents except those who were later elected president. This volume is an excellent source to use for information about those interesting individuals who have inhabited the president's home throughout the years. It will prove a useful reference in any collection. [R: BR, Sept/Oct 97, pp. 60-61]—**Nancy P. Reed**

294. Dunlap, Leslie W. **Our Vice-Presidents and Second Ladies**. Metuchen, N.J., Scarecrow, 1988. 397p. index. $35.00. LC 88-4123. ISBN 0-8108-2114-1.

John Nance Garner, one Texan vice-president, once remarked to Lyndon Johnson, another Texan vice-president, that "the vice presidency isn't worth a pitcher of warm spit." In spite of that judgment, Dunlap has produced an entertaining reference book on a seemingly unpromising subject. The book deals with vice-presidents from John Adams to George Bush. Each of the forty-three office-holders is given a biographical headnote followed by an anecdotal essay on the relationship between the vice-president and his wife. The many fascinating personal facts and stories included in this volume make it a treasure trove to browse. It turns out that the Coolidges were cruelly mistreated and snubbed by first lady Mrs. Harding. In contrast, Mrs. Coolidge was a very fine woman. The quote "What this country needs is a really good five cent cigar" was made by Thomas R. Marshall, vice-president under Woodrow Wilson, while he was presiding over the Senate during a particularly dreary speech. (Marshall, by the way, was the fourth, and so far last, Hoosier to serve as vice-president.) Unfortunately, the rambling organization of the individual essays and the book's perfunctory index preclude this work from being used as a ready-reference tool. In addition, some of the historical judgments are a bit idiosyncratic. The essay on John Tyler glosses over his very serious disagreements with the Whig Party leadership after he succeeded the deceased William Henry Harrison. Millard Fillmore also receives a surprisingly favorable assessment, although no mention is made of his widow's burning of his papers. Still, the book's focus on the marital relations of the vice-presidents makes it a unique addition for the well-stocked reference collection with an interest in American political history.—**Ronald H. Fritze**

295.   Freidel, Frank. **The Presidents of the United States of America**. 12th ed. Washington, D.C., White House Historical Association; distr., Lincoln, Mass., Sewall, 1989. 91p. illus. index. $9.95pa. LC 89-050707. ISBN 0-912308-37-0.

This joint venture of the White House Historical Association and the National Geographic Society updates the 1981 edition and exemplifies the quality that readers expect from their work. Chronologically arranged two-page spreads cover each president from George Washington through George Bush. One page provides an overview of the subject's political career; the other is a reproduction of the official White House portrait (except for President Bush, for whom a photograph is used because his portrait was not complete at the time of printing). Freidel's readable narrative of the highlights of each administration provides continuity and is useful as an overview. The table of contents lists the artist of each presidential portrait; an appendix lists the vice presidents.

Freidel's reasonably priced work will be enjoyed by readers from middle-school age through adulthood. For more informative overviews with statistical data on the presidents, their families, and their administrations, *The American Presidents* (see entry 306) by David Whitney, *Facts about the Presidents* (see entry 297) by Joseph Nathan Kane, and *The Presidents in American History* (see entry 289) by Charles A. Beard, are standard works. Still more extensive information is found in William A. DeGregorio's *The Complete Book of U.S. Presidents* (see entry 292), which includes personal and family topics, quotations, bibliographies, and information on administrations.—**Vandelia L. VanMeter**

296.   Havel, James T. **U.S. Presidential Candidates and the Elections: A Biographical and Historical Guide**. New York, Macmillan Library Reference/Simon & Schuster Macmillan, 1996. 2v. $175.00/set. ISBN 0-02-897134-5.

The emergence of Ross Perot's Reform Party in the last two presidential elections provides a rare glimpse into an electoral process that extends beyond a two-party system. Throughout U.S. history, a great diversity of candidates, political parties, agendas, and ideologies have existed in obscurity, hidden behind the current system. A number of factors, such as financial wherewithal, tradition, organizational resources, and media attention, dilute the electorate's perception that their choices consist of a Democrat, a Republican, and an occasional third-party candidate. Havel's work provides a unique point of discovery from which researchers can explore the hidden diversity within each presidential election from 1789 to 1992.

The first volume, *The Candidates*, contains an alphabetically arranged list of individuals who have sought the office of the presidency and vice-presidency, with the spectrum of diversity extending from George Bush to Lawrence Welk (Democratic presidential candidate, 1976). Entries give standard information (birth, death, education, children, organizational membership, and so forth) and a current mailing address when appropriate. As with most biographical reference tools, the length and the amount of detail contained in each entry are determined by how famous the person was. The second volume, *The Elections*, provides a summary of each election, highlighting important events, parties, conventions, and platforms. Results from primary, general, and electoral college balloting are also given. The volume begins with an introductory essay outlining the early history of the presidential nominating and election processes and concludes with a comprehensive bibliography. This reference work represents a major contribution to the understanding of both the diverse nature of presidential elections and the process that decides who leads the Executive Office. It is highly recommended for all library collections. [R: LJ, 1 Oct 96, p. 68]—**Robert V. Labaree**

297.   Kane, Joseph Nathan. **Facts about the Presidents: A Compilation of Biographical and Historical Information**. 6th ed. Bronx, N.Y., H. W. Wilson, 1993. 433p. illus. index. $55.00. E176.1.K3.973'.099. LC 93-9207. ISBN 0-8242-0845-5.

The U.S. presidency is a perennial subject for reference works, and one such book that is approaching the status of a classic is *Facts about the Presidents*. The 6th edition covers up to February 1993, the opening days of the Clinton administration.

As in previous editions, the work is divided into two parts: biographical data and comparative data. The biographical section is divided into entries for each president that are arranged in chronological order. Each entry supplies the usual biographical information: date and place of birth, religion, parents' names, a portrait, and similar facts. It also includes the convention ballot on which a president received his party's nomination, his appointments to the cabinet and the Supreme Court, presidential firsts, various outstanding or notorious events during each presidency, information about vice presidents and first ladies, and a bibliography.

The comparative section is a cornucopia of fascinating items about the presidents and the presidency. A list of presidential nicknames reveals that Grover Cleveland had the most (20) followed closely by Abraham Lincoln and Ulysses S. Grant (19 each). Books authored by presidents are also listed, with Teddy Roosevelt leading the field with 37. Presidential heights and weights are listed. Lincoln remains the tallest at 6'4", while Taft holds a commanding lead in weight. An index of subjects and personal names makes this information more accessible. No good library should be without this book. [R: SLMQ, Summer 93, p. 267]—**Ronald H. Fritze**

298. **Marshall Cavendish Illustrated History of the Presidents of the United States**. By Ruth Oakley. Freeport, N.Y., Marshall Cavendish, 1990. 8v. illus. maps. index. $149.95/set. E176.8.025. 973'.0992. LC 89-17283. ISBN 1-85435-144-3.

Presidents Washington through Bush are introduced in this set of 8 chronologically arranged 64-page volumes. Each well-bound volume includes a glossary, an index, and a brief introduction to the time period covered. Individual biographies of the presidents range from 6 to 18 pages in length and include boxed facts, a state/population map, and numerous illustrations.

This set addresses the need for a multivolume treatment of the presidents, suitable for elementary students, that supplements encyclopedia articles but is less than a monograph on each. The format of the set, with large print and adequate white space, will appeal to young readers, but they will find the writing and vocabulary uneven. The illustrations, which take up more than one-half of the space, include familiar photographs, political cartoons, drawings, and many original watercolors. Several of the pictures enhance the text, but others contribute little. In some cases illustrations or their captions are poorly placed or misleading. The glossary in each volume is useful, although some definitions are inadequate. Many pertinent terms have not been included, and those listed should have been italicized in the text for easy identification. The inclusion of "gossipy" bits about the presidents' personal lives in books for this age group is a matter of judgment, but since it was done, it should have been done consistently. For instance, Harding's and F. D. Roosevelt's extramarital romances are mentioned, but Kennedy's are not. A set of this nature could be very useful in school and public libraries, but librarians are urged to preview it before purchase. [R: RBB, 1 Mar 91, p. 1425]—**Vandelia L. VanMeter**

299. Martin, Fenton S., and Robert U. Goehlert. **The American Presidency: A Bibliography**. Washington, D.C., Congressional Quarterly, 1987. 506p. index. $75.00. LC 87-445. ISBN 0-87-187-415-6.

Martin, Fenton S., and Robert U. Goehlert. **American Presidents: A Bibliography**. Washington, D.C., Congressional Quarterly, 1987. 756p. index. $125.00. LC 86-30938. ISBN 0-87187-416-4.

Complementary but distinct, these bibliographies focus upon English-language publications from 1885 to 1986 which are "analytical, scholarly, and not merely descriptive" (pp. ix, xi). Citations are drawn from books, articles, dissertations, and research reports. Government publications are omitted. The sources searched for both bibliographies include thirty-nine indexes, *Comprehensive Dissertation Index* and *Dissertation Abstracts*, numerous bibliographies, in-print catalogs, the *National Union Catalog*, *Biographical Books*, and six databases. Directed to students and scholars, these multidisciplinary unannotated bibliographies contain more than 21,000 entries. Extensive author indexes and subject indexes, together with detailed tables of contents, provide useful access. Indexes are keyed to entry numbers.

The American Presidency considers the institution of the presidency, including its "history, development, powers, and relations with other branches of the federal government" (p. ix). It includes 8,567 entries. Thirteen broad topics are divided into more than 200 subtopics. The broad topics include perspectives, the law, organization, leadership and character, problems, and extrapresidential matters. Also included are the relationship between the president and the government, the media, foreign affairs, the world, and society. The largest number of citations, one-third of those in the volume, concern the selection and election of the president. The author and subject indexes comprise one-fifth of the volume and include access to citations relating to individual presidents.

American Presidents includes 13,150 entries. Its focus is the "accomplishments, policies, and activities of individual presidents" (p. xi). Entries are organized by president in chronological order, from Washington to Reagan. Entries for each president are grouped into five areas: biography, private life, public career, presidential years, and writings. As necessary, these are divided into subtopics, listed alphabetically. Within each area or subtopic, citations are listed alphabetically by author. Half of the citations in the volume concern the presidential years; one-fifth focus on the private lives of the presidents. The number of citations per president varies from 1,935 (Lincoln) to 24 (Pierce).

Fenton S. Martin and Robert U. Goehlert, librarians at Indiana University, have previously collaborated on bibliographies concerning policy analysis and management and the British Parliament. Their earlier work, *The Presidency: A Research Guide* (see ARBA 86, entry 679) contained 1,400 entries. It emphasized primary sources and provided explanatory text, annotations, and appendixes for research on both the presidency and the presidents.

The American Presidency and *American Presidents* were the most extensive bibliographies on these subjects when they were published. The print is readable, and they are sturdily bound. *American Presidents* is not so extensive as the projected fifty-volume annotated series, *Bibliographies of the Presidents of the United States, 1789-1989* (Meckler). However, given its availability and affordability, together with its inclusion of the relatively more accessible sources, *American Presidents*, though now dated, should be the bibliography of choice for most libraries. [R: Choice, Dec 87, p. 602; LJ, Dec 87, p. 102; RBB, 1 Dec 87, p. 612; WLB, Nov 87, p. 87]—**John Cudd**

300. **Presidential Also-Rans and Running Mates, 1758-1980**. Leslie H. Southwick, comp. Jefferson, N.C., McFarland, 1984. 722p. bibliog. index. $49.95. LC 83-25577. ISBN 0-89950-109-5.

While it is easy to find biographical information on the individuals who have attained the presidency and vice presidency of the United States, it is arduous to locate information on those who were nominated but who lost the election. This book fully satisfies the need for such information.

Arranged in chronological order by election up to 1980, the biographies are informative and readable. Details are given, yet the author attempts to portray "a human side to the candidates." The author provides an analysis of each individual's qualifications, as well as background information on family, education, personal characteristics, and public offices held. Each biography is at least 3,000 words long. A brief bibliography ends each section. In addition, dates of party conventions, popular vote, and electoral vote are provided for each election.

This book is a worthy companion to Irving Stone's *They Also Ran* (Doubleday, 1966). Stone's book includes readable sketches and is an attempt to capture "the vital essence of each man." However, it ends with the 1964 election. Although Stone's book is valuable, Southwick's provides more substantive information and should quickly become the standard reference work in the field.

Although the price of this book may seem high for smaller libraries, it should not deter any librarian from purchasing it. The book is highly recommended for all libraries.

Another title, less recent, *'If Elected': Unsuccessful Candidates for the Presidency, 1796-1968*, published by the U.S. National Portrait Gallery (Washington, D.C., GPO, 1972. 512p. $9.50. S/N 4706-0008), is a roster of names including those who became president as well as unsuccessful candidates. Major-party candidates who tried two or three times and third-party candidates are also included. Each entry contains an account of the life and philosophy of each candidate, accompanied by a portrait. [R: WLB, Dec 84, p. 293]—**Roberta R. Palen**

301. **The Presidents**. Fred L. Israel, ed. Danbury, Conn., Grolier, 1997. 8v. illus. maps. index. $259.00/set. ISBN 0-7172-7642-2.

The Presidents is an eight-volume set that details the presidencies from George Washington through the 1996 election of Bill Clinton. Coverage includes a chronology; an extensive biography; excerpts from inaugural addresses and other noteworthy speeches or documents; information about family, cabinet, and vice president; and key places associated with various presidents. The set is lavishly illustrated with both color and black-and-white photographs and drawings. A stunning full-page color portrait begins the section on each president. Entries are 20-plus pages, giving a complete overview of each administration. Although the set is easily accessible for middle school students, it will appeal to high school students and adults as well. Volume 8 includes returns for each election with color-coded maps and state-by-state voting statistics, allowing the reader to visually see the country grow. An adequate index is also provided.

The information here is more extensive than the one-volume *Facts about the Presidents* (see entry 297) or *The Presidents, First Ladies, and Vice Presidents* (see entry 293). The set under review is more readable than *The Presidents: A Reference History* (see entry 302), which does not include the 1996 election. Because of its currency, its visual appeal, and its content, this set is a must-buy for all schools and public libraries.—**Lynda Welborn**

302. **The Presidents: A Reference History**. 2d ed. Henry F. Graff, ed. New York, Scribner's/Simon & Schuster Macmillan, 1996. 811p. illus. index. $105.00. ISBN 0-684-80471-9.

A scholarly, meaty tome, Graff's reference work fills a need for a data-rich summary on each of the presidents of the United States. To the original 1984 edition (see ARBA 85, entry 448), he adds three presidencies and an article discussing the demands on First Ladies, from Martha Washington to Hillary Rodham Clinton. Each major entry provides a biography, a period history, direct citations from important speeches and interviews, an evaluation of each presidency, and a generous annotated bibliography. To the body of this incisive work, Graff appends a general bibliography; tabular data on each president, including a breakdown of Congress by party, appointments, and key events; and an overview of the expanding role of the executive branch of government.

Graff's commentary is anything but dry or predictable. To a description of Lyndon Johnson's Great Society, he quotes the president as he yells into a detractor's face the unfairness of racism; in the entry on Bill Clinton, Graff adds a touching scene in which the president, shortly before moving to Washington, D.C., returns his daughter's frog to Arkansas waters so it can live a normal life. Graff salts his text with valuable information on wars, political initiatives, and errors—for example, Ulysses S. Grant's admission that he required on-the-job training after moving from the military to the White House, and Warren G. Harding's public humiliation after *The President's Daughter* named him as the father of an illegitimate child. In describing the political scene when John Quincy Adams came to power, the text offers a tally of popular and electoral votes. The only failing of this admirable reference work is the puzzling absence of maps to indicate the size of the country in each term, action shots, or reproductions of Washington, D.C. art to show the development of the city and public appearances of presidents while in office. [R: LJ, 1 Sept 96, p. 170; RBB, 1 Sept 96, p. 170]—**Mary Ellen Snodgrass**

303. Quinn-Musgrove, Sandra L., and Sanford Kanter. **America's Royalty: All the Presidents' Children**. rev. ed. Westport, Conn., Greenwood Press, 1995. 286p. illus. index. $59.95. ISBN 0-313-29535-2.

Little research has been conducted about the lives of presidential children. In fact, in the current age of television, the media seems to treat them more as ornaments or curiosities of an incoming administration than as contributors to a president's life experience and mental well-being. This book represents a step forward in the knowledge about the offspring of the U.S. presidents and helps to illustrate the fact that with the exception of James Buchanan (the only president to never marry), the election of a new president represents not only an individual ascending to office but also a family beginning a new life.

The book begins by briefly describing the lives of six presidents who never had children, followed by a description in chronological order of the children of the presidents. This revised edition includes biographical sketches of George Bush's six children and Bill Clinton's one child, as well as changes to the text "reflecting the maturing technical or mechanical skills of this edition's author" (preface). When known, the date of birth, birthplace, date of death, age at death, cause of death, educational background, profession or occupation, name of spouse, and number of children for each child are given. The data are followed by an essay providing a detailed description of the child's life, accomplishments, and failures. A list of further readings concludes each presidential entry, although there is no list after the chapter devoted to childless presidents. The book concludes with an appendix listing shared characteristics among the presidential children, a bibliography, and an index.

This book is well written and informative, and is unique in that it describes in-depth the lives of the presidents' children. It is recommended for all libraries.—**Robert V. Labaree**

304.   **Scholastic Encyclopedia of the Presidents and Their Times**. updated ed. By David Rubel. New York, Scholastic, 1997. 232p. illus. maps. index. $17.95. ISBN 0-590-49366-3.

A revision of the 1994 edition (see ARBA 96, entry 521), this version of the *Scholastic Encyclopedia of the Presidents and Their Times* covers Bill Clinton's reelection; the assassination of Yitzhak Rabin; and the problems, physical and political, of Russia's president Boris Yeltsin. Updated maps and charts are also included.

Attractively arranged and well illustrated, each entry follows the same format. The president's name, term, and picture begin the entry. A mini-fact box containing those items dear to young researchers (e.g., the wife's name and the names of the children) and a personal tidbit—George Bush is cited for his opposition to broccoli and Theodore Roosevelt was the first president to fly in an airplane—follow. Highlights of the administration are given on the outside column of each page, with columns in the interior sections giving cultural events of the period. For example, Gibson Girls, yellow journalism, and breakfast cereals are given as part of the daily life during Grover Cleveland's term. Dates being covered are in blue numbers at the top of each page, making chronology easy to establish.

Added features of this reference book are a history of the White House and a list of presidential election results. A comprehensive index concludes the work. Throughout the essays are words highlighted in red, indicating that the subject is discussed in greater detail elsewhere. The only drawback to this system is that the topic, when found, is not in bold typeface or otherwise noted—one must read the entire page to find the information. This may be discouraging to younger students. A glossary might have been a better approach.

As an overview of the presidents, this is a valuable addition to a reference collection. The format is not overwhelming, concentrated attempts have been made to make the information engaging, and the overall effect of the book is professional and interesting. [R: SLJ, May 97, p. 162]—**Michele Tyrrell**

305.   Waldrup, Carole Chandler. **The Vice Presidents: Biographies of the 45 Men Who Have Held the Second Highest Office in the United States**. Jefferson, N.C., McFarland, 1996. 271p. illus. index. $35.00. ISBN 0-7864-0179-6.

Despite historical and contemporary denigration of its significance and value, the office of vice president of the United States is still an important government position, as the 1996 presidential election and other recent historical events have demonstrated. *The Vice Presidents* presents biographical portraits of the 45 individuals who have theoretically been "a heartbeat from the presidency." These portraits are presented in chronological order of service, from John Adams to Albert Gore Jr. Individuals profiled include vice presidents who later ascended to the presidency, such as Martin Van Buren, John Tyler, Millard Fillmore, Theodore Roosevelt, Harry Truman, and George Bush. Other vice presidents with lesser historical significance, including George Mifflin Dallas, Henry Wilson, Levi Morton, and James Sherman, are also covered.

These portraits average approximately six pages in length, covering the broad outlines of the professional and personal lives of these men. Individual entries include bibliographies, although they omit standard biographical reference sources, such as the *Dictionary of American Biography*. This work is a useful quick introduction to the lives of the U.S. vice presidents. Readers desiring more substantive analysis of the lives and careers of these individuals should consult the biographies listed in the bibliographic entries, personal papers, and government documents pertinent to the political careers of these personalities. [R: RBB, 1 Dec 96, p. 686]—**Bert Chapman**

306. Whitney, David C. **The American Presidents**. 7th ed. New York, Prentice Hall Press, 1990. 562p. illus. index. $21.95. E176.1.W6. 973'.0992. LC 89-39440. ISBN 0-13-028598-6.

According to the title page, this edition was revised and updated by the late author's wife, Robin Vaughn Whitney. It is clear that this biographical handbook was updated; the reader is brought up through the election of President Bush. However, the 6th and 7th editions appear to be exactly the same, even to the page numbers, up to the middle of the entry on Ronald Reagan. Thus the edition under review is merely an update, not a revision.

The format of this edition is the same as that of the previous editions (see ARBA 70, v.1, p. 65; ARBA 74, entry 424; and ARBA 80, entry 506), with biographical sketches comprising the largest part of the book. The sketches are easy to read and provide a balanced view of the presidents. The number of pages devoted to each president varies, but the most recent occupants of the oval office consistently receive more attention, regardless of their historical import. There are 19 pages on Gerald Ford versus 11 pages on Franklin Delano Roosevelt. Following the biographical sketches is a series of reference tables, each one treating a different aspect of the presidency, such as key facts about the presidents and presidential elections.

Anyone considering the selection of *The American Presidents* will want to compare it to Joseph N. Kane's *Facts about the Presidents* (see ARBA 90, entry 479). While the former provides useful narrative descriptions of the presidents' lives and some tabular data, the latter bulges with the kind of biographical and historical data that is requested at busy reference desks. This makes Kane's work, although twice as expensive, the book of choice for the reference library. [R: BL, 1 June 90, p. 1875]—**John P. Stierman**

307. Williamson, David. **Debrett's Presidents of the United States of America**. Topsfield, Mass., Salem House, 1989. 208p. illus. index. $27.50. E176.1.W7233. 973'.09'92. LC 87-36934. ISBN 0-88162-366-0.

It is appropriate that Debrett should create a book on U.S. presidents in the year that marks both the 200th anniversary of the presidency and George Bush's inauguration as the forty-first holder of that office. The volume was written by Williamson, who is the author of the companion volumes *Debrett's Kings and Queens of Britain* (1986) and *Debrett's Kings and Queens of Europe* (1988). His purpose is to provide a historical background for each president; to survey their lives and careers, particularly before becoming presidents; and to supply an assessment of their characters.

Each of the presidents has his own chapter, which begins with a headnote giving vital dates, place of birth, offices held, date of death, and place of burial. This information is followed by the main text, which includes black-and-white illustrations and a genealogical chart of the president's family. Many of these pictures are quite fascinating since they include some seldom-seen portraits of the presidential wives and other family members. There is a separate section of color portraits of each president. A personal name index concludes the volume.

Unlike most presidential reference books, the emphasis here is on family and personal history and not political history. The details of Andrew Jackson's duels along with the adventures and misadventures of other presidents are affectionately narrated. Williamson differs on some minor details from other authors; for example, what Zachary Taylor ate that killed him and whether Grover Cleveland was the father of Maria Halpin's child. Reasonably priced and very attractive, this book will complement most libraries' collections of presidential materials and is a suitable browsing item for the coffee table at home. [R: LJ, Jan 89, p. 82]—**Ronald H. Fritze**

308. **World Book of America's Presidents: Portraits of the Presidents**. Chicago, World Book, 1989. 288p. illus. index. $18.90. LC 88-51754. ISBN 0-7166-3213-6.

Designed primarily for students in grades 6-8 who need to write a chatty, informal report about a U.S. president, this volume does not provide enough factual information concerning the accomplishments, policies, or failures of these men. The work begins with an alphabetical listing of the presidents. This is followed by a chronological grouping of various presidents juxtaposed against a one-paragraph description of the major events of that period. A two-page chart consecutively lists each president's date and place of birth, college/university, religious preference, occupation/profession, political party, age at inauguration, term of office, death date, age at death, runner-up, and vice-president.

Most of the text is devoted to a five- to six-page biographical sketch of each president, accompanied by a full-page illustration of him and a smaller one of his wife or hostess. Additional pictures depict important events in each man's administration. A fact box furnishes biographical statistics and appropriate election results. A 90-item presidential trivia quiz and a presidential quotations section conclude the sketches. Appendixes give data regarding the presidential election process, the staff of the president, and additional reading. An index listing presidents, illustrations, major events, and laws is included.

Portraits of the Presidents presents information in an interesting manner, but its emphasis is on the personality of the president and his wife or hostess. Each sketch is liberally laced with unattributed quotations. The lack of a bibliography and source notes at the close of each profile is lamentable. Students who will use this volume are sufficiently knowledgeable to cite appropriate references when quoting and are inquisitive about additional reading. This volume provides a poor lesson in both areas. *Portraits of the Presidents* should only be purchased as a supplement to *Facts about the Presidents* (see entry 297) by Joseph Nathan Kane and *The Presidents: A Reference History* (see entry 302) by Henry F. Graff.—**Kathleen W. Craver**

States, Regions, and Cities

309.   **The Almanac of American Politics 1994: The Senators, the Representatives and the Governors: Their Records and Election Results, Their States and Districts**. By Michael Barone and Grant Ujifusa. Washington, D.C., National Journal, 1993. 1538p. illus. $59.95; $48.95pa. ISBN 0-89234-057-6; 0-89234-058-4pa.

Containing the usual information on congressional and administrative personnel and policies, this almanac starts with a useful quick-reference index of congresspeople by state, with references to the pages on which they are discussed. Thorough instructions on usage take the reader through the various categories for which data are provided: The U.S. population, ratings of Congress by lobbying groups, votes cast on major legislation, election results, and campaign financing. There is also a brief discussion of postwar politics and the current political situation. Each state section includes photographs of politicians and maps of the congressional districts, as well as an overview and factual data. Throughout the book, the narratives are not the dry, dusty recitations of fact that might be expected; for example, the overview of Colorado is evenhanded and interestingly written. This is an important resource for public libraries whose clients wish to check on their politicians' records and performance or to find basic political statistics about the United States.—**Sharon Langworthy**

310.   **Biographical Dictionary of American Mayors, 1820-1980: Big City Mayors**. Melvin G. Holli, and Peter d'A. Jones, eds. Westport, Conn., Greenwood Press, 1981. 576p. index. $69.50. LC 80-1796. ISBN 0-313-21134-5.

This directory provides brief biographies of all mayors of fifteen representative large American cities from 1820, or from the very beginnings when the office assumed a modern shape in that city, until 1980. The following cities, with starting date, which represent all regions of the country, are covered: Baltimore (1808), Boston (1822), Buffalo (1832), Chicago (1837), Cincinnati (1815), Cleveland (1836), Detroit (1824), Los Angeles (1850), Milwaukee (1846), New Orleans (1812), New York (1833), Philadelphia (1832), Pittsburgh (1816), San Francisco (1846), and Saint Louis (1823).

The biographies of 647 American mayors were prepared by over 100 scholars of American urban history, mostly professors from nearby universities who worked mainly with original sources in local city archives. Arranged alphabetically, each entry includes a list of major sources consulted and the name of the researcher. This comprehensive directory of all mayors includes many influential politicians not covered in other biographical directories; the researchers even uncovered some mayors not listed in official compilations. The twelve very useful appendixes include a chronological list of mayors by city; mayors by political party, ethnic background, religious affiliation, and place of birth; and statistical tables with selected data by decennial census on population, rank, and increase or decrease between censuses. [R: BL, 15 Dec 82, pp. 580-81; C&RL, July 82, p. 333; RQ, Summer 82, pp. 412-13; WLB, May 82, p. 699]—**LeRoy C. Schwarzkopf**

311. **Directory of Legislative Leaders 1989-90**. Denver, Colo., National Conference of State Legislatures, 1989. $20.00 spiralbound. ISSN 1051-4988.

Another in a series published by the National Conference of State Legislatures (NCSL), this title identifies legislative leaders for all 50 states and U.S. possessions. The listing includes all presiding officers as well as majority and minority leaders with their capitol and district addresses and telephone numbers. Key staff and their addresses are also included for each leadership position mentioned. This directory also notes all current NCSL officers, executive members, and chairs and vice-chairs of committees of the State-Federal Assembly.—**Frank Wm. Goudy**

312. Ritter, Charles F., and Jon L. Wakelyn. **American Legislative Leaders, 1850-1910**. Westport, Conn., Greenwood Press, 1989. 1090p. index. $125.00. E663.A46. 328.73'0922. LC 88-24734. ISBN 0-313-23943-6.

This biographical dictionary provides information on the 1,390 speakers of state houses of representatives from 1850 to 1910. Varying in length from one sentence to almost a page, the alphabetically arranged entries include useful information on birth, family, education, career before and after speakership, religious and fraternal affiliations, and death. A listing of sources consulted follows some of the entries. Arranged alphabetically by state, eight appendixes provide tabular presentation of specific characteristics of the speakers. A bibliography listing all sources consulted is arranged by state as well. The index is not particularly useful. Most index entries refer to the speakers; very few other entries appear. It is unclear what criteria were used in the indexing of contents of the biographical entries.

The 67-page introduction begins in a promising fashion by providing a scholarly overview of the history, politics, and economic issues related to state legislatures and their leaders. Unfortunately, the introduction continues with a questionable attempt at statistical analysis. As the authors admit, the sample is skewed. Nevertheless, sweeping conclusions are presented.

There are numerous editing and proofreading errors in this volume. For example, one page of the introduction has at least five errors in the numbers or percentages given in the text or in the accompanying tables. In the introduction, the authors are unable to decide if the word *data* is singular or plural. In one of the biographical entries, the subject and his brother are confused by misuse of a pronoun. On a single page of the bibliography, a place of publication is misspelled and a doctoral dissertation is not identified as such. A smaller and more carefully edited volume consisting of the beginning of the introduction, the introduction's bibliography, the biographical entries, the bibliography of sources consulted for the biographical entries, and a chronological listing of the speakers by state would be much more valuable, especially if offered at a significantly lower price.—**Carol Wheeler**

313. **State Elective Officials**. Lexington, Ky., Council of State Governments, 1976- . $45.00pa.

One of the continuing series of supplements to the *Book of the States*, this volume is particularly useful for providing information often difficult to locate elsewhere. Included are the names of elected state executive-branch officials, the judges of state courts of last resort, and state legislators. Members of state legislatures are listed by chamber. Party, district, and mailing address are given. Title of office and party affiliation of elected executive-branch officials are listed along with the names of these officials. In addition to all states, officials are listed for the District of Columbia, American Samoa, Guam, the Northern Mariana Islands, Puerto Rico, and the Virgin Islands.—**Roberta R. Palen**

314. **State Staff Directory, Summer 1997**. Alexandria, Va., CQ Staff Directories, 1997. 1919p. illus. index. $175.00pa./yr. ISBN 0-87289-129-1. ISSN 1090-7203.

CQ Staff Directories has expanded its offerings with the 1997 *State Staff Directory*. This new effort is presented with the assumption that such a guide will be increasingly useful as power continues to be shifted from the federal government to the states. This is a comprehensive guide to the 50 states of the United States with contact information and brief biographical sketches on more than 39,000 key players in state government.

Coverage for each state includes the offices of the governor, the lieutenant governor, and policy and decision makers in all departments, agencies, boards, and commissions. For smaller units, only a few names are listed, but major agencies may have 15 or 20 listings. Each listing consists of name, title, address, and telephone number. Fax numbers and zip codes are provided for the agencies as a whole. State entries also have a legislative section where each legislator is listed, complete with contact and brief biographical information and a list of committee assignments. Each state section begins with a state information page that includes historical, demographic, and budget facts.

At the end of the volume are three substantial sections. The first contains more than 800, one-paragraph biographies of key executive and legislative branch officials. The second section is a functional index: a listing of all state agencies under keywords. The third section is an index of individuals appearing throughout the volume.

This new title joins at least two similar publications: *State Legislative Leadership, Committees, & Staff* (see ARBA 92, entry 698) and *Carroll's State Directory* (see ARBA 96, entry 726). The titles vary in the level of detail provided for the many categories of information. With so much detail that is subject to constant change, it is questionable if a paper product is now the best format for another state government directory.—**Henry E. York**

315. **State Yellow Book: Who's Who in the Executive and Legislative Branches of the 50 State Governments**. Vol. V, No. 1. Imogene Akins, ed. Washington, D.C., Monitor Publishing, 1973- . illus. maps. index. $265.00pa. (4 issues). ISSN 0899-2207.

This valuable guide to state government offices and personnel is organized into four major sections: executive branches, legislative branches, state profiles, and national organizations to which state officials belong. Full addresses and direct telephone numbers for each department and its chief officers are listed in a user-friendly two-column format. Covered are the 50 states, American Samoa, Guam, Puerto Rico, and the Virgin Islands.

In the executive section, brief biographical information and a photograph of each governor appear. The legislative section includes photographs and short biographies of the speakers and presidents of state legislatures. All representatives and senators are listed, and standing committees are included, with chairpersons identified. State profiles provide a brief history and information on demographics, state symbols, the economy, education, statewide organizations, major military installations, and geography, as well as a brief bibliography. Counties are listed, with telephone numbers and statistics on population and income. The state maps showing county boundaries vary in quality; some are not very legible (e.g., Michigan). Subject and name indexes are included; the latter should be especially useful. This work is a must for public libraries.—**Sharon Langworthy**

6   Military Science

INTRODUCTION

The material in this chapter is arranged under four headings: General Works, which covers biographies of military personnel worldwide; United States Armed Forces; Australian Armed Forces; and Canadian Armed Forces. Standard works have been included in the section General Works, including *Brassey's Encyclopedia of Military History and Biography* (Brassey's, 1994) (see entry 316), which covers more than 100 biographies of military leaders worldwide, and *A Concise Dictionary of Military Biography: The Careers and Campaigns of 200 of the Most Important Military Leaders* (John Wiley, 1991) (see entry 318), which presents the careers of 200 important personalities in military history, including tribal chiefs, warrior kings, field marshals, theorists, innovators, and military administrators. Also, *The Harper Encyclopedia of Military Biography* (HarperCollins, 1992) (see entry 317) provides more than 3,000 short biographies of world military leaders and thinkers from Sun Tzu to Colin Powell.

The section United States Armed Forces includes a number of important biographical dictionaries covering individuals in the various military branches. An important source for short biographies of military biography is the *Dictionary of American Military Biography* (Greenwood Press, 1984) (see entry 323), which provides biographical information on more than 400 individuals. Two works listed provide information on African Americans who served in the United States military: *African-American Generals and Flag Officers: Biographies of over 120 Blacks in the United States Military* (McFarland, 1993) (see entry 325), and *On the Trail of the Buffalo Soldier: Biographies of African Americans in the U.S. Army, 1866-1917* (Scholarly Resources, 1995) (see entry 327). Both of these works provide information on African Americans who have not been included in other biographical dictionaries.

In 1995, John P. Dever and Maria C. Dever published *Women and the Military: Over 100 Notable Contributors, Historic to Contemporary* (McFarland, 1995) (see entry 322). This dictionary provides more than 20 in-depth biographies and over 80 shorter biographies of women who have served in the military. *Women and the Military: An Encyclopedia* (ABC-CLIO, 1996) (see entry 328), covers almost 400 women who have been involved in all aspects of the military, from the Revolutionary War to the present time.

Australia and Canada are represented with one work each. *The Oxford Companion to Australian Military History* (Oxford University Press, 1995) (see entry 330) includes many biographical entries and *Courage in the Air* (McGraw-Hill Ryerson, 1992) (see entry 331) presents brief profiles of selected Canadian airmen from World Wars I and II and the Korean War.

GENERAL WORKS

316.   **Brassey's Encyclopedia of Military History and Biography**. Franklin D. Margiotta, ed. McLean, Va., Brassey's, 1994. 1197p. illus. maps. index. $44.95. ISBN 0-02-881096-1.

The important wars of the world and the military leaders who fought them are presented in this large volume. It consists of alphabetically arranged articles drawn from the 1993 six-volume *International Military and Defense Encyclopedia* (see ARBA 94, entry 688). As such, it illustrates the expertise gained from two impressive editorial boards that served the parent publication, enhanced by a short foreword by John Keegan. Margiotta is a retired U.S. Air Force combat pilot and current author/editor of four books. Some 80 knowledgeable contributors authored the 200 articles selected for this volume.

The text begins with a four-page account of Afghanistan's invasion by the Soviet Union and ends with a four-page biography of Georgy Zhukov. There are 35 entries on wars, conquests, and so on, from classical times to the Gulf War. Of course, in the sorry history of man's combativeness, this number covers only the major engagements. There are no entries on individual battles. Some 100 biographies are well written, but interesting for their selections as well as omissions. Highlights include a 14-page discussion of terrorism, 30 pages on aircraft and air power, and such thoughtful pieces as "Armed Forces and Society," "Principles of War," "War," and "Science of War."

Although copyrighted in 1994, bibliographic citations later than 1988 are scarce. Missing, for example, is Keegan's own *The Second World War* (Penguin, 1990). Illustrations are few and trite and there are not nearly enough graphics for such articles as "American Civil War," "Punic Wars," and "Roman Empire." However, the 76-page index is excellent and all things considered, the book is worth the price, especially if the 6-volume parent publication is not available.—**David Eggenberger**

317. **The Harper Encyclopedia of Military Biography**. By Trevor N. Dupuy, Curt Johnson, and David L. Bongard. New York, HarperCollins, 1992. 834p. $65.00. U51.D87. 355'.0092'2. LC 89-46526. ISBN 0-06-270015-4.

Dupuy is one of the world's most renowned military historians. He has written more than 90 books, and his *Encyclopedia of Military History* (co-edited with his father) (see ARBA 87, entry 656) is a classic in the field. This latest volume promises to take its place alongside the *Encyclopedia* and be the standard reference on the subject.

A massive volume, it consists of profiles on more than 3,000 world military leaders and thinkers, from Sun Tzu and Julius Caesar to Colin Powell and Norman Schwarzkopf. The entries follow a common format. Most run between 200 and 1,000 words and have a brief bibliography of sources. The 32 contributors admittedly include only a few major military history scholars. Some leaders receive no more than a sentence or two. One would expect, for example, that Sun Tzu would merit more than a few lines. Although the volume includes many Asian leaders, especially Japanese, they tend to have brief listings. One assumes this is because most of the source material on these individuals is in languages that the authors cannot read. Also, the brief lists of sources at the end of each entry are far too limited, and many do not include the latest or best works. But these points aside, this is an impressive undertaking and an important contribution that should be a basic reference source in virtually every library in the country. [R: LJ, Aug 92, p. 86; RBB, 15 Oct 92, pp. 453-561]—**Joe P. Dunn**

318.   Windrow, Martin, and Francis K. Mason. **A Concise Dictionary of Military Biography: The Careers and Campaigns of 200 of the Most Important Military Leaders**. New York, John Wiley, 1991. 337p. $24.95. U51.WS3. LC 90-44696. ISBN 0-471-53441-2.

Combining factual details with clear analysis, this dictionary presents the careers of 200 of the most important personalities in military history, covering tribal chiefs, warrior kings, and field marshals, as well as influential theorists, innovators, and administrators. Here the conquests of such great leaders as Genghis Kahn and Napoleon, whose wartime successes changed the world and its maps, may be followed as well as the incompetence of others, such as George Armstrong Custer and Benedict Arnold. Popular culture heroes such as Joan of Arc and El Cid may also be investigated. Cross-cultural in design, this biographical study of careers and campaigns makes a valid effort to include great leaders of non-Western culture, such as Hideyoshi Toyotomi and Shaka. Even people such as the Baron Friedrich von Steuben and Lazare Carnot, whose careers were relatively obscure because they never held a major field command, are presented and analyzed because of their theoretical or administrative mastery of the art of warfare.

These biographical essays are fascinating studies that proceed chronologically according to major events in the subject's life. Summary remarks about the unique and significant contributions of each military leader provide important analytical information. For example, the authors point out that King Henry V of England is noteworthy not only for his considerable personal courage, sound tactical sense, and appeal to the common soldier but also for "the sense of national pride and national identity which his victories engendered among the English people of all classes." Particularly informative are the presentations of major military campaigns and the leaders involved.

Not only is this dictionary a valuable basic reference tool for anyone interested in military history, but it also makes for enjoyable armchair and bedside reading. "Coeur de Lion" Richard I,

"Law-giver" Suleyman I, John Joseph "Black Jack" Pershing, George Smith "Old Blood and Guts" Patton, Yamashita "Tiger of Malaya" Tomoyuki—they are all properly introduced.—**Colby H. Kullman**

UNITED STATES ARMED FORCES

319.   Brown, Russell K. **Fallen in Battle: American General Officer Combat Fatalities from 1775.** Westport, Conn., Greenwood Press, 1988. 243p. index. $38.00. LC 88-5644. ISBN 0-313-26242-X.

This biographical dictionary presents short entries of 200 to 300 words in length on 221 U.S. general and flag officers who have been killed since the Revolutionary War. Individuals included were officers of general or flag rank in a U.S. military unit (including the Philippine army in World War II and the Confederate army or navy) who were killed in combat or died of wounds due to enemy ion, were missing in action, or were executed or died while prisoners of war. Each entry gives particulars about the officer's life, career, and circumstances of death, as well as a list of source references. Almost three-quarters of the biographees died in the Civil War. A series of appendixes concludes the work and provides analyses of officers killed, wounded, or captured in various wars; branches of service; and battles.

The author's work is based on a variety of sources, including service, unit, and campaign accounts; newspaper articles; standard reference works; and histories. Only 30 percent of the officers cited appear in the *Dictionary of American Biography*. For those officers meeting the rigid criteria for inclusion, this is a helpful work that brings together information from many sources. On the other hand, the specialized nature of the subject and the relatively few individuals included suggest that this is not a reference work to be used in the first instance for biographical information on military figures. Libraries with strong user interest in military history will benefit from this work. [R: RBB, 1 Feb 89, p. 924; WLB, Mar 89, p. 115]—**Eric R. Nitschke**

320.   Claghorn, Charles E. **Naval Officers of the American Revolution: A Concise Biographical Dictionary**. Metuchen, N.J., Scarecrow, 1988. 363p. $35.00. E206.C53. 973.3'S. LC 87-35410. ISBN 0-8108-2096-X.

This work lists the names of some 3,260 American and 240 French naval officers and privateers active during the American Revolution. As the subtitle suggests, the biographical information is brief. Some entries are quite short ("Pierce, John. Virginia Navy, Midshipman"), but others provide information concerning ships served on or commanded, participation in battles and other actions, date of birth, commissioning, capture, and home town. In all cases entries include the state from which the individual came and the source or sources where the information was found. These sources include standard biographical dictionaries, naval histories, and naval records and documents published by the federal and state governments. The value of the work is that it brings together information from a number of diverse sources while identifying these sources for those who wish to consult them. Genealogists and historians may find this book useful in their various quests, and libraries serving these researchers will want to consider purchasing this work. [R: Choice, June 89, p. 1654]—**Eric R. Nitschke**

321.   Cogar, William B. **Dictionary of Admirals of the U.S. Navy. Volume 1: 1862-1900**. Annapolis, Md., Naval Institute Press, 1989. 217p. illus. $36.95. V11.U7C69. 359.3'31'092273. LC 89-3339. ISBN 0-87021-431-4.

The first of a projected series, this reference work provides brief biographies for the 211 officers of the U.S. Navy who attained the rank of rear admiral, vice admiral, or admiral prior to 1900. The introduction provides a short history of officer ranks in the U.S. Navy from its inception to 1900, including ranks on "non-line" staff officers (e.g., constructors, chaplains), and a chronological list of the heads of various naval administrative units to 1900.

The bulk of the book is occupied by alphabetically arranged brief biographies. Each provides a sketch of the life of the subject, naval ranks held, a summary of naval service, and remarks on highlights of the officer's service. Dates (month and day) are cited where possible. As appropriate, references are provided to publications by the officer, biographical materials, and libraries or museums where private papers are held.

This is a reference work; the presentation is terse and laden with abbreviations and dates. The introduction states that it is the first such inclusive summary of the chief officers of the U.S. Navy. (On a random check, however, the description of Charles Henry Davis, Sr., mentioned that a son, Charles Henry Davis, Jr., attained the rank of rear admiral, but the latter is not listed in the book.) The wealth of detail and the references to primary sources will make this a valuable tool for historians of the U.S. Navy.—**Bruce H. Tiffney**

322.   Dever, John P., and Maria C. Dever. **Women and the Military: Over 100 Notable Contributors, Historic to Contemporary**. Jefferson, N.C., McFarland, 1995. 163p. index. $24.95. ISBN 0-89950-976-2.

The nonspecialist authors explain that their purpose in compiling the 21 biographies and 83 briefer capsules is to demonstrate the important role that women have played in military affairs in diverse cultures from antiquity to present. Although most of the entries treat women from the United States, a few cover historical figures from Europe, Asia, and Africa. The time frame is from the ancient Israel prophet Deborah through Paula Coughlin of the Tailhook sexual harassment case.

Although the longer bibliographies have some value as a quick reference, the short profiles, many of which do little more than identify the individual, are of minimal value, and the book is not a significant contribution. More appropriate for high school and public libraries than for more scholarly collections, the volume has some utility, but libraries can let it pass without serious consequence to their reference holdings.—**Joe P. Dunn**

323.   **Dictionary of American Military Biography**. Roger J. Spiller, Joseph G. Dawson III, and T. Harry Williams, eds. Westport, Conn., Greenwood Press, 1984. 3v. index. $145.00/set. LC 83-12674. ISBN 0-313-21433-6.

Nearly 400 biographical sketches of persons prominent in American military history from the French and Indian Wars through Vietnam are presented. They include not only soldiers, sailors, and airmen but also politicians, scientists, and others who exercised significant influence on U.S. military matters. Essays, written by some 200 specialists, are arranged alphabetically, cross-referenced meticulously, and accompanied by brief bibliographies. Of particular note is the effort to accentuate the interaction between the biographee and his contemporaries, especially as it affected strategic (as opposed to tactical) results. Prose styles vary, but skillful editing assures a commendable degree of readability combined with dispassionate appraisals encountered too infrequently in the genre.

Appendixes comprise a chronology of American military developments, rank designations, military organizations, birthplaces of biographees, a roll of contributors, and an index. This latter is a paragon of comprehensiveness, listing persons, places, units, battles, campaigns, and government agencies. Its primary value lies in the numerous references that guide the reader to cogent information not completely covered in a specific biographee's entry. The *DAMB* is a superior work of scholarship and a remarkable reference source in the U.S. military history field.—**Lawrence E. Spellman**

324.   **Generals in Muddy Boots: A Concise Encyclopedia of Combat Commanders**. By Dan Cragg. Walter J. Boyne, ed. New York, Berkley, 1996. 196p. illus. $29.95. ISBN 0-425-15136-0.

Concise is an appropriate adjective for this work on combat field commanders. Not intended to be all-encompassing, this volume identifies some of the more noteworthy commanders in the history of warfare from ancient times to the Vietnam era. Entries provide a brief biography, describe military education, and discuss combat career. The alphabetic presentation eliminated the need for an index, making this a quick-reference guide. Cragg has written a more popular and anecdotal rather than a strictly scholarly work. Notable omissions from an otherwise star-studded assembly of commanders are Wilhelm Baick, Kurt Student, James Gavin, and Hasso von Manteuffel. Oversights and a lack of a more scholarly treatment aside, this is a solid, competent survey of combat commanders, and is recommended for middle school, high school, public library, and private reference collections. [R: LJ, Feb 96, p. 142; RBB, 1 May 96, p. 1519]—**Norman L. Kincaide**

325.   Hawkins, Walter L. **African-American Generals and Flag Officers: Biographies of over 120 Blacks in the United States Military**. Jefferson, N.C., McFarland, 1993. 264p. illus. index. $25.95. E181.H38.355'.0089'96073. LC 92-50886. ISBN 0-89950-774-3.

African Americans have played a significant role in American military history. Although the impediments were great, black Americans have risen to the highest ranks in the military services, with black generals as early as the Civil War. The 1- or 2-page career biographical summaries in this volume chronicle the 120 African Americans who have risen to the rank of general officer or its navy equivalent. Besides the fine summaries, the book includes a chronology of significant dates and actions in the history of blacks and the U.S. military, a list of significant firsts by blacks in the military, breakdowns of general officers by service and number of stars, listings by the states where they were born and the colleges and universities they attended, and a useful index.

Although far more specialized than the author's *African American Biographies* (see ARBA 93, entry 423), this volume also contains a tremendous amount of information. Its inexpensive price makes it affordable for a wide range of libraries. [R: RBB, Aug 93, p. 2085; WLB, May 93, p. 113]—**Joe P. Dunn**

326.   Greene, Robert Ewell. **Black Defenders of America: 1775-1973**. Chicago, Johnson Publishing Company, 1974. 415p. illus. bibliog. index. $17.95. o.p. LC 73-15607. ISBN 0-87485-053-3.

This valuable biographical dictionary covering African American soldiers who have served in the U.S. military is now out-of-print but remains a valuable source. The preface states the purpose as follows: "This partial account of Negro military personnel in the armed forces from 1775 until 1973 is presented as a reference and guide for those who want to learn the truth about America's neglected Black soldiers, sailors, marines and airmen." Using pictures and documented biographies, an attempt has been made to illustrate the black American's presence in past and present wars.

Ten separate chapters cover U.S. wars in chronological order from the American Revolution and the Indian Campaigns through Vietnam. Each chapter is introduced by a 500- to 600-word statement on the status of blacks in the military services during the particular war. Each biographical sketch cites the authority for the information. References are given at the end of each chapter. Photos appear on nearly every page. Appendix 1 is a photo album of black commissioned officers and non-commissioned officers. Appendix 2, "Black Military Milestones," is a chronology of important contributions blacks have made to U.S. military history. A small collection of documents and statistical information is provided in appendix 3. At the end is an extensive bibliography of books, articles, and government documents. An index of names completes the work. [R: BL, 1 Sept 74, p. 52; Choice, 1 Dec 74, p. 1456]—**Christine L. Wynar and Robert L. Wick**

327.   **On the Trail of the Buffalo Soldier: Biographies of African Americans in the U.S. Army, 1866-1917**. Frank N. Schubert, comp. and ed. Wilmington, Del., Scholarly Resources, 1995. 519p. $125.00. ISBN 0-8420-2482-4.

The title under consideration is a fine addition to the ranks of African American military history reference books. It is composed of thousands of entries on black soldiers for the period from the end of the Civil War to the beginning of American involvement in World War I. In these 50 years, black regiments served primarily in the West (with some service in Cuba and the Philippines), where they earned their nickname while fighting the Native Americans. Most of the alphabetically arranged entries contain only the basic information, such as birthplace, rank and unit, and a sketch of their service history, while others have much more information, with excerpts from official reports, their circumstances prior to emancipation, and relatives' names included. Virtually every entry contains a source note, and there are some cross-references. The bibliography contains citations to books, articles, newspapers, government documents, unpublished manuscripts, archival collections, military records, and Veterans Administration pension files. The appendixes list the number of black men enlisted in the army, dates of service of sergeants major of the black cavalry regiments, soldiers killed in action, recipients of the Medal of Honor, and dates and locations of the various regimental headquarters. Schubert is the Chief of the Operations History Division, Join History Office, U.S. Joint Chiefs of Staff. One can use Robert Greene's *Black Defenders of America, 1775-1973* (Johnson, 1974) and *Black Soldiers—Black Sailors—Black Ink* by Thomas Truxton Moebs (Moebs Publishing, 1994) to complement the work. This well-constructed book is well worth its price, as it presents so much information in one volume. It is recommended for military history, genealogical, African American, and general reference collections of all academic and public libraries. [R: RBB, 15 Feb 95, pp. 1111-12]—**Daniel K. Blewett**

328.   Sherrow, Victoria. **Women and the Military: An Encyclopedia**. Santa Barbara, Calif., ABC-CLIO, 1996. 381p. illus. index. $60.00. ISBN 0-87436-812-X.

Women and the Military explores the significant contributions women have made to the armed services throughout U.S. history. These include the familiar—such as the computer work of Grace Murray Hopper during World War II—as well as the less well known, such as the courageous exploits of widow "Mad Anne" Bailey during the Revolutionary War. The A to Z entries are preceded by an interesting and informative introduction that surveys the history of women's contributions to military undertakings throughout civilization and more recently in the United States.

The nearly 400 entries cover individuals, events, laws, court cases, concepts, organizations, wars, and military branches. The editors have made generous use of cross-references, and bibliographies accompany many of the longer articles. The entries, ranging in length from several sentences to a page, are current and do not shy away from the controversial, as witnessed by the lengthy article on the Tailhook incident. The intended audience for this encyclopedia is students, librarians, journalists, members of the military, and general readers. They will find *Women and the Military* a useful and welcome resource.—**G. Kim Dority**

329.   **Who's Who in World War II**. John Keegan, ed. New York, Oxford University Press, 1995. 182p. $14.95pa. ISBN 0-19-521080-8.

Keegan, defense editor of London's *Daily Telegraph* and author of many books, is one of the world's most renowned military historians. This concise, paperback volume is a useful addition to the vast number of reference works on World War II. Keegan offers brief, compactly detailed sketches on more than 300 of the most important characters in this global conflict, including the military and political leaders of all the powers involved and other notable participants. Keegan's authoritative stature and his evenhanded balance of all participant countries in the war enhance the book's status. The format is alphabetical and provides dates of birth and death and a chronological sketch of the individual's life. The entries are cross-referenced. The book's major weakness is that it does not include bibliographical references.

Although more comprehensive and more detailed, specialized sources exist on World War II, the virtue of this volume is that it is particularly valuable for the introductory student. The inexpensive price of this paperback makes it worthwhile for all libraries to acquire as a quick reference, but it is especially appropriate for secondary school, college, and public libraries.—**Joe P. Dunn**

AUSTRALIAN ARMED FORCES

330.   **The Oxford Companion to Australian Military History**. By Peter Dennis and others. New York, Oxford University Press, 1995. 692p. illus. maps. $75.00. ISBN 0-19-553227-9.

From the violence that accompanied European settlement to the 1991 Persian Gulf War, the military has figured prominently in Australian history. This history is well described in this volume, which is really an alphabetically arranged encyclopedia (one of a series of commendable Oxford companions, such as *Ships and the Sea* [see ARBA 78, entry 1549], *World War II* [see entry 329], and *Australian Literature* [2d ed.; see ARBA 96, entry 1248]).

The book has 4 authors, all with appropriate experience and expertise, and 27 distinguished contributors of the 800 entries. It is amply illustrated with 100 photographs and more than 30 maps. Entries include major battles and campaigns (Gallipoli, Kodoka); biographies of military as well as relevant civilian figures (Thomas Blaimey, Charles Bean); weapons; military units; and thematic essays on such topics as conscription, prisoners of war, and war-crimes trials. There are six pages on "Anzac Legend" describing the development of the reputation of the Australian fighting man. The term is enshrined in the annual Anzac Day of April 25.

Two criticisms can be made about this book: The articles are not signed, and the attempts at bibliography are woeful. Nevertheless, the work is highly recommended. It is well made and will serve as a valuable reference for students and the general public as well as interested specialists.—**David Eggenberger**

CANADIAN ARMED FORCES

331. Bishop, Arthur. **Courage in the Air**. Toronto, McGraw-Hill Ryerson, 1992. 307p. illus. index. (Canada's Military Heritage, v.1). $35.00. 355'.00971. ISBN 0-07-551376-5.

This volume, by a writer with a deep knowledge of his subject, both personal and professional, presents brief profiles of selected Canadian airmen from World Wars I and II and the Korean War. The entries are arranged alphabetically by conflict. As Bishop admits, the coverage is selective rather than comprehensive, but most major fighting figures (and many people distinguished for administrative services) are discussed.

The straightforward descriptions relate each man's wartime activities in varying length and detail (a few contain personal remarks that could be controversial). Every entry is followed by a citation of awards, publications, date of death, and (most valuably) the archival citations on which the accounts were based. This provides an ideal starting point for further research. Some biographies are accompanied by photographs; these are clear and of good size, but most lack captions (and one that has a caption misidentifies a German "Panther" tank as a "Tiger" tank). A few other inaccuracies were noted (e.g., no German light cruiser was sunk off Wilhlemshaven in early April 1945 by "Typhoon" attack; the "Sunderland" flying boat is repeatedly called "Sutherland" and credited with a cannon armament it did not have; the heavy cruiser KM *Prinz Eugen* is persistently designated a battleship), but these do not detract substantially from the book.

Crisply printed on good-quality paper in a sturdy binding, this is a useful initial guide to its topic. While a name index enhances its value as a ready-reference tool, the absence of an analytic index to the variety of significant historical detail it contains is regrettable.—**John Howard Oxley**

7 Psychology, Sociology, and Social Work

INTRODUCTION

The material in this chapter covers biographical dictionaries in the areas of psychology, sociology, and social work and is arranged into four sections: General Works, Aging, Psychology, and Social Work. Works directly related to the other aspects of the social sciences will be found in the chapter titled **Social Sciences**. The section titled General Works contains two works that do not fit in other sections: *American Reform and Reformers: A Biographical Dictionary* (Greenwood Press, 1996) (see entry 332), and *Key Thinkers, Past and Present* (Routledge & Kegan Paul/Methuen, 1987) (see entry 333). The section Aging provides several important biographical dictionaries, including *Profiles in Gerontology: A Biographical Dictionary* (Greenwood Press, 1995) (see entry 334), and the section Psychology includes the *Concise Encyclopedia of Psychology* (John Wiley, 1987) (see entry 336), and *The Oxford Companion to the Mind* (Oxford University Press, 1987) (see entry 337), all of which provide biographical information on psychologists and other individuals working in the area. The section Social Work concludes the chapter and includes three biographical sources: *NASW Register of Clinical Social Workers* (National Association of Social Workers, 1976-) (see entry 342), which provides information on social workers arranged by their geographical area, and Mark Lender's *Dictionary of American Temperance Biography: From Temperance Reform to Alcohol Research, the 1600s to the 1980s* (Greenwood Press, 1984) (see entry 341), which is unique in its inclusion and contains information on individuals not listed in other sources.

Other reference sources which also provide biographies in these areas include *The Social Science Encyclopedia* (Routledge, 1989), *American Men and Women of Science: The Medical Sciences* (R. R. Bowker, 1994), the *Dictionary of American Medical Biography* (Macmillan, 1996), and the *International Encyclopedia of the Social Sciences* (Macmillan, 1996). These and other sources found in the chapter titled **Social Sciences** will provide additional resources for biographical information in these areas.

GENERAL WORKS

332. **American Reform and Reformers: A Biographical Dictionary**. Randall M. Miller and Paul A. Cimbala, eds. Westport, Conn., Greenwood Press, 1996. 559p. index. $115.00. ISBN 0-313-28839-9.

This volume is far more than a biographical dictionary. The introduction includes an expanded definition of reform and an analysis of its role and context in U.S. history. Each of the 38 essays that follow combines biographical data with historical analysis of the specific reform movement for which each individual is known. The strength of the book lies in the in-depth treatment of the reform movements represented in the volume, and the importance of the role each of the biographees played in that movement.

Most of the individuals profiled in this dictionary represent reform movements of the late nineteenth through the twentieth century. Jane Addams, Cesar Chavez, John Dewey, Martin Luther King Jr., Margaret Sanger, and Russell Means are but a few examples of those included in the book. A wide range of topics includes education, unionism and labor reform, consumer rights, religious rights, and much, much more. Each of the essays is written by a notable expert in the field and provides notes and bibliographic references. A chronological chart of important events for reform movements in U.S. history from the revolutionary period to 1994 is also most helpful in understanding reform and its historical significance. An adequate index lends to its usefulness as a reference tool.

The dictionary is an excellent supplement of readings for the student or researcher of social history to anyone interested in the historical treatment of reform movements. Its basic drawback is its price. At $115.00, the work is recommended for academic libraries with strong liberal arts and social history strengths; however, this volume may only receive casual use in public libraries, precluding its purchase from all but larger libraries. [R: Choice, July/Aug 96, p. 1767; RBB, 15 Mar 96, p. 1308]—**Susan Zernial**

333. **Key Thinkers, Past and Present**. Jessica Kuper, ed. New York, Routledge & Kegan Paul/Methuen, 1987. 276p. (Social Science Lexicons). $9.95pa. LC 86-33860. ISBN 0-7102-1173-2.

This book is part of a new series of works compiled from entries reprinted from *The Social Science Encyclopedia* (see ARBA 87, entry 88). In this case, the editors selected 111 biographical essays of key social theorists, both living and dead, to create *Key Thinkers*. Each essay is approximately 500 to 2,000 words in length, including brief bibliographies of books by and about the authors. The editor's introduction does not fully explain why these 111 scholars were chosen, except to state that "the present volume offers a personalized, sometimes admittedly idiosyncratic view of the history of the social sciences, but at the same time it serves as a stimulating introduction to a great variety of theories."

The restriction of entries to the contents of *The Social Science Encyclopedia* partially explains a few anomalies, such as the inclusion of Milton Friedman (living, conservative, economist), while excluding the equally influential Robert L. Heilbroner (living, liberal, economist), or the inclusion of Ludwig J. J. Wittgenstein, but not A. J. Ayer, both of whom are distinguished linguistic philosophers.

In any event, the book is a useful tool to introduce, in brief terms, some of the most influential social theorists from Plato to Max Weber. Most of the essays are well written, concise, and accessible to the nonspecialist.

Many of the scholars included in this book are also covered in the *Biographical Supplement* (volume 18) to the *International Encyclopedia of the Social Sciences* (Free Press, 1979). This source is by far the most authoritative and is also recommended for the nonspecialist. Librarians who own *The Social Science Encyclopedia* may feel that the purchase of *Key Thinkers* is redundant, even though the price is very reasonable. [R: RBB, 15 Oct 87, p. 372]—**Richard H. Quay**

AGING

334. Achenbaum, W. Andrew, and Daniel M. Albert. **Profiles in Gerontology: A Biographical Dictionary**. Westport, Conn., Greenwood Press, 1995. $85.00. 396p. index. $85.00. ISBN 0-313-29274-4.

Profiles in Gerontology provides biographical information on more than 300 researchers, practitioners, and teachers in the field of aging. While most of the individuals represented are North Americans, there are a number from Great Britain and Europe. The work begins with an introduction by the authors that provides a brief history of the study of gerontology and some predictions for the field. Each individual's entry contains place of birth, education, prominent positions held, and a brief biography, including prominent publications and places of employment. Honors, awards, or memberships in scholarly organizations may be included.

The authors obtained the information for the volume through the use of profile questionnaires sent out during fall 1994. Several prominent gerontologists preferred not to participate and they were not included. The entries are even and provide comparable information from one gerontologist to the next.

The book is extremely useful as a biographical source, and the name and subject indexes allow for more general reference on the subject. The name index indicates the main entry for each individual along with page references in other entries. It is possible to look up colleges and universities in the subject index to find the faculty in the area of gerontology at a particular university and to trace their research efforts.

While the work is an important reference tool in the area, a complete bibliography of all works referred to in the entries and a list of individuals by specialty would have been useful. However, *Profiles in Gerontology* is still a useful source. The only other sources for information on individuals in the field that come to mind are *American Men and Women of Science: The Medical Sciences* (see ARBA 76, entry 1542), and *Dictionary of American Medical Biography* (see ARBA 85, entry 1535). Andrew W. Achenbaum's *Crossing Frontiers* (Cambridge University Press, 1995) identifies individuals who are important to the field. The work under review is strongly recommended for all medical libraries and for larger university and public library collections.—**Robert L. Wick**

PSYCHOLOGY

335.   **Biographical Dictionary of Psychology**. Noel Sheehy, Antony J. Chapman, and Wendy A. Conroy, eds. New York, Routledge, 1997. 675p. index. $130.00. ISBN 0-415-09997-8.

Biographical Dictionary of Psychology serves as a current update and expansion of information previously published in Greenwood Press's *Biographical Dictionary of Psychology* (see ARBA 85, entry 666); *A Guide to Psychologists and Their Concepts* (see ARBA 76, entry 1504); and *Women in Psychology: A Bio-bibliographic Sourcebook* (see ARBA 91, entry 918). This resource incorporates biographical information on 500-plus psychologists and individuals who have contributed to the field of psychology. The scope is international and runs from the late 1700s through the late 1900s. The methodology used by the editors in choosing entries included surveying several reference sources in the psychology literature. From that review, additional lists were created and ranked; then experts in the field were consulted and the list was reduced to its current number. It is noted that some individuals chose not to respond, so the editors were not able to produce a substantial entry, and therefore the individual was not included.

Each entry includes name; date and place of birth, and date and place of death if appropriate; nationality; main area of interest according to the American Psychological Association standards; education; principal appointments, honors, and awards; principal publications; and suggested references for further reading. The most confounding part of the entries is the lack of entries on the women who are part of the number of husband-wife teams of psychologists who have similar research interests, complement, and in most cases, enhance their husbands' research. There is not a separate or even supplemental statement about their contributions. In many cases, in the husband's entry, these contributions are not even acknowledged. Aside from this observation, the entries are clearly written using three-quarters to a full page. The only other piece of information missing is current institutional affiliation. [R: RBB, 15 Oct 97, pp. 425-26]—**Mila C. Su**

336.   **Concise Encyclopedia of Psychology**. Raymond J. Corsini and others, eds. New York, John Wiley, 1987. 1242p. bibliog. index. $74.95. LC 86-22392. ISBN 0-471-01068-5.

The full 1984 (four volumes) edition of this work (see ARBA 85, entry 669) has been described, deservedly, as "monumental" and "unique"; it was also named "Reference Book of the Year" by the American Library Association. The high cost of this outstanding work is stated as the primary reason for condensing the full set into a one-volume *Concise Encyclopedia*.

Raymond J. Corsini, the editor of the full set, did remarkably well in his difficult task of producing the abridged edition. Hans J. Eysenck, a prominent psychologist and an encyclopedist himself, states in the foreword: "Raymond Corsini has artfully boiled down an already slightly packed four-volume encyclopedia into one book that contains every entry in the prior edition and actually adds some new ones" (p. xxi). Notable among the new addition is, for example, the entry on artificial intelligence. Furthermore, several of the articles in the concise edition were updated. In order to include about 2,150 separate articles, some reductions had to be made. Nonetheless, the coverage of each entry is still signed by the original author. Biographies of living psychologists and the history of psychology in foreign countries, in particular, had to be condensed. Eliminated were case histories and detailed discussions as well as many entries from the final *Bibliography*, which is a separate part of the encyclopedia.

According to the editor, the condensed version has retained approximately 80 percent of the original substantive materials from the full encyclopedia, but only 55 percent of the original wordage. The condensation or elimination of materials from the full set was done in such a knowledgeable way that the authoritative summary of basic facts relevant to individual topics prevails.

The scope, quality, and recency of this reference work make it the best one-volume encyclopedia of psychology on the market. Also from the technical point of view, the encyclopedia is a fine piece of work; it is a sturdy volume that can readily endure heavy use as a desk copy reference. The price of this one-volume edition is less than one-third the price of the original set. [R: BL, Aug 87, pp. 1725-26; Choice, July/Aug 87, p. 1674]—**Miluse A. Soudek**

337.   **The Oxford Companion to the Mind**. Richard L. Gregory, with O. L. Zangwill, eds. New York, Oxford University Press, 1987. 856p. illus. index. $49.95. LC 87-1671. ISBN 0-19-866124-X.

The Oxford *Companions*, published in diverse fields, have acquired an excellent reputation. *The Oxford Companion to the Mind* follows this tradition. The *Companion* was written by a wide range of well-known authorities from various countries. The 216 contributors were, obviously, writing on the subjects of their particular expertise or special interests. The editor of this notable work is a British experimental psychologist and inventor, with a distinguished professional career.

The 1,001 entries in the *Companion* cover concepts and ideas related mainly to numerous branches of psychology, philosophy, and the physiology of the higher nervous system. Included also are biographies of psychologists, philosophers, and scientists from diverse countries and cultures, who contributed to the knowledge of the mind throughout the centuries. (Living personalities are excluded.) One can find biographical data on scholars such as Al-Kindi, the first Arab philosopher; Georgevon Bekesy, Hungarian physicist and physiologist; William Cheselden, British surgeon; Herophilus, Greek anatomist; Lev Semionovich Vygotsky, Soviet psychologist; Carl Wernicke, German neurologist and psychiatrist; and many others.

In the *Companion*, the concept of the mind is evidently considered in its broadest sense and, consequently, the range of topics is very wide and quite diverse. As might be expected, there are numerous entries on the structure and foundation of the human nervous system. Longer entries usually give a state-of-the-art overview of the subject. There is, for the first time in an Oxford *Companion*, a tutorial; it has over twenty pages. Its topic is the nervous system, and it can be consulted especially for definitions of some less familiar technical terms that may occur in some entries.

In addition to a great number of more traditional topics, such as consciousness; language; learning; human, animal, and computer intelligence; thinking; etc., there are also philosophical accounts concerning the mind; medical contributions; and some puzzling and intriguing, yet highly interesting, phenomena of the mind as treated, for example, in parapsychology. Moreover, as the editor admits, one can find also "various widely held beliefs which are frankly outside science, such as blood myths and the origins of powerful fantasies such as Dracula and Frankenstein" (p.vi). Astrology, the biological clock, "Clever Hans" (the famous horse), depersonalization, Egyptian concepts of mind, ethology, female sexuality, and iconic image are some examples of the diverse entries. Obviously, as can be expected in such a wide-ranging work, one can find some unexpected topics included, and at the same time wonder about the exclusion of others which one might consider more relevant.

The quality of the *Companion* is enhanced by 200 illustrations, numerous cross-references, bibliographies to individual topics, and a carefully prepared index.

The Oxford Companion to the Mind is a work ambitious in scope, done with a high degree of professional expertise. It is a work of importance that may serve as a useful reference tool in several academic disciplines, or just as highly interesting professional reading. [R: LJ, 15 Sept 87, p. 74]—**Miluse A. Soudek**

338.   **Who's Who in the Biobehavioral Sciences**. 2d ed. Barbara R. Breitbart, Sally Garson, and Ellen Leibowitz, eds. New York, Research Institute of Psychophysiology, 1987. 292p. $87.50. LC 86-62106. ISBN 0-914709-01-1.

Biobehavioral sciences integrate numerous fields of behavioral and biomedical disciplines which, in a broad sense, are related to the study of mind-body relations. The two invited essays that are part of this who's who provide an illuminating introduction to some concepts within the relatively new area of biobehavioral sciences. In "Trends and Future Applications of Biobehavioral Sciences," John V. Basmajian introduces the concept of behavioral medicine, which he considers to be one of this century's great revolutions in human health care. In order to illustrate some study areas in behavioral medicine which are related to influences on physical health and disease, he presents a list of topics, such as socio-cultural influences, including epidemiological, anthropological, and socio-logical studies; and psychosocial factors, including social psychology, personality, and psycho-physiological studies investigating behavioral, emotional, and social stresses and their conse-quences. Other topics included in his essay are health behavior, illness, and sick role behavior; cog-nitive determinants with special recognition of placebo factors; development of behavioral diagnostic techniques; pain and its regulation; research on behavioral approaches to the control of substance abuse; stress management and self-regulatory therapies such as biofeedback and relaxa-tion; and the evaluation of different types of psychotherapy and behavior change techniques. "Neuro-biological Structuring of the Mind" is a brief but quite essential essay by Jos M. R. Delgado, in which he reflects on recent spectacular advances in neurobiological knowledge. Throughout his es-say, the author stresses the importance of ethical principles whenever living nature, that until now has been a product of spontaneous development, can be modified by human manipulation.

The main part of this who's who provides biographical information on prominent professionals working in some forty-five diverse fields of biobehavioral sciences. Added to their basic biographi-cal data is information on education, past and present professional experience, concurrent positions and current activities, professional membership, honors and awards, and, finally, addresses. In com-parison to the 1st edition, this revised 2nd edition includes many new names. A new feature is the dis-cipline index listing names of professionals working in each specific discipline, such as behavioral psychology, biopsychiatry, and neurophysiology. The geographical index lists names of profession-als working in various geographic areas in the United States as well as in over forty foreign countries.

The format of this reference work provides easy access to information on administrators, re-searchers, clinicians, and other professionals working in numerous disciplines and geographic areas. Therefore, it can prove to be a useful acquisition in a variety of institutional settings. [R: Choice, June 87, pp. 1539-40]—**Miluse A. Soudek**

339. **Women in Psychology: A Bio-Bibliography Sourcebook**. Agnes N. O'Connell and Nancy Felipe Russo, eds. Westport, Conn., Greenwood Press, 1990. 441p. index. $55.00. BF109.A1W65. 150'.92'2. LC 89-25787. ISBN 0-313-26091-5.

This sourcebook provides information on 36 historical and contemporary women in psychol-ogy. The women represent a wide range of achievements in a variety of subdisciplines such as physiological psychology and personality theory. Separate chapters provide information on the indi-vidual's family background, education, career development, major achievements, and individual contributions to the field. A separate five-part bibliographic chapter identifies sources of information on women in psychology, including references to resources on 185 women who have helped shape the field. The work concludes with three appendixes (chronology of birth years, places of birth, and major fields) and an index.

Although selective in its coverage, this work should prove useful to historians of psychology as well as to individuals interested in women's history and the contributions of women in psychology. Recommended for academic and special libraries. [R: WLB, Dec 90, p. 158]—**L. L. Schroyer**

SOCIAL WORK

340. **Biographical Dictionary of Social Welfare in America**. Walter I. Trattner, ed. Westport, Conn., Greenwood Press, 1986. 897p. index. $75.00. LC 85-9831. ISBN 0-313-23001-3.

This well-executed biographical dictionary provides information on approximately 330 indi-viduals who played an active role in the field of social welfare from colonial times to the present. In-dividual sketches were written by 200 contributors chosen for their expertise in this field. Individuals selected for inclusion in this important work were chosen on the basis of active participation rather than on theoretical contributions. Excluded are living persons, labor union leaders, feminists, and abolitionists. This dictionary should be viewed as being selective rather than comprehensive.

Arranged alphabetically, each biographical essay provides a summary of the subject's life, career, and contribution to social welfare, and blends factual information with analytical com-ments. An important feature is that it provides the user with information on the major accessible sources for each entry. Also included are three appendixes: "Brief Chronology of Significant Events in American Social Welfare History," "A Listing of Subjects by Year of Birth," and a "Listing of Subjects by Place of Birth." Information about the authors and a subject index complete this reference work.

This dictionary is well prepared, easy to use, and serves as an excellent source of background information on a selective number of individuals whose activism contributed to the growth of social welfare. It should be included in the collections of large public libraries, academic institutions, and schools which sponsor various social work programs. [R: Choice, 1 Oct 86, p. 275; RBB, 1 Sept 86, p. 38]—**Anna Wynar**

341.   Lender, Mark Edward. **Dictionary of American Temperance Biography: From Temperance Reform to Alcohol Research, the 1600s to the 1980s**. Westport, Conn., Greenwood Press, 1984. 572p. index. $45.00. LC 83-12589. ISBN 0-313-22335-1.

This is a biographical encyclopedia of men and women active since the colonial period in the United States in movements related to regulating or studying drinking of alcohol. The 373 entries represent all ethnic and religious groups, both sexes, and all philosophical stances regarding drinking regulation/reform.

The arrangement is nearly identical to that of Henry Bowden's *Dictionary of American Religious Biography*. Each entry includes three parts: a who's who–type summary; a one- to one-and-a-half-page narrative, emphasizing the subject's role related to alcohol; and a bibliography. The latter may list up to six works by, and six works about, the subject (including standard general biographies). The narratives include cross-references to other entries. Access is by a subject/name/organization index. There are also lists of the biographees by birthplace and by religious affiliation.

While no detailed criteria for inclusion are given, nearly all listees died before 1980, and all are significant as leaders or intellectual contributors, or as typical of aspects of the movements.

Much of the information here parallels the biographical entries in the six-volume *Standard Encyclopedia of the Alcohol Problem* (1925-1930), although the information is fresher and the writing better. The index could have been better (e.g., nicknames rarely have entries), but it is more complete than what one usually finds in such reference works.

This would be a useful purchase for libraries with major collections or user interest in temperance, or social reform in general. [R: Choice, Oct 84, p. 250; WLB, Nov 84, p. 225]—**James H. Sweetland**

342.   **NASW Register of Clinical Social Workers**. Washington, D.C., National Association of Social Workers, 1976- . index. $60.00pa. ISSN 0277-0695.

The *Register of Clinical Social Workers* consists of a complete alphabetical listing of social work clinicians according to state and city. This listing includes descriptive information regarding each clinician's professional practice, education, and experience. In the initial section of the register, information provided includes the policy and criteria for listing in the register; a definition of "clinical social work"; a profile of the National Association of Social Workers and its code of ethics; and a listing of social work licenses, certifications, and registrations according to state. In the final section of the register, an alphabetical index of all registrants is provided. The manuscript provides the general public and human service agency employers with a guide for selection of qualified clinical social work practitioners. It also helps to clarify the distinction between different levels or types of recognition within the profession. Highly recommended for libraries serving human service educational programs and agencies.—**Maria O'Neil McMahon**

8   Law

INTRODUCTION

Subheadings in this chapter are General Works, Criminology, and Judiciary and Supreme Court. By far the largest subdivision is Judiciary and Supreme Court; and by far the preponderance of these books concern the Supreme Court of the United States. Melvin I. Urofsky has edited a book, *The Supreme Court Justices: A Biographical Dictionary* (Garland, 1994) (see entry 356), which includes justices from John Jay, the first chief justice, to Ruth Bader Ginsburg, and its review notes that the language is easy to understand and nonlegal. Another book on Supreme Court justices is *The Justices of the United States Supreme Court, 1789-1978: Their Lives and Major Opinions* (Chelsea House Publishers in association with R. R. Bowker, 1980) (see entry 355). Judicial staff is not neglected, with the publication of *Judicial Staff Directory: Containing, in Convenient Arrangement, Useful, Accurate and Timely Information . . .* (CQ Staff Directories, 1986-) (see entry 354), which includes information both on judges and on their staffs.

Biographical information on lawyers is found in many of the books listed under General Works. *The Best Lawyers in America, 1993-1994* (Woodward/White, 1983-) (see entry 346) by Steven Naifeh and Gregory White Smith contains listings for thousands of lawyers, although the reviewer notes that most are located in large metropolitan areas. *Who's Who in American Law* (Marquis Who's Who/Reed Reference Publishing, 1977-) (see entry 347) is also noted as being less than complete. Other sources to consult, noted in the reviews in this chapter, include the *Martindale-Hubbell Directory* and *United States Lawyers Reference Directory*. Two titles in this chapter concentrate on women lawyers: Rebecca Mae Salokar and Mary L. Volcansek's *Women in Law: A Biobibliographical Sourcebook* (Greenwood Press, 1996) (see entry 348), and Dawn Bradley Berry's *The 50 Most Influential Women in American Law* (Contemporary Books, 1996) (see entry 343).

Not only judges and lawyers are profiled in this chapter; individuals on the opposite side of the law are here as well, under the subheading Criminology. The FBI's most wanted criminals are in *The FBI Most Wanted: An Encyclopedia* (Garland, 1989) (see entry 349) by Michael Newton and Judy Ann Newton; while another work, William B. Secrest's *Lawmen & Desperadoes* (Arthur H. Clark, 1994) (see entry 350), gives information on people on both sides of the law.

From the distinguished to the notorious, people connected with law can be found here.

GENERAL WORKS

343.   Berry, Dawn Bradley. **The 50 Most Influential Women in American Law**. Los Angeles, Calif., Lowell House; distr., Chicago, Contemporary Books, 1996. 354p. illus. index. $30.00. ISBN 1-56565-469-2.

Nearly 50 percent of law school graduates today are women. Berry has provided an exciting array of stories about women who have overcome tremendous obstacles to influence the practice of law in the United States. These personal stories reveal the intelligence and confidence needed to overcome local and regional customs, and the pressure these women used to pave the way for far-reaching reforms in the American Bar Association, civil rights, personal liberty, and equal rights. These 50 stories provide readers with models and metaphors that will empower everyone to overcome obstacles in personal and professional development, regardless of gender. This book will inspire women who already possess self-assurance or who need to develop it to use the ambition and competitiveness necessary to succeed.

Of course, one wants to ask why these particular women were selected; many were not lawyers, and some were without higher education. The first woman profiled is Margaret Brent, who lived from 1601 to 1671, the first woman to own land in the colonies. Even though the earlier women treated practiced some law in a county bar, they were not recognized by a state bar for more than 200 years, until Arabella Babb Mansfield was admitted to a state bar in 1869 in Iowa. There are some well-known women who were not only admitted to the bar but were also highly influential. Not all of the biographees are women of the legal profession; some are women who influenced the law (e.g., biologist Rachel Carson and civil rights activist Rosa Parks). Other contemporary women include Barbara Jordan, Geraldine Ferraro, Sandra Day O'Connor, Ruth Bader Ginsburg, and Marcia Clark.

Although Berry states that her selections are subjective, she apparently gave too much thought to what would make her book sell, therefore including some contemporary people who have recently been in the headlines. Whether or not their influence is as important as her book title would indicate, only time will tell. The greatest flaw in the book is the gap in coverage between the work of Brent in 1671 and that of Elizabeth Ware Packard in 1816. Influential women of this period should have been listed, but instead Berry has loaded the book with influential women from the second half of the twentieth century. This book is a good read, not an influential reference.—**Gerald D. Moran**

344. Jacobs, William Jay. **Great Lives: Human Rights**. New York, Scribner's, 1990. 278p. illus. index. $22.95. CT215.J33. 920.073. LC 89-37211. ISBN 0-684-19036-2.

It is frequently said that young people today have no role models other than sports heroes and rock musicians. Jacobs presents alternatives in this collective biography that delineates the lives of some 30 men and women known principally for their defense of individual freedoms. Arranged in four sections that roughly cover chronological periods of American history, the work presents well-written biographies that portray the courageous struggles for freedom and justice each biographee endured. The lives of some of the 30 are fairly well known to young people (e.g., Benjamin Franklin, Martin Luther King, Jr., Eleanor Roosevelt) while others (e.g., John Peter Zenger, Sojourner Truth, Emma Goldman) are less familiar. All are portrayed not only as courageous and heroic but also as people with ordinary human frailties. The narratives are enhanced by well-chosen illustrations and by the inclusion of a bibliography and an index.

Although this is not a reference work in the strict sense of the word, it does provide some information that is not easily found elsewhere. Those working with young people should find this volume a welcome addition to their biography collection. It is both a source of information about this often-neglected group of peace and justice activists, and inspirational leisure reading for young people.—**Lucille Whalen**

345. Kornstein, Daniel J. **Thinking under Fire: Great Courtroom Lawyers and Their Impact on American History**. New York, Dodd, Mead, 1987. 243p. illus. index. $18.95. LC 86-29198. ISBN 0-396-08814-7.

Deftly profiled are ten outstanding trial lawyers, some of whom are less well known. Andrew Hamilton (not Alexander), Earl Rogers, and Robert H. Jackson may not be familiar to most readers, while Daniel Webster, Clarence Darrow, and Thurgood Marshall should be. The profiles are not brief life stories from childhood to law school to eventual triumph, but instead are courtroom glimpses, hence the title of the book. Each lawyer's most famous cases are relived but not quite dissected, which would require a set of books to do. Yet enough detail is presented for armchair visualization. Interwoven with the profiles are historical sketches of the times, and once again law and the legal climate predominate over the usual telling of history. Of interest to the general reader and the young lawyer, who is clearly targeted, the introduction is somewhat apologetic. Americans view lawyers as "contentious pettifoggers who stir up unnecessary lawsuits." These ten men were more high-minded than that. And in the summing up, "What Makes a Great Courtroom Advocate?", more lessons abound. These ten men took on cases not because the money enticed them, but because a great moral or ethical principle seized their imaginations. These men fought the just battle, and their example should instruct all of us who participate in a democracy. The writing is lofty and energetic, though not idolatrous. Legalese has been avoided. Genuine heroes every man, they are quoted so that we hear many of their own words, and their eloquence and incisive minds are easily taken to heart. It is good to read about Daniel Webster and Clarence Darrow for a second or third time because of their mastery of law, and to be introduced to new figures in the courtroom is a bonus. Recommended for all library collections as a prod to further reading of the complete biographies of these men.—**Bill Bailey**

346.   Naifeh, Steven, and Gregory White Smith. **The Best Lawyers in America**. Aiken, S.C., Woodward/White, 1983- . index. $110.00. ISSN 1067-4756.

If someone needs an attorney, this reference work is perhaps one of the first sources to consult. It is incredibly easy to use. The names of over 11,000 attorneys appear here, organized by state and listed alphabetically within each state by category (i.e., legal specialty), city, and attorney's last name. A comprehensive index of all attorneys listed concludes the work. If there is a need for a specific legal specialty, one merely need consult the category listing for the state in question.

There are, unfortunately, several difficulties with this otherwise useful directory. First, most of the "best" attorneys listed practice in large metropolitan areas. For example, more than 95 percent of the "best" attorneys in Illinois are found in Chicago. If you need recommendations in most other areas of Illinois, you are out of luck. This holds true throughout the state listings, contrary to the claim that every effort has been made to include more lawyers from outside the large commercial centers in each state. Second, recommendations from attorneys for inclusion, the voting process for inclusion, and the criteria for selection remain quite subjective. The editors acknowledge this shortcoming and note that some attorneys' names may appear more on the basis of "visibility or popularity over sheer ability." Third, many lawyers hesitate to cast negative votes for their colleagues, for a variety of reasons. It behooves anyone who consults this directory to read the brief introduction. In general, this work would begin a search for an attorney, but the search should not end here.

Other useful sources to consult for a list of lawyers, often including some indication of skill and competence, include the *Martindale-Hubbell Directory* (Martindale-Hubbell, 1931-), an annual listing of both U.S. and Canadian lawyers; *United States Lawyers Reference Directory* (Legal Directories, 1977-); and *Who's Who in American Law* (see entry 347). More specialized directories include *Law and Business Directory of Corporate Counsel* (Harcourt Brace Jovanovich, 1980-), another annual directory which lists attorneys in more than 5,000 companies; and Barry Tarlow's *National Directory of Criminal Lawyers* (University Publishers, 1979).—**Michael A. Foley and Terry Ann Mood**

347.   **Who's Who in American Law**. New Providence, N.J., Marquis Who's Who/Reed Reference Publishing, 1977- . index. $249.95. LC 77-79896. ISSN 0162-7880.

This long-standing work offers biographical sketches of "lawyers and professionals in law-related areas." The latter include educators, judges, law librarians, and legal historians. The brief descriptions include information on education, career statistics, awards and publications, *inter alia*. In addition, a fields-of-practice index enables users to locate individuals by specialty and location. The areas of practice include administrative and regulatory, admiralty, antitrust, banking, civil litigation (both federal and general), communications, criminal, environmental, family and matrimonial, general practice, insurance, personal injury, probate, product liability, securities, and taxation. There is as well a professional index that lists individuals again by state and city, grouped under categories such as arbitration and mediation, education, government, industry, and judicial administration.

The advantage of such a reference work is that it provides some direction in which to turn if one is in need of legal assistance or is uncertain, perhaps, who to contact regarding certain legal problems. The "Yellow Pages" does not constitute the best source for information regarding specialties and competencies. Unfortunately, in too many cases, neither does *Who's Who in American Law*. There are only 30,000 entries in the 1994-95 edition, yet at the time there were more than 750,000 attorneys in this country. This reviewer made a list of 20 names of both attorneys and professional educators, all of whom posses an outstanding reputation in law and legal education. Of the 20 names, not one appeared here. In the reviewer's own geographical area there was a dearth of citations. One might come here for an elementary search, but in no way should the search be confined to this one source. Recommended only for major libraries in large metropolitan areas.

An older but still potentially useful title is *Judges of the United States* (2d ed., Washington, D.C., G.P.O., 1983). Covering the eighteenth century through 1981, it provides biographical information for all judges during that time.—**Michael A. Foley and Terry Ann Mood**

348.   **Women in Law: A Bio-bibliographical Sourcebook**. Rebecca Mae Salokar and Mary L. Volcansek, eds. Westport, Conn., Greenwood Press, 1996. 376p. index. $85.00. ISBN 0-313-29410-0.

Women in Law features biographical essays on 43 women from countries in the Western legal tradition who have been prominent in the legal and related fields. Coverage is international, although limited by the editors' "inability to locate and interest specialists from some regions" (e.g., Latin America, Australia, and the Mediterranean). Subjects range from the famous (e.g., Barbara Jordan, Sandra Day O'Connor, Janet Reno) to the more obscure (e.g., Japanese legislator and activist Takako Doi and Ruwandan prime minister Agathe Uwilingiyimana).

Articles are from approximately 4 to 10 pages in length and include family background and education, career development, and achievements and contributions, as well as notes and references. They are generally adulatory and written from liberal and feminist perspectives. Depth of treatment varies, and some articles give considerable anecdotal detail. Several authors assume prior knowledge of historical events. Quality of writing ranges from adequate to excellent. The work provides a superficial introductory essay on the history of women and the law, a brief bibliography, and a subject index.

Were it not for its high price, this work might be suitable for public libraries as an inspirational work for aspiring lawyers and activists, especially women. Of limited reference use, it can be recommended as an optional purchase for circulating collections in law libraries and elsewhere where there is interest in law or women. [R: RBB, 1 Nov 96, p. 542]—**Gari-Anne Patzwald**

CRIMINOLOGY

349.   Newton, Michael, and Judy Ann Newton. **The FBI Most Wanted: An Encyclopedia**. New York, Garland, 1989. 342p. illus. index. (Garland Reference Library of Social Science, v.937). $35.00. HV6785.N48. 364.1'092'2. LC 89-11820. ISBN 0-8240-4779-6.

Reference collections have benefited greatly from the movement to encapsulate specialized information in one or several volumes. The variety of subject encyclopedias currently available represents a highwater mark in publishing, for these works form a historical record and a grand legacy for the twenty-first century. A good example of the variety is this criminal justice offering.

On March 14, 1950, FBI Director J. Edgar Hoover initiated the Bureau's "Ten Most Wanted Fugitives" program. Beginning with the first "tough guy" (and later a few "gals") and continuing to the summer of 1988, they are all here. Each biography covers known background, offenses, prison time, cohorts, and life in crime. The arrangement is chronological with a statistical analysis. The average "Top Ten" fugitive is 36 years old and male; his height is 5'9", his weight 167 pounds; and from listing of name to apprehension is 157 days, the fugitive having traveled some 969 miles between crime location and point of arrest. An appendix provides more data on each individual for easy scanning. Nearly every other page has a mug shot, an eerie reminder that there is no one criminal physiognomy. Recommended for all criminal justice collections and public libraries that have a high circulation of books about crime.—**Bill Bailey**

350.   Secrest, William B. **Lawmen & Desperadoes: A Compendium of Noted, Early California Peace Officers, Badmen, and Outlaws, 1850-1900**. Spokane, Wash., Arthur H. Clark, 1994. 343p. illus. index. $37.50. ISBN 0-87082-209-9.

Supplementing the 1992 *Encyclopedia of Western Lawmen and Outlaws* by Jay R. Nash (see ARBA 93, entry 609), which largely ignores California badmen and their legal nemeses, this volume presents extensive biographical/historical articles on approximately 50 lawmen and badmen prominent in California during the half-century shown in the title. Although the book is well researched and well written, there seems to be an overall defect in the editing, resulting in a simple lack of cross-referencing. For example, in the sketch of the notorious George Contant (also known as Sontag), there is no indication that more information may be found in other articles—some under Charles Aull (a warden at Folsom), and more under John Sontag (George's older brother) and Christopher Evans

(John's father-in-law). In a book catering to a nationwide readership, not just to California aficionados, this lack of cross-referencing is a distinct weakness in the composition of the book.

More careful editing also would have avoided some unanswered questions: The article on Contant refers to "his small book," entitled *A Pardoned Lifer*, but the author is given later as Opie L. Warner. Was he an editor? A ghost writer? No explanation is given. There is a report of the Los Angeles Rangers capturing a gang of horse thieves near La Puente, Los Angeles County, and bringing them before a local justice, who said they must deliver their prisoners to a justice in Shasta County (about 500 miles away). With no explanation, one wonders—is it a misprint? Or did the Rangers embark on a 1,000-mile journey?

The collection of biographies is well illustrated and well written, despite the author's tendency to lapse occasionally into twentieth-century slang. One reads that one desperado already had a rap before entering California; and also that Sara Hill insisted in court that she did not shack up with Senator Sharon, but was his truly wedded wife. Libraries wanting to give their readers a broader view of law and outlawry in the Far West should order this book.—**Raymond F. Wood**

JUDICIARY AND SUPREME COURT

351.   **BNA's Directory of State and Federal Courts, Judges, and Clerks: A State-by-State and Federal Listing**. 1997 ed. Judith A. Miller, with the BNA Library Staff, comps. Washington, D.C., BNA Books, 1996. 548p. illus. index. $115.00pa. ISBN 1-57018-043-1. ISSN 1078-5582.

This standard guide to the national court system begins with an overview of federal and state courts arranged by levels and types. Also included here are the District of Columbia, American Samoa, Guam, the Northern Mariana Islands, Puerto Rico, and the U.S. Virgin Islands. Entries consist of official names of the courts, clerks of the courts, and judges. Geographic jurisdictions are indicated at the third court level, with counties or cities listed alphabetically. Clerks' and judges' titles, addresses, telephone and fax numbers, and e-mail and Internet addresses are also given when available.

Each state's court structure is shown in flowchart form. Although there are four levels of courts (courts of last resort, intermediate appellate courts, general-jurisdiction trial courts, and limited-jurisdiction trial courts), the directory excludes limited-jurisdiction courts. Introductory material includes an explanatory sample entry and a map of the United States showing jurisdictional boundaries of courts of appeal and U.S. district courts. The first 3 editions of this guide were limited to state courts (see ARBA 89, entry 511, and ARBA 87, entry 552, for reviews of the first 2 editions). Federal courts were added to the 4th edition (see ARBA 93, entry 582). The directory is now published annually in order to keep up with frequent staff and other changes. BNA's World Wide Web address and the compiler's e-mail address are also provided.

Among the added features in the current edition are a directory of electronic public-access services to automated information in U.S. federal courts (which includes Internet sites for federal and state courts), a geographic jurisdiction index, and a personal-name index. The only negative feature for this reference book is the semiperforated pages, which will only encourage vandalism. A less expensive alternative (for federal courts only) is *The Sourcebook of Federal Courts: U.S. District and Bankruptcy* (see ARBA 97, entry 500). The directory under review, however, is the only comprehensive one, making it an essential purchase for all law libraries and many general collections as well.—**Gary D. Barber**

352.   Furer, Howard B. **The Fuller Court 1888-1910**. New York, Associated Faculty Press, 1986. 299p. illus. bibliog. (Supreme Court in American Life, Vol. 5). $35.00. LC 84-2873. ISBN 0-86733-060-0.

> Bindler, Norman. **The Conservative Court 1910-1930**. New York, Associated Faculty Press, 1986. 217p. illus. bibliog. (Supreme Court in American Life, Vol. 6). $35.00. LC 84-2810. ISBN 0-86733-061-9.
>
> The Supreme Court in American Life is a nine-volume series covering the court from 1787 (volume 1, *Federal Court*) to 1984 (volume 9, *Burger Court*). Other volumes include *The Reconstruction Court* (Associated Faculty Press, 1988), *The Warren Court* (Associated Faculty Press, 1987), *The Burger Court* (Associated Faculty Press, 1986), and *The Federal Court* (Associated Faculty

Press, 1986). Each begins with an identical two-page introductory note describing the historical significance of the court, followed by an editor's foreword in which the author summarizes the principal events and prevailing philosophy of that period. All volumes are divided into four parts: chronology, documents and decisions, biography, and bibliography. The four parts support each other, providing the background necessary to describe the political, economic, and sociological climate of the era. The chronology lists briefly by year and day the major national and international events, including landmark court decisions and leading statutes enacted by Congress. "Documents and Decisions" reviews, interprets, and reprints the landmark decisions with dissenting opinions, constitutional amendments, and related significant documents. The biographies are more complete than in Elliott's *A Reference Guide to the United States Supreme Court* (Facts on File, 1986) and provide official portraits from the Supreme Court Historical Society. Two pages of tables list chronologically the justices, their home states, appointer, term dates and lifespan, and replacement. The bibliography includes scholarly articles, treatises, and histories pertaining to the court and justices of the era.

The authors have succeeded in presenting a concise, authoritative insight into the impact of judicial decisions on American life in each of the nine designated periods of history. Their work does not purport to be definitive or exhaustive. It doesn't compare in depth and detail to Friedman and Israel's *Justices of the United States Supreme Court* (R. R. Bowker, 1969 and 1978) nor in erudition to Freund and Katz's *History of the Supreme Court of the United States* (Macmillan, 1974-), but this is a reliable, scholarly, compact series that will be read for pleasure as well as factual information by historians, students, and laypersons. [R: Choice, Feb 87, p. 860]—**Helen Carol Bennett**

353.   Jacobstein, J. Myron, and Roy M. Mersky. **The Rejected: Sketches of the 26 Men Nominated for the Supreme Court but Not Confirmed by the Senate**. Milpitas, Calif., Toucan Valley, 1993. 188p. $28.00. KF8776.J33. 347.73'2634. LC 93-22374. ISBN 0-9634017-4-2.

354.   **Judicial Staff Directory: Containing, in Convenient Arrangement, Useful, Accurate and Timely Information Concerning the Federal Justice System**. P. Wayne Walker, ed. Alexandria, Va., CQ Staff Directories, 1986- . maps. indexes. $89.00. ISSN 1091-3742.

The subtitle of the *Judicial Staff Directory,* 1997 edition, describes this volume quite well: "containing, in convenient arrangement, useful, accurate and timely information concerning the federal justice system of the U.S. Government with emphasis on the staffs of all the judges and all the federal courts, together with 2,200 biographies." Indeed, this shows in various ways the structure and interrelationships of the various federal courts. It lists the judges and staff members in such fairly well-known courts as the Supreme Court of the United States, the Circuit Courts of Appeal and District Courts, and Bankruptcy Courts; as well as personnel in perhaps lesser-known entities as the United States Court of International Trade and the United States Court of Appeals for the Armed Forces. Not only does this volume list personnel of these courts, but the arrangement is such that the user can see both the complexity of the U.S. court system, and how various parts of it relate to each other. Maps of each state show the various federal judicial districts within each state.

A substantial portion of the volume is devoted to biographies of both judges and staff, including such information as education, previous career, awards, and memberships. Special features include indexes of judges by the appointing president, so that one can see a list of all judges, for example, appointed by George Bush or Jimmy Carter; an index of judges by year of appointment; and information about means of electronic access to the various courts.

A final index of all names allows one to locate any person listed in this directory, in whatever section. All in all, this directory is a valuable source of information, not only to biographical information on judges and judicial staff, but to the workings of the national court system.—**Terry Ann Mood**

355.   **The Justices of the United States Supreme Court, 1789-1978: Their Lives and Major Opinions**. Leon Friedman and Fred L. Israel, eds. New York, Chelsea House Publishers in association with R. R. Bowker, 1980. 5v. $75.00/set pa. LC 69-13699. ISBN 0-87754-130-2.

Originally published in hardcover between 1969-1978 and now available in paperback (hardcover edition is o.p.), the set contains analytical and biographical essays of 109 judges written by forty-nine scholars. In the 5th volume we find re-evaluation of Chief Justice Warren Burger and Justice Thurgood Marshall (briefer evaluation was made earlier when they were relatively new to the Supreme Court). The resignations of Justices Douglas, Harlan, and Black during this period made it possible for the 5th volume to summarize their work, and to bid farewell to the era of the Warren Court. The new direction of the Burger Court may be detected most strongly from the section on Chief Justice Burger. However, the pieces on the Nixon and Ford appointees to the Court, Blackmun, Powell, Rehnquist, and Stevens, are enlightening in this regard also.

The format is the same in all five volumes. Pieces on particular justices are written by different authors, most of whom are professors of law or practicing attorneys. The writing styles differ, and so does the content, to some degree. Each piece is structured around a section devoted to personal and professional biographical information, and a section of representative opinions. It is a good combination for a reader eager to know individual contributions of justices to constitutional development.

Although an attempt is made to be even-handed in evaluating each justice, the authors are more critical of the newer justices and the chief justice. The index is for the most part quite good; it links justices with topics and also lists major topics handled by each justice separately. Each case is also indexed by name of plaintiff. Additional biographical references at the end of each article allow readers the option of pursuing research beyond the scope of this work.

Any general reference collection would benefit from this handy, concise source of biographical information for justices of the Supreme Court. The original four volumes published in 1969 won the 1970 Scribes Award as outstanding works on a legal subject.—**Barbara Van Deventer and Bohdan S. Wynar**

356.   **The Supreme Court Justices: A Biographical Dictionary**. Melvin I. Urofsky, ed. Hamden, Conn., Garland, 1994. 570p. illus. index. (Garland Reference Library of the Humanities, v.1851). $75.00. ISBN 0-8153-1176-1.

The Supreme Court Justices is a biographical dictionary of 107 men and women Supreme Court justices, from the first Chief Justice John Jay to Ruth Bader Ginsburg. The analytical and interpretive essays vary in length from 1 to 12 pages. Each essay has a picture of the justice, and a biographical sketch concentrating on legal career and significant cases. The essay is completed with a bibliography that notes important publications by the justice, information on the location of personal papers and documents, and further biographical publications. The essays are written in easy-to-understand, nonlegal language by an array of noted American legal scholars. The volume is completed by a topical index and an index of cases.

This is an excellent addition to any law library collection. Because of its readable style, the book is most suitable for any collection that needs to provide a historical overview of the development of American justice—especially any public library collection. [R: WLB, Jan 95, pp. 84-86]
—**Lorna K. Rees-Potter**

357.   **The Supreme Court Justices: Illustrated Biographies, 1789-1993**. Clare Cushman, ed. Washington, D.C., Congressional Quarterly, 1993. 576p. illus. index. $39.95. KF8744.S86. 347.73'2634. LC 93-1446. ISBN 0-87187-723-6.

This is the first single-volume illustrated reference devoted exclusively to introductory biographies of all 106 current and past U.S. Supreme Court justices. The justices are presented chronologically by appointment in essays that underscore the equal power of justices on the court regardless of historical fame or circumstance. In fact, it is the purpose of the volume to introduce the general reader to all of the justices, those fallen into obscurity as well as those better known, and to give less well known biographical information about the most famous. Because of the limitations of a single-volume biography, the appendixes and index are vital to the book. A list of the justices by chief justice and associate justice is helpful, but bibliographies that provide general and in-depth sources for each make the book and important link to information on this institution.

The biographies are too short to live up to the claim of providing full pictures of the justices, the times in which they lived, and the lives they touched. The biographies are often telegraphic in the use of unrelated facts and are by no means critical evaluations of the individuals or the periods. This leaves the reader to sort out the greater historical context of the justices. While the structure of the book implies the importance of the individual and personality in shaping history, nowhere is this view pulled together in any coherent way.

The strengths of most of the biographies are the added historical sources, views of contemporaries, and likely anecdotes. It is a useful addition to Supreme Court sources and biographies but is not a good stand-alone volume. What recommends this book most is the inclusion of comprehensive historical views of justices rarely accessible to the general reader. [R: WLB, Dec 93, pp. 83-123]—**Curtis D. Holmes**

358.　　**The Young Oxford Companion to the Supreme Court of the United States**. By John J. Patrick. New York, Oxford University Press, 1994. 368p. illus. index. $35.00. KF8742.A35P38. 347.73'26'03. LC 93-6467. ISBN 0-19-507877-2.

This book presents information concerning the U.S. Supreme Court in an encyclopedic format, with numerous aspects of the Court arranged alphabetically. Entries include biographical sketches of all 107 justices up through Ruth Bader Ginsburg; discussions of important cases, such as Dred Scott and *Roe v. Wade*; concept; terms; and constitutional information. Designed and written for ages 12 and up, it is expressly intended as a reference work for home and school, to be used for a research project or to answer preconceived questions quickly and conveniently. Critical components of the book include a full index, *see also* references, an appendix of the justices, a short essay on how to use the book, and entries for further reading after each article and a general list. The main text is enhanced by photographs, cartoons, drawings, and sidebars supplementing the entries.

Coverage of the Court is broad but unfortunately not comprehensive. The entries are well written but require fairly sophisticated research skills and previous understanding of the Court and questions about it to make full use of the information. Because of the book's concise nature, it reflects the perspective of the author on which cases to include and what information is relevant. Much is left out, and readers looking for very specific information may have to go elsewhere.

This book serves best as a complement to other material about the Court and would have been improved if the references to further reading had been listed in full along with the general list. This is not a book that teaches about the Supreme Court in any integrated way, but it can serve as an effective companion to other works. A teacher's, librarian's, or parent's guidance is imperative for younger readers. [R: BR, Sept/Oct 94, pp. 58-59; SLJ, Nov 94, p. 138; VOYA, Oct 94, p. 234]—**Curtis D. Holmes**

9   Business and Economics

INTRODUCTION

Business and economics is an area rich in biographical sources. This chapter is subdivided by a mixture of subject and geographical sections: General Works, Advertising, Australia, Banking and Finance, Canada, Europe, Great Britain, Labor, Public Relations, Scotland, Transportation, and United States. Perhaps the most general work, covering people in all fields of business, is *Business People in the* News, edited by Barbara Nykoruk (Gale, 1976) (see entry 363), a compendium of articles from a variety of newspapers and magazines. Other general sources with slightly more specific slants are various stalwart who's who books—*Who's Who in Finance and Industry* (Marquis Who's Who/Reed Reference Publishing, 1995) (see entry 379); *Who's Who in International Banking* (K. G. Saur/Reed Reference Publishing, 1992) (see entry 380); *Who's Who in World Insurance* (St. James Press, 1991) (see entry 372); and *Who's Who in Labor* (Ayer Co., 1976) (see entry 392), for those industries; and for American notables. A fairly recent publication features African American business leaders: John No Ingham and Lynne B. Feldman's *African-American Business Leaders: A Biographical Dictionary* (Greenwood Press, 1994) (see entry 365).

Other sources of international scope appear in several subdivisions. The banking industry of the Middle East is covered in *The APS Who's Who in Middle East Banking & Trade* (Gale, 1985) (see entry 376); it appears under Banking and Finance. *Dictionary of Business Biography* (Butterworth Publishers, 1984 and 1986) (see entries 387 and 388), which is limited to British business people before 1980, is of course under the heading Great Britain. *Biographical Dictionary of American Business Leaders* (Greenwood Press, 1983) (see entry 401), in the section United States, gives information on business leaders since World War II. *Who's Who in European Business* (K. G. Saur/Reed Reference Publishing, 1993) (see entry 386), in the section Europe, gives information on executives, is current to 1993, and includes people from former Soviet countries.

A somewhat quirky, hard-to-categorize, but interesting contribution is *Corporate Eponymy: A Biographical Dictionary of the Persons behind the Names of Major American, British, European and Asian Businesses* (McFarland, 1992) (see entry 370) by Adrian Room; the title speaks for itself.

For those interested in the scholars and students of business and economics, rather than in its practitioners, Mark Blaug has compiled two books of note. His *Great Economists before Keynes: An Introduction to the Lives & Works of One Hundred Great Economists* (see entry 361), and his *Who's Who in Economics: A Biographical Dictionary of Major Economists 1700-1986* (MIT Press, 1986) (see entry 371) both look at those who study the field.

The section on the United States holds both general sources, such as *Contemporary American Business Leaders: A Biographical Dictionary* by John N. Ingham and Lynne B. Feldman (Greenwood Press, 1990) (see entry 402) and more specific ones, e.g., *Encyclopedia of American Business History and Biography: Iron and Steel in the Nineteenth Century* (Facts on File, 1989) (see entry 400), and *Encyclopedia of American Business History and Biography: Iron and Steel in the Twentieth Century* (Facts on File, 1994) (see entry 399). Information on labor in the United States is in the subdivision Labor.

Transportation in the United States, both the automobile industry and the railroad industry, are covered under the subtopic Transportation, with various volumes of the *Encyclopedia of American Business History and Biography*. The volume on the automobile industry, *Encyclopedia of American Business History and Biography: The Automobile Industry, 1920-1980*, edited by George S. May (Facts on File, 1989) (see entry 395), covers the time period 1920-1980 and includes articles both on the car makers—from Henry Ford to Lee Iacocca—and the cars themselves, from the Ford and Rolls to the Stutz and the Packard. Railroads are covered in two volumes from the same series, *Encyclopedia of American Business History and Biography: Railroads in the Age of Regulation, 1900-1980*

(Facts on File, 1988) (see entry 396), and *Encyclopedia of American Business History and Biography: Railroads in the Nineteenth Century* (Facts on File, 1988) (see entry 396). Biographies are a mixed bag, with executives sharing pages with financiers, politicians, and inventors.

For those who need to make contacts with wealthy people for fundraising purposes, this chapter provides several sources. *America's Wealthiest People: Their Philanthropic and Nonprofit Affiliations* (Taft Corporation, 1984) (see entry 397); *New Fortunes 1994: Biographical Profiles of 650 of America's Emerging Wealth Holders* (Gale, 1994) (see entry 403); and *Who's Wealthy in American 1993: A Prospecting List and Directory of 102,000 Affluent Americans* (Taft Group; distr., Detroit, Gale, 1993) (see entry 404) are all aimed at those who need to contact potential donors.

GENERAL WORKS

359.   **A Biographical Dictionary of Dissenting Economists**. Philip Arestis and Malcolm Sawyer, eds. Brookfield, Vt., Edward Elgar/Gower Publishing, 1992. 628p. $139.95. HB76.B3. 330'.0922. LC 91-16267. ISBN 1-85278-331-1.

Unfortunately, the writings of numerous economists who are in substantial disagreement with basic assumptions about the nature, scope, methods, and significance of orthodox theorizing have not received adequate recognition within the economics profession. This dictionary has been compiled to provide a guide to the writings of 90 illustrious dissenting economists who have made significant attempts to broaden and deepen the understanding of economics. Although the listing is far from complete, it has some special, useful features. Some entries on living dissidents are in the form of autobiographical essays that cover how they developed their innovative thinking, the extent to which they disagree with economic orthodoxy, and the sociopolitical influences on their theories. Some dissidents asked another to write about their work. A small number declined the invitation to contribute. Most dissidents can be classified as post-Keynesian, Marxists or neo-Marxists, Sraffian, Kaleckian, institutionalists, or behaviorists, but few defy an exact categorization.

On the whole, this is a clearly written, well-organized biographical dictionary. Highly recommended to all members of the economics profession, especially those whose primary interest lies in research or the history of economic thought.—**Oleg Zinam**

360.   **Biographical Directory of the Council of Economic Advisers**. Robert Sobel and Bernard S. Katz, eds. Westport, Conn., Greenwood Press, 1988. 301p. index. $49.95. LC 86-14984. ISBN 0-313-22554-0.

The President's Council of Economic Advisers (CEA) was created by the Employment Act of 1946. Since that time forty-five distinguished economists have served on the council. This volume contains a short (two to nine pages) biographical essay on each member. The standard personal details regarding birth, education, employment, and dates of service on the council are presented, as is a distillation of key professional accomplishments and ideological bent. The authors, primarily academic economists, do an admirable job of placing each of the forty-four men and one woman council members in historical context. This is a tightly edited, concisely written, accessible work. The essays are largely free of technical jargon, demonstrating that at least some economists are literate in the English language. If there is a weakness, it is that the introductory essay describes only the events leading up to the creation of the CEA. A reader interested in the organizational and political factors that have shaped the council over the years must construct it through the lives of its individual members.—**Bruce Stuart**

361.   Blaug, Mark. **Great Economists before Keynes: An Introduction to the Lives & Works of One Hundred Great Economists**. . . . New York, Cambridge University Press, 1988. 286p. illus. index. $14.95pa. HB76.B54. 330'.092'2. LC 88-16193. ISBN 0-521-36741-7.

What at first glance appears to be just an alphabetical listing of illustrious economists looks after careful reading more like an excellently organized course in the history of economic thought. This volume is a companion to the author's previous book *Great Economists since Keynes* (Brighton, England: Wheatsheaf Books, 1985) and is more limited but much more detailed than Ludwig H.

Mai's *Men and Ideas in Economics* (Littlefield, 1975), which covered some 700 outstanding contributors to the development of economic theories in much shorter entries.

Blaug's volume is an outstanding reference source. Every entry is self-contained and self-explanatory. With few exceptions, each is embellished with its economist's portrait. The author recommends the reading of these selections in chronological order so that one can trace the logic of development in economic thought (which could be viewed as an accumulated heritage of specific ideas of individual writers). Each entry provides a biographical sketch, a historical setting of the period, the economic problems of the day, the contributions of the economist to the solution of these problems, impact on other writers, schools of thought, and the overall development of economics.

Especially valuable are numerous cross-references to other works and writers within each biographical sketch, reflecting an intricate web of intellectual cross-fertilization, interdependence, and ever-present controversies. These cross-references are summarized in the index of names (other than main entries) at the end of the volume. There is also an index of subjects. This is an excellent compendium of biographical essays of great value to all economists, especially those interested in the history of economic thought. Written in clear and concise language, this volume is highly recommended as a supplementary text for undergraduate and graduate courses in the history of economics as well as for college and public libraries.—**Oleg Zinam**

362.   Blaug, Mark. **Great Economists before Keynes: An Introduction to the Lives & Works of One Hundred Great Economists of the Past**. Atlantic Highlands, N.J., Humanities Press, 1986. 286p. illus. index. $39.95. LC 85-27083. ISBN 0-391-03381-6.

This volume gives brief summaries of the economic contributions of 100 economists written during the seventeenth through nineteenth centuries. Each of these intellectual biographies covers two to three pages (eighty-five with pictures or portraits), enough to whet a professional's appetite and to place a name in context for all students. Most economists would agree with virtually all of Blaug's selection of names for inclusion, but might differ over his sometimes strongly expressed evaluations. This volume is easy to use (and is excellent) as a quick reference, as intended; but it cannot serve (and was not intended) as a substitute for, say, Schumpeter's massive *History of Economic Analysis* (Oxford University Press, 1954). This volume "is a companion piece to (Blaug's) *Great Economists since Keynes.*" Blaug is just the right author for this reference; he is the leading living authority on the history of economic thought, analysis, and doctrine.

Blaug's audience is "those who are studying economics for the first time," and who need a quick reference when a teacher mentions the name of an economist who has made significant contributions to economics during the centuries surveyed. The result amply fulfills this goal. Not only are there summaries of the arguments of the great economists, including Smith, Ricardo, Marx, Mill, Marshall, both Keyneses, Pigou, Fisher, Schumpeter, and Walras, but Blaug includes such less well known economists as Kondratieff (business cycles), Senior (value theory and markets), and McCulloch (who spread Ricardo's analysis). Blaug also includes a paragraph or two on each economist's education and professional employment. Blaug's style is succinct, and he links each economist's contributions to contemporaneous and preceding writing.—**Richard A. Miller**

363.   **Business People in the News: A Compilation of News Stories and Feature Articles from American Newspapers and Magazines Covering People in Industry, Finance, and Labor**. Barbara Nykoruk, ed. Detroit, Gale, 1976. 402p. illus. index. (Biography News Library). $62.00. LC 76-4617. ISBN 0-8103-0044-3.

This series by Gale follows the same format and pattern as their Biography News. The biographical articles on prominent business leaders are reproduced from various U.S. magazines and newspapers. Volume 1 includes approximately 300 biographical sketches.

Because of the price and nature of this new reference series, it is most appropriate for larger libraries that need additional biographical information on business leaders—information that they have not been able to find in the standard sources. Many of the entries are included in the "Who's Who" series. [R: Choice, Nov 76, p. 115; LJ, 1 Nov 76, p. 2266; WLB, Nov 76, p. 262]—**Dwight F. Burlingame**

364.   **Contemporary Entrepreneurs: Profiles of Entrepreneurs and the Businesses They Started**. Craig E. Aronoff and John L. Ward, comps. Detroit, Omnigraphics, 1992. 488p. index. $85.00. HC102.5.A2C66. 338'.04'092273. LC 91-7637. ISBN 1-55888-315-0.

This volume gives brief discussions of 79 individuals and their 74 entrepreneurial ventures. There is little attempt at economic analysis, no synthesis or summary or conclusions, and no indication of the criteria that produced this selection of entrepreneurs. With only a few exceptions (e.g., Donald C. Burr, Steven P. Jobs), the individuals are not household names, but their products and services fall in the expected markets: computers and software, construction and building, food, clothing, and communication. Some of the products or firms are well known (e.g., Mrs. Fields' Cookies, L. A. Gear, Blockbuster Entertainment, WordPerfect, Sun Microsystems). Each entry covers basic topics: biographical information on the entrepreneur/founder, the business's origin and growth, obstacles encountered, keys to success, future vision, and entrepreneurial lessons (with a brief bibliography of relevant articles in the business press). Much of this information comes directly from the biographees. The writing is light and informative, with generous quotations, and is similar in style to the *Wall Street Journal*, *Forbes*, and *Business Week*. The entries were written by more than a dozen different authors who are identified only by initials. [R: RBB, 1 Oct 92, p. 365; WLB, Sept 92, p. 111]—**Richard A. Miller**

365.   Ingham, John No, and Lynne B. Feldman. **African-American Business Leaders: A Biographical Dictionary**. Westport, Conn., Greenwood Press, 1994. 806p. index. $99.50. HC102.5. A2152. 338.6'42'08996073. LC 93-20430. ISBN 0-313-27253-0.

This dictionary of historically significant black business leaders covers the time period from the earliest days of our country to the present, but the emphasis is on individuals who lived between 1880 and World War II. Actually, *African-American Business Leaders* is more than a dictionary. It provides encyclopedic information on the biographees that places them in a historic context appropriate to their era and their social and economic setting. Following each biographical entry is a listing of primary and secondary source materials relating to the individual. These sources range from articles in newspapers and scholarly journals and entries in collective biographies to personal papers, theses and dissertations, and oral histories. In addition to a detailed index, *African-American Business Leaders* includes appendixes of its biographees arranged by place of birth, principal place of business, and type of business. The appendix also includes a list of the nine female subjects.

The only disappointment of this work is its selectivity. The work profiles only 123 African American business leaders, most of whom lived in major cities of the southern states or in selected northern centers. This topic cries out for publication of a supplement to include persons from other geographical areas. In the food service industry alone, such current leaders as Herman Cain of Godfather's Pizza, and Larry Lundy, Pizza Hut franchisee, are worthy of inclusion. In spite of this drawback, this text should be a top priority purchase for all but the smallest school, academic, and public libraries.—**Dene L. Clark**

366.   **International Who's Who of Professional and Business Women**. 2d ed. Ernest Kay, ed. Cambridge, England, International Biographical Centre; distr., Bristol, Pa., IPS/Taylor & Francis, 1992. 702p. index. $155.00. ISBN 0-948875-85-2.

In the foreword of this work, the editor makes a special point of asserting that there is no charge or fee for inclusion in the volume, but he does not state what criteria were used. Paging through the book likewise offers no clue as to criteria. Instead, the names seem to be a rather haphazard collection, some of which are appropriate to the book's title and purpose. The reader will find such names as Corazon Aquino, Angela Lansbury, and Sandra Day O'Connor, but where are Isabel Allende, Winnie Mandela, Jeane Kirkpatrick, Agnes Varda, Gloria Steinem, and thousands of other women who have made achievements in business and professional fields? At the same time, others included are lauded for such dubious accomplishments as designing their own swimming pools.

It is interesting to note that most of the well-known names in this collection are those of women who are well past the point in their careers when they are making contributions in their given fields. In addition, the people chosen for this supposedly international directory are generally Western English speakers, a fact that is supported by examining the geographical index, where the most names occur in the sections for Australia, Canada, England, and the United States. Of the seven women selected for dedications, all are U.S. citizens, and only one was born outside of the United States. A subject index reveals further imbalances in fields represented, with educators, for instance, claiming more than a page of listings while athletes and doctors have a mere fraction of the space. Biographical descriptions in this work are limited to flat portraits that make even someone such as the late Marian Anderson, whose extraordinary career was sheer inspiration, sound tedious. Because of these deficiencies, one can only speculate about the intent and usefulness of this volume.—**Barbara Ittner**

367. Leavitt, Judith A. **American Women Managers and Administrators: A Selective Biographical Dictionary of Twentieth-Century Leaders in Business, Education, and Government**. Westport, Conn., Greenwood Press, 1985. 317p. bibliog. index. $45.00. LC 84-12814. ISBN 0-313-23748-4.

This volume arose from the need to identify twentieth-century women leaders in business, education, and government. In doing so, Leavitt compiled the biographies of 226 outstanding women managers, administrators, and leaders who have held or now hold positions of prominence. The criteria for inclusion were as follows: women who were "firsts" or who had achieved some significant accomplishment in a particular field or occupation; women who were founders of business or educational institutions; and women who have held some position of national prominence. Women who were "firsts" make up nearly half the entries in this collection.

The biographies, which vary in length, are arranged in alphabetical order. In most cases, a bibliography citing works by and about the subject follows each entry. The appendix includes an alphabetical listing by category of the women cited in the directory. The volume also includes a general bibliography and an index.

Because of its subject content, this book will be a useful reference tool in public, school, and college libraries. It will be useful for guidance and career counselors and in programs of women's studies.—**Lorraine Mathies**

368. Mai, Ludwig H. **Men and Ideas in Economics: A Dictionary of World Economists Past and Present**. Totowa, N.J., Littlefield, Adams, 1977. 270p. bibliog. (A Littlefield, Adams Quality Paperback No. 284). $11.50; $2.95pa. LC 77-9556. ISBN 0-87471-867-8; 0-8226-0284-9pa.

This volume contains brief (from a paragraph to a page) biographies of some 700 persons—mainly economists, with a few others thrown in who are important in matters of doctrine or policy (such as Lenin). One of the appendixes lists, by country, currently active economists and their principal works, and another outlines (in seven pages) a history of economic doctrine, covering the more important schools and movements and those associated with them. Although coverage is everywhere extremely summary, even economists are likely to find the work useful. They will in some cases doubtless be irritated by the shortcomings in the technical treatment of those economists whose work they know well, but they will need the work for the majority of those with whose work they have only slight acquaintance. Librarians and other laymen with an interest in matters economic will find the work very helpful for ready reference. For the money, hard to equal.

A related title is *Who's Who in Economics: A Biographical Dictionary of Major Economists, 1700-1981*, edited by Mark Blaug and Paul Sturges (MIT Press, 1983. 416p. $70.00) that covers more individuals, emphasizing primarily biographical data. [R: WLB, Dec 77, p. 345]—**John G. Williamson and Bohdan S. Wynar**

369. **Nobel Laureates in Economic Sciences: A Biographical Dictionary**. Bernard S. Katz, ed. New York, Garland, 1989. 339p. index. (Garland Reference Library of the Humanities, v.850). $75.00. HB76.N63. 330'.092'2. LC 89-1062. ISBN 0-8240-5742-2.

This book is one of a series of biographical dictionaries about Nobel laureates. The five others contain the biographies of Nobel Prize winners in literature, medicine, physics, chemistry, and peace. This volume contains a charming foreword by Paul Samuelson.

There is nothing exceptional about the quality of these biographies. The life and work of each Nobel laureate in economics is described in 10 to 15 double-column pages. Most entries rely on more authoritative biographies such as *Lives of the Laureates* by William Briet and Roger W. Spencer (MIT Press, 1986) or Robert Sobel's *The Worldly Economists* (Free Press, 1980). Yet most entries are solidly researched and written. The emphasis is on the scientific contributions of each laureate. It is not easy to condense and put into perspective the sophisticated works of these thinkers. With the focus on scientific contributions and the small amount of space allotted to each entry, these biographies appear to be condensed versions of the *Scandinavian Journal of Economics* (Stockholm: Almquist & Wiksell, 1976-) articles. Indeed, many of the biographies cite the *Scandinavian Journal of Economics* as a source.

Nevertheless, this biographical dictionary does a solid job of presenting summaries of the contributions of Nobel laureates in economics in terms that an undergraduate can understand. The book includes a brief index, and each entry has a selected bibliography.—**Elia Kacapyr**

370.   Room, Adrian. **Corporate Eponymy: A Biographical Dictionary of the Persons Behind the Names of Major American, British, European and Asian Businesses**. Jefferson, N.C., McFarland, 1992. 280p. $35.00. HC29.R66. 338.7'4'0922. LC 92-53502. ISBN 0-89950-679-8.

This work provides brief biographical descriptions of individuals whose names adorn major commercial enterprises in the English-speaking world. Room gives dates, places, family, and career history of nearly 1,000 people whose names have become familiar to us because they identify a company or product, such as Henry Ford of Ford Motor Company or James L. Kraft of Kraft cheeses. The names are presented in a dictionary arrangement. To assist in identifying similar names, a short descriptive phrase indicates the company's general area of business. Within each biography a name with its own entry is in boldface print. The 100- to 200-word biographical sketches generally supply the answer to where the name of the company originated and provide a starting point for more detailed research if desired. While the work's scope is worldwide, the majority of companies listed are of British origin. Emphasis is on names currently in use.

The introduction states that composite names are entered in all their forms with appropriate *see* references to the main entry, but this practice is executed inconsistently. For instance, Philip Morris is referred from "Morris, Philip," but Melson Wingate is not referred from "Wingate, Melson." Companies with names derived from two or more persons (e.g., Dow Jones, Merrill Lynch) are generally not cross-referenced.

A bibliography provides sources for the better-known eponyms. Also included is an exhaustive list of people who provided information about the lesser-known firms. This list is arranged by personal name, not company, which reduces its value. [R: RBB, 1 Dec 92, p. 687]—**William S. Proudfoot**

371.   **Who's Who in Economics: A Biographical Dictionary of Major Economists 1700-1986**. 2d ed. Mark Blaug, ed. Cambridge, Mass., MIT Press, 1986. 935p. index. $115.00. LC 86-2837. ISBN 0-262-02256-7.

The 2nd edition of this work includes over 300 new entries, bringing the total to some 1,400 economists from around the world. The criterion for selection among the living economists is the frequency with which their works are cited in the *Social Sciences Citation Index*. Inclusion of the deceased economists' biographical sketches was determined by an examination of names mentioned in the indexes of major works on historical economic thought.

Entries include full name, place and date of birth, current and previous positions, degrees, professional memberships and awards, major fields of interest, and a statement on their principal contributions. Two indexes are provided. The first matches the economists to their principal fields of interest. The second is an index by country of residence if not the United States. A useful title for larger academic libraries. [R: RBB, 15 Apr 87, p. 1267]—**Frank Wm. Goudy**

372.   **Who's Who in World Insurance**. Harlow, England, Longman Group; distr., Chicago, St. James Press, 1991. 280p. index. $150.00. ISBN 1-55862-168-7.

Unlike many directories that use "World" in their title, this one is truly international. It includes insurance executives from even the smallest countries and does not overrepresent either the United Kingdom, where it is published, or the United States. The major portion of the book is an alphabetical list of executives, their titles, and contact information. A few entries include brief information on qualifications, memberships, directorships, areas of expertise, and previous employment history. As a biographical dictionary, the information is generally too sketchy—or nonexistent—to be of use. However, as a way of contacting these executives, the book is quite useful, as it provides, when available, business address, telephone number, telex, fax, and cable information. The number of personnel listed per company ranges from 1 to 22. An index that lists executives and firms by specialty might enhance the usefulness of this title.

Unfortunately, the price is high in relation to the amount of information. This directory is recommended for comprehensive business collections or for insurance or international firms that can afford it.—**Susan V. McKimm**

ADVERTISING

373. **The Ad Men and Women: A Biographical Dictionary of Advertising**. Ed Applegate, ed. Westport, Conn., Greenwood Press, 1994. 401p. index. $75.00. LC 93-28040. ISBN 0-313-27801-6.

This work is a richly detailed compilation of biographical sketches of men and women who pioneered or contributed significantly to American advertising's history. The editor commissioned the 54 entries (by more than 30 scholars, researchers, and professionals) because he saw a need for a reference work that would examine the lives of creative personalities. The subjects profiled were responsible for every element of advertising as we know it today. It is fascinating to read about the originators of transit advertising, radio commercials, television spots, slogans, political sound bites, and the creative revolution in the 1960s. The collection ranges from the father of today's advertising agency to the chair of the largest minority-owned advertising agency in the United States. The work includes studies of nine females in recognition of the major contributions that women have brought to the field. In addition to copywriters and key people from major agencies, there are profiles of Walter Dill Scott, the first academic to apply psychology to advertising, and Daniel Starch, developer of the Starch Advertisement Readership Service. All entries conclude with a bibliography of works by and about the subject and a list of major clients and advertising campaigns.

Practically all of the biographical information that the contributors present is available elsewhere, but only in widely dispersed sources. This biographical dictionary is recommended for academic libraries that support programs in business, particularly advertising majors. It should also be a must-purchase for medium-size and large public libraries. [R: Choice, Oct 94, p. 255; RBB, 15 May 94, p. 1713]—**Dene L. Clark**

AUSTRALIA

374. **The Business Who's Who of Australia**. 22d ed. Janice Mayer, ed. Crow's Nest, Australia, R. C. Riddell; distr., Bristol, Pa., International Publications Service, 1988. 1v. (various paging). maps. index. $320.00. ISBN 0-947060-07-3. ISSN 0068-4503.

This volume gives basic organizational data on about 8,000 Australian business firms. Each entry includes the name of the firm (including its divisional status if appropriate); address; telephone, telex, and fax numbers; branch addresses (with manager's names); a description of products and services (including trade names); names of chief officers; names of subsidiaries and associate companies, if any; names of solicitors, auditors, and banks; names of directors; capital; sales; month of annual meeting; fiscal year; and employment. Several additional sections round out the volume: (1) general information about Australia (climate, population, exports, employment, overseas trade commissioners, diplomatic and consular representatives in Australia, and many names and addresses of Commonwealth and state parliamentarians, officers, and bureaucrats); (2) financial institutions (banks, insurance companies, and accountants); (3) an alphabetical list of individuals serving as corporate directors; (4) subsidiaries listed by parent firm; and (5) firms listed by industry. Except for the scarcity of financial information, this directory is analogous to Standard & Poor's or Moody's. It is essential to any firm planning to do business in Australia.—**Richard A. Miller**

BANKING AND FINANCE

375. **American Banker Directory of U.S. Banking Executives**. 1st ed. New York, American Banker; distr., Salem, N.H., Ayer Co., 1981. 824p. o.p.

This directory is a bargain for those who need to know names, backgrounds, and affiliations of bank executives. The gold-stamped, library-bound volume was compiled by publishers of the nation's only daily newspaper devoted exclusively to banking. *Polk's World Bank Directory* and Rand McNally International's *Bankers Directory* publish names of top managers along with data on their banks, but contain nothing like the biographical sketches provided in this first-edition *American Banker* volume. *Who's Who in Banking: The Directory of the Banking Profession* (New York, Business Press), which last appeared in 1972, contained some 8,000 biographical profiles of officers in a variety of financial institutions and regulatory agencies.

The *American Banker Directory* profiles about 15,000 bank executives, all prominent in their own milieus and many whose reputations are national and international. Biographies are alphabetically arranged, with such vital information as birth date and place; spouses and children; home address; educational background; military service; previous bank affiliations; special awards; and career, civic, political, and club affiliations. Also, banks are indexed by state, accompanied by listings of bank officers and their positions. A table of abbreviations explains shorthand such as acronyms and military rank. As in any similar work, some names are missing, presumably those who did not submit the requested data.

This volume will occupy a useful niche in the business, financial, and banking sections of reference libraries, and could benefit sales and marketing organizations dealing with upper-level executives in the commercial banking field.

A related title is *Who's Who in Banking in Europe* (4v. International Publications Service, 1983. $550.00. ISBN 0-905589-02-5) that provides brief biographical data on some 30,000 European bank executives. [R: Choice, July/Aug 81, p. 1525]—**Charles L. Hinkle and Bohdan S. Wynar**

376. **The APS Who's Who in Middle East Banking & Trade**. 3d ed. Nicosia, Cyprus, APS; distr., Detroit, Gale, 1985. 2v. maps. index. $220.00/set. LC 83-149147. ISSN 0254-2064 (v.1); 0254-2080 (v.2).

This 3rd edition of *The APS Who's Who in Middle East Banking & Trade* is divided into two volumes. The 1st volume is divided into three sections. The 1st section provides general information on each of the twenty-two Arab countries and a map for each, followed by an alphabetical listing of banks. A corporate profile is given for each bank. The 2nd section gives corporate banking information for non-Arab countries with banking interests in the Arab world.

The third section contains biographical information of individuals in the Arab or Arab-related banking world. The biographical sketches vary in length and structure. Some are very brief (name, position, and address), while others are more detailed, occupying one-quarter of a page.

Volume 2 contains three overview articles on Arab banking, the Saudi stock market, and Kuwait's al-Manakh crisis. The main part of the volume, however, is devoted to company corporate profiles in the Arab countries and biographical information on individuals, such as company executives and business leaders.

Like many other banking and trade reference books, this one has a modest number of business advertisements. The value of this set would have been enhanced by a detailed introduction offering criteria for selection of country, corporate, or individual profiles. This might have explained why Cyprus, which is not an Arab country, is included, while Turkey and Iran are not.

The major differences between the 2nd and 3rd editions are: (1) the price—the 3rd edition costs $30.00 more; (2) the distributorship—the 2nd edition is distributed by Marquis Who's Who, the third by Gale; (3) the 2nd edition covers 1983-1984, while it is unclear what years are covered in the 3rd edition. The LC number and the ISSN are identical for both editions. The similarities between the two editions are such that owners of the 2nd edition need not purchase the 3rd.—**Mary Jo Aman**

377.   **Encyclopedia of American Business History and Biography: Banking and Finance to 1913**. Larry Schweikart, ed. New York, Facts on File, 1990. 528p. illus. index. $75.00. HG2461.B33. 332.1'0973. LC 89-29581. ISBN 0-8160-2193-7.

This is the fifth volume in the *Encyclopedia of American Business History and Biography*; the others cover railroads (see entry 396), iron and steel (see entries 399 and 400), and automobiles (see entry 395). A 20-page introduction sketches the historical period, providing background and considerable cohesion to the 114 entries. (It is not, however, a substitute for a unified historical account.)

By far the strength of this volume is in its brief biographical entries. These mostly cover bankers and investment bankers: the well known (e.g., J. P. and J. S. Morgan, Hetty Green) and the less well known (e.g., W. C. Ralston, the Kountze Brothers, George Peabody). Other individuals of importance to this early history of U.S. banking are economists (e.g., Henry C. Carey, Davis Rich Dewey, George Tucker), editors (e.g., William M. Gouge, Horace White), public officials (e.g., Nelson Aldrich, Arsene P. Pujo), and some unclassifiable (e.g., John Jacob Astor, Salmon P. Chase, Dewitt Clinton, Alexander Hamilton). Each entry tells of the subject's activities relative to banking, finance, and business, as well as some personal matters (e.g., marriages, children). Omitted are figures such as Andrew Carnegie and J. D. Rockefeller, whose business dealings place them in other volumes. The remaining nonpersonal entries are sparse and predictable: banks, institutions, and issues. None seems adequate save as a starter to search the bibliography to each entry.

The intended purpose is to chronicle "America's material civilization through its business figures [people] and businesses." The expected users are students, teachers, scholars, researchers, and government and corporate officials. It serves the first and last very well, the rest only in their initial research.—**Richard A. Miller**

378.   Silver, A. David. **Who's Who in Venture Capital**. 3d ed. New York, John Wiley, 1987. 468p. index. $29.95pa. LC 86-28974. ISBN 0-471-85639-8.

Now available in an inexpensive paperback edition, *Who's Who in Venture Capital* still manages to catch and hold the attention of the avid entrepreneur. The author is very much a 1980s venture capitalist and seems truly to relish writing about this high-power field. Besides the previous editions of this work, the author has written *Entrepreneurial Megabucks* (Wiley, 1985) and *Entrepreneurial Life* (Wiley, 1983); he certainly appears to be the expert in the area. The title does not really describe the entire scope of this work. It goes beyond merely being a biographical directory of the big names in the field, including names of the capitalists, their background, education, etc.; most of them do not appear in *Who's Who in Finance and Industry* (see ARBA 83, entry 814). Beyond biography, the book tells the story of venture capital and some of its biggest successes, such as McDonald's, Mary Kay Cosmetics, and Cetus Corp.

Silver explains the "investment" equations used by venture capitalists to plan and develop strategies in easily understood terms. He even gives basics on how to dress to meet with the investment bigwigs, according to areas of the country.

The good-quality paperback has an excellent typeface and is very legible. The in-depth index provides good access to names and companies within the text. This edition is much less expensive than the prior ones, making it a handy reference addition to the library serving MBA students and to the home libraries of those interested in the growth field, those with the "itch to get rich" and an idea to help them do it. It makes an enjoyable yet useful introduction and fact-finder in the complex world of venture capital.—**Robert D. Adamshick**

379.   **Who's Who in Finance and Industry, 1996-1997**. 29th ed. New Providence, N.J., Marquis Who's Who/Reed Reference Publishing, 1995. 941p. index. $259.95. ISBN 0-8379-0330-0.

Like earlier editions, this edition of *Who's Who in Finance and Industry* includes people prominent not only in corporations but those in education, government, and media who are important in business. Information includes not only basic biography but also job history, directorships held, publications, awards, and memberships.

In other ways, the directory has changed since its 27th edition (see ARBA 93, entry 179). The number of biographies has shrunk from 25,400 to 21,000. Foreign coverage has significantly expanded, now constituting about one-sixth of the entries (reviewer's estimate). A "Professional Area Index," new to this edition, greatly enhances access. Biographees are categorized according to broad areas (e.g., finance, government, industry, law) that are in some cases subdivided (e.g., industry into manufacturing, service, trade, and so on); then they are divided geographically, ultimately at the city level. This arrangement usually produces a manageable number of entries under each city.

Admission to the directory is based upon the biographee's "reference value" as reflected by a position held or a significant achievement. This criterion encompasses principal officers of major corporations, high-level federal government officials, important labor leaders, significant scholars, and winners of major awards. To measure the directory's inclusion of principal officers of major corporations, this reviewer conducted a test using the *Forbes* annual rankings of the 500 largest publicly held companies by assets, sales, net income, and market value. To include truly major companies, only those present on the rankings every year, 1992-1995, were chosen. To allow sufficient time for their CEOs to become noteworthy, the CEO's tenure had to span the same four years. Of the 432 CEOs, 354, or roughly 80 percent, were in the directory. CEOs of Dow Jones, Oracle Systems, Pfizer, Rockwell International, and Telecommunications Inc. were among those missing.

An informal test was conducted for significant people not on the *Forbes* lists but often mentioned in the business press. The success rate was fairly high. Among those missing, however, were John Bog (chairman of Vanguard), Felix Rohatyn (investment banker), Arthur Levitt (chairman of the Securities and Exchange Commission), James Wolfensohn (president of the World Bank), and Thomas Monaght (chairman of Domino's Pizza). Although the directory passed both of these tests with high scores, Marquis Who's Who should mount a more concerted effort to improve its coverage.

Entries in this directory are also available electronically as part of *The Complete Marquis Who's Who on CD-ROM* (Reed Reference Publishing, 1996), the *Marquis Who's Who* file on DIALOG, and the PEOPLE Library/EXECDR File on LEXIS/NEXIS. This directory remains an essential purchase for business reference collections.—**John Lewis Campbell and Terry Ann Mood**

380.   **Who's Who in International Banking**. 6th ed. New Providence, N.J., K. G. Saur/Reed Reference Publishing, 1992. 625p. $225.00. HG3881.W475. 332.1'5'0922. LC 92-6406. ISBN 1-85739-040-7.

This newly revised 6th edition has two major parts: a biographical section and a bank directory. The biographical sketches appear in part 1. In the previous editions these sketches gave limited information, and no indication was given as to method of inclusion. For this new edition, entry is by invitation only and according to set criteria. Some 4,000 biographies with complete addresses, including fax numbers, are given for each entrant. Part 2 is a banking directory arranged alphabetically by country. This directory section lists key position titles and names for each bank. An additional feature is the biographical index at the end of each country section that gives the page entry number of the biographical sketch in part 1.

This is a very useful directory and a marked improvement over previous editions. However, the bank directory is not as comprehensive as *Polk's Bank Directory* (International Edition) (see ARBA 70, v. 1, p. 174) or the *Rand McNally International Bankers Directory* (see ARBA 80, entry 816). Still, it is a worthwhile acquisition for libraries that need an international banking directory and biographical information.—**Linda Suttle Harris**

381.   **Who's Who in International Banking 1990/91**. Alicja Whiteside, comp. and ed. London, International Insider; distr., Bristol, Pa., Taylor & Francis, [1991]. 1195p. $160.00. ISBN 1-85271-121-3.

This who's who covers three broad classifications: banks (individuals), bankers (as lenders, including investment banks in the United States), and borrowers (generally corporations, but including banks). For most individuals, the 4,500 or so alphabetical entries of international bankers include name, nationality, birth date, business title, address, telephone and telex numbers, previous employers, education, languages, marital status, number of children, and recreational activities. There is no indication of the criteria for individual selection; the chairpersons of Citibank, Manufacturers Hanover, and Chemical Bank are not included. The 4,400 entries of international banks (including foreign branches) in 120-plus countries include name; address; telephone, fax, and telex numbers; and selected senior officers (with titles), often limited to those officers with international lending responsibilities. The order of banks is alphabetical within the country in which the bank (or branch) operates. As expected, numerous entries occur for the United Kingdom, the United States, Switzerland, Singapore, Hong Kong, Japan, and Luxembourg. For a number of countries a single entry appears (e.g., Niue Island, Senegal, Seychelles, Andorra). The nearly 1,400 entries of international borrowers in 73 countries usually include name; address; telephone, fax, and telex numbers; and senior officers with financial (borrowing) responsibilities. An index that covers individuals, lending institutions, and borrowers might be useful, particularly as a cross-index to banks listed in several countries.—**Richard A. Miller**

CANADA

382.   **Alberta Business Who's Who & Directory**. 3d ed. Lorne Silverstein, comp. and ed. Edmonton, Alta., Alberta Business Research, 1987. 896p. illus. $59.50. ISBN 0-9692200-0-6.

A directory of business information on Alberta, two-thirds of the text of this work is biographical information on over 1,000 business leaders, including information on position, education and career background, association memberships, and personal life (sometimes including home address). Photographs accompany many entries. Also found is information on financial institutions; banks; computer consulting firms; securities and stock exchange; accountants; engineers and architects; exporting; government at the federal, provincial, and municipal levels; and native business organizations. Advertising is included and there is an advertisers' index towards the back of the text. There is a cross-index to companies with their executives names. The text would be more useful if there were a subject index, and possibly a name index, at the back of the book leading to a page reference.

Generally, this directory contains business information that is not found in other directories on Alberta or on Canada. The directory would be of use to Canadian business collections, especially any that concentrate on western Canada.—**Lorna K. Rees-Potter**

383.   **The Blue Book of Canadian Business 1987**. Edited by Canadian Newspaper Services International. Toronto, Canadian Newspaper Services International, 1987. 1300p. illus. $150.00. ISBN 0-9692531-1-7. ISSN 0381-7245.

Now in its 11th edition, this reference source has become a standard for Canadian business information. Arrangement is within three broad sections: "Profiles of Leading Canadian Companies" (134 companies), "Rankings of Major Canadian Companies" (reproduced from other sources), and the "Canadian Business Index" (approximately 2,200 companies).

Parameters for company inclusion are defined as those Canadian firms having "(1) annual revenues of $10 million or more, (2) assets of $5 million or more, or (3) 500 employees or more."

The strengths of *The Blue Book* are with its "Profiles," the 1st section. These comprehensive reports are unsurpassed in the quality of information that they provide. Standard in these profiles are lengthy sections on individual company history, activities, management philosophy, and social responsibility. Added to this detailed reporting are board of director and functional officer listings. Completing each report is an executive biography (oftentimes including photograph) profiling at least one of the chief officers from each of the 134 leading companies.

There are two indexes—a "Profile Index" and an "Executive Biography Index"—both of which apply to the 1st section only. Neither of the other two sections offers indexing.

The latter two sections, especially the "Business Index," with its brief directory listings for approximately 2,200 companies, are not unique by any means. Both the Canadian *Key Business Directory* (Dun's Marketing Services, 1975-), providing coverage of 20,000 Canadian companies, and the *Canadian Trade Index* (Canadian Manufacturers' Association, 1900-), covering 14,500 Canadian manufacturers, are far more comprehensive given the sheer number of directory listings available. The hallmark and the strong selling point of *The Blue Book* is definitely the "Profiles." The other sections appear to be more of an afterthought, and without indexing a halfhearted one at that.—**Peter B. Kaatrude**

384.   **Who's Who in Canadian Business 1989-90**. 10th ed. Kim G. Kofmel, ed. Willowdale, Ont., International Press Publications, 1989. 621p. index. $99.95. ISBN 0-920966-39-X. ISSN 0227-3411.

This tenth edition proves the usefulness of this source of information about key business people and their firms. It contains over 2,000 entries with positions and addresses, most also giving educational backgrounds. Some list interests and membership in associations. The volume includes a list of professional bodies and associations; *Canadian Business Magazine*'s top 500 Canadian companies with rank, sales, various changes, rank by income, assets and rank, debt/equity ratio, current ratio, number of employees, major shareholders, their location and proportion of shares held by them, and an index of companies and organizations. Recommended to business libraries, particularly those with links to Canada.—**Bogdan Mieczkowski**

385.   **Who's Who in Canadian Finance 1988-89**. 10th ed. Kim C. Kofmel, ed. Toronto, Trans-Canada Press; distr., International Press Publications, 1988. 629p. index. $59.95. ISBN 0-92096638-1. ISSN 0709-6305.

This volume gives brief biographies, who's who style, for over 5,000 individuals in over 1,100 institutions (banks, insurance companies, universities, government bodies, accounting and consulting firms, and especially commercial and manufacturing firms) in Canada. Usually included are the president, chief executive officer, chief finance officer, and vice president of finance. For each individual, current title and company, professional degrees and licenses, address, telephone number, education, career history, family status, and affiliations are given. The intent of the editor is to include relevant personal data on all of Canada's top financial executives. Thus this volume is akin to *Who's Who in Finance and Industry* (see entry 379) in the United States. The firms with the most representation are the largest accounting firms in Canada (Clarkson Gordon, Coopers & Lybrand, Deloitte Haskins & Sells, Thorne Ernst & Whinney, Touche Ross & Co.) and the banks (primarily the Royal Bank of Canada). Several indexes add significantly to the usefulness of this volume. One holds descriptions of 40 professional bodies and associations; another gives sectoral rankings (by size) of firms and institutions in the financial industry (e.g., venture capitalists, financial services, life insurance companies); a third alphabetically lists firms and organizations with their biographees.—**Richard A. Miller**

EUROPE

386.   **Who's Who in European Business**. Compiled by Cambridge Market Intelligence. New Providence, N.J., K. G. Saur. Reed Reference Publishing, 1993. 405p. index. $165.00. HC240. W447. 338'.04'09224. LC 93-4118. ISBN 0-86291-795-6.

This new publication was prepared as a companion volume to the *Directory of European Business* (Reed Reference Publishing, 1992) and contains biographies in English for more than 5,000 executives, arranged alphabetically by surname. There are indexes by country and by company. The information was provided and the proofs read by the entrants. Each entry contains at least the biographee's address and telephone number, and most contain more information, such as career history and directorships. The entries are up-to-date as of January 1993, when the book went to press. The entry layout is very clear and easy to read, with the name in boldface type and the mailing address and telephone and fax numbers at the end of the entry. Coverage of the country index extends to the Eastern European countries of the Czech and Slovak Republics, Estonia, Latvia, Lithuania, Poland, and Russia (filed under its former name U.S.S.R.). Under each country the biographees are listed alphabetically, with the name of the company after each.

The company index gives the name of the company and its country in boldface type, with the names of the biographees and their positions in the company in alphabetical order. This work is a solid contribution to the world of European business.—**Barbara E. Brown**

GREAT BRITAIN

387. **Dictionary of Business Biography: Biographical Dictionary of Business Leaders Active in Britain in the Period 1860-1980. Volume I: A-C**. David J. Jeremy, ed. Woburn, Mass., Butterworth Publishers, 1984. 878p. illus. $185.00. ISBN 0-406-27341-3.

The *Dictionary of Business Biography* is a substantial and authoritative contribution to British biography. Over 1,000 biographies of British businessmen from 1860 to 1980 will be contained in five volumes; there is a separately bound index volume. The 1st volume, covering the letters A to C, has now appeared. The others will follow at intervals of six months to a year.

Each of the biographies includes the name; a brief identification; a biographical sketch, sometimes as long as five pages; and a bibliography of works by and about the biographee. Many biographies are accompanied by portraits, and some have other illustrations as well. Entries are under family name, with cross-references, when necessary, to titles of nobility. For example, Lord Beaverbrook is entered under Aitken, William Maxwell.

The physical presentation is excellent: good layout, clear typeface, sharp reproduction of the portraits and illustrations, use of a heavy line to separate each biography. The binding and cover are sturdy, a necessary feature since the volume is large.

While the price is substantial (over $900 for the set), it is definitely worth the cost for those who can make use of such a valuable reference tool: large university and public libraries, historical research centers, and certain business libraries. It is highly recommended.—**Barbara E. Brown**

388. **Dictionary of Business Biography. Supplement: Indexes, Contributors, Errata**. David J. Jeremy, ed. Stoneham, Mass., Butterworths, 1986. 120p. free with *Dictionary of Business Biography*. ISBN 0-406-27346-4.

This supplement provides three indexes and the errata for the original dictionary (see ARBA 85, entry 146). There are also a list of contributors with their entries and a list of committees that gave advice on specific industries. The indexes cover industries, organizations, and personal names. The names index covers persons that are major figures in dictionary entries, but every name that appears is not indexed. It should be emphasized that the original work, which I have not seen, is a scholarly biographical dictionary of *British* business, including British subsidiaries of U.S. firms such as Kodak. This supplement seems like a useful enhancement to the original dictionary, and all who purchase the latter should make sure that they receive their free copy of this work.—**Susan V. McKimm**

389. Kay, William. **Tycoons: Where They Came from and How They Made It**. Salem, N.H., Salem House/Merrimack Publishers' Circle, 1985. 208p. illus. $16.50. LC 85-72372. ISBN 0-88162-160-9.

Tycoons is a collection of thirteen short biographical sketches of British business successes, men who have reached the top of their corporate ladder. All are millionaires, most several times over. They are between the ages of forty and sixty-three, and six are listed in the British *Who's Who*. Three, Nigel Broackes, Terence Conran, and Clive Sinclair, have been knighted. They represent business interests which vary from publishing (Robert Maxwell), to fashion (Stephen Marks), to restaurants (Michael Golden).

The author, city editor of *The Times* (London), has compiled these portraits through research and interviews. It is the latter method which makes this an interesting and worthwhile volume. Little mention is made of failure or skullduggery; the emphasis is on how each man is a self-made millionaire. Few finished formal education, and most started their own business. The sketches stop short of being laudatory, but a franker appraisal would have been refreshing. While comments are included from business associates, the reader will not find mention of competitors here. An interesting approach to business biography.—**Boyd Childress**

LABOR

390.   **Biographical Dictionary of American Labor**. Gary M. Fink, ed. Westport, Conn., Greenwood Press, 1984. 767p. index. $49.95. LC 84-4687. ISBN 0-313-22865-5.

This basic resource in the field of labor history first made its appearance in 1974 under the title *Biographical Dictionary of American Labor Leaders*. The 1984 edition promises to be even more useful. Two hundred thirty-four new sketches have been added to the 500 which appeared in the earlier edition. A special effort has been made to incorporate the biographies of women who were prominent in the labor movement. Also emphasized in the new edition are the labor leaders of the last quarter of the nineteenth century. In addition, many sketches from the 1st edition have been updated to include more recent biographical data or additional bibliographical references.

The entries in the *Dictionary* focus upon the role which each individual played in the story of American labor, whether as a trade union leader, a political radical, a labor publicist, or an academician. The sketches also touch on relevant personal information. Each entry provides a list of sources for further research.

As in the earlier edition, there are appendixes which list labor leaders by union affiliations, religious preference, place of birth, formal education, political preference, and major appointive and elective public offices.

Appearing for the first time in the 1984 edition is a seventy-seven-page introduction which offers a quantitative and qualitative examination of American labor leadership in the twentieth century. Using four sample years—1900, 1925, 1946, and 1976—the study traces the evolving characteristics of this leadership. In addition to reporting and analyzing statistical data, the introduction employs fictionalized biographies to dramatize the nature of the transitions.

The *Biographical Dictionary of American Labor* will be an important acquisition for academic libraries, labor libraries, and larger public libraries.—**Shirley Miller**

391.   **Biographical Dictionary of European Labor Leaders**. A. Thomas Lane, ed. Westport, Conn., Greenwood Press, 1995. 2v. index $225.00/set. ISBN 0-313-26456-2.

This two-volume set contains more than 1,400 biographical listings of individuals connected with the labor movement in Europe from the beginnings of industrial capitalism in the nineteenth century to the present time. All European countries are included. The editor has defined labor in broad terms and has included individuals not only from the traditional areas such as trade unions and labor ministers, but also from areas such as political parties, cooperatives, and what he refers to as "anarcho-syndicalist" groups (introduction, p.xi). Individuals from state-controlled bodies that lack any democratic procedures, such as those in the former Soviet Union and its satellites, are not included.

Each entry includes the name of the individual, birth and death dates, and a brief biography generally ranging between 150 and 300 words. Also, at the end of each biography there are references to other sources where biographical information may be obtained. There are also extensive cross-references between labor leaders of different geographic areas and different intellectual viewpoints to provide important links. In addition, the editor provides a number of useful appendixes, including a list of labor leaders by state or national/ethnic group, a selective bibliography, a detailed index, and a list of editors and contributors to the work.

The *Biographical Dictionary of European Labor Leaders* will provide a much-needed current source of information concerning many individuals who are not generally considered in other sources on labor leaders.—**Robert L. Wick**

392.   **Who's Who in Labor**. Salem, N.H., Ayer Co., 1976. 807p. bibliog. index. (Arno Press Who's Who Series). $71.50. LC 75-7962. ISBN 0-405-06651-1.

This book provides biographical information concerning over 3,800 people active in the labor movement itself, in neutral capacities (arbitration, etc.), or as government officials. Data were gathered and entries were chosen with the cooperation of the AFL-CIO, the United Mine Workers, the United Auto Workers, the American Arbitration Association, and the Federal Mediation and Conciliation Service. Also included are a list of AFL-CIO and other labor federations, national unions and employee associations, government offices serving labor, and labor studies centers. A glossary of basic labor terms is included, as is a bibliography of labor periodicals, and an index to people included, this arranged according to organization. The only other work on labor leaders is Gary Fink's *Biographical Dictionary of American Labor* (see entry 390), and both works complement and supplement each other. [R: BL, 1 Feb 77, p. 407; C&RL July 77, p. 324; Choice, Nov 76, p. 1121]—**Bohdan S. Wynar**

PUBLIC RELATIONS

393.   O'Dwyer's Directory of Public Relations Executives, 1983. Jack O'Dwyer, ed. New York, J. R. O'Dwyer, 1983. 305p. index. $70.00. ISBN 0-941424-02-2. ISSN 0191-0051.

This is the 3rd edition of this title from the publisher of several directories, including *O'Dwyer's Directory of Public Relations Firms*. The volume contains short biographies of business-related public relations executives in corporations, associations, and public relations firms. The preface states that the names of the 4,000 executives who responded to a request for information were supplemented with names from the files that the publisher had built over the years. General criteria for inclusion are: at least five years of experience in the business world, the title of manager or above at a corporation or association, or the title of account supervisor or above at an agency. Each name in the alphabetically arranged directory is followed by the name of the company for which the person works and a short professional biography that includes education, positions held, and business address. Following the main part of the work is an index that identifies the companies represented. Libraries and public relations firms should find this work easy to use and helpful. [R: BL, 1 Sept 84, p. 52]—**Peggy M. Tozer**

SCOTLAND

394.   Dictionary of Scottish Business Biography 1860-1960. Volume 2: Processing, Distribution, Services. Anthony Slaven and Sydney Checkland, eds. Aberdeen, Scotland, Aberdeen University Press; distr., Elmsford, N.Y., Pergamon Press, 1990. 447p. illus. index. $86.50. 338.6'092'2. ISBN 0-08-030399-4.

The initial volume of this series covered staple industries; this one covers processing, distribution, and services. That completes the project, based in part on voluntary labor, and the "work of love" aspect of it shows endearingly in the text. The industries covered include businesses that deal in such products and services as food, drink, and tobacco; timber and furniture; paper, printing, and publishing; electricity and water; and banking, insurance, and finance. Each industry group is introduced by a description of its main features, its history, and some personages. Some 200 biographies of leading business people in each industry are provided along with additional sources, both published and unpublished. Photographs, interesting conclusions, an index of personal names, and a subject index round out the volume. It will be valuable to economic historians and to descendants of the people named.—**Bogdan Mieczkowski**

TRANSPORTATION

395.   Encyclopedia of American Business History and Biography: The Automobile Industry, 1920-1980. George S. May, ed. New York, Facts on File, 1989. 520p. illus. index. (Encyclopedia of American Business History and Biography). $75.00. HD9710.U52A816. 338.4'76292'09730904. LC 89-11671. ISBN 0-8160-2083-3.

This is the fourth volume of an ambitious encyclopedia, each volume of which is designed to stand on its own. In the present volume there are 105 entries. The largest discuss such figures as Henry Ford II, Charles F. Kettering, and Alfred P. Sloan, Jr.; those of average length cover Edsel Ford, Lido Anthony (Lee) Iacocca, Leonard F. Woodcock, Ford Motor Company, General Motors Corporation, and Chrysler Corporation; and there are short entries on Roy D. Chapin, Jr., Pierre S. DuPont, Harold S. Vance, Jeep, Rickenbacker Motor Company, brakes, bumpers, and the Environmental Protection Agency. Included also are a few articles on major foreign presences in the United States, such as Renault, Rolls-Royce, and Volkswagen. The volume is oversized, in two columns, with a few illustrations of fair to poor quality. Articles are by 19 writers, mostly academics, several of them widely known for their work in automotive history. Publications and references are listed along with notes on archives.

The major problem with the work is the unevenness of coverage. For example, if Preston Tucker, Powel Crosley, the DuPont car, and the pre-Ford Lincoln are included, why then not Henry Leland, H. C. Stutz, the Packard, and the Pierce-Arrow? The question is only partially answered at the end of the excellent introduction, a 12-page overview of American automotive history of the period. The volume is an important one with much detail. A companion volume covering 1885-1930 has been announced for 1990 publication.—**Walter C. Allen**

396.   **Encyclopedia of American Business History and Biography: Railroads in the Age of Regulation, 1900-1980**. Keith L. Bryant, Jr., ed. New York, Facts on File, 1988. 518p. illus. maps. index. $75.00. LC 87-36493. ISBN 0-8160-1371-3.

   Encyclopedia of American Business History and Biography: Railroads in the Nineteenth Century. Robert L. Frey, ed. New York, Facts on File, 1988. 491p. illus. maps. index. $75.00. ISBN 0-8160-2012-4.

   These volumes are part of what is intended to be a fifty-volume set covering all aspects of U.S. business; if the rest of the set meets the standards set by these titles, it will become a major reference for all libraries concerned with business history.

   Written by sixty-one transportation historians (eighteen contributed to both volumes), the signed, alphabetically arranged articles include histories of individual railroad companies, biographies of railroad leaders, accounts of major federal legislation and court cases affecting railroads, and a few discussions of general topics (e.g., brakes, operating ratio). Coverage is limited to major steam railroads and the emphasis is strongly on railroad management and finance; technological developments are treated from the economic viewpoint. *Age of Regulation* biographies are exclusively of company executives; *Nineteenth Century* coverage is somewhat broader, including some financiers, inventors, politicians, etc., who were important in railroad history even though they never served as C.E.O. of a railroad company. Eugene Debs is the only labor leader included, and there are no articles on labor unions. Most of the railroad histories include maps; the biographies include portraits. Most articles include a bibliography of published sources, a list of archival collections, or both. The treatment is analytical and objective, neither an exposé nor an apology. There are comprehensive indexes of names and topics.

   The information on railroad companies is available elsewhere, but the biographical information is not; there is no comparably comprehensive and authoritative source. These volumes make an important contribution to scholarship in the field. [R: BR, Nov/Dec 88, p. 48; Choice, Oct 88, p. 288; LJ, 15 June 88, p. 53; RBB, Aug 88, p. 1901; WLB, May 88, p. 112]—**Paul B. Cors**

UNITED STATES

397.   **America's Wealthiest People: Their Philanthropic and Nonprofit Affiliations**. Benjamin Lord, ed. Washington, D.C., Taft Corporation, 1984. 78p. index. $57.50pa. ISBN 0-914756-57-5.

   From Josephine Abercrombie to Mortimer Zuckerman, this book claims to list the 500 or so wealthiest people in the United States, together with any philanthropic associations to which they may have laid claim. For each person, the compiler lists birth date, education, present employment, corporate and philanthropic affiliations, addresses, clubs, estimates of wealth, and a section called "Notes," which recounts how each person amassed his or her fortune. The amount of information varies considerably from one individual to another, reflecting, presumably, how much information about each can be found in the open press, or to put it another way, how successful each has been in keeping his or her activities hidden. The names and data are drawn from files maintained by the Taft Corporation, a Washington, D.C., firm that specializes in corporate and foundation philanthropy. Indexes are provided for state of residence, philanthropic affiliations, and broad categories (e.g., "Arts and Humanities") at which the rich may be presumed to be disposed to throw money.

   This book is aimed at fund-raisers and development officers, dangling before them the hope that knowing who the rich are will make it simpler to squeeze funds from foundations with which they are associated. To be sure, there are disclaimers: "We do not encourage you to believe that there is a scientific rationale on which you can base strategies for reaching and cultivating the people listed in this book. . ." (p. i). But the message is clear—here are the fat cats, go get them. Why else bother to publish?

The Taft Corporation has based its reputation on the notion that successful fundraising depends on knowing as much as one can about the foundation officers who make funding decisions, so that presentations can be tailored to their known inclinations. Perhaps; but the grantseeker will do well to concentrate instead on building a solid proposal as the best way to influence foundation officers. The intelligent fund-raiser will also avoid this book, whose price of $57.50 for seventy-eight meanly printed pages is plainly aimed at helping to hoist the officers of the Taft Corporation into place among the nation's wealthiest people.—**Robert Balay**

398.   **Corporate Yellow Book: Who's Who at the Leading U.S. Companies. Vol. 8, No. 3.** Laura Gibbons and others, eds. New York, Monitor Publishing, 1992. 1092p. illus. index. $185.00pa./yr. ISSN 1058-2908.

This is one of a series of "Yellow Books" from Monitor Publishing. Companies are listed alphabetically. Included for each are address; ticker symbol; telephone and fax numbers; number of employees; a brief statement about the nature of the business (including annual revenue); lists of officers and management (sometimes with telephone numbers); major subsidiaries, divisions, and affiliates (with addresses and telephone numbers); the Board of Directors (with titles); and a shareholder relations contact (with address and telephone number). There are indexes for parent company, subsidiary and division, geographical location, and name; a list of additions, deletions, and name changes is also included. This is clearly a work aimed at the business communities rather than libraries; for one thing, there is a small picture of each chief executive officer with the person's titles and academic degrees.

Updated quarterly, this title includes many more names and telephone numbers than appear in such works as *Standard and Poor's Corporation Register.* It could adequately serve any library not able to afford a comprehensive business directory. It would be a truly superb acquisition if it also included SIC (Standard Industrial Classification) codes and the names and telephone numbers of personnel departments and officers. As it stands, it is a solid work that should be seriously considered by any library that serves the business community.—**Richard H. Swain**

399.   **Encyclopedia of American Business History and Biography: Iron and Steel in the Twentieth Century.** Bruce E. Seely, ed. New York, Facts on File, 1994. illus. index. $95.00. LC 93-073377. ISBN 0-8160-2195-3.

This ninth volume of the encyclopedia is the 2nd volume about the American iron and steel industry. It provides an introductory essay on the industry since the beginning of the century, covering the development of companies, their interrelations, relations with the government and unions, and working conditions. It includes tables of production and export-import statistics. Finally, the editor briefly analyzes the pattern of executives of the industry and explains the basis for choice of the people included.

The 240 entries, organized alphabetically, conform to three models, a standard length, plus fewer major articles and short articles. Almost 60 percent are biographical, while 40 percent cover companies, organizations, and technical processes. Each biographical entry includes a brief career résumé, major accomplishments, and biography, including career assessment and community involvement. Publications, references used, and archival sources complete the entry.

A single index consolidates names, companies, organizations, laws, and technologies. Because there are no cross-references in the entries, the index provides a valuable tool for further study of a subject as well as references to industry figures who do not have their own entries. This is an important addition to the encyclopedia and a useful purchase for the business history collection of any academic or larger public library.—**Joan B. Fiscella**

400.   **Encyclopedia of American Business History and Biography: Iron and Steel in the Nineteenth Century.** Paul F. Paskoff, ed. New York, Facts on File, 1989. 381p. illus. index. $75.00. ISBN 0-8160-1890-1.

Designed to be volume 3 of the set, this title provides homogenized biographies and background articles on companies, inventions, legal decisions, and marketing innovations in historical America's iron and steel industry. Major biographical entries require about 10,000 words, while standard entries are 3,500 to 5,000 words. Where appropriate, the biographies stress individual roles in developments during three centuries of American iron and steel making. Integrated into this biomaterial are articles providing basic information about steel making and about famous companies keyed to major events in the industry. In the introduction, the volume editors provide a historical overview of the industry.

Alphabetically arranged by surname and subject in two-column format, this volume is cleanly published with black-and-white photographs and well-placed headings and captions. Biographies are introduced by brief informational career statements, followed by bibliographical references. There is an index of names, corporations, organizations, laws, and technologies.

The encyclopedia is a major academic work for the undergraduate and the research scholar alike. Clearly and concisely written, the content is unique and cannot be found in a single reference work. [R: BR, Sept/Oct 89, p. 57; LJ, Aug 89, p. 122]—**Jack I. Gardner**

401. Ingham, John N. **Biographical Dictionary of American Business Leaders**. Westport, Conn., Greenwood Press, 1983. 4v. index. $195.00/set. LC 82-6113. ISBN 0-313-21362-3.

This set contains 835 entries covering 1,100 "significant figures in American industry and commerce." All are written by the same author and reviewed by a panel of historians. Biographies range in length from a paragraph to several pages for someone such as Henry Ford. This set certainly represents a massive undertaking for one person.

The lengthy index covers company, industry, person, place, and, less extensively, general topic and catch phrase, such as "most hated woman in America." Appendixes group the biographies by industry, company, birthplace, place of business, religion, ethnicity, year of birth, and sex. These appendixes add to the book's usefulness for those doing studies of business leaders. Each entry also includes a bibliography. Many of the older biographies cite reference works that are widely available, such as the *Dictionary of American Biography* or the *National Cyclopedia of American Biography*, but people are included who were not covered in either work, such as William Webster Browne, founder of the "first all-Negro bank in America." In fact, the author has made an effort to include blacks and women who have been ignored in earlier reference works. Coverage extends to people who are still active, such as Lee Iacocca and Diane von Furstenburg, but most entries are for deceased people.

Despite the fact that the author, as he states in the preface, did not have time or resources to do primary research, the secondary research, as judged by looking at the bibliographies, seems extensive. Ingham's work fills a void, as there are a number of biographical works on contemporary business executives, but none that the reviewer is aware of to cover historically significant figures. [R: LJ, 15 June 83, pp. 1249-50]—**Susan V. Peck**

402. Ingham, John N., and Lynne B. Feldman. **Contemporary American Business Leaders: A Biographical Dictionary**. Westport, Conn., Greenwood Press, 1990. 788p. index. $99.50. HC102.5. A21534. 338.092'2. LC 89-11866. ISBN 0-313-25743-4.

This well-written, informative biographical dictionary also serves as a history and interpretation of American business development after World War II. A lengthy introduction traces the major trends in American business, key developments and their consequences for society as a whole. The introductory discussion provides the context for the highly selective inclusion of 150 people in 116 biographical entries. All are "historically significant" in business of the period, exemplifying major developments. As a result, many leaders of corporations are omitted, while some that appear are neither household names nor unqualified successes.

The alphabetically organized entries are each several pages in length and conclude with a bibliography of popular sources and full-length books by and about the individual. Appendixes provide lists of individuals by industry, company, place of business, and place of birth. There is a short list of black and female business leaders of the period. A full index lists personal, company, and product names.

Ingham's earlier four-volume *Biographical Dictionary of American Business Leaders* (see entry 401) included entries of people of the post-World War II period, none of which are reproduced in this volume. *Contemporary American Business Leaders* is highly recommended for the business and

American history collections of public, academic, or corporate libraries, although its price may restrict its purchase. [R: LJ, 1 Apr 90, p. 108; RBB, 15 May 90, p. 1838; WLB, Sept 90, p. 128]—**Joan B. Fiscella**

403. **New Fortunes 1994: Biographical Profiles of 650 of America's Emerging Wealth Holders**. Catherine M. Ehr, ed. Detroit, Gale, 1994. 350p. index. $149.00pa. ISBN 1-56995-047-4. ISSN 1066-789X.

This book identifies 650 U.S. residents who have achieved a net worth of at least $2 million or have a significant record of nonprofit or philanthropic involvement. It focuses on those who accumulated their wealth in the last 20 years. Its purpose is to provide information on the "next tier" of U.S. wealth holders. The information on each person varies considerably, but the general headings of information are as follows: full name, birthplace/year, education, residences, current employment, contact address, wealth indicators, stock holdings, background, family, charitable activities, philanthropic affiliations, club affiliations, nonprofit affiliations, corporate affiliations, additional references, and further reading. The full entries are arranged alphabetically by last name. There are indexes to place of birth, state/country of residence, alma mater, corporate affiliation, nonprofit affiliations, philanthropic affiliations, club affiliations, and personal names. The book is aimed at prospective researchers, fundraisers, financial managers, investment bankers, and marketing professionals.—**J. E. Weaver**

404. **Who's Wealthy in America 1993: A Prospecting List and Directory of 102,000 Affluent Americans**. 3d ed. Catherine M. Ehr, ed. Rockville, Md., Taft Group; distr., Detroit, Gale, 1993. 2v. index. $365.00pa./set. ISBN 1-879784-62-9. ISSN 11048-809X.

This is an updated list of the names, addresses, lifestyle interests, educational backgrounds, and other related information about more than 100,000 wealthy Americans. Lifestyle interests are defined in this directory to include such things as the ownership of yachts, aircraft, works of art, and horses, while wealth is defined to include only those individuals with a net worth of at least $1 million. The directory is organized into two volumes. The first provides an alphabetical listing, while the second identifies those listed individuals who are so-called insiders of public companies or who own securities registered with the Securities and Exchange Commission (SEC). Insiders of public companies include not only the officers and directors of those companies but also individuals who are 10 percent principal stockholders.

The directory is not intended to be an exhaustive list of relatively affluent Americans; rather, its purpose is as a sourcebook to help various organizations and philanthropic agencies find potential donors or interested individuals. Perhaps the most useful feature of this directory is its four well-organized indexes, which outline listed individuals by stock ownership, political contributions, state residency, and alma mater. The political contributions index lists candidates, political organizations, and political action committees (PACs). Collectively, these indexes not only provide a great deal of insight into the interests and backgrounds of these wealthy Americans but also, more significantly, will allow various organizations and agencies to more efficiently identify and contact potentially interested donors.—**Timothy E. Sullivan**

10 Women's Studies

INTRODUCTION

Sources in this chapter, **Women's Studies**, are those that concentrate on the discipline of women's studies—the history of women and the study of women—rather than ones that list prominent women in various fields. Sources that fit the latter category are located in their appropriate subject chapters. For example, books listing women in music will be in the **Music** chapter; books on women artists will be in one of the **Arts** chapters. The subcategories in this chapter are General Works, Canada, Great Britain, and United States. All categories indicate the rise in interest in women's studies.

The last few years have seen the publication of a number of important titles in the field of women's studies. Several of these examine feminism. The history of feminism is detailed in *Historical Dictionary of Feminism* (Scarecrow, 1996) (see entry 407), by Janet K. Boles and others, which describes various movements within feminism and gives details on people, events, documents, and organizations that have been important to feminism. An earlier effort is *Encyclopedia of Feminism* (Facts on File, 1986) (see entry 414) by Lisa Tuttle, which also presents information about many people and happenings within the movement. A more specific slant than these, which includes people and events throughout the world, is offered by Olive Banks in *The Biographical Dictionary of British Feminists*, volumes 1 and 2 (New York University Press; distr., New York, Columbia University Press, 1985; New York University, 1990) (see entries 416 and 417), giving information on the people working for women's rights between 1800 and 1945. It thus covers material concerning women's suffrage in Britain, the hunger strike, and work-related issues.

For a detailed look at working women and the issues surrounding women in the workplace, see *The ABC-CLIO Companion to Women in the Workplace* (ABC-CLIO, 1993) (see entry 405).

Several sources attempt to document women previously forgotten by standard historical sources. Beverly E. Golemba offers *Lesser-Known Women: A Biographical Dictionary* (Lynne Rienner, 1992) (see entry 409), biographical sketches of women from the seventeenth to the twentieth centuries; while Lynne Griffin and Kelly McCann present *The Book of Women: 300 Notable Women History Passed By* (Bob Adams, 1992) (see entry 410), a look at women in some unusual professions—rodeo stars, daredevils, spies, and many others. Gillian Fenwick, in her *Women and the Dictionary of National Biography: A Guide to* DNB *Volumes 1885-1985 and Missing Persons* (Scolar Press/Ashgate Publishing, 1994) (see entry 418), takes as her starting point the *Dictionary of National Biography*, which in recent years has attempted to redress what many have seen as its former emphasis on the achievements of males. In addition to gathering the sketches of women from the *DNB*, Fenwick also gives information on women who contributed to the *DNB*, who worked for it in executive or clerical capacities (the publication hired a woman typist in 1888, a very unusual step for the time), and on men who contributed articles on women. Karen L. Kinnear offers *Women in the Third World: A Reference Handbook* (ABC-CLIO, 1997) (see entry 411).

A much more specialized source on women's history is *An Annotated Index of Medieval Women* (Markus Wiener, 1992) (see entry 408) by Anne Echols and Marty Williams. This work makes "use of the recent outpouring of historical scholarship on the lives and accomplishments of women who lived between A.D. 800 and 1500." It is to be hoped that other books will follow to fill in other gaps in women's history.

Biographical sources for American women abound, and predominate in this chapter. Some cover the entire course of American history: *Portraits of American Women: From Settlement to the Present* (St. Martin's Press, 1991) (see entry 421) by O. J. Barker-Benfield and Catherine Clinton; *The Encyclopedia of Women's History in America* (Facts on File, 1996) (see entry 423) by Kathryn

Cullen-DuPont; the two volumes of *Notable American Women,* one covering 1607-1950 (Harvard University Press, 1971) (see entry 423a), the other covering 1951 to 1975 (Belknap Press/Harvard University Press, 1980) (see entry 424). Others cover a more specific time period: *Almanac of American Women in the 20th Century* (Prentice Hall Press, 1987) (see entry 422) by Judith Freeman Clark. Two states have contributed books on their own women: the Women's Project of New Jersey has produced *Past and Promise: Lives of New Jersey Women* (Scarecrow, 1990) (see entry 426), an echo of the book produced earlier by the Austin, Texas, Branch of the American Association of University Women, *Women in Early Texas* (Jenkins Publishing Co., The Pemberton Press, 1975) (see entry 427). Perhaps other states will follow suit.

Finally, an unusual but engaging offering is *Remember the Ladies: A Women's Book of Days* (University of Oklahoma Press, 1993) (see entry 412), Kirsten Olsen's collection of 380 biographical sketches, arranged throughout the calendar year and offering one or more inspirational stories of women for each day.

GENERAL WORKS

405.   **The ABC-CLIO Companion to Women in the Workplace**. By Dorothy Schneider and Carl J. Schneider. Santa Barbara, Calif., ABC-CLIO, 1993. 371p. illus. index. (ABC-CLIO Companions to Key Issues in American History and Life). $55.00. HD6095.S34. 331.4'0973. LC 93-23533. ISBN 0-87436-694-1.

This is an encyclopedic guide to the history of the paid employment of women in American society from colonial days to the present. Hundreds of alphabetically arranged entries deal with a variety of notable events, institutions, and Supreme Court decisions that have affected the availability and duties of paid employment for women. Among these entries are many interesting biographical sketches of both famous and obscure individuals who have had a significant impact on how, when, and where women have found paid employment in the American economy. Entries are also cross-referenced and typically include a brief but up-to-date bibliography for further reading. A more extensive bibliography for the entire volume can be found in an appendix. The guide also includes many useful black-and-white photographs and concludes with a practical chronology (beginning in 1714 and running through 1993) of important events in the annals of women's paid employment.

Because this reference book is intended for a wide audience, entries are informative without being too detailed. The coverage of topics, persons, and events will help make it a useful guide for a variety of users. However, there are bound to be users who are disappointed that some particular subject was not included. This does not detract from the value of this guide; indeed, this comprehensive history will encourage others to more fully appreciate and enhance our collective understanding of the role of women as skilled and unskilled workers, as professionals, or as entrepreneurs. [R: Choice, May 94, p. 1420; LJ, 1 Mar 94, p. 82: RBB, 1 Mar 94, p. 1278; SLMQ, Summer 94, p. 253; WLB, Apr 94, p. 87]—**Timothy E. Sullivan**

406.   Baldwin, Louis. **Women of Strength: Biographies of 106**. . . . Jefferson, N.C., McFarland, 1996. 242p. index. $28.50pa. ISBN 0-7864-0250-4.

Short, lively portraits of 106 women who have excelled in traditionally male fields comprise this book. Arranged chronologically by birth date, the work profiles such popular heroes as Amelia Earhart, Mother Teresa, Rosa Parks, Jane Goodall, and Wilma Mankiller. In addition, the author describes some less familiar figures, such as Rosalyn Yalow (the developer of radio immunoassay), Violeta Chamorro (president of Nicaragua), Felice Schwartz (C.E.O. of Catalyst), and Sharon Matola (a zoologist). The concise, sometimes quirky, portraits provide background information on each character and describe their achievements. An index will help readers find information in specific subject areas or about particular persons.

This slim volume would have benefited from an occasional photograph or illustration, but its real problem is one of balance. The book spans recorded history around the world, but the bias is definitely toward contemporary women from the United States. Furthermore, the author focuses on the field of journalism and the media, while such fields as sports and the arts are only thinly represented. One may also question how the position of first lady fits into a traditionally male field or why blue-collar laborers and leaders were virtually excluded. These gaps detract from what might have been an enlightening collection. Because there are numerous alternatives for women-of-achievement biographies, many with only slightly different focuses (e.g., *Prominent Women of the 20th Century*) a four-volume set published by U*X*L/Gale, and *Amazing American Women,* a softcover book published by Libraries Unlimited in 1995), those with limited resources are advised to check carefully before making a purchase.—**Barbara Ittner**

407.　Boles, Janet K., and Diane Long Hoeveler, with Rebecca Bardwell. **Historical Dictionary of Feminism**. Lanham, Md., Scarecrow, 1996. 429p. (Historical Dictionaries of Religions, Philosophies, and Movements, no. 6). $49.50. ISBN 0-8108-3042-6.

Boles and Hoeveler are coeditors of what they claim to be the "first dictionary of feminism written as a collaborative effort by faculty of one university" (p. ix). This dictionary, as with most of the productions of Scarecrow, includes much more than mere dictionary entries. The publication also contains a 21-page introduction that sketches a history of the various movements commonly grouped under the generic title "feminism," a 15-page chronology of major events ranging from the 1405 publication of Christine de Pizan's *The Book of the City of Women* to the 1995 United Nations's Fourth World Conference on Women; and an extensive 119-page bibliography that lists more than 1,000 sources grouped into some 27 content categories. Unfortunately, the 429-page volume does not include an index.

In the center of the volume are some 800 alphabetically arranged dictionary entries. The typical length of each entry is about 125 words. The entries provide an abundance of basic information on individuals, organizations, campaigns, court cases, and so on, that have had an impact on the history of feminism. The majority of the entries cover topics in American and British feminism, although no section of the world is neglected. High school and college students interested in the history of feminism will find this volume to be a useful addition to their libraries.—**Terry D. Bilhartz**

408.　Echols, Anne, and Marty Williams. **An Annotated Index of Medieval Women**. New York, Markus Wiener, 1992. 635p. $69.95. CT3220.A56. 920.72'094. LC 90-39810. ISBN 0-910129-27-4.

One of the more valuable spinoffs of the women's movement has been the attempt to revise previously male-centered history and to accommodate the growing interest in women from earlier time periods. Medieval women have recently received so much attention that an index of their names is now possible. This work is the first to make use of the recent outpouring of historical scholarship on the lives and accomplishments of women who lived between A.D. 800 and 1500.

Following an introductory section that explains how to use the book, the main listings are arranged alphabetically by first name, with variant spellings cross-indexed. Each contains a brief biographical sketch, including dates and native country, the categories (e.g., insanity, queens, politics) under which the woman might be mentioned, and an abbreviated list of sources. The biographical sketch may be too brief for many needs; many women get just a line or two, and even Joan of Arc receives only half a page.

The main listing is followed by cross-reference listings according to dates, countries, biographical categories, last names, titles, regions, and cities, and by a complete bibliography of sources with and without authors. The cross-referencing makes it possible to look for women in very specific categories, such as English women dramatists (one, Katherine of Sutton) or Italian murder victims (many). Some of the categories are too wide and should have been further subdivided. It is, for example, unnecessarily confusing to put murderers and victims in the same general category. The list of sources is extensive but not exhaustive—a situation to be expected in such a rapidly evolving field.

The serious historical researcher will find this index a handy guide. Recommended for libraries with collections on women's studies and on medieval history.—**Lynn F. Williams**

409.　Golemba, Beverly E. **Lesser-Known Women: A Biographical Dictionary**. Boulder, Colo., Lynne Rienner, 1992. 380p. index. $65.00. CT3203.G57. 920.72. LC 91-41182. ISBN 1-55587-301-4.

Golemba, a professor of sociology at Saint Leo College, has produced a dictionary that includes biographical sketches on more than 800 accomplished but lesser-known women of the seventeenth through the twentieth centuries. According to Golemba, the women are individuals who not only have made outstanding contributions within their fields of endeavor but also are representative of other women whose accomplishments have been ignored by history. The biographical entries are well written but brief, varying in length from about 100 to 250 words. The entries are arranged chronologically according to the year of the woman's most noteworthy accomplishment. The dictionary also includes several indexes that place the women by name, country, ethnicity, and profession.

While the volume contains some interesting information, the chronological (rather than alphabetical) arrangement of the entries mars its usefulness as a quick ready-reference source. Another limitation is its Anglo-American orientation: more than 6 in 10 of the women are from the United States; 3 in 4 are of either British or North American heritage. Also, while the work cites 783 sources used to produce the volume, this number includes 173 references to entries in the *Encyclopaedia Britannica* and scores of other citations from uncritical secondary sources of dubious credibility. For information on U.S. subjects, *Handbook of American Women's History* (see ARBA 91, entry 929) remains the more user-friendly and dependable reference source on lesser-known (as well as well-known) women of distinction. [R: WLB, Nov 92, p. 93]—**Terry D. Bilhartz**

410.   Griffin, Lynne, and Kelly McCann. **The Book of Women: 300 Notable Women History Passed By**. Holbrook, Mass., Bob Adams, 1992. 160p. illus. index. $10.95. ISBN 1-55850-106-1.

In *The Book of Women*, Griffin and McCann profile the lives and accomplishments of women who have largely been ignored throughout the centuries. The table of contents provides a subject list of 69 categories with 3 to 6 women listed under each. Some of the unusual topics included are rodeo stars, sting artists, daredevils, founding mothers, women who took male identities, agricultural pioneers, women who wore what they pleased, and spies. The brief biographical sketches in each category are listed chronologically. A black-and-white pen-and-ink portrait highlights one of the women from each category. The index provides an alphabetical list of those in the book, while a bibliography gives additional sources for further reading.

Readers interested in lesser-known women will find this a fascinating book. Although the authors concede they did not write this book for scholars and researchers, this concise work will be a useful addition to school and public library collections.—**Jennie S. Johnson**

411.   Kinnear, Karen L. **Women in the Third World: A Reference Handbook**. Santa Barbara, Calif., ABC-CLIO, 1997. 348p. index. (Contemporary World Issues). $39.50. ISBN 0-87436-922-3.

This book is one of the volumes in the Contemporary World Issues series. The volume describes how issues such as family relations, violence, health care, work, and politics affect the status of women in developing countries. It provides a survey of the available literature and other resources on the topic of women in the Third World. Kinnear, a professional researcher, editor, and writer with more than 20 years of experience in sociological, economic, statistical, and financial analysis, strives to offer sources for further research and opportunities to learn more about women in the Third World, their lives, and the challenges many of them face from day to day.

The book contains seven chapters: an overview of the subject including aspects of education, health, the family, work, and politics; a detailed chronology of significant events; biographical sketches of the women who have played key roles in politics, social activism, education, and other important areas; facts and statistics concerning women's lives and status in developing countries; a list of international agreements; a directory of organizations and agencies; and an annotated list of print and nonprint resources, including Internet sites. A glossary and an index also appear. The book is for students, writers, educators, researchers, professionals in the field, and women's advocacy groups.—**Vera Gao**

412.   Olsen, Kirsten. **Remember the Ladies: A Women's Book of Days**. Norman, University of Oklahoma Press, 1993. 222p. illus. index. $17.95pa. CT3202.O45. 920.72. LC 93-16868. ISBN 0-8061-2558-6.

This selective collection of 380 biographical sketches is diverse and lively. From Hypatia to Grace Hopper, Joan of Arc, and Janis Joplin, Olsen supplies an engaging collection of notable women in a format ideal for browsing. The "book of days" calendar approach is not strictly followed; although most sketches are listed under either birth or death date, so many dates are undocumented that a good proportion of the biographies are entered on arbitrary days not otherwise assigned. The sketches are short—most around 300 words—and interesting, although details such as marriages and birth or death dates are sometimes omitted. The calendar arrangement is augmented by a name index for those needing more traditional access. A highly selective bibliography is included, but there are no references at the individual entries. *Remember the Ladies* is neither as comprehensive nor as scholarly as *The International Dictionary of Women's Biography* (see ARBA 84, entry 673), although it includes a few entries not listed there.

However, it does offer a distinctive flavor, some additional details, and more than 100 portraits. The engaging style and low price make it a good choice for any library. It is especially appropriate for public and school libraries.—**Susan Davis Herring**

413.   Salmonson, Jessica Amanda. **The Encyclopedia of Amazons: Women Warriors from Antiquity to the Modern Era**. New York, Paragon House, 1991. 290p. $21.95. U51.S34. 355'.0082. LC 90-46258. ISBN 1-55773-420-5.

Most books that mention warriors claim that throughout history almost no females have occupied this role. To remedy this erroneous assertion, Salmonson, a writer with extensive publishing experience on this topic, gathered relevant information for 15 years and assembled it in this encyclopedia of "Amazons." Salmonson uses the following definition for her entries: "a woman who is a duelist or soldier, by design or circumstance, whether chivalrous or cruel, and who engages others in direct combat, preferably with some semblance of skill and honorability." Because of this limited definition and the sense that she has uncovered only the tip of the iceberg, Salmonson acknowledges that her encyclopedia is incomplete.

Although the entries are interesting, the introduction is lively, and the nine-page concluding bibliography is very useful, there are some disappointing features to this work. The entries vary considerably in length and detail. There is no explanation of the abbreviations used. Many entries have no bibliographic note, and there are some unreferenced quotations. There is occasional difficulty in distinguishing between mythical and historical figures; moreover, fictional figures are included. The writing sometimes is chatty and irreverent. There are no illustrations. Most important, there are no indexes or lists by category (although there is some cross-referencing). Thus, it is impossible, for example, to locate all Amazons who were French. Therefore, readers are able to use this intriguing collection only to browse or to learn about figures whose names they already know. [R: Choice, Dec 91, p. 578; LJ, July 91, pp. 90-92; WLB, Oct 91, p. 118]—**Shulamit Reinharz**

414.   Tuttle, Lisa. **Encyclopedia of Feminism**. New York, Facts on File, 1986. 399p. bibliog. $24.95. LC 85-31212. ISBN 0-8160-1424-8.

Written from a feminist perspective, this one-volume reference book covers titles, figures, slogans, terms, and events relevant to the women's movement both in the United States and abroad. Publications such as *Beyond God the Father*, *Les Guérillères*, *The Red Rag*; individuals such as Emily Dilke and Shulamith Firestone as well as Henry Ibsen and Sigmund Freud; and words such as *girl*, *beauty contest*, and *legal prostitution*, as well as more obscure terms like *phallogocentrism*, *gynergy*, and *labrys*, are described in entries ranging from a few sentences to a few paragraphs. Longer articles of one to three pages elaborate on the feminist view of marriage, pornography, sexuality, and the Women's Suffrage Movement, as well as the relevance of general topics—such as film, language, poets and poetry, science fiction and theater—to the feminist movement. The book is very strong on early feminists who are often left out of standard history sources. Style and content is less subjective than *A Feminist Dictionary* by Chris Kramarae and Paula Treichier. Cross-references lead the reader from one relevant entry to another (e.g., "Discrimination *see also* Sexual Discrimination, Sexism, Ageism"). The volume concludes with an extensive, up-to-date, twenty-page bibliography of titles relevant to the study of feminism. [R: WLB, Dec 86, p. 64]—**Michael Ann Moskowitz**

CANADA

415. **Making a World of Difference: A Directory of Women in Canada Specializing in Global Issues. Les Femmes s'en Melent**. Montreal, Vehicule Press; distr., Toronto and Cheektowaga, N.Y., University of Toronto Press, 1990. 314p. illus. index. $15.00pa. 300'.25'71. ISBN 0-919072-96-8.

Produced by the Women's Directory Project of the Canadian Council for International Cooperation, this is a directory of women with expertise in a wide variety of fields and positions. It is the first of a two-part project. The second part is an online database of the 250 directory listings in the printed publication, with the addition of other women with experience and expertise in global issues. This will be of help to those searching for speakers, consultants, and resource people in Canada.

Entries are arranged alphabetically by name. Each entry has the address and telephone and fax numbers of the woman highlighted, as well as special skills, areas of specialization, languages, experience, education, professional memberships, research and publications, and career highlights. Entries, prepared by the women themselves, are well written and consistent throughout the volume.

This work lists women who are community activists, economists, theologians, scientists, teachers, journalists, and feminists. Individuals range from the director of the United Nations Development Fund for Women to city counselors, members of Parliament, university presidents, ambassadors, and leaders in many disciplines. The directory includes both geographical and subject indexes that enhance its use for different regions of Canada. It is exemplary.—**Maureen Pastine**

GREAT BRITAIN

416. Banks, Olive. **The Biographical Dictionary of British Feminists, Volume One: 1800-1930**. New York, New York University Press; distr., New York, Columbia University Press, 1985. 239p. index. $55.00. LC 85-3110. ISBN 0-8147-1078-6.

This biographical dictionary is designed for persons interested in the development of the British feminist movement between 1800 and 1930. It is made up of sketches of both women and men who contributed their time, effort, and money to advancing the progress of the women's movement in Great Britain. The time limit of 1930 represents the closing of an era when women's suffrage was a primary issue. It is anticipated that descriptions of later generations of feminists who faced different problems will be included in the next volume. The subjects presented here were chosen to convey both the variety and complexity of the issues, recognizing the fact that individuals frequently changed their positions over time.

Entries in the *Dictionary* are alphabetical under the name by which the individual is most likely to be recognized, with cross-references to others in the index of names. Insofar as possible, each sketch includes a full account of the subject's life, with an emphasis upon facts and situations that affected involvement in the feminist movement. A summary of additional biographical sources of information and cross-references to other listings in the book are found with each essay.

A concise history of the feminist movement is included in the introduction. An index of topics completes this well-written work.—**Lorraine Mathies**

417. Banks, Olive. **The Biographical Dictionary of British Feminists, Volume Two: A Supplement, 1900-1945**. New York, New York University, 1990. 241p. $75.00. ISBN 0-8147-1146-4.

Volume two of this work not only brings forward the date of coverage to 1945, but adds some figures from the overlap years of 1900-1930 that were not in volume 1. Many of the women in volume two are not covered in other standard biographical works, such as the *Europa Biographical Dictionary of British Women* or the *Dictionary of National Biography*. Its detailed subject index makes this even more valuable.—**Terry Ann Mood**

418. Fenwick, Gillian. **Women and the *Dictionary of National Biography*: A Guide to DNB Volumes 1885-1985 and Missing Persons**. Brookfield, Vt., Scolar Press/Ashgate Publishing, 1994. 181p. index. $74.95. ISBN 0-85967-914-4.

Fenwick has made a career studying the *Dictionary of National Biography* (*DNB*). She has written two books: *The Contributors' Index to the Dictionary of National Bibliography 1885-1901*

(Oak Knoll Books, 1989) and *Leslie Stephen's Life in Letters* (see ARBA 94, entry 1261), as well as an article, "The Athenaeum and the *Dictionary of National Biography*" in *Victorian Periodicals Review* (vol. 23, pp. 180-88).

People in library school are taught that the *DNB* was a well-respected publication. Entry into the *DNB* was based on achievement, albeit accident of birth, rather than through paid self-promotion. Students learn that it was a product of scholarship, thorough research, and the ideals of the British Empire. Aside from the stringent standards it exercised, a person had to be a British subject as well as quite dead to be included.

Fenwick's introduction provides an excellent history of the *DNB*. Based on both secondary and primary sources, it probes the role of women in the creation of this ambitious publication. From the novelty of hiring a woman typist in 1888 to the decision to enter George Sand under her married name of Mary Ann Cross, Fenwick's essay on women as staff, contributors, and subjects is enlightening. This book goes well beyond being an index to women subjects listed in the *DNB* between 1885 and 1985 and the supplementary volume entitled *Missing Persons*. The introduction, as mentioned, provides a history of women associated with the *DNB* as well as an analysis of biography as a literary style.

The index itself is divided into four categories: an alphabetical listing of women as subjects; women contributors; male contributors (who wrote about women); and an occupations index. The headings in the occupations index tend to be more generalized and less colorful than the occupational descriptions listed in the alphabetical index. For example, Elizabeth Fenning (1792-1815) is described as "poisoner" in the alphabetical section. The occupational index holds no category for "poisoners," but rather lists the unfortunate Fenning under the sanitized and somewhat breathless category of "Law, lawyers, police, prisons, victims, criminals, impostors, witches and gamblers." Fenwick's guide to women and the *DNB* is an important and welcome addition to libraries already holding the *DNB*.—**Mary Hemmings**

419.   Sweeney, Patricia E. **Biographies of British Women: An Annotated Bibliography**. Santa Barbara, Calif., ABC-CLIO, 1993. 410p. index. $75.00. CT3320.S85. 920.72'0941. LC 93-13325. ISBN 0-87436-628-3.

More than 700 British women are featured in this ambitious annotated bibliography. Sweeney has selected women born in the United Kingdom or other parts of the British Empire who have made their fame in the United Kingdom. Émigrés to the United States, such as Mary "Mother" Jones and Lola Montez, are also included. Some 2,014 entries cover biographies more than 50 pages long that have been published from the seventh century through 1992. Included are memoirs by family members and doctoral dissertations. Autobiographical literature, however, is not listed. It is advisable to use this volume together with Sweeney's *Biographies of American Women* for women such as Lady Randolph Churchill. British authors are prodigiously represented, but there appear to be several omissions in the category of artists, such as Elizabeth Thompson (Lady Butler), whose first biography appeared in 1989. The annotations are particularly useful and accurate; they provide an indispensable guide for scholarly evaluation of research material.

Listed alphabetically, names are clearly cross-referenced and include dates. The appendix also provides a subject approach by listing women by profession or category. Titles and authors are indexed. [R: Choice, Feb 94, p. 922; SLMQ, Summer 94, p. 254]—**Mary Hemmings**

UNITED STATES

Current Biographies

420.   Garland, Anne Witte. **Women Activists: Challenging the Abuse of Power**. New York, Feminist Press at The City University of New York; distr., New York, Talman, 1988. 146p. illus. $29.95; $9.95pa. LC 88-401. ISBN 0-93531-2-79-X; 0-93531-2-80-Xpa.

The fourteen women profiled in this book are *extraordinary* "ordinary" women. Readers are unlikely to recognize any of the women's names. These are women who were catapulted into politics by personal experiences that angered them, frightened them, or assaulted their assumptions about

American justice. In most cases, there is nothing in the woman's background that would have predicted her recourse to public action. Garland singled out women activists because of her belief that women form the backbone of present-day grassroots American activism. The women's organizing efforts encompass the key issues of our times: rural development, environmental destruction, corporate power, urban renewal, nuclear power and nuclear weapons, toxic waste hazards, and automobile safety.

Bernice Kaczynski stood up to General Motors when the company convinced the city of Detroit to raze her Polish neighborhood to make way for a new Cadillac plant. Mary Sinclair became a pariah in her Michigan community when she fought to stop the building and licensing of a nuclear power plant. Cathy Hinds was spurred to action when she discovered a toxic waste dump almost in her backyard. Women of Greenham Common found that through collective resistance they could fight the fear and despair bred by the nuclear threat.

Combining the author's narrative with direct quotes, the profiles run from ten to twenty pages in length—long enough to give the reader a real sense of the women, their motivations, and the issues. Garland's interviews elicited not just the details of the women's political work, but also the women's reflections on why they became involved and how their experiences changed their own lives. The stories are as engaging as they are informative; they have much to say to anyone interested in contemporary activism and social change. *Women Activists* would be equally appropriate in school, public, and university libraries.—**Catherine R. Loeb**

Retrospective Biographies

421.   Barker-Benfield, O. J., and Catherine Clinton. **Portraits of American Women: From Settlement to the Present**. New York, St. Martin's Press, 1991. 622p. illus. $17.53pa. LC 89-62776. ISBN 0-312-03687-6.

Twenty-five women from all periods of U.S. history—2 Native Americans, 4 African Americans, and 19 European Americans—are covered in this collected biography. The book is divided into eight periods, from the Colonial era through contemporary times. Each section begins with a 10- to 12-page essay that places the subjects within their times and reviews the gender roles and expectations of the particular period. The portrait for each woman includes an artistic rendering of the subject (usually a painting or photograph), a short paragraph with highlights of her life and accomplishments, a more detailed account of the highlights, and a list of notes and sources. According to the preface, the subjects have been chosen on the basis of "significant contributions to the public realm" and accessibility to materials. Included are a religious martyr (Anne Hutchinson), a "war woman" (Nancy Ward), an abolitionist (Maria Weston Chapman), political wives (e.g., Mary Todd Lincoln), a variety of activists and reformers (e.g., Elizabeth Cady Stanton, Alice Paul, Ella Baker, Betty Friedan), an anthropologist (Margaret Mead), and an artist (Georgia O'Keeffe).

Most of the portraits are based on primary sources and have been written specifically for this book by specialists conducting ongoing biographical research, but a few are reprinted from sources published in the 1960s, 1970s, and 1980s. Gender roles and expectations are traced in each section only for Caucasians and African-Americans. Native Americans are hardly mentioned after the first two historical periods. Coverage of Asian women and Hispanic women is limited to quotations from Cherrie Moraga and Maxine Hong Kingston in the final section's introductory essay. The vast majority of the women are covered in *Notable American Women* (see ARBA 82, entry 771), *Women in Particular* (see ARBA 86, entry 869), and *Index to Women in the World* (see ARBA 91, entry 878).

This title might make a good supplementary or introductory text. Lack of indexing and the limited number of women included hinder its usefulness as a reference tool. Recommended for circulating collections in public and academic libraries.—**Linda A. Krikos**

422.   Clark, Judith Freeman. **Almanac of American Women in the 20th Century**. New York, Prentice Hall Press, 1987. 274p. illus. index. $24.95; $15.95pa. LC 86-43172. ISBN 0-13-022658-0; 0-13-022641-6pa.

Clark has produced an intriguing combination of substance and trivia in this work. Almanac-style date-and-event entries are interspersed with short essays, primarily biographical but also covering general topics such as "Early Labor Activists and Organizers," "The Baby Boom," and "The

Vietnam War." The biographies focus on women active in social change, with lesser emphasis on literary and artistic figures, scientists, sports figures, and businesswomen. Almanac entries are arranged chronologically and identified with general headings such as "Women's Issues," "Popular Culture," "Sports," "Arts and Culture," "Ideas/Beliefs," "Business," "Military," "Judicial," and "Legislative." The almanac is fun to read and educational, providing a fascinating overview of women's history during the twentieth century as well as highlighting important individuals and movements. Unfortunately, it is seriously marred as a reference work by a names-only index that makes it almost impossible to trace events or movements over time or to answer "who did what" questions when only the "what" is known. [R: LJ, Aug 87, p. 115; RBB, 15 Oct 87, p. 374]—**Susan Davis Herring**

423.   Cullen-DuPont, Kathryn. **The Encyclopedia of Women's History in America**. New York, Facts on File, 1996. 339p. index. $45.00. ISBN 0-8160-2625-4.

Cullen-DuPont (author of *Elizabeth Cady Stanton and Women's Liberty* [Facts on File, 1992]) has compiled this encyclopedia of women's history in the United States from Colonial times to the present. Apart from biographical entries, the encyclopedia includes synopses, explanations, and definitions of acts, court cases, organizations, movements, and places that have had, in the author's view, significant impact on U.S. women's lives. About 70 percent of the book is made up of entries (approximately 500 total). The last third of the volume consists of the full text of documents (such as the U.S. Constitution, *Roe v. Wade,* and passages from *Blackstone's Commentaries*); a bibliography; and a useful index.

Similar titles to the one under review include *Handbook of American Women's History*, edited by Angela Howard Zophy (see ARBA 91, entry 929), and Doris Weatherford's *American Women's History* (Prentice Hall General Reference, 1994). Cullen-DuPont's volume is most similar to Weatherford's but without the photographs. The full text of key documents alone increases its reference value, so if a library can buy only one volume on U.S. women's history, the Cullen-DuPont volume should be considered over that of Weatherford. The Zophy book, which was compiled by women's studies professionals, is a more comprehensive treatment of the subject and a better purchase than either the Cullen-DuPont or Weatherford volumes. Although the Cullen-DuPont encyclopedia is newer, it does not add significant information to the Zophy book. The encyclopedia would be beneficial for high school and college-level collections or general readers not owning the Zophy work. [R: Choice, Sept 96, p. 94; RBB, 15 Mar 96, p. 1313; SLJ, Aug 96, p. 180]—**Glynys R. Thomas**

423a.   **Notable American Women 1607-1950. A Biographical Dictionary**. Edward T. James, ed. Cambridge, Mass., Harvard University Press, 1971. 3v. $60.00. $32.50pa. LC 76-152274. ISBN 0-674-62731-8; 0-674-62734-2pa.

This biographical dictionary, the first large-scale scholarly work in its field, was prepared under the auspices of Radcliffe College. A total of 1,359 biographical sketches are included, and the entries are patterned after the well-known *Dictionary of American Biography,* which includes some 700 biographies of women out of a total of nearly 15,000 entries. According to the preface, "for each biography the editors endeavored to find an author with special knowledge of the subject or of her field. Seven hundred and thirty-eight contributors were enlisted, the scholarly community making a generous response in time and effort for which the modest honorarium was a purely token recompense. The few unsigned articles are the product of editorial collaboration. The length of the article varies according to the importance of the individual, the complexity of her career, and the availability of the material: the two longest (more than seven thousand words) are the biographies of Mary Baker Eddy, founder of the Church of Christ, Scientist, and the author Harriet Beecher Stowe; the shortest is the four hundred-word sketch of the Colonial printer Ann Timothy." It should also be pointed out that "only one group of women, the wives of the presidents of the United States, were admitted to *Notable American Women* on their husbands' credentials. For the others the criterion was distinction in their own right of more than local significance." It is worth noting that of the 706 women who appear in the *Dictionary of American Biography*, 179 were omitted in this biographical dictionary—"mostly individuals who seemed to have lost significance with the passage of time or marginal figures about whom so little material was available that there seemed no point in attempting a fresh sketch." A classified list of selected biographies is appended, including names of seventeen librarians. Highly recommended as an authoritative scholarly work for women's history.—**Bohdan S. Wynar**

424.   **Notable American Women, the Modern Period: A Biographical Dictionary**. Barbara Sicherman and Carol Hurd Green, eds. Cambridge, Mass., Belknap Press/ Harvard University Press, 1980. 773p. $45.00; $12.95pa. LC 80-18402. ISBN 0-674-62732-6; 0-674-62733-4pa.

The first three volumes of this biographical dictionary, *Notable American Women 1607-1950* (see entry 423a), appeared in 1971. This one-volume supplement, which now extends coverage to women who died between 1951 and 1975, continues in a tradition of scholarly, fascinating, and well-written articles.

An advisory board of eight leading scholars from various disciplines and the editors worked with more than 700 experts to select the 442 women who were eventually included in this directory. The criteria used for selection, as stated in the preface, were similar to those used in the first three volumes: "the individual's influence on her time or field; important or significant achievements; pioneering or innovative quality of her work; and the relevance of her career on the history of women." In addition, they considered a wide variety of fields which illustrated "the diverse ways in which women have defined themselves and made an impact on their culture. . . ." The result of this selection and outstanding research based on primary sources is a collection of 1- to 2-page signed biographies of women who have achieved recognition in both traditional and nontraditional fields. Individuals were chosen from business, science, arts, humanities, and government, as well as the more traditional disciplines of education, home economics, librarianship, and social work. Subjects such as Elizabeth Arden (business), Margaret Morse Nice (science), Maria Cadilla de Martinez (writer), Marilyn Monroe (actress), Mary McLeod Bethune (politics), and Janis Joplin (musician) are found here.

Each biographical article includes crucial dates, ancestry, birth order, education, marital status, children, and cause of death (when known). The focus of each sketch is on the woman's life and personality, and an evaluation of her career, placed in its historical framework. At the end of each article is a bibliography of primary and secondary sources. A classified list of the biographies located at the end of the work provides further access to the alphabetically arranged directory.

Although the user may find some overlap in other sources which deal with women in specific fields, or those which cover notable Americans in general, such as *Dictionary of American Biography*, this source brings together biographies of significant women from various disciplines, and treats them in a manner which is scholarly, yet engaging. [R: Choice, Jan 81, p. 640].—**Ann Hartman**

425.   Tinling, Marion. **Women Remembered: A Guide to Landmarks of Women's History in the United States**. Westport, Conn., Greenwood Press, 1986. 796p. bibliog. index. $75.00. LC 85-17639. ISBN 0-313-23984-3.

Marion Tinling has achieved that rare feat: She has written a reference book one can't put down. This treasure trove of information on U.S. women and the commemorations of their achievements makes for fascinating browsing, serves as a valuable biographical dictionary, and extends to the women's history buff a tantalizing invitation to travel.

Homes, monuments, memorials, workplaces, markers, and plaques—these are among the historic sites cataloged in this ambitious tome. Tinling organizes her material first by geographic region, then by state, city or town, and personal name. The guide is loaded with helpful details: directions for the traveler; hours that sites are open; notations identifying women included in *Notable American Women*; and sites included in historic registers. Tinling supplies additional guidance in the form of concise introductions to each geographic region, notes on sources, classified lists of women, a chronology of significant dates in women's history, a brief bibliographic essay, and an index. Photographs serve to further pique the reader's curiosity.

This work represents prodigious research. Yet most remarkable of all in this remarkable volume is the fine writing throughout. Each entry offers one to several paragraphs of background information on the woman commemorated, and these are consistently written with grace and care. Women profiled here range from the most famous (Susan B. Anthony boasts fifteen listings) to the most obscure (for example, Marie Therese Metoyer, eighteenth-century emancipated slave, Bermuda and Melrose, Louisiana). While neither the index nor the classified lists will help the user hoping to identify women from specific racial, ethnic, or religious groups, Tinling does appear to be sensitive to issues of difference and oppression. See, for example, her listing for Otahki, Cherokee victim of the "Trail of Tears" forced march in Georgia in 1838; or her comments under Hannah Dustan, an eighteenth-century white woman honored for killing and scalping her Indian captors.

It will be a rare reader who learns nothing new about his or her home town or state. At a time when many a grassroots women's history group is researching a local walking tour, most public, university, and larger school libraries will want this guide. [R: LJ, 1 Oct 86, p. 88; RBB, Dec 86, p. 636; WLB, Dec 86, p. 68]—**Catherine R. Loeb**

States and Regions

426.   **Past and Promise: Lives of New Jersey Women**. By the Women's Project of New Jersey Inc. Metuchen, N.J., Scarecrow, 1990. 468p. illus. index. $39.50. HQ1438.N5P37. 305.4'09749. LC 89-34946. ISBN 0-8108-2201-6.

Impressive, glossy, yet significantly researched, this large-format reference tool documents the lives of many women who have made significant contributions to the history of the state of New Jersey from the 1600s to the present day. It contains almost 300 biographical entries arranged in alphabetical order within four chronological sections: 1600-1807, 1808-1865, 1866-1920, and 1921 to the present. Each section includes a historical overview of the period in which each group of women lived, along with a short bibliography of sources for the period. The biographies include not only sketches of individual women but groups of women, such as Jewish farm women and the women of Lenapehoking.

The descriptive material in these biographies is substantial. The entries are not less than a page and are often two pages. Each entry is signed by the contributor and contains a short bibliography at the end. The work also includes 80 illustrations. Whenever possible, an actual photograph of the woman or group of women is reproduced.

A convenient list of biographees appears at the end of the volume. The inclusive index leads the reader to significant persons, locations, or institutions mentioned in the text. This work, although specialized, would make a significant contribution to libraries already having a substantial collection of women's studies or an interest in the history of New Jersey.—**J. C. Jurgens**

427.   **Women in Early Texas**. Evelyn M. Carrington, ed. Sponsored by American Association of University Women, Austin Branch. Austin, Tex., Jenkins Publishing Co., The Pemberton Press, 1975. 308p. illus. o.p. LC 75-27032.

This engaging book, sponsored by the Austin (Texas) Branch of the American Association of University Women as a contribution to the American Revolution Bicentennial Celebration, contains short biographical sketches of forty-two pioneer women of Texas, most of which are affectionately written by descendants, from family records and oral traditions. The trials, tribulations, and successes of these sturdy pioneer women make wonderful reading, but the book is of limited reference value.—**Paul H. Spence**

11 Ethnic Studies

INTRODUCTION

The material in this chapter is divided into seven sections: Asian Americans, African Americans, Filipino Americans, Hispanic Americans, Jews, Native Americans, and Poles. These groups represent a very small portion of the 90 or so ethnic communities in the United States. In addition to the works listed, there are many more sources mentioned in the reviews. Many additional biographical dictionaries are produced for and by ethnic communities that are not reported in standard sources, such as *Books in Print* or OCLC *FirstSearch* (online). Also, a good source for additional sources is the *American Reference Books Annual* (*ARBA*). In addition, other sources may be obtained, in many cases, by contacting particular research groups or organizations, often listed in local telephone yellow pages or on the Internet. There are several sources available that provide information on American ethnic groups, including *Ethnic Information Sources in the U.S.* (Gale Research, Inc., 1995) and *Race, Ethnicity & Self: Identity in Multicultural Perspective* (NMCI Publications, 1994). In addition, the somewhat older *Harvard Encyclopedia of American Ethnic Groups* (Harvard University Press, 1980) is a valuable tool for obtaining information on American ethnic groups.

Specific sources of note include *The Asian American Encyclopedia* (Marshall Cavendish, 1995) (see entry 430), which provides six volumes with more than 2,000 entries, many biographical; Walter Hawkins's *African American Biographies: Profiles of 558 Current Men and Women* (McFarland, 1992 and 1994) (see entry 438); *Notable Black American Women* [books I and II] (Gale, 1992 and 1996) (see entry 444), which discuss the lives of more than 800 black American women covering all occupations from the early eighteenth century to the present; *Filipino Achievers in the USA & Canada: Profiles in Excellence* (Bookhaus, 1996) (see entry 451), the first biographical reference work on Filipino Americans and Canadians published in the United States; the *Dictionary of Hispanic Biography* (Gale, 1996) (see entry 452), which provides biographical information on more than 400 Hispanic Americans from the fifteenth century to the present; *The Concise Dictionary of American Jewish Biography* (Carlson Publishing, 1994) (see entry 460), which provides biographical listings of 24,000 important American Jews; and *Ready Reference: American Indians* (Salem Press, 1995) (see entry 468), a monumental, three-volume work that provides biographical information on Native Americans on the Americas.

Two additional works are listed because they provide needed information: *Black Leaders of the Nineteenth Century* (University of Illinois Press, 1982) (see entry 435), which presents biographical essays with portraits of fifteen African Americans who have made outstanding contributions to the United States, and *Hispanic American Biography* (U*X*L/Gale, 1995) (see entry 453), which provides biographical information on more than 93 Hispanic Americans who have made important contributions to literature, music, sports, television, and film.

ASIAN AMERICANS

428. **Asian American Biography**. Helen Zia and Susan B. Gall, eds. Detroit, U*X*L/Gale, 1995. 2v. illus. index. $55.00/set. ISBN 0-8103-9687-4.

More than 130 profiles of living and deceased individuals are included in this 2-volume set for people ages 10 and above. Although it is unclear how these prominent men and women of Asian and Pacific Island descent were selected, many names are well known. Included are television (e.g., Margaret Cho) and sports (e.g., Greg Louganis) figures, along with those from academia (e.g., Ron Takaki); the arts (e.g., Maya Lin); business (e.g., Phyllis Jean Takisaki Campbell); government (e.g.,

Norman Mineta); medicine (e.g., Lillian Gonzalez-Pardo); the military (e.g., William Shao Chang Chen); music (e.g., Zubin Mehta); science (e.g., Yuan T. Lee); and technology (e.g., An Wang). Some omissions were noted. Profiles span two to three pages and most include a black-and-white photograph of the subject. Each sketch concludes with a brief unannotated bibliography of sources, and the entire work is rounded out by a field-of-endeavor index.

This set is complementary to U*X*L's three other publications: *Asian American Almanac* (1996), *Asian American Chronology* (1995), and *Asian American Voices* (1995). This biographical set will be welcomed by academic education and curriculum collections, by literacy centers helping new immigrants to learn English, and by both school and public libraries serving young readers. It is an inspiring tool, especially for young Asian Americans looking for role models.—**Ilene F. Rockman**

429. **Asian American Chronology**. Deborah G. Baron and Susan B. Gall, eds. Detroit, U*X*L/Gale, 1996. 173p. illus. index. $29.00. ISBN 0-8103-9626-0.

Asian American Chronology is another title in the impressive collection of Asian American reference books published by Gale. Other volumes on this subject include *Asian American Almanac* 429 (1996), (see entry 428) and *Asian American Biography* (see entry 428). The title under review is published under the U*X*L imprint. It is important to note that books published under this imprint are "devoted to serving the information needs of students in grades five and up" (publisher's press release). The tone and emphasis of this volume definitely indicate that it is designed for middle school students; it does not have the scholarly depth and academic apparatus of the *Asian American Almanac,* for example.

The book covers Asian Americans from 11,000 B.C.E. to C.E. 1995, and its scope includes peoples from more than 20 Asian nations and regions. Entries are arranged chronologically by year, and sometimes by month and day, and focus on important events and personalities (with appropriate photographs) in Asian American history. The biographical entries are especially informative, but where is the one for Lea Salonga? Ninety well-chosen black-and-white illustrations enhance the text; they include maps, photographs, statistical tables, and drawings.

The bibliography, while brief and not completely annotated, is compatible with the needs of the book's intended audience of young readers. The index is well structured and provides smooth access to the book's copious information. Public and school libraries will find *Asian American Chronology* to be an important addition to their collections.—**Marshall E. Nunn**

430. **The Asian American Encyclopedia**. Franklin Ng, ed. New York, Marshall Cavendish, 1995. 6v. illus. maps. index. $449.95/set. ISBN 1-85435-677-1.

This timely and helpful encyclopedia of Asian-American culture is an important addition to any reference library. The material has never been so comprehensively assembled. The 6 volumes serve as a history of this growing American culture as well as a reference to the 2,000 entries of biographical sketches, historical articles, immigration, community studies, and demographics on the 6 largest Asian-American groups. These six largest groups—Chinese Americans, Filipino Americans, Japanese Americans, Asian Indian Americans, Korean Americans, and Vietnamese Americans—are covered in great detail. The charts, tables, graphs, maps, and chronologies as well as exhaustive indexes complement the text. Lists of organizations, museums, research centers, libraries, university programs, newspapers, newsletters, magazines, and journals are helpful. Asian Americans are multicultural, and great care has been taken to be comprehensive on the various ethnic populations. These volumes are invaluable to the understanding of the history and cultural contributions of Asian Americans.—**Linda L. Lam-Easton**

431. **Notable Asian Americans**. Helen Zia and Susan B. Gall, eds. Detroit, Gale, 1995. 468p. illus. index. $65.00. ISBN 0-8103-9623-8.

Notable Asian Americans profiles 250 Asian Americans whose significant contributions in more than 130 fields have had an impact on U.S. and world culture. The biographical entries are written in an informal style by contributors who have often gathered their materials firsthand in personal interviews with their subjects. The essays are relaxed, inspirational, and conversational; they are divided into sections by subtitles, and are edited to provide a succinct introduction to each life in terms of youthful influences, education, formative experiences, and major accomplishments.

Although *Notable Asian Americans* is suitable for readers and researchers of all ages, one intention of this volume's editors is to inspire young Asian American people. The editors note the absence, up until recently, of resources available to teach the Asian-American community about the extent of its own creativity, contributions, and multiethnic vitality. This volume goes a long way toward filling the gap. As George Takei of *Star Trek* fame points out in the foreword, looking at these different lives can be a means to understanding U.S. pluralism.

The scope and range of the book are eye-opening: from Asian Indian to those of Vietnamese descent, 15 ethnic groups are represented. Weight-lifters, physicists, photographers, law enforcement officers, engineers, conductors, illustrators, poets, farmers, members of Congress, costume designers, comedians, architects, activists, and astronauts are presented in sketches that highlight personal drive and integrity. The occupation and ethnicity indexes complement the comprehensive subject index. A few notables have been overlooked, but omissions are hard to avoid in an undertaking of this size. Also, the sketches should have provided bibliographies of the noted person's works, where applicable. The oversights will no doubt be addressed in the next volume of *Notable Asian Americas*, for which lists are already being compiled.—**JoAnn Balingit**

432. **Who's Who Among Asian Americans**. Amy L. Unterburger, ed. Detroit, Gale, 1994/95- . Biennial. index. $75.00. ISSN 1075-7104.

Contemporary leaders form the backbone of what is seen as a first step in chronicling the achievements of Asian Americans. The three indexes—geographical, occupational, and ethnic origin—are particularly helpful in getting an overview of the selections. Six thousand individuals were chosen in a process that included the recommendations of 2,000 associations in business, government, colleges, and universities. Inclusion in the volume is by virtue of positions held through election or appointment to office, notable career achievements, or significant community service. For this volume, an Asian American is a U.S. resident or citizen whose ancestry is Asian or Pacific Islander and includes 20 major nationalities. This does not mean exclusively "born in the United States," which is what many definitions of the term refer to. The volume's suggested use is to serve as a reference to consult when gathering facts on a leader, locating a colleague, contacting an expert, recruiting personnel, or launching a fund-raising effort. This is a valuable volume and will become more so as future volumes increase in usage. It is well written and well documented and serves as a valuable addition to any library. [R: RBB, 1 Oct 94, pp. 363-64]—**Linda L. Lam-Easton**

433. **Who's Who in the Asian-American Community**. Marvin P. Bionat, ed. Boston, PacRim Publishing, 1994- . index. $19.00pa. ISBN 0-9642151-0-1.

This book is the 1st edition (1994-95) of what is intended to be a serial publication. It has the standard arrangement of biographical directories. A somewhat unusual feature of the criteria for inclusion allows self-nomination. This practice may raise a few eyebrows. The brief introduction traces the outlines of Asian-American history and immigration with its sociological implications in a rather cursory manner. The main section of the biographees' listings is 131 pages long. This seems rather short for such a fast-growing and dynamic segment of the U.S. population. A random check of entries for well-known Asian Americans such as I. M. Pei, Daniel Inouye, and George Takei finds them present and accounted for. But where are the entries for March Kong Fong Eu and Harry H. L. Kitano?

Next comes "Asian-American Organizations" (including social service groups that cater primarily to Asians), arranged alphabetically by state. Why does Hawaii have only one listing? A three-page unannotated bibliography follows. The last part of the book is an occupational index. Is there a need for this directory? Not really. Two Gale serials are far superior, albeit much more expensive. They are *Who's Who Among Asian Americans* (see entry 432) and *Notable Asian Americans* (see entry 431).—**Marshall E. Nunn**

AFRICAN AMERICANS

434.   **African American Biography**. Detroit, U*X*L/Gale, 1994. 4v. illus. index. $112.00/set. ISBN 0-8103-9234-8.

This four-volume biographical work profiles the lives of 300 people, both living and deceased, from all corners of the African-American experience. It joins the publisher's three-volume *African American Almanac* (1994) and two-volume *African American Chronology* (1994) in providing an integrated, curriculum-based reference set on African-American life and culture. The works are directed primarily at middle school and junior high school students.

African American Biography offers a useful collection of well-written biographical sketches on a diverse group of African Americans, from Hank Aaron to Whitney M. Young. The project's advisory board selected the biographees wisely and included a judicious mix of sports figures, entertainers, politicians, intellectuals, lawyers, judges, military persons, and civil rights activists. There are sketches, for example, of sports figures Kareem Abdul-Jabbar, the Harlem Globetrotters, Joe Louis, and Bill Russell; of entertainers Sammy Davis, Jr., Aretha Franklin, Whoopi Goldberg, and Oprah Winfrey; of politicians Marion Barry, Barbara Jordan, L. Douglas Wilder, and Coleman Young; of intellectuals George Washington Carver, Charles W. Chesnutt, W. E. B. DuBois, and Richard Wright; of lawyers Anita Hill, Thurgood Marshall, Pauli Murray, and Clarence Thomas; of military figures Benjamin O. Davis, Sr., Marcelite Harris, and Colin Powell; and of social activists Eldridge Cleaver, Jesse Jackson, Malcolm X, and Roy Wilkins.

African American Biography provides basic biographical information for each person, a quotation summarizing each biographee's philosophy, and an interpretive sketch of the person's life. A black-and-white portrait accompanies each entry. The volumes contain a cumulative subject index and a list of the biographees by field of endeavor. Unfortunately, the articles lack suggestions for further reading that might encourage young readers to go beyond the brief material included in the volumes.

Though understandably selective and eclectic in coverage, *African American Biography* provides an important, up-to-date biographical guide. While sensitive to the perspective of adolescents, the entries do not shy away from controversial issues involving gender, race, and class. Because of these strengths, it is strongly recommended for middle school and junior high school libraries. [R: BR, Sept/Oct 94, p. 57; RBB, 1 Apr 94, pp. 1472-73; VOYA, Aug 94, p. 176]—**John David Smith**

435.   **Black Leaders of the Nineteenth Century**. Loen Litwack and August Meier, eds. Champaign, University of Illinois Press, 1988. 344p. illus. bibliog. index. (Blacks in the New World). $24.95. LC 87-19439. ISBN 0-252-01506-1.

This book could be described as one of the leading volumes in the series dealing with Afro-American leaders that have been published recently. Litwack and Meier have done a fantastic job in editing those scholarly essays written by sixteen contributors who have in the past written various valuable works in the advancement of Afro-American history.

This book contains sixteen chapters of scholarly essays on selected Afro-American leaders of the nineteenth century. It serves as a supplement to two earlier volumes on a similar subject published by the University of Illinois Press. The choice of individuals selected for treatment in this book was based on their importance and significance, including the availability of adequate primary and secondary materials concerning them. This volume has attempted to include important black leaders of the nineteenth century but has left out some significant leaders and personalities such as Prince Hall, founder of the Black Masons, and Richard Allen, prominent bishop of the African Methodist Episcopal church. The reason for this obvious omission is space limitations. It is important also to mention that the individuals covered were exhaustively treated, with their pictures at the beginning of each chapter.

I recommend this book without reservations to all libraries serving scholars and students of Afro-American history, black politics, and sociology. [R: LJ, 15 May 88, p. 80]—**Felix Emer Unaeze**

436. **Contemporary Black Biography: Profiles from the International Black**. L. Mpho Mabunda, ed. Detroit, Gale, 1991- . illus. index. $45.00 for recent edition. ISSN 1058-1316.

Volume 1 of this series was first published in 1991 by Gale Research: ISBN 0-8103-5546-9. $52.00. Additional volumes with the same title include: Volume 2: 1992. ISBN 0-8103-8554-6. $52.00; Volume 3: 1992. ISBN 0-8103-8555-4. $52.00; Volume 4: 1993. ISBN 0-8103-8556-2. $52.00; Volume 5: 1993. ISBN 0-8103-8557-0. $52.00; Volume 6: 1994. ISBN 0-8103-8558-9. $52.00; Volume 7: 1994. ISBN 0-8103-8559-7. $52.00; Volume 8: 1994. ISBN 0-8103-8559-9. $52.00; Volume 9: 1995. ISBN 0-8103-8550-2. $52.00; Volume 10: 1995. ISBN 0-8103-9318-2. $52.00; Volume 11: 1996. ISBN 0-8103-9319-0. $52.00; Volume 12: 1996. ISBN 0-8103-0100-4. $52.00; Volume 13: 1996. ISBN 0-8103-0101-2. $52.00; Volume 14: 1997. ISBN 0-8103-0953-6. $52.00.

All of the volumes in this set include biographical sketches of African Americans who are currently making headlines and those who have recently died, along with a number of individuals who have died many years earlier. Also, a few individuals included are from outside the United States.

The 9th volume of Mabunda's *Contemporary Black Biography* is an eclectic reference work chronicling the lives of 71 internationally acclaimed blacks. These men and women of African heritage, according to the editor, "have changed today's world and are shaping tomorrow's" (p.ix).

The alphabetically arranged biographies include men and women of distinction, as well as lesser-known individuals "likely to be ignored by other biographical reference series" (p.xi). Some are from the fields of architecture, art, business, dance, education, fashion, film, industry, journalism, and law. Others work in the worlds of literature, medicine, music, politics and government, publishing, religion, science and technology, social issues, sports, television, and theater.

In a curious editorial decision, Mabunda chose to profile not only contemporary blacks, but also "selected individuals from earlier in this century whose influence continues to impact on contemporary life" (p.ix). Thus, in a work that provides sketches of contemporary businessman Wally Amos (b. 1937), historian David Levering Lewis (b. 1936), and talk show hostess Rolonda Watts (b. 1959), one also finds articles on such pioneer blacks as former Haitian king Henri Christophe (1767-1820), civil rights activist Archibald H. Grimké (1849-1930), cowboy Nat Love (1854-1921), politician P. B. S. Pinchback (1837-1921), bibliophile Arthur A. Schomburg (1874-1938), activist Mary Church Terrell (1863-1954), and abolitionist Harriet Tubman (1820[?]-1913). Not only have these latter figures attracted considerable historical and biographical treatment, but they fit poorly into a reference work that highlights modern figures. In addition, although the articles are signed, the editor fails to identify the contributors and to establish their credentials for the respective assignments.

On a happier note, Mabunda's work is attractively designed and well illustrated. Each article supplies sources for additional information, and the volume contains cumulative nationality, occupation, subject, and name indexes for the nine-volume set. Despite its weak conceptualization, these strengths render *Contemporary Black Biography* an attractive acquisition for public, school, and junior college collections.—**John David Smith and Robert L. Wick**

437. **Facts on File Encyclopedia of Black Women in America**. Darlene Clark Hine and Kathleen Thompson, eds. New York, Facts on File, 1997. illus. index. $29.95/volume; $329.00/set. ISBN 0-8160-3425-7 (v.1); 0-8160-3430-3 (v.2); 0-8160-3644-6 (v.3); 0-8160-3427-3 (v.4); 0-8160-3431-1 (v.5); 0-8160-3426-5 (v.6); 0-8160-3434-6 (v.7); 0-8160-3429-X (v.8); 0-8160-3436-2 (v.9); 0-8160-3435-4 (v.10); 0-8160-3428-1 (v.11); 0-8160-3424-9/set.

The 11 volumes of this set, covering the areas of pre-1900 history; literature; dance, sports, and the visual arts; business and the professions; music; education; religion and community; law and government; theater and entertainment; social activism; and sciences and health constitute a reworking and updating of Hine's impressive earlier 2-volume compilation, *Black Women in America* (see ARBA 94, entry 965). This set, however, targets a more general, less scholarly audience. Each volume contains a lengthy introduction, alphabetically arranged entries for individuals and groups pertaining to the area in question, a chronology, a brief bibliography, and an index. Each volume also repeats two lists that provide access to all other volumes, one giving entries by volume, the other an alphabetical list of entries in the whole set. The final volume also includes a master index to the entire set. Access to the readable, nicely illustrated biographies is thus provided for well.

Given considerable duplication with the earlier title, many entries are repeated verbatim, and the same photographs are featured—it is disturbing that little mention is made of a connection. Only footnotes found after the introductory essays mention that most of the latter are adapted from topical articles in *BWA*. For example, *BWA* entries on slavery and the civil rights movement were used in slightly altered form for the introduction to volume 1 describing pre-twentieth-century history. Public and high school libraries that do not own *BWA* will find this set a worthwhile purchase, and libraries serving specialized audiences may consider purchasing individual volumes. Those libraries already owning the earlier encyclopedia may want to rely on other sources for the updated portion of this expensive set and better use their dollars elsewhere.—**Willa Schmidt**

438.   Hawkins, Walter L. **African American Biographies: Profiles of 558 Current Men and Women**. Jefferson, N.C., McFarland, 1992. 490p. illus. index. $39.95. E185.96. H38. 920'. 009296073. LC 91-50938. ISBN 0-89950-664-X.

Hawkins, Walter L. **African American Biographies, 2: Profiles of 332 Current Men and Women**. Jefferson, N.C., McFarland, 1994. 367p. illus. index. $35.00. LC 93-44998. ISBN 0-89950-921-5.

These biographical dictionaries each contain biographical sketches of African-Americans residing in the United States. In the 1992 edition, Hawkins specified three criteria that he used in determining who should and should not be included in this work. First, individuals must have been born or have spent their childhood in the United States (a few exceptions are admitted). Second, they must be good role models for African-American children (an undefined quality). Third, they must not have died prior to 1969 (although Malcolm X, who was assassinated in 1965, is included). In terms of occupation, the most entries are for government employees (appointed and elected), attorneys, and educators. In spite of this, prominent African-Americans in government (e.g., Grace Hamilton, Julian Bond) and in education (e.g., Harvard's Professor W. E. B. DuBois, Henry Louis Gates, and dean of African-American historians John Hope Franklin) are excluded. The selection for other occupations, such as music and athletics, is similarly idiosyncratic. Hawkins does include entries for individuals in the military, law enforcement, and nursing, occupations not usually covered in works of this kind.

A wonderful feature of the volume is its inclusion of many sharp, small, black-and-white photographs of the biographees. In the 1994 edition, the biographical sketches are generally long, so the user gets a lot of detail about the lives of the individuals and their education, family background, and work. There is a good balance between men and women. In the back of the book there are a short biography of the author, a state-by-state listing, and an occupational listing of the entries. There is also a general index. Recommended for all reference collections. [R: VOYA, Feb 95, p. 371]—**Melvin M. Bowie and Robert L. Wick**

439.   Hedgepeth, Chester M., Jr. **Twentieth-Century African-American Writers and Artists**. Chicago, American Library Association, 1991. 323p. index. $55.00. NX512.3. A35H43. 700'.92'273. LC 90-301. ISBN 0-8389-0534-X.

The poets and composers eligible for inclusion in this reference work must have had at least 10 publications. The writers had to have at least two published novels, and the painters and sculptors must have had exhibitions in major museums. Individuals are provided biographic entries, a paragraph of criticism of their work (often quite penetrating), a partial list of works with dates, and a brief bibliography (which does not always cite the most significant titles). Although the list of consultants is extensive, there is an absence of major scholar-advisors in some areas, which might account for a few problems. The death dates are missing for Talib Hakim and William Dawson, yet provided for James Cleveland (1991). Some misspellings occur (e.g., Reigger instead of Riegger, Edward Varése rather than Edgard Varése. Contemporary figures were given the opportunity to review their entries, but—if they responded—not all errors have been corrected. One will always be surprised by the absence of expected figures in such handbooks (e.g., Richard Hunt, Olly Wilson), comforted by terse data on the giants (e.g., Langston Hughes, David Driskell), and pleased by the presence of lesser-known individuals. This work certainly merits purchase. [R: RBB, 1 Dec 91, p. 724]—**Dominique-René de Lerma**

440. Johnson, Frank J. **Who's Who of Black Millionaires**. Fresno, Calif., Who's Who of Black Millionaires, 1984. 182p. illus. index. $9.95pa. LC 83-082591. ISBN 0-915021-00-5.

This paperback offers brief biographies on 37 selected "entertainers" (perhaps Emmanuel Lewis fits that category, but not Leontyne Price), 34 "professionals and entrepreneurs" (gospel-singer Shirley Caesar is among these, while Andrae Crouch is classed with the entertainers), and 22 athletes. The sketches are designed for the very casual reader, but not the scholar (Stevie Wonder's sound system in his Rolls-Royce cost $12,000, Barry White's home has twenty-eight rooms, Michael Jackson's animals include a llama and four swans, Johnny Mathis lives in the home Howard Hughes built for Jean Harlow, Chester Washington has given a lecture tour in Sweden). The introduction provides a four-page history of black Americans' finances, and the back matter (five pages) includes a breakdown by state of the nation's 574,342 millionaires, an index to the book's main entries, photo credits, and a biography of the author.—**Dominique-René de Lerma**

441. Lee, George L. **Inspiring African Americans: Black History Makers in the United States, 1750-1984**. Jefferson, N.C., McFarland, 1991. 132p. illus. index. $14.95. CT105.L35. 920'.009296. LC 90-53503. ISBN 0-89950-576-7.

This is a collection of 170 portraits of African-Americans and a single African (Haile Selassie I) from the pen of talented caricaturist Lee. These portraits, similar to those in his previous collection, *Interesting People* (see entry 442), were originally created for the black newspaper feature "Interesting People," which Lee produced from 1945 to 1948 and from 1970 to 1986. The two books are similar in their spotty coverage of important African-Americans from a variety of fields (e.g., religion, sports, politics, entertainment, the arts). They both include individuals who are famous (e.g., Martin Luther King, Jr.) and those who are not well known (e.g., Mary T. Washington, the first black woman CPA in the United States). Each portrait has a skillful drawing and a short biographical sketch. The information presented is brief and selective. Intended to be an inspiration to young people, this book will also be a useful addition to journalism and popular culture collections. However, it will not be useful as a reference tool.—**Fred J. Hay**

442. Lee, George L. **Interesting People: Black American History Makers**. Jefferson, N.C., McFarland, 1989. 210p. illus. index. $15.95. LC 88-43542. ISBN 0-89950-403-5.

This work contains over 200 capsule biographies of prominent Afro-Americans, mostly from the twentieth century. Arranged in rough chronological order, the entries are accompanied by Lee's pen-and-ink drawings. Persons portrayed include abolitionists, politicians, athletes, musicians, civil rights leaders, and soldiers. They range from the famous (Frederick Douglass, Jesse Jackson, Martin Luther King, Jr.) to the obscure (Catherine Harris, Lelia Foley, Guion S. Bluford, Jr.). *Interesting People* highlights the Afro-American contribution to U.S. history in order to make it crystal clear to black youth that they too can succeed. Lee's message, though simple, is nonetheless powerful: Black achievement in America, despite racism, has been substantial, and with faith and determination there is good reason to believe that the future will be as bright or brighter than the past. It should also be noted that Lee's artistic skill is put to good use. His facial portraits are lifelike and the cartoons he draws can be either provocative or funny.

The list of Afro-Americans is by no means complete. Notable omissions include Booker T. Washington, W. E. B. DuBois, and William Gray. Though puzzling, these oversights do not subtract significantly from the main thrust of Lee's effort. In sum, this book provides a worthwhile compendium of Afro-American men and women of influence. Much of the information presented will not surprise university scholars, but the average reader will find a great deal that is new. Strongly recommended for public libraries as well as junior and senior high schools. [R: LJ, 15 Apr 89, p. 82]—**Richard E. Holl**

443. Lee, George L. **Worldwide Interesting People: 162 History Makers of African Descent**. Jefferson, N.C., McFarland, 1992. 134p. illus. index. $17.95. CT107.L46. 920'. 009296. LC 91-50939. ISBN 0-89950-670-4.

This book contains the likenesses, in black-and-white line drawings, of more than 100 Africans and African-Americans. Each drawing is accompanied by a brief sketch of the subject's accomplishments, with space on the page being almost evenly divided between drawings and text. This leaves the reader with little useful material. The premise behind the volume is that achievements of people of African descent have been neglected in textbooks, reference books, and other written materials to the extent that the Western world knows or cares very little about them. This volume is an attempt to remedy that situation by exposing the reader to a large number of names and faces of such people who have contributed to the world's cultural, economic, scientific, and religious progress.

While this premise is indeed noble, Lee fails in his goal, first by failing to give the reader something to read. The sketches are so brief that one is often left wondering just why a particular person has been designated "worldwide" or "interesting." Second, there is no indication about the significance of the contributions made by many of the subjects in the book. It would have been helpful to have put the contributions into some kind of context. Third, the reader is presented with facts about many "obscure" persons but is given no source for further reading and investigation. Thus, Lee fails to encourage sustained interest on the part of the reader. Fourth, the book has no apparent arrangement; personalities are not presented alphabetically, chronologically, by category, or by area of work. This makes it difficult to find a particular subject without turning to the index. Lee had deemed these personalities neglected by previous writers, but he also neglects them in his own book.—**Melvin M. Bowie**

444.   **Notable Black American Women**. Jessie Carney Smith, ed. Detroit, Gale, 1992. 1334p. illus. index. $49.95. E185 .96.N68. 920.72'08996073. LC 91-35074. ISBN 0-8103-4749-0.

Notable Black American Women, Book II. Jessie Carney Smith, ed. Detroit, Gale, 1996. 775p. illus. index. $75.00. ISBN 0-8103-9177-5.

The lives of black American women are discussed in these handsome volumes in an attempt to fill the gap in reference collections in which black women are inadequately represented. Those responsible for the work acknowledge the omission of many who could have been included. (Notably absent is Katherine Battle, the opera singer.) Criteria for inclusion in the 1992 volume hinged around the terms "pioneer," "leader," "major," "noted," "creative," or "distinguished." "The women selected as subjects of biographies do not constitute a list of the 500 most important African-American women—that would be a foolish and presumptuous goal" (introduction). Those who are included were identified by an advisory board of distinguished contemporary women who come from many areas of endeavor.

Entries cover the lives of selected women from colonial times to the present. The earliest is Lucy Terry Prince, poet (1730), and the latest is Mae C. Jemison, the only black female astronaut (1956). The range of talents and contributions cover some 200 categories. Many biographees are cross-listed under more than one category (e.g., Nikko Giovanni is listed under both "Publisher" and "Writer"; Fannie Lou Hammer is categorized as a "Sharecropper" and a "Civil Rights Activist"). Some categories overlap in meaning (e.g., "Educator" and "School Founder"; "Author" and "Writer"). It would be more helpful to standardize the list of categories to be used and then explain the reasons governing the choices.

Lengths of the biographies vary according to the amount of material available. For example, there is little known or written about Octavia Albert, who had been a Georgia slave and who wrote *The House of Bondage* in 1890, while entries about Lena Horne and Althea Gibson are lengthy and detailed. One of the best treatments is of Ada Smith, the blues singer and entertainer known from New York to Paris, who was a colleague of Duke Ellington and Cole Porter and who left a collection of her papers to James Haskin, a researcher on African-American life. A list of references accompanies each entry so that researchers and writers can have a ready place to turn. References include journal articles, books, archival materials, and special collections on the subject's life where available. When possible, contemporary biographees were given the opportunity to check over the essays written about them so that inaccuracies could be corrected. Photographs of selected subjects add considerably to the overall appeal of the volume. Entries are arranged alphabetically in a handsome typeface, with good page design and layout. In the front of the volume is an alphabetical list of all entries and lists of contributors, categories, photograph credits, and the members of the Advisory Board. A subject index is found in the back of the volume, where page references to main entries are indicated in boldface type.

The titles under review are important sources of information for both historic and contemporary black women. One can learn about Alice of Dunk's Ferry (ca. 1686-1802), an oral historian and slave; Mollie Ernestine Dunlap (1898-1977), a well-respected librarian and editor; and even Willie Mae (Big Mama) Thornton (1926-1984), who, of course, is a musician, blues singer, and songwriter familiar to many. The biographies are clearly written and detailed, but not overly long. In most cases, the bibliographies included provide useful sources for additional information.

Overall, the volumes contain well-researched material about African-American women. They should be a welcome additions to reference collections in school, public, and college libraries. Highly recommended. [R: Choice, June 92, pp. 1524-26; LJ, 1 Mar 92, pp. 84-86; RBB, 15 Apr 92, p. 1552; RQ, Fall 92, p. 121; SLJ, June 92, p. 156; WLB, May 92, p. 128]—**Melvin M. Bowie and Robert L. Wick**

445. Rogers, J. A. **World's Great Men of Color**. Edited, with an introduction, commentary and new bibliographical notes, by John Henrik Clarke. 1946-1947; repr., New York, Macmillan, 1972. 2v. illus. index. $9.95/vol. LC 73-186437. ISBN 0-02-081300-7.

Rogers' two-volume biographical work was completed in 1947 and published in a small private edition, years before black history and black studies were popularized. The long introduction by the author, an anthropologist who died in 1966, sets down his reasons for preparing the book and reflects the level of racism at the time. The purpose, as he points out, "was not to write highly critical and psychoanalytical, or even literary essays, but rather principally success stories, chiefly for Negro youth" (p. 24). Rogers maintained that knowledge of the contributions of black people had consistently been ignored and denied; his work in black history aimed to bring to light the significant accomplishments of nonwhite people and put aside the myth of black inferiority. Criteria for inclusion were based on evidence he obtained that an individual was at least one-eighth Negro.

The 200 biographical articles, arranged geographically, include Imhotep, Hatshepsut, Hannibal, Terence, Al-Jahiz, Eugene Chen, Abu Hassanali, Chaka, Alfred A. Dodds, Aleksander Pushkin, Alexandre Dumas, Samuel Coleridge-Taylor, Vicente Guerrero, Nat Turner, and Arthur A. Schomburg. Portraits of some biographees are included. A separate section gives brief mention of a selected number of great men of color who are not recognized as blacks. Clarke has added introductory matter to both volumes, surveying recent research in support of some of Rogers' findings. References at the ends of articles are updated in this new edition to include recent research on those subjects. Unfortunately, no index was added to the new edition. [R: BL, 15 June 73, p. 957; Choice, 15 June 73, p. 602; LJ, 1 Mar 73, p. 735; WLB, Apr 73, p. 701]—**Bohdan S. Wynar**

446. Salley, Columbus. **The Black 100: A Ranking of the Most Influential African-Americans, Past and Present**. New York, Citadel Press/Carol Publishing Group, 1993. 383p. illus. index. $21.95. E185.96.S225.973'.0496073. LC 92-39545. ISBN 0-8065-1299-7.

This is a list of 21 women, 81 men, and a social movement (Black Power) that Salley feels have been most influential in the struggle of African-Americans to achieve full equality. Each person is ranked for relative importance, with Martin Luther King, Jr., at number one and his Montgomery bus boycott associate, Rosa Parks, at 100. Each entry includes a photograph or other portrait, dates, and a biographical sketch. The biographies are derivative and lack sources. Moreover, although the biographical data on these individuals is covered quite well in other reference books, some errors have crept in. For example, Zora Neale Hurston's *Jonah's Gourd Vine* is classified as folklore rather than novel.

This sort of ranking is inherently subjective; there is no way to establish any validity for the hierarchy. Salley does not adequately explain why Booker T. Washington (number 3) was rated higher then W. E. B. Dubois (number 4), or why U.S. Representative Oscar De Priest and sociologist and Fisk University president Charles S. Johnson, among others, were omitted. Two jazz musicians were included but not the very influential James Brown or any musicians from the blues genre, which has been the foundation of much of the world's popular music in the twentieth century. This reviewer also questions Clarence Thomas' fit with Salley's criteria. This book will be more appropriate for browsing than as a reference tool. [R: LJ, Jan 93, p. 105; RBB, 1 Apr 93, p. 1452]—**Fred J. Hay**

447. Sammons, Vivian Ovelton. **Blacks in Science and Medicine**. New York, Hemisphere Publishing, 1990. 293p. index. $45.00. Q141.B58. 509'.2. LC 89-32934. ISBN 0-89116-665-3.

This comprehensive volume identifies black professionals in several areas of science and medicine. Each annotation contains basic biographical information along with a list of references and memberships. The book is organized as a list of individuals in specific subject areas. There are also an alphabetical index of professionals and a bibliography of sources consulted. A picture of each scientist or physician would make this work more complete. A historical approach is used to illustrate the increased participation of blacks in science and medicine. The relationship between the events of an era and the contributions of blacks during that period is shown. This work is a reference source not only for science libraries but also public, school, university, and research libraries.—**Estelle A. Davis**

448. **Who's Who Among Black Americans**. Shirelle Phelps, ed. Detroit, Gale, 1975/76- . index. $140.00 for recent edition. ISSN 0362-5753.

The lives of more than 20,000 African Americans are highlighted in the 1994 edition, an increase of 10 percent over the previous edition. The editors maintain that the volume is a logical place to turn "when gathering facts on a distinguished leader or a favorite celebrity, locating a colleague, contacting an expert, recruiting personnel, or launching a fund-raising effort" (introduction). The diversity of careers and occupations among the biographees is wide, ranging from acting to zoology. Arranged in the traditional who's-who format, each entry includes occupation, personal data, educational background, career information, organizational affiliations, honors and special achievements, military service, and home or business address. Each of these subheadings is in capital letters so that the reader can easily scan an article.

Biographical data were gleaned from books, magazines, newspapers, and other current sources. Biographees were then contacted, when possible, to confirm and supplement the information already gathered. A geographical index locates persons by city and state, and the occupational index, containing 150 categories, allows the reader to use fields of work to do the same. There is also an obituaries section that provides information about recently deceased noteworthy African Americans. As with other Gale "who's who" volumes, this one is highly recommended for all general reference collections.—**Melvin M. Bowie**

449. Williams, Ora. **American Black Women in the Arts and Social Sciences**. 3d ed. Metuchen, N.J., Scarecrow, 1994. 387p. index. $57.50. LC 93-33079. ISBN 0-8108-2671-2.

This bibliographic survey provides an invaluable resource for the study of African-American women. Williams, professor emerita of the department of English at California State University and author of the previous two editions of the work, clearly delineates her purpose in the preface. In addition to providing checklists of resources to facilitate access, the volume fulfills the larger purpose of highlighting the impressive cultural contributions of African-American women throughout history. Each edition of this work is substantially different from the others. The current edition replaces individual bio-bibliographic profiles with a focus on West Coast black women. General checklists on black women throughout the nation are grouped into categories such as reference, the literary arts, audiovisuals, and performing arts. Particularly interesting is the inclusion of culinary arts with the performing arts, as well as the care taken with this and other, less-noticed artistic fields. The resource lists are expanded and much better organized than in the previous edition. These lists include music directors and conductors; college presidents; black periodicals, newspapers, collections and resource centers; and selected ideas and achievements of black women. A general chronology and one concentrating on the West Coast trace significant dates in African-American women's history. Although not intended to be entirely comprehensive, this book provides a valuable finding tool and points out gaps in African-American studies scholarship. [R: Choice, July/Aug 94, p. 1708; RBB, 15 May 94, pp. 1713-14]—**Marie F. Jones**

450. Yount, Lisa. **Black Scientists**. New York, Facts on File, 1991. 111p. illus. index. (American Profiles). $16.95. Q141.Y68. 500'.89'96073. LC 90-19159. ISBN 0-8160-2549-5.

Eight black scientists are profiled here, including three physicians, an agriculturist, a cell biologist, two chemists, and an engineer. Three were alive at the time of publication. The author does not describe how the eight were chosen. A separate chapter is devoted to each scientist, beginning with a useful introduction that places the individual's work in context within the scientific field. Each biography includes a life history, education, and the significance of the individual's work. In addition, the author describes obstacles and challenges that are unique to the black experience. Bibliographies are found at the end of each chapter.

This work is suitable for junior high and high school libraries and perhaps freshman level college students. In a college library it would be more appropriate on the circulating shelves than in the reference collection.—**T. McKimmie**

FILIPINO AMERICANS

451.   Crisostomo, Isabelo T. **Filipino Achievers in the USA & Canada: Profiles in Excellence**. Farmington Hills, Mich., Bookhaus, 1996. 369p. illus. index. $65.00. ISBN 0-931613-11-6.

This coffee-table-format book is the first biographical reference work on Filipino Americans and Canadians published in the United States. It is an important source for this fast-growing and increasingly visible Asian American group of more than 2.2 million people. This is not a biographical dictionary. Rather, it consists of 3 parts: Part 1, "The Filipino Odyssey in North America," is a history of Filipino immigration to the United States and Canada, 1763 to date, with demographic data and sociological analysis. This useful and interesting section includes a fascinating article by Lafacadio Hern entitled "Saint Malo: A Lacustrine Village in Louisiana," which was published in *Harper's Weekly* on March 31, 1883.

Part 2, "Profiles of Filipino Achievers in the USA & Canada," is the most important and longest part of the book. It consists of 8 sections, from "Arts & Culture" to "Science and Technology"; the achievers' profiles are arranged in 69 separate chapters within each of these broad designations. Each biography is generally between three and eight pages in length, with many black-and-white photographs. Many familiar names (Lea Salonga, Irene Natividad, Ninotchka Rosca, and Loida N. Lewis) appear here. Interestingly enough, the co-author and publisher of this book, Veltisezar B. Bautista, is the subject of an addendum to part 2. It provides information on 29 biographees whose profiles for various reasons were not included in part 2. Parts 2 and 3 have a total of more than 100 biographical profiles.

Inclusion in the book was by nomination, "except for a few who were invited by the writer" (p.xii). Bautista made many contributions to the book, writing some profiles and co-authoring other parts with Crisostomo, who is the author of biographies of such well-known Philippine politicians as Ferdinand and Imelda Marcos and Corazon Aquino. The book's bibliography, in two sections, has little value because almost all of its entries lack complete bibliographic data (pagination and publication dates, most notably). There are two indexes (general and achievers'), with many personal names needlessly listed in both. *Filipino Achievers* also has an Internet Website at http://www.bookhaus.com. [R: RBB, June 96, p. 1767]—**Marshall E. Nunn**

HISPANIC AMERICANS

452.   **Dictionary of Hispanic Biography**. Joseph C. Tardiff and L. Mpho Mabunda, eds. Detroit, Gale, 1996. 1011p. illus. index. $120.00. ISBN 0-8103-8302-0.

The *Dictionary of Hispanic Biography* is a much needed, single-volume source for information concerning Hispanic individuals past and present. With more than 450 entries, this dictionary is one of the largest biographical sources available. The only other source that comes to mind that provides a larger list of names is the *National Directory of Latin Americanists: Biographies of 4,915 Specialists*, which includes not only Hispanics but also individuals who are scholars in the field of Hispanic studies. Other works, such as *Champions of Change: Biographies of Famous Hispanic Americans* and *The Hispanic 100: A Ranking of the Latino Men and Women . . .* (see entry 457) provide a much smaller listing and concentrate on Hispanics living in the United States. The *Dictionary of Hispanic Biography* includes Hispanic men and women who lived from the fifteenth century to the present, and covers all endeavors including art, business, education, entertainment, journalism, politics, religion, science, sports, and a few individuals considered in a category called "activism" (preface, p. vii). About 70 percent of the individuals listed are contemporary.

Each entry provides an in-depth biographical sketch (usually from 300 to 700 words), along with lists of the sources used to obtain the biographical information. Many of the entries have black-and-white photographs. Indexes include an Occupation Index, a Nationality/Ethnicity Index, and a Subject Index.

The *Dictionary of Hispanic Biography* appears to be well balanced in that most of the Hispanics who come to mind are included. It is always easy to go through such a source and pick out names that are not included, but in this case the compilation appears to be very satisfactory. The editors contend that their original list contained more than 700 names, and was carefully cut down to the 470 notable Hispanics chosen for inclusion.

This work is recommended for all libraries. While it is essential for all larger academic and public libraries, it is hoped that smaller public and school libraries will also consider the *Dictionary of Hispanic Biography* an important reference tool for students.—**Robert L. Wick**

453. **Hispanic American Biography**. Rob Nagel and Sharon Rose, eds. Detroit, U*X*L/Gale, 1995. 2v. illus. index. $55.00/set. ISBN 0-8103-9828-1.

This 238-page set profiles 93 well-known Hispanic American figures. Although the emphasis is on contemporary figures, some historical personalities are included. The majority of the biographies come from the fields of literature, television and film, music, and sports. The entries are arranged alphabetically in each volume, with a complete listing in the table of contents. Each entry furnishes the place and date of birth (and death, when appropriate), a quote, a two- to three-page description of the life and contributions of the figure, a black-and-white photograph, and a short bibliography.

There is a brief "Reader's Guide" in each volume identifying the scope of the work, and describing three important related reference sources: *Hispanic American Almanac* (U*X*L/Gale, 1995), *Chronology of Hispanic-American History* (see ARBA 96, entry 550), and *Hispanic American Voices* (U*X*L/Gale, 1995). Each volume also includes a useful "Field of Endeavor Index" listing the entries by subject fields.

The work is oriented toward the middle and high school level. However, it would also be appropriate for a public library audience. The presentation is attractive, the profiles easy to read and interesting. They are presented in two columns, and subdivided into sections, using various styles and sizes of typeface to facilitate easy reading. The book is a convenient source of up-to-date information on Hispanics in the United States who have made and are still making significant contributions to life today.—**Susan J. Freiband**

454. Kanellos, Nicolas. **Hispanic-American Almanac: A Reference Work on Hispanics in the United States**. Detroit, Gale, 1993. 780p. illus. index. $99.50. LC 92-075003. ISBN 0-8103-7944-9.

The purpose of this almanac is to be a source of information about a broad range of important characteristics of Hispanic life and culture in the United States. Whereas some such works specialize in a single segment of the Hispanic community, this almanac covers individuals with roots in all of them, from Mexican Americans to Spanish Americans to those from Spanish-speaking countries in Central and South America. In 25 chapters, various authors describe such aspects of the Hispanic American existence as history, education, literature, art, sports, language, religion, and family. Under science, for example, is a series of biographies of prominent Hispanic scientists. In the section on sports there is a small error; the dates following Lefty Gomez's name are 1908-1988, but the biographical text has his death date as 1989.

As an overview of Hispanics in the United States, this work will certainly serve. Serious readers, however, will note a militant point of view in many of the chapters that may seem unnecessarily unfriendly to many would-be students of Hispanic life and culture. Despite this caveat, this is a comprehensive, albeit unbalanced, resource. [R: Choice, July/Aug 93, p. 1752; JAL, July 93, p. 201; LJ, 15 Apr 93, p. 86; RBB, 15 Apr 93, p. 1536; VOYA, Oct 93, pp. 260-61]—**Isabel Schon**

455.   Meier, Matt S., with Conchita Franco Serri and Richard A. Garcia. **Notable Latino Americans: A Biographical Dictionary**. Westport, Conn., Greenwood Press, 1997. 431p. illus. index. $65.00. ISBN 0-313-29105-5.

Over the last several years, a number of reference works have been published focusing on the Hispanic American community in the United States. Meier, an author of several books on Chicano ethnic studies and history, has compiled a biographical dictionary of 127 Latinos from all walks of life who have made a significant contribution in their respective fields. Sports figures (Jose Conseco), politicians (Lincoln Diaz Balart), entertainers (Gloria Estefan), performing artists (Jose Limon), and other luminaries are given three-page entries on their personal and professional lives. The emphasis always includes the struggles or prejudices these people faced in becoming ultimately positive role models for contemporary Latino youth.

The writing style is more simplistic than that of entries appearing in *Notable Hispanic American Women* (see ARBA 94, entry 962), but is usually more detailed than biographical entries published in *The Latino Encyclopedia* (see ARBA 97, entry 337). There is approximately an 80 percent overlap in coverage with these two reference works alone. An appendix, which is arranged by professionals in the field, is a good ready reference source for determining which Latinos were dancers, artists, lawyers, etc. This work is a reasonably good choice for school, public, and community college libraries. [R: LJ, 15 Apr 97, p. 70]—**Judith A. Valdez**

456.   **Who's Who: Chicano Officeholders**. Arthur D. Martinez, comp. Silver City, N. Mex., Arthur D. Martinez, 1977/78- . illus. $24.95pa. for recent edition. ISSN 0738-4637.

This is a new edition of a work that is irregularly revised. It contains names, addresses, and telephone numbers of elected and appointed Chicano/Mexican American officeholders at the federal, state, and local levels. Also included are political party functionaries within the Democratic and Republican National and State Central Committees. Selected portraits of officeholders are given. The work is divided into nine sections: federal, state, local, political party people, nationwide Chicano civic organizations, author's remarks, political and demographic information, a dictionary of legislative terms, and a list of counties and municipalities. Some names have a short biographical paragraph describing their previous activities and affiliations. A few non-Chicano officeholders can be found (e.g., John Vasconcellos, State Representative from California).

Considerable information is provided in this compilation. However, as it is not effectively organized, it is cumbersome to use. A name index would be useful, and fax numbers should be included. If it were more frequently updated and included more information, it would be a valuable reference tool. Recommended for specialized library collections.—**Roberto P. Haro**

457.   Novas, Himilce. **The Hispanic 100: A Ranking of the Latino Men and Women**. . . . New York, Citadel Press/Carol Publishing Group, 1995. 495p. illus. index. $24.95. ISBN 0-8065-1651-8.

Novas points out in her introduction "that by the year 2000 Latinos will be the largest single minority group in the United States and account for one out of every three U.S. citizens" (p.xi). She goes on to mention that even though Hispanics represent such a large group, there still is very little known about them by mainstream America. This biographical dictionary presents 100 leading Hispanic Americans from every walk of life who have made outstanding contributions to such varied fields as entertainment, science, education, government, and labor relations. The individuals are listed in order of influence to U.S. thought and culture.

At first glance, it is difficult to determine the basic criteria for selection of the individuals included, as they come from such varied backgrounds and have made such varied contributions. Cesar Chavez is listed first, and Elizabeth Pena (the wonderful actress who appeared in such films as *Down and Out in Beverly Hills* and *The Milagro Beanfield War*) is listed last. Three criteria were used in compiling the 100 individuals listed: the heroes and heroines had to be trailblazers, legends in their own time or later, and recognized on a far-reaching or international level. For the most part, this kind of ranking is a popularity rating, but that aside, Novas' work provides valuable biographies of 100 outstanding Hispanic Americans.

Each entry contains the name, birth and death dates, a black-and-white photograph, and a biography covering the main events in the individual's life, along with important publications, plays, political positions, and other major events. The entries are written clearly and in an entertaining manner without being cute. An index is provided for both the individuals featured (because they are in order of importance, not alphabetical order) and all other names listed in the entries. The index makes the work more valuable as a reference source. *The Hispanic 100* is highly recommended for individual purchase and for academic and public libraries of all sizes. It is especially recommended for smaller public and academic collections where major biographical sources are not available.—**Robert L. Wick**

458.   Sinnott, Susan. **Extraordinary Hispanic Americans**. Chicago, Childrens Press, 1991. 277p. illus. index. $30.60. E184.S75S55. 973'.0468. LC 91-13909. ISBN 0-516-00582-0.

Sinnott modestly describes this much-needed book for children and young adults as "a maddening blend of unconnected people and events." While it is by no means comprehensive, it is filled with interesting and meaningful information about Hispanics who stand out in the history of America. (The accuracy of the term "Hispanic" is questioned by Sinnott because it glosses over the fact that there are legitimate historical differences between such groups as Puerto Ricans, Cubans, and Mexicans. Sinnott is, in most cases, careful to mention each biographee's origin.)

The organization of the book is chronological, from the European discovery of America to the modern era. Significant events or periods (e.g., the Zoot Suit Riots of 1942) are covered in brief essays, but much more information is provided in the biographical entries. There are articles on groups, such as the first Angelenos (Los Angeles's first settlers), as well as on individuals. Biographees are from a wide variety of professions, such as the military (e.g., Rafael Chacon, a captain in the Union Army), business (e.g., the Lopezes and the Riveras, colonial merchants), politics (e.g., Dennis Chavez, the first Hispanic U.S. senator), and science (e.g., Luis Alvarez, Nobel Prize winner in physics). One nice feature is the emphasis on people who are not sports figures or entertainers, although a few of these are profiled. The text is usually well written and informative, and a brief bibliography will interest those who want to explore a subject in greater detail. Illustrations, some a little fuzzy but most sharp, complement the text; they include black-and-white drawings, photographs, and reproductions of stamps. The quality of the paper and binding is excellent. Highly recommended for public and school libraries. [R: SLJ, May 92, p. 28]—**D. A. Rothschild and Dario J. Villa**

459.   **Who's Who among Hispanic Americans**. Amy L. Unterburger and Jane L. Delgado, eds. Detroit, Gale, 1991- . index. $100.00 for recent edition. ISSN 1052-7354.

Who's Who among Hispanic Americans is an important work that provides biographical information on prominent Hispanics (Latinos) in the United States. There are, however, some serious omissions and outdated data in recent editions. It is possible to identify well-known Hispanic Americans who are not included. Also, this who's who would be strengthened by including e-mail addresses and fax numbers for those listed. Electronic access to artists, business and political figures, and others is expedited by e-mail contact; long-distance telephone calls are expensive. A word of caution regarding the foreword by Ricardo R. Fernandez: Several Mexican American leaders were disappointed that Fernandez did not mention that people of Mexican origin constitute about 73 percent of the Hispanic population in the United States. The omission of such factual information about the Hispanic population does not provide a complete picture about this rapidly increasing group in our society. The work is recommended for purchase by all libraries.—**Roberto P. Haro and Robert L. Wick**

JEWS

460.   **The Concise Dictionary of American Jewish Biography**. Jacob Rader Marcus and Judith M. Daniels, eds. Brooklyn, N.Y., Carlson Publishing, 1994. 2v. $200.00/set. LC 94-20231. ISBN 0-926019-74-0.

This biographical directory is truly a labor of love by its editors. They have thoroughly extracted from more than 26 sources the biographical listings for 24,000 important American Jews, from those who lived in the Colonial period to those who died by 1985. It was no small task to compile the listings since several of the sources cited contain listings for Americans from numerous backgrounds, not just Jews (e.g., *Who's Who in America*, 1943-1985). Although the selection criteria for names included were generally left to the compilers of the sources cited by the *Concise Dictionary*, the fact that this dictionary puts these names in one place is a monumental feat.

Each person listed is given a brief biographical entry, some as brief as birth, death, and occupation, some as long as a paragraph. Each also provides references to the sources cited and in some cases a newspaper obituary citation. When conflicting data about a person were found in the cited references, both sets of data are included. Further, if there is an identity conflict about a person, both citations are quoted. These careful considerations display the thoroughness of the editors and commend the volume to libraries everywhere.

It is assumed by the editors that the persons included had all died by 1985, although some are listed without death dates because the editors could not ascertain them. Jews are defined by the editors as persons of Jewish parentage (either one or both parents) and converts. Some persons are included solely because they have Jewish-sounding names and may not actually be Jewish. With the vast research for this volume, its clear presentation, and the thoroughness of the editors, this work is appropriate for many libraries, including those that have few or none of the works cited, because the *Conuse Dictionary* stands on its own as a singularly important biographical reference work.—**Paul A. Morgan**

461.   Tapper, Lawrence F. **A Biographical Dictionary of Canadian Jewry 1909-1914: From *The Canadian Jewish Times***. Teaneck, N.J., Avotaynu, 1992. 245p. index. $35.00. F1035.J5F76. 920'.0092924071. LC 92-18521. ISBN 0-9626373-0-0.

This specialized reference work is an index of biographical data about Canadian Jews taken from the only Anglo-Jewish newspaper in Canada during 1909-1914. It consists of two parts. The first has topical entries, including bar mitzvah and confirmation announcements, biographical essays, birth announcements, deaths and obituaries, engagements and marriages, and general news items. The second and larger part includes geographical entries covering 12 cities and regions of Canada. Montreal, which contained the largest and most active Jewish community, is emphasized. The entries cover a variety of personal and family announcements, news of individual achievements, family celebrations, synagogue activities, travels, and visits. Each entry also includes the date, volume, and issue number of the *Canadian Jewish Times* from which the information was taken. An extensive name index provides quick and easy access to the people in the book. Unfortunately, except for the broad topical categories of part 1, there is no specific subject access to the data. This would have improved the usefulness of the book.

Preliminary materials include a foreword by Gerald Tulchinsky that provides an interesting historical perspective; in addition, an extensive, helpful preface by the author places the book in its historical and bibliographical context.

Tapper, a staff archivist in the National Archives of Canada, is regarded as an expert in the field of Canadian Jewish genealogy. In addition, he is contributing editor to *Avotaynu, The International Review of Jewish Genealogy.*

Advertisements from the period are interspersed throughout the text, providing needed variety and rest for the eyes. Although three columns are used to present the entries, the type is small and not easy to read. Another weak point is the short section on how to use the volume, which could have been clearer, with more detailed information about the entries, especially the cited reference to the *Canadian Jewish Times.* This would have made the book more accessible to the general Jewish reader interested in exploring family roots.

However, the book represents a unique and important contribution to Canadian Jewish genealogy and history. It is a valuable resource for reference collections in public, academic, and special libraries with an interest in these fields.—**Susan J. Freiband**

462.   Wigoder, Geoffrey. **Dictionary of Jewish Biography**. New York, Simon & Schuster Academic Reference Division, 1991. 567p. illus. $55.00. DS115.W49. 920.0092924. LC 90-29276. ISBN 0-13-210105-X.

By "Jewish biography," Wigoder means distinguished figures from the past who were Jewish. One therefore finds a combination of individuals who contributed to Jewish culture through Yiddish,

Latino, and Hebrew literature, art, and music, as well as famous people who happened to be Jewish. Thus, Mendele Moche Sforim receives coverage alongside Eric Mendelsohn. In addition, biblical and political dignitaries figure prominently in the volume. Each person receives substantial coverage; entries typically extend for at least two columns and cover background and biographical information. Minimal bibliographic references for further reading are provided. The volume is extensively illustrated and is sprinkled with quotations from writers and politicians covered. Although impressive for its scope, omissions do occur (e.g., Yiddish writer I. J. Singer, 1893-1944). Wigoder has limited entries to deceased "representative individuals," who apparently belong to what he refers to as the "Jewish elite."

Despite such restrictions and ambiguities, the reference will appeal greatly to popular and collegiate libraries. [R: RBB, 15 Nov 91, pp. 641-42; WLB, Dec 91, p. 118]—**Simon J. Bronner**

NATIVE AMERICANS

463.   **Biographical Dictionary of Indians of the Americas**. Newport Beach, Calif., American Indian, 1991. 2v. illus. index. $285.00/set. E89.B56. 920'.009297. LC 91-41400. ISBN 0-937862-29-0.

The publisher's flyer, enclosed with the review copy, states that this work has more than twice the number of entries as did the 1st (1983) edition. Checking the entries for Bs and Ps shows this claim to be correct. However, in the foreword it is stated that the 1st edition was a 1975 imprint. Moreover, this reviewer has a two-volume set from American Indian with the title *Biographical Dictionary of Indians of the Americas* that gives no copyright date, but the invoice for the review copy indicates it was shipped in 1985. Also owned is a 1978 three-volume set from Scholarly Press with the title *Dictionary of Indians of North America* (see ARBA 80, entry 29). The content of these two sets is identical. It is thus not surprising that the current compilers have trouble determining the date of the 1st edition.

A spot check shows that everything from the first editions, whatever their dates, appears in this one. In some cases the entry's sentence order has been changed, and in two sample entries one or two sentences have been rewritten. Most of the new entries are for contemporary persons. However, part of the increased entry count is for one-line entries (17 of 107 in the Ps) that are linked to illustrations—or at least they should be. For example, "Pachtuwa-chta (Arikara; fl. 19th century) was an Arikara warrior. This drawing was done in 1834. (See portrait)" (p.507). No illustration is identified as Pachtuwa-chta. On page 508, one of three illustrations lacks any identification label, so one might assume this is the person in question. For some of the twentieth-century entries that were relatively short in the earlier versions, there has been substantial increase in length. Entries for people such as Leonard Peltier, Lou Diamond Phillips, and Elvis Presley do make this a somewhat useful resource. In general the contemporary entries are accurate; however, there are occasional editorial lapses. For example, Samuel W. Brown (Yuchi) did not serve with both the Confederate and Union armies. He joined the "Loyal Creeks"; in fact, much of his later life was devoted to getting compensation for the Loyal Creek.

For nineteenth-century individuals, a better publication is *Who Was Who in Native American History* (see ARBA 91, entry 402). *Reference Encyclopedia of the American Indian* (see ARBA 91, entry 398) lists more twentieth-century personages, but the entries are shorter than those in this set. The set's price is very high, but it does contain new material and may be appropriate for some libraries with major collections of American Indian material.—**G. Edward Evans**

464.   Hauck, Philomena, and Kathleen M. Snow. **Famous Indian Leaders**. Calgary, Alta., Detselig, 1989. 90p. illus. (Following Historic Trails). $13.95pa. 970.004'97. ISBN 0-920490-99-9.

For U.S. school and public libraries with a few Native American biographical titles, this book will be a welcome addition as it contains seven short biographies of famous Canadian Indian leaders. Although Pontiac and Joseph Brant are sometimes included in such collections published in the United States, the other five (Dekanahwideh, Chief Membertou, Kondiaronk, Crowfodt, and Maquinna) are almost unknown to U.S. children. The grade level of the text is middle school to high school.

The authors prepared a balanced text that is neither stereotyped nor maudlin. A short glossary defines a few terms not fully explained in the text. Given the nature of the text, one would expect to find a list of suggested additional readings, but the selected bibliography seems to reflect the sources used by the authors rather than suggestions for reading. Few libraries will have editions of James Cook's genealogical collections in large urban public libraries. Reference collections in temple and synagogue libraries will also benefit from the acquisition of this bibliography. [R: Choice, Sept 89, p. 82]—**Susan J. Freiband**

465. **Native North American Biography**. Sharon Malinowski and Simon Glickman, eds. Detroit, U*X*L/Gale, 1996. 2v. illus. index. $55.00/set. ISBN 0-8103-9821-4.

Intended for middle and high school students, this work does not pretend to replicate the coverage of other references such as Duane Champagne's *The Native North American Almanac* (see ARBA 95, entry 439). However, it usefully profiles 112 Native North Americans from the United States and Canada, both living and deceased. The result is enjoyably browseable. Written in a somewhat journalistic style and objective in tone, the work only rarely includes controversial evaluations.

The contents are alphabetically ordered, with portraits accompanying most entries, and a list of sources at the end of each. It must have been difficult to decide what prominent Native Americans should not be included: One might have welcomed such personalities as the anthropologists Francis La Flesche (Osage) and Edward Dozier (Tewa), the painters Fritz Scholder (Luiseiio) and Harry Fonseca (Maidu), and the poets Wendy Rose (Hopi/Miwok) and Simon Ortiz (Laguna).

The front of each volume has an index by tribal groups/nations that runs into problems of terminology. Thus, the entry on Charles Alex Eastman identifies him as "Santee Sioux writer," but he is indexed only under "Dakota," while Amos Bad Heart Bull, "Oglala Sioux artist," is indexed only under "Lakota"; there is an index entry "Sioux," but no cross-referencing. Each volume ends with another index by field of endeavor, such as art, dance, or education. A more complete index—including the variant name forms for many of the personalities who are profiled—would have been useful. [R: BR, May/June 96, p. 45; SLJ, Aug 96, p. 182; VOYA, Aug 96, p. 190]—**William Bright**

466. **Notable Native Americans**. Sharon Malinowski, ed. Detroit, Gale, 1995. 492p. illus. index. $65.00. ISBN 0-8103-9638-6.

This easily readable biographical dictionary contains more than 265 men and women (70 percent contemporary, 30 percent historical) from all disciplines—activists to writers. Sketches are signed, vary in length from 1-3 pages, and often contain photographs or illustrations along with an appended bibliography.

An advisory board suggested names, and those selected are considered noteworthy by the Native American community. These names are not collectively available in any other reference source.

Prefatory materials include a provocative essay by George H. J. Abrams entitled "Race, Culture, and Law: The Quest of American Indian Identity"; a list of entries by surname, tribal group or nation, occupation or tribal role; and sketches of the contributors. A 13-page subject index rounds out the work.

Not all tribal groups are represented (there are no entries for Algonquian or Chumashan, for example), but the sketches are better written and more extensive than those in the *Reference Encyclopedia of the American Indian*, *Who Was Who in Native American History* (see ARBA 91, entry 402), and in the companion volume, *The Native North American Almanac* (see ARBA 95, entries 439 and 443). It is a useful tool for all libraries.—**Ilene F. Rockman**

467. **Ojibwa Chiefs, 1690-1980: An Annotated Listing**. John "Jake" A. Ilko, Jr. comp. Troy, N.Y., Whitston Publishing, 1995. 79p. illus. maps. $6.50pa. ISBN 0-87875-462-8.

This resource provides short biographical entries for several hundred leaders of the Ojibwa/Chippewa/Anishinaabe people in the western Great Lakes region for the historical period up to 1890. Organized alphabetically by most popular name (many chiefs were known by more than one), each entry typically includes alternate or translated names; date of birth, if known; group affiliation and places of residence; treaty signings (a major means of identification); prominent relatives; and participation in major events. No entries are longer than a paragraph, and the researcher looking for in-depth treatment of prominent chiefs will need to look elsewhere.

A preface outlines the purpose of the book and the various research problems encountered, while an introductory section discusses the nature of Ojibwa chiefly positions, types of chiefs, their authority, and activities. A center section consists of black-and-white portrait photographs of some prominent chiefs from the late nineteenth century. Four maps of place-names are poorly done and could have used more detail. Also, an index to alternate names and a chronological listing would have added to the value of this work. The resource is most appropriate for regional and Native American studies collections.—**Jeff Wanser**

468. **Ready Reference: American Indians**. Harvey Markowitz, ed. Pasadena, Calif., Salem Press, 1995. 3v. illus. maps. index. $270.00/set. ISBN 0-89356-757-4.

More than 160 U.S. scholars contributed one or more entries for this impressive 3-volume set. Entries vary in length from a few hundred words for some biographies to several pages (for example, the entry for the Arctic culture area). They are arranged in dictionary order and cover individuals, tribes, organizations, historical events, and Mesoamerica (major groups such as Maya, Aztec, and Toltec). The focus is on areas north of Mexico. Canadian material is represented, but spotty. (For example, there are no entries for Canadians such as Mary Sillett, Nelson Small Legs, Butch Smitheram, or Ralph Steinhauser.)

Each entry begins with some basic information; biographies provide birth and death dates, and who the person was or is—politician, writer, tribal leader, and so forth. Next comes tribal affiliation information and a sentence or two about why the person is important. What then follows is a narrative about the individual's life and major accomplishments. The narrative varies in length from two pages to two paragraphs. Extensive use of cross-references leads the user to related topics, and often entries provide one or two citations to more detailed material. Tribal entries supply 1990 census data and historical and contemporary information. Archaeological sites (Chaco Canyon), complexes (Mogollon), and material (Folsom point) furnish concise information and place the site or complex into the broader context of Native American history.

The more general articles, usually labeled pantribal, are of mixed content and value. For example, the article on food preparation and cooking attempts an overview of techniques across a continent in less than one full page. Needless to say, much is missing from such attempts. There are approximately 75 such "general" entries. It is unclear why some are single entries and some are more specific. Other general entries, such as "Buffalo," provide good facts but do not attempt to explore the implications. In the case of the buffalo entry, a paragraph discusses the slaughter of the herds in particular between 1870 and 1880, without commenting on why this took place. The concluding sentence of the entry will probably raise more questions than it answers: "Once the herds were destroyed, the Plains Indians were reduced to extreme poverty and had little alternative to the reservation system" (p.126). Interestingly enough, there is no cross-reference to the entry on "Reservation System of the United States." Entries for religious ceremonies cover the most widely known, such as Shalako, Shaking Tent, and Peyote Religion.

Much of the appendix directory material is better covered in other sources such as Barry T. Klein's *Reference Encyclopedia of the American Indian* (see entry 469). The four-and-one-half pages of glossary are too short, as is the mediagraphy (seven pages). The bibliography provides sound selective references. The index is helpful and makes up for the occasional lack of cross-references.

If a library already has the *Native North American Almanac* (see ARBA 95, entry 439) and *Native America in the Twentieth Century* (see ARBA 95, entry 434) and is not serving a large community interest in Native American issues, it may be difficult to justify acquiring this set. If it does not have these titles and is seeking a solid single source of information, this would be a good choice.—**G. Edward Evans**

469. **Reference Encyclopedia of the American Indian**. 4th ed. Barry T. Klein, ed. New York, Todd Publications, 1986. 2v. bibliog. index. $90.00/set. LC 86-050046. ISBN 0-915-344-08-4.

While still a two-volume set, the 4th edition of this encyclopedia contains a number of additions and changes. Volume 1 is the directory part of the set and has five new sections: "Indian Health Services" (name, address, telephone number, and type of service offered, arranged by state); "Communications" (a listing of Indian radio and television stations arranged by state); "Other Indian Tribes and

Groups" (listing of organizations representing Native American groups attempting to secure government recognition, arranged by state); "Canadian Reserves and Bands" (a worthwhile expansion to start covering Canadian Indian groups—arranged by province and reserve name, followed by band name and number of acres—no addresses or population information given); and "Federally Recognized Tribes and Bands" (an alphabetical listing by tribe followed by a list of reservations; address and population information is found in the section on reservations, as in the 3rd edition). The 3rd edition section "Associations" has been split in two here, with one section for national associations and one for state associations. The "Government Publications" section of the 3rd edition has been dropped.

As was true of the 3rd edition, there are problems of uneven treatment in the who's who bibliography sections of volume 1 and volume 2. It is difficult to know why some items from a publisher are listed when other titles, from the same publisher, are not included in the in-print bibliography. This was true for all three publishers (Scarecrow Press, Garland, and the UCLA American Indian Studies Center) I used to spot check the bibliography. Although most who's whos are dependent upon biographees returning data sheets, one expects the editors to organize carefully the data they have. One must be careful when searching for biographical information because there are problems in alphabetizing; for example, Gorman, F.; Gorman, R. C.; Gorden, P. T.; are followed by Gorman, C. N.; and Grinde, D. A.; Grobsmith, U.; are followed by Grispe, C. The new geographic index for the who's who volume (state and city) is also incomplete (for example, there is no listing for William Bright of Los Angeles). Despite these shortcomings, the set is still the best comprehensive directory for Native American-related groups, associations, and activities. If you have an earlier edition you will want to buy this new edition.—**G. Edward Evans**

470. Sherrow, Victoria. **Political Leaders and Peacemakers**. New York, Facts on File, 1994. 146p. illus. index. (American Indian Lives). $17.95. ISBN 0-8160-2943-1.

Reflecting the increasing interest in American Indian people, *Political Leaders and Peacemakers*, as part of the multivolume series American Indian Lives, presents bibliographies of 12 American Indian leaders of the past and present. From Deganawidah and Hiawatha, creators of the unique Iroquois League, to Wilma Mankiller, Principal Chief of the Cherokee Nation, these stories honor those who have led American Indian people during difficult and turbulent times. Some of those who are honored by inclusion in this book are better known than others; however, the book is not limited to famous chiefs about whom much has been written and who have traditionally formed the non-Indian conception of American Indian leadership.The photographs are valuable, as is the selected annotated bibliography.

Considerable debate is centered on the issue of whether or not non-Indians should write about American Indian peoples and cultures. The author has endeavored to research the subjects well and has listed American Indian resources. This research, quite naturally, is easier when the people are still alive, and these chapters are more interesting and more readable. Small errors in the text could have been avoided by having an American Indian edit the text. For example, a tribal powwow is not a religious ceremony as stated in the introduction. Unfortunately, these admittedly small factual errors raise doubts in the informed reader's mind and misinform the young reader—a much more serious consequence.

The chapters that involve much historical information could become confusing and even boring if the reader did not have some knowledge of this period of history or the benefit of a teacher's guidance. The book would also have been strengthened by the addition of at least one political leader who did not accept the inevitability of history and who did not earn the general appreciation of the non-Indian public.—**Karen D. Harvey**

471. Waldman, Carl. **Who Was Who in Native American History: Indians and Non-Indians from Early Contacts Through 1900**. New York, Facts on File, 1990. 410p. illus. $45.00. E89.W35. 970.004'97022. LC 89-35088. ISBN 0-8160-1797-2.

The subtitle of a book is often the key to understanding what to expect inside. That is certainly the case here; the title might lead one to think this is just about Native Americans. The 1,000-plus short biographies of individuals who played a significant role in pre-1900 Native American history are almost equally divided between Indians and non-Indians.

The alphabetically arranged entries range in length from less than 50 words (Loyola) to nearly 1,000 (Pontiac). Scholarship is at the level one would expect from this award-winning author. He provides alternate names and their spellings, indicates disputed translations of names, and includes a good cross-reference system. It appears the selection of Native Americans was partially influenced by trying to achieve some degree of geographic and tribal balance; 110 tribes have at least a single entry. Cherokee, Cheyenne, Iroquois, and Sioux have the most entries. Non-Indian entries fall into one of several broad categories: explorers and traders; frontier painters and photographers; government officials; agents and reformers; scholars and educators; and soldiers, scouts, and captives. An appendix provides tribal and band affiliation for Indian entries and lists non-Indians in the above-mentioned categories. Missionaries are categorized as either reformers or scholar/educators.

While the book is interesting, it is also disappointing. The user will find few references to other sources of information in the entries (less than 5 percent are primary publications), and there is no overall bibliography. Entries seem out of balance at times; for instance, there is a nine-paragraph entry for Christopher Columbus and only a three-sentence entry for Loyola, a Kalispel chief who converted to Catholicism. There are a number of similar entries of major historical figures already well-documented elsewhere. Other entries are for minor figures with little information given to explain their inclusion. This book is a good, but nonessential, addition to a general reference collection. [R: Choice, Nov 90, p. 468; LJ, 15 Apr 90, p. 90; RBB, 15 Sept 90, pp. 195-96; WLB, Oct 90, p. 132]—**G. Edward Evans**

POLES

472.   **Who's Who in Polish America**. 1996-1997 ed. Bolesraw Wierzbiaski and others, eds. New York, Bicentennial Publishing; distr., Hippocrene Books, 1996. 571p. index. $60.00. ISBN 0-7818-0010-1.

There are 1,962 biographies in *Who's Who in Polish America*, representing nearly 10 million Americans of Polish origin, in all walks of life. As such, the book is an important reference tool for all professionals—scholars, journalists, and librarians—in need of accurate information. The editorial work has been done over many years by Bicentennial Publishing of New York, publishers of the *Nowy Dziennik*, the largest independent Polish-language daily outside of Poland. Bicentennial also publishes *New Horizon*, a leading English-language/Polish American monthly magazine.

The candidates were selected by the publishers based on merit under the rules established by the Marquis Who's Who biographical directory series. The biographees have supplied and verified the biographical data published in the compendium. Included in each entry are date and place of birth, family members, education, career information, publications, memberships, honors, military service, languages, hobbies, and home or office address. A careful examination of the entries shows that there are some notable omissions. One hopes a future edition will include those who were not contacted or did not respond. It would also be useful in the next edition to have both geographic and occupational indexes.

This is a unique and valuable reference tool. It is especially suitable for libraries with large Slavic collections or serving communities with Polish American representation. [R: Choice, Dec 96, p. 596]—**George S. Bobinski**

12　Education

INTRODUCTION

The chapter **Education** is divided into General Works and Higher Education. The most general source is *Who's Who in American Education* (1994-95) (Marquis Who's Who/Reed Reference Publishing, 1988/89-) (see entry 476). Another is Frederik Ohles et al., *Biographical Dictionary of Modern American Educators* (Greenwood Press, 1997) (see entry 475). A more historical perspective is found in *Biographical Press Dictionary of North American and European Educationists* (Woburn Press, 1997) (see entry 474), which provides information on some 500 historical figures, from both Europe and the North American continent.

Those interested in university-level faculty can consult the *National Faculty Directory: An Alphabetical List, with Addresses, of Approximately 650,000 Members of Teaching Faculties...* (Gale, 1970-) (see entry 480), now in its 23d edition. Community and technical college personnel are covered in *Who's Who in Community, Technical, and Junior Colleges* (American Association of Community and Junior Colleges, 1991-) (see entry 481); unfortunately this has not been updated recently.

A growing interest in groups previously underrepresented in directories is evidenced by more specialized listings. *Encyclopedia of African-American Education* (Greenwood Press, 1996) (see entry 473) not only lists African American educators, but discusses places, events, educational theories, and legal cases of particular interest. *Women Educators in the United States, 1820-1993: A Bio-Bibliographical Sourcebook*, edited by Maxine Schwarts Seller (Greenwood Press, 1994) (see entry 477), includes only 66 profiles, but its bibliographies make it particularly valuable.

GENERAL WORKS

473.　**Encyclopedia of African-American Education**. Faustine C. Jones-Wilson and others, eds. Westport, Conn., Greenwood Press, 1996. 575p. index. $95.00. ISBN 0-313-28931-X.

The struggle for African Americans to achieve eductional equality is a significant issue in the history of the United States. This resource provides an overview of pertinent theories, laws, people, places, and events. Each alphabetic entry ends with a bibliography for further reading. Coverage is broad, but there are some omissions. For example, Elizabeth Koontz is not included, even though she was the first African American president of the National Education Association. The editor explains in the preface that the encyclopedia has length restrictions, and subsequently biographical entries were reduced. Instead, Greenwood Press is scheduled to issue a companion volume, *Biographical Dictionary of African-American Educators*. Other omissions are random, in an effort to provide the broadest possible scope, including local and regional information in addition to national data. Strong coverage of legal cases and numerous profiles of colleges and universities proliferate. For the history student, a chronology would have been a welcome addition. As a whole, the encyclopedia is still a useful reference tool.—**Jean Engler**

474.　Gordon, Peter, and Richard Aldrich. **Biographical Dictionary of North American and European Educationists**. Portland, Ore., Woburn Press, 1997. 528p. (The Woburn Education Series). $49.50; $25.00pa. LC 96-37182. ISBN 0-7130-0205-0; 0-7130-5025-4pa.

About 500 educationists from Europe and North America are profiled here, in entries ranging from half a page to just over a page. None of the entrants are still living. Some of the people profiled are not strictly educationists, but instead are connected with education in some way, such as psychologists whose theories contributed to change in education, or politicians who supported political reform related to education. Most of the entries contain references to other sources about the individual. Cross-references within articles to other entries within the volume are printed in bold type. A brief bibliography concludes the volume.

While the authors themselves state in their introduction that "this is not a comprehensive Biographical Dictionary," it provides information about numerous hard-to-locate historical figures in the field.—**Terry Ann Mood**

475.   Ohles, Frederik, Shirley M. Ohles, and John G. Ramsay. **Biographical Dictionary of Modern American Educators**. Westport, Conn., Greenwood Press, 1997. 432p. index. $79.50. ISBN 0-313-29133-0.

This book is a major revision of the *Biographical Dictionary of American Educators* (see ARBA 79, entry 695), originally published in 1978. The 410 bibliographic entries were selected from a list of nearly 1,500 names submitted by education agencies from the 50 states, and include many women and educators of color that may have been overlooked in the original work. Although those mentioned are not necessarily people of historical prominence, each educator included has "made a distinctive contribution to a facet of education in this country." Of the included educators, 173 were born before 1900. Among the selection criteria are a birth date before January 1, 1935, or the candidate being deceased; such criteria allow the significance of an individual's long-term contribution to education to be assessed effectively.

Each bibliographic entry includes family background, educational and career accomplishments, publications and honors, and a reference list. In addition to the alphabetic listing of comprehensive bibliographic entries, the book includes appendixes of birthplaces, states of major service, field of work, chronology of birth years, a chronological listing of important dates in American education, and a comprehensive index.

At a time when American education is confronting increasing criticism from many fronts and attempting solutions such as the implementation of national and local standards, this book provides a strong historical perspective for what has gone on before. Such concepts as implementation of driver's education classes (Amos Neyhart, 1933), a field trip consisting of an all-night bus tour through New York City as part of a social studies class (Roma Gans, 1940s), or adapting the study of physics to elementary school students (Robert Karplus, 1960s), demonstrates that much of what is good in education today has strong historical foundations.—**Craig A. Munsart**

476.   **Who's Who in American Education**. New Providence, N.J., Marquis Who's Who/Reed Reference Publishing, 1988/89- . index. $69.95. ISSN 1046-7203.

As with most of Marquis's titles, *Who's Who in American Education* is a much-needed biographical source of individuals of importance. This volume contains some 28,000 individuals, often selected from newspapers, periodicals, and professional association rosters.

Entries of each person provide much biographical data, including professional certifications, political activities, and home and office addresses. In future volumes it would be useful if e-mail addresses could be included as well. Each individual is contacted to complete that person's own biographical entry according to a standard format. For this reason the accuracy of entries is perhaps better than in some other biographical sourcebooks. For those who do not complete their own entries, the editors prepare them; these are marked with an asterisk. Inclusion is based on "reference value" (i.e., achievements) and governed selection. The position of responsibilities held and the level of achievement attained by the individual are considerations for inclusion.

As with the majority of the Marquis biographical publications, the inclusion of entrants from some institutions and organizations is uneven in quality and quantity. Many key individuals in universities, for example, cannot be found, and certain others of questionable consideration are included. The publication also includes a list of regional and national award-winning educators from various granting agencies, including professional associations and universities. It is, unfortunately, neither complete nor comprehensive. For example, the many awards by the American Library Association and its divisions are not included, and only a small handful of university awards are listed. Even without the comprehensiveness one would like in such a biographical reference work, this publication is of great value to libraries and educational administrative offices.—**Maureen Pastine and Terry Ann Mood**

477.   **Women Educators in the United States, 1820-1993: A Bio-Bibliographical Sourcebook**.
Maxine Schwarts Seller, ed. Westport, Conn., Greenwood Press, 1994. 603p. index. $99.50. LC
93-28033. ISBN 0-313-27937-3.

This volume celebrates the diversity of U.S. women educators in a series of 66 brief biographical profiles of individuals who have made significant contributions to U.S. education. The subjects of
this volume were selected because their exemplary work came during one or another of the following
periods described in an introductory essay written by the editor: "The Pioneers" (1820-1870) primarily concerns women who carved out a public service role for women either through informal or formal education; "Expanders and Reformers" (1870-1920) covers women on the front line as
educators, administrators, and activists when the takeoff of the U.S. educational system began;
"Losses and Gains" (1920-1960) deals with the women who struggled to keep from losing too much
ground during the mid-century, when men made considerable gains at the expense of women; and
"Pursuing Equality and Excellence" (1960-1993) concerns women who were the creators and beneficiaries of changes during a period of greater openness and opportunity for women.

The essays are arranged alphabetically and are evenly written, with each providing basic information on the subject's background, education, and career and the people and events that influenced
her. The average essay length is under nine pages, with over one page devoted to footnotes and a list
of works by and about the subject. The bio-bibliographic citations are an especially useful feature of
this volume, as they provide the reader with a brief, authoritative list of references for further reading.
In addition, the volume is nicely indexed and has a selected bibliography. These features, plus the
broad scope of subjects and the thoroughness of each entry, should make this a useful reference in
many collections. [R: Choice, Oct 94, p. 267; RBB, Aug 94, p. 2074]—**David V. Waller**

HIGHER EDUCATION

478.   **European Faculty Directory: An Alphabetical and Subject-Classified Listing**. . . . Detroit, Gale, 1991- . 2v. $200.00/set. ISSN 1053-640X.

The 1991 edition is the latest published, a two-volume set divided into four parts, all loaded
with information. Part 1 has a list of colleges, universities, and polytechnics from 28 Eastern and
Western European countries. The list is arranged alphabetically, first by the name of the country,
from Austria to Yugoslavia, and then by institution under each country. Every school entry includes
name, complete address, and telephone number. In addition, volume 1 begins the alphabetical list of
faculty. Over 315,000 names of faculty members from 28 countries represent 1,400 institutions of
higher learning from Europe. Each faculty entry includes name and complete office or home address;
telephone numbers are not given.

Volume 2 finishes the list of faculty members. Next comes a list of 96 subjects covered in this
publication, from African languages and literature to veterinary medicine, and over 800 cross-references. The last section of volume 2 is a subject index. Under each subject, names of faculty
members (listed with their country of origin) are arranged alphabetically. This well-prepared, comprehensive directory is an excellent addition to the literature and is recommended for all academic libraries interested in Europe. [R: Choice, July/Aug 91, p. 1757; RBB, 1 Mar 91, p. 1423]—**Ravindra
Nath Sharma and Terry Ann Mood**

479.   **Faculty White Pages: A Subject-Classified Directory**. . . . Compiled by CMG Information
Services. Detroit, Gale, 1989- . $130.00pa. ISSN 1040-1288.

This book is a directory to more than 537,000 university and college faculty in the United
States, American Samoa, Guam, Puerto Rico, the Trust Territories of the Pacific Islands, and the Virgin Islands. What makes it different from other faculty directories is its arrangement by discipline: individuals are listed alphabetically within 41 categories, from agriculture to vocational education.
Each entry contains the person's name, department, college, and telephone number. Entries can be
duplicated; for example, C. Elise Albert appears in the astronomy and the physics sections (in both
cases, her discipline is listed as physics). The front matter consists of an introduction, a how-to-use
section, a list of subjects covered, a list of abbreviations, and a roster of colleges and universities.
This last seems unusually complete, as it includes small religious colleges as well as larger institutions.

Because of the subject arrangement, it is not possible to search for someone by name unless one knows that person's field; even then, one may have to search through several related disciplines (e.g., allied health, nursing). Thus, this competently produced, attractive work is probably best used as a supplement to the larger, name-arranged faculty directories. Unfortunately, the latest edition is 1991.—**D. A. Rothschild and Terry Ann Mood**

480.   **National Faculty Directory: An Alphabetical List, with Addresses, of Approximately 650,000 Members of Teaching Faculties**. . . . Compiled by CMG Information Services. Detroit, Gale, 1970- . 3v. $710.00/set. LC 76-14404. ISSN 0077-4472.

A comprehensive guide to the individuals who teach at United States and Canadian colleges and universities, this directory contains the names, academic departments, schools and addresses of more than 650,000 people at some 3,800 institutions. All three volumes start with an introductory note, a list of abbreviations, and a roster of colleges and universities. After the prefatory material, the faculty members are listed in alphabetical order, and this information stretches through all three volumes. Only individuals who actually teach classes are included; those who are not teachers in specific subject areas and who are unlikely to adopt textbooks for class use (e.g., librarians with faculty status who do not teach) are not listed.

Data have been taken form academic course catalogs and faculty directories. Naturally, the directory is already out-of-date, but on the whole the information is accurate and reliable. This set is a necessity for all college and university libraries and many public and academic libraries.—**D. A. Rothschild and Terry Ann Mood**

481.   **Who's Who in Community, Technical, and Junior Colleges**. Washington, D.C., American Association of Community and Junior Colleges, 1991- . index. $50.00pa. ISSN 1061-8023.

This title is a companion to the *AACJC Membership Directory* (see ARBA 90, entry 321) and the *Community, Technical, and Junior College Statistical Yearbook* (see ARBA 91, entry 328). While all three annuals present accurate and up-to-date information about two-year colleges, the unique contribution of *Who's Who* is that it identifies key personnel below the level of chief executive at more than 1,200 community, technical, and junior colleges.

After briefly describing the mission, organization, and leadership of the American Association of Community and Junior Colleges (AACJC), this work lists two-year schools alphabetically by state, with additional entries for some foreign institutions. Each entry generally includes the college's name, address, telephone and fax numbers, year established, credit enrollment, number of campuses, and type of control. The name and title of the chief executive officer and names—but not titles—of those individuals responsible for administering 13 major functions are also provided. The cutoff date for data was March 28, 1991. An appendix lists state officials who oversee two-year colleges, with indexes of administrators and institutions completing the volume. *Who's Who* is very useful, but nearly all of its information about colleges and people can be located in a more comprehensive work, such as the 1987 *Higher Education Directory* (see ARBA 88, entry 358).—**Leonard Grundt**

13   Literature

INTRODUCTION

The field of literature is rich in biographical sources—and in reference sources in general—and this fact is reflected in this chapter, the longest in the book. The chapter is divided into 33 subject headings, a mix of those designating national literatures such as Turkish Literature or German Literature, and those designating genres, such as Fiction or Poetry. Both American Literature and British Literature have numerous subheadings. Most of these designate genres such as Drama or Mystery Writers, although under American Literature one can find a designation for Ethnic Minorities, Gay and Lesbian Literature, Literary Critics, Publishing, and Regional; while under British Literature, subheadings include the non-genre one of Publishing. In this arrangement, the fact of national identity takes precedence over genre; that is, a work having to do with German fiction writers is listed under German Literature rather than under Fiction; sources concerning American writers for children are listed under American Literature—Children's and Young Adult Literature rather than simply under Children's and Young Adult Literature. Under the genre headings, one can find books that transcend national lines.

Included in this chapter are the tried and true stalwart reference sources in literature, those that librarians have known, trusted, and used for many years. *Contemporary Authors* finds a listing here; as do new editions of *Contemporary Dramatists, Contemporary Novelists,* and *Contemporary Poets.* Note that *Contemporary Authors* includes more than literary authors, listing other professional authors as well, such as historians and journalists. Because it predominantly includes literary authors, and because it is used so often in that context, it is included in this chapter. However, be sure and consult other appropriate chapters for information on authors in other fields—look in the chapter **Communication and Mass Media** for sources covering journalists; or in **History** for those containing information on historians. *Benét's Reader's Encyclopedia,* 4th ed., edited by Bruce Murphy, has a new edition (HarperCollins, 1996) (see entry 483), as does the *Cyclopedia of World Authors*, edited by Frank N. Magill and others (Salem Press, 1997) (see entry 494), which has a 3rd edition.

The Dictionary of Literary Biography continues to publish volumes on various aspects of literature. These are scattered in this chapter under appropriate headings. For example, *The Bloombury Group* (Dictionary of Literary Biography Documentary Series, Vol. 10) (see entry 613) is under British Literature—General Works; *American Writers for Children, 1900-1960* (Gale, 1983) (see entry 553), *American Writers for Children since 1960: Fiction* (Gale, 1986) (see entry 554), and *American Writers for Children since 1960: Poets, Illustrators, and Nonfiction Authors* (Gale, 1987) (see entry 555) are all under American Literature—Children's and Young Adult Literature; and *Nineteenth-Century French Fiction Writers: Romanticism and Realism, 1800-1860* (Gale, 1992) (see entry 715) is under French Literature. The subheading Publishing under both American Literature and British Literature contains titles from this series: *Dictionary of Literary Biography Documentary Series: An Illustrated Chronicle, Volume Thirteen: The House of Scribner 1846-1904* (Gale, 1995) (see entry 596) and *The British Literary Book Trade, 1700-1820* (Gale, 1995) (see entry 658). Other headings also contain items from this long-standing and respected series.

Many old favorites have had supplements published. For instance, both *American Writers* and *British Writers* now have additional supplements. *American Writers* has Supplements III and IV (Scribner's, 1991 and 1996) (see entry 536), while *British Writers* has expanded to Supplements III and IV (Scribner's/Simon & Shuster Macmillan, 1996 and 1997) (Scribner's, 1997) (see entry 616).

A noteworthy development is that some standard reference sources now have CD-ROM versions. *Contemporary Authors on CD* (Gale, 1993) (see entry 491) covers *Contemporary Authors, Contemporary Authors New Revision Series*, and *Contemporary Authors Permanent Series*, although, its reviewer notes, not *Something about the Author* or *Twentieth-Century Literary Criticism* or others in the *Literary Criticism* series. Children's literature is covered on the CD *Junior DISCovering Authors* (U*X*L/Gale, 1994) (see entry 681). For other titles exploring see entries 498-500.

It is interesting to see the expansion of the literary canon, so strongly seen in high school and college/university curricula, reflected in the increased number of sources of less than traditional (or perhaps newly traditional) authors. Gay and lesbian authors are listed in *Contemporary Gay American Novelists: A Bio-Bibliographical Critical Sourcebook* (Greenwood Press, 1993) (see entry 582), and *Contemporary Lesbian Writers of the United States: A Bio-Bibliographical Critical Sourcebook* (Greenwood Press, 1993) (see entry 583). The Dictionary of Literary Biography series weighs in with several volumes on African-American writers, among them one on the Harlem Renaissance, *Afro-American Writers from the Harlem Renaissance to 1940* (Gale, 1987) (see entry 567), but other publishers do not neglect this area. Greenwood Press has *A Bibliographical Guide to African-American Women Writers* (1993) (see entry 569), while Scribner's offers *African American Writers* (1991) (see entry 562). The Dictionary of Literary Biography appears again with *Chicano Writers: First Series* (Gale, 1989) (see entry 570) and *Chicano Writers: Second Series* (Gale, 1992) (see entry 570). Native American authors are represented with *Native North American Literature: Biographical and Critical Information on Native Writers and Orators...* (Gale, 1995) (see entry 574).

Women authors have a fair share of the items in this chapter. General sources include *Great Women Writers: The Lives and Works of 135 of the World's Most Important Women Writers* (Henry Holt, 1994) (see entry 506) and *Modern Women Writers* (Continuum, 1996) (see entry 513). American women are represented in *Modern American Women Writers* (Scribner's, 1991) (see entry 545); in *American Women Writers: A Critical Reference Guide from Colonial Times to the Present* (Continuum, 1978-82) and its supplement (Unger, 1978-1994) (see entry 534); and in Jane T. Peterson and Suzanne Bennett's *Women Playwrights of Diversity: A Bio-bibliographical Sourcebook* (Greenwood Press, 1997) (see entry 561). British women authors appear in *A Biographical Dictionary of English Women Writers 1580-1720* (G. K. Hall, 1990) (see entry 612) and *The Oxford Guide to British Women Writers* (Oxford, 1993) (see entry 625). More specialized sources can be found under genre-specific headings—*Contemporary Women Dramatists* (St. James Press, 1994) (see entry 701) under Drama; or under nation-specific headings—*Japanese Women Writers: A Bio-Critical Sourcebook* (Greenwood Press, 1994) (see entry 738) under Japanese Literature.

Some national literatures are represented with new editions of surveys of the literature. Under Australian Literature is listed *The Oxford Companion to Australian Literature*, 2d ed. (Oxford University Press, 1994) (see entry 609); while under German Literature, Oxford provides *The Oxford Companion to German Literature,* 3d ed. (Oxford University Press, 1997) (see entry 725). Other national or continental literatures represented in this chapter, besides the voluminous categories of American Literature and British Literature, are African Literature, Australian Literature, Austrian Literature, Canadian Literature, Caribbean and African Literature, Chinese Literature, Cuban Literature, European Literature, Filipino Literature, French Literature, German Literature, Indian Literature, Iranian Literature, Irish Literature, Italian Literature, Japanese Literature, Latin American Literature, Oceanian Literature, Russian Literature, Slavic Literature, Soviet Literature, Spanish Literature, Turkish Literature, and Welsh Literature.

Surely in this lengthy chapter, heavy in sources, there is something for everyone, from novice—*Magill's Survey of World Literature* (Marshall Cavendish, 1995) (see entry 510) to specialist—*American Nature Writers* (Scribner's/Simon & Schuster Macmillan, 1996) (see entry 533); from history buff—*German Writers and Works of the Early Middle Ages: 800-1170* (Gale, 1995) (see entry 722) to lover of the contemporary—*Twentieth-Century Caribbean and Black African Writers, Third Series* (Gale, 1996) (see entries 673-675); from romance novels—*British Romantic Novelists, 1789-1832* (Gale, 1992) (see entry 644) to science fiction—*St. James Guide to Science Fiction Writers* (St. James Press, 1996) (see entry 760).

GENERAL WORKS

482. Bailey, Brooke. **The Remarkable Lives of 100 Women Writers and Journalists**. Holbrook, Mass., Adams Publishing, 1994. 208p. index. (20th Century Women Series). $12.00. ISBN 1-55850-423-0.

This little book provides wonderfully readable biographies of 100 U.S. women writers who worked primarily during the early to mid-twentieth century. Each of the 2-page, 700- to 750-word entries is presented in an easy, conversational style, and gives basic biographical and critical information. Up to four sources for further information are listed at the end of each biography.

The selection of women included is broadly based. Fiction writers, poets, journalists (and photojournalists, in the person of Margaret Bourke-White), screenwriters, biographers and autobiographers, and essayists are all represented. This wide range results in a broader representation than is found in many other selective collections.

As is common among alphabetically arranged reference books, this one has no table of contents. However, it also lacks any comprehensive index and the "Index by Occupation," although interesting, does not make up for this inadequacy. Poor proofreading is another, more minor, problem. Although it is fun to read, interesting, and thoughtful, this book does not present research-level information or sources. Overall, it is best suited to a high school or public library, where it should serve well as an introductory source.—**Susan Davis Herring**

483. **Benét's Reader's Encyclopedia**. 4th ed. Bruce Murphy, ed. New York, HarperCollins, 1996. 1144p. $50.00. ISBN 0-06-270110-X.

William Rose Benét's legacy lives on with this 4th edition of a classic work. Touted as "the single most complete one-volume encyclopedia" of world literature (jacket flap), this edition reflects a more diversified canon, with greater focus on African, African American, Eastern, Eastern European, Middle Eastern, South American, and women's literature. Last updated in 1987 (see ARBA 89, entry 816), the structure and type of entries remain virtually the same in the new edition. Entries cover more than just writers and works of literature—musical composers, philosophers, artists, historical and political figures, literary characters, terms, locales, folktales, mythology, and more are treated between these covers. New additions include John Cage, the Frankfurt School, and Jaime Salom. Toni Morrison's entry has been updated to reflect her winning of the Nobel Prize and the publication of her latest novel, *Jazz* (1992). That said, one must also note the entries that have not been updated. For example, Louisa May Alcott's entry does not mention the recent publication of *A Long Fatal Love Chase* (published in 1995 by Bantam Doubleday Dell). One must wonder what other recent developments in the literary world have not been recorded here. Obviously, no one-volume encyclopedia can be entirely comprehensive on such an enormous topic. However, a casual browse reveals more entries not carried over from the 3d edition than entries added to the 4th edition. Perhaps this reviewer merely looked on the wrong pages, but a perusal of several letters of the alphabet within the encyclopedia should have yielded better results. Essentially, the encyclopedia is an important work, but this long-awaited new edition could have gone even further in promoting the diversity of world literature in the 1990s. [R: C&RL, Sept 97, p. 478]—**Melissa Rae Root**

484. **Biographical Dictionary of Transcendentalism**. Wesley T. Mott, ed. Westport, Conn., Greenwood Press, 1996. 315p. index. $79.50. ISBN 0-313-28836-4.

This biographical dictionary complements the *Encyclopedia of Transcendentalism*, in which such terms as *transcendentalism* are defined, and the history of the movement prior to 1830 is given. Cross-references are to both volumes: a single asterisk for other entries in the dictionary and a double asterisk for the encyclopedia.

Following a "Guide to Abbreviations and References" of sources, 204 short biographies are alphabetically arranged in a single-column format with clear typeface and wide margins. Many of the names, such as the Quaker poet John Greenleaf Whittier, are only peripheral to transcendentalism. Most entries are a page or less in length, although there are lengthier essays for such major figures as the Alcotts, Ralph Waldo Emerson, Margaret Fuller, Henry David Thoreau, and Walt Whitman. Entries on William Wordsworth and Samuel Taylor Coleridge bear witness to the importance of

English romanticism to the movement. French and German influences are seen by the inclusion of names such as Charles Fourier, Johann Wolfgang von Goethe, Friedrich Schelling, and even Johann Gaspar Spurzheim, whose views on phrenology interested Emerson.

Readers wishing to know more about transcendentalism will be aided by a bibliographic essay as well as by the list of references at the end of each entry. The dictionary concludes with an index and pertinent information about each of the 90 contributors. The biographical dictionary is certainly a useful resource for those familiar with transcendentalism and those wishing to know more about the people associated with it. For people with a more limited knowledge, it will be necessary to also consult the companion encyclopedia.—**Charlotte Lindgren**

485. **Black Writers: A Selection of Sketches from** *Contemporary Authors*. 2d ed. Sharon Malinowski, ed. Detroit, Gale, 1994. 721p. index. $85.00. LC 81-640179. ISBN 0-8103-7788-8.

This new edition of *Black Writers* presents, in an alphabetical format, updated biographical, bibliographical, and critical data on 150 authors from the 1st edition and adds almost 250 new entries from Gale's *Contemporary Authors* series. Both editions together contain significant information on nearly 700 black authors of the twentieth century. The writers included are not only American but also African and Caribbean blacks whose works were written in or translated into English.

The biographical sketches provide essential personal information, comprehensive lists of writers' works, and useful critical sources. An interesting and usually well done feature is the "Sidelights" section that details each author's life and offers significant review materials pertaining to the writer's major works. Many of the commentaries are based on very recent scholarly criticism and are well delineated so as to reveal important perceptions and appreciations of the authors' accomplishments. Also useful are the gender and nationality indexes, along with the cumulative index to the 1st and 2nd editions.

A detracting note is the omission of article titles in the listings of journals containing critical essays on a specific author. A reader has no clue as to the particular critical topic that may be found in any one periodical entry. The collection, however, is valuable and useful and certainly ranks high in comprehensiveness, readability, and general interest. Recommended especially for those drawn to literature, education, and black studies.—**Angelo Costanzo**

486. Blain, Virginia, Patricia Clements, and Isobel Grundy. **The Feminist Companion to Literature in English: Women Writers from the Middle Ages to the Present**. New Haven, Conn., Yale University Press, 1990. 1231p. index. $49.93. LC 90-70513. ISBN 0-300-04834-8.

This is one of the most comprehensive guides to women's studies available today. Most of the alphabetically arranged entries are on women authors and include a short biography, a description of their most important writings, and a brief list of available references and studies. They have been intentionally kept short—usually under 300 words—to enable the inclusion of lesser-known women, especially writers of noncanonical works such as pamphlets, letters, and diaries. The authors have omitted entries on book titles or fictional characters, material available in more general literary companions, in favor of this broader coverage. The subject entries are also very limited; there is not one on rape, for example, although there are excellent ones on such literary topics as the Gothic, romance, science-fiction, and utopia. The alphabetical section is followed by a list of frequently cited works, a chronological index of names, and indexes of topics and cross-references.

Although the *Companion* covers all varieties of English-language writing (including that of the Caribbean, Asia, Africa, and Australia, as well as the United States and Canada), the emphasis is disproportionately on Great Britain and its colonies. This fact may limit its usefulness to American readers. Its well-researched, economical entries nevertheless supply a wealth of information that any reader interested in women's studies will find invaluable. Recommended for both university and community libraries. [R: Choice, Feb 91, pp. 912-13; RBB, 1 Jan 91, pp. 932-33; RQ, Fall 1990, p. 98]—**Lynn F. Williams**

487.   Contemporary Authors: A Bio-Bibliographical Guide to Current Writers. . . . Detroit, Gale, 1962- . $104.00. LC 62-52046. ISSN 0010-7468.

More than 98,000 authors have been represented in the Contemporary Authors series since its beginning. Writers in almost all genres—fiction, nonfiction, drama, poetry, and so forth—have been included, and prominent people in areas such as newspaper and television reporting, editing, screenwriting, and other media also appear. Three types of entries appear: sketches, brief listings, and obituaries.

Information is generally gathered from the writers through questionnaires and correspondence. If authors fail to respond to requests, material is obtained from other reliable sources. Data on living authors is sent to biographees for verification. Essays may contain personal and career information, addresses, organizational memberships, awards and honors, publications (e.g., books, articles, periodical articles), and biographical sidelights. These last may consist of critical analyses of the individual's works, interviews, or other material. Several other titles in related Contemporary Authors series have updated older volumes from this particular series. A volume update chart that follows the preface shows which of the earlier volumes may be discarded. Academic and large public libraries will want to purchase these volumes to have the most current information available on contemporary authors.—**Anna Grace Patterson**

488.   Contemporary Authors: A Bio-Bibliographical Guide to Current Writers. New Revision Series. Linda Metzger, ed. Detroit, Gale, 1981- . In progress. $85.00/vol. LC 62-52046. ISSN 0275-7176.

Gale's *Contemporary Authors* (*CA*) has tried various methods to keep information on its biographees up-to-date—the *New Revision Series* (*NRS*) is the latest effort. Libraries possessing the entire *CA* set will have three distinct sets of volumes: the basic volumes (volume 114 appeared in 1984); the *First Revision Series* (volumes 41-44 appeared in 1979); and the *CA Permanent Series* (only two volumes were published). The *Permanent Series,* abandoned after two volumes, was established to remove from the regular volumes the biographies of deceased or retired authors. The *First Revision Series* (started in 1975) combined several of the original volumes, listed the biographies in one alphabetical sequence, and offered revisions in various degrees of depth and comprehensiveness. Since not all of the entries included in the *First Revision Series* actually required revision, it became obvious that this was an inefficient and costly system.

The *New Revision Series* relieves Gale of "The need to publish entries with few or no changes," since it includes only entries that require revision. Unlike the *First Revision Series, NRS* will not replace single volumes of *CA*; libraries must keep the existing (and ongoing) volumes as well as the *NRS* volumes. The *CA* cumulative index will provide access to both sets. So far there are twelve volumes of the *NRS* in print.

Volumes of the *New Revision Series* contain updated biographical and bibliographical information on authors included in previous volumes. For deceased authors, this revision will be the final one; others may appear in later editions. Interviews are included with authors felt to be of particular interest.

Each volume of the *New Revision Series* provides a handy chart indicating which volumes of *Contemporary Authors* and of the *First Revision Series* can, in fact, be replaced by subsequent volumes.

The entries in the *New Revision Series* do not direct the user to previous volumes in which an author appeared. Instead, indexes appear in each even numbered volume of *CA*. In addition, *CA*'s *Cumulative Index* may be consulted.

All libraries having the original and the *First Revision Series* will find the *New Revision Series* valuable for its current updating of descriptions of authors who continue to be productive.—**Louis R. Ruybal and Terry Ann Mood**

489. **Contemporary Authors: Autobiography Series**. Detroit, Gale, 1962- . illus. index. LC 84-647879. ISSN 0748-0636.

This unique series was created to fill a gap in literary reference works: there have been no brief autobiographies of current writers collected in one source. For most of these writers, many of whom have only recently been recognized, autobiographical information is unavailable elsewhere. As stated in the preface, this work provides "an opportunity for writers . . . to let their readers know how they see themselves and their work, what carefully laid plans or turns of luck brought them to this time and place, what objects of their passion and pity arouse them enough to tell us." Volume 6 concentrates on novelists and poets, including Nikki Giovanni, D. Keith Mano, and Dee Brown. Volume 7 covers, among others, Andrew Greeley, Jamake Highwater, and David Ray. As in the main *Contemporary Authors* set, the writers represented here are not only fiction writers, but fall into a broad range of categories, including literary criticism, nonfiction, drama, film, and television.

Each of these volumes contains sixteen essays, although other volumes in the series have a greater number. The scope and style were left entirely to the authors. As a result, some are chatty and entertaining, others are introspective, matter-of-fact, or poetic. Some are chock full of facts, names, and dates; others leave the reader with a "feeling" for the author's thoughts about life and literature. Karl Shapiro's is written in the third person, and Arnold Wesker's is a "mini autobiography in three acts and a prologue." All of them make for fascinating reading.

Each essay is accompanied by photographs supplied by the writer. The only feature added by the editorial staff is a bibliography of book length works for each writer. The index provides adequate access to names or titles mentioned in this or previous volumes. Some of the other Gale literary series index one another. While *Contemporary Authors: Autobiography Series* is indexed in several other Gale sets, its own index is limited to volumes within the series.

An autobiography series is a great idea, and this particular one is an interesting and unusual companion to existing sources for literary biography and criticism.—**Emily L. Werrell and Terry Ann Mood**

490. **Contemporary Authors Bibliographical Series**. Detroit, Gale, 1986-1989. index. ISSN 0887-3070.

The *Contemporary Author Bibliographical Series (CABS)* is designed as a companion series to Gale Research's *Contemporary Authors* bio-bibliographical series. In this, the 2nd volume of *CABS*, the focus is on eleven major post-World War II poets: John Berryman, Elizabeth Bishop, James Dickey, Robert Hayden, Randall Jarrell, Robert Lowell, Howard Nemerov, Charles Olson, Theodore Roethke, Anne Sexton, and Richard Wilbur. No indication is made regarding criteria for the inclusion of these poets and the omission of others.

Each chapter, written by a specialist, is devoted to a particular poet and is divided into three sections. First is a bibliography listing the poet's major works. Next is a section that lists works about the poet and his or her works. Last is an analytical bibliographical essay in which the critical works are discussed. The volume concludes with two indexes: a cumulative index to authors, and a cumulative index to critics. Both indexes include authors and critics found in volumes 1 and 2 of *CABS*.

The method used in *CABS* of creating an annotated bibliography by tying the citations together in an essay is one that works very well, especially for literary works. It provides the user with a good evaluation of the critical works themselves. Furthermore, it gives the user guidance on how to proceed in studying and analyzing works of both poet and critic. Additional volumes in *CABS* are anticipated. They will include foreign as well as U.S. authors. This present volume and future ones will be of great value to collections focusing on contemporary literature.—**Marjorie E. Bloss**

491. **Contemporary Authors on CD**. Detroit, Gale, 1993. Minimum system requirements: IBM or compatible XT; MS-DOS CD-ROM Extensions 2.0 or higher (or MSCDEX 2.1 or higher with MS-DOS 4.0 or higher); MS-DOS or PC-DOS 3.1 or higher; 640K RAM (500K available); 1MB hard disk space. $795.00.

At last, no more looking up authors in the various printed sets of *Contemporary Authors*! At last, patrons can find author information instantly! These statements are right, but there is a caveat.

Contemporary Authors on CD (CA-CD) covers only the original *Contemporary Authors* (see ARBA 93, entries 1108-09), volumes 1-140; *Contemporary Authors New Revision Series*, volumes 1-41; and *Contemporary Authors Permanent Series*, volumes 1-2. This is acceptable, although one would prefer all the other author series, such as *Something about the Author* and *Twentieth-Century Literary Criticism,* on the same disc. The new ways to search the set through Boolean logic—even subject searching, no less—are wonderful, as are the almost instant access, the ability to save to disc and print, and the ability to jump easily within an entry to the beginning of the entry or to mark portions for further study. Even the author entries have been updated, so that if in the original volumes there were three entries (an original sketch, a revised sketch, and an obituary), they have now been merged and updated. But there is a flaw that requires a double-step look up that patrons will miss if they use only the CD version. Gale publishes the *Contemporary Authors Cumulative Index*, which is the first stopping place for any search. It will refer a person to author information in the complete Gale authors series, but the CD version will not. There are some cross-references to other titles, but they are not complete. This means that Gale did not merge the helpful information in its cumulative index file with this CD file before publication. It would have made a one-stop search a complete one.

Of course, the problem for most libraries is that they already have a complete set of *Contemporary Authors* in print form and wonder if they can justify another $800 to convert to CD. What do you do with the paper edition? What will it cost to keep *CA* current? (This information was not supplied to the reviewer.) Will an expanded version including the Gale authors series be forthcoming? What will it cost to update *CA-CD* annually? These are sticky questions about all reference works on CD, and libraries will need to make some hard decisions as they move away from the print world. Of course, for libraries that do not own the complete set, this product's price is a steal.

Taking all these factors into consideration, and with the hope that Gale will add the complete cross-reference structure in future editions, this CD is certainly a tempting purchase. If your library does a lot of author queries, then there is no question: This product is a must-purchase. [R: Choice, Oct 94, pp. 267-68; RBB, July 94, pp. 1968-70; VOYA, Oct 94, p. 238; WLB, Nov 94, pp. 113-14]
—**David V. Loertscher**

492. **Contemporary Popular Writers**. Dave Mote, ed. Detroit, St. James Press, 1997. 528p. index. (Contemporary Writers Series). $130.00. ISBN 1-55862-216-0.

No longer simply entertaining and diverting, contemporary popular literature has become serious, instructive, and important, even as it continues to please readers on a large scale. From Cleveland Amory, Isaac Asimov, and Margaret Atwood to Barbara Tuchman, Alice Walker, and Tom Wolfe, this useful reference tool provides copious information about 309 writers of popular fiction and nonfiction. Primarily American and British in its coverage, this volume includes novelists and short story writers, biographers, historians, humorists, playwrights, poets, social commentators, and psychologists who have been active in the field of popular literature since the early 1960s.

Each alphabetized author entry begins with nationality; birth and death dates; education; military service; family; career; awards; memberships; agent; and address followed by a list of publications (with publishers and dates), divided into genres. In many entries, bibliographies and critical studies are also listed. Concluding each entry is a signed, well-written critical commentary of varying length, usually a half-page, addressing various personal and professional highlights. A helpful preface outlines the raison d'être, content, and progress of popular literature from its beginnings in mid-century to the present. Nationality, genre, and title indexes, along with notes on advisers and contributors, conclude the volume.

Although the price is high, this well-bound, typographically pleasing text will be sought after frequently by users of public, academic, and, perhaps, high school libraries. It will have a long shelf life until the revised edition arrives. [R: RBB, 1 Mar 97, p. 1183]—**Charles R. Andrews**

493. **Contemporary World Writers**. Tracy Chevalier, ed. 2d ed. Detroit, St. James Press, 1993. 686p. $135.00. PN51.C6235. 809'.04. LC 93-5352. ISBN 1-55862-200-4.

Anyone comparing this work with the 1st edition, published in 1984 as *Contemporary Foreign-Language Writers* (St. Martin's Press), will be struck by the significant increase in the number of writers included: approximately 340 living authors representing more than 60 countries, some 200 more than the previous edition. The key criterion for inclusion remains: living writers whose work has been translated, in whole or in part, into English. Among the diversity of nationalities represented are Cameroonian, Faroese, Ivorian, Macedonian, and Sudanese.

For each entry a biographical sketch concludes with a current address of the writer or the person's literary agent. This is followed by a bibliography listing verse, fiction, plays, and other works, the titles arranged chronologically within each category. The bibliographies are composed mostly of books but may include for some, especially Japanese, Russian, and *samizdat* writers from Central and Eastern Europe, works initially published in journals. Original editions are cited in the original language along with the first British and United States editions of English translations. For works not translated into English, a literal English translation of the title is supplied in brackets.

The primary bibliography is supplemented by a roster of secondary sources that may include published bibliographies and critical studies in English if available. Signed essays critique the writer's work. In some entries, writers comment on their own work, although this is not a significant feature. Pseudonyms are cross-referenced to the author's main entry.

An important new feature of this edition is a nationality index listing writers under current as well as past nationality. The title index includes only those from the fiction, play, and verse sections and may exclude titles that fall into the category of other works. Collections in comparative literature as well as large public libraries will want to acquire this up-to-date survey of contemporary writers, both for the bio-bibliographical information and as a tool for collection development in modern literatures.—**Bernice Bergup**

494.   **Cyclopedia of World Authors**. 3d ed. Frank N. Magill, McCrea Adams, and Juliane Brand, eds. Pasadena, Calif., Salem Press, 1997. 5v. index. $350.00/set. ISBN 0-89356-434-6.

This 5-volume encyclopedia of more than 2,000 authors from Aesop (3d century B.C.E.) to Sherman Alexie (born 1966) has dual purposes: to combine, revise, and expand the 2 previous sets, *Cyclopedia of World Authors* (1974) and *Cyclopedia of World Authors II* (see ARBA 91, entry 1105); and to complement *Masterplots* (2d ed.; see ARBA 97, entry 906). The revisions are substantial: 25 percent of the entries are new to this edition. Although the greatest number of entries still come from the anglophone world, this edition includes new essays in major ethnic areas—African American, Latino, Asian American, Native American—and women's literature. The sketches consistently average a page in length, regardless of the writer's reputation, stressing biography over literary criticism.

Unlike other sources of this type, the *Cyclopedia* includes two unique aspects: writers whose primary claim to fame is not literary (Thorstein Veblen and Elizabeth Cady Stanton, for example), for whom this source may not be the most obvious or intuitive choice for information, and one-hit wonders, such as Shelby Steele, Harriet Wilson, and Darryl Pinckney. The searcher is furthermore rewarded with ready access to contemporary writers (approximately 25 percent of the authors are still living). The 1997 copyright date, furthermore, reflects current biographical data, such as the recent death of Jose Donoso. In addition, most of the lists and bibliographies of authors' works have been updated, if not expanded. As previously, the lists of works are sorted by the genre in which the writer is best known; the bibliographic sources were selected on the basis of availability, timeliness, and usefulness, with a heavy slant toward English-language materials. The lack of page references for periodical citations, however, inhibits the effectiveness of the tool somewhat.

New to this edition are two indexes, one by a birth date timeline and one by where the writer flourished or was born. The geographic index inspires some caveats; for example, the cases of Albert Camus and Jacques Derrida, who are listed under both Algeria and France, are symptomatic of several duplications. Galicia, Silesia, and Numidia are designated as separate geographic entities. The master list of authors in volume 5 merely replicates the table of contents from each of the individual volumes; there is no additional index to names embedded within entries. All entries are signed, but an unusually high proportion of the contributors to this edition (nearly 15 percent) are designated as "independent scholar" under affiliation.

Although the set is almost beyond comparison in terms of sheer numbers of entries, its coverage is more superficial than that of Scribner's European, Ancient, British, American, and Latin American Writers sets (see ARBA 97, entry 961). *Cyclopedia*'s approach is more biographical and less interpretive than *Contemporary World Writers* (2d ed.; see ARBA 94, entry 1144). Its style is less colorful, but scholarship is more current than all but the most recent Wilson Authors series (see ARBA 97, entry 887). All in all, the set is a useful stepping-stone for works by and about the most influential and studied writers in today's curriculum.—**Lawrence Olszewski**

495. **Dictionary of Literary Biography**. Matthew J. Bruccoli, ed. director. Detroit, Gale, 1978- . In progress. $85.00/vol.

The Dictionary of Literary Biography, started in 1978, is a multi-volume series designed to fill a significant gap in literary biographical scholarship. Each volume in the DLB series focuses on a specific period or literary movement. It is projected that the entire series, when completed, will ultimately encompass all authors who made significant contributions to literature in the United States, Canada, England, and other countries. Individual volumes are edited by recognized scholars with contributions by subject specialists.

Each volume follows a similar format. Major biographical-critical essays are presented for the most important figures of each era. Each of these master essays includes a career chronology, list of publications, and a bibliography of works by and about the subject for easy reference. The main portion of each essay is a chronologically arranged personal and career summary with discussions of all major works. Entries for lesser figures deal with each subject's life, work, and critical reputation, all chronologically arranged in one section. All entries are arranged in a single alphabetic sequence.

Many of these volumes are reviewed separately in this work by our subject specialists.—**Bohdan S. Wynar**

496. **Dictionary of Literary Biography Documentary Series: An Illustrated Chronicle**. Margaret A. Van Antwerp, ed. Detroit, Gale, 1982- . In progress. (A Bruccoli Clark Book). $92.00/vol. LC 82-1105.

Designed to complement the biographies in other volumes of the Dictionary of Literary Biography, each volume in the *Documentary Series* includes selected photographs, manuscript facsimiles, letters, notebooks, interviews, and contemporary reviews of major books for a few authors of prominence. Volume 1 covers Sherwood Anderson, Willa Cather, John Dos Passos, Theodore Dreiser, F. Scott Fitzgerald, Ernest Hemingway, and Sinclair Lewis. Revealing glimpses of authors' perceptions and contemporary critical opinions abound. For this reviewer, Willa Cather's comments on her research for *Death Comes for the Archbishop* and her angry denunciation of those who would make literature subservient to propaganda were particularly rich in human interest.

Scholars and doctoral students will need to go far beyond the samples here, but undergraduates writing term papers and faculty preparing lectures for survey courses will find much of value. So, of course, will reference librarians seeking to help these clients. Each selection on a given author begins with a cross-reference to the appropriate biographical volumes of DLB and a short bibliography. Contributors are identified in the "acknowledgments" section.

The 2nd volume makes readily available contemporary evidence concerning the works of seven authors: James Gould Cozzens, James T. Farrell, William Faulkner, John O'Hara, John Steinbeck, Thomas Wolfe, and Richard Wright.

With volume 3, the focus becomes more contemporary. Of the six representative and influential post-World War II writers chosen, five have had long and distinguished careers. Saul Bellow, winner of the Nobel Prize for Literature in 1976, published his first novel in 1944; Norman Mailer began in 1948 with *The Naked and the Dead*; John Updike's first short story appeared in 1954; and Kurt Vonnegut's debut as a novelist was in 1952. Vladimir Nabokov was a special case; writing novels in Russian in the 1920s, first publishing in English in 1941, and dazzling critics until his death in 1977. The remaining figure in the volume, Jack Kerouac, was essentially limited to the Beat Movement of the 1950s. There are, of course, other significant postwar writers who could have been included in this volume (e.g., Baldwin, Capote, Cheever, or Malamud), but these six form a splendidly diverse, and eclectic, group.

Unlike the previous three volumes in this series, volume 4 (published in 1984) focuses exclusively on one writer: Tennessee Williams. It is intended as a concise illustrated biography, presenting in chronological order documents that illustrate specific events in the author's literary and personal life (i.e., diverse "materials that have heretofore been accessible to a limited group of researchers"). However, most of the materials reprinted here are readily available to scholars. Many reviews of the plays, novels, and poems are taken from major New York papers; most of the interviews (eighteen) are also available in other published sources. Three brief interviews are printed for the first time, but add little to our understanding of the man or his work. Of eleven reprinted letters, four are from the published Williams/Donald Windham correspondence, and all but three of the remainder are from newspapers or other published collections. Most disappointing is the lack of examples showing corrected manuscript copy.

The hundreds of illustrations (photographs, dust jackets, playbills) are of interest. However, the reduction of some of the printed illustrations makes them difficult to read.

The volume does not make an important contribution to Williams scholarship and, like the author's *Memoirs*, concentrates too much on biographical information and not enough on the plays. However, there is more emphasis here on the plays than there is in *Memoirs*. Smaller libraries with limited newspaper and periodical holdings will make good use of this collection of documents. Students of Williams will continue to start with Dreway W. Gunn's *Tennessee Williams: A Bibliography.* [R: Choice, Dec 82, p. 554; Choice, May 83, p. 1263; Choice, July/Aug 83, p. 1593; LJ, 15 Sept 82, p. 1744; LJ, 1 Mar 83, p. 489; WLB, Oct 82, pp. 171-72]—**Milton H. Crouch and A. Robert Rogers**

497.   Dictionary of Literary Biography Yearbook. Detroit, Gale, 1980- . illus. index. (Dictionary of Literary Biography). ISSN 0731-7867; 1730-3793.

This is the 16th yearbook of the Dictionary of Literary Biography (DLB) series. Each yearbook reviews the events of the literary year in poetry, fiction, literary biography, drama, and children's books. The 1995 annual has 20 articles by contributors from academia and publishing, varying in length from 5 to 55 pages. Some of the longer articles deal with such matters as the World War II Writers' Symposium, book reviewing in the United States, primary bibliography, and Nobel Prize winner Seamus Heaney. Lists of literary awards announced in 1995, a necrology, and a two-page checklist of contributions to literary history and biography round out the volume.

The articles in the DLB *Yearbook* are generally well written and interesting, especially for literary scholars and followers of publishing trends. However, the yearbook has slight reference value, considering its cost, especially for libraries that already subscribe to the *Bowker Annual*. Larger libraries may purchase the DLB *Yearbook* for their circulating collections.—**Jonathan F. Husband**

498.   DISCovering Authors: Biographies & Criticism on 400 Most-Studied Canadian & World Authors. Canadian ed. [CD-ROM]. Toronto, Gale Canada, 1996. Minimum system requirements: IBM or compatible 286 (386 or faster recommended). ISO 9660-compatible CD-ROM drive with cables, interface card, and MS-DOS CD-ROM Extensions 2.1 (double speed or faster recommended). MS-DOS 3.3. 640K RAM. 10MB hard disk space. VGA monitor and graphics card. Mouse (optional). Printer (optional). $750.00. ISBN 0-8103-9955-5.

DISCovering Authors provides fast access to biographical, bibliographic, and critical information on the most well-known authors from ancient times to the present. More than 400 writers from all over the world have been included in the database. This version of *DISCovering Authors* includes biographies and criticism of more than 70 Canadian authors. In addition, 250-plus portraits are included.

Each entry in the biography section provides an introduction to the author; a portrait (if available); a full-text biography (usually approximately 1,000 words); personal background data including family, education, awards received, and so forth; a bibliography of the author's work; any media adaptations of the author's works (i.e., movies, television programs, books on tape); and any additional sources of information. In addition, there is a criticism section that consists of selected critical essays on the author's best-known works. These criticism entries supply subject headings that make it possible to search them and the bibliographic citation indicating the source. Additional features of the CD-ROM include a copy of the 10th edition of *Merriam-Webster's Collegiate Dictionary*, a glossary of literary terms, research paper topics, a timeline of literary and world events, and something called a "notepad editor" that allows the user to personalize the search to some extent. Much of the information included on this CD-ROM has been obtained from the Gale literary and biography series entitled Contemporary Authors, Contemporary Literary Criticism, Twentieth-Century Literary Criticism, the Dictionary of Literary Biography, Black Literature and Criticism, and others. The publisher contends that this information has been updated and corrected when necessary, but it appears that much of the material has been entered as it was in the original Gale publications.

The database is easily set up and used. It is possible to use it on local area networks with multiple users or as a stand-alone system. Search times are quick, and the printing setup is adequate. (The number of pages printed in one search session can be limited when the program is set up.) This disc is recommended for larger public and academic libraries (especially ones in Canada), and for libraries that do not already own many of the Gale biographical publications that provide the basic information. It is not recommended for smaller public and academic libraries because of the cost.—**Robert L. Wick**

499. **DISCovering Authors: Biographies & Criticism on 300 Most-Studied Writers**. [CD-ROM]. Detroit, Gale, 1993. Hardware requirements: IBM XT, AT, PS/2, or compatible; MS-DOS or PC-DOS 3.1 or higher; MSCDEX version 2.0 or higher; 640K RAM; hard disk drive with 1M free space or floppy diskette. $500.00. ISBN 0-8103-5057-2.

From Aristophanes and Maya Angelou to Paul Zindel and Emile Zola, *DISCovering Authors* is an excellent resource for almost any library. This CD-ROM version of selections from the Gale series includes a wide range of authors from a variety of cultures, genres, and time periods selected by a committee of librarians, teachers, and editors. Each entry generally includes four to seven excerpted essays from other Gale series. The search menus are very easy to use, and the commands are standard mnemonics or very intuitive. The full citation can be printed, or any portion of the text may be selected to be printed or saved to disk.

One of the particularly nice features of this CD-ROM, in addition to the fact that it is extremely user-friendly, is the ability to search the personal data on authors in any field contained in the record, including dates, nationality, politics, religion, avocational interests, genre, and even media adaptations (thus identifying writers for students to contrast or compare). When searching the "Personal Data on Authors," a function key will display a list of words or phrases that may be searched, allowing any number of these to be selected and linked by Boolean operators, even using truncation and proximity operators. First-time users like the clear screens, easy scrolling and selection, abundant function keys, main menu toggle, and on-screen help. The disc is accompanied by a concise reference guide with easy-to-follow directions for installation and configuration, full search directions, a complete index, and a laminated help card. Of particular value in instructional planning is the appendix, which lists all the subject terms and cross-references used, such as "African-American Life and Thought," "Class Structure," "Fatalism," "Individual and Society," "Materialism," "Rebellion," and "War." Users want more authors included and ask when other authors would be available.

Gale has addressed the only criticism of the reference guide by shipping all new products with a printed list of authors covered on the disc. The toll-free technical support number is either staffed or a call is returned promptly. The disc is reasonably priced for a stand-alone station, and there is a sliding price scale for network versions for up to eight simultaneous users. All Gale products are available for a 30- or 60-day trial period. The release of a Macintosh version has been announced. [R: Choice, Nov 93, p. 442; LAR, Sept 93, p. 517; RBB, 1 May 93, pp. 1616-18; RQ, Summer 93, pp. 557-58; SLJ, May 93, p. 46]—**Betty Bankhead**

500. **DISCovering Authors Modules**. [CD-ROM]. Detroit, Gale, 1996. Minimum system requirements: IBM or compatible 286 (386 or higher recommended). ISO 9660-compatible CD-ROM drive with cables, interface card, and MS-DOS CD-ROM Extensions 2.1 (double-speed or faster drive recommended). MS-DOS 3.3. 640K RAM. 10MB hard disk space. VGA monitor and graphics card. Mouse (optional). $600 (first module); $300 (each additional module). ISBN 0-8103-5104-8.

This revised and expanded CD-ROM offers much of the same kind of information found in many of Gale's printed literary criticism sources. Each entry gives an overview of the author's work, biographical and bibliographical information, excerpts from one or more critical sources, sources of additional information, and suggested paper topics. Some entries also include a portrait of the author. Purchasers can choose to install any combination of six modules provided: Most-Studied Authors,

Multicultural Authors, Dramatists, Novelists, Poets, and Popular and Genre Authors. The entire set covers more than 1,200 authors, with many authors appearing in more than 1 module. In comparison, version 1.0 covered only 302 of the most-studied authors (see ARBA 94, entry 1146). As noted in that review, the disc is easily installed and features attractive screen designs and easy-to-use navigation through a series of on-screen menus and clearly labeled buttons on the screen. An inexperienced user should be able to find information easily, although some of the more sophisticated features, such as the use of Boolean operators, will probably require instruction.

It is unfortunate, however, that such an attractive product has several serious flaws. As with any such tool, one might question the criteria for inclusion or exclusion, but the absence of such classic authors as James Fenimore Cooper and Jules Verne stands out. There are more serious problems, however, some of which might be attributable to the search software and some to editorial control. In many cases, the user is led to marginal or totally irrelevant material. For example, clicking on either "Afghanistan" or "Khyber Pass" as a subject leads the user to Jay McInerney's *Bright Lights, Big City*, a novel about New York City. If one reads the entire entry for McInerney, Afghanistan is briefly mentioned in a discussion of another of his books, *Ransom.* A search for "Jondalar," a character in the novels of Jean Auel, yields four titles under her name, none of which were actually written by her. However, clicking on any one of those titles does take the user to Auel's entry. A search on "pilot" in the career category yields, among other names, that of Thomas Tryon, the actor turned author. Examination of his entry shows that he once appeared in "Moon Pilot." While perhaps technically correct, this sort of result is misleading and would be confusing to someone who may be legitimately expecting to find references to authors who also had the occupation of pilot. Use of the character list is made more difficult by the apparent editorial choice not to standardize entries. Therefore, a character search for "Dracula" does not retrieve the classic Bram Stoker novel. To find that, one must enter "Count Dracula." Similarly, there are two formats for most personal titles: "Dr." and "Doctor," "Sgt." and "Sergeant," "Rev." and "Reverend." Editorial control seems to have been lax in general. Misspellings and typographic errors can be found throughout, including errors such as stating that Alexandre Dumaspere (1802-1870) worked as a librarian for the Duc d'Orleans from 1923 to 1930.

Such sloppiness is unacceptable and unexpected from such a company as Gale. It is a shame that such a promising, potentially useful product is so flawed. Libraries contemplating purchase should take full advantage of the 45-day trial period in order to assess these problems in light of their specific situations and user communities. [R: RBB, 15 May 96, p. 1606; VOYA, Dec 96, p. 296]—**Barbara E. Kemp**

501. **Eighteenth-Century British and American Rhetorics and Rhetoricians: Critical Studies and Sources**. Michael G. Moran, ed. Westport, Conn., Greenwood Press, 1994. 318p. index. $85.00. PE1405.G7E43.808'.0017'041. LC 93-35838. ISBN 0-313-27909-8.

The theories of and biographical facts about 33 eighteenth-century rhetoricians make this volume both an introduction to the field and a handy reference for serious scholars of rhetoric. The title is slightly misleading: Most of the subjects are British. While there are three influential French writers (one from the seventeenth century) listed, only two rhetoricians are American: John Witherspoon, born and educated in Scotland, and Noah Webster, primarily a lexicographer and educator. Strangely, English lexicographer Samuel Johnson was omitted. Two women are included, although Margaret Askew Fell, who died in 1702, did her writing in the seventeenth century, and both she and Mary Wollstonecraft are more concerned with the right of women to speak than with formal theory.

The general introduction divides the theories of the rhetoricians into six classifications—neoclassical, stylistic, elocutionary, belletristic, psychological-philosophical, and women's rhetoric—recognizing that there is often an overlap. The major section of the book lists each rhetorician alphabetically, giving for each a brief biography and a description of rhetorical theory (the two longest, John Locke and Robert Watson, are about 14 pages in length). Each concludes with a bibliography of primary sources, biographies, critical studies, and secondary sources. There is a lengthy general bibliography divided into such topics as elocutionary movement, influence of rhetoric on education, rhetoric and other disciplines, and social contexts of rhetorical theory. The index is detailed. Information about the editor and each of the 32 contributors is provided at the end. This volume should prove useful to students of rhetoric and experts in the field.—**Charlotte Lindgren**

502. **The Encyclopedia of Language and Linguistics**. R. E. Asher, ed. Tarrytown, N.Y., Pergamon Press, 1994. 10v. illus. maps. index. $2,975.00/set. P29.E48. 403. LC 93-37778. ISBN 0-08-035943-4.

The Encyclopedia of Language and Linguistics (*ELL*) is the most comprehensive and ambitious work of its kind ever produced. While there are several fine, one- to four-volume dictionaries and encyclopedias in the discipline available (e.g., *International Encyclopedia of Linguistics* [see ARBA 93, entry 1050]), this monumental work contains more than 2,000 articles totaling more than 5 million words, by more than 1,000 contributing editors representing 75 countries. *ELL* succeeds in covering every imaginable topic in linguistics and related subject areas. It also succeeds in meeting its aim of being authoritative, up-to-date, comprehensive, and international in scope. All 34 members of the editorial board acted as subject editors; some of the celebrated members of the honorary editorial board are Noam Chomsky, Dwight Bolinger, John Lyons, and M. A. K. Halliday.

Although the editorial board is largely from the United Kingdom, the house style follows the American standard in respect to spelling, using Merriam-Webster dictionaries.

The set is almost 6,000 pages long. The large-format pages are generously laid out with two columns of text and illustrated in black-and-white, including diagrams of grammatical trees, photographs, maps, and other drawings. The alphabetical entries have cross-referencing and individual bibliographies. In addition to the extensive glossary of more than 3,000 definitions and a comprehensive three-level subject index, there are also name and contributor indexes. Finally, a thematic guide is provided, further facilitating access to the large range of subject areas.

While the work is intended for the greater academic community, it would be quite useful to readers who know little about the discipline. The articles are mostly signed—the exception being only the very short articles—and vary in length from a few sentences to more than 10, two-column pages. The coverage includes linguistics (e.g., foundations, history, current theories, research developments), interdisciplinary applications of linguistics and language studies (e.g., anthropology, religion, philosophy, psychology, sociology, media, topics in applied linguistics), and global communication, including writing systems. In addition to the expected general topics of linguistics and language studies, such as semantics (150-plus articles), syntax (130-plus articles), phonology (70-plus articles), morphology (50-plus articles), and pragmatics (100-plus articles), other topics include languages by geographic region or country, translation (20-plus articles), speech technology (20-plus articles), lexicography (40-plus articles), and sign language (19 articles). Of special note are the signed biographies (740-plus articles) on leading world figures in language studies and linguistics, complete with bibliographies. The area of history of linguistics covers Painian linguistics through the work of the Neogrammarians to Chomskyan linguistics and beyond. The study of language, so often controversial in opposing theories, is presented from various approaches in an objective and informed manner, avoiding polemics.

A random check of topics in the index produced entries for such diverse languages as Estonian, Malayaiam, Navajo, Quechua, Samoan, Tibetan, Totonac, Urdu, and Yoruba. There are three entries for machines translation, covering general principles and historical aspects in Europe and North America. Among the useful features of particular interest are the full list of languages of the world with variant names, an extensive list of abbreviations, and a long list of major language and linguistic journals.

This work will become the reference of choice for meeting the needs of a wide range of users, including specialized researchers and instructors as well as students of language studies and linguistics. This magnificent set fills a long-standing void in reference collections. Enthusiastically recommended for all academic and large public libraries. [R: Choice, June 94, p. 1552; WLB, June 94, p. 94]—**Edward Erazo**

503. **Encyclopedia of Transcendentalism**. Wesley T. Mott, ed. Westport, Conn., Greenwood Press, 1996. 280p. index. $75.00. ISBN 0-313-29924-2.

Seventy contributors have written 145 alphabetically arranged entries covering the major philosophical concepts, themes, genres, periodicals, organizations, and places associated with transcendentalism, especially the New England Renaissance between 1830 and the Civil War. European and Asian influences are also included, from classical names (e.g., Plutarch, Plato, and Virgil) and the Hindu Bhagavadgita to Emanuel Swedenborg, Benedict de Spinoza, Jean-Jacques Rousseau, and even such remote connections as William Shakespeare and John Milton. There is an extremely useful 15-page chronology from the birth of Ralph Waldo Emerson in 1803 up to 1917.

The volume is a companion to the *Biographical Dictionary of Transcendentalism* (see entry 484), which gives brief biographies of major figures associated with the movement. References to these are marked by a double asterisk; cross-references within the volume at hand are indicated by a single asterisk. The encyclopedia discusses the major movements of the times from abolitionism to Unitarianism, places from Brook Farm to Walden Woods, and journals from the *Atlantic Monthly* to the *Western Messenger.* It gives a coherent definition of transcendentalism, an elusive concept.

Each entry is followed by a list of references. In addition, the volume has a five-page, up-to-date bibliography of important book-length studies of the transcendental movement organized by areas of interest, such as literature, theology, nature, reform, and transcendental periodicals. An index and a list of contributors complete this volume, which is an essential reference for anyone interested in nineteenth-century American thought.—**Charlotte Lindgren**

504.	**Feminist Writers**. Pamela Kester-Shelton, ed. Detroit, St. James Press, 1996. 641p. index. $130.00. ISBN 1-55862-217-9.

Bio-bibliographic encyclopedias of women writers are today in fortunate abundance. Kester-Shelton's compilation strives for uniqueness by focusing on female (and a few male) writers of fiction, poetry, nonfiction, and journalism who espouse a "feminist viewpoint." Although most of its 290 entrants have written in the twentieth century, pertinent figures from all periods (e.g., Aphra Behn, Mary Wollstonecraft, Susan B. Anthony) are included, as are non-English-language writers if their works are available in English. Entries contain biographical facts, a list of publications by genre, a selection of critical studies, and a critical essay signed by one of a lengthy list of mostly academic scholars. Helpful are indexes by nationality of author, by subject/genre, and by titles mentioned in entries; lists of additional print and other resources, including electronic ones, are also useful. Hortense Spillers's foreword, "Feminist Writings: At Century's End," is aimed at aficionadas/os rather than the students and general public the editor claims as the book's intended audience.

A related work, *The Feminist Companion to Literature in English* (see ARBA 92, entry 1095), contains more than 2,700 entries, including many of the names found in the present volume. Disadvantages of the earlier title are briefer coverage and emphasis on British and Commonwealth women. Also, *Feminist Writers* includes writers of very current interest—such as Barbara Ehrenreich, Susan Faludi, or Camille Paglia—not found in the *Companion.* At less than one-half the cost, however, the earlier work may suffice for many libraries; those that can pay this volume's hefty price will find it a useful supplement.—**Willa Schmidt**

505.	Fenton, Jill Rubinson, and others. **Women Writers: From Page to Screen**. New York, Garland, 1990. 483p. index. (Garland Reference Library of the Humanities, v.687). $45.00. PN1997.85.W58.016. 79143'75'082. LC 89-23479. ISBN 0-8240-8529-9.

Fenton and her co-authors survey the novels, plays, and short stories of over 800 English and American female authors whose writings have been adapted into theatrical and television motion pictures. Spanning over 75 years of cinema history, some 2,200 film titles are offered that cover everything from 4-reel silent films released in 1913 to television movies produced as late as 1988.

Arranged alphabetically by author, each entry supplies the title and type of literary work and the title, production company, and date of the film. Numerous cross-references link pseudonyms, and all collaborating authors are credited, with female authors receiving separate entries. Indexes to film titles and literary sources further enhance the reference value of this work. Also supplied is a 116-item bibliography of film and literary sources consulted in the compilation of this catalog. Included is A. G. S. Enser's highly regarded *Filmed Books and Plays* (see ARBA 86, entry 1075), which this work expands and complements.

In the preface (which through an apparent printer's error ends abruptly) Fenton notes that the materials produced by these women "offer interesting insights into the values and dreams of their times" (p.ix). This observation rightfully implies that where an author was born and the time period in which she wrote had a direct influence on her writing. Yet Fenton offers no biographical information on these women. This could easily have been confined to noting the author's country of origin, and birth and death dates. Even the inclusion of this minimal information would have expanded the book beyond merely being an impressive list of literary-to-film adaptations. Recommended for college and university libraries supporting collections in women's history, literary history, and film.—**David K. Frasier**

506. **Great Women Writers: The Lives and Works of 135 of the World's Most Important Women Writers**. . . . Frank N. Magill, ed. New York, Henry Holt, 1994. 611p. index. $40.00. PN471.G74. 809'.89287. LC 93-47648. ISBN 0-8050-2932-X.

This new bio-bibliography from Magill is an alphabetical listing of 135 women authors, including principal works, achievements, biographical details, analyses of major works, and short, selective bibliographies. A brief, generic essay on women writers serves as an introduction.

As do many of Magill's reference books, this one promises more than it delivers. The book is much more limited than the subtitle suggests. Although not acknowledged in the title or introduction, all the authors are fiction writers, poets, or dramatists; writers in other genres are ignored. Of the 135 authors presented, 109 are either U.S., British, or Canadian, and only 5 are not Western; 110 are from the twentieth century. As just one example of the book's limited scope, the only Japanese author represented is Murasaki Shikibu, the eleventh-century novelist and poet. Despite the focus, many important Western authors are excluded. Aphra Behn, although cited in the introduction, is not listed in the text.

Perhaps the best that can be said of *Great Women Writers* is that it is a good, although limited, introductory reference source. It would be a justifiable purchase for school or public libraries with little else in the area, or for academic libraries beginning to build a collection in women's studies. [R: BR, Nov/Dec 94, p. 58; Choice, Nov. 94, p. 428; RBB, 1 Sept 94, p. 70; SLJ, Dec 94, p.146; WLB, Nov 94, pp. 91-92]—**Susan Davis Herring**

507. **Great Writers of the English Language**. New York, Marshall Cavendish, 1989. 14v. illus. index. $399.95/set. PR85.G66. 820'.9. LC 88-21077. ISBN 1-85435-000-5.

According to writer and literary critic Anthony Burgess, the criterion for inclusion in this lavishly illustrated 14-volume series is that a writer's works "are enjoyable." While this sole measure is subjective, the 56 authors chosen are still revered as great writers in their native tongue. Literary critics might suggest James Fenimore Cooper and Washington Irving as enjoyable writers whose works typify "the frontier, the pioneer spirit and the democratic outlook" instead of Walt Whitman and his *Leaves of Grass.* They might also question the absence of James Joyce and W. B. Yeats as examples of the modern period. Yet the omission of these authors does not seriously mar an excellent series.

The set consists of 13 volumes of text and a 4-part index volume encompassing separate lists of writers, titles, and subjects, and a literary-terms glossary. Each volume, with the exceptions of volumes 3 and 13, presents 4 authors arranged within a chronological or thematic framework. For example, volume 1, *Early English Writers,* provides information about William Shakespeare, John Bunyan, Samuel Pepys, and Henry Fielding. Volume 2, *Exotic Journeys*, contains information about Charles Darwin, Herman Melville, Joseph Conrad, and E. M. Forster. Volume 3, one of the unusual volumes, is devoted to only two authors, Charles Dickens and Thomas Hardy, because of the quantity and literary significance of their work. The other unusual volume, *The Great Poets* (volume 13), profiles 11 poets within thematic groups, such as the Romantic poets—William Wordsworth, Samuel Coleridge, Lord Byron, Percy Shelley, and John Keats—and the War poets— Robert Brooke, Siegfried Sassoon, Wilfred Owen, and Isaac Rosenberg. Every volume has a table of contents, a bibliography that includes recommended histories and biographies, and an index.

Each chapter about a writer is divided into four sections arranged for the perspective they provide about the author's life and work. The 1st section furnishes biographical facts about an author emphasizing major events that influenced his or her works. The 2nd section presents a summary of one of the writer's major works, providing annotated descriptions of characters and an analysis of the literary themes and issues that made it a classic. In the same section is a discussion of the themes and significance of the writer's other works and literary accomplishments. The 3rd section explores the literary devices and themes involved in the creation of that particular genre of literature. The last section conveys through writing and illustration various contemporary events (e.g., war or the industrial revolution) that were influential in a writer's life.

The distinctive feature of this useful series is the illustrations. Starting with a full-page portrait of each writer, the corresponding chapter contains between 40 and 50 reproductions of paintings, photographs, posters, and character sketches designed to evoke the social life and customs, political events, and environment that influenced the writer's works. The illustrations help illuminate the sources of characters, images, and narration. They reanimate the sights, smells, and tastes of an era and provide the reader with an instant comprehension of the desolate beauty of a wild moor or "Egdon Heath."

Unfortunately, *Great Writers of the English Language* cannot substitute for the H. W. Wilson or Gale Literary Criticism series. Because of the small amount of text vis-à-vis the illustrations, this series should be considered a supplementary one for high school libraries. It will definitely be used for term papers and could be used as a complementary source when book-talking the classics. The price for this set makes it a reasonable additional purchase. [R: Choice, July/Aug 90, p. 1805; RBB, 15 Feb 90, p. 1186]—**Kathleen W. Craver**

508. Legat, Michael. **The Illustrated Dictionary of Western Literature**. New York, Continuum, 1987. 352p. illus. (part col.). $29.50. LC 87-19991. ISBN 0-8264-0393-X.

For the purposes of this nicely illustrated literary dictionary, "Western" includes writers from every continent and almost every country with the exception of the Middle East and Far East. Thus, Russian writers are included, as are African, Latin American, American, and European writers. As would be expected, the 2,000 entries in the dictionary are arranged alphabetically. Length of the articles varies from one sentence to up to one page. Most entries cover authors and specific works; movements and literary terms are covered only minimally. There are two appendices: the first provides examples of various kinds of verse, such as heroic verse, sonnets, and lyrics; the second is a list of authors included in the dictionary, arranged chronologically by birth date. While some biographical entries are quite lengthy, most are short, listing major works and dates, and neglecting any comment on literary style, importance, or themes. There are almost no additional references or cross-references to other entries. In addition to the lack of cross-references, terms appear in some definitions which should be defined elsewhere but are not. For example, Kingsley Amis is defined as one of the "angry young men" and Roland Barthes is described as a "leading member of the Structuralist movement." Neither *angry young men* nor *Structuralist* is defined in the dictionary, and an interested reader would be forced to find the definition in a more comprehensive work. Although the book is nicely illustrated, on at least one occasion (a painting of D. H. Lawrence) the author has failed to credit the artist (whose name does, however, appear in the painting itself). This dictionary will be of greatest interest to general readers and beginning students of literature, but will not replace standard literary dictionaries or encyclopedias. [R: RBB, 1 Apr 88, p. 1322]—**Jean M. Parker**

509. **Literary Exile in the Twentieth Century: An Analysis and Biographical Dictionary**. Martin Tucker, ed. Westport, Conn., Greenwood Press, 1991. 834p. index. $99.30. PN493.L43. 809'.8920694. LC 89-23920. ISBN 0-313-23870-7.

Tucker defines literary exile as "the experience of rejection from one's native land" (p.xiv). With only a few exceptions it means physically or psychologically leaving one's native land, either by deportation, banishment, voluntary flight, or psychic distancing.

Following a lengthy introduction is a section of 19 group entries that focus on such topics as American expatriates in Europe, francophone African writers, holocaust writing, and gay and lesbian writers. Primarily the contributions of other scholars, these articles vary widely in content, approach, and length. American expatriates are discussed in two paragraphs, the second composed mostly of names. Hungarian writers are listed alphabetically and briefly identified. However, three pages of analysis are devoted to Armenian writers and almost six to Iranian writers.

The body of the work consists of some 330 biographical articles on individual writers. Articles are signed; those unsigned are by Tucker, a scholar, writer, and literary editor. Depending on length, the articles also analyze and critically assess the writer's work; again, the treatment varies. Penny Lernoux receives 10 lines; Thomas Mann gets 7 pages. Some authors, such as Else Lasker-Schuler, are discussed by more than one contributor. Most articles conclude with a list of selected titles and some critical references.

A separate appendix lists rather sketchily, by geographic region, major twentieth-century historical events that influenced writers. Other appendixes list by country the places from which writers were exiled and the places that gave haven. Another enables the user to identify writers by category (e.g., those exiled for political reasons). A general bibliography directs the reader to additional scholarly sources, most published within the last 30 years, some as recently as 1990.

Overall, the work provides representative coverage worldwide for twentieth-century writers, including many contemporary authors. Although the treatment is uneven and sometimes inconsistent, Tucker's achievement is remarkable both in its range and its geographic scope. Scholarly in tone and execution, its riches are quite accessible to serious students of the subject. [R: Choice, Oct 91, p. 262; RBB, 13 Oct 91, pp. 464-66]—**Bernice Bergup**

510. **Magill's Survey of World Literature**. Frank N. Magill, ed. North Bellmore, N.Y., Marshall Cavendish, 1995. 2v. illus. index. $134.95/set. ISBN 0-7614-0104-0.

It is wonderful to meet an old friend in the reference book world, and this two-volume supplement to the six-volume 1993 set of *Magill's Survey of World Literature* (see ARBA 94, entry 1158) is indeed such a friend. How one remembers discovering the treasures hidden in these works when trying to write school research papers or critical papers—Magill's always reaffirmed one's assessments. In the 6-volume set, some 215 of the world's writers were initially written about; this 2-volume supplement updates and extends that original by some "seventy-nine contemporary or hitherto neglected writers who have had a substantial effect on the evolution of world literature." All varieties of literature are included: fiction, nonfiction, poetry, drama, and short stories. Many postcolonial writers are treated as well.

Biographical sketches are presented, followed by an analysis of the author's themes, styles, and other characteristics. A bibliography is attached to each entry as well, providing lists of further reading for the serious researcher. Full-page photographs are given, and this set, as the others, is designated for middle school and high school libraries, although college and university undergraduates will find the information both current and useful for their own research.

Each work is "boxed" and set off, so that researchers can easily locate the work they are searching for under each author's listing. Not all of the entries are contemporary: One finds Sappho with David Storey, and Hans Christian Andersen with Kobo Abe, or Aphra Behn with Brendan Behan, and Anita Desai with Isak Dinesen. This is a solid general reference work to major world literature authors, and one that will be welcomed.—**Anne F. Roberts**

511. **Major 20th-Century Writers: A Selection of Sketches from** *Contemporary Authors*. Bryan Ryan, ed. Detroit, Gale, 1991. 4v. index. $293.00/set. LC 90-84380. ISBN 0-8103-7766-7.

This encyclopedia could also have been titled "The Concise Contemporary Authors," as it contains over 1,000 biographical essays culled from that series. The editors have been selective in choosing which writers to include. Among the authors chosen are well-known and established twentieth-century novelists and short story writers, dramatists, poets, essayists, and philosophers. As with the parent series, entries are arranged alphabetically and contain biographical information that includes family, address, career highlights, memberships, awards and honors, a bibliography of primary works, a biocritical essay, and sources for additional reading. Only a few entries are signed, although all the entries in *Contemporary Authors* (*CA*) are. Each appears to contain the same information as in the *CA* essays, with slight changes in format. Some have been revised to include new information and dates. The set concludes with two indexes: nationality and genre/subject. The straightforward arrangement and concise entries make this a useful and accessible literary reference source for small and medium-sized libraries not subscribing to the series. [R: Choice, May 91, p. 1462; LJ, 1 Feb 91, pp. 72-74; RBB, 13 Mar 91, p. 1323; WLB, Mar 91, p. 129]—**Jean M. Parker**

512. **Medieval Women Writers**. Katharina M. Wilson, ed. Athens, University of Georgia Press, 1984. 366p. $30.00; $12.50pa. LC 82-13380. ISBN 0-8203-0640-1; 0-8203-0641-Xpa.

Researching women writers from the Middle Ages is no simple task. However, with the publication of this critical anthology, and a few scattered articles and similar anthologies, women writers from the Middle Ages are becoming more accessible to the interested student and scholar.

This volume covers fifteen women writers from seven centuries and many nationalities. The writers included are Dhuoda, Hrotsvit of Gandersheim, Marie de France, Heloise, Hildegard of Bingen, Castelloza, Mechthild of Magdeburg, Hadewijch, Marguerite Porete, Saint Bridget, Saint Catherine of Siena, Julian of Norwich, Margery Kempe, Florencia Pinar, and Christine de Pizan. The editor provides the historical context from which the "religious, didactic, and visionary genres" of the women writers come. Each of the fifteen chapters is written by a different noted literary or historical scholar. Biographical and critical material, selections of the women's works in translation, and bibliographies are included for each writer. The anthology is extremely valuable because it introduces some outstanding, but obscure, women writers of the Middle Ages, providing an in-depth understanding of the literary achievements of both religious and secular women writers. [R: LJ, Jan 84, p. 94]—**Maureen Pastine**

513. **Modern Women Writers**. Lillian S. Robinson, comp. and ed. New York, Continuum Publishing, 1996. 4v. index. (A Library of Literary Criticism). $95.00/v; $285.00/set. ISBN 0-8264-0813-3 (v.1); 0-8264-0814-1 (v.2); 0-8264-0815-X (v.3); 0-8264-0920-2 (v.4); 0-8264-0823-0 (set).

Eight years in the making, and a part of Continuum Publishing's Library of Literary Criticism series, *Modern Women Writers* (*MWW*) provides excerpts of criticism on writers of the twentieth century. The writers profiled are all women, although the slant of their work need not be feminist; the author must have attracted some critical attention to be discussed. For those women who have been included in previous volumes or sets of the series, the same critical excerpts may be employed, with new criticism as available.

Entries consist of anywhere from 2 to 10 excerpts of criticism concerning the author under discussion. Criticism can be either positive or negative as long as it reflects an important aspect of the individual writer's oeuvre. No biographical information is supplied, as that is not the intent of this work, but such data can be found in other sources (e.g., certain volumes of the Dictionary of Literary Biography series). Each excerpt lists an author; the source of the critical assessment (whether book or journal); and other bibliographic information, such as publisher, issue, and page number, where pertinent. A few typographical errors turn up, but one must wonder if these are present in the original critical essay or a result of the current editing. The particular strength of *MWW* is its value for students, who may need a starting point for researching critical responses to certain writers.

A list of authors covered in the set (complete with country/ethnic designations) precedes the main text. Volume 1 expands this list to cover all 4 volumes; the other volumes only list those writers appearing in that particular text. An acknowledgments document (in place of a bibliography) appears at the end of volume 4, as does an index to critics. The critics index furnishes information on which author(s) the critic wrote about, the volume number, and the page number. Many critics are famous writers in their own right (and many are profiled in this set): Margaret Atwood, Louis Auchincloss, James Baldwin, Willa Cather, W. E. B. DuBois, T. S. Eliot, Langston Hughes, Bobbie Ann Mason, V. S. Naipaul, Joyce Carol Oates, Philip Roth, Susan Sontag, Amy Tan, Gore Vidal, and Eudora Welty are but a few examples. Despite the usefulness of the lists of authors covered and the critics index, one misses the "authors as critics" index present in *Modern Black Writers* (see ARBA 96, entry 1157).

In comparing *MWW* with two other works on women writers—*Masterplots II: Women's Literature Series* (see ARBA 96, entry 949) and *Third World Women's Literatures* (see ARBA 96, entry 946)—some interesting points emerge. More than 15 percent of the entries in *MWW* are found in *Third World,* indicating the editor's effort to encompass post-colonial writers. *MWW* covers women from Leila Abouzeid to Nikki Giovanni, Oba Minako to Mayy Ziyadah. Approximately 25 percent of the writers are also profiled in *Masterplots,* which has a much greater scope time-wise. However, those twentieth-century authors appearing in *Masterplots* but not in *MWW* are easily justified omissions in most cases. Sandra Gilbert, Susan Gubar, Juliet Mitchell, Elaine Showalter—all stray from the primarily fiction focus of the work under review. For Laura Esquivel, Susan Howe, Barbara Kingsolver, Terry McMillan, Ayn Rand, and Jade Snow Wong, one could say that there is not a strong enough critical base from which to pull excerpts (although this seems somewhat suspect in a few instances).

In conclusion, even those libraries already possessing the *Masterplots* volumes should purchase *MWW*. Its focus on contemporary writers, its accessible format, and its truly global approach make the set a valuable acquisition for public and academic libraries alike. [R: LJ, 15 May 96, p. 54; RBB, 1 Nov 96, pp. 538-39]—**Melissa Rae Root**

514.   **Nobel Laureates in Literature: A Biographical Dictionary**. Rado Pribic, ed. New York, Garland, 1990. 473p. index. (Garland Reference Library of the Humanities, v.849). $75.00. PN452.P7.809'.04. LC 89-11803. ISBN 0-8240-5741-4.

This work contains an interesting biographical sketch of Alfred Nobel and the Nobel Foundation, with emphasis on the development of the Nobel Prize in Literature. It is followed by a chronology of award winners, a list of contributors to this volume, and an alphabetical presentation of essays on each laureate. Although the essays vary greatly in length, each contains a useful selected bibliography of primary and secondary sources.

This work covers much of the same ground as many other publications, notably *Nobel Prize Winners* (see ARBA 88, entry 32), *Who's Who of Nobel Prize Winners* (see ARBA 88, entry 33), and the more extensive *Nobel Prize Winners: Literature* (see ARBA 89, entry 988). Garland's promotional literature claims that its series "takes the middle ground between exhaustive tomes and sketchy biographical dictionaries." While Garland has certainly provided an easy-to-digest biography, this ground has already been well covered not only in similar works but also in many standard biographical dictionaries and directories. This book presents a useful and interesting, but not essential, addition to research tools in this well-documented subject. [R: Choice, June 90, p. 1660; LJ, 1 Mar 90, p. 88; RBB, 1 May 90, p. 1749]—**Elizabeth Patterson**

515.   **The Nobel Prize Winners: Literature**. Frank N. Magill, ed. Englewood Cliffs, N.J., Salem Press, 1987. 3v. illus. index. $210.00/set. LC 88-6469. ISBN 0-89356-541-5.

This set is the first in a projected series about Nobel laureates in all areas, so subsequent volumes will cover peace, physics, chemistry, physiology or medicine, and economics. Volume 1 of this set begins with an interpretive essay tracing the sometimes quite controversial history of the Nobel Prize for Literature, first awarded in 1901. A table is also provided listing the winners' names, dates of birth, death, and award years, as well as the nationalities and literary genres for which the laureates are best known. Most of the rest of the set is then devoted to separate essays in chronological order on each laureate through Joseph Brodsky, the winner in 1987. Preceding each article is a photograph of the laureate. The articles, each about 3,500 words long, are arranged in a standard format. To facilitate ready-reference, at the head of each article are the winner's name, place and date of birth and death, language(s) in which he or she wrote, and major genres. A brief one- or two-sentence summary of why the laureate won the prize is given in italics (in words taken from the official citation). The text of each article then covers (1) a synopsis of the points made by the presenter of the award and a summary of the laureate's Nobel lecture or acceptance speech (including Jean Paul Sartre's letter explaining his refusal of the award); (2) a survey of international reactions to the choice; (3) a brief biography; (4) a review of the laureate's major works; and (5) a list, by genre, of principal works by the laureate, as well as some significant critical works about him or her. A separate author/title index allows readers to locate laureates by country and genre, and each volume begins with a complete alphabetical list of the laureates.

This set will be very useful to students tracing patterns among various laureates. It will also be valuable for information about now-obscure laureates. Readers just seeking information about well-known winners, such as Kipling or Faulkner, do not, of course, need this set, since so many other sources provide that information in greater depth. But readers wanting to know why these writers won the Nobel Prize, or who need information about less well-known writers—such as Sully Prudhomme and Vernervon Heidenstam—will welcome this set.

Readers interested in sources devoted to all of the Nobel winners may want to consult the following: *Nobel Prize Winners: An H. W. Wilson Biographical Dictionary* (see ARBA 88, entry 32) and *The Who's Who of Nobel Prize Winners* (see ARBA 88, entry 33). [R: RBB, 15 Nov 88, p. 555]—**David Isaacson**

516.   **A Reader's Guide to Twentieth-Century Writers**. Peter Parker and Frank Kermode, eds. New York, Oxford University Press, 1996. 825p. $35.00. ISBN 0-19-521215-0.

Poignant, intriguing snippets fill this volume on twentieth-century writers, a companion text to *A Reader's Guide to the Twentieth-Century Novel,* published in 1995 and produced by the same editorial team. Those profiled are all English-language writers, predominantly from the United States and Great Britain; but some authors from Australia, India, the Caribbean, and other locales are also treated. Novelists, poets, playwrights (less fully covered because of the nature of their genre), and short story writers are all discussed in this educational and entertaining book. Select crime and mystery writers have earned a place in the text; solely nonfiction writers are not included.

The writers are listed alphabetically by the name under which they wrote. The entries provide biographical details as well as a critical assessment. Following an entry, which is usually a column and a half in length, is a bibliography of works by that writer, broken down by genre. A biographical work about that author is commonly provided as well. The entries consist of minutiae not always found in a scholarly work. Biographical details range from the mundane to the oftentimes bizarre. Much of the information is interesting, but some is questionable (e.g., do readers really want to know about Joseph Conrad developing an anal abscess?). The writing is sometimes a bit convoluted; for example, the entry for Ernest Hemingway states, "While in war hospital, he conceived the passion . . .," and later, "He contrived to become involved . . ." (p.324).

Despite these criticisms, the work is recommended for most libraries. The entries entice the user to want to learn more, and the bibliographies and biographies help with that goal. A bibliography of works about the authors in question would have served the public even better, but for ascertaining quick biographical and critical data, this volume serves its audience well. [R: RBB, 1 Sept 96, pp. 170-71; SLJ, Aug 96, p. 183]—**Melissa Rae Root**

517.   **Reference Guide to World Literature**. 2d ed. Lesley Henderson and Sarah M. Hall, eds. Detroit, St. James Press, 1995. 2v. index. $260.00/set. ISBN 1-55862-332-9.

First published as *Great Foreign Language Writers* (see ARBA 86, entry 1088), this 2d edition increases coverage from 253 to 490 writers. The historical range covers ancient Greece through the present day, although living authors are few and far between, as 350 living writers are discussed in a similar publication, *Contemporary World Writers* (see ARBA 94, entry 1144). This reference begins with an editors' note, followed by a lengthy contributor's list, and lists of writers and works treated in the two-volume set—in both alphabetic and chronological order. Entries on authors include biographical information, primary works, awards and honors, a critical overview, and bibliographies. The works discussed run the gamut from novels, short stories, poems, and plays to television and radio scripts, essays, travel writing, memoirs, letters, and theoretical works. Anonymous writings, such as the epic of Gilgamesh, and collaborations, such as the Bible, are also given entries. No American or British writers are profiled here.

As stated in the review of the initial edition, the critical overviews consist of only one or two pages and only serve as introductory assessments (indeed, as much information can be found in any Norton anthology). Differing slightly in content from the previous edition, occasional references to foreign-language critical studies are found in the bibliographies, but often in English translation. Coverage of women writers is surprisingly inadequate.

The set is completed by a couple of indexes. New to this edition is the language index, which lists writers under their primary language. A title index follows (no author index is necessary due to the alphabetic format of the main text). A list of advisers and contributors, complete with affiliations and publications, concludes the 2nd volume. While it is refreshing to see a set concerned solely with world literature, and having said information at hand in two volumes is useful, much of the data can be found elsewhere. The bibliographies and lists of critical studies are still woefully remiss—more fulfilling lists can be found online. The benefits of this set do not live up to its price.—**Melissa Rae Root**

518. **The Schomberg Center Guide to Black Literature from the Eighteenth Century to the Present**. Roger M. Valade III, with Denise Kasinec, eds. Detroit, Gale, 1996. 545p. illus. index. $75.00. ISBN 0-7876-0289-2.

This volume on black literature is an ideal guide for people seeking quick access to key information on black fiction and nonfiction writers. Most of the authors are from the United States, but the alphabetically arranged reference tool also includes data on international black artists whose works are available in English. Other entries deal with plot summaries of 460 major literary pieces; cross-references of characters to the works in which they appear; and concise information on topics, terms, genres, and literary movements relating to black writing during the past 3 centuries.

The guide is handsomely done and is designed to attract high school and university students who are beginning to delve into black literary studies. There are photographs of nearly 100 authors and reproductions of about half as many dust jackets, title pages, book covers, and manuscript pages. The information is useful, brief, and adequate. Those desiring more comprehensive and in-depth information are given references to other works for further study, especially to volumes in the Gale family.

The book is introduced by a short, interesting essay concerning the history of the Schomberg Center for Research in Black Culture. The introduction also provides a chronological list of the major biographical and historical events relevant to black literature. A significant feature of this reference is the addition of numerous minor or little-known (but still worthy) creative artists, such as Chester Himes, Ida B. Wells, and Eric Walrond. Also, the book ably shows the worldwide connections of black writing by including coverage of authors outside the United States. *The Schomberg Center Guide* is excellent for finding key information on black literary subjects, but it should be used as a starting point for more serious study or as a fascinating place to browse for facts about a rich field of creative work. [R: Choice, May 96, p. 1459; RBB, 15 Feb 96, pp. 1045-47]—**Angelo Costanzo**

519. **Who's Who at the Frankfurt Book Fair 1989**. Edited by the Frankfurt Book Fair. Munich, New York, K. G. Saur, 1989. 487p. $35.00pa. ISBN 3-598-21889-3.

The annual Frankfurt Book Fair is the major international publishing trade show. It is the premier place to negotiate for foreign rights to adult books. This directory lists individuals and firms registered at the 1989 fair. The entries for individuals identify each person's employer, title, and languages spoken; some also identify the individual's Frankfurt hotel. The entries for firms identify booth numbers, mailing addresses, telephone and fax numbers, and key officers.

This book is essential for individuals attending the fair. After the fair, it has some value for those who negotiate for international rights and permissions. The book is too specialized for most libraries, which are better served by *Literary Market Place* and *International Literary Market Place*. It is suitable only for highly specialized collections.—**Jerome K. Miller**

520. **Wilson Author Biographies on Disc 1995**. [CD-ROM]. Bronx, N.Y., H. W. Wilson, 1994. Minimum system requirements: CD-ROM drive. $299.00. ISBN 0-8242-0865-X.

Wilson Author Biographies is the CD-ROM version of five publications in the Wilson Author series, covering some 4,300 writers who lived from 800 B.C. until the early twentieth century. It includes authors from many parts of the world. Contemporary authors are not included. It is similar to other Wilson CD-ROM products, and uses the same software. If one presently has Wilson products on disc, with Wilson disc 3.0 or higher, this will run. For those who do not have 3.0 or higher, installation is reasonably simple.

Like other Wilson products, this has three levels for searching: name and title; Wilsonsearch mode, which allows the user to search multiple subject terms; and Wilsonline, which allows sophisticated search methods such as truncation and Boolean operators. By using the author/title mode and typing in either an author's name or the title of a work, the user immediately retrieves the author biography requested, as it appears in the appropriate Wilson publication. In multiple subject search, the user can type in more than one word for retrieval, and also use various qualifiers such as century, nationality, or genre. Truncation also is allowed in this mode. Searching by subject word, however, is done only as a keyword search: If the word searched appears in a certain biographical sketch, that sketch is retrieved. No assigning of subject terms has been done.

Searching on Wilsonsearch is clearly the most powerful. In that mode, the user retrieves all mentions of the author searched, including many bibliographical citations. The use of the "neighbor" command in Wilsonsearch is especially helpful, as it allows one to expand a search term and see all nearby terms. Thus, searching (Charles) Dickens with a neighbor command reveals that the system holds records relating to "Dickens—stage adaptations" and "Dickens—sources," among others. Exploring one of those terms usually reveals a list of further sources on the topic.

This is an easy-to-use CD-ROM, especially at the author/title search level, and especially for those already familiar with Wilson products. Unfortunately, the more powerful modes will be seldom used; most will use the author/title search to display what can easily be retrieved in book form. Of course, using the disc allows one to search all five titles simultaneously, obviously an advantage. Whether that advantage is enough to justify its purchase—or whether a library's clientele will make sufficient use of the sophisticated search mode—must be an individual decision. This is a fine source if it will be used.—**Terry Ann Mood**

521. **Women Writers of Great Britain and Europe: An Encyclopedia**. Katharina M. Wilson, Paul Schlueter, and June Schlueter, eds. New York, Garland, 1997. 571p. illus. (Garland Reference Library of the Humanities, v.1980). $95.00. ISBN 0-8153-2343-3.

This impressive collection of essays provides a rich resource for readers interested in short introductions to the histories of hundreds of British and European women writers. Reaching back in time to Sappho in the seventh century B.C.E., the encyclopedia discusses women writers through the years, such as Nossis (third century B.C.E.), Hélïse (twelfth century), Dames des Roches (sixteenth century), Jeanne-Marie Leprince de Beaumont (eighteenth century), and Virginia Woolf (twentieth century).

The entries begin with the vital statistics: pseudonym (if applicable), birth date, birthplace, death date, place of death, genres, and languages. After a discussion of the writer, the entry concludes with a list of the author's works. The entries may be written by one of the editors or by one of more than 100 contributors. Because of this, the style varies widely, with some entries quite intriguing and others merely factual.

Occasional photographs and drawings enliven the text; more photographs would have been appreciated. Useful indexes include pseudonyms, a list of entries by countries, and a list of entries by centuries. Historians, women writers, students, and general readers will enjoy browsing this resource.—**Suzanne I. Barchers**

522. **World Authors 1900-1950**. Martin Seymour-Smith and Andrew C. Kimmens, eds. Bronx, N.Y., H. W. Wilson, 1996. 4v. illus. (Wilson Authors Series). $395.00. ISBN 0-8242-0899-4.

The World Authors series is well known to librarians for its concise but informative biographical and critical essays on important writers. This four-volume work comprises a comprehensive rewriting of two of its most popular titles, *Twentieth Century Authors,* first published in 1942, and *Twentieth Century Authors First Supplement*, published in 1955. This edition includes nearly all of the 2,500 writers from the original work plus others added to reflect significant authors who came into prominence post-1955.

Entries retain the first-person sketches written in the authors' own words found in the previous editions. All entries have been updated to reflect recent scholarship and current critical thinking about each author's works. In all, *World Authors 1900-1950* lives up to the literary biography standards set by this series for critical evaluation; lively anecdotal narratives; and extensive, authoritative biographical information.—**G. Kim Dority**

523. **World Authors 1980-1985**. Vineta Colby, ed. New York, H. W. Wilson, 1991. 938p. illus. (Wilson Authors Series). $80.00. PN431.W672. 809'.04048. LC 90-49782. ISBN 0-8242-0797-1.

The latest edition of *World Authors* carries on the tradition of *World Authors 1950-1970* (see ARBA 76, entry 1217), *World Authors 1970-1975* (see ARBA 81, entry 1239), and *World Authors 1975-1980* (see ARBA 86, entry 1080). The 1970-75 edition contained profiles of 348 authors; that for 1975-80, 370. This presents brief but useful biographical and critical essays on 322 authors who became active or came into prominence from 1980 to 1983. Authors were selected for inclusion based on literary merit, popularity, and the availability of their work. While most listed authors come from the "imaginative" literature—poets, novelists, short story writers, dramatists; a number of people from other fields—literary criticism, science, history, philosophy, and journalism—are also included. The growing awareness of non-Western writers and the increasing availability of their work in translation are shown by the appearance of many authors from Africa, Latin America, South America, the Mid-East, and the Far East, although the largest percentage of entries still represents North America and Europe.

Each of the two- to four-page essays has a short biography of the author, a discussion of the author's approach and philosophy, a summary of major works with brief critical analyses, and lists of principal works (or works in translation) and selected references. Photographs are included for almost all entries. About one-third of the entries include a statement contributed by the author. This series continues to be an enriching supplement to other biographical and critical sources for the general reader. [R: RD, Summer 91, p. 13; WLB, May 91, p. 144]—**Susan Davis Herring and Terry Ann Mood**

524.   **The Writers Directory**. Detroit, St. James Press, 1973- . ISSN 0084-2699.

The 13th edition (1998-2000) of this fine reference work provides pertinent information on more than 15,000 living writers from the English-speaking nations of the United States, United Kingdom, Australia, New Zealand, Canada, South Africa, and Ireland. Writers represented have written at least one full-length book in English. The individual entries include the writer's full name, any pseudonyms, nationality, birth year, genre or writing category in which the author chiefly works, career background information, list of publications, and address. A separate section lists obituaries of writers who appeared in previous editions of *The Writers Directory* and whose passing has occurred since the publication of the last edition. In this new edition, boldface rubrics or signals have been added to entries to highlight such particulars as genre, career, publications, and address. This new feature greatly enhances the speed and ease of the search for pertinent information about subjects. An extensive index to writing categories is color-coded and lists writers alphabetically by genre or category such as "Mystery/Crime/Suspense" and "Economics." A guide to abbreviations used in the entries is also provided.

The Writers Directory is especially useful to media specialists and teachers who wish to share biographical data about a vast array of contemporary authors with students. The listing of contact addresses is a boon to all who wish to engage in inquiries or further research.—**Jerry D. Flack and Terry Ann Mood**

AFRICAN LITERATURE

525.   **African Writers**. C. Brian Cox, ed. New York, Scribner's/Simon & Schuster Macmillan, 1997. 2v. index. $220.00/set. ISBN 0-684-19651-4.

This two-volume reference collection of essays offers an introduction to the richness and diversity of late-nineteenth- and twentieth-century literature from the African continent. The editor has chosen to feature those writers who were born or spent a good deal of their lives in Africa. He treats writers who have received international recognition for their achievement and made significant contributions to the literature of their countries. Although not entirely comprehensive, the editor's selection of 65 authors does include 4 writers awarded the Nobel Prize in literature: Albert Camus (1957), Nadine Gordimer (1991), Naguib Mahfouz (1988), and Wole Soyinka (1986). Not to be exclusionary, both women and men are represented in the collection. The diversity within the literature is shown by the inclusion of writers of everything from poetry to literary criticism.

The set is well organized. Following the table of contents, there is an index in which the authors are grouped according to the present-day African countries with which they are most frequently associated. In most cases, the countries are the lands in which the writers were born, grew up, and developed their reputations. This index includes a brief paragraph about the writer, which is quite useful. The writers discussed in this collection use many different languages. In general, those from Ghana, Kenya, Nigeria, and South Africa write in English; those from Algeria, Cameroon, Guinea, and Senegal write in French; those from Angola and Mozambique write in Portuguese; and Egyptian authors write in Arabic. A few write in indigenous African languages, such as Akan, Yoruba, and Kikuyu, and some write in more than one language. Most of the non-English works discussed in this collection are available in English translations. When this is the case, the published English titles appear in italics in parentheses following the original title.

A nice aspect of this set is a chronological table of African history from 1830 to 1996, which precedes the alphabetic essay entries. Biographical in nature and written by a number of contributors, these essays analyze the works of these world-renowned African writers. At the end of each entry is a selected bibliography of the publishing history of each writer and selected secondary sources. Volume 2 concludes with biographical sketches of the contributors and a comprehensive index for the set. This reference set is highly recommended for any library having a world literature collection or an explicit interest in global writers.—**Judith A. Valdez**

AMERICAN LITERATURE

General Works

526. **American Authors 1600-1900. A Biographical Dictionary of American Literature**. Stanley J. Kunitz and Howard Haycraft. New York, H. W. Wilson, 1938. 846p. $33.00. LC 38-27938. ISBN 0-8242-0001-X.

This is a standard work for more popular audiences, now in its seventh printing (1977). It includes readable biographies of nearly 1,300 authors who contributed to the development of American literature from the first English settlement at Jamestown to the close of the nineteenth century, which makes this volume an essential reference work on the period. Lists of principal works and critical and biographical sources follow each sketch; portraits accompany 400 of these entries. Highly recommended for all school and public libraries.—**Bohdan S. Wynar**

527. **American Colonial Writers, 1606-1734**. Emory Elliott, ed. Detroit, Gale, 1984. 415p. illus. bibliog. index. (Dictionary of Literary Biography, Vol. 24). $80.00. LC 83-20577. ISBN 0-8103-1703-6.

The first of three volumes in the Dictionary of Literary Biography series that are devoted to early American writers, *American Colonial Writers, 1606-1734* contains biographical and critical essays concerning 95 of the writers of the period. Lengthy, in-depth articles on major writers (such as William Bradford, Anne Bradstreet, William Byrd II, Jonathan Edwards, Benjamin Franklin, Cotton and Increase Mather, Samuel Sewall, Edward Taylor, and Roger Williams) are supplemented with information commentaries about many lesser-known and recently discovered writers of the colonial period.

Following the standard DLB format, essays include a list of the author's separate publications, basic bibliographical and career information, and notes on the locations of the author's collected papers. Often including representation comments from earlier sources, critical commentary reflects the most recent interpretations. Entries normally include illustrations from the author's life, facsimile title and text pages, manuscript pages and letters, and an author portrait.

Providing ready access to the wealth of materials relating to the literary activities of colonial New England as well as the Middle and Southern colonies, *American Colonial Writers, 1606-1734* contributes to a more complete understanding of the complex nature of the literary achievement of the colonial writers. As an information source, it is basic enough to provide general information for a high school or college student writing a term paper and specific enough to lead the specialist scholar to valuable primary and secondary source materials. [R: WLB, May 84, p. 673]—**Colby H. Kullman**

528. **American Colonial Writers, 1735-1781**. Emory Elliott, ed. Detroit, Gale, 1984. 421p. illus. bibliog. index. (Dictionary of Literary Biography, Vol. 31). $82.00. LC 84-13533. ISBN 0-8103-1709-5.

Anyone with the least interest in American literature will find this book irresistible. From the most famous to the most obscure, this 31st volume of Dictionary of Literary Biography covers 62 American writers in the period 1735 to 1781 with wit and authority. The ideas of six eighteenth-century philosophers that influenced American thought during this period are also profiled.

Major writers are treated in lengthy essays beginning with standard biographical and bibliographic information in outline form and followed by notes on references, biographies, papers, and letters. The essays chronicle the subjects' writing careers with critical commentary from historical and contemporary perspectives. Obscure facts and tidbits of information about the writers' quirks lend interest and often humor without detracting from the text's authority.

Dealing with a period in which writing and politics were, for the most part, inextricable, the editors wisely chose an American studies approach. Reading several entries, one gains not divorced glimpses of the individual careers and talents of colonial writers but an overview of the political, philosophical, social, cultural, and artistic scheme of the times. Drawings, portrait reproductions, and facsimiles of manuscripts enhance the overview.

The book is generally readable and accurate, although the writing is sometimes unclear and a typo in the first entry sets the publication date of some John Adams letters 100 years too late. Regardless, the volume will be of use—and, just as important, of interest—to students on a general introductory level, as well as advanced scholars interested in the commentary and bibliographic information.—**Constance Hardesty**

529. **American Diversity, American Identity: The Lives and Works of 145 Writers Who Define the American Experience**. John K. Roth, ed. New York, Henry Holt, 1995. 709p. index. $45.00. ISBN 0-8050-3430-7.

What does it mean to be a citizen of the United States? What does the term "American" say about a person's identity? This reference work strives to answer these questions, emphasizing that the "American identity" is not a "one-size-fits-all" pattern, and attempts to portray the U.S. identity in all its complexity, diversity, and, the editor hopes, cohesion. The book covers 145 writers that Roth feels epitomize the various aspects of the "American experience."

The text is organized into 13 sections, based on regionalism, ethnicity, gender, and sexual preference; one section discusses writers who concentrate on life during wartime. Each section provides an introduction to the topic at hand and then proceeds to profile individual authors who embody the approach. Each essay supplies a biography of the author, including principal fiction written; achievements; an analysis of how the writer promotes the viewpoint in question; and a bibliography for further reading. The primary text is followed by "A Categorized Listing of Writers" and a comprehensive index by titles of works and names of authors. The bibliographies at the ends of the essays are helpful, as is the categorized list of authors.

Interesting as this work is, there are problems. Some authors transcend the boundaries under which they have been placed, while others seem to be questionably distinguished. Writers such as Mark Twain, James Baldwin, Toni Morrison, Alice Walker (why put Walker under "Bearers of the African American Tradition" and Morrison under "Renewing Visions of America," but neither under "Women's Voices"?), Barbara Kingsolver, Audre Lorde, and Adrienne Rich could be placed in different categories than the ones they are assigned. Interestingly, the categorized list at the end of the text provides names of other writers who fit these categories, and places individuals in more than one category as they fit. Another flaw concerns the lack of visions based on religious experience beyond Jewish American voices (which goes beyond mere religious identity)—Do not different religions also contribute to the American identity? Also, no mention is made of Canadian authors, although the broad definition of "American" includes them, and many Canadians also live the "American experience."

The format and goal of the book seem best suited for a high school library, where students could be exposed to new authors and ideas. However, the language used may be a bit advanced for many high school students; it seems more appropriate for undergraduate or graduate institutions. Therefore, the audience to whom this book is directed is questionable; libraries should carefully consider their patrons' needs before purchasing the volume.—**Melissa R. Root**

530. **American Expatriate Writers: Paris in the Twenties**. Matthew J. Bruccoli and Robert W. Trogdon, eds. Detroit, Gale, 1997. 378p. illus. index. (Dictionary of Literary Biography Documentary Series, v.15). $146.00. ISBN 0-8103-9971-7.

In 1980, *American Writers in Paris, 1920-1939*, the 4th volume of the Dictionary of Literary Biography (DLB) series, offered in-depth biographies of 99 writers, journalists, and publishers of the *belle epoque* of American letters in Paris. This volume, in the well-established companion documentary series, provides access (in facsimile or transcription, of course) to primary materials associated with the brightest stars of that incredibly creative expatriate society. Writers such as Ezra Pound, Ernest Hemingway, Gertrude Stein, F. Scott Fitzgerald, and John Dos Passos, whose works continue to provide pleasure and food for thought for new generations of readers, are included. It also covers the group's principal publishers—Sylvia Beach, William Bird, Robert McAlmon, and Edward Titus, as well as lesser luminaries whose work still sparkles for scholars and others who seek out the era's fuller literary record. In addition, chapters treat the "Lost Generation's" key literary magazines—*The Little Review*, *The Transatlantic Review*, and *This Quarter*—and the milieu in which their café society flourished.

Typical chapters reproduce sample pages from drafts of major works as well as their book jackets or title pages. They also reprint letters, introductions to others' books, newspaper pieces, journal articles, and excerpts from books. The result is an inevitably incomplete mosaic—incomplete, that is, if viewed from the perspective of a scholar or a biographer who seeks to find and fit every piece together. However, this fragmentary view of these writers and publishers works, especially when multiple chapters are used to get a sense of the era rather than of just one writer, will look much more complete for the popular student audience for whom this is intended. Members of that audience will take from this book a richer, fuller understanding of the aesthetic ideas and ideals of these writers, the ways in which their personal interaction produced creative synergy, and the range of their work beyond the best known novels of Hemingway and Fitzgerald. Furthermore, the cumulative index covering both the Dictionary of Literary Biography Series and this documentary series will help them connect the in-depth critical biographies in other volumes with the selected documentary information in this volume.—**James Rettig**

531. **American Literary Biographers: First Series**. Steven Serafin, ed. Detroit, Gale, 1991. 401p. illus. index. (Dictionary of Literary Biography, v.103). $108.00. LC 91-23854. ISBN 0-8103-4583-8.

This follows the format of preceding volumes, which have focused on particular themes, genres, or periods. However, it just as readily stands on its own as a separate reference resource. It covers more than 30 individuals who have been recognized primarily as biographers of literary subjects. Each signed entry lists the author's major works and selected writings in periodicals or other publications, followed by an essay on the life and works of that biographer. Entries vary greatly in length and include photographs and related illustrations. A checklist for further reading in the art of biographical writing and research is included, as is a cumulative index to the Dictionary of Literary Biography (DLB) and its companion publications, the DLB *Yearbook* (see ARBA 91, entry 1101) and DLB Documentary Series (see ARBA 91, entry 1176).

This work focuses almost exclusively on twentieth-century writers and provides an interesting, if brief, overview of some of the major biographers of today and their subjects. Although narrowly focused and of use to a specialized audience, as part of the larger DLB series it helps create a useful and detailed introductory resource to the field of British and American literature.—**Elizabeth Patterson**

532. **American Literary Biographers: Second Series**. Steven Serafin, ed. Detroit, Gale, 1991. 399p. illus. index. (Dictionary of Literary Biography, no. 111). $108.00. LC 91-26672. ISBN 0-8103-4591-9.

Libraries with standing orders to the Dictionary of Literary Biography series have probably already realized that Gale will never exhaust its supply of literary groups to include in this series for undergraduate collections. This recent offering is the 2nd volume in a subseries on American literary biographers. As did the previous volume, this work provides well-written bio-bibliographical essays by recognized scholars. Thirty-five biographers born in the first half of this century are the subjects of articles of about ten pages each. Although any of the best-known biographers (e.g., Richard Ellman, Edwin H. Cady) appeared in the first volume, this continuation includes important writers such as Virginia Spencer Carr, Walter Harding, Richard S. Kennedy, and Stanley Weintraub. The relation between biographer and subject is a theme that runs through all the articles, with particular emphasis on the circumstances that led the writer to delve into another person's life. It becomes clear that the task of the biographer entails not only an enormous amount of research but also a true sense of devotion—to the subject, regardless of how many years or centuries might separate the two. If biography is a form of voyeurism, these essays, which obviously use the techniques of the biographer to describe them, are doubly voyeuristic, for one sees into the lives of those who look into the loves of people one admires.—**Valerie R. Hotchkiss**

533.   **American Nature Writers**. John Elder, ed. New York, Scribner's/Simon & Schuster Macmillan, 1996. 2v. illus. index. $220.00/set. ISBN 0-684-19692-1.

Nature writing has only recently come into its own as a distinct literary genre. The genre is, of course, writing about nature, but it has a strong, reflective, personal element absent in scientific discourse. The writing is a blend of science and an appreciation of the beauty and value of physical creation and humankind's place in it. The genre's maturity has been marked by an increase in the number of popular books, anthologies, magazines, and articles reflecting a heightened environmental awareness.

Although American nature writing has been around since Henry David Thoreau, there has been no single source of information about its leading practitioners. Much of that void is now filled by this elegant set with its 70 alphabetically ordered, bio-bibliographic essays on prominent American nature writers, past and present. The essays, each with a picture of its subject, run from 10 to 20 pages in length, including bibliographies by and about its subject. Chronological coverage is from William Bartram (1739-1823) to Rick Bass (1958-). Nearly two-thirds of the entries are historical, and by reading the essays in chronological order, a reader would, in effect, have a history of the subject from Thoreau and Ralph Waldo Emerson through John Burroughs and John Muir to Peter Matthiessen and Barry Lopez. Women nature writers from Susan Fenimore Cooper to Diane Ackerman also receive their due.

The bio-bibliographic essays are supplemented by a dozen "general topic" articles, in such subjects as Afro-Americans and nature writing, nature in Native American writing, contemporary ecofiction, literary theory and nature writing, modern bird-watching literature, nature poetry, and so on. Although nature writing has now become mainstream and includes some of the best American writers, the field still suffers from critical neglect. This sumptuously produced reference set is a unique and valuable resource.—**D. Barton Johnson**

534.   **American Women Writers: A Critical Reference Guide from Colonial Times to the Present**. Vols. 1-4 and Supplement. New York, Frederick Ungar, 1978-1994. LC 78-20945. ISBN 0-8044-3151-5 (vol. 1); 0-8044-3152-3 (vol. 2); 0-8044-3153-1 (vol. 3); 0-8044-3155-8 (vol. 4). LC 78-20945. ISBN 0-8264-0603-3 (Supplement).

This pioneering work offers articles on women who made literature their career as well as women who wrote seriously about their work in history, psychology, theology, home economics, and other fields. It also brings to public attention many unjustly neglected writers, whose stories, journals, and poetry reflected their world. Each entry provides biographical information, a summary of the writer's career, and an examination of her works, with helpful bibliographies. A comprehensive index is included in volume 4.

Though *Notable American Women* (Edward T. James, Janet Wilson James, and Paul S. Boyer, eds., 1951) provides some overlap, *AWW* is a substantially different source because it concentrates exclusively on writers: "those who are known and read, and those who have been generally neglected or undervalued because they were women." Each critical biography meticulously assesses the writer's contribution; provides the basic biographical information, including married and maiden names, pseudonyms, and aliases that often elude even diligent searchers; and lists complete bibliographies (the first such compilations for many of the women included). Every biography is signed by a scholar or editor working in the fields of literature, women's studies, or American studies, which may account for the excellent overall quality of the entries. The range of writers represented is considerable—from little-known names to the contemporary literary luminaries. Elizabeth Bishop, Harriette Arnow, and Louisa May Alcott are, not surprisingly, here, but so are the newer names—Olga Broumas, E. M. Broner, and Rita Mae Brown. Nor is this work confined to poets and fiction writers. Diarists, journalists, anthropologists, historians, and academicians figure into the unparalleled resource, too.

One can always find cause to quarrel with the editors' selection in a work such as *AWW*. This reviewer was disappointed by the limited attention paid to minority writers. It is perplexing not to find black writers of the caliber of Audre Lorde, June Jordan, and Ntozake Shange, and Indian writers such as Joy Harjo, Wendy Rose, and Paula Gunn Allen. The abridgment of course shrinks the coverage still further, eliminating some writers included in the full set (e.g., Leslie Marmon Silko, Alice Walker, Toni Morrison, Maya Angelou, and Maxine Hong Kingston). In the introduction to the 1st edition, the editors admit to not doing justice to black and lesbian writers but argue that this can be justified by the fact that "these contemporary writers are getting adequate attention—they are being read, anthologized, taught. We concluded that such women writers could most easily be omitted in this 1st edition and best be covered in a supplementary volume." The editors did make an effort to include more minority women in the 1994 supplement.

Entries are brief—some three or four pages in most cases; and readers may use this source mostly as a place to begin research. However, references to other sources allow for further investigation.—**Catherine R. Loeb and Terry Ann Mood**

535.   American Women Writers: Bibliographical Essays. Maurice Duke, Jackson R. Bryer, and M. Thomas Inge, eds. Westport, Conn., Greenwood Press, 1983. 434p. index. $39.95. LC 82-6156. ISBN 0-313-22116-2.

Twenty-four major American women authors, often neglected in scholarly treatments of our national literature, are the focus of this collection of bibliographical essays. This authoritative guide to women novelists, dramatists, and poets is highly selective, excluding authors who have been given similar scholarly treatment elsewhere. The essays, prepared by well-known critics of the authors, include brief introductory statements about each author and sections on bibliography, editions, manuscripts and letters, biography, and criticism, in a format similar to those of Floyd Stovall's *Eight American Authors* and *Sixteen Modern American Authors,* edited by Jackson R. Bryer (Duke, 1974). Beginning with Anne Bradstreet, the coverage extends to Sarah Orne Jewett, Gertrude Stein, Kate Chopin, Margaret Mitchell, Flannery O'Connor, Carson McCullers, Anais Nin, Zora Neale Hurston, Anne Sexton, and others. Historical and technical innovations in literature by women writers are reflected in choice of authors. The volume is a major accomplishment, noting areas where further research is needed. Perhaps it will promote similar efforts for coverage of other significant women writers. [R: BL, 1 Dec 83, p. 547; Choice, Oct 83, p. 270; LJ, 1 Feb 83, p. 196; WLB, June 83, p. 880]—**Maureen Pastine**

536.   American Writers. A Collection of Literary Biographies. Leonard Unger, ed.-in-chief. New York, Scribner's, 1971-1996. 8v. $495.00/set. **Supplement I**. 2v. $130.00/set. **Supplement II**. 2v. $130.00/set. (May be purchased separately.) LC 73-1759. ISBN 0-684-17322-0 (set). **Supplement III**. 2v. index. $150.00/set. ISBN 0-684-19196-2. **Supplement IV**. 2v. index. $199.00/set. ISBN 0-684-19785-5.

The eight-volume set that inspired the *British Writers, Ancient Writers*, and *European Writers* series, this basic set of *American Writers* contains 156 critical studies of notable poets, novelists, short-story writers, playwrights, critics, historians, and philosophers from the seventeenth century to the present day. Each article is the work of a distinguished scholar, who provides a basic account of the writer's life but focuses on a discussion of literary style, genre, and place within established or emerging literary tradition.

The 97articles in the original 4-volume parent set were selected from a series of pamphlets published by the University of Minnesota Press. They were re-edited, bibliographies were updated, and a comprehensive index was added. Among the contributors are Louis Auchincloss ("Henry Adams," "Ellen Glasgow," "Edith Wharton"), Leon Edel ("Henry James," "Henry David Thoreau"), Granville Hicks ("James Gould Cozzens"), Mark Schorer ("Sinclair Lewis"), Charles E. Shain ("F. Scott

Fitzgerald"), Lawrence Thompson ("Robert Frost"), Leonard Unger ("T. S. Eliot"), and Philip Young ("Ernest Hemingway").

All the essays are well documented with a selected bibliography of works by and about a given author. A brief biographical sketch is provided in each essay, but the emphasis is on the critical evaluation and analysis of the writer's literary achievements.

As is to be expected, the supplementary volumes in this series continue the basic plan of the primary volumes. Unger's intention here has been to fill gaps in the primary set and to continue the coverage of major figures down into the twentieth century. He cites the major gap being filled as that of the omission of the Schoolroom Poets (the "bearded trinomials"), with the exception of Longfellow. That has been corrected here, with essays on each of the major figures in that grouping. Coverage in the supplements also includes more women and minority writers, as well as literary critics and some writers from earlier times who have only recently begun to be appreciated. Some 30 persons are covered in the first supplement; 29 in the second; another 29 in the third; and 35 in the fourth. Essays are lengthy (20 pages seems a minimum). They tend to delve very heavily into individual works, and students with no knowledge of the author's entire work may be a bit put off by having *everything* dissected and explained before it's ever been encountered. However, that appears to be the fashion.

Each entry has a selected bibliography attached, one listing for works and the other of criticism. Especially in the case of contemporary authors, listing works (including essays and uncollected works) can be very helpful, as they often get so easily lost or go unnoticed in the contemporary publishing swirl of activity. The layout is handsome and easy on the eye, and the books will be used for some time to come. [R: Choice, Sept 79, p. 795; WLB, June 79, p. 721-22]—**Bohdan S. Wynar and Terry Ann Mood**

537. Barstow, Jane Missner. **One Hundred Years of American Women Writing, 1848-1948: An Annotated Bio-bibliography**. Pasadena, Calif., Salem Press and Lanham, Md., Scarecrow, 1997. 333p. index. (Magill Bibliographies). $42.00. ISBN 0-8108-3314-X.

This annotated bio-bibliography provides a valuable summary of the flood of critical attention paid to women writers since the beginning of the women's movement in 1970. Intended for a general audience rather than specialists, the work nevertheless contains ample useful information for the student or teacher embarking on a study of U.S. women's writing.

Barstow has chosen 66 representative writers who published most of their work between 1848, the year of the Seneca Falls Convention on Women's Rights, and 1948, when Simone de Beauvoir began her groundbreaking *The Second Sex*. Their work has been reissued in new editions and attracted considerable critical interest. The book is divided into sections by period, genre, and ethnicity (many categories overlap), each beginning with an introduction and an annotated list of general works. Individual entries, arranged in alphabetic order, contain a brief biography, a list of major works in modern reprints, and a selected and annotated bibliography of criticism since 1970. The annotations are economically written but provide a useful and generally accurate summary of the contents. Two appendixes, arranged by birth date and by ethnicity, contain more names for further research.

Although this book does not claim to cover all U.S. women writers, it provides an excellent overview of well-chosen material. It will have a permanent place on this reviewer's reference shelf and belongs in every school and university library.—**Lynn F. Williams**

538. **Biographical Dictionary of Contemporary Catholic American Writing**. Daniel J. Tynan, ed. Westport, Conn., Greenwood Press, 1989. 341p. index. $49.95. PS153.C3B5. 016.81'09'9222. LC 88-38488. ISBN 0-313-24585-1.

This inventory of contemporary Catholic American writers contains 135 biographical-critical essays on such literary luminaries as Flannery O'Connor, Walker Percy, Tennessee Williams, Robert Lowell, Eugene O'Neill, and Joyce Carol Oates. Also profiled are dozens of popular novelists and playwrights and lesser-known poets and essayists. Appended to each entry is a complete list of the author's works and a bibliography of books, critical articles, and significant book reviews.

In a long and provocative introduction, the editor explores the diversity of belief on the part of the authors chosen for inclusion. However, one can easily carp over his inclusions and exclusions.

About all the biographees have in common is that they were baptized into the church. More than half of those listed are not what might be called "Incarnational Catholic-Christians." It is somewhat misleading to include indifferent, nonpracticing, and even vehemently anti-Catholics in such a collection. On a positive side, the entries (written by some 80 critics and scholars of contemporary American literature) do now and then refer to aspects of Catholicism—favorably or unfavorably—in the lives and works of the figures listed. [R: LJ, 1 Oct 89, p. 86; RBB, 15 Nov 89, p. 688]—**G. A. Cevasco**

539. **Biographical Dictionary of North American Classicists**. Ward W. Briggs Jr., ed. Westport, Conn., Greenwood Press, 1994. 800p. index. $115.00. PA83.B53. 480'.092'27. LC 94-4785. ISBN 0-313-24560-6.

As one might expect in a volume compiled by a respected classicist under the auspices of the American Philological Association, the *Biographical Dictionary of North American Classicists* is a model of clarity and careful scholarship. It begins with overviews of classical scholarship in the United States by William Calder III and in Canada by Alexander B. McKay. These essays, which contrast the strong pro-Germanic focus of U.S. scholars with the French tradition in Canada and detail the anti-Semitism and contempt for women that hindered the careers of many scholars, are far from dull and could be read with profit by many outside the field of classics. They are followed by bio-bibliographical entries on more than 600 scholars; indexes arranged by chronology, educational institution, and last degree earned; and a general index and a bibliography. The biographies assess the importance of the work and teaching of deceased scholars from the time of George Sandys (who arrived here in 1611 as a shareholder in the Virginia Company) to 1993. Entries on the most recent generation often contain warm expressions of appreciation for their *humanitas*.

This volume is clearly a labor of love for its editor and contributors and a reminder of the *temporis acti* when a knowledge of the classics was considered an essential part of education. Despite its quality, however, its high price and specialized subject make it suitable only for large university research libraries.—**Lynn F. Williams**

540. **The Cambridge Handbook of American Literature**. Jack Salzman, ed. New York, Cambridge University Press, 1986. 286p. bibliog. $19.95. LC 86-2586. ISBN 0-521-30703-1.

Arranged in alphabetical order, the *Cambridge Handbook* is an excellent and informative guide to American writers, literary movements, and magazines, in brief form. The entries, although brief, summarize with excellence subject matter which would elsewhere be less elegantly or less appropriately expressed. Entries contain brief summaries of plots of major works of American literature, or literary, biographical, and bibliographical details of importance. There is ample evidence that, as stated in the preface, deliberate effort has been expended to avoid reflecting personal opinions, and "to reflect received historical attitudes" when rendering critical commentary.

Also included in this work are a side-by-side "Chronology of American History" and "Chronology of American Literature," and a "Select Bibliography" of important critical works published during the fifty-year period prior to 1983.

Although the *Cambridge Handbook* is only one-third the length of the *Oxford Companion to American Literature,* 5th edition (Oxford University Press, 1983), it compares favorably. Both works contain a "chronology," but because of its brevity the *Cambridge Handbook* omits authors of importance (Vardis Fisher) one would like to see included. On the other hand, Thackery is included in the *Oxford Companion* on the strength of two visits to the United States, the conclusion of *Henry Esmond* and *The Virginians*. [R: WLB, Dec 86, p. 63]—**M. David Guttman**

541. **The Confidence Woman: 26 Women Writers at Work**. Eve Shelnutt, ed. Atlanta, Ga., Longstreet Press, 1991. 392p. illus. $17.95. LC 90-063897. ISBN 0-929264-91-6.

The editor of *The Confidence Woman* chose women whose work she admires and invited each "to write an essay about your career, shaping it in any manner you like." The writers whose responses are collected here have been, with a few exceptions, born in the United States and are almost exclusively Caucasian. In this sense, the book is considerably more limited than it might have been. Yet the women are not, on the whole, well known, and this fact, plus their diverse manners of responding to the editor's invitation, makes the book a refreshing change from the predictability of many such collections.

The essays tend to focus on such influences on the writers' careers as family, education, early reading, and the developing sense of self as a writer. Some—Patricia Goedicke is a good example—use their lives and excerpts from their poetry or prose to illuminate each other. The quality of the essays is somewhat uneven, ranging from the rather ordinary and sometimes clichéd to the passionate, vibrant, and even humorous. (Debora Gregor's essay is a series of drawings.) A bibliography is included for each writer. As many of the writers featured here have not been included in other such works, this book should be a useful addition, especially to libraries with interests in creative writing, contemporary American literature, or women's studies.—**Robin Riley Fast**

542. **American Transcendentalist**. Joel Myerson, ed. Detroit, Gale, 198p. illus. bibliog. (Dictionary of Literary Biography Documentary Series: An Illustrated Chronicle). 473p. index. $95.00. LC 82-1105. ISBN 0-8103-2639-6.

Ralph Waldo Emerson and Henry Thoreau are perhaps the only American transcendentalists whose names are recognized by most educated people today, but many other individual thinkers influenced and were influenced by these two luminaries. Volume 5 of the Dictionary of Literary Biography Documentary series reprints some of the less known writings of this group: literary criticism by Margaret Fuller and Orestes A. Brownson; philosophical essays by James Freeman Clarke and Theodore Parker; and personal reminiscences by Nathaniel Hawthorne, Louisa May Alcott, and Henry Thoreau. Two short sections of the book are devoted to the experimental communities associated with this movement, Brook Farm and Fruitlands. An essay on transcendentalism by Alexander Kern discusses the ideas and writings of more than 30 individuals who contributed to the introduction and development of the transcendentalist movement in America. A wide selection of illustrations of people, places, and texts break up the solid, double-column pages, while a list of further readings and a cumulative index to the series round out the volume. Although the format of the volume is rather forbidding for casual browsing, this book provides students with many important texts of the period and will be a useful addition to both public and university library collections.—**Adele M. Fasick**

543. **A Directory of American Poets and Fiction Writers**. 1995-1996 ed. New York, Poets & Writers; distr., Pushcart Press/W. W. Norton, 1995. 318p. index. $25.95pa.; $30.95pa. (institutions). ISBN 0-913724-47-0. ISSN 0734-0605.

This work contains the names and addresses of approximately 7,000 poets and fiction writers whose work has been published in the United States and who have applied to be included in the directory. The purpose of the work is to list contemporary writers, many of whom give readings or performances based on their work. The 1995/1996 edition has information about 4,000-plus poets, nearly 2,000 fiction writers, and more than 1,000 individuals who produce both poetry and fiction. Playwrights, nonfiction writers, translators, critics, biographers, journalists, and authors of children's books are not included.

The entries are arranged alphabetically by the state of the writer's home address. Each listing provides the writer's name (with pseudonyms cross-indexed), address, telephone number, type(s) of writing, and a representative sample of the publications in which the writer's work has been published. According to the publishers, the information was correct as of June 1, 1994; readers are given a telephone number to call for updated information.

Poets & Writers is a nonprofit service organization that supports writers' professional efforts. With the aid of grants from the Literature Program of the National Endowment for the Arts and other sources, it publishes a bimonthly magazine and other reference books in addition to the title under review. Inclusion in the directory does not constitute any sort of endorsement. Those wishing to contact contemporary writers personally will find this unique book valuable; however, most others will continue to rely on other, more inclusive, reference books.—**Kay O. Cornelius**

544. **Magill's Survey of American Literature**. Frank N. Magill, ed. North Beilmore, N.Y., Marshall Cavendish, 1991. 6v. illus. index. $369.95/set. PS21.M34. 810.9'0003. LC 91-28113. ISBN 1-85435-437-X.

Contrary to its title, in both its scope and its organization, this work presents a survey of American writers rather than of American literature. Coverage encompasses "190 American writers from the seventeenth to the late twentieth centuries whose lives and work are significant in the literary world of our time" (preface). The editors have made an effort to be multicultural in their selection; they have included Native American, African American, Asian American, Mexican American, immigrant, and women writers. Young adult authors, science fiction writers, and detective and western fiction writers are also present. The genres represented include long and short fiction, poetry, drama, and nonfiction.

The work is organized alphabetically by author. The entries, contributed by 130 subject specialists, are signed, and almost all include a full-page photograph of the profiled writer. Arranged to provide a ready-reference function, entries lead off with boxed introductory material that gives birth and death dates and a one-sentence summary of the writer's "principal literary achievement." (Unfortunately, it is nearly impossible to impart meaningful information about a writer's influence on American literature in one sentence, so this is perhaps the weakest point in an otherwise solid publication.) Three sections follow the introductory material: biography, analysis, and an overview of the writer's major work. The biography presents "a chronological overview of the author's life, with an orientation toward his or her literary endeavors"; the analysis section considers the author's "style, themes, and literary characteristics."

The section covering the writer's works is organized by genre, then chronologically within each genre. Boxed introductory material (date of publication, type of work, and a one-sentence plot synopsis) leads off each of these overviews. One- to two-page analyses then discuss the work in terms of plot, themes, relationship to the writer's overall growth and development, and impact on American literature. Each entry concludes with a multi-sentence summary of the writer and his or her position within the American literary environment, and a bibliography (not annotated) of 5 to 10 citations. The writing style of these profiles is academic but reasonably informative and accessible; the work is appropriate for a ready-reference situation when the primary goal is to provide information rather than insight or passion.

The strengths of this work are its practical, ready-reference arrangement, the multicultural nature of its selections, and the informative and thoughtful writing of its contributors. Its weaknesses are a 200-item glossary whose definitions range from very clear and useful to vague, and the lack of a chronology that would enable the reader to place the writers profiled in a historical context. If, in fact, the editors do intend this excellent work to be a survey, then both of these areas need to be addressed in a future edition. For now, however, most libraries at the public, high school, and academic level will find that this literary resource provides their patrons and students a helpful starting point from which to explore further.—**G. Kim Dority**

545.   **Modern American Women Writers**. Lea Baechler and A. Walton Litz, eds. New York, Scribner's, 1991. 583p. index. $85.00. PS151.M54. 810.9'9287'03. LC 90-52917. ISBN 0-684-19057-5.

There is an increasing amount of information available on women writers, which is a boon to many researchers. This collection of essays on major modern American women writers is an outstanding addition to the field. The book includes entries on 41 twentieth-century writers, from Frances Ellen Watkins Harper (1825-1911) to Alice Walker (1944-). The essays, averaging about 14 pages in length, and written by recognized scholars in American literature, are comprehensive, thoughtful, critical surveys of the writers' lives and works. Each entry also includes a list of primary works and a selection of biographical and critical studies. The introduction by Elaine Showalter gives an overview of the history and tradition of women's literature. An added feature is an interesting chronology of major American women writers and important events in American women's history from 1640 to 1990.

Much of the information given here is available elsewhere. *American Women Writers* (see ARBA 84, entry 1152, and ARBA 80, entry 1239) has short biographical sketches of the writers, and essays on all of them can be found in the Dictionary of Literary Biography series. However, by bringing scholarly essays and bibliographies on these authors together into one easily accessible volume, this work provides an outstanding reference source for all high school, college, and public libraries. [R: Choice, Sept 91, pp. 64-66; LJ, 15 June 91, p. 70; RBB, Aug 91, p. 2169; WLB, June 91, p. 130]—**Susan Davis Herring**

546. **The New Consciousness, 1941-1968.** Detroit, Gale, 1987. 539p. illus. (Concise Dictionary of American Literary Biography). $58.00. LC 86-33657. ISBN 0-8103-1822-9.

The New Consciousness is the first volume in a new series, *Concise Dictionary of American Literary Biography* (CDALB). Gale plans to publish five more volumes, covering American authors of literary periods from 1640 to 1987. Author entries are selected from those already appearing in Gale's Dictionary of Literary Biography (DLB) series and are reprinted in full with some updating and revisions. The new series was developed in response to requests from high school and junior-college teachers and librarians from small and medium-sized libraries for a smaller, more affordable set than the DLB series, which at the end of 1986 consisted of nearly 80 volumes, the most recent of which is priced at around $90.00. The CDALB, then, has the same goal as the DLB: "to make our literary heritage more accessible" (p.vii).

The 36 author entries in *The New Consciousness* are arranged chronologically. Each article begins with a diagram summary of the author's places of residence, influences and relationships, literary movements and forms affecting and reflected in his or her work, major themes, and cultural, artistic, social, and economical influences. This is one feature which the DLB volumes lack that is very useful, giving a quick overview of the important aspects of an author's life and works. Next, basic data such as date and place of birth and death, education, marriages, and awards and honors are listed, followed by a bibliography of all the author's works. The text itself consists mainly of biographical information, a description of his or her literary works, and critical reaction to those works, and is accompanied by several black-and-white photographs. Last, a list of sources for additional information is given at the end of each article.

No index is provided, only a list of contributors, comprising those who wrote the original articles and/or revised them for this volume. This information is also cited at the beginning of each entry, along with the number and name of the original DLB volume.

Judging from this first volume, the CDALB promises to be an excellent source for students and others and may be more accessible to them because of the smaller size and cost.

The New Consciousness provides up-to-date bibliographies for additional reference, covers a variety of important writers, and offers concise, complete information about these authors, enhancing the text with interesting photographs and easy-to-read diagram summaries. [R: RBB, 15 Sept 87, p. 124; WLB, Sept 87, p. 92]—**Kari Sidles**

547. **Nineteenth-Century American Women Writers: A Bio-bibliographical Critical Sourcebook.** Denise D. Knight, ed. Westport, Conn., Greenwood Press, 1997. 534p. index. $99.50. ISBN 0-313-29713-4.

This readable collection of essays profiles more than 70 U.S. women writers of the nineteenth century. Some names, such as Louisa May Alcott and Frances Hodgson Burnett, will be familiar. Other writers, such as Angelina Grimké, who addressed issues of slavery and abolitionism, are now generally unfamiliar. Yet, many of these writers held major roles through their writing. For example, Marietta Holley is credited by essayist Kate H. Winter as having helped gain the vote for women through her pen.

Although the essays are written by various (mostly women) authors, the underlying structure gives this resource cohesion and accessibility. Each essay begins with a biography that usually provides some family background; the writer's interests, activities, and accomplishments; and the context of the times. The next section, "Major Works and Themes," provides insights into the motivations of the writer. "Critical Reception" addresses the popularity, criticism, and general response to the writer's corpus of works. Some reviewers also address modern-day criticism when appropriate. The last sections detail the works cited, a bibliography of the author's works, and studies of the author. This is a particularly fine resource for those who are interested in a starting point for research or who simply want the pleasure of learning about some of the heritage of women writers.—**Suzanne I. Barchers**

548.   Otfinoski, Steven. **Nineteenth-Century Writers**. New York, Facts on File, 1991. 122p. illus. index. (American Profiles Series). $16.95. PS201.08. LC 90-20107. ISBN 0-8160-2486-3.

Nineteenth-Century Writers launches this new biographical series, designed to give middle and high school students accessible information on notable Americans and their achievements set against the backdrop of major historical periods and movements. The 10- to 15-page essays are intended as introductions only, so a brief list of additional titles and a basic chronology follow each entry. The present volume introduces 10 giants of nineteenth-century American literature (e.g., Edgar Allan Poe, Herman Melville, Emily Dickinson). After a brief introduction that summarizes the significance of the nineteenth century and its important literary trends, the essays offer biographies—of each author and analyses of their oeuvres. Otfinoski's portraits are nuanced and detailed, doing justice to the complicated personalities under consideration, yet having all the simplicity and straightforward-ness required by the targeted audience.

The contents, the format, the simple and direct style, and the affordable price make this book a welcome addition to most school library collections and public libraries. If forthcoming titles in the series prove to be as well written as this volume, American Profiles deserves every suc-cess.—**Zsuzsa Koltay**

549.   **The Oxford Companion to American Literature**. 6th ed. By James D. Hart. Revised by Phillip W. Leininger. New York, Oxford University Press, 1995. 779p. index. $49.95. ISBN 0-19-506548-4.

Recently an editor of the rival *Benét's Reader's Encyclopedia of American Literature* (see ARBA 92, entry 1155), Leininger has revised the late Hart's work to produce the first revision of this well-known title in a dozen years (see ARBA 84, entry 1159, for a review of the 5th edition). Nearly 200 new entries are incorporated in this edition; fewer than half of these were derived from notes left by Hart in 1990. The chronological index has been enlarged as well, appending the major literary and social events from 1983 to 1994.

Notable newcomers debuting in this volume include contemporary writers Amy Tan, Jim Har-rison, Gloria Steinem, Larry McMurtry, and Amy Clampitt. Redressing previous editions' over-sights, Leininger has written entries for Charlotte Perkins Gilman and Henry Roth. An unspecified number of 5th edition entries have been condensed, truncated, or dropped. Many deleted items are on obscure subjects (e.g., Hiram Chittenden, Moses Coit Tyler). Some writers' statures, however, would seem to warrant longer entries than they are accorded. A few omissions are questionable, such as those of entries treating the literary associations of certain U.S. cities and presidents.

Significant twentieth-century writers remain underrepresented in *The Oxford Companion*. For example, only 4 percent of personal entries for names beginning with A through D are of women born since 1900. Modern male authors who are missing include Harlan Ellison, Andre Dubus, and Lowell Thomas. Coverage is generally superior, however, in terms of the updated entries carried for-ward from the 5th edition. The revised article on William Gaddis has been tripled in length, and the Philip Levine entry lists no fewer than five works that appeared since *Oxford*'s previous edition.

Several comparisons with *Benet's* yield telling results. The entry in *Benet's* for each of the fol-lowing literary icons is more than twice the length of its *Oxford* counterpart: Herman Melville, Edgar Allan Poe, Mark Twain, James Fenimore Cooper, and William Faulkner. Yet, the breadth of the work under review is creditable in terms of embracing expatriates, explorers, colonists, and foreign discours-ers on American matters (e.g., Kay Boyle, Richard Hakluyt, Samuel Sewell, and Charles Dickens).

However, more could be written on Latin American and Canadian literature. Besides offering substantive overview essays on these literatures, *Benet's* offers entries on internationally acclaimed writ-ers whose works are readily available in English translation, such as Jorge Luis Borges, Pablo Neruda, and Octavio Paz. Also, unlike *Oxford*, *Benet's* treats such Canadian luminaries as Margaret Atwood, Robertson Davies, and Michael Ondaatje. For such giants as these, it is unfortunate that the researcher us-ing *Oxford* has to consult a supplementary source, whether it be *Benet's* or the Canadian (see ARBA 85, entry 1138) or Spanish (see ARBA 80, entry 1310) volumes in the Oxford Companion series.

Finally, the reduction of typeface size since the 5th edition may prove irritating to librarians us-ing this book on a regular basis. While the praises to be sung for *The Oxford Companion to American Literature* are considerable, one would be better served by employing *Benet's*, except involving more obscure areas of U.S. literature. [R: Choice, Mar 96, p. l096]—**Jeffrey E. Long**

550. **Sixteen Modern American Authors**. **Volume 2: A Survey of Research and Criticism since 1972**. Jackson R. Bryer, ed. Durham, N.C., Duke University Press, 1989. 810p. index. $57.50; $24.95pa. PS221.S625. 810.9'0052. LC 89-11789. ISBN 0-8223-0976-9; 0-8223-1018-Xpa.

This indispensable research book updates the previous edition published in 1973 (see ARBA 75, entry 1338). Evaluative bibliographical essays discuss significant scholarship and criticism up to 1985; frequently, material up to mid-1988 has been added. When possible the same contributors were asked to update the earlier edition. The bibliographical material covers the same 16 authors from the first half of the twentieth century as the earlier editions (although the original 1969 volume, *Fifteen Modern American Authors* [see ARBA 70, v.2, p. 71] dealt with only 15 writers). These are Sherwood Anderson, Willa Cather, Hart Crane, Theodore Dreiser, T. S. Eliot, William Faulkner, F. Scott Fitzgerald, Robert Frost, Ernest Hemingway, Eugene O'Neill, Ezra Pound, Edwin Arlington Robinson, John Steinbeck, Wallace Stevens, William Carlos Williams, and Thomas Wolfe.

Under each author there are sections on bibliography, editions, manuscripts and letters, biographies, criticism, and usually an updating supplement. Some of the essays are more exhaustive than others and include articles as well as major works. The perceptive evaluations clearly indicate biographies and critical works that are derivative, inaccurate, or controversial as well as those that cover new ground. Controversial material, such as Lawrence Thompson's psychological assessment of Robert Frost, and differences in critical approach, such as that of Helen Vendler versus the philosophical critics on Wallace Stevens, are discussed.

At the beginning of the volume is a key to abbreviations of journals. Notes on contributors and an extensive index conclude the work. Scholars of modern American literature will find this new edition an invaluable tool.—**Charlotte Lindgren**

551. **The Twenties, 1917-1929**. Detroit, Gale, 1989. 326p. illus. index. (Concise Dictionary of American Literary Biography). $60.00. PS129.C66. 810'.9'0054. LC 86-33657. ISBN 0-8103-1824-5.

This is the fourth published volume of the projected six-volume series covering the span of American literary history. Like the other volumes in the series, the book updates and expands information originally appearing in the comprehensive Dictionary of Literary Biography, but emphasizes fewer writers. This volume covers 16 major writers of the 1920s, including F. Scott Fitzgerald, Robert Frost, Ernest Hemingway, and Sinclair Lewis.

The format is primarily the same as the parent set, with articles in alphabetical order by author. The articles provide basic biographical data, awards and honors, lists of published literary works, books about the writer listed in chronological order of publication, and a lengthy bio-critical essay. At the end of each essay is a secondary bibliography divided into sections for letters, interviews, bibliographies, biographies, books about the author, and locations of manuscripts. Unique to this series are full-page charts at the beginning of each article that schematically outline themes and influences of each writer. However, the information provided here is too sketchy to be of much value.

The work is aimed at the junior high through junior college audience, but articles have not been condensed or rewritten for the intended audience. Black-and-white photographs of the writers, important places in their lives, and related subjects add interest to the text. On the whole this is a reliable, up-to-date, and well-written reference source which will meet the budget requirements of smaller libraries.—**Marilyn Strong Noronha**

Children's and Young Adult Literature

552. **American Writers for Children before 1900**. Glenn E. Estes, ed. Detroit, Gale, 1985. 441p. illus. bibliog. index. (Dictionary of Literary Biography, Vol. 42). $88.00. LC 85-15990. ISBN 0-8103-1720-6.

A companion volume to John Cech's *American Writers for Children, 1900-1960* (Detroit, Gale, 1983), this volume has the same excellent coverage and format. For each of 52 authors from the nineteenth century, there is a list of "Selected Books," a portrait, an interestingly written bibliographical account, illustrations from the author's books, and additional helps such as listings under bibliography, biography, references, and papers. Included are such well-known writers as Jacob Abbott, Louisa May Alcott, Horatio Alger, Joel Chandler Harris, Helen Hunt Jackson, Howard Pyle, and

Kate Douglas Wiggin. At the end of the volume are two useful sections: "Checklist for Further Reading" and a cumulative index of the first 42 volumes of Dictionary of Literary Biography, the Dictionary of Literary Biography *Yearbooks,* 1980-1984, and the Dictionary of Literary Biography Documentary series, volumes 1-4. A list of contributors is also provided.

Biographical accounts interweave life events and commentaries on literary works. Random reading indicates the contributors and editor have successfully made this a uniform characteristic. The companion volumes are reminiscent of Anne Commire's *Yesterday's Authors of Books for Children* (Detroit, Gale, 1977), and *Something about the Author* (Detroit, Gale, 1971). However, while the two volumes of *American Writers for Children* are more literary and readable in style, they are not so inclusive in coverage as the Commire titles.

A strong binding, good quality paper, excellent print, and clear reproductions of photographs and illustrations make this an inviting book for users, especially for libraries. *American Writers for Children before 1900* is strongly recommended for all who are interested in children's authors.—**Ruth E. Bauner**

553. **American Writers for Children, 1900-1960**. John Cech, ed. Detroit, Gale, 1983. 412p. illus. bibliog. index. (Dictionary of Literary Biography, Vol. 22; A Bruccoli Clark Book). $78.00. LC 83-14199. ISBN 0-8103-1146-1.

This title in Gale's Dictionary of Literary Biography series focuses on "Childhood's Golden Era" in the United States. From 1900 to 1960 there was an awakening interest in and development of literature for children. "The intent of this volume is to present many of the major figures—as well as important though perhaps less well known writers and author-illustrators" of U.S. children's books published between 1900 and 1960. Forty-three authoritative and readable entries give the subject's name, dates, portrait, and a selected bibliography of the subject's work. This is followed by a narrative containing biographical information and a description and critique of the subject's major contributions to children's literature. Such well-known authors and illustrators as Lynd Ward, Robert McCloskey, Margaret Wise Brown, and E. B. White are deservedly included. Less well-known people who contributed to or significantly influenced the development of children's literature over these six decades are also included, for example, William McCay and Watty Piper. Discussions of the author's or illustrator's work include such things as the controversy over the black-and-white rabbits in Garth Williams's *Rabbits' Wedding* and the importance of the double-page spread in Virginia Lee Burton's work. In the back, a good bibliography lists titles for further reading.

Although not appropriate for in-depth research, this volume can serve well as a quick reference to some of the more important people involved with children's literature during these years. It is a good tool for an academic library supporting children's literature courses, or any other libraries that can afford it. [R: BL, 15 Apr 84, p. 1196]—**Carol A. Doll**

554. **American Writers for Children since 1960: Fiction.** Glenn E. Estes, ed. Detroit, Gale, 1986. 488p. illus. bibliog. index. (Dictionary of Literary Biography, Vol. 52). $88.00. LC 86-14885. ISBN 0-8103-1730-3.

In the 1960s, social realism found its way into children's fiction as authors began to write frankly and freely about the problems not only of growing up, but also of living in a culturally diverse society. Although this realistic writing brought with it numerous attempts at censorship, many of the writers who pioneered in this field have produced works which have found a lasting place in children's literature.

The 44 biographees included in this biographical dictionary are authors of realism as well as the writers of historical fiction and fantasy who worked in the years 1960-1986. Many of them are award winners, such as Lloyd Alexander, Judy Blume, Robert Cormier, Katherine Paterson, Judith Viorst, and Paul Zindel, to name a few.

Each biographical essay, written by a scholar or expert, depicts the author's life and work, incorporating critical quotes from published reviews wherever feasible. Supplementing each essay are bibliographies of works by and about the author. Heavily illustrated with portraits and facsimile title and text pages, the volume is attractive and readable.

An afterword by Perry Nodelman of the University of Winnipeg critically reviews the literature of the period and provides a fitting conclusion to this useful reference work. A cumulative index to the entire Dictionary of Literary Biography is found at the end of the volume.

Anyone interested in current trends in children's literature and biographical information on today's important authors with perceptive descriptions of their works will find this volume an invaluable resource.—**Sara R. Mack**

555. **American Writers for Children since 1960: Poets, Illustrators, and Nonfiction Authors**. Glenn E. Estes, ed. Detroit, Gale, 1987. 430p. illus. bibliog. index. (Dictionary of Literary Biography, Vol. 61). $92.00. LC 87-14352. ISBN 0-8103-1739-7.

Containing thirty-two biographies of illustrators, poets, and nonfiction writers for children, this volume complements the (DLB) volume *American Writers for Children since 1960: Fiction* (see ARBA 87, entry 1091). Illustrators are the focus of most of the four- to fifteen-page biographies, which relate the subjects' backgrounds and describe many of their works in some detail. Each contains a bibliography of the subject's works and most include a short list of references for further information. There are many illustrations which reproduce the dust jackets of the various books in black-and-white, facsimile reproductions of pages from the authors' original typescripts, and a photograph of each author or illustrator.

The table of contents reads like a children's literature hall of fame. Included are biographies of such noted children's writers and illustrators as Tomie de Paola, Eve Merriam, Maurice Sendak, Steven Kellogg, Marcia Brown, Chris Van Allsburg, and Nancy Larrick.

An appendix lists the winners of fifteen awards and prizes given for children's books, including the Caldecott and Newbery Medals. There is a "Checklist of Further Readings" for more information about children's literature in general. Finally, the volume includes the usual cumulative index to DLB volumes 1-61, as well as the DLB *Yearbook* volumes for 1980-1986, and the *Documentary Series* volumes 1-4.—**Nancy Courtney**

556. **Children's Books and Their Creators**. Anita Silvey, ed. New York, Houghton Mifflin, 1995. 800p. illus. index. $40.00. ISBN 0-395-65380-0.

The editor, with the help of several hundred contributors, has compiled an encyclopedic overview of authors and illustrators (creators) working in the field of children's and young adult literature in the United States over the past hundred years. Silvey's compilation is devoted almost entirely to creators working in the twentieth century, but it also includes some creators from the nineteenth century, due to their continued relevance and popularity in this century (e.g., Mark Twain and Louisa May Alcott). The stated intent for the collection is fourfold. First of all, it is to present the creators working in the twentieth century. Second is to treat the subjects broadly by offering biographical information on the creators; evaluations of the entries; and historical information about the trends, themes, and genres being used at the time. Next, the reference is to be entertaining in its presentation, offering some of the creativity and spontaneity that are evident throughout children's literature. Finally, it is to present a different perspective by featuring various creators speaking for themselves.

Silvey has more than accomplished her desired goal by presenting information that is not only accurate when compared to the *Something about the Author* series but also with the added perspective of comments supplied by the creator. Although there are only 75 such interviews, interspersed throughout the text and encased in a black border for easy identification, they offer a new dimension to the text beyond the usual biographical and critical evaluations. There are also mostly black-and-white illustrations throughout the book (with 15 pages of color plates), reprinted from the books being discussed, which further add to the understanding of children's literature.

This wide-ranging, although purposely not comprehensive, presentation of children's literature creators during the past century is an excellent addition to any size of public or school library. The text, consisting of 800 pages, gives interesting and accurate information, presented in an entertaining fashion. It will be useful for teachers, librarians, parents, and students either studying children's literature or looking for information on a favorite author. [R: BR, Mar/Apr 96, p. 47]—**Bridget Volz**

557. Rollock, Barbara. **Black Authors & Illustrators of Children's Books: A Biographical Dictionary**. 2d ed. Hamden, Conn., Garland, 1992. 234p. illus. index. (Garland Reference Library of the Humanities, v.1316). $35.00. Z 1037. R63. 809'. 89282. LC 91-37402. ISBN 0-8240-7078-X.

Adding some 35 new authors and illustrators to the lineup of African American writers included in the initial edition, this work contains short biographical sketches of some 150 personalities, both living and dead, in the field of children's literature. While any biographical work related to a field in such popular demand as multicultural literature is useful, a few limitations of this work need to be pointed out.

Coverage of biographees is not always even, with birth dates sometimes left out. Many include quoted introductory material, but in the majority of articles this has been omitted. Also, article length does not appear proportional to the importance of the author or illustrator discussed. For example, while Glennette Turner, who has only done a handful of books, is certainly an up-and-coming author, her biography is almost two-and-a-half pages long, while John Steptoe, who illustrated 16 works, including a 1985 Caldecott Honor Book, has slightly more than a page devoted to him.

Noteworthy features of the work, however, are numerous: a simple-to-use dictionary arrangement; a clean, readable format; more than 85 pictures of the authors and illustrators as well as some of their better-known works; and an index of 500 book titles. Appendixes contain a list of children's award and honor books for the authors and illustrators included, with all Coretta Scott King Award recipients given, and a useful list of black children's publishers' series. School districts, school and public libraries, and children's literature collections should all have this useful biography reference tool. [R: Choice, Sept 92, p. 90]—**Carol Truett**

Drama

558. **American Women Playwrights, 1900-1930: A Checklist**. Frances Diodato Bzowski Diodato, comp. Westport, Conn., Greenwood Press, 1992. 420p. (Bibliographies and Indexes in Women's Studies, no.15). $59.50. Z1231.D7B95. 016.812'52099287. LC 92-12301. ISBN 0-313-24238-0.

The reasons for Bzowski's choice of the period surveyed are interesting. The beginning of the twentieth century, she points out, offered women playwrights a unique opportunity: it accepted their right to express themselves at a time when there was a concurrent strong little-theater movement across the country. However, the depression brought women's social freedoms to an end until the women's movement reemerged in the 1970s. (The plays written by women in that period will be the subject of another bibliography.) Given the output of some 12,000 plays by American women during the period, the fact that this bibliography was compiled by one person represents an impressive achievement. Limitations of time and energy, however, have led Bzowski to skimp on certain aspects, notably biographical data on the writers. Also, her vague information that certain plays were "probably published, but not located" is not really helpful without any indication of the evidence on which that judgment was made. Overall, this bibliography maintains the high standard of scholarly thoroughness of the earlier volumes in the series. [R: Choice, Dec 92, p. 598]—**John B. Beston**

559. **Contemporary American Dramatists**. K. A. Berney and N. G. Templeton, eds. Detroit, St. James Press, 1994. 771p. index. $40.00. ISBN 1-55862-214-4.

This volume is part of the St. James Press Contemporary Literature series that also contains *Contemporary British Dramatists* and *Contemporary Women Dramatists*. The focus of this work is on the best English-language writers for the stage who are currently active. It also includes many who have died since 1950 but whose reputations remain essentially contemporary.

An introductory essay discusses the influences and movements of the last four decades on, and addresses the current state of, the American theater. Nearly 200 playwrights (including women) from George Abbott to Paul Zindel are listed alphabetically. Each entry contains a biography; a complete list of plays, screenplays, and radio and television writing; recordings; theatrical activities; and other published works. Also included are a list of bibliographies and critical studies on the writer and a signed essay. In some cases the writers also furnished comments on their work. The entries conclude with addresses where the living writers may be reached. A title index is also provided.

Selecting the writers to be featured in such a volume is always problematic. One might argue that older writers like O'Neill and Wilder, about whom much is already available, should have been omitted in the interests of adding more truly contemporary artists, such as Robert Schenkkan, who is mentioned in the introductory essay but is otherwise unaccountably missing. However, on balance, this work has a great deal of information to offer on its subject, much of which would not be available in any other single volume.—**Kay O. Cornelius**

560.   Gavin, Christy. **American Women Playwrights 1964-1989: A Research Guide and Annotated Bibliography**. Hamden, Conn., Garland, 1993. 493p. index. (Garland Reference Library of the Humanities, v.879). $75.00. Z1231.D7G38. 016.812'54099287. LC 92-42768. ISBN 0-8240-3046-X.

Limited to works by and about women playwrights active during the 25-year period from 1964 to 1989, Gavin's bibliography is thorough and well researched. The tone of the introduction and some of the annotations, however, betray her aversion to traditional theater, which she views as dominated by Caucasian males. For example, her claim that plays by women, such as Marsha Norman's *'night Mother* and Wendy Wasserstein's *The Heidi Chronicles,* have been ignored by the theatrical community, academia, and the general public is unfounded, because both plays won Pulitzer Prizes (as Gavin admits) and had very successful runs in New York City. Elsewhere, Gavin further distinguishes among female playwrights by singling out "multicultural" playwrights for special attention.

Despite the lapses into subjectivity, Gavin has produced a well-organized work, dividing it into three sections: an introductory bibliographical essay; an annotated list of general works on the topic; and, by far the largest section, an annotated bibliography of works by individual playwrights and secondary literature about the women and their plays. The author index is useful, but a list of multicultural playwrights without page references serves no obvious purpose. Recommended for theater collections. [R: Choice, Oct 93, p. 266; RBB, 1 Oct 93, p. 377]—**Valerie R. Hotchkiss**

561.   Peterson, Jane T., and Suzanne Bennett. **Women Playwrights of Diversity: A Biobibliographical Sourcebook**. Westport, Conn., Greenwood Press, 1997. 399p. index. $79.50. ISBN 0-313-29179-9.

This work includes more than 100 women playwrights writing from and about the ethnic and cultural diversity in the United States in the 1990s, encompassing African American, Asian American, Latina, and lesbian/bisexual writers, both established and emerging. The sourcebook was produced as a resource for theater practitioners and teachers of dramatic literature and women's studies courses. The works included here have been written since 1970. Recommendations for inclusion were from community theater groups, drama critics, and selected scholars and teachers of marginalized women playwrights. The criteria for selection were existing production records of the writers and the potential for production on and off Broadway. Production values, such as appeal to a diverse audience; audience response to characters; the writer's understanding of the stage; the attraction of the works by directors, designers, and actors; the worth of the dramatic piece; and the piece's distinctive voice were considered in the selection process. The authors were particularly drawn to plays that would have an attraction for performance by other than the original creators. The list of playwrights is a selective one and thus does not include all ethnic and lesbian writers of import today, but it is representative of a broad and growing diversity in theater productions.

The volume includes an introduction by Bennett, followed by critical essays, the first on African American women playwrights by Sydne Mahone; the second on Asian American women playwrights by Chiori Miyagawa; the third on Latina drama by Tiffany Ana Lopez; and the fourth on lesbian playwrights by Jill Dolan. The major section of the book is devoted to separate entries about each playwright, arranged in alphabetical order by dramatist's surname. The entries include a brief biographical note, descriptions of important plays, a selected production history of each work, grants and awards won by the playwright, and a selected bibliography of critical works. Some of the playwrights included are Sydne Mahone, who wrote *for colored girls*; Wakako Yamauchi, who wrote *And the Soul Shall Dance*; Caridad Svich, who wrote *Any Place but Here*; and Jane Chambers, who wrote *Quintessential Image*.

There are 4 appendixes to the volume, the 1st with listings of key playwrights' names by cultural/ethnic grouping, the 2d a list of additional playwrights by the same cultural/ethnic group; the 3d a list of nominators associated with theaters from San Francisco to New York; and the last a list of nominators' names. A brief but important selected bibliography for further research is provided. It includes general reference works, collections of plays, and critical works. An index, arranged alphabetically by dramatist and title of work, leads back to the entries with page numbers in bold typeface referring to main entries.

The introduction, the essays, and the entries are well written and provocative, leading one to a greater understanding of the impact and importance of women dramatists of color and varying sexual orientation. Much of the information presented is difficult to identify and locate in traditional reference resources, thereby bringing new works to light and highlighting many others that have or will have a major impact on valuing cultural and ethnic diversity in the theater. [R: LJ, 1 Apr 97, p. 84]—**Maureen Pastine**

Ethnic Minorities

562.   **African American Writers**. Lea Baechler and A. Walton Litz, eds. New York, Scribner's, 1991. 544p. index. $85.00. PS153.N5A344. 810.9'896073. LC 90-52918. ISBN 0-684-19058-3.

This new volume presents 34 critical essays on the lives and works of African American writers, from Olaudah Equiano (1745-1797) to Alice Walker (1944-). The work represents an effort to compensate for the underrepresentation of African American writers in the popular American Writers series. It appears that the editors have also consciously endeavored to recognize women writers—a group often slighted in literary reference works—by treating an equal number of male and female authors. The articles are written by established scholars (e.g., Henry Louis Gates on Ishmael Reed, Arnold Rampersand on Langston Hughes) and offer not only bio-bibliographical data but also some original literary criticism. Each essay includes a discussion of the author's life and contributions to literature, as well as some treatment of literary reception and a selected bibliography of primary and secondary works. If applicable, the location of the author's manuscripts and papers is also given. The articles seem to be intended for the serious high school student or undergraduate, but more advanced scholars will also find these essays useful and thought-provoking.

Although this reference work makes no claim to be comprehensive, the diversity of the authors represented offers a fine overview of the many and varied contributions of African American writers to American literature. Indeed, many (although not all) of these authors can be found in other literary reference works. This volume is significant, however, for its focus on the African-American experience as portrayed in the works of these important authors. [R: Choice, Oct 91, p. 253; LJ, 1 June 91, p. 124; BL, Aug 91, p. 2169; WLB, June 91, p. 130]—**Valerie R. Hotchkiss**

563.   **Afro-American Fiction Writers after 1955**. Thadious M. Davis and Trudier Harris, eds. Detroit, Gale, 1984. 350p. illus. bibliog. index. (Dictionary of Literary Biography, Vol. 33). $82.00. LC 84-18724. ISBN 0-8103-1711-7

Volume 33 of the Dictionary of Literary Biography features bio-bibliographies of 49 Afro-American fiction writers who have gained prominence since 1955. Some, like James Baldwin, have produced a lengthy bibliography, while others, such as George Cain, are known for one novel.

Each signed biocritical essay discusses the author's development as a writer as well as his or her growth in reputation. Most sketches include personal experiences that shaped the author's vision and work. The articles are exceptionally well written; unlike many biographical works, this one is hard to put down! The illustrations, which run from portraits to reproductions of book jackets and edited pages of typescript, enhance the already handsome volume's esthetic appeal.

The DLB series is expensive, but worth its price. The entries in each volume are consistently well written and edited; the criticism alone is of enormous value to students in college and graduate literature courses. To budget-conscious libraries, however, there may be too great an overlap between the DLB and *Contemporary Authors*. Forty-one of the 49 profiles in volume 33 also appear in *CA*, although only 17 of them have earned space in *Contemporary Literary Criticism*. Still, when finances permit, the series is a good one, and *Afro-American Fiction Writers after 1955* is no exception to its predecessors.—**Diane J. Cimbala**

564. The Afro-American Short Story: A Comprehensive, Annotated Index with Selected Commentaries. Preston M. Yancy, comp. Westport, Conn., Greenwood Press, 1986. 171p. (Bibliographies and Indexes in Afro American and African Studies, No. 10). $35.00. LC 85-27132. ISBN 0-313-24355-7.

More than 800 short stories, written between the socially significant years of 1950 and 1982 by 300 authors, are the subject of this guide. The 1st section is a chronological register, with titles arranged alphabetically within the year, each assigned its own index number for subsequent reference. The 2nd part treats anthologies and collections, with bibliographic citations under the editor's name and with contents provided. Third are commentaries on selected stories, headed by an appropriate category (e.g., comic, personal experience, protest, militant) and a statement regarding the role of race. The commentaries themselves give a summary of the story.

The author index, which makes up the 4th section, lists the authors and refers to five biographical encyclopedias which include information on them. These listings include a works list, a statement about which voice the story is written in, a bibliographic citation, a terse explanation of the plot, and the aforementioned reference number. That number is also provided in the concluding title index. Quite apart from reference to this volume as a finding tool (which aspect might have been intensified with the inclusion of an index of themes—and there are some commonalities revealed in the summaries), one is encouraged to see the social change over the 32-year period are revealed by these writers. [R: Choice, July/Aug 86, p. 1662; RBB, Aug 86, p. 1671; WLB, May 8, p. 60]—**Dominique-René de Lerma**

565. Afro-American Writers after 1955: Dramatists and Prose Writers. Thadious M. Davis and Trudier Harris, eds. Detroit, Gale, 1985. 390p. illus. bibliog. index. (Dictionary of Literary Biography, Vol. 38). $85.00. LC 85-1673. ISBN 0-8103-1716-8.

Focusing on those writers whose careers developed after the *Brown* vs. *the Board of Education* decision in 1954, this collective biography includes information for many lesser-known black authors. Like other books in the DLB series, this volume offers biographical information, plot summaries, and bibliographies of published works by each author. Photographs play an important part throughout this set. Reproductions of dust jackets abound, and there are many face-on views of the 35 authors included. However, none of these photographic portraits are dated and many are of poor quality. There is neither a subject index nor an author-title index serving to identify influential works and writers mentioned by biographees or helping to identify an author included here when one knows only the title of a work. Most essays include a list of references. However, many published articles and interviews referred to in the text are not cited among the references given. This omission will frustrate some users. Some essays concentrate on an author's work, giving a critical review that is insightful and original; others, like the one on Charles Fuller, consist almost entirely of quotations taken from other published sources. An appendix contains six reprinted articles concerning black theatre, including a preliminary listing of black theatres and theatre organizations in the United States.—**Milton H. Crouch**

566. Afro-American Writers before the Harlem Renaissance. Trudier Harris and Thadious M. Davis, eds. Detroit, Gale, 1986. 369p. illus. index. (Dictionary of Literary Biography, Vol. 50). $88.00. LC 86-12121. ISBN 0-8103-1728-1.

Thirty-three individuals are treated in this elaborately produced volume, the oldest being Jupiter Hammon (born in 1711), the youngest being Joseph Cotter, Jr. (born in 1895). Among the best-known figures are Frederick Douglass, W. E. B. DuBois, Paul Laurence Dunbar, and Phillis Wheatley. Each entry is written by a specialist, following the editors' format. After the vital statistics comes a bibliography of the books and other publications by the writer. The biographical sections are detailed and include criticism and an evaluation of the writer's place in history. The entries conclude with reference to significant literature about the individual and identification of the location of the writer's papers. Photographs and facsimiles are abundantly provided in the main body of the volume, which concludes with five appendices (mainly reprints of critical commentary) and a cumulative index for the entire series. This is a monumental undertaking which will be of major value to researchers.—**Dominique-René de Lerma**

567. **Afro-American Writers from the Harlem Renaissance to 1940**. Trudier Harris and Thadious M. Davis, eds. Detroit, Gale, 1987. 386p. illus. bibliog. index. (Dictionary of Literary Biography, Vol. 51). $90.00. LC 86-26954. ISBN 0-8103-1729-X.

This monumental series now provides biographical data (in the same excellent format) on 34 new figures. The earliest included here is James Weldon Johnson, also one of the best known, born in 1871. The youngest is Helene Johnson, born in 1907. Arna Bontemps, Countee Cullen, Jessie Fauset, Langston Hughes, Zora Neale Hurston, Georgia Douglas Johnson, Walter White, and Jean Toomer are among those included in this volume, with a contrast in racial attitudes particularly evident in those of George Schuyler and Claude McKay. As before, this is a fine source for information on the lives of these figures, but there are also excellent criticism of their work and very valuable aids which will lead to additional data. The appendix treats Alain Locke and Carl Van Vechten. [R: Choice, May 87, p. 1371]—**Dominique-René de Lerma**

568. **Afro-American Writers, 1940-1955**. Trudier Harris and Thadious M. Davis, eds. Detroit, Gale, 1988. 389p. illus. bibliog. index. (Dictionary of Literary Biography, vol. 76). $95.00. LC 88-21423. ISBN 0-8103-4554-4.

This "sixth and final volume in the [DLB] series devoted exclusively to Afro-American writers" (p.xi) covers 26 novelists, poets, playwrights, biographers, screenwriters, and essayists who published significant works between 1940 and 1955. Other volumes in the subseries cover fiction writers after 1955 (see ARBA 85, entry 1056), dramatists and prose writers after 1955 (see ARBA 86, entry 1132), poets after 1955 (see ARBA 86, entry 1155), writers before the Harlem Renaissance (see ARBA 87, entry 1069), and writers from the Harlem Renaissance to 1940 (see ARBA 88, entry 1158). The essays in this volume begin with a list of works by each writer followed by discussions (punctuated with photographs) of each writer's life and works, and conclude with selected references to critical works (not linked to the text) and locations of papers. Essay length varies for each author based on his or her renown (e.g., 3 pages for William Blackwell Branch, 23 for Richard Wright). References are often insufficient (e.g., 2 references for J. Saunders Redding, 3 for Melvin Tolson, 4 for Margaret Walker), although the entry for Ralph Ellison has 81 references. The essays are well written, some critical, some simply descriptive, by little-known scholars (although Robert Farnsworth composed the Tolson entry), and all significant authors of the period are covered (e.g., Gwendolyn Brooks, Robert Hayden, Chester Himes, Ann Petry). Three additional essays describe the Hatch-Billops Collection, the Moorland Spingarn Research Center, and the Schomburg Center. A superfluous reprint of the readily available December 1950 issue of *Phylon* expands the text by 62 pages, space that could have been better used for an analytical index. The work concludes with a 46-item general bibliography and the usual DLB cumulative index.—**Robert Aken**

569. **A Bibliographical Guide to African-American Women Writers**. Casper LeRoy Jordan, comp. Westport, Conn., Greenwood Press, 1993. 387p. index. $65.00. Z1229.N39J67. 016.8108' 09287'08996. LC 93-6561. ISBN 0-313-27633-1.

Compiled by a former librarian and library school educator, this bibliography lists writings by and by and about African-American women writers through 1991. The approximately 900 creative writers, biographers, essayists, and critics included range chronologically from the eighteenth-century poet Lucy Terry to Lorene Cary, whose first novel appeared in 1991. In addition to such major writers as Maya Angelou, Gwendolyn Brooks, and Alice Walker, the bibliography covers numerous lesser-known and obscure figures, many of whom are not generally included in standard sources.

Arranged alphabetically by author, the entries identify primary works first, followed by a section for secondary sources. References to critical and other secondary works include books, articles in popular magazines and scholarly journals, chapters in books, and dissertations. Book reviews are excluded. Due to an extension of the cut-off date for the bibliography, publications from 1988-1991 appear in separate sections at the end of an author's entry. A separate supplementary section near the end of the volume covers writers whose first publications appeared between 1988 and 1991. Additional chapters list anthologies of black writings and general biographical and critical works. The index includes not only the authors treated but also the authors, editors, translators, and compilers of secondary works cited.

Substantial portions of this bibliography overlap the coverage of previous bibliographies, such as *Black American Women in Literature* (see ARBA 90, entry 858) and *The Pen Is Ours* (see ARBA 92, entry 1150). Unfortunately, comparison with both of those works and with *Toni Morrison: An Annotated Bibliography* (see ARBA 89, entry 1080) and *Zora Neale Hurston: A Reference Guide* (see ARBA 88, entry 1177) reveals that Jordan has omitted a significant number of titles. However, due to its breadth of coverage, it can serve as a starting point for research on Afro-American women writers, particularly for minor and previously neglected figures. [R: Choice, Nov 93, p. 423; RBB, 15 Dec 93, p. 774; WLB, Nov 93, p. 98]—**Marie Ellis**

570. **Chicano Writers: First Series**. Francisco A. Lomelí and Carl R. Shirley, eds. Detroit, Gale, 1989. 388p. illus. index. (Dictionary of Literary Biography, v.82). $98.00. PS153.M4C48. 810'.9'86872. LC 88-36536. ISBN 0-8103-4560-9.

Chicano Writers: Second Series. Francisco A. Lomelí and Carl R. Shirley, eds. Detroit, Gale, 1992. 417p. illus. index. (Dictionary of Literary Biography, v. 122). $140.00. LC 92-29057. ISBN 0-8103-7599-0.

These volumes in the Dictionary of Literary Biography series include biographical essays on 116 Chicano writers, 52 in the *First Series*; 64 in the *Second*. Visual materials such as photographs of the writers and their families, manuscript pages, sketches, and book jackets add to the immediacy of the text. Beginning with a brief look at Chicano history, each appendix also contributes useful information. In the *First Series*, an appendix on Chicano language is followed by another on non-Hispanic authors writing about the Mexican American experience. Such works, called *literatura chicanesca,* or chicanesque literature, date from 1826. The *Second Series* contains an appendix on Miguel de Quintana (1671-1748), considered a forerunner on Chicano literature.

As the editors point out, critics do not agree on a definition of Chicano literature. In the foreword to the *First Series*, in fact, Luis Leal argues that the Chicano canon must include authors who wrote when the southwestern United States was part of Mexico because their "sensibility . . . is different from that of the writers of Central Mexico." On the other hand, the preface indicates 1848, the year that the United States acquired most of the southwestern states, as their dividing point. Despite this inconsistency, these books provide important information about literature and literary criticism by and about Americans of Mexican descent.—**Renee B. Horowitz and Terry Ann Mood**

571. **Contemporary Jewish-American Novelists: A Bio-Critical Sourcebook**. Joel Shatzky and Michael Taub, eds. Westport, Conn., Greenwood Press, 1997. 506p. index. $85.00. ISBN 0-313-29462-3.

With 63 alphabetic entries on novelists whose birth years range from 1874 to 1954, this volume focuses on works published after World War II. (The entry on Gertrude Stein, who died in 1946, is a curious exception.) Much earlier fiction by American Jews dealt with European experiences or trials of early immigrants rather than the subject emphasized here—problems resulting from assimilation into American culture. Except for Mordecai Richler, a Canadian, all the writers covered were born or are based in the United States. Most entries (the one for Lionel Trilling varies slightly) contain five sections: biographical sketch, analysis of major works and themes, summary of the writer's critical reception, listing of primary works, and bibliography of criticism. Discussion of major authors (Saul Bellow, Bernard Malamud, and especially Philip Roth) is thorough and incisive, but the editors choose to give slight attention to novels by authors of Jewish origin when those works reflect little ethnic concern (e.g., some popular novels by Norman Mailer). Potentially more useful, because they provide information not readily available elsewhere, are entries on lesser-known writers. Here the editors have included several women, some gay writers (Judith Katz and Lev Raphael), and one author, Art Spiegelman, whose narratives take the form of comic strips.

Directed toward both students and scholars of Jewish American literature, this work supplements and sometimes overlaps two earlier publications—*Jewish American Women Writers: A Bio-bibliographical and Critical Sourcebook* (Greenwood Press, 1994) and *Twentieth-Century American-Jewish Fiction Writers* (see ARBA 85, entry 1064). The book at hand contains a perceptive introduction to Jewish fiction by Sanford Marovitz, an appendix with minimal information about 25 Jewish women writers, and a general bibliography.—**Albert Wilhelm**

572.   Holte, James Craig. **The Ethnic I: A Sourcebook for Ethnic-American Autobiography**. Westport, Conn., Greenwood Press, 1988. 210p. index. $39.95. LC 87-23650. ISBN 0-313-24463-4.

Descriptive studies and criticisms of major autobiographical works by 29 ethnic American writers comprise the contents of this sourcebook. The work begins with a brief essay, "Introduction: Personal Voices from the New World," in which Holte discusses the particular conventions of the autobiography as a literary genre, emphasizing its ability to combine both history and literature as well as the objectivity of facts and the subjectivity of the perceptions of personal experience.

Holte also points out two major approaches taken to the ethnic autobiography: (1) as a chronicle of the transformation or conversion of the ethnic or immigrant from outside the dominant culture to an accepted, often successful, insider; and (2) as recorded observations of instances in which the majority culture has not included individuals who, because of race, sex, class, language, or their own volition, failed to be assimilated into the mainstream of society. He points out that, in either case, the writer may have experienced some kind of transformation, and says that "the very language used to describe ethnic and immigrant experience underscores the notion of change and conversion" (p.6).

Autobiographies described that represent the first success story of conversion include those of writer Mary Antin, steel maker Andrew Carnegie, and film director Frank Capra. Some that exemplify rejection of the individual of or by the American community include personal narratives of Emma Goldman, Black Elk, and Malcolm X.

The 29 accounts included represent a wide range of personal experiences, from well-known and popular works (e.g., Nicky Cruz's *Run, Baby, Run*; *Jacocca;* and Booker T. Washington's *Up from Slavery*) to those that are less familiar, or even obscure, such as black writer Zora Neal Hurston's *Dust Tracks on a Road: The Autobiography of Mary Jane Hill Anderson*. The titles cover a period of over 150 years, from the personal recollections of Mary Jane Hill Anderson, who was born in 1827, to contemporary accounts of *The Woman Warrior* (1976) by Maxine Hong Kingston, and Lee Iacocca's *Jacocca* (1984).

Entries are arranged alphabetically by author and include a brief biographical sketch of the writer; descriptive comments about his or her autobiography, including selected excerpts; a critical analysis of the work; and a bibliography of further references. The work is not indexed, but is concluded with a "Bibliographical Essay" examining ethnic and immigrant writing in American literature as a growing field of intellectual investigation. While the amount of coverage given to literary criticism is rather limited in each of these narratives, the descriptions of the ethnic American's emotions and experiences are rich and vivid, making this a unique source book for readers from a historical, sociological, and literary perspective.—**Lois Buttlar**

573.   **Modern African American Writers**. New York, Facts on File, 1994. 92p. index. (Essential Bibliography of American Fiction). $18.95; $9.95pa. Z1229.N39M63. 016.813'509896. LC 93-8643. ISBN 0-8160-2998-9; 0-8160-2999-7pa.

This bibliography contains up-to-date listings of significant primary and secondary works pertaining to nine major figures in twentieth-century African-American literature. The book is designed for convenient and easy use in high schools, community colleges, and general libraries. The foreword is by the well-known scholar Keneth Kinnamon, who provides an interesting sweep of the general accomplishments of Black literary creativity. Through it the reader receives a deep appreciation of the remarkable work produced by numerous writers of the African American experience. The plan of the entries for each literary figure includes, in addition to the primary material by the writer, lists of bibliographies, manuscript and archival collections, biographies, and critical studies in books and journals.

The volume's focus is on the most important scholarly work associated with a select group of writers: James Baldwin, Charles W. Chesnutt, Ralph Ellison, Zora Neale Hurston, Toni Morrison, Ishmael Reed, Jean Toomer, Alice Walker, and Richard Wright. Unfortunately absent from the list is a major poet; a good choice for inclusion would have been Langston Hughes. There are other sections that give essential information on general critical sources, such as guides to research, literary dictionaries, and journals containing materials on African American writers.

This book will prove useful to persons of many different educational levels because of its simplicity of presentation, uncluttered format, and complete informational listings. An improvement would have been to include brief annotations for some of the most important entries. Instead, the reader is told to go to other works that contain annotated items. However, a helpful device in the bibliography is the use of an asterisk to denote those critical studies that are considered the most accessible and influential ones. [R: Choice, July/Aug 94, p. 1704; RBB, 1 Apr 94, p. 1476]—**Angelo Costanzo**

574. **Native North American Literature: Biographical and Critical Information on Native Writers and Orators**.... Janet Witalec, ed. Detroit, Gale, 1995. 706p. illus. index. $99.00. ISBN 0-8103-9898-2.

The reading public has had two new major guides to Native American literature appear within six months of one another. *Dictionary of Native American Literature* appeared first (see ARBA 95, entry 1175). There are certainly many similarities in the structure and content between this publication and the *Dictionary,* as one would expect due to subject matter. Both encompass oral and written literature, as well as having biographical essays about some of the leading individuals in the field. This volume provides in-depth essays on 78 people, 4 entries under oral autobiography: Black Elk, Black Hawk, Maria Chona, and Lame Deer; and 4 entries under oratory: Chief Joseph, Chief Seattle, Sitting Bull, and Tecumseh. The balance of entries are for writers, most of whom are actively writing. The oral literature section has a 45-page introduction that discusses the character of the oral literature as well as exploring the differences between stories, myths, and song.

Biographical entries are long, a minimum of four pages, meaning excellent depth. The volume is selective, but one finds entries for all of the major contemporary Native American authors (e.g., Vine Deloria, Joy Harjo, N. Scott Momaday, Duane Niatum, and Leslie Marmon Silko). There is also a good selection of authors whose works are readily available, if one goes to a first-rate bookstore or places a special order. Witalec also included a reasonable cross section of deceased authors.

Each entry provides basic biographical information; a biographical essay; a chronological list of major works; a discussion of the criticism of the individual's works excerpted from published reviews, articles, and books (also arranged chronologically); and a "sources for further study" section. There is an explanatory notes section with the criticism material that enables users to place the material in a broader context, such as who the critic was and the purpose of the criticism. Separate genre and title indexes provide additional useful means of access. If a choice must be made, this volume provides more biographies and excerpts of criticism; the *Dictionary* has more essays about Native American literature. Libraries with large reference collections, as well as those serving communities with a strong interest in Native Americans, should have both titles.—**G. Edward Evans**

575. Peterson, Bernard L. Jr. **Contemporary Black American Playwrights and Their Plays: A Biographical Directory and Dramatic Index**. Westport, Conn., Greenwood Press, 1988. 625p. bibliog. index. $75.00. LC 87-17814. ISBN 0-313-25190-8.

The main entries in this valuable reference work are by individuals active in writing for the stage (spoken and musical), television, radio, and film, since 1950, even if some works have remained unpublished and unperformed. The biographical sketches which follow are terse but informative, and include current addresses. The plays are described by genre (drama, tragicomedy, domestic comedy, etc., although it can be anticipated these terms do not come from a list of standardized terms), date of production, synopsis of plot, location of the scripts (including films and recordings), and other information of value. The foreword is by James V. Hatch, a highly respected archivist in the field. Appendices cover additional materials deposited in special collections and works by other writers about which insufficient information has been located. The bibliographic aids are excellent.

Although a new edition is already projected, this initial venture provides significant data not available elsewhere. As a stimulus for research, perhaps the next edition will add a topical index to the existing ones (titles and general) so that one might be led to consider the treatment of recurring themes, such as bicultural values, miscegenation, sexual orientation, and domestic issues. Because this publication appears not to have been produced by computer, the cut-off date seems to be 1984. Producers, theater devotees, cultural historians, and Americanists will welcome this acquisition.—**Dominique-René de Lerma**

576.   Roses, Lorraine Elena, and Ruth Elizabeth Randolph. **Harlem Renaissance and Beyond: Literary Biographies of 100 Black Women Writers 1900-1945**. Boston, G. K. Hall, 1990. 413p. illus. index. $45.00. PS153.N5R65. 810.9'9287'03. LC 89-38731. ISBN 0-8161-8926-9.

This collection of 100 biographical essays fills a gap in the history of black American women writers flourishing between 1900-1945. This well-documented reference source, relying heavily on archival documents and oral testimony, is a convenient springboard for in-depth research into the lives and work of a significant body of writers.

These biographies profile, for the most part, formally educated, published writers who achieved some national recognition during the period in which they wrote or after their deaths. Each biography averages from one to eight-and-a-half pages in length and contains selected bibliographies of both primary and secondary sources. Many contain photographs.

The work contains four appendixes that classify the writers by literary genre/profession (i.e., autobiographies, poets, essayists, biographies), location, date of birth, and titles. A more extensive bibliography of secondary sources appears at the end. This work is recommended for all medium to large academic libraries with collections of black and women's studies. [R: Choice, May 90, p. 1484; RBB, 15 Jan 90, 904, pp. 1042-44; RQ, Fall 90, p. 123]—**J. C. Jurgens**

577.   **Southern Black Creative Writers, 1829-1953: Bio-bibliographies**. M. Marie Booth Foster, comp. Westport, Conn., Greenwood Press, 1988. 113p. (Bibliographies and Indexes in Afro-American and African Studies, No. 22). $29.95. LC 88-5595. ISBN 0-313-26207-1.

This publication contains bio-bibliographical information on nearly 200 Southern black writers. While the names one expects to see—Arna Bontemps, Frank Yerby, Frances Harper, W. E. B. DuBois—are included, other writers who have not been so felicitously dealt with by time—Alice Dunbar-Nelson and Mary Weston Ford come to mind—also appear. The volume opens with an essay on the historical periods covered: 1829-1865, Reconstruction to 1912, 1913-1928, and "Oppressed, Depressed, Suppressed, but Determined 1829-1953" (this latter turns out to be a typographical error for 1929-1953, *cf.* pp. xiv and 81). Following this essay are the entries themselves. It is sometimes difficult to read this section because the authors' names appear in a typeface identical to that of the entry itself, set apart only by blank lines above and below. Moreover, the information contained in the entries seems sometimes to have been brought over wholesale from another source without much editorial adjustment. Compare, for example, Abram Hill's entry in *Southern Black Creative Writers* (*SBCW*) (p. 36) with the one in Edward Mapp's *Directory of Blacks in the Performing Arts* (see ARBA 79, entry 1016), a directory cited as a source for *SBCW* (p.109). *SBCW* states that Hill earned his bachelor's degree in 1937 from Lincoln University. To my certain knowledge, there are Lincoln universities in Tennessee, Missouri, and Pennsylvania—but to my consternation, *SBCW* does not distinguish between them. The fact that Mapp does not include the state name is really no excuse for Foster. The criterion for inclusion in *SBCW* is birth date, birth place, and race. Thomas Ward, for example, who was born in 1908 in Louisiana, is included (p.67), although he left the South at thirteen, and all of his creative life seems to have been spent in the North.

In the back of the volume are author listings sorted by date and state. Authors can be listed more than once here. W. E. B. DuBois, for example, appears under 1866-1912 (p.79) as well as under 1913-1928 (p.80).

This work's editorial control is truly insufficient. One can only hope that this material will be handled more seriously in the future.—**Judith M. Brugger**

Fiction

578.   **American Novelists, 1910-1945**. James J. Martine, ed. Detroit, Gale, 1981. 3v. illus. bibliog. index. (Dictionary of Literary Biography, Vol. 9; A Bruccoli Clark Book). $240.00/set. LC 81-6834. ISBN 0-8103-0931-9.

The period 1910 to 1945, encompassing World War I, the Great Depression, and World War II, a period of conflict and turmoil in American history, gave rise to eighteen major, and more than 100 lesser-known, American novelists. These novelists and their works are critically examined in this three-volume set of Gale's Dictionary of Literary Biography series. Among the major writers discussed are Sherwood Anderson, Willa Cather, John Dos Passos, Theodore Dreiser, William Faulkner, F. Scott Fitzgerald, Ernest Hemingway, Sinclair Lewis, Henry Miller, John O'Hara, John Steinbeck, Edith Wharton, and Thomas Wolfe. In all, 125 writers are covered in *American Novelists, 1910-1945.*

Entries are arranged alphabetically and begin with a listing of the author's work, followed by critical essays about the author and his or her writings, and listings of other relevant readings and reference material. The length of the entries varies, the editors state, depending on the writer's influence and size of canon. The shorter essays run 2 to 3 pages; the longer ones go up to 20 pages.

Illustrative material includes photographs of the authors, early drafts of their novels, and edited manuscripts. Appendixes provide additional useful information, including articles giving an "Overview of U.S. Book Publishing, 1910-1945" and examining "Southern Writers between the Wars," the "Proletarian Novel," "American Fiction and the 1930s," and "Tough-Guy Literature."—**Patty Wood**

579.   **American Novelists since World War II**. Jeffrey Helterman and Richard Layman, eds. Detroit, Gale, 1978. 557p. illus. bibliog. (Dictionary of Literary Biography, Vol. 2; A Bruccoli Clark Book). $80.00. LC 77-82804. ISBN 0-8103-0914-9.

American Novelists since World War II, Second Series. James E. Kibler, Jr., ed. Detroit, Gale, 1980. 404p. illus. index. (Dictionary of Literary Biography, Vol. 6; A Bruccoli Clark Book). $80.00. LC 80-22495. ISBN 0-8103-0908-4.

American Novelists since World War II, Fifth Series. James R. Giles and Wanda H. Giles, eds. Detroit, Gale, 1996. 379p. illus. index. (Dictionary of Literary Biography, v.173). $140.00. ISBN 0-8103-9936-9.

The first volume of the three covers some eighty figures of prominence who have established themselves since the end of World War II. It continues the series's pattern of long essays (18) as well as some shorter ones. Here, long essays are given on Baldwin, Barth, Cheever, McCullers, Nabokov, Pynchon, Updike, Vonnegut, Penn Warren, and Welty, among others. There are also bibliographies.

Here, despite the apparent attempt to follow the general pattern, the essays are overly long. This book has 80 sketches and fills 557 pages; the Myerson first volume, by contrast, covers 98 figures in less than half the space—224 pages. Long sections of each essay are devoted to exegesis of individual works, sometimes detailed examination, and it seems too much here. Instead of saying, "Hey, here's a good book!," the essay reduces the books to playthings, sometimes resembling hardcover Cliff Notes.

The *Second Series* provides material on many lesser-known literary figures, many of whom are still developing their reputations. While it is easy to find data on Vladimir Nabokov, James Agee, and Ray Bradbury (all treated in the 1978 edition), this volume offers the user background on such writers as Mark Steadman, a "patient craftsman" who has produced two novels since 1971, and Joan Williams, who has done three since 1961. Essays vary in length.

The *third series* covers twenty writers, many of whom were covered in earlier volumes in the series. In some cases, this is justified, when the author is still producing (Philip Roth, E. L. Doctorow). In the case of deceased authors (Carson McCullers, Jean Stafford), this is less justified.

These volumes will be added by those libraries which subscribe to the series, and will be wanted by libraries with an interest in contemporary fiction.[R: Choice, July/Aug 79, p. 645; LJ, 1 Apr 79, p. 938; WLB, June 79, pp. 722-23]—**Koert C. Loomis, Jr. and Terry Ann Mood**

580.   **American Realists and Naturalists**. Donald Pizer and Earl N. Harbert, eds. Detroit, Gale, 1982. 486p. illus. index. (Dictionary of Literary Biography, Vol. 12; A Bruccoli Clark Book). $70.00. LC 82-9258. ISBN 0-8103-1149-6.

This volume, highly useful in itself, is an important addition to the DLB series. *American Realists and Naturalists* would be valuable if it merely confined itself to presenting somewhat traditional biographies; however, the editors have made sure the volume goes much further than that. Authors are not only treated within the context of their age, but also studied as participants in an American culture that would bear their impress. As a result, the intersections of European thought, American intellectual life, and the promise of the future become underlying themes of many of the biographies. In fact, the reader wishes that the essays would somehow be longer—a sign of how fulfilling each study actually is.

The entries have a common format: citations for birth, education, death, awards, etc.; a list of selected books; and lists of bibliographies, biographies, letters, seminal critical works, papers, and the like. While these critical references are, in instances, highly selective, and I think, partisan (one person's acclaimed biography is another's unimaginative reading), they often do great justice to the subject. The entries are fleshed out with photographs of the writer, a reproduction of a page from a manuscript, or the picture of a book-jacket. In short, the essays seek to make their subjects accessible and timely. Finally, the essays themselves are quite readable; they are free from literary jargon and tight in their focus. If they are not necessarily daring, they are thoughtful and always informative.—**Lewis Fried**

581.   **Modern Classic Writers**. New York, Facts on File, 1994. 99p. index. (Essential Bibliography of American Fiction). $18.95; $9.95pa. Z1231.F4M63. 016.813'509. LC 93-8641. ISBN 0-8160-3002-2; 0-8160-3003-0pa.

Volumes in this series, "largely adapted from author entries" in *Facts on File Bibliography of American Fiction 1919-1988* (see ARBA 92, entry 1162) and *Facts on File Bibliography of American Fiction 1866-1918* (see ARBA 94, entry 1229), are intended for high schools, community colleges, and general libraries. The authors are William Faulkner, F. Scott Fitzgerald, Ernest Hemingway, John Steinbeck, Robert Penn Warren, and Thomas Wolfe. Each entry begins with a brief author profile; these do not add to the reference value of the bibliography. However, George Garrett's foreword provides a good explanation of the reasons for selecting these authors. Entries for the six authors separate their original production from criticism and their letters and interviews from secondary biographical sources. Critical studies are divided into books, collections of essays, special journal titles (*The Faulkner Journal* and special issues of standard critical titles), citations to chapters in books, and (the most important set of sources for students), journal articles. There are no annotations.

Citations to most of the sources included here are complete; however, many references to chapters cited from books are dead-ends and, for many theses, there are no entries included in the index. Another problem for serious users is the lack of descriptions given for manuscript collections. Discussion is limited to listing the library. One pleasant surprise is finding a list of concordances for Faulkner and Fitzgerald. The index is nothing more than a selected list of book titles and author entries; users are not provided subject references to compensate for the lack of annotations. This is not an essential purchase for any library's reference collection. [R: Choice, July/Aug 94, pp. 1704-05; RBB, 1 Apr 94, p. 1476]—**Milton H. Crouch**

Gay and Lesbian Literature

582.   **Contemporary Gay American Novelists: A Bio-Bibliographical Critical Sourcebook**. Emmanuel S. Nelson, ed. Westport, Conn., Greenwood Press, 1993. 421p. index. $69.50. PS374.N63C66. 813'.54099206642. LC 92-25762. ISBN 0-313-28019-3.

A remarkable compilation of bio-bibliographical information on 50-plus novelists, this work is likely to be used over and over by students, researchers, and others looking for information on the authors included. Each writer is treated by a different essayist who provides basic biographical information and discussions of major works and themes, critical reactions, and primary and selected secondary bibliographical information. Essays average 4 to 20 pages, and each is a solid treatise on its particular author. The work is prefaced by an introduction that explains the parameters and tenets of gay literature and the perception of gay literature over time. An appendix provides a list of small presses and selected journals that regularly publish gay fiction. A separate index and biographical profiles of essayists are included.

There is no current work with which this title can be compared. For the present it stands alone as a comprehensive sourcebook to gay authors. One hopes that it will serve as a model for other editors and publishers. Any public or academic collection with strengths in American literature and the literary tradition would benefit from this work. [R: Choice, July/Aug 93, p. 1745; LJ, Jan 93, p. 94; RBB, 1 Apr 93, p. 1454; RQ, Fall 93, pp. 120-21]—**Edmund F. SantaVicca**

583. **Contemporary Lesbian Writers of the United States: A Bio-Bibliographical Critical Sourcebook**. Sandra Pollack and Denise D. Knight, eds. Westport, Conn., Greenwood Press, 1993. 640p. index. $99.50. P5153.L46C65. 810.9'9206643. LC 92-39468. ISBN 0-313-28215-3.

Contemporary Lesbian Writers is a welcome addition to a growing body of resource tools documenting the gay and lesbian experience. This collection of 100 biographical sketches of contemporary "women-identified" writers focuses upon known and less well known U.S. writers of poetry, fiction, and drama. The emphasis is upon those writers whose lesbianism has had a profound impact on their writing. Although lesbian writers have been included in general references about women literary figures, such as the multivolume *American Women Writers* (see ARBA 84, entry 1152, and ARBA 80, entry 1239), this is one of the first ready-reference tools devoted exclusively to lesbian writers of the twentieth century. It complements *Contemporary Gay American Novelists,* edited by Emmanuel S. Nelson (Greenwood Press, 1993), and similar works.

Contemporary Lesbian Writers includes such familiar names as Marilyn Hacker, Adrienne Rich, Jane Chambers, May Sarton, and Audre Lorde, as well as the more unfamiliar Kitty Tsui, Mary Wings, Sara Schulman, Ruthann Robson, and Sapphire. Each entry contains a brief biography, a summary of the author's major works and themes, and how the author was critically received in the media. A complete bibliography of the author's works is provided, as well as a list of selected secondary readings in difficult-to-locate sources. An excellent introduction titled "Deconstructing the Absolute—Reality and Difference" traces the history of the genre and the difficulties and struggles in bringing a unique, often-challenged perspective into print. The volume also contains a list of publishers of lesbian works, a list of selected periodicals and journals pertaining to lesbian writers, and a bibliography of selected nonfiction on lesbian issues. This volume is a welcome addition to any public or academic library. [R: LJ, 15 Sept 93, p. 68; RBB, 1 Nov 93, p. 561]—**Jane Jurgens**

Humor

584. **American Humorists, 1800-1950**. Stanley Trachtenberg, ed. Detroit, Gale, 1982. 2v. illus. index. (Dictionary of Literary Biography, Vol. 11; A Bruccoli Clark Book). $156.00. LC 81-20238. ISBN 0-8108-1147-X.

One of the advantages of the Dictionary of Literary Biography (DLB) is that each volume (which in this case consists of two parts) can be evaluated and purchased separately; the differences in the series are notable enough that not all libraries will want all volumes. A disadvantage is the price, made especially manifest in this two-volume set, which costs nearly $0.20 per page!

Even with the price, however, this item will be hard to resist, for here we have a very useful collection of biographical and critical essays on 72 notable American humorists, complete with fascinating photographs, cartoons, bibliographies of the writers' works, and references for further reading. Major humorists—such as George Ade, Robert Benchley, Finley Peter Dunne, Ring Lardner, Ogden Nash, Dorothy Parker, S. J. Perelman, James Thurber, Mark Twain, and E. B. White—are accorded master essays of 15 to 30 pages, whereas lesser figures, many of them indeed obscure, are treated more briefly. All are considered to be *literary* figures, rather than performers, newspaper columnists, or cartoonists. Writers such as Ambrose Bierce and William Faulkner are included where there is deemed to be a "significant body of humorous writing." Appendixes embrace a historical survey by regions of the country, humorous book illustrations, newspaper syndication of American humor, a selection of humorous magazines illustrated by their covers, a supplementary reading list, and a cumulative subject index of volumes 1-11 of DLB.

A useful compendium of information and illustration on American humor, *American Humorists, 1800-1950* belongs in all libraries that can afford it. [R: Choice, Nov 82, p. 405; LJ, 15 Oct 82, p. 1978]—**Edwin S. Gleaves**

585. **Encyclopedia of American Humorists**. Steven H. Gale, ed. New York, Garland, 1988. 557p. index. (Garland Reference Library of the Humanities, Vol. 633). $75.00. LC 87-8642. ISBN 0-8240-8644-9.

This book does not pretend to be an all-inclusive reference on every American humorist who ever penned a line. So one will find omissions, and perhaps a favorite funny man is missing from these pages. For instance, there are no articles on Richard Bissell, George Shepard Chappell (Captain Traprock), Bill Cosby, or Lewis Grizzard, and the only one of the colonial "Connecticut Wits" included is John Trumbull. In his preface, the editor reveals the processes, and problems, of selecting those writers who are included.

This will be a useful volume, with its information on 135 American and Canadian humorists from colonial times to the present. It includes newspaper columnists, stand-up comedians, and script writers as well as book-length authors. It is alphabetically arranged from Franklin P. Adams through Matthew Franklin Whittier. Vital statistics, a biographical sketch, a literary analysis, a bibliography, and a list of secondary sources are given for each humorist. Each article is signed by the contributor. Following the text there is an alphabetical list of contributors with curriculum vitae and area of expertise. The length of the articles varies, with a few receiving longer entries than might be warranted (e.g., Erma Bombeck with three pages and Woody Allen with six-and-a-half pages, versus four columns for Garrison Keillor). The text is presented in a two-column format, with good typography and adequate leading contributing to legibility. It is well indexed, well bound, and lies flat when opened so that the researcher need not wrestle with the book while copying information. [R: Choice, June 88, p. 1532; LJ, 1 May 88, p. 71; RBB, Aug 88, pp. 1901-2; WLB, June 88, p. 140]—**Frank J. Anderson**

Literary Critics

586. **American Literary Critics and Scholars, 1800-1850**. John W. Rathbun and Monica M. Grecu, eds. Detroit, Gale, 1987. 406p. illus. bibliog. index. (Dictionary of Literary Biography, Vol. 59). $92.00. LC 87-11828. ISBN 0-8103-1737-0.

With volume 59, the Dictionary of Literary Biography begins a three-part series on nineteenth-century literary critics and scholars. Although most of the entries are not well-known figures, they were selected on the basis of "their critical attitudes and goals and their relations to the critical scenes of the time." This criterion is an important one because these scholars and critics were primarily concerned with social rather than aesthetic values.

Entries concentrate on the writer's work but include photographs and other graphics to suggest each writer's ambiance. Graphics and layout enrich the text, providing a pleasurable experience as well as a reference work for readers. For example, the William Hickling Prescott entry provides portraits of Prescott, a reproduction of the title page of one of his essay collections, and a page from the manuscript of his *History of the Conquest of Peru.*

Each entry concludes with a list of references, and the volume also features a checklist of further readings. Another useful section is the *Cumulative Index* of the dictionary's 59 volumes, the *Yearbook*, and the 4-volume *Documentary Series.*

This volume looks at the critical writings of Ralph Waldo Emerson, Edgar Allan Poe, and Henry Wadsworth Longfellow. It is more valuable, however, as a source of information about those early-nineteenth-century critics and scholars we rarely encounter.—**Renee B. Horowitz**

587. **American Literary Critics and Scholars, 1880-1900**. John W. Rathbun and Monica M. Grecu, eds. Detroit, Gale, 1988. 374p. illus. bibliog. index. (Dictionary of Literary Biography, Vol. 71). $95.00. LC 88-10879. ISBN 0-8103-1749-4.

This volume in the well-known Dictionary of Literary Biography series is the last in a three-volume study of American literary critics and scholars of the nineteenth century. Among the 36 authors covered in the book are Ambrose Bierce, Hamlin Garland, Henry James, Frank Norris, and George Santayana.

As with all the volumes in the DLB, the essay covering each person studied provides biographical and critical information, a list of major writings, and a secondary bibliography noting biographies, significant periodical articles, and the location of the writer's personal papers and manuscripts.

Although advanced students will naturally have to supplement their research with more in-depth material, beginning researchers can find a great deal here that will be of interest—as can the reference librarian desiring to help these patrons.

All libraries carrying the DLB will probably add this volume, although the ever-rising cost of each book, along with Gale's proliferation of inevitable spin-offs (*Documentary Series*, *Yearbooks*, and now *Concise Series*), will eventually cause acquisition librarians to look hard at each purchase. Another problem is the rather sloppy indexing. Although each volume in the DLB contains a cumulative index, if the name of a person included in an essay is not in the article's title, then access to that name can be found only through a broad, hard-to-find generic heading. For example, researchers wanting information on mystery writers Dashiell Hammett or Raymond Chandler will look through the index in vain unless they are familiar with the entry "Tough-Guy Literature."—**Jack Bales**

588. **Modern American Critics, 1920-1955**. Gregory S. Jay, ed. Detroit, Gale, 1988. 384p. illus. bibliog. index. (Dictionary of Literary Biography, Vol. 63). $92.00. LC 87-25138. ISBN 0-8103-1741-9.

This volume, like others in the series, may be used profitably by itself, although some of the essays are interconnected with other volumes in the series. Devoted to analyses of the major writings of modern American critics who flourished between 1920 and 1955, it includes essays ranging in length from ten to twenty pages on 25 literary and cultural critics. These include figures with a worldwide, secure reputation, such as T. S. Eliot, Kenneth Burke, H. L. Mencken, Edmund Wilson, Lionel Trilling, Ezra Pound, Lewis Mumford, Allen Tate, John Crowe Ransom, and Cleanth Brooks, as well as less well-known critics, such as R. S. Crane and Waldo Frank. Some of these men, such as Mencken, Mumford, and Wilson (no women are included—a judgment that, it can be argued, does not reflect sexism but rather the relative paucity of influential women critics in this period), are significant for their cultural, not simply their literary, commentary. Others are, or were, well-known creative writers as well as critics, such as Eliot, Pound, Ransom, and Tate. Some of these figures were considerably more influential during their lifetimes or earlier in their careers than they are today, such as Irving Babbit, Randolph Bourne, Van Wyck Brooks, and Vernon Parrington. Some have been very prolific, such as Van Wyck Brooks, Burke, Mencken, Mumford, Trilling, and Wilson. Others, while less prolific, have made very important contributions with one or a few books, such as F. O. Matthiessen with his *American Renaissance* and Parrington with the three volumes of *Main Currents in American Thought*.

Each of these essays provides an introductory discussion of the lives and ideas of these critics, with greater emphasis, appropriately, on the ideas. Most of the critics here are responsible for creating academic criticism, although a few, like Kenneth Burke, have made brilliant contributions without obtaining a college degree or holding a regular academic job. Each of the 25 writers of these essays presents balanced assessments, not hagiography. All of the essays sampled by this reviewer assume that the reader is at least somewhat familiar with literature, though the editor has been careful to see that a general, literate audience will find these critiques accessible. Each essay begins with a summary paragraph describing the most significant contributions of the critic, so one does not have to read the whole essay if one only needs a quick overview. A brief bibliography of the critic's most important works, a selected list of works about the critic, and the location of his papers are also provided. A well-chosen photograph or two also accompanies each entry. A special glossary of literary terms frequently used by these critics will be included at the end of the 2nd volume devoted to these twentieth-century American critics.

While it is not difficult to obtain biographical and analytical information about the more famous of these men in other literary reference tools, this volume is handy because it brings these 25 together. Although there is no summary essay attempting the admittedly difficult task of categorizing these sometimes very diverse thinkers, many of these essays make comparisons to other critics covered in this volume. Recommended especially for academic audiences. [R: Choice, May 88, p. 1384]—**David Isaacson**

589.   **Modern American Critics since 1955**. Gregory S. Jay, ed. Detroit, Gale, 1988. 397p. illus. bibliog. index. (Dictionary of Literary Biography, Vol. 67). $92.00. LC 87-30283. ISBN 0-8103-1745-1.

Covering individuals who have played a prominent role in contemporary American literary criticism, this volume complements *Modern American Critics, 1920-1955*, which is published as volume 63 of the Dictionary of Literary Biography series. Other volumes of the DLB treat American literary critics of the nineteenth century.

By focusing on the major proponents of contemporary literary theories, *Modern American Critics since 1955* reflects the various trends in interpreting literature that have developed during the past several decades, such as theoretical criticism, feminist criticism, Afro-American criticism, and deconstruction. Among the twenty-seven critics it treats are M. H. Abrams, Harold Bloom, Northrop Frye, Alfred Kazin, Adrienne Rich, and Susan Sontag.

Following the format established in previous volumes of the DLB, entries are arranged alphabetically by individual. The signed essays, which average about ten pages each, usually include some biographical information; however, the major emphasis is on the individual's career and the literary theories espoused in his or her writings. A bibliography of the critic's books, edited works, and periodical articles appears at the beginning of each entry, and a brief list of secondary references follows most of the essays. In addition, each article is accompanied by one or more photographs.

Supplementing the text is a useful glossary that provides explanations of the principal terms, schools, concepts, and movements (e.g., reader-response criticism, semiotics, deconstruction) associated with modern literary criticism. An additional appendix reprints three papers addressing "The Limits of Pluralism," written by Wayne C. Booth, M. H. Abrams, and J. Hillis Miller, who represent differing critical views.

A selective list of works recommended for additional reading precedes the cumulative index, which cites entries contained in all the DLB volumes published to date as well as the DLB *Yearbook* and the DLB *Documentary Series*. This index would be more useful if topical articles were indexed under their subjects rather than their titles. For example, "An Interview with Peter S. Prescott" is listed under "Interview" rather than "Prescott," while "A Field Guide to Recent Schools of American Poetry" is entered under "Field" rather than "American Poetry."

Although *Contemporary Literary Critics* (see ARBA 83, entry 1140) covers over four times as many individuals, it surprisingly does not include eleven of the critics treated in this volume, nor does it provide the detailed assessment offered by this work. This will be an important addition to academic and other libraries that support scholarly research in the field of literary criticism. [R: Choice, May 88, p. 1384]—**Marie Ellis**

Mystery Writers

590.   **Dictionary of Literary Biography Documentary Series: An Illustrated Chronicle. Vol. Six: Hardboiled Mystery Writers: Raymond Chandler, Dashiell Hammett, Ross Macdonald.** Matthew J. Bruccoli and Richard Layman, eds. Detroit, Gale, 1989. 383p. illus. index. $98.00. PS129.D48. 810'.9. LC 82-1105. ISBN 0-8103-2781-3.

This volume compiles significant literary documents chronicling the writings and careers of Raymond Chandler, Dashiell Hammett, and Ross Macdonald. It includes photographs, manuscript facsimiles, letters, notebook and diary entries, interviews, and contemporary assessments. Roughly half of the book is devoted to Hammett, with the remainder equally divided between Chandler and Macdonald. The arrangement and format is similar to that of the other Dictionary of Literary Biography volumes.

Most of the textual material on Chandler and Macdonald can be found in the average research library, but the reproductions of original book jackets and facsimiles of manuscript pages are not available elsewhere. The Hammett material was drawn from more obscure sources and much of it is not readily available from alternative works. Neither Hammett nor Chandler is covered in the series. Macdonald has appeared in two previous volumes, but there is little duplication in the far more substantial article in the present work.

Like the other volumes in this respected series, this is a handsome book with high-quality illustrations, paper, and binding. It was personally edited by noted literary scholars Matthew Bruccoli and Richard Layman, who are the editorial directors for the entire Dictionary of Literary Biography series. The selected documents are well chosen and provide an accurate representative sampling of the authors' lives and works. This volume is admirably suited for scholars and laypersons and for reference and circulating collections.—**Dennis Dillon**

Poetry

591. **American Poets, 1880-1945. Second Series**. Peter Quartermain, ed. Detroit, Gale, 1986. 510p. illus. bibliog. index. (Dictionary of Literary Biography, Vol. 48). $88.00. LC 86-7550. ISBN 0-8103-1726-5.

Forty-five poets of the modern era appear in this second DLB installment on American poets from the first half of the twentieth century. The more prominent names are accorded 20-page essays (in double columns) with the usual selective bibliography of primary and secondary works. The volume includes splendid family snapshots of poets at play as well as reproductions of poems in draft form. A ten-page bibliography and a cumulative index to the first 48 volumes of the series cap off this handsome book.

This volume is an important selection not only because of the intrinsic merit of the essays, but also because of the period under consideration. Students are likely to need more help with the themes, styles, and careers of poets like Hart Crane, Robert Penn Warren, E. E. Cummings, and John Berryman than with writers from a less fragmented time. Other significant figures appearing here are Delmore Schwartz, Langston Hughes, Randall Jarrell, Muriel Rukeyser, May Sarton, Thomas Merton, and Stanley Kunitz, an old friend of reference librarians everywhere.

The essays reinforce and reconstruct reputations, as necessary. Eliot's influence, Schwartz's confessional style, and Allen Tate's critical praise infuse many of these lives. Praise should also be paid to the editor for raising the profile of such deserving poets as Countee Cullen and Arna Bontemps. A full dozen of the poets assayed here are not to be found in a standard source like the *Oxford Companion to American Literature* (5th ed. Oxford University Press, 1983; see ARBA 84, entry 1159).—**John P. Schmitt**

592. **American Poets since World War II, Fourth Series**. Joseph Conte, ed. Detroit, Gale, 1996. 377p. illus. index. (Dictionary of Literary Biography, v.165). $135.00. ISBN 0-8103-9360-3.

American Poets since World War II, Fifth Series. Joseph Conte, ed. Detroit, Gale, 1996. 404p. illus. index. (Dictionary of Literary Biography, v.169). $140.00. ISBN 0-8103-9932-6.

The 165th and 169th volumes of the Dictionary of Literary Biography (DLB) are recent additions to the ongoing series that records the achievements of the world's most influential literary figures. Each volume is devoted to a specific topic, period, or genre and is organized and written by experts in their respective fields.

Volume 165 includes 20 poets (e.g., John Ashbery, Robin Blaser, Gwendolyn Brooks, Hayden Carruth, Lyn Hejinian, Michael Heller, Li-Young Lee, Denise Levertov, James Merrill, Kenneth Rexroth, Armand Schwerner, Gary Snyder, and Louis Zukofsky) who represent 3 generations in this century. Zukofsky, for example, represents the first postmodernist generation (i.e., writers who dealt with the social, political, and personal concerns of their generation). The second generation—poets of the 1950s and 1960s—challenged the precepts of modernism, added new concepts to the encyclopedia of poetics, founded postmodern schools of poetry, and enjoyed the largest and broadest readership for poetry in the twentieth century. Finally, the third generation, the baby boomers, do not identify with postwar movements and feel only slightly indebted to former generations. They may be subdivided into four interest groups: traditional, experimental, identity politics, or personal lyricist.

In selecting the entries for DLB volume 165, the editor gave special consideration to its relation to prior volumes in the DLB series that treat U.S. poetry after 1945. He was particularly interested in the poets included in the two-volume *American Poets since World War II, First Series* (see ARBA 81, entry 1264). In the years since the appearance of that set, a number of poets included in that volume have produced major new works or have since been the beneficiaries of extensive critical studies, providing grounds for a fresh appraisal. Finally, DLB volume 165 presents several poets whose work was still in a gestational stage in 1980 or who appear in the DLB for the first time.

Volume 169 includes both lesser knowns such as Jean Burden and Wsyatt Prunty, and greats such as Robert Lowell and Elizabeth Bishop.

The authors of articles on individual poets in both volumes are themselves recognized authorities in the poetry field. Virtually all are well represented by contributions to scholarly journals listed in the *MLA International Bibliography*. This DLB volume is an indispensable critical appraisal of leading U.S. poets of the twentieth century and therefore belongs in every university or research library's Americana collection.—**Mark Padnos and Terry Ann Mood**

593.   Boswell, Jeanetta. **Spokesmen for the Minority . . . A Bibliography of Sidney Lanier, William Vaughn Moody, Henry Timrod, Frederick Goddard Tuckerman, and Jones Very with Selective Annotations**. Metuchen, N.J., Scarecrow, 1987. 296p. index. $29.50. LC 86-24828. ISBN 0-8108-1944-9.

The "minority" of the title refers to the minor status of these five American poets of the late nineteenth century, each of whom—with the exception of Jones Very—died early in his career. As Boswell says in her preface, their productivity was cut short by "illness, madness, or other forms of tragedy." Lanier and Timrod were Southerners, Tuckerman and Very New Englanders, and Moody essentially a Midwesterner.

Each of the five parts is divided into a small chronologically arranged section of anonymous reviews of the poems, followed by a larger alphabetically arranged (by author) section of criticism, biography, and dissertations. Slightly more than half of the 1,700 entries are devoted to Lanier. Beginning each part is a brief biographical commentary on the poet. A useful subject index concludes the volume.

Most academic libraries will want this modestly priced, meticulously organized bibliographical study, for these " 'pre-modern American writers of fading and/or never very glowing poetic reputation . . .' should not be allowed to slip out of the canon of American literature because . . . they said something worth saying and they said it well."—**Charles R. Andrews**

594.   **Dictionary of Literary Biography Documentary Series: An Illustrated Chronicle. Vol. Seven: Modern American Poets**. Karen L. Rood, ed. Detroit, Gale, 1989. 397p. illus. index. $98.00. PS129.D48. 810.'9. LC 82-1105. ISBN 0-8103-1112-7.

This volume continues the two-fold purpose of making significant literary documents accessible to students and scholars and supplementing individual entries on authors contained in the Dictionary of Literary Biography volumes. The poets covered here are the Americans James Dickey, Robert Frost, and Marianne Moore. Of the three, Dickey and Frost are well represented with around 120 pages each, but Moore is covered by a mere 75 pages.

The work first lists the authors' major books, translations, bibliographies, interviews, poetry concordances, exhibition catalogs, and—perhaps most significantly—the location of archives. The remainder of each author treatment provides a chronological presentation of the poet's artistic life in the form of either published or unpublished journal entries, correspondence, book reviews, and photographs of the poet's family and manuscripts.

The section on Dickey is perhaps the most promising. The author, Ronald Baughman, provides a greater number of previously unpublished items than are found in the two articles on Frost and Moore. He gives excerpts from Dickey's World War II Army Air Corps combat mission log, journal entries from the early 1950s ("sketch for the building of the rational poem"), an application for the 1953 Sewanee Review Writers Fellowship, and correspondence and speaking schedules. Additionally, Baughman includes the usual published book reviews by Dickey, important published correspondence (especially with Ezra Pound), reviews of Dickey's works, and photographs of poem drafts.

Rood's article on Frost presents an unpublished biographical and genealogical manuscript by Frost's father, a photograph of the *Lawrence High School Bulletin,* Frost's high school valedictory address, and numerous photographs of his manuscripts and poetry booklets. The periodical articles from Frost's early career are of interest, but the reviews of his works are easily found elsewhere. This is also true of the correspondence published here—virtually all of it is from Frost's *Selected Letters.*

Willis's contribution on Marianne Moore provides previously unpublished items only in the form of Moore's drawings. These are, of course, related to her poetry. All the other entries are periodical articles or published correspondence. A number of the early photographs of Moore (from her childhood and Bryn Mawr periods) are of great interest and appear here for the first time; the others have been published elsewhere.

Reviews of previous volumes in this series have been mixed. The present volume can be recommended on the basis of the Dickey article alone. Collection development librarians will have to purchase cautiously in this series, since the price is prohibitive.—**Mark Padnos**

595.   Jason, Philip K. **Nineteenth Century American Poetry: An Annotated Bibliography**. Pasadena, Calif., Salem Press, 1989. 257p. index. (Magill Bibliographies). $40.00. Z1231.P7J37. 016.811'309. LC 89-10804. ISBN 0-89356-651-9.

Prepared for the high school student and general undergraduate rather than the English major, the graduate student, or the scholar, this annotated bibliography leads to the more important criticism of 16 major American poets of the nineteenth century. The introduction is clear and concise in explaining the scope and limitations. The poets include Bryant, Longfellow, Poe, Lowell, Whitman, Tuckerman, Dickinson, Lanier, Dunbar, and others. Primary emphasis is on Whitman and Dickinson. The author does not intend to be comprehensive, but rather to focus on frequently anthologized poems and major secondary sources in critical books and journals.

The introduction includes a list of general material, excellent critical works on nineteenth-century American writings, and brief commentary on the poets covered in this work. The body of the book is arranged by author, and under each a list of general critical works precedes criticism about specific poems.

As can be expected, only a few poems of each author are treated—those most often studied by high school and undergraduate students. Moreover, authors with minimal literary output or of lesser reputation have fewer poetic entries and criticisms.

Because the work is not intended for in-depth scholarly inquiry, the focus is not on new or unique scholarship. This bibliography is not a necessity, but it could prove an easy guide for introductory American poetry study. The author points out that few critical works focus on just nineteenth-century American poetry; thus, because these poets tend to be prominent in classroom texts and course syllabi, the work may be of greater use than other guides to secondary literature. [R: LJ, 15 Apr 90, p. 86; WLB, May 90, p. 124]—**Maureen Pastine**

Publishing

596.   **Dictionary of Literary Biography Documentary Series: An Illustrated Chronicle. Volume Thirteen: The House of Scribner 1846-1904**. John Delaney, ed. Detroit, Gale, 1995. 442p. illus. index. $128.00. ISBN 0-8103-5706-2.

The House of Scribner is part of the respected Dictionary of Literary Biography *Documentary Series.* However, it can also stand alone outside the set. The *Documentary Series* uses such documents as letters, photographs, contracts, interviews, and newspaper articles to bring a particular author or subject into focus and to place that person or subject in a larger context. In this case, the subject is the publishing house of Charles Scribner's Sons.

The volume covers the years 1846-1904; a second volume is planned which will cover 1905 through 1984, when Scribner's merged with the Macmillan company. The 1st section of the volume consists of a lengthy history of the company, written by Charles Scribner III, the fifth Charles Scribner in 1978. Scribner details the beginnings of the company and the various changes wrought not only by the strong personalities of the succeeding Charles Scribner's, but by the exigencies of the times. This history is followed by a chronology of major events in the company's history.

Delaney adds chronicles of a dozen major authors associated with Scribner's. He included particular authors because of their importance to the publishing house at the time; indeed he states in his Preface that these authors "were major reasons for its [Scribner's] success."

In addition to the chronicles of specific authors, Delaney details the history of the various magazines which Scribner's published, including *Scribner's Magazine* and *St. Nicholas*, their children's magazine.

All sections are copiously illustrated and documented. Most of this archival material came from the archives of Charles Scribner's Sons, housed at Princeton University.

This book is many things: the history of a particular publishing house, a detailed look at the careers of various authors, a history of some magazines important in American publishing history, and a look at the publishing industry in general during the latter half of the nineteenth century. Libraries with an interest in the history of books and publishing will want to purchase this, even if they are not subscribers to the series.—**Terry Ann Mood**

Regional

597. Contemporary Poets, Dramatists, Essayists, and Novelists of the South: A Bio-Bibliographical Sourcebook. Robert Bain and Joseph M. Flora, eds. Westport, Conn., Greenwood Press, 1994. 642p. index. $95.00. ISBN 0-313-28765-1.

Describing and assessing the achievements of 49 modern Southern writers of poetry, drama, essays, and novels, this bio-bibliographical sourcebook presents a preliminary report on the excellent work these authors have produced during the last 3 decades. Although none of those whose careers are highlighted here have the reputation of William Faulkner, Eudora Welty, or Tennessee Williams, many of them are already well-known heroes and heroines of Southern literary culture: Maya Angelou, Beth Henley, William Morris, Ishmael Reed, and Tom Wolfe. Only time will tell whether or not the fame of the other authors will last well into the twenty-first century. A companion volume, *Contemporary Fiction Writers of the South: A Bio-Bibliographical Sourcebook* (see ARBA 94, entry 1222), works along with this literary guide as the number of Southerners writing well exceeds that which can be treated in-depth in a single book.

Editors Bain and Flora observe that "unlike the writers of the Southern Renascence, most of whom were white males and from the upper middle class, many contemporary poets, dramatists, essayists and novelists come from the middling or rising middle classes." Of course, "formidable work by women and Black authors plays a much more important role in the current flowering than it did in the Renascence" (p.xviii). Also clearly evident in the work of this diverse group of Southern writers are their responses to such radical changes in the South as the decline of rural living; the rise of urban and suburban environments; the influence of mass media and popular culture (such as sports events, shopping malls, hunting traditions, and auto racing); the preoccupation with gaining wealth; and the social mobility that comes once it is achieved. Faulkner's eternal verities of love, honor, courage, and sacrifice are omnipresent, but so also are themes emphasizing the importance of place, the values of religion and politics, a fascination with the comic grotesque, and the impact of the past on the present.

Each entry includes five parts: a biographical sketch, a discussion of the author's major themes and forms, an assessment of reviews and scholarship, a chronological list of the author's works, and a bibliography of selected criticism. This reference guide will be of help to casual readers as well as lifelong scholars of Southern literature and culture. In its coverage of modern trends in poetry, drama, essays, and fiction, it goes beyond its Southern focus and will be of interest to modernists of every age, race, class, and gender.—**Colby H. Kullman**

598. Fifty Southern Writers after 1900: A Bio-Bibliographical Sourcebook. Joseph M. Flora and Robert Bain, eds. Westport, Conn., Greenwood Press, 1987. 628p. index. $75.00. LC 86-19460. ISBN 0-313-24519-3.

The editors have provided an outstanding biographical-bibliographical, and critical sourcebook for information about the Southern Renascence writers who published between 1919 and mid-century (including such diverse writers as Thomas Wolfe, Richard Wright, Ellen Glasgow, Alan Tate, and Eudora Welty) as well as for the new generation of Southern writers who have published within the last three decades (Harry Crews, Doris Betts, Ernest Gaines, Reynolds Price, and Ann Tyler).

Written by a knowledgeable scholar, each article contains five parts: a biographical sketch, a discussion of the author's major themes, an assessment of the scholarship, a chronological list of the author's works, and a bibliography of selected criticism. The editors wisely recommend that readers working with this bio-bibliography (and its companion volume *Fifty Southern Writers before 1900* (see entry 599) complement their study by also reading *The History of Southern Literature,* edited by Louis D. Rubin, Jr. (Louisiana State University Press, 1985).

The eight-page introductory essay provides an excellent condensed overview of Southern literature of the twentieth century by discussing Southern writing before and after the turn of the century; by presenting those authors who first questioned the "moonlight and magnolias" genteel tradition; and by explaining the significance of the Fugitive Era, the Agrarians, and black Southern writers as well as the importance of individual authors (James Weldon Johnson, Thomas Wolfe, Richard Wright, William Faulkner, and Ellen Glasgow).

Detailed information about these and many other twentieth-century Southern writers who have achieved regional and national reputations may be found in the first-rate essays that follow this introductory history. This reference book is highly recommended for community as well as university libraries.—**Colby H. Kullman**

599. **Fifty Southern Writers before 1900: A Bio-Bibliographical Sourcebook**. Robert Bain and Joseph M. Flora, eds. Westport, Conn., Greenwood Press, 1987. 601p. index. $75.00. LC 86-31832. ISBN 0-313-24518-5.

A companion volume to *Fifty Southern Writers after 1900, Fifty Southern Writers before 1900* takes as its province "the work of half a hundred Southerners whose careers ended before 1900 or thereabouts, whose works often appear in anthologies of Southern and American writing, and whose books figure prominently in the history of Southern letters." Beginning with Captain John Smith and ending with Grace King and Charles W. Chestnut (who both died in 1932), this volume confronts historical events from 1607 to 1900, including the first settlements, the introduction of slavery, the Revolutionary War, the adoption of the Constitution, the Southern expansion across the mountains and into the Old Southwest, the growing controversy over slavery and secession, the devastating War between the States and equally devastating Reconstruction, and the rocky road to reunion. The range of writers covered includes major authors (William Byrd, Thomas Jefferson, Edgar Allan Poe, Mark Twain, and Kate Chopin, to mention a few) as well as lesser-known Southern authors (such as Robert Beverley, William Alexander Caruthers, and Augusta Jane Evans Wilson).

Focusing mostly on those nineteenth-century authors whose works give a sense of the long background behind the Southern Renascence, this volume offers students and teachers an overview of the writers' lives and works. Each essay is divided into five sections: a biographical sketch, a discussion of the author's major themes, an assessment of the scholarship on each writer, a chronological list of the author's works, and a bibliography of selected criticism. A comprehensive index provides easy access to authors and their works as well as to major themes, literary movements, and historical events.

Written by knowledgeable scholars, the essays and bibliographies in this volume (and its companion) are so carefully researched and aptly detailed that they are of value to the specialist in Southern studies as well as the student looking for useful introductory materials about a specific author or work.—**Colby H. Kullman**

600. Flora, Joseph M., and Robert Bain. **Contemporary Fiction Writers of the South: A Bio-Bibliographical Sourcebook**. Westport, Conn., Greenwood Press, 1993. 571p. index. $75.00. P5261.C565. 813'.5409'03. LC 92-36515. ISBN 0-313-28764-3.

Explore the world of Pat Conroy's "Lowcountry," discover the "boomerang return motion" that is built into Barry Hannah's fiction, view the Southern racial situation as it is found in Ellen Douglas's stories of the South in the early and mid-twentieth century, study Larry Brown's ability to fuse Vietnam fiction and a Southern novel in *Dirty Work*, watch Ellen Gilchrist's female protagonists struggle for self-knowledge and self-recognition, and find out why John Kennedy Toole was a Southern Catholic writer for whom the loss of faith was critical. Reporting on the many good books Southerners have written within the last thirty years, *Contemporary Fiction Writers of the South* presents a flowering of talent comparable to the Southern Renascence in the first four decades of this century. Maintaining that none of the authors discussed has yet earned the reputation of a William Faulkner, a

Eudora Welty, a Flannery O'Connor, or a Robert Penn Warren, but that many have already achieved international reputations, Flora and Bain highlight 49 Southern writers of fiction who have either stayed at home to write or who rank among those expatriates who live outside the South but still draw on their heritage for their fiction. Influenced by World War II, the Vietnam War, the civil rights movement, new understandings of race and cultures, changing roles for women, and sexual freedoms afforded by the age of the pill, this new generation of Southern writers record their responses to "such radical changes in the South as the decline of rural living and the rise of cities and towns, the influence of television and shopping malls, Southerners' obsession with sports and cars, the preoccupation with getting rich, and the social mobility that comes with wealth" (p.xii). The powerful voices of all classes of society, as well as the formidable talents of blacks and women, are more significant to this second Renascence than they were to the first.

To be included in this valuable study of contemporary Southern fiction, each author needs to have written at least four books (one exception is Alex Haley), to have been reviewed widely, and to have achieved critical recognition outside of the South. Written by knowledgeable scholars, each essay contains five parts: a biographical sketch, a discussion of the author's major themes, an assessment of reviews and scholarship, a chronological list of the author's works, and a bibliography of selected criticism. Love and honor and courage and sacrifice, a sense of place, the importance of religion, a celebration of the gothic and the grotesque, the respect for art and letters, the complexity of family relationships, the influence of the past on the present, and a sense of being different from the rest of the nation—all are to be discovered in this book. [R: RBB, 15 Nov 93, p. 649]—**Colby H. Kullman**

601. **A Literary History of the American West**. J. Golden Taylor and others, eds. Fort Worth, Texas Christian University Press; distr., College Station, Texas A & M University Press, 1987. 1353p. illus. bibliog. index. $79.50. LC 85-50538. ISBN 0-87565-021-X.

This massive volume provides not only a synthesis of the many movements, trends, and genres of Western literature, but also gives good biographical and literary analysis of several hundred writers of narrative, fiction, poetry, drama, and film scripts, from early oral traditions and folklore to the work of the recently deceased Louis L'Amour. No aspect of literature is overlooked—travel, romance, heroic fiction, poetry, drama, film, and essays.

The major divisions of the work are: "Encountering the West," subdivided into such topics as "Across the Wide Missouri" and "Precursors of the Western Novel"; the next division, part 2, is subdivided geographically, with excellent biographies and criticism of over forty major writers—Mark Twain, Mary Austin, and others in the Far West; J. Frank Dobie and Paul Horgan as examples in the Southwest, Willa Cather, Mari Sandoz, and others for the Middle West, and Vardis Fisher and Bernard De Voto as typical of the Rocky Mountain region. The final major division is entitled "Rediscovering the West" and includes such essays as "Indian Poetry," "Contemporary Western Drama," and "Western Movies since 1960," with a final essay on modern trends in western radio, television, film, and print.

Each of the more than 80 essays is by a different author, usually an established authority in that field. Each is followed by an excellent bibliography of both primary and secondary sources. A list of contributors, giving affiliation and listing a few of the person's writings, a list of 126 "Major Reference Sources" for the book as a whole, and an excellent index of names and subjects are included. This is a monumental work which should be in every library with a collection dealing with the West. [R: LJ, 15 Apr 88, p. 33]—**Raymund F. Wood**

602. Reisman, Rosemary M. Canfield, and Christopher J. Canfield **Contemporary Southern Women Fiction Writers: An Annotated Bibliography**. Metuchen, N.J., Scarecrow and Pasadena, Calif., Salem Press, 1994. 225p. index. (Magill Bibliographies). $32.50. Z1251.S7R44. 016.813'54099287'0975. LC 93-6549. ISBN 0-8108-2832A.

Twenty-eight regional authors are included in this annotated bibliography, which contains published criticism and major reviews. Titles selected for inclusion are those studies that comment on an author's style, themes, and tone and, if possible, that serve to reflect a critic's point of view. Recent studies have been included as frequently as possible; however, many of these authors have not received sustained critical attention over time. Then, too, some recent publications have not yet been evaluated by literary scholars; in such cases, newspaper and journal reviews are cited.

Annotations average fewer than 100 words. Citations are complete and, fortunately for students needing information, criticism contained in published secondary works is preferred to that in more easily located journal or newspaper articles. A strong feature of the bibliography is the general studies section. Here, some of the major books on the South—literature and social history—are suggested as important background reading. This section serves as an excellent selection aid for librarians needing to develop a good small collection of important literary works on the region. Users must read an entire section to locate criticism about a specific novel or short-story collection. Because individual bibliographies average 24 or 30 entries, this is not a hardship.

There is no subject index to help users locate themes or tones unique to contemporary Southern women fiction writers, but the names of critics are included in the index for those wishing to locate comments by important scholars such as Louis D. Rubin. An interesting introduction attempts to justify the need to separate women from men and to focus on regionalism.—**Milton H. Crouch**

603.   Sadler, Geoff. **Twentieth-Century Western Writers**. 2d ed. Chicago, St. James Press, 1991. 848p. $105.00. 823.914. LC 91-61857. ISBN 0-912289-98-8.

This bio-bibliographical work of 450 Western fiction writers extends the work of *Western Writers* by James Vinson (St. James Press, 1981), which included approximately 90 bio-bibliographies of writers. The focus is on works by Western fiction writers active during the twentieth century. Western poets, dramatists, and authors of nonfiction are not included unless they also wrote fiction that merited inclusion.

The fascinating prefaces to both editions are included, and a reading list of about 180 of the best books and articles on Western fiction is provided in the front of the volume. Entries are arranged in alphabetical order by author. Each includes a biography, a bibliography of works, the location of manuscripts in library special collections (if known), published critical studies, and a signed critical review. Living authors were invited to add comments, and many have done so. The bibliographies list writings according to the categories of Western fiction and other publications; Western writing is further subdivided into lists of works published under pseudonyms. The list of works includes all British and United States editions of books; other editions are listed only if they are the first editions. In addition to novels and works in anthologies, uncollected Western short stories published since the entrant's last collection have been listed. The biographies and the comments are very well written, and the length of the biography seems to correspond to the importance of the writer.

The work covers novels and stories set in or related to the frontier experience of the last century, or works that embody that experience in a modern setting. This includes classics, formula Westerns, modern treatments of the Western theme, and fictional accounts of domestic life on the frontier that present the female viewpoint of the Western experience. It does not include contemporary novels that are located in the Western states but that have no other obvious connection with Western writing. This edition includes more works by Native Americans, Afro-Americans, Hispanics, and women whose contributions form an essential part of the story of the West. Both editions include established literary giants and lesser-known figures. Writers are from the United States and around the world. The time period covered most extensively is 1940 to 1980, although there are entries from the late nineteenth century and recent years.

By perusing this substantive work, it is possible to gain an in-depth understanding of the variety and style of literature in the Western genre. Although there are a few minor typographical errors scattered throughout the volume, this work is one of the best of its kind.—**Maureen Pastine**

604.   **Twentieth-Century Western Writers**. James Vinson, ed.; D. L. Kirkpatrick, associate ed. Detroit, Gale, 1982. 941p. index. $95.00. ISBN 0-8103-0227-6.

The actual coverage of this book is less than is implied in its title, being limited to authors of novels, short stories, plays, and occasional essays. Within these limits, however, the coverage is very good, far better than that provided for similar writers in *Southwestern American Literature: A Bibliography* (Swallow, 1980). For example, for the prolific writer S. Omar Barker, the bibliography cited above devotes only one-half page, mixing nine titles of novels, verse, and short stories, without differentiation; the work under review gives five pages to Barker, with a complete listing of titles, differentiating among novels, collected short stories, short stories in magazines, verse, juveniles, and "others."

Each entry starts with a brief biographical sketch and ends with a longer, signed critical essay. Bibliographical data are categorized by type—Western writings first, then (if any) those of other regions, such as Willa Cather's *Shadows on the Rock*. Under each type the works are then differentiated (e.g., novels, short stories, etc.). Under the heading "Other" are sometimes listed autobiographies or critical works. Manuscript locations are sometimes given. Pseudonyms are listed but refer the reader to the author's proper name. An index of titles (nearly 100 pages) completes this valuable bibliography.

Chronologically the book is limited to the twentieth century. Although the writings of Bret Harte and Helen Hunt Jackson are acknowledged in the preface, neither they nor Mark Twain are included in the book itself. [R: Choice, July/Aug 83, pp. 1578-79; LJ, 15 May 83, pp. 993-94; RQ, Summer 83, pp. 429-30; WLB, May 83, pp. 789-90]—**Raymund F. Wood**

Short Stories

605.   **American Short-Story Writers, 1880-1910**. Bobby Ellen Kimbel, with William E. Grant, eds. Detroit, Gale, 1989. 402p. illus. index. (Dictionary of Literary Biography, v.78). $98.00. PS374.S5A39. 813'.01'09. LC 88-30994. ISBN 0-8103-4556-0.

This volume, like others in the Dictionary of Literary Biography (DLB) series, consists of separate biographical-critical essays on writers related by topic, period, or genre. Each volume is a self-contained whole. However, since some writers are treated in more than one volume (e.g., Jack London is treated in this volume as a writer of short stories, in volume 8 as a writer of science fiction, and in volume 12 as American realist), readers will need to consult the most recent volume for the cumulative index to the whole series.

This volume is the 2nd in the DLB to focus on short-story writers. It covers an especially productive period in American literature and a frenetic period in American history. The 30 years between 1880 and 1910 represent a transition between the end of the Victorian and the beginning of the modern age. The 31 authors covered in this volume include a few who were major figures in their lifetime and continue to be significant today, such as Willa Cather, Stephen Crane, Jack London, and Edith Wharton. Quite a number of other writers were popular while alive but are not well known today, such as Gertrude Atherton, Mary Austin, James B. Connolly, and Margaret Deland.

Each essay begins with a brief summary of the major contributions of the writer and weaves together a biography, descriptions of specific short stories, and an assessment of literary significance. Major writers receive longer treatment than minor ones. Essays include bibliographies of major works by and about each author as well as the locations of their papers. One of the most attractive features of the book is the generous number of photographs.

The essays are consistently well written. In many cases, contributors make a good argument for renewed popular and scholarly interest in such writers as Hamlin Garland and Brander Matthews, whose work has been unjustly labeled as mere local color. This book will be useful to both scholars and readers first encountering these authors.—**David Isaacson**

606.   **American Short-Story Writers, 1910-1945**. **First Series**. Bobby Ellen Kimbel, ed. Detroit, Gale, 1989. 386p. illus. index. (Dictionary of Literary Biography, v.86). $98.00. PS374.S5A396. 813'.0109. LC 89-34227. ISBN 0-8103-4564-1.

American literature was in a dramatic state of flux between World War I and World War II. Many of America's finest writers found the short story to be the genre best fitted to experimentation with plot, language, and theme. This new entry in the dependable Dictionary of Literary Biography (DLB) covers 25 American short-story authors active between 1910 and World War II. Included are such major voices as Sherwood Anderson, F. Scott Fitzgerald, Damon Runyon, William Saroyan, Gertrude Stein, and William Carlos Williams. In addition, there are essays on less well known writers, such as Ring Lardner and William March, and welcome coverage of two Harlem Renaissance authors, Langston Hughes and Zora Neale Hurston.

Along with the detailed essays, which combine social history and biography with basic literary criticism, the reader will find photographs, illustrations, manuscript pages, lists of works by each author, and short bibliographies. A wide-ranging introduction gives an overview of the period, emphasizing the radical changes in language, style, and structure that marked literature of the time. A list of books for further reading serves as an addendum. This new volume of the DLB provides an important introductory source for study of the period, especially for students at the high school and college levels.—**Susan Davis Herring**

607. **American Short-Story Writers, 1910-1945: Second Series**. Bobby Ellen Kimbel, ed. Detroit, Gale, 1991. 472p. illus. index. (Dictionary of Literary Biography, v.102). $103.00. LC 91-24164. ISBN 0-8103-4582-X.

One of the latest additions to a solid, basic, and easy-to-use series, this volume has biographical and bibliographic information on some 37 writers who have contributed to the development and repertoire of the American short story genre. Each profile is by a different contributor and provides author's full name; birth and death dates; cross-references to additional information found in other DLB volumes; a list of works by the author (pertinent to the genre), including collection; a 7- to 10-page summary review and evaluation of the author's work; and bibliographic citations to primary and secondary source material such as letters, interviews, bibliographies, and biographies. Also included are a statement regarding the general plan of the series; a foreword written by the editor, which includes an overview of the short story; a list of books for further reading; a list of contributors with their academic affiliations; and a cumulative index encompassing three DLB series.

As a basic introduction to the authors and as a beginning guide to additional resources, this volume and series are especially useful to lower-division undergraduates and other patrons who need only summary information. One of the strengths of this series is its heavy use of photographs, which generally capture the authors at different periods. Recommended for undergraduates and high school libraries.—**Edmund F. Santa Vicca**

608. **American Short-Story Writers since World War II**. Patrick Meanor, ed. Detroit, Gale, 1993. 419p. illus. index. (Dictionary of Literary Biography, v.130). $125.00. LC 93-078551. ISBN 0-8103-5389-X.

This volume, like the others in the series, is an important reference book for serious students and scholars of literature. Its subject, twentieth-century American short fiction, is arguably the most neglected of all of the literary genres, especially by the custodians of the American literary establishment—university professors and the publishing industry. As Meanor points out in his introductory essay, prior to the 1950s writers could make a living by publishing their short stories in such "large-circulation magazines" as *The Saturday Evening Post* and *Collier's*. By the 1950s interest in the short story declined as television displaced reading as a popular form of entertainment. The short story writer was similarly displaced, from the local cafés where much of American intellectualism once fermented to the "sometimes-insular atmospheres" of such prestigious institutions as the University of Iowa's Writers' Workshop. Meanor attributes what he feels is a renewed interest in the short story to the fact that short story writers-turned-university professors now have access to an important vehicle for their work: the university press. The problem is that, unlike popular magazines, academic journals have a very limited circulation. Hence, the short story as a popular literary genre may well be a thing of the past.

Of the 40 writers represented here, roughly half are either products of creative writing programs or have been, at some point in their careers as writers, involved with them. Some of them—Charles Bukowski, Fielding Dawson, Robert Kelly, and Joyce Carol Oates—are prodigious in their output. Others, like Lee K. Abbott, Wanda Coleman, Mary Robinson, and Elizabeth Tallent, are younger and less well known, but have nevertheless begun to make an impression on academic literary circles. Most of the essays about the authors were written by university professors. All of them, without exception, are excellent and are easily accessible to the general reader.

This work concludes with a short list of books for further reading and a welcome index that includes the names and dates for all of the authors in the 130-volume series. The index alone makes this a valuable resource for librarians, researchers, and others interested in European and American literature.

The editors for this series should be commended for undertaking such an ambitious and useful literary project. [R: Choice, May 94, p. 1407]—**Sandra Adell**

AUSTRALIAN LITERATURE

609.   **The Oxford Companion to Australian Literature**. 2d ed. By William H. Wilde, Joy Hooton, and Barry Andrews. New York, Oxford University Press, 1994. 833p. $79.00. ISBN 0-19-553381-X.

This substantially expanded edition is every bit as good as the 1st (see ARBA 88, entry 1233). New entries, including major articles on crime fiction and the immigrant experience, as well as entries for a new generation of writers, bring the total to 3,050 entries. All existing entries have been reviewed and updated with a special emphasis on writers who were in mid-career when the 1st edition was prepared.

This continues to be a splendid companion not just to Australian literature, but to many other aspects of Australian culture and history as well. Many of the entries remain relatively brief, but there are some lengthy essays on major topics that are outstanding expositions of a theme (e.g., the Aborigine in white Australian literature). Arranged alphabetically by author, character, literary work, or topical subject, this volume is so easy to use that the lack of an index is no handicap at all. Libraries with only an incidental interest in Australian literature may be tempted to make do with the 1st edition; however, the strength of this companion as the major reference source in its area, and the quantity and quality of the additions in the 2d edition, suggest that purchase of the new edition is fully warranted.—**Norman D. Stevens**

610.   **Who's Who of Australian Children's Writers**. 2d ed. Port Melbourne, Australia, D. W. Thorpe/Reed Reference Australia; distr., New Providence, N.J., Reed Reference Publishing, 1996. 205p. $35.00pa. ISBN 1-875589-77-5.

This biographical dictionary of living Australian children's authors is based on a national database created by sending questionnaires to published authors. Those writers who have written at least one work for children were selected from the larger database. This 2d edition makes corrections on the 1st and adds new names, but there is no change in format.

The information contained in the entries is factual and basic. Each entry gives the author's birth date, pseudonyms, education, employment history, books, types of writing, recreations, memberships, awards, availability for appearances or work, and well-known relatives. Publications in which the author's articles appear are given, but no specific bibliographic details are included.

Space considerations, say the editors, have obliged them to abbreviate almost every entry except titles. This book would not be suitable for children or their parents who wanted to know a little about the author because of the time required to check these excessive abbreviations. For librarians or serious researchers inquiring about Australian children's authors, the information is detailed and useful. Purchase is recommended only for academic libraries, or libraries that have a special children's-literature research collection. For other libraries, the *Something about the Author* series is much more detailed and readable, and a number of Australian children's authors are described.—**Joann H. Lee**

AUSTRIAN LITERATURE

611.   **Austrian Fiction Writers, 1875-1913**. James Hardin and Donald G. Daviau, eds. Detroit, Gale, 1989. 405p. illus. index. (Dictionary of Literary Biography, v.81). $98.00. ISBN 0-8103-4559-5.

Literature from Austria more often than not gets thrown in with surveys covering that of its more eminent cousin Germany; thus it is overshadowed undeservedly, given the smaller land's very different history and outlook. The Dictionary of Literary Biography is therefore to be applauded for devoting several volumes to Austrian fiction writers alone. The present compilation focuses on those whose published works appeared before 1914. (A future volume will treat more recent fiction writers.) Twenty-seven names are included, updating in part Frederick Ungar's *Handbook of Austrian Literature* (see ARBA 74, entry 1412). Well-known fin de siecle Viennese Hofmannsthal,

Schnitzler, and Hermann Bahr appear, as do residents of the greater Austro-Hungarian Empire such as Kafka, Rilke, and Ebner Eschenbach. Not all these people are best known for their fiction, and a few, such as Franz Nabl and Marie Eugenie delle Grazie, are not well known at all.

As is customary for the series, the essays are detailed and informative, illuminating their subjects' lives by means of thoughtful, interesting presentations of their works. Each is accompanied by a bibliography of primary and secondary literature as well as information about the author's archives; most are enhanced by photographs and other illustrations. An up-to-date supplementary reading list is appended. If a library can afford the price, its patrons will be well served by purchase of this volume.—**Willa Schmidt**

BRITISH LITERATURE

General Works

612. Bell, Maureen, George Parfitt, and Simon Shepherd. **A Biographical Dictionary of English Women Writers 1580-1720**. Boston, G. K. Hall, 1990. 298p. $29.95. PR113.B46. 820.9'9287'03. LC 89-26844. ISBN 0-8161-1806-X.

Although there are other reference works on women in the seventeenth century, this one is by far the most inclusive for the period. The authors uncovered a surprising number of interesting women from all backgrounds and classes, with a large number coming from the middle class after 1640. Over one-third are Quakers. Most of these women were not "writers" in the modern sense; what they produced were diaries, religious tracts, prophecies, letters, and petitions. The dictionary attempts to cover all writing by women, even brief quotations from letters and epitaphs. The alphabetical list includes, when available, the writer's place of residence, religion, social status, and husband. Very few of the entries are complete; it is fortunate that there is any knowledge of these women at all.

The dictionary is followed by a series of critical appendixes that survey the historical and social conditions under which these women wrote. These point out the importance of the Quakers, the modes of writing (e.g., petitions, letters) not usually noticed by literary critics, the role of men as "gatekeepers" censoring and controlling women's writing, and the function of women in the printing trade.

This book makes a major contribution to women's studies. Any library with an interest in feminism or in seventeenth-century literature will wish to purchase it. [R: WLB, Nov 90, p. 147]—**Lynn F. Williams**

613. **The Bloomsbury Group**. Edward L. Bishop, ed. Detroit, Gale, 1992. 369p. illus. index. (Dictionary of Literary Biography Documentary Series, Vol. 10). $113.00. LC 82-1105. ISBN 0-8103-7581-8.

Continuing the format of the preceding titles in the Dictionary of Literary Biography *Documentary Series*, this volume on the Bloomsbury Group comprises an eclectic collection of photographs, facsimiles of manuscripts, paintings, letters, diaries, reviews, and miscellaneous archival documents. Covered are the nine principal members of that varied group of talented, eccentric, independent, and creative intellectuals who met in the Bloomsbury section of London from roughly 1905 to 1940 and whose influence was so powerful in the world of literature, art, politics, and economics. These include three figures who have had previous entries in the DLB (E. M. Forster, Leonard Woolf, and Virginia Woolf) and six who have not (Clive Bell, Vanessa Bell, Roger Fry, Duncan Grant, John Maynard Keynes, and Lytton Strachey). A typical entry is that for Virginia Woolf's *To the Lighthouse*, which includes two letters, a diary entry, a book review, a manuscript facsimile, and a reproduction of the dust jacket. In all there are 60 entries, followed by checklists for each person, which include a bibliography of the person's writings, a list of biographies, and the location of the person's archives. There is also a bibliography of works about the Bloomsbury Group.

Due to the vast range of intellectual and artistic achievement of the Bloomsbury Group, this is a somewhat less cohesive book than previous volumes in this series, but there is much that is new, interesting, or difficult to find here. Taken as a whole, it is a valuable addition to Bloomsbury literature. The only disappointing feature is the often-mediocre quality of the reproductions, difficult to excuse in a book this expensive.—**Jeffrey R. Luttrell**

614.   **British Reform Writers, 1789-1832**. Gary Kelly and Edd Applegate, eds. Detroit, Gale, 1996. 465p. illus. index. (Dictionary of Literary Biography, v.158). $128.00. ISBN 0-8103-9353-0.

British reform writers of the late eighteenth and early nineteenth centuries defy neat categorization because their writing took so many forms, including journalism; essays; poetry; fiction; and political, religious, and pedagogical tracts. The common thread connecting their works—some widely published, but many ephemeral—is the broad themes of political, economic, religious, and social reform. The introduction establishes the historical setting and summarizes issues of concern to reform writers.

Most of the 47 writers included here are not well-known literary figures, although Thomas Paine, Percy Bysshe Shelley, and Mary Wollstonecraft will be familiar to most undergraduate readers. The writers were selected not just for their contributions to the various reform movements, but also each writer "should have been remarkable or representative in some way as a writer and not just as a voice for one reform cause or another" (p.xii).

For those writers also covered in other Dictionary of Literary Biography (DLB) volumes, cross-references are provided. The standard components one expects to find in DLB volumes are present here: For each writer, a primary bibliography, a portrait and other illustrations, a biographical essay, bibliographies of published letters and secondary material, and location of papers are furnished. A general bibliography of recommended reading follows the entries, as does a cumulative index of the entire series. Because the subject of this volume is so specialized, despite its accessibility for the general reader, it will be most useful in those libraries serving advanced literature or history students. [R: Choice, May 96, p. 1446]—**Emily L. Werrell**

615.   **British Women Writers: A Critical Reference Guide**. Janet Todd, ed. New York, Continuum; distr., New York, Harper & Row, 1989. 762p. index. $59.50. PR111.B75. 820'.9'9287. LC 88-34424. ISBN 0-8044-3334-8.

This work is a biographical/critical dictionary (the most comprehensive to date) of some 400-plus women writers from the Middle Ages up to about 1987. Entries are primarily British with some Commonwealth writers such as Fleur Adcock and Germaine Greer. The editor selected some writers for their innovation, others for their popularity or because of their representation of special groups such as the working class of particular regions or the privileged class. The focus is on women's contributions to British literary history.

Entries in the main section of the book are arranged alphabetically by surname, followed by dates and places of birth and death (if applicable). The entries include whether the writer is best known as a novelist, poet, essayist, or other kind of writer. There are basic biographical data, data on the writer's names and pseudonyms, and a selective list of works by and about the author at the end of each entry. These entries range from 600 to 2,500 words in length. Each author's works are assessed with a description of major writings and themes.

The comprehensive index not only includes each author's name in boldface type (along with page number) but also headings such as "abolitionists," "escapist fiction," and "scandal novel." Many of the index headings are further subdivided so that the user can look under a major heading such as "women in literature" and find a subheading such as "constraints on" women in literature.

This reference work is one of the best of its kind, demonstrating care in editing and expertise in writing. It will prove to be a highly valuable work in the study of British women's literature. [R: Choice, Oct 89, p. 280; RBB, 15 Nov 89, p. 688]—**Maureen Pastine**

616.   **British Writers, Supplement III: James M. Barrie to Mary Wollstonecraft**. George Stade and Carol Howard, eds. New York, Scribner's/Simon & Schuster Macmillan, 1996. 576p. index. $110.00. ISBN 0-684-19714-6.

British Writers, Supplement IV. George Stade and Carol Howard, eds. New York, Scribner's/Simon & Schuster Macmillan, 1997. 668p. index. $120.00. ISBN 0-684-80496-4.

Two earlier supplements to *British Writers* have been published, *British Writers, Supplement I: Graham Greene to Tom Stoppard* (Scribner's, 1987) (see ARBA 93, entry 1191) and *British Writers, Supplement II: Kingsley Amis to J. R. R. Tolkien* (Scribner's, 1992) (see ARBA 88, entry 1199). Like the others, these two supplements continue to fill in major gaps in coverage. While the first two concentrated on twentieth-century figures (e.g., Agatha Christie, Doris Lessing, Elizabeth Bowen, Barbara Pym), these volumes cover more older, previously neglected writers than they do contemporary figures, as well as writers not immediately recognized as British, such as Salman Rushdie and Roald Dahl.

Of the 25 writers covered in *Supplement III,* only 2 were still alive at the time of publication—the playwright Christopher Fry and the eminent man of letters V. S. Pritchett. The others selected cover a wide span of years, from Aphra Behn (1640-1689) to Angela Carter (1940-1992), with writers from the nineteenth and twentieth centuries most prevalent. The philosopher David Hume is included, as is the humorist P. G. Wodehouse. The creators of Dracula (Bram Stoker) and Frankenstein (Mary Shelley) are profiled, as well as Shelley's influential mother, Mary Wollstonecraft. On a gentler note, the creators of Peter Pan (James M. Barrie) and Peter Rabbit (Beatrix Potter) are also found within this volume.

The major writings of the authors are highlighted within each 17- to 20-page entry, and many titles are discussed in specific subsections of the text. In addition to basic biographical and critical information, a substantial bibliography of primary and secondary sources is provided for each writer. The book includes a "Complete British Writers Chronology," which lists historical events, publications, and births and deaths of prominent writers from 1325 to 1995 (a shorter "Chronological Table," covering 1835 to 1991, appeared in *Supplement II*). Also, there is a master index of the entire *British Writers* set that lists names and writings. The series remains a useful reference source for academic and large public libraries.

Supplement IV includes a chronology of British literature from 1901 to 1997, and a master index of the entire series. [R: RBB, 15 Apr 96, p. 1460]—**Thomas A. Karel and Terry Ann Mood**

617.   **Contemporary Writers, 1960 to the Present**. Detroit, Gale, 1992. 582p. illus. index. (Concise Dictionary of British Literary Biography, v.8). $65.00. ISBN 0-8103-7988-0.

This is the last of the eight-volume Concise Dictionary of British Literary Biography set. Entries have been selected from the Dictionary of Literary Biography (DLB) series to meet the needs of libraries that do not have the budget to purchase the more than 100 volumes in the DLB. Each of these eight volumes spans a different chronological period, beginning with a volume covering the Middle Ages and the Renaissance. The series is directed toward high school and beginning college students. Every volume consists of alphabetically arranged biographical entries devoted to major authors. Each entry, which is essentially the same as the essay on which it is modeled in the DLB, has the same format: a chronological list of the author's works, a biography focusing on major events in the author's career, a discussion of major works reflecting the most important critical interpretations of these works, and a selected list of interviews and critical works. Each entry includes photographs of the author, reproductions of typescript or manuscript pages of key works, and at least one dust jacket of a representative book.

Few scholars or general readers could quarrel with the 27 authors selected for this 582-page volume. The adjective *contemporary* in the title reflects the fact that the authors (with the exception of the poet/librarian Philip Larkin and the playwright Joe Orton) are alive and writing. Genres include detective and mystery fiction (e.g., P. D. James, John le Carre, Len Deighton, John Mortimer), fantasy (e.g., Doris Lessing), fiction (e.g., Anthony Burgess, Iris Murdoch, V. S. Naipaul), poetry (e.g., Seamus Heaney), and drama (e.g., Harold Pinter, Arnold Wesker, Peter Shaffer).

Entries in this volume, as in others of the set and in the parent volumes of the DLB, may serve the general reader as an introduction to an author, or they may be consulted by a more advanced reader for basic biographical facts. This reviewer's experience as Humanities Librarian confirms that this set is very popular with both beginning college students and high school students, although the level of writing is occasionally beyond that which some of these students can appreciate.—**David Isaacson**

618.　Eighteenth-Century British Literary Biographers. Steven Serafin, ed. Detroit, Gale, 1994. 370p. illus. index. (Dictionary of Literary Biography, v.142). $125.00. LC 94-076614. ISBN 0-8103-5556-6.

This volume in the Dictionary of Literary Biography (DLB) series treats 71 British literary biographers of the "eighteenth century" (several did their biographical work in the early decades of the nineteenth century). Among the 18 men and 3 women, only Samuel Johnson, James Boswell, and perhaps Robert Southey are likely to be familiar to contemporary readers as biographers, although one or two others (e.g., Oliver Goldsmith, William Godwin) are remembered for literary productions of a different sort. Twelve of the 21 subjects are treated in DLB volumes emphasizing other aspects of their literary careers. Two eighteenth-century collective biographies, *Biographia Britannica* and *Lives of the Poets* (not the Johnson *Lives*), are covered in appendixes.

Format and treatment are no different from other volumes in the DLB. Each subject receives a biographical and critical essay of 6 to 20 pages (Johnson is allotted 46 pages), with a primary and secondary bibliography and illustrations (usually a portrait or reproduction of a title page). Contributors of essays are U.S., Canadian, and British academics. Many of these biographers languish in deserved oblivion. Others, such as Edmond Malone and Mary Hays, deserve more recognition. The essays dealing with these lesser-known figures are likely to be the most comprehensive and detailed to be found in all but the largest and most specialized library collections. Treatment is readable and reliable, if generally uninspired.

Many libraries subscribe to the DLB. Other libraries will probably find the price a bit stiff unless they desperately need material on literary biographers.—**Jonathan F. Husband**

619.　An Encyclopedia of British Women Writers. Paul Schlueter and June Schlueter, eds. New York, Garland, 1988. 516p. index. (Garland Reference Library of the Humanities, Vol. 818). $75.00. LC 88-21393. ISBN 0-8240-8449-7.

This biographical dictionary covers approximately 400 women writers who spent a major portion of their lives in the British Isles. Thus, it includes not only British-born authors such as Jane Austen and Virginia Woolf but also writers like Mary Lavin and Ngaio Marsh, who were born in other countries but produced a significant body of their work while living in England. Although medieval and Renaissance personalities are included, the majority of the writers treated are from the eighteenth through twentieth centuries. Coverage of contemporary British authors, such as Fay Weldon and Anita Brookner, is especially strong.

The alphabetically arranged entries combine biographical information with a critical overview of each writer's work. Contributed by subject specialists, the signed articles range in length from one-half to three-and-one-half pages. The scope encompasses not only creative writers such as novelists, poets, dramatists, and children's authors but also critics, biographers, diarists, translators, and other prose writers. Some of these women (e.g., Florence Nightingale and Ellen Terry) are better known for careers other than writing.

Bibliographies at the end of each entry provide a chronological list of the author's published works and a selective list of secondary sources. Among the latter are abbreviated citations to standard biographical and literary reference works that include entries on the individual. The secondary references do not provide the titles of articles, nor do they include pagination, a particularly serious omission when the citations are to newspaper or periodical articles. However, the bibliographies are commendably up-to-date, often including citations to 1987 publications.

The index includes all authors covered and provides cross-references from pseudonyms and other alternative forms of their names. It also selectively indexes topics discussed in the entries. A particularly useful feature is the detailed breakdown of genre headings. For example, the "fiction" entry is further subdivided into over 30 categories, ranging from "adventure" to "working class."

Similar in concept to *American Women Writers* (4v., Ungar, 1979-1983), this work complements that set and enlarges upon the coverage of *A Dictionary of British and American Women Writers, 1660-1800* (see ARBA 86, entry 1079). Most libraries that support in-depth research in British literature or history or in women's studies will want to add this volume to their collections.—**Marie Ellis**

620. **Late Nineteenth- and Early Twentieth-Century British Literary Biographers**. Steven Serafin, ed. Detroit, Gale, 1995. 367p. illus. index. (Dictionary of Literary Biography, v.149). $128.00. ISBN 0-8103-5710-0.

This is the 3d volume on British literary biographers in the Dictionary of Literary Biography series (others are *Eighteenth-Century British Literary Biographers* [volume 142] and *Nineteenth-Century British Literary Biographers* [volume 144; see ARBA 95, entry 1204, and entry 1226, respectively]). Format and treatment are the same as in other DLB volumes: Each subject receives a 6- to 24-page biographical and critical essay preceded by a primary bibliography, and ends, in most cases, with a secondary bibliography accompanied by 1 or 2 illustrations—usually a portrait or a title page reproduction. An appendix includes essays on the writing of literary biography by Sidney Lee, Harold Nicolson, Virginia Woolf, and Lytton Strachey, and a 120-plus item "Checklist of Further Readings." A cumulative subject index to the entire DLB set is included.

Twenty-seven biographers are treated, the majority of them forgotten except by specialists. Most of the exceptions, such as G. K. Chesterton and Herbert Read, are covered by other DLB volumes. Strachey is probably the only biographer whose books are still read and who is not covered elsewhere in the DLB. The essays, written by American and British academics, are generally readable, but pedestrian. A few minor errors were noted (e.g., John Masefield is referred to as "Maysfield" twice on p. 86). Larger public and academic libraries already subscribe to the DLB. Most other libraries will not feel the need to pay for material on such writers as George Paston, Charles Harold Herford, and Edward Tyas Cook.—**Jonathan F. Husband**

621. **Late Victorian and Edwardian Writers, 1890-1914**. Detroit, Gale, 1991. 434p. illus. index. (Concise Dictionary of British Literary Biography, v.5). $65.00. ISBN 0-8103-7985-6.

This volume of selected entries from Gale's Dictionary of Literary Biography (DLB) series is part of a series of eight, each devoted to a particular historical period. It is designed for libraries that need a smaller, less expensive alternative to the complete DLB. The entries on the 21 British late Victorian and Edwardian writers have been updated by the same scholars who prepared the originals.

Arranged alphabetically from Barrie to Yeats, the volume is easy to use. Names are followed by dates of birth and death; brief notes on each contributor; extensive lists of selected works by the authors; and cogent essays, varying in length from 5 pages on H. H. Munro (Saki) to 54 pages on Yeats, that summarize major events in the authors' lives, the reception of their works, and some critical evaluation. These are followed by bibliographies of works about the authors and the places where their papers are archived. No women are included. While Lady Gregory is mentioned in several of the essays, her own work is not discussed. Illustrations include portraits of the authors; pictures of their homes, wives, and friends; manuscript pages that show handwriting and corrections; and dust jackets of selected editions.

The index has all people, places, and works mentioned in this volume. A cumulative index of author entries lists the authors featured in all eight volumes. A complete list of Gale books on literary biography, British and American, is given on the end pages. The Concise Dictionary of British Literary Biography series is a useful addition to any library. [R: VOYA, Dec 92, p. 318]—**Charlotte Lindgren**

622. **Major Tudor Authors: A Bio-bibliographical Critical Sourcebook**. Alan Hager, ed. Westport, Conn., Greenwood Press, 1997. 514p. index. $95.00. ISBN 0-313-29436-4.

The Tudor era in Great Britain (1485-1603) is known as a time of political and intellectual radicalism, complexity, and ambiguity. The authors of this period are among the most creative and challenging in British literary history, including such greats as Edmund Spenser, William Shakespeare, John Donne, and Elizabeth I. This new bio-bibliography provides a wide-ranging introduction to almost 100 authors, including dramatists, poets, religious writers, political figures, science writers, and music composers. They are primarily British, but many Irish, Scottish, and influential Europeans are also covered. A good collection of women authors is included.

Each author entry gives a brief biography, a discussion of major works and themes, a summary of the critical reception, and a bibliography of primary and secondary works. Entries vary in length from 3 to 10 pages, depending upon the importance of the figure. Bibliographies range from just a few entries to two to three pages. A brief, general bibliography and an index complete the volume.

The entries were written by over 50 contributors, primarily academics. As is typical in such a compilation, the writing is somewhat inconsistent, but the treatments are generally comprehensive and well written, providing interesting introductions and summaries. With few exceptions, the discussions of works, themes, and criticism are nicely balanced. One major exception is the "Critical Reception" section on John Donne, which, unfortunately, devolves into a critique by the author of the entry. The book could also be strengthened by the inclusion of a single, comprehensive listing of all authors, internal cross-references from variant forms of authors' names, and improved subject entries in the index.

Overall, Hager has compiled an important reference source on this exciting period in British literary history. This book will be a valuable addition to any academic library or public library and to larger high school collections.—**Susan Davis Herring**

623.   **Modern Writers, 1914-1945**. Detroit, Gale, 1991. 480p. illus. index. (Concise Dictionary of British Literary Biography, v.6). $65.00. ISBN 0-8103-7986-4.

Similar to its companion series, the Concise Dictionary of American Literary Biography, this eight-volume series on prominent British writers is intended primarily for use in small academic, public, and secondary school libraries (those libraries that are unlikely to own the more comprehensive corresponding volumes of the Dictionary of Literary Biography [DLB] series). As an alternative reference source to the DLB, the concise series scores high marks for its selectivity and the quality of its biographical essays. Most of these are updated versions of essays originally published in the DLB, although some have simply been reprinted without revision. A complete list of the writer's works and a selected bibliography are included, as are several relevant photographs and illustrations.

The eight volumes of this series are arranged chronologically and trace the development of British literature from the Middle Ages to the present. The individual volumes, however, are not being published chronologically. Volumes 4, 5, 6, and 7 appeared in 1991, with the remainder scheduled for publication in 1992. Most volumes contain 20 to 25 biographical entries; the two volumes that cover 1945 to the present have the most entries. This particular volume, which covers a transitional period in British literature and spans World War I, the Great Depression, and World War II, features a number of truly major writers: W. H. Auden, H. M. Forster, Robert Graves, Aldous Huxley, James Joyce, D. H. Lawrence, Somerset Maugham, G. B. Shaw, Evelyn Waugh, H. G. Wells, and Virginia Woolf. Of somewhat lesser stature, but nonetheless representative of the period, are Rupert Brooke, Joyce Cary, Agatha Christie, Noel Coward, Sean O'Casey, Wilfred Owen, J. B. Priestley, Dorothy Sayers, and P. G. Wodehouse.

With compilations such as this series, one can always quibble about the selection criteria and wish that the volumes or the series were longer and more inclusive. Many writers could have been placed in more than one volume. In volume 6, for example, one looks in vain for George Orwell, who wrote most of his work prior to 1945; he is found in volume 7. Among the names completely missing from the series are V. S. Pritchett, David Storey, Salman Rushdie, and David Lodge. Still, this is a useful series and is highly recommended for any library that lacks the resources to invest in the complete DLB. [R: LJ, Jan 92, p. 110; VOYA, Dec 92, p. 318]—**Thomas A. Karel**

624.   **Nineteenth-Century British Literary Biographers**. Steven Serafin, ed. Detroit, Gale, 1994. 387p. illus. index. (Dictionary of Literary Biography, v.144). $128.00. ISBN 0-8103-5558-2.

Continuing the coverage of biographers begun with *Eighteenth-Century British Literary Biographers* (see ARBA 95, entry 1204), this volume focuses on 26 nineteenth-century writers whose works include biographies of literary figures. Also covered in the appendixes are 2 major biographical sources conceived during the nineteenth century: the *Dictionary of National Biography* and the 39-volume first series of *British Men of Letters*, published by Macmillan. Additional literary biographers associated with the Victorian era are treated in yet another volume, *Late Nineteenth- and Early Twentieth-Century British Literary Biographers*.

Eighteen of the writers in this volume are also included in one or more of the previous volumes of the Dictionary of Literary Biography (DLB). The majority of these are authors who are better known for their writings in other genres, such as Thomas Carlyle, Elizabeth Gaskell, and Sir Walter

Scott. Among the eight individuals for whom this volume marks the first appearance in the DLB series are Lucy Aikin, John Forster, George Gilfillen, and George Trevelyan.

Following the now-familiar format of other volumes in this series, the signed essays, which range in length from 7 to 20 pages, provide both biographical information and critical analysis. Each essay is preceded by a bibliography of primary works and followed by a selected list of secondary sources. Locations of manuscript collections are also noted. The cumulative index covers volumes 1-144 of the DLB, its *Yearbook* through 1993, and its *Documentary Series* through volume 11.

Because so many of these authors have been the subject of articles in other DLB volumes, libraries that are purchasing this series selectively may not need to add this volume. It will be of interest primarily to academic libraries that support graduate programs in English literature.—**Marie Ellis**

625.　**The Oxford Guide to British Women Writers**. By Joanne Shattock. New York, Oxford University Press, 1993. 492p. $30.00. PR1 11.S48. 016.8208'09287. LC 92-47232. ISBN 0-19-214176-7.

This compact volume is intended as an introduction for the general reader rather than as a comprehensive and detailed work for the specialist. The selection of British women is to some extent arbitrary; "British" turns out to be a term that allows for the inclusion of Anne Bradstreet, usually considered the first American poet, and writers like Katherine Mansfield and Sylvia Plath, who were not born in Great Britain but who did much of their best work there. Twentieth-century women are included only if their writing was primarily creative rather than political or historical. The cutoff date seems to be somewhere in the 1980s.

The alphabetical entries include articles on relevant aspects of literature, such as albums, the Gothic novel, and "The New Woman," as well as biographies of the writers themselves. Pen names are listed, with real names cross-referenced. A selected bibliography of secondary works on women writers follows, divided into pre- and post-1920 sections. Even selected (it could have been 10 times as long), it is a strong reminder of how much valuable work has been done on women's writing in the past two decades. There is no index, however.

The entries, all apparently written by Shattock and none longer than a couple of pages, contain a brief account of the authors' lives and publications followed by a short list of recommended secondary sources. In comparison to reference works such as *The International Dictionary of Women's Biography* (see ARBA 84, entry 673), *The Feminist Companion to Literature in English* (see ARBA 92, entry 1095), or *British Women Writers: A Critical Reference Guide* (see ARBA 90, entry 864), which cover similar ground, the writing is livelier and more concerned with details of each author's personal life and her relationship with the life of her time. This distinctive voice and low price make the book an ideal choice for a school or community library.—**Lynn F. Williams**

626.　**Seventeenth-Century British Nondramatic Poets. Third Series**. M. Thomas Hester, ed. Detroit, Gale, 1993. 434p. illus. index. (Dictionary of Literary Biography, v.131). $125.00. LC 93-8481. ISBN 0-8103-5390-3.

　　Sixteenth-Century British Nondramatic Writers. First Series. David A. Richardson, ed. Detroit, Gale, 1993. 466p. illus. index. (Dictionary of Literary Biography, v.132). $125.00. LC 93-8480. ISBN 0-8103-5391-1.

　　Sixteenth-Century British Nondramatic Writers, Third Series. David A. Richardson, ed. Detroit, Gale, 1996. 385p. illud. index. (Dictionary of Literary Biography, v. 167). $140.00. ISBN 0-8103-9362-X.

　　Sixteenth-Century British Nondramatic Writers, Fourth Series. David A. Richardson, ed. Detroit, Gale, 1996. 377p. illus. index. (Dictionary of Literary Biography, v.172). $140.00. ISBN 0-8103-9935-0.

These four volumes, all part of the long-running and respected Dictionary of Literary Biography (DLB) series, cover the sixteenth and seventeenth centuries, a time of great literary and political ferment in England. Those libraries that subscribe to the series will of course receive these volumes; other libraries might want to consider their purchase for several reasons. One reason is the excellence of the introductory essays and the bibliographies of further reading; another is the quality of the essays on individual authors. A third is the fact that concise, connected information on the whole of this period is somewhat sketchy, so these volumes fill a gap.

The introductory essay to each volume acts as a literary history of the period, identifying major authors as well as major literary and political trends that influenced those authors. They set the authors in context and make the reader acquainted with the authors' world. Those who know the series will know the general arrangement of each volume: a series of critical/biographical essays on authors, each of which includes a list of the author's works, and a list of critical works. Most essays are lavishly illustrated with portraits of the author, the author's family and home, facsimiles of title pages and manuscript pages—anything that further serves to give the flavor of the time. The editors have seen to it that these volumes include not only the major, well-known figures of the time—John Dryden, Andrew Marvell, Philip Sidney, and the like—but also others, mainly women, who have recently been added to the canon. Aphra Behn, whose complete works are now being published by Ohio State University Press, is here, as are Margaret Lucas Cavendish, Duchess of Newcastle, and Anne Killigrew. Each volume contains an index to the entire DLB. Gale provides cross-indexing not only to these volumes but also to many of their other sets.

The bibliographies of further reading reveal an interesting lack of up-to-date criticism of these periods. Only a few of the books listed date from the late 1980s; most are much earlier. One key source on the period, *English Literature in the Sixteenth Century, Excluding Drama*, which is volume 3 of the Oxford History of English Literature, was published in 1954. With such a lack in comprehensive reviews of the period, these DLB volumes are most welcome. They are still too scholarly—and probably too pricey—for many small libraries and high school libraries. These might prefer the eight-volume *Concise Dictionary of British Literary Biography,* which includes the volume *Writers of the Middle Ages and Renaissance before 1600* (see ARBA 93, entry 1199). Others, however, will want to take a close look at these sources.—**Terry Ann Mood**

627. **Twentieth-Century British Literary Biographers**. Steven Serafin, ed. Detroit, Gale, 1995. 413p. illus. index. (Dictionary of Literary Biography, v.155). $128.00. ISBN 0-8103-5716-X.

This is the third Dictionary of Literary Biography (DLB) volume on British literary biographers. Both earlier entries were published in 1994 *Eighteenth-Century British Literary Biographers* (see ARBA 95, entry 1204) and *Nineteenth-Century British Literary Biographers*. Now, literary biographers of the twentieth century receive the standard DLB treatment, and happily, the group of 40 chosen for this volume is much more noteworthy (and familiar) than the earlier groupings. Scholars, novelists, poets, and popular writers dominate the selection; among them are Peter Ackroyd, Quentin Bell, Humphrey Carpenter, Margaret Drabble, P. N. Furbank, Victoria Glendinning, Ian Hamilton, Ronald Hingley, Elizabeth Longford, Nigel Nicolson, Peter Quennell, A. L. Rowse, Norman Sherry, Julian Symons, John Wain, A. N. Wilson, and Angus Wilson. Several of the writers are also covered in other DLB volumes.

While the study of biography as a literary art may be blossoming, this remains an area that is pretty much ignored by students of literature. Therefore, this volume (and its predecessors) will have a limited audience, and it will be a marginal purchase for most academic libraries despite the high quality of writing and research found on its pages.—**Thomas A. Karel**

628. **Victorian Writers, 1832-1890**. Detroit, Gale, 1991. 516p. illus. index. (Concise Dictionary of British Literary Biography, v.4). $65.00. ISBN 0-8103-7984-8.

Anyone curious about the collective quality of the 21 biocritical essays in this book need look no further than the pages of past volumes of ARBA, for all of the essays have been reprinted in full with updates to the bibliographies of secondary works from various volumes of the Dictionary of Literary Biography (DLB) series. The borrowings from *Victorian Novelists before 1885* (see ARBA 84, entry 1187); *Victorian Novelists after 1885* (see ARBA 85, entry 1130); *Victorian Poets before 1850* (see ARBA 86, entry 1096); *Victorian Poets after 1850* (see ARBA 86, entry 1097); *Victorian Prose Writers before 1876* (see ARBA 88, entry 1201); *Victorian Prose Writers after 1867* (see ARBA 88, entry 1202); and *British Mystery Writers, 1860-1919* (see ARBA 89, entry 1097) naturally carry the strengths and weaknesses identical to the originals. As literary biographies and career summaries, they provide excellent introductory overviews of these writers' lives and works. As biocritical essays, they are less successful, providing less critical than biographical insight, particularly because critical comments tend to come from the authors' contemporaries rather than latter-day readers. Numerous illustrations, many of them portraits of the writers and people closely associated with them, strengthen the biographical element. Where an author has been treated in more than one volume of the DLB, this volume reprints the essay from the volume covering that author's principal genre (e.g., the essay on Matthew Arnold as prose essayist rather than as poet). A volume-specific index made up mostly of proper names and titles of literary works adds value to the essays.

The intent of this volume and the set of which it is a part is analogous to that of the Concise Dictionary of American Literary Biography—to make available to libraries that cannot afford the entire DLB those essays that cover the principal, most frequently studied authors of a nation's literary heritage. The eight volumes of this set, when complete, will span English literature from the Middle Ages to the present. Among the writers covered, one can question only the inclusion of Wilkie Collins, whose contributions to mystery fiction, while indisputably significant, have been eclipsed by more artful masters of the genre.

With their emphasis on biography and their generous use of illustrations, these volumes will serve a wider audience than the more analytical essays in *British Writers* (see ARBA 80, entry 1268) and its supplements (see ARBA 88, entry 1199). Although libraries that have the DLB source volumes have no need of *Victorian Writers, 1832-1890*, other libraries can now obtain a sample of its most important essays at a price designed to meet the needs of smaller budgets. [R: LAR, Aug 92, p. 533]—**James Rettig**

629. **Writers after World War II, 1945-1960**. Detroit, Gale, 1991. 420p. illus. index. (Concise Dictionary of British Literary Biography, v.7). $65.00. ISBN 0-8103-7987-2.

This eight-volume series is designed primarily for high school and junior college students, for use especially in small or medium-sized libraries. It takes its origins in a reduction of the multi-volumed Dictionary of Literary Biography (DLB) (now composed of more than 100 volumes), which covers literary biographies in many languages. The focus in the Concise Dictionary of British Literary Biography is, as indicated in the title, specifically on British literature.

The eight volumes are organized, the editors maintain, in chronological sequence, but their chronological divisions work best prior to this century. The three volumes dealing with this century cover, respectively, 1914-1945 (volume 6), 1945-1960 (the volume under review), and 1960-present (volume 8). No rationale is offered for the division of the twentieth century into these periods, which are curiously uneven; the bounds of this present volume, only 15 years, seem oddest of all. What do these 15 years represent in the long lives of the writers included here: their early publications or the years of their most important productions? No clear answer emerges. And on what principle is Muriel Spark included in this volume while her contemporary, Iris Murdoch, is deferred until the next volume?

The entries are taken complete from the DLB, without abridgment, and all entries are accompanied by a bibliography of the author and a list of critical references. The selection of author entries is traditional and patriarchal; few women are included in any of the volumes. Only 3 of the 25 entries in this volume are of women. And in the three volumes that cover this century, the most glaring omissions are of women: Katharine Mansfield in volume 6, Stevie Smith in this volume, and Barbara Pym in volume 8.—**John B. Beston**

630. **Writers of the Middle Ages and Renaissance before 1660**. Detroit, Gale, 1992. 436p. illus. index. (Concise Dictionary of British Literary Biography, v.1). $65.00. ISBN 0-8103-7981-3.

Designed for school and small public libraries, this is the first in an eight-volume selective version of Gale's expensive and massive Dictionary of Literary Biography (DLB) series. The entries chosen for inclusion are identical to those in the DLB. The series concentrates on British literature in chronological sequence from the Middle Ages to the present. As in the DLB, this series provides illustrated biographies and bibliographies of major authors in 10- to 20-page signed articles that focus on the author's literary development and influence without ignoring biographical detail. A list of secondary sources follows each article, and references to editions of personal correspondence, bibliographies, and biographies are provided when possible.

This particular volume contains essays on the anonymous poem *Beowulf* and 17 well-known male writers, such as Geoffrey Chaucer, Thomas Malory, Ben Johnson, William Shakespeare, and Edmund Spencer. Conspicuously absent are Julian of Norwich, Margery Kempe, Elisabeth Cary, and other notable women writers who have finally found their way into the literary canon. In the 8 volumes in this series, there are fewer than 20 women out of almost 200 authors. Nonetheless, the figures included certainly number among the most illustrious in British literature and the most often read in American schools.—**Valerie R. Hotchkiss**

631.   **Writers of the Restoration and Eighteenth Century, 1660-1789**. Detroit, Gale, 1992. 580p. illus. index. (Concise Dictionary of British Literary Biography, v.2). $65.00. ISBN 0-8103-7982-1.

As are the seven other volumes in the series, volume 2 of the Concise Dictionary of British Literary Biography is an abbreviated version of part of the monumental Dictionary of Literary Biography (DLB) series. It is intended for high school and small community libraries unequipped with the more than 100 volumes of the longer version.

As in the rest of the series, the entries are essentially the same as those in the DLB and have the same format: a list of works in recommended editions; an account of the author's life; summaries of major works; and an updated list of material on the author, including letters, bibliographies, biographies, and critical works. The entries are profusely illustrated in rather muddy black-and-white. All the major male writers of the period from 1660 to 1789, including John Milton, are included, but minor writers such as James Thomson and William Cowper are not; and there are no women authors at all, an unfortunate omission for a work published in 1992.

The intended readers of the Concise Dictionary are high school and undergraduate students, who will find this material useful and informative. Recommended for libraries without the complete DLB.—**Lynn F. Williams**

632.   **Writers of the Romantic Period, 1789-1832**. Detroit, Gale, 1992. 468p. illus. index. (Concise Dictionary of British Literary Biography, v.3). $65.00. ISBN 0-8103-7983-X.

The eight volumes of the Concise Dictionary of British Literary Biography, of which this is the third, are an attempt to make some of the material in the Dictionary of Literary Biography (DLB), the standard reference work for large libraries, available to a wider audience. An emphasis on biography is still current in high school teaching, so this abridgment is an appropriate choice for high school, college, and small public libraries that cannot afford (and may not need) the more than 100 volumes of the parent work.

The entries are essentially unabridged from DLB but have been updated through 1990. As in DLB, they are arranged alphabetically within the volume. Each article begins with a list of works in recommended editions, then continues with the author's life and fairly detailed summaries of major works. Although some account is given of a work's reception at publication, critical judgments are kept to a minimum. The articles are generously illustrated, but the black-and-white reproductions are often muddy, a particularly annoying fault when an important manuscript is too out of focus to be readable. An extensive bibliography of secondary works completes the entry.

The volume covers all the major romantic writers who lived long enough to be considered a Victorian, from Robert Burns and William Blake to Thomas Carlyle. It includes Mary Wollstonecraft and Jane Austen but omits Anne Radcliffe, Dorothy Wordsworth, Robert Southey, and John Clare, among others. The decision to reprint the DLB entries unabridged retains the original scholarship but means that this short version is limited to major authors, omitting less well known ones whose lives might have interested some readers. Nevertheless, within its limitations this series will provide a valuable resource for smaller libraries and is recommended for those without the complete DLB. [R: RBB, 1 Feb 92, p. 1058; VOYA, Dec 92, p. 318]—**Lynn F. Williams**

Children's and Young Adult Literature

633. **British Children's Writers, 1800-1880**. Meena Khorana, ed. Detroit, Gale, 1996. 428p. illus. index. (Dictionary of Literary Biography, v.163). $135.00. ISBN 0-8103-9358-1.

Hooray, hooray! Children's writers are making it into standard reference works, and one no longer has to rely on the Something about the Author series (see entries 688-689) or *The Oxford Companion to Children's Literature* (see ARBA 85, entry 1034) for biographical information on authors across the water. Gale is to be commended for adding this contribution to its series of the Dictionary of Literary Biography (DLB). The focus is on the "golden age" of children's literature, which flowered in the nineteenth century.

Khorana, editor of this volume and well known in the field of children's literature, has done a masterly job of putting together crucial information on these nineteenth-century writers of books for children. Khorana posits that the theories of education, coupled with the theories of raising children, were in part responsible for this incredible outpouring of talent. Some 41 writers are included, with essays following the biographical information on the authors that are authoritative, well written, and provide thoughtful insights into the reasons for the extraordinary works that were written between 1800 and 1880 for children. Superb facsimiles of photographs or tin types and other types of prints are also included in this 428-page volume, providing realistic images from the time period.

British Children's Writers, 1800-1880 is an excellent addition to the ever-growing body of reference material that is becoming available for serious scholars of children's literature. This volume of the DLB gives information and resources for teaching courses in the field and is an excellent source. [R: Choice, Dec 96, p. 586]—**Anne F. Roberts**

634. **British Children's Writers, 1880-1914**. Laura M. Zaidman, ed. Detroit, Gale, 1994. 390p. illus. index. (Dictionary of Literary Biography, v.141). $125.00. LC 94-076443. ISBN 0-8103-5555-8.

This volume contains 24 alphabetically arranged entries on writers and illustrators who played a dominant role in children's book publishing during the late Victorian and Edwardian periods. An appendix discusses minor illustrators, and an introduction provides an overview of the political, social, and cultural factors that influenced children's book production. A bibliography of critical and historical studies and a cumulative index complete the book.

Each entry contains a bibliography of primary sources, an essay analyzing the subject's life and work, and a list of biographical sources and works cited. Although the essays follow a pattern by analyzing a subject's works chronologically, the best essays seem far from mechanical. Those on J. M. Barrie, Frances Hodgson Burnett, Kenneth Grahame, Rudyard Kipling, and E. Nesbit do not break new critical ground, but they are ideal introductions to these writers. Among the entries for minor writers, that on G. A. Henty is notable because it effectively selects items from Henty's vast output to reveal plotting formulas and underlying ideological assumptions. In comparison to the studies of writers, the essays on illustrators are disappointing; they seldom explain what makes pictures meritorious and how pictures complement texts. The entry on Kate Greenaway is an exception; those on Beatrix Potter and Arthur Rackham also offer meaningful information.

Although awkwardness or intellectual thinness mars a couple of essays, this volume is extremely useful. It should be the first place both scholars and general readers search when they want reliable information about the figures it covers.—**Raymond E. Jones**

635. **British Children's Writers, 1914-1960**. Donald R. Hettinga and Gary D. Schmidt, eds. Detroit, Gale. 1996. 422p. illus. index. (Dictionary of Literary Biography, v. 160). $128.00. ISBN 0-8103-9355-7.

British Children's Writers, 1914-1960 follows the general format of the series: lengthy critical articles on particular authors, with a bibliography of the author's works and a list of further reading. What makes this particular volume of interest beyond the series is the choice of genre, a genre that has received less critical attention than have others. All the authors profiled—some 40—were popular and influential during their time. Most have retained that popularity, either with their primary market of children (A. A. Milne, P. L. Travers, Mary Norton), or with the second-hand and rare book collector market (Elfrida Vipont, many of the school story series).

As is usual with this series, the essays are thoughtful and well researched, discussing the author's development and the changing critical reception of the works. Most essays make the point that even the most formulaic of these authors, those who wrote books in series or books with repetitive plots and reappearing characters, provided a world of stability for children growing up in a time of turmoil, a time of two world wars, economic insecurity, and deep and disorienting societal changes.

Bibliographies of further reading are uneven in length, but this is no doubt a reflection of how much is available on a given author. The bibliography on J. R. R. Tolkien, for example, is extensive, while only a few items are mentioned for the lesser known Alison Uttley.

Two appended essays treat two particular subgenres: the school series, and the pony story, that specifically British story of a country world of riding clubs, horse shows, and children's contests. Libraries with a clientele interested in children's literature will want this volume, even if they are not subscribers to the Dictionary of Literary Biography series.—**Terry Ann Mood**

636. **British Children's Writers since 1960, First Series**. Caroline C. Hunt, ed. Detroit, Gale, 1996. 394p. illus. index. (Dictionary of Literary Biography, Vol. 161). ISBN 0-8103-9356-5.

Thirty children's authors are profiled in *British Children's Writers since 1960. First Series*, an addition to the Dictionary of Literary Biography series. Most of the authors included were born well before World War II, but produced the bulk of their work during the 1960s, 1970s, and 1980s.

The format is similar to other works in the series; each profile begins with a list of the author's works, is followed by a biographical/critical essay, and ends with a list for further reading. Most of the essays give fairly complete descriptions and plot summaries of many of the author's works. The articles are heavily illustrated, not only with a portrait of the author, but with pictures of title pages and dust jackets of the authors' books, with pictures of the authors' homes, or with photographs of the settings used in the stories. In this way this volume of the Dictionary of Literary Biography continues its tradition of setting an author in a world context.

An introductory essay discusses the development of children's literature in general during this time. For the most part, the authors profiled in this volume followed predictable patterns from the past: they wrote books in series, including an immensely popular series with two generic characters, Peter and Jane; family stories; animal stories; updated versions of the school story; and fantasy stories. The immense social changes of the 1960s wrought a great change in publishing for children. Later in their careers, these authors continued with the same patterns, but in an updated form. Historical fiction became more realistic; family stories incorporated different configurations of family; the problem novel became more popular.

British Children's Writers since 1960 is a valuable addition to the bibliography of children's literature.—**Terry Ann Mood**

Drama

637. **British Playwrights, 1880-1956: A Research and Production Sourcebook**. William W. Demastes and Katherine E. Kelly, eds. Westport, Conn., Greenwood Press, 1996. 457p. index. $95.00. ISBN 0-313-28758-9.

This comprehensive sourcebook will be useful for teachers, directors, scholars, and general readers who wish to enhance their knowledge of British drama in one of the most restless and volatile periods in the history of modern literature. Among the 40 authors covered are such major figures as Max Beerbohm, Noel Coward, and T. S. Eliot, and also minor authors such as Cicely Hamilton, Allan Monkhouse, and St. John Hankin.

Each entry provides a concise biographical overview, a list of important plays, and a list of critical receptions of the plays. Also included for each figure is substantial bibliographic material (e.g., lists of scholarly and critical works on the author), as well as listings of locations housing unpublished material.

There is also information on adaptations and productions of the plays and on previously published bibliographies on the playwright. Each section contains a brief but thorough assessment of the playwright's career. Also furnished are a thorough index and a detailed list of contributors.

The editors of *British Playwrights, 1880-1956* are well qualified for their task. Professor of English at Louisiana State University, Demastes is series editor of Greenwood Press's Research and Production Sourcebooks. Among his own books are *Beyond Naturalism: A New Realism in American Theatre* (1988) and *Theatre of Chaos*. Kelly is associate professor of English at Texas A&M University. She is the author of *Tom Stoppard and the Craft of Comedy* (1991) and the general editor of *Modern Drama by Women, 1880s-1930s: An International Anthology* (1996).

British Playwrights is an indispensable tool for the researcher or the professional. Even for the layperson, it is useful as an introduction and a guide to a fascinating period of British drama.—**Peter Thorpe**

638. **British Playwrights, 1956-1995: A Research and Production Sourcebook**. William W. Demastes, ed. Westport, Conn., Greenwood Press, 1996. 502p. index. $95.00. ISBN 0-313-28759-7.

The Midas marked the beginning of a new energy and realism on the British stage, according to the editor of *British Playwrights, 1956-1995*; such plays as Samuel Beckett's *Waiting for Godot* and John Osborne's *Look Back in Anger* turned British theater on its head, replacing the upper-class "genteel comedy of manners" with a "radical social consciousness" (p.ix). Editor Demastes, professor of English at Louisiana State University, and 31 others (mostly professors of English or theater) have contributed chapters on 36 British playwrights active between 1956 and 1995. All but five are still alive, and many have produced work as recently as the 1990s. Included along with Beckett and Osborne are Harold Pinter (considered by some critics to be the greatest English-language playwright of the twentieth century), Pam Gems (the first woman playwright produced by the Royal Shakespeare Company), Peter Shaffer (of *Amadeus* fame), Louise Page (the youngest playwright in the book), and Tom Stoppard (whose *Arcadia* is still touring the United States).

This book presupposes some familiarity with the playwrights' original works. Its purpose is to present the history of each writer's career and critical reception and provide references for further research. Each chapter has a brief summation and assessment of the playwright's career, a production history, a primary bibliography (the playwright's published works and interviews), and a secondary bibliography (reviews and other criticism). Although the focus is on the major plays, mention is also made of their other work, such as motion picture adaptations, translations, television productions, and other prose writing. A selected bibliography of sources on British theater and drama, an index of names, and an index of titles are useful for quick reference.

A few misspellings and typographic errors were noted. The chapter on Gems at first indicates her adaptation of *The Blue Angel* is based on Thomas Mann's novel and, three pages later, on Heinrich Mann's novel (the latter is correct). These quibbles aside, *British Playwrights* will serve well in literary criticism and theater collections of academic libraries.—**Lori D**. **Kranz**

639. **Contemporary British Dramatists**. K. A. Berney and N. G. Templeton, eds. Detroit, St. James Press, 1994. 886p. index. $40.00. ISBN 1-55862-213-6.

At first glance, *Contemporary British Dramatists* and its kin, *Contemporary American Dramatists* and *Contemporary Women Dramatists*, seem logical redefinements of the successful standard reference *Contemporary Dramatists*, now in its 5th edition (see ARBA 94, entry 1467). *Contemporary British Dramatists* claims to cover 210 of "the best and most prominent of contemporary playwrights from the United Kingdom and Ireland (those who are currently active, as well as some who have died since 1950, but whose reputations remain essentially contemporary)" (p.vii). The 1950 cutoff, in fact, permits inclusion of Sean O'Casey, Noel Coward, T. S. Eliot, and Agatha Christie, whose stage successes date from the 1920s. Other deceased notables include Brendan Behan, Joe Orton, Samuel Beckett, and Graham Greene; prominent living playwrights include John Arden, Edward Bond, Caryl Churchill, Michael Frayn, Brian Friel, Harold Pinter, and Tom Stoppard. Most of the playwright entries are recycled from *Contemporary Dramatists*'s 5th edition, with about 20 others taken from previous editions. It seems that fewer than a dozen entries (e.g., those for Eliot, O'Casey, Orton, and Behan) are original to the volume. Playwright entries typically give brief biographical data and "a complete list of published and/or produced plays and all other separately published books, [and] a selected list of bibliographies and critical studies" (p.vii), with one- or two-page analyses of major individual plays and broad assessment of dramatic stature. Even in entries for

Coward and Christie, this mostly amounts to updating previously published bibliographies, with little revision of the analyses. Bibliographic information for primary works and for bibliographies and critical studies is allusive at best: Imprint information is always incomplete; titles of bibliographies and critical studies are abbreviated. Besides the few original entries already mentioned, all that is really new in *Contemporary British Dramatists* are the more in-depth essays (often 2-plus pages) on some 34 notable contemporary plays, ranging from O'Casey's *Juno and the Paycock* (1924) to Timberlake Wertenbaker's *Our Country's Good* (1988). Essays for works, like analyses in the playwright entries, consistently offer wonderfully pointed and very quotable comments on dramatic elements, both specific and general. None of the essays or entries, however, references acts, scenes, and lines, nor footnotes critical sources. Like *Contemporary Dramatists* before it, *Contemporary British Dramatists* is mainly useful as a companion or starting point for research. One would like to see progress toward something more.—**James K. Bracken**

640.   **Elizabethan Dramatists**. Fredson Bowers, ed. Detroit, Gale, 1987. 492p. illus. bibliog. index. (Dictionary of Literary Biography, Vol. 62). $92.00. LC 87-19779. ISBN 0-8103-1740-0.

    Elizabethan Dramatists, volume 62 of Dictionary of Literary Biography, focuses on 19 dramatists, including Shakespeare, George Chapman, Thomas Dekker, Ben Jonson, Thomas Heywood, and Christopher Marlowe, as well as several selected minor figures. *Elizabethan Dramatists* was compiled by a number of experienced scholars under the supervision of Fredson Bowers and is well equipped to meet the needs of students and scholars alike.

    Each biography includes a list of first or early productions of the dramatist's plays, modern editions of his works, a section on the life and works of the dramatist, and a bibliography and list of references. The length of the literary biographies ranges from four pages on the minor dramatist Thomas Preston to John Andrews's massive essay, nearly 100 pages long, on Shakespeare, which incorporates up-to-date information on Shakespeare's biography as well as an assessment of Shakespeare's works. But the biographies of Shakespeare's contemporaries deserve the highest commendation: they are impressively and carefully put together by a cadre of scholars.

    Equally valuable are the three appendices: "The Theater in Shakespeare's Time," prepared by the theater historian Andrew Gurr; "The Publication of English Renaissance Plays," by Fredson Bowers; and "Sources for the Study of Tudor and Stuart Drama," by Albert H. Tricomi. The numerous illustrations, including copies of title pages of 1st editions, make this a handsome work that is appealing to the experienced reader, the student, and the general public. The Dictionary of Literary Biography in general and this superb volume in particular are among the best reference works of their kind.—**Geraldo U. de Sousa**

641.   **Jacobean and Caroline Dramatists**. Fredson Bowers, ed. Detroit, Gale, 1987. 370p. illus. index. (Dictionary of Literary Biography, Vol. 58). $92.00. LC 87-8645. ISBN 0-8103-1136-2.

    This volume of bio-bibliographic essays on Jacobean and Caroline dramatists, as well as a companion volume on the Elizabethans, has been edited by the University of Virginia's Fredson Bowers, probably America's foremost bibliographic scholar of the drama of the sixteenth and seventeenth centuries. Bowers has collected 27 essays by 21 fine scholars (including Cyrus Hoy, also of the University of Virginia) covering many of the major and minor playwrights active during the years after the death of Elizabeth I in 1604 to the closing of the theaters in 1642 (but continuing on, in the entry on Davenant, into the Interregnum and the Restoration). The contributors to this volume have a good sense of the literary atmosphere of the era as well as an appreciation of the contributions made by the lesser lights of the contemporary literary scene, as the quality of the essays on the greatest names of the era (Beaumont and Fletcher, Ford, Massinger, Middleton, Webster, etc.), as well as the most obscure, are consistently excellent. Unfortunately, the book does not contain entries for all of the great playwrights active at this time—Shakespeare, for instance, produced much of his most mature work after the death of Elizabeth, as did his rival Jonson (who is most conspicuous in his absence, considering his influence on the generation of playwrights focused on here), yet neither are present. Both are included in the volume on the Elizabethans. Each entry contains lists of original production as well as known publications (both contemporary and modern); all of the entries are illustrated, but the photographs are at times poorly reproduced (especially in Bowers's foreword) and sometimes not properly attributed. As this book constitutes volume 58 of the Dictionary of Literary Biography, a cumulative index for the set is appended at the end.

As excellent as the volume is, it will not replace Bentley's *The Jacobean and Caroline Stage* (Oxford University Press, 1941-1968) or Chambers's *The Elizabethan Stage* (Clarendon Press, 1923), nor does it even improve substantially on these standard sets. Libraries that own those sets and are not committed to the Dictionary of Literary Biography series may wish to forego this volume and the one on the Elizabethans, as the cost is not inconsiderable. [R: Choice, Dec 87, p. 601]—**James Edgar Stephenson**

642.   Mann, David D., and Susan Garland Mann, with Camille Garnier. **Women Playwrights in England, Ireland, and Scotland 1660-1823**. Bloomington, Indiana University Press, 1996. 417p. $57.50. ISBN 0-253-33087-4.

Prior to the mid-1980s when feminist scholars began in earnest to recover the works of women writers, women playwrights received scant attention from drama critics and theater historians alike. Now, with the publication of this volume, a more comprehensive picture of the role women played in the development of English drama begins to take shape. Covering the period from 1660 (when women were first allowed on London's and Dublin's theater stages) to 1823, the authors have compiled biographical information about more than 150 women playwrights and written summaries of many of their plays.

Arranged alphabetically according to the title of the plays and the authors' names, some of the entries are about plays whose authorship has not been established with certainty. As the authors explain in their introduction, women playwrights were rarely taken seriously and were often publicly ridiculed for their efforts to stage their works. To avoid criticism, they sometimes used pseudonyms or simply signed their plays with "By a Lady." Several of the playwrights included here wrote only a single play; others wrote "closet plays," that is, plays that were never intended for production. Also included are more prolific playwrights, such as Aphra Behn, Susannah Centlivre, Elizabeth Inchbald, Mary Pix, and Jane Scott, all of whom managed to sustain a fairly visible presence in English theater. The chronological list of plays in the appendixes helps to place the playwrights in a historical context, as does the authors' excellent introduction.

This groundbreaking book is filled with information on women who for too long have remained behind the scenes. Scholars, researchers, and general readers will all find this book easy to use and enjoyable to read. It is highly recommended. [R: Choice, Mar 97, p. 1140]—**Sandra Adell**

643.   **Restoration and Eighteenth-Century Dramatists: First Series**. Paula R. Backscheider, ed. Detroit, Gale, 1989. 397p. illus. index. (Dictionary of Literary Biography, v.80). $98.00. PR701.R4.822'.009. LC 89-1070. ISBN 0-8103-4558-7.

Solid, high-quality, and informative best describe the essays in this collection, the first of three volumes on Restoration and eighteenth-century playwrights. Biocritical studies of 18 writers born between 1621 and 1666 are included. John Dryden, "the dominant dramatist of his generation," and William Wycherly receive the most attention. Essays for George Etherege; Thomas Otway; George Villiers, second duke of Buckingham; Nahum Tate; Thomas Shadwell; and John Vanbrugh are less extensive. Three women are discussed—Aphra Behn, Delariviere Manley, and Mary Pix. Other writers included are John Banks, Roger Boyle, John Crowne, Thomas Durfey, Nathaniel Lee, Peter Anthony Motteux, and Thomas Southerne.

Although each essay certainly represents good scholarship, each is also rather formulaic. Little new information is provided in them. Emphasis is largely on the plays rather than their writers; each play generally gets two to three paragraphs that indicate central themes and describe actions of major characters. Greater attention is given to the lives of those playwrights for whom substantial biographical information exists, such as Dryden and Buckingham. The essay for Lee, on the other hand, almost exclusively reflects modern critical interpretations of the plays.

Checklists of the earliest productions and published texts, with references to modern scholarly editions, begin the essays; checklists of secondary works (bibliographies, biographies, critical studies, and manuscript resources) conclude them. In addition, the volume reprints a selection of 28 prologs, epilogs, prefaces, and dedications from editions of plays by these and other contemporary writers. Both the selections and their topical arrangement (on authorship, audiences, history of the theater, and the like) are rather arbitrary. A separate index of playwrights represented in this selection would be helpful. The cumulative index references the essays contained in other Dictionary of Literary Biography (DLB) volumes and series. As in its 79 antecedents, essays in this DLB volume offer students and scholars solid bases for further research.—**James K. Bracken**

Fiction

644. **British Romantic Novelists, 1789-1832**. Bradford K. Mudge, ed. Detroit, Gale, 1992. 438p. illus. index. (Dictionary of Literary Biography, v.116). $112.00. LC 92-9153. ISBN 0-8103-7593-1.

It is interesting to note that 17 of the 33 major and minor novelists included in this volume are female. Mudge points out in the introduction that when circulating libraries made books available to the middle classes, increasing numbers of popular novels were written by and for women and were condemned as dangerous to cultural standards.

The entries, which appear alphabetically from Jane Austen to Edward Trelawny, vary considerably in length, from 40 pages on Sir Walter Scott to 5 pages for little-known Irish writer John Banim, but they are nearly always informative and entertaining. Each literary biography appears under the author's name with dates of birth and death and full bibliographic information on novels and editions. At the end of each essay are listed letters, biographies of the writer, and reference works. Locations of the papers and manuscripts are also given. The iconography is exceptional, with illustrations of the writers, their families and homes, manuscript pages, frontispiece drawings, and title pages of 1st editions. A checklist of further reading suggests 45 useful reference works on the Romantic novel. A list of the contributing scholars and the colleges with which they are associated concludes the volume.

Each volume in the series contains a cumulative index that lists the names to be found in all volumes of the Dictionary of Literary Biography and its related series, citing the appropriate volume and page number. Each volume provides a treasury of information within its special framework.—**Charlotte Lindgren**

645. **British Short-Fiction Writers, 1800-1880**. John R. Greenfield, ed. Detroit, Gale, 1996. 402p. illus. index. (Dictionary of Literary Biography, v.159). $128.00. ISBN 0-8103-9354-9.

British Short-Fiction Writers, 1800-1880, examines 31 writers of the time period. It is a recent volume of the long standing and respected series, Dictionary of Literary Biography. In format it is similar to earlier volumes. Material on an author begins with a list of the author's works. Then follows a critical essay on the author's life, works, and influence, and a list of further sources. All essays are illustrated by portraits of the authors at various stages of their lives, by illustrations from their works, and pictures of their homes and families. This is in keeping with the DLB's Advisory Board's belief that authors should be studied in context rather than in isolation.

Many of the authors are well known and have been examined in previous volumes of the DLB series: Trollope, Mary Wollstonecraft Shelley, Wilkie Collins. This is also in keeping with DLB tradition: Writers fit into more than category and their accomplishments and influence can be examined from more than one perspective. Other authors are perhaps less well known, but all contributed greatly to the expansion of the short fiction genre during this time period.

An added plus to most volumes in the series, and certainly to this one, is the introductory essay. This one discusses the various changes in society which led to the flowering of this literary form, and mentions many of the periodicals and literary annuals which flourished at the time and which provided an outlet for short fiction.

Libraries with the entire ongoing set will of course purchase this addition. Others will find this a helpful addition to criticism of short story authors.—**Terry Ann Mood**

646. **Late-Victorian and Edwardian British Novelists**. **First Series**. George M. Johnson, ed. Detroit, Gale, 1995. 420p. illus. index. (Dictionary of Literary Biography, v.153). $128.00. ISBN 0-8103-5714-3.

Although for decades the writings of Thomas Hardy, William Makepeace Thackeray, and the Brontës have undergone continual appraisal and reappraisal by successive waves of literary critics, hardly any significant scholarship has focused on the works of such deserving contemporaries of theirs as E. F. Benson, Richard S. Hitchens, or Beatrice Harraden. Strides to redress this oversight have now been made with this collection of biocritical essays and bibliographies. Although volumes 18, 34, and 36 of the Dictionary of Literary Biography (DLB) have previously touched on the works of some of these figures, 20 of the writers discussed in the book have heretofore received no treatment in the series.

Johnson, in his 13-page introduction, displays an informed appreciation of these unheralded authors. Herein he explores the cultural biases (including the ever-present disdain of the literari toward the popular writer) that have obscured such classics as George du Maurier's *Peter Ibbetson* or William Hope Hodgson's *The Nightland* from the view of generations of readers. The 35 articles contained in this volume reflect a refreshingly wide array of critical perspectives held by an international field of scholars who are affiliated with universities in the United States, Canada, Great Britain, the Netherlands, and Portugal. Indeed, only about half of the contributors are tied to U.S. institutions. Also, in this work it is pleasing to encounter such heaven-sent matches of scholar and subject as the study of W. H. Hudson by George Woodcock.

As is customary with the DLB, each article contains a black-and-white illustration of the writer under consideration, usually accompanied by reproductions of manuscript leaves, title pages from 1st editions, and so forth. Extensive (if not comprehensive) bibliographies of books, play productions, and appearances of shorter works in periodicals and collections precede each biocritical essay; citations for such suggested reading and scholarship sources as letters, interviews, biographies, and papers conclude the study of each writer. A forthcoming companion volume is promised, which would treat neglected writers from this period who are realists as opposed to the mostly neo-romantic writers included in the present work. Libraries serving appreciable numbers of college students should consider purchasing this excellent book.—**Jeffrey E. Long**

647. Sutherland, John. **The Stanford Companion to Victorian Fiction**. Stanford, Calif., Stanford University Press, 1989. 696p. index. $60.00. LC 88-61462. ISBN 0-8047-1528-9.

This work's intent is to bring to more popular attention "a lost continent of English literature" that extends beyond the familiar works of Dickens, the Brontës, Eliot, and Hardy. First published in 1988 as the *Longman Companion to Victorian Fiction* (London, Longman), it consists of biographies of 878 novelists (including those noted above), synopses of the plots and publications of 554 novels, and historical notes on magazines and periodicals, publishers, schools of writing (e.g., "Silver Fork Fiction"), illustrators, and miscellaneous items of significance to Victorian publishing and reading (e.g., "Mudie's Circulating Library"). The biographies note important facts and summarize successes and failures. The entries for novels provide the details and dates of publication (typically first in serial and later in multivolume form), and note illustrators and variant titles. Appendixes link proper names with pseudonyms and maiden with married names. A tight rein on the book's scope wisely excludes entries on persons such as Matthew Arnold, Leslie Stephen, and Henry James, who were closely involved with Victorian fiction but whose inclusion would make the work unwieldy.

For sheer quantity of information and informed critical evaluation, the *Companion* is peerless. Sutherland's terse style and occasional dry wit suits the often intersecting lives and plots he recounts. [R: Choice, July/Aug 89, p. 1821; LJ, June 89, p. 100; RBB, 1 Sept 89, p. 108]—**William S. Brockman**

Humor

648.   **Encyclopedia of British Humorists: Geoffrey Chaucer to John Cleese**. Steven H. Gale, ed. New York, Garland, 1996. 2v. index. (Garland Reference Library of the Humanities, v.906). $150.00/set. ISBN 0-8240-5990-5.

This two-volume set spans the entire history of British literature, from *Beowulf* to John Cleese (of Monty Python fame) and will assist anyone interested in humor. Almost any person of significance born or writing among the nations of the British Isles—England, Ireland, Scotland, and Wales—is included. It should be noted that stand-up comedians, comic actors, and joke writers have been excluded, thus individuals such as Benny Hill will not be found in these volumes.

The set contains 203 entries listed alphabetically by author, covering 206 humorists (there are 3 pairs of duo-authors), written by 118 scholars from 7 different countries. There are indexes of authors, titles, and subjects. A chronological index and a list of pseudonyms are provided at the start, as some authors are listed by given name and some by pseudonym, depending on which is more popularly recognized. Most entries contain a brief biography, a bibliography of sources, a literary analysis, and summary remarks. Entries average about six full pages and provide rich detail and examples. Most major humorists are featured in addition to several minor authors. Also, some authors who are not primarily known for humor are included because they wrote some humorous materials; for example, Winston Churchill and C. S. Lewis. In such cases, only the humorous material is considered.

These volumes, six years in the making, were written to assist both the scholar and the interested layperson. Analysis is insightful and focuses on the humorist's technique and contribution to the field of humor, yet avoids the academe penchant for dry minutiae. Some knowledge of literary history is helpful when using these volumes. Still, providing generous samples of humor, from the ironic to the absurd, the encyclopedia is simply fun to look through. [R: Choice, Oct 96, p. 250; RBB, Aug 96, pp. 1922-24]—**Brad R. Leach**

Mystery Writers

649.   **British Mystery Writers, 1860-1919**. Bernard Benstock and Thomas F. Staley, eds. Detroit, Gale, 1988. 389p. illus. bibliog. index. (Dictionary of Literary Biography, Vol. 70). $95.00. LC 88-11465. ISBN 0-8103-1748-6.

Ever since the discovery of crime, people have relished stories of suspense and intrigue. *British Mystery Writers, 1860-1919* is the 70th volume in the biographical-bibliographical series known collectively as the Dictionary of Literary Biography. It is also the first volume of that series to be devoted to the roots of mystery fiction. Subsequent volumes will cover the "Golden Age of British Mysteries" and trace the development of the genre up to the present.

During the later half of the nineteenth century, Britain was the breeding ground for a new style of writing, which grew out of the Gothic novel into a middle-culture literary style that forever blurred the line between serious literature and popular fiction. The writers of this period were the foundation builders for modern mystery fiction, which has, in its many manifestations, gone on to become both a popular form as well as a means of serious literary expression.

Familiar members of the genre such as Sir Arthur Conan Doyle, Sax Rohmer, and H. G. Wells are covered as well as some of the less well-known ground breakers: Angus Reach, Fergus Hume, and Charles Dickens. Well-written biographical and critical essays focus on 35 writers covered by this volume. As the foreword explains, "just as an author is influenced by his surroundings, so is the reader's understanding of the author enhanced by a knowledge of his environment." Each signed essay is accompanied by a bibliography of the author's major works and articles, a short list of critical works and the location of their collected papers.

Following the traditional DLB format, *British Mystery Writers, 1860-1919* is copiously illustrated with portraits, scenes from the author's life, illustrations, book jackets, and stills from films based on their works. The volume contains a cumulative index for the entire series and a list of contributors. A "Books for Further Reading" section lists 75 titles on the art, history, style of crime, and detection fiction.

An excellent addition for libraries with strong mystery collections or for reference collections supporting research in popular literature.—**Steven J. Schmidt**

650. **British Mystery Writers, 1920-1939**. Bernard Benstock and Thomas F. Staley, eds. Detroit, Gale, 1989. 4l4p. illus. index. (Dictionary of Literary Biography, v.77). $95.00. LC 88-30048. ISBN 0-8103-4555-2.

The mystery is considered to have come of age between the two world wars, when the form found a vast and enthusiastic audience. A continuation in the Dictionary of Literary Biography series on British mystery writers (see ARBA 89, entry 1097 for a review of the volume covering 1860-1919), the present work covers 45 authors who wrote from 1920 to 1939 when mystery solidified as a genre. Some of the favorites include Nicholas Blake (alias C. Day Lewis), Dorothy L. Sayers, Graham Greene, C. P. Snow, Agatha Christie, Ngaio Marsh, and J. B. Priestly.

Entries contain chronological bibliographies of the writers' works (including screenplays, short stories, and articles) and photographs of authors, dust jackets, and program and magazine covers. The biographies focus on the period when the works were written and under what circumstances, as well as on content, style, and imagery. Important events and people are also covered. Article lengths range from a few pages (Ethel Lina White) to almost 20 (Dorothy L. Sayers). An up-to-date list of books for further reading on mystery, detective, and espionage stories and a cumulative index for the DLB series conclude the volume.

In contrast, the biographical dictionary *Twentieth-Century Crime and Mystery Writers* (see ARBA 86, entry 1123) contains 600-plus entries. Yet this DLB biography of mystery writers concentrates on a particular era and dimension of the genre, making it valuable to the study of popular literature. [R: Choice, May 89, p. l484]—**Patricia M. Leach**

Poetry

651. **Eighteenth-Century British Poets: Second Series**. John Sitter, ed. Detroit, Gale, 1991. 385p. illus. index. (Dictionary of Literary Biography, v.109). $108.00. LC 91-19801. ISBN 0-8103-4589-7.

The authors covered in this volume were born after the death of Queen Anne in 1714. Their publishing careers ranged from the 1740s to the early years of the nineteenth century. Generalizations about them and their works are limited. Although there seems to be a continuing attempt to impose unity on their diversity, to label them as poets of "sentiment" or "sensibility" or as "pre-Romantics" is hardly profitable. To designate them as belonging to the "Age of Johnson" has some merit, but Samuel Johnson was essentially a prose writer without the distinctive voice of a poet.

As with previous volumes in the Dictionary of Literary Biography (DLB), this one has an illustrated biocritical essay written by a leading eighteenth-century scholar, a specialist on one of the 24 authors represented. Among those profiled are the well-known Robert Burns, Thomas Chatterton, Oliver Goldsmith, and Thomas Gray; the lesser known Anna Laetitia Barbauld, John Langhorne, and William Whitehead are also covered. Each essay typically contains a chronological discussion of the poet's life and literature, which is followed by a primary bibliography of books and major articles, a secondary bibliography of critical works, and information about published letters.

Favorable remarks made about previous DLB volumes can be duly echoed about *Eighteenth Century British Poets*. Large reference libraries will want to obtain this latest addition for their collections. Those that have the entire series will find an appended 70-page cumulative index especially useful since it provides a complete alphabetical list of all authors represented in the DLB (v.1-109), the DLB *Yearbooks* (1980-1990), and the DLB *Documentary Series* (vols. 1-8).—**C. A. Cevasco**

Prose

652. **British Prose Writers, 1660-1800: Second Series**. Donald T. Siebert, ed. Detroit, Gale, 1991. 434p. illus. index. (Dictionary of Literary Biography, v.104). $108.00. LC 91-6630. ISBN 0-8103-4584-6.

Siebert's other volume, *British Prose Writers, 1660-1800: First Series* (1991), covered a core of prominent literary figures, including Daniel Defoe, John Dryden, Henry Fielding, Alexander Pope, and Jonathan Swift. The present volume is notable for coverage of writers of wider-ranging interests. Significant among them are philosopher and historian David Hume, historian Edward Gibbon, artist Joshua Reynolds, political economist Adam Smith, evangelist John Wesley, antiquary Thomas Percy, biographer James Boswell, and feminist Mary Wollstonecraft. Also included is Samuel Johnson, who perhaps personifies the period's diversity and versatility.

In general, as in other volumes in the Dictionary of Literary Biography (DLB), the individual essays balance biography and criticism, providing sympathetic introductions to author's lives and works without extensive detail or analysis. A welcome exception to this pattern is Donald Livingston's rather lengthy aside on the complex ideas underlying Hume's A *Treatise of Human Nature* (pp.162-70). Primary and secondary bibliographies accompany the essays. Heavily illustrated with portraits of the writers (many by Joshua Reynolds), engravings from contemporary publications, and facsimiles of manuscripts and title pages, the volume is a solid addition to the DLB. And, similar to many others in the series, this volume will be useful to a wider audience than students and researchers in English literature.—**James K. Bracken**

653. **British Romantic Prose Writers, 1789-1832: Second Series**. John R. Greenfield, ed. Detroit, Gale, 1991. 431p. illus. index. (Dictionary of Literary Biography, v.110). $108.00. LC 91-27535. ISBN 0-8103-4590-0.

This volume of the Dictionary of Literary Biography lives up to its predecessors. In a second series of British Romantic prose writers, it focuses on those writers born after 1775 and whose major works were written between 1810 and 1845. To create a sense of the intellectual climate and concerns of that age, it includes prose essayists, journalists, polemicists and political writers, writers known for works in other genres but who have significant prose works, writers known for their friendships with other writers, and popular or important writers now forgotten. Each entry provides biographical information in conjunction with the history of that author's writing and reputation. In the appendix, articles discuss the treatment of literature in some of the important quarterlies and magazines of the age. Each author's entry is copiously (and often amusingly) illustrated and includes a primary bibliography and bibliographies of letters, of bibliographies, and of secondary sources, as well as the location of the writer's papers. The journal articles include secondary sources. The volume ends with "Books for Further Reading" and a cumulative index to the series. Each entry, be it author or journal, is well written and informative, and the book is satisfying to mind and hand. It provides plenty of helpful information without the aura of unimaginative scholarship.—**Rebecca Jordan**

654. **British Travel Writers, 1837-1875**. Barbara Brothers and Julia Gergits, eds. Detroit, Gale, 1996. 437p. illus. index. (Dictionary of Literary Biography, v.166). $135.00. ISBN 0-8103-9361-1.

How many people have sat as children with large, old, often disintegrating books of engravings of far-off places in their laps, books that came to their parents from their parents? How many have watched movies on weekend afternoons, the scripts for which were fed by accounts of Victorian travelers? Many people have complex, albeit often inaccurate, preconceptions of foreign nations and cultures based on the original works of nineteenth-century travel writers.

This current volume of the Dictionary of Literary Biography (DLB) does an admirable job of presenting a cross section of 38 authors from this once popular genre. Included are names that will be recognized as "legendary" in travel writing (David Livingstone, Sir Richard Burton, Lucie Duff-Gordon), several major literary and scientific figures (Charles Darwin, Francis Galton, Edward Lear, Charles Dickens), and several authors that still stand as popular culture icons of travel and work abroad (Florence Nightingale, and Anna Leonowens of *Anna and the King of Siam* fame). Each of the 38 entries includes a bibliography of the author's works; a signed critical essay; a list of biographical sources; and, where possible, a section locating the author's papers. The entries are followed by two bibliographies: The first, entitled "Travel Writing, 1837-1875," is a list of works by authors not included in the body of the volume; the second, a "Checklist of Further Readings," is a bibliography of secondary sources on travelers and travel writing. Each entry is also accompanied by clearly identified black-and-white illustrations, including maps, portraits of the authors, book illustrations, pages from authors' sketchbooks, and photographs ranging from grave sites to the authors in native dress. The volume concludes with an index cumulating the contents of all of the DLB volumes, the 1980-1995 volumes of the DLB *Yearbooks*, and the 13 volumes of the DLB *Documentary Series*.

Any academic library serving an undergraduate or graduate population studying nineteenth-century history should have this volume. Any large public library that has a historical collection of works of nineteenth-century travelers should also consider purchasing it.—**Caroline M. Kent**

655. **Modern British Essayists, First Series**. Robert Beum, ed. Detroit, Gale, 1990. 421p. illus. index. (Dictionary of Literary Biography, v.98). $103.00. LC 90-39010. ISBN 0-8103-4578-1.

This volume and its companion (volume 100 of the series) cover 32 out of 63 modern British essayists, practitioners of the formal and the informal essay. Among the more familiar writers are D. H. Lawrence and William Butler Yeats, while Holbrook Jackson and Elizabeth Wordsworth are perhaps less well known. The essayists selected cover a broad range within the genre. Although some were literary critics, those primarily engaged in analytical criticism are excluded.

As with other volumes in the Dictionary of Literary Biography series, the emphasis on biography varies with individual volumes. For example, Yeats appears in volumes 10 and 19, the former on him as dramatist, the latter on him as poet. The latter study goes into detail about Yeats' personal life. The present volume sketches the author's life in four scant paragraphs; the bulk of the discussion is a commentary on his work as an essayist. Thus, there is little duplication among the studies.

Following a brief history of the essay in the foreword, each entry begins with a list of the author's works. A critical discussion of the essayist's contributions is interspersed with black-and-white photographs of the author and other key figures, and occasionally of a manuscript or typescript. Where applicable, published correspondence, bibliographies, biographies, selected secondary sources, and the location of an author's papers are cited.

This volume, as others in the series, will prove very useful, especially to undergraduate students of literature, who will benefit from these accessible studies by literary scholars. However, while the cumulative index is convenient, it takes 60 of the 421 pages. One questions whether some other means of access might be devised. Certainly the practice contributes to the high cost of the volume and may dissuade smaller collections from purchasing it. [R: Choice, May 91, p. 1464]—**Bernice Bergup**

656. **Victorian Prose Writers after 1867**. William B. Thesing, ed. Detroit, Gale, 1987. 571p. illus. bibliog. index. (Dictionary of Literary Biography, Vol. 57). $90.00. LC 87-336. ISBN 0-8103-1735-4.

Planned, although not written to formula, each volume of the Dictionary of Literary Biography treats a genre (e.g., prose, poetry, fiction, history, children's literature) during an age (e.g., the post-World War II period, the period between the World Wars, the Restoration and eighteenth century) and of a nation (Great Britain, the United States, Canada, Ireland, or recently, Germany). Each also identifies the genre's principal artificers in that age and nation and ranks them in two categories. Those in a select minority receive extensive bio-bibliographical treatment covering as many as twenty-five pages, while the others receive space, usually eight or ten pages, indicative of their second-tier stature. Regardless of length, each entry opens with a selective list of the author's books and other works, and concludes with a more selective bibliography of secondary works. Illustrations, usually portraits, family group photographs, and facsimiles of manuscript pages, illustrate the volumes and break the otherwise monotonous appearance of double-columned page after double-columned page of print. Some volumes, this among them, include extensive appendices reprinting key passages from some of the subjects' works or those of their contemporaries to convey in part their own interpretation of their genre in their own time. In all respects, this volume's plan fits the formula.

A companion to *Victorian Prose Writers before 1867* (see entry 657), volume 55 of the Dictionary of Literary Biography, this volume singles out five for extended treatment. Each of these five, Matthew Arnold, Charles Darwin, William Morris, Walter Pater, and Oscar Wilde, is certainly deserving. Not only did each of these men challenge the intellectual order and societal assumptions of mid- and late-Victorian Britain, each continues to influence thinkers. Among the other 25 treated are William Gladstone, Gerard Manley Hopkins, George Meredith, George Saintsbury, Herbert Spencer, Leslie Stephen, and Arthur Symons. The 132-page appendix prints selections from 19 authors.

A diligent reader could devour this entire appendix and deduce from these diverse pens and minds criteria for judging the era's prose. That reader could then read additional selections of prose by the authors treated in the body of the book and apply the criteria deduced from the appendix to these selections. Alas, in most cases this is the only way that the reader can use this book to evaluate the prose of the thirty featured writers. The essays themselves, fundamentally bio-bibliographical in nature, rarely venture into criticism or analysis of their subjects' prose as prose. All analyze and delineate the arguments of major works and trace an author's intellectual development through the course of his or her life, relating it to significant personal events. But few characterize style or place it in the context of the development and purposes of prose in Victorian British society. Even when they do, as in the essay on Hopkins's prose, the critical technique they employ is quoting contemporaries, in this case Hopkinson Hopkins. This widespread lack of critical evaluation of the authors does not diminish the book's usefulness as a source of intellectual biography. However, this lack signals the volume's limitations, limitations made up only in part by excerpts of criticism available in Gale's *Nineteenth-Century Literature Criticism* (see ARBA 82, entry 1270). The volume's usefulness would be that much greater if it included more criticism along with the history and biography of these prose writers.—**James Rettig**

657. **Victorian Prose Writers before 1867**. William B. Thesing, ed. Detroit, Gale, 1987. 379p. illus. bibliog. index. (Dictionary of Literary Biography, Vol. 55). $90.00. LC 86-25837. ISBN 0-8103-1733-8.

Victorian Prose Writers before 1867 continues the fast-growing Dictionary of Literary Biography series, which consists not only of the 55 bio-bibliographical guides (grouped by period, topic, or genre), but 4 volumes of "documentary" information and some yearbooks (through 1985). In truth, the biographies are more thorough than the bibliographies and are enhanced by excellent illustrations.

This volume is intended to be used along with previously published volumes in the series (18, 21, 32, and 35) that treat Victorian novelists and poets and the companion volume, *Victorian Prose Writers after 1867* (see entry 656). The emphasis in these two volumes is on nonfiction prose, including letters, journals, diaries, sermons, speeches, reviews, biographies, autobiographies, and travel writings, as well as historical, philosophical, political, critical, and scientific books and essays.

Of the 28 writers covered in DLB 55, five are accorded extended treatment: Thomas Carlyle, Thomas Babington Macaulay, John Stuart Mill, John Henry Newman, and John Ruskin. (The editors express their doubts about Macaulay's future place in this select group, but they include him anyway.) The article on Carlyle, to take one example, is more than 10,000 words long and contains 7 photographs and 2 copies of pages of his manuscripts, plus a bibliography of his writings and a brief bibliography of secondary works (all books). Other articles are of lesser, but still substantial, length. Well-known writers such as Dickens, George Eliot, and Thackeray are seen in this volume from the point of view of their nonfiction writings, and are treated more fully in other volumes of DLB. Among others in the current volume are Thomas Arnold, George Borrow, Jane Welsh Carlyle, Benjamin Disraeli, Harriet Martineau, A. Welby Pugin, Samuel Smiles, and Queen Victoria herself (whose 22-volume journal was destroyed by her daughter Beatrice). The volume concludes with a brief general bibliography and a not-so-brief (51 pages) cumulative index of the complete set to date.

The DLB continues to be an excellent series for the public, high school, and college library. This volume may not be the most popular of the lot, but it deals effectively with an important body of the writings of those eminent Victorians who, as much as the novelists and poets of the time, set the Victorian temper.—**Edwin S. Gleaves**

Publishing

658. **The British Literary Book Trade, 1700-1820**. James K. Bracken and Joel Silver, eds. Detroit, Gale, 1995. 366p. illus. index. (Dictionary of Literary Biography, v. 154). $128.00. ISBN 0-8103-5715-1.

As noted in the editors' 2,000-word introduction, this volume complements Dictionary of Literary Biography (DLB) volumes 106 and 112 (Gale, 1991), which examine British literary publishers who achieved prominence between 1821 and 1965. The book at hand focuses on the transitional period that witnessed the merging of such ancillary trades as printer, bookseller, and stationer into the monolith of the publishing house. Disclaiming any intent toward exhausting their subject, Bracken and Silver have overseen the production of 37 essays (by 28 academics) on such representative individuals and firms as William Blake; Edmund Curll; William Blackwood and Sons, Ltd.; and the Strawberry Hill Press. Most entries run 5-10 pages in length. Where applicable, the evolving variants of businesses' names appear at the head of the article. Anne Dodd is the only featured woman, although Mary Jane Godwin receives her due attention in the piece on the publishing house named after her by William Godwin (her spouse and the company's principal operator).

Black-and-white pictures and facsimiles of title pages and frontispieces are scattered throughout the text. Each essay concludes with a list of references and a list of institutions holding papers about the publisher under review. Back matter includes an appendix on British copyright developments and a bibliography of 32 recent titles. An index to the names of specific major authors or works published by the firms encompassed by this survey would have added to the work's usefulness. A subsequent volume—covering aspects of Britain's seventeenth-century book trade—is scheduled to be published. In summary, this work of composite scholarship makes a solid contribution to an often-neglected period of publishing history. [R: Choice, Apr 96, p. 1281]—**Jeffrey E. Long**

Short Stories

659. **British Short-Fiction Writers, 1880-1914: The Realist Tradition**. Detroit, Gale, 1994. William B. Thesing, ed. 442p. illus. index. (Dictionary of Literary Biography, v.135). $125.00. LC 93-35683. ISBN 0-8103-5394-6.

The period from 1880 to 1914 saw the passing of the Victorian Age, emerging social reform movements, and a proliferation of short fiction in literary magazines. A contributor to this volume estimates the readership of the *Strand* at 500,000 in the 1890s. The 37 writers described represent the tastes, causes, forms, and subject matter followed by the literary realists of the age. The editor includes essays on prominent writers such as Thomas Hardy, May Sinclair, Arnold Bennett, and George Gissing, as well as a number of less well known figures who appealed to the popular tastes of their time.

The well-written essays describe each author's biographical details, literary influences, themes, and forms and provide useful synopses of their more important stories. The bibliography includes all primary works, select secondary sources, biographies, bibliographies, and papers. The introduction to the volume contains an excellent discussion of literary realism and its problems. The subtitle "The Realist Tradition" and statements in the introduction indicate plans for another volume dealing with the romantic tradition.

Already there are four Dictionary of Literary Biography volumes that overlap British fiction writers from this period. Bennett and George Moore appear in all four, Hardy in three. The high quality of the series notwithstanding, librarians will need to decide what the saturation point is for their reference collections.—**John P. Schmitt**

660. **British Short-Fiction Writers, 1880-1914: The Romantic Tradition**. William F. Naufftus, ed. Detroit, Gale, 1996. 499p. illus. index. (Dictionary of Literary Biography, v.156). $128.00. ISBN 0-8103-5717-8.

The latest volume of the Dictionary of Literary Biography (DLB) acts as a companion volume to volume 135, which covers the realistic short fiction of the same period (see ARBA 95, entry 1209). Profiled are the late Victorian and Edwardian writers who established a tradition of tales of fantasy, high adventure, and romantic love that to this day give British popular fiction a quite different tone from American fantasy and science fiction primarily derived from pulp literature. The authors include the well known, such as Arthur Conan Doyle and H. G. Wells, such writers as Olive Schreiner and Rudyard Kipling who are now returning to critical attention, and those (e.g., Ouida and Frank Harris) better known for their interesting lives than for their artistic achievements. A regrettable omission in both volumes is that of Katherine Mansfield, who was born in New Zealand but did most of her work in England. The DLB solves the problem of such multigenre writers as William Butler Yeats or Kipling by duplicating much of the bio-bibliographical material in other DLB volumes.

The arrangement of this volume follows that of earlier DLB volumes: an introduction surveying the literary, political, and social trends of the period; alphabetic entries on each author; and a useful cumulative index. Each entry contains a bibliography of the author's work; a brief biography; a discussion of the author's short fiction; a critical assessment of his or her achievements and literary reputation; and finally a bibliography of letters, biographies, collections, and other secondary material. The entries, written by different authors, are generally accurate, readable, and well researched.

The DLB is an invaluable resource that belongs in any well-equipped library. Smaller community and school libraries that cannot afford its considerable expense may prefer to purchase the eight-volume *Concise Dictionary of British Literary Biography*. [R: Choice, Apr 96, pp. 1281-82]—**Lynn F. Williams**

661.   **British Short-Fiction Writers, 1915-1945**. John H. Rogers, ed. Detroit, Gale, 1996. 444p. illus. index. (Dictionary of Literary Biography, v.162). $135.00. ISBN 0-8103-9357-3.

This monumental Gale series has split into so many subcategories that it now resembles less a biographical dictionary than an encyclopedia of literary forms and time periods. This is the 5th volume dealing with British short fiction writers, and many of the subjects covered here are far better known for their contributions to the novel. The biographical information is sometimes brief, as a full account of the writer's life appears in one or more of the other Dictionary of Literary Biography volumes. James Joyce, for instance, now appears in four volumes; D. H. Lawrence is in five.

There is no denying that the short story occupies a place of distinction in the literature of the twentieth century, but what may be debatable is the editor's assertion that the British short story began in 1877, specifically with Robert Louis Stevenson. This would seem to negate Gale's *British Short Fiction Writers, 1800-1880*, which includes, among others, Charles Dickens. Nonetheless, this period of literary modernism, postwar disillusionment, declining empire, and ascendant Irish nationalism is amply reflected in the short story genre.

The 30 authors selected for this volume are a diverse group. They include Irish writers, such as Joyce, James Stephens, and Seán O'Faoláin; traditionalists, such as Evelyn Waugh, John Galsworthy, and E. M. Forster; experimental writers, such as Virginia Woolf and Katherine Mansfield; and writers who were born or traveled extensively in the old British colonies. Some, such as P. G. Wodehouse, were prolific but slight writers. Others were like Joyce, who published only one short story collection but was tremendously influential. One common thread for many of these writers is that they turned to the short story to lift themselves out of poverty between novels.

Each essay describes the author's life and principal influences, both personal and literary. In most cases, there is a synopsis and some analysis of individual short stories, with occasional excerpts from literary critics. Each entry contains a primary bibliography, indicates the location of the author's papers, and provides a select list of criticism, bibliographies, and biographies. Exceptional photographs and reproductions of manuscripts enhance the book. The contributors lend a particularly valuable service by giving a good sense of each writer's initial reception and contemporary reputation. The work concludes with a running index of names for the earlier volumes of the series. [R: Choice, Nov 96, p. 426]—**John P. Schmitt**

CANADIAN LITERATURE

662. **Canadian Writers and Their Works**. Robert Lecker, Jack David, and Ellen Quigley, eds. Toronto, ECW Press; distr., Toronto, University of Toronto Press, 1983-1996. $50.00/vol. ISBN 0-920802-43-5 (set).

This is a 24-volume set containing essays on major Canadian fiction and poetry writers of the last 2 centuries and their works, each volume covering 4 or 5 authors. Separate essays treat the prose and poetic works of those writing in both genres (e.g., Margaret Atwood). Most essays are written by recognized critics and authorities on Canadian literature, such as George Woodcock, and the quality of the contents is generally very high.

Each essay is divided into sections: a brief biography, a discussion of the tradition and milieu that influenced the author, an overview of published criticism, an analysis of the author's major writings, and a selected bibliography of the author's works and criticism. This compartmental approach leads to some repetition and hinders the interrelating of the topics covered (e.g., life and milieu, works and criticism), but this is, at most, an inconvenience. The essays contain extensive quotes from both the author's works and from critical sources.

As with other works of this type, the essays vary in focus and character. Some contain considerable biographical information, others little. Some relate criticism in a substantive way that is useful in itself; others serve as guides to critical works, leading the user to the original sources. A name and title index is included in each volume.

This series will be useful to advanced undergraduate and graduate students. Although considerably greater in depth, this series is similar in scope to the Canadian literature volumes of the Dictionary of Literary Biography series. Libraries owning the latter should consider carefully whether interest warrants the acquisition of this excellent, but expensive, new series. Another source of interest is *The Annotated Bibliography of Canada's Major Authors*, published by the same press between 1979 and 1985. Selective purchase of individual volumes may be appropriate for some collections.—**Gari-Anne Patzwald and Terry Ann Mood**

663. **Canadian Writers, 1920-1959: First Series**. W. H. New, ed. Detroit, Gale, 1988. 417p. illus. index. (Dictionary of Literary Biography, Vol. 68). $95.00. LC 88-724. ISBN 0-8103-1746-X.

The 68th volume in the Dictionary of Literary Biography is the first of two volumes on Canadian writers who established their reputations between 1920 and 1959. It begins with an excellent introductory essay by editor W. H. New. The following sections on individual authors begin with lists of works by the subjects. These cover all major works but are not exhaustive (e.g., books by Gabrielle Roy are included but not her contributions to periodicals). Essays, written by scholars, emphasize the subject's professional development and describe major works. These essays are professionally written and informative, if frequently subjective, and careful editing has made them remarkably similar in scope. Where available, selected interviews, biographies, critical works, and manuscripts are included. The black-and-white photographs of authors may be useful, but the numerous reproductions of dust jackets serve only to pad the volume. A supplementary reading list is appended.

To use this volume effectively, one will need access to its proposed companion volume and to the volumes covering the previous and subsequent periods of Canadian literature. Although valuable for its inclusion of literary figures not often bound elsewhere (e.g., editor Alan Crawley), due to its somewhat subjective nature, its limitations as a ready-reference source, and its high price, this volume's potential usefulness should be carefully assessed before purchase is considered by all but libraries serving specialists in Canadian studies. [R: Choice, Nov 88, p. 456]—**Gari-Anne Patzwald**

664. **Canadian Writers since 1960: First Series**. W. H. New, ed. Detroit, Gale, 1986. 445p. illus. bibliog. index. (Dictionary of Literary Biography, Vol. 53). $88.00. LC 86-14892. ISBN 0-8103-1731-1.

This is the 1st volume of a four-volume set in the Dictionary of Literary Biography to cover Canadian writers who use English or French as the language of artistic expression. This and a 2nd volume will cover the period after World War I up to 1959 and the period prior to 1918. Like other volumes in the DLB, both biographical and bibliographical information on writers is included.

Entries are arranged alphabetically by surname. Each entry is signed and includes birth and death dates when known, listings of works by the author, a biocritical narrative, and a listing of published interviews and bibliographical and other references about the author and the author's works. Most entries include black-and-white photographs of the author as well as photographs of handwriting samples or sample dust jackets from the author's works.

A supplementary reading list on Canadian literature is provided at the end of the volume. The contributors to the volume and their institutional affiliation are given. This volume contains a cumulative index to DLB, volumes 1-53; to DLB *Yearbook*, 1980-1985; and to DLB *Documentary Series*, volumes 1-4.

This volume is an excellent follow-up to Gordon Ripley and Anne Mercer's *Who's Who in Canadian Literature 1985-86.*—**Maureen Pastine**

665.   **The CANSCAIP Companion: A Biographical Record of Canadian Children's Authors, Illustrators, and Performers**. Barbara Greenwood, ed. Markham, Ont., Pembroke, 1991. 296p. illus. $24.95pa. 700'. 92'2. ISBN 0-921217-58-7.

The Canadian Society of Children's Authors, Illustrators, and Performers (CANSCAIP) has produced a biographical directory of its 262 members. Each entry gives name, address, telephone number, date and place of birth, marital status, and number of children. The subject's career is described in one or two paragraphs, followed by a list of works (only the most recent for the more prolific), awards, and professional memberships, as well as a statement of availability for programs. Most entries include a black-and-white photograph of the subject. Appendixes provide lists of artists by craft (e.g., author, illustrator, performer) and region, a directory of relevant organizations, and a list of major Canadian literary awards.

The directory has the disadvantage of all such works in that it lists only the members of the organization. However, this problem is greatly alleviated by the tendency of Canadian creative artists to join together to promote common interests; thus, most major artists are included. While the more prominent of those listed can be found in standard biographical sources, this relatively inexpensive guide will be useful to those wanting information on newer and less well known artists and for schools and libraries with limited budgets. It will be an essential tool for those seeking children's authors, illustrators, or performers for programs. Recommended for all Canadian schools and public and academic libraries, and for other libraries where interest warrants. [R: EL, Nov/Dec 91, p. 43]—**Gari-Anne Patzwald**

666.   **Contemporary Canadian Authors, Volume 1: A Bio-bibliographical Guide**. . . . Robert Lang, ed. Toronto, Gale Canada, 1996. 488p. $170.00; $125.00 (U.S.). ISBN 1-896413-08-0. ISSN 1203-2816.

Gale's premier volume of *Contemporary Canadian Authors* follows the same general principles and format of the *Contemporary Authors* series in providing bio-bibliographic information on writers of Canada from a wide range of fields, including media in numerous formats as well as more traditional literary publications. Entry sketches provide a nominal heading, including the most complete form of the author's name (with any variations or pseudonyms), personal information as available with pertinent points of contact, a career summary, and inclusion of awards/honors/memberships as appropriate. Writings are listed chronologically with date, edition, and adaptation notes and works in progress if known. A "sidelights" section furnishes a diverse blend of historical background, philosophy, and commentary by or about the author and may contain critical evaluations or interview materials. Concluding each entry is a list of source materials as a basis for further research.

Although not as comprehensive in coverage as individual inclusions in Gale's Dictionary of Literary Biography series, this initial volume provides a much broader framework of references and wider definition of authorship for Canadian writers. As a reference series, it will be an ongoing source of current information on Canadian literary endeavors. Access will be further enhanced if entries are to be included in Gale's *Contemporary Authors* cumulative index.—**Virginia S. Fischer**

667.   Machaiski, Andrew. **Hispanic Writers in Canada: A Preliminary Survey of the Activities of Spanish and Latin-American Writers in Canada**. Ottawa, Department of the Secretary of State of Canada, 1988. price not reported. ISBN 0-662-16031-2.

Commissioned by the Multicultural Sector, this report is part of a series intended to survey literary activities of ethnic groups. Sending questionnaires and conducting interviews across Canada, the author attempted to provide a summary of current work and an overview of "present and potential contribution to Canadian culture and literature" (p.3). Prominent among the Hispanics are Europeans teaching at Canadian universities and a large group of Latin Americans, mostly Chilean, who came to Canada during the last two decades.

The first part of the report sets out methodology, then provides excerpts from answers to the objective/quantitative questions that 20 of the writers completed. Part 2 consists of bio-bibliographies, ranging in length from I line to 2 pages, of 70 Hispanic writers. Periodicals and collections cited in the entries are gathered into a list with place and date of publication identified for almost all. Admittedly modest, this useful report expands Canada's literary community for researchers and book selectors.—**Patricia Fleming**

668.   Pivato, Joseph. **Italian-Canadian Writers: A Preliminary Survey**. Ottawa, Department of the Secretary of State of Canada, 1988. 53p. free looseleaf without binder. ISBN 0-662-16034-7.

One in a series of reports commissioned by the Canadian government's Multicultural Sector, Department of the Secretary of State, this survey is just that: an initial attempt to gather information for a field in which basic sources are either incomplete or totally lacking. Series editor Michael Batts's foreword outlines the magnitude of the problems encountered in ethnic literature, which range from nonconformance with deposit requirements at the National Library to absence of bibliographic, biographic, and critical sources in the field. The hope is that the series will stimulate research and understanding of multicultural Canadian society.

In his preface Pivato expands on the difficulties confronted in his study of Italian-Canadian authors for whom neither a listing nor bibliography exists. He refers to his use of the "snowball" method to compile basic groundwork in the field. He was unable to examine all the works included and indicates that the research is, by nature, ongoing.

Part 1 is an excellent overview of the Italian-Canadian sociocultural experience that touches on specific historic antecedents of the present literary environment. Pivato emphasizes the differences in language as a determining factor in literary activity as well as economic conditions which preclude opportunity. He notes that the major themes of the group have continued to be the immigrant experience, although many of the works deal with more universal aspects of the human condition.

The bibliographic sources that comprise the second and major portion of the report are divided into five sections—abbreviations, periodicals, general works, collections, and a bio-bibliography of writers. In this final section, an alphabetical listing of authors includes birth date and place, year of settlement in Canada, and bibliographic data for all known publications and unpublished works. One must rely on the author's completeness and accuracy in this preliminary effort and hope that further research into this aspect of Canadian culture will be encouraged.—**Virginia S. Fischer**

669.   Ripley, Gordon, and Anne Mercer. **Who's Who in Canadian Literature**. Teeswater, Ont., Reference Press, 1984- . 369p. $35.00pa. 810'.9'005. ISSN 0715-9366.

This biennial was originally published in 1983. It includes information about living Canadian poets, playwrights, story writers, novelists, children's writers, critics, editors, and translators. The majority of data came from questionnaires sent to writers. Secondary sources were also used. All in all, more than 1,100 individuals are described briefly as to birth date and place, parents, education, spouse, children, memberships, awards, publications, works in progress, anthologies, mailing addresses, sources of critical information, and the like. Not included are journalists, and historians (unless they have written "letters").—**Dean Tudor and Terry Ann Mood**

670.   Schwab, Arnold T. **Canadian Poets: Vital Facts on English-Writing Poets Born from 1730 through 1910**. Halifax, N.S., School of Library and Information Studies, Dalhousie University, 1989. 100p. (Occasional Papers Series, no.47). $17.50pa. 81 l'.009. ISBN 0-7703-97344.

This work provides a biographical dictionary for those authors who meet the stated criteria. No attempt was made to include those born after 1910, although the cutoff date does not have any literary or historical significance; it seems to be related to previous research interests.

The book comprises 3 alphabetical lists and totals 100 pages. The first and most extensive list includes deceased poets with complete vital facts. This is followed by a much briefer section of "deceased(?)" poets with incomplete facts. The final section includes poets who are assumed to be still living as of a given date and their last-known residences. In all entries, poets are listed by full/married name and pen name with cross-references. Birth date and place are followed by death date, place, and age.

A quick check of the *Dictionary of Canadian Biography* reveals that the author included several individuals who do not appear in those volumes. Many obscure poets were omitted for lack of sufficient data, but the author maintains that every well-known and important poet has been included on one of the lists. By defining *poet* and *Canadian* in the broadest possible sense, he has made some questionable inclusions, listing several authors far better known for their work in other literary genres. Similarly, Schwab elected to include authors with brief or seasonal connections to Canada. However, the effect has been to make the work all the more complete. For researchers of basic biographical source material in this limited area of Canadian literature, this compilation will be an asset.—**Virginia S. Fischer**

671.   **Who's Who in the League of Canadian Poets**. 3d ed. Stephen Scobie, ed. Toronto, League of Canadian Poets, 1988. 227p. illus. bibliog. $19.95pa. ISBN 0-9690327-4-9.

Each entry submitted by more than 200 professionally published and performing poets includes a photograph, a biographical sketch, awards, major publications, a selection of anthologies in which the poet's work is included, and excerpts from critical comments and reviews. Although a membership directory cannot be comprehensive, this one includes most of English Canada's major poets as well as new voices from across the country. A useful appendix identifies 69 current poetry magazines and 49 publishers of poetry, all with addresses. Since the previous edition was published in 1980, book selectors will welcome the title lists in this handy biographical directory.—**Patricia Fleming**

672.   **Who's Who in the Writers' Union of Canada: A Directory of Members**. 3d ed. Toronto, Writers' Union of Canada, 1988. 483p. illus. $16.95pa. ISBN 0-9690796-2-1.

With almost as many entries as the 1st and 2nd editions combined, this edition offers concise information on nearly 500 writers, all of whom have at least one book in print. Entries consist of a photograph; a biographical sketch; selected publications (with ISBN); awards; critical comment; availability for readings, lectures, and workshops; and mailing address. Very few French-Canadian writers are included. The volume concludes with a name list of more than 100 hundred additional members and notes on the union and its activities. Even though not all Canadian writers are members, and not all members are represented in the detailed entries, TWUC's directory provides information which cannot be found in any other source.—**Patricia Fleming**

CARIBBEAN AND AFRICAN LITERATURE

673.   **Twentieth-Century Caribbean and Black African Writers. First Series**. Bernth Lindfors and Reinhard Sander, eds. Detroit, Gale, 1992. 406p. illus. index. (Dictionary of Literary Biography, v.117). $112.00. LC 92-8972. ISBN 0-8103-7594-X.

This work adheres strictly to the format established in previous volumes of the Dictionary of Literary Biography (DLB) series. Individually authored chapters on 31 writers (19 African and 12 Circum-Caribbean) are arranged alphabetically by writer's name. All authors featured in this volume are of the twentieth century, with the exception of Old Equine, and all are from former British colonies and write in English. Individual chapters begin with a bibliography of the writer's publications and end with a bibliography of published interviews with the writer and critical and biographical works about the person. They are also illustrated with photographs of the authors and of dust jackets from their books. The lengths of chapters vary from slightly more than 4 pages on Jamaican John Hearne to 22 pages on St. Lucian Nobel laureate Derek Walcott. The chapters vary in quality; some of the longer ones tend to be uneven and rambling. As do all volumes in the DLB, this one contains a cumulative index to this and related series. This work complements another recent Gale publication, the three-volume *Black Literature Criticism*. That set presents a succinct and balanced critical overview of the authors' work, while DLB's coverage is a more in-depth view.—**Fred J. Hay**

674. **Twentieth-Century Caribbean and Black African Writers. Second Series**. Bernth Lindfors and Reinhard Sander, eds. Detroit, Gale, 1993. 443p. illus. index. (Dictionary of Literary Biography, v.125). $120.00. LC 92-41196. ISBN 0-8103-5384-9.

The present volume, together with volume 117 of the Dictionary of Literary Biography (see ARBA 93, entry 1110), is a bio-bibliography of 34 major anglophone writers, almost all of whom are bilingual or multilingual, from Africa and the Caribbean. This second series concentrates on writers from Kenya, Uganda, Sudan, Somalia, Barbados, and Trinidad and Tobago. The 1st series dealt with writers from Gambia, Ghana, Guyana, St. Lucia, and Africa. Another volume is planned for Caucasian South African writers.

The writers, selected on the basis of influence and reputation, represent a wide spectrum of literature—novelists, dramatists, and poets—dealing with the colonial past as well as contemporary social and political issues. V. S. Naipaul (Trinidad) and Wole Soyinka (Nigeria) may be more familiar to users; less so are such writers as Numddin Farah (Somalia) and Richard Rive (South Africa). Preceded by bibliographies of the writer's work, essays focus on critical aspects and are reproductions of drafts and manuscripts. Critical analysis varies. The entry for Andrew Salkey gives capsule summaries for most of his works; by contrast, Es'kia (Ezekiel) Mphahlele's work is discussed in greater detail and depth. Such unevenness is often a hazard in composite works such as this. However, this volume, along with its companion in the series, highlights what is called in the introduction "The internationalization of English." They can usefully serve collections focusing on expanding world literatures.—**Bernice Bergup**

675. **Twentieth-Century Caribbean and Black African Writers, Third Series**. Bernth Lindfors and Reinhard Sander, eds. Detroit, Gale, 1996. 461p. illus. index. (Dictionary of Literary Biography, v.157). $128.00. ISBN 0-8103-9352-2.

The 157th volume of the Dictionary of Literary Biography (DLB) contains essays on 33 writers from Africa and the Caribbean and adds to the 65 writers found in the 2 previous volumes: DLB volume 117 (see ARBA 93, entry 1110) and volume 125 (see entry 674). Entries contain photographs of authors and selected dust jackets as well as other illustrations. As with other volumes in the acclaimed DLB series, the biographical information and critical examination of the authors' works are thorough. Researchers will appreciate that entries also include complete lists of the authors' works, bibliographic references, and references of interviews.

The authors represent a younger generation primarily from the same top three countries represented in the first two volumes: Nigeria, South Africa, and Jamaica. In the introduction, the editors explain that the selection of authors was based on influence and reputation: Most of the authors selected have only recently made their reputations in the broader area of post-colonial literature. Unlike their predecessors in the previous volumes, who explored the colonial experience and the past, writers of the baby-boom generation have tended to look into post-colonial life at home.

As anglophone literature by these fine writers becomes increasingly well known and read within the larger, English-speaking community, more of their work will be studied and enjoyed. This reference is highly recommended for academic and public libraries. [R: Choice, May 96, p. 1458]—**Edward Erazo**

CHILDREN'S AND YOUNG ADULT LITERATURE

676. **Author Profile Collection**. Worthington, Ohio, Linworth Publishing, 1992. 106p. illus. $24.95pa. ISBN 0-938865-12-9.

Twenty-one children's and young adult authors and illustrators are presented here, ranging from Arnold Adoff to Jane Yolen and from David Wiesner to Daniel and Susan Cohen. The three- to six-page accounts include some biographical information and noncritical discussions about the author or illustrator's work. Final sections include two articles on author visits, one article about whole language, a chronological list of birthdays for authors and illustrators, and a short section of instant art.

Overall, these sketches are quite readable and are appropriately illustrated with pictures of the people and their books. Bookmark bibliographies, ready to photocopy, are an added bonus. The three-ring notebook format does facilitate the use of the material. The problems with this collection primarily arise from the fact that the profiles included have been lifted directly from the pages of the *Book Report* and *Library Talk*, and citations to those profiles are not given. Comparisons between this collection of reprints and the originals show no changes or updating. An address is given for those who wish to write John Steptoe, who died in 1989, and David Wiesner's Caldecott book *Tuesday* is not mentioned. The quality of the photographs in the original material is much better than in these reproductions, which look like poor photocopies. The birthday list in the back does not include all of the people profiled in the book.

There are many useful bibliographic tools for librarians, media specialists, teachers, and young readers to use. This collection of author and illustrator sketches needs some revision and rewriting before it can be recommended. [R: BL, July 92, p. 1946]—**Carol A. Doll**

677. **Authors & Artists for Young Adults**. Detroit, Gale, 1989- . 253p. illus. index. $81.00. ISSN 1040-5682.

This guide to artists of interest to young adults follows the format of previous volumes (see ARBA 95, entry 1144; ARBA 92, entry 1126; and ARBA 90, entries 1091 and 1092). Each entry lists biographical and career information, and provides bibliographies of publications, adaptations, works cited, works in progress, and suggestions for further reading. Most entries are illustrated with photographs. The main section, "Sidelights," is actually a biocritical sketch.

Design and content problems weaken this attractive volume. Two typographical lapses are particularly annoying. First, in some entries, a space comes between a hyphen and the word following it. Second, the asterisk indicating that the subject has not examined an entry is confusingly placed with the last item listing further readings. The major weakness, however, is the book's inclusiveness. In addition to writers for young adults, entries cover classic writers studied in high school (Arthur Conan Doyle and Edgar Allan Poe); popular writers read by adolescents (John Grisham and Peter Benchley); photographers (Ansel Adams and Dorothea Lange); movie directors (Tim Burton and Harold Ramis); journalists (Dave Barry and Frank Deford); a film composer (Danny Elfman); a fantasy illustrator (Frank Frazetta); and a nonfiction writer (James S. Haskins).

Although the entries lean to biography rather than criticism, they are well-written and entertaining introductions. Nevertheless, the indiscriminate inclusiveness is disturbing. Too many entries cover artists who do not produce works specifically for young adults or, worse, are of questionable significance. The six member editorial board, consisting of teachers, librarians, and people representing young adults, needs to reexamine the inclusion of film directors, columnists, and cartoonists, and to readdress the question of what constitutes artists for young adults.—**Raymond E. Jones and Terry Ann Mood**

678. Drew, Bernard A. **The 100 Most Popular Young Adult Authors: Biographical Sketches and Bibliographies**. rev. ed. Englewood, Colo., Libraries Unlimited, 1997. 531p. $55.00. ISBN 1-56308-615-8.

This collection covers 100 popular contemporary and classic young adult authors. Novelists are predominately American, with several British and other nationalities represented. It includes a few upper middle school authors, such as Judy Blume, Betsy Byars, and Phyllis Reynolds Naylor, and several adult authors read by young adults—V. C. Andrews and Stephen King. The genres covered range from science fiction and historical fiction to recent horror authors like Christopher Pike and R. L. Stine.

The entries are listed alphabetically by surname of the writer. Each author's entry is listed with a genre type, birth date, date of death, birthplace, and most recognized works of fiction. The text includes a brief biography of the author; critical comments on his or her works from magazines, interviews, and other reference sources; a list of titles written; series information; and bibliographic information suggesting further reading about the author.

The entries represent an adequate list of authors read by the designated age group, but as a reference tool it is lacking in consistency and organization. The biographical information is too brief and lacking in substance. The writing careers of the individuals portrayed through interviews and critical sources are not organized chronologically and are difficult to follow. Criticism of specific works by the novelists is not mentioned uniformly or skillfully. The title contains some useful, consise information about the authors, but a more complete source such as the *Something about the Author Autobiography* series would be a more helpful tool.—**Marlene M. Kuhl**

679.   **High-Interest Books for Teens: A Guide to Book Reviews and Biographical Sources**. 2d ed. Joyce Nakamura, ed. Detroit, Gale, 1988. 539p. index. $95.00. LC 81-6889. ISBN 0-8103-1 830-X.

Over 3,500 fiction and nonfiction titles by 2,000 authors, of special interest to junior and senior high school students, with sources of critical reviews about them are listed in this reference tool aimed at librarians, classroom teachers, and reading tutors. This 2nd edition updates and expands the first edition published by Gale in 1981.

Titles included have been recommended in reading lists by educators, librarians, and publishers as especially appropriate for enticing students with learning disabilities, or those who need to improve their reading skills, to read. They have been identified as "high interest/low-readability level" materials and include both contemporary works and favorite classics by familiar authors.

In the main body of the work, "Guide to Book Reviews and Biographical Sources," entries are arranged by author (or pseudonym), with dates of birth and death (if applicable) indicated. At least one citation to a source of further biographical information follows. For individual books by each author, a list of citations to evaluations of the title in reviewing periodicals is provided. Subject headings and cross-references to name variants/pseudonyms, and co-authors/adapters or authors of adapted works under which other books have been written and reviewed are also indicated. Two brief sections, "Book Review Sources Cited" and "Biographical Sources Cited," give complete names of biography and review sources indicated by abbreviations or codes in the entry. In addition to a title index, the 2nd edition has included a very useful subject index with over 500 categories popular with young adults, such as adventure stories, mystery and detective stories, sports, occult sciences, motorcycles and motorcycle racing, rock music and musicians, and family life and family problems. Subject headings are those used by the Library of Congress and also from the *Sears List of Subject Headings*.

While recommended lists for students whose chronological age exceeds their reading ability are not hard to find, a tool that identifies in one place all sources of reviews for each title is a definite asset. [R: RBB, Aug 88, p. 1903; VOYA, Aug 88, p. 153]—**Lois Buttlar**

680.   **International Directory of Children's Literature Specialists**. Leena Maissen, ed. Munich and New York, K. G. Saur, 1986. 263p. index. $49.00. ISBN 3-598-10623-8.

The International Board on Books for Young People (IBBY) has compiled for UNESCO a useful listing of specialists in children's literature throughout the world. The purpose, as stated in the introduction, was to seek people "who are able to communicate their experience and knowledge in children's literature to others, who can make a professional contribution in a seminar or a workshop." The areas in which specialists were sought included writing, translating, illustration, publishing, book selling, libraries, school, reviewing, research, and teaching. The resulting list of 405 specialists from 32 countries covers a wide range of expertise. Many of the experts listed have backgrounds in library work or teaching; a somewhat smaller number are editors, translators, or writers. The entry for each individual includes information about experience and publications as well as the crucial facts of language facility. Four categories of fluency are included: mother tongue, teaching ability, ability to discuss, and ability to understand. Information about the length of time for which each individual is available for giving seminars or lectures is also included, although often in vague terms. Entries for American experts include many well-known names, but others are inexplicably missing, and it is not clear exactly how the listees were chosen by the national sections of IBBY. North American librarians and educators will find this volume useful chiefly as a way of finding out about children's literature experts in countries with which they are not familiar. A subject index gives a listing of experts in particular aspects of children's literature. Although no plans for updating are mentioned, periodic revisions would be useful.—**Adele M. Fasick**

681.   **Junior DISCovering Authors**. [CD-ROM]. Detroit, U*X*L/Gale, 1994. Minimum system requirements: IBM or compatible (80386 or faster recommended). CD-ROM drive with MSCDEX 2.0. DOS 3.1. 640K RAM with 480K available. 1MB hard disk space or floppy diskette drive. $250.00 (single user version); $350.00 (network of up to 8 users). ISBN 0-8103-5896-4 (single user); 0-8103-5850-6 (network). [Also available in Macintosh version.]

For many years, Gale has published the popular but expensive *Something about the Author* (*SATA*) series (see ARBA 91, entry 1119), which covers both children's and young adult authors, but as school budgets declined, fewer libraries were able to afford it. Recently, Gale issued a subset of *SATA* entitled *Major Authors and Illustrators for Children and Young Adults* (see ARBA 94, entry 1187), which includes 300 sketches. Now, aimed at the middle and junior high school age, *Junior DISCovering Authors* selects another 300 author subset and presents it in CD-ROM format.

If one has used any other Gale CD-ROM product, then one will be familiar with the search engine for this product. It is excellent and fast (depending on hardware), and it allows searching by subject, title, text contents, and so forth. Thus, it is vastly superior to the print product (in addition to photographs) and it allows the user to save text or print it out easily.

A comparison of the first 10 authors in *Junior DISCovering Authors* versus *Major Authors* gives a quick comparison of coverage for the age group:

Junior	*Major Authors*
Aaseng, Nathan	Aardema, Verna
Adams, Douglas	Aaron, Chester
Adler, C. S.	Aaseng, Nathan
Adoff, Arnold	Achebe, Chinua
Aiken, Joan	Adams, Harriet Stratemeyer
Alcock, Vivien	Adams, Richard
Alcott, Louisa May	Adkins, Jan
Alexander, Lloyd	Adler, Carole Schwerdtfeger
Angell, Judie	Adler, David A.
Armstrong, William H.	Adler, Irving

One may question inclusion versus exclusion, but for the most part there are enough authors included to make the disc worth the price. Middle schoolers are often sensitive about "baby" books and authors, so this work provides fewer children's authors to wade through before one gets to the upper levels.

Information included in each sketch follows that exactly from *SATA*, and where several sketches are in the *SATA* volumes, the information has been merged into a single comprehensive article. For libraries serving the middle and junior high age group and needing biographical information, this disc is a great first purchase. Highly recommended. [R: RBB, 15 May 94, pp. 1710-13; SLJ, Aug 94, p. 92; VOYA, Oct 94, pp. 238-39]—**David V. Loertscher**

682. Kovacs, Deborah, and James Preller. **Meet the Authors and Illustrators: 60 Creators of Favorite Children's Books Talk after Their Work**. Ontario, Scholastic Canada, c1991, 1992. 142p. illus. $9.95pa. 810.9'9282. ISBN 0-590-74291-4.

This book differs from other author-and-illustrator biographical sources in that the focus here is on the process each person goes through in creating a book or illustration. The 60 subjects are well known and well loved and represent broad cultural diversity.

The book is divided into two parts: the creators of picture books and the creators of intermediate books. Only brief biographical information is provided within each two-page author or illustrator profile, the thrust of the material being the description of the creative process, the discipline techniques, and the struggles experienced by each subject. Most of this information was gathered through direct interviews. Details of childhoods and adult lives are described only as they have influenced that creative process. An activity to extend children's learning is included with each profile; often these activities have been suggested by the author or illustrator. The profile is completed with a photograph of the subject and a list of selected titles. A series of creative literary extension activities is appended along with an extensive bibliography of source material.

This work complements standard biographical sources, such as *Something about the Author* (see ARBA 91, entry 1119). For teachers and librarians engaged in whole language activities and for those who want to encourage children's creative efforts, this will provide grist for the mill.—**Joanne Kelly**

683. **Major Authors and Illustrators for Children and Young Adults: A Selection of Sketches from *Something about the Author***. By Laurie Collier and Joyce Nakamura. Detroit, Gale, 1993. 6v. illus. index. $265.00/set. LC 92-073849. ISBN 0-8103-7702-0.

In an attempt to provide a more affordable biographical source on children's authors, Gale has pulled together sketches from its *Something about the Author* (see ARBA 91, entry 1119) set, on more than 800 of the most popular authors and illustrators, into a single set of six volumes. Multiple entries for the same person were edited for this set, and 60 percent of the sketches were recorrected by the biographees themselves. A board of school and public librarians selected the people to be included by mail ballot, and emphasis is upon United States, Canadian, and United Kingdom coverage. As expected, entries are identical in format to the parent volumes and include a biographical sketch, a picture of the author (if available), a bibliography of writings by and about the author, sidelight anecdotes and sample illustrations from the author's works if appropriate, and a list of sources consulted. As with the original volumes, the user can expect accuracy and authority in the sketches.

The problem for librarians is, of course, whether they should purchase this set. For those that have complete holdings of *Something about the Author*, the answer is probably no. New collections could substitute this set in place of older volumes and begin their subscription to *Something about the Author* with the 1993 volumes. Libraries that hold incomplete runs should consult the set or its advertising, which lists the authors covered, before making a decision. At current prices, this set is a little more expensive than a single-year subscription to the main volumes—another factor that will help one weigh value versus coverage. For all libraries including children's literature, one of the two sets is a basic purchase. [R: Choice, May 93, p. 1444; RBB, 1 Jan 93, p. 826; SLJ, May 93, p. 136; VOYA, June 93, pp. 125-26; WLB Mar 93, p. 112]—**David V. Loertscher**

684. McElmeel, Sharron L. **An Author a Month (for Dimes)**. Englewood, Colo., Teacher Ideas Press/Libraries Unlimited, 1993. 185p. illus. index. $23.50pa. Z718.1.M368. 027.62'S. LC 92-21381. ISBN 0-87287-952-6.

This 3rd volume in the *Author a Month* group is a resource for teachers following the whole-language philosophy of connecting books to achieve broad curriculum goals. Similar to its 1988 and 1990 predecessors, it focuses on nine authors or illustrators (Martha Alexander, Caroline Arnold, Graeme Base, Byrd Baylor, Jan Brett, Anthony Browne, Joanna Cole, Eric Kimmel, and Janet Stevens) and provides abbreviated capsule units on three more (Demi, Keiko Kasza, and Patricia Polacco). Each chapter includes a reproducible author poster and large-type biography; an overview for the teacher; suggested introductory strategies; and an "Idea Cupboard," an annotated alphabetical bibliography that contains suggested activities. A cumulative index of McElmeel's *Author a Month* and *Bookpeople* (see ARBA 93, entry 1142) collections and a full index complete the book.

The summaries are useful selection guides, but the suggested activities vary markedly in quality. McElmeel notes that teachers must implement her basic ideas themselves, but more examples, such as a story map for a cumulative tale, would have made this work vastly more useful. Furthermore, too often, as with Anthony Browne's *Gorilla,* the emphasis on factual research ignores central thematic and literary elements. In addition, because of the alphabetical arrangement of the "Idea Cupboard," teachers will have to devise programs to make the author units workable. These units, however, are the least significant element of this book, which is more useful for suggesting connections between the annotated titles and books by other authors. Teachers looking for a "canned" program will be disappointed; those willing to explore will find some useful suggestions for thematically connecting a wide variety of books. [R: SLMQ, Summer 93, p. 265]—**Raymond E. Jones**

685.   McElmeel, Sharron L. **Bookpeople: A Multicultural Album**. Englewood, Colo., Libraries Unlimited, 1992. 170p. illus. index. $23.00pa. PN497.M34. 809'.89282. LC 92-13252. ISBN 0-87287-953-4.

Spotlighting 15 children's book authors and illustrators who deal with multicultural concerns, this work offers suggestions to teachers and media specialists who want to develop a multicultural focus in their schools. Biographical sketches and photographs of authors or illustrators are given, and their works are introduced. Discussion questions to be used with the books are suggested, and related titles by other authors are listed and annotated. Among the artists included are Mitsumasa Anno, Donald Crews, Mem Fox, Paul Goble, Jamake Highwater, Nicholasa Mohr, and Laurence Yep. Individuals selected are either members of a minority culture (whether or not their books are about that culture) or have written or illustrated books about such a culture. This broad scope has enabled McElmeel to include artists who will appeal to children at various grade levels. The suggestions for further reading and the discussion questions are appropriate for a wide range of children and should spark interest in the books. To accompany a reading of Ashley Bryan's *All Night, All Day,* for example, children are encouraged to illustrate one of the spirituals included; for Mem Fox's *Night Noises,* children are asked to interview their grandmother or grandfather and write down some of the memories shared. Imaginative teachers and media specialists will be able to build on the suggestions presented here. *Bookpeople* will be a valuable addition to both classrooms and media centers.—**Adele M. Fasick**

686.   Rollock, Barbara. **Black Authors and Illustrators of Children's Books: A Biographical Dictionary**. New York, Garland, 1988. 130p. illus. bibliog. (Garland Reference Library of the Humanities, Vol. 660). $25.00. LC 87-25748. ISBN 0-8240-8580-9.

Black authors and illustrators (115) from the United States, Africa, Canada, and Great Britain whose works have been published in the United States are profiled in this biographical dictionary. Intended to "represent those black authors who have made or are making literary history in the world of children's books" (p.xi), the collection includes subjects whose works were published as early as the 1930s, although most are from the 1970s and 1980s.

Each profile includes a biographical sketch plus a bibliography of the subject's work for children. The sketches range in length from about 30 to 350 words; most are very brief. "Bibliographical Sources and References" (p.xiii) lists 17 sources for more information. Also included in the collection are 51 black-and-white photographs of people and book covers.—**Nancy Courtney**

687.   **Seventh Book of Junior Authors & Illustrators**. Sally Holmes Holtze, ed. Bronx, N.Y., H. W. Wilson, 1996. 371p. illus. index. $50.00. ISBN 0-8242-0873-0.

Some 235 entries for authors and illustrators of children's and young adult books each give the name, the birth date, a brief autobiographical or biographical sketch, a list of selected works, and often a photograph and reproduction of the person's signature. An initial list of about 1,000 candidates was compiled based on the recommendations of reviewers and critics. Winners of awards and honors voted on by professionals in the area of children's and young adult literature were included as well. In addition, popularity of the author or illustrator was considered. An advisory committee of seven "prominent professionals" in the area of youth literature voted on the initial list and made additional selections, which resulted in the names included in this volume. A cumulative index contains all names and pen names for people in any of the seven volumes of this series.

In general, this is a broad, balanced collection of biographical sketches that continues the work of the *Sixth Book of Junior Authors & Illustrators,* published in 1989. It treats both people who have established their careers and those just getting started during the intervening years. More importantly, each sketch tends to have only a few references to sources of additional information about these people. The *Contemporary Authors* (see ARBA 96, entry 1150) and *Something about the Author* series (see ARBA 97, entries 926-930) are the most frequently cited sources; however, some entries are more limited. For example, an article in *People Weekly* is the only reference given for Reeve Lindbergh. This is one indication that the editors have succeeded in identifying authors and illustrators who are not already included in other sources.

Two editorial concerns are not explained adequately in the book. First, there is a discrepancy of 100 names between the number chosen by the advisory committee (135) and the total number of entries (235) included in the book. This discrepancy may be a typographic error, or it may be a real difference; it is not explained in the preface. Second, the preface states that the author or illustrator wrote a brief autobiographical entry whenever possible. In some cases where entries have been made posthumously, it is evident why the entry is biographical instead. For other entries, readers can only wonder.

Overall, this volume is a competent addition to the series of *Junior Authors & Illustrators* titles, and it will be useful to all library collections having the previous volumes. Moreover, it provides information that will be helpful in academic and public libraries and in school library media centers.—**Carol A. Doll**

688.   **Something about the Author Autobiography Series**. Detroit, Gale, 1986- . illus. index. $85.00. LC 86-641293. ISSN 0885-6842.

This continuing well known series contains autobiographical sketches of authors and illustrators of books for children and young adults. The works of those covered include fiction, nonfiction, and poetry, by authors writing for preschool through young adult. The autobiographies are intended not as comprehensive stories of the individuals but as vehicles for young readers, students of their literature, teachers, and librarians to "personally" meet their favorites. Each essay runs about 18 pages and attempts to convey its author's view ". . . that is shaped by their own choice of materials and their own manner of storytelling," while answering many commonly asked questions, such as who and what influenced their early lives and how they began their careers. All essays follow a similar format, which includes a highly personalized mini-autobiography, old family photographs, and, for illustrators, some representative selections of their work. Bibliographies compiled by the series staff conclude each article.

The index at the end of the volume is cumulative for all volumes in the series; thus, those who have been buying the series all along will want to add this update to their reference collection. Highly recommended for those libraries serving children or young adults or those who work with them and their literature, since the series fills an important biographical niche.—**Carol Truett and Terry Ann Mood**

689.   **Something about the Author: Facts and Pictures about Authors and Illustrators of Books for Young People**. Detroit, Gale, 1971- . illus. index. $92.00. ISSN 0276-816X.

This excellent series by Gale focuses on authors and illustrators of works for young people and has been cited as an "Outstanding Reference Source" by the Reference and Adult Services Division of the American Library Association. Biographies range from less than one page to six pages in length and follow a fairly standard format. Most, but not all, include a portrait of the individual and also such details as personal data, address, brief career highlights, awards and honors received, a bibliography of writings or works illustrated, work in progress, sidelights of the person's life, and sources for the biography. The extensive references attest to the meticulous research done for each person, and where the biographees themselves could not review the listing, the entry is marked with an asterisk.

Strengths of this series include the excellent format, large readable typeface, ease of use, and sample book illustrations found in many of the biographies. Also helpful is that there is both an illustration and an author index at the end of alternate, odd-numbered volumes, which include references to previous volumes in this series, plus three other Gale titles—*Yesterday's Authors of Books for Children,* Children's Literature Review series, and *Something about the Author Autobiography Series.* Obituaries are also included, and the series attempts to include emerging and lesser-known authors and illustrators.

The only disadvantage of this work would be cost, because with two volumes in 1995 and three in 1996, many libraries and media centers (unfortunately) probably cannot afford the series. Yet for those public, school, and academic libraries that can, this work is highly recommended for its well-researched and interesting insights into the world of young people's literature.—**Carol Truett and Terry Ann Mood**

690.   **Speaking for Ourselves, Too: More Autobiographical Sketches by Notable Authors of Books for Young Adults**. Donald R. Gallo, comp. and ed. Urbana, Ill., National Council of Teachers of English, 1993. 235p.   illus. $14.95pa. PS 129.S644. 813'.54099283. LC 92-44193. ISBN 0-8141-4623-6.

This companion volume to *Speaking for Ourselves* (see ARBA 91, entry 1118) profiles 89 additional writers for young adults. Adhering to a format similar to that of the first volume, selected authors disclose interesting details about their lives and writing careers. Their comments are personal and engaging. Students will discover, for example, that Brock Cole had an almost parent-free childhood, moved from school to school, and enjoyed it all; and Sonia Levitan decided at the age of twelve to become a writer, loves it still, but hates rejection. Each sketch averages one to two pages in length and is accompanied by a photograph and a bibliography of the author's works.

Throughout the book, in profile after profile, two patterns emerge. First, the majority of the authors express a love of reading. Second, they encourage perseverance when embarking on a writing career. Potential young authors could not receive more valuable advice for this profession or many other related ones.

For students needing comprehensive biographical information about contemporary authors, these brief profiles will not satisfy them. They will need to consult the *Sixth Book of Junior Authors & Illustrators* (see ARBA 90, entry 30). Librarians who regularly book talk these authors, however, will find it a treasure. It offers just the right amount of chatty, intimate detail about a writers' lives that sheds light upon their writing themes, styles, and characters. It is also very helpful for preparing public relations posters, brochures, and handouts prior to an author's visit. School and public libraries should definitely acquire copies of both volumes. Their costs make them reference bargains. [R: SLMQ, Fall 93, p. 58]—**Kathleen W. Craver**

691.   **Twentieth-Century Children's Writers**. 4th ed. Laura Standley Berger, ed. Detroit, St. James Press, 1995. 1272p. index. (Twentieth-Century Writers Series). $132.00. ISBN 1-55862-177-6.

Using a panel of experts, the editor of *Twentieth-Century Children's Writers* has again chosen thousands of English-language authors of fiction, nonfiction, poetry, and drama to chronicle. Since the publication of the 3d edition of this work, a companion, *Twentieth-Century Young Adult Writers* (see ARBA 95, entry 1147), has been published, so the contents of this volume have been adjusted more toward the younger set. The writers included are, for the most part, those writing in the twentieth century, although a section on nineteenth-century greats is covered in the appendix. The entry for each author consists of a biography, a complete list of published works, and a signed critical essay. Information is accurate when compared to works such as *Something about the Author* (see ARBA 96, entries 1172-1174). Coverage is mainly of British and U.S. writers; however, a number of Australian and Canadian authors are included, as are a smattering of Third World authors.

For a one-volume quick source for information about children's authors, this is the best source. Addresses of the authors or their agents are particularly valuable for those wishing to correspond with these people. There are no references to further information about the authors, so *Something about the Author* or *Biographical Index to Children's and Young Adult Authors and Illustrators* (see ARBA 93, entry 1144) will need to be consulted. Because this source is rather expensive, it begs to be compared to the CD-ROM product *Junior DISCovering Authors* (see entry 681), although that product only covers 300 authors. If the library has the right technology, the CD-ROM product would be attractive because of its lengthier biographical sketches, photographs of the authors, and references to further information. However, if the library is still fairly print-oriented, cannot afford *Something about the Author*, and wants extensive coverage, then *Twentieth-Century Children's Writers* is the perfect source. Larger libraries will want all the biographical sources possible to provide the best coverage. Owners of the previous edition will want to add this volume for the additional names and current addresses.—**David V. Loertscher**

692. Ward, Martha E., and others. **Authors of Books for Young People**. 3d ed. Metuchen, N.J., Scarecrow, 1990. 780p. $59.50. PN497.A97. 809.8'9282. LC 90-32569. ISBN 0-8108-2293-8.

This is a revision of Martha E. Ward and Dorothy A. Marguardt's long-standing effort to provide brief biographical information on authors and illustrators for young people. (See ARBA 80, entry 1203, and ARBA 72, entry 158, for reviews of the earlier editions.) This edition contains 3,708 entries, 297 more than the previous edition and its supplement.

The strength of this work is that it identifies more names than any other one-volume source. A typical entry provides name, birth and death years, a few sentences about the author, and references to several titles. Information in the source has been extracted from Gale's *Contemporary Authors* series (which is much too expensive for a small library to own) and, evidently, from promotional material, news articles, and other personal sources available to the authors.

The work has several major flaws. The presentation of birth dates and places is inconsistent, even when contained in the original source. The authors seem to have been more intent upon varying the style of prose in the entry than in supplying consistent information. In checking entries against more thorough sources, there are a number of factual errors. Other sources, such as H. W. Wilson's *Junior Book of Authors* series and Gale's *Something about the Authors* series, are more authoritative. It is unfortunate that the authors limited themselves to the *Contemporary Authors* series for much of their data. Using the other series mentioned would improve their work immeasurably. If a library can afford only one source, *Twentieth-Century Children's Writers* (see entry 691) is recommended over this book.—**David V. Loertscher**

693. **Writers for Children: Critical Studies of Major Authors since the Seventeenth Century**. Jane M. Bingham, ed. New York, Scribner's, 1988. 661p. index. $90.00. LC 87-16011. ISBN 0-684-18165-7.

"A critical guide to selected classics in children's literature . . . important writers from the seventeenth century to the first part of the twentieth century. It includes eighty-four original critical essays, alphabetically arranged with selected bibliographies" (introduction). Beginning with Louisa May Alcott and ending with Charlotte Mary Yonge, each essay is by a named, often noted, contributor, and while entries vary in length, most cover the subject quite fully.

There are a listing of contributors with their backgrounds and credentials and a full index of important persons, titles, and events mentioned.

This extremely interesting and well-written reference work is aimed at scholars and critics in the field of children's literature, and is obviously of great interest and value to children's librarians, students, and researchers in the field as well as those who are concerned with this delightful and important area of literature. Useful (maybe even essential) for academic libraries as well as public and school libraries of any size. [R: Choice, Feb 88, p. 890; WLB, Jan 88, pp. 98-99]—**Eleanor Elving Schwartz**

694. **Writers for Young Adults**. Ted Hipple, ed. New York, Scribner's/Simon & Schuster Macmillan, 1997. 3v. illus. index. $235.00/set. ISBN 0-684-80474-3.

This 3-volume set is a great addition to secondary school libraries and the young adult section of public libraries, especially those that cannot afford Gale's *Authors & Artists for Young Adults*. Robert Cormier's foreword should be read. Signed articles cover 129 classical and contemporary authors, with the emphasis on the latter category. Teachers and students looking for background information will vie to use this set. It is also a browser's delight.

Each article includes the author's picture or illustrations, biographical information, critiques or interpretations of the author's important books, a selected bibliography of the author's works, works about the author, and how to contact the author. Many articles include a note indicating that quotations are from current correspondence with the writer. Even though the articles provide typical information about the authors, each article is slightly different. This gives each entry a unique feel and lets the author discussed shine. The articles are written with young adults in mind.

The easy-to-read page layout includes outside margins used for definitions, brief explanations, suggestions for other authors to read who write in a similar vein, and so on. The list of contributors gives affiliations and articles written. The category index lists titles alphabetically by genre and theme; it certainly aids in reading list preparations. The general index lists authors and titles. In typical Scribner's fashion, the authors' names are listed on the spine of the book. There is a similar list on the back cover. These user-friendly additions ensure no fumbling with a table of contents, although the one for this set is well laid out. This set will definitely be requested at report-writing time. [R: RBB, 15 Oct 97, p. 430]—**Esther R. Sinofsky**

695.   **Writers of Multicultural Fiction for Young Adults: A Bio-Critical Sourcebook**. M. Daphne Kutzer, ed. Westport, Conn., Greenwood Press, 1996. 487p. index. $75.00. ISBN 0-313-29331-7.

Here is a reference book that all librarians and teachers of children's literature will embrace; 51 authors, many relatively unknown and many who write about ethnic groups not their own, are given prominence in this most solid and sane reference work. The editor is to be highly commended for both her selection of authors and her choice of good writers to profile the authors. Labeled as a "bio-critical sourcebook," *Writers of Multicultural Fiction for Young Adults* contains many of today's multicultural authors—Gary Soto, Laurence Yep, Walter Dean Myers, Nicholasa Mohr, Julius Lester, Alice Childress, Rosa Guy, Jamake Highwater, and James Berry—but it also includes lesser-known contemporary authors, such as Andrew Salkey and Cynthia Kadohata, and several "forgotten" older writers, such as Florence Crannell Means, Ann Nolan Clark, Laura Adams Armer, and Evelyn Sibley Lampman.

Each entry presents a brief biographical sketch, followed by a section on major works and themes, one on critical reception, and a complete bibliographic listing of the writer's works and some selected secondary sources on the author. Significantly, Kutzer includes authors who write about ethnic groups that are not from that ethnic group; she stresses that she wants to "ensure a historical context for the issues raised by multiculturalism, and the sections on the critical reception of each author addresses [sic] such important issues as the authority and authenticity of the writer to comment on a different culture." Kutzer also defines "young adults" as those people ages 12 or above, although occasionally they may be as young as 10. Kutzer maintains that "multicultural literature *is* American literature, not merely a category." This is an excellent addition to the field. [R: BR, Sept/Oct 96, p. 57; Choice, July/Aug 96, p. 1780]—**Anne F. Roberts**

696.   **Yesterday's Authors of Books for Children: Facts and Pictures after Authors and Illustrators of Books for Young People, from Early Times to 1960**. Anne Commire, ed. Detroit, Gale, 1977-1978. 2v. illus. index. $62.00/vol. LC 76-17301. ISBN 0-8103-0090-7.

Yet another children's authors series—this one devoted exclusively to authors and illustrators of children's books who died before 1961. *YABC* complements Gale's *Something about the Author* series, which covers authors and illustrators now living or deceased since 1961. Each volume of *YABC* covers about 40 figures. Unfortunately this project stopped with the publication of volume 2.

Entries range from Andy Adams to Kate Wiggin and vary in length from 1 to over 16 pages (Wiggin). Each entry includes the following categories of information: personal; career; writings; adaptations; sidelights; and references to biographies, obituaries, and other sources. The "sidelights" category consists of excerpts from letters, diaries, memoirs, and autobiographies, arranged chronologically. A portrait of each biographee and numerous black-and-white illustrations from each subject's books or adaptations are included. Omitted are references to book reviews. The editors do not provide any critical assessment of an author's work or position in the world of children's writing. This is especially puzzling in view of the editor's claim that the cutoff date of 1961 makes it possible "to offer thorough overviews of their life and work."

In selecting biographees, primary attention is given to those authors who are still being read by children; no other criteria or sources used in choosing the entrants are provided. Attractively printed and designed, the set can be expected to be popular with young people and children's librarians. [R: JAL, Nov 77, p. 298; WLB, Nov 77, p. 262]—**Christine L. Wynar**

CHINESE LITERATURE

697. **Modern Chinese Writers: Self-Portrayals**. Helmut Martin and Jeffrey Kinkley, eds. Armonk, N.Y., M. E. Sharpe, 1992. 380p. illus. index. (Studies on Modern China). $55.00; $22.00pa. PL2277.M65. 895.1 09'0052. LC 91-31578. ISBN 0-87332-816-7; 0-87332-817-5pa.

This volume contains extraordinary autobiographies of 43 modern Chinese writers. They are meant to convey the "hopes, fears, and everyday problems of China's writers." Those published here were selected from a longer list of more than 100 writers, part of a Chinese-German joint venture that came to an abrupt halt in 1986-1987 due to what the editors describe as a deteriorating political climate in China. A Chinese version, however, appeared in 1989 but omitted Bei Dao, Cong Weixi, Liu Binyan, Wang Ruowang, and Wu Zuguang, among others. The volume reviewed here includes not only these controversial figures but also authors from Taiwan and one from Hong Kong. The emphasis is on serious rather than popular authors, but some space is devoted to tensions between literary and mass-market writers. The original titles of all autobiographies are given in both Chinese and English, along with the bibliographical references to where they first appeared. Some have been abridged for the purposes of this anthology, and minor errors have been corrected.

The German version of this book carries a more expressive title: *Bittere Traume*—"Bitter Dreams," although a loose translation of the Chinese title, *Chuangzuotan*, "Casual remarks on the creative process," describes what each of the authors provides in the self-portraits they have written of their lives and thoughts as writers. Each self-portrait is accompanied by a brief introduction about the author, along with a photograph. A glossary of Chinese terms, names, major political events, and literary landmarks will help readers unfamiliar with China's history and contemporary literature to orient themselves to the most important names, dates, places, and events referred to in the book. Martin offers a thoughtful retrospective introduction on the subject of "enforced silence or émigré uncertainties, in which he considers the fate of Chinese writers in the aftermath of the Tiananmen Square massacre of June 4, 1989.

As Kinkley says in his introduction, this book shows "how Chinese society and its creative writing have supported, competed, and fought with each other for the past forty years and more, on both sides of the Taiwan Strait." Most of the selections translated here, he stresses, were meant "for Chinese eyes; they reveal political treachery and social cowardice with a directness that is by turns hair-raising and humorous."—**Joseph W. Dauben**

CLASSICAL LITERATURE

698. **Classical Scholarship: A Biographical Encyclopedia**. Ward W. Briggs and William M. Calder III, eds. New York, Garland, 1990. 534p. illus. index. (Garland Reference Library of the Humanities, v.928). $75.00. PA83.C58. 880'.092'2. LC 89-23294. ISBN 0-8240-8448-9.

Treated in this biographical/critical compendium are 50 significant classical scholars from the modern period (here defined as 1777 to 1987). The editors acknowledge that their selection is subjective and that these persons in no way "represent our view of the fifty greatest classicists of the era" (p.ix). Rather, the subjects were chosen because their lives and works provide a framework for reviewing the history of the discipline during the past 200 years. The preface notes a number of other eminent scholars who were considered for inclusion but for one reason or another do not appear. While the work is international in scope, Germans inevitably predominate, reflecting their dominant role in "Altertumswissenschaft" itself. No living persons are included.

The alphabetically arranged essays, written by an impressive group of today's most influential classicists, vary considerably in length, style, and the balance between coverage of the subjects' lives and their works (although the majority are more critical than biographical in focus). Each has a portrait and a bibliography covering both the subjects' major publications and the principal sources used by the essay writers. All publications include complete lists of books, but lists of journal articles vary in completeness. There is also a short subject index.

This is a work of impressive scholarship that does not duplicate any other currently available reference work. Its audience, however, will doubtless be limited to academic libraries in those institutions where the classics are still taught. [R: C&RL, Sept 90, p. 432; Choice, July/Aug 90, p. 1802]—**Paul B. Cors**

CUBAN LITERATURE

699.   Maratos, Daniel C., and Marnesba D. Hill. **Cuban Exile Writers: A Biobibliographic Handbook**. Escritores de la diáspora cubana: Manual Biobibliográfica. Metuchen, N.J., Scarecrow, 1986. 391p. index. $35.00. LC 85-31756. ISBN 0-8108-1878-7.

This book is an excellent bio-bibliography of approximately 1,400 literary works written by about 420 Cuban writers living in exile since 1959. This work, which lists almost exclusively books, supplements Alberto Gutierrez de la Solana's *Investigacion y critica literaria y linguistica cubana* (Senda Nueva de Ediciones, 1978), which registers mainly articles and essays in periodicals and professional journals. Generally, only authors who left Cuba during the period since 1959 or, in a few instances, in the two- or three-year span preceding that date, were considered. However, included are some writers who are detained in Cuba against their will, but whose works have been published abroad. The entries, organized in alphabetical order, are in Spanish and English. Each entry consists of vital statistics and bio-bibliographic information about the author in question.

Researchers as well as general readers in the fields of Hispanic literature and peripheral disciplines would find this book extremely useful. All academic and those public libraries which serve Hispanic communities are advised to acquire it.—**Antonio Rodriguez-Buckingham**

DRAMA

700.   **Contemporary Dramatists**. 5th ed. K. A. Berney, ed. Detroit, St. James Press, 1993. 843p. index. $130.00. ISBN 1-55862-185-7.

Containing more than 300 entries for individuals writing in English, this edition of *Contemporary Dramatists* lists playwrights from previous editions who are not included in this volume by citing within the text the most recent edition of *Contemporary Dramatists* that contains an entry on them. This makes it extremely important to have all five editions on the reference shelf. Information for each writer consists of a biography, a complete list of produced or published plays and all other separately published books, and a signed essay. In addition, the entrants were invited to comment on their work. Rick Cluchey, for example, tells how he became involved with the theater for the first time while serving time at San Quentin.

Original British and United States editions of all books are listed, as are other 1st editions. The very first production, first productions in both Great Britain and the United States, and first productions in London and New York are also presented. Cited in the critical studies section are all books written about the playwright as well as reviews and essays that have been recommended by the entrant.

Why are Jerome Lawrence and Robert E. Lee, of *Inherit the Wind* fame, so often referred to as "the thinking man's playwrights"? In what ways is Robert Anderson's *Tea and Sympathy* a subtle indictment of the witch-hunt as well as a perceptive commentary on the failure of compassion in a society that demands conformity as the price for acceptance? In his third play and first professionally produced drama, *Dutchman,* how did Amiri Baraka achieve the cultural revolution of the black man in white America? In what ways does death hold a unique place in Wole Soyinka's dramatic world? Before his skyrocketing journey into prominence with his two-part, roughly seven-hour production of *Angels in America,* what previous plays had Tony Kushner written and had produced? The answers to thousands of significant questions such as these are just a few moments away with *Contemporary Dramatists* at hand. Celebrating contemporary playwrights who work in English, this outstanding reference tool awaits the pleasure of all persons interested in the theater. It will be helpful to the casual browser as well as to the serious scholar.—**Colby H. Kullman**

701.   **Contemporary Women Dramatists**. K. A. Berney and N. G. Templeton, eds. Detroit, St. James Press, 1994. 335p. index. $30.00. ISBN 1-55862-212-8.

Covering 84 English-language contemporary women dramatists, the primary section of this volume includes alphabetical entries by surname, brief biographical information that also includes literary agent's name and address of the entrant, publications with dates, comments the dramatist has made about her own work, types of writing and influences on her writing, a selected list of bibliographies and critical studies on the writer, and a signed essay for each entrant. The focus is on the best and most prominent of women playwrights from the twentieth century, a few of whom are deceased. Women included range from Djuna Barnes to Susan Yankowitz. The next most important section is a section of essays on 21 works, such as Shelagh Delaney's *A Taste of Honey* and Lorraine Hansberry's *A Raisin in the Sun*. The volume also includes an eight-page introduction discussing women's drama versus women's theater, a historical overview of women's drama, contemporary women dramatists from 1968 to the present, publication and production, expanding the "canon" (or the classics) of theater with a few plays by different types of women, themes and issues in women's drama, and contributions of women dramatists today. The work concludes with an index of plays, radio plays, television plays, and screenplays, arranged alphabetically by title and including dramatist's name and date of publication or performance.

Of the 84 dramatists included, 18 are also included in Brenda Coven's *American Women Dramatists of the Twentieth Century* (see ARBA 83, entry 964). Both this volume and the earlier Coven work are crucial to this subject. This volume includes only writers who have published plays, primarily dramatists whose work was done after 1968—unlike the Coven work, which includes dramatists with unpublished work and a number of early-twentieth-century dramatists. Many of the dramatists included in the St. James volume are better known than some of the unpublished female dramatists in the Coven book.—**Maureen Pastine**

702. **Critical Survey of Drama**. rev. ed. Frank N. Magill, ed. Pasadena, Calif., Salem Press, 1994. 7v. index. $425.00/set. PR623.C75. 822.009'03. LC 93-41618. ISBN 0-89356-851-1.

Neither the title pages nor the spines of these volumes indicate that this revision is of the six-volume *Critical Survey of Drama: English Language Series* published in 1985 (see ARBA 86, entry 1092). In expanding and updating that set, Magill incorporated articles on the 29 English-language dramatists who were covered in the 1987 *Critical Survey of Drama: Supplement* (see ARBA 88, entry 1136) and included essays on an additional 11 playwrights who are completely new to this series. Among the latter are Tina Howe, David Hwang, Wendy Wasserstein, and August Wilson, but, surprisingly, not Tony Kushner. The majority of the playwrights treated are English or from the United States, but African, Australian, Canadian, Irish, and West Indian writers are also represented.

Volumes 1-6 contain alphabetically arranged essays on 240 dramatists, ranging from Joseph Addison to Paul Zindel. According to the publisher, 22 of these articles are completely new, while 77 have been substantially revised or edited. In addition, new annotated bibliographies of secondary sources have replaced the original, unannotated bibliographies at the end of each essay. The signed articles consist of eight sections: place and date of birth and death (when appropriate); a chronologically arranged bibliography of principal plays; a discussion of other literary forms for which the author is noted; a summary of major achievements; a biography; an analysis of the playwright's style, themes, and major plays; a bibliography of major works in other genres; and a brief, annotated secondary bibliography.

Volume 7 includes 21 essays devoted to various periods of British drama, the drama of the United States and other English-speaking countries, and types of drama (e.g., musical, television). With the exception of the omission of the essay on cinema and drama, the subjects of these essays correspond to those in the previous edition, although 2 are by different authors and 12 have been updated. Unfortunately, the useful bibliographies that originally accompanied these essays have been dropped. This final volume also includes a glossary of dramatic terms and movements and a bibliography of critical, historical, and technical works pertaining to drama. An index covers playwrights, titles of plays accorded considerable discussion, and topics covered in the essays.

Titles in the *Critical Survey* series are generally noted for the readability of their essays and the uniformity of the information that they provide. This set is no exception. Libraries that have the earlier edition and its supplement will probably want to add this updated version for its more extensive coverage of contemporary playwrights and for the convenience of its single alphabetical sequence. [R: BR, Nov/Dec 94, p. 61; Choice, Nov 94, p. 424; LJ, 1 Sept 94, p. 172]—**Marie Ellis**

EUROPEAN LITERATURE

703.   **An Encyclopedia of Continental Women Writers**. Katharina M. Wilson, ed. New York, Garland, 1991. 2v. (Garland Reference Library of the Humanities, v.698). $175.00/set. PN481 ES. 809'. 89287'03. LC 91-6930. ISBN 0-8240-8547-7.

A two-volume ready-reference with an ambitious scope, this work contains biographical sketches of known and less well known European (non-British) women writers from antiquity to the present. Its more than 1,800 entries seem to be balanced between countries and eras. The lack of an index or even a list of the included authors makes it difficult to evaluate the scope. The work includes poets, essayists, novelists, and dramatists from countries such as France, Portugal, Germany, Sweden, Russia, and Greece. A cross-section of languages is also represented, including Provencal, Yiddish, and Arabic. The entries range from about one-half to three pages in length and include a list of the author's major works and a short bibliography of secondary literature. The dates, genre, and language of the author are given at the beginning of each essay. The major themes in the author's works are briefly discussed.

Information on non-British European women writers is often difficult to uncover. Despite its lack of an index or list of authors, this is a convenient set for most academic and public libraries to have on hand. If the budget allows, libraries should consider purchasing more comprehensive dictionaries and resource tools on these writers as they become available. [R: Choice, Oct 91, p. 256; LJ, 1 June 91, p. 126; WLB, Sept 91, p. 120]—**J. C. Jurgens**

704.   **European Writers: Selected Authors**. George Stade, ed. New York, Scribner's, 1992. 3v. index. $250.00/set. PN501.E9. 809'.894. ISBN 0-684-19583-6.

Aimed at high school students and undergraduates, this compilation includes 68 of the 261 essays that appeared in the 14-volume *European Writers* (see ARBA 92, entry 1231). Selected on the basis of a survey of school and college librarians regarding the authors most frequently studied, the alphabetically arranged articles are unabridged, averaging 20 pages in length. Six articles treat genres or themes (e.g., "Arthurian Legend," "Medieval Drama"); two cover the poems *Beowulf* and *Romance of the Rose*; and the remainder are devoted to major writers, ranging chronologically from St. Augustine to Gunter Grass. In addition to prominent literary figures such as Miguel de Cervantes and Victor Hugo, the compilation also features significant writers in history, philosophy, religion, and other disciplines (e.g., Rene Descartes, Martin Luther). The well-written essays focus on the authors' lives and works within the context of their times and provide critical analyses of major works and discussion of principal themes. Bibliographies of selected primary and secondary works follow each article. As the bibliographies on earlier figures were compiled more than 10 years ago, it would have been useful if they had been updated for this edition.

Each volume includes a table of contents for the set, and volume 3 contains a detailed index to authors, titles of works, themes, genres, and topics. Index references note page number and column but unfortunately do not include the volume number. Because inclusive pagination is not indicated on the spines of the volumes, this omission hampers efficient access to the set. Volume 3 also includes sections that categorize the writers chronologically and by language as well as a complete list of essays in the parent set. For libraries that need greater depth than that provided by Stanley J. Kunitz and Vineta Colby's *European Authors 1000-1900* (H. W. Wilson, 1967) but cannot afford the 14-volume edition of *European Writers*, this abridged version offers a welcome alternative. [R: Choice, June 93, p. 1600; LJ, 1 June 93, p. 104; SLJ, Nov 93, p. 145]—**Marie Ellis**

705.   **European Writers**. George Stade and others, eds. New York, Scribner's, 1983-1991. 14v. index. $1,060.00/set. PN501.E9. 809'.894. LC 83-16333. ISBN 0-684-19267-5.

The publication of a comprehensive index as the 14th volume of this series marks the completion of a significant literary reference work. Begun in 1983, the set was designed to complement Scribner's other compilations devoted to world authors: *American Writers* (last reviewed in ARBA 82, entry 1322), *British Writers* (last reviewed in ARBA 85, entries 1092-93), and *Ancient Writers: Greece and Rome* (see ARBA 83, entry 1240). More recently, the three-volume *Latin American Writers* (see ARBA 90, entry 1208) was added to the series.

The first 13 volumes of *European Writers* are divided into 4 chronologically arranged subsets: volumes 1-2, *The Middle Ages and the Renaissance* (see ARBA 85, entry 988); volumes 3-4, *The Age of Reason and the Enlightenment* (see ARBA 85, entry 997); volumes 5-7, *The Romantic Century* (see ARBA 86, entry 1084); and volumes 8-13, *The Twentieth Century* (see ARBA 90, entries 1200-01 for reviews of volumes 8-9). Stade, a professor of English at Columbia University, served as general editor of the series, while the late William T. Jackson edited the volumes on the Middle Ages and the Renaissance, and Jacques Barzun edited those dealing with the Romantic period.

The series contains a total of 261 essays, 248 of which treat individual writers who range chronologically from the fourth-century Christian poet Prudentius to the twentieth-century Czechoslovakian writer Milan Kundera. Four essays cover anonymous works (e.g., *Beowulf*), and the remaining nine essays focus on themes and genres (e.g., "The Cid in Epic and Ballad," "Renaissance Short Fiction"). In identifying individuals for inclusion, the editors chose not only prominent creative writers, such as Aleksandr Pushkin, Miguel de Cervantes, Johann Wolfgang von Goethe, and Sidonie-Gabrielle Colette, but also noted scholars and thinkers in such disciplines as history, religion, philosophy, music, psychology, and literary criticism. Thus, persons such as Martin Luther, Rene Descartes, Richard Wagner, and Sigmund Freud are among those featured.

The 1st volume of each subset includes an introductory essay and a chronology of the period covered. Signed articles on individual writers, contributed primarily by scholars associated with academic institutions in the United States and Great Britain, then appear in chronological sequence by the author's date of birth. These essays, which average about 15,000 words in length, do not follow a prescribed format or style. Generally, however, the articles discuss the authors' lives and works against the broader backdrop of the social, political, and cultural milieu in which they lived. In addition, the essays provide critical analyses of the writers' major works and discuss their style, thematic concerns, and literary relationships with other authors. Although scholarly, the highly readable essays are written on a level appropriate to the general audience for which this set is intended. Following each essay is a selective bibliography of primary and secondary works.

Volume 14, the index to the entire set, includes entries for authors, titles, themes (e.g., utopia, nature), genres (e.g., detective fiction, pastoral poetry), literary devices (e.g., hyperbole, parody), and other topics. Cross-references guide the user from both original and translated titles to the appropriate author and subheading. Index references locate the pertinent passage by volume, page number, and column. The extensiveness and detail of the index make it a valuable source for identifying interrelationships among writers. For this reason it can be useful for finding information on authors who do not fall within the scope of this set (e.g., Charles Dickens, Walt Whitman, Plutarch) but whose work influenced individuals who are covered.

Prefacing the index are a volume-by-volume table of contents to the set; an alphabetical list of all the writers and other subjects accorded separate essays; and a list that categorizes the authors and anonymous works by language. In addition, the index volume includes a seven-page bibliography of general works arranged according to the chronological periods covered by the subsets.

The essays in this series provide excellent introductions to the writings and ideas of the foremost European authors and thinkers for 16 centuries. Thus, the set is a particularly valuable resource for academic and large public libraries. Since the *Twentieth Century* subset includes no authors born after 1929, librarians can only hope that supplementary volumes extending coverage to more contemporary European writers will be published. [R: Choice, Oct 91, p. 258; RBB, 15 May 91, p. 1831; WLB, June 91, p. 130]—**Marie Ellis**

FICTION

706.   Bold, Alan, and Robert Giddings. **Who Was Really Who in Fiction**. Chicago, Longman Trade, 1987. 383p. index. $13.95. ISBN 0-582- 89251-1.

This is an expanded version of the authors' *True Characters: Real People in Fiction* (Longman, 1984). The original edition covered 309 characters, while the revision identifies the real-life counterparts of over 600 characters from novels, songs, poems, films, and other creative works. Entries are not limited to characters, however, since some identify other fictional elements, such as Manderley, the setting for *Rebecca*.

Arranged alphabetically, letter by letter, under the character's surname, the volume is easy to use since entry headers are placed in the outer margin of each page. In addition to the header, the marginalia also include the author who created the character, the work or works in which the individual appeared, the name of the person on whom the character was based, and, usually, one or more references to sources containing further information. The body of the entry provides a description of the character that places the character in the context of the work in which he or she appear and an explanation about the real person on whom the character was based.

Included in the index are references to the authors and titles of the works in which the characters covered are depicted, as well as entries for the names of their real-life counterparts. The latter are distinguished by boldface type, a system of identification which facilitates use except in the case of authors (such as Charles Dickens and D. H. Lawrence) who also served as models for characters. Although these authors are listed in boldface type, there is no distinction between page references that refer to works by them and those that identify them as the basis for a character in another writer's work.

Who Was Really Who in Fiction is not nearly as comprehensive as William Amos's *The Originals: An A-Z of Fiction's Real-Life Characters* (see ARBA 87, entry 1113), which covers almost 3,000 characters. However, the amount of duplication between the two titles is not as extensive as might be expected. A comparison of the listings under "D" and "O" in the two works revealed that the subjects of 12 of the entries under "D" and 11 of those under "O" in *Who Was Really Who in Fiction* are not covered by *The Originals*. In addition, the entries in *Who Was Really Who* are generally much more detailed, providing fuller information about both the character and the real individual.

Entertainingly written and fun to browse, this work would be an appropriate addition to collections that support literary research.—**Marie Ellis**

707. **Contemporary Novelists**. 5th ed. Lesley Henderson and Noelle Watson, eds. Chicago, St. James Press, 1991. 1053p. (Contemporary Writers). $115.00. 823'.914'09. ISBN 1-55862-036-2.

Covering 589 living English-language novelists, this latest edition of a now-standard work follows the same format as the preceding edition (see ARBA 87, entry 1074). Among the 74 writers new to this edition are James Clavell, Louise Erdrich, Bobbie Ann Mason, John Mortimer, Bharati Mukherjee, and Tom Wolfe. Of the 80 individuals who have been dropped, most are now deceased (e.g., James Baldwin, Samuel Beckett, Graham Greene). An advisory panel composed of such noted figures as Malcolm Bradbury, Margaret Drabble, David Lodge, and Anthony Powell was responsible for recommending the entrants, but the editors do not divulge the criteria that were used in the selection process.

The alphabetically arranged entries include brief biographical information, an extensive bibliography of the author's publications (including any uncollected short stories), and a signed critical essay. In addition, most entries contain a bibliography of critical works, and some incorporate comments provided by the writers themselves. Locations of manuscript collections are also noted. Primary bibliographies are up-to-date through mid-1991, citing such recent novels as Anita Brookner's *Brief Lives* and Don DeLillo's *Mao II,* while many secondary bibliographies include 1990 publications. A number of the critical essays have been revised to include commentary on works published since the last edition, and a few authors (e.g., Ruth Prawer Jhabvala, Alison Lurie, John Updike) have been accorded entirely new critiques. Regrettably, however, some essays on writers who have produced major works during the past five years (e.g., Kingsley Amis, Gail Godwin, Peter Taylor, A. N. Wilson) remain unchanged. A title index includes all novels and short story collections cited in the primary bibliographies.

Almost all of the writers in this volume are also covered in Gale's *Contemporary Authors* series. However, *Contemporary Novelists* is valuable for its more extensive and uniformly up-to-date primary bibliographies, its signed critical commentaries, and the convenience of its single-volume format. Most academic and public libraries will want to add this latest edition to their collections.—**Marie Ellis**

708. **Postmodern Fiction: A Bio-Bibliographical Guide**. Larry McCaffery, ed. Westport, Conn., Greenwood Press, 1986. 604p. bibliog. index. (Movements in the Arts, No. 2). $75.00. LC 85-17723. ISBN 0-313-24170-8.

McCaffery introduces postmodernism in its own language as "not a unified movement but a term that serves most usefully as a general signifier rather than as a sign with a stable meaning." It extends to certain writers who have established their careers since the 1960s. These include Ursula K. Le Guin, Stanislaw Lem, and Roger Zelazny, who have expanded upon the genre of science fiction; commercially successful authors such as Günter Grass, John Fowles, and John Irving; Latin American writers such as Julio Cortázar, Carlos Fuentes, and Gabriel Garcia Márquez; regular contributors to *The New Yorker* Ann Beattie and Donald Barthelme; and Yale critics J. Hillis Miller, Paul de Man, Harold Bloom, and Geoffrey Hartman. Part 1 of the book offers 15 well-documented overview articles which examine the modes of postmodern fiction and criticism. Part 2 contains over 100 short (1- to 3-page) biographical and critical entries on individual postmodern writers and critics. Each of the overview articles and the individual entries includes primary and secondary bibliographies. A "Selected Bibliography of Postmodern Criticism" enumerates some 150 general sources.

The 88 contributors (identified as mostly well-published scholars and a handful of independent writers) approach their topics with conviction, authority, and imagination. As a work which manages to define (as any reference work must do) literary postmodernism, to examine writers which fall into its purview, and to serve as a guide for further study, this volume is unparalleled.—**William Brockman**

709. **Short Story Writers**. Frank N. Magill, ed. Pasadena, Calif., Salem Press, 1997. 3v. illus. index. (Magill's Choice). $175.00/set. ISBN 0-89356-950-X.

Short Story Writers, a three-volume set, is the first title published under Salem Press's new series, Magill's Choice. This set surveys approximately 100 authors of short fiction whose inclusion is based on, according to the publisher's note, being "the most taught, most read, most acclaimed, and most researched in the American library." Essays in this work appeared first in the larger Salem Press reference, *Critical Survey of Short Fiction* (rev. ed.; see ARBA 94, entry 1215). The contents of this work focus primarily on the modern short story. However, earlier works, including Boccaccio's *Decameron*, Geoffrey Chaucer's *The Canterbury Tales*, and Jacob and Wilhelm Grimm's *Fairy Tales*, are treated as forerunners of modern short fiction. Although other countries are represented, more than half of the authors surveyed are from the United States.

Essays are arranged alphabetically in the three volumes, and pagination is continuous. The text is divided into four sections: other literary forms, achievements, biography, and analysis. The section on analysis examines several of the author's works. For the most part, the coverage is brief, but it is a good springboard for more serious and detailed examination. The sections are followed by a list of other major works and a bibliography. Each essay begins with the author's name, birth date and death date where appropriate, and a chronological list of major publications of short fiction. In many, but not all instances, a photograph of the author is included. Volume 3 contains both a glossary and an index. This is a useful reference tool for school, public, and undergraduate collections.—**Mary L. Bowman**

710. **Twentieth-Century Romance and Historical Writers**. 3d ed. Aruna Vasudevan, ed. Detroit, St. James Press, 1994. 890p. index. $132.00. ISBN 1-55862-180-6.

This edition of *Twentieth-Century Romance and Historical Writers* closely follows the format of the previous edition, published in 1990 (see ARBA 91, entry 1136). Approximately 100 entries have been added, while about 85 have been dropped; some of these include gothic writers who will be profiled in a future St. James Press title. Unfortunately, there is no indication as to which of the dropped authors will appear in the alternate title.

The book opens with prefaces by Kay Mussell and Alison Light on the history of and current trends in historical and romance fiction. The biographical entries are arranged alphabetically by the author's real name or primary pseudonym, with cross-references from variant pseudonyms. Entries include a capsule biography, with address; lists of publications arranged by date, in categories for romance and historical publications, other publications, film adaptations, and critical studies; comments from the author (in a minority of entries); and a signed, critical review of the author's work. These reviews are well written, concise, and frequently very insightful.

Some authors in this volume, such as John Barth and E. L. Doctorow, have received plenty of critical attention elsewhere. Most of the authors, however, are popular mostly with their devoted fans; genre romance novelists in particular get little respect from the literary community. The comprehensive lists of publications, combined with the critical reviews, will prove invaluable in reader's advisory work. Therefore, this book is highly recommended for public libraries. Academic Libraries should also consider it to support programs in literature, popular culture, and women's studies.—**Beth Clewis**

FILIPINO LITERATURE

711.   Valeros, Florentino B., and Estrellita Valeros-Gruenberg. **Filipino Writers in English (A Biographical and Bibliographical Directory)**. Quezon City, Philippines, New Day; distr., Detroit, Cellar Book Shop, 1987. 236p. $11.75pa. ISBN 971-10-0285-X.

This excellent reference source contains biographical and bibliographical information on Filipino writers in English, past and present, at home or abroad. It includes sketches of both purely literary as well as non literary writers (such as historians, sociologists, and journalists), and this feature enhances its value.

The entries are arranged in alphabetical order by author's last name and include a wide variety of data: "name, type of writer, year and place of birth, work experience starting from the latest and working back in time, education including schools, honors and awards, published works with place and date of publication, and prizes and awards won. In some cases excerpts from critics' comments have been included" (p.vii).

The style is informal, almost chatty, and is easily readable. The entries are enriched by frequent critical comments on various aspects of the writers' lives and works.

Filipino Writers in English is the only guide of its kind and is packed with interesting and valuable information. Interestingly enough, the two well-qualified authors are a father and daughter writing team.—**Marshall E. Nunn**

FRENCH LITERATURE

712.   **French Novelists, 1900-1930**. Catharine Savage Brosman, ed. Detroit, Gale, 1988. 381p. illus. bibliog. index. (Dictionary of Literary Biography, vol. 65). $95.00. LC 87-25822. ISBN 0-8103-1743-5.

French Novelists, 1930-1960. Catharine Savage Brosman, ed. Detroit, Gale, 1988. 478p. illus. bibliog. index. (Dictionary of Literary Biography, Vol. 72). $95.00. LC 88-16462. ISBN 0-8103-4550-1.

French Novelists since 1960. Catharine Savage Brosman, ed. Detroit, Gale, 1989. 413p. illus. index. (Dictionary of Literary Biography, v.83). $98.00. PQ671.F69. 843'.914'09. LC 89-1127. ISBN 0-8103-4561-7.

These three volumes of the popular, well-established reference series, DLB, include about eighty biocritical essays that trace the novelists' lives, writings, influences, and reputations. The entries provide excellent summaries and starting points for studies by undergraduates, the general public, and scholars. The length of each entry is related to the quantity and critical reception of the author's writings, for example, 25 pages for Colette, 14 for Yourcenar, 36 for Proust, and 4 for Maurice Genevoix. Each entry includes a list of the author's works and usually several photographs, a list of references (many in French), and the location of collections of manuscripts and letters.

In the foreword the editor discusses the scope of the volumes, the selection of authors, and the characteristics of twentieth-century French fiction. At the end of the book a short bibliography of books for further reading lists bibliographies, histories, and criticism of French literature. All three, like all DLB volumes, have a cumulative index to the main entries in the volumes published to date in the DLB, the DLB *Yearbook,* and the DLB *Documentary Series.* Whereas this index is handy at times, a serious inconvenience is the lack of an index of the many persons, titles, and concepts in each volume.—**Joyce Duncan Falk**

713. **French XX Bibliography: Critical and Biographical References for the Study of French Literature since 1885**. Selinsgrove, Pa., Susquehanna University Press; distr., Cranbury, N.J., Associated University Presses, 1940- . 1v. (various paging). $78.00pa. LC 77-648803. ISSN 0085-0888.

The basic format of this annual bibliography has not changed since it was first reviewed in ARBA 79 (see entry 1266). Over 9,000 citations to biographical and critical material relating to French literature since 1885 are listed in one of three parts: general subjects, author subjects, and cinema. As can be seen, literature is broadly defined and entries are found for both theatrical and film directors and actors. Entries also identify the source of information or the library in which the item was examined. Items not verified are identified as an indirect reference. Although the bibliography offers impressive coverage of its field, there are a few drawbacks. A first-time user is likely to be confused by the lack of explanation of how the volume in hand is related to those of previous years. After some examination the user gets the idea that paging in the series is continuous and that references to certain citation prefix letters appear in earlier volumes, but this is not stated in the volume. In comparison to the revised format of the *MLA International Bibliography,* the *French XX Bibliography* lacks the enhanced access points that let the *MLA International Bibliography* user more quickly and accurately identify relevant citations, but the extensive coverage provided by the *French XX Bibliography* still makes it a valuable resource for research libraries.—**Barbara E. Kemp**

714. **French Women Playwrights of the Twentieth Century: A Checklist**. Cecilia Beach, comp. Westport, Conn., Greenwood Press, 1996. 515p. index. (Bibliographies and Indexes in Women's Studies, no.24). $79.50. ISBN 0-313-29175-6.

This checklist extends the work of Beach's preceding volume, *French Women Playwrights before the Twentieth Century*, published by Greenwood Press in 1994 (see ARBA 95, entry 1405). Its scope is limited to plays written by French women and published or performed in France between 1900 and 1990. Excluded are plays written by women in other francophone countries; translations or adaptations; and puppet theater, music hall, and cabaret works. Very few other restrictions apply, so that playwrights are included regardless of their critical reception or their relative fame or obscurity.

Each entry indicates the location of at least one copy of the play, in either published or manuscript form, at a Parisian library or archive. Entries are brief, arranged by playwright's name or pseudonym, with variant names and a list of plays with places and dates of publication and first performance. Biographical information is unevenly provided, consisting of a few words indicating an author's origin, affiliations, other occupations, or other genres.

A selected bibliography cites general works on French theater/French women writers, catalogs of collections, bibliographies, and periodicals. A play title index is included. One desirable but missing feature is an index of the many varying names—maiden names, married names, patronyms, titles, and pseudonyms—that complicate the researcher's task. Users may wish for more critical and biographical information about the lesser-known playwrights here, but the compiler has succeeded admirably in her stated goal of creating a comprehensive list of twentieth-century plays written by French women. [R: Choice, Nov 96, p. 425]—**Emily L. Werrell**

715. **Nineteenth-Century French Fiction Writers: Romanticism and Realism, 1800-1860**. Catharine Savage Brosman, ed. Detroit, Gale, 1992. 415p. illus. index. (Dictionary of Literary Biography, v.119). $112.00. LC 92-17232. ISBN 0-8103-7596-6.

This volume discusses 19 major French writers whose work appeared in the first half of the nineteenth century. The essays, ranging in length from 8 to 30 pages, are detailed enough to provide an understanding of the political, social, cultural, and creative influences on each writer's work. They also succinctly describe and characterize that work while generally eschewing the jargon of literary criticism. They will thus serve as solid background reading for undergraduates and other general users.

Preceding the text of each essay is a bibliography of primary works, including collections. Following the essays are references to published correspondence, bibliographies, biographies, and other secondary materials. The locations of the writers' papers—diaries, letters, manuscripts, and the like—are also provided. Brosman's 17-page introduction contributes a useful overview of the period, the evolution of the novel in France, romanticism and realism, and critical responses to and interest in nineteenth-century French fiction.

Completing the volumes are a bibliography of books for further reading and a cumulative index to all the Dictionary of Literary Biography (DLB) volumes. Volume 119 will be a valuable addition to the reliable and respectable DLB series. [R: Choice, May 93, p. 1445]—**Emily L. Werrell**

GERMAN LITERATURE

716. **German Baroque Writers, 1661-1730**. James Hardin, ed. Detroit, Gale, 1996. 492p. illus. index. (Dictionary of Literary Biography, v.168). $140.00. ISBN 0-8103-9363-8.

This valuable addition to Gale's Dictionary of Literary Biography series covers 46 notable writers of the later German baroque period. Following the standard format of the series—consisting mainly of primary bibliography, illustrated bio-bibliographic essay, and secondary bibliography—its articles are clearly and concisely written and exhibit a high standard of scholarship. A sequel to *German Baroque Writers, 1580-1660* (see entry 719), it is the work of competent and distinguished specialists, including some of the contributors to its predecessor. The choice of authors for coverage reflects an intelligently broad understanding of the term "literature"; in addition to persons known primarily as novelists, dramatists, and lyric poets, one finds the philosopher Gottfried Wilhelm Leibniz, the folklorist writer Johannes Praetorius, the polyhistor Samuel Pufendorf, the educator and jurist Christian Thomasius, and the religious writer Nikolaus Ludwig von Zinzendorf. Perhaps in order to balance page counts, some "later" authors were covered in the earlier volume. This edition features all of the major literary figures of the latter part of the period, plus a balanced selection of others.

Dates of coverage for the individual bibliographies vary. Although some include matter published in 1994, others cease rather earlier. In several of the latter instances, important material from the early 1990s has been missed. Among the bibliographies whose usefulness has been compromised by this editorial decision are prominent writers such as Abraham a Sancta Clara, Daniel Casper von Lohenstein, and Johann Jacob Christoffel von Grimmelshausen. It is also unfortunate that either article author or editor failed to correct the opaque "Salluste" (p.118) into "du Bartas" and the curious "Cassius Dion" (p.277) into "Cassius Dio" or "Dio Cassius." Such errors detract from the high standard of editing established by earlier volumes in the series.

Despite the work's cost, which is about the same as that for obtaining similar books published in Germany, this volume is highly recommended for college and university libraries supporting strong programs in German literature, comparative literature, or German history. Major public libraries in German settlement areas of North America may also find it useful.—**John B. Dillon**

717. **Contemporary German Fiction Writers: First Series**. Wolfgang D. Elfe and James Hardin, eds. Detroit, Gale, 1988. 413p. illus. bibliog. index. (Dictionary of Literary Biography, Vol. 69). $95.00. LC 88-11164. ISBN 0-8103-1747-8.

This volume of the now familiar Dictionary of Literary Biography series covers West German, East German, and Swiss-German fiction writers who established their literary reputations in the decade following World War II. A companion volume surveys writers who achieved notoriety after the mid-1950s. Post-war Austrian authors will be covered in yet another volume of the series.

As with other German literature titles in the DLB series, the articles in this volume are solid, informative, and generally well written. Each provides an overview of the author's life and works, which are described within the larger context of recent German literary history. The volume as a whole documents several important characteristics of post-war German literature, including its attempt to come to terms with the Nazi past and the war, the different directions taken by literature in East and West Germany, and the role of "Gruppe 47."

One problematic aspect is the volume's inclusion of a number of writers who now are virtually forgotten. Of the 43 authors covered, seven have no entries in the *Oxford Companion to German Literature* (see ARBA 88, entry 1246), and as many as half are unlikely to receive noticeable attention from American readers.

The scope of the volume is also problematic. Several of the authors are primarily known as poets, dramatists, or essayists, and, despite the editor's insistence that the focus is prose fiction, the articles that cover these writers include discussions of their nonfiction works. One wonders if much of this material will be duplicated in future series volumes on German poetry, drama, and prose.

The main value of *Contemporary German Fiction Writers* for American audiences will be the coverage it provides of the better-known literary figures. While information on these authors is easily available—for example, the *Encyclopedia of World Literature in the 20th Century* (for reviews of volumes 3 and 4, see ARBA 84, entry 1103, and ARBA 85, entry 992) includes eighteen of the writers—this volume provides excellent and substantive survey articles and bibliographies. Librarians will need to decide if these advantages justify the $95.00 price.

For additional comments on the DLB series, see *German Fiction Writers, 1885-1913* (see entry 720). [R: Choice, Dec 88, p. 624]—**Ray English**

718. **Contemporary German Fiction Writers: Second Series**. Wolfgang D. Elfe and James Hardin, eds. Detroit, Gale, 1988. 367p. illus. bibliog. index. (Dictionary of Literary Biography, Vol. 75). $95.00. LC 88-23267. ISBN 0-8103-4553-6.

This volume is the fourth in the Dictionary of Literary Biography series to deal with German fiction writers and the second to feature contemporary writers (i.e., those whose reputations were established after World War II). The subjects of *Contemporary German Fiction Writers: First Series* (see entry 717) were adults during the Hitler period and World War II and for the most part achieved renown in the post-World War I decade. The *Second Series* provides a continuation, highlighting significant authors who were born between 1917 and 1946 and who gained recognition between the mid-1950s and the mid-1970s.

Thirty-nine writers are included. Of these, 4 are Swiss and 14 are East German. (Austrian writers are covered in entry 611.) Some, such as Gunter Grass, Martin Walser and Christa Wolf are internationally famous; others, Ludwig Fels and E. Y. Meyer, for example, are little known outside their own countries. Feminist writers such as Gabriele Wohmann and Irmgard Morgner are represented somewhat sparsely: only seven of the names belong to women. Writers of varied genres appear, such as Michael Ende (fantasy) and Willi Heinrich (popular literature). Prose fiction is emphasized, though some writers, such as Johannes Bobrowski and Sarah Kirsch, are better known for other genres.

As usual, an excellent bio-bibliographical essay and lists of primary and secondary literature are provided for each author by an established scholar in the field. Photographs and other pertinent illustrations enhance the book. Two appendices contain reprinted articles on efforts of postwar German writers to deal with their recent pasts and immediate futures. Highly selective as it is, this compilation provides an attractive, useful tool for introducing English speakers to modern German literature. The cost may keep all but the largest libraries from purchasing the series, however.—**Willa Schmidt**

719. **German Baroque Writers, 1580-1660**. James Hardin, ed. Detroit, Gale, 1996. 459p. illus. index. (Dictionary of Literary Biography, v.164). $135.00. ISBN 0-8103-9359-X.

This excellent addition to the Gale Dictionary of Literary Biography (DLB) series covers 45 major or notable writers of the German baroque period. As the period is usually considered to extend into the eighteenth century (Hardin, the volume's editor, dates it from roughly 1580 to roughly 1720), the terminus of 1660 announced in the title is significant. Although a few figures whose productivity at least largely postdates 1660 have been treated (Daniel Georg Morhof, Philipp Jakob Spener, Caspar Stieler, Paul Winckler), most of the later baroque writers of note, including Hans Grimmelshausen, are absent. All of the really important literary authors of the earlier part of the period are featured, while the selection of others to go with them is balanced and fair.

The volume follows the standard DLB format of primary bibliography, illustrated biobibliographic essay, and secondary bibliography (including location of personal papers when known). The bibliographies, exhibiting varying degrees of thoroughness, cease as a rule in or before 1992. As with other German literature volumes in this series, the contributors are competent and often distinguished specialists, the selection of authors covered reflects an intelligently broad view of what constitutes "literature," and the standard of editing is high. Despite its cost (about the same as that of similar books published in Germany), this volume is highly recommended for college and university libraries supporting strong programs in German literature, comparative literature, or German history. Major public libraries in German settlement areas of North America may also find it useful.—**John B. Dillon**

720.   **German Fiction Writers, 1885-1913**. James Hardin, ed. Detroit, Gale, 1988. 2pts. illus. bibliog. index. (Dictionary of Literary Biography, Vol. 66). $190.00/set. LC 87-29300. ISBN 0-8103-1744-3.

This latest volume in the expansive Dictionary of Literary Biography covers 38 German novelists and short fiction writers who were born during the second half of the nineteenth century and whose first significant literary works were published between 1885 and 1913. About a third of the entries are for noted literary figures; the remainder are either less known or obscure.

Following the standard format of the series, entries include full primary bibliographies, extensive biographical and critical articles, selective secondary bibliographies, and notes on the location of manuscripts and papers. Also included are an appendix of seven reprinted essays on German culture and history, a glossary of German historical terms, and a checklist of additional readings.

The essays for each author are substantive, generally well written, and contain much more than simple biography. Most succeed in conveying a sense of the author's *oeuvre* and its importance within the larger context of German literary history. They often also include surprisingly full discussions of individual works. For the less known figures, these articles will in many instances be the most extensive treatment available in English. Some of them may prompt critical revaluation.

Those libraries considering this set should weigh the excellent quality of its contents against several other factors. First, biographical and critical material on the prominent authors it covers is readily available in English. Patrons of libraries other than those which serve active graduate programs in German literature are unlikely to be interested in the more obscure figures that are included. Finally, the set is very costly, due in part to a large amount of nonessential material. Approximately half of the set's space is taken up by illustrations, reprinted essays, and a cumulative index for the series.

The cost of existing DLB volumes now totals over $7,000, and no end to the series is in sight. Libraries should therefore evaluate carefully the need for this and each future volume in the series. The publisher should also consider whether or not libraries and their patrons would be better served by a series—at least for the foreign-language literatures—of leaner, more modestly illustrated volumes that cover only more significant authors and larger time spans. [R: Choice, July/Aug 88, p. 1675]—**Ray English**

721.   **German Fiction Writers, 1914-1945**. James Hardin, ed. Detroit, Gale, 1987. 382p. illus. bibliog. index. (Dictionary of Literary Biography, Vol. 56). $90.00. LC 87-216. ISBN 0-8103-1734-6.

This volume marks the beginning of a new direction for the Dictionary of Literary Biography, which during its first nine years of existence has devoted itself exclusively to North American and British writers. Turning now to modern European, specifically German, literature, the editors have stayed with the unique idea of organizing their detailed, illustrated biobibliographies not simply alphabetically but by topic, period, or genre. *German Fiction Writers, 1914-1945* includes German and Swiss authors "whose first significant prose work appeared in or after 1914 and whose chief literary activity took place between the world wars" (p.xi). Of the 33 names chosen some, such as Brecht and Remarque, are world-renowned; others—Ludwig Hohi or Marieluise Fleisser, for example—are virtually unknown to readers of English. The selection is occasionally puzzling: one wonders why Fritz von Unruh and Gottfried Benn, known primarily for other genres, are found here to the exclusion of important prose fiction artists Hermann Hesse or Alfred Dublin. Perhaps the latter will be included in a promised companion volume to cover twentieth-century writers who began their careers before 1914. (Other volumes will treat German-Swiss prose writers after 1945, Austrian writers from 1900 to the present, and eventually all of German literature from 1700 on.)

Since German writers, especially recent ones, are still not as well known as they could be to the English-speaking world, this volume renders a great service. It provides interesting, readable essays on its subjects' lives and works in addition to good basic bibliographies of primary and secondary literature for each. Other recent works which are at all similar are invariably in German. Also, all entries are prepared by established scholars who are experts in the field. Undergraduates and researchers needing a review will take delight in the information presented here. [R: WLB, Sept 87, p. 92]—**Willa Schmidt**

722.   **German Writers and Works of the Early Middle Ages: 800-1170**. Will Hasty and James Hardin, eds. Detroit, Gale, 1995. 414p. illus. index. (Dictionary of Literary Biography, v.148). $128.00. ISBN 0-8103-5709-7.

Volume 148 of the distinguished Dictionary of Literary Biography (DLB) series deals with significant German writers and anonymous works from 800 to 1170. Where little is known about an author, entries stress the author's work. In addition to providing essential biographical and bibliographical information, authors are assessed in the light of the critical reception of their works. The treatment of the works provides readers with a sense of their atmosphere, language, and significance. Works are discussed individually and in chronological order, rather than thematically.

The Germanists who have written chapters for this work are, generally speaking, leaders in the field. For example, Hasty, one of the volume's editors, is the author of a dissertation on the theme of adventure in the German court epic. He has also written articles on the medieval German love epic and Andreas Gryphius. Robert Levine, who covers the Archpoet and Einhard, is an accomplished medieval literary scholar, whose articles discuss Latin literature in England, Geoffrey Chaucer's *Troilus and Cnseyde*, Wolfram von Esehenbach, and *Gawain and the Green Knight.*

Each entry is headed by the full name by which the author is generally known, or the title of the anonymous work. Dates of birth and death appear below the author's name; in the case of an anonymous work, the approximate date of the work's composition appears below the work's title. The author's major works are listed in chronological order with their approximate dates of composition. The titles are listed as they generally appear in standard editions and are italicized. The title of a work is followed by a brief description of the age and location of significant manuscripts. In general, disputes on the merits of various manuscripts of a work are not given much space. The first printing dates, standard or critical editions of the original Middle High German text, modern German editions, and English translations follow. Each essay assesses the author's or anonymous work's place in the literary history of the period. Biographical information on medieval German authors is provided wherever possible. All quotations are in the original, accompanied by parenthetical idiomatic translations. Each entry concludes with a reference section of representative writings on the author or work. At the end of the volume, a list of books for further reading in the field of early German literature is provided.

This DLB volume, edited by Hasty and Hardin, is nothing less than an outstanding collection of well-organized essays on early German authors and anonymous works. It is all the more significant because the editors have so successfully attempted to keep everything in the volume comprehensible to a reader unfamiliar with German language, history, and culture. It is highly recommended for all German and medieval literature collections in university libraries, as well as major public libraries.—**Mark Padnos**

723.   Hardin, James, and Christoph E. Schweitzer. **German Writers in the Age of Goethe, 1789-1832**. Detroit, Gale, 1990. 435p. illus. index. (Dictionary of Literary Biography, v.90). $103.00. PT311.G47. 830.9'006. LC 89-23646. ISBN 0-8103-4568-4.

Conforming to the format of earlier volumes in the Dictionary of Literary Biography series, this work offers brief accounts of the lives and letters of 47 German writers (40 men, 7 women) from the *Sturm und Drang* period through Romanticism. The articles are written by established American Germanists (e.g., Jeffrey L. Sammons, Lawrence Ryan) and are arranged alphabetically. Each entry is headed by a reproduction of the author's likeness and a chronological list (sometimes selective) of works. The four- to eight-page articles concentrate on the author's literary development and influence without ignoring biographical detail. All German quotations and titles within the text are translated. A list of secondary sources follows each article, and references to editions of personal correspondence, bibliographies, and biographies are provided when possible. In addition, each entry ends with information about the location of the papers or archives of the author.

Although the treatment of the literary works remains cursory, the critical observations generally avoid the danger of becoming clichéd or superficial. The even quality and style of the articles—a mark of good editorial direction—make this a very readable and coherent reference work. Indeed, this collection of literary biographies addresses the needs of several types of users; it is accessible to high school and undergraduate students with little knowledge of German, yet useful (particularly for its bibliographies and archival information) for the more advanced researcher.—**Valerie R. Hotchkiss**

724.   **Nineteenth-Century German Writers, 1841-1900**. James Hardin and Siegfried Mews, eds. Detroit, Gale, 1993. 533p. illus. index. (Dictionary of Literary Biography, v.129). $125.00. LC 92-44546. ISBN 0-8103-5388-1.

The nineteenth century was a time of social and political upheaval in German-speaking Europe, and writers selected for the present volume (which brings to a dozen those in the series devoted to German-language literature) reflect that unrest. Representing a plethora of viewpoints and genres, the 42 names included range from pre-March radicals Karl Marx and Friedrich Engels to realist novella masters Theodor Storm and Gottfried Keller, to *Grunderzeit* novelists Gustav Freytag and Theodor Fontane. Otto von Bismarck the statesman is here, as are Friedrich Nietzsche the philosopher, early women's advocates Fanny Lewald and Louise Otto-Peters, Jewish editor and prose writer Karl Emil Franzos, and prolific adventure-yarn spinner Karl May. Many of the names are virtually unknown to readers of English; the editors' introduction provides justification for the inclusion of most of them along with a useful survey of this portentous era.

As usual, the bio-bibliographical essays have been prepared with competence and care by established scholars and embellished with lists of primary and secondary bibliography and attractive illustrations. A brief checklist of further readings and a cumulated index to the whole series complete the volume, which is highly recommended for all collections that serve adults interested in German literature and that can afford the stiff price. [R: Choice, May 94, pp. 1419-20]—**Willa Schmidt**

725.   **The Oxford Companion to German Literature**. 3d ed. By Henry Garland and Mary Garland. New York, Oxford University Press, 1997. 951p. $75.00. ISBN 0-19-815896-3.

This companion marks the 3d edition of a title first published by Henry and Mary Garland in 1975 (see ARBA 77, entry 1263), then revised by Mary Garland alone in 1986 (see ARBA 88, entry 1246). Mary Garland, who died shortly before the book went to press, has updated this work through the mid-1990s to reflect Germany's reunification, as well as the burgeoning crop of new authors, titles, and literary trends of the past decade. A further purpose is to increase representation of the neglected women writers of all periods.

Eighty new entries have been added and over 200 existing ones revised. Among the new entries are those for contemporary authors such as Elfriede Jelinek, Monika Maron, and Gunter de Bruyn; and recent titles such as Thomas Bernhard's final novel *Ausloschung* (1986) and Gunter Grass's 1996 tome *Ein weites Feld*. Also new and welcome are articles on anti-Semitism and the Yiddish language. One wishes similar attention had been given to topics such as feminism or the flourishing literary output of Germany's new ethnic groups. Entries on living persons have been brought up-to-date and sometimes totally revised, such as in the case of Christa Wolf; new editions for writers of all periods have been duly noted. Geographic entries, such as Berlin or Potsdam, have been updated, and two current maps are included. The current period seems to have been slighted somewhat in order to retain almost all existing entries; important writers such as Sten Nadolny, Gerhard Roth, and Helga Konigsdorf receive no mention. However, enough new information is presented here to make the book's purchase worthwhile.—**Willa Schmidt**

726.   **Twentieth-Century German Dramatists, 1889-1918**. Wolfgang D. Elfe and James Hardin, eds. Detroit, Gale, 1992. 388p. illus. index. (Dictionary of Literary Biography, v.118). $112.00. LC 92-19190. ISBN 0-8103-7595-8.

Each entry in this volume begins with the rubric "PLAY PRODUCTIONS," listing the first performances of each drama. This is followed by a primary bibliography of the author's works, the most important section of which is a chronological list of all of the author's book publications. The text of the entry is a thorough account of the dramatist's life that attempts to place the person in proper perspective within the history of German drama and theater. A secondary bibliography and a statement about the author's literary estate end the entry.

The volume covers dramatists from Hermann Bahr (1863-1934) through Stefan Zweig (1881-1942), with essays on such significant authors as Gerhart Hauptmann, Hugo von Hofmannsthal, Arno Holz, Karl Kraus, Heinrich Mann, Arthur Schnitzler, Fritz von Unruh, and Frank Wedekind. The contributors to the volume, chiefly Germanists from the United States, Canada, and Great Britain, are experts on their respective authors. The appendix contains an essay by Roy C.

Cowen on the development of German drama and theater from the advent of naturalism in 1889 to the Nazi takeover of Germany in 1933. Cinematic productions by the dramatists are touched on in the entries, as are the contributions of many dramatists as drama critics. A list of books for further reading appears at the end of the volume.

This volume is recommended for undergraduate and graduate German collections. Small college libraries may find its price prohibitive.—**Mark Padnos**

727. **Twentieth-Century German Dramatists, 1919-1992**. Wolfgang D. Elfe and James Hardin, eds. Detroit, Gale, 1992. 567p. illus. index. (Dictionary of Literary Biography, v.124). $113.00. LC 92-26833. ISBN 0-8103-5383-0.

Companion to *Twentieth-Century German Dramatists, 1889-1918* (Gale, 1992), the present volume spans a significantly greater time period and covers almost twice as many writers. The 50 German, Austrian, and Swiss-German playwrights highlighted include representatives of 1920s expressionism, such as Ernst Toller and Franz Werfel; a selection of *Neue Sachlichkeit* authors; and an array of National Socialist, exile, and postwar dramatists that includes Hanns Johst, Bertolt Brecht, Heiner Muller, Gunter Grass, Friederich Duerrenmatt, and Peter Weiss. Eight of the 50 were born after 1940. Some, such as Else Lasker-Schuler or Hermann Broch, are better known for other genres and have also appeared in earlier series volumes.

The usual DLB entry format of primary bibliography, illustrated bio-bibliographical essay, and secondary bibliography is followed here with one helpful addition: A list of first performances of the author's dramas opens each entry, preceding the list of published works. An introduction by the editors divides years and persons covered chronologically, and an essay on the German radio play and a brief bibliography of related works conclude the volume. Undergraduates and English speakers looking for an introduction to recent German drama will find this an excellent resource.—**Willa Schmidt**

728. **Women Writers of Germany, Austria, and Switzerland: An Annotated Bio-Bibliographical Guide**. Elke Fredereiksen, ed. Westport, Conn., Greenwood Press, 1989. 323p. index. (Bibliographies and Indexes in Women's Studies, no.8). $49.95. Z2233.5.W6W66. 016.8309'9287. LC 89-7503. ISBN 0-313-24989-X.

A selective guide to the lives and works of 185 women prose writers from German-speaking countries, this book includes such nontraditional genres as diaries, letters, and polemics. While not comprehensive, it is extensive, covering medieval to current writers. Each entry includes name and pseudonyms (if any), country, dates, biographical information, and a list of works, some with annotations. Entries were prepared by 36 contributors, all with academic credentials, who are identified by initials at the end of each entry. Frederiksen's introduction provides a good overview of the concept and history of *Frauenliteratur* in Austria, Switzerland, and the Federal Republic of Germany.

A major aggravation is the lack of running heads; the only way to establish where one is alphabetically is to scan each page. Another problem appears in the title index, where the initial English articles *a* and *an* are considered in the alphabetizing of the entries. The biographies and annotations are very uneven in both approach and coverage.

These weaknesses, however, are fairly minor compared to the value of this work to researchers. It is the only source covering women's literature in German to this extent, and should be available in any academic library supporting a program in German literature. [R: Choice, Dec 89, p. 618]—**Susan Davis Herring**

INDIAN LITERATURE

729. **Writers of the Indian Diaspora: A Bio-Bibliographical Critical Sourcebook**. Emmanuel S. Nelson, ed. Westport, Conn., Greenwood Press, 1993. 468p. index. $85.00. PR 9485.45.W75. 820.9'891411. LC 92-27898. ISBN 0-313-27904-7.

Biographical dictionaries are very useful sourcebooks for researchers and information seekers. There are many such dictionaries on authors available, but this is the first time that a biographical dictionary deals with authors of Indian descent. A total of 58 entries are arranged alphabetically by the last name of the author. Many individuals included are major international figures, such as Kamia

Markandaya, Ved Mehta, V. S. Naipaul, Raja Rao, Santha Rama Rau, and Salman Rushdie. A majority of the writers are from India, but a few are from Bangladesh, Canada, Pakistan, Sri Lanka, the West Indies, and other parts of the world. Each chapter has been divided into various subject headings, such as biography, major works and themes, critical reception, and works by and about the author (in a chronological order that includes both primary and secondary works). Biographical information on all writers is up-to-date, reliable, and detailed. It includes their education, major life achievements, and a summary of their major works. Writers who write and publish in non-English languages are not included. All 58 biographies have been written by well-known authors. An appendix lists writers with their place of birth and places of domicile.

This is an excellent book that fills a major gap in the literature. Its price is very high, but it is recommended for all reference collections.—**Ravindra Nath Sharma**

IRANIAN LITERATURE

730.   Green, John. **Iranian Short Story Authors: A Bio-Bibliographic Survey**. Costa Mesa, Calif., Mazda, 1989. 250p. index. $29.95. Z3369. L5G74. 016.891'5530108. LC 89-12432. ISBN 0-939214-64-4.

The title of this book implies that it includes all Iranian authors who have published short stories, regardless of where the works appeared. In fact, it includes only those authors who have published collections of short stories in monograph form. No reference is made to individual stories published by these authors in journals or newspapers, but Green supplies a full list of their other works—biographies, other works of nonfiction, novels, translations of foreign materials, and collections of poetry. The biographical side of the compilation varies considerably; for many authors no such in formation is available, while for a very few others there is as much as half a page. Both pseudonyms and real names are listed in the index.

Green used all the major Iranian and North American bibliographic tools to identify authors and materials. Where possible he also provided information concerning which U.S. libraries hold particular titles. Full bibliographic information is supplied for most of the short story collections, although some are identified as being listed only because a publisher announced them. When full information is available, a complete list of the table of contents is provided, together with the length of each story. The spelling for authors' names follows the rules set by the Library of Congress, as does the transliteration system for the titles of the various works listed.

The compiler concludes his preface with the statement that it is now time to search out the book production of those authors who have not published books of short stories and, following that, to index all of the Persian literary journals. It is hoped that he will address the first two recommendations himself since he has established a sensible format for producing such a bibliography. [R: Choice, Mar 90, p. 1114]—**Margaret Anderson**

IRISH LITERATURE

731.   **Dictionary of Irish Literature**. rev. ed. Robert Hogan and others, eds. Westport, Conn., Greenwood Press, 1996. 2v. index. $135.00/set. ISBN 0-313-29172-1.

This dictionary could have been more appropriately called *Dictionary of Irish Authors*. Containing more than double the entries of the premier edition (see ARBA 80, entry 1300), it continues the process of discussing important Irish writers and their works both biographically and critically. The structure of the dictionary remains basically the same. An introductory essay, "Gaelic Literature" by Seamus O'Neill, is reprinted from the 1st edition. This is followed by a new essay written especially for this set, "Contemporary Literature in the Irish Language" by Alan Titley. These articles attempt to fill a gap, as much of the great Irish literature (and much of the subject matter in the dictionary) has been written in English as the Irish language slowly dies. The main dictionary segment is followed by a chronology of Irish history and literature; a bibliography focusing on general discussions of Irish literature or certain aspects of it; and a comprehensive index (a rarity in a work in dictionary format) keyed to the dictionary proper as well as to the introductory articles.

As previously mentioned, the entries are mainly on authors. A few general articles appear, but on a highly selective basis. Individual works of literature are only given their own entry if the author is unknown; otherwise they are found under the author's name, making the index very important for finding titles quickly. If one knows the title of the work but not the author, a quick check in the index will lead to the correct place. The length of the entries ranges from a short paragraph to several pages. Some other-than-Irish writers are included if they have made significant contributions to the promotion of Irish literature. Most of the original entries have been revised and expanded, often by the original contributor. A great attempt has been made to include recent writers who have cropped up in the 15 years since the publication of the premier edition. The sexist language used in the introduction (e.g., "The qualities that have formed the Irish writer are the qualities that have formed the Irish man") is not mirrored in the main text in terms of content—many women writers are herein profiled. Entries end with (in many cases extensive) bibliographies that in and of themselves would make the dictionary a worthy acquisition.

All in all, this two-volume set is a worthwhile addition to any library collection. Libraries that own the original dictionary will benefit from the updated entries and new additions; those without that 1st edition will benefit from the well-written, scholarly, and interesting entries on some of the best-known writers in the world.—**Melissa Rae Root**

732. Etherton, Michael. **Contemporary Irish Dramatists**. New York, St. Martin's Press, 1989. 253p. illus. index. (Modern Dramatists). $24.95. PR8789.E8. 822'.914'0989162. LC 88-6646. ISBN 0-312-01695-6.

In this latest contribution to the Modern Dramatists series, Etherton traces recent developments in the Irish theater, with emphasis on the past two decades. He analyzes plays, playwrights, and modern dramatic themes from both the North and South, but rightly finds that this geographic distinction is not the critical one. The important dichotomy in contemporary theater in Ireland is between the urban cultures of Dublin and Belfast and the rural traditions of the western part of Ireland. Etherton maintains that the theater of the cities embraces the heritage of Yeats and Synge and their European sensibilities, while the drama in the west, although not specifically about Ireland or using an Irish viewpoint, touches upon issues and ideas that need to be explored by Irish audiences. Commercially unnoticed until recently, the theater of the rural west is "the real locus of contemporary Irish drama."

Etherton focuses his criticism on several important authors and their works. The plays of Thomas Murphy, Brian Friel, and Margaretta D'Arcy and John Arden are analyzed in depth, especially Friel, who the author feels is "one of the most accomplished playwrights writing in English today." Etherton explores the ideas of Irish identity, Irish nationalism, neocolonialism, emigration, communication, and family relationships and how the authors weave these themes through their works. He also examines the difference, particularly important for Irish playwrights, between criticism of the written work as opposed to that of the performance of the play. His explications are detailed and insightful, excellent analyses of the dynamic changes in recent Irish theater. A useful bibliography of primary and secondary sources and an index are included.—**Robert Neville**

733. **Irish Playwrights, 1880-1995: A Research and Production Sourcebook**. Bernice Schrank and William W. Demastes, eds. Westport, Conn., Greenwood Press, 1997. 454p. index. $95.00. ISBN 0-313-28805-4.

The establishment of Irish drama as a recognized genre begins with the founding of the Abbey Theatre in 1897 as the Irish Literary Theatre by Lady Gregory, Edward Martyn, and William Butler Yeats. As the chronological limits in the title indicate, this reference book contains the 32 playwrights who were prominent at the founding of the theater and those who have emerged subsequently. The entries are arranged alphabetically from Samuel Beckett to Yeats. In addition to these two playwrights, other prominent names (e.g., Sean O'Casey, George Bernard Shaw, John Millington Synge, and Oscar Wilde) receive extensive treatment. Also included in the listing are lesser-known playwrights (e.g., Austin Clarke, Teresa Deevy, and Donagh MacDonagh). Perhaps it is the information on these latter figures that proves the greatest value of the volume.

Each entry is written by an expert contributor and includes a brief biographical sketch, production histories for major works, a critical assessment of the playwright's career, and extensive bibliographic information. Of particular usefulness is the list of archival sources for further reference. The sourcebook concludes with a selected, general bibliography that serves as an aid to locating general works on Irish drama. This reference book is characterized by careful scholarship and succinct, but thorough, entries. Its value to a reference collection in dramatic literature is apparent.—**Jackson Kesler**

734.   **Modern Irish Writers: A Bio-Critical Sourcebook**. Alexander G. Gonzalez, ed. Westport, Conn., Greenwood Press, 1997. 457p. index. $95.00. ISBN 0-313-29557-3.

Even though the "Irish Literary Revival" began c1885 and lasted through the Great Depression, the "Irish Renaissance" continues into the present. This creative surge has included some of the world's finest authors. The writers found in *Modern Irish Writers* range from familiar names, such as Padraic Colum and William Butler Yeats, to more exotic Celtic-language writers like Nuala Ní Dhomhnaill. Each of the book's 75 entries has been written by an expert on that particular author.

According to the editor, Irish scholar Gonzalez, this volume is intended as a reference for both the novice and more experienced researcher in the field of modern Irish literature. Each of the alphabetically arranged entries contains a brief biography; a concise, detailed discussion of the author's major works and themes; a review of the author's critical reception; and a bibliography of both primary and secondary sources. End matter includes an extensive bibliography, divided into "Literary History," "General," "Fiction," "Drama," and "Poetry," along with an index and an annotated list of the volume's 54 contributors.

An introductory essay makes the distinction between the terms "Irish Literary Revival" and "Irish Renaissance" and traces the history of scholarship on the subject. The editor cites the continuing interest in studying Irish literary culture as evidence that the subject is not soon likely to be exhausted. For that reason, this well-thought-out volume would be a valuable addition to any world literature collection.—**Kay O. Cornelius**

ITALIAN LITERATURE

735.   **Dictionary of Italian Literature**. rev. ed. Peter Bondanella, Julia Conaway Bondanella, and Jody Robin Shiffman, eds. Westport, Conn., Greenwood Press, 1996. 716p. index. $99.50. ISBN 0-313-27745-1.

The 1st edition of this work (see ARBA 80, entry 1302) was strongly endorsed by the *American Reference Books Annual* reviewer, and this new edition will surely continue to be a basic information source in all libraries where there is any interest in Italian literature. More than 80 new entries have been added, and many of the original articles have been updated. The timeline in the appendix has been extended through 1995.

Roughly two-thirds of the alphabetically arranged entries deal with individual authors, with the rest treating more general topics, such as time periods, literary movements, genres, and aspects of criticism (worth noting are extended new articles on feminism, literature and art, and literature and film). All entries include bibliographies. The contributors are scholars at North American universities; the articles are signed (except those written by the editors), and if an entry from the 1st edition has been revised by someone other than the original author, both writers are identified. A brief bibliography of reference aids, a good index, and an annotated list of the contributors are included. The one factual error noted by the reviewer of the 1st edition has been corrected, but his recommendation to add an entry for Gaetano Moroni has not been followed.—**Paul B. Cors**

736.   **Italian Women Writers: A Bio-Bibliographical Sourcebook**. Rinaldina Russell, ed. Westport, Conn., Greenwood Press, 1994. 476p. index. $89.50. PQ4063.I88. 850.9'9287. LC 93-49535. ISBN 0-313-28347-8.

The 51 writers treated in this work range chronologically from Caterina da Siena (1347-1380) to Dacia Maraini (b. 1936), although it is clear that the sixteenth and twentieth centuries have been especially productive periods for Italian women of letters. They wrote in all the major literary forms, and some wrote in Latin as well as Italian. While a few are well known and adequately documented elsewhere, many have been unjustly neglected and are not easily found in other reference works; a few, indeed, appear to be examined critically here for the first time. The alphabetically arranged articles consist of three sections: a biography, a discussion of the major themes in the author's works, and a review of published criticism. Each includes a bibliography listing the author's works, currently available English translations (when applicable—not all of these authors are in print in English), and a selected list of recent criticism. A general introduction by the editor provides the context for the individual articles; the work also includes a general bibliography, a detailed index, and an annotated list of contributors.

The writers of the articles are recognized scholars (mostly faculty at North American universities), and the quality of the contributions is consistently high. The writing is insightful, fresh, and scholarly but not pedantic. There is a consistent feminist viewpoint (most of the contributors are women), but it does not become polemic. This important work, effectively presenting a wealth of new material, is suitable for all Italian literature and women's studies collections.—**Paul B. Cors**

737.   **Twentieth-Century Italian Poets**. **First Series**. Giovanna Wedel De Stasio, Glauco Cambon, and Antonio Illiano, eds. Detroit, Gale, 1992. 417p. illus. index. (Dictionary of Literary Biography, v.114). $125.00. LC 92-44162. ISBN 0-8103-7591-5.

Twentieth-Century Italian Poets. **Second Series**. Giovanna Wedel De Stasio, Glauco Cambon, and Antonio Illiano, eds. Detroit, Gale, 1993. 462p. illus. index. (Dictionary of Literary Biography, v.128). $125.00. LC 93-12732. ISBN 0-8103-5387-3.

First Series treats 36 poets who were active during the period from the beginning of this century to the end of World War II; *Second Series* covers 50 individuals who wrote mostly in the second half of the century (most of them still active). In each volume, the alphabetically arranged entries include a list of the poet's works, a portrait (usually), an essay containing both biographical data and critical assessment (e.g., the subject's place in Italian literature), and a bibliography of sources. In *Second Series,* because most of the poets are still writing, it would be premature to attempt to assess their permanent places in Italian literature; therefore, the articles tend to be shorter than those in *First Series.* All the articles are signed by the authors, who are principally faculty members at U.S. universities. A general bibliography, a list of contributors and their affiliations, and a cumulative index to the series are appended.

The quality of the individual essays is consistently good; the writing is scholarly but generally not stuffy. Excerpts from the poets' works are given both in the original Italian and in idiomatic English verse translations. The length of the articles is appropriate to the relative importance of the subjects. Because many of the poets covered have not, regrettably, been widely published in English translation, they will not be familiar to those who cannot read Italian. The set's audience, therefore, will largely be limited to academic libraries supporting programs in Italian literature.—**Paul B. Cors**

JAPANESE LITERATURE

738.   **Japanese Women Writers: A Bio-Critical Sourcebook**. Chieko I. Mulhern, ed. Westport, Conn., Greenwood Press, 1994. 524p. index. $95.00. PL725.J37. 895.6'099287. LC 94-617. ISBN 0-313-25486-9.

This volume is designed to serve a tandem purpose "as a bio-critical reference book to provide cultural and literary insights into the lives and works of major Japanese women writers, and as a guide to comparative studies of Japanese women from various perspectives." Altogether, 19 contributors, most of them professors at institutions for higher education in Japan and the United States, introduce a total of 58 Japanese women. They include poets, novelists, essayists, television and movie scriptwriters, and journal editors. Forty-three of the women who had been selected for coverage in this book lived after the Meiji reform, while the rest date from between the ninth century and the modern era. The criteria for inclusion in this volume were that the works of the women authors have been translated into English; they have been the subject of study by Western scholarship; their works are likely to be translated into Western languages; and they may provoke interest among Western scholars and readers. Each contributor presents each subject in an article-length chapter of about five to nine pages. In it the contributor begins with the subject's biography, with contemporary social and political environments that might have influenced her personality and works; provides synopses of her major works; discusses and evaluates them; and lists a bibliography at the end of the informative presentation. A brief discussion of the history of Japanese literature by Mulhern in the preface is a good guide to the volume. The book concludes with a chronology, a bibliography, an index, and the list of contributors. Recommended for college and public libraries.—**Seiko Mieczkowski**

739.	Lewell, John. **Modern Japanese Novelists: A Biographical Dictionary**. New York, Kodansha America, 1993. 497p. illus. $50.00. PL747.55.L48. 895.6'3409. LC 92-11324. ISBN 4-7700-1649-2.

Lewell provides annotated bibliographies of 57 well-known modern Japanese writers, 47 of whom are men, and 10 women. His chronological coverage extends from S. Tsubouchi (1859-1935) to Y. Tsushima (1948-).The ideological backgrounds of these writers represent a spectrum from naturalism, socialism, proletarianism, and existentialism to new school and the like. Lewell produced this dictionary using exclusively English translations and describes the process by which he produced it. The dictionary thus can guide English-speaking readers in their approach to and appreciation of Japanese novels and stories, although it is useful to readers with knowledge of Japanese as well. Coverage of writers varies in length from 3 to 20 pages. Lewell provides a biography of each writer and evaluates the main works. His evaluations are thoughtful and sensitive and show creative insights. At the end of each entry, Lewell provides a list of works translated into English and references to critical studies about each writer. Sources listed under general reading discuss modern Japanese novelists and offer a good introduction to Japanese literature; the glossary is also useful. The volume is recommended for all public, college, and university libraries, and it may also be helpful to instructors of Japanese studies. [R: Choice, Nov 93, p. 436; RBB, 1 Nov 93, p. 568]—**Seiko Mieczkowski**

740.	Miner, Earl, Hiroko Odagiri, and Robert E. Morrell. **The Princeton Companion to Classical Japanese Literature**. Princeton, N.J., Princeton University Press, 1985. 570p. illus. maps. index. $55.00. LC 83-24475. ISBN 0-691-06599-3.

The classical period designates the long period from the beginning of Japanese literature to the Meiji Restoration of 1867-1868. In the preface to this new and only guide to this period of Japanese literature in English, the authors state: "Information is provided in considerable variety, consisting of things that we ourselves feel we need to know, to remember, and to have available. In the process, we have used narrative, charts, series, figures, maps or pictures—in short, whatever seemed most useful and economical of space." First, there is a short history of defined literary periods within this time period. This most interesting and informative section is also beautifully and succinctly written, filled with evaluative comments such as "Mokuami is a better poet than Namboku, but he lacks the corrupt or—perhaps rather—the shuddering energy of Namboku." The several chronologies, the review of geography and place names, the discussion of social groups, the sections devoted to arts and architecture (including a well-illustrated section on clothing, housing, arms, and armor), all contribute to an understanding of the period. Reference use may center on two sections: "Major Authors and Works" and "Literary Terms." Here, entries provide pertinent information, and are as long as necessary to cover the subject. For example, the Murasaki Shikibu entry is of essay length. The section on literary terms is organized with the English-speaking user in mind, and begins with a most helpful glossary that also serves as a subject guide to literary terms. This section of the companion answers many questions about literary allusions.

The companion complements a recent work devoted to rare books of the period, Kogoro Yoshida's *Tanrokubon, Rare Books of Seventeenth Century Japan* (Tokyo, 1984). The book is printed on quality paper and is carefully bound to withstand the heavy use it should receive at universities offering a program in Japanese literature. The companion provides a rich picture of a tumultuous period, and the material presented is based on an exhaustive study of sources. Highly recommended. [R: Choice, Sept 86, p. 88]—**Milton H. Crouch**

LATIN AMERICAN LITERATURE

741. Bhalla, Alok. **Latin American Writers: A Bibliography with Critical and Biographical Introductions**. New York, Envoy Press; distr., New York, Apt Books, 1987. 174p. index. $22.50. LC 87-80661. ISBN 0-938719-20-3.

This bibliography covers 18 major Spanish-American literary figures. Brazilian writers are not included, although the title and the preface (by referring to original works in Portuguese [p.v]) imply that they are. The entry for each author includes a biographical and critical introduction, and bibliographies of the author's original works, his works in English translation, and criticism in English.

The introductions combine biographical data (sometimes scant, as in the case of Jose Lezama Lima) with rather subjective discussions of the philosophical or ideological viewpoints which inform the writer's literary efforts, and summaries of or comments on major works. The cut-off date for the accompanying bibliographies is about 1985, although a very few 1986 imprints were noted.

This work suffers from careless editing; misspellings are common. Two glaring errors which were repeated were the spelling of Argentina as Argentinia (pp.10 and 41 in the section headings), and that of the last name of the Nicaraguan dictator, Anastasio Somoza, as Samoza (p.27, twice in the same paragraph). The quality of the printing is rather poor, and diacritics in Spanish-language words are totally lacking.

Although this work does not provide any information which cannot be pieced together by consulting other sources, it does supply bibliographic data for English translations and criticism in English in one place for the limited number of Latin American authors that it covers. It is therefore a useful tool for libraries supporting teaching and research in Latin American literature.—**Ann Hartness**

742. **Biographical Dictionary of Hispanic Literature in the United States: The Literature of Puerto Ricans, Cuban Americans, and Other Hispanic Writers**. Nicolas Kanellos, ed. Westport, Conn., Greenwood Press, 1989. 357p. index. $49.95. PQ7420.2.K3. 016.86'09'973. LC 88-37288. ISBN 0-313-24465-0.

This work presents to the English-speaking reader a selection of significant contemporary Hispanic literary figures—novelists, poets, and dramatists—who have contributed to "multiethnic letters in this country." The book includes primarily Puerto Rican and Cuban writers but also lists some from Central and South America. Cuban writers are limited to those active in the United States from 1959 to the present. Mexican-American writers (already covered in other reference tools) are excluded.

The arrangement is alphabetical by name of writer. Each entry includes a brief identification of the writer, a biographical sketch (two to three pages), a short discussion of major themes in the author's work, a brief survey of criticism, and a bibliography of works by and about the author. The entries are signed. Most of the contributors are professors of literature, Spanish, foreign languages, and Hispanic studies at U.S. universities. There is a nine-page introduction presenting the context of the book and providing an overview of Puerto Rican and Cuban American/Cuban exile literature. The book also contains a three-page general bibliography on Hispanic literature of the United States, an author-title index, and a listing (with brief descriptions) of contributors. The editor is a well-known figure in Hispanic literary circles, publisher (Arte Publico Press), author, and professor of Hispanic and classical languages at the University of Houston.

It is important to remember that the 50 writers included in this dictionary represent a limited selection of the wealth of contemporary Cuban, Puerto Rican, and Latin American literary figures. For example, well-known Puerto Rican writers such as Abelardo Diaz Alfaro, Emilio Diaz Valcarcel, Joseemilio Gonzalez, and Edgardo Rodriquez Julia, comparable in stature to those found in this book, are not included. Reasons for their omission are not clearly stated. Given this limitation, however, the dictionary is a useful tool for students, teachers, and researchers interested in Hispanic literature, and is an important addition to reference collections in academic, public, and secondary school libraries serving Hispanic users or supporting programs in Hispanic literature or Hispanic studies. [R: RBB, 1 Nov 89, p. 600]—**Susan J. Freiband**

743. **Contemporary Spanish-Speaking Writers and Illustrators for Children and Young Adults**. Isabel Schon, with Lourdes Gavaldon de Barreto, eds. Westport, Conn., Greenwood Press, 1994. 248p. index. $49.95. PQ7082.C48C66. 860.9'9282'098. LC 93-11529. ISBN 0-313-29027-X.

Schon, noted author and long-standing advocate for Hispanic literature for children, has created the first biographical dictionary of Spanish-speaking children's writers. The title is descriptive of the scope of this unique work. It contains contemporary, not historical, persons; authors who are native Spanish speakers (almost no natives of the United States); and those who write or illustrate for children (Octavio Paz is not included, for example). The only U.S. authors covered are Pura Belpré, Cecilia Bustamante deRoggero, Carmen Lomas Garza, and Gary Soto.

More than 200 persons from countries such as Argentina, Bolivia, Chile, Costa Rica, Cuba, Uruguay, Venezuela, Mexico, Peru, and Spain are included. The information was collected directly from the authors and bibliography of books written or illustrated for children, sidelights (personal comments), and a bibliography of further sources of information. The dictionary is arranged alphabetically by author/illustrator, and there is an index to names by country of birth or citizenship.

In comparing the coverage of this volume with the over 2,000 biographical sources indexed in *Biographical Index to Children's and Young Adult Authors and Illustrators* (see ARBA 93, entry 1144) almost no overlap could be found. Thus, the Schon contribution is unique. Any library building Spanish-language collections for children or needing biographical information for these people should classify this as a must-purchase. [R: Choice, July/Aug 94, p. 1699; RBB, 1 June 94, pp. 1872-74; RQ, Fall 94, pp. 104-5; SLJ, Dec 94, p. 37; SLMQ, Summer 94, p. 249; WLB, June 94, p. 90]—**David V. Loertscher**

744. Flores, Angel. **Spanish American Authors: The Twentieth Century**. Bronx, N.Y., H. W. Wilson, 1992. 915p. $100.00. PQ7081.3F57. 860.9'868. LC 92-7591. ISBN 0-8242-0806-4.

This is an extraordinarily useful bio-bibliographical dictionary of twentieth-century Spanish American authors. Following a biography, often compiled from data in letters to Flores, are critical comments on the author. The bibliography is divided between a list of the author's books (sometimes with their English translations) and a list of books and articles about the author. There was an editorial board of 6 scholars and an advisory committee of 17 scholars; 66 scholars wrote the biographies and critiques. However, the scholar responsible for the entry is usually not identified, and while many of the entries have been translated from Spanish, the names of the translators often do not appear.

Better editing would have resulted in greater consistency. The Pablo Neruda bibliography by Woodbridge and Zubatsky is duplicated (588-589). Only one reference appears in the "About" section for Paco Ignacio Taibo II. The reference to the *Diccionario de escritores mexicanos* (1967), should be replaced by *Diccionario de escritores mexicanos: siglo xx* (Mexico: UNAM, 1988), 333-343 (189). In the Rulfo entry, UNED does not appear in the list of abbreviations.

Yet these are microscopic blemishes on a work that will be of inestimable value to librarians and students of Spanish American literature, for nothing like it now exists in a single volume. (It would be nice if a companion volume on Brazilian authors could be produced that used this volume as a model.) The sketches run from the nine on Neruda to two pages for Taibo I. Every effort has been made to provide accurate biographical data; for example, the correct date of Rulfo's birth is given. The data on English translations should be useful to those who either do not have access to the original Spanish or who cannot read this language. The bibliographies are a tribute to Flores's vast knowledge of the field; many 1990, 1991, and 1992 publications are listed. Although now dead, Flores lives on through the reference books, critical studies, and translations that he compiled, edited, wrote, and produced during his lifetime. Hispanists owe him a debt of gratitude for his contributions to their field. [R: Choice, May 93, p. 1443; JAL, Mar 93, p. 57; RBB, 1 Apr 93, p. 1460; RQ, Summer 93, p. 578; SLJ, Nov 93, p. 142; WLB, Apr 93, p. 124]—**Hensley C. Woodbridge**

745. **Hispanic Writers: A Selection of Sketches from Contemporary Authors**. Bryan Ryan, ed. Detroit, Gale, 1990. 514p. index. $75.00. LC 90-83635. ISBN 0-8103-7688-1.

This important work "provides students, teachers, researchers, and interested readers with biographical and bibliographical information on more than 400 authors who are a part of twentieth-century Hispanic literature and culture in the Americas" (p.vii). Coverage includes authors from

Mexico, the Spanish-speaking countries of Central and South America and the Caribbean area, and the United States. Additionally, 31 influential authors from Spain are included. Most of the authors' works are available in English translation.

Updated entries from Gale's *Contemporary Authors* series comprise about 40 percent of *Hispanic Writers*, while the remaining entries have been written specifically for it. The authors covered represent four categories: major literary figures, social and political figures, scholars and journalists, and lesser-known writers not covered in other sources. Each entry provides personal and career data, addresses, memberships, awards, writings, works in progress, sidelights (comments by the author, a profile of the author's literary development, and notes on critical reception), and biographical and critical sources. There are no portraits. An index by author nationality completes the work.

This is a useful source of information about Latin American and major Spanish authors. It is well balanced in terms of country coverage. Mexico and Argentina rightfully receive the largest number of entries (60 and 47 respectively) because of their strong literary and intellectual contributions, although all of the Spanish-speaking Latin American countries are represented. Its strong coverage of U.S. Hispanic authors (128 entries plus an additional 46 for Puerto Rico) also makes it a valuable tool for readers interested in U.S. Hispanic culture. [R: Choice, Feb 91, p. 914; RBB, 1 Jan 91, pp. 953-54; SLJ, Feb 91, p. 107]—**Ann Hartness**

746. **Jewish Writers of Latin America: A Dictionary**. Darrell B. Lockhart, ed. New York, Garland, 1997. 612p. index. (Latin American Studies, v.9; Garland Reference Library of the Humanities, v.1794). $75.00. ISBN 0-8153-1495-7.

The editor states that this dictionary is the first that focuses on the contributions of Jewish writers as a category of Latin American literature. He points out that its purpose is two-fold: to provide greater recognition of the contribution made by Latin American Jewish writers and to stimulate further critical attention on their work. Fifty scholars contributed the approximately 120 entries in the work, representing ten Latin American countries (although most are from Argentina, Brazil, and Mexico). Also appearing in the editor's introduction is a list of works cited, as well as a lengthy, selective bibliography.

The signed entries start with the name, year of birth, and country associated with the author (not necessarily his or her country of birth or residence). Each entry also includes a brief biography and a general overview—focusing on those details that pertain to Jewish identity—plus primary and secondary bibliographies. Entries vary in length; most are from 1 to 4 pages, but some are as long as 5 to 10 pages. An excellent index makes finding author entries and references easy.

This reference, a fine addition to Garland's Latin American Studies series, would make a solid addition to any library collection on Latin American and Caribbean literature. It fills a real void in reference material used in the study of the subject. The dictionary is recommended, especially for large public and academic libraries.—**Edward Erazo**

747. **Latin American Writers**. Carlos A. Solé and Maria Isabel Abreu, eds. New York, Scribner's, 1989. 3v. index. $250.00/set. PQ7081.A1L37. 860'.9'98. LC 88-35481. ISBN 0-684-18463-X.

This three-volume set, totaling 1,497 pages, traces the literary history of Mexico, Central America, the Spanish-speaking Caribbean, and South America from the colonial period to the present through critical essays about the writers representing the best of Latin American literary tradition. The essays—arranged in chronological order by date of birth of the writers—begin with Bartolomé de las Casas (1474-1565), the Spanish Dominican missionary whose writings on the Indies and their indigenous inhabitants played an important historical role, and end with Reinaldo Arenas (1943-), the contemporary Cuban novelist. A total of 176 writers—poets, novelists, playwrights, journalists, states people, clergy, diarists, and others—are covered. In addition to including biographical data, the essays attempt to place the writers in their political and social contexts, to trace literary movements influencing their work, and to provide selected bibliographies of their writings, of translations of those writings into English, and of biographical and critical studies about them.

The countries of Spanish America are represented by 146 writers, and Brazilian writers are the subjects of 49 essays. Only 16 of the writers included are women. Although one could quibble about the inclusion of some authors and the omission of others, the selection generally serves to advance the stated primary goal: "to offer a panoramic view of Latin American literary history, beginning with its origins in the colonial period and continuing to the present" (p.xv).

The essays, which vary in length from 2,500 to 10,000 words, were written by distinguished contributors from Latin America, the United States, and Europe. The majority of the 135 contributors are university professors, although writers, literary critics, and intellectuals such as diplomats are also represented. The overall quality of the essays is high, both in terms of content and of writing—a significant achievement, considering the number of contributors and the translation of many of the essays into English from Spanish or Portuguese. The editors are to be congratulated for compiling a work of such excellent and even quality.

Each of the editors contributed to an introductory essay that discusses Spanish-American literature and Brazilian literature. This serves as a useful overview preceding the material devoted to individual authors. A chronology incorporating political, social, intellectual, and literary events and landmarks into one table is also a useful feature. The index is very complete in its coverage, including authors, names of other literary figures mentioned, titles, countries, literary movements, and other entries. There are extensive subject breakdowns under the authors' names. Geographical and alphabetical lists of authors covered and a list of contributors provide additional useful information.

This work is a major contribution to the study of Latin American literature for English-speaking readers. Although the basic biographical and bibliographical information is available in scattered sources—including some in English, such as the *Oxford Companion to Spanish Literature* (see ARBA 80, entry 1310), the valuable works by David William Foster (*Dictionary of Contemporary Latin American Authors* [Center for Latin American Studies, Arizona State University, 1975], *A Dictionary of Contemporary Brazilian Authors* [Center for Latin American Studies, Arizona State University, 1981], and others), and the literary dictionaries of individual Latin American countries, this work will serve to introduce Latin America and its literature to the novice and may provide new insights and food for thought for those with more knowledge. Highly recommended for libraries serving readers with an interest in world literature. [R: LJ, 15 Nov 89, pp. 76-80; RBB, 15 Dec 89, p. 856; WLB, Dec 89, p. 147]—**Ann Hartness**

748.   **Modern Latin-American Fiction Writers. Second Series**. William Luis and Ann Gonzalez, eds. Detroit, Gale, 1994. 413p. illus. index. (Dictionary of Literary Biography, v.145). $128.00. ISBN 0-8103-5559-0.

The editors' main concern, according to their introduction, is to make this second series collection a complement to the 1st volume by veering attention from the "boom" and its literary giants. Instead, the collection focuses on the inclusion of well-known figures from underrepresented and marginalized groups or nations. The 39 bio-bibliographical essays—each executed by a different scholar—include a short biography; a list of works; a look at major novels or short story collections; and a selected bibliography on authors born between 1900 and 1951, from 19 nations. Although on a three-to-one ratio in men's favor, women are well represented.

Apart from the well-crafted analytical summaries of each author's major works, an attractive and humanizing touch is the inclusion of photographs of the authors and covers of their books' editions. The look at works of authors such as Lino Nova's Calvo, Demetrio Aguilera Malta, and Alfredo Pareja Diezeanseco, who are often overshadowed by high-profile or young writers and overlooked by recent criticism, enriches this collection. Despite a deficient job of proofreading, the volume offers novices a look at an interesting variety of Latin American writers across North, Central, and South America. The essays on lesser-known figures from small nations, and the carefully selected bibliographies, provide a useful tool for proficient scholars in the field.—**Stella T. Clark**

749.   **Spanish American Women Writers: A Bio-Bibliographical Source Book**. Diane E. Marting, ed. Westport, Conn., Greenwood Press, 1990. 645p. index. $85.00. Z1609.L7S6. 016.8609'9287. LC 89-27283. ISBN 0-313-25194-0.

The result of the joint effort of the editor and more than 50 contributors and translators, this work consists of analytical and bibliographical studies of 50 of the most important women writers of Latin America from the seventeenth century to the present, representing most Spanish-speaking

American nations and a variety of literary genres (p.ix). Entries, averaging about 12 pages in length, are composed of four major sections covering each writer's life and career, major themes of her work, a survey of criticism, and a bibliography. Two essays, "Indian Women Writers of Spanish America" and "Latina Writers in the United States," cover material not included elsewhere in this work. A bibliography of bibliographies and general criticism; appendixes listing the writers by birthdate, country, and genre; and title and subject indexes complete this work.

This is Marting's second contribution as an editor to the knowledge of Spanish-American women writers, her first being *Women Writers of Spanish America* (see ARBA 88, entry 1253). Since the aim of that book was to be as inclusive as possible, it covered more writers with shorter entries in a dictionary format. It did not provide information on criticism of the writers' works and often cited only titles, omitting place and date of publication. The bibliographical data in *Spanish American Women Writers* is a marked improvement.

A good complementary source in English about some of the same writers is *Latin American Writers,* edited by Carlos Sole and Maria Isabel Abreu (see ARBA 90, entry 1208). However, since only 16 women writers are included in its 3 volumes, Marting's work must be considered the first choice for information. This work is highly recommended for libraries with clienteles interested in Latin American literature, comparative literature, and women's studies. [R: Choice, Dec 90, p. 616]—**Ann Hartness**

750. **Women Writers of Spanish America: An Annotated Bio-Bibliographical Guide**. Diane E. Marting, ed. Westport, Conn., Greenwood Press, 1987. 448p. (Bibliographies and Indexes in Women's Studies, No. 5). $49.95. LC 86-33552. ISBN 0-313-24969-5.

Two intersecting trends are reflected in this work: "The relatively recent 'boom' in Latin American literature and the growth of women's studies and women's literature courses in particular [which] have dramatically increased the interest in Spanish-American women writers" (p. ix). It covers Spanish-American women authors of creative literature from twenty-one countries, including U.S. Hispanic women who write principally in Spanish. Most of the works cited were published no later than 1980.

Seventy-two contributors prepared the two types of entries included. The annotated ones include name, country of origin, life dates, brief biographical data, and a listing of selected literary works with bibliographical and descriptive information about each one. Remaining entries provide less information, including only the author's name, country, and life dates when known, along with an unannotated list of works. Unfortunately many of the entries in the latter category omit bibliographical data about the books that they list, citing only their titles—a major defect in any bio-bibliography. Neither type provides comprehensive bibliographies for the authors in question: non-literary works are usually excluded, as are all works published in periodicals. Literary criticism is not within the scope of this work. As might be expected in a work with many contributors, the annotations are uneven in content and quality.

The appendixes include lists of anthologies, translations and bilingual editions, authors born before 1900, dramatists, and authors by country. The first two lists are partially annotated, but do not duplicate information in the annotations of two important earlier publications contributing to the knowledge of Spanish American women writers: *Women Writers in Translation, 1945-1982: An Annotated Bibliography* (see ARBA 85, entry 987) and *Women in Spanish America: An Annotated Bibliography from Pre-Conquest to Contemporary Times* (G. K. Hall, 1977), by Meri Knaster.

This work meets a real need in spite of some weaknesses, and those interested in Spanish literature and in women's studies will find it very useful.—**Ann Hartness**

OCEANIAN LITERATURE

751. Simms, Norman. **Writers from the South Pacific: A Bio-Bibliographical Critical Encyclopedia**. Washington, D.C., Three Continents Press, 1991. 184p. illus. maps. index. $35.00; $17.00pa.

Despite being mistitled and often poorly executed, this volume does have merits. Simms inexplicably includes the Southeast Asian nations of Malaysia and Singapore in the "South Pacific" but excludes the more southern and Pacific nations of the Philippines and Indonesia. Had the book been restricted to the geocultural area of its title, this reviewer's complaints would have been far fewer. Authors from Singapore and Malaysia (comprising about one-third of the alphabetical entries) suffer from minimal entries, as if their contributions consisted only of having been included in an anthology rather than major works. If Malay, authors are sometimes entered under their fathers' names (e.g., Muhammad Haji Salleh and Shanon Ahmad). Important reference sources—even in English—for correct information on these authors (e.g., *A Biography of Malaysian Writers* [Kuala Lumpur, Dewan Bahasa dan Pustaka, 1985]) are omitted from the minimal bibliography.

The strength of the volume lies in its treatment of the South Pacific, including non-European authors from Australia and New Zealand. Moreover, with a number of these authors (and a few from Singapore), Simms engages in a dialog that attempts to present their thinking on the relationship of writers to their societies. These lengthier entries somewhat compensate for Simms's lamentable decision "to work as much as possible *not* from pre-existing information or 'dead data' " (p.7, emphasis added), despite the general unavailability of the latter. Although this work is seriously flawed, the paucity of information on South Pacific writers makes it a useful addition to larger or literary reference collections.—**K. Mulliner**

POETRY

752.   **Contemporary Poets**. 5th ed. Tracy Chevalier, ed. Chicago, St. James Press, 1991. 1179p. index. $115.00. 821.914. LC 90-63664. ISBN 1-558-62035-4.

One wonders why a reference work of this magnitude and price is accorded only 10 lines of editorial explanation, especially in light of its preceding 4 editions. Indeed, the previous editions receive no more than passing mention in the editor's note. More the pity, for the body of the work, with or without explanation, is an impressive compendium of information on English-language poets from around the world. Each of the 800 entries, selected by an international board, typically consists of a brief biography, a bibliography of works published by the poet, and a few paragraphs of critical commentary by one of the contributors. Some entries also include comments by the poet in question. Poets are listed alphabetically in the main body of the work, and their published books (over 8,000) are also gathered in an index that shows publication dates and authors. Biographical information on the critics appears at the end of the book.

In preceding editions of *Contemporary Poets,* coverage of authors changed from edition to edition by approximately 10 percent; the percentage of essays that underwent revision was somewhat higher. In any case, the changes have not been significant enough to make purchase of all editions advisable for any but the most affluent libraries. However, all academic and many public libraries will find at least one edition of this work to be a useful complement to Gale's various *Contemporary Authors* titles. [R: BR, Nov/Dec 91, p. 59; RBB, July 91, pp. 2065-66]—**Edwin S. Gleaves**

753.   **International Who's Who in Poetry and Poets' Encyclopedia**. 7th ed. M. J. Shields, ed. Cambridge, England, International Biographical Centre; distr., Bristol, Pa., IPS/Taylor & Francis, 1993. 430p. $150.00. ISBN 0-9488-7501-1.

Formerly a part of *The International Authors and Writers Who's Who* (see ARBA 94, entry 1147), this title now appears as a reference work in its own right. It is arranged alphabetically by author, with see references from pseudonyms or name-variants to main entry. The more than 3,500 entries vary in size, depending upon the eminence of the poet. Each entry includes place and date of birth (usually), profession, spouse or family, education, appointments, publications and contributions, honors, memberships, and current address. Following the 381-page biographical section are 14 appendixes, including poetic forms and rhyme schemes, noted poets of the past, poets laureate, prize winners, and poetry magazines. These, along with a concluding geographical index of poets, constitute the "Poets' Encyclopedia" part of the title. Although convenient, the information can easily be found elsewhere.

There is little question that this is a comprehensive, useful, and easy-to-use volume, despite its small print. The price, however, is staggering, even for libraries with ample book budgets. Reference departments with the *Contemporary Authors* series (see ARBA 93, entries 1108 and 1109), *Contemporary Poets* (see entry 752), and *Writers Directory 1992-1994* (see ARBA 93, entry 1118) probably do not need this expensive addition.—**Charles R. Andrews**

RUSSIAN LITERATURE

754. **Early Modern Russian Writers, Late Seventeenth and Eighteenth Centuries**. Marcus C. Levitt, ed. Detroit, Gale, 1995. 465p. illus. index. (Dictionary of Literary Biography, v.150). $128.00. ISBN 0-8103-5711-9.

For most people, modern Russian literature begins with Aleksandr Pushkin in the 1820s. In fact, Russian literature has a substantial tradition starting from the mid to late seventeenth century and flourishing in the reign of Catherine the Great (1762-1796). This crucial period saw the transition of Russia from an isolated medieval state to one adopting Western models. Although there are two standard literary histories in English—William E. Brown's *A History of Russian Literature of the Romantic Period* (Ardis, 1986) (volumes on the seventeenth and eighteenth centuries), and Harold B. Segel's history-cum-anthology *Twentieth Century Russian Drama* (Johns Hopkins University Press, 1993) for the latter period—as well as various more specialized studies, there are virtually no general-purpose English reference works. This gap has now been filled.

Admirably edited by Levitt (University of Southern California), 20-odd North American and Russian scholars provide solid bio-bibliographical articles on 49 writers. Levitt's introduction surveys the historical context, and judiciously presents the issues raised by differing scholarly assessments of the period and its literature. Each of the alphabetically ordered entries opens with a bibliography of the subject's books, followed by an interpretive essay. Lists of biographies, references, and, where available, archival resources are appended to the handsomely illustrated essays. Most of the references are, perforce, in Russian, but English publications are also cited, where possible. The volume concludes with a "Checklist of Further Readings," which constitutes a model bibliography for the field. The attractively printed and durably bound volume is a major addition to the relatively modest repertoire of books devoted to this area of Russian cultural studies.—**D. Barton Johnson**

755. Kasack, Wolfgang. **Dictionary of Russian Literature since 1917**. New York, Columbia University Press, 1988. 502p. index. $55.00. LC 87-20838. ISBN 0-231-05242-1.

This volume is a translation of Wolfgang Kasack's *Lexikon der russischen Literatur ab 1917* (1976) and its supplement (1986), which have been recognized as an excellent reference source for post-1917 Russian literature. They contain more authors for this period than either Victor Terras's *Handbook of Russian Literature* (see ARBA 86, entry 1221) or Harry B. Weber's *Modern Encyclopedia of Russian and Soviet Literatures* (Academic International Press, 1977-1984). Note that this is not a dictionary of Soviet literature, but Russian literature: Kasack has subordinated national boundaries to language. The dictionary contains only authors, not critics, literary scholars, or translators, unless they have produced belles lettres as well. The 619 author entries are divided into a biographical section and a section dealing with the author's work (primary and secondary sources). The biographical portion includes data expected in such entries, as well as father's occupation, course of study, beginning of literary activity, membership in the Communist Party, date of emigration when applicable, pseudonyms used, and position in writers' unions. The translated entries are well executed and read smoothly; the bibliographic apparatus is accurate and easily decipherable. The dictionary also has 87 subject entries that include journals, literary circles, movements, etc. Access to the volume is enhanced by both name and subject indexes.

This volume is a major reference work for modern Russian literature and will serve as a reliable source for many years to come.—**Robert H. Burger**

756. Stevanovic, Bosiljka, and Vladimir Wertsman. **Free Voices in Russian Literature, 1950s-1980s: A Bio-Bibliographical Guide**. New York, Russica, 1987. 510p. ("Russica" Bibliography Series, No. 4). $87.50. LC 84-61344. ISBN 0-89830-090-8.

The phenomenon known as *samizdat*—self-publishing—began to emerge with Khruschchev's ascent to power and rising hopes for greater freedom of individual expression. When these hopes were dashed and censorship returned, writers were forced to circulate their works privately, and copies eventually found their way to the West, where they were published by the émigré press. This body of "unofficial" Russian writing has attained major importance in world literature. The emphasis in

Free Voices is on the writers who have produced it. It includes biographical and bibliographical data on over 900 authors who live, or lived in the Soviet Union. It is not intended as a comprehensive guide to Soviet political dissidents or to Russian *samizdat* literature, but is limited to those authors whose work, regardless of genre or literary or political affiliation, was rejected by the censor, smuggled out of the country, and published in the émigré press. It was compiled exclusively from Russian-language publications that appeared in the West between 1937 and 1985. The work is arranged alphabetically by author. Each entry includes birth and death dates when available and a brief description, which may include educational background and political and publication activities. This is followed by a list of published writings. An effort was made to obtain biographical information directly from the authors now living in the West; where this was not possible, information was drawn from any other available source. The identity of those authors using pen names was revealed only when this information was public knowledge, or with the author's consent. A similar bibliographical work is Josephine Woll's *Soviet Dissident Literature: A Critical Guide* (see ARBA 84, entry 1217). Her emphasis is on the writings, rather than the authors, so there is little biographical information; however, she also includes English-language publications, as well as works which may have been published officially but in censored form, or may have circulated underground before being published officially. Scholars of modern Russian history and literature will find in these two works a very comprehensive guide to this important body of Russian literature. [R: Choice, Jan 88, p. 752]—**Sara J. Richardson**

SCIENCE FICTION, FANTASY, AND HORROR

757.   Green, Scott E. **Contemporary Science Fiction, Fantasy, and Horror Poetry: A Resource Guide and Biographical Directory**. Westport, Conn., Greenwood Press, 1989. 216p. index. $35.00. Z1231.Q7G74. 016.811'50801. LC 89-16966. ISBN 0-313-26324-8.

Although many readers may not consider science fiction, fantasy, and horror poetry a major genre literary form, this reference book is dedicated to the belief that such poetry plays an important part in these genres. This book focuses on American poets and their publishers and attempts to cover every appearance of poetry published in contemporary genre magazines and anthologies.

Green begins with a brief history of science fiction (SF) poetry in America, from John Campbell's refusal to print any to the efforts to improve literary quality evident in *The Magazine of Fantasy and Science Fiction* and Great Britain's *New Worlds*. The guide then attempts to cover every poem published in magazines, both commercial and small press; in key anthologies, including Edward Lude Smith's landmark *Holding Your Eight Hands;* other anthologies; and single-author collections. This is followed by an excellent directory of poets that includes their addresses, a short biographical sketch, lists of publications and awards, and an index. The section on anthologies is the weakest part; Green has missed a number of anthologies such as Dick Allen's *Science Fiction: The Future* (Harcourt Brace Jovanovich, 1983) and Roger Elwood's *Future City* (Pocket Books, 1973) that print some poetry along with prose.

In other aspects, however, this is a thorough job of research, a labor of love in an obscure and difficult field. Although this reference work is probably too specialized for the general library, those with holdings in contemporary poetry or in SF genre material will find it of interest.—**Lynn F. Williams**

758.   **Reader's Guide to Twentieth-Century Science Fiction**. Marilyn P. Fletcher, comp. and ed. Chicago, American Library Association, 1989. 673p. index. $55.00. PN3433.8.R44. 809.3'876. LC 88-7815. ISBN 0-8389-0504-8.

This work adds a collection of biographies and plot summaries for selected modern writers to the general reference books on science fiction. It is more limited in scope than Neil Barron's *Anatomy of Wonder* (see ARBA 89, entry 1042), since it concentrates almost entirely on Anglo-American literature with the addition of a few Eastern bloc authors (Lem, Strugatsky, and Zamiatin) whose works are available in English translation. However, unlike the brief entries in *The Anatomy of Wonder*, the entries for the authors in *Reader's Guide* contain summaries of lives and works, discussions of the authors' themes and styles, plot summaries of what the editors consider major works, and brief bibliographies of critical works. An appendix supplies a list of magazines and journals in the field and of Nebula and Hugo winners.

The entries, mostly prepared by librarians rather than writers within the science fiction community, are uneven. Some are insightful and knowledgeable with useful critical comments, but others are unsophisticated and awkwardly written. There are many misprints and misspellings. The general reader and undergraduate looking for basic information on a favorite writer will find this compilation useful, but it is too limited for the serious researcher. [R: VOYA, Dec 89, pp. 312-13]—**Lynn F. Williams**

759. **St. James Guide to Fantasy Writers**. David Pringle, ed. Detroit, St. James Press, 1996. 711p. index. $95.00. ISBN 1-55862-205-5.

The *St. James Guide to Fantasy Writers* is the first of a planned two-volume set. The 2nd volume is to be titled *St. James Guide to Horror, Ghost, and Gothic Writers*. The *St. James Guide to Fantasy Writers* lists more than 400 fantasy authors who wrote between the late seventeenth century and the present time. While the majority of the authors listed wrote in English, a few foreign-language authors are also included, such as Hans Christian Andersen, Anatole France, Charles Perrault, and Jakob and Wilhelm Grimm. The volume is arranged alphabetically by author with each entry including the nationality of the author, date and place of birth, current address, address of an agent if available, a list of works with the dates of publication, a brief biography, and a signed critical essay concerning the author. The biographies range from about 300 words to more than 1,500 words for more well-known authors.

Many of the authors listed are known for works generally not considered fantasy, but have been included based on one or two works in the genre. The editor points out that "there is no such a thing as 'purity' in the matter of literary genres, least of all in a field as protean as fantasy . . . nevertheless, fantasy as a perceived type of modern fiction, [as] regarded by most readers is quite distinct from horror and science fiction" (editor's note, p. vii).

The book has some interesting appendices in addition to the alphabetical list of biographies, including a list of works on the genre of fantasy (96 items), a nationality index that lists each author by nationality, a title index, and notes on advisers and contributors to the volume.

Though the work is somewhat uneven in its coverage of the various authors, it is generally well done and provides a much-needed source of information on writers in the fantasy genre. It is recommended for all academic and larger public libraries.—**Robert L. Wick**

760. **St. James Guide to Science Fiction Writers**. 4th ed. Jay P. Pederson and others, eds. Detroit, St. James Press, 1996. 1175p. index. $135.00. ISBN 1-55862-179-2.

Since its 1st edition (see ARBA 83, entry 1164) through its 3d edition (see ARBA 93, entry 1159), this superlative bio-bibliography (formerly titled *Twentieth-Century Science-Fiction Writers*) has been a staple in most medium- to large-size academic and public libraries with modest science fiction collections. Alphabetically arranged by author, this new edition lists 649 writers of science fiction—from the early nineteenth to the late twentieth centuries—as well as writers of fantasy, horror, and other forms of speculative fiction that have had an impact on the SF field.

Each entry consists of a brief biography, including pseudonyms, nationality, birth and death dates, education, family, career, agent, and address; a complete list of published works; and a signed, critical essay. These essays, varying in length, are helpful and interesting introductions to the writers. For example, one may not remember that Arthur Conan Doyle, Marge Piercy, and Edward D. Hoch—better known for other genres—have also been SF contributors. This heavy, attractively formatted volume also includes H. Bruce Franklin's preface on the history of SF, nationality and title indexes, and a useful six-page reading list.

Larger libraries will most likely want to purchase this 4th edition with its updatings and additions. In spite of its steep price, it nicely complements the various SF handbooks and guides and is a trove of information for even the beginning SF reader.—**Charles R. Andrews**

761. **Twentieth-Century Science-Fiction Writers**. 3rd ed. Noelle Watson and Paul E. Schellinger. Chicago, St. James Press, 1991. 1016p. $123.00. 823.087609. ISBN 1-55862-111-3.

This massive tome is the 3d edition of a reference book previously edited by Curtis C. Smith (whose work goes unaccountably unmentioned in the introduction). Covering more than 600 English-language science fiction writers, with an appendix on another 38 foreign-language writers, this is by far the most inclusive biocritical guide to the field. It should not be confused with the much less useful *Twentieth-Century American Science-Fiction Writers* (see ARBA 82, entry 1301) or *Reader's Guide to Twentieth-Century Science Fiction* (see ARBA 90, entry 1108). It includes not only well-known writers but also minor figures who have written only one or two science fiction books.

Each entry begins with a brief biography that is followed by chronological lists of science fiction novels and short stories, other publications, bibliographies, and critical studies. Pseudonyms are included, as are non-science fiction works. The most substantial section contains a critical discussion of the author's work, often introduced by a brief commentary supplied by living authors. The length varies greatly and is not always in proportion to the importance of the writer. There is also a reading list of critical works, a list of the writers, and an index of book titles.

Many of the 166 contributors to this volume are well-known professionals in the science fiction field. As is inevitable with so many different critics, the entries are uneven and sometimes unreasonably laudatory, but are on the whole well written and authoritative. However, while the book is more carefully edited than the previous editions, there are many errors in the bibliographical material. For example, two of C. J. Cherryh's short story collections are mislabeled. Despite its faults, this is still the most useful and up-to-date guide to science fiction writers and their work. Most large and medium-sized libraries will want it.—**Lynn F. Williams**

762. Yntema, Sharon K. **More Than 100 Women Science Fiction Writers**. Freedom, Calif., Crossing Press, 1988. 193p. $44.95. Z5917.S36Y58. 016.8093'876. LC 88-3600. ISBN 0-89594-301-8.

Readers interested in the increasingly important role played by women writers in science fiction will welcome the appearance of this volume, as it is intended to fill a major need. Unfortunately, many will be disappointed by the omissions and inconsistencies in this book, which provides a brief biography and reading list for 104 women writers of science fiction and fantasy (no clear distinction is made between the two genres).

Perhaps incompleteness is to be expected in a pioneering work like this, but far too many of the entries lack date and place of birth and other relevant information. Some entries are much more complete than others, with their length not clearly related to the importance or productivity of the writer. Some lists include writing that is not SF (science fiction); others do not. The criteria for inclusion in the list of 104 writers seem quite arbitrary. A number of well-known women, including Patricia McKillip, Katherine Kurtz, and Zenna Henderson, are relegated to a brief listing in an appendix, evidently because Yntema considers them insufficiently feminist, while many who have written only one SF book receive the full treatment. Cynthia Ozick and Monique Wittig are omitted entirely.

A number of appendixes list dates of birth, places of birth, who was deceased by 1988, the addresses of writers' agents, and recommended reading. All but the last could have been more economically and usefully incorporated into the main text.

Nevertheless, this book contains a great deal of useful information. Libraries with a special emphasis on feminism or science fiction may be willing to pay the rather high price for this slim volume. [R: RBB, 15 Feb 89, pp. 984, 986]—**Lynn F. Williams**

SLAVIC LITERATURE

763. **South Slavic Writers before World War II**. Vasa D. Mihailovich, ed. Detroit, Gale, 1995. 368p. illus. index. (Dictionary of Literary Biography, v.147). $128.00. ISBN 0-8103-5708-9.

The South Slavs include the Slovenes, Croatians, Serbs, Macedonians, and Bulgarians. All were part of the Ottoman or Austro-Hungarian Empires prior to World War I, when all but the Bulgarians were incorporated into the newly established Yugoslavia. Although the Croatians can trace the origins of their belletristic tradition to the sixteenth century and the Serbs to the eighteenth, the "classic" fiction of the South Slavic peoples really begins in the mid- to late nineteenth century. Of the 43 figures profiled in this volume, 32 died in this century–1 as recently as 1991. Apart from Nobel Prize winner Ivo Andrić', almost none of the writers is familiar to English readers. Editor Mihailovich has made an evenhanded selection: Croatian and Serbian writers are represented by about 13 entries each, while the less numerous Bulgarians and Slovenes rate about half that number.

The volume observes the standard Dictionary of Literary Biography format. Each handsomely illustrated profile begins with a list of the author's works, including English translations, and concludes with a critical bibliography. Essays open with a brief estimate of the writer's place in his or her national literature, followed by a biographical sketch, a chronological survey of works, and a summation. The entries assume only a general knowledge of historical circumstances. An introductory thumbnail sketch of the national literatures is provided. End matter contains a checklist of histories of the national literatures, a bibliography of English-language collections of each literature, and a chronology of major historical and literary data.—**D. Barton Johnson**

SOVIET LITERATURE

764. **The Modern Encyclopedia of Russian and Soviet Literatures (Including Non-Russian and Emigre Literatures). Vol. 9: Gorin, Grigorii Izrailevich-Holovko, Andrii Vasyl'evych.** George J. Gutsche, ed. Gulf Breeze, Fla., Academic International Press, 1976- . 248p. $37.00. ISBN 0-87569-038-6.

Planned in 50 volumes, this comprehensive encyclopedia was originally edited by Dr. Harry Weber of the University of Iowa, with some 1,700 entries included in volumes 1 to 8. Volume 9 was edited by Professor George Gutsche; volume 10 by Peter Rollberg. As is the case with *The Modern Encyclopedia of Religions in Russia and the Soviet Union* (Academic International Press, 1988) and *The Modern Encyclopedia of Russian and Soviet History* (Academic International Press, n.d.), this ambitious project contains a mixture of articles, some original and some reprinted and translated, with contributions by more than 140 Western scholars. For example, a short article on Soviet Ukrainian poet and prose writer Andrii Holovko (1897-1972) was written by L. N. Kovalenko, a Soviet literary critic. An article on Hrushevsky (in volume 10) will be written by a Western scholar. All in all, the coverage is uneven, but nevertheless very comprehensive.—**Bohdan S. Wynar**

SPANISH LITERATURE

765. **Twentieth-Century Spanish Poets: First Series.** Michael L. Perna, ed. Detroit, Gale, 1991. 400p. illus. index. (Dictionary of Literary Biography, v.108). $108.00. LC 91-15266. ISBN 0-8103-4588-9.

Twentieth-Century Spanish Poets: Second Series. Jerry Phillips Winfield, ed. Detroit, Gale, 1993. 410p. illus. index. (Dictionary of Literary Biography, v. 134). $146.00. LC 93-26861. ISBN 0-8103-5393-8.

These two volumes together contain biographical, critical, and bibliographical sketches of 60 twentieth-century Spanish poets, 29 in the *First Series*; 31 in the *Second*. There is no indication as to the criteria for their selection. The biographical-critical sketches are all by authorities on the individual poets. Each begins with a chronological list of the poet's works, works edited by the poet, and translations by the poet. English translations are provided with the treatment of the Spanish title, and translations in the form of anthologies follow the list of the Spanish titles. The sketches vary in length from 7 pages to almost 30 pages.

The biographical information appears to be accurate; the critic describes the poet's place in twentieth-century Spanish poetry, ideology, contribution to literary theory and development, and poetic technique. The bibliographies that conclude each sketch follow a similar pattern. That on Federico Garcia Lorca is divided into letters, interviews, bibliographies, biography, references, and papers. As is the other data, the bibliographies are very up-to-date. The only slight criticism of this work is that these volume seems to be chiefly intended for the monolingual English speaker, and fuller bibliographies whose references were mostly in English would have been desirable.

These volumes are excellent sources for biographical, critical, and bibliographical data on these poets. They belong in every library with an interest in contemporary Spanish literature.—**Hensley C. Woodbridge and Terry Ann Mood**

766. **Women Writers of Spain: An Annotated Bio-Bibliographical Guide**. Carolyn L. Galerstein, ed. Westport, Conn., Greenwood Press, 1986. 389p. index. (Bibliographies and Indexes in Women's Studies, No. 2). $45.00. LC 86-379. ISBN 0-313-24965-2.

Under the direction of Carolyn L. Galerstein, approximately eighty individuals have collaborated on producing his bio-bibliographical dictionary of Basque, Galician, Catalan, and Spanish women authors. Writers are not included if these eighty twentieth-century scholars have been able to add nothing to what has already been published in Manuel Serrano y Sanz's *Apuntes para una biblioteca de escritoras españotas desde el año 1401 al 1833*. The introduction by Galerstein discusses previous attempts to catalog Spain's women authors, while Kathleen McNerney discusses the problems that arise when an attempt is made to list those who have written in Basque, Catalan, and Galician.

An attempt is made to provide brief biographical data on each author and an annotated list of her belles lettres contributions in book form. Editing has not always provided consistency in the annotations. Thus, we find both Milan and Milano in the imprint data for several items. Some contributors, apparently not realizing that most academic libraries are members of a cataloging network, indicate locations in one or more U.S. libraries. However, I wonder how valuable such comments as "the book is in hardback form and is not easily available through interlibrary loan" (p.9) are.

There are four appendices: authors by birth date, authors in Catalan, authors in Galician, and translated titles, which are followed by a title index.

Except for its printing errors, this volume should be of great value to those interested in the contributions of women to the belles lettres of Spain. I would have appreciated a brief bibliography of critical studies on each author. Perhaps this idea can be considered for future volumes in this series that will include a volume on Spanish-American women authors. [R: Choice, Oct 86, p. 289]—**Hensley C. Woodbridge**

TURKISH LITERATURE

767. Mitler, Louis. **Ottoman Turkish Writers: A Bibliographical Dictionary of Significant Figures in Pre-Republican Turkish Literature**. New York, Peter Lang, 1988. 203p. (American University Studies, series 19, General Literature, v.15). $31.50. PL213.M48. 894'.35109. LC 87-21514. ISBN 0-8204-0633-3.

A number of anthologies of Turkish literature in translation exist, but this is the first biographical dictionary of Ottoman Turkish writers to be written in the English language. The Ottoman period extended from the fourteenth century to the end of World War I and included lands from Caucasia and Persia to the Danube, south to Cairo and the Persian Gulf. The volume covers nearly 100 writers, and the author included certain writers who lived prior to this period, such as Nasreddin Hoca and Mevlana, because of their stature in world literature.

The arrangement of the volume is alphabetical, with the entry for each writer being under the best-known form of his or her name. Entries contain a brief biography with reference to important historical events that occurred during the writer's life, as well as translations of brief passages from his or her work or a summary of plot elements from a well-known title. A selected bibliography of works both in English and Turkish completes the entry. Care has been taken to reproduce the Turkish names accurately, and the author includes a guide to pronunciation of the Turkish alphabet. The book is well designed, but the binding is quite poor and will not withstand heavy use.

This work fills a gap in the study of Turkish literature and will be valuable as a starting point for the study of any of these writers. It is an excellent overview of a literature inaccessible to many.—**Shirley Lambert and Ahmet Yücel**

WELSH LITERATURE

768.   **The Oxford Companion to the Literature of Wales**. Meic Stephens, comp. and ed. New York, Oxford University Press, 1986. 682p. $32.00. LC 85-7095. ISBN 0-19-211586-3.

This latest addition to the *Oxford Companion* family continues the tradition of excellence that has become a hallmark of titles in this series. Covering the sixth century to the present, this compilation consists of 2,825 alphabetical entries, almost half of which pertain to authors. Although emphasis is on writers in the Welsh language, selected Welsh nationals known for their writings in English or Latin are also included, as are authors from other countries whose works are set in Wales. In addition to creative writers, entries cover other individuals involved in literary pursuits, such as historians, critics, lexicographers, and editors. Writers born after 1950 are excluded.

According to the preface, the next largest category of entries deals with other aspects of literature, such as literary genres, motifs, characters, and titles of major literary works and periodicals. In a departure from general practice, characters are listed under their first names rather than their surnames. Headings for Welsh titles are always followed by English translations.

The dictionary also includes numerous entries for historical figures, events, and movements, and for societies, buildings, customs, folklore, institutions, and other topics likely to be alluded to in Welsh literature. *See* references are used frequently, and an asterisk before a term in the text indicates that a separate entry exists for that subject. Entries vary in length from a brief paragraph to three columns (one-and-one-half pages), and many list suggested sources for additional information. A guide to the pronunciation of Welsh appears near the front of the volume, and a chronology of the history of Wales is provided at the end.

The editor is to be commended for the consistency and clarity of style he achieved in synthesizing the work of over 200 contributors. His accomplishment is even more remarkable considering that he simultaneously prepared a Welsh edition, which has been published by the University of Wales.

The Oxford Companion to the Literature of Wales serves not only as a guide to Welsh and Anglo-Welsh literature but also as a handbook to the broad spectrum of Welsh culture and history. It will be a valuable resource for public, academic, and research libraries. [R: Choice, Oct 86, p. 284; RBB, 15 Oct 86, pp. 338-39]—**Marie Ellis**

14   Applied Arts

INTRODUCTION

Applied arts is a subject that does not quite fit in fine arts or crafts, and because of that, it is being listed here as a separate chapter including Decorative Arts, Fashion, Photography, and Type Designers. The section Decorative Arts contains books on designers in general, such as *Contemporary Designers* (St. James Press, 1990) (see entry 769), which provides biographical information on more than 600 designers in the areas of interiors, display, textile, fashion, product, industrial, graphic, and other design fields, and *The International Dictionary of Women Workers in the Decorative Arts: A Historical Survey from the Distant Past to the Early Decades of the Twentieth Century* (Scarecrow, 1981) (see entry 770), which, though now somewhat older, still provides information on women in the applied arts and design throughout the ages. One recent source of note for biographies in the field of fashion design is *Contemporary Fashion* (St. James Press, 1995) (see entry 772), which covers 1945 to the present with access to information on more than 400 clothing and accessory designers.

There is a new and important biographical dictionary in the area of photography. The 3rd edition of *Contemporary Photographers* (St. James Press, 1995) (see entry 775), provides biographical information on contemporary photographers worldwide, and remains an important source. In addition, we have included the older *American Photographers: An Illustrated Who's Who . . .* (Facts on File, 1989) (see entry 774), which provides biographies on over 1,000 photographers living and working today, and finally, one of the only sources for African American photographers is *An Illustrated Bio-Bibliography of Black Photographers, 1940-1988* (Garland, 1989) (see entry 777), which is a companion book to *Black Photographers, 1840-1940* (Garland, 1986).

DECORATIVE ARTS

769.   **Contemporary Designers**. 2nd ed. Colin Naylor, ed. Chicago, St. James Press, 1990. 641p. illus. $135.00. 756'092'2. ISBN 0-912289-69-4.

This is an expanded and updated edition of a major reference work. The careers and accomplishments of over 600 designers are covered with biographic data, bibliographic information, and highly relevant commentary. The result is an authoritative, comprehensive survey of the major figures in the 1990s. Leading international designers are presented along with many who are deceased but still influential. The fields of design covered are architecture, interiors, display, textile, fashion, product, industrial, graphic, and stage and films. The principal designers are all here, including Halston, Edith Head, the Chermayeff Associates, Erte, Michael Graves, Tschichold, Herman Zapf, Chwast, Lenica, Emilio Ambasz, Bernard Leach, Japanese designers by the score, and hundreds more from around the world.

This is a gigantic undertaking, with 225 design critics and historians contributing the essays. As with similar publications from St. James Press, the value of the information is greatly enhanced by statements from many of the designers. This primary source opinion and information, the well-prepared biographies and bibliographies, and the crisp black-and-white photographs of specific creations and products present unique and worthwhile entries of value to students, librarians, feature writers, and researchers. This is an essential reference book for individuals and institutions involved in the complex world of design. [R: BR, May/June 91, p. 59; RBB, 15 Feb 91, p. 1245]—**William J. Dane**

770.   **The International Dictionary of Women Workers in the Decorative Arts: A Historical Survey from the Distant Past to the Early Decades of the Twentieth Century**. Alice Irma Prather-Moses, comp. Metuchen, N.J., Scarecrow, 1981. 200p. bibliog. index. $15.00. LC 81-8947. ISBN 0-8108-1450-1.

This is an alphabetical dictionary of women throughout the ages who were known for their work in the decorative arts. It includes textile workers, metal and ceramic workers, architects, jewelers, and assorted other crafts people. In most cases, the biographies are quite brief, short paragraphs which give an account of the woman's career, her major works and/or exhibitions, and limited material on her personal life. The introduction traces women's involvement in the decorative arts scene from prehistoric times to the present, and Prather-Moses also provides a large bibliography and subject index. While undeniably presenting the reader with a wealth of previously inaccessible information, this rather specialized work will be an essential purchase only for major art and all-inclusive university collections.—**Deborah Hammer**

771.   **Who's Who in Interior Design**. Laguna Beach, Calif., Barons Who's Who, 1988- . index. $145.00 for recent edition. LC 89-081540. ISSN 0897-5914.

Worldwide in coverage, this directory profiles more than 3,000 professional designers currently active in some 61 countries, republics, and principalities. The scope of their work includes architecture, contract health care, hospitality, industrial, residential, and transportation design. A select number of interior design editors and educators are also listed.

Such factors as education, career experience, awards and honors, publication of projects, major projects completed, memberships, and community services were all major criteria for inclusion. Great effort was made to ensure the accuracy of the profiles, including careful nomination, independent research of leading interior-design publications, and verification of each biographical profile by the biographee.

Although the geographical coverage is heavily focused on North America, Western Europe, and Asia's Pacific Rim, there are numerous entries from Africa, the Middle East, South America, and Inner Asia. In some cases information was dependent upon government cooperation, and in areas such as Eastern Europe this was not always forthcoming.

Each entry includes the biographee's name, specialization, birthplace and date, family data, education, career, awards, memberships, projects and projects published, political and religious affiliations, avocations, address, and telephone number. Alphabetical in arrangement, the 412-page profile section is supplemented by a geographical index by country, which is then broken down by city. Designers are listed within each city. For the United States the listing is by state, then by city and designer. Thus the user has easy worldwide geographical access to the interior design profession. There is also a section listing and describing major interior design organizations. Aimed at other interior-design professionals, business and civic leaders, researchers, biographers, librarians, educators, and students, this directory should admirably fulfill any reference or research need.—**G. Joan Burns**

FASHION

772.   **Contemporary Fashion**. Richard Martin, ed. Detroit, St. James Press, 1995. 575p. illus. index. $135.00. ISBN 1-55862-173-3.

Contemporary Fashion is a much-needed addition to the area of biographical fashion reference. It is international in scope, providing access to more than 400 clothing designers, accessory designers, and design houses. Each entry furnishes a personal and professional biography, including awards, exhibitions, and an address; a bibliography of books and articles by and about the designer; a critical essay by a scholar in the field; and in some cases, a designer statement about work and design philosophy.

The scope of this work is 1945 to the present, and it covers early designers such as Fortuny, Elsa Schiaparelli, Rodier, and Liberty of London, to current designers such as Vivienne Westwood and Issey Miyake. This source is illustrated with handsome black-and-white photographs, exemplifying the work of the designers. The editor, the curator of the Costume Institute of the Metropolitan Museum of Art, has assembled an excellent group of fashion experts as contributors. A nationality and a name index are also included. *Contemporary Fashion* is an essential purchase for any library collection fielding questions in the area of fashion.—**Monica Fusich**

773.   Stegemeyer, Anne. **Who's Who in Fashion**. 3d ed. New York, Fairchild, 1995. 300p. illus. index. $22.50. LC 95-061081. ISBN 0-56367-040-7.

The 3rd edition of this biographical dictionary emphasizes designers with an established track record, although it also includes influential persons in related fields and some up-and-coming stars. The author has made several changes to the 3rd edition to aid in its relevance as a reference source. Its new arrangement combines entries on foreign and American designers into one alphabetical listing. Only the "Names to Know" section is separated, as it was in the 1st edition. This separate section is much condensed from its predecessor, as many of the names from the 1st edition have been inserted into the main alphabetical part of the volume.

The majority of the entries are illustrated with photographs of the designers and their creations. Most entries are fairly short, but the bibliography gives the reader numerous suggestions for further sources. Some of the better-known designers do warrant a full page or more and several illustrations. Recommended for all types and levels of libraries.—**Laurie Saboll and Robert L. Wick**

PHOTOGRAPHY

774.   **American Photographers: An Illustrated Who's Who**.... Les Krantz, ed. New York, Facts on File, 1989. 352p. illus. index. $40.00. o.p. TR139.K73. 770'.92'273. LC 89-1435. ISBN 0-8160-1419-1.

This comprehensive reference source chronicles America's top living photographers. Up-to-date and visually beautiful, the volume surveys the lives and works of more than 1,000 photographers, from the superstars of the fashion and advertising worlds to Pulitzer Prize-winning photojournalists. To be included, photographers had to have a minimum of five years professional experience and had their work reproduced in at least five media in 1988.

The book is arranged alphabetically and provides easy access to biographical information on each artist that includes name, address, and telephone number; major exhibitions and awards; fields of specialization; and a concise history. Included are an extremely practical index that cross-references photographers by location and specialty, a listing of stock photograph agencies, and an index of illustrations.

This is a very special reference source lavishly printed on quality paper with over 300 exquisite black-and-white photographs and 109 in color. It is an indispensable reference work for laymen, art directors, public relations specialists, librarians, and students. [R: LJ, 15 Nov 89, p. 76]—**Thomas L. Hart**

775.   **Contemporary Photographers**. 3d ed. Martin Marix Evans, ed. Detroit, St. James Press, 1995. 1234p. illus. index. $160.00. ISBN 1-55862-190-3.

By all positive standards, the 3d edition of this worldwide survey is a remarkable compilation for its depth of coverage as well as for a truly extraordinary gathering of facts and expert opinions. The contemporaneity of the material is stressed up front in a note from the editor, which informs us that more than 140 new entrants have been prepared for this 1995 edition and that photographers who died before 1975, along with some who have not added significantly to their corpus since the 2d edition (see ARBA 89, entry 891) are not included. This is important information for those who now own the 1987 edition, for they should most certainly hold onto it if they are seriously interested in biography and history of the art of photography.

Each entry covers copious material, with many giving a summary of the philosophy and objectives of their work in the photographer's own words. This is frequently followed up with a cogent article by an authority on the photographer's art and career. The text is immensely rewarding and highly readable as it covers the earlier generation—for example, André Kertész, Gyula Brassaï, Ansel Adams, Gordon Parks, Man Ray—through newer and prominent photographers such as Sandy Skoglund and the Bechers. The many contributions by women to the field are frequently noted, and entries are provided for Eve Arnold, Ruth Orkin, Jill Krementz, and Judith Joy Ross, as well as sometimes controversial practitioners such as Andres Serrano and Larry Clark.

The survey is universal, with a nationality index noting entries for scores of nations. The celebrated works of painter/photographers are also recognized with extensive text on David Hockney,

Robert Rauschenberg, Ed Ruscha, and Andy Warhol. The richness of the current state of the art of photography when viewed from a global perspective is astounding as revealed in 1,200-plus pages of text and illustration. Electronic innovations including digital manipulation in the realm of photography will undoubtedly change the future of this art as it is known today. However, this publication serves as a definitive reference source for the next decade and well into the next century. —**William J. Dane**

776.   **Photographers on Disc: An International Index of Photographers, Exhibitions, and Collections**. [CD- ROM]. New York, G. K. Hall/Simon & Schuster Macmillan, 1996. Minimum system requirements: IBM or compatible. CD-ROM drive with Microsoft CD-ROM Extensions 2.0. 512K RAM. $495.00.

Price is the first detail one notices about this CD-ROM. To pay $495.00 for a DOS-based CD-ROM is perhaps a bit disconcerting for most librarians. The product itself is straightforward. It contains three files: an alphabetic list of photographers, with birth and death dates and nationality noted, as well as address if applicable; a list of institutions with collections in photography; and a list of exhibitions of the photographer's work. Searching is also straightforward and typical of CD-ROM products. One can search using Boolean techniques—combining terms and using Boolean limiters. Thus, a search on Ansel Adams can be done and combined with a term such as *Yosemite*. The result is a list of places that house those works by Adams. One can also directly search any index. Thus, one can go into the institution index, search directly for the name of a particular institution, and retrieve its name and address. Display and print functions are easily learned.

Some of the information on this disc is available in other standard sources such as *The Photographers Market, 1998* (see ARBA 98, entry 936) for biographical information on contemporary photographers, or *Index to American Photographic Collections* (Hall, 1995) for information on photography collections. This CD-ROM, however, also lists historical photographers in addition to ones currently active.

More unusual, and perhaps more helpful, is the list of exhibitions. The standard way to identify exhibitions that have been held on a photographer's work is to look through past editions of photography magazines and newsletters. Similarly, to locate upcoming exhibitions, one has to subscribe to or have access to these same publications and be willing to keep them up-to-date. This list of exhibitions, if updated on subsequent discs, should prove helpful. This brings us back to the original question: Is $495.00 too much to pay to have organized access to this information? It is a question that librarians will have to answer for themselves, considering their own situations, needs, and budgets.—**Terry Ann Mood**

777.   Willis-Thomas, Deborah. **An Illustrated Bio-Bibliography of Black Photographers 1940-1988**. New York, Garland, 1989. 483p. illus. (Garland Reference Library of the Humanities, v.760). $85.00. TR139.W55. 770'.92'2. LC 88-11200. ISBN 0-8240-8389-X.

This book is a companion volume to the author's *Black Photographers, 1840-1940: An Illustrated Bio-Bibliography* (see ARBA 86, entry 998) and includes over 300 black Americans who have worked as studio owners, photojournalists, and commercial and fine art photographers during the past 50 years. The work is extremely useful and thoughtfully researched, and is a valuable tool containing some difficult-to-find information. Willis-Thomas's perseverance and determination in collecting information about contemporary artists is commendable.

The entries are alphabetical and include the artist's name and dates of activity or geographic location of work. Better-documented photographers have brief biographical notes or comments on work, lists of exhibitions and collections, and bibliographies. A general bibliography of books and journal and newspaper articles is added, as well as a list of exhibits of black American photography from 1969 to 1987.

The book is physically attractive, with dignified page design and effective decoration. Over 300 pages beautifully reproduce the photographers' works and are worth the proverbial 1,000 words. [R: LJ, 15 June 89, p. 54; RBB, 1 Sept 89, p. 106; RQ, Winter 89, pp. 293-94]—**Linda A. Naru**

TYPE DESIGNERS

778.   Eason, Ron, and Sarah Rookiedge. **Rookiedge's International Handbook of Type Designers: A Biographical Directory**. Carshalton Beeches, England, Sarema Press; distr., Wakefield, R.I., Moyer Bell, c.1991, 1993. 209p. illus. $19.95. 686.220922. ISBN 1-55921-092-3.

Typography is a broad term that can mean different things to different people. All typography is creative; no design problem can be resolved without thoughtful and imaginative treatment of type forms. Interpreting the meaning of words through the manipulation of typefaces is the work of type designers. The lives and careers of more than 175 of these individuals are profiled here in an alphabetical arrangement, from Adobe Systems to Gundrun Zapf-von Hesse. Some 700 text typefaces are discussed, beginning with Gutenberg and proceeding to present-day designs. Sparsely illustrated with photographs of designers, typefaces, and alphabet samples, this book offers relatively obscure and narrowly focused information.

While this volume does not attempt fresh research, it does bring together, in a convenient format, information from a range of sources to stimulate interest in type and in those who have made it their life's work. There may be some debate on the merit of the designers selected for inclusion, but the brief entries will clear the shroud of anonymity surrounding most type designers. A subject index and typeface list provide invaluable access for scholars, designers, typographers, and graphic artists.

Other brief biographies of type designers do exist, generally buried within works such as *Twentieth Century Type Designers* (Taplinger, 1987) and *Modern Encyclopedia of Typefaces 1960-90* (Van Nostrand Reinhold, 1990), but this entertainingly presented biography is unique. It may strengthen one's sensitivity to letter forms and their creators and help dispel the mystery that surrounds this intriguing subject.—**Judy Gay Matthews**

15 Fine Arts

INTRODUCTION

Biographical works on persons involved in the fine arts, including graphic artists, architects, designers, painters, sculptors, computer artists, engravers, and topologists, are included in this chapter. The biographies are organized into broad categories of General Works Current Biographies (Retrospective Biographies), Architects and Designers (General Works, United States, Australia and New Zealand, and Great Britain), Graphic Artists, Canada, China, Greece, Latin America, Netherlands, Nigeria, Russia, Spain, Scotland, and United States (Current Biographies and Retrospective Biographies.

The biographical sources have been broadly selected, including *Contemporary Artists* (St. James Press, 1996) (see entry 780), which provides brief biographies of more than 800 artists; *Who's Who in American Art* (R. R. Bowker/Reed Reference Publishing, 1936/37-) (see entry 784), a standard source with over 600 entries kept up-to-date with yearly editions; and the *Encyclopedia of Living Artists: A Catalog of Works by Living Artists . . .* (ArtNetwork Press, 1993) (see entry 781), which should be extremely useful to a great number of people: art buyers, exhibitors, book editors, and art lovers, who will find the book itself worth keeping and consulting.

On the other end of the spectrum, a number of sources have been included that are much more specific, such as Richard Kostelanetz's *Dictionary of the Avant-Gardes* (Independent Publishers Group, 1993) (see entry 782), which provides biographies of a wide variety of avant-garde creators; *Folk Artists Biographical Index . . .* (Gale, 1987) (see entry 790), which includes artists who have been overlooked in dictionaries and encyclopedias focusing on biography; *North American Women Artists of the Twentieth Century: A Biographical Dictionary* (Garland, 1995) (see entry 794), a much-needed reference source that provides information on more than 1,500 women artists from Canada, Mexico, and the United States; and *Contemporary Architects* (St. James Press, 1994) (see entry 800), an excellent and classic reference source that covers architects and architectural partnerships of the past 50 years and includes 585 entries, 70 of which are new.

The section on graphic artists contains works that list graphic artists specifically and includes a wide variety of sources, such as Ron Goulart's *The Great Comic Book Artists* (St. Martin's Press, 1986) (see entry 815), which is for the public or high school library patron seeking a brief introduction to the world of comic book artists; *Artists of the Page: Interviews with Children's Book Illustrators* (McFarland, 1992) (see entry 819), which is filled with insights into the careers and lives of 30 children's book illustrators; and *A Biographical Dictionary of Science Fiction and Fantasy Artists* (Greenwood Press, 1988) (see entry 821), which includes nearly 280 artists and illustrators whose creations grace the covers and interiors of science fiction/fantasy books and magazines.

The geographical sections end with the United States, which includes current and retrospective sources such as Paul Cummings's *Dictionary of Contemporary American Artists* (St. Martin's Press, 1994) (see entry 833), which provides 900 biographies of individuals prominent in art; *Who's Who in American Art* (R. R. Bowker/Reed Reference Publishing, 1936/37-) (see entry 784), which includes nearly 12,000 representatives from all segments of the visual arts profession in North America; and Patrick Lester's *The Biographical Directory of Native American Painters* (University of Oklahoma Press, 1995) (see entry 836), which provides a valuable list of Native American artists. Also, a number of biographical sources from Canada, China, Greece, Latin America, Netherlands, Nigeria, Russia, Spain, and Scotland are included.

General encyclopedias of art, though not included here, are also good sources for biographical information, including *The Grove Dictionary of Art* (Dictionary of Art, 1996), which provides one of the largest lists of artists available; the *Oxford Companion to Twentieth-Century Art* (Oxford University Press, 1988); and the now somewhat older *Praeger Encyclopedia of Art* (5v. Praeger, 1971), which still provides valuable biographical information on artists.

Finally, it is important to remember that biographies on specific artists can be searched using index services, including the *Art Index: A Cumulative Author and Subject Index to a Selected List of Fine Arts Periodicals and Museum Bulletins* (H. W. Wilson, 1933-), the *Index to Art Periodicals* (11 vols.; Supplements; G. K. Hall, 1962), the *Index to Artistic Biography* (2 v. Scarecrow, 1973), and Jack Robertson's *Twentieth-Century Artists on Art: An Index to Artists Writings, Statement, & Interviews* (Macmillan Pub. Co., 1985). Also, there are two other indexes that are worth consulting: *Artist Biographies Master Index: A Consolidated Index to More Than 275,000 Biographical Sketches of Artists Living and Dead . . .* (Gale, 1986) and *Biographies of Creative Artists: An Annotated Bibliography* (Garland, 1991).

GENERAL WORKS

Current Biographies

779.   **St. James Guide to Black Artists**. Thomas Riggs, ed. Detroit, St. James Press, 1997. 625p. illus. index. $155.00. ISBN 1-55862-220-9.

The *St. James Guide to Black Artists* contains biographical and career information on 400 of the most well-known black artists worldwide. Approximately 75 percent (around 300 artists) were alive at the time of publication, and the remainder were active in the early part of the twentieth century. The research for the volume was done with the assistance of the New York Public Library's Schomburg Center for Research in Black Culture. A few of the artists included were active in the nineteenth century. Although the entries vary from a few remarks about the individual to complete essays detailing his or her life, the coverage is generally adequate, and in some cases extensive. In addition, there are more than 300 illustrations (mostly portraits of the artists covered).

Even though there is no shortage of biographical dictionaries of black artists in print, the *St. James Guide* is unique not only in its depth of coverage but its inclusion of a number of artists from Africa, the Caribbean, Brazil, and other countries that have not had good coverage. Several works already available will complement this work, including Robert Doty's *Contemporary Black Artists in America* (Whitney Museum of American Art, 1971); David Driskell's *Two Centuries of Black American Art* (Los Angeles County Museum of Arts, 1976); and the Albany Institute of History and Art's compilation titled *The Negro Artist Comes of Age: A National Survey of Contemporary American Artists* (1945). In addition, there have been some notable works covering black women artists, including *Gumbo YaYa: Anthology of Contemporary African-American Women Artists* (Midmarch Arts Press, 1995).

Each entry in the present publication includes a brief biographical sketch; a timeline showing exhibitions, collections, and publications; and a biographical essay covering the individual's life and work. Some of the essays are "critical" in the sense of critiquing some of the works of the artists. The illustrations, even though all black-and-white, are nicely produced and generally quite interesting. The *St. James Guide to Black Artists* is highly recommended for all larger academic and public libraries with specialized collections, and at the same time it should be of value to smaller academic, public, and school libraries that wish to select a good biographical source for black artists. [R: RBB, 15 Oct 97, pp. 429-30]—**Robert L. Wick**

780.   **Contemporary Artists**. 4th ed. Joann Cerrito and others, eds. Detroit, St. James Press, 1996. 1340p. illus. index. $160.00. ISBN 1-55862-183-0.

The 4th edition of this biographical dictionary is a welcome update to the 3d edition, published in 1989 (see ARBA 90, entry 948). Profiles of more than 800 individuals representing all areas of the fine arts are arranged alphabetically. The editor notes that for this edition a special effort was made to include artists working in the fields of video and computer art. Selection criteria continue to be a record of exhibitions in major galleries or museums that have attracted significant critical attention. Entries for deceased artists are included only when they are perceived to be a continuing influence on current practice, although no artist who died before 1965 has been included (as opposed to 1960 for the 3d edition).

Entries include biographical data, a list of individual exhibitions and selected group exhibitions, collections, sites of permanent public installations (a new feature), an artist's statement when supplied, bibliographies of publications by and about the artist, and a signed critical essay. Black-and-white photographs of representative works accompany many of the entries. As a source of in-depth information on the most prominent of contemporary artists, this title remains an essential acquisition for all art libraries.—**Michael Weinberg**

781.	**Encyclopedia of Living Artists: A Catalog of Works by Living Artists.** . . . 7th ed. Constance Franklin-Smith, ed. Renaissance, Calif., ArtNetwork Press, 1993. illus. index. $17.95pa. ISBN 0-940899-22-1.

This remarkable publication should be extremely useful to a great number of people: art buyers, exhibitors, book editors, and art lovers, who will find the book itself worth keeping and consulting. The entries, all in full color, range from abstract art to impressionistic renditions to academically precise watercolors, all the way down to plain kitsch. A separate section is devoted to sculpture. As might be expected in a collection of this kind, some works are derivative, but most are highly original. A notable segment is the extensive chapter devoted to computer art, which presents several astoundingly inventive and attractive works of art. (Some of these, in addition to dimensions, carry their measurements in pixels.) Artists from the United States and Canada are featured, but there are also a number of artists from Holland, Norway, the Dominican Republic, Mexico, Germany, Argentina, and Singapore. All are supplied with addresses and telephone numbers (in the case of most of the foreign artists, their U.S. agents are listed). The back of the book contains concise biographical sketches of all included artists, their previous exhibitions, and brief descriptions of their style.—**Koraljka Lockhart**

782.	Kostelanetz, Richard. **Dictionary of the Avant-Gardes**. Chicago, A Capella Books; distr., Chicago, Independent Publishers Group, 1993. 246p. illus. $16.95pa. NX456.K67. 700'.9'04. LC 93-17793. ISBN 1-55652-202-9.

In his preface Kostelanetz points out that his "principal reason for doing a book of this title would be to defend the continuing relevance of the epithet 'avant-garde,' which frequently appears in my own critical writing. A second reason is that I enjoy reading dictionaries myself. . . ." This is precisely what one wants to do with this dictionary: read it from cover to cover. Kostelanetz's work is a biographical dictionary of the avant-garde creators, not specifically the avant-garde movement. The introduction provides a lengthy definition of the avant-garde as "art that is ahead of its time—that is beginning something—while decadent art, by contrast, stands at the end of a prosperous development."

Much of the charm of the book lies in the opinionated and sometimes irreverent comments found in the text of the entries. Kostelanetz often cuts directly to the point, as in his entry on John Cage, where he points out that Cage "was among the rare artists whose statements about his own work were more true and insightful than his critics' writings." Or in his comment about Dave Morice, who is referred to as "one of the few writers . . . to have an M.F.A. from the mass-production lines of the Writer's Workshop at the University of Iowa." Other individuals included in the work are Northrop Frye, who "belongs in [the] book less for his major theories, which remain influential, than for passing insights into avant-garde writing that remain freshly persuasive"; Conlon Nancarrow, the jazz trumpeter, who studied composition with Nicholas Slonimsky, who is also listed; Laszlo Moholy-Nagy (of the Bauhaus school); Robert Moog (who popularized the electronic music synthesizer); Buster Keaton; and Roy Lichtenstein of pop art fame.

The source of information for each entry is listed at the end of the item, and a bibliography of the dictionaries is included in the postface (20 items). [R: LJ, 15 Feb 94, p. 152; RBB, 1 Apr 94, p. 1474; WLB, June 94, p. 93]—**Robert L. Wick**

783.   Smith, V. Babington. **Dictionary of Contemporary Artists**. Santa Barbara, Calif., ABC-Clio Press, 1981. 451p. index. $47.50. ISBN 0-903450-46-1.

The *Dictionary of Contemporary Artists* is the first of a planned annual series to be published by ABC-Clio Press on beginning and little-known living and working artists whose work is now exhibited in galleries and museums around the world. Unfortunately, no more volumes have been published in this series since 1981. Entries are alphabetical by artist, providing brief bibliographical and biographical information, including exhibition details. All artistic disciplines are covered, including ceramicists, jewelers, painters, printmakers, and video artists. The most useful feature of the work is the inclusion of full addresses for over 700 exhibiting galleries and museums which publish catalogs and brochures on artists and their works. This biographical dictionary could well become the easiest and fastest method to trace biographical and exhibition details on contemporary artists. [R: Choice, Nov 81, p. 355; RQ, Fall 81, pp. 92-93]—**Maureen Pastine**

784.   **Who's Who in American Art**. New Providence, N.J., R. R. Bowker/Reed Reference Publishing, 1936/37- . index. $189.00 for recent edition. ISSN 0000-0191.

Nearly 12,000 representatives from all segments of the visual arts profession in North America are profiled in this annual publication. The book covers artists, administrators, historians, educators, lecturers, collectors, librarians, publishers, critics, consultants, curators, and dealers. Entries are arranged alphabetically and cite vital statistics, professional titles, education and training, and mailing addresses. Also given is a description of professional activities that may include works in public collections; commissions; exhibitions; publications; positions held with schools, museums, or organizations; memberships in art societies; honors and awards; an interest or research statement; media; and the dealer. All entries are indexed by geographical location and professional classification. In addition, a necrology is provided, which is cumulative from 1953.

Criteria for selection are not thoroughly discussed, but the editor states that new names were obtained through nominations of current entrants, and subsequently went through a selection process based on "works in public collections, commissioned works, and exhibitions of an international, national and wide regional scope in noncommercial galleries and museums." Non-artists were chosen on the basis of position and experience in the field. Thus, while some accomplished artists and art professionals are not included, lesser-known individuals may receive full citations. In spite of its inevitable weaknesses, this is an informative work and should be considered for all large public and academic libraries.—**Barbara Ittner and Robert L. Wick**

785.   **Who's Who in Art**. London: The Art Trade Press, Ltd. 1927- . illus. $90.00 for recent edition.

This standard British biographical source has been published since 1927, although its appearance was irregular until about 1980; it is now published biennially. The work includes names of British artists for the most part. A number of artists who also live and work in the United States and elsewhere are included. Included are biographies of leading men and women in the world of art today—artists, designers, craftsmen, critics, writers, teachers, collectors and curators, with appendices of signatures. Recent editions include more than 3,000 names of living artists. A typical entry in the alphabetically arranged section includes the artist's name, memberships and honors, art specialty, place and date of birth, parentage, marriage, education, exhibits, work in permanent collections, studio address, and how work is signed. Listings vary in length from 4 or 5 lines to a half page, with most entries being about 10 lines long. An appendix of artists' signatures is interesting and potentially useful.—**Frank J. Anderson and Robert L. Wick**

Retrospective Biographies

786.   Bailey, Brooke. **The Remarkable Lives of 100 Women Artists**. Holbrook, Mass., Adams Publishing, 1994. 207p. index. (20th Century Women Series). $12.00. ISBN 1-55850-360-9.

Whereas Frank N. Magill's *Great Lives from History: American Women Series* presents its information in a highly structured, consistently formatted manner appropriate to ready-reference work, this book instead focuses on the stories of the women's lives. Entries generally are one- to two-page narratives that attempt to recount the essential and influential events, people, and ideas that informed each artist's "unique personal vision." Bailey has thrown a wide net, encompassing architects, archivists of indigenous American music, blues performers, classical composers, collage artists, concert pianists, filmmakers, folk dancers, illustrators, jazz singers, muralists, photographers, sculptors, and even a trapeze performer among her women artists. Although each entry concludes with a very brief list of resources "to find out more," this delightful work has been designed more for inspiration than reference-desk duty.—**G. Kim Dority**

787. **A Biographical Dictionary of Artists.** rev. ed. Lawrence Gowing, ed. New York, Facts on File, 1995. 784p. illus. index. $50.00. ISBN 0-8160-3252-1.
This well-designed and handsomely printed volume was edited by Gowing, himself a painter and Slade Professor of Art at London University. The length of each of the 1,340 alphabetical entries usually matches the relative importance of the artists (although Vincent van Gogh is given more space than Leonardo da Vinci, and Holman Hunt more than Henri-Marie-Raymond de Toulouse-Lautrec), and each provides a clear, vivid, and perceptive synthesis of both the life and the work. Francis Bacon's "handling of paint [is] heavily worked in smears to suggest the vulnerability and flexibility of flesh and blood"; Goya's *Disasters of War,* which depicts "the inhumanity to which all classes in Spain had been reduced, contrasts with the self-confident sentimentality of official military art in Napoleonic France." Many, although not all, of the entries include an essential bibliography. There are also an extensive chronology, a glossary, and an index. The essays are more elaborate than those in *The Oxford Companion to Art* (see ARBA 71, entry 1079), and much broader in scope than the more individualistic pieces in *Lives of the Great Twentieth Century Artists* (see ARBA 88, entry 1010). The only errors noticed are minor: [Diego Rodriguez de Silva] Velasquez is misspelled in the Bacon essay, Wyndham Lewis went blind in 1951 (not 1950), and Kenneth Clark's *Leonardo da Vinci* was published in 1939 (not 1967).
The only significant artist missing from the book (and supplementary index) is the Italian surrealist Leonor Fini. The volume emphasizes, quite reasonably, English artists and illustrations from British museums. The essays on Jacques Callot, Vittore Carpaccio, Albrecht Dürer, Hans Holbein, Andrea Mantegna, Henry Moore, and Edvard Munch are especially good; and there are also useful articles on critics and impresarios such as Charles Baudelaire, Emile Zola, and Sergey Pavlovich Diaghilev. The illustrations—many of them full- or half-page color plates—are superb, and the book's low price is astonishing.—**Jeffrey Meyers**

788. **Dictionary of Women Artists.** Delia Gaze, ed. Chicago, Fitzroy Dearborn, 1997. 2v. illus. $250.00/set. ISBN 1-884964-21-4.
Another star is born in the fields of art research and women's studies with the publication of *The Dictionary of Women Artists* from Fitzroy Dearborn. This two-volume reference work is a welcome addition to the above-mentioned fields.
Arranged alphabetically by name of artist, each article is a scholarly overview of the artist's life, including training/biographical information as well as critical and stylistic interpretations of her works. Two indexes enhance this alphabetic arrangement. One is an alphabetic list of all artists (name only), and the other is a chronological list. These lists are included at the front of both volumes. As stated in the foreword, no one born since 1945 is included; this dictionary is a historical survey. The dictionary is also international in scope. Several factors were used in determining what artists were to be included, which are detailed in the foreword as well. However, the concentration is on the fine arts (painting, sculpture, photography, and the like) as opposed to the applied arts. Even though the volume presents scholarly entries, many different users, from high school age through graduate-level researchers, can use it.
In comparing this title to the recently published *Dictionary of Art*, it becomes obvious that the two works complement each other. For example, the bibliographies are quite different. The bibliographies in *Dictionary of Women Artists* are arranged chronologically and are composed of the key works relating to the entry. They vary in comprehensiveness. For example, the bibliography for Frida Kahlo contains 25 items. The bibliographies in the *Dictionary of Art* are alphabetic by main entry, are

selective, and tend to focus on the core primary sources. The Kahlo bibliography here consists of seven items, three of which are not included in the formerly mentioned bibliography.

There are 11 introductory surveys that cover the full range of art history, beginning with an essay entitled "Women as Artists in the Middle Ages" and ending with "Feminism and Women Artists." All of these are comprehensive and add immense value to this work. The only noticeable flaw is the illustrations, which appear only in black-and-white. Also, there is a wide range in the quality of the illustrations. Some are clear and well reproduced; others are dreadful. This difference in reproduction quality may have to do with the originals used at the source. This flaw is minor given the overall excellence of the work, especially because there are many sources for illustrations. *Dictionary of Women Artists* is highly recommended for most academic and larger public libraries.—**Roland C. Hansen**

789.   Ergas, G. Aimée. **Artists: From Michelangelo to Maya Lin**. Detroit, U*X*L/Gale, 1995. 2v. illus. index. $38.00/set. ISBN 0-8103-9862-1.

This 2-volume reference work designed for children 10 and up, or grades 5 and up, is an excellent biographical guide to 62 well-known North American and European artists (sculptors, painters, architects, photographers, illustrators, and designers) who have changed the face of art from the Renaissance to the present. It includes many women and minority artists as well. Artists covered range from Ansel Adams to Mary Cassatt, Paul Cezanne, Marc Chagall, Vincent van Gogh, El Greco, Edward Hopper, Maya Lin, Michelangelo, Georgia O'Keeffe, Pablo Picasso, Faith Ringgold, Diego Rivera, and Titian.

Artists are first arranged alphabetically by name with birth and death dates when applicable, followed by the major section, divided first by fields and media, and then alphabetically by artist. This section provides many black-and-white photographs of the artists and selected works. Fields and media treated range from architecture to collage, etching, furniture design, lithography, needlework, photography, sculpture, and wrap art.

The biographical entries attend to the personal experiences, motivations, and social and artistic climates that impacted the artists. Entries are from 5 to 10 pages in length; they are clear and informative. Boxed sidebars are frequently furnished to denote the importance of movements, events, or processes such as impressionism and composition.

A glossary defines such key terminology as abstract art, fauvism, pointillism, rococo, still life, surrealism, and woodcuts. The prefatory pages in each volume include some key times for events in art and history. The end of each volume has a selective reading list for further information, along with a comprehensive index of biographees and illustrations.—**Maureen Pastine**

790.   **Folk Artists Biographical Index: A Guide to over 200 Published Sources of Information on Approximately 9,000 Folk Artists**. . . . George H. Meyer, George H. Meyer, Jr., and Katherine P. White, eds. Detroit, Gale, 1987. 496p. $40.00. LC 86-15029. ISBN 0-8103-2145-9.

As we move rapidly towards the twenty-first century, more research is being done on all aspects of American art history as curators, collectors, and the art world in general continuously evaluate our stunning visual heritage. Folk artists have been overlooked in dictionaries and encyclopedias focusing on biography in the area of the fine arts. With this publication, the director of the Museum of American Folk Art documents biographical data on over 9,000 folk artists, including birth and death dates, type of work, period of activity, and bibliographic citations to other printed sources. The diversity of the art fields covered is complex, and includes sculpture, furniture, calligraphy, trade signs, pottery, painting, fabrics, and specific items such as canes, weather vanes, decoys, mourning samplers, coverlets, quilts, and circus banners.

Approximately 210 publications were culled to glean the biographic information recorded for each artist, and these titles were thoroughly searched page-by-page for relevant material by the editor and his research staff. A broad definition of folk art was considered when searching for the individual artists to be recorded. The major part of the book is devoted to an alphabetical listing of individuals, but five specific indexes add greatly to the reference function of the book. These indexes were compiled using a computer database format, and list artists by the name of the museum owning their works, by ethnic origin, by media, and by type of work produced. The last index, which records the eclectic and highly imaginative materials created by the American folk art community, presents a clear picture of the staggering diversity of objects which were produced from coast to coast from the seventeenth century right up to the present.

The editor quite frankly states that there is considerable room for future editions to be expanded, corrected, and revised. However, this initial publication brings a sense of organization and order to the folk art tradition in our nation. The thousands of living artists as well as those interested in historical aspects will benefit from the massive amount of information which has been carefully compiled in this single volume. [R: BL, 1 Sept 87, p. 38; Choice, Nov 87, p. 454]—**William J. Dane**

791. **Great Artists of the Western World**. Clive Gregory and Sue Lyon, eds. Freeport, N.Y., Marshall Cavendish, 1987. 10v. illus. (part col.). index. $299.95/set. LC 86-23863. ISBN 0-86307-743-9.

New ways to introduce the general public to the joys of art history continue to be produced, though there never seems to be any shortage of books on the market for this audience. The latest contender for public attention is an attractive ten-volume hardcover set called the *Great Artists of the Western World*, published originally in England.

The organizational principles of the series are based on the identification of a significant art historical period and the selection of four artists, primarily painters, from the pre-Renaissance through modern periods. Each of the painters chosen is analyzed in a series of five subsections covering biography, methods and style, cultural background, contemporary events, and a "gallery" of works. Short bibliographies and a general index are also provided. While the text is clearly and interestingly written, the abundance of color illustrations on every page should be the strongest selling point for the set.

For the casual reader or the home student, *Great Artists* will be an easy way to learn about major European and American artists and important concepts, but libraries should have reservations about paying the $300.00 price this series carries. The selection of periods and artists is idiosyncratic at best, neglecting styles like post-Impressionism, French Romanticism, and the Italian Baroque. Van Gogh, Cezanne, Caravaggio, Bernini, Delacroix, and most twentieth-century artists get only cursory mention. The lack of art historians in the credits for this series is also a problem and damages the credibility of the text for academic consideration. Therefore, with the Metropolitan Museum in New York issuing a similar set in 1988, the prudent librarian may choose to wait before purchasing *Great Artists of the Western World.*—**Stephanie C. Sigala**

792. **International Dictionary of Art and Artists**. James Vinson, ed. Chicago, St. James Press, 1990. 2v. illus. index. $120.00/v. 700. ISBN 1-55862-001-X (Art); 1-55862-000-1 (Artists).

This work seeks to explain art history by presenting biographical sketches of artists and critical essays on important works of art. Volume 1 is an alphabetically arranged group of short biographies of the Western world's most important artists since the thirteenth-century painter Cimabue. Within each entry an excellent arrangement allows the reader to quickly find the information needed. For each artist 4 sections are given: a paragraph of facts about the artist's life, location of the artist's major works, a bibliography, and a critical article of up to 2,000 words.

Volume 2 is a chronologically arranged series of essays on artwork of importance, starting with Cimabue's *Santa Trinita Madonna* and continuing to Andy Warhol's *Gold Marilyn Monroe*. Each work is pictured in black-and-white; naturally, some works have reproduced better than others. Ambrogio Lorenzetti's *Good and Bad Government,* for example, suffers from the extreme reduction needed to reproduce a room-sized fresco onto a book page.

The well-written essays concentrate on explaining the work, putting it in historical context, and describing its influence on later artists. The articles in both volumes are written mainly by art historians, and in most cases the writer of the artist's biography has written the critical article on the artist's work in volume 2 as well. Since volume 2 is arranged chronologically, an index of artists helps to identify specific works. An index of artwork locations is helpful because it allows the reader to learn about works in a specific museum before visiting the institution.

It would be helpful to cross-reference the works in volume 2 within the biographies in volume 1. Since the work does not include any Eastern or African artists or any classical art, it might better be called a dictionary of Western art. Further, it does not define any art movements or techniques. However, as a source for information about Western artists and their work, and as an overview of Western painting and sculpture, it is an excellent supplement to the now-aging *Encyclopedia of World Art* (McGraw-Hill, 1959-1968). [R: WLB, Dec 90, p. 152]—**Linda Keir Simons**

793.   Lucie-Smith, Edward. **Lives of the Great Twentieth Century Artists**. New York, Rizzoli, 1986. 359p. illus. (part col.). bibliog. index. $45.00. LC 86-3195. ISBN 0-8478-0722-3.

Edward Lucie-Smith, a British art critic who has written at least thirty-five books about art and artists, has created a highly unusual reference work. Stating that it is "impertinently modeled on the greatest classic of Renaissance art history, Giorgio Vasari's *Lives of the Artists*" (Introduction). Lucie-Smith has collected intimate, even gossipy, biographies. They are arranged not alphabetically, but roughly chronologically. The lives of 101 artists are described in twenty-seven chapters which reflect major trends in the art of this century. Beginning with "Towards the Modern," "The Fauves," "Cubism," "Futurism," and "German Expressionism," the volume ends with a chapter titled "The Artist Not the Art-Work," which discusses Yves Klein and Joseph Beuys. Each chapter has a succinct introduction describing the style or movement, followed by lively illustrated biographies of some of the outstanding artists.

All of the entries, while concise, are written in a more fully narrative and anecdotal style than that found in *Contemporary Artists* (2d ed. St. Martin's Press, 1983), for example, which not only gives biographical information, but lists works and references for over 1,000 artists in a straight alphabetical arrangement. Lucie-Smith's work is highly selective, and most of the artists included are indeed "great" artists: Picasso, Braque, Miro, Magritte, Arp, Dali, Duchamp, Modigliani, Mondrian, Schiele, Soutine, and Tanguy, etc. There are only five women included, and some of the men may be unfamiliar to Americans: David Bomberg, Mikhail Larinov, and Paul Nash, for example. While seven Russian and three Mexican artists are included, most are from Western Europe and the United States.

The artistic development is certainly discussed in the context of each biography, but the emphasis is upon the personal life of each artist. There are excellent portraits and reproductions of art included, but the family relationships, education, friendships, artistic growth, and life experiences are stressed. Although the arrangement is stylistic and chronological, it is not a scholarly survey such as H. H. Arnason's *History of Modern Art* (2d ed. Abrams, 1977).

There are a bibliography and an alphabetical list of artists at the back of the book. However, there is no true index, and the many other artists and various subjects mentioned cannot be easily located. The bibliography would have been far more useful if appropriate references had been appended to the individual artists' biographies or to each chapter.

Very scholarly art libraries may not need or want this volume. However, many public and undergraduate library patrons will enjoy this book, which brings a more "human" dimension to the great artists of this century.—**Sydney Starr Keaveney**

794.   **North American Women Artists of the Twentieth Century: A Biographical Dictionary**. Jules Heller and Nancy G. Heller, eds. Hamden, Conn., Garland, 1995. 612p. illus. index. (Garland Reference Library of the Humanities, v.1219). $125.00. ISBN 0-8240-6049-0.

This much-needed reference source provides information on more than 1,500 women artists from Canada, Mexico, and the United States. Each entry includes concise biographical and exhibition information and a brief bibliography. To be included in this dictionary, an artist must have been born before 1960, have lived or worked in the United States, Canada, or Mexico, and have shown a serious commitment to the arts as proven by participation in exhibitions and a body of literature about that artist. Well-known artists such as Imogen Cunningham, Frida Kahlo, and Georgia O'Keeffe are covered, as well as lesser-known artists such as Grace Medicine Flower, a Native American potter, and Ulayu Pingwartok, a Canadian Inuit graphic artist. A variety of fields are represented, such as painting, performance art, sculpture, printmaking, ceramics, fibers, metals, and photography. More than 100 black-and-white illustrations, revealing the abundance of North American women's artistic output, are included. This is an excellent and timely reference work, filled with important information on women artists. It is an important and basic addition to any art collection.—**Monica Fusich**

795. **The Oxford Dictionary of Art**. Ian Chilvers and Harold Osborne, eds. Consultant editor, Dennis Farr. New York, Oxford University Press, 1997. $39.95. ISBN 0-19-86008-4-4.

Every academic and public library will want a copy of the *Oxford Dictionary of Art*, but some libraries may want to order an extra for the ready-reference librarian. A successor to the Oxford *Companion* titles on art (1970), decorative arts (1975), and twentieth-century art (1981), the 3,000 new volume entries have been rewritten extensively, shortened, and updated for quick consultations. Like other one-volume comprehensive guides to art, the majority of the entries in the new work describe the significance of individual artists. Most of the entries are two or three paragraphs, however, so the sort of factual detail one might find in a biographical dictionary has been eliminated in favor of well-considered, but succinct, historical assessment. New in this work are hard-to-find descriptions of contemporary art historical terms ("luminism," or "School of Paris") that have come into general use only in the last decade.

Some things are missing from the dictionary. Long articles on national art histories familiar from the *Oxford Companions* are now banished, as are pictures and bibliography. Architects and architecture are only discussed in relation to other media, and non-Western artforms are ignored unless they have affected European art traditions. Because of these subject limitations, one might wish for another less inclusive title, but what this dictionary sets out to do it does well; it will become a reference standard.—**Stephanie C. Sigala and Robert L. Wick**

796. Petteys, Chris, and others. **Dictionary of Woman Artists: An International Dictionary of Women Artists Born before 1900**. Boston, G. K. Hall, 1985. 851p. bibliog. $49.95. LC 84-22511. ISBN 0-8161-8456-9.

This new comprehensive international biographical dictionary of more than 21,000 women painters, sculptors, printmakers, and illustrators born before 1900 is the most important publication on women artists to date. Photographers, architects, crafts workers, and designers are excluded. Entries include full name, married name, and pseudonyms (all cross-referenced), birth and death dates, the medium in which the artist worked, and subject matter for which she is known, place of residence, other artists in the family, formal education and teachers with whom she studied, exhibitions and awards, and further bibliographical references. The references given direct the scholar to collection locations and further materials on the artists included. An extremely valuable asset is the provisions of references consulted for each entry leading the researcher to even more information. Many individuals and publications provided source material, most notably the 36 volumes of Thieme Becker's *Aligemeines Lexicon der bildenden Künstler von derAntike bis zur Gegenwart*.

Used in conjunction with publications by Donna G. Bachmann and Sherry Piland, *Women Artists: An Historical, Contemporary, and Feminist Bibliography* (Scarecrow, 1978); Charlotte Streifer Rubenstein, *American Women Artists: From Early Indian Times to the Present* (G. K. Hall, 1982); Anne Sutherland Harris and Linda Nachlin, *Women Artists: 1550-1950* (Museum/Knopf, 1977); and similar works, this massive volume extends the ability of artists, art historians, art teachers, women's studies scholars, librarians, and others to investigate women's role in our artistic and cultural history. It will also be of inestimable value to art collectors and dealers, art galleries, and museums. The guide to bibliographical references is a superb listing of major references for student and scholar.—**Maureen Pastine**

797. **St. James Guide to Black Artists**. Thomas Riggs, ed. Detroit, St. James Press, 1997. 625p. illus. index. $155.00. ISBN 1-55862-220-9.

The *St. James Guide to Black Artists* contains biographical and career information on 400 of the most well-known black artists worldwide. About three-fourths (around 300 artists) were alive at the time of publication, and the rest were active in the early part of this century. The research for the volume was done with the assistance of the New York Public Library's Schomburg Center for Research in Black Culture. A few of the artists included were active in the nineteenth century. While the entries vary from a few remarks about the individual to complete essays detailing their lives, the coverage is generally adequate, and in some cases, extensive. In addition, there are more than 300 illustrations, mostly portraits of the artists covered.

While there is no shortage of biographical dictionaries of black artists in print, the *St. James Guide to Black Artists* is unique not only in its depth of coverage, but its inclusion of a number of artists from Africa, the Caribbean, Brazil, and other countries that have not had good coverage. Several works already available will complement this work, including Robert Doty's *Contemporary Black Artists in America* (Whitney Museum of American Art, 1971), David Driskell's *Two Centuries of Black American Art* (Knopf, 1976), and the Albany Institute of History and Art's compilation entitled *The Negro Artist Come of Age: A National Survey of Contemporary American Artists*. (Albany Institute of History and Art, 1945). In addition, there have been some notable works covering black women artists, including *Gumba Ya Ya: Anthology of Contemporary African-American Women Artists* (Midmarch Arts Press, 1995).

Each entry in the present publication includes a brief biographical sketch, a time line showing exhibitions, collections, and publications and concluding with a biographical essay covering the individual's life and work. Some of the essays are "critical" in the sense of critiquing some of the works of the artists. The illustrations, while all black-and-white, are nicely produced and generally quite interesting.

The *St. James Guide to Black Artists* is highly recommended for all larger academic and public libraries with specialized music collections, and at the same time, it should be of value to smaller academic, public, and school libraries that wish to select a good biographical source for black artists.—**Robert L. Wick**

798.   **The Thames and Hudson Dictionary of Art and Artists**. rev. ed. Herbert Read and Nikos Stangos, eds. London, Thames and Hudson, 1984; distr., New York, W. W. Norton, $19.95. 352p. illus. $19.95. LC 84-50342. ISBN 0-500-23402-7.

Attempting to be comprehensive in its coverage of the fine arts, this work is limited in scope to painting, sculpture, drawing, and prints; to various artists; and to a selection of technical and conceptual terms relevant to art and art history. Most of the entries included were originally written for *The Encyclopaedia of the Arts* (Meredith Press, 1966). Some have been revised; others have not. Three hundred seventy-six black-and-white illustrations (somewhat dark) accompany more than 2,500 entries.

As a quick reference source for high school and small public libraries, this work may prove sufficient. There is however, an evident lack of consistency in entries and cross-references—a quality which will limit usefulness in the academic setting. Non-Western art is given cursory treatment, with the noticeable absence of information on Indian art. Other areas overlooked are American Indian art, folk art, crafts, and photography. Mayan, Aztec, and Incan art are included in a general entry for Pre-Columbian art, yet cross-references appear only under "Maya art" and "Aztec art." "Earth art" and "Ecological art" have separate entries with similar definitions, yet neither is cross-referenced to the other. Definitions are presented for "Graphic arts" and "Drawing," yet none appear for *painting* or *sculpture*.

A work of uneven quality, this dictionary might reasonably be selected when all others are out-of-print, and no encyclopedia can be located.—**Edmund F. SantaVicca**

799.   Wingfield, Mary Ann. **A Dictionary of Sporting Artists 1650-1990**. Wappingers Falls, N.Y., Antique Collectors' Club, 1992. 354p. index. $89.50. ISBN 1-85149-140-6.

The Antique Collectors' Club operates to provide prices for and information about a wide range of collecting pursuits and hobbies. Formed in 1966, the Club is British and, in addition to monographs, publishes the well-known monthly *Antique Collecting*. The dictionary listings in this work are mostly for British artists who painted "at least one good sports painting" during their careers. When that is the case—one painting up to a handful—only the title, date, and size are given for each. Otherwise, the entry is longer and establishes the artist as a certain kind of genre painter.

The introduction makes clear there never was a British school of sporting painters. Rather, the artists painted sports scenes as the whim struck them, not as a singular pursuit. The sports index reflects predominately British interests: angling, coursing, cricket, croquet, curling, dog fighting, donkey racing, dressage, equestrian, fencing, ferreting, fox hunting, lawn bowls, lawn tennis, the National Hunt, rugby, and shooting. Some unusual entries are for the Eton Wall Game, jousting, pig sticking, ratting, and tent-pegging. To appeal to an American audience, American football and what the Club calls "real" tennis are included. The artists lived from around 1650 to the present and may have painted many sports scenes. Still, as noted, the Club's criterion for inclusion in this work is that the artist painted at least one good sports painting. Knowing monetary value as it does, the Club bases its decision on sales records and ownership. Recommended for either sports or art collections with strong British holdings.—**Bill Bailey**

ARCHITECTS AND DESIGNERS

General Works

800. **Contemporary Architects**. 3d ed. Muriel Emanuel, ed. Detroit, St. James Press, 1994. 1125p. illus. index. (Contemporary Arts Series). $149.00. ISBN 1-55862-182-2.

The 3d edition of this excellent and classic reference source covers architects and architectural partnerships of the past 50 years and includes 585 entries, 70 of which are new. These entries are written by an impressive list of contributors. The scope of this international work has been broadened to embrace not only architects, but also engineers, theorists, and landscape architects who have influenced twentieth century architecture. Each entry contains biographical information; awards received; lists of works and projects; major exhibitions; publications by and about the architect; and an evaluative essay by an architectural historian or academic. A black-and-white photograph of a major work is included with each entry. Cross-references to architects in earlier editions are included, which is helpful. Additionally, there is an index of major buildings arranged geographically by country. This is an essential purchase for all libraries supporting research in architecture and art history.—**Monica Fusich**

801. **Encyclopedia of Architecture, Design, Engineering & Construction**. Joseph A. Wilkes, ed. New York, John Wiley & Sons, 1990. 4166p. illus. index. $200.00. ISBN 0-471-63243-0.

With volume 5 this set is now complete. It is a comprehensive and widely acclaimed encyclopedia which has been six years in preparation. Volume 5 also contains a supplement of more than 200 pages of new and late submitted subjects. In addition there is an index which provides access to all 5 volumes. This encyclopedia is of interest to all who research or work in the area of architecture and design. Also included are a large number of biographies of architects and designers both living and deceased.—**Robert L. Wick**

802. Gray, A. Stuart. **Edwardian Architecture: A Biographical Dictionary**. Iowa City, University of Iowa Press, 1986. 421p. illus. index. $55.00. LC 85-51111. ISBN 0-87745-136-2.

A. Stuart Gray's handsome volume on Edwardian architecture satisfies a long-standing desire for a comprehensive overview of both the period and its practitioners. An extensive introduction acquaints the reader with many of the general topics addressed by Edwardian architects, city planners, and reformers, such as housing for the poor, the innovation of the Garden Suburb, the influence of the Art Worker's Guild, the emergence of Art Nouveau, and the impact of the London Tube Railways. The emphasis is clearly upon those London-based architects who came to prominence during the reign of Edward VII (1901-1910). Gray, a distinguished architect himself, is careful to provide social and political background so that students of the period understand not just what was built, but why. The main body of the book consists of over 300 biographical entries for Edwardian architects, sculptors, and painters. Meticulous cross-referencing through these entries enables the reader to follow an architect's career influences via references to other designers, firms, and buildings. Listings typically include place of birth, family background, educational information, chronologies of collaborations, and descriptions of major works. Major talents such as Sir Edwin Lutyens, Charles Rennie Mackintosh, C. F. A. Voysey, and landscape architect Gertrude Jekyll receive listings in detail, including concise examinations of their personal and artistic philosophies. The entire text is enriched with some 400 masterful black-and-white photographs shot especially for the book by Nicholas Breach. Photographs are complete with addresses so that extant buildings can be easily identified. Architects, sculptors, painters, buildings, and works of art are thoroughly indexed. This volume is certain to become the standard reference for architects, preservationists, and general enthusiasts of the Edwardian age. [R: RBB, 15 June 86, pp. 1512-14]—**Octavia Porter Randolph**

803.   **The Illustrated Encyclopedia of Architects and Architecture**. Dennis Sharp, ed. New York, Whitney Library of Design/Watson-Guptill, 1991. 256p. illus. index. $39.95. NA40.I45. 720.3. LC 91-710. ISBN 0-8230-2539-X.

A notable feature of this reference volume is its two-part format. Part 1 is a biographical dictionary of over 350 historical and contemporary architects. Short biographies, evaluations, bibliographies, and occasional photographs of outstanding work are given. Part 2, "Architecture and the History of Ideas," is a collection of visual essays on the history of architecture from the ancient world to the present. The black-and-white and color photographs have been well selected to illustrate short statements on architectural styles, movements, and influences on both Western and non-Western culture throughout the ages. Important architects mentioned in part 2 are cross-referenced to their biographies in part 1. There are also an index and a glossary of terms, movements, and abbreviations. The editor is executive editor of the international journal *World Architecture,* and the credentials of the various contributors are impressive. However, the essays and biographies are too short to be satisfying. The architects selected are mostly European or British; some well-known U.S. architects have been lumped under firm names rather than having entries of their own.—**Robert J. Havlik**

804.   **International Dictionary of Architects and Architecture**. Randall J. Van Vynckt, ed. Detroit, St. James Press/Gale, 1993. 2v. illus. index. $250.00/set. NA40.I48. 720'.9. LC 93-13431. ISBN 1-55862-089-3.

If weight were the only criterion, the combined 15.5 pounds of these two volumes would make them very important. But weight is only one impressive statistic about this important set. Featured in these volumes are essays by some 220 experts that cover 523 architects and 467 buildings and sites that have figured prominently in Western architectural history. Volume 1 is devoted to architects, and volume 2 covers buildings and sites. The architect volume gives a short biographical outline of the architect, followed by a concise chronology of the architect's major built works. Then there is a chronological list of books and articles by and about the person and the works, followed by a signed critical essay averaging about 1,000 words. Architects are listed alphabetically by name. The architecture volume features dates of construction, architect (if known), and a selected list of books and articles about the building or site, followed by a critical essay. The buildings and sites are listed by country, then town, and then name, under three major groups: classical sites and monuments, Europe, and the Americas. Both of the volumes are well illustrated with some 1,133 photographs and floor plans. Indexing and cross-referencing are important in a set such as this, so there is a building index in volume 1 and an architect index in volume 2. There are also extensive notes on the contributors of the essays.

Comparison can be made of these volumes with the five-volume *Encyclopedia of Architecture*, which began publication in 1988. (See ARBA 91, entry 1026 for a review of volume 5.) These two volumes are more limited in scope, but the entries are more detailed and informative because of the emphasis on chronological and bibliographical references. [R: JAY, Nov 93, pp. 346-47; LJ, 15 Sept 93, p. 68; WLB, Nov 93, p. 103-5]—**Robert J. Havlik**

805.   Johnson, Donald Leslie, and Donald Langmead. **Makers of 20th Century Modern Architecture: A Bio Critical Sourcebook**. Westport, Conn., Greenwood Press, 1997. 387p. illus. maps. index. $89.50. ISBN 0-313-29353-8.

Frank Lloyd Wright said that architecture must always be in transition. This sourcebook, intended for a wide audience, combines biographies with extensive but selective bibliographies. "Whither We Went," an introductory philosophical and historical essay on the evolution of modern architecture, explores how late-nineteenth-century architecture influenced the twentieth century. Central to the avant-garde movement was Wright. Accordingly, he is given a lengthy biography and is discussed in more than half of the introduction, linking him to several other architects.

The dictionary includes several concepts and groups, such as Archigram, Congress Internationaux d'Architecture Moderne (CIAM), Coop Himmelblau, futurism, and metabolism, and major firms like Skidmore, Owings, and Merrill. Coverage is worldwide, including Hassan Fathy (Egypt), Arata Isozaki (Japan), Ieoh Ming Pei (China), Denise Scott Brown (Zambia), and Luis Barrag (Mexico). Each of the more than 80 biographies addresses the architect's life and and works, followed by a three to five part bibliography: writings by the architect, biographical works, assessment articles about their work, and bibliographic and archival sources for further research. Fifty-two plates, from drawings to photographs, illustrate the varied styles.

A chronology and list of founders provide further links between contemporary architects. Two indexes complete the book, one by personal names/concepts and one by place-names. Both authors, with previous contributions to the scholarship of architecture, have created a source essential for architecture libraries and interdisciplinary collections.—**Ralph Hartsock**

806. **Who's Who in Interior Design**. John L. Pellam, ed. Laguna Beach, Calif., Barons Who's Who, 1988- . illus. index. $175.00 for recent edition. ISSN 0897-5914.

This publication covers more than 3,000 individuals from 90 countries. It is timely, for we are constantly reminded that we "live in a designer's world." The editorial advisers cover a wide range of expertise and include talented interior-design professionals involved with architectural, contract, health care, hospitality, industrial, residential, and transportation design. The qualifications for the entries were very well established and carefully considered. The criteria emphasize professionalism, with weight given to education, experience, awards and honors earned, major completed projects, community service rendered gratis, and publications and membership in major organizations in the field. Among the specifics requested were political and religious affiliation and avocations. (Many designers did not provide this information.)

Most of the entries originate in North America, Europe, and the Pacific Rim. However, the editors tried to include representation from Africa, the Middle East, South America, and Inner Asia. This explains in part why there is only one representative designer from Berlin as well as single entries for Fiji, Iran, Latvia, Morocco, and Sri Lanka. Hong Kong, London, Mexico City, Milan, and Tokyo have dozens of listings, but there is no entry from St. Petersburg, where renovation and remodeling are visibly active aspects of daily life. It would appear that the goal of the directory—worldwide coverage—is not practical. However, coverage for Canada and the United States is impressive, with centers such as Toronto, San Francisco, Los Angeles, Miami, and Chicago well represented. No one will be surprised to note that New York City leads the field in the variety and number of design professionals in residence or with offices there.

In most entries, the information is ample and generous, providing potential clients and researchers with solid information in their searches for the best-qualified individuals or firms to undertake specific design projects. The directory also includes concisely edited data on the six leading professional associations for interior designers and a geographic index. Another bonus is a solid binding that will hold up well after frequent use. Major value is found in the many entries for North American interior designers, with somewhat less success in global coverage.—**William J. Dane**

United States

807. Doumato, Lamia. **Architecture and Women: A Bibliography Documenting Women Architects, Landscape Architects, Designers, Architectural Critics and Writers and Women in Related Fields Working in the United States**. New York, Garland, 1988. 269p. illus. index. (Garland Reference Library of the Humanities, Vol. 886). $40.00. LC 88-17698. ISBN 0-8240-4105-4.

Architects are so little known among the general American populace that few citizens can name one beyond Frank Lloyd Wright. Given this lack of public profile, how much greater is the shadow of obscurity in which women architects languish. The compiler of this bibliography states as her goal the encouragement of research on the history of American women in architecture and its related fields. This volume brings to light the names of 128 American women, past and present, who are notable as architects, landscape architects, critics, garden writers, reformers, and planners. The volume begins with a list of extant published bibliographies, and continues through listings of monographs, dissertations and theses, exhibition catalogs, and periodical articles. This last category is drawn from publications as refreshingly diverse as *The Ladies Home Journal* and *Architectural Record*. The main body of the book comprises an alphabetical listing of the women themselves, including birth and death dates (if known), a simple title such as "Architect" or "Planner," a list of primary and secondary works, and exhibitions, if any. Twenty crisp black-and-white photographs illustrate the work of women designers of this century and the last. The alphabetical table of contents makes locating citations on a given woman quick and simple.—**Octavia Porter Randolph**

808.   Krantz, Les. **American Architects: A Survey of Award-Winning Contemporaries and Their Notable Works**. New York, Facts on File, 1989. 301p. illus. $40.00. NA736.K7. 720'.92'273. LC 89-1466. ISBN 0-8160-1420-5.

This summary focuses upon some 400 architects who have won a variety of awards and whose prominence in architecture encompasses a wide variety of building types. The final selection was made from more than 12,000 firms and is not intended to be a list of the best 400 architects in the country. The arrangement is a simple alphabetical one of individual architects. Where a firm name is listed, it refers the user to the individual architect-designer entry. Each entry includes the architect's specialties, location, telephone number, date of birth, education, and a listing of awards and notable works. Believing that buildings best express the architect's concepts and philosophies, each entry includes one or more paragraphs describing several projects.

Although the work contains over 150 illustrations, 27 of them in color, a number of the architects are represented by two or more illustrations, consequently narrowing the scope of visual representation of award-winning projects. There is also a certain carelessness in editing; for example, "Hardy Holaman Pfeiffer Associates" is listed as an entry, while in the text "Holaman" becomes Holzman, the correct spelling of his name. The title and foreword imply that all the listed architects are living, yet George Nelson and Minoru Yamasaki are both deceased. Nor does the title prepare one for the inclusion of the number of Canadian practitioners and projects listed.

These objections aside, this is a useful reference tool for a quick survey of a wide number of successful architects and designers whose work encompasses many diverse design philosophies from modernism to regionalism to contextualism. There is a very practical "Architects Cross-Referenced by Specialties" listing that includes building design, exhibition design, facility planning, historic preservation, interior architecture, landscape architecture, planning, and urban design with a geographical breakdown under each category and architects listed where appropriate. The ease of access and the broad scope of the survey make it a welcome addition to ready reference biography and special subject collections.—**G. Joan Burns**

809.   **ProFile: The Official Directory of The American Institute of Architects**. Topeka, Kans., Archimedia; distr., Grosse Point, Mich., Moonbeam, 1983- . $175.00 for recent edition. ISSN 0190-8766.

As the "official" directory of the American Institute of Architects (AIA), it contains the entire list of members, emeritus members, and associate members as of August each year. In addition, separate listings are given for architects in education, in government, and in industry; fellows and honorary fellows of the AIA; AIA medal and award winners; presidents; the Board of Directors; headquarters staff; state architectural registration boards; and organizations of related interest.

The body of the volume contains profiles of more than 18,000 architectural firms by state, with indexes by firm name and by principals. Among the information given are address, telephone number, year established, principals and responsibilities, personnel by discipline, work distribution by percent of gross income, geographical distribution of work, minority/women's business enterprise designation, and award-winning projects. Information is submitted by the individual firms, and the editors "accept" the correctness of that information. A "special effort" has been made to include new and previously unlisted firms and to exclude firms no longer in existence or that lack AIA member principals.

While the reliability of this source has been questioned (because of the survey methodology), it is a valuable tool to architects, job seekers, students, suppliers, freelance designers, and others interested in contacting architectural firms. The price is steep, especially considering the newsprint quality of the paper. It is, however, a unique reference tool recommended for all architectural libraries and most other large reference collections.—**Jay Schafer and Robert L. Wick**

Australia and New Zealand

810. **The Dictionary of Australian Artists: Painters, Sketchers, Photographers and Engravers to 1870**. Kerr, Joan, ed. New York, Oxford University Press, 1992. 889p. illus. $195.00. 709.94. ISBN 0-19-553290-2.

The early art history of Australia has many things in common with the early art history of the U.S. Midwest. Both are characterized by embryonic activity and ill-documented itinerant artists until permanent art galleries and schools began to be established in the 1860s. Just as in the U.S. Midwest, it has been hard to find information about the pioneers of culture in the antipodes until relatively recently.

Containing information about 2,500 painters, sketchers, photographers, and engravers, this hefty volume is a landmark of cooperative research. It appears that anyone who claimed artistic credentials is included, from the humble daguerreotypist to the artist formally trained in the latest British techniques. Each is documented in a readable essay written by one of 195 contributors. Many essays include bibliographical references and photographs of the artists or their work. In addition, a useful summary of art historical trends in Australia to 1870 is contained in Kerr's introduction, while a list of major art exhibitions of the period completes the volume.

This book has all the components of a great reference work: It is thorough, well edited, attractively designed, and full of hard-to-find information. A comparable treatment of U.S. pioneer artists would be welcome. [R: Choice, Nov 93, p. 428]—**Stephanie C. Sigala**

Great Britain

811. Colvin, Howard Montagu. **A Biographical Dictionary of British Architects, 1600-1840**. rev. and enlarged ed. New York, Facts on File, 1980. 1080p. index. $75.00. ISBN 0-87196-442-2.

Titled *A Biographical Dictionary of English Architects, 1660-1840* in its 1st edition (1954), this superior work contains biographical sketches of significant architects who practiced in England, Scotland, and Wales during the seventeenth, eighteenth, and early nineteenth centuries (from Inigo Jones, 1573-1632, to Sir Charles Barry, 1795-1860). This revision expands coverage to include Scotland and Wales and an additional sixty years. Most Victorian architecture is excluded. The lengthy and informative introduction of the 1st edition has been reprinted in this enlarged edition.

Every building (and some projects that were never executed) considered by the author to be significant and for which the architect can be identified is listed, along with its date of erection and demolition, its style, and references to published descriptions. Each architect's work is given in chronological order, with an evaluation of his contributions to British architectural history. All British architectural publications appearing between 1600 and 1840 are listed by author. Thorough building and name indexes facilitate access to the dictionary's contents. [R: BL, 15 Nov 81, p. 460; Choice, Apr 81, pp. 1069-70]—**Bohdan S. Wynar**

812. Harvey, John. **English Mediaeval Architects: A Biographical Dictionary Down to 1550**. rev. ed. Gloucester, England, Alan Sutton; distr., New York, St. Martin's Press, c.1984, 1987. 479p. illus. index. $35.00pa. ISBN 0-312-01600-X.

The presentation of the revised version of this work to an eager audience renders an inestimable service to the modern scholar and to the medieval architects it chronicles. Architects, for the purposes of this book, include master masons (who very often functioned as chief designers for entire projects), carpenters, carvers, and building contractors. Rescued at last from obscurity, the great achievements of those who created the masterworks of medieval England are finally linked with names and personal histories. Piecing together information from receipts, ledgers, diaries, wills, and court accounts, the authors present an illuminating record of the lives of individual designers, beginning with Edward and Thuruerd, architects of St. Benet Holme Abbey in 1020, and ending with Henry Bullock and John Russell, designers of a fountain at Windsor Castle in 1558. Tables of remuneration enlighten the modern reader about payment received by past masters (e.g., in 1393, Richard Lattlebury, resident mason of works at Barton Oratory, received as annual payment 10 shillings, a gown, food, and feed for his horse). The indexes are jewels of information: they include a complete topographical index; a county by county index; an "at a glance" chronological table listing commencement of construction, building by building, with architect; a subject index of structures by building type (e.g., bridges, castles, mills, etc.); and an exhaustive general index of names, places, architectural terms, obscure tools, and so on.—**Octavia Porter Randolph**

GRAPHIC ARTISTS

813.   Castagno, John. **Artists as Illustrators: An International Directory with Signatures and Monograms, 1800-Present**. Metuchen, N.J., Scarecrow, 1989. 625p. $127.50. NC961.63.C37. 741.6'092'2. LC 88-34832. ISBN 0-8108-2168-0.

Although illustrators have occasionally received recognition as fine artists, the fine art painter has more frequently crossed over the line into illustration. However, with the growing acceptance of illustration as fine art, galleries, museums, and individuals are establishing illustration collections, while auction houses are holding sales of illustrations with prices climbing into the hundreds of thousands of dollars. In support of this trend, the 14,000-plus biographical entries found in this directory provide a comprehensive listing of illustrators, sculptors, and fine artists whose work has appeared as illustrations in books, magazines, booklets, book and record covers, and posters. As such it serves as a valuable tool for reference and research.

Each entry includes the artist's full name, nationality (with a dual listing when the artist is claimed by more than one country), dates of birth and death, and biographical sources. In addition, approximately 4,000 facsimile signatures are shown under appropriate entries. The 90-plus biographical sources given include the standard titles one expects in such a reference book, but it is well supplemented by many volumes focusing on cartoons, posters, magazine covers, graphic annuals, and illustrations. Many of the popular magazines of the early twentieth century are also cited as valuable sources.

The brief introduction in English, French, German, Italian, and Spanish states that the author intends to publish supplements in the future. As it stands the present volume should prove to be a highly useful ready-reference tool to any fine arts library, museum, dealer, or collector, and any further updating volumes should be welcome. [R: RBB, 1 Sept 89, pp. 98-99]—**G. Joan Burns**

814.   **Comic-Book Superstars**. Don Thompson and Maggie Thompson, eds. Iola, Wis., Krause Publications, 1993. 255p. illus. $16.95. LC 93-77544. ISBN 0-87341-256-7.

Few reference books on the individuals who create comics have focused on the modern scene. Most cover historical figures, with a few current figures thrown in almost as an afterthought. Others deal primarily with the writers and artists of strips, neglecting the body of people whose work is confined to comic books. On the surface, *Comic-Book Superstars* fills this reference need by including "creators whose work has appeared in what we could determine were comic books which received wide potential distribution throughout the comic book direct market" (introduction). Entries, which are based on questionnaires and are thus not always complete, try to provide the person's name, address (personal, office, or agent), birth date and place, college or other advanced training, comics-related education, biggest creative influences, 1993 comics projects, past projects, favorite comics from other people, and dream project. While most of the individuals did answer all the questions, the amount of information they provided varies widely. The inclusion of photographs and self-portraits from some of the entrants is a nice touch, although they too vary in quality, some being sharp, others blurry. The book concludes with birthday lists of people born in each month.

This work has two problems, one minor, one major. The minor problem is that the questions asked are not overly informative. While it is nice to know about the dream projects of cartoonists, such knowledge provides few insights into what makes these people tick. Users would find biographical questions more interesting and revealing (e.g., why did they become involved with comic books? Do they do anything else to support themselves? Have they encountered any difficulties in their work?). The book's major problem is its omission of a host of important figures in the genre, such as Art Spiegelman and Francoise Mouly, Rob Liefeld, and Alan Moore. The

Thompsons acknowledge this problem—which, after all, is a hazard of questionnaire-based directories—in the introduction, but one wonders if they could have provided some basic information on significant individuals, as is done in the Marquis Who's Who books.

Overall, this book is not perfect, but it is the only work that provides data on many of these people. Its price is attractive for a hardcover and helps recommend it to public and college libraries, as well as fans and comic book store owners. It is hoped that a subsequent edition will address the problems mentioned.—**D. A. Rothschild**

815.   Goulart, Ron. **The Great Comic Book Artists**. New York, St. Martin's Press, 1986. 128p. illus. bibliog. $12.95pa. LC 86-3711. ISBN 0-312-34557-7.

For the public library or high school library patron seeking a brief introduction to the world of comic book artists, this work might prove useful. Goulart provides capsule summaries of the careers of some sixty artists who have met his criteria for inclusion: "I've tried to produce a balanced book, but I must admit I slipped in a few highly subjective choices." The scope is both historical and contemporary, with each of the one-page essays accompanied by a single page of representative artistic work from the comic *oeuvre* of the artist.

Useful in a limited environment, Goulart's work falls short of being a solid reference tool in a number of ways. First, the entries on individual artists are too brief. Second, the subjectivity of editorial license provides no guarantee that an individual artist will be included. Instead, we are tantalized by the writer into hoping there might be a sequel to this volume. Third, all reproductions of comics included are black-and-white, somewhat diminishing the effectiveness of the art itself, and the consequent understanding of some points made in reference to the artist.

Most academic libraries will want to pass over this work. Biographical material on the artists included can be located through standard biographical and periodical indexes. For the patron seeking samples of an artist's work, referral to a local retail outlet specializing in sales of comic books is currently the best route. [R: LJ, 15 June 86, p. 63]—**Edmund F. SantaVicca**

816.   Houfe, Simon. **The Dictionary of 19th Century British Book Illustrators and Caricaturists**. rev. ed. Wappingers Falls, N.Y., Antique Collectors' Club, 1996. 367p. illus. $79.50. ISBN 1-85149-193-7.

Although *The Dictionary of 19th Century British Book Illustrators and Caricaturists* remains an important reference tool, the publishers missed the opportunity of creating a visually interesting as well as useful tool worthy of the subject. This 2d and "extensively revised" edition adds 250 new artist entries, but for a subject wealthy in color and imagination, one would expect to see more samples of the artists' work. The 30 color plates, placed within the informative opening essay, "A Century of Illustration," fall short of what one would expect to see for the price asked. Another aggravating feature is the lack of information provided for the "minor artists and amateurs." Some of the artist entries are of limited use because the only information provided is the year the artist contributed to a certain publication.

The appendix of monograms in interesting and pertinent, but the other appendixes seem to be an afterthought. For example, appendix B lists "Specialist Illustration" yet divides the artists into only two subjects, "Fairy Artists" and "Special Artists." "Special Artists" seems to refer to those artists who provided art for specific publications and repeats information already given in the artist's biographical sketch. Despite these bothersome idiosyncrasies, the dictionary remains the only source available on the subject. One hopes that the 3d edition will include more samples of the artists' illustrations. The title is recommended for most library reference collections.—**Elizabeth A. Ginno**

817.   Hunnisett, Basil. **An Illustrated Dictionary of British Steel Engravers**. Brookfield, Vt., Scolar Press/Gower, 1989. 180p. illus. $75.00. NE625.H86. 769.92'2. LC 88-4696. ISBN 0-85967-740-0.

There are 644 entries in this updated and corrected edition that covers major as well as relatively obscure British steel engravers who flourished in the nineteenth century. Each engraver is classified by the principal type of subject matter for which he or she is noted, such as architecture, figures, history, landscapes, portraits, or sculptured works. Some biographies are brief, as recorded data is scant and information sketchy, but the longer entries include quantities of valuable information. The author used scores of special sources to gather the facts on these graphic artists. These sources include the English periodicals *Art Union* (1839-1848) and *Art Journal* (1849-1912) as well as the notable print holdings in London's British and Victoria and Albert museums and those in provincial art centers. This revised dictionary has reference value to graphic art and illustrated book collections as well as the growing audience of those involved with the history and customs of the Victorian era.—**William J. Dane**

818.   Livingston, Alan. **The Thames and Hudson Encyclopedia of Graphic Design and Designers**. New York, Thames & Hudson, 1992. 215p. illus. $12.95. ISBN 0-500-20259-1pa.

This little volume is packed with information concerning typography, grahic design, and other aspects of design and designers. While most of the entries are extremely brief, it does provide for quick reference on a number of subjects including journals, design organizations, typefaces, and other technical information. The biographies do include a number of individuals not included in other sources. There is an especially interesting list of biographies of typographic designers.

Also included is an interesting if somewhat confusing 150 year chronology tracing the evolution of graphic design beginning in 1840 and continuing through to the present time.

This work is mainly of use for individual libraries and for collections in larger public and academic libraries that attempt to purchase everything available in the area of graphic design.—**Robert L. Wick**

819.   Marantz, Sylvia, and Kenneth Marantz. **Artists of the Page: Interviews with Children's Book Illustrators**. Jefferson, N.C., McFarland, 1992. 255p. index. $29.95. NC965.M34. 741.6'42'0922. LC 91-50951. ISBN 0-89950-701-8.

Warm and inviting in its conversational tone, this work is filled with insights into the careers and lives of 30 children's book illustrators. Through interviews with the artists we learn of their backgrounds, training (both formal and informal), working styles, influences, and philosophies. Some of the most talented members of an exclusive fraternity appear in this volume, so this work is a significant contribution to a field that has had slight coverage in existing reference works. Arranged alphabetically, each chapter has a sampling of works in print by the artist, a brief background sketch, and several pages devoted to the actual interview—a distillation of conversations with the artists. The articles have been reviewed and occasionally edited for greater clarity by the artists themselves. An update appears at the end of the chapter for many individuals. A brief bibliography and an index to names and books completes the work, which will complement what little information there is on the topic of children's artists and authors. Highly recommended for any public, school, or academic setting. [R: BL, July 92, p. 1948; SLJ, Aug 92, p. 91]—**Gregory Curtis**

820.   **Talking with Artists**. Pat Cummings, comp. and ed. New York, Bradbury Press/Macmillan, 1992. 96p. illus. $18.95. NC975.T34. 741.6'42'092273. LC 91-9982. ISBN 0-02-724245-5.

Cummings has illustrated several popular picture books. Because of her interest, she has traveled around the country meeting school children and adults who are interested in art. These people tend to ask her similar questions, such as how an artist works, how an illustrator was first assigned a book, and what were some of their childhood influences. Interest from these groups led her to write this book. She has conversed with 14 favorite children's book illustrators, including Leo and Diane Dillon, Stephen Kellogg, and Chris Van Allsburg, asking them the same 8 questions but getting many different answers. The questions asked are: Where do you get your ideas? What is a normal day like for you? Where do you work? Do you have any children or pets? What do you enjoy drawing the most? Do you ever put people you know in your pictures? What do you use to make your pictures? How did you get to do your first book?

A childhood photograph and a current photograph are included for each illustrator, along with artwork from both eras. A glossary and a bibliography of five favorite books illustrated by each artist conclude the volume. The large print and simple language of these personal stories will have appeal to both children and adults.—**Kathleen J. Voigt**

821. Weinberg, Robert. **A Biographical Dictionary of Science Fiction and Fantasy Artists**. Westport, Conn., Greenwood Press, 1988. 346p. bibliog. index. $49.95. LC 87-17651. ISBN 0-313-24349-2.

Nearly 280 artists and illustrators whose creations grace the covers and interiors of science fiction/fantasy books and magazines are described in this volume. The entries (with a few exceptions) are more detailed and the coverage is more comprehensive than that offered by *The Encyclopedia of Science Fiction and Fantasy* (see ARBA 75, entry 1330, and ARBA 79, entry 1204), *The Visual Encyclopedia of Science Fiction* (see ARBA 79, entry 1202), or *The Science Fiction Encyclopedia* (see ARBA 80, entry 1212). The author's background combines extensive research in the science fiction/fantasy field with experience as an art dealer.

Prefatory material includes an introduction, an explanation of how to use the book, and a list of abbreviations. A brief history of science fiction art is followed by the artist biographies (arranged alphabetically with cross references and *see* references), an overview of still-existing art materials, and a list of the art awards in science fiction. A select bibliography is provided, along with an index of the biographical entries and a general index.

While some of the entries provide only a brief description of the artist, most provide a biographical sketch, an estimate of the artist's influence, notes on techniques used, and quotations from the artists concerning their work. The writing is crisp and clear, with emphatic critical evaluations. Particularly valuable is the appended indicative listing of published work for most artists (divided into hardback and paperbound covers, and magazine illustrations). A representative test sample of the data prove accurate.

The dictionary is admittedly incomplete. Major missing artists include P. Bruillet, H. R. Giger, J. Giraud, Jack Kirby, and K. Thole. As another measure of comprehensiveness, about 40 percent of the artists whose illustrations appear in *The Science Fiction Encyclopedia* are not given entries. The coverage is occasionally uneven (despite the fact that John Berkey is described as "the American master of science fiction hardware art," his entry occupies less than one-quarter of a page), and the occasional misspelling or missed cross-reference was noted. Overall, however, these flaws do not detract from the substance of this work, although its value could be enhanced considerably if a representative illustration of each artist's work had been included.

In summary, this volume, clearly printed on good-quality paper in a sturdy binding, fills a major gap in science fiction studies, and can serve effectively both as a ready-reference source and as a scholarly index to materials which otherwise would be difficult (if not impossible) to find. [R: LJ, 15 June 88, p. 53; RBB, Aug 88, pp. 1896, 1898]—**John Howard Oxley**

CANADA

822. **Biographical Dictionary of Saskatchewan Artists: Men Artists**. Marketa Newman, comp. and ed. Saskatoon, Sask., Fifth House; distr., Toronto and Cheektowaga, N.Y., University of Toronto Press, 1994. 281p. index. $55.00. ISBN 1-895618-45-2.

Drawing on her years as the fine arts librarian at the University of Saskatchewan, Newman has completed a second guide to the lives and works of Saskatchewan artists. A companion volume on women artists was published in 1990 (see ARBA 92, entry 969). Her dictionary provides the documentation of regional art that every user, whether student, teacher, collector, curator, dealer, administrator, or researcher, hopes to find, perhaps in a well-thumbed card file or here in a neat handbook. Using an inclusive definition of Saskatchewan (as the place of birth, studies, teaching, or career) and a specific time span (born between 1872 and 1950) predating the creation of the province in 1905, Newman presents 188 painters, printmakers, sculptors, and installation artists. Some work in holography and video, while others are creating murals and icons or preserving folk and Plains Cree traditions.

Entries were launched by a questionnaire, then developed with searches of catalogs, gallery records, books, articles, and interviews. The completed entry was then submitted for checking to the artist or a close relative; entries so verified (an overwhelming majority) are marked with an asterisk. The format is standard: biographical note; education and experience; patents; gallery; a statement (sometimes quoted) of media, style, and subject; chronological lists of exhibitions, collections, commissions, memberships, and awards; and selected bibliographies of publications and interviews by and about the artist. No cutoff date is stated; some entries list 1993 events, others end in 1991 or 1992. The work closes with a general bibliography and two name indexes by artists and folk artists. Competent and streamlined, this dictionary is recommended for fine art reference collections.—**Patricia Fleming**

823. **Biographical Dictionary of Saskatchewan Artists: Women Artists**. Marketa Newman, with Eva Jana Newman, comps. and eds. Saskatoon, Sask., Fifth House; distr., Toronto and Cheektowaga, N.Y., University of Toronto Press, 1990. 309p. illus. $45.00. 709.7124. ISBN 0-920079-66-0.

This welcome addition to biographical information on North American artists covers two areas about which very little has been written. The first is the art of the Canadian prairie region, and the second is the focus on 130 women artists of the province. Surveys of Canadian art generally concentrate on the more populated centers in eastern Canada. The work concentrates on painters, printmakers, sculptors, and installation artists whose birth dates fall between 1872 and 1950. For many entries, the artists themselves filled out questionnaires that were augmented by original research in depth; this has resulted in quantities of precise data. For example, there are nearly seven pages on Dorothy Knowles and five pages on the life and art career of Rota Cowled. The systematic plan for the information on each artist includes her education, related experience, dealers, media, subjects and style, records of group and solo exhibitions, commissions, awards, writings, collections, and selected bibliographies, all of which are most useful.

Although this dictionary is restricted to women artists working and living in only one central Canadian area, it is a welcome reference tool in art biography as it is so well researched, and it is presented with infinite care. The information is in a solid publication with easily readable data in a lasting format. In addition, this type of scholarly art reference publication encourages other regional compilers to issue biographic surveys, as reliable information on artists is in great demand by collectors, dealers, curators, writers, and other researchers. See entry 822 for coverage of male artists from the vast Saskatchewan area. [R: Choice, July/Aug 91, p. 1754]—**William J. Dane**

824. Kobayashi, Terry, and Michael Bird. **A Compendium of Canadian Folk Artists**. Erin, Ont., Boston Mills Press, 1985. 241p. illus. bibliog. $14.95pa. ISBN 0-919783-32-5.

This is a biographical dictionary to some 500 Canadian folk artists from a period of approximately 300 years in Canada. It is extremely useful for libraries, especially since it includes some rare and unique biographical details that are generally hard to find elsewhere. Each entry has name; life dates; place of work; medium; a paragraph or more on the artist's work; source references (articles, exhibitions, interviews); and collection notes of museums, libraries, galleries, archives, and so forth, where the artist's work can be found.

The authors, of course, have extensive files about Canadian folk artists; they have published at least four other books dealing with folk art in Canada and Ontario, and they also promise to update this biographical tool in the years ahead. Some of their previous works have included *Ontario Fraktur* (Feheley, 1977), *A Splendid Harvest: Germanic Folk and Decorative Arts in Canada* (1981), *Canadian Folk Art* (Oxford University Press, 1983), and *Folk Treasures of Ontario* (1985). As an added bonus in this book, there are black-and-white illustrations throughout.—**Dean Tudor**

CHINA

825. Sullivan, Michael. **Art and Artists of Twentieth-Century China**. Berkeley, University of California Press, 1996. 354p. illus. index. $65.00. ISBN 0-520-07556-0.

In this book, Sullivan, a world-recognized leading scholar of Chinese art with numerous publications on the subject, provides an in-depth look at the development of modern Chinese art. The theme of the book is "the rebirth of Chinese art in the twentieth century under the influence of Western art and culture" (p. xxvii), and he aptly demonstrates how Western influence was necessary to revitalize Chinese art. Although the author offers the book as a personal view developed during 50 years of observation, his scholarship is evident throughout the work, making this an essential work for advanced undergraduates, graduate students, and faculty in this area of art history. Despite the difficulties of finding accurate, unbiased information and gaining access to historical documents, Sullivan's knowledge of the country and its art enables him to make sense of its complexly intertwined history and art from the late 1800s into the 1990s. The book received a special mention from the 1997 George Wittenborn Memorial Book Award Committee of the Art Libraries Society of North America.

Sullivan provides a fascinating panorama of modern Chinese art, primarily painting and sculpture, from the early intense debates between traditionalists and reformers through the struggles of the Cultural Revolution to the exodus in the 1980s of young artists seeking the greater freedom of the West, to attempts by those who remained in China to push back the limits of the Communist Party's tolerance, and to the new challenges faced after Tiananmen Square. His insights are profound and so well formed that they seem to flow quite naturally through the historical discussions. The book is well written, with events lucidly set out in logical progression and well placed in context. From the beginning, the reader is aware of the depth and breadth of the author's knowledge and understanding of his subject, an awareness that enriches the experience of reading the book.

The high quality of the text is maintained in and complemented by the supplementary material. In the 94 color plates and 278 black-and-white illustrations, the author has included not only recognized major works but also works that illustrate an unfolding historical process. The extensive end notes provide rich supplementary information in addition to citations of sources and are complemented by the selected bibliography that organizes both Chinese- and Western-language sources for ease of access. Although the author points out the impossibility of the biographical index being either complete or completely accurate, it is nonetheless an important and much-needed resource, with numerous cross-references, that may be used on its own as well as with the text. The 20-page index to the text includes names of artists and institutions as well as subjects and is well supplied with cross-references, a necessity considering the several different ways it is possible to romanize a name. This substantial work likely will be a standard reference for years to come, coming as it does before the amount of material becomes too unwieldy to allow for a comprehensive general survey.—**Kristin Doty**

GREECE

826. Livas, Haris. **Contemporary Greek Artists**. New York, Vantage Press, 1993. 569p. illus. index. $40.00. LC 91-91135. ISBN 0-533-10045-3.

Livas knows a lot about twentieth-century Greek artists and exhibitions; *Contemporary Greek Artists* serves as a vivid personal memoir of personalities and events. The immediacy of the narration is both a strength and a weakness, making this volume colorful as background reading but poor as a reference book. Some 170 modern Greek artists are included. Each merits a dated essay (e.g., 1977), with a personal opinion of the artist's work at that time, much in the manner of a newspaper review for a Greek newspaper. The style is journalistic, with each essay peppered by statement like "What I see in Hatzis' art is . . ." (p. 119). There is no reference to the artist's birth date, education, or previous exhibition history. Some artists' work is illustrated by a black-and-white full-page photograph, but no photographer credit, location, or title is given for the work included.

Even the structure of the book is idiosyncratic. There are five unequal sections. Section 1 is the largest, with essays on 81 artists (not in alphabetical order). Section 2 covers five folk artists and includes a chapter on "Agricultural Life in Contemporary Greek Popular Painting" dating from 1983. Other sections cover 11 sculptors, 3 Byzantine-style artists, and 3 Cypriot artists and are interrupted by digressions into the quality of art collections and group exhibitions. There seems to be no alphabetical or chronological rationale for the structure of the book. Nor is there a bibliography to direct other reading on these artists.

Given the crying need for biographical data on twentieth-century European artists, *Contemporary Greek Artists* is a disappointment. There is still a gap in art reference collections waiting for a high-quality, systematic treatment of modern Greek art.—**Stephanie C. Sigala**

LATIN AMERICA

827.   **Contemporary Latin American Artists: Exhibitions at the Organization of American States 1941-1964**. Annick Sanjurjo, ed. Lanham, Md., Scarecrow, 1997. 506p. index. $75.00. ISBN 0-8108-3281-X.

This is the 2d volume of a 2-volume set that together records some 750 exhibitions by more than 2,000 artists covering the years 1941 to 1985 at the Museum of Modem Art of Latin America of the Organization of American States in Washington, D.C. The volume under review here deals with about 320 exhibitions of the work of approximately 950 artists between the years 1941 and 1964.

Information on the exhibits is inserted in chronological order, including professional résumés and curricula vitae of those artists whose information was available to the editor. Recognizing that the chronological scheme for the entries alone would make it difficult and even tiresome to look up individual artists or works from any given country, the editor included two useful indexes: an index of artists and an index of exhibitions by country.—S. D. **Markman**

NETHERLANDS

828.   **Dutch Art: An Encyclopedia**. Sheila D. Muller, ed. New York, Garland, 1997. 489p. illus. index. (Garland Reference Library of the Humanities, v.1021). $125.00. ISBN 0-8153-0065-4.

Dutch art, from the luminous flesh tones of a Rembrandt portrait to the meticulous detail of a Gerrit Dou genre painting, from the mathematical precision of a Piet Mondrian painting to its equivalent in a Gerrit Rietveld chair, has always held a special place in the canon of art history. This work, a compilation of essays by more than 100 recognized scholars in the field, offers a tripartite approach to the vast topic; one part devoted to biographies (Pieter Aertsen through Lambertus Zijl); one to a historical narrative; and the other to specific concepts, both stylistic and developmental. The arrangement appears to be a simple alphabetic format, but the reader must be aware of the somewhat hierarchical organization peculiar to this work: There are preliminary lists of themes in a variety of groupings, which include asterisked items suggested as an introduction to a topic. It is therefore of primary importance to thoroughly read the "Reader's Guide and Bibliographical Note" to understand just how best to proceed in using this reference.

Each entry ends with a *see also* reference that leads to further information on specific topics. Many of the artists for whom biographical information appears to be lacking can be located in topical articles by consulting the index. The bibliographies provided contain literature in a variety of languages, reflecting the current spate of Netherlands research arising from sources closer to both the origins as well as the sites of the current collections. The plates, with a small number in color, are quite good. However, they are gathered in three groupings that require a bit of referring back and forth, but this may well be secondary to useful book design and practical binding.

The work is a sound survey of a profoundly important and enormously interesting topic; its comprehensive coverage, essentially from the mid-fifteenth century to the present, makes it a valuable addition to any research library. The volume is highly recommended with one caveat—access is neither as quick nor as simple as is suggested in its press release; but the extra effort proves worthwhile.—**Paula Frosch**

NIGERIA

829.   **Nigerian Artists: A Who's Who & Bibliography**. Bernice M. Kelly, comp., and Janet L. Stanley, ed. New Providence, N.J., published for the National Museum of African Art Branch, Smithsonian Institution Libraries, Hans Zell/Reed Reference Publishing, 1993. 600p. index. $175.00. N7399.N5K46. 709'.2'2669. LC 92-40052. ISBN 0-905450-82-5.

Works by prolific bibliographer Stanley have radically transformed the information landscape of African art in the last decade. Here she collaborates with Kelly to produce the continent's first artist biography. Some 350 twentieth-century Nigerian artists are covered in great detail, including directory information, career summary, education, exhibition history, commissions, awards, publications, and a personal bibliography. While a few individuals (e.g., Sokari Douglas Camp) have exhibited in English-speaking countries, others are less well known to Westerners; Kelly's diligent research on them is particularly useful.

The volume is exemplary in many ways. Although the artist biographies make up the core of the volume, they are not its only valuable component. For students, the introduction to and chronology of Nigerian art give clear and useful summaries of modern movements in that country. End matter includes a four-part annotated bibliography of modern Nigerian art, listing books, theses, and magazines; exhibition materials and reviews; audiovisuals; and archival collections A subject index, an index of artists by name, and an index of artists by media conclude what will be the standard work on Nigerian art at least until the end of the decade. [R: Choice, Dec 93, p. 587]—**Stephanie C. Sigala**

RUSSIA

830. Milner, John. **A Dictionary of Russian and Soviet Artists 1420-1970**. Wappingers Falls, N.Y., Antique Collectors' Club, 1993. 483p. illus. $99.50. ISBN 1-85149-182-1.

With the thawing of the Cold War has come a new opportunity to learn about artists of the former Soviet Union. Drawing on sources in English and Russian, British art historian Milner has put together as important biographical dictionary that sheds light on artists from virtually the whole art history of Russia up to 1970. Each artist merits an entry arranged in order by the established Western form of the name; there are many name cross-references to aid the researcher. The entries vary in length from a paragraph to several pages and may include a detailed chronology of activity in Russia, lists of theater designs and collections, literature citations for the artist, and some commentary on an important work. In many cases, access to new information for Western readers has been dramatically improved over standard reference sources for artist biographies. In the case of Cubist painter Aristarkh Lentulov, for example, the Milner volume gives five columns of information and a picture, while Emmanuel Benezit's venerable *Dictionnaire des Peintres* (Librairie Grund, 1976) contains a mere paragraph. Another major strength of the volume is its abundance of illustrations, many of large size and in color, which provide an attractive visual summary of Russian art history, and appendixes that give a Cyrillic-Roman alphabet transliteration chart and a short bibliography listing general sources in Russian and English. [R: LJ, 1 June 94, p. 100; RBB, July 94, pp. 1972-73]—**Stephanie C. Sigala**

SPAIN

831. **Spanish Artists from the Fourth to the Twentieth Century: A Critical Dictionary**. New York, with Frick Art Reference Library, G. K. Hall/Simon & Schuster Macmillan, 1993, 1996. 4v. index. $140.00/vol. ISBN 0-8161-0164-2 (v.1); 0-8161-0656-5 (v.2); 0-5161-0657-6 (v.3); 0-7838-8037-5 (index); 0-8161-0614-2 (set).

Spanish Artists, produced in conjunction with the Frick Art Reference Library, lists approximately 10,000 painters, sculptors, drafts people, printers, architects, and applied artists, covering 1,600 years of Spanish art. The artists included were either born in Spain or worked chiefly in Spain. Artists born in 1920 and after are not included. The original project began as a 3-volume annotated checklist with a chronological list of artists and a complete bibliography of all sources used in the compilation. The completed project includes 3 volumes from A to Z and the 4th volume, the bibliography. It is based on the Authority File of Artists, an internal resource of the Frick Art Reference Library.

This critical dictionary is more comprehensive in scope than any other record in English of Spanish art. The introduction and guide to use are given in English, Spanish, French, and German. Entries are listed under authority names and include all the alternative names used by the artist. Each entry contains authority name, alternate names, dates of birth or death or documented activity, national school when nationality is questioned, fields of artistic endeavor when not exclusively a painter, notes when clarification is necessary, and bibliographic references. Volumes 1 and 2 are divided into 2 parts: artists' records and bibliography, and volume 3 contains artists' records only. Volume 4 consists of the general bibliography, a chronological index, and a comprehensive index of authority and alternate names. This set is a must for every public library art collection and art museum, even though it is an expensive title.—**Kathleen J. Voigt**

SCOTLAND

832.   McEwan, Peter J. M. **Dictionary of Scottish Art & Architecture**. Wappingers Falls, N.Y., Antique Collectors' Club, 1995. 626p. illus. $99.50. ISBN 1-85149-134-1.

McEwan clearly outlines the ambitious scope of his superb dictionary in its introduction: "The intention has been to provide the most relevant details of all painters, engravers and etchers who met a comprehensive range of criteria, and all architects, carvers, designers, draughts men, embroiderers, illustrators, jewelry designers, masons, photographers and stained glass window designers who met slightly more rigorous criteria."

McEwan's definition of *Scottish* for the purposes of this work is broad indeed. He covers artists who are Scottish by birth, ancestry, or marriage. However, he expands his parameters by including artists having an important association with Scottish art, or who exerted some influence on the country's artistic tradition. Additionally, all artists listed in the dictionary have exhibited in a major public institution or executed at least one work of repute.

The resulting volume is a detailed and comprehensive reference work on Scottish art with more than 11,000 entries, the majority of which are biographical. Entries range from a single line to several paragraphs and include birth and death dates where appropriate. Selected bibliographies on the artists are provided with details of their major exhibits and where their work may be seen. In addition, McEwan traces the development of artistic movements along with the schools of art that inspired them and provides brief histories of national academies, art societies, and other organizations. The quality of the work is enhanced by the inclusion of black-and-white reproductions of portraits or self-portraits of 86 artists. This book will be a welcome addition to arts and humanities collections, essential to art dealers and collectors, and useful to anyone interested in the artistic heritage of Scotland.—**Jennifer Comi Ellard**

UNITED STATES

Current Biographies

833.   Cummings, Paul. **Dictionary of Contemporary American Artists**. 6th ed. New York, St. Martin's Press, 1994. 786p. illus. index. $85.00. N6512.C854. 709'.2'273. LC 93-46372. ISBN 0-312-08440-4.

This edition of the *Dictionary of Contemporary American Artists* deletes 27 artists and adds 41 to achieve the most extensive revision since its first publication in 1966. Presented alphabetically, each of the 900 entries delineates where and with whom the artist studied; teaching experience; participation in the Federal Art Project; commissions executed; scholarships and awards; spouse (only if prominent in art); address and dealers of record; important one-person retrospective and group exhibitions; and a bibliography. Where repetition occurs, as in group exhibitions, a series of keys are employed for brevity. Much information, such as museum names, is abbreviated and codified in an index/key. Inclusion in the dictionary and information presented are based on questionnaires, personal interviews, and intensive research. The criteria for selection are as follows: representation in museum, public, and private collections; representation in major U.S. and international exhibitions; influence as teachers; and recognition received from fellow artists, dealers, critics, and others with a professional interest in fine arts.

This dictionary is well research and well presented. It will be of use to art historians, dealers, museums, and professional organizations. It also has the potential to serve as a tool in guiding young artists seeking to establish themselves.—**Linda L. Lam-Easton**

834.   **Who's Who In American Art 1995-96**. 21st ed. New Providence, N.J., R. R. Bowker/Reed Reference Publishing, 1995. 1521p. index. $189.00. ISBN 0-8352-3571-8. ISSN 0000-0191.

Nearly 12,000 representatives from all segments of the visual arts profession in North America are profiled in this annual publication. With some 600 entries new to this edition, the book covers artists, administrators, historians, educators, lecturers, collectors, librarians, publishers, critics, consultants, curators, and dealers. Entries are arranged alphabetically and cite vital statistics, professional titles, education and training, and mailing addresses. Also given is a description of professional activities that may include works in public collections; commissions; exhibitions; publications; positions held with schools, museums, or organizations; memberships in art societies; honors and awards; an interest or research statement; media; and the dealer. All entries are indexed by geographical location and professional classification. In addition, a necrology is provided, which is cumulative from 1953.

Criteria for selection are not thoroughly discussed, but the editor states that new names were obtained through nominations of current entrants, and subsequently went through a selection process based on "works in public collections, commissioned works, and exhibitions of an international, national and wide regional scope in noncommercial galleries and museums." Non-artists were chosen on the basis of position and experience in the field. Thus, while some accomplished artists and art professionals are not included, lesser-known individuals may receive full citations. In spite of its inevitable weaknesses, this is an informative work and should be considered for all large public and academic libraries.—**Barbara Ittner**

Retrospective Biographies

835.   Dunford, Penny. **A Biographical Dictionary of Women Artists in Europe and America since 1850**. Philadelphia, University of Pennsylvania Press, 1989. 340p. illus. $89.95. N6757.D86. 709.2'2. LC 89-16663. ISBN 0-8122-8230-2.

Dunford's book provides short biographical sketches of female artists working in Europe or America after 1850. It thus includes more than 750 biographies of both living and deceased artists. Dunford's purpose in compiling the book is not just to present the facts of these women's lives, but also to show the perseverance and success of women under difficult circumstances. To illustrate her point she augments standard biographical details, such as place and date of birth, education, and prizes won, with details of each woman's personal life. A bibliography and a list of institutions holding examples of the artist's work are appended to each entry. Dunford includes both well-known artists such as Kathe Kollwitz, Lee Krasner, and Georgia O'Keefe, and lesser-known women whose art is worthy of study. A lively style makes the biographies interesting reading, and the book is attractively illustrated with examples of the artists' works.

Most of the nineteenth- and early-twentieth-century women covered in this book are also in Chris Petteys's *Dictionary of Women Artists* (see ARBA 86, entry 1013), a work which covers 21,000 artists. Dunford offers more information in a more attractive style, and she includes women born after 1900, such as political artist Sue Coe and feminist artist Judy Chicago. Her work is a useful supplement to Petteys's more comprehensive work and to standard works such as *Who's Who in American Art* (see ARBA 88, entry 1011). [R: Choice, June 90, p. 1650; LJ, 15 June 90, p. 108; RBB, 1 Sept 90, p. 80]—**Linda Keir Simons**

836.   Lester, Patrick D. **The Biographical Directory of Native American Painters**. Tulsa, Okla., SIR Publications; distr., Norman, University of Oklahoma Press, 1995. 701p. index. $49.95. ISBN 0-8061-9936-6.

Biographical information on Native American painters is always difficult to find. The only other attempt at such a listing was Jeanne Snodgrass-King's *American Indian Painters: A Biographical Directory* published in 1968. While Ms. Snodgrass-King's compilation was, and still is, a useful directory, many of the younger Native American painters are not listed. This directory begins with the Snodgrass-King directory and brings it up-to-date with a number of format changes; for example, references to private collections have been deleted, and all references to specific biographical publications have also been deleted. In addition, the format of the entries has been changed somewhat in the update. An artist's spouse and children are no longer listed, and some of the abbreviations have been made more clear.

Each entry contains the artist's name, the name of his or her tribe (including the prior European name and the current official tribe name), birth and death dates, residence, education, occupation, media, a list of published works, illustrations appearing in books, commissions, works in public collections, exhibits (which are coded and must be looked up in another list), awards, and honors. While there is no biographical narrative as such, the tradition established by Ms. Snodgrass-King of including a narrative in the margins of the work has been continued. These narratives vary in content, but are generally biographical in nature. They are direct quotes from individuals familiar with the artist and are signed.

One question that always surfaces in such a compilation by ethnic background is what the author calls "the question of 'Indian-ness'." Mr. Lester points out that it is not his "responsibility to define 'Indian,' nor [does he] intend to become embroiled in the Indian Arts and Crafts Act of 1990 definition of 'Indian-ness'." He goes on to point out that he has accepted each artist's "attestation as to his or her Indian heritage, whether or not he or she is on a particular tribal roll" (Preface, x).

The Biographical Directory of Native American Painters is an important reference source. It will, no doubt, be welcomed by researchers, collectors, museum personnel, and admirers of the many important American Indian artists who provide us with such wonderful art. It is recommended for all library collections, especially larger academic and public libraries. And, because of its relatively low price ($49.95), it should be considered for smaller public and school libraries. In addition, anyone interested in Native American painters will find it a useful addition to their private collections.—**Robert L. Wick**

837.   **Mantle Fielding's Dictionary of American Painters, Sculptors and Engravers**. 2d ed., newly rev. and enlarged. Glenn B. Opitz, ed. Poughkeepsie, N.Y., Apollo Book, 1986. 1081p. bibliog. $85.00. ISBN 0-938290-04-5.

This is the latest of several revisions and republications of an important reference work originally written and published privately by Mantle Fielding in Philadelphia in 1926. For many years it was the most exhaustive source for information about American artists, particularly lesser-known artists. There were approximately 5,000 entries, although the information was often sketchy and incomplete.

The book was reprinted in 1960 by Paul A. Strook in a limited edition. Then in 1965, another edition was published, edited by James Carr with a 93-page addendum with 2,500 2-line entries. In 1974, Genevieve C. Doran edited yet another version (Modern Books and Crafts). None of these corrected some obvious mistakes in the original (Benjamin West's birth date given as 1828, for example) or integrated the new names into one alphabet with the original.

In 1983, Glenn B. Opitz published a "new completely revised, enlarged and updated edition" which included in one alphabet nearly 11,000 entries. It apparently merged the original and the 1929 *American Art Annual* (reprinted, edited by Opitz, published also by Apollo Book, under the title *Dictionary of American Artists 19th & 20th Century*) In addition, many contemporary artists were added. Sources, however, have not been given in the entries, and no bibliography is included. The editor explains in the preface that he attempted to make the entries more uniform, but many are obviously incomplete. For early-twentieth-century artists, the entries end: "address in 1926 . . ." or "address in 1929. . . ." Obviously, many of these artists are deceased, but no death date has been found.

This 1986 "second newly-revised, enlarged and updated edition" now contains entries for nearly 13,000 American artists. It is far handsomer than the 1983 edition, being typeset with boldface for names and headings instead of a copy of the product of a word-processor (which the 1983 version apparently is). Many new dates have been found or corrected, such as West's, and a bibliography is included (although some of the citations are from the 1926 edition, and are incomplete). The researcher would wish that more death dates had been established, and that references were included in each entry as they were in the scholarly *New York Historical Society's Dictionary of Artists in America 1564-1860* by George C. Groce and David H. Wallace (Yale University Press, 1957). Despite the number of bibliographical resources published in the past years and the explosion of interest in American art, nothing matches the coverage of this new edition. Most other biographical dictionaries are limited to "important" or well-known artists and lack the breadth of this resource. Even the recently published *Who Was Who in American Art,* edited by Peter H. Falk (Sound View Press, 1985) which boasts nearly 25,000 entries taken from the *American Art Annual* (37v. American Federation of Arts, 1898-1948), is limited in coverage to late-nineteenth- and early-twentieth-century artists only. Thus, this new edition is a necessary addition to most research libraries, or any libraries concerned with American art.—**Sydney Starr Keaveney**

838. Sharylen, Maria. **Artists of the Pacific Northwest: A Biographical Dictionary, 1600s-1970**. Jefferson, N.C., McFarland, 1993. 252p. index. $45.00. N6528.S52. 709'.2'2795. LC 92-56693. ISBN 0-89950-797-2.

Drawing on published materials and general biographical dictionaries for artists, Sharylen has produced the first biographical guide to artists in Oregon, Washington, Idaho, Alaska, and British Columbia. Following scattered pioneering efforts in the northwest in the seventeenth and eighteenth centuries, organized artistic activity began in this area in the 1890s; the 4,000 artists documented were thus mostly active in the early and mid-twentieth century.

Despite the quantity of artists included, the quality of information about each one is disappointing. Readers often must be satisfied with a frustratingly sketchy career chronology. This is understandable for elusive local artists, but less so for some nationally recognized names. There is no evidence that Sharylen consulted periodicals, newspapers, or city directories (usually considered to be gold mines of artistic data). Although an appendix provides addresses of art museums, schools, and organizations in the northwest, nowhere does Sharylen cite information from any art or local history collection. In fact, there is no indication, either in the entry or in the *very* selected biography, where information on an individual artist came from or where more information can be found. Students and researchers will want to know more than this amateur effort provides. Not recommended.—**Stephanie C. Sigala**

839. Shipp, Steve. **American Art Colonies, 1850-1930: A Historical Guide to America's Original Art Colonies and Their Artists**. Westport, Conn., Greenwood Press, 1996. 159p. illus. index. $69.50. ISBN 0-313-29619-7.

Art colonies are not a modern concept. For generations, artists have gathered together for support, inspiration, and a sense of community. This book examines the American interpretation of the late-nineteenth-century European idea of shared aesthetic experiences and does so in terms of the settings and the actors involved. The lists of names are long; some are familiar, some less so, and some are of interest only to art historians of the period.

Each chapter deals with a specific colony, from East Hampton to Santa Fe, Old Lyme to Laguna. It describes the colony, its development along philosophical and aesthetic lines, and the importance of its geographic location: For some artists the colony was a temporary escape from a city; for others, a departure to "unspoiled" areas. This section is followed by short biographical sketches of the major figures. The information supplied is particularly useful for the lesser-known artists and is based on multiple sources.

The use of an asterisk to mark those artists whose biographies follow is less than felicitous to the reader's eye, and a change in typeface may have been a better tool for this indication. The bibliography is excellent, including periodicals, and the index seems errorless. This is a useful work, both for its own content and for its sources for further study.—**Paula Frosch**

840. Soria, Regina. **American Artists of Italian Heritage, 1776-1945: A Biographical Dictionary**. Cranbury, N.J., Fairleigh Dickinson University Press; distr., Cranbury, N.J., Associated University Presses, 1993. 178p. illus. $38.50. N6538.I8S67. 709'.2'273. LC 91-55130. ISBN 0-8386-3425-7.

An inclusive biographical study of more than 350 artists of Italian descent working in America, this work chronicles much of the artistic shaping of our visual environment. Forgoing the traditional view of artists, the author includes individuals who worked in a variety of media: stone workers, marble workers, scenic and commercial artists, figurine and stucco decorators, puppet makers, wood carvers, carousel figure makers, cabinetmakers, bronze casters, and iron mongers. This comprehensive view covers many diverse craft areas instrumental in understanding the development of our visual culture but not typically dealt with in artistic biographies. Although the title offers 1776 as a beginning date, the majority of the artists listed were either born or worked during the latter half of the nineteenth and the first half of the twentieth centuries. This is not surprising, because a significant number of listed individuals came to this country as part of the mass immigrations from Europe. Most entries include birth and death dates, career highlights, education, major works and exhibitions, memberships, names or parents, and references for further study; they average approximately a quarter of a page in length. Many black-and-white illustrations of works by the artists are also included.

This work will find use in academic, special, and public libraries fielding questions on American art and culture or Italian heritage. The well-researched information will prove invaluable to the study of the developing visual climate and the contributions of artists of Italian heritage. It would be an interesting comparison to chronicle American artists of other heritages and develop a series of volumes with the same structural format as the current work. [R: Choice, Mar 94, pp. 1104-6]—**Gregory Curtis**

841.   **North American Women Artists of the Twentieth Century: A Biographical Dictionary**. Jules Heller and Nancy G. Heller, eds. Hamden, Conn., Garland, 1995. 612p. illus. index. (Garland Reference Library of the Humanities, v.1219). $125.00. ISBN 0-8240-6049-0.
This much-needed reference source provides information on more than 1,500 women artists from Canada, Mexico, and the United States. Each entry includes concise biographical and exhibition information and a brief bibliography. To be included in this dictionary, an artist must have been born before 1960; have lived or worked in the United States, Canada, or Mexico; and have shown a serious commitment to the arts as proven by participation in exhibitions and a body of literature about that artist. Well-known artists such as Imogen Cunningham, Frida Kahlo, and Georgia O'Keeffe are covered, as well as lesser-known artists such as Grace Medicine Flower, a Native American potter, and Ulayu Pingwartok, a Canadian Inuit graphic artist. A variety of fields are represented, such as painting, performance art, sculpture, printmaking, ceramics, fibers, metals, and photography. More than 100 black-and-white illustrations, revealing the abundance of North American women's artistic output, are included. This is an excellent and timely reference work, filled with important information on women artists. It is an important and basic addition to any art collection.—**Monica Fusich**

842.   Watson-Jones, Virginia. **Contemporary American Women Sculptors**. Phoenix, Ariz., Oryx Press, 1986. 664p. illus. index. $125.00. LC 84-42713. ISBN 0-89774-139-0.
There seems to be an unprecedented number of prominent American women sculptors at work today. Among those who come to mind are Louise Nevelson, Marisol, Nancy Grossman, Lynda Benglis, and Lee Bontecou. This reference book includes these and over 300 additional artists. It is a very useful source, with information about "established and emerging artists." In the introduction the author refers to the book as a "study . . . offering previously unpublished information for those who wish to gain insights into the careers of women who pursue art through sculpture." She also explains that the artists were chosen by means of questionnaires sent to art historians, museums, art associations, and other sources, identifying artists in all fifty states. The format is attractive, with a double spread for each artist and a large black-and-white reproduction of one of the artist's works included. There is brief biographical, bibliographic, and chronological in formation, as well as a statement by each artist. Many of these artists, while professional sculptors, are not included in the current edition of *Who's Who in American Art* (R. R. Bowker, 1984). Thus, it is a valuable tool, although the price is prohibitive. [R: Choice, Oct 86, p. 288; RBB, 15 Dec 86, p. 632; RQ, Fall 86, p. 111; WLB, Sept 86, p. 79]—**Sydney Starr Keaveney**

843.   **Who Was Who in American Art**. Peter Hastings Falk, ed. Madison, Madison, Conn., Sound View Press, 1985. 744p. illus. $115.00. LC 85-050119. ISBN 0-93208-700-0.
Nearly 25,000 entries are included in this work, compiled from the original thirty volumes of the *American Art Annual* (1898-1933) and four subsequent volumes entitled *Who's Who in American Art* (1935-1947). Biographies are entered for painters, sculptors, printmakers, illustrators, photographers, cartoonists, critics, curators, educators, and crafts people active from the 1890s through the 1940s. Each entry includes the name, profession, last known address, birth and death dates, where the subject studied, where his or her work is preserved, a record of exhibitions and awards, memberships, and the last volume of the *Annual* or the *Who's Who* in which the subject is listed.
Florence N. Levy, founding editor of the *American Art Annual*, collected data by sending questionnaires to the subjects; she also examined exhibition catalogs and association membership lists. Falk's work for the present volume included examining the last *Who's Who in American Art* (1947), preparing a file of entries, then adding and editing additional bits of information from previous volumes—a process that necessitated cross-checking more than 120,000 entries.

Possessed of an obvious enthusiasm for this gargantuan task, the compiler occasionally adds information not readily available for most subjects. He notes, for example, that Birtley Canfield (1866-1912), a sculptor who specialized in dogs, died from being bitten by one of his subjects. Charles Basing (1865-1933) died in Morocco from blood poisoning after a camel stepped on his foot. Jefferson Chalfant (1856-1931) painted a one-dollar bill in such meticulous detail that it was confiscated by the U.S. Government.

Rarely does one reference source combine as many excellent qualities as does this one. It is eminently useful, saving library users many hours of laborious searching; it is physically durable and typographically pleasing; it is most affordable, especially for such a comprehensive source. A superb choice for art libraries and for large public and academic libraries, its special contribution is an ability to supply biographical details about little-known subjects. [R: LJ, 15 Nov 85, p. 88]—**John Mark Tucker**

16   Music

INTRODUCTION

This chapter on biographical dictionaries of musicians and composers is divided generally by musical genre. It begins with general works both current and retrospective and then continues with Composers, Instrumentalists (General), Jazz, Opera, Popular and Country/Western Music, and Religious Music. These divisions are somewhat arbitrary since many musicians would fall into more than one category. The arrangement has been driven by the major subject inclusions of the biographical dictionaries being considered. While most of the sources are recent, a number of older, and sometimes out of print, dictionaries have been included due to their importance or unique coverage. A few of the older but still important general works dictionaries include *Women Composers, Conductors, and Musicians of the Twentieth Century: Selected Biographies* (Scarecrow, 1988) (see entry 847), which provides information on a number of women composers and musicians not included elsewhere; *Who's Who in American Music: Classical* (Bowker, 1985) (see entry 848), with more than 6,800 entries; which provides 56 interviews based on interviews with each woman composer; and *The Jazz Singers: From Ragtime to the New Wave* (Sterling Publishing, 1988) (see entry 879), which includes some jazz singers not usually found in other sources. Of course, *The New Grove Dictionary of Music & Musicians* (Grove's Dictionaries, 1980) (see entry 858) is now more than eighteen years old but still an important source for biographical information on musicians.

A number of new general biographical dictionaries on musicians, conductors, and composers have also been included. These include updates of some old standards, such as *The Harvard Biographical Dictionary of Music* (Harvard University Press, 1996) (see entry 853), which has been published periodically for many years and includes more than 5,500 brief biographies; *The Portable Baker's Biographical Dictionary of Musicians* (Simon & Schuster, 1995) (see entry 862), which is an abridged version of the larger *Baker's Biographical Dictionary* (Schirmer Books, 1991), and *The Penguin Dictionary of Musical Performers* (Viking Penguin, 1990) (see entry 860), which provides a handy smaller reference for general biographies.

The section Composers includes several important sources, such as *International Encyclopedia of Women Composers* (Books & Music, 1987) (see entry 865), which is now somewhat older but still provides a very large list of women composers; *The Lives of the Great Composers* (W. W. Norton, 1997) (see entry 869), which was in the process of being updated as this book went to press and includes a large number of biographies of composers; and Bull Storm's *Index to Biographies of Contemporary Composers* (Scarecrow, 1987) (see entry 864), which, while not providing a great deal of biographical information, does direct the reader to more than 13,500 composers found in other sources. Several important sources on opera may be found in this chapter, including the recent *International Dictionary of Opera* (St. James Press/Gale, 1993) (see entry 886), which covers a large number of opera performers and composers with brief biographical sketches, and *The New Grove Dictionary of Opera* (Grove's Dictionaries of Music, 1992) (see entry 887), which is one of the more recent Grove's dictionaries and has become an invaluable tool for information on opera.

Both jazz and popular music have been fully represented. *The Harmony Illustrated Encyclopedia of Jazz* (Harmony Books/Crown, 1986) (see entry 877) lists 100 jazz musicians and provides in-depth biographies for each; the *Encyclopedia of the Blues* (University of Arkansas Press, 1992) (see entry 883), first published in French, is translated into English and covers most of the mainstream blues performers; and, of course, *The New Grove Dictionary of Jazz* (Grove's Dictionaries of Music, 1988) (see entry 885), which is the definitive source for information on the jazz world including several hundred biographies. Popular and country/western music has been combined into one section with more than 10 biographical sources. Of particular note are *Contemporary Musicians:*

Profiles of the People in Music (Gale, 1989) (see entry 893), which, as part of a series still being published, provides biographies of more than 80 popular musicians, and *The Da Capo Companion to 20th-Century Popular Music* (Da Capo Press, 1995) (see entry 894), which provides profiles on more than 2,000 popular performers and composers.

GENERAL WORKS

Current Biographies

844.   **Contemporary Composers**. Brian Morton and Pamela Collins, eds. Chicago, St. James Press; distr., Detroit, Gale, 1992. 1019p. $125.00. 780.922. ISBN 1-55862-085-0.

As described in the editors' foreword, this is a summary of almost 500 living composers, not necessarily the most prominent. All were living at the start of this project, around 1989, although a few have died since that time. Following a who's who-style biography, the works of each composer are listed along with the dates of composition and first performance. The third portion of the listing is a description of the entrant's style and manner of composition and place in the vast spectrum of contemporary classical composition. This appears to be the justification for the project, and it succeeds in achieving this goal, although it may possibly suffer from the omission of some prominent names from the list. It is hoped that future revisions will rectify the omission.

No close parallel to this work is apparent. Only among living composers listed in Grove's standard work; in the most recent edition of *Baker's Biographical Dictionary of Musicians*, edited by Nicholas Slonimsky (Schirmer Books/Macmillan, 1992); or in Greene's *Biographical Encyclopedia of Composers* (see ARBA 87, entry 1223) can one find a list of current composers even close to this one. Only one typographical error was found and that in the necrology, probably the most difficult part to keep up-to-date in a work of this kind. Recommended for any extensive reference library. [R: Choice, Dec 92, p. 598; RBB, 1 Dec 92, pp. 686-87; WLB, Oct 92, p. 104]—**Arthur R. Upgren**

845.   **Contemporary Musicians: Profiles of the People in Music**. Michael LaBlanc, ed. Detroit, Gale, 1989- . (twice yearly). illus. index. $49.95 for recent edition. ISSN 1044-2197.

Contemporary Musicians has been published twice yearly beginning in 1989. The latest volume is vol. 18 (1997). Each volume covers between 80 to 100 well-known musicians and groups in all areas of popular music as well as a handful of crossover classical artists. Each of the signed entries incorporates an essay of around 2,000 words, a biographical data section, a selective discography, and a bibliography. Sources rely heavily on periodicals, while other reference tools, such as *The New Grove Dictionary of American Music* (see ARBA 88, entry 1277), are largely ignored. The bibliographies are selective; any patron with access to InfoTrac, for example, will almost always generate additional relevant references. The discographies are inconsistently supplemented by lists of films and compositions, even for composers such as Henry Mancini or Philip Glass. A subject index arranges the entries by categories which may prove helpful (e.g., African, conductors, film scores, harmonica, performance art, rockabilly) and the musicians index usefully includes members of groups.

Because the musicians covered are so well known (perhaps half of the entries have been covered at one time or another in *Current Biography*), they are almost always represented in other reference sources, although rarely in this detail. As with *Current Biography*-like serials, it will take a number of volumes before coverage is sufficient to ensure that any particular person or group has been included in *Contemporary Musicians*.—**Robert Skinner and Robert L.Wick**

846.   **International Who's Who in Music and Musicians' Directory (in the Classical and Light Classical Fields)**. David M. Cummings, ed. Cambridge, England, International Biographical Centre; distr., Bristol, Pa., IPS/Taylor & Francis, 1935- . $165.00 for recent edition. ISSN 0083-9647.

Although this title was first published in 1935, it was only with the 5th edition in 1969 that new editions began appearing every couple of years. The latest editions have become significantly more rigorous in their criteria for inclusion, unlike some of the earlier ones, in which the piano teacher down the road was more likely to be included than an internationally recognized concert pianist. All of the 8,000-plus persons covered are practitioners of Western art music. Format of entries is typical of who's who-type resources, with heavy emphasis on significant career dates. As in the previous editions, seven appendixes cover such areas as names and addresses of orchestras, major competitions, and musical organizations. These are largely superfluous, as similar lists are available in a variety of other publications, and one has to wonder what the purpose is of the U.S. portion of the libraries appendix, which is restricted entirely to public libraries. Regardless, this series remains an essential purchase for larger music collections.—**Robert Skinner and Robert L. Wick**

847.   LePage, Jane Weiner. **Women Composers, Conductors, and Musicians of the Twentieth Century: Selected Biographies**. Volume III. Metuchen, N.J., Scarecrow, 1988. 323p. illus. index. $32.50. LC 80-12162. ISBN 0-8108-2082-X.

This book follows two other volumes of the same title (see ARBA 81, entry 1038, and ARBA 84, entry 884). Like the previous volumes, it offers biographies of women musicians, in this case Orazyna Bacewicz, Betty Beath, Anne Boyd, Sylvia Caduff, Ann Carr-Boyd, Gloria Coates, Selma Epstein, Nicola LeFanu, Priscilla McLean, Elizabeth Maconchy, Mary Mageau, Ursula Mamlok, Priaulx Rainier, Shulamit Ran, Ruth Schonthal, Margaret Sutherland, Joan Tower, and Gillian Whitehead. The articles are based on interviews with each musician (or a family member) as well as writings, often newspaper articles, about the women and reviews of their works. A list of compositions selected by the composer accompanies each appropriate article, as do a discography, a list of publishers, and a list of record companies. Although interesting and informative, the articles on these musicians are very informal and chatty in style, often colored by the author's views. A useful addition to this volume would have been a bibliography of other sources containing information on these musicians.—**Allie Wise Goudy**

848.   **Who's Who in American Music: Classical**. 2d ed. Edited by Jaques Cattell Press. New York, R. R. Bowker, 1985. 783p. index. $124.95. ISBN 0-8352-2074-5. ISSN 0737-9137.

This volume is a significant expansion of the 1st edition (1983). It now contains over 9,000 entries (6,800 taken over from the 1st edition) for "currently active and influential contributors to . . . serious music in America." Information comes mainly from questionnaires submitted by the individuals included, although some entries were prepared from other sources. The information provided includes most of the following: name (and professional name, if different); a "professional classification" (up to three categories); educational background; significant performances (up to seven); recordings; roles; a career outline (usually a listing of formal positions); teaching experience; selected listings of honors, awards, and articles or books about the individual (up to three); memberships; research interests; a list of up to six publications; an artist's manager; and mailing address.

Although the editorial work seems to have been done mainly by computers (a number of errors from the 1st edition have been carried over), many of the significant omissions in that edition have been rectified. Still, this is an expensive work, and only those libraries that have extensive music reference collections will need every edition. Other libraries should purchase editions selectively; and, as already stated, the 2nd edition is a better bargain than the first. [R: WLB, May 86, p. 66]—**George R. Hill**

Retrospective Biographies

849.   **American Musicologists, c. 1890-1945: A Bio-Bibliographical Sourcebook to the Formative Period**. Curt Efram Steinzor, comp. Westport, Conn., Greenwood Press, 1989. 286p. index. (Music Reference Collection, no.17). $49.95. ML1 28.M8S73. 01 6.78'092'2. LC 88-38549. ISBN 0-313-26197-0.

The first generation of American musicologists had to go to Europe to study. European wars both made our scholars more independent and brought many European musicologists to our shores. The establishment and growth of musicology in the United States is chronicled here by a study of the 35 most important and influential American musicologists of its first phase. While 19 of them were American-born, such as Theodore Baker, Gustave Reese, and William Oliver Strunk, 16 were transplanted Europeans, including Willi Apel, Alfred Einstein, Paul Henry Lang, and Curt Sachs. Their contributions to musicology are of great importance, and their students have carried their interests, ideas, and methods forward into succeeding generations of music scholars, establishing this country as a potent contributor to international musicology.

Steinzor has gathered basic research materials together by giving short biographical entries for each musicologist, chronological lists of their writings, and sources for material about them. The author stops here, but his brief but fascinating introduction hints that he has learned more and drawn more conclusions than he is willing to share.

For many, the most useful feature of the book will be the lists of the writings of these musicologists. The period covered predates *Music Index*, which makes the classified subject index of major importance. It could have been more detailed and specific rather than limited to broad headings such as "History of Music" and "Musicians—Lives and Works," especially since the author went to such lengths to ferret out these articles. A list of sources and a selected list of literature on the subject are provided and should be used for those wanting more information on the basic subject. [R: Choice, Oct 89, p. 294]—**George Louis Mayer**

850.   **Baker's Biographical Dictionary of Musicians**. 8th ed. Revised by Nicolas Slonimsky. New York, Schirmer Books/Macmillan, 1992. 2115p. $125.00. ML105.B16. 780'.92'2. LC 91-24591. ISBN 0-02-872415-1.

This work contains information on musicians of all genres, times, and places. At the age of 97, the Russian-American musicologist Slonimsky continues to entertain with his sharp wit and inform through his detailed research in music. In this edition he has added 1,100 new entries and has revised 1,300 others. The additional entries include a wider coverage of popular music, women composers, and ethnomusicologists than did the 7th edition (see ARBA 86, entry 1232). Most entries contain brief biographical information, a list of works and writings, and a bibliography. Items in the bibliography are arranged in chronological order; some are as recent as 1990. Although the information about each person is brief, it serves as an excellent starting point for further research. This work remains one of the core resources for music reference collections. [R: LJ, Jan 92, p. 104; RBB, 1 Feb 92, p. 1052; SLJ, May 92, p. 32; WLB, Mar 92, pp. 113-14]—**Margaret A. Grift**

851.   **Baker's Biographical Dictionary of Twentieth-Century Classical Musicians**. Nicolas Slonimsky, comp. Laura Kuhn and Dennis McIntire, eds. New York, Schirmer Books/Simon & Schuster Macmillan, 1997. 1595p. $90.00. ISBN 0-02-871271-4.

This is the first single-volume work on twentieth-century classical composers and musicians. John Vinton's *Dictionary of Contemporary Music* (see ARBA 75, entry 1143) covered fewer composers, although it treated terminology, but is becoming dated. *Contemporary Composers* (see ARBA 93, entry 1255) is selective in coverage. Editor Kuhn described the 8th edition of the more general *Baker's Biographical Dictionary of Musicians* (see ARBA 93, entry 1244) as "literally bursting its seams." *Baker's Biographical Dictionary of Twentieth-Century Classical Musicians* is physically husky, only 500 pages smaller than the more general work; 60 percent of its materials is new.

Kuhn, no stranger to lexicography, assisted the late Slonimsky with the biographical dictionary and the most recent edition of *Music since 1900*. She and McIntire maintain the standards so ably set by the former editor. One visual improvement to the volume is bold typeface to highlight works and genre sections of the biographies and bibliographies. Limiting the volume to one century has allowed for more complete works lists for composers. Composers and performers who are known primarily for jazz but made a contribution to classical music are included, such as George Gershwin, Duke Ellington, Irving Berlin, Max Roach, and Wynton Marsalis. There are brief entries for Richard Rodgers and Frederick Loewe, but not George M. Cohan. For composers of band music, such as Henry Fillmore, *The Heritage Encyclopedia of Band Music* (see ARBA 93, entry 1283) still provides more information. Other entries have seen significant expansion from the 8th edition of *Baker's*, such as Morton Feldman, Samuel Barber, and Leonard Bernstein, with recent bibliographic entries. A glossary explains many of the forms and styles of avant-garde music, with links to specific composers. This volume will undoubtedly be an essential resource for study of twentieth-century classical musicians.—**Ralph Hartsock**

852. **The Concise Baker's Biographical Dictionary of Musicians**. By Nicolas Slonimsky. New York, Schirmer Books/Macmillan, 1988. 1407p. $35.00. LC 87-32328. ISBN 0-02-872411-9.

The 7th edition of *Baker's Biographical Dictionary* (see ARBA 86, entry 1232) included approximately 13,000 entries and was published in an unwieldy single volume of 2,577 pages, an increase of over 400 pages from the 6th edition. This concise version of *Baker's* 7th edition has been reduced by over 1,100 pages, and the number of entries has been reduced to about half that of the parent volume. No changes in content have been made in the entries, although a necrology has been included to update death dates. Rather, entries for secondary figures, such as music critics, church organists, librarians, theorists, and commentators have been eliminated, as have those of minor composers and popular music idols not deemed to be of lasting value.

Baker's, of course, is a basic music reference tool. For those libraries which do not own the 7th edition and find it difficult to afford, for general reference collections, and for librarians needing a desk copy (such as catalogers), the *Concise Baker's* is a bargain. For libraries already owning the 7th edition, and not needing an additional, smaller, less expensive resource, the purchase of this volume seems unnecessary.—**Allie Wise Goudy**

853. **The Harvard Biographical Dictionary of Music**. Don Michael Randel, ed. Cambridge, Mass., Belknap Press/Harvard University Press, 1996. 1013p. illus. $39.95. ISBN 0-674-37299-9.

Based on *The New Harvard Dictionary of Music* (see ARBA 87, entry 1231), *The Harvard Biographical Dictionary of Music* provides authoritative biographical information on more than 5,500 figures in the world of music, including performers, composers, instrument makers, and music theorists. Randel points out in the preface that the *Harvard Biographical Dictionary* "concerns primarily the history of concert music in the Western tradition. That is, the musicians whose biographies it includes are first and foremost composers of Western concert art music from the earliest times to the present . . . [and] includes jazz musicians and at least some of the more prominent exponents of popular music." The individual entries follow the standard form used in the other Harvard dictionaries (i.e., name, birth and death dates and places, and a brief biography covering the major events in the individual's life). Each entry also contains a list of works by the individual and a brief bibliography of major books and articles about the individual. In a few cases, there are black-and-white photographs of more prominent individuals, but they are rare and appear to be used in a random manner.

As in the case of *The New Harvard Dictionary of Music*, the scholarship in this biography spin-off is meticulous, and the information provided is to the point and covers the major elements of the individuals' lives. The biographies are written by more than 70 of the most prominent musicologists today. Also, in most cases, the prose of the biographies is lively and easily read.

The major competition for this work is, of course, *Baker's Biographical Dictionary of Musicians* (8th ed.; see entry 850), which has been the standard source for brief biographies for at least 30 years. The 8th edition of *Baker's* provides slightly more than 2,500 biographies, far fewer than the *Harvard* title. In addition, the entries in *Baker's* tend to be shorter than those found in *Harvard*, and *Baker's* does not furnish photographs. Of course, *The New Grove Dictionary of Music and Musicians* (see ARBA 81, entry 1016) supplies a large number of individual biographies of musicians and composers that are usually very detailed, but it does not replace the ease of use of the smaller dictionaries of biography.

The Harvard Biographical Dictionary of Music is highly recommended for all library collections. Its large number of biographies of individuals in non-Western classical music is especially welcome.—**Robert L. Wick**

854. **International Who's Who in Music and Musicians' Directory (in the Classical and Light Classical Fields)**. 13th ed. David M. Cummings, ed. Cambridge, England, International Biographical Centre; distr., Bristol, Pa., IPS/Taylor & Francis, 1992. 1357p. $165.00. ISBN 0-948875-11-9.

Although this title was first published in 1935, it was only with the 5th edition in 1969 that new editions began appearing every couple of years. The latest editions have become significantly more rigorous in their criteria for inclusion, unlike some of the earlier ones, in which the piano teacher down the road was more likely to be included than an internationally recognized concert pianist. All of the 8,000 persons covered are practitioners of Western art music, and 2,000 of these are new to this edition. Format of entries is typical of who's who-type resources, with heavy emphasis on significant career dates. As in the previous editions, seven appendixes cover such areas as names and addresses of orchestras, major competitions, and musical organizations. These are largely superfluous, as similar lists are available in a variety of other publications, and one has to wonder what the purpose is of the U.S. portion of the libraries appendix, which is restricted entirely to public libraries. Regardless, this series remains an essential purchase for larger music collections.—**Robert Skinner**

855.   Mender, Mona. **Extraordinary Women in Support of Music**. Lanham, Md., Scarecrow Press, 1997. 309p. index. $48.00. ISBN 0-8108-3278-X.

Occasionally, writers of reference books fill a slot that was not obviously gaping. Mender's *Extraordinary Women* is just such a filler. Opening with a preface explaining her intent to celebrate women in the secondary role of supporting the arts, she begins chapter 1 with a masterly capsulized history of music in the Western tradition that highlights the service of nuns, feudal homemakers, and the subdued objects of the troubadour's plaint. Specific supporters fall into roughly six categories: patronesses and salon mistresses, mates, teachers, administrators, family members, and choreographers. The addition of five pages of notes, more than six pages of sources, an index of proper names, and a brief author's biography undergirds the work with helpful scholarly connections. A more thorough index might have listed musical eras, genres, and individual musical instruments (e.g., baroque, hymnody, and pipe organ).

Entries are balanced biographies filled with insightful commentary and generous citations. Mender stresses the strengths, character, tastes, and passions of female music supporters, for example, Aspasia's wit, Diane de Poitiers's grounding in the arts, Eleanor of Aquitaine's intelligence, Alma Werfel's self-confidence, Isabela d'Este's generosity toward Renaissance performers, and Maria Mozart's dedication to her brilliant brother. Some of the 63 subjects were themselves musicians, as is the case with opera diva Beverly Sills, cellist Marta Casals, vocalist Rildia Cliburn, conductor Sarah Caldwell, and composer Clara Schumann.

With compassion and regret, Mender expresses the yearnings of pre-feminist music lovers and the philosophies of their eras that relegated them to the background of the art world. Of teacher Nadia-Juliette Boulanger, she notes that women were required to have a chaperone when attending public concerts. Counter to those who were muzzled by patriarchy, Mender celebrates the female love of life, as found in George Sand's embrace of public issues, Mary Louise Zimbalist's altruism, and Martha Graham's tribute to human reproduction through dance. Altogether, Mender's work is a surprisingly delightful compendium.—**Mary Ellen Snodgrass**

856.   **Musical Americans: A Biographical Dictionary 1918-1926**. Mary DuPree, ed. Berkeley, Calif., Fallen Leaf Press, 1997. 303p. index. (Fallen Leaf Reference Books in Music, no. 23). $37.95. ISBN 0-914913-13-1.

Musical Americans consists of reprints of 414 biographies originally published in the magazine *Musical America* between February 1918 and January 1926. The editor provides an eight-page introduction describing *Musical America* and its relationship to the contemporary musical scene. She also describes the influence the magazine's editor, John Freund, had in selecting the chosen musicians. His selection features composers, singers, and instrumentalists, and he makes a point of including women in almost equal numbers with men. Many of the featured subjects are not found in standard music biographical tools. The biographies are arranged alphabetically, with two columns per page, and at the end of each entry the date of the original issue appears. In back are listings of musicians by date of article and by birth date. A substantial index listing topics, corporate entities, musical works, and persons concludes the work.

The index comprises about one-third of the book and has a one-page introduction. It is unusual in that it refers directly to the names of the musicians (given in parentheses) rather than to pages. To users unfamiliar with this technique and who expect to see numerical references, either to pages or to article numbers, the absence of numbers may be mistaken for a production error. Actual errors found were the misspelling of Clough-Leighter and the misnumbering of footnotes 9 and 10 in the introduction.

Fallen Leaf Press has created a sturdy, attractive book, which will be a welcome source for historians of music and Americana as well as for those preparing program notes for concerts and recordings. The index itself constitutes a rich source of information and makes the work worthy of consultation for a wide range of historical topics. Because the original publication is likely to be difficult to obtain, this reproduction is welcome. The production format also lends itself to bedtime reading for avid connoisseurs of early-twentieth-century American music.—**Ian Fairclough and Robert L. Wick**

857. **The New Grove Dictionary of American Music**. H. Wiley Hitchcock and Stanley Sadie, eds. New York, Grove's Dictionaries of Music, 1986. 4v. illus. $495.00/set. LC 86-404. ISBN 0-943818-36-2.

It is difficult to imagine the library that will not have purchased *The New Grove Dictionary of American Music* as a matter of course, in light of the reputation enjoyed by *The New Grove Dictionary of Music & Musicians* (see ARBA 81, entry 1016) and *The New Grove Dictionary of Musical Instruments* (see ARBA 86, entry 1252). Those that have not should consider whether they can afford to remain without so important a resource at any price. For while sins of omission and commission in so broad an undertaking will echo in the critical press for some time, let it be said at the outset that the book under review is an unequivocal triumph, a national dictionary not likely to be equaled or surpassed in our lifetime.

Amerigrove addresses the music of the United States proper, whether created by Americans themselves or by foreigners living or visiting here. It does not purport to cover the music of the Americas in general. Helmut Kallmann's *Encyclopedia of Music in Canada* (see ARBA 83, entry 930) already provides excellent treatment of the music of that country, while Latin America must await some future army of determined lexicographers. Articles with their attendant worklists and bibliographies follow the stylistic guidelines employed so successfully in the *New Grove*, yet *Amerigrove* is far more than a spinoff from its distinguished parent. With minor exceptions, articles carried over from the *New Grove* were extensively revised and updated, and nearly 1,000 scholars contributed the vast amount of entirely new material.

Entries for individual composers comprise approximately two-thirds of *Amerigrove*'s 5,000 articles. The editors envisioned a "critically organized repository of historically significant information" (v. 1, p. ix) rather than a comprehensive directory, and the selectivity inherent in the term *historically significant* has been responsibly exercised. After composers, performers (both individuals and groups) enjoy the most thorough coverage, followed by a rich miscellany of conductors, choreographers, lyricists, impresarios, educators, patrons, publishers, instrument makers, and others. Hundreds of terms, from *break dancing* and *chicken scratch* to work songs, are clearly and concisely identified.

Perhaps the most impressive achievement of *Amerigrove* lies in its deep understanding of indigenous traditions far removed from the heritage of European art music. In addition to outstanding articles on the music of Afro-Americans and native Americans, virtually all aspects of jazz, rock, popular, country, and gospel music are explored in rich detail. Broad topical articles survey Asian-American music, women in music, and the music of religious denominations. Genre headings such as *chamber music* and *musical theater* evaluate uniquely American contributions to individual repertoires.

Miscellaneous articles, including many one might expect to fall outside the scope of a music dictionary, are a continuing source of useful and unusual information. Entries on awards and festivals, copyright, college songs, periodicals, and the music industry will be frequently consulted by librarians, as will the articles on major cities, educational institutions, and libraries themselves.

The larger physical format and handsome Garamond typeface of the four-volume *Amerigrove* are an improvement (to these eyes) over its predecessors. The 600 or so photographs and drawings are adequately reproduced, and the volumes seem destined to stand up to the heavy use they will undoubtedly receive. With the announcement of a dictionary of jazz close on the heels of this important milestone, one awaits the next efforts of the seemingly indefatigable *New Grove* team with renewed admiration and anticipation. [R: Choice, Jan 87, pp. 724-25]—**Ross Wood**

858. **The New Grove Dictionary of Music & Musicians**. Stanley Sadie, ed. 6th ed. Washington, D.C., Grove's Dictionaries of Music, 1980. 20v. illus. bibliog. $2,100.00/set. LC 79-26207. ISBN 0-333-23111-2.

The 6th edition of the standard multi-volume music encyclopedia in English was published in 1980, and its new title reflects a major revision, the most thorough since the work was first published in the nineteenth century. The 9-volume 5th edition (1954) had a very strong British bias and was still aimed quite frankly at the musical amateur. By contrast, this new edition is designed for both the informed layperson and the professional musicologist. It seeks an international scope and perspective, by and large successfully. Clearly, the conception of the set has been influenced strongly both by the *New Encyclopaedia Britannica* and by *Die Musik in Geschichte und Gegenwart* (*MGG*), a 16-volume work with signed articles written by specialists from throughout the world.

Volumes of *The New Grove* average well over 750 pages each. According to the publisher's prospectus, the set contains approximately 18 million words, 22,500 articles and 7,400 cross-references, 3,000 illustrations (occupying about 7 percent of the total space), and 2,500 musical examples. It is claimed that 97 percent of the text is new. With a few exceptions (mainly entries for families of musicians), arrangement of the encyclopedia is alphabetical. Volume 20 contains an index of approximately 9,000 terms used in non-Western and folk music, with references to the articles in which they occur.

Twice the size of the 5th edition of *Grove's Dictionary*, this new edition both extends its scope to new areas and expands the treatment of most traditional subjects. Important new areas of emphasis include popular music, jazz, non-Western music, and dance. Articles on early music (European music before the mid-eighteenth century) and contemporary music have been greatly amplified. Latin America, Spain, Portugal, and Eastern Europe are much more thoroughly covered. As might be expected, less enduring aspects of the nineteenth century in general, and of Victorian England in particular, receive less space than in previous editions. Those libraries concerned with supporting historical research will want to retain all earlier editions.

Most signed articles are written by well-known authorities and are highly reliable. More than a third of the contributors are American, and approximately a fifth are from Britain. The prospectus explains the relatively smaller representation of authors from the world's other most important musicological center, the German-speaking community, by noting that they had contributed heavily to *MGG*.

The senior editors and consultants responsible for the planning, solicitation, and review of articles are recognized scholars. Undoubtedly in part because of the team approach, *The New Grove* does not seem to have major gaps in coverage. It must be said, however, that the junior editorial staff was not always up to the job. This can be seen in minor slips and inconsistencies of various sorts, which generally result from insufficient knowledgeable checking. Reliability thus depends in no small part on the care with which individual authors read galleys and were able to follow through in the correction process. In a work of this size, naturally some articles are perfunctory or inadequate, but in general, coverage of assigned topics is thorough and the level quite high.

The encyclopedia is printed in double-column format in a legible typeface on paper with a reasonable opacity. The volumes for the first part of the alphabet were printed in Hong Kong; the others, in the United States; and the quality of printing in these latter volumes is noticeably higher. Reproductions of illustrations (all are black-and-white) vary in quality from acceptable to poor. Many are too gray and too small to show the required detail clearly. Illustrations in *MGG* are far superior. The binding is handsome and appears serviceable.

The New Grove represents a major advance over earlier editions. Any library that answers even casual questions about music should have it available in the reference section. *MGG* contains many biographies and by far is the most important source for information on this subject. For example, earlier-twentieth-century composers are all included in this set. In addition, many younger men and women and even minor composers are also represented with short biographies. Major biographical articles include not only actual material, but also stylistic criticism and numerous critical comments from recognized authorities. [R: BL, 1 Oct 80, p. 273; LJ, 15 Dec 80, p. 2562]—**George R. Hill and Bohdan S. Wynar**

859.   **The Norton/Grove Concise Encyclopedia of Music**. Stanley Sadie and Alison Latham, eds. New York, W. W. Norton, 1995. 909p. illus. $40.00. ISBN 0-393-03753-3.

Published in England by Macmillan as *The Grove Concise Dictionary of Music*, this offshoot of *The New Grove Dictionary of Music and Musicians* (see ARBA 81, entry 1016) shares the same editor (Sadie), uses its parent work as its primary source of information, and employs the efforts of some two dozen contributors (although their work is not signed). The 1995 edition of the *Norton/Grove* offers music lovers and students more than 10,000 short entries for composers, performers, instruments, musical terms, genres, musical works, music publishing, instrument makers, acoustics, and non-Western music. An apt comparison can be made to Michael Kennedy's *The Oxford Dictionary of Music* (Oxford University Press, 1985), similar in size and design to *Norton/Grove*. Kennedy is stronger on historical persons. Kennedy gives only years of births and deaths, while *Norton/Grove* gives complete dates. More non-English terms are included in Kennedy, but *Norton/Grove* covers more instruments. Notable features of *Norton/Grove* include extended (up to a page or two) entries for major topics such as criticism, opera, and symphony; line drawings of families of instruments; and selective worklists for major composers. In breadth, balance, and authority, this is a valuable resource which complements similar one-volume reference works on music. [R: Choice, Mar 89, p. 1128; LJ, Jan 89, p. 80; RBB, 1 Apr 89, p. l360]—**William S. Brockman and Robert L. Wick**

860.   **The Penguin Dictionary of Musical Performers**. By Arthur Jacobs. New York, Viking Penguin, 1990. 25Op. $21.95. ISBN 0-670-80755-9.

This is a good, basic guide to the major performers of the distant and near past. However, as with so many books of this kind, The author does not include up-and-coming names no matter how promising their career. One would expect to find an entry for the 19-year-old Russian pianist Evgeny Kissin, who has been hailed as an extraordinary talent on the international scene since he was 12. But his name and those of many others that users of this book might expect to find are omitted. This is a pity since the short and informative style of the author is attractive.

Entries for chamber groups such as the Juilliard Quartet are important inclusions. An entry gives the year the group was founded, original personnel, and changes that have occurred since. This is often hard-to-find information (especially in a one-volume dictionary likely to appear in small, nonspecialized reference book collections). The work is useful as far as it goes. One wishes it went further. [R: LJ, Aug 90, p. 104; RBB, 15 Oct 90, pp. 474-75]—**George Louis Mayer**

861.   Pilkington, Michael. **Campion, Dowland and the Lutenist Songwriters**. Bloomington, Indiana University Press, 1989. 179p. index. (English Solo Song). $25.00. ML128.S3P54. 016.78242'0942'09031. LC 89-11006. ISBN 0-253-34695-9.

Pilkington, Michael. **Gurney, Ireland, Quilter and Warlock**. Bloomington, Indiana University Press, 1989. 194p. index. (English Solo Song). $25.00. ML2831.P54. 782.42168'092'242. LC 89-11024. ISBN 0-253-34694-0.

These two books by Pilkington, a teacher at the Guildhall School of Music and a compiler and editor of music publications, are the initial volumes in the English Solo Song series. As such they are organized similarly. The first volume, *Campion, Dowland and the Lutenist Songwriters* (hereafter *Campion*), includes the songs of 32 lutanist songwriters whose songs have been published in collections currently in print. *Gurney, Ireland, Quilter and Warlock* (hereafter *Gurney*) covers songs with piano accompaniment by these four British composers who worked primarily in the first half of the twentieth century. Extensive information is provided for each song listed in both volumes: title, poet if known, tonality, the collection in which the song appears, range of vocal line, meter, duration, difficulty, appropriate voice types, subject of song, description of the vocal line, description of the accompaniment, additional comments often noting variations between the text of the poetry and the song, arrangements of the song, and qualitative notes as well.

Both volumes include a selected bibliography of general sources, anthologies, and sources about the poets whose texts were set. *Gurney* includes an index to titles and first lines, while *Campion* has only an index to first lines. *Gurney* contains an index to special categories such as cycles, sets,

Christmas songs, drinking songs, and program finishers, as well as an index to songs by voice types, features not included in *Campion*. These indexes are especially useful and should be continued in future volumes.

This repertoire, although relatively unknown, deserves greater recognition and appreciation. By highlighting it through these volumes, Pilkington provides that opportunity. This reviewer eagerly awaits additional volumes.—**Allie Wise Goudy**

862. **The Portable Baker's Biographical Dictionary of Musicians**. By Nicholas Slonimsky. Richard Kostelanetz and Michael Stutzman, eds. New York, Schirmer Books/Simon & Schuster, 1995. 291p. index. $20.00pa. ISBN 0-02-871225-0.

Baker's Biographical Dictionary of Musicians is approaching its 100th birthday. It was first published by G. Schirmer in 1900 and has since gone through several major revisions. The 8th edition was published in 1991 (see ARBA 93, entry 1244) and contained more than 2,000 pages and some 2 million words. *Baker's*, as it is known to music students and professionals, is still the major source for biographical information on musicians and other music professionals. The problem has been that it has only been available in larger libraries due to its size and cost. Kostelanetz and Stutzman have put into one small volume the major entries of the larger *Baker's*. In some cases entries have had to be abridged to keep the volume small, but most of the original flare of Slonimsky's writing has been retained. Also, much of the additional material found in the larger *Baker's* is missing (e.g., the large bibliographies, prefaces, and lists of compositions).

For the most part the selections from the larger work appear to be good ones. Most of the well-known musicians and composers can be found, including some popular music performers such as Janis Joplin and Elvis Presley. While many of the entries are abbreviated from the larger work, they provide valuable information concerning the life of the individual, place of birth, positions held, and an analysis of major works. The narrative form of the original *Baker's* has been maintained, along with many of the witty comments.

The Portable Baker's makes an ideal reference for home and office, and it will delight all music enthusiasts, from the casual concert goer to the professional musician. While it probably is not a logical purchase for academic and public libraries that already own the larger *Baker's*, smaller branches and special music collections not owning the larger title will find it a useful addition.—**Robert L. Wick**

863. Turner, Patricia. **Dictionary of Afro-American Performers: 78 RPM and Cylinder Recordings of Opera, Choral Music, and Song, c.1900-1949**. New York, Garland, 1990. 433p. illus. (Garland Reference Library of the Humanities, v.590). $45.00. ML156.2.T87. 016.78' 08996073'00266. LC 89-17102. ISBN 0-8240-8736-4.

Considering the large number of recording studios and record labels that existed in the early years of the phonograph industry, it is almost a wonder that there are persons brave enough to compile discographies. Turner notes in her preface that she desired to fill the gap in the existing discographies created by "the exclusion from many surveys and histories of American classical music [of] the Afro-American participation in the classical music tradition." With this challenge Turner has admirably embraced the extensive research required to complete a reference work of this nature.

In identifying recordings made between roughly 1900 and 1949, the dictionary encompasses the era from the acoustical (preelectric) period until well into the electric period. The alphabetical lists include composers, vocalists, instrumentalists, vocal groups, musicals, and operas. A few spoken word recordings are also included. Three record companies—Black Swan Records, George W. Broome Records, and Paramount Records—that pioneered Afro-American recordings are listed under separate entries. The inclusion of a small number of studio and advertisement portrait photographs provides a visual insight into the composers and artists of this era.

Individual entries consist of a short biography, a bibliography, and a discography. Included in the discographies are record labels, record numbers, composers, matrix numbers (these were the numbers of the "master" recordings), accompaniment, and dates of issue. Also cataloged in the case of reissues are long-playing album record labels and numbers and reissue dates. The author provides an extensive bibliography of books and articles, printed library catalogs, periodicals, journals, recording company catalogs, and newspapers.

A complete general index would be desirable. Nevertheless, for the most part, the information provided in this work is not available elsewhere, and the dictionary should be added to the collection of those libraries serving music and theatrical patrons. [R: Choice, Nov. 90, p. 462]—**Louis G. Zelenka**

COMPOSERS

864.   Bull, Storm. **Index to Biographies of Contemporary Composers**. Volume III. Metuchen, N.J., Scarecrow, 1987. 854p. $62.50. LC 64-11781. ISBN 0-8108-1930-9.

The first volume, from 1964, covered composers active between 1900 and 1950 who were alive at the time of printing. The 2nd volume (1974) covered ten more years, adding more than 2,000 names. The present volume has culled 13,500 names from 98 generally newly published sources; included in the latter are national directories from probably every country that has one. The scope is thus international. This is a very helpful volume for one needing to find sources for information on specific composers. Along with the composer's name are given designation of national origin, birth and death dates, name variants, and a register of the sources for the data. It can thus be helpful in the development of a librarian's authority file, and certainly for the researcher. The one obstacle is the source abbreviations. Eileen Southern's *Biographical Dictionary of Afro-American and African Musicians* (see ARBA 83, entry 961), as an example, is cited as AFR, and Bjarne Korsten's *Contemporary Norwegian Piano Music* becomes NPM. Not very mnemonic. But these sources would make a good acquisition list for libraries wishing to intensify their music reference collections, and even the small music collection will benefit from this directory.—**Dominique-René de Lerma**

865.   Cohen, Aaron I. **International Encyclopedia of Women Composers**. 2d ed. New York, Books & Music (USA), 1987. 2v. illus. bibliog. $125.00/set. LC 86-72857. ISBN 0-9617485-2-4.

The 1st edition of this valuable reference work (see ARBA 83, entry 945) has been out of print for several years, and it is good to have an expanded, two-volume version available costing less than the original. The new edition contains over 1,230 pages (over 600 pages longer than the original) and covers 1,200 more composers. It includes 572 photographs. The original appendices listed lacuna; composers arranged by various criteria including country, century, instrument, occupation; an extensive bibliography; and other information. Cohen has added lists of operas by women, compositions influenced by Shakespeare, pseudonyms, and a discography of LPs. Although the 1st edition was generally well received, the compiler and his staff have taken a number of criticisms to heart. It is particularly gratifying to see female composers (most notably, Amy Marcy Beach) listed first under their own names rather than their husbands' names. Although this set will not replace other more specialized resources (especially those dealing with popular music), it belongs in every music collection. [R: Choice, Sept 88, p. 76]—**Robert Skinner**

866.   **Flute Music by Women Composers: An Annotated Catalog**. Heidi M. Boenke, comp. Westport, Conn., Greenwood Press, 1988. 201 p. bibliog. index. (Music Reference Collection, No. 16). $37.95. LC 88-21317. ISBN 0-313-26019-2.

The publication of this catalog adds another volume to the growing list of books concentrating on women's role in music. This particular book presents flute compositions—solo, concertos, chamber works—written by women composers from all over the world. The vast majority of composers are from the twentieth century. The author has included any composition she could find, even if complete information was unavailable. Most of the entries, however, which are alphabetically arranged by composer, include brief biographical information about the composer, a list of flute compositions with instrumentation, publisher, and date of publication. Also included, when available, are a record number and date, an OCLC number, and an item number from the *National Union Catalog*. Indexes are provided which allow access by instrumentation and title. These are useful, although the instrumentation index would be improved if several of the categories, such as "Duets," "Flute and Strings," "Other Small Ensembles," and "Other Large Ensembles," were subarranged by specific instruments. Users will appreciate the thoroughness of the information within the entries. The book is recommended to conservatory libraries, large and medium-sized academic music collections, and larger public libraries needing specialized resources.—**Allie Wise Goudy**

867.   Grattan, Virginia L. **American Women Songwriters: A Biographical Dictionary**. West-port, Conn., Greenwood Press, 1993. 279p. illus. index. $39.95. ML106.U3G73. 782.42'092'273. LC 92-32211. ISBN 0-313-28510-I.

Grattan has compiled a useful tool for anyone wishing to study the role of women as creators of American popular song during the last two centuries. Neither a history nor a critical evaluation of the literature—nor even a particularly scholarly work—this book provides biographies, ranging in length from a half page to five pages, of women composers and lyricists, the majority active since 1920. For convenience the author groups the entries under several categories: pop/rock, motion pic-tures, musicals, blues, jazz, folk, country, hymns, and gospel, and adds a section on women writers of nineteenth- and early-twentieth-century parlor songs. After a stripped-down history of each type of song, each section presents, in alphabetical order, biographies of up to 30 women. At the end of each bi-ography is a list of materials to be consulted for further information. Although Grattan's writing is at best journalistic and often colloquial, her manner is well suited to her subjects and her potential readers.

Comparison of Grattan's biographies with those in *The New Grove Dictionary of American Music* (*NGA*) (see ARBA 88, entry 1277) illuminates several areas where she has something of an edge over that most scholarly source. First, she includes many women whom the editors of *NGA* con-sidered too unimportant to mention. Moreover, Grattan is more likely than *NGA* to provide material of a personal or anecdotal nature, which the general reader will enjoy, and to list more items in her bibliographies. Yet Grattan and *NGA* give conflicting information on many women listed in both sources (e.g., *NGA* disagrees with Grattan on the year of Madonna's birth, and Peggy Lee may have written more than 200 songs [Grattan] or more than 500 songs [*NGA*]). This is not to say that *NGA* is invariably correct, but simply to point out that such conflicts can only be resolved by consulting addi-tional sources of information.

More disturbing is Grattan's lack of clarity in stating exactly what her subjects have contributed to American popular song. Some were composers, others were lyricists, while still others wrote both tunes and lyrics; but it is difficult to determine which women belong in which category. One also can-not be sure whether a composer actually wrote the music down or whether she simply sang her tunes to someone capable of notating them and adding harmony and orchestration. Some women also col-laborated with other poet-composers on specific songs, but the nature of the collaboration is seldom described. Grattan has provided a good starting point in the search for materials on women songwrit-ers, but her book is inadequate as a sole source of information. [R: Choice, Nov 93, p. 432; LJ, 15 Mar 93, p. 68; RBB, July 93, p. 2000; RQ, Winter 93, p. 279; SLMQ, Fall 93, p. 58]—**Karin Pendle**

868.   Jezic, Diane Peacock. **Women Composers: The Lost Tradition Found**. New York, Femi-nist Press; distr., New York, Talman, 1988. 250p. illus. $29.95; $12.95pa. ML390.J37. 780'.92'2. LC 88-31052. ISBN 0-935312-94-3; 0-935312-95-1pa.

This volume presents the lives and works of 25 Western women composers from the eleventh century to the present. Arranged chronologically, it is divided into five periods of music history. The chapter on each composer includes a biographical summary, discussion of her life and work, very brief analysis of one or more compositions, selected discography, and brief bibliography. Six appen-dixes provide further information on women composers and conductors, music textbooks, and re-cording companies. A very useful bibliography completes the work.

Jezic created this resource as a result of the poor coverage of women composers in music appre-ciation textbooks. She designed the book to be suitable for use in both music appreciation and women's studies courses. Cassettes presenting all of the analyzed compositions have been specially produced and are available separately.

While there is reference value in Jezic's offering, especially the bibliography, it will be of more value as a classroom text or additional reading for students. It cannot compare with either edition of Cohen's *International Encyclopedia of Women Composers* (see ARBA 83, entry 945, and ARBA 89, entry 1199) as a general reference source. Cohen's 1st edition provides biographies, more complete listings of compositions, and bibliographies on 3,700 women composers from all periods and all parts of the world; the 2nd edition includes even more women composers. *Women Composers* will be more appropriately placed and better appreciated in the circulating collection than in reference. [R: LJ,15 Apr 89, p. 70]—**Carol Wheeler**

869. Schonberg, Harold C. **The Lives of the Great Composers**. 3rd ed. New York, W. W. Norton, 1997. 653p. illus. bibliog. index. $24.95. LC 80-15058. ISBN 0-393-03857-2.

This work was updated and enlarged in the 1997 edition. Some of the material in this book originally appeared in his weekly *New York Times* column and as *Times* magazine pieces and is presented here in a revised and amplified version. There are chapters on nationalistic schools and light classical composers such as Offenbach, Johann Strauss, Jr., and Sullivan. Schonberg has not missed many composers. They are presented chronologically, and the *life* of each composer is stressed rather than his output. Detailed descriptions of the composers' works will not be found here, although a large bibliography (over 400 items) is included so that the person who desires to look at a composer in more depth is given guidelines for a search. *The Lives of the Great Composers* is light reading and anecdotal in concept, but it does capture the interest of the readers, so that they might read on and discover other composers.—**Robert Palmieri and Robert L. Wick**

870. Sonevyts'kyi, Ihor, and Nataliia Palidvor-Sonevyts'ka. **Dictionary of Ukrainian Composers**. New York, Union of Ukrainian Composers, 1997. 335p. index. $25.00pa.

As the only dictionary of Ukrainian composers published in English, this work fills a definite need. Presented in alphabetic order, all entries consist of three parts: biographical information; a comprehensive list of the composer's major works; and a bibliography of articles and books, if available, about the composer. Ihor Sonevyts'kyi, a noted composer in his own right, and his wife Nataliia spent many years on this important project, consulting all available sources published abroad and some reference sources published in the former Soviet Union (e.g., *Sovetskiie Kompozitory i Muzykovedy* [Moscow 1978-1981] and *Spilka Kompozytoriv Ukrainy* [Kiev, 1968]). In addition, questionnaires were used as sources of information for those Ukrainian composers living abroad.

A spot-check of the entries listed under "A" and "B" was conducted to evaluate the coverage of this work. A number of names were found here that are not listed in standard Soviet sources (e.g., *migr* composers and those composers who were censored under the Communist regime). Some examples of those covered in the Sonevyts'kyis' book are Mykola Arkas, Virko Baley, Volodymyr Boltarovych-Stone, Vasyl Barvins'kyi, and Maksym Berezovs'kyi. It is unfortunate that not all reference books published in the Soviet Union were available to the Sonevyts'kyis. For example, *Soiuz Kampozytoriv Ukrainy: Spravochnik* (Kiev, Musychna Ukraina, 1984) is not mentioned along with other sources consulted. A number of composers can be found in this Soviet publication that are not mentioned in the Sonevyts'kyis' work (e.g., S. Alekseeva, O. Amautov, L. Archimovych, V. Ban'kevych, V. Barabasov, S. Bedusenko, M. Bilins'kaia, V. Borysov, and others). Obviously, not all of those omitted are prominent names; anyhow, it is difficult to trace the biographies of scholars, musicians, artists, or even politicians in Soviet reference works. One hopes this situation will improve over time.

In spite of the obstacles, these authors have performed a valuable service for Ukrainian scholarship. *Dictionary of Ukrainian Composers* is a scholarly and useful work that should be found in all music collections.—**Bohdan S. Wynar**

871. Tischler, Alice. **A Descriptive Bibliography of Art Music by Israeli Composers**. Warren, Mich., Harmonie Park Press, 1988. 424p. index. (Detroit Studies in Music Bibliography, no.62). $50.00. ML120.I75 T57. 016.78175694. LC 88-38301. ISBN 0-89990-045-3.

The purpose of this bibliography is to encourage the performance and study of music by Israeli composers. The music of 63 composers who have created over 3,200 works since 1910 and have lived in the geographic area that is now Israel is methodically recorded in an alphabetical listing. A compact biography of each composer with current address (if living) appears at the beginning of each entry. This is followed by information on the reference sources which were consulted, titles (in English and Hebrew), medium, author and language of the text, information on publication, performance time for the composition, location of scores, performance history, recordings, and miscellaneous notes. Some of the categories listed above are not filled in for a number of compositions because the data are not known or do not apply. The author established a large collection of scores and recordings at the Music Library of Indiana University, and this location frequently appears as a source for Israeli music along with the Library of Congress and four libraries in New York City, including the New

York Public Library and the Hebrew Arts School Birnbaum Library. The scores included have an international background in that many composers were born in other parts of the world before emigrating to Israel. As expected, Germany, Poland, and Russia are often cited as the birthplace for many entrants, but Israel's current musical heritage includes composers originally from Chile, Romania, the Ukraine, Austria, Hungary, Macedonia, Latvia, and Canada. Wide margins and clearly delineated categories facilitate use of this new reference work. Four essential indexes add considerably to the reference value of this specialized publication. Of particular value are the listings for type of music (e.g., bagatelle, cantata, fugue, and march) and instrumentation (e.g., harp, harpsichord, trombone, woodwind trio, and xylophone). The other indexes are for the authors of texts which have been put to music, plus transliterated Hebrew and multilingual titles. All in all, this is a well-organized compilation on a subject not previously available in the literature of twentieth-century music. [R: Choice, July/Aug 89, p. 1821]—**William J. Dane**

INSTRUMENTALISTS

General

872.   Campbell, Margaret. **The Great Cellists**. North Pomfret, Vt., Trafalgar Square/David & Charles, c.1988, 1989. 352p. illus. index. $24.95. LC 88-50782. ISBN 0-943955-09-2.

This very readable history of cellists and cello playing is similar in format and style to the author's earlier book *The Great Violinists* (Doubleday, 1981). It fleshes out details in the lives of influential performers and teachers in a way that makes it informative and entertaining for laypersons and musicians alike. It attempts to trace schools of playing from baroque to modern times by creating a "family tree" of noted cellists and their accomplished pupils.

The book is arranged more or less chronologically, beginning with Bononcini and ending with Harrell, Foster, Ma, and du Pré. Within each era, cellists are grouped by country and by association (as teachers, students, and colleagues). The author has provided notes for each chapter, a selected bibliography, a list of the principal cello concertos cited, a chronological list of cellists, and a name index.

The author includes extensive quotations from books, articles, and her interviews with performers. For readers who prefer a less folksy approach to biography, there are still van der Straeten's *Story of the Violoncello . . . with Biographies of All the Most Eminent Players of Every Country* (1971 reprint of the London 1914 edition), though this is limited to pre-twentieth-century artists; Julius Bachi's *Beriihmte Cellisten* (2d edition, Zurich, 1973), that, however, discusses fewer performers; and name entries in *Baker's Biographical Dictionary of Musicians* (see ARBA 86, entry 1232) and the *New Grove Dictionary of Music and Musicians* (see ARBA 81, entry 1016). But for those who want to find information that is current, in English, and in one source, Campbell's book is the one to read. It certainly fills a gap in the literature and will be welcomed by all types of libraries. [R: LJ, 1 June 89, p. 106]—**Carole Franklin Vidali**

873.   Gillespie, John, and Anna Gillespie. **Notable Twentieth-Century Pianists: A Bio-Critical Sourcebook**. Westport, Conn., Greenwood Press, 1995. 2v. illus. index. (Bio-Critical Sourcebooks on Musical Performance). $125.00/set. ISBN 0-313-25660-8.

The idea of interviewing musical artists—in this case pianists and pedagogues—has become a popular part of keyboard magazines and journals. People want to know everything about a celebrity; therefore, there is interest in this type of essay. The work discussed here is not based on interviews, but is a compilation of detailed examinations of 100 pianists, with information derived from years of library research and correspondence. Authors John and Anna Gillespie, in their 2-volume set *Notable Twentieth-Century Pianists*, delve into the lives, performances, and recordings of 100 notable twentieth-century pianists. Those chosen to be included were first named on a list compiled by pianists and pedagogues in music conservatories and colleges throughout the United States. The authors then tabulated the results and supplied their own choices as well.

The Gillespies admit that the final list of 100 pianists could not possibly please everyone, but the list does cover the major pianists of this century, from the earliest (by date of birth) pianist listed—Francis Planté (1839-1934)—to the latest pianist—Barry Douglas (b. 1960). This source-book contains biographical material; style analyses (taken from reviews, recordings, articles, and the like); references and reviews; and a representative discography. The material in the volumes makes for fascinating reading, as it not only discusses the artists' backgrounds but also looks into their performance styles, which can vary greatly from artist to artist.

The volumes include a preface, a general bibliography for the set, illustrations, and a name index (in volume 2). *Notable Twentieth-Century Pianists* will be of interest to pianists and pedagogues and should be included in reference sections of music conservatory libraries and university/college music libraries.—**Robert Palmieri**

874. Gregory, Hugh. **1000 Great Guitarists**. San Francisco, Calif., GPI Books/Miller Freeman, 1994. 164p. illus. index. $19.95pa. LC 94-75867. ISBN 0-87930-307-7.

This resource is touted as a comprehensive guide to the world's greatest guitarists. It covers every style from rock to classical and jazz. The author derived this information from research that included searching guitar magazines as well as 60 books, which are listed in the bibliography at the end of the work.

The guitarists are listed alphabetically by surname. Brief biographies and evaluations are provided along with lists of key instruments used and suggested best recordings. The gray text is interspersed with a series of full-color pages in which the careers of 12 selected guitar masters are described in detail.

This is a valuable but brief introduction to the named guitar players. In-depth studies of individuals will require further research. This book is recommended for public and music libraries. The unusual, broad range of coverage of musical styles and the price make it a valuable addition for any size of library. [R: RBB, Aug 94, p. 2073]—**James M. Murray**

875. Meckna, Michael. **Twentieth-Century Brass Soloists**. Westport, Conn., Greenwood Press, 1994. 291p. index. (Bio-Critical Sourcebooks on Musical Performance). $75.00. ML399. M4. 788.9'092'2. LC 93-23943. ISBN 0-313-26463-6.

This book provides two- to four-page entries on 99 brass instrument soloists active in this century. Though the earliest birth date is that of Herbert Clarke (1867), most of the performers were born after 1900, and many young, still active players are included (e.g., Wynton Marsalis, Christian Lindberg). The author's criteria for inclusion were that the performer had a solo career, recorded frequently, made a unique artistic contribution, and influenced both musicians and laypeople. Classical, jazz, and popular music performers are included, slightly more than half being classical. Almost half are trumpet players; 20 hornists, 18 trombonists, and 13 tubists compose the remainder.

Each entry begins with biographical background, including the circumstances of the performer's early training, the positions held, career highlights, and any honors or awards received. There follows a discussion of the performer's style and technique, with comparisons to other players. A selected discography and bibliography concludes each entry. There is a bibliography of general sources and an index that usefully includes all the names of the numerous performers, teachers, and instrument makers mentioned in the text but not given their own entries. Photographs of 30 of the performers are included.

Though the best known of these performers will have entries in standard music reference works, the rest have brief or no entries. This work is valuable for bringing together so much biographical and discographical information and stylistic commentary in one place on a class of musicians often neglected by standard music scholarship. Recommended for all music collections. [R: Choice, Sept 94, p. 74; RBB, 15 Dec 94, p. 773]—**Steven J. Squires**

876.   Rehrig, William H. **The Heritage Encyclopedia of Band Music: Composers and Their Music**. Westerville, Ohio, Integrity Press, 1991. 2v. index. $110.00/set. LC 91-73637. ISBN 0-918048-08-7.

The backbone of the research for this work is Robert Hoe's series of LP band records, described in appendix 9. In contrast to the American scope of the LPs, the encyclopedia's goal is international—to document all music for concert and military bands, with biographies of composers, source references, and work lists. Certain limits apply: brass band music is excluded on the laudable grounds that this genre is sufficiently specialized to merit a work of its own; South America and Africa are not represented as it was too hard to find information from those areas; and some materials are not included because publishers declined to be of assistance. Bands themselves do not fall within the work's scope.

Rehrig has created an impressive tool. Biographies for composers not likely to be in other sources are given to the extent of information available; better-known composers are treated more briefly. Appendixes include histories of American band music and publishing practices, with instructions for substituting modern instruments for historical ones; lists of publishers, distributors, and band journals; special instructions for performing foreign band music in America; a list of marches; notes on possible repositories of band music (a section that could well be expanded in a subsequent edition); and research journals. The title index refers to composers and gives some indication of genre; it has running titles, which partially mitigate the tiny typeface in use throughout the work.

With its superior physical production, this work could become the tool of first recourse for information on band music. But it does not displace other publications. Users will still wish to consult, among others, *Band Music Notes* by Norman Smith and Albert Stoutamire (Kjos West, 1979) for program descriptions of specific pieces, and David Whitwell's *The History and Literature of the Wind Band and Wind Ensemble* (Winds, 1984) for primary sources, as well as for many other composers and works. Any library that holds these titles should acquire *Heritage Encyclopedia*. It is appropriate for all libraries that collect in music and popular culture. Also, a *Supplement to the Heritage Encyclopedia of Band Music: Composers and Their Music,* edited by Paul E. Bierley, was published in 1996 (Westerville, Ohio, Integrity Press, 1996. $90.00. LC 96-77526. ISBN 0-91804-12-5). [R: Choice, Apr 92, p. 1212; LJ, Jan 92, p. 110; WLB, Jan 92, p. 127]—**Ian Fairclough and Robert L. Wick**

JAZZ

877.   Case, Brian, and Stan Britt. **The Harmony Illustrated Encyclopedia of Jazz**. Revised and updated by Chrissie Murray. New York, Harmony Books/Crown, 1986. 208p. illus. (part col.). index. $22.95; $13.95pa. LC 86-15040. ISBN 0-517-56442-4; 0-517-56443-2pa.

This 3rd edition of *The Illustrated Encyclopedia of Jazz* (see ARBA 79, entry 996) retains the large format and plethora of photographs of musicians and album jackets that visually distinguished the earlier edition. The text now includes over 450 entries for jazz musicians as well as several for subjects such as "Blue Note" (the record label) and "British Jazz." Biographical entries assess subjects' contributions, and often highlight significant recordings or tracks. Entries conclude with selective discographies of LP releases, listed in chronological order. An appendix includes brief entries for about 100 musicians for whom "lack of space" is cited as preventing more extended treatment. The index lists musicians given full entries or cited within entries in both sections.

The encyclopedia's inclusion of jazz-rock fusion stars such as Jamaaladeen Tacuma and of British musicians such as Phil Seamen differentiates it from other comprehensive biographical dictionaries of jazz. But it shows an imbalance in giving full entries for these while relegating such important musicians as Philly Jo Jones, Bobby Hackett, and Kenny Clarke to the appendix. The lack of precise dates, particularly of births and deaths, and the failure to include dates or issue numbers for the LPs listed limit its use as a reference work. Yet, while it offers no new insights into its subjects' lives and music, and too liberally uses superlatives such as "great" or "brilliant," it gives informed assessments of figures throughout the history of jazz.—**William Brockman**

878. Chilton, John. **Who's Who of British Jazz**. Herndon, Va., Mansell/Cassell, 1997. 370p. $29.95pa. ISBN 0-304-33910-5.

Chilton is a respected jazz researcher and historian whose previous work in this format, *Who's Who of Jazz: Storyville to Swing Street* (1970), is a standard reference work in the field. Chilton has also written books on such musicians as Billie Holiday, Sidney Bechet, and Coleman Hawkins. An Englishman himself, he devotes the present work exclusively to British jazz musicians, making it the first of its kind. Some 850 entries are presented here—covering all jazz styles and musicians who played in the 1920s, as well as the young players active today. At two or three entries a page, the information includes the musician's professional name and original name (if different), date and place of birth and death, instruments played, and a brief professional chronology. Despite the occasional and inevitable lapse—implying that pianist Derek Smith performed simultaneously on both the Johnny Carson Show (1967-1974) and the Tonight Show (1968-1975), when both names refer to the same program—Chilton is a knowledgeable and careful researcher. With the number of British musicians who are having an impact on jazz worldwide continuing to grow, this book is an important addition to reference shelves of most libraries.—**A. David Franklin**

879. Crowther, Bruce, and Mike Pinfold. **The Jazz Singers: From Ragtime to the New Wave**. London, Blandford Press; distr., New York, Sterling Publishing, c.1986, 1988. 224p. illus. bibliog. index. $12.95pa. ISBN 0-7137-2047-6.

This is an interesting and readable account of the jazz singer in music. Some 200 vocalists who have performed on disc from the turn of the century up through the modern jazz age are described. Covered are such unique artists as Louis Armstrong, B. B. King, Ma Rainey, and Billie Holiday, in a narrative text, usually in chronological chapters. Unfortunately, this book is not a reference book in dictionary arrangement style. Access to the individuals is through the entries in the index, and many performers are scattered throughout the book. All of the page references must be tracked down.

On a larger level, there are more important things remiss in this book. One is that the definition of "jazz singer" is wide-ranging, for it embraces blues, soul, popular and stage singers, and big-band vocalists. Only the latter can be regarded as anywhere near being "jazz." I am not being picky over the criteria for inclusion, but I do wish to draw librarians' attention to the fact that data about blues, soul, and popular and stage performers are available elsewhere and in better shape (i.e., dictionary arrangement). All Crowther and Pinfold have done is provide a context for the better-than-bland singers. There are some photographs, some recommended discs (with no reasons or choices made for specific titles), and some additional reading. Curiously, Henry Pleasants's major epic, *The Great American Popular Singers* (Simon & Schuster, 1974), is missing from this bibliography. *The Jazz Singers* is a useful and enjoyable book to read, but slight to consult.—**Dean Tudor**

880. Cunningham, Lyn Driggs, and Jimmy Jones. **Sweet, Hot and Blue: St. Louis' Musical Heritage**. Jefferson, N.C., McFarland, 1989. 245p. illus. index. $35.00. ML394. C86. 780'.92'2. LC 88-27353. ISBN 0-89950-302-0.

This book contains a curious mixture of data about 124 musicians (mostly jazz) who were born in St. Louis and its suburbs. For each musician there are stage names, life dates, and career biographies that are mainly band affiliations, clubs and concerts, and recordings. However, the information is not given consistently. Sometimes the entries are incomplete, such as the one on Olive Brown. Needed are more details about her Detroit album, such as song titles, recording personnel, label number, and recording dates, as well as some facts about how she died. Some entries have interviews that were conducted by Cunningham, and these consume too much space. In the entry on Miles Davis there is a reference to "Billy Eckstein." Of course, it should be Billy Eckstine. The style is a bit gushy, even verging on boosterism for St. Louis, and without much discussion about the St. Louis style of jazz, influences, and so on.

There is a 186-item glossary for an explanation of jazz slang, and an index is useful for showing linkages among the musicians. Overall, however, the book has limited value, particularly in view of the price.—**Dean Tudor**

881.   Feather, Leonard, and Ira Gitler. **The Encyclopedia of Jazz in the Seventies**. New York, Da Capo Press, c.1976, 1987. 393p. illus. bibliog. $16.95pa. LC 87-517. ISBN 0-306-80290-2.

Feather's encyclopedias of jazz remain an unsurpassed resource for biographical information. These two Da Capo editions reprint those originally published by Horizon in 1966 and 1976, respectively (see ARBA 78, entry 915), both of which update and supplement *The Encyclopedia of Jazz* (Horizon Press, 1960). Entries in all volumes summarize subjects' professional activities (often using quotations from the subject, other musicians, or reviewers), and list compositions, television appearances, and recordings.—**William S. Brockman**

882.   Gilmore, John. **Who's Who of Jazz in Montreal: Ragtime to 1970**. Montreal, Vehicule Press; distr., Toronto and Cheektowaga, N.Y., University of Toronto Press, 1989. 318p. illus. (Dossier Quebec Series). $15.95pa. 785.42'092'2. ISBN 0-919890-92-X.

This companion to the author's *Swinging in Paradise* (Vehicule Press, 1988) gives short biographies of over 200 musicians and bands who resided in Montreal prior to 1970. Among them are well-known Canadian figures such as Oscar Peterson, Paul Bley, and Maynard Ferguson, and exiled Americans such as Sadik Hakim. Entries, which cover events into the 1980s, trace careers in abbreviated fashion, including birth and death dates and places (when available), education, tours, major performances, recordings and awards.

Gilmore's concise style includes other biographical details only when pertinent. He offers little musical commentary beyond identifying the instruments a musician played or the repertoire and style of a band. Some entries cite sources and discographies. A number of black-and-white photographs are included.

Geographically specialized as the work is, it shows that Montreal has had a rich and fluid musical history. It is important as the only easily accessible source of information for most of the musicians included.—**William S. Brockman**

883.   Herzhaft, Gerard. **Encyclopedia of the Blues**. Fayetteville, University of Arkansas Press, 1992. 513p. illus. index. $32.00; $16.95pa. ML102.B6H4313. 781.643'03. LC 92-7386. ISBN 1-55728-252-8; 1-55728-253-6pa.

Just about everybody can name a few blues musicians, present or past (do the names Ray Charles and B. B. King ring a bell?), but there is so much fusion and crossover in American musical forms that it is possible to locate blues musicians equally in rock, gospel, or other genres. This title, originally a French-language work known as *Nouvelle Encyclopedie du Blues* and recently translated into English, contains a single alphabetical arrangement of people, places, and instruments, all connected with the blues, a uniquely American musical form that grew out of the appalling conditions of life among rural African-Americans in the early decades of this century. There is virtually no front matter, just a rudimentary preface in which Herzhaft (an obvious aficionado) thanks and acknowledges those who furnished assistance to his project. He then launches into his alphabet, without so much as a definition of the musical form he is discussing (but maybe that is just as well, as nobody has ever defined the blues to everyone else's satisfaction).

Among the performer entries are discussions of common blues instruments (e.g., harmonica [aka "blues harp"]), guitar, and piano, and geographical locations noted for having spawned a type of blues or a number of exponents (e.g., Louisiana, Mississippi, Memphis, St. Louis, Chicago). An interesting entry for "White blues" launches into a serious debate (without conclusion) over whether Caucasians deserve to be considered blues singers or merely imitators. The uninitiated will be struck by some of the nicknames blues musicians have chosen for themselves (e.g., Gatemouth, Cripple, Scrapper, Howlin' Wolf, Homesick, Leadbelly, Smokey Hogg). Then there are repetitive descriptive or evocative nicknames (e.g., lots of people named Little, Big, Sonny, Slim, or Blind).

The work is sprinkled with half-page, black-and-white photographs and concludes with some valuable reference material, including a bibliography, a selected discography, an index by instrument, and a general index. Music collections will probably want this title, but one cannot help wishing that some general discussion of the "birth of the blues" had been provided. [R: Choice, May 93, p. 1442; RBB, 1 Jan 93, p. 825]—**Bruce A. Shuman**

884.   Lees, Gene. **Jazz Lives: 100 Portraits in Jazz**. Willowdale, Ont., Firefly Books, 1992. 216p. illus. index. $39.95. 781.65'092. ISBN 1-895565-12-X.

While the typical biographical guide to jazz musicians provides the requisite basic information, this one goes a step farther. It adds valuable insights acquired through Lees's personal acquaintance with his subjects throughout a long and varied career in jazz that has included editing *Down Beat* magazine, publishing his own highly respected *Jazzletter*, and setting lyrics to music composed by the likes of Antonio Carlos Jobim. Lees's commentary accompanies 100 candid duotone photographs of musicians in their private moments taken over a four-year period by award-winning Canadian photographer John Reeves. The musicians profiled have participated in and, in some cases, made major contributions to the history of jazz from the early 1920s to the present. Several outstanding Canadians are included. Although well-known figures such as Benny Carter, Artie Shaw, the Modern Jazz Quartet, Dave Brubeck, and Dizzy Gillespie are present, such lesser-known major talents as Bill Challis—Paul Whiteman's chief arranger in his glory days—and Bill Holman—who served in a similar capacity for Stan Kenton in the 1950s—are also included. All are treated warmly and respectfully both by the photographer and by the author, so their brief profiles assume a human dimension frequently lacking in standard reference works.—**A. David Franklin**

885.   **The New Grove Dictionary of Jazz**. Barry Kernfeld, ed. New York, Grove's Dictionaries of Music, 1988. 2v. illus. $350.00/set. ML102.J3N48. 785.42'03. LC 87-25452. ISBN 0-935859-39-X.

Long noted in the music world for scholarly excellence, Grove has added another dictionary to its growing list of definitive music reference works. Similar in format to the earlier *New Grove Dictionary of American Music* (see ARBA 88, entry 1277), *The New Grove Dictionary of Jazz* gathers together a vast amount of information, much of which was previously unavailable or scattered throughout various sources, and presents it in a scholarly yet readable fashion.

The work is comprehensive in scope, focusing on all aspects of jazz and reflecting its evolution from its American origins to its current worldwide status. In keeping with this, more than one-fourth of the entries are on non-American topics and almost one-half of the contributors are from outside the United States, giving the work a decidedly international flavor. Although some of the articles in *Jazz* draw upon material previously published in earlier Grove sources, this accounts for less than 10 percent of the total, and much of that material has been extensively rewritten.

The 4,500 entries include a broad variety of categories covering individuals, groups and bands, styles, topics and terms, instruments, record companies and labels, and institutions. As with other Grove sources, the entries range in length from one sentence to many pages. Most articles are signed, and selected lists of books, recordings, and arrangements are provided when appropriate. The dictionary proper is preceded by a preface, introduction, and four separate lists of abbreviations. It is concluded by two appendixes, one a bibliography of bibliographies and reference sources, discographies, other books, and periodicals; the other, a list of contributors.

It would be too much to expect that a work of this size and scope be either error-free or totally comprehensive; and, indeed, it is not. Contributing experts do not always agree, and there are a few surprising omissions. Nevertheless, it is a work of monumental proportions, providing easy access to a wealth of research information. Comprehensive, scholarly, and accessible, this source should be considered a mandatory acquisition for music library collections and a highly recommended purchase for most academic and public libraries, especially those with a strong music, American history, or popular culture emphasis. [R: BL, 15 Dec 89, p. 780; Choice, Apr 89, p. 1310; LJ, 1 Feb 89, pp. 61-62; LJ, 15 Apr 89, p. 41; RBB, 15 Apr 89, pp. 1438, 1440; WLB, Feb 89, p. 116]—**Kristin Ramsdell**

OPERA

886.   **International Dictionary of Opera**. C. Steven Larue, ed. Detroit, St. James Press/Gale, 1993. illus. index. $250.00/set. ML102.O616. 782.1'03. LC 92-44271. ISBN 1-55862-081-8.

Part of the introduction to this splendid two-volume dictionary sums it up best: "[It] provides students, teachers, researchers, and opera enthusiasts with a comprehensive source of biographical, bibliographical, and musicological information on people and works important to the history and development of opera." Some entries usually found in dictionaries of this kind are not included here (e.g., items on individual cities, opera houses, and companies), but the ones selected have been presented in a wonderful new way. Performing artists past and present all start with a brief biographical sketch, followed by signed essays on their artistry, strong points, and even weak points—the latter often presented with total (and hard-to-find) honesty and objectivity. Composer entries are followed by a thorough list of compositions, with librettist and premiere information attached.

An opera lover will find this dictionary extremely hard to lay aside, because it brims with intelligent, readable, and fair assessments in every category it covers. The publication is backed by an impressive advisory board, and the 200 contributors/writers come from academia, music writing, newspapers, and magazines. Printed on heavy coated stock, the reproductions are of a quality rarely found nowadays. In addition, most of the selected illustrations are striking, often rare and unusual, although contemporary productions shots seems to lean heavily on the British side (e.g., Covent Garden, Glyndebourne), which is somewhat understandable in view of the British provenance of the dictionary. This reviewer, an editor with a peculiar knack for spotting typographical errors, has not been able to find a single such mistake in several extended periods of browsing through this excellent set of volumes. If one cannot afford *The New Grove Dictionary of Opera* (Stockton Press/Grove's Dictionaries of Music, 1992) (and even if one can) and wants a bit more than *The Oxford Dictionary of Opera* (Oxford University Press, 1992) can provide, this publication will provide the perfect answer. Highest possible recommendation. [R: Choice, Oct 93, p. 267: LJ, 1 May 93, pp. 82-83; RBB, Aug 93, p. 2092; RQ, Winter 93, pp. 288-89]—**Koraljka Lockhart**

887.   **The New Grove Dictionary of Opera**. Stanley Sadie, ed. New York, Grove's Dictionaries of Music, 1992. 4v. illus. $850.00/set. ML102.O6N5. 782.1'03. LC 92-36276. ISBN 0-935859-92-6.

In the preface, the editor is firm in making the point that this work bears very little relationship to the coverage of opera that appeared in *The New Grove Dictionary of Music and Musicians* (see ARBA 81, entry 1016), which is now more than a decade old. He claims that close to 90 percent of this set is new or newly written by the best available author for each entry. The scope is vast, covering singers, conductors, directors, authors, and composers, and a huge number of subjects, such as translation, libretti, recordings, opera glasses, and super titles. Performers and composers receive coverage of their operatic activities, not their careers as a whole. Operas have entries with some historical information and excellent plot summaries that vary in length and detail according to importance. Non-Western musical stageworks with a different kind of history and performing tradition are excluded.

A book with approximately 1,300 authors cannot be expected to have one standard, one viewpoint, or one level of quality. No editor, not even the skillful Sadie, could achieve that, but a high quality and a prevailing consistency are almost always in evidence. The long articles on composers and subjects always command respect. Certainly, most of the big names of the distant and recent past are here, and the entries are usually written by well-known specialists. General assessment, usually right on target, is given along with the career facts. The shorter entries on singers and others raise, as always in a book of this kind, the question of why some are included and others excluded. Recently established singers, such as Cecilia Bartoli, Ben Heppner, and Thomas Hampson, are included, but Renee Fleming and Sharon Sweet, perhaps too new, are not. Usually, it is possible to justify choices to one's own satisfaction, but some seem downright capricious. Why, among prominent American-based opera directors, did Tito Capobianco get in and Frank Corsaro stay out? And why, of the two Russian baritones now having great international careers, is Sergey Leiferkus in and Vladimir Chernov out? Among writers and editors some major American figures, such as Irving Kolodin and Robert Jacobson, would seem to qualify for inclusion, as others of less importance are to be found in these pages. Some decisions for entries of cities and places also seem arbitrary. The major Wagner festival of the 1920s and l930s in Zoppot (then Germany, now Poland) gets a brief entry with no bibliography, whereas Santa Cruz, Wilmington, and many other cities with limited operatic histories get good coverage. Why some entries are unsigned (e.g., those on Teresa Stratas, Charles Kullman, and Marcella Sembrich) is a mystery.

Errors are inevitable (but few in number). For example, Mirella Freni never sang Suzel at the Metropolitan. Marie Powers, who made a specialty of the role of Madame Flora in Menotti's *The Medium* is credited as having sung the New York premiere, but she did not; she sang the revised version on Broadway a year after it was first produced. Yet Claramae Turner is correctly given credit for creating the role in her entry. (Both articles are written by the same author.) The entry for the conductor Maurice Abravanel states that he conducted Weill's *Knickerbocker Holiday* (1938), with Marian Anderson as soloist. It appears that a line or two of type disappeared to combine two events into this fictitious one.

The one real weakness of the work is in the inconsistencies and omissions in the bibliographies for the performer entries. Some, such as the one for Kathleen Ferrier, are models that list all important and up-to-date book sources; some have poor lists; some have none; and some omit major books while listing sources of lesser importance. For example, autobiographies of Rita Hunter and Rosa Ponselle and a major biography of Grace Moore are not listed. This is the only element of this work that exhibits no sense of quality control. Major subject entries, on the other hand, have superb bibliographies.

The illustrations deserve special praise. Although not too well reproduced, the choices are excellent; unfamiliar prints, paintings, engravings, and photographs abound. Appendixes cover role names, first-line and title entries for arias and ensembles, a list of contributors, and illustration acknowledgements.

This is a major reference work with a serious and scholarly approach to a subject often considered frivolous and treated accordingly. It can generally be consulted with confidence and read with pleasure. [R: Choice, July/Aug 93, pp. 1752-53; LJ, 15 Feb 93, pp. 160-62; LJ, 15 Apr 93, pp. 61-62, RBB, 1 Apr 93, p. 1452]—**George Louis Mayer**

888. **The Oxford Dictionary of Opera**. By John Warrack and Ewan West. New York, Oxford University Press, 1992. 782p. $40.00. ML102.06W37. 782.1'03. LC 92-6730. ISBN 0-19-869164-5.

For years, opera enthusiasts and professionals have used the Rosenthal-Warrack *Concise Oxford Dictionary of Opera* (Oxford University Press, 1986) as a kind of an opera bible. The present volume is an outgrowth of the same, but it is considerably expanded, containing 4,500 entries, which include 750 composer etches; 600 opera entries with all relevant cast, premiere, synopsis, and performance details; 900 singer biographies; and more. The opera synopses are no longer thumbnail summations of the plot; for example, Lo Forrza del Destino was previously told in 49 words, and now it takes up 250. (The reader who finds value in short opera plots should keep the old volume by the side of the new one.) Being a British publication, the book includes some spelling peculiarities common to Great Britain (e.g., "Rakhmaninov," "Shalyapin"). The dictionary is extremely detailed in its listings of operas based on works by famous writers; its Shakespeare section alone covers an exhaustive array of works written between 1692 and 1991.

A few mistakes have crept in. Hans Hotter is listed as retired, although he continues to perform, and vital statistics for Tiana Lemnitz say "(b. Metz, 26 Oct. 1897; d?)," although the legendary singer celebrated her 95th birthday with great fanfare in 1992. In preparing the new edition, Warrack and West discarded a number of entries that pertained to relatively obscure singers of yesteryear (e.g., Claire Dux, Leopold Sachse, Albert Saleza), a somewhat questionable decision in a reference book of this kind. Among the singers of the younger generation, one can find Cecilia Bartoli but not Dolora Zajick, Cecilia Gasdia, Sharon Sweet, or Neil Shicoff, all artists of considerable international repute. Still, this dictionary will prove of immense value to anyone who deals with opera. [R: RBB, 15 Feb 93, pp. 1082-84; SLJ, May 93, pp. 139-40]—**Koraljka Lockhart**

889. Smith, Eric Ledell. **Blacks in Opera: An Encyclopedia of People and Companies, 1873-1993**. Jefferson, N.C., McFarland, 1995. 236p. illus. index. $49.95. ISBN 0-89950-813-8.

The difficulties of compiling any specialized encyclopedia are staggering to contemplate. The best of such works are marked by a consistency from entry to entry using the same format and covering the same data, as well as by the accuracy of the information provided. This work is too inconsistent and incomplete in the way the entries are handled to be a successful guide to its subject. Its fullest entries are reserved for the most famous, which is a pity because it is not hard to locate solid information about the careers of singers such as Leontyne Price or Kathleen Battle. The entries for the famous include birth dates (frequently incomplete) and sections devoted to education, awards, opera companies and orchestras with which the singer has appeared, debuts, a repertoire, videos, recordings (without label information) reviews, a bibliography, and an obituary. Almost no entries contain all of these sections, and the review section is often left out.

Information provided in each of the sections is often spotty. The entry for Grace Bumbry's repertoire excludes any mention of the soprano roles that dominated the last half of her career and is limited to the mezzo soprano roles of her early years. The recordings section for Marian Anderson gives no indication of her huge output of recordings, which have remained in print in their original 78 format through LP and current CD compilations. Some important singers are all but passed over. Ella Lee, a soprano with a distinguished career, receives note of her birth in Texas, appearances with three opera companies, one review, and one bibliographical entry. More should be mentioned about Altonell Hines than her birth and death dates, where she studied, and the fact that she created an important role in *Four Saints in Three Acts*. She is on the original recording of excerpts, which is not mentioned despite its historical importance as having been conducted by composer Virgil Thomson.

This work will certainly be useful to many users. The range of its coverage, including composers, directors, conductors, and others in the opera world, is impressive. The frustration lies in the lack of information about many of the artists discussed in the work. It certainly gives an impressive overview of just how strong and important the black gift to the world's opera houses has been and continues to be. The book does have a superb index that leads the reader to information within the entries perfectly. The encyclopedia is useful as far as it goes.—**George Louis Mayer**

890.   Steane, J. B. **Singers of the Century**. Portland, Oreg., Amadeus Press/Timber Press, 1996. 271p. illus. index. $34.95. ISBN 1-57467-009-3.

Connoisseurs of fine singing who have as much interest in the great artists of the past and their recordings as they do in those currently active in the opera house and concert hall must all know of Steane by now. As author of one of the great books on recorded voices, *The Grand Tradition: Seventy Years of Singing on Record 1900 to 1970* (the 2d edition is available in the United States from Amadeus Press), and as a regular contributor to *Gramophone* and other periodicals, the author has proven to have an exceptionally well-tuned ear for vocal quality and the mechanics of singing as well as uncompromising standards for musical interpretation. Steane helps the listener to hear what is important about a singer and to help place him or her among contemporary and historical performers of the same repertory. Because passing judgment on a fine singer is such a subjective enterprise, not everyone can always agree with Steane's verdicts, but one always knows what standards have been employed in presenting evidence and forming opinions.

Most of Steane's writings are about singers performing specific music. This book is something of a departure by its broader, more generalized discussions of singers' lives, careers, and performances. These are the first 50 articles of an ongoing series of 1,500-word pieces written for the periodical *Opera Now*. They are collected in the order in which they were published, which is to say haphazard, because the choice of a certain singer at any specific time may have been prompted by a timely event, such as a farewell recital or a death. The expected "golden age" singers such as Adelina Patti, Luisa Tetrazzini, and Fyodor Ivanovich Chaliapin are, of course, covered, as well as many mid-century singers, such as Kirsten Flagstad, Victoria de los Angeles, and Kathleen Ferrier, and some who came a bit later, such as Joan Sutherland and Birgit Nilsson. No young, currently active singers have yet made it into this series.

Although not designed as a reference book, the individual articles do present clear overviews of great singers' careers and help to explain them better than most reference books. A separate section, "Dates, Books and Records," has entries for each of the singers in the book, this time alphabetically arranged, adding facts not covered in the essays and making excellent suggestions as to what to read and listen to for further insights. Every singer in the book can be heard on recently issued historical CD-ROMs. *Singers of the Century* is highly recommended. [R: Choice, Jan 97, p. 776]—**George Louis Mayer**

891.   **Who's Who in British Opera**. Nicky Adam, ed. Brookfield, Vt., Scolar Press/Ashgate Publishing, 1993. 339p. $59.95. ML102.06A3. 782.1'092'245. LC 93-12314. ISBN 0-85967-894-6.

As in other who's who publications, the reader is provided basic personal and professional information about 493 individuals associated with British opera today. The men and women included represent virtually all aspects of opera production and performance—singers, conductors, designers, directors, and critics, to name a few. All the people are living and are currently active in the British opera world. British is defined not only as English but also as Scottish and Welsh. Inclusion is very specific to opera. Being a classical singer of some note in the United Kingdom does not guarantee an entry; it appears opera credentials are necessary. Probably because of the relatively small number of entries, the format is much more readable than one would expect in this kind of publication. The type is clear, with usually no more than two or three entries on each page. The only complaint regarding format—and this is from a U.S. reader—is the lack of a comma between the surname and the first name of each entry. Following the name entries are three appendixes of varying value. The first is headed "Cross References" and lists the individuals by occupation. The second lists operas and their composers, with the third providing acronyms for record labels listed.

This book does well what it sets out to do, but due to the subject matter, it is expected the audience will be limited. Thus, it will be the library with a significant music collection that will find this book to be a necessary addition. [R: Choice, Mar 94, p. 1087]—**Phillip P. Powell**

POPULAR AND COUNTRY/WESTERN MUSIC

Music/Popular and Country/Western Music

892.   **Artists of American Folk Music: The Legends of Traditional Folk, the Stars of the Sixties, the Virtuosi of New Acoustic Music**. Phil Hood, ed. New York, William Morrow, 1986. 159p. illus. index. $12.95pa. LC 85-63796. ISBN 0-688-05916-3.

The last great (excepting a boomlet in the late seventies) American folk music revival occurred in the late fifties and early sixties. The Kingston Trio; Peter, Paul, and Mary; and Bob Dylan emerged as leaders in the troubadour tradition during this revival. Their names and those of their legendary predecessors—Woody Guthrie, Pete Seeger, Leadbelly, Earl Scruggs, and others—are the subjects of the biographical sketches and interviews in this assemblage. Thirty-one artists or groups are included. Selected discographies are included for each artist. Most of the pieces originally appeared in *Guitar Player* and *Frets* magazines, the latter of which is edited by Phil Hood, also the editor of this collection. While there is a slight bias here toward instrumentation, at the expense of songwriting, interpretation, and performance, it does not detract from the interest which the nicely written profiles maintain in their three to six pages. All the writers represented in this rather uniform collection have lent to their work an air of authority that reflects their firm grasp of the folk "scene." This work can be looked upon as a supplement to Irwin Stambler's *Encyclopedia of Folk, Country & Western Music* (see ARBA 84, entry 920): a few of the less well known folk artists profiled in the pages of this new book (Elizabeth Cotten, Tom Paley, John Herald, and others) were not included in the more comprehensive encyclopedia. In addition, this book's introduction and epilog form a compact overview of the folk genre. It is a strong choice for the reference or circulating popular music library. [R: BL, 15 June 86, p. 1490]—**Randall Rafferty**

893.   **Contemporary Musicians: Profiles of the People in Music**. Suzanne M. Bourgoin, ed. Detroit, Gale, 1989- . (twice yearly). illus. index. $63.00 for recent edition. ISSN 1044-2197.

Written in the same format as previous volumes in the series, *Contemporary Musicians* profiles personalities who create or influence the music heard today. The information for each person or group includes a photograph, a brief biography, and a history of career highlights with examples of critical response to the artist's work. A selected discography of recordings and sources of additional information in books and periodical articles are also listed for each biographee. A wide range of musical talent is presented, from Lawrence Welk to Easy-E, including band leaders, rock groups, and opera singers.

Most of the major contributors to the popular music scene are found here and easily located through the cumulative index in the back of all volumes. A cumulative subject index classifies the information by type, such as instrument, kind of music, and occupation (conductor, producer, and so forth). The advantage of this series is that a great deal of information can be found easily in one source. It is easy to read and entertaining. The information is not exhaustive, as much information will also be available elsewhere, and serious researchers will have to use other sources. However, this source will satisfy the information needs of most people. Some listees have been on the music scene long enough to have new and revised listings (which began with volume 11). This series will be appreciated in every library where information is sought about the makers of contemporary music.—**Marilyn Strong Noronha and Robert L. Wick**

894.	**The Da Capo Companion to 20th-Century Popular Music**. rev. ed. By Phil Hardy and Dave Laing. New York, Da Capo Press, 1995. 1211p. index. $29.50pa. ISBN 0-306-80640-1.

This revised edition of *The Da Capo Companion to 20th-Century Popular Music* contains profiles of more than 2,000 recording artists who have contributed to popular music in the twentieth century. Individuals listed include singers, band leaders, instrumentalists, vocal groups, and some important figures who are generally behind the scenes in the popular music industry. Individuals from all branches of popular music have been included—pop, jazz, old time, rock and roll, easy listening, and so on—and groups are listed in addition to individual members.

This edition has more than 200 new entries, generally of individuals who became prominent in the 1980s or 1990s. Each entry contains the name of the individual or group, date and place of birth, lists of recordings, and a brief biography. In addition, boldfaced items in each entry indicate that they may be looked up in the *Companion* for additional information. The connections between genres and individuals make this volume unique in music reference works, and the writing is entertaining and exceptionally readable. Appendixes include a glossary of styles and genres, an index of entries and cross-references, and an index of song and album titles.

The premier edition of this work was published as *The Faber Companion to 20th-Century Popular Music* (1990) and immediately became a standard reference work in the field. Hardy and Laing have improved the volume with this edition, which is destined to become even more important as a reference work in the area of popular music. It is recommended for personal libraries and is especially recommended for smaller academic and public libraries where each music reference book must provide as much information as possible.—**Robert L. Wick**

895.	DiMartino, Dave. **Singer-Songwriters: Pop Music's Performer-Composers, from A to Zevon**. New York, Billboard Books/Watson-Guptill, 1994. 306p. illus. index. (Billboard Hitmakers Series). $21.95pa. ISBN 0-8230-7629-6.

While there is no shortage of biographical reference works on popular musicians, this work is a notable addition to the field. The author has managed to identify performers who have attained some measure of stability and endurance in a profession that is accustomed to transitory fame. DiMartino is refreshingly candid about this selection process. To begin, he focused only on singer-songwriters who are pop artists as opposed to those who perform R & B or country. They must also have made solo recordings, be regarded as solo artists, write a majority of the songs they sing, and enjoy some commercial success or have made a significant contribution to the field of songwriting. Even after a candidate survived this winnowing process, the author exercised a measure of personal discretion to pare the list to 208 artists.

Thankfully, this is not another list of top-selling artists with only the scantiest data on each personality. Because of the author's selection process, he is able to devote an average of one-and-a-half double-column pages to each performer. The writing style is informal but not without authority, typical of the author's other venues, which include *Musician, Entertainment Weekly, Rolling Stone*, and *Village Voice*. The insightful details and evaluative commentary in most entries place this work above other similar reference tools. In addition to biographical information and a discussion of the subject's artistic development, each entry includes a profile of the artist's significant songs and albums. These titles are gleaned from *Billboard* charts and provide label name and year of release. Most entries are accompanied by a generously sized black-and-white photo of the singer. A copious index allows users to locate quickly a favorite song and the singer who wrote it. This work should prove valuable to any public, college, or university library.—**Gregg S. Geary**

896. **Encyclopedia of Rock**. rev. ed. By Phil Hardy and Dave Laing. Revised by Stephen Barnard and Don Perretta. New York, Schirmer Books/Macmillan, 1988. 480p. illus. $50.00. ISBN 0-02-919562-4.

The original mid-1970s edition of this fine encyclopedia was published only in Great Britain, so it was not widely available in the United States. Revised and updated to include developments of the last 10 years, the present work provides over 1,500 entries on solo artists, bands, musical styles, and historical events. The 300-plus photographs are fairly routine publicity shots, but the photo captions are often noteworthy for cleverly summing up the artist with a single phrase.

Approximately 50 contributors composed the entries, but despite the expected unevenness, the quality is generally high, the opinions well founded, and the historical details thoroughly researched. Sensitivity to the nuances of the music is everywhere apparent, from Johnny Mathis's "ethereal but schmaltzy voice," to an articulate description of Joan Baez's "stunning projection, clear-as-glass intonation . . . a focus many a schooled conservatory singer would envy." The inclusion of performers like Mathis and Baez is typical of the pleasantly eclectic selection throughout. The writers effectively assess the artists' careers and the moods of the times that shaped them. Entertaining gossip is also well covered, such as Rod Stewart's flamboyant lifestyle and liaison with actress Britt Ekland. Consistently knowledgeable, important technical concepts like Phil Spector's "Wall of Sound" are duly noted.

Unfortunately, there are no discographies appended to each entry, as in the *Harmony Illustrated Encyclopedia of Rock* (see ARBA 85, entry 1215), a similar work with a similar title and also British, with which this volume compares favorably. *Harmony* does have bigger and more exciting color photographs, which make for better browsing. Absent from *Harmony* but provided here are topical entries covering subjects like radio in the United States and the United Kingdom, the 1960s folk revival, and cover versions, but most entries by far are on the artists and groups.

The British perspective on rock and roll is always instructive to American readers, but unfamiliarity with stateside acts occasionally results in bizarre statements like calling Gladys Knight and the Pips "One of Motown's great triumvirate of girl groups." Of course, Gladys is the only girl—the three Pips are male! [R: Choice, May 89, p. 1492; RBB, 15 June 89, pp. 1802-3; RQ, Summer 89, pp. 566-67]—**Richard W. Grefrath**

897. Ewen, David. **American Songwriters**. Bronx, N.Y., H. W. Wilson, 1987. 489p. illus. index. (H. W. Wilson Biographical Dictionary). $50.00. LC 86-24654. ISBN 0-8242-0744-0.

This is the latest (and presumably last) volume to be completed by David Ewen (1907-1983), one of the most prolific authors of music reference works in recent decades. Superseding (and similar in format to) Ewen's *Popular American Composers* (1962) and *Popular American Composers: First Supplement* (see ARBA 74, entry 1104), this compilation, covering 146 composers and lyricists, contains references to "more than 5,500 songs." Early songwriters such as John Hill Hewitt (1801-1890) and Henry Clay Work (1832-1884) stand at one side of the chronological spectrum, while several born at the end of the 1940s or the beginning of the 1950s—Billy Joel, Lionel Richie, Bruce Springsteen, Stevie Wonder—stand at the other. The core of the work concerns those writers who attained fame during the period from the 1920s to the 1950s.

Much attention is paid to the critical reception of individual songs or musical shows and the performers associated with them. Entries are liberally sprinkled with statistics on successive Broadway performances, numbers of appearances on *Your Hit Parade*, and quotations from prominent newspapers. Portraits and brief bibliographies accompany the articles. A song index is provided, but a performer index, which would have been useful, is lacking. Typographical lapses are not infrequent: For example, the outbreak of the Civil War is given as 1860 (instead of 1861) on page 169, and the tenor Jan Peerce has become Jan Pearce on page 225. Those who do not require the last word in scholarship may possibly feel comfortable with this work; others may wish to double-check details in *The New Grove Dictionary of American Music* (see entry 857) or the latest edition of *Baker's Biographical Dictionary of Musicians* (see entry 850). [R: Choice, June 87, p. 1530]—**John E. Druesedow, Jr.**

898.   Gregory, Hugh. **Who's Who in Country Music**. London, Weidenfeld and Nicolson; distr., North Pomfret, Vt., Trafalgar Square, 1993. 262p. index. $22.95pa. ISBN 0-297-81343-9.

Who's Who in Country Music is a sincere, ambitious attempt to improve the image of, and knowledge about, country music in the United Kingdom, which makes its use to North American audiences limited. Artists, producers, and songwriters are listed alphabetically, along with any recordings available in the United Kingdom. A strong point is the inclusion of many "fringe" acts from bluegrass, zydeco, Cajun, and Tex-Mex, formats rarely covered in depth or well by mainstream North American publications. Many names are left out, however, and some choices for inclusion can be debated, such as the Rolling Stones.

For most entries the facts are correct as far as they go. Occasionally they do not go far enough (material goes up to only early 1992, leaving out many recent deaths and personal and professional separations), or they make one wonder about Gregory's sources (e.g., Dottie West did not die from cancer but from a car accident). While appreciating what is attempted here, this reviewer cannot recommend this book when there are more accurate, up-to-date North American books available. [R: BL, July 94, p. 1910]—**R. S. Lehmann**

899.   **The Harmony Illustrated Encyclopedia of Rock**. 6th ed. New York, Harmony Books/Crown, 1988. 208p. illus. $14.95pa. ML102.R6C6. 784.5'4'00321. LC 88-21473. ISBN 0-517-57164-1.

Reviews of previous editions have noted the book's highlights, but proofreading, editorial, and factual problems remain. Because the book lacks an index, one will not find Iggy Pop unless browsing. His biography is alphabetized by his first name, so he is sandwiched between Billy Idol and INXS. Careless proofreading has resulted in numerous grammatical and stylistic errors.

Egalitarian Bruce Springsteen will be pleased to note that his career warrants only as much space as does his much lesser known friends Southside Johnny and the Asbury Jukes. The now-defunct Police and their six albums are given a two-page spread while Prince and his ten albums are relegated to barely a half page. Not to deny the tremendous successes of old guard rockers like the Rolling Stones, Elton John, and the Who, but do any of them need a two-page spread, especially when their entries have not changed significantly from previous editions? The extra space could be devoted to artists such as Marshall Crenshaw, the Replacements, and Graham Parker. In the introduction, the editors mention Live Aid, the huge 1985 concert that was held simultaneously in London and Philadelphia. However, Bob Geldof, a member of the Boomtown Rats and one of the driving forces behind Live Aid, is nowhere to be seen. The Bo Deans, Lone Justice, and Midnight Oil have been overlooked in favor of Richard Marx, Barry Manilow, Leo Sayer, and Perry Como. Also left out are such idiosyncratic but popular musicians as the Pogues, T-Bone Burnett, and Lyle Lovett. Innovators such as Grandmaster Flash and the Furious Five, Laurie Anderson, and Brian Eno, and early rock influences and legends such as Lead Belly, Woody Guthrie, and King Curtis, are covered only in the book's appendix with a sentence or two explaining their careers. There seems to be no principle guiding the editors' decisions on who to cover.

Useful features of the 1986 edition that enhanced the reference value of this book have been removed. Previously there were appendixes of management and promotion personalities, directories of record companies and musical instruments, and an index to performers. Without the appendixes there is no access to Leo Fender, Malcolm McLaren, John Hammond, Norman Whitfield, or other visionaries.

In summary, this encyclopedia only belongs in libraries that have comprehensive rock music literature collections. Its reference value is negligible. [R: RBB, 15 June 89, pp. 1802-3; VOYA, June 89, pp. 136-37]—**Laurie Saboll**

900.   **Rock Movers & Shakers**. Barry Lazell, ed., with Dafydd Rees and Luke Crampton. New York, Billboard, 1991. 585p. illus. $19.95pa. ML385.R736. 784.5'4'00922. ISBN 0-8743-6661-5.

This work is a rock 'n' roll reference book with a twist. Instead of presenting the personal opinions, anecdotes, and quotations found in other rock sources such as the *Encyclopedia of Pop, Rock and Soul* (see ARBA 90, entry 1298), this book contains straight facts about the lives, careers, and recordings of U.S. and U.K. artists from the 1950s through 1990. It contains nearly 1,000 alphabetical entries, each a chronological listing of events in the artists' careers. Every entry is arranged by year, month, and exact day (when possible). Entries for bands include the names of the original (or best-known) members.

Noticeably absent from this book are an appendix, an index, and a bibliography, sections that appear in most other rock reference guides. The only mention of bibliographic material appears in the introduction. The editor lists seven publications that he used as source material and discounts the rest as "miscellaneous U.S. and U.K. rock magazines and books."

Another missing element is the criteria used to select the material for this compilation. Rock enthusiasts have varied opinions about which styles of music should and should not be labeled as rock 'n' roll; the editor never addresses this. Furthermore, he does not explain why he considers certain artists to be "movers and shakers" apart from stating that they have had an influence on rock music.

In spite of the book's drawbacks, readers may find that its novel approach to rock 'n' roll history outweighs its flaws. The work is informative, easy to read, and fun to thumb through.—**Lisha E. Goldberg and Robert L. Wick**

901. Stambler, Irwin. **Encyclopedia of Pop, Rock & Soul**. rev. ed. New York, St. Martin's Press, 1989. 881p. illus. $35.00. ML102.P66S8. 784.5'0092'2. LC 88-29860. ISBN 0-312-02573-4.

This 2nd edition of Stambler's work updates and adds to the excellent biographical essays that appeared in the 1st edition (see ARBA 76, entry 1030). Over 500 entries aim "to reflect all of the pivotal influences in the evolution of today's popular music spectrum" (p. ix) by focusing on superstars and groups, both representative and influential. Alphabetically arranged entries (averaging 800 to 1,000 words) give birth date and place of all individuals and biographical essays (including interview quotations) with often only selective discographies. Length of entry seems to coincide with importance, but it is hard to accept five-and-a-half columns on Abba and nearly four on Be Bop Deluxe while Jackson Browne gets only two and the Beatles not quite six (although individual members of the Beatles do have separate entries). Notable exclusions include America, John Hiatt, and REM. For substantial overviews of the major artists, however, Stambler's work surpasses the shorter but more numerous entries of Mike Clifford's *The Harmony Illustrated Encyclopedia of Rock* (see ARBA 87, entry 1268) and *The Rolling Stone Encyclopedia of Rock and Roll* (Summit, 1983) (which does include complete discographies), as well as the broader chronological coverage of Donald Clarke's *The Penguin Encyclopedia of Popular Music* (Viking, 1989). [R: LJ, 15 Feb 89, p. 156; RBB, 15 June 89, pp. 1802-3]—**Robert Aken**

902. Stancell, Steven. **Rap Whoz Who: The World of Rap Music**. New York, Schirmer Books/Simon & Schuster Macmillan, 1996. 339p. illus. index. $22.95pa. ISBN 0-02-864520-0.

This is a welcome addition to the relatively sparse literature on an influential genre of music. It contains basic data on many of the performers, producers, record labels, and promoters; data that should be easily available but has not been until the publication of this book.

Organized alphabetically, it contains articles on individuals as well as groups. Each article provides a brief history, a selected discography, and comments on their role in the world of Rap. The length of the articles reflects the importance of each topic. Afrika Bambaataa, Def Jam Recordings, Grandmaster Flash, and N. W. A., for example, are treated in greater depth. Scattered throughout the book are useful sidebars on various topics, including the definition of Rap terms; interviews with major figures, such as Afrika Bambaataa; performance and recording techniques, such as sampling and the art of MC Oing; and sympathetic discussions of political and moral issues, such as the relationship between violence and Rap. Photographs and a detailed index round out the book.

The author, who writes a regular column in the *New York Beacon on Rap*, introduces the book with a brief but informational and sympathetic history of the genre. The book is written in an informal and accessible style. This book is highly recommended for anyone who is interested in the history, people, techniques, and language of Rap. [R: Choice, Jan 97, p. 776]—**Howard Spring**

903.   Sumrall, Harry. **Pioneers of Rock and Roll: 100 Artists Who Changed the Face of Rock**. New York, Billboard Books/Watson-Guptill, 1994. 307p. illus. index. (Billboard Hitmakers Series). $21.95pa. ML102.R6S85. 781 .66'092'2. LC 93-44847. ISBN 0-8230-7628-8.

Identifying artists with the greatest impact on rock and roll is inherently controversial, as the task of defining "pioneer" and "rock and roll" is very subjective. Some readers may object to the definition of, or the inclusion or exclusion of, an artist as "most influential." Others may question the boundary set for the rock-and-roll genre. Noted rock critic Sumrall's entrants include "artists" with commercial or aesthetic impact rather than "performers, musicians, or acts." This accounts for the exclusion of the many who may have achieved commercial success but otherwise lacked significance. Individual artist profiles are arranged alphabetically, and there is an index of people, song and LP titles, and other artists mentioned in the text. Each entry in cludes a chronological list of the artist's significant songs and albums, complete with the name of the record label, year of release, and peak *Billboard* chart position. Entries are evenly written, with each including a discussion of the artist's career and an analysis of music and impact that explains the pioneer status. This last feature is the true strength of the volume, one that distinguishes it from more comprehensive indexes of popular music or others arranged thematically by style. Many of the potential criticisms inherent in such a project as this are quickly put to rest by the analytical discussion of the included artists' influence on others. This is especially so in the case of artists who have had greater aesthetic impact than commercial success.

As a reference source, this relatively inexpensive volume will be most useful for those interested in the impact of artists on the broad mainstream of popular music. It will be a valued addition to many collections.—**David V. Wailer**

RELIGIOUS MUSIC

904.   **Sing Glory and Hallelujah! Historical and Biographical Guide to Gospel Hymns Nos. 1 to 6 Complete**. Samuel J. Rogal, comp. Westport, Conn., Greenwood Press, 1996. 229p. index. (Music Reference Collection, no. 49). $79.50. ISBN 0-313-29690-1.

At first glance it may be somewhat confusing as to what exactly Mr. Rogal is covering in this guide, but he makes it clear in the Introduction. He points out that his analysis is of a series of hymn books published in the late nineteenth century which culminated in a work titled *Gospel Hymns Nos. 1 to 6 Complete*, published by the Biglow and Main Company and the John Church Company in 1895. This work incorporated two earlier works, titled *Gospel Hymns and Sacred Songs* (1975) and *Gospel Hymns* (published serially in six volumes from 1976 through 1891). The combined work *Gospel Hymns Nos. 1 to 6 Complete* contained 739 hymns and "more than 125 standard hymns and tunes of the church" (Introduction, xi).

Sing Glory and Hallelujah! Historical and Biographical Guide to Gospel Hymns Nos. 1 to 6 Complete provides an analysis of the hymns and their composers and authors. Section one, titled "Authors of the Hymns," lists all of the authors of the hymns alphabetically. Each entry contains the name of the author, birth and death dates, a brief biography, and the author's hymn(s) by the original number used in the *Gospel Hymns* volumes. (Each hymn listing includes title, date, Bible verse, and first line, along with the name of the composer of the music.) The 2nd section, titled "Composers of the Music," is an alphabetical listing of the composers and contains similar information with the exception of the detail concerning the hymn, which can be found under the author section. Additional sections include a list of works cited and consulted (31 items), and an index to titles and opening lines.

Sing Glory and Hallelujah! is the only research tool in print that provides complete information concerning these standard American hymns. It is an important research source for information concerning the hymns and, at the same time, provides valuable information for the study of popular culture in the United States during the last half of the nineteenth century. Additional indexing would have been useful (e.g., a list of the hymns by the original numbers for easy cross-referencing), and a list of the hymns by original date of publication would provide a more historical view. The work is recommended for all larger academic and public libraries, and for music collections that emphasize hymnody. It could also provide useful information for clergy who wish to research the older hymns still used for services.—**Robert L. Wick**

905.   Smith, Jane Stuart, and Betty Carlson. **Favorite Men Hymn Writers**. Wheaton, Ill., Crossway Books/Good News, 1993. 127p. index. $6.99. BV325.S55. 264'.2'0922. LC 93-17452. ISBN 0-89107-754-5.

The authors of *Favorite Men Hymn Writers* point out that "nearly every good hymn has a story behind it, a story worth knowing about, and that is why [they] have written this book" (prelude)—and this little volume certainly has some interesting stories. About 30 hymns and hymn writers are included, ranging from the rather obscure (e.g., Joseph Scriven, 1819-1886) to the well known, including John Bunyan, William Cowper, and John Milton. Most of the accounts take only two or three pages, but the writing is clear, simple, and packed with information. The authors, while recounting wonderful tales, are careful to point out what can or cannot be verified.

Favorite Men Hymn Writers probably has little place in the great religious literature, but it is fun to read. Even if one's interest in Christian hymns is rather limited, the tales are fascinating. The entries are not documented, but there is a bibliography (15 items) at the end, along with an index to the hymns. The composers are listed in the table of contents. The book would most likely serve private hymnology collectors best but could be a source for worship services, sermon illustrations, small group discussions, and general home reading or private devotions.—**Robert L. Wick**

INTRODUCTION

This chapter covers film, journalism, public speaking, television/cable/radio, and general works in communication. By far the greatest number of entries lie in the Film category, which is subdivided into General Works; Actors and Actresses; Directors, Cinematographers, Designers, and Songwriters; and Screenwriters. Film buffs have a plethora of sources to choose from, either to use as true reference sources, or simply to browse through. General works cover all segments of the film industry. *Variety's Who's Who in Show Busines*, rev. ed. (R.R. Bowker, 1989) (see entry 916), edited by Mike Kaplan, for example, provides information on 6,500 show business personalities; while Roy Pickard's *Who Played Who on the Screen* (Hippocrene Books, 1989) (see entry 914) gives information on both real and imaginary characters. Two specialized sources of interest are Gary D. Keller and Estela Keller's *A Biographical Handbook of Hispanics and United States Film* (Bilingual Press, 1997) (see entry 911) and the intriguing *Who's Who of Victorian Cinema: A Worldwide Survey*, edited by Stephen Herbert and Luke McKernan (British Film Institute, 1996) (see entry 921).

The category Actors and Actresses gives the most scope. Some cover all types of actors and actresses, such as David Ragan's *Who's Who in Hollywood: The Largest Cast of International Film Personalities Ever Assembled* (Facts on File, 1992) (see entry 934); while others concentrate on subgenres such as cowboys, horror film stars, character actors, or child actors. *The Oscar Stars from A-Z* (Trafalgar Square, 1996) (see entry 930) covers Oscar winners—in the acting categories—from the beginning of the sound era in 1929 to 1996.

For people seeking information on directors, cinematographers, songwriters, or designers, there are a host of sources. A number are international in scope, such as John Wakeman's two-volume set, *World Film Directors* (Wilson, 1987 and 1988) (see entry 950), which covers 1890-1985 and which compiles information published previously in other sources; *Michael Singer's Film Directors,* 12th ed. (Lone Eagle, 1997) (see entry 947), which covers world film directors of feature, documentary, or telefilms; or the *International Dictionary of Films and Filmmakers, Volume 2: Directors,* 2d ed. (St. James, 1991) (see entry 944), whose entries were written by film critics and other experts in the field. Others cover the filmmaking efforts of various regions; there are directories of Indian, Spanish, Soviet, and African filmmakers.

Only a few books are listed in the television category. One, however, Tim Brooks's *The Complete Directory to Prime Time TV Stars: 1946-Present* (Ballantine/Random House, 1987) (see entry 967), contains thousands of entries for both major and supporting players in television shows. Moreover, the review for this title refers to two other titles containing biographical information: one is *International Television and Video Almanac* (Quigley Publishing, 1987), which includes behind-the-scenes personnel as well as performers; the other is an earlier work by Brooks, *The Complete Directory of Prime Time Network TV Shows* (Ballantine, 1981).

The category Public Speaking has some specialized sources. Greenwood Press contributes two: *Women Public Speakers in the United States, 1800-1925: A Bio-Critical Sourcebook* (Greenwood Press, 1993) (see entries 964-965); and Richard W. Leeman's *African-American Orators: A Bio-Critical Sourcebook* (Greenwood Press, 1996) (see entry 961).

The printed word is also covered in this chapter, with directories of journalists and other authors. Excepted are literary authors; works listing them are in the chapter **Literature**, as are works listing both literary and non-literary authors. As in so many areas, the Dictionary of Literary Biography proves helpful for the field of journalism, offering several historical sources: *American Magazine*

Journalists, 1741-1850 (vol. 73) (Gale, 1988) (see entry 954) and *American Magazine Journalists, 1850-1900* (vol. 79) (Gale, 1989) (see entry 955).

GENERAL WORKS

906.   **Who's Who in Mass Communication**. 2d ed. Sylwester Dziki, Janina Maczuga, and Walery Pisarek, eds. Munich, New York, K. G. Saur, 1990. 191p. index. $110.00. ISBN 3-598-10884-2.

This work is a revised edition of *World Directory of Mass Communication Researchers* (Krakow: Press Research, 1984), which was a more accurate title for this directory. The core of individuals listed in the directory come from the attendees of a biennial conference of the International Association for Mass Communication Research. Other individuals are also included, but for an international, comprehensive listing of communication researchers, this work is scanty, with only 1,124 entries and an index. In addition, it is disturbing to find someone listed who died in the mid-1980s.

With good editing and expansion, future editions will prove useful for academic libraries with communication majors and larger public libraries. Until then, this volume does not replace current membership directories for key communication organizations.—**Glynys R. Thomas**

FILM

General Works

907.   Bogle, Donald. **Blacks in American Films and Television: An Encyclopedia**. New York, Garland, 1988. 510p. illus. index. (Garland Reference Library of the Humanities, Vol.604). $60.00. LC 87-29241. ISBN 0-8240-8715-1.

Bogle is the leading historian of black portrayals and performances in the entertainment industry. His reputation was established by *Toms, Coons, Mulattos, Mammies & Bucks: An Interpretive History of Blacks in American Films* (Viking, 1973) and *Brown Sugar: Eighty Years of America's Black Female Superstars* (Harmony Books, 1982). Here he offers facts about and highly charged critical evaluations of over 260 Hollywood and independent films and more than 100 television series, specials, and movies. All have featured black performers and, in Bogle's opinion, reflected racial attitudes. A "Profiles" section looks at and critiques the careers of about one hundred black performers and a handful of directors. Good illustrations abound. There are an up-to-date bibliography and a substantial index. My only real criticism concerns the decision to organize the volume as an alphabetical encyclopedia with a skimpy nine-line table of contents. Given the importance of an historical perspective, it would have been more useful to arrange the films and programs chronologically and to include a detailed listing of titles and "Profiles" in the table of contents. This is a meaty volume crammed with facts and strong opinions. It is sure to be a valued reference book in public and academic libraries. [R: Choice, Sept 88, p. 74; LJ, 1 Sept 88, p. 161; RBB, 1 Oct 88, p. 223]—**Joseph W. Palmer**

908.   **Encyclopedia of European Cinema**. Ginette Vincendeau, ed. New York, Facts on File, 1995. 524p. illus. index. $55.00. ISBN 0-8160-3394-3.

Published to coincide with the medium's 100th anniversary, this encyclopedia was created to recognize and summarize the accomplishments of Europe's film industry since 1895. The entries were written by 90 contributors representing different countries, most filmmaking specialties, and various academic disciplines. Entries are of four kinds: national essays (surveying the breadth and history of a country's cinema); personnel (mainly directors and actors); critical (to explore topics such as *New Gennan Cinema* or *animation;* and institutional (film schools, festivals, and companies). The entries range in length from a few sentences to half a page or more, with articles on individuals predictably being briefer than the critical and national essays. Cross-references are used when necessary, and an index to names and terms is provided. Four pages of graphs list annual film production figures and annual audience figures, by country, for the period 1945-1993. An introductory essay explains how the expansion of the U.S. film industry (the country's second-biggest exported product) has caused the decline of European cinema.

The popularity of videocassette recorders has created an abundance of printed film guides that limit their reviews to feature films available on videocassette. The purpose of this book is to survey all of Europe's cinema, to discuss films as art and as cultural history. It is an admirable effort, unique in focus and scope, but with some slight failings. Filmographies are lengthy but only occasionally comprehensive. There are no entries for two of Europe's finest (and in the latter case, most prolific) actresses: Falconetti and Bulle Ogier. Respected director Alain Jessua is ignored. Despite the lapses, Vincendeau has filled agap with this publication. It is more comprehensive than either *Halliwell's Film Guide 1995* (see ARBA 96, entry 1385) or such video guides as *Roger Ebert's Video Companion* (see ARBA 95, entry 1362). This is an indispensable source for students of Europe's sizable film history. [R: Choice, July/Aug 96, p. 1771; RBB, 1 May 96, pp. 1519-20]—**Ed Volz**

909.   **International Motion Picture Almanac**. New York, Quigley Publishing, 1929- . $109.00. ISSN 0074-7084.

A great deal of information regarding the entertainment industry, and the personalities in it, is provided by the *International Motion Picture Almanac*. Although much of this guide is a who's who, containing thousands of brief biographies of people currently active in films and television, other chapters are involved with the behind-the-scenes workings of the industry.

An index of subjects promotes access to the text and precedes a summary of last year's activities and its releases from major film companies. The biographical listing includes the person's work in theater, film, and television, and is followed by the year's obituaries and chapters on awards, services, major studios, corporations, and organizations enabling the entertainment industry to flourish. "Feature Pictures of 1980-1994" includes production company, year, and cast. Also available is information about the industry in select foreign countries.

Such an almanac is a helpful reference tool, containing up-to-date information regarding a major national and international industry. Future annual editions will ensure the volume's continued usefulness.—**Anita Zutis and Terry Ann Mood**

910.   Karsten, Eileen, with Dorothy-Ellen Gross. **From Real Life to Reel Life: A Filmography of Biographical Films**. Metuchen, N.J., Scarecrow, 1993. 475p. index. $52.50. PN1995.9.B55K37. 016.79143'651. LC 93-9160. ISBN 0-8108-2591-0.

Filling an overlooked reference niche is *From Real Life to Reel Life,* a filmography of commercially produced English-language biopics. This comprehensive volume (listing more than 1,000 entries) also includes foreign features and documentaries available with English subtitles or dubbing. Each entry provides filmographic details and may be accessed through the many indexes. Although *From Real Life* is an excellent first outing that breaks new ground, many elements of it could be improved. Karsten recognizes the importance of made-for-television films in the development of the biopic but does not differentiate them in the filmography. Works of fiction are included and treated as fact (e.g., *Badlands* does *not* depict Charles Starkweather's life). Entries for couples are listed under only one name, but there is no consistency as to which partner gets the entry (e.g., for Clyde Barrow *see* Bonnie Parker; for Nancy Spungen *see* Sid Vicious). Strong on historical figures, weak on contemporary ones, and probably offering unique coverage of television true-crime movies, this volume will serve the needs of public libraries. [R: Choice, Dec 93, p. 587; JAL, Sept 93, p. 274; RBB, 15 Sept 93, p. 187; WLB, Oct 93, pp. 88-89]—**Megan S. Farrell**

911.   Keller, Gary D., with Estela Keller. **A Biographical Handbook of Hispanics and United States Film**. Tempe, Ariz., Bilingual Press, 1997. 322p. illus. index. $49.00; $28.00pa. ISBN 0-927534-65-7; 0-927534-56-8pa.

This is the 2d volume of a 2-volume set by Gary Keller that began with *Hispanics & United States Film* (Bilingual Press, 1994). This work provides both biographical and filmographic information on Hispanic actors and filmmakers active in the U.S. film industry from 1894 to the present. The work at hand consists of biographical entries that include given and stage names, date and place of birth, and information about the films in which the individual participated. These entries are interspersed with 20 photographic themes that do little to enhance the usefulness of the work (e.g., "History as a Function of Interracial Sex" is not adequately explained by three photographs [p. 76]). The author uses Spanish-language diacritical marks within the majority of the text. He does make exceptions in those cases in which the American-style pronunciation is so common that adding diacritics would confuse the reader.

A weakness in this work's companion volume is addressed here by the inclusion of a comprehensive 43-page bibliography. The bibliography is divided into four sections: "Periodicals, Trade Journals, and Newspapers"; "Exhibition Programs, CD-ROMs, Videotapes, and Software Programs"; "Archival Materials at the Library of Congress and Elsewhere"; and "General Bibliography." The author includes two cumulative indexes that differentiate between the two volumes by using Roman numerals. There is an index for individual and group names and an index for film and television show titles. It is also noted in the introduction that spelling errors made in the 1st volume are corrected within the indexes. Keller has produced an excellent reference source that will be useful in both film collections and Hispanic studies collections. [R: LJ, 1 Mar 97, p. 70; RBB, 1 Mar 97, pp. 1183-84]—**John R. Burch Jr.**

912.   MacCann, Richard Dyer. **The First Tycoons**. Metuchen, N.J., Scarecrow, 1987. 259p. bibliog. (American Movies: The First Thirty Years). $22.50; $12.50pa. LC 86-22064. ISBN 0-8108-1949-X; 0-8108-1950-3pa.

This title is one in a series of books which will deal with the history of the motion picture industry and the people who fostered and prospered from it. *The First Tycoons* begins with Edison's kinetoscope (c.1894) and ends around the time that *Ben Hur*, starring Ramon Novarro and Francis X. Bushman, premiered in 1925. The text is composed of excerpts from books, journal articles, and speeches by and about the pioneers of those days.

According to the author, it was his intent to portray more of the flavor of the times using anecdotal narrative rather than a more conventional form of information transmittal. The results are a composite picture which is rambling and jerky, much like those early silent films.

There is no index, but there are several bibliographies, the first giving the sources of the excerpts, the second listing additional reading, and the third listing the films mentioned in the text, along with information on availability. While the format precludes its inclusion in a general reference library, libraries specializing in the history of the film may find this title useful.—**Mary Jo Aman**

913.   Monaco, James. **Who's Who in American Film Now**. 2d ed. New York, New York Zoetrope, 1987. 388p. $39.95. LC 87-43024. ISBN 0-918432-63-4.

This book covers 6,000 films, made between 1975 and 1986, and over 11,000 people who worked on those films. It is arranged in thirteen chapters by the craft of the individuals who worked on the films. The chapters are arranged in the sequence usually followed in the stages of movie production. Thus, the first chapter is given to the writers; then are listed producers of all sorts; directors; actors and actresses; production designers; art directors; etc.; costume designers; cinematographers; sound on the set and off; recording and editing; choreographers; music; special effects; and finally, the editors. The entries within each chapter are alphabetically arranged by surname with the titles of the films and the date made listed in chronological order.

Unfortunately, there is not a master index for all thirteen chapters, and so, for individuals who do a great variety of things with a movie, such as Woody Allen, Mel Brooks, or Harold Ramis, one will have to go through all the chapters to gather complete information. An introductory chapter is included that deals with the salaries paid to film people. The information in this publication is taken from BASELINE, a comprehensive database for the film and television industry, which was started by the author. Even thought here is no biographical information about the people included, this should prove to be a useful source for relatively current information on the activities of individuals in the American film industry. [R: RBB, 1 Jan 88, p. 770]—**Robert L. Turner, Jr.**

914.   Pickard, Roy. **Who Played Who on the Screen**. New York, Hippocrene Books, 1989. 351p. illus. $37.50. ISBN 0-87052-789-4.

First published in the United Kingdom in 1988, this updated and expanded version of the author's earlier *Who Played Who in the Movies* is an alphabetical reference guide to nearly 800 real persons (e.g., Joy Adamson, Emile Zola) and fictional characters (e.g., Nick Adams, Zorro) who have been portrayed on film. Each entry starts with a chatty paragraph about the person or character with interesting tidbits about their movie incarnations. This is followed by a chronological listing of sound films in which he or she was portrayed, giving the full name of the actor playing the role, the name of the film in its country of origin, the last name of the director, the country of origin, and the year of release. More often than not this is followed by a paragraph in which silent screen and television impersonations and important allied characters are identified. For instance, under Batman are given the names of the actors who played Robin in the 1943, 1949, and the 1966 movies as well as those who played the Penguin, Joker, Riddler, and Catwoman in the 1966 film.

It was surprising to find *Andy Warhol's Frankenstein* missing from a list of 26 Frankenstein movies and listings that call Martin Scorsese's *The Last Temptation of Christ,* "The Passion" but this is nit-picking. One cannot help but be impressed by the research that has resulted in a book with entries for persons as famous as Lincoln, Beethoven, and Geronimo, and as obscure as British horror writer "Chetwynd-Hayes," and which tells who played the title role of *Charley's Aunt* in American, British, French, German, Argentine, Italian, Danish, Spanish, and Swedish productions.

A beautifully designed volume printed on high quality (but not acid free) paper, the book is enhanced by over 300 gorgeous production stills. Cinemaphiles, scholars, and trivia buffs will find this book chock full of information and great fun to browse. [R: BL, 1 Oct 89, p. 251]—**Joseph W. Palmer**

915.   Stewart, John. **Italian Film: A Who's Who**. Jefferson, N.C., McFarland, 1994. 812p. index. $95.00. PN1998.2.S74. 791.43'092'245. LC 93-38733. ISBN 0-89950-761-1.

This is an encyclopedic reference to 4,991 people, both Italians and foreigners, who have been active in Italian film since 1896. It is divided into two parts: a who's who and a film index. The entries in the who's who give very brief biographical information, such as the person's role in films (e.g., actor, director, producer) and approximate birth and death dates as well as extensive filmographical information. The index is to the who's who section and is not meant to be an exhaustive list of Italian movies. The numbers in the index section are often followed with a one-letter code so that one can pick out a producer, director, or the like without having to look at each entry. However, there are some inconsistencies. For example, not all the actors are listed for the films indexed. It would seem to be a rational assumption that the complete cast would be included in the who's who section; in at least one case this is not so. There is no discussion of who is included and who is not. Still, this is a tremendous resource for Italian cinema. The author has included the very famous and the not-so-famous, those who made many films, and those who made only one. It is a very handy sourcebook and should be in all film collections. It would have been even more helpful if the author had also included an annotation of each film. However, that could be another work. [R: Choice, Oct 94, pp. 265-66; LJ, 1 June 94, p. 100]—**Robert L. Turner, Jr**.

916.   *Variety's* **Who's Who in Show Business**. rev. ed. Mike Kaplan, ed. New York., R. R. Bowker, 1989. 412p. $49.95. LC 85-20578. ISBN 0-8352-2665-4.

A revised edition of the 1983 volume, this work continues to present biographical data of important figures in the entertainment industry. After this edition the work will be issued annually. The selection of personalities and compilation of information is overseen by *Variety*, the main newspaper of the entertainment industry. Information is complete up to November 30, 1988. Persons deceased prior to June 30, 1988, are not included, but information about them is available in other volumes. This is the 1st edition to list persons from around the world.

More than 6,500 names are found here. Each entry provides a minimum of personal information on birth date, birthplace, and education, with a listing of professional activities on stage, screen, television, music, and dance. For extensive information the researcher will have to look elsewhere. However, this is a valuable source to quickly locate the credits of show business personalities currently alive or active in the industry.—**Marilyn Strong Noronha**

917.   Vazzana, Eugene Michael. **Silent Film Necrology: Births and Deaths of over 9000 Performers, Directors, Producers**. . . . Jefferson, N.C., McFarland, 1995. 367p. $55.00. ISBN 0-7864-132-X.

Vazzana is lending his voice to documenting the lives and deaths of silent film figures. More than 9,000 actors, directors, producers, animators, publicists, scenarists, writers, and even Thomas A. Edison, the co-inventor of the motion picture camera, appear in this biographical dictionary of silent film, an era that came to an end in the late 1920s. A surprising number of these actors lived until recent years, such as Lillian Gish (1893-1993). Others died under mysterious or obscure circumstances much earlier in their career, which Vazzana attempts to document with historical and contemporary citations. The subjects usually had some connection with the U.S. film industry, although some figures such as Emil Jannings or Charles Pathé were best known in Europe. Some figures are known primarily for their sound pictures or television careers (e.g., Walter Brennan, Ruth Gordon, Charles Farrell), but are included here because of their early years in silent pictures.

Each entry attempts to indicate the individual's birth and death date and place; given name; spouse(s); studio affiliation; and citations to biographies, autobiographies, and obituaries. Vazzana does not list film credits. The author notes instances when biographical information is not available or is in doubt. In addition, Vazzana cites news articles and other notices from sources such as *The New York Times*, *Variety*, and a few dozen film reference books, updating the bibliographical information to recent years. Some details extend beyond what one would expect from a work such as this; for example, by providing the name and address of fan newsletters, citing film tributes and documentaries, including the headlines of obituary notices, and indicating the cause of death.

There is no index or bibliography to *Silent Film Necrology*. Instead, it stands as an index to film industry papers, newspapers of the day, and subsequent film reference works. It also stands on its own, as a thorough, well-researched biographical dictionary of the prominent and lesser-known figures from the three decades when pictures moved but did not speak.—**John P. Schmitt**

918.   Waldman, Harry. **Hollywood and the Foreign Touch: A Dictionary of Foreign Filmmakers and Their Films from America, 1910-1995**. Lanham, Md., Scarecrow, 1996. 3l6p. $49.50. ISBN 0-8108-3192-9.

This title is described by the author as a "catalog, a listing, and a discussion of significant foreign filmmakers who worked in Hollywood and America between 1910 and 1995." Although the selection criteria are somewhat vague, the work apparently focuses on foreign filmmakers, especially lesser knowns, who came to the United States, made a film (or several), and then went back to their homelands rather than staying on in the States. Additionally, there are separate entries for significant (if little-known) films made by these foreign filmmakers.

Written in a popular rather than academic or scholarly style, the 527 entries range in length from several sentences to 1-1/2 pages. The entries are strictly biographical and include no evaluation of the films or the filmmakers' careers. There are no supplementary materials that would support further research, such as lists of recommended reading. However, this is not really meant as a scholarly resource. It is instead the work of an amateur film enthusiast who has done a substantial amount of research in a neglected area of film history. Waldman's work will be a welcome supplement to the literature of film history.—**G. Kim Dority**

919.   **Who's Who in Canadian Film and Television. Qui est Qui au Cinema et à la Television au Canada**. Waterloo, Ont., Wilfrid Laurier University Press; distr., Atlantic Highlands, N.J., Humanities Press, 1986- . $49.95pa. 791.43'025'71. ISSN 0831-6309.

First published in 1986, this comprehensive directory of the Canadian production community provides information on thousands of film and television directors, picture editors, writers, producers, cinematographers, art directors, composers, production managers, costume designers, sound personnel, and publicists. Professional and biographical information in the entries is based on data supplied by those responding to a form sent to them by the Academy of Canadian Cinema and Television. Entries appear in English or French depending upon the language used by the respondent to answer the form. Explanatory texts are in both English and French.

Personnel entries are grouped under 14 alphabetically arranged job designations, from art directors to writers. Each entry contains union, guide, or association membership; home or work address; and telephone number. The subsections titled "Types of Production and Credits," "Genres," "Biography," and "Selected Filmography" complete the entry and identify the individual's principal areas of professional endeavor. Entries are rife with abbreviations that some users may find cumbersome, but a complete list of these is offered, and their use is uniform. A name index provides access to entries alphabetically listed under the 14 job designation sections. Also included is the text of the Canadian government's "Canadians First Employment Policy." Recommended for academic libraries with strong television and film collections. [R: Choice, June 92, p. 1530]—**David K. Frasier and Terry Ann Mood**

920. **Who's Who in the Motion Picture Industry: Directors, Producers, Writers, Cinematographers, Executives**. . . . Beverly Hills, Calif., Packard Publishing, 1984- . index. $18.95pa. LC 81-64574. ISSN 0278-6516.

This reference work is needed. It is handy to have information on the people in the motion picture industry. Included, as suggested by the subtitle, are directors, producers, writers, cinematographers, executives, major studios, production companies, and distribution companies. There is also a name index.

However, the work is often incomplete and sloppily edited. For example, in the writers' section one is told that Harold Ramis wrote *Animal House* with Douglas Kenney and Chris Miller. Neither are included separately in the section on writers or in the index. The same entry says that Ramis wrote *Back to School* with Steven Kampmann and Will Porter. There was actually a fourth writer, Peter Torokvei, listed in the movie credits. In fact, the various entries for the four writers give credit for that movie to differing combinations of the writers; only in Torokvei's entry are all four mentioned. The section on writers lists Ramis's office address and telephone number, but his entry in the directors' section omits them. Similar problems exist throughout the volume. One hopes that future editions will be more complete and correct.—**Robert L. Turner, Jr.**

921. **Who's Who of Victorian Cinema: A Worldwide Survey**. Stephen Herbert and Luke McKernan, eds. London, British Film Institute; distr., Bloomington, Indiana University Press, 1996. 178p. illus. index. $59.95. ISBN 0-85170-539-1.

When Queen Victoria died in January 1901, just five years had elapsed since the Lumière brothers first exhibited a program of projected motion pictures to a paying audience. Although movies in 1901 were still a crude novelty found mostly on music hall bills and in cheap amusement arcades, they represented the culmination of decades of effort by investors and entrepreneurs who had worked first to perfect and then to exploit the new medium.

In order to provide a convenient and reliable source of information on persons who were involved with film prior to 1901, the British Film Institute commissioned 21 film scholars to research and compile this biographical dictionary. It includes short but well-written articles on more than 250 individuals, including inventors, camerapeople, businesspeople, and actors. There are even entries for prominent public figures who appeared in early films (e.g., President William McKinley) and for several individuals (e.g., the Sultan of Morocco and Winston Churchill) who were merely film aficionados. Portraits accompany articles dealing with persons who were especially significant in the development of film, and articles often debunk myths that have grown up about these individuals, thus correcting misinformation found in other sources.

Each entry has its own bibliography, but there is also an annotated bibliography at the back of the book that cites and describes the merits of 56 books dealing with nineteenth-century film. Indexes to personal names and to the names of inventions are available, but, alas, no indexes to corporate names, film titles, or geographic locations appear. The last is regrettable because the book is international in scope and there are articles (sometimes hard to locate) on pioneers in such diverse places as Russia, Denmark, Italy, Hungary, Japan, Venezuela, and Mexico. Authoritative and informative, this is a valuable addition to the film scholar's reference shelf. [R: Choice, Mar 97, p. 1144]—**Joseph W. Palmer**

Actors and Actresses

922.   Doyle, Billy H. **The Ultimate Directory of the Silent Screen Performers: A Necrology of Births and Deaths and Essays on 50 Lost Players**. Metuchen, N.J., Scarecrow, 1995. 346p. illus. $49.50. ISBN 0-8108-2958-4.

Doyle offers an extensive and useful index to the vital statistics of approximately 7,500 performers of the silent screen. The foreword, written by Anthony Slide, provides details of the research methodology employed by Doyle to supply accurate information on the dates of each performer's birth and death as well as where the person died. Along with the short entries of the main section described above, the book contains essays furnishing fuller biographical information on 50 of the performers who intrigued the author the most. Included are such long-forgotten names as Anita Stewart's sister, Lucille Lee Stewart, who worked with Ethel Barrymore and Norma Talmadge; and "rugged outdoorsman" William Stowell, who was killed in a train accident at the peak of his leading-man career in 1919. Each of the essays describes background information on the actors in addition to a filmography and details of their death. This work will be a good first step in research on those silent film actors not commonly included in other film sources (such as *Who Was Who on Screen* by Evelyn M. Truitt [abridged ed. R. R. Bowker, 1984] and John T. Weaver's *20 Years of Silents, 1908-1928* [Scarecrow, 1971]). An invaluable resource to film researchers and enthusiasts, this work is recommended for most libraries.—**Elizabeth A. Ginno**

923.   Dye, David. **Child and Youth Actors: Filmographies of Their Entire Careers, 1914-1985**. Jefferson, N.C., McFarland, 1988. 310p. illus. bibliog. index. $24.95. LC 87-46441. ISBN 0-89950-247-4.

To be included in this book, an actor or actress had to have at least two performing credits. The entry for each person contains the person's name (both assumed and real), the date and place of birth, death date, series information, chronological listing of roles, and trivia notes. Included in the chronological listing are movies (general releases), including year released, title of the movie, production, company, and the character portrayed; movies (made for television), including year released; title of the movie; station (followed by TVM, made for television); segment title, if needed; and character portrayed; series, including the year released, title of the series, station, date (month and day) that the episode was aired, and the character portrayed; and any work on the stage, including year, title of the production, name of the theater, city in which it was performed, and the character portrayed. An asterisk precedes the title of a movie or series in which the person was scheduled to appear but did not. There is a bibliography, as well as a title index of movies, plays, television series, and made-for-television movies.

There are errors in this book. For example, for the movie *Andy Hardy's Private Secretary*, the date of release is given as 1940 for one of the actors and 1941 for all the others, and one of the characters in the movie, Polly Benedict, is misnamed Polly Hardy. In the entry for Kurt Russell, many of his movies for the Disney studios were not listed. However, this is an interesting and worthwhile addition to the reference collection, since much of this information would be fairly difficult to find. [R: Choice, Nov 88, p. 458; LJ, 1 Sept 88, p. 162; VOYA, Dec 88, p. 258]—**Robert L. Turner, Jr.**

924.   Ellrod, J. G. **Hollywood Greats of the Golden Years: The Late Stars of the 1920s Through the 1950s**. Jefferson, N.C., McFarland, 1989. 222p. illus. index. $27.50. PN1998.2.E45. 791.43'028'092273. LC 89-42713. ISBN 0-89950-371-3.

The Golden Age of Hollywood is personified here by 81 portraits of actors and actresses from the late 1920s to the mid-1950s. These individuals were stars in the true Hollywood sense, possessing those elusive qualities that endeared them to the public. Another criterion used in selection was that they were deceased as of 1989.

Alphabetically arranged, each entry contains a very short biography followed by a listing of the star's feature films. Numerous black-and-white stills illustrate the entries. An index provides additional access to the main entries, listing not only the names of those profiled but also names mentioned in the stars' biographies.

This anthology purports to stir the reader's memories of the stars and movies of an important period in film history and to inspire further research into this era. It presents a brief overview of three decades in American motion picture entertainment.—**Anita Zutis**

925.   Holston, Kim. **Starlet: Biographies, Filmographies, TV Credits and Photos of 54 Famous and Not So Famous Leading Ladies in the Sixties**. Jefferson, N.C., McFarland, 1988. 299p. illus. bibliog. index. $39.95. LC 87-43209. ISBN 0-89950-307-1.

Promoted as future stars, the fifty-four women profiled here all gained popularity in the 1960s. All were leading ladies at one time, but only a few, like Natalie Wood or Jane Fonda, went on to attain superstardom. Each entry contains black-and-white illustrations consisting of publicity shots and stills from the individual's movies, and details the starlet's career development. Among the sources used are co-workers, critics, and the women themselves. A filmography and a list of television credits complete the portrait.

A general bibliography and individual ones, including reviews, letters, interviews, articles, and monographs, follow. Additional access points are provided by the index. Insight into the last decade of Hollywood's "star system" is obtained through fifty-four accounts of women who have experienced it. This compendium sheds new light on a period of radical change in American cinema.—**Anita Zutis**

926.   Katchmer, George A. **Eighty Silent Film Stars: Biographies and Filmographies of the Obscure to the Well Known**. Jefferson, N.C., McFarland, 1991. 1067p. illus. index. $75.00. PN2285. K34. 791 .43'028'092273. LC 90-28262. ISBN 0-89950-494-9.

This work provides information on actors and actresses who might otherwise be no more than footnotes in the history of the cinema. It focuses not on those whose names remain known, such as Mary Pickford, Douglas Fairbanks, and Rudolph Valentino, but on those whose faces may only be barely remembered from the many films they appeared in. The entries are arranged alphabetically, from Art Acord to Guinn "Big Boy" Williams, and numbered. Despite the passage of time, the frequent dearth of reliable information, and the contradictory stories created by publicity, self-promotion, or scandal, every entry provides the most accurate and complete biography and list of films possible for each actor. The biographies range in length from two to several pages and include date and place of birth if known; original name; family background; reason for becoming an actor; key events and films; anecdotes and favorite sayings; personal and professional problems; and information about deaths, funerals, and survivors. The filmographies are arranged chronologically and list studio, director, writer, length, and cast. The sources for this information are included in the section of notes on the filmographies. The index lists other actors and actresses mentioned in the main biographies and references to the main entries elsewhere in the text. For fans of silent films, this volume will recall a vanished world, and the biographies are generally interesting, if somewhat informal. [R: Choice, May 92, p. 1370; RBB, 1 Mar 92, p. 1305]—**Rebecca Jordan**

927.   Nowlan, Robert A., and Gwendolyn Wright Nowlan. **Movie Characters of Leading Performers of the Sound Era**. Chicago, American Library Association, 1990. 396p. $47.50pa. PN1995.9.C36N69. 791 .43'09'0927. LC 88-37686. ISBN 0-8389-0480-7.

The Nowlans have produced a useful paperback guide to over 20,000 movie roles portrayed by some 450 actors and actresses they consider to be leading performers of the sound era. Defining same as those who helped carry the story of the movie in which they appeared, their selection criteria is admittedly subjective but generally defensible. Unlike many guides to film characters, for instance, Susan Lieberman and Frances Cable's *Memorable Film Characters: An Index to Roles and Performers, 1915-1983* (see ARBA 86, entry 1324), this book is arranged solely by performer. Each entry consists of brief biographical information, a descriptive sampling of the performer's key roles, and a chronological list of the actor's other film roles. The main sources of information consulted were the *New York Times* movie reviews and *Variety*, although the biographical sketches suggest exhaustive readings in other sources.

The decision to arrange the text by performer has its strengths. The browser will enjoy its well-written capsule biographies, which are filled with obscure facts and amusing anecdotes. Likewise, the brief descriptions of the performer's key roles are informative, if opinionated. The inclusions of the film's director and releasing studio are invaluable. Another nice touch is the addition of the performer's birth name (when applicable) to the entry.

The lack of character or film title indexes to augment the book's biographical structure is a drawback. One must know that Humphrey Bogart portrayed Fred C. Dobbs in *The Treasure of the Sierra Madre* in order to find the entry listed among the actor's key roles. With over 20,000 films and characters cited, a complete index may be impractical, but certainly an index to key roles would greatly enhance the work's reference value. The book will be most effectively used in conjunction with other movie character indexes such as the one previously cited and Roy Pickard's *Who Played Who in the Movies* (see ARBA 82, entry 1120).

An unavoidable criticism, and one acknowledged by the authors, is the inevitable disagreement over who should or should not have been included. While most major stars are well represented, there are some glaring omissions. It seems strange to include Betty Field while excluding horror greats Boris Karloff and Bela Lugosi. Still, the authors promise another edition of this work to update the roles of currently active performers and to rectify any such omissions. [R: LJ, 1 June 90, p. 120; RBB, 15 June 90, p. 2032]—**David K. Frasier**

928. Palmer, Scott. **A Who's Who of Australian and New Zealand Film Actors: The Sound Era**. Metuchen, N.J., Scarecrow, 1988. 171p. bibliog. $20.00. LC 87-32215. ISBN 0-8108-2090-0.

"Who's who" leads you to expect more than you get from this little book. "Who Was in What?" would be a more accurate title, since the work merely consists of names of film actors of Australian/New Zealand origin or citizenship and lists of films in which they appeared. Some of the actors are unexpected (and well covered in other reference books): Errol Flynn, Judith Anderson, silent comedians Snub Pollard and Billy Bevan, 1930s comedian Leon Errol. Others are obscure: Frederick Esmelton, Marshal Crosby, Anouska Hempel. Information given is minimal: name, sometimes year of birth and death, a brief blurb ("Australian leading lady of films and television of the eighties"), and a chronological list giving titles and years of films in which they appeared (*High Rolling* 1977, *My Brilliant Career* 1979). Hollywood, British, and television films are included. Indeed, they seem to far outnumber Australian films although there is no way to know since there is no indication of which films are which. The value of the book is enhanced by a twenty-eight-page introductory essay which chronicles the development of the Australian film industry between 1896 and 1983 (with a couple of paragraphs on the 1986 film *Crocodile Dundee* tossed in at the end) and by a bibliography of twenty-five relevant monographs published between 1964 and 1984. I am not sure there is much need for this little volume, but cinema collections should find it of some value.—**Joseph W. Palmer**

929. Parish, James Robert, and Don Stanke. **Hollywood Baby Boomers**. Hamden, Conn., Garland, 1992. 670p. illus. index. (Garland Reference Library of the Humanities, v.1295). $75.00. PN2285.P333. 791.43'028'092273. LC 91-38768. ISBN 0-8240-6104-7.

Hollywood baby boomers are defined in this biographical dictionary as actors and actresses born between 1946 and 1964. Because of space limitations, only a few members of the baby boomer generation—50 men and 30 women—are portrayed. The names range from Glenn Close and Mel Gibson to Gregory Harrison and Mandy Patinkin.

Every biography begins with a quotation from the featured individual that gives the reader a glimpse into that person's mind set (e.g., "I would never take a part irresponsibly, knowing that the media so strongly affects our society" [Lindsay Wagner]). The biographies continue to define their subjects by relaying aspects of their lives that have given them their direction, such as childhood incidents, personal interests, and acting accomplishments. Each biography is accurate as of March 1991. The entries conclude with complete filmographies and lists of television series, albums, and future releases. A complete index concludes the text and includes a listing of actors and actresses who are not featured but who are mentioned throughout.

The use of footnotes would have given validity to the text. Most quotations are cited with a resource, but some are unsubstantiated, making the accuracy of the statement debatable (e.g., "One bio revealed that his mood swings ranged from aloofness, when he chose to be remote, to friendliness and conviviality" [Tom Berenger]). Included with each biography is a movie still of the personality.

While most are characteristic of the individuals, a few do not give fair representations of the celebrities. The photograph of Cybill Shepherd, for example, is from the movie *The Heartbreak Kid* and displays a profile view of her, with most of the picture consisting of her co-stars. With their extensive background in the writing of Hollywood biographies, the authors have delivered well-researched and thought-provoking biographies that are informative as well as entertaining.—**Deborah A. Taylor**

930.   Pickard, Roy. **The Oscar Stars from A-Z**. London, Headline; distr., North Pomfret, Vt., Trafalgar Square, 1996. 433p. illus. index. $29.95. ISBN 0-7472-1638-X.

As the author boasts in his all-too-brief preface, this is a "bright and breezy 'read and dip' " into Oscarland, listing all 717 nominees A to Z. Limited to performers only and to the period after the birth of sound (1929) to 1996, *The Oscar Stars* provides lively entries à la *Variety* that place nominations within the context of stars' careers. Pickard does not hesitate to make frank judgments about the winners and the professional impact of being a nominee. He also relates bits of fascinating trivia, among them oldest winner, Jessica Tandy at 82; youngest winner, Tatum O'Neal at 10; only director to direct his father and daughter to Oscars, John Huston; most honored Oscar actress and actors, Katharine Hepburn, 4 wins and 8 other nominations, Jack Nicholson and Laurence Olivier, 10 nominations each; only woman playing a man to win an Oscar, Linda Hunt in *The Year of Living Dangerously*; only star to win for a role where his face was behind a grotesque mask, John Hurt in *Elephant Man*; or only star to win without speaking a word of dialogue, Holly Hunter in *The Piano*.

Other interesting data can be gleaned from the entries, such as family nominees of the Fondas, the O'Neals, the Masseys, the Redgraves (father Michael and daughters Lynn and Vanessa), Paul Newman and Joanne Woodward, and Judy Garland and Liza Minelli; nominees with other claims to fame, such as Frank Sinatra, Robert Preston, Bobby Darin, Peggy Lee, Michael Chekhov (nephew of Anton Chekhov), and Melina Mercouri (Greek culture minister); or the hundreds of non-American nominees, 119 of whom hailed from the United Kingdom.

A chronology listing all nominees by year in the categories of best film, director, actor, actress, supporting actor, and supporting actress, and an index of films add to the book's usefulness. *The Oscar Stars* has something for everyone: film researchers, fans, and trivia buffs. [R: RBB, June 97, p. 1764]—**John A. Lent**

931.   Pitts, Michael R. **Horror Film Stars**. 2d ed. Jefferson, N.C., McFarland, 1991. 464p. illus. index. $24.95pa. PN1995.9.H6P55. 791.43'028'0922. LC 90-53707. ISBN 0-89950-507-4.

The original (1981) edition of this title covered the filmographies and careers of 43 actors and actresses. This edition not only expands and updates the coverage of the original 43, but also contains a total of 66 entries, arbitrarily divided into 17 "stars" and 49 somewhat lesser known individuals, called "players." By way of definition of what constitutes horror films, Pitts seems to prefer to be vague. About all that can be gleaned from his introduction is that if a film is "scary," it qualifies. The list of biographees covers well-known genre actors such as Bela Lugosi, Boris Karloff, Vincent Price, and the Lon Chaneys (pere et fils). However, while filmographies are complete for stars, only genre parts are included for players.

Horror always has been, and ever shall be, open to interpretation; consider the difference between the subtle horror of Alfred Hitchcock's movies and the explicit, graphic "splatter" of some of today's cheap exploitation films. While Pitts scatters his opinions liberally, readers who seek steamy, gossip/tidbits, such as those that pervade similar treatments, are going to be disappointed. The entries say little of a truly biographical nature, as the focus is on screen contribution rather than on formative years or private life. The book is salted with half-page and full-page black-and-white photographs, with all performers clearly identified. Entries vary in length; those on John Carradine and Vincent Price run about 15 pages each, while a couple of performers have only a single page, including the photograph.

Not all of the people profiled in this genre-specific treatment are from the bygone era of cinematic thrillers. Among the many players written up are Donald Pleasance, Jack Palance, and Jamie Lee Curtis. Since appearing in genre films tends to lead to permanent typecasting, it is not surprising that the same names and faces keep cropping up again and again. For creature-feature buffs (and every library's community has them), this work is recommended browsing, as well as a handy guide to the on-screen work of some of the movies' most memorable players.—**Bruce A. Shuman**

932.   Quinlan, David. **Quinlan's Illustrated Directory of Film Character Actors**. new ed. London, B. T. Batsford; distr., North Pomfret, Vt., Trafalgar Square, 1995. 384p. illus. $35.00. ISBN 0-7134-7040-2.

The author, a British film critic of long standing, has done a great service to the lesser-known actors whose "... names remained a secret between them and their friends, their agents and those producers and directors wise enough to hire these ever-reliables when their image became familiar" (p. 5). The book is composed of entries for 1,110 actors and actresses whose faces are known but whose names elude all but the most obsessive readers of movie credits. It updates and expands a 1985 edition (see ARBA 87, entry 1286). Each entry contains a black-and-white photograph, a brief career assessment, and a filmography. The last is the most comprehensive this reviewer has seen; it includes not only the standard feature film appearances and television movies, but also short subjects and even narrations done. Directorial stints (rare for this group) are noted. Birth and death dates are complete to April 1, 1995. The roster of subjects appears to have an unsurprising partiality for British actors over Americans of equal regard.

Browsers will appreciate the droll and incisive descriptions Quinlan makes of his subjects: Dudley Foster is described as "cadaverous"; Richard Masur is "tall, shambling, [and] benign"; Brenda Frickeris "dumpling-homely." Reading such descriptions while looking at the adjacent photographs makes one appreciate Quinlan's wit and insight. As with most books of this kind, a solid familiarity with the subject matter exponentially increases one's appreciation of the text.

Access is challenging in a directory whose subjects are known by their faces and not their names. The photographs, taken at the approximate time of an actor's greatest success (to ease recognition), are crucial to the use and value of this resource. Nonetheless, without a film title index to narrow the searching process, using this book to identify individual actors will be time-consuming. As it stands, this directory's usefulness is in its impressive filmographies and as browsing material for film fans with a dry sense of humor. It is advisable for film collections with a breadth extending beyond titles on superstars. [R: Choice, Apr 96, p. 1292]—**Ed Volz**

933.   Quinlan, David. **Quinlan's Illustrated Directory of Film Comedy Actors**. New York, Henry Holt, 1992. 302p. illus. $35.00. PN2285.Q56. 792'.28'092273. LC 92-12512. ISBN 0-8050-2394-1.

Film journalist Quinlan has given us a pithy treatment of almost 300 film comedians, from the days of Ben Turpin (1868-1940) to Whoopie Goldberg. He states his intention "to inform and to entertain," an aim he reaches with succinct analyses of acting careers and talents. He profiles mainly American and British comics, although an occasional figure such as Jacques Tati shows up too. The articles range from a half-column (e.g., John Belushi) to three pages (e.g., Charlie Chaplin, Buster Keaton), with women accounting for about one-sixth of the subjects. Each entry concludes with a fairly extensive filmography, usually more complete for contemporary actors than for those of the silent era. The work is well illustrated with promotional shots, stills, and portraits.

Because many of these actors had overlapping careers on stage and in television, Quinlan devotes space to describing these other areas. Occasionally, as with Chaplin, the discussion of the London music hall days is very informative. At other times the subject's television career considerably outweighs film achievements, as in the case of Sid Caesar. Selectivity means making choices, and Quinlan has done a commendable job; but one wonders whether he really intended to omit Michael J. Fox and Madeline Kahn. Occasional Britishisms crop up, as in the author's description of Mickey Rooney as "a human catherine-wheel." Quinlan does not hesitate to make judgment calls, but readers will find them balanced and perceptive.—**John P. Schmitt**

934.   Ragan, David. **Who's Who in Hollywood: The Largest Cast of International Film Personalities Ever Assembled**. New York, Facts on File, 1992. 2v. $135.00/set. PN1998.2.R34. 791.43'028'0922. LC 90-2980. ISBN 0-8160-2011-6.

The cast referred to is indeed large—more than 35,000 entries reflect the history of the motion picture industry from 1893 to 1991. Anyone who ever appeared on the silver screen—stars, legends, international figures, and bit players—may be included. Film scholars, students, and movie buffs are the book's intended audience.

Living performers' birth dates, places, and current residences are noted, along with a selection of their motion picture credits. For deceased players, the year and age at death and titles of significant films are listed. It is stated that movie credits are not complete but constitute a "telescoped sampling" of the person's work. Winners of Academy Awards and of special Oscars are noted. Scattered throughout the volumes are short biographies and insights into the lives of the players. A brief bibliography lists other compendiums of film history.

Of course, the sheer volume of coverage precludes detailed profiles of all the performers. Entries range in length from one word to almost a page. Although the work would be even better if some of the individual entries were more informative, it can serve as a starting point for further research. A more complete edition with expanded coverage is promised for the future. [R: BR, Nov/Dec 92, p. 38; Choice, June 92, p. 1526; RBB, 15 Apr 92, pp. 1555-56; WLB, Apr 92, p. 128]—**Anita Zutis**

935.   Rainey, Buck. **Heroes of the Range: Yesterday's Saturday Matinee Movie Cowboys**. Metuchen, N.J., Scarecrow, 1987. 334p. illus. index. $37.50. LC 85-2071. ISBN 0-8108-1804-3.

The action and adventure-packed Hollywood Westerns of decades past continue to excite young and old. The good guys wore white hats, triumphed over evil, and won the girl's heart in the end. Though the actors who starred in these hay burners were folk heroes in their own time, today many are almost unknown even though their Westerns are rerun on cable and independent television stations.

Buck Rainey has compiled the present work along the lines of his *Saddle Aces of the Cinema* (see ARBA 82, entry 1122) in order to immortalize fifteen of these Western heroes. Each chapter begins with an excellent biography of the actor, featuring all kinds of delightfully obscure episodes in his life. Buddy Roosevelt, for instance, loved to throw knives and bayonets at trees at his mountain cabin, and after a few rounds of bathtub gin (Prohibition being then in force), guests would often invite him to throw knives around them and pin them to a tree. Fortunately his brother always hid the knives to prevent a mishap on occasions when the spirits flowed too freely! These biographical pieces are all about a half-dozen pages long and include appropriate references to films made along the way, relating each to the actor's life and career. Finally, each chapter concludes with a detailed filmography, "from his earliest walk on to his last fade-out." Among the actors featured are Buster Crabbe, Johnny Mack Brown, Jack Hoxie, Tom Tyler, and Charles Starrett. Large, half-page movie stills and lobby cards are liberally interspersed throughout and enhance the enjoyment of this fine volume.

The author is a college professor in the field of business education, yet he is a well-known authority on Westerns and his enthusiasm and clever insights make this lively and entertaining reading. Indexes by personal name and film title facilitate access. The filmographies are the result of careful research and will be of value to film historians.—**Richard W. Grefrath**

936.   Segrave, Kerry, and Linda Martin. **The Continental Actress: European Film Stars of the Postwar Era: Biographies, Criticism, Filmographies, Bibliographies**. Jefferson, N.C., McFarland, 1990. 314p. illus. index. $35.00. PN2570.S4. 791.43'028'09224. LC 89-13878. ISBN 0-899505104.

In order for an actress to be included in this work, she had to have become prominent after the end of World War II; been born in, or done much of her work in, continental Europe; and been recognized as an international star in the North American press. Forty-one actresses from Italy, Greece, France, Germany, and the Scandinavian countries met those qualifications. Together they appeared in 1,799 movies, many rarely seen in the United States since American audiences prefer English-language films rather than dubbed or subtitled ones.

The entry on each actress consists of a biography that critically discusses her work, career, and off-screen life. These essays try to give the reader a well-rounded view of the actress as a person. There are also a complete filmography with foreign as well as translated titles of the works and a bibliography that only uses English-language sources from North America. Two pictures of each actress are also included in her essay. Some are publicity photographs while others are film stills. This work will be useful for those who need in-depth information about these actresses and their works.—**Robert L. Turner, Jr.**

937.   Segrave, Kerry, and Linda Martin. **The Post-Feminist Hollywood Actress: Biographies and Filmographies of Stars Born after 1939**. Jefferson, N.C., McFarland, 1990. 313p. illus. index. $39.95. PN1998.2.S44. 791.43'028'09227. LC 90-42755. ISBN 0-89950-387-X.

This publication is an exposition of the second-rate status of the Hollywood film actress over the past 30 years. The introductory essay argues that male control of the American film industry has hardly been affected by the rise of modern feminism. Extensive quantifiable data, such as the number of lead roles for women (versus men) and the percentage of major roles portrayed by women, are cited to document this thesis. The essay concludes with a list of sources heavily weighted with references to articles in *USA Today, Mademoiselle, Glamour, Esquire,* and *Variety.*

The remainder of the book profiles 50 American and English actresses born in 1940 or after who rose to professional acclaim during the feminist era. They are presented in four special categories: "Superstars," "Leading Ladies," "New Screen Stars," and "Up and Coming Actresses." These distinctions seem somewhat arbitrary, as the authors admit "the line with separates Superstars from the lesser rank & is a thin one . . . that is not very easy to explain." This division of actresses dates the book. Kathleen Turner, Jessica Lange, and Meryl Streep are considered "New Screen Stars," while Glenn Close, Darryl Hannah, and Rosanna Arquette are considered "Up and Coming Actresses." A number of women are omitted, including Karen Allen, Geena Davis, Dolly Parton, and Dianne Wiest.

The authors introduce each of the categories with a decidedly profeminist statement. They delight in sweeping generalizations, such as "Hollywood's preferred way to display an actress was, and remains, disrobed" (p. 2), and they are judgmental of the stars they profile. For example, they state that "Karen Black's talent has been sadly wasted" (p. 70) and "Mia [Farrow] did little more than play herself in *Hannah and Her Sisters*" (p. 44). Nevertheless, the essays on the individual actresses, which range from three to six pages, are filled with interesting information about their personal and professional lives. Each piece includes a black-and-white photograph, filmography, and list of sources.

This work would be more appropriate in the circulating collection than in the reference section of most libraries. Those seeking ready-reference or more objective data would do well to consult *Actors and Actresses,* volume 3 of the *International Dictionary of Films and Filmmakers* (see ARBA 88, entry 1346), *Contemporary Theatre, Film and Television* (see ARBA 87, entries 1318-20), or *Theatre, Film and Television Biographies Master Index* (Gale, 1982). [R: LJ, Jan 90, p. 103; RBB, 1 May 90, p. 1750]—**Michael Ann Moskowitz**

938.   Wise, James E., Jr., and Anne Collier Rehill. **Stars in Blue: Movie Actors in America's Sea Services**. Annapolis, Md., Naval Institute Press, 1997. 316p. illus. index. $29.95. ISBN 1-55750-937-9.

Some of the names are quite familiar: Spencer Tracy, Kirk Douglas, Jack Lemmon, Henry Fonda. Some are fodder for crossword puzzles and trivia games: Wayne Morris, John Howard, Logan Ramsey. Others are real surprises: Jack Benny, Bill Cosby. What they all have in common is the fact that they led two lives. All of the people in this book were (or are) movie stars, and all served in the Navy or Coast Guard. Just about all of them portrayed military personas at some time in their careers, and after reading of their exploits, it is interesting to see how they applied their firsthand knowledge to their screen characters. Many of them won combat medals, and some of the stories are downright harrowing. Eddie (*Green Acres*) Albert saved more than a dozen Marines on the bloody beaches of Tarawa, Tom (*The Seven Year Itch*) Ewell criss-crossed the Atlantic on merchant ships, and Kirk Douglas was a gunnery officer on a ship that saw frequent action in the Pacific.

Wise is a naval aviator who rose to the rank of captain and who has written several other military books. His coauthor is a writer, editor, and publisher. They have produced a well-researched, tightly written book on a unique subject, and their efforts to show readers the military career behind the movie star are successful. There are some omissions (Jason Robards, for example), and coverage of women's contributions to the war effort is confined to a chapter titled "The Ladies Do Their Bit," but overall, this is a solid work that will prove popular in most public libraries and certainly in military history collections.—**Joseph L. Carlson**

Directors, Cinematographers, Designers, and Songwriters

939. Barson, Michael. **The Illustrated Who's Who of Hollywood Directors. Volume 1: The Sound Era**. New York, Noonday/Farrar, Straus & Giroux, 1995. 530p. illus. index. $27.50pa. ISBN 0-374-52428-9.

Containing more than 150 essays 2 to 8 pages in length, Barson gives the reader a slightly opinionated and very knowledgeable view of Hollywood film directors whose careers began before 1975. Candid photographs, portraits, movie posters, and promotional shots are used to highlight the insightful essays. This book delves deeper into its subjects than do other film encyclopedias. Each director is given a complete career retrospective, with plot summaries and critical overviews for each of their films. The on-set photographs are gems not likely to have been published elsewhere, whether it is a shot of Mike Nichols sitting with Orson Welles in *Catch-22* or Fritz Lang coaching George Raft in *You and Me*.

The directors are not given equal attention. Logically, career length and degree of prestige affect the extent of coverage warranted. The careers of horror-meister William Castle and funnyman Mel Brooks are surveyed in two pages; John Ford and John Huston are treated in eight-page appraisals. Brief overviews of 44 lesser-known directors follow the main text, and an index to names and film titles ends the book.

Barson has degrees in American culture and popular culture; he has written extensively about Hollywood films. What he has created here is not a book just for director name or film title verification, although it could serve that function. The real values of this resource are its illustrations and plentiful (although individually brief) film summaries. Students would find Barson's book to be an engaging starting point for their research. Fans of a particular director would likely be pleased with this single source.—**Ed Volz**

940. **Directory of African Film-Makers and Films**. Keith Shiri, comp. and ed. Westport, Conn., Greenwood Press, 1993. 194p. index. $79.50. PN1993.5.A35S48. 016. 79143'0233'09226. LC 92-22105. ISBN 0-313-28756-2.

Most movie-going Americans can name very few African films and may find it startling to learn just how many have been made in the past 65 years. *African*, in the context of this book, refers to every nation on the continent, not (as is often intended by the term) Africa south of the Sahara. In all, directors from 29 nations are represented, from Algeria to Zimbabwe. Thus, in addition to significant filmmakers from the "Black" African countries, there are numerous contributors from the Arabic-speaking world. English and French are the principal languages of African film, but other languages represented include Afrikaans; Arabic; Portuguese; Italian; and native tongues such as Amharic, Bambara, Dyula, Hausa, Malagasy, and Swahili.

The principal arrangement of the entries is alphabetical by director's surname, with brief biographical sketches provided from returned questionnaires and supplemented, where available, by other sources. Each named person has a filmography that gives titles and years. It would be nice if some descriptive information were provided about the films, but all that is given is title, title translated into English (where necessary), alternative titles (where extant), and year. The biographical information is uneven, depending on what was supplied, and emphasizes the film-related aspects of the director's life. Annoyingly, some titles vary considerably; it is not unusual for a film to have three or four different names. The second part of the work consists of several cross-indexes, in which film titles, educational institutions, film organizations, and mentioned people are separately listed. To the film-literate, but nonspecialist, Westerner, there will be few familiar names or titles (except, perhaps, for the celebrated *The Gods Must Be Crazy* and its sequel), but Shiri, who works at the African Centre in London, has done a good job of organizing the filmic output of an entire continent over 65 years. Because this book covers such an esoteric subject and is priced so high, libraries and special collections will want to evaluate it for purchase based on need. [R: Choice, Mar 93, p. 120]—**Bruce A. Shuman**

941.   **Directory of Indian Film-Makers and Films**. Sanjit Narwekar, comp. and ed. Westport, Conn., Greenwood Press, 1994. 500p. index. $85.00. PN1998.2.N37. 791.43'0233'092254. LC 93-44642. ISBN 0-313-29284-1.

Which nation leads the world in annual output of feature films? India; yet the preponderance of Indian films escapes the attention of Western filmgoers and critics alike. Almost from the beginning of modern cinema, Indian directors have been putting out their products in astonishing numbers, the national output topping, in recent years, 900 films annually. Narwekar, a journalist, author, and screenwriter whose studies at the University of Bombay led to a lifelong career in film criticism, faced numerous daunting problems in gathering this information. He points out that recorded information about films is difficult to obtain in India, not only because some prolific directors may be working on 8 to 10 films at once and lack the time to document anything, but also because many are superstitious, concerned that written records may visit bad fortune on the director or his or her various projects. Another problem is language: The films listed here are rendered in 19 languages (including English).

Arrangement is alphabetical by director's name, which creates another problem. While many of the 363 directors are listed by surname, some go by their given names, while still others use patronymics, geographics, or honorifics as identification. Each entry gives biographical information on the filmmaker's life and career, together with a filmography consisting of titles and dates. Two indexes are supplied, one general and one of film titles. Altogether, there are more than 15,000 entries. Finally, a selected bibliography provides sources of further information about Indian filmmakers and their films.

One cannot help wishing that this treatment were not so "bare-bones," and that there were some information about the films themselves, but that is not Narwekar's purpose. Under the circumstances, he has performed an astonishing feat of scholarship just to do what he has accomplished. Recommended, therefore, but only for Western libraries with the largest collections of writings on the cinema. [R: Sept 94, p. 74—**Bruce A. Shuman**

942.   Fischer, Dennis. **Horror Film Directors, 1931-1990**. Jefferson, N.C., McFarland, 1991. 877p. illus. index. $75.00. PN1995.9.H6F5. 791.43'616. LC 91-52510. ISBN 0-89950-609-7.

Fischer, a Los Angeles-based film critic, has been writing about films for a dozen years. His work is an exhaustive study of the major directors of horror films of the past 60 years or so, including for each director a complete filmography, a career summary, a roundup of critical assessments, some unusual behind-the-scenes information, and Fischer's own judgments. After a brief but informative introduction that attempts both to define the genre and to explain its appeal, Fischer covers his selection of 50 "major" directors (e.g., Brian DePalma, Roman Polanski) in depth in part 1. Part 2, aptly entitled "The Hopeless and the Hopeful: Promising Directors, Obscurities, and Horror Hacks," provides Fischer's highly seasoned, subjective evaluations of the bit players in this directorial cast of thousands. Sound pejorative? It is, and Fischer's barbed commentary effectively skewers numerous "wannabees" whose work, he thinks, does not deserve to take its place with true horror cinema. In this section Fischer is careful to distinguish the truly frightening from the repulsive, the cheap, and the tasteless. An appendix briefly notes classic horror films by nonhorror directors, and an annotated bibliography finishes this impressive tour de force of film scholarship.

While we are all film critics, in a sense, and should feel free to differ with the published prejudices of a particular scholar of the genre, Fischer is astute, witty, and generally fun to read. This book, therefore, belongs in all larger film literature collections.—**Bruce A. Shuman**

943.   **Handbook of Soviet and East European Films and Filmmakers**. Thomas J. Slater, ed. Westport, Conn., Greenwood Press, 1992. 443p. index. $69.50. PN1993.5. R9H28. 791.43'0947. LC 91-9255. ISBN 0-313-26239-X.

This is an exhaustive survey of filmmaking in the Soviet Union, Poland, Czechoslovakia, Yugoslavia, Hungary, East Germany, Romania, and Bulgaria. Aimed primarily at the scholar, it covers all of the major movies (accent on "major"; not every film ever made in these countries is listed) and movie makers from the Eastern bloc in the past 100 years. In addition, a historical essay puts the film industry of each country into proper perspective, providing a geographical and political overview as well as an accurate appraisal of the origins and development of the film industry. The appendix features a chronological list of major historical, cultural, and film events in the former Soviet Union and Eastern Europe between 1890 and 1990. The volume is rounded out by a subject index and a film index. The titles in the latter are given in English translations, followed by original (mostly transliterated) titles. Strangely enough, no indications are given as to whether the films are in black-and-white or color. Spelling is mostly accurate, no mean feat in a book with a myriad of foreign titles and names that feature just about every diacritical mark known in Europe.

The book is not for the casual browser or movie buff; persons seeking brief movie synopses will not find them here, and some categories, such as music, are given short shrift. For instance, Shostakovich and Dunayevski made it into the book, but one of the most prolific and talented contemporary composers who wrote a number of Soviet film scores, Alfred Schnittke, did not, except for one dry listing in a Klimov film. Sergei Prokofiev (Eisenstein's *Alexander Nevsky and Ivan the Terrible*) does not rate a separate entry either. Still, students and scholars of the genre will find this volume a valuable resource. [R: Choice, June 92, p. 1520]—**Koraljka Lockhart**

944.   **International Dictionary of Films and Filmmakers. Volume 2: Directors**. 2d ed. Nicholas Thomas, ed. Chicago, St. James, 1991. 958p. illus. $115.00. 791.43. LC 90-64265. ISBN 1-55862-038-9.

When the initial edition of this work appeared in 1984, an ARBA reviewer commented that the set (of which *Directors* is volume 2) "promises to become a standard source for film studies" (see ARBA 86, entry 1321). The 2d edition, begun in 1990 with volume 1, *Films*, and projected to conclude in 1992 with volume 4, *Writers and Production Artists*, fulfills that promise. This greatly expanded edition discusses 480 international directors whose inclusion is based upon recommendations from a distinguished board of advisors. Some 80 new entrants include such popular American directors as Roger Corman, Oliver Stone, and John Waters. Over 60 directors previously included have been dropped due to critical reassessment or space considerations. Of that number, animators (e.g., Chuck Jones, Tex Avery) will be included in volume 4.

Each entry consists of a brief biography; a complete filmography; a selected bibliography of works by or on the entrant; and a signed expository essay that discusses, among other topics, the major themes in the filmmaker's work. The short essays are written by film critics, scholars, and other experts in the field. All bibliographies have been updated and provide an excellent starting point for further study. Unique to this edition is the inclusion of photographs for most of the directors discussed. The new, larger-paged format makes the source more attractive and readable.

The only comparable source to this essential reference tool is the two-volume set entitled *World Film Directors* (see ARBA 89, entries 1269-70). Allegedly "world" in scope, the source actually covers around 400 directors from primarily English-speaking countries. While the essays are much lengthier and more detailed than those in *Directors*, the bibliographies suffer by comparison. Whether purchased as part of the set or individually, this volume deserves to be in any academic library that supports a film studies program.—**David K. Frasier**

945.   **International Directory of Cinematographers, Set- and Costume Designers in Film. Vol. 10: Czechoslovakia (from the Beginnings to 1989)**. Alfred Krautz, ed. Munich, New Providence, N.J., K. G. Saur, 1991. 281p. index. $45.00. ISBN 3-598-21440-5.

This directory contains a comprehensive chronological list of feature film credits for over 600 Czech cinematographers and set and costume designers. The film's director is noted after each title. Biographical information, if given at all, is very brief and may contain birth/death dates and places; where the artist trained or studied; and other types of work, such as documentary film, theater, or television. There are some minor spelling and grammatical errors in these entries. For individual artists who may have credits in films outside Czechoslovakia, the editors have cross-referenced other volumes in the International Federation of Film Archives series. There are indexes for directors and for film titles. The titles are listed in the original language with no English translation.

This specialized reference work contains information that is not available in any other source. It is appropriate for libraries with film research collections.—**Deborah V. Rollins**

946.   Lacy, Robin Thurlow. **Biographical Dictionary of Scenographers: 500 B.C. to 1900 A.D.** Westport, Conn., Greenwood Press, 1990. 762p. $69.50. PN2096.A1L33. 792'.025'0922. LC 90-14004. ISBN 0-313-27429-0.

A scenographer's work is perhaps the most ephemeral aspect of a theatrical performance. Whereas an actor receives cast credit, the work of a set designer or a scenery painter is seldom publicly noticed. Until fairly recent years, scholars of theatrical history have also paid little attention to the scenographer's art. Lacy's work is therefore groundbreaking as well as fine scholarship.

The dictionary provides brief biographical information for all known scenographers working in the Western tradition from ancient Greece to the beginning of the twentieth century. Theatrical practitioners from Japan, China, Indonesia, and other Eastern traditions receive no mention. (Greenwood's publicity incorrectly claims that the book presents information on scenographers from all of "those countries with major theatre traditions.") Each entry includes a three-digit number that is keyed to a useful bibliography of sources; an appendix arranges all names in a geographical-chronological list. A surprising element is the inclusion of many artists and architects who are better known in the fine arts, making this dictionary an adjunct reference source for art history as well. Recommended. [R: Choice, Apr 91, p. 1291]—**James Edgar Stephenson**

947.   **Michael Singer's Film Directors, 1997: A Complete Guide**. 12th ed. Michael Singer and Bethann Wetzel, comps. and eds. Los Angeles, Calif., Lone Eagle, 1997. 798p. index. $75.00pa. ISBN 0-943728-85-1. ISSN 0740-2872.

World film directors active in feature, documentary, and telefilm production are the focus of this hefty directory. Entries provide three distinct types of information: personal (date and place of birth); current contact information (agent, city, and telephone number); and film credits. The inclusion of contact information alone is worth the purchase price. "Active" directors are defined as those who have released a film in the past 10 years. Credits appear complete but concise, listing film title, distributor, and year. Supplementary materials include a section on notable directors of the past and indexes of foreign-based directors, guilds (worldwide), agents and managers (mostly from the United States), and a list of Academy Award nominees and winners.

With its emphasis on current directors (including documentary and television), the guide differs from other popular directories typically found in libraries, including the *International Motion Picture Almanac* (67th ed.; see ARBA 97, entry 770) and the *International Dictionary of Films and Filmmakers*. As such, its purchase complements existing holdings while providing a one-stop source for difficult-to-track information.—**Megan S. Farrell**

948.   Miller, Lynn Fieldman. **The Hand That Holds the Camera: Interviews with Women Film and Video Directors**. New York, Garland, 1988. 271p. illus. (Garland Reference Library of the Humanities, Vol. 688). $27.00. LC 87-32871. ISBN 0-8240-8530-2.

The premises that "the hand that holds the camera" determines the images of women in films and that there is a "women's culture expressed through the minds and experiences of women" are the subject of the book's short introduction. It details the characteristics of the work of the women interviewed, selected as examples of how a woman's direction makes a difference. The directors, some quite young and some more experienced, are Doris Chase, Michelle Citron, Kavery Dutta, Tami Gold, Amalie Rothschild, Meg Switzgable, and Linda Yellen. Of the seven interviews, one was done in 1987 and six from 1982 to 1985. Each one is accompanied by a photograph of the artist, a brief biographical-professional sketch, and a list of her films and videos. There are an additional nineteen photographs.

Besides providing insights into issues about women in films and filmmaking, the interviews are sources for historical and critical studies and offer opinions and practical information for young artists on the direction, production, business, and technical aspects of making films and videos. Perhaps interviews were the only way to capture these insights and information, but they also try the reader's patience and waste space on inane remarks such as: "everyone suggests that women be teachers" (p. 20); "You should send her a letter. . . . Oh, I did. You did?" (p. 142); and "I don't want to take up too much of your time" (p. 270).

Woefully lacking is any index, which is needed to locate the many references to persons, titles, institutions, and issues in the interviews.—**Joyce Duncan Falk**

949.   Parish, James Robert, and Michael R. Pitts. **Hollywood Songsters**. New York, Garland, 1991. 826p. illus. index. (Garland Reference Library of the Humanities, v.1164). $75.00. ML400.P295.782'.0092'2. LC 90-41110. ISBN 0-8240-3444-9.

Hollywood Songsters is a testament to the national preoccupation with those performers who have had an impact as both film stars and singers. While not attempting to be all-inclusive, this book contains over 100 sketches of personalities dating from the introduction of sound to movies in the late 1920s. Entries consist primarily of a four- to seven-page biography supplemented by a filmography, lists of shows, and an album discography. Each is illustrated by a black-and-white still from one of the performer's films. An extensive general index and a song and album index follow the main section. Title access is provided by the former to movies, shows, and books, and by the latter to musical productions.

A bibliography would be a helpful addition to this biographical dictionary, enabling readers to obtain more detailed information on past stars and new developments in the future of present ones. The volume does, however, profile a variety of popular performers, ranging from Tex Ritter to Madonna, and will serve to supplement the authors' abundant collection of works that research the world of entertainment. [R: Choice, May 91, p. 1464]—**Anita Zutis**

950.   **World Film Directors. Volume I: 1890-1945**. John Wakeman, ed. Bronx, N.Y., H. W. Wilson, 1987. 1247p. illus. $90.00. LC 87-29569. ISBN 0-8242-0757-2.

   World Film Directors. Volume II: 1945-1985. John Wakeman, ed. Bronx, N.Y., H. W. Wilson, 1988. 1205p. illus. $90.00. LC 87-29560. ISBN 0-8242-0763-7.

By providing introductions to the work and lives of about 400 of the world's best-known film directors from the beginning of cinema to the present, *World Film Directors: 1890-1945* and *1945-1985* succeed in doing for filmmakers what *Twentieth Century Authors* (H. W. Wilson, 1955), *World Authors* (see ARBA 86, entry 1080), and other works in the Wilson Company's authors series do for writers. Making no claims to original research, this two-volume work brings together in one place information previously scattered throughout many reference books, monographs, histories, critical essays, reviews, and interviews.

Whether the user seeks a definition of George Cukor's style, information about Sergio Leone's best and worst "spaghetti Westerns," commentary on Vittorio de Sica's view of each script as a highly structured artifact, an analysis of the use of color in Jean Renoir's 1951 film adaptation of Rumer Godden's *The River*, an explanation for the tremendous success of Ken Russell's 1969 adaptation of D. H. Lawrence's *Women in Love*, or a reason for the celebration of Stanley Kubrick's *Lolita* as an "epic comedy of frustration rather than lust," the answers to tens of thousands of such queries may be easily found in this monumental pair of reference books.

Arranged alphabetically, the entries in *World Film Directors* provide a 1,500- to 8,000-word essay on each director and offer a summary of the director's films, an analysis of the filmmaker's early development, a commentary on significant influences on the artist, a discussion of the major films directed, information on casting and production, a complete filmography of the director, and a selected bibliography of relevant books and articles. Each article is often highlighted with first-person statements by the directors themselves, the deliberations of academic critics, and the spontaneous responses of good reviewers.

Well aware of the difficulty of providing "a fair summation of representative critical response," the authors of the articles have skillfully charted the "dazzling flux" of reputations that "have soared or plummeted with sobering abruptness," trying to be as comprehensive and objective as "time, space, and patience" allow. In order to keep the project to a manageable size, editor John Wakeman interprets "directors" rather strictly and excludes figures who are best known as animators or producers. He also admits that in selecting directors he has favored those who have films that can be seen in the United States, Great Britain, and other English-speaking countries. Consequently, the "emerging or flourishing cinemas of the Third World have perhaps received less attention than they deserve."

Although intended primarily for students and moviegoers, these volumes will also be an invaluable aid to scholars, for nowhere else is so much information about filmmakers available in a reference guide. Individuals and libraries interested in any aspect of film will find *World Film Directors* a much-used companion. [R: BR, May/June 88, p. 49; Choice, Apr 88, p. 1226; LJ, 15 Apr 88, p. 75; RBB, 15 Nov 88, p. 548; WLB, Mar 88, p. 104]—**Colby H. Kullman**

Screenwriters

951. **American Screenwriters**. Robert E. Morsberger, Stephen O. Lesser, and Randall Clark, eds. Detroit, Gale, 1984. 382p. illus. index. (Dictionary of Literary Biography, vol. 26). $80.00. LC 83-25414. ISBN 0-8103-0917-3.

Purists may quibble about the inclusion of two volumes (see also entry 952) on screenwriters in the Dictionary of Literary Biography series, yet this is a genre that deserves serious critical examination. A screenwriter is essentially a dramatist, once-removed from the legitimate theatre. Thus, it is not surprising to find a number of important American playwrights included in the 1st volume (e.g., Clifford Odets, Robert E. Sherwood, Sidney Howard, Ben Hecht). The editors, however, attach new significance to screenwriters. They feel that "the screenplay has emerged as a new form of literature" in the past decade, justifying a close examination of the careers of the important screenwriters, present and past.

In this 1st volume, 65 such "major" writers are discussed in separate, signed essays, which average between five and six pages in length. This group is composed of those "who wrote primarily for the screen or who had noteworthy film achievements while writing in other media." Many of the writers found here will be familiar to anyone with a moderate knowledge of the American cinema: Charles Brackett, I. A. L. Diamond, Philip Dunne, Jules Furthman, Nunnally Johnson, Ring Lardner Jr., Anita Loos, Herman Mankiewicz, Stirling Silliphant, Donald Ogden Stewart, Dalton Trumbo. A few of the major screenwriters were also prominent directors: John Huston, Preston Sturges, Billy Wilder (Wilder "never directed a film he did not write"). In addition to the playwrights mentioned above, several important television writers are represented (Rod Serling, Reginald Rose, Horton Foote), as are a few novelists (James Agee, Budd Schulberg, Daniel Fuchs). The essays here on these writers are good supplements to the fuller accounts found in previous volumes. Excluded are those novelists, like Faulkner and Fitzgerald, who wrote part-time for films, and playwrights who have primarily adapted their own work for the screen (Neil Simon).

Of the two volumes, the second may be the more accessible for the casual moviegoer. Another 64 names are treated here, including some who are better known as performers (Woody Allen, Charlie Chaplin, W. C. Fields, Mae West). Most of this volume is devoted to influential writer-directors (such as Robert Benton, Richard Brooks, Francis Ford Coppola, Paul Mazursky, John Milius, Paul Schrader, and Robert Towne) and highly successful and respected screenwriters (Robert Bloch, William Goldman, Ernest Lehman, Joseph L. Mankiewicz, Abby Mann, Eleanor Perry, Waldo Salt, and Calder Willingham). Also, the early years of the American cinema are well represented: Lenore J. Coffee, Jeanie MacPherson (who wrote many of Cecil B. DeMille's films in the 1920s), Frances Marion, June Mathis, Arthur Ripley, Casey Robinson, and Ernest Vajda.

The biographical essays in both volumes contain a photo of the writer and, usually, several film stills (most are half a page in size). There is a short list of references at the end of most essays, plus an extensive list titled "Books for Further Reading," which fills nine pages in the back of the volume. This particular volume also contains a cumulative index to the entire DLB series to date.

There is no comparable reference work available on American screenwriters; Richard Corliss's *Talking Pictures: Screenwriters in the American Cinema, 1927-1973* (Overlook Press, 1974) provides similar coverage, but only 38 writers are discussed. Even though this DLB volume is more comprehensive, there are many important omissions (e.g., Ernest Lehman, S. J. Perelman, Walter Bernstein, William Goldman, Woody Allen), though that may be rectified in a projected second volume on screenwriters. Despite the inclusion of Stanley Kubrick and Buck Henry, most of the new generation of screenwriters (Robert Towne, Robert Benton, Elaine May, Nancy Dowd, et al.) are not covered. Nonetheless, this will be a popular volume in the DLB series—informative, readable, and great for browsing. [R: Choice, Nov 84, p. 397]—**Thomas A. Karel**

952.   **American Screenwriters: Second Series**. Randall Clark, ed. Detroit, Gale, 1986. 464p. illus. index. (Dictionary of Literary Biography, vol. 44). $88.00. LC 85-31221. ISBN 0-8103-1722-2.

This companion volume to volume 26, *American Screenwriters* (see ARBA 83, entry 1239), in effect completes the Dictionary of Literary Biography's treatment of this genre. The *Second Series* adds sixty-four newly listed screenwriters to the sixty-five covered in the 1st volume. The format is identical, with screen credits, illustrations, and references included for each writer. Most of the writers I noted as missing in my review of the 1st volume are found in this new compilation, and it is hard to think of a major screenwriter, past or present, who has now been overlooked by the series.

Of the two volumes, this may be the more accessible for the casual moviegoer. Many more familiar names are treated here, including some who are better known as performers (Woody Allen, Charlie Chaplin, W. C. Fields, Mae West). Most of this volume is devoted to influential writer-directors (such as Robert Benton, Richard Brooks, Francis Ford Coppola, Paul Mazursky, John Milius, Paul Schrader, and Robert Towne) and highly successful and respected screenwriters (Robert Bloch, William Goldman, Ernest Lehman, Joseph L. Mankiewicz, Abby Mann, Eleanor Perry, Waldo Salt, and Calder Willingham). Also, the early years of the American cinema are well represented: Lenore J. Coffee, Jeanie MacPherson (who wrote many of Cecil B. DeMille's films in the 1920s), Frances Marion, June Mathis, Arthur Ripley, Casey Robinson, and Ernest Vajda.

Among the highlights of this volume (in addition to the many fine and sometimes rare photos) are a nine-page discussion of William Faulkner's screen work which nicely supplements the Faulkner entries in volumes 9 and 11 of the DLB (likewise, S. J. Perelman is briefly considered here, complementing the much longer entry on him in volume 11, *American Humorists, 1800-1950*); a concise evaluation of Woody Allen's films through *The Purple Rose of Cairo* (1983); a lengthy survey of Charlie Chaplin's career; a longer-than-expected treatment of John Sayles's work (*Return of the Secaucus Seven*, etc.); and a brief account of the rather mysterious career of Carol Eastman (aka Adrien Joyce), who is probably best known for two Jack Nicholson films, *Five Easy Pieces* and *The Fortune*.

While this is an essential purchase for those libraries owning volume 26, it is also highly recommended for libraries supporting course work in the American cinema or housing large film collections.—**Thomas A. Karel**

953.   **International Dictionary of Films and Filmmakers. [Volume] 4: Writers and Production Artists**. 2d ed. Samantha Cook, ed. Detroit, St. James Press, 1993. 836p. illus. $115.00. ISBN 1-55862-040-0.

The making of a feature film entails the collaborative efforts of hundreds, sometimes thousands, of people. While some people can name who starred in a film, and the cognoscenti can supply the director's name, how many know the name of the person who made all those neat horror masks in the last fright flick or wrote the pounding score that made the chase scenes seem even scarier? This 4th volume of a revised five-volume set honors those unsung heroes of the film industry: production artists. The term is intentionally vague, encompassing many specialized fields, including (but not limited to) art directors, animators, cinematographers, costume designers, composers, arrangers, lyricists, editors, choreographers, stunt coordinators, special effects personnel, and sound technicians. This large tome contains 530 entries, each supplied with a brief biographical reference, a complete filmography, a selected bibliography of articles about the person, and a dissertative critical essay by a specialist in the field. There are 62 new entrants in the work, and all the other information has been updated and revised since the publication of the 1st edition. One definitional change: Animators, once classed, curiously, with directors, are now included as production artists, which seems only right and fitting.

For non-English film titles (of which there are many in this book), translations (or alternate translations, where there is discrepancy) and transliterations are furnished. Throughout the tiny-print glossy pages are scattered frequent black-and-white photographs of persons discussed or stills and lobby cards of the actors in their movies. Not surprisingly, few of these names are household words, or ever were, but that is the special value of this volume. A cross-reference index from personal names to film titles would have made it ever better. The whole set is recommended as essential for both the serious film scholar and for the settling of bar bets about who gave the Creature from the Black Lagoon that mangy costume and such a silly grin.—**Bruce A. Shuman**

JOURNALISM

954. **American Magazine Journalists, 1741-1850**. Sam G. Riley, ed. Detroit, Gale, 1988. 430p. illus. bibliog. index. (Dictionary of Literary Biography, Vol. 73). $95.00. LC 88-17586. ISBN 0-8103-4551-X.

The first of a 3-part set in the Dictionary of Literary Biography series, this work covers 46 American magazine journalists whose lives and careers spanned the period from 1741 to 1850. Among the distinguished personalities included are Ralph Waldo Emerson, Benjamin Franklin, Thomas Paine, Edgar Allan Poe, and Noah Webster. Entries include major positions held, a four- to six-page essay highlighting the journalist's life and career, a bibliography of secondary sources, and information on which libraries or historical societies have special collections about the journalists. A black-and-white photograph or painting of each journalist is provided, along with many other interesting photographs which enhance the text. In the back of the volume are a two-page checklist of further readings on early American periodical publication and a cumulative index of all the persons included in all volumes of DLB to date. The table of contents contains the names of all the journalists found in the work. The volume is well researched and the writing is clear and lively, making it an excellent addition to this distinguished series.—**Marilyn Strong Noronha**

955. **American Magazine Journalists, 1850-1900**. Sam G. Riley, ed. Detroit, Gale, 1989. 387p. illus. index. (Dictionary of Literary Biography, v.79). $98.00. ISBN 0-8103-4557-9.

The second part of a 3-volume set on American magazine journalists, this publication covers a pivotal period in the history of the American magazine during which important new titles—such as the *Atlantic Monthly* and *Harper's New Monthly* emerged. The excellent foreword by Riley relates magazine publishing trends to the political, social, and economic developments of the latter half of the nineteenth century.

The arrangement and format of the volume are similar to ones in the Dictionary of Literary Biography (DLB) series. In addition to the main biographical sketch, data for the journalists include the main positions they held in magazine publishing and their individual publications, as well as lists of bibliographies, biographies, references, and papers about them. Entries include photographic portraits of the journalists as well as pictures of title pages and other relevant illustrations. A note at the beginning of each sketch refers the reader to other volumes in the series for additional information.

The volume concludes with a list of further readings on the evolution of the American magazine and a list of contributors to this volume and their academic affiliations. A cumulative index refers to volumes 1 through 79 of the DLB series, the *Dictionary of Literary Biography Yearbook 1980-87*, and the Dictionary of Literary Biography *Documentary* series, volumes 1 through 4. Volume 79 represents a significant and useful addition to the DLB series. [R: Choice, Sept 89, p. 75]—**Michael Ann Moskowitz**

956. **Biographical Dictionary of American Journalism**. Joseph McKerns, ed. Westport, Conn., Greenwood Press, 1989. 820p. index. $95.00. PN4871.B56. 070'.92'2. LC 88-25098. ISBN 0-313-23818-9.

Here are 500 biographical sketches and bibliographies of American journalists who have lived since 1690. The format is that of the *Dictionary of American Biography*: life dates, a paragraph summarizing achievements, a chronological narrative of the subject's life, a bibliography by and about the subject, and a signed contributor. There are 133 contributors, mainly academics.

The biographies read well and the indexes are extremely useful. The general index includes subject matter, names of publications/broadcast companies (e.g., *New York Times,* ABC) so that a user can trace various journalists who have worked for one particular company, and specific subjects of interest such as "alternative journalism." The appendix is really another series of indexes that list the biographees according to media (e.g., newspaper, magazine, radio), professional fields of interest such as foreign correspondents or women in journalism, and Pulitzer prizes. It is a simple matter to then look up the name in the main sequence. The only real problem in dealing with the book is the selection of names, the criteria for closure (dead or retired), and the truly "mass" nature of the media. There are many columnists and correspondents here primarily because they are known (or were known) throughout the land. Similarly, in the area of broadcasting, not only are many of the pioneers still alive and contributing, but they are also celebrities by virtue of nightly exposure on the national airwaves. This does not make them better journalists; it simply makes them better known. The regular editors and local paper/station journalists who toil in the vineyards are not here, and there may not be anything that can be done to include them, for celebrity is the nature of the beast in the "mass" field. [R: LJ, 15 June 89, p. 50; RBB, 1 Sept 89, pp. 99-102; WLB, Nov 89, p. 114]—**Dean Tudor**

957.   Downs, Robert B., and Jane B. Downs. **Journalists of the United States: Biographical Sketches of Print and Broadcast News Shapers**.... Jefferson, N.C., McFarland, 1991. 391p. index. $39.95. PN4871 .D68. 070'.92'273. LC 91-52634. ISBN 0-89950-549-X.

A brief overview of U.S. journalism introduces this work. Particular attention is given to censorship, muckraking, humorists, women and black journalists, and war correspondents. Basic histories of journalism and general biographies of journalists are listed in a selected bibliography. Biographies are arranged alphabetically, and each includes place and date of birth and death date. Training, careers, and noteworthy accomplishments of each journalist are captured in biographies that range in length from a brief paragraph to a page. Biographies of colonial journalists, such as William Bradford and Samuel Adams, are included as well as those of electronic media journalists, such as Morley Safer and Charlayne Hunter-Gault. There is a general index of personal names, titles of newspapers and periodicals, organizations, and topics.

This work is a remarkably thorough overview of American journalism and journalists. The biographical sketches are economically and gracefully written, without obvious bias. This book would be a welcome addition in any small to medium library that does not have the resources to purchase an extensive biographical and historical collection on journalism. Larger libraries will find it useful as a quick reference tool for names of journalists, publications, or broad topics.—**Margaret McKinley**

958.   Edwards, Julia. **Women of the World: The Great Foreign Correspondents**. Boston, Houghton Mifflin, 1988. 275p. illus. index. $17.95. LC 87-37593. ISBN 0-395-44486-1.

This engaging book gives a highly readable overview of American women who have served as foreign correspondents, spotlighting the leading journalists. It serves not only as a reference tool, but also as a source of inspiration for anyone striving to follow in the footsteps of these intrepid women.

Edwards does not give in-depth biographies; they range from passing references to chapter-long sketches which cover the individual's life and work, with information coming from biographies, writings, personal correspondence, and interviews. The chapter references at the end of the book are excellent. The index is quite thorough, which is extremely important considering the ambiguous chapter headings.

Although the biographies of some of the women included in this book can be found in other sources, such as the Dictionary of Literary Biography series, no other source offers the coordinated, comprehensive, personal coverage provided here. The lively, conversational style, open admiration, and solid research combine to produce a work suitable for any library collection. [R: LJ, Aug 88, p. 155]—**Susan Davis Herring**

959.   Nimmo, Dan, and Chevelle Newsome. **Political Commentators in the United States in the 20th Century: A Bio-Critical Sourcebook**. Westport, Conn., Greenwood Press, 1997. 424p. index. $95.00. ISBN 0-313-29585-9.

In 40 essays, the life and contribution to U.S. political commentary of 42 key personalities (2 essays treat 2 persons each, Robert MacNeil and James Lehrer and Martha Rountree and Lawrence Spivak) are set forth. The entries are alphabetic by the names of the commentators, one-half of whom are deceased. As explained in the introduction, the book traces political commentary through four phases: that of newspaper columnists, 1914-1928; radio commentators, 1929-1946 (the "golden age of radio"); the entertainment phase of television, 1949-1980; and the era of "opinionated commentary that invites expressive behavior among audiences," 1981 to the present. The introduction also points out the highly selective nature of the work (a selection [Walter Cronkite, Larry King, Rush Limbaugh, Dan Rather, and Bernard Shaw are among the living ones included] from the hundreds of commentators this nation has produced in this century) as well as listing standard, general biographical and media-specific biographical sources consulted.

Coverage is current enough to include John Chancellor's death on July 12, 1996, but not David Brinkley's departure as anchor of "This Week" the following November. Each well-written essay usually concludes with three types of selected reference material: works by the commentator, critical works about him or her, and general works. A selected bibliography and an index of persons; newspapers and periodicals; radio and television shows; radio and television stations and networks; government agencies; places; and historic events, such as the Vietnam War, Watergate, and the two World Wars, conclude the book.

The authors (a political scientist at Baylor University and a communications teacher/researcher at California State University, Sacramento) state that the purpose of *Political Commentators* is to "portray the careers of key political commentators of the era and, through their lives and works, to illustrate the rise and decline of political commentary across the century." In this goal they have succeeded. This book can be recommended for medium-sized and large public and academic journalism/mass communications collections. [R: LJ, 15 Mar 97, p. 57]—**Wiley J. Williams**

960. Riley, Sam G. **Biographical Dictionary of American Newspaper Columnists**. Westport, Conn., Greenwood Press, 1995. 411p. index. $79.50. ISBN 0-313-29192-6.

Covering the Civil War era to the present, this volume treats 600 U.S. newspaper columnists, ranging from Eugene Field, Joel Chandler Harris, and James Thurber to Erma Bombeck, Hodding Carter, and Anna Quindlen. Riley, a professor of communication studies who has compiled a number of reference works pertaining to print journalism, profiles not only nationally syndicated and self-syndicated columnists but also those who write for only one newspaper. His primary focus is on writers of general interest, political, lifestyle, and humor columns. Although he includes well-known advice, etiquette, and society columnists, he excludes other special interest columnists, such as those writing about finance, gardening, or hobbies.

Varying in length from a few brief paragraphs to more than a page, the alphabetically arranged biographical sketches concentrate on the individuals' careers rather than details of their personal lives. When appropriate, entries conclude with bibliographical references to works by and about the columnist. In addition, a selective bibliography of sources relating to newspaper columns and columnists appears near the end of the volume. An excellent index provides access to the columnists treated, individuals mentioned within entries, and other proper names (such as titles of newspapers, periodicals, and columns; awards; and names of organizations).

Although the four volumes of *American Newspaper Journalists* (see ARBA 87, entry 880; ARBA 85, entries 781-782; and Gale, 1984), which cover 1690 to 1950 and are part of the Dictionary of Literary Biography series, offer much greater depth, they treat only a small percentage of the columnists in Riley's compilation. This work also complements other recent biographical sources on journalists, such as the *Biographical Dictionary of American Journalism* (see ARBA 90, entry 905), which provides more detailed biographical information but includes only 75 of the columnists identified by Riley. Especially valuable for its coverage of outstanding local columnists and those just beginning their ascent to national prominence, this dictionary will be particularly useful in academic libraries that support programs in journalism and mass communication.—**Marie Ellis**

PUBLIC SPEAKING

961. **African-American Orators: A Bio-Critical Sourcebook**. Richard W. Leeman, ed. Westport, Conn., Greenwood Press, 1996. 452p. index. (Bio-Critical Sourcebooks on American Orators). $95.00. ISBN 0-313-29014-8.

Public speaking has long played a central role in the African American heritage; the voices of influential orators such as Martin Luther King Jr., Sojourner Truth, and Frederick Douglass have echoed throughout U.S. history down to the present day. Leeman, a professor of communication studies, has assembled this collection of critical bio-bibliographies of notable African American speakers in order to convey to readers the vibrancy of this form of communication, to engender appreciation for the ideas and ideals expressed therein, and to act as a catalyst for further research in this area. The volume is intended for broad interdisciplinary use by students, teachers, activists, and general readers in college, university, institutional, and public libraries.

An informative introduction emphasizes themes common to the orators treated: the quest for freedom and equality of treatment, the upholding of U.S. ideals, and black pride. The body of the work includes entries on 43 representative orators from the mid-nineteenth century to the present, contributed by speech communication faculty members from a variety of U.S. universities. Each alphabetic entry consists of a biographical essay, a critical analysis of the orator's speeches, a list of information sources, and a chronology of major speeches. Information sources include research collections and collected speeches, selected critical studies, and selected biographies. The chronology of speeches lists the title, date, and source of the text for the speech. The number of orators covered was restricted in order to enable the essays to be as comprehensive as possible. The book is indexed by personal name and by subject.

Well written, this book is successful on many levels: in providing information on a specific aspect of American history, in providing insightful analyses of African American rhetoric, and in being an unusually interesting and inspiring reference work. Part of the Greenwood Press series Bio-Critical Sourcebooks on American Orators, it differs from other volumes in the series in that it is not a summary of conclusions of the discipline but is intended as a prologue to research yet to come in an area previously neglected. The sourcebook is recommended for a general audience as well as specialists.—**Jeanette C. Smith**

962.   **American Orators before 1900: Critical Studies and Sources**. Bernard K. Duffy and Halford R. Ryan, eds. Westport, Conn., Greenwood Press, 1987. 481p. index. $75.00. LC 86-33610. ISBN 0-313-25129-0.

The spoken word has always held an important place in American social and political discourse. The eighteenth and nineteenth centuries were particularly blessed with practitioners of oratory, that most democratic form of mass communication. Listeners need only be at the right place at the right time to hear the likes of Frederick Douglass, William Lloyd Garrison, Elizabeth Cady Stanton, or Sojourner Truth. *American Orators before 1900* brings together in one volume biographical and bibliographical information about fifty-five of the best, and most persuasive, public speakers of that tumultuous period.

The arrangement, alphabetically by orator, is mildly problematic as it mitigates against following the development of American oration either thematically or chronologically. In part this problem is addressed by the inclusion of a subject index that allows the reader to locate all mention of women's suffrage by individual speakers as well as topics addressed by a particular speaker in a given speech. A second index lists orators and names of speeches referenced in the text.

The main body of the work consists of signed essays on each of the 55 orators. The introductory paragraphs contain brief biographical information, but is most useful for setting the individual in his or her historical context. The remainder of the entry discusses the content and style of some of the individual's major speeches.

A brief, highly selective list of "information sources" following each entry is divided into three parts: research collections and collected speeches, selected critical studies, and selected biographies. The last item included with each entry is a chronology of major speeches, keyed to the research collections. For those unfamiliar with the art (and science) of oratory, the editors have kindly provided a glossary of rhetorical terms to help lay readers decipher some of the more technical language that occasionally appears in the text.—**Ellen Broidy**

963.   **American Orators of the Twentieth Century: Critical Studies and Sources**. Bernard K. Duffy and Halford R. Ryan, eds. Westport, Conn., Greenwood Press, 1987. 468p. index. $65.00. LC 86-10003. ISBN 0-313-24843-5.

The first two entries in this biographical and critical compilation of twentieth-century orators are Spiro T. Agnew and Ti-Grace Atkinson. Each was active and influential during the period of the late 1960s and early 1970s, though certainly representing widely divergent views. Their inclusion in this volume is an immediate indication of the range of individuals selected and the political focus of the compilation. Major political figures are abundant here. In addition to each U.S. president since

Theodore Roosevelt (except, not surprisingly, Harding and Coolidge), there are entries for the likes of William Jennings Bryan, Frank Church, Mario Cuomo, Everett Dirksen, Sam Ervin, Huey P. Long, Joseph McCarthy, George Wallace, and Henry Wallace. Black oratory is also well covered: Shirley Chisholm, W. E. B. DuBois, Marcus Garvey, Jesse Jackson, Barbara Jordan, Martin Luther King, Jr., and Malcolm X. Other influential figures include Cesar Chavez, Betty Friedan, Clarence Darrow, Eugene V. Debs, John L. Lewis, and Douglas MacArthur.

An important and continuing component of American oratory has been its religious or evangelical orientation. Indeed, the compilers define political oratory as "discourse that treats the constitutional, social, theological, moral and partisan political concerns of the American people." Thus, in addition to many of the black orators listed above, religious figures are nearly as plentiful as politicians. Among the most familiar names are Charles E. Coughlin, Jerry Falwell, Billy Graham, Billy James Hargis, and Fulton J. Sheen.

Each essay is written by a qualified academician, with professors of speech, communications, and politics predominating. For each orator, a brief biographical sketch is followed by a longer analysis of particular oratorical skills (e.g., style, delivery, use of vocabulary, persuasive techniques). The authors also assess the impact of the orators on American society, politics, and values. Appended to each essay are key information sources—research collections, collected speeches, selected critical studies, and biographical works—as well as a chronology of major speeches. There are also a concluding bibliographic essay, "Basic Research Sources in American Public Address," a glossary of rhetorical terms, a subject index, and an index arranged by speaker and speeches.

This is a reference source which students in a variety of disciplines will find useful. It is recommended for public and academic library collections; many high school libraries might also want to consider this volume. A companion volume, *American Orators before 1900* (see entry 962), is forthcoming. [R: RBB, 15 June 87, p. 1572]—**Thomas A. Karel**

964. **Women Public Speakers in the United States, 1800-1925: A Bio-Critical Sourcebook**. Karlyn Kohrs Campbell, ed. Westport, Conn., Greenwood Press, 1993. 509p. index. $75.00. HQ1412.W67. 305.42'092'2. LC 92-14615. ISBN 0-313-27533-5.

Although recent years have seen a growing number of reference books devoted to women as writers, less attention has been paid to women as orators and rhetoricians. This new biocritical sourcebook devoted to women as public speakers is thus very welcome as it chronicles the struggles of women "to be heard and to be heeded in the face of the hostility of the church, the courts, the professions, and the press" (introduction).

The sourcebook describes the lives and accomplishments of 37 women, including social reformer Jane Addams; educator Emma Willard; Clara Barton, founder of the American Red Cross; abolitionist Sojourner Truth; radical Emma Goldman; and many of the famous women who devoted their lives to women's rights and women's suffrage. The contributors are experts in their field; their entries are well written and well researched. Campbell has evidently allowed them a good deal of freedom in their choice of material: Some devote space to their subject's career and achievements, while others emphasize the rhetorical strategies the women employed as speakers. However, each entry does contain background material, a critical discussion of the subject's speeches, and a conclusion summarizing the importance of her work. The bibliography that follows includes library collections, biographies, critical sources, and a chronology of major speeches and writing. There is an index as well. This excellent book should be useful to libraries with collections on both women's studies and public speaking. [R: Choice, June 93, p. 1612; RBB, 1 Sept 93, p. 92]—**Lynn F. Williams**

965. **Women Public Speakers in the United States, 1925-1993: A Bio-Critical Sourcebook**. Karlyn Kohrs Campbell, ed. Westport, Conn., Greenwood Press, 1994. 491p. index. $75.00. HQ1412.W68.305.42'092'2. LC 93-21145. ISBN 0-313-27535-1.

The 1st volume of this bio-critical guide on women speakers before 1925 appeared in 1993. This second volume brings it up to the present, covering the lives and accomplishments of 31 more influential women speakers, including Margaret Sanger, Eleanor Roosevelt, Phyllis Schlafly, and Geraldine Ferraro. Since these are the women who have played a major role in American life and politics, this volume will prove useful to anyone interested in rhetoric, politics, or the contemporary women's movement. The alphabetical arrangement is the same as in the 1st volume. The contributors vary in their choice of material, but all provide a biography, a critical discussion of the subject's speeches, a summary of her work, and a substantial bibliography including critical material and a chronology of major speeches and other works. Both volumes are essential for libraries with holdings in women's or communications studies. [R: Choice, Dec 94, p. 583]—**Lynn F. Williams**

TELEVISION, CABLE, AND RADIO

966.   Adir, Karin. **The Great Clowns of American Television**. Jefferson, N.C., McFarland, 1988. 260p. illus. bibliog. index. $25.95. LC 88-42642. ISBN 0-89950-300-4.

Though quite a bit of material has been produced on the great clowns of the cinema, such as Charlie Chaplin, W. C. Fields, and Buster Keaton, very little can be found that documents the lives and work of the prominent comedians of television. Labeled "a labor of love" by the author, this is a collection of biographies of eighteen funny men and women of the small screen: Lucille Ball, Milton Berle, Carol Burnett, Sid Caesar, Imogene Coca, Tim Conway, Jackie Gleason, Danny Kaye, Ernie Kovacs, Olsen and Johnson, Martha Raye, Soupy Sales, Red Skelton, Dick Van Dyke, Flip Wilson, Jonathan Winters, and Ed Wynn.

The only criterion for the selection of these individuals is the fact that they have been prominent "clowns" of television during the past thirty-five years. For those individuals not included, such as Don Knotts, Johnny Carson, and Rowen and Martin, the author simply states that "perhaps he or she will turn up in the next volume." The coverage is rather uneven, ranging from three to twenty-seven pages in length per individual, but the sketches are well written and provide information on the early years of the comic figure, marriages and personal challenges, anecdotes, the characters they created, styles, and a representative dialog or sketch description. Black-and-white photographs are included. An index directs the reader to other comic figures mentioned within the sketches.

Despite its shortcomings, the book provides quite a bit of insight into the lives of these clowns of television and is easily read from cover to cover. It would be an interesting addition to many collections.—**Susan R. Penney**

967.   Brooks, Tim. **The Complete Directory to Prime Time TV Stars: 1946-Present**. New York, Ballantine/Random House, 1987. 1086p. bibliog. index. $14.95pa. LC 86-92108. ISBN 0-345-32681-4.

During the past four decades, television has been used as a medium for thoughtful expression, heated political debate, popular entertainment, and sometimes a mixture of the above. It has created the thousands of stars in this directory, encompassing major and supporting players who appeared as regulars on any nighttime network series. Principals of late-night shows and top-rated miniseries are also included.

An introduction defining the directory's format precedes the main section, listing prime-time stars alphabetically. Series appeared in, parts played, awards won, and biographical notes are in each personality's listing, which can vary in length from one line to one page, depending on the information available. Four appendices contain stars' birthplaces and birthdays, as well as a short "know your stars" quiz. A bibliography and an index of television productions follow.

Other attempts to document people in the field of television have had a broader scope, including "behind the scenes" personnel, such as producers and directors and covering other media in addition to television (e.g., the *International Television and Video Almanac*, Quigley Publishing, 1987).

This unique directory, focusing on the performers in the most pervasive medium of this century, serves as a companion volume to the author's previous work, *The Complete Directory of Prime Time Network TV Shows* (Ballantine, 1981). The current book attains the right blend of trivia and researched facts to appeal to a wide range of fans, critics, and scholars. It is, as the author proclaims, the "first comprehensive 'Who's Who' of the thousands of stars, big and small" who have appeared on the small screen since the 1940s.—**Anita Zutis**

968. DeLong, Thomas A. **Radio Stars: An Illustrated Biographical Dictionary of 953 Performers, 1920 through 1960**. Jefferson, N.C., McFarland, 1996. 306p. illus. index. $59.50. ISBN 0-7864-0149-0.

As radio became more familiar to thousands of U.S. homes in the 1920s, the people behind the voices became almost members of the family. This work provides biographies of some 950 radio performers from the period 1920 through 1960. Many of these people are household names, while others have disappeared into the time warp of the past. Reading this volume brings back many memories and opens vistas into an age that will never return. Aside from providing the standard biographical information on personalities of the period, insight can be obtained into the life and times of the period covered.

Historians will find this work appealing because of the scenes into the past the entries provide. Each person's story is told as completely as possible, given the obvious space constraints of a volume such as this. In addition, an emphasis is placed on why the individual was memorable in the field of radio broadcasting. For example, Wendell Hall's entry states, "Ukulele-playing vocalist, he popularized that stringed instrument among flappers and sheiks in the 1920s." DeLong's style of writing makes this work all the more important and memorable to the reader. The work is extensively illustrated.

This volume is bound in a sturdy library binding. Most reference collections will find it invaluable.—**Ralph Lee Scott**

969. Lieberman, Philip A. **Radio's Morning Show Personalities: Early Hour Broadcasters and Deejays from the 1920s to the 1990s**. Jefferson, N.C., McFarland, 1996. 204p. illus. index. $29.95. ISBN 0-7864-0037-4.

The title of this volume pretty much tells it all. The volume contains 33 biographies of major morning radio talk show personalities as well as brief listings of several hundred other prominent morning personalities. From *Rambling with Grambling* to Howard Stern, the author covers the important a.m. radio jocks who shaped this uniquely American form of morning entertainment. The biographies roughly parallel the development of this radio genre starring "morning men" who at first talked to their listeners, then graduated to playing recorded music, and finally ending with the current target audience "shockjock" type of show characterized by Stern. (While in the classic era, there were no major women morning radio show personalities, several women radio personalities are listed in the "other prominent" section.) Covered are such deejays as Gene Rayburn, Bob Elliott, Ray Goulding, Arthur Godfrey, Buffalo Bob Smith, Don Russell, Wolfman Jack, John Leslie, Joe Roberts, and Don Imus.

The volume is well constructed and interesting to read. The entries give a lively and accurate picture of each personality. A number of the entries contain show dialogues, thereby giving the real flavor and humor of each deejay. The author spent four years doing research and conducting live interviews with a number of personalities. Libraries with patrons interested in early and current radio will find this volume both a quick reference and a useful history.—**Ralph Lee Scott**

970. Slide, Anthony. **Some Joe You Don't Know: An American Biographical Guide to 100 British Television Personalities**. Westport, Conn., Greenwood Press, 1996. 271p. illus. index. $59.95. ISBN 0-313-29550-6.

Contained in this guide are short biographical profiles of approximately 100 British performers who have turned up on television in the United States, principally on PBS stations or Arts & Entertainment cable. Indeed, many British shows have also been recycled on other cable networks, thus exposing these artists even more. Both drama and comedy are covered, from the 1950s up to the modern times (although the entry for Inspector Morse's John Thaw does not mention his role in *A Year in Provence*, seen on A&E two years before the entry's publication date). Also provided is a short history of British programming on American television, which really began in 1969 with the *Forsythe Saga* on PBS, followed by *Masterpiece Theatre* and *Upstairs Downstairs*.

Each biography has a listing of credits, along with dates and a bibliography for further reading. There are 24 not-very-well-reproduced, black-and-white photographs (only one in four can be visualized). Prominent names include Stephen Fry and Hugh Laurie (both of whom played Jeeves),

Jennifer Saunders of *Ab Fab* (but not her partner Dawn French of *French and Saunders*), Rowan Atkinson, Jeremy Brett, Dame Edna Everage, David Frost, David Suchet, and Joan Hickson from Agatha Christie shows. The price seems a little steep for 248 pages of entries, but there is a plus in that there is an index to names of shows and other actors who do not have a separate entry. [R: Choice, June 96, p. 1623]—**Dean Tudor**

971.　Watson, Elena M. **Television Horror Movie Hosts: 68 Vampires, Mad Scientists and Other Denizens of the Late-Night Airwaves.** . . . Jefferson, N.C., McFarland, 1991. 242p. illus. index. $29.95. PN1992.8.F5W37. 791 .45'616. LC 91-52642. ISBN 0-89950-570-8.

Thirty-one hosts of television horror movies are portrayed in this book. They range from 1954's Vampira (Maila Nurmi), who was reportedly the first such host, to Grampa Munster (Al Lewis), a recent addition to cable television. Factual information is provided, but the material is largely anecdotal. Much of the text is written somewhat tongue in cheek. Most of these hosts have had movie careers, and their film achievements are noted. The many black-and-white photographs will no doubt delight fans. Quite a few are full-page and awash in ghoulishness. There is a reasonably good index to names and titles, although not everyone mentioned is indexed. A filmography-discography of the hosts is appended, as is a brief bibliography.

This work will help answer many of the questions asked about this genre. It is a must for public and school libraries, but academic libraries may want to pass on it.—**Helen M. Gothberg**

18 Performing Arts

INTRODUCTION

This chapter on performing arts contains works that do not fit into the larger chapters of Music, Communication and Mass Media, or Literature, which includes written dramatic works as opposed to theatre. **Performing Arts** includes the sections General Works, Dance, and Theatre. General Works brings together a number of useful sources, such as *Performing Artists* (U*X*L*/Gale, 1995) (see entry 978), encompassing comedy, drama, film and television, and music biographies; *Performers and Players* (Facts on File, 1998) (see entry 973), with its 400-plus biographical entries. In addition, more unusual biographical sources may be found, including *Obituaries in the Performing Arts: Film, Television, Radio, Theatre, Dance, Music, Cartoon, and Pop Culture* (McFarland, 1996) (see entry 974); *Great Jews on Stage and Screen* (Jonathan David, 1987) (see entry 975); Tom Ogden's *Two Hundred Years of the American Circus: From Aba-Daba to the Zoppe Zavatta Troupe* (Facts on File, 1993) (see entry 977); and *Funny Women: American Comediennes, 1860-1985* (McFarland, 1987) (see entry 981).

By far the most numerous sources in this chapter are those on theatre. They include the *Concise Oxford Companion to American Theatre* (Oxford University Press, 1987, 1990) (see entry 984), which provides short biographies of leading figures in the theatre; the *Cambridge Guide to American Theatre* (Cambridge University Press, 1996) (see entry 985), which has more than 2,000 biographical sketches; and the *International Dictionary of Theatre—2: Playwrights* (St. James Press, 1994) (see entry 988), with its 485 biographical entries. Another important work of theatre biographies listed is the *Contemporary Theatre, Film, and Television: A Biographical Guide. . .* (Gale, 1984-) (see entry 972), which provides more than 400 biographies for performers, directors, writers, producers, designers, managers, choreographers, composers, executives, dancers, and critics working in theatre, film, and television. Finally, two very important and long-lasting theatre sources are included: *Who's Who in the Theatre: A Biographical Record of the Contemporary Stage* (Gale, 1912-) (see entry 999), which provides biographies of major theatre individuals; and *Theatre World* (Crown, 1945-) (see entry 1000), which provides a complete list of Broadway productions and personnel, including actors, replacements, producers, directors, authors, composers, costume designers, lighting technicians, press agents, and opening and closing dates for plays.

GENERAL WORKS

972. **Contemporary Theatre, Film, and Television: A Biographical Guide Featuring Performers, Directors, Writers.** Terrie M. Rooney, Brandon Trenz, and Lynn M. Spampinato, eds. Detroit, Gale, 1984- . index. $125.00 for recent edition. ISSN 0749-064X.

Contemporary Theatre, Film, and Television (CTFT) continues the biographical reference series' coverage of the lives and work of performing arts professionals. This volume brings the total number of references in *CTFT* to about 6,600 and is intended for researchers in general readers. More than 400 entries cover performers, directors, writers, and producers, as well as other specialists in the theater, film, and television industries in the United States and Great Britain. While emphasis is given to individuals who are currently active in these fields, obituaries are included, as are revisions of previous entries.

Entries list biographical and career information, awards, memberships, title-by-title credits, recordings, writings, and sources for further information. Entries vary in length from one column to several pages. A cumulative index provides access to previous volumes in the series, and to Gale's *Who's Who in the Theatre* and *Who Was Who in the Theatre*. This ongoing publication gathers information on a wide range of people in the entertainment field and makes it easy to locate.—**Anita Zutis and Robert L. Wick**

455

973.   Franck, Irene M., and David M. Brownstone. **Performers and Players**. New York, Facts on File, 1988. 196p. illus. bibliog. index. (Work Throughout History). $16.95. LC 87-30340. ISBN 0-8160-1443-4.

This volume presents a comprehensive survey of persons who participate or perform in fields usually referred to as entertainment, such as actors, athletes, dancers, directors, musicians, puppeteers, racers, and variety entertainers. Included for each occupation are the history of the vocation, its socioeconomic status, the specific tasks performed, and the changes technology and society have wrought.

In addition to the easy to read text, illustrations, a comprehensive index, and suggestions for further reading enhance this volume as a reference work.

Part of the series entitled Work Throughout History, this is for young readers 10 and up. The entire set explores occupations as they have evolved and are executed throughout the world. It will be a valuable addition to middle and high school libraries.—**Sara R. Mack**

974.   Lentz, Harris M., III. **Obituaries in the Performing Arts: Film, Television, Radio, Theatre, Dance, Music, Cartoons, and Pop Culture**. Jefferson, N.C., McFarland, 1994- . illus. $25.00pa. for recent edition. PN1583.O25. ISSN 1087-9617.

These reference works combined contain nearly 1,100 obituaries of people from both show business and the performing arts, including film, television, sports, radio, theater, music, and dance. Entries begin with date, place of death, and cause of death, followed by career highlights and other biographical information. Entries range in length from under 50 to several hundred words. Most entries also include periodical references to the reports of the death, from newspapers such as *The New York Times*, *Variety*, the *Los Angeles Times*, *The Washington Post*, and *Times* (London), and from such magazines as *People*, *Newsweek*, and *Time*. More than half of the entries also supply black-and-white photographs of the deceased. Filmographies are provided with the entries of television and motion picture performers. A brief introduction and a 26-book reference bibliography are also included in each volume.

This work is part of a series of reference works from McFarland. The author has written obituaries of film personalities for more than 20 years, in addition to several significant reference works. These useful additions to the biography reference shelf are recommended.—**Edward Erazo and Robert L. Wick**

975.   Lyman, Darryl. **Great Jews on Stage and Screen**. Middle Village, N.Y., Jonathan David, 1987. 279p. illus. index. $19.95. LC 87-4214. ISBN 0-8246-0328-1.

Defining a Jew as "anyone who was born of a Jewish mother or who converted to Judaism," Lyman presents 100 biographies of Jewish performers from the theater, film, and television. Each one- to three-page biography includes a biographical sketch; a large black-and-white photograph; and a list of the biographee's "selected performances" on stage, film, radio, and television. These major biographies are followed by 25 pages of thumbnail sketches of Jewish performers, including many—such as Isaac Stern, Paul Simon, Bob Dylan, and Roberta Peters—that one would expect to find in Lyman's companion volume, *Great Jews in Music* (1986).

Although most of the information presented in this volume will be readily found in *Current Biography* and/or standard entertainment biographies, these sketches are very easy to read and provide an ethnic overview that is not available in other sources. On the other hand, how many readers looking for information on Erich von Stroheim, Dinah Shore, or Marilyn Monroe would know to consult this book? Lyman does not explain why some entertainers are given major biographies and others only a one- or two-sentence sketch. For instance, Stella Adler, Anouk Aimee, Sara Bernhardt, and Alvin Epstein are all reduced to thumbnail sketches, while Henry Houdini, who is certainly not remembered for his six film roles, is presented in a three-page major biography. [R: RBB, Aug 88, p. 1903]—**Michael Ann Moskowitz**

976. Mapp, Edward. **Directory of Blacks in the Performing Arts**. 2d ed. Metuchen, N.J., Scarecrow, 1990. 594p. index. $57.50. PN1590.B53M3. 791'.08996073. LC 89-30477. ISBN 0-8108-2222-9.

Expanded by 150 pages, this edition contains concise data on more than 1,000 performers (including producers, broadcasters, choreographers, and agents) categorized by career. The entries from the previous edition (see ARBA 79, entry 1016) have been updated, but the real value of this book rests in the inclusion of figures who have become prominent in the past dozen years. The sources for the data must extend beyond the few references cited in the bibliography, only a third of which were published after 1978. It is reassuring to find 1989 deaths reported (e.g., Alvin Ailey, Undine Moore); however, some earlier information has not been corrected. Although those using this reference will wish to verify critical data in other sources, it is a pleasure to find an old companion rejuvenated and ready for new applications. No matter what the inevitable shortcomings are, this remains a valuable biographic tool. [R: Choice, Nov 90, p. 462; LJ, July 90, p. 88; RBB, 1 Dec 90, p. 776]
—Dominique-René de Lerma

977. Ogden, Tom. **Two Hundred Years of the American Circus: From Aba-Daba to the Zoppe Zavatta Troupe**. New York, Facts on File, 1993. 402p. illus. index. $50.00. GV1815.033. 791.3'03. LC 92-31880. ISBN 0-8160-2611-4.

This handbook and guide to 200 years of the American circus, as distinguished from British or Continental, covers just about everything one might want to know. Entries vary in length from a few lines to several pages, with many cross-references in the text and many *see also* references at the end of important articles. About one-third of the entries are biographical, such as those for P. T. Barnum, Joseph Gatti, Annie Oakley, Jenny Lind, and other lesser-known personalities that either organized or performed under the big top from about 1793 to 1993. Another portion contains subject entries on such topics as clowns, cyclists, circuses, the flying trapeze, horses, midgets, passing leap, push pole, and other terms known to the public. Interspersed with them are items of circus jargon, such as dukey run (a two-day engagement with only a box lunch, a dukey, on the second day), gennie (a portable generator), giraffe (an extra-high unicycle), and kinker. Also, there are historical articles on all of the great circus companies whose names have become synonymous with circus life in the United States, such as Ringling Brothers, Buffalo Bill's Wild West, and Sells-Floto Circus.

This book does not give much space to magical tricks or escape artists, although some have appeared in circuses. Harry Houdini is not listed, but famous elephants, such as King Tusk (50 years old in 1992 but still on the road), are given as much space as their trainers or fellow performers. An especially valuable article deals with some 75 movies that portray, in whole or in part, some aspects of circus life. Besides cross-references, whenever a main-entry word or name is mentioned in the articles, the text is printed in boldface type to indicate further information. There are many black-and-white illustrations throughout. In addition, there are a good bibliography and a full index. This is an excellent reference work on a little-known topic. [R: LJ, Aug 93, p. 96; RBB, 1 Dec 93, p. 717]—**Raymund F. Wood**

978. **Performing Artists**. Molly Severson, ed. Detroit, U*X*L/Gale, 1995. 3v. illus. index. $57.00/set. ISBN 0-8103-9868-0.

Bubbling with the names, multiracial faces, and performances of living artists in the youth arena, this sensibly priced, three-volume biographical encyclopedia is attractive, informative, and inviting. The layout offers maximum coverage, beginning with a table of contents listing names by volume and by field of endeavor, encompassing comedy, drama, film and television, and music. For young readers, the appeal is instantaneous: Editors establish the validity and dedication of favorites, unfortunately limited to black-and-white photographs, from Snoop Doggy Dogg, Anthony Hopkins, Alvin Ailey, and Gloria Estefan to Janet Jackson, Raul Julia, Arnold Schwarzenegger, Paula Abdul, Ice-T, and the Red Hot Chili Peppers. A concise three-paragraph reader's guide concludes with another upper for young researchers—an address and a telephone number requesting user input on future volumes.

The strongest feature of this set is attractive fonts, wide margins, and clean layout; the work demystifies research by supplying simplified sources, meaningful subheads, consecutive numbering, lively citations by critics and fellow professionals, and sidebars quoting insightful glimpses of the personality and vision of the subjects. For example, under a fluid shot of Axl Rose, Danny Sugerman speaks to the humanistic necessity for celebration of life and art. A cutline under the picture of Maria Tallchief partnering with Jacques d'Amboise connects her with an appropriate honor: a White House performance of *Sylvia*. The index lists titles, performers, and performances followed by volume and page number and boldface to indicate main entries. U*X*L's dedication to racially balanced, stimulating writing provides human models—warts and all—for users to study, learn from, admire, and emulate.—**Mary Ellen Snodgrass**

978a.   Bailey, Brooke. **The Remarkable Lives of 100 Women Artists**. Holbrook, Mass., Adams Publishing, 1994. 207p. index. (20th Century Women Series). $12.00. ISBN 1-55850-360-9.

Whereas Frank N. Magill's *Great Lives from History: American Women Series* presents its information in a highly structured, consistently formatted manner appropriate to ready-reference work, this book instead focuses on the stories of the women's lives. Entries generally are one- to two-page narratives that attempt to recount the essential and influential events, people, and ideas that informed each artist's "unique personal vision." Bailey has thrown a wide net, encompassing architects, archivists of indigenous American music, blues performers, classical composers, collage artists, concert pianists, filmmakers, folk dancers, illustrators, jazz singers, muralists, photographers, sculptors, and even a trapeze performer among her women artists. Although each entry concludes with a very brief list of resources "to find out more," this delightful work has been designed more for inspiration than reference-desk duty.—**G. Kim Dority**

979.   Sampson, Henry T. **The Ghost Walks: A Chronological History of Blacks in Show Business, 1865-1910**. Metuchen, N.J., Scarecrow, 1988. 570p. illus. index. $47.50. LC 87-27973. ISBN 0-8108-2070-6.

The history of black American entertainment, from its origins at the end of the Civil War to the first decade of the twentieth century, is traced in this illustrated chronology. Original source material, obtained mostly from libraries, includes newspaper reviews, playbills, theater programs, letters, biographical sketches, and critical commentary. Rare photographs, from abroad as well as from the United States, enhance the narrative.

Entries document the development of black entertainment from minstrel shows to involvement with all facets of popular entertainment, such as burlesque, circus, vaudeville, and musical comedy. The business of show business is included as well; it led to the formation of a black film industry years later. An index is provided.

This work serves as a prolog to the author's previous books, *Blacks in Blackface* (see ARBA 81, entry 1059) and *Blacks in Black and White* (see ARBA 78, entry 950). The chronology links the first fledgling efforts of blacks to the achievements of the emerging stars of the 1920s.

While entries are detailed, bibliographical annotations are often lacking, and no bibliography exists for those wishing to do further research. Such information would add to the usefulness of this historical account.—**Anita Zutis**

980.   Sonneborn, Liz. **Performers**. New York, Facts on File, 1995. 112p. illus. index. (American Indian Lives). $17.95. ISBN 0-8160-3045-6.

Performers is part of a multivolume series, American Indian Lives, written for young readers. In presenting the stories of Native American dancers, actors, and singers, the book fills a void in the literature by combining the engrossing stories of American Indian people in the performing arts with an enlightening picture of their audiences and the society in which they performed. The traditional role of performer was to ensure the continuity of the culture; the contemporary role has been as a representative of American Indian cultures to non-Indian cultures. Both roles have great responsibility.

Each biography is carefully crafted to engage the young reader in the power and excitement of each story, and the photographs and selected annotated bibliography contribute to the readability and usefulness of the book. Young readers are likely to be drawn to the life stories of those contemporary performers that they know, such as Graham Greene or John Trudell, but they will be attracted also to the stories of those who are not as well known but whose powerful stories of ambition, training, and persistence are compelling. Through the biographies, the reader will develop a greater understanding of how American Indian performers have confronted both positive and negative stereotyping in their roles and prejudice in the entertainment industry, and how they have helped to shape the perceptions of American Indians through their work. They bring their Indian traditions and values to their work, enriching everyone. The book expands understanding of American Indians in a manner that has been ignored in the past and makes a valuable contribution to the field.—**Karen D. Harvey**

981. Unterbrink, Mary. **Funny Women: American Comediennes, 1860-1985**. Jefferson, N.C., McFarland, 1987. 267p. illus. bibliog. index. $19.95. LC 85-43595. ISBN 0-89950-226-1.
    This is a collection of brief biographical career summaries, which range in length from less than one page to six or seven pages. As the author points out, any reader might question the inclusion or absence of particular individuals, but the intent here is to provide examples of comediennes, who represent different periods of American entertainment history and trends in humor.
    The sketches are grouped into eight chapters: "The Early Days (1860-1930)," "Vaudeville Legends," "Funny Women of Radio," "Early Stand-Up Comics," "Funny Women of Television," "Familiar Faces," "Writers and Directors," and "Rising Stars." Certainly these categories create overlap, since many comediennes have found fame in several of these arenas. Also, the time period of "The Early Days" obviously covers vaudeville and radio and even extends to the stand-up comics included. An index of personal names, titles, and awards does help the user find all the appropriate references.
    Funny Women must be compared to *Women in Comedy* by Linda Martin and Kerry Segrave (Citadel Press, 1986). *Funny Women* has more entries than the earlier work, but *Women in Comedy* generally has more informative entries, which go beyond presentation of facts and provide more analysis of the comedic styles and impacts of the women profiled. *Women in Comedy* also has a strictly chronological arrangement, which prevents confusion and overlap of categories. Not surprisingly, though, both works have relied heavily on popular magazines, newspapers, and interviews for information. Naturally, they cover many of the same women, but *Funny Women* is stronger in its coverage of the new comediennes. While only time will reveal the longevity of these newcomers, *Funny Women* does provide a useful compilation of biographical material which might otherwise be hard to find. Not strictly a reference work, it will be an asset in biography searches. [R: Choice, Dec 87, p. 606]—**Barbara E. Kemp**

DANCE

982. Billman, Larry. **Film Choreographers and Dance Directors: An Illustrated Biographical Encyclopedia**.... Jefferson, N.C., McFarland, 1997. 652p. illus. index. $110.00. ISBN 0-89950-868-5.
    Seeking to make the public more aware of the achievements and importance of dance directors and choreographers in U.S. cinema, Billman has compiled a biographical dictionary of the creators and directors of dance sequences in both musical and non-musical motion pictures. The majority of this volume consists of an alphabetic listing of more than 900 choreographers. In his introduction, Billman writes of the difficulty of obtaining information on many choreographers. Indeed, many films do not even list the choreographer's name in the credits. The book's entries, therefore, vary in size and detail. Entries are much longer and more complete for such famous dance designers as Hermes Pan (creator of many dances for MGM and Warner Brothers musicals), Fred Astaire, Gene Kelly, and Agnes DeMille than for other lesser-known choreographers. When the information is available, Billman provides a short biography; a list of book-length biographies; and lists of credits for work in theater, ballet, television, video, and film.
    Preceding the biographical entries is Billman's history of cinema choreography, arranged into chapter roughly by decade, and extending from 1893 to the early 1990s. Each chapter provides a quick overview of the decade, but no one film is covered in much detail. Each chapter concludes with a selected filmography (movie title, choreographer, studio name, date of release, video release information, and short annotation). Throughout the book, black-and-white photographs depict rehearsals, publicity shots, and other behind-the-scenes action. An appendix lists films alphabetically with their

choreographers. Because choreography credits are hard to find, this part of the volume will be especially useful to librarians and dance historians. The book's index provides reliable access to people, films, plays, places, and selected subjects. Billman, a dancer and choreographer himself, has done the world of dance a service with the compilation of this book.— **Linda Keir Simons**

983.   **Minor Ballet Composers: Biographical Sketches of Sixty-Six Underappreciated Yet Significant Contributors to the Body of Western Ballet Music.** By Bruce R. Schuenenman. William E. Studwell, ed. Binghamton, N.Y., Herewith Press, 1997. 133p. index. $39.95. ISBN 0-7890-0323-6.

Schuenenman's compendium of brief biographies of composers of ballet music charges a steep price for the value offered. Featuring clear typefaces and attractive layout, the work opens with an adequate introduction to ballet history and purpose and follows with a note on *Les Six*, which introduces the members and time frame of this short-lived coterie of French composers. The selection in the main text is Eurocentric and stresses the contribution of female composers. Nationalities cover musicians from England, France, Russia, Austria, Germany, Romania, Denmark, Scotland, Norway, Czechoslovakia, Hungary, Sweden, Italy, Egypt, and the United States. The 79-page text cites life span, places of birth and death, a terse summary of professional career, influence of mentors and collaborators, and titles and dates of significant ballet scores. The glossary of 20 choreographers is similarly spare. An index of ballet titles alphabetizes the 518 works covered in the text. A bibliography offers nearly six pages of notes, which establish the quality of the research. A 15-page index provides an additional list of titles along with composers and choreographers.

Schuenenman's style and depth are major stumbling blocks to the effectiveness of this work. Information is uneven in quality and coverage and is formatted and written at a grade-school level, for example, the 3-line summary of August Strindberg's *Miss Julie* on page 71 and the quick gloss of giants of the ballet world, notably Frederick Ashton, Agnes de Mille, George Balanchine, and Martha Graham. Overall, sentence structure is simplistic in the extreme and relies heavily on colorless verbs. The writer tends to omit or ignore causality, motivation, effect, and critical reputation and excludes commentary on awards and achievements. Information on the scoring of ballets for film is also skimpy. An index of entries by country would be a helpful addition.—**Mary Ellen Snodgrass**

THEATRE

984.   Bordman, Gerald. **The Concise Oxford Companion to American Theatre**. New York, Oxford University Press, 1987. 451p. $24.95. LC 86-33294. ISBN 0-19-505121-1.

When Gerald Bordman's *Oxford Companion to the American Theatre* (Oxford University Press) appeared in 1984, it quickly established itself as the standard one-volume reference on the American stage. This 1987 abridgment of the massive original volume eliminates many entries on minor plays and figures, while it preserves those articles that are of the widest general interest.

Hundreds of biographical sketches and summaries of individual plays illuminate the major achievements of playwrights such as William Dunlap, Eugene O'Neill, Elmer Rice, Lillian Hellman, Arthur Miller, William Inge, David Mamet, David Rabe, and Sam Shepard. Also included are essays on significant performers, directors, and producers (ranging from Edwin Booth to Joseph Jefferson, Colleen Dewhurst to James Earl Jones, Sidney Kingsley to Joseph Papp). While extensive coverage is given to the great tradition of the American musical, the often neglected achievements of the nineteenth century are also represented. Here one may find information on American theater companies (such as Houston's Alley Theatre, the Dallas Theatre Center, and the Oregon Shakespeare Festival Association), theater structures (Charleston's Dock Street Theatre, New York's Lyceum Theatre, and Philadelphia's Arch Street Theatre, for example), and types of theater (mime, theater-in-the-round, off-Broadway theater).

Updated information on contemporary topics as well as many new articles make this concise edition of more than 2,000 entries an excellent companion to the 1984 volume. An outstanding resource for theater scholars, it is also an enjoyable text for anyone interested in the world of theater, as the articles are clearly written and well informed.—**Colby H. Kullman**

985. **Cambridge Guide to American Theatre**. updated ed. By Don B. Wilmeth, with Tice L. Miller. New York, Cambridge University Press, 1996. 463p. index. $49.95; $24.95pa. ISBN 0-521-40134-8; 0-521-56444-1pa.

First published in 1993 (see ARBA 94, entry 1479), this updated edition provides an encyclopedic history of U.S. theater that is essential to any library from secondary schools upward. It contains more than 2,300 cross-referenced entries that are noteworthy for accuracy, succinct presentation, and suggestions for further reading on the respective topic. The entries are drawn from historical as well as the latest contemporary artists, theaters, plays, and topics. Particularly noteworthy in this edition are the expansions of entries dealing with the theater of diversity and social issues. The topics are drawn from popular areas, such as burlesque and puppetry, as well as the more scholarly areas of criticism and theory and everything in between. There is a biographical index of more than 3,000 names in addition to an extensive bibliography of 1,000-plus sources. This guide represents an essential source for students and scholars of U.S. theater.—**Jackson Kesler**

986. **The Facts on File Dictionary of the Theatre**. William Packard, David Pickering, and Charlotte Savidge, eds. New York, Facts on File, 1988. 556p. $24.95. LC 88-28379. ISBN 0-8160-1841-3.

This reference volume attempts to cover the development of world drama from its earliest beginnings to the present day. The more than 5,000 entries are chosen from a variety of areas: biographies of performers, playwrights, and figures from all aspects of theater; major plays; historical dramatic styles, innovations, and genres; technical design terminology; and theatrical companies, schools, and organizations. The formidable task of selecting the entries for inclusion is completed with satisfactory results. The next task concerning the content of the entries is not handled as successfully—the brevity of the information severely limits the usefulness of the volume. The information capsules present only the most basic of facts with little elaboration. A regrettable omission is a bibliography for further reference.

Volume 5's usefulness can be found in its generally broad scope. It can also be used to verify basic information, but a reader consulting the volume for anything further would be greatly disappointed. [R: BR, Sept/Oct 89, p. 57; Choice, June 89, p. 1660; LJ, 1 Apr 89, pp. 84-85; RBB, 15 June 89, p. 1804]—**Jackson Kesler**

987. Highfill, Philip H., Jr., Kalman A. Burnim, and Edward A. Langhans. **A Biographical Dictionary of Actors, Actresses, Musicians, Dancers, Managers & Other Stage Personnel in London, 1660-1800. Vols. 1–16.** Carbondale, Southern Illinois University Press, 1973- . illus. $60.00 for recent edition. PN2597.H5. 790.2'092'2. ISBN 0-8093-1802-4.

A masterful work begun some 20 years ago has now ended, with the final two volumes having been published. Scholars will continue to appreciate the exhaustive research that is evident in these volumes. From the most minor to the most major personalities, the authors present a series of profiles that detail the accomplishments and professional work of those individuals. Anecdotes are included throughout, as are excerpts and interpretations. Entries range from a mere two lines for individuals whose names have been recorded in a docket or diary somewhere, to pages and pages for major characters such as Catherine Tofts (singer); James Tokely (comedian); Barbara Van Beck (bearded lady and harpsichordist); and Margaret Woffington (actress, singer, dancer), whose entry is accompanied by nine portraits! Bibliographers and theater historians will appreciate the detail of these entries, as particular performances and manuscripts are identified for posterity and research. The many illustrations (black-and-white) are of high quality and were selected for their unique or representative value.

Highly recommended for addition to serious theater history archives.—**Edmund F. Santa-Vicca and Robert L. Wick**

988. **International Dictionary of Theatre-2: Playwrights**. Mark Hawkins-Dady, ed. Detroit, St. James Press, 1994. 1218p. illus. index. $120.00. ISBN 1-55862-096-6.

Following on the heels of a remarkable volume on plays (see ARBA 93, entry 1391) that profiles individual dramatic works, this second volume focuses on playwrights—their life, works, criticism, and interpretation. Each of the 485 entries includes brief biographical information (e.g., dates, education, marriage, awards, honors). This is followed by a list of the writer's works, divided into the following categories: collections, stage works, screenplays, television plays, radio plays, fiction, verse, memoirs and letters, and miscellany. Where relevant, the entry continues with lists of bibliographies and criticism (including selected foreign-language titles) about the writer. Excluded are works of a general literary nature, those that focus on the nondramatic writings of the author, most works that treat an individual play, and any article less than five pages in length. The entry concludes with a brief critical essay regarding the writer's contributions, significance, and so forth, to the world of the stage. Where appropriate, cross-references are made to individual plays treated in volume 1. Each essay is signed by one of the many contributors to the volume. Black-and-white illustrations and photographs are located throughout the volume. This substantial work is worthy of inclusion in most performance, drama, and literary collections. [R: LJ, Aug 94, p. 74; RBB, 1 Sept 94, p. 72]—**Edmund F. SantaVicca**

989.   **International Dictionary of Theatre-3: Actors, Directors, and Designers**. David Pickering, ed. Detroit, St. James Press, 1996. 829p. illus. $130.00. ISBN 1-55862-097-4.

This, the 3d and final volume in the *International Dictionary of Theatre,* joins its predecessors, volume 1, on plays (see ARBA 93, entry 1391), and volume 2, on playwrights (see ARBA 95, entry 1421), and nicely completes the series by focusing on actors, directors, and designers. While the earlier volumes are well done and contain much useful information, this latest addition, with its inclusion of less-often covered directors and designers, makes the entire set just that much more helpful and appealing. International and historical in scope, this source covers theater from classical Greece to the present and includes plays written in 20 languages and theater personnel of various cultures and nationalities.

Following a brief introductory editor's note and a list of advisers and contributors, the work continues with an integrated alphabetic listing of generally notable actors, directors, and designers. Each entry will vary with the individual being discussed and may include a brief biography; a chronological list of selected productions or roles; sections on achievements in films, television, and radio; relevant publications authored by the entrant; a bibliography; and a critical essay written by the appropriate contributor. The volume is concluded by two sections—"Notes on Advisers and Contributors" and "Picture Acknowledgments."

Clearly written and organized, nicely formatted, and filled with much useful information, this resource is accessible to a wide range of readers. It will be a welcome addition to most academic and public library reference collections. [R: Choice, May 96, p. 1450; RBB, 15 Mar 96, p. 1315]—**Kristin Ramsdell**

990.   Leiter, Samuel L. **The Great Stage Directors: 100 Distinguished Careers of the Theater**. New York, Facts on File, 1994. 340p. illus. index. $35.00. PN2205.L44. 792'.0233'0922. LC 93-33380. ISBN 0-8160-2602-5.

This volume provides succinct, alphabetically arranged descriptions of 100 stage directors. By expanding the study historically and beginning with the earliest directors—Garrick, Goethe, and George II—and continuing to the most recent—Mark Lamos and Jerry Zaks—the author has produced a volume that is international in scope and comprehensive in historical perspective. Each of the entries contains biographical information, an analysis of the person's working methods and styles, summaries of the major productions, and selections for further reading. The entries are significant in their presentation of an artistic sense of the subject as opposed to concentrating only on biographical data. Also, through reading the entries one achieves a true understanding of the development of the role of the director, a knowledge of the many styles of theater that each practices, and an insight into the skills of a director. There are 88 black-and-white photographs plus an index and a bibliography. This is a highly useful and recommended volume. [R: Choice, Dec 94, p. 577; RBB, July 94, pp. 1974-75; SLJ, Dec 94, p. 146; WLB, Oct 94, p. 80]—**Jackson Kesler**

991.   **Notable Women in the American Theatre: A Biographical Dictionary**. Alice M. Robinson, Vera Mowry Roberts, and Milly S. Barranger, eds. Westport, Conn., Greenwood Press, 1989. 993p. index. $99.50. PN2285.N65. 792'.082. LC 89-17065. ISBN 0-313-27217-4.

Paging through this volume provides the reader with an overview of women's contributions to the American theater and shows how notable and substantial these have been. Including some 325 individuals either born in the United States or associated with the American theater, the selection is limited to women whose achievements were important, influential, and pioneering. Biographies of 145 actresses summarize the stage careers of America's foremost performers from the eighteenth century to the present. Perhaps even more revealing are the narratives describing and evaluating the careers of agents, critics, designers, directors, educators, playwrights, producers, managers, and administrators. These serve as reminders that women made important contributions to all aspects of the American theater.

Entries, written by 181 contributors, are consistent and well organized. Biographical data is followed by a summary of significant career achievements, and each entry concludes with a brief bibliographical essay identifying the most important primary and secondary sources pertinent to the individual. A moderately useful appendix listing individuals by place of birth is followed by a listing by profession. The index is a useful guide to individuals and subjects not treated in separate entries. This volume is an essential reference tool for women's and theater studies. [R: Choice, May 90, p. 1482; RBB, 1 Feb 90, p. 1116; RQ, Fall 90, pp. 130-31]—**Joyce Duncan Falk**

992.   Owen, Bobbi. **Costume Design on Broadway: Designers and Their Credits, 1915-1985**. Westport, Conn., Greenwood Press, 1987. 254p. illus. index. (Bibliographies and Indexes in the Performing Arts, No. 5). $49.95. LC 87-7515. ISBN 0-313-25524-5.

Many diverse talents combine to achieve the unique art form that is the theater. One of the least appreciated groups, costume designers, only gained union recognition in 1936, but gradually their contributions were acknowledged and documented. In this compilation, 1,021 designers who worked on Broadway in the seasons between 1915 and 1985 are profiled.

Biographical sketches, describing a designer's background, together with Broadway credits, are followed by 100 black-and-white renderings of selected designs. Only one criterion for inclusion was used—that at least one costume was designed for a Broadway production. The illustrations all represent costumes in their original state.

Three appendices cover the major awards in this field, including the Tony, Marharam, and Donaldson, with recipients and plays listed chronologically. An index of plays provides designers' names associated with that particular play, enhancing access.

Theater is a singularly collaborative medium, where the desired result can never be achieved by one or two types of artists. In order to broaden our understanding of it, it is necessary to document the contributions of myriad groups. *Costume Design on Broadway* is taking an important step in that direction.—**Anita Zutis**

993.   Owen, Bobbi. **Lighting Design on Broadway: Designers and Their Credits, 1915-1990**. Westport, Conn., Greenwood Press, 1991. 159p. index. (Bibliographies and Indexes in the Performing Arts, no.11). $39.95. PN2091.E4094. 792'.025'09227471. LC 91-24007. ISBN 0-313-26533-X.

This publication is Owen's third volume in an attempt to list all Broadway designers and their credits from 1915 to 1990. The focus of the book is on lighting designers; more than 400 are listed alphabetically and profiled with a biographical sketch. Also given is a chronological list of Broadway credits for lighting and for scenic and costume design when relevant. An introduction briefly surveys the development of the professional Broadway lighting designer since the earliest attempts at illumination in indoor theaters. Appendixes list winners of the three major awards in the field: Tony, Marharam, and American Theatre Wing Design. There is a selective bibliography on lighting design. The index provides access from play title to designer's name and, in doing so, indicates every play for which a lighting designer was credited. This is a comprehensive volume that enhances the author's other volumes on theater. It will be valuable to researchers and professionals in lighting design, related design areas, and theater history in general.—**Jackson Kesler**

994.   Owen, Bobbi. **Scenic Design on Broadway: Designers and Their Credits, 1915-1990**. West-port, Conn., Greenwood Press, 1991. 286p. illus. index. (Bibliographies and Indexes in the Performing Arts, no.10). $55.00. PN2096.A1094. 792'.025'09227471. LC 91-25254. ISBN 0-313-26534-8.

This volume continues the author's valuable and extensive project of profiling the designers who have worked on Broadway between the 1915-1916 and 1989-1990 seasons. This book follows the first volume, which was devoted to costume designers. There are more than 900 biographies of scenic designers arranged alphabetically, each of which contains a chronological list of credits in scenic design. Also listed are credits in lighting and costume design. An introduction surveys professional scenic design in the twentieth century, with attention devoted to the development of American design from the "New Stagecraft." The four appendixes list winners of the Tony, Maharam, American Theatre Wing Design, and Donaldson awards. There are a selected bibliography, an index of plays, and a section of 12 original renderings that span the period of the study.

This book is significant for its unique subject, careful research, and concise presentation of extensive data. Unquestionable, it will be a valuable source for those researching this period of American scenography. [R: Choice, Apr 92, p. 1212]—**Jackson Kesler**

995.   Smith, Ronald Lande. **The Stars of Stand-up Comedy: A Biographical Encyclopedia**. New York, Garland, 1986. 227p. illus. (Garland Reference Library of the Humanities, Vol. 364). $39.93. LC 84-48408. ISBN 0-8240-8803-2.

"A fellow walked up to me, he said, 'You see a cop around here?' I said, 'No,' He said, 'Stick 'em up.' " (Henny Youngman, p. 223). If Henny Youngman is not your favorite stand-up comic, keep looking through this book—it provides information on a comprehensive range of comics known in the United States and you should be able to find your favorites. This work is limited to stand-up comics, and the author notes that he excluded such people as "Jackie Gleason, Sid Caesar, and Danny Kaye, who have performed monologues or solo sketches on occasion; but are not stand-up specialists" (p.vii). Smith's book is comprehensive, although he admits that out of the 101 comics or comedy teams included, "the average reader may agree with 90 of my selections . . . but recall a few comics who deserve mention over some others. They have a legitimate case" (p. vii).

Arranged alphabetically, each entry includes a picture (sometimes a few); birth date and place; a listing of records, television, videos, and films; book biographies; any books written by the comedian or the comedy team; and a discussion, usually averaging two to three pages, of background, philosophy, and type of humor. The strength of this volume lies in the interesting, informative, and readable text; one could have an enjoyable time flipping from one entry to another, culling facts not only about the comics but also about social mores, history, and the American character. Not all of the comics tell PG jokes, however, and the reader should be warned that some of the entries, in relating the humor of the comics they discuss, could be offensive.

Comics included range from old timers such as Moms Mabley, Groucho Marx, and Smith and Dale, to currently popular figures such as Eddie Murphy, Lily Tomlin, Richard Pryor, and Bill Cosby. The "Sick-Niks," such as Lenny Bruce, Tom Lehrer, and Shelley Berman, are well represented, as are more mainstream and well-known figures, such as Bob Hope, Phyllis Diller, Sam Levensen, and Steve Allen. The information seems well researched and reliable, although two Woody Allen movies were mentioned in the text but omitted from the list of movies. As a one-volume, sturdily bound reference to a topic often discussed only as a subgrouping of vaudeville, variety shows, or film, this work would be a most useful-and-fun purchase.—**Gloria Palmeri Powell**

996.   **Stage Deaths: A Biographical Guide to International Theatrical Obituaries, 1850 to 1990**. George B. Bryan, comp. Westport, Conn., Greenwood Press, 1991. 2v. index. (Bibliographies and Indexes in the Performing Arts, no.9). $135.00/set. Z5781.S76. 791'.092'2. LC 91-10304. ISBN 0-313-27593-9.

Much of the history of the theater is a reflection of the lives of its artists. While biographical sources are readily available on well-known personalities, obituaries are often the only sources of information on more obscure lives. They are a unique feature of this guide, which encompasses actors, directors, playwrights, composers, and other theater participants who died between 1850 and 1990. Each entry contains biographical data: alternate names, family information, birth and death dates, and theatrical work done. Sources of obituaries and death notices in selected Anglo-American newspapers and any book-length biographies in English are included. Extensive cross-references lead readers to the main citation of interest.

Such a compilation represents a contribution to regional theater history by providing access to sources of information about lesser-known figures comprising that history. These volumes are intended for theater and reference collections and will be corrected and augmented by future editions. [R: Choice, Dec 91, p. 578; RBB, 15 Oct 91, p. 468]—**Anita Zutis**

997. **Theatrical Directors: A Biographical Dictionary**. John W. Frick and Stephen M. Vallillo, eds. Westport, Conn., Greenwood Press, 1994. 567p. index. $85.00. PN2205.T54. 792'.0232'0922. LC 93-1138. ISBN 0-313-27478-9.

This volume is a compilation of alphabetically arranged biographical sketches of over 300 individuals, both historical and contemporary, who have distinguished themselves as stage directors. Information about each person includes a succinct overview of the subject's life; a list of accomplishments, awards, and productions; and a bibliography. The author of each entry is identified. There are two appendixes: a chronological list of directors, and directors listed by the countries in which their primary stage work was done. A selected bibliography and an index of names and plays complete the volume.

The most formidable task facing the editors of any such compilation is the selection of the subjects. An advisory board assisted the editors in this process. Inevitably, users of the volume will discover that some of their favorites were overlooked. Nevertheless, there is no question that the directors included merit notice. The entries are well written, and even though the data could be obtained from other sources, it is most helpful to have them compiled in this one accessible volume. Most students and theater generalists will find this book useful. [R: Choice, Nov. 94, p. 438; LJ, 1 Feb. 94, p. 71; RBB, 15 Mar. 94, p. 1395; RBB, July 94, p. 1967; WLB, Oct. 94, p. 80]—**Jackson Kesler**

998. **Theatrical Designers: An International Biographical Dictionary**. Thomas J. Mikotowicz, ed. Westport, Conn., Greenwood Press, 1992. 365p. index. $65.00. PN2096. A1AM54. 792'.025'03. LC 91-28086. ISBN 0-313-26270-5.

This volume presents biographical and analytical data on the editor's selection of the 270 most important set, costume, and lighting designers and theater architects from the fifteenth century to the present. The entrants are international in scope, but an emphasis is placed on United States and Western European subjects. Entrants are designated as to the particular fields of design in which they excelled and their dates, countries of birth, biographical sketches (including professional experience), and awards, plus suggestions for further reading when available. The author of each entry is identified. An entry's length reflects the designer's importance and available data. The alphabetically arranged listing is preceded by a historical survey on the evolution of theatrical design. There are three appendixes: a list of the designers chronologically by birth date; a list by country of birth; and periodicals and theater collections. There are an index and an annotated general bibliography on theatrical design and designers.

The value of this volume is found in the wide scope of its entrants, the concise presentation of vital data, and its unique subject. Researchers will undoubtedly find it useful as a quick reference and guide to sources for more in-depth investigation.—**Jackson Kesler**

999. **Who's Who in the Theatre: A Biographical Record of the Contemporary Stage**. Edited by Ian Herbert, with Christine Baxter and Robert E. Finley. Detroit, Gale, 1912- . 2v. index. $200.00/set for recent edition.

Who's Who in the Theatre is published in two folio-sized volumes and published by Gale; the title becomes a companion volume to *Notable Names in the American Theatre,* published by James T. White Company, later co-distributed by Gale, and still in print. The arrangement for the biographical entries had always been the same for the Who's Whos covering the two worlds of the English-speaking stage, but now the uniformity of all phases of the publications leads one to suspect a future melding in which two massive volumes might cover the entire English-speaking stage.

The *Playbills* volume has fifteen sections. Although the London and New York lists are the most useful and include off-West End and fringe, and off- and off-off-Broadway, the Shakespeare festivals lists, the several long-run lists, and the theatre buildings lists are valuable additions to a remarkable compilation.

This volume can be supplemented by *Theatre World* (Crown, 1946- . Annual. $60.00) edited by John Willis. *Theatre World* provides a record of performances, casts, and other information primarily for New York theatre, and includes many biographical sketches of actors and actresses.—**Richard M. Buck and Robert L. Wick**

1000.   Willis, John. **Theatre World**. New York, Crown, 1945- . illus. index. $35.00 for recent edition. ISSN 0032-1559.

Theatre World continues to provide a complete list of Broadway productions and personnel, including actors, replacements, producers, directors, authors, composers, costume designers, lighting technicians, press agents, and opening and closing dates for plays presented between 1 June and 31 May each year. Also included are numerous photographs of the plays and their players, and hundreds of short biographies. Off-Broadway, touring companies, and regional theater productions are included as well. The entire work is tied together with a thorough index.

Virtually any question involving who does what in the theater world can be answered with this volume. A standard reference work, recommended for performing arts reference collections.—**Daniel Uchitelle and Robert L. Wick**

19 Folklore and Mythology

INTRODUCTION

All entries in this chapter fall under the heading General Works, with no subdivisions. A major new title in the folklore field is *American Folklore: An Encyclopedia* (Garland, 1996) (see entry 1002), edited by Jan Harold Brunvand, a respected scholar in the field of folklore. This title combines information on real people in the field of folklore, such as storytellers, scholars, and musicians, with information on the mythological and folklore characters themselves.

Oxford University Press covers the world of mythology with two titles, Michael Grant and John Hazel's *Who's Who in Classical Mythology* (Oxford University Press, 1993) (see entry 1003) and Egerton Sykes's *Who's Who in Non-Classical Mythology*, revised by Alan Kendall (Oxford University Press, 1993) (see entry 1005). A more specialized, narrowly focused title is *Who's Who in Egyptian Mythology*, 2d ed., by Anthony S. Mercatante (Scarecrow, 1995) (see entry 1006).

Some other recent titles, though not strictly biographical and thus not included in this volume, can also be helpful in finding information about figures in folklore. Among them are *Dictionary of World Myth* by Peter Bently (New York, Facts on File, 1996) and *The Larousse Dictionary of World Folklore* by Alison Jones (New York, Larousse, 1995).

GENERAL WORKS

1001.   Aghion, Irène, Claire Barbillon, and François Lissarrague. **Gods and Heroes of Classical Antiquity**. New York, Flammarion; distr., Abbeville Press, 1996. 317p. illus. index. (Flammarion Iconographic Guides). $45.00. ISBN 2-08013-581-3.

Gods and Heroes of Classical Antiquity is intended for readers who love art, as well as individuals simply curious about the subject. Originally published in French (in 1994) under the title *Héros et Dieux de l'Antiquité*, it is a handsomely presented iconographic guide to the most famous themes in Greek and Roman myth and history as represented in ancient and modern art since antiquity. *Gods and Heroes* provides ready if preliminary access to the narrative content of numerous works of art that readers are likely to encounter in either books or museums. Authors Aghion, Barbillon, and Lissarrague reach beyond the art (illustrated with beautiful color and black-and-white photographs) and back into the legends and tales that served as a source of inspiration for the artists themselves.

With that in mind, the tales are arranged alphabetically to assist readers looking for particular information. Latin spellings are used throughout, although some Greek names are retained when deemed absolutely essential. Cross-references are used where Greek names differ from Latin, as with Athena/Minerva or Dionysius/Bacchus. Translation of the names is also provided in the principal European languages. Multiepisodic legends with many characters are broken down, with episodes and characters receiving individual treatment. Each character entry entails a brief account of the relevant tradition, with particular attention paid to important features that help clarify the work of art. Mythic representation is discussed, with distinctions made between ancient and modern. In some instances, entries end with a list of attributes, cross-references to other entries, sources, and a concise bibliography. The section on sources, for example, notes the texts from which modern works of art derive, rather than all the texts that allude to a specific character and that the reader can find elsewhere in specific encyclopedias. Although books and articles about the iconography of a specific character are sometimes cited at the end of an entry, the principal iconographic repertories are placed in the general bibliography.

The authors of *Gods and Heroes of Classical Antiquity* have aimed for a modest and practical guide for the reader with a will to explore and learn something new. Their volume will clearly meet that goal. [R: Choice, May 97, p. 1471]—**Arthur Gribben**

1002.   **American Folklore: An Encyclopedia**. Jan Harold Brunvand, ed. New York, Garland, 1996. 794p. illus. index. (Garland Reference Library of the Humanities, v.1551). $95.00. ISBN 0-8153-0751-9.

Packed with entries on folklorists, multiracial performers, crafts, music, and academic discussion, this comprehensive folklore encyclopedia is useful, accessible to most readers, and informative. The layout offers wide columns, pleasant typefaces, guide words, and simple pagination. The editor excels at inclusion of customs from many racial and ethnic backgrounds. Coverage is thorough—from maritime folklore and zydeco to verse, quilts, baskets, proverbs, odori, riddles, and folkways; from Mormon and Jewish lore to Burl Ives, John Lomax, Johnny Appleseed, Austin Fife, and Leadbelly (Huddie Ledbetter).

Above all, the encyclopedia is scholarly. Based on the work of 263 experts from mostly U.S. communities, independent scholars and lecturers, colleges, universities, the Smithsonian Institution, and the Library of Congress, signed entries consist of topic, discussion, and references. Photographs—although grainy and blurred in the case of antique sources—are broad-based, ranging from powwows, roughnecks, and cross-dressers to a Russian Sunday school, xeroxlore, the jitterbug, checkers, street preaching, and Elliot Wigginton's Foxfire writers rebuilding a mountain cabin. Most entries are succinct, lively, and substantiated with anecdotes, lyrics, jokes, advertisements, models, and dialogue.

However, a modest entry on Mark Twain is surprisingly poor; information on Joel Chandler Harris fails to mention the Walt Disney film *Song of the South,* which uses a beloved beast fable in the first cinema blend of acting and animation. The absence of Calamity Jane, Jackie Torrance, and Datsolali is puzzling; also wanting is commentary on Paul Green and Kermit Hunter, founders of outdoor historical pageants. The editor could further strengthen this work with clearer illustrations, a few maps, pronunciation guides, and cross-referencing, but overall, the encyclopedia reads well in its current form. [R: Choice, Oct 96, p. 247; RBB, Aug 96, pp. 1920-21; VOYA, Dec 96, p. 298]—**Mary Ellen Snodgrass**

1003.   Grant, Michael, and John Hazel. **Who's Who in Classical Mythology**. New York, Oxford University Press, 1993. 367p. $14.95pa. BL715.G68. 292.1'3'03. ISBN 0-19-521030-1.

Who's Who in Classical Mythology is a reprint of the 1973 volume published in England under the same title and in the United States as *Gods and Mortals in Classical Mythology* (see ARBA 74, entry 1205). It provides well-written descriptions of the major characters of Greek and Roman mythology. Major figures receive entries of up to a few pages in length, although most entries are a paragraph long. No illustrations are included, unlike the original edition, but a set of family trees and a brief bibliography are appended. The book will serve popular and ready-reference usage, but it lacks scholarly apparatus, such as references to the classical texts.

Libraries already owning more substantial books, such as *Crowell's Handbook of Classical Mythology* (see ARBA 71, entry 1351) or Pierre Grimal's *Dictionary of Classical Mythology* (see ARBA 87, entry 1275), will find little new in Grant and Hazel's work. *Crowell's* and Grimal's dictionary additionally contain more detail, exact references to the classical literature, maps, and pronunciation guides.—**Christopher W. Nolan and Terry Ann Mood**

1004.   Monaghan, Patricia. **The New Book of Goddesses and Heroines**. 3d ed. Saint Paul, Minn., Llewellyn, 1997. 371p. illus. $19.95pa. ISBN 1-56718-465-0.

The stated purpose of this book is "to tell goddess myths and to describe goddess symbols." Monaghan pursues this goal with an alphabetical list of some 1,500 goddess figures and mythical heroines from around the world and throughout history. Written for the general reader, the entries provide basic information about the figures that is often presented in narrative, or story, form. Herein lies the weakness of the book, for the author does not pursue her subject in a detailed or scholarly manner. For example, the relatively lengthy entry on the Egyptian deity Isis summarizes a number of stories about the goddess, but does not convey her importance as creator of all things or her relationship to other mythologies and deities in ancient Mediterranean cultures (e.g., to the story of Mary's Egyptian journey).

A section new to this edition, "Culture of the Goddess," provides background material on the cultures from which the goddesses arose. Again, the material is very general, and one would be hard put to explain a practical application for the information. Another new section, "Names of the Goddess," cites some (but not all) of alternative spellings and names for many of the figures. There is also a list of "Feasts of the Goddess," a bibliography, and a topical section on "Symbols of the Goddess." Black-and-white photographs from Chicago's Field Museum of Natural History illustrate the text.

In a work this general, it would be helpful to cite sources for further study on each entry; however, that is not done. There is no index, nor are there cross-references. These omissions and the general nature of the book hamper its usefulness as a reference, but public libraries may want to consider it as a purchase for general readers interested in the topic.—**Barbara Ittner**

1005.   Sykes, Egerton. **Who's Who in Non-Classical Mythology**. Revised by Alan Kendall. New York, Oxford University Press, 1993. 235p. $14.95pa. BL303.S9. 291.1'3. ISBN 0-460-86136-0.

Sykes's dictionary, originally published in 1952 as *Everyman's Dictionary of Non-Classical Mythology,* has been minimally revised in this edition with the addition of some entries, some minor textual changes, and some unexplained deletions of entries. The volume's entries are quite short—usually one or two sentences long. Most of the text is helpful, but some entries do not indicate the nationality or cultural origin of the topic. The title is somewhat misleading, as there are entries not only for names of personal figures but also for places, customs, and creation legends. The range of mythologies covered is quite wide, although European and Near Eastern myths receive the largest amount of space. A good bibliography of narrative sources is provided.

The work does a good job of briefly describing the story behind mythological figures and is easy to use, unlike some topically oriented sources such as *Larrousse World Mythology* (Hamlyn, 1965). Sykes's volume exists in a subject having fewer good sources of this type and might be more useful, although other good works include *Dictionary of World Mythology* (see ARBA 81, entry 1132, for review of an earlier edition) and the eclectic but uneven *Facts on File Encyclopedia of World Mythology and Legend* (see ARBA 89, entry 1250).— **Christopher W. Nolan and Terry Ann Mood**

1006.   **Who's Who in Egyptian Mythology**. 2d ed. By Anthony S. Mercatante. R. S. Bianchi, ed. Metuchen, N.J., Scarecrow, 1995. 231p. illus. $32.50. ISBN 0-8108-2967-3.

Bianchi, the editor and reviser of this edition, "decided against a revision . . . and . . . made only those slight changes" needed to reflect more recent scholarship (p. vii). Thus, the comments by the reviewer of the 1st edition (see ARBA 80, entry 1091) still stand. The modifications for this edition occur in the annotated bibliography and involve the elimination of some truly outdated materials (e.g., the works of E. A. Wallis Budge), while adding materials published since 1978. In these revisions, the editor neglected, however, to correct the spelling of Serge Sauneron's name, to add the important 3d volume of Miriam Lichtheim's *Ancient Egyptian Literature* (University of California Press, 1973-1980), and to note that both Alan Gardiner's *Egyptian Grammar* (Oxford University Press) and James Pritchard's *Ancient Near Eastern Texts Relating to the Old Testament* (Princeton University Press) each appeared in 3d editions with significant changes in 1969. Most important, the revised bibliography includes no translation of the *Book of the Dead* (R. O. Faulkner's *Book of the Dead* [1972] being a good example).

Although a library can certainly benefit from having Mercatante's book in either the 1st or 2d edition, George Hart's *Dictionary of Egyptian Gods and Goddesses* (Routledge, 1986), though lacking the annotated bibliography and the full narratives of various tales, provides a better compendium of the mythological world of the ancient Egyptians.—**Susan Tower Hollis**

20   Philosophy and Religion

INTRODUCTION

Only a few titles are included under Philosophy in this chapter. Two major ones are general directories of philosophers, one with an international scope, one limited to American philosophers: *International Directory of Philosophy and Philosophers* (Philosophy Documentation Center, Bowling Green State University, 1965-) (see entry 1010) and *Directory of American Philosophers* (Philosophy Documentation Center, Bowling Green State University, 1962-63) (see entry 1010). Both are serials. Of course, a major source not included in this bibliography also contains much biographical information: the old and respected *Encyclopedia of Philosophy* (Macmillan, 1967; supplement, 1996).

In the Religion category, there are many more offerings, sources that cover specific religions, denominations, religious leaders, and historical figures. Several international directories are reviewed in this chapter, many of them offering international coverage. *Who's Who in Religion* (Marquis Who's Who/Reed Reference Publishing, 1975/76-) (see entry 1019) has basic biographical information on 15,600 figures in a standard Who's Who format. Smaller in scope, but giving what the reviewer calls "chatty" entries, which provide some sense of the personality as well as biographical facts, are *Seeds in the Wilderness: Profiles of World Religious Leaders* by Marty Gervais (Quarry Press, 1994) (see entry 1014) and *Who's Who of World Religions* (Simon & Schuster Academic Reference Division, 1991-) (see entry 1020), which—again according to the reviewer—gives more space than do other directories to religions other than Christianity.

American religious personalities are covered in *Dictionary of American Religous Biography*, 2d ed. (Greenwood Press, 1993) (see entry 1013), with sketches of 550 people, all of them deceased before July 1, 1992.

Books devoted to bible studies, religious denominations, and saints are also listed in this chapter. Under The Bible and Biblical Studies, both old and new testament figures have books devoted to them: *Who's Who in the New Testament* by Ronald Brownrigg (Oxford University Press, 1993) (see entry 1021) and *Who's Who in the Old Testament, Together with the Apocrapha* by Joan Comay (Oxford University Press, 1993) (see entry 1022). Denominations with directories include Baptist, Presbyterianism, Judaism, and Catholicism, while the Holiness-Pentacostal movement within African-American churches also merits a separate book: *Biographical Dictionary of African American, Holiness-Pentacostals 1880-1990*, edited by Sherry Sherrod DuPree (Middle Atlantic Regional Press, 1989) (see entry 1026).

Books about saints abound in this edition. One is by Oxford University Press: *The Oxford Dictionary of Saints*, edited by David Hugh Farmer, 3d ed. (Oxford University Press, 1992) (see entry 1045). Another compilation of saints is by the Benedictine Monks of St. Augustine's Abbey, Ramsgate, *The Book of Saints: A Dictionary of Servants of God* (Morehouse, 1989) (see entry 1041).

PHILOSOPHY

General Works

1007.   Bales, Eugene F. **A Ready Reference to Philosophy East and West**. Lanham, Md., University Press of America, 1988. 289p. index. $24.50. ISBN 0-8191-6640-4.

"Ready-reference" can mean a multitude of things, but here it refers to an outline history of philosophy that mainly strings together brief summaries of individual philosophers and, to some extent, schools of philosophy. These summaries are comparable in length and content to the alphabetically arranged entries typically found in single-volume philosophical dictionaries, notably Antony Flew's *Dictionary of Philosophy* (see ARBA 80, entry 1086), although Bales includes more individuals than Flew or any other current dictionary. To this extent, then, Bales's "ready-reference" might function somewhat similarly to a dictionary, with the advantage of placing each summary within its appropriate historical context. This function, moreover, is facilitated by two "quick alphabetical indexes" placed in the front, one to philosophers and another to philosophical theories and movements. On the other hand, it is possible to describe this as simply an exceptionally compressed history, and not necessarily to be treated as a reference work. Aimed at undergraduate philosophy students and the general reader, it is competently done, though it lacks the authoritative touch of most compact histories turned out by more "mainstream" publishers. The inclusion of Eastern philosophy (here confined to Indian and Chinese) along with Western philosophy in a single volume is a fairly unusual benefit, as is the attention to Russian philosophy under twentieth-century Western philosophy. This is the sort of work that comes in handy now and then, even if it cannot be recommended as a priority acquisition for most libraries. [R: Choice, May 88, p. 1378]—**Hans E. Bynagle**

1008. Collinson, Diané. **Fifty Major Philosophers: A Reference Guide**. New York, Croom Helm/Methuen, 1987. 170p. $29.95; $11.95pa. LC 87-8929. ISBN 0-7099-3466-1; 0-7099-4871-9pa.

For general readers unfamiliar with philosophical inquiry and terminology, this volume serves a useful purpose. The author has designed a reference guide with the modest ambition of helping the reader "briefly to share something of the point of view of each philosopher" (preface). The fifty philosophers selected span more than 2,000 years of the Western tradition, beginning with Thales in the sixth century B.C. and concluding with Sartre in the latter half of the twentieth century.

A brief biography follows an initial statement of the philosopher's thought. Each entry is restricted to discussing only one or two aspects of a philosopher's thought, and mentioning the relationship to other philosophical work. The emphasis is on piquing the nonspecialist's curiosity to pursue further inquiry. Following each entry are a "Notes" list, cross-references to other philosophers in the text, a description of the philosopher's major writings, and a brief list of "Further Readings." The text itself is readable, concise, and nontechnical. A glossary of about fifty terms assists the reader with some basic philosophical concepts.

Within this framework the guide should prove functional for its users.—**Bernice Bergup**

1009. Collinson, Diané, and Robert Wilkinson. **Thirty-Five Oriental Philosophers**. New York, Routledge, 1994. 205p. $65.00. ISBN 0-415-02596-6.

As Collinson and Wilkinson admit in their introduction to this slim volume, the term *Oriental* tends to conflate the meaning of several distinct philosophical traditions, suggesting that they all, in some manner, share a common mode of philosophical thought. Apart from a central concern with ethics, however, such is not the case, as this volume, with its brief descriptions of the thought of the main figures of Asian philosophy, will attest.

Divided into five main sections, this work covers representative philosophers from the various Islamic, Indian, Tibetan, Chinese, and Japanese traditions. Each entry provides a three- to five-page elaboration and discussion of a particular philosopher's views. Technical philosophical terms are highlighted within the text, and a glossary is included at the end of the volume to further explain the meaning of these terms. Brief two- to four-item primary and secondary bibliographies are included at the end of each entry. There is, as well, a general bibliography at the end of the volume.

The main attraction of this work is its concise and readable nature. Its main detractions include a limit to the number of philosophers covered (a few thinkers are conspicuously absent, e.g., Chuang Tzu) and the high price levied by the publishers for this relatively short work. The book is recommended for undergraduate collections in philosophy and religion, but probably is not needed for graduate collections.—**Mark Cyzyk**

1010.   **Directory of American Philosophers**. Bowling Green, Ohio, Philosophy Documentation Center, Bowling Green State University, 1962/63- . index. $109.00. ISSN 0070-508X.

International Directory of Philosophy and Philosophers. Bowling Green, Ohio, Philosophy Documentation Center, Bowling Green State University, 1965- . index. $89.00. ISSN 0074-4603.

These two works intend to provide current information on "philosophical activities" and are companion volumes, the first covering the United States and Canada and the second encompassing Europe, Central and South America, Asia, Africa, and Australia. Both are organized alphabetically by country under the same five categories (universities, centers and institutes, societies, journals, and publishers) and were compiled by collecting responses to questionnaires. Recent editions of the two works differ from their predecessors in that they include a complete list of names and addresses of philosophers. Each concludes with five indexes, one for each of the five categories treated. The type is clear and the binding sturdy. The list of names and addresses of philosophers should prove especially useful to reference librarians, as should the listing of faculty with their specializations for each university or college department in which philosophy is taught. Similarly, there is a wealth of information included about journals that are devoted to the study of philosophy (e.g., editor, aim, sponsoring organization, details for manuscript submission, subscription data). Both directories are updated and published biennially.

Although both works may be recommended (primarily to college and university libraries), they suffer from what may be a too-mechanical method of compilation. For example, is it necessary to include extensive lists of graduate assistants in the major university programs (e.g., Duke University), or the one faulty member who teaches general studies in a small technical school (e.g., Forsyth Technical College), or the religion faculty of schools with little orientation to philosophy (e.g., Abilene Christian University)? By the same token, while some schools of theology are included, many significant ones are not (e.g., Candler School of Theology), in spite of the fact that they often include renowned faculty who teach philosophy of religion or other theological subjects that are largely philosophical in nature. Consequently, the directories are unnecessarily large, include the names of people who by no means consider themselves primarily as philosophers, and neglect important scholars who specialize in philosophy.—**M. Patrick Graham and Terry Ann Mood**

1011.   Kersey, Ethel M. **Women Philosophers: A Bio-Critical Source Book**. Westport, Conn., Greenwood Press, 1989. 230p. index. $49.95. B105.W6K47. l09'.2'2. LC 88-24615. ISBN 0-313-25720-5.

Kersey's book fills the need for a work that brings together biographical information about women who have written and taught in the field of philosophy. Kersey defines philosophy to include traditional areas such as ethics, metaphysics, epistemology, and aesthetics, but omits writers on the philosophy of women, since there is other literature on them. Kersey's work is primarily historical, and thus few women born since 1920 are included. Almost all the women fall within the tradition of Western thought.

In the preface Kersey clearly delineates the scope of the work, and her introduction provides an historical essay characterizing the main themes of women philosophers. The work is organized alphabetically by the name of the philosopher, and includes a name index and an outline of the women by historical period, country, and discipline or subject of writings. A list of reference sources is also provided. Each biographical entry includes birth and death dates (where applicable), educational background, a listing of works by and about the philosopher, and some details of her life. The main body of the entry is a well-written synopsis of the philosopher's main ideas in the context of the thought of her time.

Kersey's discussion of her criteria for inclusion in the sourcebook leaves open the question of whether the definition of philosophy itself will change as more women become involved in the discipline. A further volume covering contemporary thought may well include feminist writers in philosophy because the boundaries of the field will change thanks to these very writers. This excellent resource belongs in all academic and larger public library collections and will be useful to those interested in philosophy and in women's studies.—**Joan B. Fiscella**

United States

1012.   **Directory of American Philosophers**. Bowling Green, Ohio, Philosophy Documentation Center, Bowling Green State University, l962/63- . index. $59.00; $99.00 (Institutions). ISSN 0070-508X.

This well-established biennial directory has been in continuous publication since 1963, and its organization has changed little over the years (see ARBA 91, entry 1406). Philosophy departments in the United States and Canada are arranged by state or province. Each entry lists the department's address, type of university it is affiliated with, enrollment, highest degree offered, and telephone number. Next, the faculty are listed with degrees, rank, and specialties. Professors emeriti are the final element in the department's listing. This is followed by sections on assistantships, centers and institutions, societies, journals, and publishers. Names and addresses of philosophers are in separate listings, divided into those with and without institutional affiliation. There is also a brief statistical table that summarizes the data in the volume. Each section is thoroughly indexed. This directory remains a useful, well-organized, attractively presented, and up-to-date reference source.

See also the review of *International Directory of Philosophy and Philosophers* (entry 1010) in this chapter.—**Jeffrey R. Luttrell and Terry Ann Mood**

RELIGION

General Works

1013.   Bowden, Henry Warner. **Dictionary of American Religious Biography**. 2d ed. Westport, Conn., Greenwood Press, 1993. 686p. index. $75.00. BL72.B68. 209'.2'2. LC 92-35524. ISBN 0-313-27825-3.

The first edition of this dictionary (see ARBA 78, entry 999) contained biographies of 425 significant American religious figures who had died prior to July 1, 1976. In this revision Bowden has added 125 biographies and extended the terminus *ad quem* for inclusion to July 1, 1992. Among the new names are William F. Albright, Edgar Cayce, Fanny Crosby, L. Ron Hubbard, and Alan Watts. All of the original articles were retained, and 350 of them were at least slightly revised in content or in the bibliographies following each article. Two other changes were made: the addition of a selected general bibliography at the end of the volume, and the separation of the alphabetical sections of the dictionary.

Bowden attempts to be pluralistic in his choices of people to include, and biographies are entered for not only clergy (although clergy predominate), but for laypeople as well; not only whites but blacks, Asian-Americans, and Indians; not only members of standard denominations but free thinkers, theists, and cult members.

As with the first edition, the articles are well written, and they are just long enough to summarize the interesting and important facets of the biographees' lives and to whet the reader's appetite for more. The biographical references listed at the end of each article direct the reader to additional (usually fuller) sources, when these are available. In some cases there are few, if any, sources listed because a particular person is not included in the standard reference sources chosen by Bowden. This scarcity of information on some of the individuals makes one wish that the author had increased his pool of standard sources. This, however, is not a major complaint and in no way detracts from the overall value and utility of the dictionary. Recommended. [R: Choice, Nov 93, pp. 423-24; RBB, 15 Oct 93, p. 470]—**Craig W. Beard and Terry Ann Mood**

1014.   Gervais, Marty. **Seeds in the Wilderness: Profiles of World Religious Leaders**. Kingston, Ont., Quarry Press, 1994. 277p. illus. $19.95pa. ISBN 1-55082-110-5.

Gervais's book on religious leaders fills a felt need for more of this kind of information. The book is better than *Who's Who in Religion* (see ARBA 94, entry 1510) but not as good as *Religious Leaders of America* (see ARBA 92, entry 1402). Gervais's book is different from the latter in that it covers a more intentional flavor of candidates, but far fewer and is far more subjective.

Contained herein are leaders such as Rabbi Kahane, Jerry Falwell, Mother Teresa, Charles Templeton, Chuck Colson, Pope John Paul II, Norman Vincent Peale, and more. The net to seine these depths is fathomless: Dr. Benjamin Spock is a religious leader, as are Desmond Tutu and Nancy Manahan and Rosemary Curb (of the Lesbian Nuns) and Andrew M. Greeley (he of the "sex as religious expression" club). The book's strength and weakness are in its chattiness.

These are not scholarly sketches, but they are thoughtful ones. The book may serve collections better as a supplement as one reporter's view of public figures, some of whom are religious, than as a bona fide biographical reference tool.—**Mark Y. Herring**

1015.   Holte, James Craig. **The Conversion Experience in America: A Sourcebook on Religious Conversion Autobiography**. Westport, Conn., Greenwood Press, 1992. 228p. index. $59.95. BV4930. H65. 291.4'2. LC 91-32173. ISBN 0-313-26680-8.

Holte, an Associate Professor of English at East Carolina University, has produced a concise, eloquently written, and scholarly volume that deserves a much wider readership than its price is likely to allow. His work contains 5- to 10-page alphabetically arranged entries on 30 American religious autobiographers who have written about their conversion experiences. Each entry is subdivided into 4 sections: "Biography" (a 200-600 word introduction to the life and times of the autobiographer), "The Autobiography" (a 1,000-2,000 word discussion of the narrative), "Criticism" (a 200-500 word summation of how scholars have interpreted and assessed the significance of the piece), and "Bibliography" (an unannotated listing of related sources about the subject). The volume concludes with a brief bibliographic essay and index.

While the volume covers 350 years of conversion narratives, it is weighted in favor of twentieth-century writers. Seventeen of the thirty subjects published their works this century, and 11 were born in the quarter-century between 1915 and 1940. This modern focus gives the volume a mass-market appeal but limits its usefulness for readers interested primarily in American religious autobiography during the seventeenth through nineteenth centuries. The work includes entries on men and women from a wide variety of ethnic and religious backgrounds. Seven of the subjects are female; nine are minority voices.

Twenty-two belong to a Protestant denomination; four are Roman Catholic; the remaining four represent the black Muslim, Shaker, Native American, and Buddhist religious traditions. Taken together, the entries demonstrate the great diversity of American conversion experiences. Recommended for college, university, and community libraries. [R: Choice, Nov 92, p. 444]—**Terry D. Bilhartz**

1016.   **National Directory of Christian Artists**. 1986 ed. By Fred Littauer. Eugene, Oreg., Harvest House, 1985. 264p. illus. index. $9.95pa. LC 85-80487. ISBN 0-89091-490-2.

A first effort of its kind, this directory lists and describes approximately 235 individuals and groups-all of whom have "received Jesus Christ as Lord and Savior" (p. 11). Entries are arranged, one to a page, alphabetically within five categories: speakers, evangelists, individual musicians, musical groups, and visual artists. More than half appear in the first category, though many having dual gifts are entered in more than one category in the index, which is enhanced by the additional classifications of authors and comedians.

Most entries appear by personal name, though some individuals are listed by corporate name, and generally include a small promotional photo, address and telephone number, brief biographical sketch, preferred audience, titles or subjects of possible presentations, publications or recordings, quotations from testimonials of previous engagements, the geographical area of ministry, range of fees (indicated by code), and names, addresses, and telephone numbers for up to three references. The entries naturally vary in the amount of data included.

The people listed in this work represent a wide array of available "born again" performers, suitable for churches, schools, and related groups needing inspirational programming. A testimonial letter printed at the beginning suggests that many are lesser known performers who are looking for wider exposure and full-time employment. Some, perhaps many, are undistinguished outside of fundamentalist circles, but others are better known. The president of Campus Crusade for Christ's theological schools is there, as is "a former fashion coordinator, model and pageant winner" who helps others "discover their Total Image in Christ." Surprises in the listings include basso Jerome Hines, pianist Ken Medema, illusionist Andre Kole, and the popular musical group Liberated Wailing Wall—all of which have achieved notable success by any standard. Since the biographical sketches were apparently written by the respondents themselves, they abound with the typical hype of a public relations release. A number of artists are associated with C.L.A.S.S. Speakers (not explained), which has the same address as the editor in San Bernardino, California.

This work will be of some use to churches and other organizations requiring religious entertainment.—**Donald G. Davis, Jr.**

1017.   **Twentieth-Century Dictionary of Christian Biography**. J. D. Douglas, ed. Grand Rapids, Mich., Baker Book House, 1995. 439p. $24.99. ISBN 0-8010-3031-5.

This work contains approximately 800 signed brief biographical sketches of "Christians who lived during, or whose lives extended into, the present century" (p. 12). It includes people, both living and dead, who by profession are (or were) ministers, theologians, and missionaries, as well as lawyers, social reformers, educators, historians, scientists, writers, and so forth. In addition to presenting the basic biographical facts, the writers also evaluate the individual's impact on the world of his or her time. Major writings (if any) are mentioned within each sketch, and when there is a published biography, it is listed at the end of the entry.

Any biographical dictionary that is this brief—even one that is as limited in scope as this one is—cannot discuss everyone who might be designated a twentieth-century Christian. Even among famous or important individuals, choices must be made. No doubt, everyone who looks at this dictionary can find someone who might have been chosen but was not. The editors acknowledge this. However, within the constraints of size, there is fair representation of the theological spectrum. Conservatives and liberals; Catholics and Protestants; and people from the First, Second, and Third Worlds are profiled.

The sketches are well written. Some of them—especially those by general editor Douglas—are even lively. There is one glaring technical omission—no cross-references. Even though mention of one included biographee is frequently made in the entry for another, readers cannot tell immediately if a sketch on the former is included in this dictionary. Also, a factual error was noted: No mention is made of C. Everett Koop's stepping down as surgeon general in 1989.

Biographical information on some of the people chosen for inclusion in this work can be found in other reference volumes, such as *New 20th-Century Encyclopedia of Religious Knowledge* (see ARBA 92, entry 1417); *Dictionary of American Religious Biography* (see ARBA 94, entry 1509); and *Handbook of Evangelical Theologians* (see ARBA 95, entry 1461). In addition, the entries in the latter two—especially *Handbook*—have more information than the work under review. However, the *Twentieth-Century Dictionary of Christian Biography* will serve as a supplemental source. —**Craig W. Beard**

1018.   **Twentieth-Century Shapers of American Popular Religion**. Charles H. Lippy, ed. Westport, Conn., Greenwood Press, 1989. 494p. index. $65.00. BL2525.T84. 291'.092'2. LC 88-15487. ISBN 0-313-25356-0.

Objective reporting that includes the negative as well as the positive aspects of the biographees' lives makes this a most interesting reference volume. It reads easily, enticing the reader by the inclusion of realities which make some of the shapers very human indeed.

The editor points out the difficulty of selection of who to include in this work. It appears that a good selection has been made since 64 major figures in popular religion are here, even those recently vilified by personal peccadilloes. Included in this array are some who have been influential rather than directly involved, such as Sinclair Lewis (*Elmer Gantry*), Morris West, and John Foster Dulles. Each entry includes a biography, an appraisal of the person's contribution and importance to the field, and a survey of criticism. A bibliography of the writings by and about each person is an added benefit. The articles are brief but thorough. Each is written and signed by a knowledgeable scholar in the field; most of them are professors in institutes of higher education. A table of contents identifies the biographees and a complete index assists in finding specific information in the book.

Although expensive, the work is recommended for any library. It will have particularly valuable application in public library reference departments where questions about these individuals arise. [R: Choice, Sept 89, p. 96; LJ, 15 Mar 89, p. 69; RBB, 15 June 89, p. 1807]—**Edward P. Miller**

1019. **Who's Who in Religion**. New Providence, N.J., Marquis Who's Who/Reed Reference Publishing, 1975/76- . $129.00. LC 76-25357. ISSN 0160-3728.

This directory profiles living religious leaders—church officials, clergy, religious educators, and lay leaders—throughout the world. Individuals chosen for *Who's Who in Religion* are selected by the Marquis editorial staff, who examine "literature, communications media, and other available data sources" (preface) and solicit nominations from a 41-member board of advisers. Then the staff determines whether a person's religious work or achievement merits inclusion.

The following information is presented for each person when available and applicable: name, occupation, vital statistics, parents, marriage, children, education, professional certification, career, writings and creative works, civic and political activities, military service, awards and fellowships, professional and association memberships, clubs and lodges, political affiliation, home address, office address, and thoughts on life. Most of this information is supplied by the biographees. When they did not provide the information, it was researched and compiled by the editorial staff. These entries are identified by an asterisk.

When a work has proved to be as beneficial in meeting an information need as this one has, it almost seems petty to criticize it. However, one observation might be allowed. Although it would be impossible to include *all* current religious leaders, and some names will inevitably be left out, it is unclear why a number of "outstanding individuals" (preface) were not included (e.g., Robert Alter, Kurt Aland, Walter Brueggemann, Elizabeth Achtemeier). It is all the more baffling in light of the appearance of many relatively unknown names. That aside, *Who's Who in Religion* is still a recommended purchase for libraries with religion or extensive biographical collections.—**Craig W. Beard and Terry Ann Mood**

1020. **Who's Who of World Religions**. John R. Hinnells, ed. New York, Simon & Schuster Academic Reference Division, 1992. 560p. maps. index. $75.00. BL72.W54. 291'.092'2. LC 91-36866. ISBN 0-13-952946-2.

Biographical dictionaries abound for biblical and Christian notables but are hard to find for other religions. That palpable gap is filled to some extent by this volume, with its coverage from African religions to Zoroastrianism, and people from the mists of legend (e.g., Gilgamesh) to such contemporary religious leaders as the Maharishi, Sun Myung Moon, and Pope John Paul II. Not surprisingly, Christians take up most of the work, but an attempt has explicitly been made to provide balance by emphasizing non-Western Christians, and the terms C.E. and B.C.E. are used in place of B.C. and A.D.

Each entry provides full name, dates, indication of religious subject group, references to the extensive bibliographies, and a biographical sketch. Initials indicate the author of the entry, who can be found among the list of scholarly contributors in the front. Cross-references are somewhat haphazard. For example, Children of God's Moses David is found under his real name, David Berg, but there is no cross-reference, while there is from Khomeini, Ayatollah to Khumayni, Ayat Allah Ruh Allah (but not from Ayatollah Khomeini). Altogether, a nice balance is provided, not only among religions but also between teachers or founders of religions (e.g., Buddha, L. Ron Hubbard); the poets, artists, or singers of religions (e.g., J. S. Bach, Giotto); and between men and women (e.g., Sarah as well as Abraham; Nefertiti as well as Akhenaten). [R: Choice, June 92, p. 1531; LJ, 1 Feb 92, p. 82; RBB, 15 Mar 92, p. 1406; RQ, Summer 92, pp. 583-84]—**Johan Koren**

The Bible and Biblical Studies

1021. Brownrigg, Ronald. **Who's Who in the New Testament**. New York, Oxford University Press, 1993. 286p. $13.95pa. BS2430.B67. 225.9'22. ISBN 0-19-521031-X.

Similar to Joan Comay's *Who's Who in the Old Testament* (Oxford University Press, 1993), to which this is a companion volume, Brownrigg's book is a reprint of the original 1971 publication (see ARBA 72, entry 1194). The extensive illustrations of the first printing have been eliminated, but otherwise the entries are unchanged. Articles on major figures are long, and recount various scholarly opinions, thus presenting an objective view. Libraries with standard biblical dictionaries and encyclopedias or those with a serviceable copy of the 1971 edition will have no need for this softcover version. Serious students and scholars will turn to the major biblical dictionaries, especially the recently published *Anchor Bible Dictionary* (Doubleday, 1992), for a more serious and occasionally more extensive treatment of these names, rather than rely on this volume, which is based on thin and now very much dated scholarship.—**Harold O. Forshey and Terry Ann Mood**

1022. Comay, Joan. **Who's Who in the Old Testament, Together with the Apocrypha**. New York, Oxford University Press, 1993. 398p. $15.95pa. BS570.C64. 221.9'2. ISBN 0-19-521029-8.

This is a softcover printing of a 1971 publication (see ARBA 72, entry 1198) without the extensive illustrations that appeared in the older work. Save for the deletion of the illustrations and acknowledgments related to them, the book is unchanged. Hence, the limited scholarship on which this work is based is now more than 20 years out-of-date. Particularly noticeable is the inconsistency and unreliability of the frequent translations of the names into English (e.g., the name "Abital," although borne by a woman, is translated as "father of dew"). Only libraries lacking some of the standard biblical dictionaries and a serviceable copy of the original printing would find this a useful addition. The recently published six-volume *Anchor Bible Dictionary* (Doubleday, 1992) is one of several more reliable and comprehensive alternatives. The companion volume by Ronald Brownrigg, *Who's Who in the New Testament* (see entry 1021), has simultaneously been republished in a softcover edition.—**Harold O. Forshey**

1023. Duchet-Suchaux, Gaston, and Michel Pastoureau. **The Bible and the Saints**. Paris, Flammarion; distr., New York, Abbeville Press, 1994. 360p. illus. (Flammarion Iconographic Guides). $24.95pa. ISBN 2-08013-575-9.

Christian art has been full of symbolism from its beginning, and those symbols can be bewildering in their number and complexity. Fortunately *The Bible and the Saints*, the first volume in the Flammarion Iconographic Guides series, has appeared to fill the need for a comprehensive introductory guide. Entries are arranged alphabetically and consist of saints, biblical personages, episodes from the Old and New Testaments, plants, animals, objects, allegorical figures, and ecclesiastical offices. Individual entries begin with alternative forms of the name (e.g., Magi followed by Three Kings and Three Wise Men). Entries are then divided into two main parts. The first part consists of either "Life and Legend" for saints or "Tradition" for biblical persons or scenes, and provides the historical or legendary background.

The second part is called "Representation and Iconography," which supplies various uses of the hagiographical or biblical scene through the ages and describes the motifs evolution. A list of cross-references and a brief bibliography conclude the entry. Black-and-white and color photographs of relevant works of art are generously scattered throughout the text. Numerous *see* references also guide the reader. A list of "Attributes and Their Associated Figures" and a bibliography conclude the volume. *The Bible and the Saints* is a well-organized and clearly written work that belongs in any library interested in religion and art history. It is also an attractive browser's delight that many individuals will want to purchase. [R: Choice, Feb 95, p. 914]—**Ronald H. Fritze**

1024. **Who's Who in Biblical Studies and Archaeology**. 2d ed. Washington, D.C., Biblical Archaeology Society, 1993. 360p. index. $39.95. LC 93073150. ISBN 1-880317-06-0.

This edition contains biographical information on around 2,000 "women and men of superior achievement and status" in contemporary biblical scholarship (introduction). Beyond this brief statement, there is no indication of the criteria for inclusion. In most cases the information was provided by the individual. Otherwise, data were gathered by the compilers. As one would expect, based on the title, the entries are sketches that list academic degrees, employment, memberships, publications, and the like. Rounding out the volume are indexes listing biographees by specialization and geographical location.

Those familiar with the fields of biblical study and biblical archaeology will recognize many of the names included here. They will also notice that several noted scholars are missing. A cursory examination revealed no entries for Elizabeth Achtemeier, Walter Brueggemann, Robert Gundry, Caal Holladay, William Lane, Peter O'Brien, Richard Oster, John Rogerson, Douglas Stuart, Mary Ann Tolbert, Hugh Williamson, John Willis, and several others. In addition, there are other things that escaped the editorial eye. There is apparently some material missing after line 21 of the entry for Scott Banchy. Leander Keck, who has been at Yale Divinity School since 1979, is shown to be still at Candler School of Theology, although his New Haven address is given and he is listed under Connecticut in the geographical index. Kikup Matsunaga is actually Kikuo Matsunaga.

There is, however, something positive to say about this work. A comparison of the "A" and "M" sections of *Who's Who in Biblical Studies and Archaeology* and *Who's Who in Religion 1992-1993* (see ARBA 94, entry 1510) revealed entries for 210 individuals that were unique to the former (many of whom are well known) and only 58 that appeared in both. Thus, despite the omissions and editorial oversights, this work provides data on biblical and archaeological scholars that are available in no other single source. If the compilers correct errors, add omitted names, and publish future editions on a more timely basis, this work will be a useful addition to religious studies reference collections.—**Craig W. Beard**

Denominations

1025.   Balmer, Randail, and John R. Fitzmier. **The Presbyterians**. Westport, Conn., Greenwood Press, 1993. 274p. index. (Denominations in America, no.5). $49.95. BX8935.B355. 285'.1. LC 92-17840. ISBN 0-313-26084-2.

A recent addition to the publisher's Denominations in America series, this volume follows the now familiar Greenwood Press formula. The authors begin with a very readable, narrative essay that historically surveys the Presbyterian tradition in the United States. This essay is remarkably well balanced, carefully documented, and thoughtfully succinct as it is, especially in the early and middle periods; however, the final section of the essay seems to tilt toward the ecumenical interests and trendy concerns of, and to neglect the contributions of, evangelicals within and without the principal denomination.

The biographical dictionary of Presbyterian leaders includes entries for 96 mostly deceased figures of varying importance to the denomination, such as Jane Addams and John Witherspoon. Ironically, the dissident Carl McIntire is the only living person to merit inclusion. Following the essential historical facts for each entry, the authors present a brief essay assessing the person's achievements and significance and conclude with references to the figure's major works and biographical references. A short denominational chronology, a helpful bibliographical essay, and an index conclude the volume.

This volume and series will be useful in collections serving collegiate religious and American studies programs, as well as to the general public where regional and local interests warrant. Research and theological libraries may well find these efforts convenient syntheses for review purposes. [R: Choice, Sept 93, p. 73]—**Donald G. Davis Jr.**

1026.   **Biographical Dictionary of African-American, Holiness-Pentecostals 1880-1990**. Sherry Sherrod DuPree, ed. and comp. Washington, D.C., Middle Atlantic Regional Press, 1989. 386p. illus. index. $39.95; $23.95pa. BX8762.Z8D86. 289.94'092'273. LC 89-12590. ISBN 0-9616056-0-X; 0-961-6056-9-3pa.

This paperback is an excellent addition to a growing body of literature on black religion. It contains over 1,000 biographical sketches of Americans from 1880 to 1990 who have contributed to the Holiness-Pentecostal movement among blacks. The overwhelming majority of the biographies are of black preachers, religious educators, lay leaders, missionaries, and musicians, but a few Caucasians are also cited, such as Charles Fox Parham, a major figure in Pentecostalism.

Arranged alphabetically and accompanied in many instances by a photograph, the entries vary in length from only a sentence or two to a full-page account, depending upon the reliability of available information. DuPree conducted approximately 300 interviews and journeyed to 27 states to examine church records, private collections, and newspapers. When all else failed, she relied upon obituaries.

While a brief opening essay by E. Myron Noble summarizes the Holiness-Pentecostal movement and provides context for the biographies, DuPree points researchers toward other avenues of investigation by listing dissertations and papers on the subjects. Without doubt, this compilation will be indispensable to all scholars of American religion, particularly those interested in blacks and the Holiness Pentecostal tradition. An adequate index makes for easy usage. [R: Choice, Apr 90, p. 1297]—**John W. Storey**

1027. Brackney, William Henry. **The Baptists**. Westport, Conn., Greenwood Press, 1988. 327p. index. (Denominations in America, No.2). $49.95. LC 87-15047. ISBN 0-313-23822-7.

This work consists of two major parts. The first is a thematic approach which gives rather lengthy essays on various phases of Baptist history: "An Overview of Baptist History," "The Bible: Authority or Battleground?," "A New Vision for the Church," "Sacraments/Ordinances: Signs of Faith," "A New Way: Voluntary Religion," and "The Struggle for Religious Liberty"; and the second covers biographies of Baptist leaders, both those of earliest times and some of the outstanding ones who are still active.

There are copious footnotes at the conclusion of part 1, and at the end of each biography are bibliographies that will be appropriate for those seeking more detailed information about these personalities. Following part 2 are two appendices, one a chronology of dates beginning with John Smyth in 1609 and ending with Jerry Falwell in 1979. The second of the appendices is "The International Baptist Family," which lists in tabular form the number of churches and their membership in the United States, Canada, Europe, Africa, Asia, and Latin America. Also of value is the bibliographic essay on pages 296-315. Finally, there is a detailed index.

William Brackney is vice-president, dean, and professor of the history of Christianity at the Eastern Baptist Theological Seminary. He is also an editor of the *American Baptist Quarterly*, has written three other books on Baptists and American religious history, and has contributed numerous articles to professional journals. He has also served as executive director of the American Baptist Historical Society.

The Baptists will find a welcome place in all seminary, church, and church-related libraries. Its excellent bibliographies will lead the scholar of religion and religious history to more exhaustive materials. [R: Choice, Sept 88, p. 146; RQ, Winter 88, pp. 264-65]—**Jefferson D. Caskey**

1028. Carey, Patrick W. **The Roman Catholics**. Westport, Conn., Greenwood Press, 1993. 375p. index. (Denominations in America, no.6). $55.00. BX1406.2.C346. 282'.73. LC 93-20125. ISBN 0-313-25439-7.

This work presents a history of Catholicism in the United States and about 145 biographical sketches of the major figures who shaped the religion in this country. Each of the eight chapters of the narrative history is followed by extensive bibliographical notes, and a bibliographical essay is included at the end of the work. The biographies are about a page in length and include bibliographies of works by and about each person. A large number of the subjects are women. Both the narrative history and the biographical sketches are clearly written and do not avoid controversial aspects of U.S. Catholicism. A chronology of U.S. Catholic history and an index are also included. —**James P. McCabe**

1029. **Dictionary of Baptists in America**. Bill J. Leonard, ed. Downers Grove, Ill., InterVarsity Press, 1994. 298p. $16.99pa. ISBN 0-8308-1447-7.

The focus of this fine reference work is the largest U.S. Protestant community, the Baptists. The dictionary uses a historical approach and contains many biographical sketches of important figures in the Baptist Church. Some entries are taken from the *Dictionary of Christianity in America* (see ARBA 91, entry 1444). This is not an encyclopedic compilation, but rather the first one-volume reference work done on this denomination in America. Additional information may be found by using the helpful bibliographical references at the end of each article. Following the preface is a simple guide to using the dictionary that includes an explanation of the many cross-references found within the entries. The introduction to the dictionary contains an easily readable history of the Baptist community in the United States.

This valuable reference work should be a part of collections in college, university, and public libraries. Useful in answering the general reference question, the dictionary is also a helpful guide for the beginning researcher looking for additional information and details. [R: RBB, 15 Feb 95, p. 1109]—**Bruce H. Webb**

1030. **Encyclopedia of African American Religions**. Larry G. Murphy, Gordon Melton, and Gary L. Ward, eds. Hamden, Conn., Garland, 1993. 926p. index. (Religious Information Systems, v.9; Garland Reference Library of Social Science, v.721). $125.00. BR563.N4E53. 200' .89'96073. LC 93-7224. ISBN 0-8153-0500-1.

This encyclopedia includes approximately 1,200 entries written by the editors or one of 32 contributors. Entries vary in length from a paragraph to essays exceeding 12 large, double-column pages, and each includes a bibliography. Contributed pieces are signed. Individuals (more than 800), denominations, churches, organizations, schools, and movements of relevance to African-American religious life are included. The encyclopedia also includes excellent prefatory essays on African-American religion, Martin Luther King Jr., and black feminist theology; a chronology; an alphabetical list of entries; a selected, classified bibliography; a directory of African-American churches and religious organizations; a biographical cross-reference index by religious tradition; and an index.

Typographical errors have crept in (e.g., Rolling Fork, not "Fort," Mississippi; Jesse Jackson was born in South Carolina, not North Carolina), as well as errors of fact (e.g., John Coltrane did not "author" *My Favorite Things*). The book's greatest deficiency is what is omitted: preachers (e.g., C. L. Franklin), visionary artists (e.g., James Hampton), gospel musicians (e.g., Blind Willie Johnson), scholars (e.g., Sterling Stuckey), religious communities (e.g., Adat Beyt Moshe), and imported Afro-Caribbean religions (e.g., Santeria). Conjure/Hoodoo is not included, nor is Cornel West, Afrocentrism, or John Work. The bibliography lacks a section on music, and the index does not include proper names that occur in the text. In spite of these omissions, this is a monumental achievement and one that is essential to a core reference collection in African-American religion. [R: WLB, Dec 93, p. 77-78]—**Fred J. Hay**

1031. Nadell, Pamela S. **Conservative Judaism in America: A Biographical Dictionary and Sourcebook**. Westport, Conn., Greenwood Press, 1988. 409p. bibliog. index. (Jewish Denominations in America). $55.00. LC 87- 31782. ISBN 0-313-24205-4.

This book documents the lives and careers of the most important leaders in the Conservative Jewish movement in the United States. It also provides a brief history of the movement and its central institutions. The majority of the work consists of biographical sketches of some 130 key conservative leaders, mostly rabbis. Each entry includes, in addition to the essential biographical data, an evaluation of the figure's contributions to the development of American conservatism, a bibliography of the individual's major writings, and selected references about him or her. The preface discusses the approach toward the selection of leaders who are included in the dictionary. In addition to the biographical dictionary, three essays (based on printed sources) present the history, ideology, and organization of Conservative Judaism. The Jewish Theological Seminary of America, the Rabbinical Assembly, and the United Synagogue of America are discussed in these essays. Each includes extensive bibliographical notes. The book concludes with a series of appendices listing the names and dates of the leaders of the most important Conservative and Reconstructionist associations. There are also a glossary of Hebrew terms, and a sixteen-page bibliography of resources for further study. The bibliography, arranged by types of materials, includes both primary and secondary sources. There is an extensive subject index, including cross-references. The author is Associate Professor of Jewish

Studies and History at American University, and a specialist in modern American Jewish history. The book is an important contribution to American Jewish scholarship. It serves as a valuable resource for students and scholars in understanding the Conservative movement, and would be an excellent addition to reference collections in the area of Jewish studies in academic, public, and special libraries. It is also especially important for Judaica collections in temple, synagogue, community center, and day school libraries.—**Susan J. Freiband**

1032.   **The Official Catholic Directory**. Wilmette, Ill., P. J. Kenedy; distr., Wilmette, Ill., Marquis Who's Who, 1913- . $129.00. LC 1-30961. ISSN 0078-3854.

Every year since its initial publication in 1817, this directory has improved its format, arrangement, and features. Today no other single volume contains such a plethora of information about the Roman Catholic Church in America. Not only does it contain countless ecclesiastical statistics of the Church in the United States, Puerto Rico, the Virgin Islands, Agana, Caroline and Marshall Islands, foreign missionary activities, Canada, and Mexico, but it also contains dozens of other specific and helpful features. To cite a few: it enumerates the governing bodies in Vatican City; supplies the names and addresses of each archdiocese and diocese in America and their bishops, priests, brothers, sisters, and lay administrators; details every seminary, school, college, university, convent, hospital, nursing home, interfaith center, and institute; and provides an alphabetical list of the entire American clergy plus a separate necrology of prelates and clergy who have died since the last issue of the directory. Of added interest are maps, charts, and fold-out general summary sheets. To keep the price of this large, clearly printed, well-stitched, and beautifully bound volume at a reasonable cost, its editors have accepted hundreds of classified advertisements, many illustrated in brilliant color. Even advertisements of such things as liturgical art, missals, and clerical clothing and vestments have their value, since all advertisers were selected rather than solicited.—**C. A. Cevasco**

1033.   **Reform Judaism in America: A Biographical Dictionary and Sourcebook**. Kerry M. Olitzky, Lance J. Sussman, and Malcolm H. Stern, eds. Westport, Conn., Greenwood Press, 1993. 347p. index. (Jewish Denominations in America). $75.00. BM750.R39. 296.8'346 '0973. LC 92-25794. ISBN 0-313-24628-9.

This biographical dictionary is the second in a set of three covering the major branches of American Judaism. Unlike the earlier volume, *Conservative Judaism in America* (see ARBA 89, entry 1031), which was authored by one writer, this volume contains entries by a variety of scholars and rabbis. Approximately 170 important American Reform leaders from the period 1824-1976 are profiled in this work. Several essays on the history of Reform Judaism and its major institutions are also included, as well as historical lists of the major officers of Reform organizations.

The core of the dictionary is the alphabetically arranged entries of one to two pages on each of the figures, covering their religious contributions and basic life events, such as birthplace and children. The tone of the pieces is consistently objective, avoiding obvious bias in descriptions of theological or political controversies. Primary and secondary bibliographies are appended to all of the entries. The secondary sources are especially useful, as they frequently list newspaper articles, obituaries, theses, and other references less accessible to the average researcher. A bibliography on Reform Judaism is appended to the dictionary; it lists a large number of synagogue histories, memoirs, and unpublished sources in addition to the standard monographic and journal literature.

This work provides useful and comprehensive biographies of leaders in an important American religious tradition. Many of these leaders are difficult to find in other religious biographical sources, so this work fills a useful niche. Additionally, the lengthy bibliography on Reform Judaism provides access to a large realm of unpublished materials. [R: Choice, Nov 93, p. 438]—**Christopher W. Nolan**

1034.   **Who's Who in Jewish History: After the Period of the Old Testament**. 2d ed. By Joan Comay; revised by Lavinia Cohn-Sherbok. New York, Oxford University Press, 1995. 407p. index. $15.95pa. ISBN 0-19-521079-4.

This revision of a work first published in 1974 offers brief biographical information on figures of importance in Jewish history from 135 B.C. to the present. Most are deceased. Introductory material includes a glossary of historical terms, a chronology of events and historical figures, and maps of the journeys of Paul of Tarsus and Benjamin of Tudela, as well as of the Russian Pale of Settlement and Israeli-held territory after the 1967 and 1973 wars.

The alphabetical entries range in length from a few sentences to one page. They discuss people from all over the world who have contributed to Jewish life and culture. Non-Jews who have influenced Jewish history also appear. Cross-references to related entries are in small capital letters. Among those covered are scholars (Moses Maimonides, Leo Baeck, Eliezer Ben-Yehudah); authors (Saul Bellow, Marcel Proust, Amos Oz); musicians (Aaron Copland, Otto Klemperer, Isaac Stern); political leaders (Benjamin Disraeli, Golda Meir, Teddy Kollek); and scientists (Richard Feynman, Elie Metchnikoff, Selman Waksman).

Non-Jews include Paul, Jesus, Yasir Arafat, Adolf Hitler, and Tomás de Torqucmada. Oddly, there is no entry for Levi Strauss, although British clothing manufacturer Montague Burton has one. Supreme Court Justice Abe Fortas, who died in 1982, is listed as still living. A subject index completes the work. The brevity of the entries and the lack of bibliographies make this work of limited use for large reference collections, but it is an appropriate ready-reference tool for school and synagogue libraries.—**Barbara M. Bibel**

Religious Leaders

1035.   Brosse, Jacques. **Religious Leaders**. New York, Chambers Kingfisher Graham, c.1988, 1991. 234p. illus. index. $9.95pa. ISBN 0-550-17006-5.

Guided by strict criteria, Jacques Brosse has sifted through antiquity, Judaism, Christianity, Islam, Hinduism, and Buddhism for entrants in this compact reference to the world's religious leaders. The traits he looked for were absolute selflessness, a lack of concern for worldly status, association with a major religious tradition, and an awareness that one's own path was not necessarily the only avenue to God. (According to Brosse, genuine leaders are concerned only with guiding others to the truth and are uninterested in material rewards.) Given this volume's enormity of scope and brevity of space, Brosse has had to be highly selective. Even so, some of his choices are puzzling. Should Socrates, Plato, and Epicurus be regarded as religious leaders? If Joseph Smith of the Church of Jesus Christ of Latter-day Saints and George Whitefield are included, why not Alexander Campbell of the Church of Christ and Billy Graham? The study is far from exhaustive.

Such questions notwithstanding, this is a useful paperback reference. Most of its 163 entries, which average one to two pages of relatively small print, are on individuals, but several deal with groups, such as the Sikhs and Neoplatonists, and some describe sacred writings, such as the Vedas and the Book of the Dead. Enhanced by illustrations, a brief glossary, and an adequate index, this work will be helpful to people seeking general information about major religions and their principal leaders. [R: LJ, 1 Nov 92, p. 76]—**John W. Storey**

1036.   **Great Leaders of the Christian Church**. John D. Woodbridge, ed. Chicago, Moody Press, 1988. 384p. illus. (part col.). maps. bibliog. index. $22.95. LC 87-34974. ISBN 0-8024-9051-4.

Presented here are brief biographies of sixty-four persons considered to be "some of the most important leaders of the Christian church" (p. 9). They span the history of Christianity from the first to the twentieth century and include biblical figures (Peter, Paul, and John), popes (Leo the Great, Gregory the Great, and Innocent III), reformers (Luther, Zwingli, and Calvin), and evangelists (C. H. Spurgeon, D. L. Moody, and Billy Graham). Each chapter consists of a one-page sketch (most with a chronology) and the biography proper. Timecharts and topical essays interspersed throughout the text supplement the biographies. A select bibliography suggests sources of material by and about the biographees for further study.

A work of this sort must necessarily be selective, and this one is. However, the selection criteria are not spelled out and the reader is left wondering why certain individuals are included and others are not (e.g., why William Wilberforce and not Martin Luther King?). In spite of this, there can be little disagreement over those chosen for inclusion.

The quality of the work varies, as it will with multi-author products, but overall, both text and illustrations are very good. The biographies are marked by fairness and well-rounded presentation (with the exception of the treatment of Calvin, which borders on eulogy). They also have generally overcome a major problem of condensed treatments, that of clarity. There are occasions, though, when lay persons will need to go elsewhere for clarification of unfamiliar terminology and concepts.

Biographical information on most of the biographees can be found, often in concise form, in other sources. So, where is this volume's niche? It will serve the smaller libraries which are unable to afford the several larger works through which the material is scattered. For them it will provide a high-quality alternative.—**Craig W. Beard**

1037. **Handbook of Evangelical Theologians**. Walter A. Elwell, ed. Grand Rapids, Mich., Baker Book House, 1993. 465p. illus. $29.99. BR1640.H363. 230'.046. LC 93-5606. ISBN 0-8010-3212-1.

The essays in this volume present information about the lives and contributions of 33 twentieth-century evangelical theologians, from Augustus H. Strong (1836-1921) to Alister E. McGrath (1953-). Among them are those that are well known—B. B. Warfield, Francis Schaeffer, and Carl F. H. Henry—and some that are perhaps not so well known—Francis Pieper, Charles W. Carter, and J. Rodman Williams. The individuals included represent various points along the evangelical spectrum. Some critics might argue that some of them are so far from the center of the spectrum that they do not even belong. However, considering the scope and purpose of the handbook, the editor has chosen well. The purpose of the volume is to paint as full and accurate a picture as possible of evangelicalism (which Elwell identifies in broad terms) for those inside the movement as well as those outside. Thus it was necessary to provide a cross-section of evangelical thought, both chronologically and theologically.

Each contributor to this volume was selected because of knowledge of a particular theologian or access to appropriate primary and secondary material. As is often the case with collections of essays by different authors, the quality is somewhat uneven, although by no means low. However, while *all* the essays are informative and generally well written, some of them are quite engaging while others are flat.

Elwell deserves much credit for bringing together portraits of those who have helped shape modern evangelicalism. (Some readers may be surprised to find that it is not a monolith and that it possesses great breadth and depth.) It is also to his credit that he, unlike many other editors, spells out the purpose and scope of the work in the preface. Thus, readers (and reviewers) know what to expect from the outset. Recommended.—**Craig W. Beard**

1038. Kennedy, Leonard A. **A Catalogue of Thomists, 1270-1900**. Houston, Tex., Center for Thomistic Studies, University of St. Thomas; distr., Notre Dame, Ind., University of Notre Dame Press, 1987. 240p. index. $29.95. LC 86-72913. ISBN 0-268-00763-2.

Kennedy provides a sort of biographical checklist of Thomists, that is, theologians and philosophers who follow the thought of St. Thomas Aquinas. He has included those thinkers who claimed to be (or are described as) Thomists, as well as those whose book titles seemed to indicate Thomistic work. The entry for each of the approximately 2,000 people listed includes birth and death dates, if known, up to three titles of works written by that person, and an indication of what sources provide fuller biographic or bibliographic information. The thinkers are arranged chronologically by century, then by religious order, and finally by country of origin. The table of contents contains a tabulation of the number of entries in each category, allowing one to get an overview of the interest in Thomas's thought during different eras and among different religious groups. A name index concludes the volume.

This work may be useful to those doing historical research on less-known figures in the Thomistic school, principally for identification. But it will probably be peripheral for those researching the major figures of the tradition, on whom much more comprehensive reference materials are available. The amount of information provided on any figure here is quite minimal. Also, the author notes that difficult to pursue items were often omitted, so the potential use of this as a comprehensive catalog of a major intellectual school is diminished.—**Christopher W. Nolan**

1039. Melton, J. Gordon. **Religious Leaders of America: A Biographical Guide to Founders and Leaders of Religious Bodies, Churches, and Spiritual Groups**. . . . Detroit, Gale, 1991. 604p. index. $79.95. ISBN 0-8103-4921-3. ISSN 1057-2961.

This collection of 1,000-plus biographical sketches of North American religious leaders since 1865 is the most recent of Melton's numerous publications in the field of religion. The work covers a wide range of religious groups and makes a special effort to include women, African-Americans, and Native Americans. An introduction and user's guide, as well as several indexes and appendixes, enhance the book's usefulness.

Articles supply the subject's date of birth (and death, if deceased), affiliation/occupation, an account of life and achievements, and a brief bibliography. The entries are clearly written and generally uniform in length (e.g., Martin Luther King, Jr. is given no more space than obscure persons). Margins are narrow, but the typeface is clear.

The justification for including most of the persons treated is evident, although one may legitimately question the rationale for some (e.g., the article on Geronimo fails to establish his religious significance). Moreover, while most treatments seem evenhanded, there are occasional lapses; for example, compare the entries on Billy Graham and Jesse Jackson with those in the *Dictionary of Christianity in America* (see ARBA 91, entry 1444). For the most part, however, Melton's work succeeds in its aim and will surely fill a niche in American religious biography for academic, public, and theological libraries. [R: LJ, 1 Nov 91, p. 90; RBB, 15 Nov 91, pp. 650-51]—**M. Patrick Graham**

1040. **A Photo Directory of the United States Catholic Hierarchy**. Jacquelyn M. Murphy, ed. Huntington, Ind., Our Sunday Visitor, 1993. 134p. illus. $19.95pa. ISBN 0-87973-700-1.

This directory, as its title indicates, is a list of the almost 400 cardinals, archbishops, and bishops of the church in the United States. Alongside each black-and-white facial photograph is a brief biography. The factual information, current as of August 1993, details the man's date and place of birth; educational institutions attended; date of ordination to the priesthood; date of episcopal consecration; episcopal appointments; and, where appropriate, date of retirement or resignation.

Entries are arranged alphabetically, running from Alfred L. Abromowicz, auxiliary bishop of Chicago, to Paul A. Zipfel, auxiliary bishop of St. Louis. The value of this compendious volume lies less in the listing and photographs of prominent U.S. churchmen and more in the inclusion of lesser-known members of the hierarchy, about whom basic information is not readily available elsewhere. An updated edition of this directory will not be available until the fall of 1996.—**G. A. Cevasco**

Saints

1041. **The Book of Saints: A Dictionary of Servants of God**. 6th ed. Compiled by the Benedictine Monks of St. Augustine's Abbey, Ramsgate. Wilton, Conn., Morehouse, 1989. 60p. illus. $34.95. BX4655.2. B66. 282'.092'2. LC 89-33515. ISBN 0-8192-1501-5.

This respected biographical dictionary of saints has been revised and updated to reflect changes in the Roman Calendar promulgated since the last edition (1966). By more than doubling the number of entries to 10,000, the focus has been broadened, with less emphasis on English saints. Each entry includes the saint's name, appellation, feast day, dates, liturgical group, hagiographic rank (saint or blessed), religious order, and a short description of the saint's life.

Concise and informative descriptions outline important dates, positions, and events in the saint's life. Those who were removed from the General Calendar in 1969 are included, but their questionable authenticity is noted. On occasion, the tone of entries for undocumented saints seems unnecessarily harsh, as in the description of the bearded female saint Wilgefort is. Her legend is described as "a worthless romance abounding in absurdities." Such outbursts, however, are relatively rare.

This new edition is illustrated with pictures of saints and symbols from all eras of Christian art. There is also an index of emblems that notes saints by attributes or symbols. A list of patron saints offers a representative sample, but it is not comprehensive. Finally, the supplementary list of sibyls complements the main entries since these pre-Christian prophetesses were often associated with saints in Christian art.

The enhanced scope of this edition makes it one of the best single-volume reference works on hagiography. Moreover, because it follows the revised General Calendar and includes those saints recently canonized or beatified, it is the most current and accurate source for hagiographic information available.—**Valerie R. Hotchkiss**

1042.   Heffernan, Eileen. **Fifty-Seven Saints**. 2d ed. Boston, St. Paul Books & Media, 1994. 543p. illus. index. $10.95pa. ISBN 0-8198-2656-1.

This title provides colorful narratives on a small selection of saints chosen for their ability to teach children moral lessons. Written from a traditional Roman Catholic perspective, the six- to eight-page entries are composed of stories with imagined dialogue that deal with pivotal moments of the saints. Each story ends with a homily intended to show children how to emulate some behavior of that particular saint. The text is reasonably entertaining and accessible for grade-school-aged children.

Each entry includes the known birth and death dates of the saint and the feast day usually associated with the saint. A nice black-and-white portrait of each saint is also pictured. Otherwise, there is no background on the history of the saint, her or his process of canonization, questions concerning historical evidence, or additional sources to read for further information. Obviously, the purpose is not to offer any sort of critical judgment. Consequently, the reference utility of this title, even in a juvenile literature collection, is quite limited. The extremely small number of saints covered is also a serious drawback for reference use. Those looking for brief dictionaries of Catholic saints that have some reference value may wish to consider *Penguin Dictionary of Saints* (2d ed.; see ARBA 85, entry 1312) or *Oxford Dictionary of Saints* (3d ed.; see ARBA 94, entry 1527). The first has lengthier entries, but the latter provides references to other literature on most saints.—**Christopher W. Nolan**

1043.   Jones, Alison. **Saints**. New York, Chambers Kingfisher Graham, 1992. 243p. illus. index. $9.95pa. ISBN 0-550-17014-6.

That individuals whose lives of faith and virtue are worthy of commendation is obvious from the number of books written about them. This latest addition to an ever-increasing bibliography is a useful one-volume guide to men and women of exemplary holiness, immovable morality, and extraordinary ability. Among them are monarchs, monks, lawyers, teachers, martyrs, and common folk. A few have been virtually forgotten; others have become legendary and have inspired poets and painters.

The 200 or so saints profiled in this volume have been drawn from all levels of society and varied national groups. They range from the earliest days of the church up to contemporary times. Their entries run about 500 words, state the essential facts (distinguishing between pious fictions and historical records), list the feast days, and indicate the relative importance of each biographee.

Other hagiographical volumes may be better researched, more complete, better illustrated, and more specialized in one way or another. But any library that does not shelve *The Who's Who of Heaven* (see entry 1044), *The Oxford Dictionary of Saints* (see ARBA 88, entry 1424), or *A Calendar of Saints* (see ARBA 88, entry 1423) should obtain this handy reference tool. The moderate price makes it a worthwhile addition to all reference collections.—**G. A. Cevasco**

1044.   Kleinz, John P. **The Who's Who of Heaven: Saints for All Seasons**. Westminster, Md., Christian Classics, 1987. 334p. bibliog. $12.95pa. LC 87-071420. ISBN 0-87061-136-4.

Before Vatican Council II, collections of lives of saints and biographies of individual saints were prominent on Catholic publishers' lists. Today there are not so many of these items, but books about saints written in recent years are invariably of better quality from the historian's and theologian's perspective. *The Who's Who of Heaven* is a good example of this "new hagiography." Painstaking research (supported by over a dozen pages of notes) here records the lives of those saints considered to have the most modern appeal, those saints whose lives demonstrate that sanctity is remarkably varied and readily capable of imitation—even in today's world.

An introduction delves into the question "What is a saint?" and explains why such individuals are worthy of veneration. The first and longest chapter concentrates on Mary, the Queen of Saints; treats the myriad of ways Catholics honor her; explains the origin of various Marian hymns;

and concludes with a history of popular Marian shrines. Among the seven chapters that follow are those devoted to remarkable men and women who should serve as role models for priests, nuns, and all Christians; to missionaries who were martyred in the Americas, Africa, China, Japan, and New Guinea; to foundresses of viable religious congregations; to certain medieval saints; and to several contemporaries who someday may be beatified and canonized.

Although this volume lacks an index, it does have a detailed table of contents and a six-page bibliography. *Who's Who of Heaven* actually is more of a spiritual reader than a ready-reference tool, but is still of value to large theology collections. [R: BL, 1 Jan 88, p. 732]—**G. A. Cevasco**

1045. **The Oxford Dictionary of Saints**. 3d ed. David Hugh Farmer, ed. New York, Oxford University Press, 1992. 530p. $13.95pa. BR1710.F34. 270'.092'2. LC 92-6722. ISBN 0-19-283069-4.

This edition of a useful work has been revised and expanded to include approximately 1,500 saints. Entries are brief—about half a page in length—and include bibliographical references. The selection of saints includes all English saints, most well-known saints from other countries, and recently canonized saints. Appendixes include a list of patronages (i.e., the patron saint of ...), a list of principal iconographical emblems, an index of place-names, and a calendar of feast days. This work should be in most reference collections, but it cannot substitute for more comprehensive works.—**James P. McCabe**

21   Library and Information Science

INTRODUCTION

This section on library and information science biography covers librarians in the United States, Canada, and the United Kingdom. The first section, General Works, includes several sources that provide biographical information worldwide, including the *International Biographical Directory of National Archivists, Documentalists, and Librarians* (Scarecrow, 1997) (see entry 1047), which includes brief biographies on librarians worldwide; *Who's Who in Special Libraries* (Special Libraries Association 1980- .) (see entry 1048), which provides biographical sketches on more than 28,000 individuals in over 17,000 institutions, and *Who's Who in the European Information World 1995-96* (TFPL, 1995) (see entry 1049), which lists librarians by country of origin.

The major listing of librarians in the United States is the *American Library Directory* (R. R. Bowker, 1978-) (see entry 1053), which provides only basic information on librarians by state; the *Directory of Library & Information Professionals* (American Library Association by Research Publications, 1988) (see entry 1054), which is published in cooperation with the ALA and is also available on CD-ROM; and, finally, the *Encyclopedia of Library and Information Science* (Marcel Dekker, 1968-) (see entry 1055), which provides biographical information on a large number of librarians mainly in the United States.

Finally, biographical dictionaries on Canadian librarians, librarians in the United Kingdom, and Spanish-speaking librarians are represented. Sources include the recently published *Directory of College and University Librarians in Canada* (Toronto Ontario College and University Library Association/Ontario Library Association, 1996) (see entry 1050), which includes more than 1,700 librarians in colleges and universities in Canada.

GENERAL WORKS

1046.   **Biographical Directory of National Librarians**. Frances Laverne Carroll and Philip J. Schwartz, eds. London, Mansell; distr., Rutherford, N.J., Publishers Distribution Center, 1989. 134p. index. $50.00. Z720.A1C37. 020'.92'2. LC 88-28779. ISBN 0-7201-1875-1.

The purpose of this publication is to furnish biographical information about those individuals who currently hold executive positions in national libraries of the world. The volume is a useful directory to people working in the areas of cultural affairs, education, and international librarianship. Information was collected via a survey to individual libraries and supplemented by an examination of relevant guides and directories. To be eligible for inclusion, national libraries must conform to the Unesco definition of libraries that are "responsible for organizing and conserving copies of all significant publications published in the country and functioning as deposit libraries." More than one library serves as the national library in some countries.

The *Biographical Directory of National Librarians* is arranged alphabetically by country. Individuals, libraries, and countries are listed in the index. Each main entry includes extensive information about the biographee organized under the following headings: name; official title; address (home and professional); birth date; spouse; education; certificates; career; military service; publications; honors and awards; fellowships; professional memberships; civic and political activities; religious groups, social clubs, and lodges; languages; and recommended sources of the history and description of the library. About 25 percent of the 198 entries contain only the name and address of the director. Future editions should concentrate on these nonrespondents. Recommended as a useful and unique companion to better-known biographical sources.—**Arthur P. Young**

1047. **International Biographical Directory of National Archivists, Documentalists, and Librarians**. Frances Laverne Carroll, ed. Susan Houck, comp. Lanham, Md., Scarecrow Press, 1997. 225p. index. $45.00. ISBN 0-8108-3223-2.

This directory brings together data gathered directly from surveys sent to executive officers of national archives, documentation centers, and libraries as well as information from several specialized biographical sources. Information for 192 countries is included. The completeness of data provided is inconsistent because of differences in organization and staffing of facilities in the countries treated. Most entries give substantial biographical information on executive officers as well as addresses and telephone and fax numbers for the facilities. E-mail addresses are available for a few. Separate indexes for places, institutions, and persons make the book easy to use. The directory will have a limited audience, but those with a need to contact international archivists, documentalists, and librarians will appreciate the scope and accuracy of this carefully compiled volume. [R: LJ, 15 April 97, p. l26]—**Ahmad Gamaluddin**

1048. **Who's Who in Special Libraries**. Washington, D.C., Special Libraries Association, 1980- . maps. index. $25.00pa. for recent edition. ISSN 0278-842X.

The membership directory of the Special Libraries Association remains a valuable too for accessing information on individuals in special libraries. The first section may be correctly termed an organizational handbook. Among other items of interest, this section includes names, addresses, and telephone numbers of the current board of directors, a list of association staff members, information about the organizational structure, the complete bylaws, history, honors and awards, and past presidents. This section also includes the locations and dates of future meetings, the location of SLA student groups with names and telephone numbers of faculty advisors, and the names and addresses of all division and state chapter officers.

As much routine information is repetitive and identical to the previous year, change is accomplished by inclusion of additional information as opposed to revision. The division, chapter, and business indexes are in reality alphabetical listings of the membership by subject division, state chapter affiliation, and organizational affiliation. The alphabetical listing of the more than 12,000 members of the association includes organizational affiliation, addresses, and telephone numbers when known, and comprises one-half of the volume. Until 1980, *Who's Who in Special Libraries* was published as the annual directory issue of *Special Libraries*, the official journal of the association. This is a useful and informative work. Mailed without charge to members of the association, *Who's Who in Special Libraries* would be of interest to vendors, suppliers, and all who have an interest in activities of the Special Libraries Association.—**Robert M. Ballard and Robert L. Wick**

1049. **Who's Who in the European Information World 1995-96**. 2d ed. Jorund B. Nordin, comp. and ed. Washington, D.C., TFPL, 1995. 899p. index. $230.00. ISBN 1-870889-51-7.

This directory provides information on personnel working in the information industry and in special libraries in Europe. The eastern countries of the former Soviet Union are not included. The information industry is widely defined to include online and CD-ROM database producers; automated library systems vendors; faculty teaching in library or information science fields; information brokers; consultants; and relevant personnel in public, national, or academic libraries. As such, the directory provides a useful source of contacts.

At the beginning of the directory there is a listing of international and Pan-European professional associations. Each country also has its national professional associations listed. The main part of the directory is a listing by country of information professionals. Within each country, names are listed alphabetically. A full entry provides the name and address of the organization for which the person currently works, the person's position in the organization, and how long they have held the position. Telephone and fax numbers, e-mail addresses, total years of work experience, previous positions, main areas of professional activity, languages spoken, personal interests and hobbies, and memberships in professional associations are listed. Not all entries are full, due to the fact that entries are self-submitted. The entries are clear and easy to read.

The directory contains three indexes: an organizations index that lists each organization alphabetically with its employees; an activities index following a modified UK Standard Industrial Classification (SIC92) system (organizations and their employees decided themselves to which category they belong, and there is much cross-listing); and a surnames index that does not refer back to a page number, but lists the country under which the individual is entered.—**Linda Main**

CANADA

1050.   Leckie, Gloria J., and Kim G. Kofmel. **Directory of College and University Librarians in Canada. Répertoire des Bibliothécaires des Collèges et Universités du Canada**. 2d ed. Toronto, Ontario College and University Library Association/Ontario Library Association, 1996. 173p. index. $18.95 spiralbound. ISBN 0-9699462-1-X.

Many people need to contact Canadian academic librarians but, until the appearance of this welcome volume, have not had one source where most names and addresses could be found easily. This directory, the 1st edition of which appeared in 1995, provides a listing of approximately 1,740 librarians at 27 colleges and universities in Canada; the roster is fairly complete, but inclusion remains voluntary. Entries are arranged by province or territory, and then by institution. A mailing address is given for each institution, and the entry for each librarian at that school contains the person's name, title, telephone and fax numbers, and e-mail address. Institutional and name indexes greatly ease access to information in the directory.

If it is to provide "a current, comprehensive and accessible listing of college and university librarian from across the country" (p. 2), the directory will have to be updated annually and expanded to include all academic librarians. The name index, which supplies each librarian's institutional affiliation, could also be improved by adding the page number where an individual's entry appears. As it is, one has to go through the intermediary step of turning to the institutional index. These concerns can easily be addressed in the next edition. In the meantime, this handy reference source belongs on the desk of every academic librarian in Canada and in all Canadiana, research, and large public collections.—**John D. Blackwell**

UNITED KINGDOM

1051.   Munford, W. A. **Who Was Who in British Librarianship, 1800-1985: A Dictionary of Dates with Notes**. London, Library Association; distr., Chicago, American Library Association, 1987. 91p. bibliog. $30.00. ISBN 0-85365-976-1.

Biographical information can often be difficult to find when it concerns those various groups of people who have traditionally been considered insignificant, such as librarians. Fortunately that situation has been changing recently, and the appearance of *Who Was Who in British Librarianship* provides an example of just how good the products of that change can be. W. A. Munford has sketched the careers of the approximately 2,000 people who served as senior librarians in the United Kingdom after 1800 and who died before December 1985. Each entry supplies the birth and death dates and the dates and duration of professional appointments when available. In the case of those more famous and accomplished librarians, the entry includes a biographical annotation ranging in length from 25 to 350 words (e.g., Sir Anthony Panizzi), which annotation is sometimes accompanied by a brief bibliography. Among the librarians receiving biographical annotations are Henry Bradshaw (1831-1866), chief librarian of the Cambridge University Library, and Barbara Kyle (1913-1966), a leader of Aslib and an editor of the *Journal of Documentation*. While entries for most librarians simply contain the brief facts of vital dates and professional service, that is all this pioneering volume ever intended to do. It provides quick (once one has read the brief "Elucidation" section on page x) access to basic information from which further research can proceed if needed. All of that comes in an attractive and relatively inexpensive volume. This publication helps to make up for the absence, until relatively recently, of an ongoing series of current biographical reference publications about librarians. [R: LAR, 9 Sept 87, p. 473]—**Ronald H. Fritze**

1052. **Who's Who in the UK Information World**. Jorund B. Nordin, comp. and ed. Washington, D.C., TFPL, 1990- . index. $155.00pa. for recent edition. ISBN 1-870889-50-9.

Task Force Pro Libra (TFPL), a British company offering employment services and training programs in the United Kingdom, publishes two directories of information professionals, one for the United Kingdom (reviewed here) and one for Europe. Criteria for inclusion include three years' working experience in a special library or information department, and status as a senior public librarian, a senior academic librarian, the manager of a special library or information department, an information broker, or an active board member of a professional body in the information sector. Not all British librarians or information professionals qualify, but the majority could be included, and the publication solicits qualified entrants with a notice at the bottom of each page and an entry form in the back of the directory. It appears that there are many more entries for special libraries than academic or public libraries.

The work has a brief introduction including criteria for entry, a description of the format of entries, and a description of the indexes. The body of the work includes 468 pages of entries in alphabetical order. Entries contain name, current position, contact address and numbers, relevant qualifications and memberships, library- or information science training institution attended, years of professional experience (total and in current position), names of the two most recent positions held, foreign languages spoken, and brief descriptions of current responsibilities and interests. There are three indexes: employing organization employing organization main area of activity, and library- and information science institution attended. The indexes improve the utility of the publication, and similar indexes may profitably be included in U.S. directories of librarians and information professionals.

The work is paperbound and includes advertisements for other TFPL publications and programs and for Whitaker Bibliographic Services. While a specialized publication aimed at a British audience, this work should prove useful for academic, public, and special librarians looking for contacts in the United Kingdom. It would thus be an excellent addition to the libraries of schools of information and librarianship. Also, the organization activity index makes it a useful resource for researchers in the information business.—**Richard H. Swain**

UNITED STATES

1053. **American Library Directory**. New York, R. R. Bowker, 1978- . 2v. index. $164.95/set for recent edition. ISSN 0065-910X.

Pertinent factual information on over 34,000 U.S. and Canadian libraries is included in this two-volume biennial edition (1997-98). Almost every type of library is covered; however, the directory still lacks a listing of school libraries. Entries are comparable to previous editions and provide not only addresses and personnel information, but collection size, expenditures, and a wide variety of other information about the library. Arrangement is by state or province and then alphabetically by city. An index by library name is provided. Information is supplied by the libraries listed.

Special sections give added value to the volumes. Included are lists of networks, library schools (not just ALA accredited), libraries of the handicapped, state libraries, Army libraries, and USIA centers. Spinoff publications include the entire database available on DIALOG and access to mailing labels from the publisher. Thus, libraries who cannot afford the price can access the information contained through electronic means.

American Library Directory is an indispensable and current tool for all who need information about libraries, including library professionals, publishers, and the general public who want to learn about libraries available not only in their local area, but in areas where they will be traveling.—**David V. Loertscher and Robert L. Wick**

1054. **Directory of Library & Information Professionals**. Woodbridge, Conn., with American Library Association by Research Publications, 1988. 2v. index. $345.00/set. ISBN 0-89235-125- X. ISSN 0894-7031.

This directory was designed by its publisher in cooperation with ALA to replace *Who's Who in Library and Information Services* (1982). The idea was to publish a work that would be not only more comprehensive than its predecessor, but also machine-readable on CD-ROM. Computerization also provided many different access points to the professionals other than by name. The arrangement of volume 1 is alphabetical by the person's name. Volume 2 provides indexes to names by specialty, employer, consulting expertise, and geographical area.

Information was gathered by massive mailings to the professionals of twenty library and information societies. Self-reports included detailed information on education and positions but restricted prolific writers to three publications of interest. A single follow-up mailing and some telephone solicitation was done to include as many persons as possible. Individual listings were edited by the publisher but were not returned to respondents for proofreading.

The effort to provide a wider listing of professionals is a great one. However, this publication is full of errors and lacks the comprehensive coverage originally intended by its designers. Its cost to produce both in-print and CD-ROM formats is evident from the price, which puts it out of range of most libraries and library professionals in the country. One would almost wish that the alphabetical access to persons in volume 1 had been published as a separate publication at less than half the price, with access by other database fields being limited to an online search or to the CD-ROM application alone. Users of volume 2 will quickly come to the conclusion that access by computer and self-reporting of a single item such as library specialty leads to the most confusing maze of terminology for the same specialty. For example, there are at least fifty different titles which school librarians gave themselves, and the computer generates them as reported. Is computer access to a hodge-podge of information of value? This publication is a good example of what computerization is doing to publishing. Quality standards and information access needs should be evaluated before we drown the world in a morass of information from which we may never recover.

Conclusion? If the person you are looking for responded to the questionnaire, the source is valuable, but don't expect miracles. [R: Choice, Nov 88, p. 458; JAL, May 88, p. 111; LJ, 1 May 88, p. 64; RBB, 1 Apr 88, p. 1319; WLB, Mar 88, pp. 96-97; WLB, June 88, p. 124]—**David V. Loertscher**

1055.   **Encyclopedia of Library and Information Science**. Allen Kent, ed. New York, Marcel Dekker, 1968- . illus. $55.00 for recent edition. LC 68-31232. ISBN 0-8247-2041-5.

Allen Kent, who remains the executive editor of this set, has described the purpose of the *Encyclopedia of Library and Information Science* updates as follows: To update articles in the main set; to add new articles on topics currently important in the field; to include recently deceased prominent librarians; and, finally, to include article and originally commissioned for the main set but not received in time for inclusion.

The impact of technology on the field of library science in the last ten years has been felt by all of us. This work has taken more than one and one-half decades to produce. Indeed, they are well written, but there will be no end to these supplements if we continue in this fashion. In other words, the editor and his editorial staff still have to resolve this important problem—how much to update and whom to add. Perhaps a master plan of some nature shared among the members of our profession is in order.—**Bohdan S. Wynar and Robert L. Wick**

22 Science and Technology

INTRODUCTION

This chapter contains 12 subject divisions, including General Works, Anthropology, Aviation and Aerospace, Botany, Chemistry, Computer Science, Energy and Nuclear Science, Engineering and Technology, Environmental Science, Mathematics, Physics, and Physiology. By far the largest number of biographical dictionaries can be found in the General Works category, with more than 30 sources. Other sections range from a single source for the subject to one or two sources. The section General Works includes a number of important sources, such as *American Men & Women of Science: A Biographical Directory* (R. R. Bowker/Reed Reference Publishing, 1998-) (see entry 1056), which provides biographical information for more than 120,000 individuals; the *Dictionary of Scientific Biography* (Scribner's, 1990) (see entry 1059), which is the latest volume in a more than 16-volume work that has included more than 417 biographies of prominent scientists; and *Notable Twentieth-Century Scientists* (Gale, 1995) (see entry 1063), which provides brief biographies of more than 1,300 scientists. Other sources of note include the work by Nathan Aaseng titled *Twentieth-Century Inventors* (Facts on File, 1991) (see entry 1072), which provides a good source of biographies of scientists for K-12 students. The *Biographical Encyclopedia of Scientists* (Philadelphia, Institute of Physics Publishing, 1994) (see entry 1077) has recently been updated and remains an important source, and the *McGraw-Hill Multimedia Encyclopedia of Science & Technology* (McGraw-Hill, 1994, 1996) (see entry 1081), which is a recently published CD-ROM based on the older paper edition of the same title and contains a separate biography index, provides biographies of more than 250 scientists.

The section Anthropology contains five biographical sources, including the *Biographical Directory of Anthropologists Born before 1920* (Garland, 1988) (see entry 1089), which is now somewhat older but still a valuable source, and the *International Dictionary of Anthropologists* (Garland, 1991) (see entry 1091), which provides brief biographies for more than 700 anthropologists and other individuals related to the field of anthropology.

Aviation and Aerospace contains three sources, of which the most notable is the work by Douglas Hawthorne titled *Men and Women of Space* (Univelt, 1992) (see entry 1095), which is a complete and comprehensive biographical source of all individuals who have traveled in space.

The section Chemistry lists several newer works, including *American Chemists and Chemical Engineers* (Gould Books, 1994) (see entry 1098), which covers more than 250 individuals who have made significant contributions in addition to the original volume, which included more than 500 biographical entries; and *The Nobel Prize Winners: Chemistry* (Salem Press, 1990) (see entry 1100), which provides detailed biographies of the laureates in chemistry.

Computer Science, Engineering and Technology, and Environmental Science contain only several sources each. The recently published *International Biographical Dictionary of Computer Pioneers* (Fitzroy Dearborn, 1995) (see entry 1102) is an important source for information on several hundred individuals who played an important role on the development of computers, and the *Biographical Dictionary of the History of Technology* (Routledge, 1996) (see entry 1105) offers researchers handy information on inventions and inventors. Several sources are included that provide biographical information on environmental scientists, including *The Environmentalists: A Biographical Dictionary from the 17th Century to the Present* (Facts on File, 1993) (see entry 1108) and *Who Is Who at the Earth Summit, Rio de Janeiro, 1992* (Vision Link Education Foundations, 1992) (see entry 1109), which includes more than 30,000 participants of this important meeting.

Finally, though there are few new sources in the areas of mathematics, physics, and physiology, some unique sources are included. In Mathematics, the *Biographical Dictionary of Mathematicians* . . . (Scribner's, 1991) (see entry 1112) is a subset of the *Dictionary of Scientific Biography* (Scribner's, 1990) (see entry 1059) and provides more than 1,000 biographies of mathematicians and other scholars related to that field; the major biographical source is the *Combined Membership List of the American Mathematical Society* . . . (American Mathematical Society, 1954-) (see entry 1113), which includes information on more than 50,000 mathematicians. In Physics, the *McGraw-Hill Dictionary of Physics* (McGraw-Hill, 1996) (see entry 1116) covers all aspects of physics, including a very large number of brief biographies. In Britain, there are two biographical sources for physiologists, including W. J. O'Connor's *British Physiologists 1885-1914* . . . (St. Martin's Press, 1991) (see entry 1118) and *Founders of British Physiology* . . . (St. Martin's Press, 1988) (see entry 1119), which covers an even earlier period from 1820 through 1885.

GENERAL WORKS

Current Biographies

1056.   **American Men & Women of Science: A Biographical Directory**.... New Providence, N.J., R. R. Bowker/Reed Reference Publishing, 1998- . 8v. index. $850.00/set for recent edition. ISSN 0192-8570.

This set provides personal and professional data on more than 120,000 individuals working in the fields of the biological and physical sciences, engineering, mathematics, statistics, and computer science. Persons covered must have exhibited significant contributions to their disciplines, especially through publications, research activities, and attainment of high professional positions. Currently active scientists are covered; those who have died since the last edition have references to that edition. Retrospective or historical coverage requires libraries to maintain previous editions of this title.

This source certainly ranks among the best titles in its field. Biographies have been verified through contact with the persons discussed and entries show careful proofing. Searches by name are easy, but subject searching is somewhat limited. The index volume lists entrants under one or more of subject specialties (such as inorganic chemistry), subdivided by state of residency. A more detailed keyword index by research interests would facilitate more precise subject searches.

Also interesting are the statistical tables and graphs in the index volume that break down the people by discipline and geographical location. The inclusion of gender as a category here would have been quite useful. However, these minor quibbles should not detract from the status of this title as a standard in the field.—**Christopher W. Nolan and Robert L. Wick**

1057.   **The Biographical Dictionary of Scientists**. 2d ed. Ray Porter, ed. New York, Oxford University Press, 1994. 891p. illus. index. $85.00. Q141.B528. 509.2'2. LC 94-10982. ISBN 0-19-521083-2.

Over 1,200 men and women, major contributors to science, are profiled in concise biographies, some with figures or examples. For each of seven disciplines (astronomy, biology, chemistry, engineering, geology, mathematics, and physics), essays review major developments and recent events (e.g., test-tube babies) but fail to identify future trends. Basic biographical information is recounted in entries along with a discussion of each scientist's landmark contributions. Although many familiar scientists appear (e.g., Einstein, Cousteau), some notable women do not (e.g., Rosalind Franklin), and the criteria for inclusion are not delineated. The unsigned biographies, which vary in length, stress important historical and scientific contexts. Although the editor is a well-known scientific historian, contributor qualifications and sources consulted are not indicated. An extensive glossary and appendix of Nobel Prize winners complete the volume.

The comprehensive index to biographies and topics (e.g., DNA, ecology), without page numbers, refers to the alphabetical arrangement. The index hinders rather than facilitates the searching process when a topic (e.g., transition metals) refers to a scientist (e.g., G. Wilkinson) whose entry leads to a joint one (e.g., Fischer and Wilkinson) that is out of order amongst similarly named individuals.—**Sandra E. Belanger**

1058. **Biographies of Scientists for Sci-Tech Libraries: Adding Faces to the Facts**. Tony Stankus, ed. Binghamton, N.Y., Haworth Press, 1992. 228p. (*Science & Technology Libraries,* vol.11, no.4). $29.95. Q141.B535. 509.2. LC 91-31241. ISBN 1-56024-214-0.

This volume contains a variety of essays that identify sources of biographical information on scientists. The editor's intent is that the listed titles will go beyond the merely scientific contributions of the scientists to explore some of the drama of their lives, thereby making science look more appealing to those considering such a career. Consequently, consistency of approach and comprehensiveness of coverage are not goals. The scientists represent both U.S. and foreign figures, almost all from the nineteenth and twentieth centuries. The essays, each covering one discipline, vary considerably in style. Some are lists of key figures with brief biographies and lists of references included; some are general bibliographic essays; and one is a mixture of the history of the discipline with a hodgepodge of tables, including Library of Congress subject headings and classification numbers, as well as lists of periodical indexes and monographic series.

This work succeeds only so far as each essay does. Some, such as that on animal scientists and the editor's introduction, provide their biographees with lively annotations that emphasize the excitement of science. Others, such as those on computer science and physics, are less selective in their sources and fail to indicate which titles might be especially engaging.

This is a monographic reprint of a volume of the serial *Science & Technology Libraries,* and the publishers have elected to include several articles unrelated to the title and purpose of the book. Additionally, no index is provided, so reference use of the work is severely limited. Most of the scientists covered are sufficiently famous to appear in other reference works, such as the classic *Dictionary of Scientific Biography* (see entry 1059), which also contains extensive bibliographies. The volume under review might be useful in circulating collections to pique student interest in science, but it does not offer much to a reference collection that owns other biographical sources in the sciences. [R: LJ, July 92, p. 133]—**Christopher W. Nolan**

1059. **Dictionary of Scientific Biography**. Frederic L. Holmes, ed. New York, Scribner's, 1990. iv. (various paging). index. $160.00/set. Q141.D5. 509'.2'2. LC 80-27830. ISBN 0-684-19178-4.

With volume 19, supplement II, the *Dictionary of Scientific Biography* focus on international twentieth-century scientists, updating the limited coverage in the original 16-volume reference work. Biographies of 417 leading scientists, the majority of whose lives ended between 1970 and 1981, are presented. The selection criteria for the sciences are not stated. As in the original volumes, the scientific areas of the scientists are limited to mathematics, astronomy, physics, chemistry, biology, and Earth sciences.

The 265 international contributors continue the scholarly reputation of the work. The signed biographies (2 columns to over 18 columns long) contain birth and death locations and dates, scientific field, and a bibliography of each scientist's original works and secondary literature. Very few diagrams are used in the text, and there are no photographs or portraits of the scientists. The biographies are well written and reflect special knowledge of each scientist's activities. Volume 18 contains an excellent, detailed subject index to the two supplements and a list of scientists by discipline.

As stated in the preface, future supplements will continue to include eligible scientists not appearing in earlier volumes. It is also noted that relatively few female scientists are represented. The board feels that future volumes will rectify this deficiency. It is also aware of specialty areas in the natural sciences and social sciences and medicine that are not included in this reference work. With the success of the work, the board hopes that similar ventures into these areas will be published. This will be needed since there are more scientists living now than in the whole of time. This biographical dictionary is a monumental project and an excellent reference work in the history of science. [R: RBB, July 90, p. 2113]—**Anne C. Roess**

1060. Hackmann, W. D. **Apples to Atoms: Portraits of Scientists from Newton to Rutherford**. Wappingers Falls, Antique Collectors' Club, 1991. 88p. illus. bibliog. $11.95pa. ISBN 0-904017-72-9.

In the autumn of 1986, the Science Museum in London held an exhibition of portraits from the National Portrait Gallery titled "Science's Image and Its Relations with Art." This is the catalog from that exhibition. The portraits are of members of Britain's scientific community from the seventeenth century to the present day. They were selected to show their personal attributes, but also to illustrate how the setting and symbols chosen by subject and artist linked the scientist to his or her world. For example, the subject might be portrayed as sitting in front of a blackboard covered with mathematical equations, or working in a laboratory.

Each of the portraits is accompanied by an account of the subject's scientific contributions, written by Willem Hackmann, Assistant Curator of the Museum of the History of Science in Oxford. The main text is preceded by an introductory essay by Roy Porter, of the Wellcome Institute of the History of Medicine. Porter discusses science's impact on society during the time covered, and how science was viewed by nonscientific writers and thinkers (many saw it as threatening). He also discusses the significance of portraiture, and how the genre in general has depicted the scientist.

The portraits are reproduced in black-and-white, with eight also reproduced in color. The book makes for fascinating browsing, but its value to a collection would depend largely on how extensively the library collects in the history of science: the textual information will be available from other sources likely to be in the collection, but the portraits may not be.—**Donald J. Marion and Robert L. Wick**

1061. Kessler, James H., and others. **Distinguished African American Scientists of the 20th Century**. Phoenix, Ariz., Oryx Press, 1996. 382p. illus. index. $49.95. ISBN 0-89774-955-3.

While most people can list without difficulty the names of eminent black Americans in politics, sports, music, movies, law, and literature, they cannot with equal ease list the names of famous African Americans in physics, mathematics, chemistry, or medicine. Yet, numerous black Americans have worked actively and successfully in the various sciences, many achieving recognition and eminence in their fields. Given unfortunate racial stereotypes and misperceptions, it is important that black children and adults, as well as other Americans, learn about them.

The book under review serves this important purpose. It presents to the reader the lives and achievements of 100 African Americans who have reached the highest academic levels in such diverse fields as anthropology, physics, mathematics, and endocrinology. The brief biographies are based on information gathered from a variety of sources, in many cases including material provided by the subjects themselves. This is most valuable as readers are able to see reflections of some of the personal struggles these outstanding individuals went through in order to accomplish what they did.

One fine example of the people profiled is young scientist Mae C. Jemison, who became the first African American woman astronaut. Among the others who are listed are George Carruthers, who developed a far UV camera/spectrograph that was used in the Apollo missions to the moon; J. Ernest Wilkins, who received his Ph.D. in mathematics from the University of Chicago when he was barely 19 years old; and Meredith Gourdine, the Olympic medalist and engineering physicist who invented many things and established his own company. Many women scientists are discussed as well. Important to note is the fact that between 1870 and 1900, black inventors had more than 400 patents to their names. Because the book limits itself to the twentieth century, such men as Benjamin Banneker, the self-taught black mathematician of the eighteenth century who studied astronomy and wrote an almanac based on his calculations, and Edward A. Bouchet, the first black Ph.D. in physics who graduated from Yale University in the late nineteenth century, are not mentioned. Fortunately, George Washington Carver, who became one of the most eminent agricultural chemists of his time, has found a place here.

Children should remember that many of the people mentioned in this book grew up under difficult economic constraints, social injustices, and racial prejudices, with little encouragement from the outside. However, they were individuals with enormous determination and a sense of self-worth who struggled against obstacles. Black students have countless role models to draw inspiration from, and this book offers insight into the lives of many such heroes. [R: LJ, 1 Apr 96, pp. 74-76; RBB, 15 Feb 96, p. 1042; SLJ, May 96, p. 146; VOYA, Aug 96, p. 190]—**Varadaraja V. Raman**

1062. **Larousse Dictionary of Scientists**. Hazel Muir, ed. New York, Larousse Kingfisher Chambers, 1994. 595p. index. $35.00. ISBN 0-7523-0002-4.

This compact 1st edition provides access to an impressive amount of biographical information at an affordable price. More than 2,200 descriptions of eminent natural scientists, averaging about

200 words each, are included. Emphasis is given to physics, chemistry, biology, astronomy, and the earth sciences, although mathematics and medicine are well represented also. A selection of ancient natural philosophers and modern technologists completes the work. In its scope and contents, this dictionary is comparable to the *Biographical Encyclopedia of Scientists* (see ARBA 95, entry 1484), but is more compact, less costly, and generally more focused upon the professional accomplishments of the subjects than on personal details.

The dictionary is not completely free of errors; occasional typographical errors and inconsistencies exist (e.g., the famous Biot-Savart law of magnetism is mentioned in Felix Savart's entry but not in Jean-Baptiste Biot's), as well as significant mistakes (such as incorrect first names for Sonya Kovalevskaya and Bernd Matthias). A potentially valuable feature is the subject index, which links important topics to the individuals described in the book. In principle, this would allow readers to easily identify the leading exponents of a scientific subdiscipline. However, the current version of the index is poorly done. For example, having 10 subcategories related to X-rays but just 1 for vision seems unreasonable. Heike Kamerlingh Onnes, the patriarch of low-temperature physics, is not listed under the heading for that field; neither Biot nor Savart appears under magnetism. To make matters worse, the index is difficult to read because the entries and headings are set in nearly indistinguishable fonts. Despite these shortcomings, the volume promises to be a useful reference, and is a welcome addition to the splendid Larousse collection of publications. [R: Choice, Feb 95, pp. 917-18; LJ, Jan 95, p. 89; RBB, 1 Feb 95, p. 1028]—**John U. Trefny**

1063.   **Notable Twentieth-Century Scientists**. Emily J. McMurray, Jane Kelly Kosek, and Roger M. Valade III, eds. Detroit, Gale, 1995. 4v. illus. index. $295.00/set. ISBN 0-8103-9181-3.

Biographical information is always in demand and often difficult to find, particularly when the subject is a living scientist or one who has made relatively recent contributions. For these reasons, *Notable Twentieth-Century Scientists* is a welcome and much-needed addition to any reference collection. This reference work features nearly 1,300 scientists from all over the world and covers the natural, physical, and applied sciences, from biology, mathematics, and chemistry to computer science, ecology, and engineering. Entries include prominent figures, such as Albert Einstein and Marie Curie, as well as lesser-known contemporary scientists working in significant, cutting-edge areas of research. Of particular note is the emphasis on women (17 percent of all profiles), minority (12 percent), and non-Western (6 percent) scientists. Indexes by gender and nationality/ethnicity are especially helpful.

The advisory board for this work, consisting of librarians, academics, and individuals from organizations and associations, developed a comprehensive list of scientists for inclusion according to the following criteria: discoveries, overall contributions, or impact on scientific progress in the twentieth century; receipt of a major science award (e.g., Nobel Prize, National Medal of Science); involvement or influence in education, organizational leadership, or public policy; familiarity to the general public; and notable "first" achievements, including degrees earned and positions held. The biographical sketches are written by over 150 contributors, although it is unclear whether they are scientists or have backgrounds in science. These contributors gathered the biographical information from published sources when available; in many cases, however, a lack of published data required telephone interviews and correspondence with the scientists or with their institutions or families.

Entries are arranged alphabetically by surname and begin with a heading that includes the full name, dates of birth and death, nationality, and area of specialization. The biographical essay then follows, ranging from 400 to 2,500 words. The sketches are of consistently high quality and often well written and well organized. Each entry describes the scientist's personal and professional achievements in a lively and interesting style that is accessible to readers without a background in science. Cross-references to entries on the scientist's colleagues, predecessors, and contemporaries are noted in boldface type. A list of selected writings by the scientist and reference sources for additional information follow the essay. About one-third of the entries provide photographs of the scientists.

Each of the four volumes is prefaced by an alphabetical list of the scientists profiled in all four volumes and by a chronology of important scientific events from 1895 to 1993. In addition to the gender and ethnicity indexes, volume 4 contains a comprehensive subject index to scientific terms used in the text (e.g., *complex analysis* and *computer-aided design*) and a field-of-specialization index. Not surprisingly, biochemistry, chemistry, engineering, mathematics, medicine, and physics receive the largest number of entries.

Notable Twentieth-Century Scientists complements other biographical sources by offering a number of unique and valuable features. First, it strives to be comprehensive and succeeds by covering scientists who are not well known. Second, its biographical sketches are longer and more complete than many other resources, such as biographical directories or the *Biographical Encyclopedia of Scientists*. Third, the essays are written by contributors, not by the scientists themselves, as in *Modern Scientists and Engineers* (McGraw-Hill, 1980). Therefore, the sketches are more consistent in quality and format and less prone to personal bias. For example, professional setbacks and controversies are discussed forthrightly, as in the essay on Robert Gallo. Finally, *Notable Twentieth-Century Scientists* is the first source of comprehensive scientific biography to recognize and strive to more fully represent the diversity behind scientific achievements. Overall, this reference work is an excellent contribution to scientific biography. Highly recommended! [R: WLB, Feb 95, p. 70] —**Janice M. Jaguszewski**

1064.   **Notable Women in the Physical Sciences: A Biographical Dictionary**. Benjamin F. Shearer and Barbara S. Shearer, eds. Westport, Conn., Greenwood Press, 1997. 479p. illus. index. $49.95. ISBN 0-313-29303-1.

Essays in this nicely compiled volume highlight the contributions of women scientists from the United States and a few from Europe, Canada, China, and India. Fields covered include physics, astronomy, physical chemistry, and chemistry, but not applied sciences, such as engineering and materials science. This volume complements other reference works providing biographical information about women scientists—such as Marilyn Bailey Ogilvie's *Women in Science: Antiquity through the Nineteenth Century* (see ARBA 88, entry 1441) and Martha J. Bailey's *American Women in Science* (see ARBA 96, entry 1486)—by its emphasis on twentieth-century scientists whose work is continuing. Editors Benjamin and Barbara Shearer also produced the earlier work, *Notable Women in the Life Sciences* (see AREA 97, entry 1231), to which this volume is certainly a welcome companion.

Each entry includes a straightforward biography of 1,000 to 1,500 words, a chronology, and a bibliography comprising both primary works of the scientist and secondary sources. Reviews are signed, and an appendix gives short descriptions of the contributors, who include scientists, librarians, and researchers on women. Essays note if a scientist received a starred entry (denoting outstanding work) in the *American Men of Science* (Jacques Cattell Press, 1906, 1968), a detail to help researchers tracing the historical treatment of women scientists. Useful appendixes include a list of scientists by specialty and a compilation of prize-winners. Photographs accompany approximately half of the entries—an excellent addition considering that some of these women scientists are not well known.

Necessary limitations to this volume include the lack of critical analysis in the brief essays and the selective rather than comprehensive approach to inclusion of scientists. Still, this work should be added to collections in high school, public, and academic libraries as a quick reference and first stop for research.—**Jean C. McManus**

1065.   **Who's Who in European Research and Development**. New Providence, N.J., Bowker-Saur/Reed Reference Publishing, 1995- . index. $400.00. ISBN 1-85739-097-0.

This significant work is one of three parts of the new European Research and Development database (ER&D) that exists as two CD-ROMs and two printed titles. The first CD-ROM lists 20,272 organizations and their 120,000-plus staff members who completed the supplied entrant forms asking for 18 categories of information. The second CD-ROM analyzes the above information for the top categories of staff (totaling 10,000 names). This leaves 110,000 remaining names dispersed in CD-ROM I. However, a hypertext link between the CDs can be exercised so as to obtain an enhanced entry having both organizational and total staff information.

First of the printed works is the two-volume *Dictionary of European Research and Development* (DER&D), which is reviewed in ARBA 96, entry 1504. Next is the 800-page, softbound *Who's Who in European Research and Development 1995* (WWER&D), with an entry load comparable to

Who's Who in America and alphabetical order for the same 10,000 staff members as DER&D and 2 indexes. The preliminary pages are most useful, especially an outstanding statistical study of the database by Jeremy Howells of the Center for Business Research, Cambridge University, and the staff of the European Community. The "Key to Biographical Entries" lists 18 categories of data that can best be summarized as having the elements of an academic promotion memorandum plus communication links. (Listees were expected to respond in English, too.)

In addition to checking organizations and personnel of wide renown and a "Must" category (Nobel Prize winners, Fellows of the Royal Society), the compilers checked organizations in lists of "Small-to-Medium" private businesses. Another concern is the stated prevalence of nonfunded research and development groups in certain Eastern European countries where the staffs no longer reported for work. A point where input personnel evidently erred are the instances of staff of international organizations serving in Geneva invariably listed as being of Swiss nationality. There are about 15 biographical entries per 3-column page; a somewhat larger typeface would have been welcomed for extended-use sessions.

There is a wide range in the names shown per country: Iceland has 2 names, Portugal has 143, and Russia has 443. An even wider range exists in subject specializations, partly because one could list more than a single topic. Overall, the 786 specializations averaged 65 researchers each.

A major consideration in purchase decisions is the 110,000 biographies only on the CD-ROMs. Marketing studies of a less-than-definitive nature could get by with the paper copies, but Fortune 500-type studies would need the CD-ROM regularly.—**Eugene B. Jackson**

1066. **Who's Who in Science and Engineering**. New Providence, N.J., Marquis Who's Who/Reed Reference Publishing, 1992/93- . index. $259.95 for recent edition. ISSN 1063-5599.

After all of these years, the Marquis Who's Who series has settled into a fairly standardized entry for those people who are included. This format requires no new evaluation. The variation, however, is in the collection of new groups of individuals by different subjects or interests, and the compilation of various indexes to the work.

This compilation, which is composed of biographies of living scientists and engineers throughout the world, is one of their newer products. To round out this volume, the publishers have included persons not only in the physical and life sciences and medical technologies, but also in selective "soft" sciences such as sociology, economics, and psychology.

Altogether, this collection includes more than 26,000 individuals in 110 distinct specialties. Its three primary indexes are a geographic index, professional area index listings, and the major honors and awards organized by fields and by professional organizations within the fields. One of the major benefits of the work will be its assistance to universities and corporations in recruiting new faculty and staff.—**Robert J. Havlik**

1067. **Who's Who in Science in Europe: A Biographical Guide to Science, Technology, Agriculture and Medicine**. London, Cartermill International; and New York, Stockton Press, 1967- . 2v. index. $950.00/set for recent edition. ISSN 0083-968X.

As a subset of the World Research Database, *Who's Who in Science in Europe* provides biographic references to more than 60,000 individuals at 30,000-plus institutions in 36 European countries, including Turkey but excluding the former Soviet Republic. This work has become a standard over the years. The scientists selected come from the areas of education government, agriculture, industry, and technology.

The entries furnish the individual's name, year of birth, present job, employer and year appointed, main professional and research interests, higher education and degrees (including the degree-granting institutions), previous professional experience with length of service, current telephone and fax numbers address, and a list of professional organizations and societies to which the person belongs. In addition, major publications are listed, but full bibliographies of works are not included. While narrative biographic references, are not supplied, the facts listed provide a high level of information concerning the individuals. The scientists profiled are self-selected in that the editors send forms to various institutions and societies requesting the information (the forms are not sent directly to the individual scientists). Entries that are derived from printed sources or from third parties and not verified by the individual are marked with an asterisk.

As a companion volume to *European Research Centres*, *Who's Who in Science in Europe* is the most comprehensive listing of biographical profiles of European scientists. Both works are also available on CD-ROM. While the subject index is detailed, the directory would benefit from additional appendixes listing scientific areas, scientists by research center or laboratory, or even major research grants obtained. It would appear that because the information is in machine-readable form, generating these additional appendixes would be relatively simple. *Who's Who in Science in Europe* is an important selection for all larger public and academic libraries and could be considered essential for important scientific collections. The price of the volumes probably makes the work an unlikely purchase for individual scientists.—**Robert L. Wick**

1068.   **Who's Who in Technology**. Kimberley A. McGrath, ed. Detroit, Gale, 1986- . index. $195.00 for recent edition. ISSN 0877-5901.

This large and impressive work contains biographical descriptions of more than 25,000 North American scientists and engineers. Each entry includes personal and employment data as well as affiliations, honors, awards, and special achievements in the individual's areas of expertise. The listed biographees have been selected by virtue of their technical contributions, positions of responsibility, and nominations from professional associates. As no selection process is perfect, it is certainly possible to question numerous entries and omissions in the present work. Nevertheless, the cross-section of "technologists" represented here seems reasonable and undoubtedly improves with each new edition.

Several special sections are provided to aid the reader; for example, lists of entries by geographical location, by employer, and by field of expertise. Another separate section furnishes obituaries of listed individuals who have died since the previous edition. Neither these sections nor the main entries themselves are perfectly up-to-date given the continual changes within the professions. Even so, the attempts to organize the information in multiple ways is a welcome improvement. The work is available in various electronic formats as well as in print. It is a useful complement to other biographical collections for anyone needing to identify the technological leaders of the times.—**John U. Trefny and Robert L. Wick**

1069.   **Who's Who in Theology and Science: An International Biographical and Bibliographical Guide**. . . . Compiled by the John Templeton Foundation. New York, Continuum Publishing, 1996. index. $59.50. ISBN 0-8264-0874-5.

This guide contains four directories and five indexes, all designed to direct users to individuals, rganizations, and publications "active in the dialogue between religion and science, or between religion, spirituality, and faith on the one hand, and science and technology on the other." Directory A, consisting of 465 pages, lists individuals publishing in the field, about 30 percent of whom reside in the United States. Each entry provides a basic résumé, listing current addresses, educational history, positions held, and areas of interest, along with selected publications. Directory B is limited to individuals actively interested in the field and runs slightly less than 100 pages. Additional directories are devoted to organizations, journals, and newsletters. The book ends with a brief description of John Marks Templeton, founder and trustee of the John Templeton Foundation, which underwrote publication of this book. His statement, "The Theology of Humility," is also reprinted. The John Templeton Foundation is devoted primarily to furthering research and publication by scientists "related to the creative and purposive activities of God."

The major shortcoming of this directory is that it includes only individuals who responded to a questionnaire circulated by the foundation. Thus, the only information provided is that solicited from individuals who wished to be included in this "who's who." Consequently, many scholars who have actively studied and contributed to the field of science and religion are noticeably absent. Still, as a reference work for anyone interested in this subject in general, but with no other resources at hand, this guide is a helpful starting place from which to begin a search for more detailed information concerning individuals and organizations interested in the subject of science and theology.—**Joseph W. Dauben**

1070. **Who's Who of British Scientists**. Dorking, Surrey, England Simon Books; distr., New York, St. Martin's Press, 1969/70- . $75.00 for recent edition. ISBN 0-312-87433-2.

Although the first and second editions of *Who's Who of British Scientists* were published in 1969 and 1971, it took nine years for the 3rd edition to appear. This meant that the new edition had to practically start from scratch and suffer a few compromises in the process. Since the editors had to rely upon voluntary submission of entries, biographies of recent winners of Nobel prizes in science, as promised, are scarce. Also, they had to abandon plans for a cross-reference list of scientists by scientific specialization. The book, however, is a wealth of information on over 6,000 scientists in universities, polytechnics, research establishments, and industry, mostly under the age of fifty. Documented are the birth dates, current position, past appointments, selected publications, professional interests, and current address for each entry. The selected publications, although limited, give shortened citations, but they are sufficient for most librarians to track down. Abbreviations and lists of research establishments, scientific societies, and professional institutions in Great Britain are also given. Larger reference libraries will find this volume useful.—**Robert J. Havlik**

1071. Yount, Lisa. **Contemporary Women Scientists**. New York, Facts on File, 1994. 124p. illus. index. (American Profiles). $16.95. Q130.Y65. 509.2'273. LC 93-26821. ISBN 0-8160-2895-8.

Contemporary Women Scientists contains profiles of 10 women who have been recognized as having made important contributions to some field of scientific inquiry. The articles are arranged chronologically by the year of birth of the subjects, with Helen Brooke Taussig (1899) the oldest, and Flossie Wong-Staal (1946) the youngest. Each article contains a picture, a biographical chronology, and a bibliography of titles of and about the subject's work. The women chosen represent a balance and variety of scientific fields, from astronomy to AIDS research. The omission of female astronauts is valid, given the greater publicity that these women scientists have received.

This book is designed to meet the needs of middle and high school girls who might consider a career in science. Yount says that if a girl finds science fun, she should not let anything or anyone stop her from pursuing a scientific career. She states, "All the women in this book became first-class scientists while leading full personal lives. There's no reason you can't do the same." However, the book also makes it clear that while more women are in scientific disciplines today than ever before, they still are less likely to be promoted and rewarded on the same basis as men and much more likely than the general population to be divorced. While one might want to see more entries, *Contemporary Women Scientists* is a valuable addition to the scant material available on the topic. [R: SBF, Aug/Sept 94, p. 173; VOYA, Oct 94, pp. 237-381]—**Kay O. Cornelius**

Retrospective Biographies

1072. Aaseng, Nathan. **Twentieth-Century Inventors**. New York, Facts on File, 1991. 132p. illus. index. (American Profiles Series, 2). $16.95. T39.A37. 609.2'2. LC 90-46547. ISBN 0-8160-2485-5.

Invention is currently one of the most popular topics in the K-12 curriculum. *Twentieth-Century Inventors* will lead students in middle and high school to inventors whose names are not, for the most part, well known, but whose works have dramatically changed the way twentieth-century citizens live. One of the most fascinating and valuable sections of Aaseng's book is his introductory chapter, in which he explains why inventors in the twentieth century tend to be much less well known than their nineteenth-century counterparts. Indeed, the only inventors in this volume likely to be familiar to students are Orville and Wilbur Wright. Other inventors and inventions included are Leo Baekeland (plastic), Vladimir Zworykin (television), Chester Carlson (xerography), and Wilson Great Batch (the implantable pacemaker). Aaseng provides a solid background profile of each inventor, including insightful information about their formative years. Of particular value is the emphasis on the perseverance, tenacity, and task commitment of these men. Students will leave these profiles with the notion that success comes through hard work and sacrifice. Most of the products created by these inventors are highly technical, yet Aaseng's handling of scientific information is such that it can be understood by most lay readers.

If there is any fault to be found with this work, it is that no women or minority inventors are represented. One hopes this omission is redressed in *Black Scientists* and *Women Scientists,* two forthcoming companion volumes. On balance, *Twentieth-Century Inventors* is an excellent resource book that should be available to students in all middle and high school libraries and should also be in science classrooms.—**Jerry D. Flack**

1073.   Number not used.

1074.   Bailey, Martha J. **American Women in Science: A Biographical Dictionary**. Santa Barbara, Calif., ABC-CLIO, 1994. 463p. illus. index. $60.00. ISBN 0-87436-740-9.

American Women in Science concentrates specifically on women working in the sciences before 1950. The dictionary is derived from numerous sources, including *American Men & Women of Science* (see ARBA 93, entry 1438; ARBA 90, entry 1420; and ARBA 87, entry 1380), *Women Scientists of America* (Johns Hopkins University Press, 1995), *The Dictionary of American Biography*, *Women Scientists from Antiquity to the Present* (see ARBA 87, entry 1381), and others. Other sources used to compile the dictionary included women listed in other sources who started their employment prior to 1950, women selected for recognition by the National Academy of Sciences, women scientists identified as working for federal or state agencies, and other women who contributed to the development of various sciences in the nineteenth and early twentieth centuries working for companies, museums, arboretums, or associations. In all, more than 400 women scientists are listed in Bailey's work.

Each entry contains the area of scientific specialization, education, an employment record, a brief biography, a list of awards and specific accomplishments, and a bibliography of the sources of information concerning the scientist. When available, a photograph of the scientist is also provided. Appendixes furnish a select bibliography, illustration credits, and an index.

American Women in Science is a welcome addition to the biographical literature in the sciences. The women's entries in *American Men & Women of Science* were all too brief, and often failed to provide vital information. This work contains much more detailed and accurate information on women scientists. It is recommended for libraries on all levels. The dictionary is especially useful for personal collections, and smaller school and public libraries where the larger biographical dictionaries are not collected. [R: BR, Jan/Feb 95, p. 59]—**Robert L. Wick**

1075.   **Biographical Index to American Science: The Seventeenth Century to 1920**. Clark A. Elliott, comp. Westport, Conn., Greenwood Press, 1990. 300p. (Bibliographies and Indexes in American History, no.16). $55.00. Q141.B533. 509.2'2. LC 90-31735. ISBN 0-313-26566-6.

This work presents basic biographical data for approximately 2,850 American scientists who died prior to 1921. The volume supplements the author's *Biographical Dictionary of American Science: The Seventeenth through the Nineteenth Centuries* (see ARBA 80, entry 1324). The entries are much briefer in the present work, but there are three times as many persons listed. While not intended to be comprehensive, this work provides a cross-section of scientists from all disciplines, including those on the periphery of the scientific community.

Entries in the main section are arranged alphabetically by last name. Data includes birth and death years, major disciplines and occupations, entry numbers for works by or about the scientists listed in the *National Union Catalog of Manuscript Collections* (Chadwyck Healy, 1988), and references to other biographical sources. An index of names by scientific fields completes the volume. Fields range from the broad, such as chemistry, to the specific, such as almanac making. Individuals may be listed under more than one field.

The book is sturdily bound and easy to use. Its real value may be as a tool for identifying more specific information sources on obscure individuals who contributed to the transitional years from classical to modern science. The general scope of the work allows the inclusion of persons who might normally have been omitted from more selective reference works. At the same time, selection of entries is somewhat irregular. For example, one finds an entry for Eli Whitney but none for Cyrus McCormick. The user may also become frustrated by not being informed of a person's main achievements and the need to check other biographical sources for more specific data. [R: Choice, Nov 90, p. 450; RBB, 1 Nov 90, p. 559]—**Andrew G. Torok**

1076.   Cocks, Elijah E., and Josiah C. Cocks. **Who's Who on the Moon: A Biographical Diction-ary of Lunar Nomenclature**. Greensboro, N.C., Tudor, 1995. 600p. illus. maps. $45.00. ISBN 0-936389-27-3.

The moon is the second brightest object in the Earth's sky, next to the sun. The fact that varia-tions of its surface are visible to the unaided eye has made the moon a source of lore and fascination. Some of the largest features were given names by various mapmakers of Europe beginning early in the seventeenth century, reflecting mostly European interests. With the development of the tele-scope, these features were seen in greater detail, and the lunar nomenclature became more confused. The International Astronomical Union (IAU), established in 1921, set out to standardize the naming of lunar features, resulting in 681 names. With the early lunar orbiters of the 1960s, the number of identifiable features dramatically increased. The United Nations, working with the IAU, sanctioned the naming of 1,993 lunar features. Of these, 1,586 are named for historical individuals.

The authors have compiled in this single volume a collection of biographical sketches of these 1,586 individuals. Included is the type, size, and location of the feature on the moon's surface. A sec-tion of photographs of the moon, with coordinates and features labeled, is provided, although the names are difficult to read. The five different lists found in the appendix are particularly helpful. The first is a list of women honorees. The next two lists are sorted, first by professions, and then by countries of origin. The last two are lists sorted by location and by size. The biographies provide only the very briefest information, which is reasonable within the purpose of this book. This resource would be an as-set in any general reference collection. [R: Choice, Feb 96, pp. 924-26]—**Margaret F. Dominy**

1077.   Daintith, John, and others. **Biographical Encyclopedia of Scientists**. 2d ed. Philadelphia, Institute of Physics Publishing, 1994. 2v. illus. index. $190.00/set. o.p. ISBN 0-7503-0287-9.

This handsome set is the 2d edition of a work first published in 1981. Approximately 10 percent of the more than 2,000 entries are new. Most of these are taken from basic sciences such as physics, chemistry, biology, and astronomy. Fields such as medicine, mathematics, engineering, some social sciences, and even philosophy are covered to a lesser extent. Winners of the Nobel Prize and similar recognitions are included, as one would expect. Others seem to have been selected because of peer recognition or even public notoriety. Each entry is headed by the subject's full name, birth and (if ap-plicable) death dates and locations, nationality, and major field. The narrative is typically a brisk sev-eral hundred words long, basically accurate, and usually delightful. Unlike many encyclopedias, this one is fun to read. One can scarcely turn past more than one or two pages without being stopped by a biography of compelling interest. Chronologically, the range is impressive—from the early Greeks to individuals of recent accomplishments, like George Smoot (cosmology) and Edward Witten (string theory). Though the emphasis is clearly on scientific achievement rather than on the lives or circumstances of the subjects, there is a significant amount of commentary about their personalities (e.g., the skepticisms and individual styles of Geoffrey Burbidge and Fred Hoyle) or controversies (e.g., those surrounding David Baltimore and Robert Gallo). Scientific contributions are described only in simple, qualitative terms.

Although errors are relatively scarce, there are a few serious ones. Paid Chu's famous super-conducting compound has a stoichiometry described b $Y_1Ba_2Cu_3O_{7-x}$ rather than the strange variation given in his entry. Biased Josephson junctions, described in the section on Brian Jo-sephson, have currents that alternate at frequencies proportional to the bias voltage, not inversely proportional to it. The word "semiconductors" rather than "superconductors" is unfortunately used in the same article. Also, the history of "spin" is confusing, with credit for its discovery correctly given to Samuel Goudsmit and George Uhlenbeck but *also to* Wolfgang Pauli, who, in fact, ini-tially discouraged the idea. There are inevitable selections or omissions with which one might be inclined to argue. For the most part, the editors seem to have used good judgment, although it is hard to see how the discredited names of Martin Fleischmann and Stanley Pons (for example) be-long here among so many others of enduring accomplishment. The encyclopedia ends with several appendixes of questionable value: a chronology, a brief and hardly complete listing of significant scientific institutions, and a short bibliography. Subject and name indexes (the latter confusingly contains only individuals who are mentioned in the text but who do not themselves have entries) complete the work. [R: Choice, Oct 94, p. 256]—**John U. Trefny**

1078.   **Dictionary of Scientific Biography**. Charles Coulston Gillespie, ed.-in-chief. New York, Scribner's, 1989-90. 18v. $695.00/set. ISBN 0-684-151448.

The set, over seventeen years in preparation, comprises eighteen basic volumes, a supplement, and the index. The *DSB,* edited under the auspices of the American Council of Learned Societies, is a comprehensive reference work in the history of science. Some 5,000 biographies of mathematicians and natural scientists cover all regions and historical periods, including such topics as Japanese, Egyptian, Mesopotamian, Indian, and pre-Columbian sciences. The biographies, ranging in length from 500 to 20,000 words, were written by 1,500 authors from 90 countries. *DSB* had the full cooperation of the Academy of Sciences of the USSR. All articles were specially commissioned for *DSB,* and cover scientists from antiquity to the mid-twentieth century.

In terms of selection, this dictionary is patterned on the *Dictionary of National Biography*; it lists well-documented biographical sketches of scientists no longer living, and the selection criteria are influenced by "contributions to science . . . sufficiently distinctive to make an identifiable difference to the profession or community of knowledge." The scope is international, but, as indicated in the preface, some countries (India, China, Japan) will not be as well represented as their Western counterparts.

This highly praised work is completed by the index, which contains over 75,000 entries. Eight indexers worked for ten years preparing it. References to biographees comprise only a small portion of this comprehensive work. All but the most trivial and isolated references to other individuals are indexed. Periodicals, societies, universities, museums, medals, lectureships, and prizes are accessed. When a topic is pertinent to a particular country, the country is indexed. Scientific topics and concepts are fully indexed, including chronological and topical subheadings. The index is both logical and legible, and is in itself a contribution to scientific scholarship. Since its appearance in 1970, the *Dictionary of Scientific Biography* has been an invaluable tool; its completion makes it indispensable. [R: Choice, July 73, p. 754; Choice, Dec 73, p. 1526; LJ, 19 Sept 76, p. 1845; LJ, 1 June 80, p. 1292; WLB, June 80, pp. 669-70]—**Bohdan S. Wynar and Robert L. Wick**

1079.   Franck, Irene M., and David M. Brownstone. **Scientists and Technologists**. New York, Facts on File, 1988. 212p. illus. bibliog. index. (Work throughout History). $14.95. LC 87-19959. ISBN 0-8160-1450-7.

One of a fifteen-volume set, this book describes developments in science and technology from ancient times to the present day. Most notably, physicists, astronomers, mathematicians, engineers, chemists, alchemists, and biologists are included here, as are a few others.

Each occupation is introduced with a brief definition and a broad statement about its very early beginnings. Developments, famous scientists, and the accomplishments through the ages and in many lands are described in language that is far too sophisticated for the intended juvenile audience. The authors talk about the "vulnerability of the Ptolemaic model" in geography, and the "existence of . . . a symmetrical inverse of the Compton effect (wave-particle dualism), when [Louis de Broglie] showed that there was also a particle-wave dualism." This is difficult material to understand, but is especially so in the case of this book because few terms are defined in the text, and no glossary is provided. The chapters vary widely in length, from the mere four paragraphs that describe the work of cartographers to the twenty-four-page chapter on astronomers.

There are other shortcomings. While it is only to be expected for authors to have cross-references to related occupations in the other volumes of the series, to cite these referenced volumes as "forthcoming" will only confuse the reader, especially once they are available. The skimpy annotated bibliography has limited use. The annotation for another Facts on File publication reads: "A valuable new survey"—a less than valuable annotation. In addition, smaller public and school libraries are not likely to have the works cited here by scholarly publishers such as Oxford University Press. The illustrations are adequate, consisting mostly of woodcuts and black-and-white photographs. The index, which is printed in a small and difficult to read typeface, has few cross-references. Leonardo da Vinci is listed under "Vinci, Leonardo da," with no cross-reference under "da Vinci."

Already published titles in the Work Throughout History series are *Artists and Artisans, Builders, Clothiers, Financiers and Traders, Harvesters, Healers, Helpers and Aides, Leaders and Lawyers, Manufacturers and Miners, Performers and Players, Restaurateurs and Innkeepers, Scholars and Priests*, and *Warriors and Adventurers*. For high school and public libraries. [R: BR, May/June 88, p. 42; VOYA, Aug 88, p. 145]—**Kerry L. Kresse**

1080. **McGraw-Hill Encyclopedia of Science and Technology**. 7th ed. New York, McGraw-Hill, 1997. 20v. illus. (part col.). index. $1,600.00/set. LC 86-27422. ISBN 0-07-079292-5.

With the publication of the 7th edition, the *McGraw-Hill Encyclopedia of Science and Technology* continues to provide high school and college students with current, understandable information about all major areas of science and technology. First published in 1960, the set was slightly revised in 1966. Reviews of the following 3d, 4th, and 5th editions can be found in ARBA 71 (entry 1520), ARBA 78 (entry 1210), and ARBA 83 (entry 1267).

This edition has been expanded since the one published in 1982, from fifteen to twenty volumes. Four hundred fifty entries have been added, 500 deleted, and 1,600 revised, for a total of 7,700 articles. Computers, nuclear engineering, psychology, telecommunications, and genetics are a few of the twenty-eight main subject areas in which most of the revision has taken place. Also, 1,900 illustrations are new and 2,000 are revised, comprising about 15,000 illustrations altogether. Other changes occurring in this edition are an easier to read typeface and the addition of hundreds of new contributors, twenty of whom are Nobel Prize winners, including Hans Bethe and Henry Taube.

Articles appear alphabetically by subject, and many include cross-references to more specific topics. They are written in pyramid style, beginning with a dictionary-type definition and expanding into more detailed information. All are signed.

The extensive index cumulated in volume 20 consists of four parts: a list of contributors, scientific tables and style notations, a topical index, and an analytical index. The topical index merely lists names of topics under the seventy-seven main subject headings, with no page numbers or cross-references. The analytical index cites the volume number and page number where an article on a specific topic can be found. Subentries are indicated with an asterisk.

For an encyclopedia, *McGraw-Hill* is relatively current. For instance, an account of the space shuttle *Challenger* disaster can be found in the "Space shuttle" article, and the "Halley's comet" entry makes note of the 1986 sighting. Also, new fields of inquiry such as acid rain, supercomputer, AIDS, and computer-integrated manufacturing are now being scrutinized.

Coverage of topics is objective and up-to-date. The entry for "Death," for example, discusses such contemporary issues as organ transplantation, moment of death (is it when the mind or body dies?), and prolonging life artificially. The article is also very interesting to read and contains six cross-references within its five pages.

In comparison to other current publications, *McGraw-Hill* holds its own in terms of currency, coverage, and readability. For example, the article on cancer in *The Facts on File Scientific Yearbook 1987* (Facts on File, 1987) is less technical (partly because its audience is primarily high school students) and also less objective than *McGraw-Hill's*. The latter merely names the seven warning signs of cancer, while *Facts on File* recommends: "A mole or any other spot on the skin with any of these signs should always be examined immediately by a physician" (p. 45). *Facts on File's* commentary on the *Challenger* is also nonobjective and makes assumptions such as "the American people had become increasingly blasé about the launches" (p. 147) and "with each successful launch, NASA worried less, not more, about the O-rings, hoping that their luck would hold" (p.147). *Facts on File* has more sensational photographs than *McGraw-Hill,* in keeping with the tone of its articles, but *McGraw-Hill* is obviously a better-written, more objective source, providing more solid information in a concise but interesting fashion.

Another comparable publication is the *Encyclopedia of Physical Science and Technology* (Academic Press, 1987). Its audience includes (advanced) high school students and college students, as does *McGraw-Hill's,* but is also directed towards science professionals. The sections on air pollution and air pollution control have short glossaries at the beginning (as do all the articles) and read more like textbook chapters than *McGraw-Hill's.* The *Encyclopedia of Physical Science and Technology* (*EPST*) also contains more references to math equations and tables, while *McGraw-Hill* has more than twice the number of illustrations and graphs in its similarly lengthy, if not shorter, articles. The bibliographies for the two air pollution entries in *EPST* and in *McGraw-Hill* are similar in size and currency, *EPST* listing a total of fourteen books and articles and *McGraw-Hill* twelve. The majority of copyright dates in both works' bibliographies are from the 1980s, though *McGraw-Hill* includes a few older titles. The *McGraw-Hill* articles do contain several more cross-references than *EPST*'s.

In conclusion, the *McGraw-Hill Encyclopedia of Science and Technology* is an excellent source of science and technology information that is comprehensive and easy to use and understand. [R: LJ, Aug 87, pp. 116-17; RBB, 15 Sept 87, pp. 118-19; WLB, Sept 87, pp. 94, 96]—**Kari Sidles and Robert L. Wick**

1081. **McGraw-Hill Multimedia Encyclopedia of Science & Technology**. [CD-ROM] New York, McGraw-Hill, 1994, 1996. System requirements: IBM or compatible 386. 150-9660 CD-ROM drive. Windows 3.1. 4MB RAM. 3MB hard disk space. VGA or SVGA monitor and graphics card. $1,300.00. ISBN 0-07-046759-5.

This multimedia product is a compilation of eight interrelated databases using one standard search interface. The most comprehensive of these databases are the encyclopedia, containing the text of the printed *McGraw-Hill Encyclopedia of Science and Technology,* 7th ed. (see ARBA 93, entry 1446); the dictionary, based on the *McGraw-Hill Dictionary of Scientific and Technical Terms,* 5th ed. (see ARBA 90, entry 1428, for 4th edition review); and the illustrations. Additional small databases of animations, biographies, and maps are included.

The encyclopedia text, evaluated in the earlier review, is generally well written and authoritative. The articles contain words that serve as hypertext links to related subjects and figures, making browsing quite simple. If an illustration, map, or animation for the topic is available, users can select an icon to display it. A nice feature is a reverse cross-reference button, which permits the user to *display* articles that reference the present text.

The dictionary, containing over 100,000 terms, is broad in coverage though brief in explanation. Unlike the printed dictionary, illustrations are not provided (though many concepts are illustrated in the separate encyclopedia database). The biography database of 250 famous science-related people also has very brief entries, but *all* include relevant cross-references to topical articles in the encyclopedia.

A multimedia encyclopedia should be distinguished in its use of nonprint materials. In this area, this CD-ROM is inconsistent in quality. The encyclopedia's 530 illustrations are clear, attractive, and useful; however, one wonders why the multimedia version contains less than 10 percent of the number of illustrations found in the printed source. The 22 maps only cover large regions and contain little detail, making them less useful than inexpensive CD-ROM atlases. Finally, the 39 animation sequences are generally instructive and interesting, though some (e.g., a volcanic eruption) use somewhat crude graphics. Many animations are intolerably slow on a single spin CD-ROM player, though quite acceptable using double-spin drives. In total, this CD product, while appealing to use, provides only a limited additional amount of utility over its print parents, while omitting some of their media materials. The high cost makes this an expensive supplement or a questionable replacement to the originals. [R: RBB, 1 Oct 94, p. 359; SLJ, Oct 94, p. 60; WLB, Nov 94, p. 113]—**Christopher W. Nolan**

1082. McKissack, Patricia, and Frederick McKissack. **African-American Scientists**. Brookfield, Conn., Millbrook Press, 1994. 96p. illus. index. $17.90. ISBN 1-56294-372-3.

These two volumes make excellent gift books, especially for people who are culturally sensitive and who appreciate finding out about less-known biographies of U.S. citizens. Both books are attractive in design, printed on good quality paper, and have indexes and bibliographies. Writing gift books, however, may not be the objective of the authors—who testify to the difficulty of writing these books—but they do not clearly state their objective. Evidently, it is not to write a comprehensive history of African-American scientists and inventors. More apparent is that these books are intended to honor great African-American achievers and to dispel misleading myths about African Americans as incapable in science and creative projects. Unfortunately, these books do not suffice individually or jointly to fulfill either objective.

Only a few of the achievers covered are honored with descriptive essays of their achievements. This unintended slight is augmented by the failure of the authors to explain the selection process for inclusion, and for going beyond a mere mention of the individual to honor as an achiever. On the other hand, noting the achievement of a few individuals over the last two or three centuries of African-American history cannot dispel any negative myth that has been ingrained in that history. Given that they have suffered from discrimination in the form of underendowment, underutilization, and underrewarding, removing such myths would necessitate showing that the frequency of achievement among African Americans is similar to that of people faced with similar constraints. Even more convincing would be an attempt to show that the percentage of African Americans who had an opportunity to achieve in science and technology and were able to do so is comparable to the percentage of others.

The authors could have provided more comprehensive bibliographies of science and creativity than they have. They also could have provided biographical essays of *all* the achievers mentioned in their books. There is an evident bias toward medicine at the expense of other fields of science, though physicists, chemists, entomologists, and other life scientists are sparingly included. These books would be more effective in promoting African-American achievements by listing more achievers and by presenting more detailed essays rather than utilizing space for a history of patents. All this is not to undermine the value of these two attractive and easy-to-read books, but to suggest that they could have been more forceful in promoting the proud heritage of the African American.—**Elias H. Tuma**

1083.   Noonan, Jon. **Nineteenth-Century Inventors**. New York, Facts on File, 1992. 114p. illus. index. (American Profiles). $16.95. T39.N66. 609'.2'273. LC 91-13584. ISBN 0-8160-2480-4.

This slim volume provides brief biographies on eight important nineteenth-century inventors of the United States. Although no criteria for inclusion are given, all eight created important devices still valuable today (e.g., the computer, the telephone, the telegraph). The book, written for young adults, gives generally serviceable biographies, introductions to the importance of the inventions, life chronologies, and lists of further readings (which usually consist of other young adult-oriented titles).

The text of the biographies is somewhat uneven and at times convoluted, especially considering the intended audience. However, most of the entries are sufficiently clear, if not particularly engaging. The inventions are explained in a non-technical manner that should be accessible to students. Noonan successfully elucidates the implications of the inventions for the larger social context in which they occurred. The chronologies may have some use, but they are quite brief and could have been expanded without risking unnecessary detail.

Each of the eight figures is Caucasian and male. The publisher includes volumes on black and women scientists in this series to offset this bias. Overall, this work may be of some use to school or public libraries wishing to supplement general encyclopedias' basic biographical data on the history of technology. [R: BR, Jan/Feb 92, p. 51]—**Christopher W. Nolan**

1084.   **Notable Women in the Life Sciences: A Biographical Dictionary**. Benjamin F. Shearer and Barbara S. Shearer, eds. Westport, Conn., Greenwood Press, 1996. 440p. illus. index. $49.95. ISBN 0-313-29302-3.

The 97 distinguished women scientists listed in this biographical work were selected according to certain criteria: Their names were starred in the 1st editions of *American Men of Science* (R. R. Bowker, 1906), and they won awards such as the Nobel Prize and the Lasker Prize. The emphasis is on the twentieth century, although the time period covered is from antiquity to the present. Living and deceased scientists are included. All major areas of biology and medicine are covered.

Each biographical entry supplies a brief chronology covering dates of birth and death, education, employment, and awards. The text describes important events in the life of each biographee; how each advanced in her career, including her teaching and interactions with students; major scientific achievements; and how mentors aided her advancement. Portraits of some of the scientists are furnished.

An excellent book such as this one, covering women scientists, is most welcome, as there are not many comparable titles. This dictionary is extremely readable, and the personal lives of the scientists come through in each biography. It should be in the reference collections of academic, school, and public libraries. [R: RBB, 1 Sept 96, p. 168; SLJ, Nov 96, pp. 138-39]—**John Laurence Kelland**

1085. Ogilvie, Marilyn Bailey. **Women in Science: Antiquity through the Nineteenth Century: A Biographical Dictionary with Annotated Bibliography**. Cambridge, Mass., MIT Press, 1990. 272p. index. $25.00. ISBN 0-262-65038-X.

A compilation of almost 200 biographical sketches, primarily limited to Western scientists, this reference work is a significant contribution to the biographical literature. Covering women who made major contributions in a wide variety of scientific fields, *Women in Science* is arranged alphabetically by last name with entries ranging from one paragraph to more than eight pages in length. Standard data include birth and death dates, birthplace, parents, branch of science, nationality, education, professional positions, husband(s) name(s), and sources of additional information in standard biographical sources and in the annotated bibliography in this work.

The length of each entry depends on the person's impact and available written information. Those women for whom the author had limited data are included in a special appendix. There are a name index and a table of all subjects showing period (e.g., antiquity, nineteenth century, etc.), field, and nationality. Appropriate for reference collections in academic and some school and public libraries, this work's scope is broader than *Profiles of Pioneer Women Scientists* by Elizabeth M. O'Hern (Acropolis, 1985) and is more detailed. [R: Choice, May 87, p. 1382; RBB, 1 June 87, p. 1509; RQ, Summer 87, pp. 527-28; WLB, Apr 87, p. 69]—**Robert A. Seal and Robert L. Wick**

1086. Stanley, Autumn. **Mothers and Daughters of Invention: Notes for a Revised History of Technology**. Metuchen, N.J., Scarecrow, 1993. 1116p. index. $97.50. T36.S73. 305.43'6. LC 92-42054. ISBN 0-8108-2586-4.

The neglect of women inventors in historical research is widespread and pernicious; only recently has any real attempt been made to recognize their many contributions. Stanley has spent many years gathering the information on women inventors that is presented in this massive work. Divided into general subjects—agriculture, health and medicine, sex and fertility, tools and machines, and computers—the book presents a wide but detailed view of women's inventions from prehistory through the twentieth century, emphasizing the diversity and importance of women's inventions, whether officially recognized (i.e., patented) or not. Inventions are described, and brief profiles are given for women inventors when biographical information is available. The book closes with an impressive 125-page bibliography.

Some weaknesses are apparent. Stanley's research is extensive but has been superseded in places. For example, it is amusing to read that the ubiquitous portable hair dryer is "a minor but possibly commercially interesting invention." Although she names nearly 2,000 women inventors, she also misses several notable ones, such as Stephanie Kwolek, inventor of Kevlar. The bibliography, while extensive, excludes some important sources, including the U.S. Patent Office's Buttons to Biotech. Her definition of technology is broad, ranging from agricultural implements to computer languages; however, the inclusion of fields such as exercise programs (e.g., Jazzercise) is somewhat questionable. The focus on U.S. women, although enhanced by some British, French, and Russian examples, is limiting, and the failure to include patent numbers is a real detriment to the serious researcher.

However, despite its drawbacks, this is a unique and invaluable source that belongs in any library. No other book covers the subject as thoroughly or in as much detail.—**Susan Davis Herring**

1087. **Women in Chemistry and Physics: A Biobibliographic Sourcebook**. Louise S. Grinstein, Rose K. Rose, and Miriam H. Rafailovich, eds. Westport, Conn., Greenwood Press, 1993. 721p. index. $99.50. QD21.W62. 540'.92'2. LC 92-40224. ISBN 0-313-27382-0.

This work profiles 75 women who achieved prominence in the fields of chemistry or physics. Covering nearly three centuries, it is limited in scope to those who were born prior to 1933 or who are deceased. The foreword emphasizes the struggle that women have had in obtaining scientific educations and careers. Those profiled achieved success in various ways, including publications, editing, teaching, professional leadership, or overcoming societal or familial obstacles in gaining an advanced degree. The chapters average about eight pages, and each is divided into three sections. A biographical section details family background, education, career development, and important influences upon career direction. This section tends to be quite personal. The work section covers significant contributions to the chosen field, such as research, problems solved, service, and honors. The bibliography section denotes works by or about the person profiled. This section ranges in length from a few references to more than 100. Appendixes provide entry by places and years of birth, fields of interest, and countries of work. Short biographies of contributors are included, and the index is by subject and name. This work is very consistent in quality despite the fact that nearly all the biographies are written by different authors. Highly recommended for academic libraries.—**T. McKimmie**

ANTHROPOLOGY

1088. Babcock, Barbara A., and Nancy J. Parezo. **Daughters of the Desert: Women Anthropologists and the Native American Southwest, 1880-1980**. Albuquerque, University of New Mexico Press, 1988. 241p. illus. $39.95; $19.95pa. E78.S7B15. 979'.00497. LC 88-2979. ISBN 0-8263-1087-7; 0-8263-1083-4pa.

A "translation" of an exhibit to book form, this richly illustrated catalog is designed to show the impact that female anthropologists, scholars, activists, and philanthropists have had on understanding Native American cultures of the Southwest. It presents vignettes of 45 women, most of whom began their careers before 1940, who worked with the indigenous cultures of New Mexico and Arizona. In a "patchwork of words and images," each vignette encapsulates aspects of the woman's background and contributions to Southwestern research.

Each of the book's three sections relates to a specific theme. "Discovering the Southwest" concentrates on pioneers such as Matilda Coxe Stevenson and Elsie Clews Parsons who laid the groundwork for women to do research in the Southwest and establish it as a field for study. "Understanding Cultural Diversity" deals with the roles that women such as Ruth Benedict and Ruth Bunzel played in interpreting the diversity of four of the major cultures of the Southwest. "Interpreting the Native American" covers women's contributions to archaeology, applied anthropology, ethnomusicology, folklore, and arts and crafts as well as their efforts to preserve the Native American Southwest. A selected Southwest bibliography concludes the volume. The photographs and text give life to women whose contributions are marginalized or subordinated in historical and disciplinary accounts.

The volume serves to recapture and remember the achievements of women in the Southwest, to demonstrate how history often ignores women's accomplishments, and to "rewrite a story that needs retelling." Unfortunately, it omits the role of women who worked with Hispanic populations in the Southwest. Nevertheless, the book is a well-organized and beautifully presented array of courageous women who dared to deal with a harsh terrain. It is a valuable addition to gender studies, the history of anthropology, and feminist research. [R: Choice, June 89, p. 1717]—**Suzanne G. Frayser**

1089. **Biographical Directory of Anthropologists Born before 1920**. Compiled by Library-Anthropology Resource Group. Thomas L. Mann, ed. New York, Garland, 1988. 245p. illus. index. (Garland Reference Library of the Humanities, Vol. 439). $45.00. LC 87-29219. ISBN 0-8240-5833-X.

This directory, compiled by the Library-Anthropology Resource Group (LARG), contains biographical information of people from various professions and geographic areas born before 1920 who have contributed to the field of anthropology. Each of the 3,488 entries contains such data as time of birth and death, birthplace, and major publications as well as published sources of bibliographical information. For the purpose of this compendium, anthropology is broadly defined as the study of humankind. Anthropology as a discipline is an outgrowth of numerous contributions of a large number of scholars from various professions and countries.

Despite extensive efforts to make this directory as complete as possible, some eligible persons might have been inadvertently omitted. Therefore, a revised edition is planned to add the missing biographies. The compilation of the directory started in 1971 by means of a systematic search through anthropological journals, histories of anthropology, bibliographical reference works, directories, and subject catalogs. Before completing this volume, LARG produced three closely related publications: two editions of *Serial Publications in Anthropology* (1973 and 1982) and *Anthropological Bibliographies: A Selected Guide* (1981).

This volume is a significant contribution to anthropological research, as it will greatly facilitate the search for existing contributions and bibliographical data in the field. Among the entries are 889 archaeologists, 555 anthropologists, 464 ethnologists, 202 folklorists, 188 historians, 157 orientalists, 140 linguists, 138 priests, 105 missionaries, and several hundreds from other fields and professions. A subject index enhances the value of this excellent reference volume, which is highly recommended for college and public libraries. [R: Choice, June 88, pp. 1529-30; WLB, Apr 88, p. 98]—**Oleg Zinam**

1090. **Directory of Europeanist Anthropologists in North America**. Susan Carol Rogers, David D. Gilmore, and Melissa Clegg, comps. Washington, D.C., American Anthropological Association, 1987. 106p. maps. bibliog. index. $6.00pa. ISBN 0-913167-20-7.

This is the premier project of the Society for the Anthropology of Europe (SAE) of the American Anthropological Association. The SAE identified a need for networking and communication among Europeanist anthropologists. The directory is an excellent vehicle for meeting these needs. This listing for the directory was developed from a survey, which is presented in the appendices. The directory list of 340 entries is arranged alphabetically by last name. Each entry includes basic demographic information, including address, title, and institution. Academic information is also provided for each individual and includes degree awarded,

awarding institution, and date of award. Background information in the list also provides geographic specialty, field research sites, and topical specialties. The entries are concise and provide useful information for networking. There are twenty-four topical entries for several areas of interest (aging, class, ecology, etc.), as well as listings by geographic area.

In addition, the directory contains many access points to the main list. The several indexes are arranged by country, European region, non-European area specialty, and topical specialty. Another useful tool is the section of maps illustrating the location of each field research site. One of the most productive networking and communications items in the work is the bibliography of publications written by the individuals listed in the directory. The directory is well formatted to assist in the utilization of the access points.

Although the *Directory of Europeanist Anthropologists in North America* is designed for a select audience, college and university libraries will find it a useful reference tool. The work is a basic item for professionals in European anthropology.—**Warren G. Taylor**

1091. **International Dictionary of Anthropologists**. Compiled by Library-Anthropology Resource Group (LARG). Christopher Winters, ed. Hamden, Conn., Garland, 1991. 823p. index. (Garland Reference Library of Social Science, v.638). $75.00. GN20.I5. 016.301'03. LC 91-4782. ISBN 0-8240-5094-0.

This comprehensive reference is the first major international dictionary of anthropologists born before 1920. Winters states in his preface that the "Dictionary's chief purpose is not to serve as a history of the discipline but rather to provide readily accessible concise biographical information about some major contributors to anthropology." The work attempts to build a bridge between two distinct models of the history of anthropology: the so-called "central periphery model" with its assumption that anthropology "was almost entirely the creation of Americans and Britons" (p. xii), and the "parallel-schools model" with its emphasis on independent anthropological national schools. It seems that this synthetic approach by the editorial board is justified in the historical coverage of all major contributors to various anthropological disciplines. Over 300 scholars from various countries have written the biographical entries and provided relevant background material.

The dictionary contains 725 biographical entries on anthropologists, travelers, curators of museums, and other individuals from over 50 countries who contributed to this field. Each entry contains a brief biography, a list of major works, and sources with information pertaining to the scholarly activity and biography of the listed anthropologist. There is also a brief glossary that contains major terms not explained in the text. A comprehensive index includes references to personal names, institutions, and geographical and ethnic names. Some country designations are incorrect. For instance, the entry for Alexander Goldenweiser states that he was "Born in Kiev (Ukraine, Russia)" (p. 244). Kiev is the capital of Ukraine and is not located in Russia.

Previously, the Library-Anthropology Resource Group published *Biographical Directory of Anthropologists Born before 1920* (see ARBA 89, entry 332), which had about 3,500 entries with brief biographical information and sources. To a certain degree, *International Dictionary of Anthropologists* may serve as a companion volume to that directory. It will remain a permanent and durable reference source for all major libraries.—**Lubomyr R. Wynar**

1092.   **Women Anthropologists: A Biographical Dictionary**. Ute Gacs, and others, eds. Westport, Conn., Greenwood Press, 1988. 428p. bibliog. index. $55.00. LC 87-11983. ISBN 0-313-24414-6.

This is a collection of biographies of fifty-eight female anthropologists, mostly American, but a few of British or other nationalities, born between 1835 and 1935. Most are cultural or social anthropologists; some are archaeologists or physical anthropologists. Individual biographies are three to seven pages in length, and are accompanied by a selected list of works by the anthropologist and, usually, also by a list of references and works about the anthropologist.

The biographies are often based on interviews with the subjects or with people who knew them, as well as on written sources. In addition to the usual items covered in biographies (information on birthplace, parents, career highlights, etc.), the biographies are "intended to reveal something of the special nature of being female in the domains of fieldwork, research, formal higher education or training, and public life" (p. xv). Both advantages and disadvantages of being a female in the field of anthropology are noted. Most of the biographies are sympathetic (some writers even acknowledge the support and/or help of their subjects).

Although the experiences of selected female anthropologists have been chronicled previously, this book is unique in its breadth of coverage, making it a very useful contribution. [R: Choice, July/Aug 88, p. 1679]—**Joseph Hannibal**

AVIATION AND AEROSPACE

1093.   Cassutt, Michael. **Who's Who in Space: The First 25 Years**. Boston, G. K. Hall, 1987. 311p. illus. index. $35.00. LC 86-26988. ISBN 0-8161-8801-7.

The tragic demise of the *Challenger* space craft and its crew in January 1986 was a sad close to twenty-five years of exciting history of humanity in space. From Yuri Gagarin to Christa McAuliffe there has been a steady stream of U.S., Soviet, and international space travelers pushing forward the frontiers of space exploration. This interesting and readable book is the first collective biography of over 250 U.S., 73 Soviet, and 58 international space travelers.

The biographies cover personal and educational backgrounds, career histories, and facts and statistics on the flights in which they were involved. There are over 360 individual photographs plus crew photographs and a collection of photographs on U.S. crew patches. There is also a section on X-15 pilots who flew higher than fifty miles above the Earth. The introductory essays give a rather candid insight on the selection of astronauts, and the biographies also reveal candid facts on personality clashes and disciplinary problems in both the U.S. and Soviet programs, as well as giving some little known facts about some of the historical flights. This all makes the book worth reading on its own in addition to its value as a ready-reference book. The logs of flights and launch data given in the various appendices tie the biographies into a grand overall picture of humanity in space. [R: RBB, 15 June 87, p. 1584; WLB, Sept 87, p. 97]—**Robert J. Havlik**

1094.   Cassutt, Michael. **Who's Who in Space: The International Space Year Edition**. New York, Macmillan, 1993. 439p. illus. index. $75.00. TL788.5.C37. 629.45'0092. LC 92-19275. ISBN 0-02-897092-6.

This book, a revised edition of the author's first work, *Who's Who in Space: The First 25 Years* (see ARBA 88, entry 1587), is a classified biographical dictionary of the first 31 years of space exploration. Data are provided for individuals from the U.S. space program, the Soviet space program, and the 23 other countries that have sent people into space. Entries include the astronaut's name, birth date and place, childhood, education, service record, contribution to space program, and current status. Most entries are illustrated by photographs. While a few of the Soviet photographs are rather crude, they are most likely the best available. Additional useful tables include space acronyms and abbreviations; manned space flights, 1961-1992; X-l5 flights; a chronological log of space flights; manned time-in-space log; U.S. and Soviet mission flight crews; teacher-in-space candidates; and journalist-in-space candidates. There is an index to the biography section, but it does not reference the tables. Also included is a center photograph section that illustrates NASA mission crew patches, group photographs of U.S. astronauts the author feels are pioneers, and a much smaller section of Soviet pioneers. The volume is hardbound and is attractive in design and layout.

This volume compares favorably with Douglas Hawthorne's *Men and Women of Space* (see entry 1095) (Univelt, 1992). However, the entries in the Hawthorne volume contain more information and are better and more accurate. For example, Cassutt gives Yuriy Sheffer's birth date as June 3, 1947, when it is in fact June 30, 1947; and he fails to record the death of Alexandr Shchukin in a plane crash on August 18, 1988. While the Cassutt volume is better illustrated, and hence more appealing, Hawthorne's work is better edited and more comprehensive in scope. Libraries not wanting to purchase both would do better to stick with *Men and Women of Space*. [R: Choice, Nov 93, p. 424; LJ, Aug 93, p. 90; RBB, 1 Nov 93, p. 571; RQ, Winter 93, p. 298; SLJ, Nov 93, p. 140; WLB, Sept 93, pp. 124-27]—**Ralph Lee Scott**

1095.   Hawthorne, Douglas B. **Men and Women of Space**. San Diego, Calif., Univelt, 1992. 904p. $90.00. ISBN 0-912183-08-X.

Men and Women of Space is a complete and comprehensive biographical dictionary of individuals who have traveled in space. Russian cosmonauts, United States test pilots, and people from "all space-faring nations of the world" are listed. Biographical information is comprehensive, including the date and circumstances of the individual's death (e.g., "On a railroad bridge at Ippolitovka . . . while undergoing 'a serious spiritual crisis' and in a state of intoxication, [Grigoriy Nelyubov] threw himself under a train"). Typical entries include current status in space program, nickname, date and place of birth, military and marital status, children, education, publications, memberships, decorations and awards, physical description, recreational interests, life experience, space experience, space flight assignments, place and manner of death (if deceased), and an extensive bibliography on the person. The volume is well written. The layout, typeface, and binding are attractive. There are, alas, only two illustrations (the cover and the frontispiece); more photographs would have helped break up the long text entries. But the work contains some 650 biographies, which may account for the lack of illustrations. Most reference collections will find this work useful. Highly recommended for young adults.—**Ralph Lee Scott**

BOTANY

1096.   Desmond, Ray. **Dictionary of British and Irish Botanists and Horticulturalists: Including Plant Collectors, Flower Painters, and Garden Designers**. rev. ed. London, Natural History Museum; and Bristol, Pa., Taylor & Francis, 1994. 825p. index. $250.00. ISBN 0-85066-843-3.

A little different than other directories, this one covers people who worked in the horticultural world as far back as the 1500s. It attempts to be as exhaustive a compilation of British and Irish people involved with plants as possible. This revision of the 1977 edition has more than 3,700 entries. It includes added information for already existing biographical entries and the new categories of flower- and botanical-artist sand-garden designers.

The body of the work is arranged in alphabetical entries by name. These range in length from three to four lines to one column, depending on the information available on the individual. To the best of the author's effort, each entry contains the person's name; birth, death, or flourishing dates, where known; education and qualifications; honors and offices held; brief career details; selected publications by the person; locations of any plant collections, herbaria, manuscripts, or portraits; any commemorative plants; and finally, citation information.

Three interesting indexes are included, the first a list of professions (e.g., artists, bryologists, nursery people) with appropriate names. The second is a list of particular plants that each person is associated with, and the third is a list of geographical locations where individuals worked with or studied flora. Anyone in the plant world would love to own this dictionary, but it is a really important tool for any institution engaged in the study of botany or horticulture.—**Lillian R. Mesner**

1097. Isely, Duane. **One Hundred and One Botanists**. Ames, Iowa State University Press, 1994. 351p. illus. index. $32.95. ISBN 0-8138-2498-2.

Isely has selected 98 male and 3 female botanists extending chronologically from Aristotle to Winona Hazel Welch (1896-1991). For each scientist, Isely has prepared a three- to five-page essay briefly placing the scientist in history, mentioning any verified personal facts, and his or her major contribution, closing with a three- to five-item bibliography about the subject. Isely stresses the paucity of definitive biographies, eschews autobiographies and obituaries lauding their subjects, and finds published reviews of books by these botanists helpful. Beyond the expected profiles such as Theophrastus, Gregor Mendel, and Adolf Engler, Isley has included both different people such as Nicholas-Theodore de Saussure, the first plant chemist, and unexpected aspects of familiar botanists. For example, Charles Bessey negotiated microscopes for laboratory courses at Iowa State University and stipulated their purchase as a condition for his moving to the University of Nebraska. One disappointment is the omission of Barbara McClintock (1902-1992), awarded the 1983 Nobel Prize for her contribution to maize cytogenetics. Two indexes complete this work, which is enthusiastically recommended for interested amateurs, undergraduates, and botanical historians seeking brief overviews.—**Helen M. Barber**

CHEMISTRY

1098. **American Chemists and Chemical Engineers**. Wyndham D. Miles and Robert F. Gould, eds. Guilford, Conn., Gould Books, 1994. 365p. index. $20.00. QD21.A43. 540'.92'2. LC 76-192. ISBN 0-9640255-0-7.

This is a complement to a book that appeared in 1976 (see ARBA 78, entry 1257). It adds biographical listings for 269 men and women who have made significant contributions to chemistry or chemical engineering in this country to the 517 entries in the original edition. The 40 contributors who have written these biographies not only present conventional information but also include anecdotes that show the human side of these scientists. For example, one learns that Alfred Dohme staged a "Chemical Ballet" at the 1939 American Chemical Society meeting; that Aden King was a dedicated gardener who developed a new strain of orchid; that Edward Renouf was an amateur mountain climber who taught himself to roll cigarettes in his pocket with one hand while waiting to be rescued from a serious fall; and that Bradley Dewey's leadership of the synthetic rubber program during World War II was marked by a prominent New York ecdysiast who, when she reached her girdle, "took it off for Bradley Dewey."

The selection criteria furnish a broad representation of chemists and those in related fields. Most of these individuals are less prominent than those in the first volume, but the editors have also taken advantage of this opportunity to correct omissions from the first volume and add well-known chemists who have died recently. Each biography includes a brief list of sources of information, and an index is provided. This volume will be welcomed both by libraries that wish to add a useful supplement to the previous volume and by those who wish to read some delightful stories about U.S. chemists. [R: LJ, 1 Sept 94, p. 168]—**Harry E. Pence**

1099. **Nobel Laureates in Chemistry, 1901-1992**. James K. Laylin, ed. Washington, D.C., American Chemical Society, 1993. 798p. illus. index. (History of Modern Chemical Sciences). $69.95; $34.95pa. QD21.N63. 540'.92'2. LC 93-17902. ISBN 0-8412-2459-5; 0-8412-2690-3pa.

Since their inception in 1901, the Nobel awards in chemistry have increasingly been recognized to represent the highest level of scientific accomplishment in the field. Although not all the outstanding chemists of the twentieth century have received this award, those who have represent many of the leading contributors to the field. Thus, this compendium of short biographies both summarizes the careers of those who received the Nobel Prize and also provides a chronicle of the changing direction and emphasis of chemistry during this century.

The individual articles are long enough to include not only the major achievements of each scientist but also comments and stories that give a more rounded impression of each individual. The international panel of contributors includes a number who were colleagues or former students of the Nobel laureate. Each biography includes a helpful bibliography and a photograph of the subject. This volume is a useful supplement to the standard biographical works and also includes information on a number of contemporary chemists who are less likely to be covered in the standard sources. [R: Choice, Mar 94, pp. 1100-1102]—**Harry E. Pence**

1100. **The Nobel Prize Winners: Chemistry**. Frank N. Magill, ed. Pasadena, Calif., Salem Press, 1990. 3v. illus. $210.00/set. QD21.N64. 540'.79. LC 90-8092. ISBN 0-89356-561-X.

In this third of six series covering the Nobel Prize categories, Magill undertakes the noble task of consolidating a great deal of information into three handy volumes. There are other reference works about Nobel Prize winners, but none are equal to the exhaustive and organized nature of these volumes.

One hardly needs to examine the publisher's note in volume 1 because the three volumes are arranged in strict chronological order from 1901 to 1989. However, it does provide complete explanations about the set, namely the history and an overview of the Nobel Prize in chemistry. In these are included the insightful biographical view of Alfred Nobel and the establishment of the foundation to award the prize that came to bear his name. Following this essay is a timeline that lists in tabular form essential information about all 113 of the laureates.

Each entry is preceded by a display page listing the laureates in other disciplines for the same year, a photograph of each chemistry laureate, and a 3,500-word article giving basic biographical information and areas of concentration in chemistry. Particularly impressive are the overviews of the laureates' Nobel lectures and the direct linkage of each scientist's career to the ultimate winning of the award. There is a bibliography of primary and secondary sources, and all entries are signed by the contributing authors.

As with many definitive works, the inclusion of a comprehensive index in the third volume is a strong feature. Each volume also contains the complete alphabetical list of laureates. The attractive and sturdy binding and the clear print make this set a good purchase for most reference collections. Strongly recommended. [R: WLB, Oct 90, p. 131]—**J. H. Hunter**

COMPUTER SCIENCE

1101. Cortada, James W. **Historical Dictionary of Data Processing: Biographies**. Westport, Conn., Greenwood Press, 1987. 321p. index. $49.95. LC 86-31805. ISBN 0-313-25651-9.

This volume is one of a trilogy; the other two volumes are subtitled "Technology" (see entry 1703) and "Organizations" (see entry 1702). Topics and people in the three volumes are tied together by a notational system: a single asterisk indicates that the topic is treated in the technology volume; two asterisks, elsewhere in the present (biography) volume; and a dagger, in the organization volume.

More than 150 individuals whom the author has identified as being key figures in the history of data processing are dealt with in some detail. Each article has bibliographical references appended. While one might quibble with a few of the selections (e.g., Fourier, the mathematician, and A. B. Dick, the mimeograph entrepreneur), most are indeed appropriate selections. The volume is exhaustively indexed, and two appendices list the biographees by birth date and profession.

This volume stands alone; the other two volumes, while perhaps useful, are not required to justify this handy compilation of brief biographical information about key figures in the history of computing and data processing. It is likely to find frequent use in most public libraries and in many academic libraries. [R: WLB, Nov 87, pp. 93-94]—**Edwin D. Posey**

1102. **International Biographical Dictionary of Computer Pioneers**. J. A. N. Lee, ed. Chicago, Fitzroy Dearborn, 1995. 816p. illus. index. $75.00. ISBN 1-884964-47-8.

This excellent reference book provides information on several hundred people who played an important part in the growth and development of the computer industry. Many of the names have been drawn from the *Annals of the History of Computing*, in particular from the work done for the 10th anniversary issue; other sources were also used. The editor has tried to include not only pioneers—defined as those whose contributions were central to the field of computing—but also managers, educators, and financiers. It is unclear when the cutoff date is; for example, Steve Jobs and Steve Wozniak are included, but Bill Gates is not.

Each entry tries to set the person in the context of computer developments of the time and show the impact or influence of the person on the field of computing. The entries are uneven in their completeness, depending on the role of the person and the amount of information the compilers were able to locate. The fullest entries have a brief biographical statement, followed by education, professional experience, and honors and awards. Many of the entries contain articles written by people who personally knew the subject of the entry; these articles have been selected because they help set the people in context and show their importance to the field of computing. The individual bibliographies contain biographical references and lists of significant publications by the person profiled. Some entries have pictures and a quotation from the biographee.

The appendix lists collections of biographies and memoirs. It also references oral interviews conducted for the Charles Babbage Institute Oral History Collection (June 1992). Furnished in the appendix are lists of professional society awards, including the Association for Computing Machinery, IEEE Computer Society, American Association for Artificial Intelligence, American Federation of Information Processing, Computing Research Association, and the Inamori Foundation. The index is comprehensive, and all the biographical entries are also listed alphabetically in the table of contents. This is a useful reference source. It supplies information about lesser-known figures in the field of computing, but it also contains fascinating insights into many of the better-known figures.—**Linda Main**

1103.   Slater, Robert. **Portraits in Silicon**. Cambridge, Mass., MIT Press, 1987. 374p. illus. bibliog. index. $24.95. LC 87-2868. ISBN 0-262-19262-4.

This book is a stimulating and exciting collection of portraits about historical and present-day individuals who have made significant contributions to the computer industry. These individuals are pioneers through their efforts and talents in different facets of the computer revolution. The book begins with the conceptualizers who laid the foundation of computing, the early inventors who built the first machines, and the early entrepreneurs who commercialized the computing industry. The book continues with those who made the computer smaller and more powerful, the hardware designers, and the software specialists. The book ends with those who brought the computer to the masses and a pioneer in computer science. There are a total of 31 portraits. The author discusses early figures such as Watson and Perot and their efforts in founding commercial computer companies. There are also biographies of Gates and Jobs, whose endeavors have made computers available to the general public. Each portrait is about eleven pages long and covers the challenges and crucial events leading to the particular contribution of the pioneer, in an unbiased, journalistic manner. Many of the portraits are written from direct interviews with the persons themselves and hence carry the flavor of the inventor's point of view. This book is non-technical in nature and is written for the general public. It is highly recommended for all libraries. [R: SBF, Jan/Feb 88, p. 137]—**John Y. Cheung**

ENERGY AND NUCLEAR SCIENCE

1104.   *Financial Times* **Who's Who in World Oil & Gas 1996**. 14th ed. New York, Groves Dictionaries, Inc., 1995. 546p. index. $295.00. ISBN 1-561-59183-1.

This reference book contains biographical information on more than 4,000 executive personnel working in companies, consulting firms, government agencies or departments, and universities and research organizations involved in the oil and gas industries. This includes CEOs, presidents, vice presidents, directors, managers, partners, and ministers. The biographical data includes current and previous appointments, business address and telephone number, personal details (e.g., birth date, nationality), qualifications, professional memberships, honors and awards, and publications. Company and geographical indexes list all personnel under each company or country.

What is the editorial policy for the selection of names? Most of the key companies listed in the companion publication *Financial Times Oil and Gas International Year Book* (1993 edition) (see ARBA 93, entry 1748) are included, but the number of names varies for the same companies. For example, Enron Corporation has only 3 names listed in *Who's Who,* while in the *Oil and Gas International Year Book* there are more than 20 names listed, some of which would fit into the categories for the former publication. This situation seems to continue with the 1995 edition. The majority of the listings are for personnel in companies, and biographical information varies greatly among the entries.

This reference book has been used by the oil and gas industries for a long time. Its information is certainly useful, but it would be much more useful if it included the names of many personnel now excluded.—**Anne C. Roess and Robert L. Wick**

ENGINEERING AND TECHNOLOGY

1105.   **Biographical Dictionary of the History of Technology**. Lance Day and Ian McNeil, eds. New York, Routledge, 1996. 844p. index. $125.00. ISBN 0-415-06042-7.

This concise, well-organized compendium offers schools, libraries, museums, and businesses a handy source of facts about inventions. Arranged alphabetically by inventor, this upgrade of the 1990 volume opens with a preface expressing the editors' aim, selection criteria, and method of presentation, including a claim to fairer representation for the accomplishments of African Americans. The acknowledgments page lists 23 contributors who covered female, Asian, and Islamic technologists. The body of the text concludes with an index arranged by subject areas (for example, agriculture and food, mining and extraction, ports and shipping, recording, steam and internal combustion engines, and synthetic materials). Additional indexes compile names of particular inventors and topics, such as bridges, printing, pumps, railways, weapons, and shipbuilding.

Biographical entries follow a simple arrangement of name; dates and places of birth and death; and a brief summary of contributions, as in "Scottish cotton spinner and textile machine maker." The text of each brief entry precedes principal honors and distinctions, a bibliography, a list for further reading, and the initials of the contributor. Where appropriate, *see also* notations direct the user to additional data (e.g., from Samuel Thomas von Soemmerring to Samuel Finley Breese Morse).

Overall, coverage is disappointing. For example, the list of entries on electronics mentions Benjamin Franklin and Nikola Tesla, but omits the massive number of patents General Electric derived from the work of Charles Proteus Steinmetz, especially his contributions to electric streetcars. Of the many women who have contributed to the Industrial Revolution, the volume omits Sarah Mather's submarine light and telescope; Katherine Burr Blodgett's invisible glass and plane-wing deicer; Hedy Lamarr's coding system and remote-control torpedo; Grace Hopper's computer language; Bessie Cary Evinrude's motor designs; Mary Engle Pennington's frozen food containers; and Rosalyn S. Yalow's radio immunoassay. [R: Choice, Nov 96, p. 456; RBB, 1 Apr 96, p. 1387]
—**Mary Ellen Snodgrass**

1106.   **Who's Who in Engineering**. Gordon Davis, ed. Washington, D.C., American Association of Engineering Societies, 1977- . index. $200.00 for recent edition. ISSN 0149-7537.

The stated objective of this directory is to list members of the engineering profession who have "distinguished themselves in the practice of engineering, the development of engineering resources, or the promotion of technological innovation." Individuals listed must be living and satisfy one or more of the following qualifications: have a degree in engineering; be registered as an engineer in one or more states; be a member of the National Academy of Engineering; be a president, dean, tenured faculty member, or department head of an engineering college; be a principal of a consulting firm or head of a major division within a consulting firm or governmental agency that includes at least twenty engineers.

Most of the book consists of a biographical listing in alphabetical order. Each entry generally consists of business and home address, degrees, awards, previous and current employers, area of specialization, and society affiliations. The other sections include a listing of the major engineering societies and their awards; also included are listings by specialization and by state. Each award listing includes a brief description of the award and a listing of recent recipients. Listings by specialization and state are arranged alphabetically. Both of these additional access points are useful. However, they might have been more useful if the larger states were broken down by either city or region and if some of the areas of specialization were broken down a bit further. For example, the California listing consists of over eighteen columns of single-spaced names and the specialization list of electrical engineering consists of eleven columns.

Both of these are minor points. This is a well-produced directory of basic information on approximately 15,000 living American engineers. The directory more than meets its stated goal of "promoting greater public awareness of the importance of engineering and the people who perform this essential role." This should be found in any library where biographical information on engineers is needed.—**Susan B. Ardis**

1107. **Who's Who in Technology.** (North American ed.). Woodbridge, Conn., Research Publications, 1986- . 7v. index. $545.00/set. ISSN 0877-5901.

Now in its 5th edition, and formerly titled *Who's Who in Technology Today,* this multi-volume set serves as a major source of biographical data on scientists, researchers, and even executives in engineering and technology. The biographical sketches, each about one paragraph long, are arranged into the following volumes: "Electronics & Computer Science"; "Mechanical Engineering and Materials Science"; "Chemistry & Physics"; "Civil Engineering, Earth Sciences & Energy"; "Physics & Optics"; and "Biotechnology."

Except for volume 7, the master index, each volume is arranged identically: the biographical sketches, followed by an index of expertise and a name index. The biographical data are very brief and include current position and address, past positions, summary of publication activity, expertise, significant contributions to the field, patents, awards, professional memberships, and personal data.

The last volume contains a master index of expertise and a master index of names for all the volumes in the set. In all, there are 36,500 entries including 4,800 new entries. Two-thirds of the information in the previous edition has been updated. The set will be useful to librarians and researchers, primarily in special and university libraries, and perhaps in some large public libraries.—**Robert A. Seal**

ENVIRONMENTAL SCIENCE

1108. Axelrod, Alan, and Charles Phillips. **The Environmentalists: A Biographical Dictionary from the 17th Century to the Present**. New York, Facts on File, 1993. 258p. illus. index. $45.00. S926.A2A94. 363.7'0092'2. LC 92-38773. ISBN 0-8160-2715-3.

Although talked about as a new trend, environmentalism is a thing of not only our present but also our past. How far past is a debatable issue, but for the authors of *The Environmentalists*, the seventeenth century is past enough. More than 600 individuals are included in this biographical dictionary, along with key organizations and agencies that have affected the environment, both negatively and positively. The emphasis is placed on U.S. figures, but the coverage is international. The criterion for inclusion is that an individual's contributions are generally acknowledged as landmarks in the development of ecology. This allows for both Charles Darwin and Ronald Reagan to be included. Organizations must have proved themselves as crucial to the field of ecology, as well as representative of its various facets, such as the National Rifle Association or the International Whaling Commission. Entries for people include brief biographical backgrounds, along with their contributions to the ecology movement. An individual's important publications are sprinkled throughout the text, and, when available, a bibliography of further reading about a person is given. Some black-and-white photographs are included. The volume is served by a very good index. All in all, this dictionary will provide a good jumping-off point for those interested in the people and organizations behind the Green movement. [R: RBB, 15 Dec 93, p. 776]—**Angela Marie Thor**

1109. **Who Is Who at the Earth Summit, Rio de Janeiro, 1992**. Tucson, Ariz., Terra Christa Communications; and Waynesville, N.C., Vision Link Education Foundation, 1992. 481p. illus. $30.00pa. ISBN 0-9628405-3-X.

In 1992, the United Nations Conference on Environment and Development, commonly called the Earth Summit, brought together in Rio De Janeiro more than 30,000 participants to discuss the future of our planet. The meeting of 100-plus heads of state and more than 1,400 non-governmental organizations represented an unprecedented gathering of those who are concerned with the need to balance economic development against environmental costs. Thus, the roster of those who attended the conference is a unique directory of environmental leaders and policy-makers throughout the world.

The book is well organized, making the information easily accessible. The main register, by country, includes not only names and addresses but also some telephone and fax numbers. Alphabetical cross-indexing by individual names and organizations provides more resources for accessing the main list.

This document is a worthwhile resource for those who wish to conduct research involving the international environmental movement. Even though normal turnover may soon make the list of individual names outdated, this book could be useful for some time as a source of addresses.—**Harry E. Pence**

1110.   **Who Is Who in Service to the Earth: People, Projects, Organizations, Key Words**. Hans J. Keller and Daniel Maziarz, eds. Waynesville, N.C., VisionLink, 1991. 524p. $19.95pa. ISBN 0-9628405-1-3.

This is an unusual book. Part 1 consists of a set of "41 Visions of a Positive Future." The writers of these essays do indeed take a positive view, although they express alarm about what humans have done, are doing, and appear to be continuing to do to the environment. There seems to be no regular arrangement of these essays, but a detailed table of contents provides adequate access. The writers are all included in part 2, which provides directories of people, projects, and organizations, as well as a list of key words. The criterion for the inclusion of people is that their "sincere and effective efforts in Service to the Earth make them worth knowing." The list introduces environmentalists and others, both the well known and the obscure, from all over the world. There are no full biographies, just each person's name, address, organization, and projects. The next section lists organizations with a contact person (who appears in the list of individuals, along with the organization's address) and a statement of purpose. The projects section is arranged alphabetically, again requiring the user to look up the contact person in the people list for access to information on organization and address. The keyword section serves as an index. Six order forms and four forms for data on individuals, organizations, and projects not included in the volume are appended. The price of the book is a pleasant surprise. Recommended for any library that wants a positive treatment of the Earth's environment and future. [R: Choice, Mar 92, p. 1050]—**Edward P. Miller**

1111.   **World Who Is Who and Does What in Environment & Conservation**. Lynn M. Curme, comp. Nicholas Polunin, ed. New York, St. Martin's Press, 1997. 592p. $75.00. ISBN 0-312-17448-9.

This valuable reference book profiles 1,300 major figures from around the world in environment and conservation. Persons included were selected by recommendations of the World Conservation Union, World Wildlife Fund International, United Nations Environment Programmer, and other organizations. Biographies were prepared from detailed questionnaires sent to each person profiled. Each includes career and achievement information, relevant publications, language capabilities, willingness to consult, address, and telephone and fax numbers. There is a detailed appendix by specialty: Examples are advocacy, environmental; fish, early life history; fisheries; flows, hydraulic research of; forestry; nature conservation; nutrient cycling; rehabilitation, environmental; sustainable agricultural development; taxonomic botany; whale conservation; wilderness; wildlife (plant and animal); wind energy; and women. Even some unusual specialties are noted (e.g., "Zen teaching" for Peter Matthiessen). There is also an appendix by country, which is broken down by state for the United States.

Although this reviewer found herself wondering why some individuals considered notable were not included, there is no way the book could be complete, especially in its premier edition. This is a useful book for libraries and for the many organizations and agencies that need to know who's who in environment and conservation.—**Marquita Hill**

MATHEMATICS

1112.   Biographical Dictionary of Mathematicians: Reference Biographies from the *Diction-ary of Scientific Biography*. New York, Scribner's, 1991. 4v. index. $175.00/set. QA28.B534. 510'.92'2. LC 90-52920. ISBN 0-684-19282-9.

This work is a subset of the *Dictionary of Scientific Biography* (see ARBA 91, entries 1461 and 1462). Each of the 1,023 biographies includes the name of the contributor; some are collaborative efforts. Biographies of well-known persons whose work crossed over disciplines are written by a team of contributors, each focusing on a specific aspect of their subject's work.

The mathematicians selected span history from ancient times to the mid-twentieth century. No living individual is included. In the selection of subjects, the editors not only focus on individuals whose work falls well within the disciplines of mathematics but also those better known in other fields, such as Plato, Omar Khayyam, and Leonardo da Vinci. Although it is interesting to read of the contributions to mathematics and related fields made by these scientists, this dictionary would not be the first source of data for some. On the other hand, their mathematical efforts are not usually given as thorough a treatment in more general encyclopedias. The cultural distribution of subjects seems uniform, with a significant number of Asian and Arab mathematicians. Also included is the nonperson Nicolas Bourbaki (the pseudonym of an influential group of French mathematicians).

The articles vary in length from a single column to as many as 20 pages. They present a comfortable blend of information about the early life of the subject and analysis of the scientific contribution, giving the latter considerably more emphasis. A list of the subject's major publications and secondary literature about the person concludes each article. The contributors of the articles are either mathematicians—typically in the same field as the subject—or scientific historians. These articles are written for an audience familiar with college-level mathematics and science. In many cases the original notation is provided accompanied by the modern equivalent or explanation.

Three indexes in the fourth volume cover all volumes. The first sorts the mathematicians into broad fields: algebra; analysis and differential equations; arithmetic, computing, and number theory; astronomy, geodesy, and trigonometry; foundations, logic, and set theory; geometry and topology; history, philosophy, and dissemination of knowledge; mechanics, physics, and technology; and probability and statistics. The second index is a selected chronology; the third is a subject/name index.

Although it appears that the editors determined to produce a culturally balanced work, there seems to be a gender bias. Despite the fact that their contributions to mathematics rival those of many of their male colleagues, the dictionary contains no entry for Nina Bari, a leader of early-twentieth-century Soviet mathematics; Ada Lovelace, one of the earliest contributors in the field of programming; Grace Young, the first woman to receive a doctorate in Germany in any field, who (with her husband, William Young) produced over 200 mathematical articles and several books; or Charlotte Scott, an early organizer of the *American Mathematical Society*, an editor of the *American Journal of Mathematics*, and the instigator of the College Entrance Examination Board. The lives of these mathematicians fall well within the limits of this dictionary.

Biographical Dictionary of Mathematicians is highly recommended for mathematics collections that might be distantly located from a general collection. Even if the main library or general collection has the larger and inclusive set of the *Dictionary of Scientific Biography,* the duplication would be warranted.—**Margaret F. Dominy**

1113.   Combined Membership List of the American Mathematical Society, Mathematical Association of America, and the Society for Industrial and Applied Mathematics. Providence, R.I., American Mathematical Society, 1954- . $36.00pa. for recent edition.

This membership list published by the American Mathematical Society includes the names and addresses of all current (as of June 1 each year) members of the American Mathematical Society (AMS), the Mathematical Association of America (MAA), and the Society for Industrial and Applied Mathematics (SIAM). A limited number of advertisements are included in the publication.

The publication is divided into three sections. The first is an alphabetical listing of members. The entries include name, society affiliation, mailing address, a title or position when available, place of employment, telephone numbers, and e-mail listings.

The second section is a geographic listing. Members from the United States are listed first by state and then by city. Foreign listings follow divided by country and then by city. The third section lists academic and institutional members. The division is by states within the United States. These entries list the appropriate departments within each member institution and include main switchboard numbers, department numbers, and societal affiliation. Abbreviation listings precede the main entries.

A useful addition to future editions might be the inclusion of each member's area of expertise, which would increase the directory's usefulness as a reference tool for libraries. This directory will be welcome in academic library collections, particularly those serving mathematics, computer science, engineering, and statistics departments as well as selected corporate library collections.—**Joanne M. Goode and Robert L. Wick**

PHYSICS

1114.   **American Men and Women of Science: A Biographical Directory of Today's Leaders in Physical, Biological and Related Sciences**. Edited by Jaques Cattell Press. New York, R. R. Bowker, 1989/90- . 8v. index. $595.00/set. ISSN 0192-8570.

It seems remarkable that, in the more than 90 years since its inception as *American Men of Science,* this standard reference work has documented the lives and accomplishments of more than 300,000 scientists. Scientists from North America, especially from the United States, are the primary entries, with non-citizens included if they have worked in the United States or Canada for an extended period.

While all the different areas of the natural sciences are represented, it is not feasible to list all American scientists. For the purpose of this edition, inclusion is limited to living scientists in the physical and biological sciences, the health sciences, engineering, mathematics, statistics, and computer science. Criteria were established to limit the number of candidates. The prospective entrants are considered by those listed in previous editions, and also those in charge of various research programs throughout the country. The seventeen members of the advisory committee represent most areas of science, and the majority are directors or executive directors of prestigious associations such as the American Chemical Society, the American Institute of Physics, the American Geological Association, the American Psychological Association, and Argonne National Laboratory. In order to be selected, a scientist must have considerable achievements in research, which may or may not have been published in the literature (in order not to exclude those whose work is classified by either government or industrial restrictions); research activity of high quality; or have reached a key position of responsibility that requires a scientific background.

The format of the entries is unchanged from the previous editions. Because the published information is solicited from the individuals, there are variations in length and content. Those who returned the questionnaires have the longest and most complete entries. Those who did not are listed in one of two ways. If their current position can be verified by means of secondary sources, the entry from the previous (15th) edition is repeated. If no position can be found and the person is presumed to be still active in research, a cross-reference to the previous edition is given. Those known to be deceased are listed as such. The care that has been taken by the editorial staff for completeness and accuracy is obvious.

A separate volume for the set contains a discipline (subject) index. The classification outline follows guidelines set forth by the National Science Foundation in the Taxonomy of Degree and Employment Specialties. The theory behind the use of this classification is sound, though it leaves a bit to be desired in practice. While consistency in classification is a quality that taxonomists and librarians make careers out of, the subject classification is often too broad to be useful. In most cases, it may not be helpful to look under "Organic chemistry" and find more than 8,100 names without addresses. A feature of this sort is better used in computer format, where one could sort by research specialty, and then print out hundreds or even thousands of names that include addresses, all in one step.

The discipline index can be used to determine the numbers of researchers in each subject area. Because names are repeated under different headings, reflecting different areas of research, these numbers can be misleading. Despite the shortcomings of this particular evaluation technique, some areas seem to have been short changed when relative numbers of entries are compared. The area of computer science is sparsely represented. Aeronautical and astronautical engineering are listed together, yet despite obvious similarities, scarcely 1,000 names are listed.

In short, *American Men and Women of Science* is an indispensable reference tool. It is one of a handful of reference works whose updated editions are eagerly awaited by both patron and librarian alike. All academic libraries are obliged to purchase at least one copy. Large public libraries will also need to purchase a copy, though smaller ones may be daunted by the price in these times of fiscal shortages.—**Kerry L. Kresse and Robert L. Wick**

1115.　**Energy & Nuclear Sciences International Who's Who**. 3d ed. New York, Groves Dictionaries, Inc., 1983- . index . (Reference on Research). $550.00 for recent edition. ISBN 0-561-59120-3.

The 1st edition (1983) of this directory was entitled *International Who's Who in Energy and Nuclear Sciences.* With the 2d edition (1987), the title was changed to the *Energy & Nuclear Sciences International Who's Who.* The 3d edition, like the first two, is divided into two parts. The major portion is devoted to brief biographical profiles of more than 3,500 energy and nuclear engineers and scientists in academe, research institutes, and industry in some ninety countries worldwide. The directory is a companion to the latest editions of *World Nuclear Directory: A Guide to Organizations and Research Activities in Atomic Energy* and *World Energy Directory: A Guide to Organizations and Research Activities in Non-Atomic Energy,* also published by Longman and presumably the source for biographees' names. Two-thirds of directory entries are based on questionnaires returned by biographees. Complete profiles, where information was available, include full name, year of birth, degree earned, current job, employer and date of hire, previous employment, membership, major publications, areas of interest, telephone number, and complete address. Some entries (flagged by asterisks) consisting only of name, job, and address are derived from unindicated recently published sources. The second part of the directory, the country and subject index, is actually an alphabetical listing of countries sub-arranged alphabetically, as appropriate, by fifteen subject categories: civil and structural, electrical, and electrical power engineering; energy conservation, planning, and storage; fuel production; fusion technology; geothermal, wind, and/or ocean energy; nuclear sciences; geophysics and hydrology; geology and mineral technology; and high and low energy physics followed by names of approximately 40 percent of the biographees in alphabetical order. Biographees marked with asterisks are, of course, not included, nor are administrators or those whose interests do not fall within the designated categories. The highest concentration of index entries is in energy planning and nuclear sciences. Only the United Kingdom is represented in all fifteen categories; a third of the indexed biographees are European, the largest number being British, followed by the Federal Republic of Germany and Poland. Of the 1,800-plus directory profiles which include birth date, about 80 percent are for engineers and scientists born before or in 1940 and about 40 percent were born after 1940. The format is attractive and the type easily read; this is for specialized collections which can afford the publication price.—**Virginia E. Yagello and Robert L. Wick**

1116.　**McGraw-Hill Dictionary of Physics**. McGraw-Hill Staff, eds. New York, McGraw-Hill, 1996. 656p. $16.95pa. LC 96-046186. ISBN 0-07-052429-7.

The *McGraw-Hill Dictionary of Scientific and Technical Terms* is packaged separately in this inexpensive paperbound physics dictionary. By its very nature, this specialized dictionary is as authoritative as the parent dictionary from which it is derived. Areas of classical physics such as acoustics, electricity, mechanics, and optics are represented, as well as areas such as particle physics, quantum mechanics, and solid state physics.

Entries for terms consist of designations of the particular fields of physics to which the terms belong followed by concise, technical definitions varying in length and complexity as determined by their subject content. There are numerous, useful cross-references from abbreviations, acronyms, variant spellings, symbols, and synonyms to the entry terms where definitions are given. Not all technical terms used in entry definitions are defined in the dictionary, and even when they are, no linkage between entries is made.

Other dictionaries to which this dictionary may be compared are *A New Dictionary of Physics*, edited by H. J. Gray and Alan Isaacs, and the *Concise Dictionary of Physics and Related Subjects*, edited by James Thewlis. Both of these dictionaries include terms from related subject areas and contain tables of useful supplementary information. Gray uses more tables but Thewlis covers a greater number of related subject areas. Definitions in the Gray volume are lengthier, more detailed and explanatory of concepts involved, and are frequently illustrated by diagrams. Brief biographies of famous physical scientists are interspersed with the definitions. This work more closely corresponds to the McGraw-Hill dictionary, giving shorter definitions largely limited to a single concept. The McGraw-Hill dictionary does not replace either of these earlier dictionaries; its usefulness lies largely in its inclusion of additional physics terms and the updating of entry information where advances in knowledge have been made.—**Virginia E. Yagello**

1117.   **The Nobel Prize Winners: Physics**. Frank N. Magill, ed. Pasadena, Calif., Salem Press, 1989. 3v. illus. index. $210.00/set. QC15.N63. 530'.092'2. LC 89-6409. ISBN 0-89356-557-1.

Probably the most complete, up-to-date reference on the Nobel Prize in physics, this three-volume set includes information on physics prize winners from the first award through 1988. The set is the second in a series that will cover each of the Nobel Prizes. Beginning with an introductory chapter on the history of the Nobel Prizes, the prize selection process, a timeline, and quick summaries of the physics awards, the body of the work is organized chronologically and consists of a chapter for each prize winner. Each signed chapter consists of biographical information, a description of the winning achievement, and summaries of the Nobel Committee's presentation speech and the Nobel lecture. The four- to nine-page chapters end with a bibliography of several primary and secondary sources. The writing is consistently interesting and clear.

One of the best features of the set is the attempt to provide a context for each year's physics prize and its winners. The other Nobel awards for the year are listed at the beginning of the chapter. Also included are a summary of the critical reception of the award and a segment on the winner's pre- and post-Nobel career. These sections make interesting additions to the chapters, revealing the controversy sometimes associated with the award and helping to dispel the notion that Nobel winners work in brilliant isolation. Completing the set is an index that lists only page numbers. The addition of volume numbers would save users time and frustration.

At more than $200 a set, the price of the entire six-set series may be prohibitive for smaller libraries. Although there is no truly comparable work on the Nobel Prize in physics alone, a good but much less thorough treatment of the subject can be found in *Nobel Prize Winners* (see ARBA 88, entry 32). But the volume under review is highly recommended for public, high school, and academic libraries. [R: RBB, 15 Nov 89, p. 698; RQ, Winter 89, pp. 297-98; WLB, Oct 89, pp. 140-42] —**Kathleen Kenny**

PHYSIOLOGY

1118.   O'Connor, W. J. **British Physiologists 1885-1914: A Biographical Dictionary**. New York, Manchester University Press; distr., New York, St. Martin's Press, 1991. 382p. index. $90.00. QP25.027. 612'.0092'241. LC 90-8666. ISBN 0-7190-3282-2.

Reading British medical literature often rewards the reader with magical turns of phrase while providing practical and valuable information on a specific topic. O'Connor's works are no exception. This dictionary presents biographical notes of some 350 physiologists in Britain from 1885 to 1914. It continues a previous work by the same author: *Founders of British Physiology* (see ARBA 89, entry 1535).

As with its predecessor, this work's biographical notices are grouped under the university or medical school where the physicians worked. There are 13 chapters. The first examines physiologists and physiology in general, while the next 10 deal with medical schools and their famous physiologists whose work made them legends in the field of medicine. A chapter also covers physiologists outside medical schools and institutions. The last chapter provides a helpful list of important books on physiology published at that time.

The book presents scholarly introductory essays and concise, well-written biographical information. The individual entries are chronologically arranged within each section. Because of this, the general index becomes even more important. To help the reader, the index of physiological topics resembles the subject index of the *Journal of Physiology*. It is an important feature in clarifying semantic ambiguities. This book is well worth reading by anyone interested in medical biography, physiology, or the history of medicine.—**Nancy L. Herron**

1119.   O'Connor, W. J. **Founders of British Physiology: A Biographical Dictionary, 1820-1885**. Manchester, England, Manchester University Press; distr., New York, St. Martin's Press, 1988. 278p. index. $49.95. ISBN 0-7190- 2537-0.

The core of this book consists of the biographical sketches of over 100 most important British physiologists in Victorian England. The principal source of these sketches is the obituaries of the individuals covered that appeared in the scientific periodicals of the time. To be sure, these are not critical or interpretative sketches, but they do reveal the prevailing opinion of the listed individuals' scientific contributions and the relevant basic facts about the sequence of their progression through their professional careers. The individual entries are not arranged alphabetically, and as such this is not strictly a dictionary as the book's subtitle implies; rather, they are grouped into the period in which the listed physiologists worked and into the institutions to which they were attached. Part 1 of the book covers the period 1820-1835, when physiology was still part of anatomical and clinical medicine. Part 2 covers the period 1835-1870, when physiology became a discipline taught in medical schools and hospitals. Part 3 covers the period 1870-1885, when experimental physiology emerged and flourished as a new discipline of scientific information. A short explanatory essay introduces each period covered and each of the institutions covered. These interpretative essays are easily discerned by their larger typeset, are scholarly, and taken together form a concise history of the development of physiology in Britain during that critical period when physiology established itself as an independent discipline within the medical sciences. This book is well worth reading, not only by those interested in British physiology but also by anyone concerned with the history of medicine and the development of physiology. [R: Choice, Oct 88, p. 294]—**Garabed Eknoyan**

23   Health Sciences

INTRODUCTION

The material in this chapter is arranged under three headings: Medicine, Psychiatry, and Public Health and Health Care. There are several important general sources listed under Medicine, including the *Biographical Dictionary of Medicine* (Facts on File, 1990) (see entry 1120), which provides brief biographies on more than 500 individuals ranging from ancient herbalists to modern medical scientists; and *The Official ABMS Directory of Certified Medical Specialists* (Marquis Who's Who & Reed Reference Publishing, 1993-) (see entry 1130), which lists physicians by their fields of speciality and provides a very large retrospective list of individuals from the seventeenth century to 1977. More specialized is the *Nobel Laureates in Medicine or Physiology: A Biographical Dictionary* (Garland, 1990) (see entry 1128), which includes Nobel laureates in medicine from 1901 through 1989.

Only two sources are listed under Psychiatry: *American Psychiatric Association Membership Directory 1995* (American Psychiatric Association, c.1994) (see entry 1132), which is published yearly and in 1994 lists more than 38,000 APA members; and *The Encyclopedia of Psychiatry, Psychology, and Psychoanalysis* (Henry Holt, 1996) (see entry 1133), which provides brief biographies of individuals working in these areas.

The final section, Public Health and Health Care, provides biographical sources including *Who's Who in American Nursing* (Marquis Who's Who/Reed Reference Publishing, 1984) (see entry 1140), which provides biographies of more than 27,000 nurses, heads of nursing colleges, nursing directors of major hospitals, officials of state departments of public health, and heads of major associations; *The National Directory of Chiropractic* (One Directory of Chiropractic, 1992) (see entry 1139), which provides biographical information on chiropractors by region; and the *Directory of Hospital Personnel: All Hospitals Plus over 180,000 Key Decision Makers* (Medical Economics Data, 1985) (see entry 1137), which lists individuals working in hospitals throughout the United States.

MEDICINE

1120.   Bendiner, Jessica, and Elmer Bendiner. **Biographical Dictionary of Medicine**. New York, Facts on File, 1990. 284p. index. $40.00. R134.B433. 610'.92'2. LC 89-23604. ISBN 0-8160-1864-2.

Man's continuing progress in understanding and treating his own ills has been the result of remarkable individuals, from ancient herbalists to medical scientists. This fascinating new reference describes the lives of over 500 of the most important persons in the history of medicine. Biographies range in length from a paragraph to several pages. Many of these men and women have been all but forgotten; the authors have done an excellent job of bringing their contributions to light.

Compared to the standard in the field, *A Biographical History of Medicine* (see ARBA 72, entry 1677), this newer work is less scholarly, more accessible to the lay person, and includes more of the medical researchers working today. The authors have tailored this book for the popular reader, both in language and choice of subjects (e.g., the biography on pioneering podiatrist William Scholl, "Dr. Scholl" to corn and fallen-arch suffers the world over). Several appendixes—a chronology of medical history from the year 2838 B.C. to the present, a selected bibliography, a name index with cross-references, and a subject index—make it particularly useful as a reference tool. [R: BR, May/June 91, p. 59; Choice, Apr 91, p. 1284; RBB, 1 Mar 91, p. 1420; SLJ, Dec 91, p. 152]—**Carol L. Noll**

1121. **Canadian Medical Directory**. Don Mills, Ont., Seccombe House: Southam Communications, Ltd., and the Canadian Medical Association, 1955- . 1v. (various paging). $169.00 for recent edition. 610.69'52'02571. ISSN 0068-9203.

Divided into three sections, this directory offers a main alphabetical listing of physicians; a second section grouped by general practice and specialty; and a third general section of miscellaneous information such as hospitals, associations, universities, and names of recent graduates in medicine. In recent editions the section on general practitioners and specialists has been reorganized according to province and city. This section requires some analysis by the user before it can be useful. A recommendation for future editions is the use of indented tabs for each of the three sections to indicate a clearer definition of categories. This directory, nonetheless, maintains its reputation for comprehensiveness, excellence, and accuracy.—**Mary Hemmings and Robert L. Wick**

1122. **Canadian Medical Directory on CD-ROM, 1996**. [CD-ROM]. Don Mills, Ont., Southam, 1996. Minimum system requirements: IBM or compatible, Intel-compatible 386. CD-ROM Drive. MS-DOS 3.0. Windows 3.1. 4MB RAM. 1MB hard disk space. VGA monitor. Microsoft-compatible mouse. $335.00/single user.

The disc under review is primarily a database of 56,000 Canadian physicians that can produce more than 20 categories of lists according to specialty, geographic location, hospital and other affiliations, and by year of graduation. These lists can be annotated and used to create personalized listings in a shadow file called an infobase. Furthermore, the infobase can be manipulated into word processing programs or printed directly from the program. The disc loads effortlessly (it was tested on a Windows 95 platform using a Pentium 75). The program was designed using Folio VIEWS, making it slick, powerful, and visually appealing. A brief 36-page pamphlet accompanies the disc and serves as an introductory self-training guide. In addition, the software help screens are useful and free of "dead end" information.

Hypertext features within the database records offer a variety of links. For example, a physician's affiliated hospital is linked to a database record for the hospital itself. Information is current and accurate in both records tested. Abbreviations for degrees and fellowships are hyperlinked to "pop-up" definitions. Shadow files created by the individual user are easy to tag and edit, especially for users familiar with Microsoft products or Word Perfect 6.1. Boolean operators and phrase searches are also easy to use once the user learns some of the necessary protocol through the help screens. The protocol, such as enclosing a phrase search in quotations, is easy to remember.

Printing results is an easy process. The software setup automatically detects printer configuration and accommodates color printing. Saving results to DOS files is also a simple process and within the menu prompts. Supporting 20-plus search criteria, this is a useful tool that produces defined subsets of Canadian physicians, as well as subsets of more than 1,300 hospitals.—**Mary Hemmings**

1123. **Directory of Physicians in the United States**. 35th ed. Chicago, American Medical Association, 1996. 4v. $545.00/set. ISBN 0-89970-827-7.

> **Directory of Physicians in the United States**. 35th ed. [CD-ROM]. Chicago, American Medical Association, 1996. Minimum system requirements: IBM or compatible 386 DX/33 MHz (486DX/66MHz recommended). Double-speed CD-ROM drive. Windows 3.0. 4MB RAM (8MB recommended). 2MB hard disk space. 256-color monitor. $745.00/single user; $1,145.00/networks. ISBN 0-89970-830-7/single user; 0-89970-831-5/networks.

The 35th edition of this standard medical reference tool is produced by the American Medical Association (AMA) in both a 4-volume book and a CD-ROM format. Both formats present difficult-to-find information on more than 723,000 MDs and DOs who are AMA members, living in the United States, the Virgin Islands, Puerto Rico, some Pacific islands, or temporarily out of the United States as of May 1996. This information has been obtained directly from the practitioners and has been verified by material provided by medical schools, the American Board of Medical Specialists, and state licensing boards. The MDs listed include both members and nonmembers of the AMA.

In the traditional book format, volume 1 alphabetically lists all the names found in the other 3 volumes, giving city locations for each name. Volumes 2 through 4 are arranged geographically, by state and then by city. The biographical information for each individual contains, when available, the following items: home/business address, medical school attended and graduation date, board certification, year of licensure, type of specialty practice, and whether the practitioner has received the Physician's Recognition Award for continuing medical education. There are no listings for the doctors' telephone numbers, residency training, academic appointments, or hospital affiliations. This additional information can be found in *The Official ABMS Directory of Board Certified Medical Specialists*. However, that reference work only covers 487,306 practitioners, thus making the current work by far the most comprehensive for basic information about U.S. physicians.

The CD-ROM format, although quite expensive and lacking sufficient instructions for the computer-challenged, does provide worthwhile additional search capacities. This format allows patrons to formulate a search strategy combining any or all of the following criteria: name, city, state, region, primary specialty, and type of physician. The search feature is the major reason to purchase this expensive software. By double-clicking on the physician's name, the system presents the same information about this individual as appears in the book format.

All academic, large public, and health-related libraries must have this key reference tool. The cost for the CD-ROM format may require many libraries to purchase only the print version.
—**Jonathon Erlen**

1124. **The Medical Directory**. Harlow, England, Longman; distr., Chicago, St. James, 1845- . 2v. index. $150.00/set for recent edition. 610.69'52'02541. ISSN 0305-3342.

Published annually since 1845, this work is primarily an alphabetical list of physicians registered with the General Medical Council (of Great Britain). Also included are physicians outside Great Britain in Commonwealth countries. Each entry provides an address, professional data, education, and some publications. The directory also includes a local list of practitioners in London by postal district and a list of practitioners under postal towns in England, Wales, Scotland, the Channel Islands, the Isle of Man, Northern Ireland, and the Republic of Ireland. There are several other lists including hospitals, universities and medical schools, medical societies and associations, and government and statutory bodies. A similar publication is the *Medical Register* (London: General Medical Council, 1858-), inclusion in which gives physicians a legal right to practice.—**Theodora Andrews**

1125. **Medical Sciences International Who's Who**. Vol.7. New York, Groves Dictionaries, Inc., 1996. (Reference on Research). $595.00/set. ISBN 0-561-59206-4.

This work was previously published as *International Medical Who's Who* (see ARBA 82, entry 1599). The present title was used for the 1987 and more recent editions. The present edition contains capsule biographical entries, including information on education, employment, and address and telephone number, for more than 10,000 "senior" (usage not defined) medical and biomedical scientists around the world. Entries are based on questionnaires, or when these were not returned, other sources. The latter are clearly labeled. In addition, there is a geographic index, by country and then by specialty. This work is useful only when one knows the name of the person about whom information is sought. Searching by city or institution, for example, is difficult, if not impossible. Judging from the geographical index, the work may have somewhat of a bias toward Great Britain and the Continent. One certainly finds a bias against the Soviet Union: only three researchers from that country are listed, exactly as many as for Ethiopia. Perhaps this is due to difficulty in identifying and corresponding with scientists in the USSR. In any event, some comment on the matter ought to appear in the volume, and does not. The introduction identifies *Medical Research Centres* as a companion to this set.—**Philip A. Metzger and Robert L. Wick**

1126. Naifeh, Steven, and Gregory White Smith. **The Best Doctors in America 1994-95**. Aiken, S.C., Woodward/White, 1994. 1131p. index. $60.00. R712.A1N25. 610'.25'73. LC 92-223. ISBN 0-913391-05-0.

Patients and their physicians are often confronted with the problem of finding the best specialist to consult for a particular medical problem. This volume, from the publishers of *The Best Lawyers in America* (1992), is meant to assist in that search. Doctors have been chosen by recommendation and review by their peers. Most of the initial contacts were made at major medical centers, such as the

Mayo Clinic and Johns Hopkins, and, as can be expected, most of the physicians included are at universities and research centers throughout the country. All, however, are clinicians, not just engaged in research.

The book is arranged by general medical fields, then subspecialties. Information on physicians includes name and address, academic and hospital affiliations, telephone numbers, and sometimes further treatment specialization. Close to 4,000 doctors are listed, with representatives from all areas of the United States and a substantial number from Canada. However, one should not assume that only those doctors listed are fine physicians; the methodology used has given a definite preference to doctors who work in high-profile fields and in well-known institutions. [R: LJ, 15 Sept 92, p. 62]—**Carol L. Noll**

1127.   **National Health Directory**. Betty Ankrapp and Sara Nell Di Lima, eds. Gaithersville, Md., Aspen, 1977- . maps. $99.00pa. for recent edition. ISSN 0147-2771.

Librarians working in a well-funded library that has a constant need for questions involving government officials at all levels may want to consider the *National Health Directory*. Otherwise, they should not spend $99 a year for a book that is probably out-of-date by the time it is received. The *National Health Directory* lists the names, titles, addresses, and telephone numbers of "key information sources on health programs and legislation at all levels" (p. v). The table of contents is extremely brief and lacking in detail and, worst of all, there is no index to the entire book.

Almost all the information on a national level can be found in the *United States Government Manual* (Bernan Press, annual) or the *Washington Information Directory* (see ARBA 96, entry 734; ARBA 93, entry 743; and ARBA 90, entry 702), both of which are easier to use. The maps of state congressional districts can also be found in many other places. The only information not available elsewhere would be that on the local or state level. For the occasional questions most public and academic libraries would get in this area, librarians are better off calling their local health departments rather than spending this amount of money on a book that is most likely valid for only nine months. Only larger medical centers and government libraries need consider this directory.—**Natalie Kupferbert and Robert L. Wick**

1128.   **Nobel Laureates in Medicine or Physiology: A Biographical Dictionary**. Daniel M. Fox, Marcia Meldrum, and Ira Rezak, eds. New York, Garland, 1990. 595p. index. (Garland Reference Library of the Humanities, v.852). $95.00. o.p. R134.F69. 610'.92'2. LC 90-13907. ISBN 0-8240-7892-6.

Probably the most biographical questions concerning medically related individuals are asked about those few who have won Nobel prizes in the fields of medicine and physiology. While these people have been portrayed in various biographical reference works, this current compilation is by far the most useful.

Fox and his fellow editors have selected a renowned group of scholars to research and write biographies for each Nobel laureate in medicine or physiology from 1901 through 1989. These biographies range in length from three to over five pages and include the personal side of these famous individuals as well as their major scientific contributions. Following each biography is a valuable bibliography that cites key publications by these individuals and useful additional biographical studies. The only information not provided is the location of illustrations of these scientists. Despite this flaw, this biographical guide will be a welcome addition to all reference collections.—**Jonathon Erlen**

1129.   **The Nobel Prize Winners: Physiology or Medicine**. Frank N. Magill, ed. Pasadena, Calif., Salem Press, 1991. 3v. illus. index. $210.00/set. R134.N63. 610'.92'2. LC 91-12143. ISBN 0-89356-571-7.

This set is fourth in a series of six works that cover the Nobel laureates in all categories. Magill has consolidated a great deal of information in an easy-to-read and easy-to-use format that will be of more value to general readers than the various other works available on Nobel Prize winners.

Volume 1 provides an excellent history and overview of the Nobel Prize in physiology and medicine, written by Stephen L. Wolfe. A timeline follows this essay and lists information about all

151 laureates. Similar to the preceding set, *The Nobel Prize Winners: Chemistry* (see ARBA 91, entry 1765), this work has separate essays in chronological order. An attractive display page precedes each laureate's entry and lists prize winners in other disciplines for the same year. The articles in each volume are written by experts in their respective fields and provide comprehensive information on the laureate's life and career. Each essay concludes with a two-part bibliography to provide readers with sources for further study. The large photograph of each winner at the beginning of an article adds a human element to the listed accomplishments of each person. Researchers who need a more scholarly presentation of prize winners prior to 1980 can find additional materials in the *Dictionary of Scientific Biography* (see ARBA 91, entries 1461-62). An alphabetical index appears at the end of the third volume and includes the prize winners, countries, discoveries, theories, and key terms. Boldface type in the index helps one find the primary articles on each laureate. Since this is a three-volume set, the index could be improved by adding volume numbers to the page numbers.

Alkaline paper, sturdy binding, and clear print further enhance the value of this reference work. Written at an undergraduate level, this work is highly recommended for large public and all academic libraries. [R: Choice, Dec 91, p. 576]—**Diane J. Turner**

1130.   **The Official ABMS Directory of Board Certified Medical Specialists**. New Providence, N.J., Marquis Who's Who/Reed Reference Publishing, 1993- . 4 vols. index. $439.95/set for recent edition. ISSN 0000-1406.

This four-volume set was formed by the merger of Marquis's *Directory of Medical Specialists* and the American Board of Medical Specialists' *Compendium of Certified Medical Specialists*. Issued annually, it is the most comprehensive listing of physicians available. The most recent edition contains profiles of more than 466,000 retired and practicing specialists on its nearly 9,000 pages. Profiles include medical school and year of degree, place and date of internship, place and date of residencies, fellowship training, academic/hospital appointments, professional associations, type of medical practice, and address information. Physicians are listed geographically within specialities, with a single name index at the end of volume 4. A separate necrology index lists physicians who have died since the publication of the directory's previous edition.

With such a comprehensive list of specialities included—even "Family Physician" is employed as a kind of catch-all category—one would be hard-pressed not to find a particular U.S. physician in this reference set. While brief, the individual profiles provide sufficient data to get some sense of a specialist's background. Evaluative/critical information is not the role of this resource; it is a directory only. The various specialty boards are listed preceding the list of physicians in that area of practice. Board members' names and addresses are listed, and board history, policy statements, and general information are provided.

Libraries desiring a comprehensive resource of this kind will either need to buy this title or live without an adequate resource. It stands alone and will be an automatic purchase for libraries with a demand for medical directory information.—**Ed Volz**

1131.   **The Oxford Companion to Medicine**. John Walton, Paul B. Beeson, and Ronald Bodley Scott, eds. New York, Oxford University Press, 1994. 2v. 800p. illus. $65.00/set. ISBN 0-19-262355-2.

Described as a comprehensive reference book concerned with the theory, practice, and profession of medicine, this title includes more than 200 major entries, each written by an authority, on topics ranging from forensic medicine to art and medicine. In addition, there are entries on topics such as medical and nursing practice, medical education, and computers in clinical medicine. Entries on communication between doctors and patients, ethics of medical experimentation, and the organization of medicine and its relation to the government and the law in Britain and in America, elucidate the relationship between medicine and society at large. Entries are listed in a simple letter-by-letter alphabetical order. The longer entries normally include references as well as titles for further reading.

In addition to these major entries, there are over 1,000 biographies of medical women and men, mainly those who have made significant contributions to medicine but also those who have achieved distinction (or notoriety) in other activities or in fiction. To complete the encyclopedic coverage of the *Companion*, there are more than 5,000 short entries that explain many medical terms, such as particular diseases, drugs, and medical abbreviations.

Two of the editors (John Walton and Paul Beeson) saw the project through to completion after Sir Ronald Bodley Scott's death early in the publication process. During preliminary discussions it was decided that this book would be not "just another medical dictionary" but rather an encyclopedia of medicine. Although it would include short definitions of selected terms, it was not intended to be as comprehensive as a dictionary. Rather, the intention was to include major essays on a variety of topics so that the volume would be "meaningful to students and practitioners of medicine whatever their specialty, for instance, a plastic surgeon wishing to learn more about the role and responsibilities of a psychiatrist might turn with profit to the article on psychiatry to seek the information he required." Further, contributors were asked to discuss the historical development of their subject as well as "its major emphases in the present day"; to undertake to make entries "useful to nurses and other health care professionals seeking more detailed information about disciplines relevant to medicine"; and to ensure that essays be written in "language sufficiently clear and simple to make them meaningful to the intelligent layman." In fact, all of these aims have been met in the two-volume work.

The *Companion* was compiled with the help of about 150 contributors from Britain and North America. The list of names is very much a who's who of distinguished medical practitioners.

Two appendices complete the work. One is titled "Major Medical and Related Qualifications," which gives the abbreviations and complete names for various medical titles (e.g., KCMG, which stands for "Knight Commander of the Order of St. Michael and St. George"). The second appendix is a list of medical abbreviations with their meaning spelled out in full.

This two-volume set is an excellent complement to the *International Dictionary of Medicine and Biology*. The latter specifically set out to be an exhaustive dictionary, while, as noted above, the *Companion* was intended to serve an encyclopedic function. Another balance struck between the two works is that the *Companion* has a decided British flavor, while the *International Dictionary* is more predominantly American in tone. Finally, the *Companion* treats topics in terms of historical underpinnings, with illustrations tending to be historical prints, while the *International Dictionary* is more concerned about currency. Both titles deserve a place in medical reference collections. [R: Choice, Dec 86, pp. 608-9]—**Sherrilynne Fuller and Robert L. Wick**

PSYCHIATRY

1132. **American Psychiatric Association Membership Directory 1995**. Washington, D.C., American Psychiatric Association, c.1994. 783p. index. $55.00. ISBN 0-89042-187-0pa.

Listing more than 38,000 American Psychiatric Association members, this directory provides basic biographical information including name, address, phone number, date of APA membership, and a code describing specialties and other key professional information. It is possible with this directory to determine through the geographic indexes where a particular psychiatrist is located. The work also provides information concerning the constitution and bylaws, and a list of the councils of the organization.

This work is a valuable companion to the *ABMS Directory of Board Certified Medical Specialists* (American Board of Medical Specialists, 1992). The work is recommended for all larger medical collections, and for special libraries in the medical arts.—**Robert L. Wick**

1133. **The Encyclopedia of Psychiatry, Psychology, and Psychoanalysis**. Benjamin B. Wolman, ed. New York, Henry Holt, 1996. 649p. index. $135.00. ISBN 0-8050-2234-1.

This single-volume resource is a product of the same editorial team that produced the *International Encyclopedia of Psychiatry, Psychology, Psychoanalysis, and Neurology* (see ARBA 78, entry 1367), which won the Dartmouth Medal from the American Library Association. That 12-volume set was lauded for its comprehensiveness and currentness. The volume under review not only abridges the larger work but also revises and updates the entries, and it endeavors to cover the advancements of the past 20 years of the topics at hand. Neurology has been omitted from this encyclopedia but will be the topic of a separate volume.

Adhering to the A to Z format found in the larger encyclopedia, this volume provides articles on a variety of topics, from abortion to human immunodeficiency virus and acquired immunodeficiency syndrome, to stimulus-response theories in social psychology. The entries are signed by one of the nearly 700 contributing authors, many of whom hold Ph.D.s or M.D.s. Scope of the articles covers studies conducted (with the year), important statistics, people active in that particular study, and related concepts. They cover basic ground without delving too deeply into complex ideas. Much of the biographical information is brief, so brief as to be of little value to most users. A useful bibliography complements the body of the encyclopedia. The index is functional, providing *see also* references to related terms.

The intended audience for this one-volume encyclopedia is professionals in the fields discussed and graduate students or postdoctoral scholars. For its ready-reference value, one can easily see that audience making good use of the volume. It is doubtful that professional psychiatrists or psychologists would have a need for this volume beyond ready-reference; the same holds true for students. The articles are not in-depth enough for the book to serve as a textbook or as an answer-all encyclopedia. However, for quick answers to questions involving psychology, psychiatry, and psychoanalysis, this somewhat reasonably priced encyclopedia will be helpful to that audience not having access to the full 12-volume set.—**Melissa Rae Root**

PUBLIC HEALTH AND HEALTH CARE

1134.   Bullough, Vern L., Olga Maranjian Church, and Alice P. Stein. **American Nursing: A Biographical Dictionary**. New York, Garland, 1988. 358p. illus. o.p. (Garland Reference Library of Social Science, Vol. 368). $60.00. LC 87-29076. ISBN 0-8240-8540-X.

Bullough, Vern L., Lilli Sentz, and Alice P. Stein, eds. **American Nursing: A Biographical Dictionary**. **Volume II**. Hamden, Conn., Garland, 1992. 389p. illus. (Garland Reference Library of Social Science, Vol.368-). $95.00. RT34.A44. 610.73'092'2. LC 87-29076. ISBN 0-8240-720-4.

Two volumes of a projected three-volume set have been published to date. The first volume lists 175 women and two men, all but one deceased, who made significant contributions to nursing, not always as "trained" professionals. While the *American Journal of Nursing* and the early *Trained Nurse and Hospital Review* often carried obituaries of these nurses, personal data were usually lacking; few were included in the who's who or current biography types of reference books; and nursing history texts were rarely known outside the schools. The feminist movement has focused attention on nursing as a research area. As the editors point out, further research could well be done on almost all of the figures included here, as well as on the large number who it is hoped will appear in a projected second volume. They also acknowledge that the group is "heavily weighted toward the East and Midwest."

The articles follow a pattern in which each author (there are seventy contributors) tries to state in the first paragraph exactly who the biographee was and what she accomplished for the nursing profession or American society in general. This is followed by what personal information is known, career activities and honors, the books and articles written by the person, a bibliography, and the contributor's name. Indexes list persons under decades of birth, beginning with "before 1840"; first nursing school attended; areas of special interest or accomplishment (e.g., Sanger is under "public activity"); and states or countries of birth.

The second volume includes biographies of significant American nurses, born in 1915 or before and mostly deceased. A few retirees are listed, but today's active professional leaders will have to wait until the third volume, due in 1997 or 1998. Considerable overlapping exists with volume 1, but both volumes are necessary for a comprehensive view of the development of nursing in this country, as seen through the contributions of those who lived it—391 individuals, only 9 of them men.—**Harriette M. Cluxton and Robert L. Wick**

1135.   **Dictionary of American Nursing Biography**. Martin Kaufman, ed. Westport, Conn., Greenwood Press, 1988. 462p. index. $49.95. LC 87-25454. ISBN 0-313-24520-7.

With the recent emergence of the scholarly discipline of the history of nursing, there is a need for quality reference tools in this field. Martin Kaufman's new nursing biographical dictionary, an outgrowth of his 1984 publication covering American physicians, is a useful reference work for anyone interested in the history of nursing.

This volume contains one- to five-page biographical sketches of 196 nineteenth- and twentieth-century pioneers who contributed to American nursing. Selection criteria included the significance of the individual's contributions to nursing and the ability of the research team to find fairly complete biographical material about the person. Only individuals who died prior to 31 January 1987 and who met the selection criteria are included. The biographical sketches cover nursing leaders in a variety of nursing fields, such as education, public health, administration, and the military. For those persons selected, the following information is provided: education, family background, career highlights, contributions to the evolution of nursing, and a list of their main publications and locations of additional bibliographic material. Unfortunately, this last segment does not include recent journal articles about these noteworthy pioneers in nursing. Appendices which list these nursing leaders by place of birth, state where they worked during most of their careers, and their nursing specialty, along with a comprehensive index, provide easy access to the useful information in this book. [R: Choice, Oct 88, p. 283]—**Judith A. Erlen and Jonathon Erlen**

1136. **The Directory of Health Care Professionals**. Baltimore, Md., HCIA, 1993- . 2v. $299.00pa./set for recent volume. ISSN 1049-9253.

This work provides information about more than 7,000 hospitals in the United States. The information is supplemented by HCIA's hospital database, which contains detailed financial and operating information compiled from each hospital's annual Medicare cost report. The directory is divided into two volumes: Volume 1: *Hospitals and Health Care System Professionals*, and Volume 2: *Index to Professionals*. Section A of volume 1 lists more than 183,000 hospital professionals by hospital. These hospitals are arranged alphabetically by city within each particular state. The information provided covers: names of the hospitals; addresses and zip codes; main telephone and fax numbers; number of beds (most listings); system affiliations (if the hospital is affiliated with a health care system, the system name and location are listed); listings of chief administrative officers and chief medical officers; administrative/financial services; clinical services department/units; and support service departments with their direct telephone numbers. Support service departments include nutrition services, safety and security, and engineering.

Section B consists of two indexes: an alphabetic hospital index and the health care system headquarters index, listing more than 500 system headquarters and more than 3,000 health care system professionals. Entries list the addresses and zip codes; main telephone and fax numbers; lists of chairpersons, CEOs and other health care system officers, as well as participating member hospitals.

The Directory of Health Care Professionals provides data similar to that in *The Register of North American Hospitals* (American Preeminent Registry Publications, 1995) and the *Hospital Phone Book* (U. S. Directory Service, 1993). This work is recommended for college and university libraries and medical libraries.—**Marilynn Green**

1137. **Directory of Hospital Personnel**. Heidi M. Siegenthaler Garrett, ed. Montvale, N.J., Medical Economics Data, 1985- . 1v. (various paging). index. $310.00. for recent edition. ISSN 0885-9671.

Directory of Hospital Personnel is an in-depth profile of hospitals in the United States. The profiles are arranged alphabetically by city within state. They include name, address, telephone number, teaching affiliations, number of interns and residents, nursing students, employees licensed, actual beds, rehabilitation facility, and Joint Commission on Accreditation of Healthcare Organizations (JCAHO) approval indicators. Also listed are department heads or key decision makers organized by title. The type of insurance plans accepted and health care group purchasing membership information are provided where available. Cross-references are made to parent hospitals (e.g., Humana Hospital/see Michael Reese).

Directory of Hospital Personnel is more comprehensive than the *Hospital Phone Book* (U.S. Directory Service) but provides fewer names than the *Register of North American Hospitals*. Recommended for college, university, and medical libraries.—**Marilynn Green and Robert L. Wick**

1138.   **Merriam-Webster's Medical Dictionary**. Springfield, Mass., Merriam-Webster, 1995. 771p. $6.99pa. ISBN 0-87779-914-8.

This paperback medical dictionary is an abridged version of *Merriam-Webster's Medical Desk Dictionary*. It contains 35,000 of the most frequently used words in both human and veterinary medicine. The vocabulary includes common abbreviations, Latin and English names of plants and animals, and generic and brand names for drugs. Compiled for lay users, terms in the lexicon encompass sports terms such as *abs*, *pecs*, and *delts* for common muscle groups, and brief biographical information on important historical figures such as Louis Pasteur and Rudolf Virchow.

The dictionary is easy to use. Entries are in alphabetical order, letter by letter, with main entries in boldface. Entries list syllabication, pronunciation, variant spelling and pronunciation, hyphenation, and definitions. Functional labels, inflected forms, and capitalization and usage notes are part of the text, but etymology appears only in entries for abbreviations and eponyms. Scientific plant and animal names follow the New Latin vocabulary. These entries are at the genus level, with higher orders listed in the definitions. Cross-references in small capitals direct readers to related materials. Common prefixes and suffixes have their own entries so that readers may use them to determine the meaning of words not in the lexicon. An appendix contains graphic scientific and medical symbols that are not in the main body of the dictionary.

The text is arranged in two columns with guide words at the top of each page. The typeface is small but not difficult to read. The margins are adequate. Although this dictionary lacks the breadth, detail, and illustrations of larger medical dictionaries such as *Dorland's* (27th ed.; see ARBA 889, entry 1538), *Stedman's* (see ARBA 91, entry 1664), and *Mosby's* (2d ed.; see ARBA 87, entry 1627), it contains the vocabulary that lay users need. This dictionary is inexpensive and well suited for home use. It will also be useful for students, court reporters, and transcribers who need portable dictionaries.—**Barbara M. Bibel**

1139.   **The National Directory of Chiropractic**. 3d ed. Olathe, Kans., One Directory of Chiropractic, 1992. 333p. $95.00pa.

This directory is divided into three sections. The first section is composed of advertisements for providers of equipment, supplies, and services to the chiropractic profession. The next section lists chiropractors by state and city. Entries provide the physician's name, address, telephone number, college attended, year of graduation, and chiropractic techniques used. Not all entries are complete. An alphabetical name index follows the geographical listings. The third section provides information on the practice of chiropractic in each state, including the scope of practice, licensure eligibility requirements, a general description of the licensing examination, and names and addresses of state chiropractic organizations.

While this last section may be useful in some libraries, the information in the directory is readily available elsewhere and at less cost. This work will primarily be of use to chiropractors in locating suppliers and in referring patients to other chiropractors who use specific therapeutic techniques.—**Gari-Anne Patzwald**

1140.   **Who's Who in American Nursing**. New Providence, N.J., Marquis Who's Who/Reed Reference Publishing, 1984- . index. $139.00 for recent edition. ISBN 0-8379-1002-1.

Originally published by the Society of Nursing Professionals, *Who's Who in American Nursing* lists more than 27,000 (1995 edition) biographical entries. Concentration on formal education, progressive career track, and organizational involvement enabled the society to target those individuals active in the field. Information comes from the biographees. Selection is judged on either the position of responsibility held or the level of attainment achieved by the individual. Admissions based on position include heads of colleges, nursing directors of major hospitals, officials of state departments of public health, or heads of major associations. Admission for individual achievement is based on qualitative criteria, including education, career advancement, contributions to the nursing literature, awards and fellowships, civic activities, and organizational leadership roles. Information contained within each entry is similar to all other *Who's Who* publications. The professional area index categorizes the nursing professionals by state and city within their specialties, including administration, community health, consultation, critical care, education, gerontology, maternal and women's health, medical and surgical, midwifery, occupational health, oncology, pediatrics, psychiatry, rehabilitation, and research.

While not comprehensive, the directory does provide access to a group of professionals who have been ignored in the past, but who may well become one of the most important participants in health care reform. Health sciences libraries, in particular those that serve schools of nursing and large medical centers, should add this to their collections.—**Vicki J. Killion**

24   Sports and Recreation

INTRODUCTION

This chapter on sports and recreation is divided into seven sections, including General Works, Baseball, Basketball, Chess, Football, Hockey, and Wrestling. There are a number of important sources listed in General Works, including the *Biographical Dictionary of American Sports* (Greenwood Press, 1995) (see entry 1142), represented here by the 1992-1995 supplement, which includes more than 600 entries on various sports figures; and *Chase's Calendar of Events* (Contemporary Books, 1988-) (see entry 1145), which provides biographies of more than 400 sports figures, including coaches, broadcasters, journalists, and stars. Three newer sources cover women in sports, including Robert J. Condon's *Great Women Athletes of the 20th Century* (McFarland, 1991) (see entry 1146), which provides biographical sketches of 50 of the most prominent female athletes of the twentieth century; the *Encyclopedia of Women and Sports* (ABC-CLIO, 1996) (see entry 1156), which includes more than 600 biographies of women athletes; and *Outstanding Women Athletes: Who They Are and How They Influenced Sports in America* (Oryx Press, 1992) (see entry 1163), which provides detailed biographical studies of 60 women who represent 19 sports.

Biographies of Olympic athletes are found in *The Lincoln Library of Sports Champions* (Encyclopaedia Britannica, 1993) (see entry 1152), which includes sketches of almost 500 athletes from 50 different sports around the world; and the somewhat older but still valuable *Black Olympian Medalists* (Libraries Unlimited, 1991) (see entry 1153), which is a biographical dictionary of African American Olympians who date back to 1904.

Several works of note are contained in the chapters on specific sports. The section on baseball contains nine sources, including *The Ballplayers: Baseball's Ultimate Biographical Reference* (William Morrow, 1990) (see entry 1164), which includes biographies of players who had long careers in baseball; and Rich Westcott's *Diamond Greats: Profiles and Interviews with 65 of Baseball's History Makers* (Meckler, 1988) (see entry 1170), which includes biographies of the greats of the sport. Basketball includes one comprehensive work, titled *Basketball Biographies: 434 U.S. Players, Coaches and Contributors to the Game, 1891-1990* (McFarland, 1991) (see entry 1173), which includes short biographies of more than 400 players. Football is represented with four sources: the *Biographical Dictionary of American Sports: Football* (Greenwood Press, 1987) (see entry 1175), which includes biographical information on more than 500 players throughout the game's history; *Who's Who in the Super Bowls: The Performance of Every Player in Super Bowls I to XX* (W. W. Norton, 1986) (see entry 1177); and *The Pro Football Bio-Bibliography* (Locust Hill Press, 1989) (see entry 1178), which provides sketchy information on football players. Also, it should be noted that there is a *Cumulative Index to the "Biographical Dictionary of American Sports"* (David L. Porter, comp. Westport, Conn., Greenwood Press, 1993), which covers all of the volumes in this series from 1987 through 1992.

GENERAL WORKS

1141.   **African-American Sports Greats: A Biographical Dictionary**. David L. Porter, ed. Westport, Conn., Greenwood Press, 1995. 429p. illus. index. $59.95. ISBN 0-313-28987-5.

Despite the plethora of recent books on African-American and black sports figures, this is the first all-sport collection of biographies that is exclusively devoted to the greatest African-American athletes. In the recent past, there have been histories of black athletic development and biographies of U.S. sports greats and Olympic sports heroes, all of which have included African Americans among the biographees. However, none has covered all sports and all places and times in the United States.

The editor has had some experience in this field. Here he has marshaled the contributions of many people who come from a variety of backgrounds. The entries, two to three pages in length, are written to a standard that is perhaps a testimonial to his previous work: the six-volume *Biographical Dictionary of American Sports*. The 166 men and women profiled in the work under review represent figures from the early days (boxer Jack Johnson) to the present day (football player Emmitt Smith), as well as some administrators and coaches.

Porter's approach is fresh and satisfying. He insists on presenting a picture of the whole person. If there are difficulties in an athlete's private life, the editor does not shirk from dealing with them, although always in an unemotional and factual way. The sensational murder case involving football and sports personality O. J. Simpson is included (the book is current through mid-1995), but the event is placed in the context of his life. The same can be said for boxing great Mike Tyson, in that his legal troubles and turbulent life are examined. Entries are about 800 to 1,000 words in length; use quotations liberally from knowledgeable people; and cover the subject's family, education, personal struggles, career achievements and records, and awards and honors. Each entry concludes with a bibliography of books and articles on the biographee.

This biographical dictionary is a fine contribution to the literature. Any U.S. sports fan would enjoy it, and it is well suited for school, public, and some academic libraries. It is sturdily bound in an attractive cover and printed on permanent paper. Photographs and appendixes are provided. **—Randall Rafferty**

1142.   **Biographical Dictionary of American Sports: 1992-1995 Supplement for Baseball, Football, Basketball, and Other Sports**. David L. Porter, ed. Westport, Conn., Greenwood Press, 1995. 429p. index. $89.50. ISBN 0-313-28431-8.

This is the second supplement to the four-volume set that appeared in 1987-89 (see ARBA 90, entries 757 and 769; ARBA 89, entry 735; and ARBA 88, entry 798); a first supplement came out in 1992 (see ARBA 93, entry 817) and a separate cumulative index in 1993. The format remains unchanged: signed articles of 200-600 words arranged by sport, each with several bibliographical references. The subjects include not only players, but also managers, coaches, league administrators, broadcasters, and others who have achieved prominence in American sports. Of the 616 entries in this volume, the majority (383) are from baseball and football; the next greatest is basketball, with 58 entries. While some of the subjects have gained fame only since the late 1980s, most of them were active at an earlier time, suggesting that they probably do not rank as highly in importance as the subjects of the earlier volumes.

While there are numerous contributors, the entries are stylistically similar and the quality of the writing is uniformly good. There is an alphabetical index of all subjects, as well as listings of entries by subject's place of birth, women athletes by sport, major U.S. sports halls of fame, and sites of Olympic games. A cumulative index of subject names would have been a desirable feature. Libraries owning the earlier volumes will obviously wish to add this supplement; others should seriously consider purchasing the entire set.**—Jack Ray**

1143.   **Biographical Dictionary of American Sports: Outdoor Sports**. David L. Porter, ed. Westport, Conn., Greenwood Press, 1988. 728p. index. $75.00. LC 87-31780. ISBN 0-313-26260-8.

This is an interesting and much needed reference work, although the title may be misleading. Many think of outdoor sports in terms of hunting and fishing, but this book concerns itself with athletic activities that take place outdoors—auto racing, golf, horse racing, lacrosse, skiing, soccer, speed skating, tennis, and track and field. Football and baseball have been covered in separate volumes. This work contains a total of 519 entries selected according to three general criteria: the individual must have been born or spent childhood years in the United States, had an exceptional career in the particular sport, and made a major contribution to that sport. A number of additional factors, which are explained in the preface, were also weighed in the selection process. Judging by the entries for soccer, the selection process was a sound one. However, as is usually the case in works such as this, the quality of individual entries varies. Some contributors clearly spent considerable time on their work; this is evidenced by the bibliographies accompanying their entries and the soundness of the coverage. Others apparently treated subjects in a somewhat perfunctory fashion, providing basic information but not the depth one would have liked. On the whole, however, the work is well done, and special praise is due the ten appendixes and solid index. This is a reference work which belongs in any library supporting interests in sport history, physical education, or indeed a sporting audience with strong reading inclinations. [R: Choice, Apr 89, p. 1300; LJ, 1 Apr 89, p. 84; RBB, 15 Jan 89, p. 845; WLB, Mar 89, pp. 112-14]—**James A. Casada**

1144.   Brownstone, David, and Irene Franck. **Sports People in the News**. New York, Macmillan Library Reference/Simon & Schuster Macmillan, 1995- . illus. index. $85.00 for recent edition. ISSN 1090-6681.

This new series is scheduled to be an annual, as is *People in the News*, from which it is modeled. The volumes contain biographies of more than 400 sports figures, such as coaches, broadcasters, journalists, and stars, both professional and amateur, drawn from baseball, basketball, boxing and wrestling, figure skating, football, golf, gymnastics, hockey, racing, swimming and diving, tennis, and track and field. Recently deceased sports-related figures are also included.

Selection is based on current activities and importance, not on past achievements or celebrity status alone. Entries include the person's role in sports from spring 1995 through May 1996, a brief career summary, and a short descriptive summary, and conclude with a further reading list. More than 300 of the 400 profiles include black-and-white photographs.

Although the volume is arranged alphabetically, there are two indexes, by name and by sport, which will cumulate in future volumes, making it valuable for reference.—**Kathleen J. Voigt and Robert L. Wick**

1145.   **Chase's Calendar of Events**. Chicago, Contemporary Books, 1988- . illus. index. $29.95pa. for recent edition. ISSN 1091-2959.

Who knows that August 15 is the birth anniversary of Charles Comiskey, or that he was born in 1859 and died in 1931? Who knows that August 15 is also the anniversary of the first woman in pro football, the anniversary of major league baseball's "Forfeit by Ground Crew," and the anniversary of "Three Men on Third"? *Chase's Calendar of Events* supplies this information and much, much more. The listing for August 15 includes six events scheduled to take place in 1997 as well. Also listed for each day of the year are the birthdays of living athletes, emphasizing baseball, basketball, football, and hockey players, but additionally treating sportscasters, actors noted for sports films, and other sports-related figures.

This book comes in an easy-to-read, 8-by-11-inch format with readily recognizable boldfaced headings. The useful index not only lists each name and event alphabetically, but organizes the entries by sport as well. These features make *Chase's* easy to use. The day-by-day calendar listings are supplemented by separate listings of league and team addresses, halls of fame, annual sports award winners, U.S. national champions, and a directory of sports organizations.—**David A. Doman and Robert L. Wick**

1146.   Condon, Robert J. **Great Women Athletes of the 20th Century**. Jefferson, N.C., McFarland, 1991. 180p. illus. index. $25.95. GV697.A1C68. 796.092'2. LC 91-52633. ISBN 0-89950-555-4.

Condon presents biographical sketches of 50 female athletes of the twentieth century. Each biographical essay is two or three pages long and is accompanied by a black-and-white photograph. The work does not include footnotes or other bibliographic citations.

Condon's writing style is simple and easy to follow. In most essays he does a good job of describing the historical and situational contexts of an athlete's life and accomplishments. A few historical and factual errors appear but do not constitute a major problem. For instance, in discussing the pioneers of women's marathon running, Condon mistakenly says that Katherine Switzer was ejected from the Boston Marathon course in 1967. He also fails to mention that in 1966, Roberta Gibb Bingay became the first woman to complete the Boston race. The entry on Katarina Witt states that Olympic figure skating competition now includes a compulsory figures competition. In fact, 1988 marked the last time that compulsory figures appeared in the Olympics.

The entries are well chosen. Readers may wonder why basketball star Cheryl Miller and volley-ball player Flo Hyman are omitted, but there is no question that all of the entries deserve inclusion. This book will serve as a useful source of concise biographical information on many of the top female athletes of this century. [R: BR, Nov/Dec 92, pp. 59-60; Choice, Mar 92, pp. 1119-20; SLJ, May 92, pp. 28-29]—**Wayne Wilson**

1147.   Condon, Robert J. **The Fifty Finest Athletes of the 20th Century: A Worldwide Reference**. Jefferson, N.C., McFarland, 1990. 152p. illus. index. $20.95. QV697.A1C67. 796'.092'2. LC 89-43643. ISBN 0-89950-374-8.

Sports biographies and reference books are common, but there are few good biographical dictionaries. This volume begins to fill that gap by presenting brief biographies for 50 athletes of the twentieth century. Only four women are included. The coverage is intended to be international, but only five non-Americans appear. The sports covered are baseball, basketball, boxing, football, golf, hockey, horse racing, ice skating, soccer, swimming, tennis, and track and field. However, the concentration is on professional baseball, basketball, and football, so that the majority of athletes presented are male Americans. The title and subtitle are thus misleading.

The choices of athletes are the author's, and there is only a brief rationale as to why individuals were selected. They are divided, for reasons that are not explained, into the top 20 and the runners-up. In each case the entries are arranged alphabetically, so there is no further distinction as to relative standing. A second article on Babe Ruth concludes the book, as he has been selected as the greatest of the lot. The biographies are brief, averaging about two pages, and each is accompanied by one or more black-and-white photographs, usually of the athlete in action. The biographies are reasonably good and provide detailed facts and figures about performance, as well as background information. Because of the stature of the biographees, biographical and statistical information about them is readily available in other reference sources. The book seems to be intended for an adult audience but may prove to be more popular with teenagers and young adults. [R: Choice, Apr 91, p. 1287; VOYA, June 91, pp. 138-40]—**Norman D. Stevens**

1148.   **Great Athletes**. Pasadena, Calif., Salem Press, 1992. 20v. illus. index. (Twentieth Century). $400.00/set. GV697.A1 G68. 796'.092'2. LC 91-32301. ISBN 0-89356-775-2.

As the first in a series that is intended to give young adults a broad perspective on the events, ideas, and people of the twentieth century, *Great Athletes* gets things off to a sound start. Its multivolume, oversized format, with only about 35 entries per volume, seems, at first glance, inappropriate for a reference set. In fact, the set is most likely to be used either as a source for student papers or simply for entertainment. Under those circumstances, a set of large volumes with text that is easy to read and that can be used by several students at once is a distinct advantage. On the other hand, while the price per volume seems reasonable, the decision to publish the set in so many volumes has probably driven the price up to the point where many libraries, especially school libraries (to whom the set is targeted), will think carefully about adding it to their collection.

Great Athletes has much to recommend it. It provides brief (typically two-page) biographical sketches of 738 outstanding athletes who were active in this century. Every entry is accompanied by a full-page black-and-white photograph and a separate body of tabular materials. Each sketch is broken down into basic biographical information, initial career development, contributions that made the person a superstar, and later career developments and other aspects of the person's life. The texts, which have been written by experts who have strong academic credentials, are carefully organized and highlight the challenges and opportunities that motivated the biographees. This kind of balanced presentation—coupled with the representation of 61 different major and minor sports and the inclusion of men and women from 42 different countries—makes *Great Athletes* a set of substantial value that should find wide acceptance and use.

The individuals covered represent the best in their fields. Each volume includes the name, sport, and country index for the entire set, making it easy for a student using one volume to locate information in others. The final volume contains an excellent glossary that explains sport-specific terminology (e.g., chip shot) used in the entries that is not likely to be found in a standard dictionary. It also includes a less useful timeline section that simply lists each of the individuals chronologically by their date of birth. Unfortunately, this feature often fails to reveal much about rivals or stars who were active at the same time. All in all, *Great Athletes* offers a comprehensive, diverse, and useful series of biographical sketches of a splendid body of athletes. Despite its seemingly high price, it represents a sound purchase. [R: BR, Sept/Oct 92, p. 72; RBB, July 92, pp. 1960-61; WLB, June 92, p.112]—**Norman D. Stevens**

1149.   **Great Athletes. Supplement 21-23: The Twentieth Century**. Pasadena, Calif., Salem Press, 1994. 3v. illus. index. $75.00/set. ISBN 0-89356-819-8.

This set updates and broadens the coverage of the original 20-volume edition by examining the lives and careers of 106 athletes, many of whom have risen to prominence since the 1st edition's publication in 1992. The final volume lists recent major accomplishments by and recent deaths of athletes profiled in the 1st edition.

As previously, each article is uniform in its format, averaging about four pages long, and includes a photograph of the athlete, ready-reference data, early life, the road to excellence, the emerging champion, continuing the story, and a summary. Each entry is supplemented by tabular materials that contain information such as career statistics, honors and awards, records set, and other individual milestones.

The supplement volumes continue the volume-and-page numbering of the original edition. New in the final volume is a year-by-year chart of highlights in world sports during the century. The indexes and timeline have been updated, and each references all 23 volumes. These works have a clear, readable format for middle school students, and also are conducive to browsing by adults.—**Kathleen J. Voigt**

1150.   Jacobs, Timothy. **100 Athletes Who Shaped Sports History**. San Francisco, Calif., Bluewood, 1994. 112p. illus. index. $7.95pa. ISBN 0-912517-13-1.

Sports have played an important part in history, and to this end, *100 Athletes Who Shaped Sports History* encompasses 100 athletes whose birth dates range from 558 B.C. through 1966.

Arranged in chronological order, male and female athletes of various multicultural backgrounds are presented in one-page descriptions. Each page includes an athlete's name in bold capital letters, the dates of birth and (if applicable) death, the sport in which he or she excelled, and a locator map to show birthplace. The biographical sketches address each athlete's personal and unique talent. There is also a line drawing of each athlete. Cross-references to other athletes in the book are included. These are in boldface print for easier reference.

This book has a timeline cross-referenced to each athlete and an extensive index arranged by name, sport, and organization to assist the reader. For extra fun, the author includes a trivia quiz. The answers to the questions are given as clues.

With just enough writing for explanation, this compact and concise book will be a valuable addition to a middle school collection, both as a reference source as well as a part of the regular nonfiction collection.—**Barbara B. Goldstein**

1151.   Lee, George L. **Interesting Athletes: A Newspaper Artist's Look at Blacks in Sports**. Jefferson, N.C., McFarland, 1990. 165p. illus. index. $14.95pa. GV697.A1L37. 796'. 092'2. LC 89-29306. ISBN 0-89950-482-5.

Designed more for the casual reader than the scholar, this is a collection of reprinted did-you-know-type newspaper cartoons from the past four decades. Many come from issues of the *Defender* and *Chicago Tribune*, with which Lee was long affiliated. The earliest was drawn in 1935, when Lee covered the first professional boxing match of Joe Louis. The coverage is primarily Chicago-based with an emphasis on boxing, although other sports are given attention. Data are provided on many figures (all indexed), from Bill Richmond (1763-1829), who taught boxing to Lord Byron, through Kareem Abdul Jabbar, Arthur Ashe, and O. J. Simpson. Although an interesting document of a historical aspect of journalism, this would be of peripheral reference value.—**Dominique-René de Lerma**

1152. **The Lincoln Library of Sports Champions**. 6th ed. Columbus, Ohio, Frontier Press; distr., Chicago, Encyclopaedia Britannica, 1993. 14v. illus. index. $399.00/set. LC 92-75323. ISBN 0-912168-14-5.

First published in 1974, this extensive set of biographical sketches of famous sports figures is still aimed at elementary and junior high school students. It has undergone substantial changes since the 2nd edition was reviewed in ARBA 1980 (see entry 684). That 20-volume edition contained sketches of almost 500 athletes in 50 different sports, including 85 football and 82 baseball players, as well as a sports glossary. The current edition contains sketches for 297 athletes in 25 sports, and the glossary has been eliminated. The mixture of figures has changed over the years, but many of the old favorites, such as Babe Ruth and Jim Thorpe, are still here, and new favorites, such as Bonnie Blair and Shaquille O'Neal, have been added. There are some anomalies, such as the inclusion of Arnold Schwarzenegger as a bodybuilder when he is seldom considered an athlete in recent years.

Arranged alphabetically by athletes' names, each volume contains about 20 entries. Each entry consists of a brief capsule summary of the person's career, which is accompanied by a black-and-white or brown-and-white head shot. This is followed by a longer sketch that runs between 4 and 10 pages depending on the fame and career of the person. Representatives of minor sports such as swimming, and younger athletes whose careers are just beginning, typically are given less coverage than the big-name figures whose athletic careers are behind them. In every case the entry is accompanied by many color and black-and-white action photographs. The entire set contains nearly 2,400 pictures, including 425 in color. The text, which is simply written, concentrates on the person's athletic career but in many cases, especially with the most famous figures, also discusses the person's private life, most often focusing on the person as a potential role model.

The first volume lists an extensive array of individuals and associations as educational advisers and major contributors, and acknowledges support from many others, but the sketches appear to have been produced through a consistent editorial process that gives them a certain sameness. The first volume contains a table of contents arranged by sport, and the final volume contains an index to the main entries. The final volume also contains a supplementary reading list of both general titles and appropriate works on each of the sports represented by the athletes.

This biographical encyclopedia warrants close comparison with *Great Athletes* (see ARBA 1993, entry 816), which is similar in size, price, arrangement, and content. *Great Athletes* provides somewhat shorter entries (of about 2 pages each) and fewer photographs for 738 athletes from 42 different countries. It represents a greater balance of men and women and nationalities than *Sports Champions*, which includes only 25 non-North American figures and 72 women. The entries in *Great Athletes* are attributed to individual contributors, although they have also been edited for consistency of approach, content, and style. The major difference is that *Great Athletes* is intended for a slightly higher grade level, probably junior high to high school, as is reflected in language of the entries, the use of fewer photographs, and the inclusion of a greater number of less-popular people and less-popular sports.

Depending on the level of the school or the abilities of its students, either of these sets represents a reasonable buy, with *Great Athletes* having a slight edge because it includes more individuals. *Great Athletes* is also probably a better choice for public libraries because it is more likely to appeal to, and be useful for, adults. For libraries where budget constraints preclude the purchase of either *Great Athletes* or *Sports Champions*, the inexpensive, one-volume *Fifty Finest Athletes of the 20th Century* (see ARBA 1992, entry 768) is an acceptable alternative that will provide basic information as a starting point for anyone interested in knowing more about sports figures.—**Norman D. Stevens**

1153. Page, James A. **Black Olympian Medalists**. Englewood, Colo., Libraries Unlimited, 1991. 190p. illus. index. $27.50pa. GV697.A1P284. 796'.092'2. LC 90-6660. ISBN 0-87287-618-7.

Page has compiled a biographical dictionary of black Olympians who date back to 1904. While American athletes predominate, African-descended athletes from throughout the world are represented in 465 brief biographical sketches. Basic information such as full name, date and place of birth, country represented, events, medals won, and times and distances is provided. The biographical sketches vary in length and are informal in style, highlighting the major achievements of each athlete both on and off the field. A list of sources is given after each entry, but one must refer to the bibliography in the back of the book for the full citations. In the case of newspaper articles, dates are given but page numbers are omitted.

In addition to the bibliography, Page provides a series of useful statistical tables broken down by event, and when applicable, by sex. He also gives two tables by place and date, one for U.S. medalists and one for international medalists, and a full list of athletes by sponsoring country. Of added interest is a section of group profiles, which includes the "Tiger belles" of Tennessee State University and East African middle-and long-distance runners. Page also supplies a profile of black management in U.S. professional sports. While this profile emphasizes a controversial and important issue, its inclusion does not contribute to the book's usefulness as a reference on black Olympic medal winners.

In compiling this reference, Page has done a service for those interested in the history of the Olympic Games. He has produced an easy-to-use source of information on these medal winners that not only answers questions about individual athletes but also points out the significance of black achievement in the Olympic Games. This book is particularly suited for public and school libraries and may be of interest to college libraries. [R: Choice, July/Aug 91, p. 1764; LJ, 15 June 91, p. 83; VOYA, Oct 91, p. 278]—**Tom Gilson**

1154. Pare, Michael A. **Sports Stars**. Detroit, U*X*L/Gale, 1994. 2v. illus. index. $38.00/set. GV697.A1P32, 796'.092'2. LC 94-21835. ISBN 0-8103-9859-1.

This biographical dictionary of 80 current active or recently retired top performers is a handy and relatively inexpensive source of information about those figures that will have considerable appeal to young readers. The entries are arranged alphabetically by player, but a brief guide also provides a listing by 17 sports. Each entry includes a section on "growing up" that deals with the athlete's early life and motivations, followed by one called "superstar" that highlights the career. Numerous boldface headings break the text into readable segments. A scoreboard sidebar, which highlights a few major accomplishments, and a black-and-white photograph add visual appeal. The address at which an athlete can be contacted, a brief bibliography of further readings, and a short index are especially useful.

The chief limitation of this set is that it covers only 80 athletes. Of those, about 40 are baseball, basketball, and football players. Other sports, such as horse racing or speed skating, generally have only one or two athletes included. In an effort to achieve balance, more women than men may be included from sports in which both participate. One of the three criteria for inclusion is that the person is a "role model who [has] overcome physical obstacles or societal constraints." The inclusion of more women and of role models may be noble goals, but neither results in the inclusion of popular personalities who may have greater appeal. Teenage auto racing fans, for example, are likely to be disappointed that Emerson Fittiipaldi and Lyn St. James are the only two entrants from that sport. Either this set or the one-volume *Fifty Finest Athletes of the 20th Century* (see ARBA 1992, entry 768) is a good choice for public or school libraries with budgetary limitations. For libraries with greater resources *Great Athletes* (see ARBA 1993, entry 816), which covers 738 people, or *The Lincoln Library of Sports Champions* (Encyclopaedia Britannica, 1993) which covers 297 people, will provide students with a much greater choice of athletes.—**Norman D. Stevens**

1155. Pare, Michael A. **Sports Stars, Series 3**. Detroit, Gale, 1997. 342p. illus. index. $34.00. ISBN 0-7876-1749-0.

This readily accessible reference provides profiles and photographs of 30 amateur and professional athletes. Featured athletes must meet one or more criteria for inclusion: currently active in amateur or professional sports, considered top performers in their field, and role models who have overcome physical or societal obstacles to reach the top of their professions. Both sexes, various cultures, and a wide variety of sports—including auto racing, baseball, basketball, bicycle racing, boxing, figure skating, football, golf, gymnastics, hockey, horse racing, skiing, soccer, speed skating, swimming, tennis, track and field, and yachting—are represented.

Each profile opens with a thumbnail sketch. Following is a section titled "Growing Up," which is further subdivided into important aspects of the athlete's life, and a section titled "Superstar," which is subdivided into highlights of the athlete's sports career. Each profile includes at least one black-and-white photograph, and many include additional photographs of the athlete in action. Sidebars provide interesting details or anecdotes, and each profile concludes with a list of sources and an address to write to for further information.

Arranged alphabetically, there are two tables of contents: one in order of appearance of the entries and the other listed by type of sport. A comprehensive index is included. Generous margins, an easy-to-read typeface size, and an eye-catching cover add to the appeal of this resource.—**Dana McDougald**

1156. Sherrow, Victoria. **Encyclopedia of Women and Sports**. Santa Barbara, Calif., ABC-CLIO, 1996. 382p. illus. index. $60.00. ISBN 0-87436-826-X.

Laws and societal pressure have discouraged women from participating in sports around the world for centuries. Chronicling the history of women athletes and the barriers that they have faced and overcome is the focus of the *Encyclopedia of Women and Sports.*

The introduction guides readers through a fascinating overview of the history of women and sports, beginning with the first Olympic Games in Ancient Greece, where not only were women banned from competition, but were also banned from watching the games at all. This is a readable, enlightening introduction that describes societal beliefs of the "weaker sex," the negative attitudes of "unfeminine" women, sexism, and the "experts" who deemed that sports would be detrimental to a woman's health. The first acceptable sports for women—golf, croquet, and archery—helped to make athletic pursuits more permissible for women, and the arrival of the bicycle had a great impact on society. It provided an important form of transportation as well as a popular pastime, but the bicycle also presented a problem with women's attire: How were women to ride with long skirts without getting them tangled in the spokes? Amelia Bloomer and her supporters suggested a freer style of dress consisting of wide pants beneath a loose-fitting dress. Thus, the arrival of the Bloomer in 1851. "Both cycling and bloomers came to symbolize a new spirit in America and were linked to the broader social efforts of the suffragist movement as women struggled for the right to vote" (p. xii). The introduction also chronicles minority women and the struggles they overcame, women athletes who defied society and helped to change common thinking, the fight for Olympic participation, athletic scholarships, and the media role models who encouraged the message that sports could be "feminine."

More than 600 alphabetically organized entries highlight key individuals who have participated in or advanced the cause of women in sports and include related topics, such as sexual and racial discrimination, tournaments, organizations, leagues, awards, health issues, segregation, sport history, scholarships, and officiating. The volume not only records athletic achievements but chronicles other accomplishments as well. Tenley Albright, for example, overcame polio to become a gold-medal figure skater in the 1936 Olympics, graduated from Harvard Medical School, became a surgeon, and served as the first woman on the U.S. Olympic committee.

Encyclopedia of Women and Sports underscores the progress women have made not only as athletes but as coaches, officials, teachers, administrators, sportscasters, sportswriters, and women's rights advocates. Current as of the 1996 Summer Olympic Games, entries are concise, interesting, and readable with *see also* and bibliographical references. A timeline of events from 776 B.C.E. to 1996 gives a clear overview of progress. A bibliography and an index complete the work. The encyclopedia is highly recommended.—**Deborah A. Taylor**

1157. Siegman, Joseph. **Jewish Sports Legends: The International Jewish Sports Hall of Fame**. 2d ed. Hemdon, Va., Brassey's (U.S.), 1997. 222p. illus. $29.95. ISBN 1-57488-128-0.

Jewish people have been an integral part of the American and world sports scene for decades. Well-known Jewish athletes like baseball's Sandy Koufax, basketball's Dolph Schayes, and Olympic swimmer Mark Spitz are recognized by sports fan of any era. In a concise, highly illustrated, and rather expensive volume, Siegman (who founded the International Jewish Sports Hall of Fame in Jerusalem) writes brief biographies of these and 250 other less recognized Jewish sports stars. The sketches are arranged alphabetically by sport: baseball, football, and others—and include athletes of several nationalities from the modern era as well as names dating back to the eighteenth century (bowling's John Brunswick, for example). Virtually every entry includes a photograph or illustration.

The book includes few statistical records of athletes—we do not know how many total games Koufax won, for example—and there is little information that cannot be located in some standard source. The price is high, and useful information is at a premium. Libraries with a strong emphasis on sports collections may want to add this title to their collection, but most will find it easy to pass on it as a purchase.—**Boyd Childress**

1158. Silverman, Buddy Robert S. **The Jewish Athletes Hall of Fame**. New York, Shapolsky, 1989. 205p. illus. $16.95. GV697.A1SS2. 796.089'924'073. LC 89-32618. ISBN 0-944007-04-X.

The Jewish athlete has excelled in many sports—boxing, baseball, basketball, football, and swimming. This volume celebrates Jews in sports in brief sketches, interviews, and photographs. Included are 71 male and female athletes and 21 executives. Familiar names highlight the pages—Sandy Koufax, Dolph Schayes, Sid Luckman, and Brad Gilbert, to mention a few. Records and statistics are included in a few cases.

Interestingly, compiler Silverman rates these sports stars; for example, former Detroit Tiger and Hall of Famer Hank Greenberg is rated first among the "Jewish Magnificent Seven," and 1972 Olympic champion swimmer Mark Spitz is ranked 11th among Jewish sports figures. While unique, the volume is unexceptional, but it does serve to illustrate the athletic prowess of several dozen Jews.—**Boyd Childress**

1159. Sparhawk, Ruth M., and others, comps. **American Women in Sport, 1887-1987: A 100-Year Chronology**. Metuchen, N.J., Scarecrow, 1989. 149p. index. $20.00. GV583.A64. 796'.0194. LC 89-6150. ISBN 0-8108-2205-9.

Adequate documentation would make this first attempt at a chronology of American women in sport even better. The chronology is divided into four timeframes: pre-organizational era, 1887-1916; organizational years, 1917-1956; competitive period, 1957-1971; and Title IX era, 1972-1987. It is then further divided by year followed by a listing of names and feats. Many, if not most, of the names will be unknown to the general reader. Because of this some of the entries appear to be only footnotes at best, and perhaps even uninteresting next to the likes of legendary stars such as Mildred "Babe" Didrikson Zaharias or Billie Jean King. The same, of course, would apply to a chronology of American men in sport; names that live for a brief moment without becoming historical fixtures lose their luster quickly. If the compilers had cited sources for each entry, then the lesser-known female athletes would come alive. Directing the reader to a newspaper or magazine article, a chapter in a book, or even a page in a book would be of great assistance. Indexes by name and sport tie the work together; there is a bibliography at the end. Recommended as a testimonial to all women in sport who made a mark in male-dominated arenas. [R: LJ, 15 Sept 89, p. 104]—**Bill Bailey**

1160. **Sports Stars: Series 2**. Michael A. Pare, ed. Detroit, U*X*L/Gale, 1996. 2v. illus. index. $44.95/set. ISBN 0-7876-0867-X.

Sports Stars: Series 2 presents biographies of 60 amateur and professional athletes, including 2 sports teams—the women's baseball team the Colorado Silver Bullets and the yachting team Mighty Mary. According to the reader's guide (the first section of the book), the athletes meet one or more of the following criteria: They are currently active in amateur or professional sports, are considered top performers in their field, and are role models who have overcome physical obstacles or societal constraints to reach the top of their professions. Other critical selection criteria, which this reviewer tested with the neighbor kids (two middle school boys who do not like to read), are the popular appeal of the athletes chosen and the readability and ease of use as perceived by this kind of reader. Some of the interesting and convenient features consist of the listing of the athletes by sports; a wide range of sports covered, including the less popular (bicycle racing, golf, horse racing, speed skating, yachting); a "Scoreboard Box" listing the athlete's top awards; a "Growing Up" section presenting the early life and motivations of the person or team; a "Superstar" section highlighting the athlete's career; a "Where to Write" section with an address to contact the athlete; and a list of sources for further reading.

As one would expect, fewer women are listed than men, for sports are male-dominated, but the editor has taken care to profile many women. Their struggles to be successful in these male bastions have been accurately portrayed. The athletes presented, because of the very nature of the field, encompass a realistic range of ethnicity. The reading level is appropriate for middle school students, and the text is down-to-earth, describing what actually happened in these athletes' lives— divorce, illness, failure, disappointment, personal problems, racial conflict—making it more interesting to the age group targeted. Interesting sidebars and many photographs are provided. Finally, each profile is just eight pages in length, which is attractive to many less-skilled readers.

Teachers and parents struggle to get young people, particularly active boys, to read. They also strive to find suitable role models for kids, particularly girl athletes, and to locate engaging reference materials for budding writers and researchers. This series answers many needs of students and their teachers and builds a bridge from the typical interests of young people to books.—**Karen D. Harvey**

1161.   Sugar, Bert Randolph. **The 100 Greatest Athletes of All Time: A Sports Editor's Personal Ranking**. New York, Citadel Press/Carol Publishing Group, 1995. 446p. illus. index. $24.95. ISBN 0-8065-1614-3.

Greatness, as defined by Sugar, "is a combination of things, an equation that includes dominance, perceived greatness, consistent performance, accomplishments that transcend time, and overall excellence" (p. xiii). With this definition, and a dose of "Sugar," comes this ranking of the 100 greatest athletes of all time. Conducting his research at "watering holes," gathering nominees from new acquaintances, reading and rereading yellowed newspapers and clips of bygone eras, Sugar has ranked the 100 greatest athletes according to their contribution to sports history.

Each ranking is accompanied by a photograph and an insightful biography of the athlete. The biographies range from two to six pages each and are succinctly written with a summary of the biographee's childhood, college achievements, amateur and professional accomplishments, and statistics. Although there is a profusion of information in each biography, Sugar also manages to capture the essence of the personal side of the athlete.

The rankings encompass athletes from around the world, and from all eras of the twentieth century. They have been pulled from predominately U.S. sports, such as baseball, boxing, football, golf, and tennis. To the casual observer, the list includes anyone and everyone worthy to be among the greatest 100, but in the addendum titled "101," Sugar lists another 250 athletes who could have easily made the cut.

Sugar has covered the sports scene for more than three decades, both in print and on television. He wrote this book to be the source of endless arguments among sports fans. He does not seek to convince the reader, as there is no such thing as objective truth, but merely to stimulate. This book belongs in the library of every sports fan, and it can be considered a benchmark for those sports figures who are deemed to be "great."—**Deborah A. Taylor**

1162.   **Twentieth-Century American Sportswriters**. Richard Orodenker, ed. Detroit, Gale, 1996. 439p. illus. index. (Dictionary of Literary Biography, v.171). $140.00. ISBN 0-8103-9934-2.

Although biographies of sportswriters have been published separately or have appeared in other compilations, this book is devoted entirely to the genre. Forty writers, flourishing from the early part of the twentieth century to 1970, have been chosen to represent various styles and decades. Some, such as Roger Kahn and Grantland Rice, are well known in the field. Others, such as Paul Gallico and Damon Runyon, are perhaps better known in other genres. The majority, however, will be unfamiliar to most readers.

The alphabetic entries follow the familiar Dictionary of Literary Biography (DLB) format: birth and death dates as appropriate; references to entries in other DLB volumes; major positions held; a bibliography of the individual's publications; the biographical essay; a list of further readings, if available; and the location of the individual's personal papers, if appropriate. The entry focuses on the sports writing career and achievements of the subject. Additional features, which enhance the value of the work, include a brief introduction that gives an overview of sports literature and sports writing in general and a checklist of further readings. Combining convenient access and readable essays, this is a welcome addition to a major reference work that is a standard in libraries of all types and sizes.—**Barbara E. Kemp**

1163. Woolum, Janet. **Outstanding Women Athletes: Who They Are and How They Influenced Sports in America**. Phoenix, Ariz., Oryx Press, 1992. 279p. illus. index. $39.95. GV697.A1W69. 796'.0 1 94'0922. LC 92-199. ISBN 0-89774-713-5.

Woolum's work is the latest, and probably the best, of new books featuring biographical sketches of women athletes. It is certainly superior to Robert J. Condon's *Great Women Athletes of the 20th Century* (McFarland, 1991). Besides providing sketches of 60 women who represent 19 sports, *Outstanding Women Athletes* includes a brief history of American women's sports and women's Olympic participation, a bibliography, a directory of some relevant organizations, and a list of all female Olympic medalists by sport.

Having all this data under one cover is excellent. However, this is not primarily a scholarly reference. As the quotation on the back cover indicates, it is intended for young readers. The bibliography, which contains numerous scholarly monographs, is therefore inappropriate. The biggest problem, however, is with the biographies themselves. Unlike standard biographical dictionaries, which have for every entry standard facts such as birth date, parentage, education, marriage, divorce, offspring, and career, this book is uniform only on the first two. For example, entries for Patricia McCormick and Joan Benoit Samuelson mention that they became pregnant and had children, but their husbands are never mentioned. Worse, many women appear to have no life beyond the pool or gym, and many significant achievements are ignored. Better biographies of many of these women are available elsewhere, including in the 20-volume *Great Athletes* (Salem Press, 1992), which is also intended for the youth market and lists the victories and records for each athlete. Woolum's book is a worthwhile addition to public school and public libraries but not for colleges. [R: RBB, 1 Nov 92, pp. 552-54]—**Mary Lou LeCompte**

BASEBALL

1164. **The Ballplayers: Baseball's Ultimate Biographical Reference**. Mike Shatzkin, ed. New York, William Morrow, 1990. 1230p. illus. $39.95. GV665.A1B323. 796.357'092'2. LC 89-77086. ISBN 0-87795-9846.

The Ballplayers has its flaws but largely succeeds in its billing as "Baseball's Ultimate Biographical Reference." Length of career is the first criterion that makes a player eligible for inclusion here, then fan interest. Thus, short careers are given short shrift (not counting the one of Eddie Gaedel, a midget who once pinch-hit for the St. Louis Browns).

Famous fans, such as leather-lunged, cowbell-ringing Hilda Chester of Brooklyn Dodgers fame, receive their due. So do managers; executives; minor leaguers; and notable Japanese, Mexican, and Negro League players. The book was created under the auspices of SABR, the Society for American Baseball Research, which is making a point of researching and re-creating the Negro League records.

The facts and statistics are flawless, their presentation less so. Editing and proofreading errors creep in. A ballplayer is described as "increasingly sager," and the entry on Commissioner Bart Giamatti makes it sound as if he died immediately upon taking office, not five months after doing so. Also, the entries should be cross-referenced. There is an interesting story about a fan named Eddie Mifflin, who was instrumental in persuading Ted Williams to remain in the majors until he compiled statistics that would ensure his entrance into the Hall of Fame. Yet this is not mentioned in the entry on Ted Williams, and fans could miss this wonderful story.

Most of the entries are utilitarian, but there are occasional gems, such as a loving portrait of gentle fast ball pitcher Walter Johnson. Some entries reach a little too far, such as trying to recap all of World Series history in six pages. Still, this is a worthwhile book for its statistical compilations or for browsing. Recommended. [R: Choice, Sept 90, p. 68; LJ, 1 Apr 90, p. 106; RBB, 1 June 90, p. 1921; WLB, Sept 90, p. 126]—**R. S. Lehmann**

1165. **Biographical Dictionary of American Sports: Baseball**. David L. Porter, ed. Westport, Conn., Greenwood Press, 1987. 713p. index. $75.00. LC 86-12091. ISBN 0-313-23771-9.

A supplement to this work was published in 1995: *Biographical Dictionary of American Sports: 1992-1994, Supplement for Baseball, Football, Basketball, & Other Sports* (Westport,

Conn., Greenwood Publishing Group, Inc.). The supplement brings the information up-to-date. This volume is part of Greenwood's *Biographical Dictionary of American Sports*. It contains over 500 biographical sketches of "extraordinary baseball figures," including players, managers, coaches, officials, executives and administrators, and rules developers. Coverage extends from the mid-nineteenth century to 1987, although some players with noteworthy achievements in 1986 are not included. Each essay concentrates on the life and achievements of its subject, rather than on statistics, which can be found in *The Baseball Encyclopedia* (see ARBA 86, entry 758), *The Sports Encyclopedia: Baseball* (see entry 797), and other statistical publications. The essays, which range in length from 200 to 900 words, include interpretation and analysis of each biographee's accomplishments and his significance to the sport. Extensive cross-references are utilized and a bibliography of works by and about the subject (including journal articles and audiovisual materials) concludes each sketch. All entries are signed. The writing is readable and on a level understandable by middle-grade students and up.

Appendixes list entries by main category (such as "Player"), main position played, and place of birth. Other listings include Negro League entries, major and Negro leagues, and members of the National Baseball Hall of Fame.

One unfortunate characteristic of this volume, which will perhaps be rectified in succeeding books in the series, is the replacement of a biographical sketch by a cross-reference when a person is profiled in another volume of the *Biographical Dictionary*. For example, Peter Ueberroth is mentioned a number of times throughout the volume, but does not have his own entry, nor does R. Cal Hubbard, elected to the Hall of Fame in 1976. Both will be in future volumes. The student or researcher needing information should not have to go to separate sources. Nonetheless, this is a well-done biographical dictionary with a different focus and more comprehensive coverage than some other works available. [R: Choice, Dec 87, p. 595; RBB, 15 Nov 87, p. 547; WLB, Dec 87, p. 90]—**Shirley Lambert and Robert L. Wick**

1166. Freese, Mel R. **Charmed Circle: Twenty-Game-Winning Pitchers in Baseball's 20th Century**. Jefferson, N.C., McFarland, 1997. 347p. index. $35.00pa. ISBN 0-7864-0297-0.

How many people know that, of all the pitchers who have pitched in the major leagues since 1901, about 1 in 15 have won 20 games in a season? That information is the most important fact imparted in this book that is not readily found in *The Baseball Encyclopedia* (see ARBA 94, entry 830, for a review of the 9th edition, and ARBA 96, entry 803, for a review of the 1995 update). This book does include summations of the careers of all pitchers who ever won 20 games in a season and reflections on many who never won 20. Many interesting conclusions are drawn by the author. However, not all of these conclusions are completely buttressed with statistical analysis. *Charmed Circle* also supplies an appendix listing pitchers by how many times they won 20 or more games in a season.

Charmed Circle is an interesting book, but it does not really belong in a general library reference collection. Libraries with major baseball collections will want to include the volume, and some serious fans will buy it.—**David A. Doman**

1167. Honig, Donald. **The Greatest Catchers of All Time**. Dubuque, Iowa, Wm. C. Brown, 1991. 118p. illus. index. $18.95. LC 90-83085. ISBN 0-697-12806-7.

Honig, Donald. **The Greatest Pitchers of All Time**. New York, Crown, 1988. 168p. illus. index. $18.95. LC 87-32960. ISBN 0-517-56887-X.

Honig, Donald. **The Greatest First Basemen of All Time**. New York, Crown, 1988. 148p. illus. index. $18.95. LC 87-22208. ISBN 0-517-56842-X.

Honig's ongoing series of brief commentaries on the baseball players whom he considers the best at their position is a useful addition to strong sports reference collections. His choice of the best catchers, pitchers, and basemen is based on his personal judgment, not a statistical analysis. However, his picks seem reasonable, although there is (as always) room for argument. The balanced selection of players from different eras helps the reader understand how the game has changed over time.

The relatively brief statistical compilation of the career records of the players provides information that is readily available in larger and more comprehensive compilations. The short biographies and commentaries and the considerable assortment of good black-and-white photographs are what make these volumes valuable, especially since information about individual players is not readily available in other sources. Honig's writing is simple and straightforward and seems to be aimed primarily at a young adult audience. While not an essential text, these volumes offer another perspective on America's pastime that will appeal to the dedicated baseball fan.—**Norman D. Stevens and Robert L. Wick**

1168.   Kelly, Robert E. **Baseball's Best: Hall of Fame Pretenders Active in the Eighties**. Jefferson, N.C., McFarland, 1988. 200p. bibliog. index. $16.95pa. LC 88-42507. ISBN 0-89950-352-7.

Each year, millions of baseball fans speculate on who, among retired players, will receive baseball's highest honor, election to the Hall of Fame (HOF). The HOF, in Cooperstown, New York, is a shrine to professional baseball; and only a select few are chosen by ballot each year, which makes the honor infrequent, coveted, and controversial.

Robert E. Kelly, who has written analytical essays for several national baseball magazines, here ventures his predictions and analyses of the chances of (1986 season) active players of making the HOF, based on their prior and projected achievements. Kelly's analyses, written at the completion of the 1986 season, may be affected by subsequent events and records, but this cannot be helped short of publishing an annual edition.

Calling those with a fair shot at HOF election "pretenders," Kelly discusses specific players and their chances of election, individually and in groups by position. Analyses are provided, with performance and position/classification charts, short biographies, a history of the HOF, a discussion of how selection juries are formed and operate, and the intriguing chapters "The Fairness Issue" and "The Neglected Ones."

Picking away at Kelly's methodology, one might say that he is strongly subjective, despite attempts to be statistical and analytical. His criteria for rankings (production per at bat, earned run average) are supposed to buttress his contentions with the appearance of objectivity, which is nowhere in evidence in his prose. One must, however, give him credit for attempting to be fair towards the players he discusses, despite perhaps unavoidable omission or dismissal of other people's favorites. Kelly has simply chosen what he calls "the best" for entry into his group of pretenders. The problem lies not in who is a good player, but rather with how Kelly decided on who is *better* (and thus more deserving) than whom.

Updated editions would help (the 1986 season seems so long ago now), but there is much readable information, accompanied by calculations and justifications, in this little volume, which should please most baseball fans, while infuriating the rest. Recommended for sports collections in larger public libraries.—**Bruce A. Shuman**

1169.   *The Sporting News* **Official Baseball Register**. Sean Stewart, Kyle Veltrop, and John Duxbury, eds. St. Louis, Mo., Sporting News Publishing, 1886- . $13.95pa. for recent editions. ISSN 0038-805X.

Probably the oldest sports registry, for many years this work was published under the title of *The Official Baseball Register*, but the publisher's name was added, making it *The Sporting News Official Baseball Register*. This is the book to find statistics on everyone who appeared in at least one major league game and on other players who did not appear in a game in the last year but were listed on a 40-man major league roster as of the end of December each year. The *Register* is an exhaustive listing of the names in the game today. Each entry provides minor league as well as major league records; personal information (including any high school, junior college, and college the player attended); transactions the player was involved in; records and honors; and any other item of statistical or miscellaneous interest (e.g., "tied for A.L. lead with three balks in 1995" or "led A.L. with 32 sacrifice hits in 1989").

The *Register* has all players listed in a single alphabetic volume, and pitchers and other players are listed together, which makes it easier to use. However, the National League pitchers' entries do not furnish hitting statistics. Some additional interest is provided by the football records for those few individuals who have played both games (Brian Jordan of the St. Louis Cardinals and Deion Sanders, who is a free agent in major league baseball, for example). The section on major league managers supplies each individual's minor and major league playing statistics, as well as their minor and major league managing records. The *Register* is an essential book for reference collections and serious baseball fans.—**David A. Doman and Robert L. Wick**

1170.   Westcott, Rich. **Diamond Greats: Profiles and Interviews with 65 of Baseball's History Makers**. Westport, Conn., Meckler, 1988. 389p. illus. $22.50. LC 87-24023. ISBN 0-88736-220-6.

In this collection of short biographies, each player is either interviewed or covered by a short five-page sketch written by Westcott.

This is only marginally a reference book. There is no index. Westcott had no real criteria for which players he included and which he excluded. Some of the players are in the Hall of Fame, some were Most Valuable Players, some were outstanding hitters or pitchers, and some performed memorable feats. Because the table of contents is arranged neither alphabetically, chronologically, nor by position played, it is difficult to locate who is included and who is not: Babe Ruth, Ty Cobb, and Pete Rose are not included; Lou Brock, Ted Williams, and Minnie Minoso are.

The selections are fascinating and well written, giving both a picture of the times and of the men who lived them. There is no comparable collection of short baseball biographies, but because of the small number of players included and the idiosyncratic selection criteria, this work is better suited to the general collection than for reference.—**Dennis Dillon**

BASKETBALL

1171.   **Biographical Dictionary of American Sports: Basketball and Other Indoor Sports**. David L. Porter, ed. Westport, Conn., Greenwood Press, 1989. 801p. index. $75.00. GV697.A1B494. 796'.0973. LC 88-17776. ISBN 0-313-26261-6.

This book is the fourth of four companion volumes containing biographies of notable American sportsmen and sportswomen published by Greenwood Press (see ARBA 88, entry 798, and ARBA 89, entry 735). This volume contains 558 entries covering basketball, bowling, boxing, diving, figure skating, gymnastics, ice hockey, swimming, weight lifting, wrestling, and a few miscellaneous sports. Amateur and professional athletes, coaches, club officials, administrators, and referees are the subjects of sketches ranging in length from 200 to 900 words. Although most biographees are deceased or retired, several were currently active as of January 1989.

Each signed essay contains the subject's full name, date and place of birth and death, background of parents, formal education, names of immediate family members, and significant accomplishments. A brief bibliography of works by and about the subject follow each entry. Several appendixes and a comprehensive general index make this a useful biographical source of indoor sports personalities. Information in the appendixes is presented according to place of birth, women athletes by type of sport, married women athletes and their maiden names, ring names and real names of boxers, major U.S. sports halls of fame, and major indoor sporting events.

Although some cross-references are made to individuals whose biographical sketches appear in other volumes of the series and some minor indoor sports are not covered, these limitations do not detract meaningfully from the value of this book for historians, educators, and librarians. [R: Choice, Nov 89, p. 456]—**Dennis J. Phillips**

1172.   *The Sporting News* **Official NBA Guide**. Alex Sachare and Dave Sloan, eds. St. Louis, Mo., The Sporting News, 1981- . illus. index. $10.95pa. for recent edition. ISSN 0078-3862.

The Sporting News is the long-standing sports statistics leader, and the *Official NBA Guide* is an annual example of its excellence. The volume includes a statistical summary of the past season, present season rosters and schedules, NBA records and award winners, and season-by-season team records since the 1946-1947 season. These records include team and individual records, making this volume an indispensable source for NBA information. When compared to the *NBA Register* (see entry 610), the *Guide* provides the same information with a different approach. Since the *Register* includes information on players from the past season and present season, the *Guide* is the only source for information on greats of the game like Connie "The Hawk" Hawkins, who is not listed among the greats in the *Register*. When hard purchasing decisions have to be made, the *Guide* is the preferable choice.—**Boyd Childress**

1173.   Taragano, Martin. **Basketball Biographies: 434 U.S. Players, Coaches and Contributors to the Game, 1891-1990**. Jefferson, N.C., McFarland, 1991. 318p. illus. index. $45.00. GV884.A1T37. 796.323'092273. LC 91-52761. ISBN 0-89950-625-9.

This handy collection of basketball biographies will be a useful item in high school and public library collections. Taragano has pulled together short information pieces on 434 players, coaches, and a few others who have contributed significantly to the game. Entries are in alphabetical order. There is a good index with references to entries other than the player's own. The narratives provide career information, statistics, and a discussion of the individual's contribution to the sport. Taragano has based his choices on high career scores, All-Star selections, career top-l0 leaders in one or more statistical categories, longevity, number of games played, defensive prowess, leadership in assists, or making a unique contribution. College players were chosen mostly on the basis of All-American status and being a significant member of a championship team. Coaches and others were chosen for their contributions throughout their careers.

Given these criteria, the book will stimulate discussion on who should not have been chosen and who has been omitted. (To begin the discussion, this reviewer protests the omission of Gene Keady.) As a quick reference tool for short questions, it will have somewhat limited value, since a user would need to read the entire entry to locate information. A statistical summary of each player's career would have been useful. For high school students who need a place to start, this work will be valuable.—**Susan Ebershoff-Coles**

CHESS

1174.   Gaige, Jeremy. **Chess Personalia: A Bio-bibliography**. Jefferson, N.C., McFarland, 1987. 505p. index. $45.00. LC 86-43123. ISBN 0-89950-293-8.

For about 14,000 chess players and problemists, the author, a well-known chess archivist and journalist, provides name (including nickname, maiden name, or pseudonym, if appropriate), date and place of birth, date and place of death (if applicable), chess titles won, and selected references to sources for further information. This incredible work took twenty-five years to research, and its high quality is evident from the sources cited, the detailed explanations about its preparation, and its over-all excellence. The appendix consists of an index of all the obituaries found in the *British Chess Magazine* from its origins in 1881 through 1986. Truly a solid addition to chess reference books, this impressive volume will become a standard source. Highly recommended for public and academic libraries, as well as special collections of sports and games materials.—**Bonnie Gratch**

FOOTBALL

1175.   **Biographical Dictionary of American Sports: Football**. David L. Porter, ed. Westport, Conn., Greenwood Press, 1987. 763p. index. $75.00. LC 86-29386. ISBN 0-313-25771-X.

This biographical dictionary lists more than 500 players, coaches, and executives who have had significant achievements relating to football and have had impact on the history of the sport. Arranged alphabetically and averaging about one page in length, the signed entries provide basic background information about the biographees, with primary emphasis on their sports careers. Each entry also has a brief bibliography of other sources of information. There are several appendixes: entry by main category (player, coach, or executive); entry by main position played; players by place of birth; biographees who have or are playing professional football; members of the College Football Hall of Fame; members of the Pro Football Hall of Fame; and a list of college and professional football conferences, leagues, and associations. There is a general index, which provides access to information within the essays but which, unfortunately, has some minor errors.

As evidenced by the bibliographies provided, much of the factual information found in this book can be found in other sources, but having such information and the analyses of impact in one volume will be very useful to reference librarians, researchers, and football fans. [R: Choice, Apr 88, p. 1219; LJ, 15 Apr 88, p. 31]—**Barbara E. Kemp**

1176.   Chestochowski, Ben. **Gridiron Greats: A Century of Polish Americans in College Football**. New York, Hippocrene Books, 1997. 300p. illus. index. $24.95. ISBN 0-7818-0449-3.

Both college football and books on the sport are consistently popular among people of the United States. As one of these books, *Gridiron Greats* presents a unique and unusual look at some 250 players and coaches of Polish descent who have played (or coached) college football since 1893. Chestochowski profiles these Polish Americans in sketches averaging one-half to two-thirds of a page in length. The biographical sketches feature college and professional statistics, records, and awards. The arrangement includes All-Stars, an all-academic team, an all-Polish future team, and distinguished coaches. To qualify, an individual must have either a father or mother who is Polish. Included are such All-American players as Johnny Lujack and Leon Hart of Notre Dame, Jack Ham and Ted Kwalick of Penn State, Vic Janowicz of Ohio State, and Dan Marino of Pittsburgh. Lujack, Hart, and Janowicz were Heisman Trophy winners. Coaches include Hank Stram; Forest Evashevski; and Joe Restic, recently retired Harvard coach. An index and a brief bibliography conclude the book. The unusual ethnic nature of the book makes it a one-of-a-kind reference volume but also severely limits the potential audience. This is a selection for libraries with exhaustive sports collections only.—**Boyd Childress**

1177.   Sabljak, Mark J., and Martin H. Greenberg. **Who's Who in the Super Bowls: The Performance of Every Player in Super Bowls I to XX**. New York, Dembner Books; distr., New York, W. W. Norton, 1986. 261p. illus. $22.50; $14.95pa. LC 86-6208. ISBN 0-934878-80-3; 0-934878-81-1pa.

In Super Bowl play, who scored the first touchdown? Who holds the record for most fumbles? Which team scored the most points? The answer to these and almost any other questions a person might have about Super Bowls I to XX can be found in *Who's Who in the Super Bowls*. Divided into three sections, "Players, A to Z," "The Games, I-XX," and "Game Records," this volume is a must for anyone who has ever tried to answer the Monday morning quarterbacks' queries.

Each entry in the A to Z listing of players contains the player's name, team, position, height, weight, college, and whether the player was a starter or reserve. *Who's Who in the Super Bowls* also details significant plays the pros participated in, as well as pertinent statistics such as touchdowns, interceptions, fumbles, and yards gained. Over 1,100 football pros played in the first twenty Super Bowls, and all appear in this reference book. The second section devotes one page to each Super Bowl, I to XX. Statistics are given in detail for each game. The final chapter, "Game Records," lists individual and team records for all Super Bowls combined. Recommended for reference collections and football fanatics alike!—**Janet R. Ivey**

1178.   Smith, Myron J., Jr. **The Pro Football Bio-Bibliography**. West Cornwall, Conn., Locust Hill Press, 1989. 288p. $25.00pa. Z7514.F7S63. 016.796332'64'0973. LC 88-37741. ISBN 0-933951-23-X.

Smith has gathered a bibliography of articles from magazines, books, league publications, team yearbooks, and commercially published annuals on over 1,400 players, coaches, and other people connected with professional football. Newspaper articles are not included. Arrangement is alphabetical by individual and contains brief player data (teams, position played, and years) followed by article citations printed through late 1988.

The work provides an index to longer and more significant copy than a periodical or newspaper index might and thus is more valuable for the serious researcher. It is, however, mistitled. The "bio" in bio-bibliography does not really belong since only playing information (and that very sketchy) is given. No birth dates, personal data, or educational and other attainments are given. Even with this drawback, the bibliography provides valuable access to information for any library that serves the football enthusiast. [R: RBB, Aug 89, p. 1960; Choice, July/Aug 89, p. 1820]—**David V. Loertscher**

HOCKEY

1179. *The Sporting News* **Hockey Register**. Larry Wigge, ed. Frank Polnaszek, comp. St. Louis, Mo., Sporting News, 1984- . $9.95pa. for recent edition. ISSN 0090-2292.

The *Hockey Register* is a companion volume to another Sporting News annual volume, the *Football Register*. Its intent is similar: to present up-to-date personal data and statistics on active players in the National Hockey League. It includes information on players who participated in at least one NHL game in the 1983-1984 season as "selected invitees to training camps" (p. 2).

The main section of the book is a roster of forwards and defensemen, alphabetically arranged by name. Each entry lists personal data, positions played, and a year-by-year statistical summary of the player's hockey career. The same format is repeated for the smaller section on goal keepers. This volume is a must purchase for most libraries.—**Marshall E. Nunn**

WRESTLING

1180. Lentz, Harris M., III. **Biographical Dictionary of Professional Wrestling**. Jefferson, N.C., McFarland, 1997. 373p. index. $55.00. ISBN 0-7864-0303-9.

Lentz has done a thoughtful job of assembling brief biographical information about virtually every professional wrestler of any note who plied his or her trade in the twentieth century. Entries are arranged alphabetically by the wrestler's best-known name, with ample cross-references to the many other names he or she may have used, and start with basic information about the person's life. Lentz is careful to point out how unreliable much of that information, which is supplied by promoters, may be. He also provides detailed information about each person's professional career, including titles; affiliations with other wrestlers (which shift frequently); major bouts; and, in some cases, other activities such as appearances in films.

As the first standard biographical dictionary dealing with this sport/entertainment, the dictionary is a major contribution to knowledge in the field. The volume can, in most respects, serve as an abbreviated history of professional wrestling until such a badly needed history is finally written. It would be all too easy for public and school librarians to dismiss this biographical dictionary as not worthy of being added to their collections whether for snobbish reasons or because they feel that library users are not likely to be wrestling fans. That judgment would be a mistake because, for all of its flaws, professional wrestling does attract wide audiences, including many young people, from a diverse range of backgrounds. Because there is a real shortage of serious and useful books on professional wrestling, this biographical dictionary deserves a place in public and school libraries.—**Norman D. Stevens**

Author/Title Index

Numbers refer to entry numbers. Titles with an (n) indicate annotations.

Subject Index

Numbers refer to entry numbers unless otherwise indicated by a (p), which refers to page numbers. Numbers with an (n) indicate annotations.